The Oxford Handbook of Retirement

OXFORD LIBRARY OF PSYCHOLOGY

Editor in Chief PETER E. NATHAN

Editor, Organizational Psychology STEVE W. J. KOZLOWSKI

The Oxford Handbook of Retirement

Edited by

Mo Wang

OXFORD

UNIVERSITY PRESS

OXFORD
UNIVERSITY PRESS

Oxford University Press, Inc., publishes works that further Oxford University's
objective of excellence in research, scholarship, and education.

Oxford New York
Auckland   Cape Town   Dar es Salaam   Hong Kong   Karachi
Kuala Lumpur   Madrid   Melbourne   Mexico City   Nairobi
New Delhi   Shanghai   Taipei   Toronto

With offices in
Argentina   Austria   Brazil   Chile   Czech Republic   France   Greece
Guatemala   Hungary   Italy   Japan   Poland   Portugal   Singapore
South Korea   Switzerland   Thailand   Turkey   Ukraine   Vietnam

Oxford is a registered trade mark of Oxford University Press in the UK and certain other countries.

Published in the United States of America by
Oxford University Press
198 Madison Avenue, New York, NY 10016

Library of Congress Cataloging-in-Publication Data
The Oxford handbook of retirement / edited by Mo Wang.
      p. cm.—(Oxford library of psychology)
   ISBN-13: 978–0–19–974652–1
   ISBN-10: 0–19–974652–4
   1. Retirement.   2. Retirement—Planning.   3. Retirement income.   4. Retirement—United States.
   I. Wang, Mo.
   HQ1062.O96 2013
   306.3'8—dc23
   2012015031

9 8 7 6 5 4 3 2 1
Printed in the United States of America
on acid-free paper

I dedicate this volume to my wife, Jing Zheng, and my daughter, Zoe Wang, who make my life interesting and meaningful.

SHORT CONTENTS

The *Oxford Library of Psychology,* a landmark series of handbooks, is published by Oxford University Press, one of the world's oldest and most highly respected publishers, with a tradition of publishing significant books in psychology. The ambitious goal of the *Oxford Library of Psychology* is nothing less than to span a vibrant, wide-ranging field and, in so doing, to fill a clear market need.

Encompassing a comprehensive set of handbooks, organized hierarchically, the *Library* incorporates volumes at different levels, each designed to meet a distinct need. At one level are a set of handbooks designed broadly to survey the major subfields of psychology; at another are numerous handbooks that cover important current focal research and scholarly areas of psychology in depth and detail. Planned as a reflection of the dynamism of psychology, the *Library* will grow and expand as psychology itself develops, thereby highlighting significant new research that will impact on the field. Adding to its accessibility and ease of use, the *Library* will be published in print and, later on, electronically.

The *Library* surveys psychology's principal subfields with a set of handbooks that capture the current status and future prospects of those major subdisciplines. This initial set includes handbooks of social and personality psychology, clinical psychology, counseling psychology, school psychology, educational psychology, industrial and organizational psychology, cognitive psychology, cognitive neuroscience, methods and measurements, history, neuropsychology, personality assessment, developmental psychology, and more. Each handbook undertakes to review one of psychology's major subdisciplines with breadth, comprehensiveness, and exemplary scholarship. In addition to these broadly conceived volumes, the *Library* also includes a large number of handbooks designed to explore in depth more specialized areas of scholarship and research, such as stress, health and coping, anxiety and related disorders, cognitive development, or child and adolescent assessment. In contrast to the broad coverage of the subfield handbooks, each of these latter volumes focuses on an especially productive, more highly focused line of scholarship and research. Whether at the broadest or most specific level, however, all of the *Library* handbooks offer synthetic coverage that reviews and evaluates the relevant past and present research and anticipates research in the future. Each handbook in the *Library* includes introductory and concluding chapters written by its editor to provide a roadmap to the handbook's table of contents and to offer informed anticipations of significant future developments in that field.

An undertaking of this scope calls for handbook editors and chapter authors who are established scholars in the areas about which they write. Many of the nation's and world's most productive and best-respected psychologists have agreed to edit *Library* handbooks or write authoritative chapters in their areas of expertise.

For whom has the *Oxford Library of Psychology* been written? Because of its breadth, depth, and accessibility, the *Library* serves a diverse audience, including graduate students in psychology and their faculty mentors, scholars, researchers, and practitioners in psychology and related fields. Each will find in the *Library* the information they seek on the subfield or focal area of psychology in which they work or are interested.

Befitting its commitment to accessibility, each handbook includes a comprehensive index, as well as extensive references to help guide research. And because the *Library* was designed from its inception as an online as well as a print resource, its structure and contents will be readily and rationally searchable online. Further, once the *Library* is released online, the handbooks will be regularly and thoroughly updated.

In summary, the *Oxford Library of Psychology* will grow organically to provide a thoroughly informed perspective on the field of psychology, one that reflects both psychology's dynamism and its increasing interdisciplinarity. Once published electronically, the *Library* is also destined to become a uniquely valuable interactive tool, with extended search and browsing capabilities. As you begin to consult this handbook, we sincerely hope you will share our enthusiasm for the more than 500-year tradition of Oxford University Press for excellence, innovation, and quality, as exemplified by the *Oxford Library of Psychology.*

Peter E. Nathan
Editor-in-Chief
Oxford Library of Psychology

ABOUT THE EDITOR

Mo Wang

Dr. Mo Wang, a tenured Associated Professor at University of Florida, specializes in research and applications in the areas of retirement and older worker employment, occupational health psychology, cross-cultural HR management, leadership, and advanced quantitative methodologies. He has received Academy of Management HR Division Scholarly Achievement Award (2008), Careers Division Best Paper Award (2009), and Erasmus Mundus Scholarship for Work, Organizational, and Personnel Psychology (2009) for his research in these areas. He also received Early Career Achievement Awards from SIOP (2012), Academy of Management's HR Division (2011) and Research Methods Division (2011), and Society for Occupational Health Psychology (co-sponsored by the APA and NIOSH, 2009). He currently serves as an Associate Editor for *Journal of Applied Psychology*. He also serves on the Editorial Boards of *Personnel Psychology, Journal of Management, Organizational Research Methods, Journal of Occupational Health Psychology,* and *Journal of Business and Psychology.* He is the co-director of the Human Resource Research Center at Warrington College of Business Administration in University of Florida.

CONTRIBUTORS

Gary A. Adams
College of Business
University of Wisconsin, Oshkosh
Oshkosh, WI

Victoria A. Albright
RTI International
Research Triangle Park, NC

James T. Austin
Center on Education and Training
for Employment
College of Education and Human Ecology
The Ohio State University
Columbus, OH

Derek R. Avery
Department of Human Resource
Management
Fox School of Business
Temple University
Philadelphia, PA

Boris B. Baltes
Department of Psychology
Wayne State University
Detroit, MI

Terry A. Beehr
Industrial and Organizational Psychology
Program
Central Michigan University
Mount Pleasant, MI

Nathan A. Bowling
Department of Psychology
Wright State University
Dayton, OH

Kevin E. Cahill
Sloan Center on Aging & Work
Boston College
Chestnut Hill, MA

Christina L. Causey
Harvard Law School
Cambridge, MA

Jeanette N. Cleveland
Department of Psychology
The Colorado State University
Fort Collins, CO

Eileen M. Crimmins
Andrus Gerontology Center
University of Southern California
Los Angeles, CA

Lorraine T. Dorfman
School of Social Work and Aging Studies
Program
The University of Iowa
Iowa City, IA

Jesse Erdheim
NSF Academy
National Science Foundation
Arlington, VA

Ryan Fehr
Department of Management and
Organization
Michael G. Foster School of Business
University of Washington
Seattle, WA

Daniel C. Feldman
Terry College of Business
University of Georgia
Athens, GA

Gwenith G. Fisher
Institute for Social Research
University of Michigan
Ann Arbor, MI

William T. Gallo
School of Public Health and Graduate
Center
City University of New York
New York, NY

Michael D. Giandrea
Office of Production and
   Technology
U.S. Bureau of Labor Statistics
Washington, D.C.

Barbara Griffin
Department of Psychology
Macquarie University
Sydney Australia

James Grosch
National Institute for Occupational
   Safety and Health
Cincinnati, OH

Douglas T. Hall
School of Management
Boston University
Boston, MA

Jerry W. Hedge
RTI International
Research Triangle Park, NC

Kène Henkens
Netherlands Interdisciplinary Demographic
   Institute (NIDI)
The Hague, The Netherlands
Department of Sociology
University of Amsterdam
Amsterdam, The Netherlands

Douglas A. Hershey
Department of Psychology
Oklahoma State University
Stillwater, OK

Beryl Hesketh
School of Computing, Engineering, and
   Mathematics
University of Western Sydney
Penrith, Australia

Man Huang
College of Information Studies
University of Maryland
College Park, MD

Charles L. Hulin
Department of Psychology
University of Illinois at Urbana-Champaign
Champaign, IL

Juhani Ilmarinen
Finnish Institute of Occupational Health
Juhani Ilmarinen Consulting, Ltd.
Helsinki, Finland

Joy M. Jacobs-Lawson
Graduate Center for Gerontology
University of Kentucky
Lexington, KY

Jacquelyn Boone James
Sloan Center on Aging & Work
Boston College
Chestnut Hill, MA

Gahyun Jeon
Department of Psychology
University of Illinois at
   Urbana-Champaign
Champaign, IL

Steve M. Jex
Department of Psychology
Bowling Green State University
Bowling Green, OH

Najung Kim
Carroll School of Management
Boston College
Chestnut Hill, MA

Joanna N. Lahey
The Bush School of Government and
   Public Service
Texas A&M University
College Station, TX

John Laitner
Department of Economics and
   Institute for Social Research
University of Michigan
Ann Arbor, MI

Michael A. Lodato
ICF International
Fairfax, VA

Vanessa Loh
Department of Psychology
Macquarie University
Sydney, Australia

Aleksandra Luksyte
Department of Management
University of Western Australia
Perth, Australia

Sarina M. Maneotis
Department of Psychology
The Pennsylvania State University
University Park, PA

Russell A. Matthews
Department of Psychology
Louisiana State University
Baton Rouge, LA

Karoline Mortensen
Department of Health Services
Administration
University of Maryland, College Park
College Park, MD

Daniel A. Newman
Department of Psychology
University of Illinois at
Urbana-Champaign
Champaign, IL

Deborah A. Olson
Department of Management and
Leadership
University of La Verne
La Verne, CA

José Maria Peiró
IDOCAL Research Institute
University of Valencia
IVIE Research Institute
Valencia, Spain

Haoran Peng
Lingnan College
Sun Yat-sen University
Guangzhou, China

Kristina Potočnik
Business School
University of Edinburgh
Edinburgh, UK

Joseph F. Quinn
Department of Economics
Boston College
Chestnut Hill, MA

Barbara L. Rau
College of Business
University of Wisconsin, Oshkosh
Oshkosh, WI

Cort W. Rudolph
Department of Psychology
Florida International University
Miami, FL

Meline Schaffer
Department of Psychology
Clemson University
Clemson, SC

Kenneth S. Shultz
Department of Psychology
California State University, San Bernardino
San Bernardino, CA

Amanda Sonnega
Institute for Social Research
University of Michigan
Ann Arbor, MI

Maximiliane E. Szinovacz
Gerontology Institute and Department
University of Massachusetts, Boston
Boston, MA

Mary Anne Taylor
Department of Psychology
Clemson University
Clemson, SC

Núria Tordera
IDOCAL Research Institute
University of Valencia
Valencia, Spain

Hendrik P. van Dalen
Netherlands Interdisciplinary Demographic
Institute (NIDI)
Department of Economics and CentER
Tilburg University
Tilburg, The Netherlands

Hanna van Solinge
Netherlands Interdisciplinary Demographic
Institute (NIDI)
The Hague, The Netherlands

Jennifer Villani
School of Public Health
University of Maryland, College Park
College Park, MD

Sabrina D. Volpone
Department of Human Resource
Management
Fox School of Business
Temple University
Philadelphia, PA

Monika E. von Bonsdorff
Gerontology Research Center and
Department of Health Sciences
University of Jyvaskyla
Jyvaskyla, Finland

Mo Wang
Department of Management
University of Florida
Gainseville, FL

Ivan Watkins
College of Information
University of Texas at Austin
Austin, TX

Felicia Wheaton
Andrus Gerontology Center
University of Southern California
Los Angeles, CA

Robert J. Willis
Institute for Social Research and
Department of Economics
University of Michigan
Ann Arbor, MI

Paul Wink
Department of Psychology
Wellesley College
Wellesley, MA

Bo Xie
School of Nursing & School of
Information
University of Texas at Austin
Austin, TX

Xiang Yao
Department of Psychology
Peking University
Beijing, China

Yujie Zhan
School of Business and Economics
Wilfrid Laurier University
Waterloo, Ontario, Canada

Michael J. Zickar
Department of Psychology
Bowling Green State University
Bowling Green, OH

CONTENTS

PART 1

General Introduction

Retirement: An Introduction and Overview of the Handbook

Mo Wang

Abstract

This opening chapter introduces the motivation and approach for developing the current handbook. It offers a brief review of the current state of retirement research, especially the important progress that has been made in the field over the past two decades. It also provides an overview of the current handbook's organization and content.

Key Words: retirement, the process view of retirement, work experience

Demographic projections have shown that by 2018, nearly 23.9% of the total U.S. work-force will be age 55 or older, almost doubling the 12.4% in 1998 and representing a sizable increase from 18.1% in 2008 (Toossi, 2009). This rapid trend of labor force aging continues to lead to an increase in the number of people who will transition into retirement in the next decade. This reflects the fact that the population as a whole is getting older due to several factors, including the aging of the large baby-boom generation, lower birth rates, and longer life expectancies (Alley & Crimmins, 2007). These demographic and labor force change patterns were also demonstrated by data from other countries and regions (e.g., Western Europe, Japan, China, and India; Tyers & Shi, 2007), suggesting that retirement is an area of global significance that influences the sustainable economical and social development of countries and societies. Further, at the individual level, retirement has been viewed as a major life-changing event that poses significant adjustment challenges for older employees (Quick & Moen, 1998). For example, maladjustment to the retirement process has been shown to lead to increased alcohol use (e.g., Perreira & Sloan, 2001) and decreased mental health (e.g., Wang, 2007).

In addition, the context within which employees retire has changed significantly in the past twenty years. For example, employees who retire now have to work longer to receive the full Social Security benefit than those retiring twenty years ago. This policy change has occurred not only in the United States but also in other developed countries, such as Germany and France. In addition, most employers in the private sector have replaced defined-benefit pensions with defined-contribution plans, which put investment risks on the employees' side. Most employers are also eliminating health care benefits for retirees, thus requiring retirees to rely on the much less generous Medicare system for their growing health care needs. In 2005, the U.S. Department of Commerce also reported that the private saving rates have been decreasing over the past two decades and reached an all-time low since the Great Depression. However, there is evidence that this declining trend has been reversed since the recent economic depression hit the world in 2008 (McCully, 2011). Changes such as these that have occurred in the past twenty years have generated abundant research to address questions and issues related to retirement.

Despite the obvious importance of retirement to employees, their families and employing organizations, and the larger society, as well as the significant accumulation of knowledge on its related topics, the last handbook of retirement, *The Columbia Retirement Handbook* (Monk, 1994), was published in 1994, almost two decades ago. Therefore, there is a pressing need to create a new volume of handbook that offers comprehensive, up-to-date, and forward-thinking summaries of contemporary knowledge on retirement. To accomplish this goal, I have assembled a collection of leading scholars in this field and asked them to describe the work in their area not only to present the depth and breadth that would capture their area, but to present it in a way in which those outside the field could appreciate the latest thinking in their area of interest. I believe that they did this very well—and did it in such a way that this resulting handbook can serve to inform and guide retirement research in the coming ten to fifteen years.

Specifically, the current handbook provides a comprehensive examination of retirement and its related topics. The approach is interdisciplinary, spanning human resource management, organizational psychology, development psychology, gerontology, sociology, public health, and economics. It covers conceptualizations of retirement from multiple disciplines, reviews existing theoretical perspectives and research findings on retirement, explores current and future challenges in retirement research and practice, and provides corresponding recommendations and suggestions. It also incorporates an international perspective, surveying knowledge and findings across countries, regions, and entities that are governed by different socioeconomic policies.

Before I provide a more detailed overview of the content of this handbook, I first briefly review the current state of retirement research, especially the important progress that has been made in the field over the past two decades. I believe that this brief review can provide a useful background for readers to further approach the specific topics covered in the current handbook and facilitate a better understanding about the organization and content of this handbook.

Advances in Retirement Research

In the past two decades, retirement researchers have made several important advances in this field, including (1) moving beyond using only the economic perspective and social structural perspective to analyze and understand retirement; (2) generating better knowledge about the individual-level process of retirement and the impact of retirement; and

(3) understanding more about how work experience pre- and post-retirement shapes the retirement process. Although all these advances are covered or hinted throughout the chapters included in this volume, I am highlighting them here to provide readers with a brief overview of the current orientation of the field.

First, more and more researchers have recognized that retirement is not just a one-time decision-making event. Rather, it represents a process through which workers decrease their psychological commitment to work and behaviorally withdraw from the workforce (Wang & Shultz, 2010). As such, the traditional economic perspective and social structural perspective merely tell one side of the story by emphasizing financial conditions and societal policies as major driving forces behind retirement (Beehr & Adams, 2003). To contrast, the process view of retirement argues that it is not the decision to retire but the characteristics of the retirement process embedded in this decision that are most important to understand (van Solinge & Henkens, 2008). In other words, people may make the same decision to retire, yet the timing of the decision, the preparation for the decision, the resources associated with the decision, and the amount of the activity change led by the decision may be very different. Therefore, conceptualizing retirement as a process emphasizes investigating the fine-grained nature of retirement rather than the simple decision content (Szinovacz, 2003). Further, this process view recognizes retirement as a longitudinal developmental process characterized by adjustment, which provides a more realistic depiction of retirement and guides the selection and investigation of retirement outcomes (Wang, 2007; Wang, Henkens, & van Solinge, 2011).

Adopting this process view of retirement has inspired broader investigations about predictors and outcomes of retirement, going beyond economic factors and financial consequences. Further, it has encouraged researchers to incorporate theoretical frameworks that are capable of describing the longitudinal adjustment process (i.e., both retirement transition and post-retirement development) and informing the antecedents and outcomes of this longitudinal process. To date, three theoretical frameworks are most frequently used in association with this process view of retirement. They are the life course perspective (Elder, 1995; Elder & Johnson, 2003), continuity theory (Atchley, 1989; Atchley, 1999), and role theory (Barnes-Farrell, 2003).

Jointly, employing these theoretical perspectives has facilitated systematic examinations of effects from individual attributes, job and organizational factors, family factors, and socioeconomic factors on the retirement process (Shultz & Wang, 2011; Wang & Shultz, 2010).

Second, researchers now know significantly more about the individual-level process of retirement. In particular, the temporal progression model, which includes retirement planning, retirement decision making (including early retirement), bridge employment, and retirement transition and adjustment, has been established as the general framework to understand the dynamic mechanisms underlying the retirement process (Shultz & Wang, 2011). Specifically, retirement typically begins with a somewhat distal pre-retirement preparation and planning phase where individuals begin to envision what their retirement might entail and begin discussing those plans with friends, family members, and colleagues. Next, as retirement becomes more proximal, one begins the retirement decision-making process, taking into account a wide variety of factors, including the current economic and employment contexts, as well as family and personal considerations. Finally, as individuals make the transition from full-time worker to retiree, they begin the retirement and life adjustment process. This may include engaging in bridge employment (i.e., temporary or part-time work) to help smooth the transition to full retirement. Thus, viewing retirement from this temporal progression perspective allows researchers to investigate retirement as it unfolds over time from one phase to another, better capturing and matching the process view of retirement.

Further, we also know significantly more about the impact of retirement on people. In the past, the literature has demonstrated a noticeable heterogeneity of findings in terms of the impact of retirement. Some research has found that retirees, in comparison with workers, tend to report greater depression and loneliness, lower life satisfaction and happiness, a less positive view about retirement, and lower activity levels (e.g., Kim & Moen, 2002; Richardson & Kilty, 1991). In contrast, other research has found that most individuals tend to look forward to retirement (e.g., Dorfman, 1992) as well as report being satisfied with retirement (e.g., Calasanti, 1996). Finally, retirement has been shown to be a benign event with no apparent impact on an individual's well-being (e.g., Gall, Evans, & Howard, 1997). Minimal differences in measures of mental health, coping, and health behaviors were reported between workers and retirees within a similar age range (e.g., Wu, Tang, & Yan, 2005).

To reconcile these inconsistent findings, Wang (2007) hypothesized that multiple forms of retirement transition and adjustment coexist in the retiree population. Using longitudinal data from two nationally representative samples obtained by the U.S. Health and Retirement Study and the growth mixture modeling technique (Wang & Bodner, 2007), he was able to consistently demonstrate that over an eight-year period of retirement adjustment process, about 70% of retirees experienced minimum psychological well-being changes; about 25% of retirees experienced negative changes in psychological well-being during the initial transition stage but then showed improvements afterward; and about 5% of retirees experienced positive changes in psychological well-being. These findings suggest that retirees do not follow a uniform pattern of retirement adjustment.

Wang's (2007) findings were further corroborated by Pinquart and Schindler (2007). They used a nationally representative sample of German retirees from the German Socioeconomic Panel Study and found that during retirement transition and adjustment, about 75% of German retirees experienced trivial changes in life satisfaction; about 9% of German retirees experienced significant decrease in their life satisfaction during the initial transition stage but continued on a stable or increasing life satisfaction trajectory thereafter; and about 15% of German retirees experienced significant increases in their life satisfaction.

Taken as a whole, both Wang (2007) and Pinquart and Schindler (2007) suggest that multiple longitudinal change patterns of retirees' psychological well-being exist during the retirement adjustment process, and these patterns correspond to different subpopulations of retirees. As such, these findings support the multiple-pathway nature of retirement adjustment, illustrating that the same retirement decision may lead to different adjustment processes in retirement for different retirees, directly supporting the process view I mentioned earlier (Wang & Shultz, 2010; Wang et al., 2011).

Third, in the past two decades, researchers have paid substantial attention to understanding the important association between pre-retirement and post-retirement work experience and retirement-related phenomena, which has been previously neglected. In particular, researchers have examined a broad range of work-related variables (e.g., employment history, job characteristics, job attitudes, career attachment, age stereotypes at work, and flexible job options) on retirement decision making, bridge employment, and retirement transition and adjustment. For example, regarding retirement decision making, researchers have found that workers in jobs with higher substantive complexity are less likely to retire, while workers in jobs with greater physical and psychological demands or those dissatisfied with their job are more likely to choose retirement (Gobeski & Beehr, 2008; Wang, Zhan, Liu, & Shultz, 2008) or intend to retire early (Elovainio et al., 2005; Lin & Hsieh, 2001). Several studies have also reported that those who report simply "being tired of work" are likely to decide to retire as well (Beehr, Glazer, Nielson, & Farmer, 2000; Bidwell, Griffin, & Hesketh, 2006). In addition, Adams and his colleagues (e.g., Adams, 1999; Adams & Beehr, 1998; Adams et al., 2002) have shown that a sense of attachment or commitment to various facets of work, such as the organization where one is employed and one's career, is negatively related to the decision to retire. Finally, recent research from blue-collar workers indicated that work conditions (e.g., heavy lifting at work) and busy work schedules were related to increased risks for leaving the workforce before the nationally mandated age of retirement (Szubert & Sobala, 2005).

Regarding bridge employment, Weckerle and Shultz (1999) found that older workers who wanted to continue with bridge employment had flexible jobs and felt the decision to retire would be voluntary. Their findings were corroborated by Rau and Adams's (2005) findings that scheduling flexibility and equal employment opportunity were likely to attract older workers to engage in bridge employment. Using actual bridge employment decisions as outcomes, Kim and Feldman (2000) found that job tenure was positively related to the extent of bridge employment for retirees. In another study, Kim and DeVaney (2005) found that retirees who were self-employed were more likely to engage in bridge employment. Finally, Wang et al. (2008) found that retirees who experienced less work stress and higher job satisfaction at pre-retirement jobs were more likely to engage in bridge employment than full retirement.

Regarding retirement transition and adjustment, retirees' work role identity (e.g., Quick & Moen, 1998; Reitzes & Mutran, 2004) has been shown to be negatively related to retirement transition and adjustment outcomes, whereas work stress (e.g., Wang, 2007), psychological and physical job demands (e.g., Quick & Moen, 1998; Wang, 2007), job challenges (e.g., van Solinge & Henkens, 2008), job dissatisfaction (e.g., Wang, 2007), and unemployment before retirement (e.g., Marshall, Clarke, & Ballantyne, 2001; Pinquart & Schindler, 2007) have been shown to be positively related to retirement transition and adjustment outcomes. Further, working after retirement has been shown to be positively related to retirees' retirement and life satisfaction (Kim & Feldman, 2000), psychological well-being (Wang, 2007), and physical and mental health (Zhan, Wang, Liu, & Shultz, 2009). Dendinger, Adams, and Jacobson (2005) showed that the psychological outcomes of working after retirement might depend on retirees' reasons for working bridge jobs. Specifically, they found that the generative reason for working (i.e., working for teaching and sharing knowledge with the younger generation) was positively related to retirees' bridge employment satisfaction and attitude toward retirement, whereas the social reason for working was negatively related to retirees' attitude toward retirement.

Taking all these research findings together, the important association revealed between pre-retirement and post-retirement work experience and retirement-related phenomena suggests that we need to go well beyond demographic, health, and wealth factors to understand the retirement process at the individual level.

The Organization and Content of the Handbook

The chapters assembled in this handbook are organized into five parts. Part I (General Introduction) offers a set of chapters that set the stage by reviewing the scope of the handbook, identifying basic concepts and defining them in historical and demographic contexts, and setting up retirement research in a background of multidisciplinary views. Specifically, besides the opening chapter, this section also includes a review of the evolving history of retirement, a demographic overview on population aging and retirement, and a survey of multiple ways of defining and studying retirement.

Part II (Retirement Process: Theoretical Perspectives) examines extant and emerging theoretical perspectives that explicate the retirement process. The chapters cover the adult development perspective (i.e., the life course perspective, continuity theory, and the theory of selective optimization of compensation), career development perspective (i.e., the protean career model), organizational and management perspective (i.e., retirement as a part of human resource management), and economic perspective (i.e., economic theories of retirement). At the end of that section, a multilevel perspective for retirement research is introduced to connect macro-, meso-, and micro-levels of constructs that are related to retirement and their reciprocal relationships with the retirement process.

Part III (Retirement Research) offers a collection of chapters that report and summarize retirement research in multiple aspects of the retirement process and retirement-related phenomena. This part starts with a chapter that provides a detailed review of research methods that are often used in conducting retirement research, including sampling, design, missing data treatment, and quantitative vs. qualitative methods. It also discusses ways in which retirement research methods have evolved and offers recommendations for future methodological practice. The research methods chapter is followed by a chapter that attends to important demographic variables (i.e., age and gender) that influence the retirement process. The next two chapters consider research regarding the employer's perspective on retirement and workers' retirement attitudes—both are topics that have not been systematically reviewed in the retirement literature. The remaining chapters in this part review retirement research along the time course of the retirement process, following the order of pre-retirement (i.e., retirement planning), making retirement decisions (i.e., retirement decision making and early retirement), and post-retirement (i.e., bridge employment, retirement adjustment and satisfaction, physical health and health behavior in retirement, and leisure activities in retirement). This part ends with a chapter that examines how retirement and family life intertwine throughout the retirement process.

Part IV (Retirement Practice) surveys retirement-related practices that are important for shaping the retirement process and ensuring the quality of retirement. This part of the handbook starts with a chapter that reviews the old-age security systems of four countries (i.e., the United States, Germany, China, and India), including social security, pension systems, and retirement savings, and analyzes the major issues and challenges faced by retirement institutions established in these countries. This chapter is followed by a chapter exploring how legislation and government regulations could impact retirement outcomes, such as encouraging and discouraging work at later ages and affecting well-being during the retirement process. The remaining chapters in this part focus on practices at more micro-levels (e.g., individual and organizational levels), such as the preparation for retirement (i.e., effective financial planning for retirement), utilizing and managing the aging workforce (i.e., retaining and recruiting older workers and designing early retirement incentive packages), health care and health insurance in retirement, and further knowledge and skill development (i.e., learning and training in retirement, technology use, and retirement life). This part ends with a chapter that comprehensively examines how organizations influence individual transition to retirement in different societies by implementing various types of human resource practices.

Part V (Future Trends and Conclusion) is the concluding section that directs readers to several new topics in retirement research and practice. Specifically, the first chapter in this part deals with the continuously changing nature of work and how it may influence the retirement process. The second and third chapters of this part focus on dealing with the structural changes in demographics caused by immigration and aging and examine how these phenomena may impact retirement for certain subpopulations. The fourth chapter focuses on examining retirement through the lens of creativity research and exploring how retirement can exert a positive impact on retirees through the provision of novelty. Finally, the handbook concludes with a chapter that reflects on the challenges faced by retirement researchers and offers a systematic strategy to move retirement research forward.

In sum, the chapters of this volume are meant to provide a comprehensive summary on the knowledge domain of retirement and to describe the material in a way that is useful both for first-time readers (e.g., students) and for those whose work is more focused on this field (e.g., retirement researchers). It is expected that some will read the whole volume, whereas others will turn only to particular chapters that address their concerns. Indeed, the authors have written the chapters so that each chapter can stand alone. I trust that the volume will serve readers across the spectrum of retirement knowledge. I also expect that practitioners in the fields of public policy administration, labor market analysis, business administration, human resource management, organizational development, career and financial counseling, and older worker and retiree advocacy (e.g., AARP) will find this handbook useful.

References

Adams, G. A. (1999). Career-related variables and planned retirement age: An extension of Beehr's Model. *Journal of Vocational Behavior, 55,* 221–235.

Adams, G. A., & Beehr, T. A. (1998). Turnover and retirement: A comparison of their similarities and differences. *Personnel Psychology, 51,* 643–665.

Adams, G. A., Prescher, J., Beehr, T. A., & Lepisto, L. (2002). Applying work-role attachment theory to retirement decision-making. *International Journal of Aging & Human Development, 54,* 125–137.

Alley, D., & Crimmins, E. (2007). The demography of aging and work. In K. S. Shultz & G. A. Adams (Eds.), *Aging and work in the 21st century* (pp. 7–23). New York, NY: Psychology Press.

Atchley, R. C. (1989). A continuity theory of normal aging. *The Gerontologist, 29,* 183–190.

Atchley, R. C. (1999). Continuity theory, self, and social structure. In C. D. Ryff & V. W. Marshall (Eds.), *Families and retirement* (pp, 145–158). Newbury Park, CA: Sage.

Barnes-Farrell, J. L. (2003). Beyond health and wealth: Attitudinal and other influences on retirement decision-making. In G. A. Adams & T. A. Beehr (Eds.), *Retirement: Reasons, processes, and results* (pp. 159–187). New York, NY: Springer.

Beehr, T. A., & Adams, G. A. (2003). Introduction and overview of current research and thinking of retirement. In G. A. Adams & T. A. Beehr (Eds.), *Retirement: Reasons, processes, and outcomes* (pp. 1–5). New York, NY: Springer.

Beehr, T. A., Glazer, S., Nielson, N. L., & Farmer, S. J. (2000). Work and nonwork predictors of employees' retirement ages. *Journal of Vocational Behavior, 57,* 206–225.

Bidwell, J., Griffin, B., & Hesketh, B. (2006). Timing of retirement: Including delay discounting perspective in retirement model. *Journal of Vocational Behavior, 68,* 368–387.

Calasanti, T. M. (1996). Gender and life satisfaction in retirement: An assessment of the male model. *Journal of Gerontology: Social Sciences, 51B,* S18–S29.

Dendinger, V. M., Adams, G. A., & Jacobson, J. D. (2005). Reasons for working and their relationship to retirement attitudes, job satisfaction and occupational self-efficacy of bridge employees. *International Journal of Aging & Human Development, 61,* 21–35.

Dorfman, L. T. (1992). Academics and the transition to retirement. *Educational Gerontology, 18,* 343–363.

Elder, G. H. (1995). The life course paradigm: Social change and individual development. In P. Moen, G. H. Elder, & K. Luscher (Eds.), *Examining lives in contexts: Perspectives on the ecology of human development* (pp. 101–139). Washington, DC: American Psychological Association.

Elder, G. H., & Johnson, M. K. (2003). The life course and aging: Challenges, lessons, and new directions. In R. A. Settersten, Jr. (Ed.), *Invitation to the life course: Toward new understandings of later life* (pp. 49–81). Amityville, NY: Baywood.

Elovainio, M., Forma, P., Kivimaki, M., Sinervo, T., Sutinen, R., & Laine, M. (2005). Job demands and job control as correlates of early retirement thoughts in Finnish social and health care employees. *Work and Stress, 19,* 84–92.

Gall, T. L., Evans, D. R., & Howard, J. (1997). The retirement adjustment process: Changes in the well-being of male retirees across time. *Journal of Gerontology: Psychological Sciences, 52B,* P110–P117.

Gobeski, K. T., & Beehr, T. A. (2008). How retirees work: Predictors of different types of bridge employment. *Journal of Organizational Behavior, 37,* 401–425.

Kim, H., & DeVaney, S. A. (2005). The selection of partial or full retirement by older workers. *Journal of Family and Economic Issues, 26,* 371–394.

Kim, J. E., & Moen, P. (2002). Retirement transitions, gender, and psychological well-being: A life-course, ecological model. *Journal of Gerontology: Psychological Sciences, 57B,* P212–P222.

Kim, S., & Feldman, D. C. (2000). Working in retirement: The antecedents of bridge employment and its consequences for quality of life in retirement. *Academy of Management Journal, 43,* 1195–1210.

Lin, T., & Hsieh, A. (2001). Impact of job stress on early retirement intention. *International Journal of Stress Management, 8,* 243–247.

Marshall, V. W., Clarke, P. J., & Ballantyne, P. J. (2001). Instability in the retirement transition: Effects on health and well-being in a Canadian study. *Research on Aging, 23,* 379–409.

McCully, C. P. (2011). Trends in consumer spending and personal saving, 1959–2009. *Current Survey of Business, 91,* 14–23.

Monk, A. (Ed.). (1994). *The Columbia retirement handbook.* New York, NY: Columbia University Press.

Perreira, K. M., & Sloan, F. A. (2001). Life events and alcohol consumption among mature adults: A longitudinal analysis. *Journal of Studies on Alcohol, 62,* 501–508.

Pinquart, M., & Schindler, I. (2007). Changes of life satisfaction in the transition to retirement: A latent-class approach. *Psychology and Aging, 22,* 442–455.

Quick, H. E., & Moen, P. (1998). Gender, employment, and retirement quality: A life course approach to the differential experiences of men and women. *Journal of Occupational Health Psychology, 1,* 44–64.

Rau, B. L., & Adams, G. A. (2005). Attracting retirees to apply: Desired organizational characteristics of bridge employment. *Journal of Organizational Behavior, 26,* 649–660.

Reitzes, D. C., & Mutran, E. J. (2004). The transition into retirement: Stages and factors that influence retirement adjustment. *International Journal of Aging and Human Development, 59,* 63–84.

Richardson, V., & Kilty, K. M. (1991). Adjustment to retirement: Continuity vs. discontinuity. *International Journal of Aging and Human Development, 33,* 151–169.

Shultz, K. S., & Wang, M. (2011). Psychological perspectives on the changing nature of retirement. *American Psychologist, 66,* 170–179.

Szinovacz, M. E. (2003). Contexts and pathways: Retirement as institution, process, and experience. In G. E. Adams & T. A. Beehr (Eds.), *Retirement: Reasons, processes, and outcomes* (pp. 6–52). New York, NY: Springer.

Szubert, Z., & Sobala, W. (2005). Current determinants of early retirement among blue collar workers in Poland. *International Journal of Occupational Medicine & Environmental Health, 18,* 177–184.

Toossi, M. (2009). Labor force projections to 2018: Older workers staying more active. *Monthly Labor Review, 132,* 30–51.

Tyers, R., & Shi, Q. (2007). Demographic change and policy responses: Implications for the global economy. *The World Economy, 1,* 537–566.

van Solinge, H., & Henkens, K. (2008). Adjustment to and satisfaction with retirement: Two of a kind? *Psychology and Aging, 23,* 422–434.

Wang, M. (2007). Profiling retirees in the retirement transition and adjustment process: Examining the longitudinal change patterns of retirees' psychological well-being. *Journal of Applied Psychology, 92,* 455–474.

Wang, M., & Bodner, T. E. (2007). Growth mixture modeling: Identifying and predicting unobserved subpopulations with longitudinal data. *Organizational Research Methods, 10,* 635–656.

Wang, M., Henkens, K., & van Solinge, H. (2011). Retirement adjustment: A review of theoretical and empirical advancements. *American Psychologist, 66,* 204–213.

Wang, M., & Shultz, K. S. (2010). Employee retirement: A review and recommendations for future investigations. *Journal of Management, 36,* 172–206.

Wang, M., Zhan, Y., Liu, S., & Shultz, K. (2008). Antecedents of bridge employment: A longitudinal investigation. *Journal of Applied Psychology, 93,* 818–830.

Weckerle, J. R., & Shultz, K. S. (1999). Influences on the bridge employment decision among older U.S.A. workers. *Journal of Occupational and Organizational Psychology, 72,* 317–330.

Wu, A. S., Tang, C. S., & Yan, E. C. (2005). Post-retirement voluntary work and psychological functioning among older Chinese in Hong Kong. *Journal of Cross-Cultural Gerontology, 20,* 27–45.

Zhan, Y., Wang, M., Liu, S., & Shultz, K. (2009). Bridge employment and retirees' health: A longitudinal investigation. *Journal of Occupational Health Psychology, 14,* 374–389.

The Evolving History of Retirement within the United States

Michael J. Zickar

Abstract

In this chapter, I review the history of retirement as it has evolved from ancient times to today. Throughout the chapter, I focus on the history of retirement within the United States, though not exclusively. I show that retirement as it currently exists is a relatively new phenomenon brought about by changing demographics, improved economic situations, and social reform legislation. I break this review into separate time periods, focusing on a review of the cultural attitudes toward retirement, economic practices, and legislative efforts. There are several lessons to learn from the review of this history. First, older workers in previous eras experienced the end of their working life in ways that would seem alien to today's workers. Second, the study of retirement requires an interdisciplinary approach that includes economics, gerontology, sociology, and psychology. Finally, the review of retirement history makes one appreciate that there is still much more to learn!

Key Words: history of retirement, Social Security, social welfare, pensions, aging, economic history

You work hard for a living until you get old
And sometimes they push you right out in the cold.
When you're working times through, you don't want charity.
You'd like to retire with some dignity.
Who will take care of you? How will you get by?
When you're too old to work and too young to die.[1]

Joe Glazer's folk song reflects the hard realities of early American industrial life in that many older workers were too old to be successful in the coal mines, steel mills, or lives as itinerant salesmen; yet they might have had many enjoyable years traveling to exotic locales or tending to their grandchildren if they could only have afforded to retire. Unlike the current American workforce, which expects to spend their retirement years in sunny Florida and Arizona beginning at a somewhat early age, the notions and expectations of retirement were much different throughout history.

In this chapter, I review the history of retirement, focusing on a variety of dimensions. Although I focus on retirement within the United States, I consider other countries as well at times. The goal is to place retirement in a historical context that will help readers understand better the phenomena of retirement as it exists today. To do so, I review economic, legislative, and cultural history as it relates to the intersection of aging, working, and leisure. Given the space limits of a chapter, this is an idiosyncratic review that focuses on topics that I found interesting and illuminating. In today's world, where new college graduates are already encouraged to put money into 401(k) plans and dream of retiring at 50, it is important to remember that for workers referenced in Glazer's song, such advances would have seemed more like utopian fantasy than anything else.

The notion of retirement has changed along with the changing demographics of America. To get a sense of the changing nature of retirement, it is enlightening to examine the percentage of men who retire from the workforce by the age of 65. In 1850, around 75% of all men aged 65 or over were still participating in the labor force. Since that time, the labor participation rates have dropped significantly and nearly continuously throughout U.S. history, although there is some thought that rates will increase given the current economic crisis. For example, at age 65 the labor participation rate went from 58% still employed in 1930 down to less than 20% in 1990. This pattern of declining labor participation rates holds across other countries with historical data (i.e., Great Britain, Germany, and France) (see Costa, 1998), though there has been an increase in labor participation since the 1990s that will be discussed later in this chapter (see Johnson & Kaminski, 2010).

In addition to decreasing labor participation rates among older workers, the United States (along with the rest of the world) has continued to age. For example, the Centers for Disease Control estimated that the life expectancy within the United States was 77.7 in 2006, whereas the expectancy was 49.2 in 1900 (Arias, 2010). As can be seen in Figure 2.1, 4.1% of all Americans in 1900 were 65 or older; that percentage has steadily increased to 13.0% in 2010 and is projected to be 20.2% by 2050 (Administration on Aging, 2010).

As the population has aged, societies have had to cope with how to provide for the health and welfare of the aged, as well as to incorporate older adults into and out of the workforce. As I will describe throughout this chapter, these demographic changes are responsible for changing many of this country's attitudes and policies and practices related to retirement. In addition, it is likely that much of our country's legislation and changing practices has worked to influence these demographic changes as well.

Although there are many different ways to structure a historical review (e.g., thematically, chronically, focusing on important individuals), I chose to structure this review along chronological lines, with a focus (though not exclusively) on the history of retirement within the United States. Throughout each section, I will concentrate on legislative changes as well as cultural and economic trends that influenced our notions of retirement. For more complete treatments of the history of aging and retirement within the United States, the reader is encouraged to consult Achenbaum (1978), Costa (1998), Fischer (1978), and Graebner (1980). As will be evident

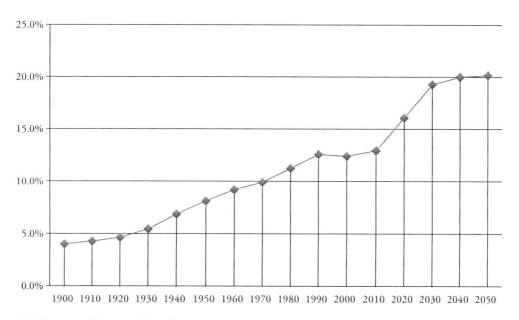

Figure 2.1 Percentage of Americans 65 or older
Note. From Administration on Aging, 2010.

throughout this chapter, I relied on these sources greatly as well.

Ancient History of Retirement (Ancient to 1700)

The issue of retirement was likely nonexistent in prehistoric days, as people did not live very long. An analysis of Paleolithic skeletons showed that very few people lived to the age of fifty (Cook, 1972). These studies estimate that 100% of all Neanderthals were dead by the age of 50, 90% of all Cro-Magnons died by the same age, and 97% of all Mesolithics as well. For these societies, members died before their physical bodies gave out; they were dead before they would need to worry about having others take care of their food and security needs. The concept of retirement had to be established as large portions of the population began to reach older ages. The Romans, for which during the late Roman Empire at least 20% of their population reached 55, created *gerocomeia*, which were nursing homes for the elderly (Fischer, 1978). Some emperors would tour the Empire's gerocomeia, paying respect to the retired. In the Old Testament, the Levites (a Hebrew tribe that served religious functions) were instructed: "But at the age of fifty years they shall retire from service in the work and not work any more" (Numbers, 8: 24–26, New American Standard Bible, 1995). Romans and Greeks were required to retire at age 60 from the military, though commanders were exempted (Shahar, 1997). These policies show that at least in some occupations, retirement policies were established.

In the Middle Ages, the historical records show that very few individuals had the luxury of retiring (see Shahar, 1997). Occasionally, wealthy landowners and royalty would provide pensions for older servants as those servants grew old. In addition, royalty and wealthy landowners might provide money for their aging servants in their wills to support them after their deaths. Wealthy individuals might themselves retire to a monastery or nunnery, where they would pay a large donation that would cover the cost of their upkeep. At the monastery or nunnery, some of the retirees were active in the religious order; others were not. Most individuals, though, were never able to retire. They worked on their farms or in their workshops until they were unable to physically complete their work. At that point, they depended on the goodwill and care of their family members. Outside of the religious orders, there were few institutions and systematic support networks that helped individuals transition from their life of work to retirement.

As cultures developed and humans mastered their environments and began to live longer, institutions were developed to attend to the needs of the elderly. In the society with the most documentation (the Romans), the elderly were treated with respect and given positions of authority. As life span lengthened, societies were forced to learn how to adapt to the aged. In many societies, the aged became leaders and were given positions of respect. The Roman Senate (derived from *senex*, which meant aged) and the Spartan Gerusia (from *gera*, which meant old) were legislative institutions that were ruled by councils of elders (see Fischer, 1978). The elderly had a special place in society due solely to their ability to survive into old age. Throughout the next phase, that respect for the elderly seemed to be an important characteristic.

1700 to 1920s

Early American society placed a high value on its aged population, which was consistent with the Calvinistic idea that people who lived long lives were blessed in the eyes of God. People who lived long lives were more likely to be of the "chosen few" that Calvinists believed would be saved by God. People looked to the aged as role models on how to live their lives. One historian demonstrated the respect for the elderly by determining, based on church congregation records, that older people were given more privileged pews (Fischer, 1978). The respect for the elderly can be seen in many other ways as well.

Although many people worked until they died, there were cases of retirement, either forced or voluntary, though they were rare. An analysis of 35 New England clergymen between 1635 and 1700 showed that 32 died while still holding office and that only three retired (Fischer, 1978); similar results were found for leaders in colonial government. Working until you die may have been somewhat easier for jobs such as clergy or municipal official, in which the physical toil of the work was relatively minimal compared to other occupations. Some historians (Ransom & Sutch, 1986) note that older workers "retired" from work in subtle and gradual ways. For example, a worker in a physically challenging job such as glassblower might have changed jobs to a less demanding job such as bottle packer. Many older workers adapted to work by changing the nature of work instead of retiring completely from paid employment.

During this time, the amount of legislation at the state or federal level related to old age and retirement was minimal, although American Revolutionary Thomas Paine might have been the first to propose a retirement pension in his work *Agrarian Justice* (Paine, 1797). Paine proposed that all Americans over the age of 50 be paid the sum of 10 pounds annually; his plan, which was funded by a tax of estates, would give this annual sum to everyone, regardless of income level. In addition, his plan considered the needs of the blind and the lame, individuals who could no longer work. Although his plan never seemed to be given serious consideration, as we will see, many of its principles were similar to the Social Security legislation enacted many years later.

The first major old-age pension system created in the United States covered Union army veterans from the Civil War. In 1862, Congress passed the General Law pension system, which provided pensions for veterans who could prove that they were disabled during the war and provided medical screening procedures for determining these disabilities. This was important legislation that was passed to help bolster recruiting efforts and provide guarantees to soldiers that they would be taken care of if injured. Disabled soldiers were given $8 per month if they were deemed unable to perform manual labor; smaller amounts were given if the disability was viewed as not totally debilitating. The pension amount was raised in 1866 to $20 per month for total disability, and to $24 by 1872. This was a substantial amount that was roughly 75% of the wages of a typical laborer (see Costa, 1998). In 1890, Congress passed legislation that granted any Union service member an old-age pension that ranged from $6 to $12 per month. These pension laws provided significant stability for Union Civil War veterans, and given the high percentage of military involvement by males in the Civil War, nearly 25% of all men over 64 in 1900 were covered by these laws, which accounted for about 30% of the federal budget at the time (Costa, 1998). Incidentally, the veterans from the Confederacy were ineligible for the federal legislation; some received payments from state governments, though the amounts were generally much smaller than the federal pensions. The nation's first pension laws, although created initially out of military expediency, were the first large-scale programs that provided stable income for older Americans.

Due to the demands of industrialization, attitudes about the elderly began to change from the previous Calvinist-dominated era. In 1882, the famous British novelist Anthony Trollope published the dystopian (i.e., anti-utopian) novel *The Fixed Period*, about a fictional former British colony, Britannula, which had just passed legislation that required the euthanasia of all adults at the age of 68. The "Fixed Period" legislation was passed to improve the efficiency of society, to save the aged from the miseries and pains of old age, and to allocate resources that would have gone to serving the aged to the education of the young and improving the country's infrastructure. Trollope writes, "It [the Fixed Period legislation] would keep us out of debt, make for us our railways, render all our rivers navigable, construct our bridges, and leave us shortly the richest people on God's earth!" (Trollope, 1882, p. 12). The novel ends when the protagonist—the leader of the country and the architect of the legislation—gets dethroned by a group of British soldiers who were sent by the Crown to stop what is viewed as legislation contrary to "God's will."

Throughout the novel, there is discussion on the value of old people. One of the conflicts within the novel is that the first person who was set to be executed under the law was a hale and productive sheep farmer. Trollope wrote, "The poor fellow to whom nature has been unkind, departs from us decrepit and worn out at forty; whereas another at seventy is still hale and strong in performing the daily work of his life" (Trollope, 1882, p. 223). Trollope's fictional and satirical observations throughout the novel highlight the difficulties in applying one fixed policy that would apply equally to all. And although it is clear at the beginning of the novel that the "Fixed Period" legislation was presented as an alternative to scare individuals, it is also clear that Trollope desired the reader to think more closely about the difficulties of growing old and the need for society to come up with rationale policies for utilizing the talents of the aged as well as minimizing the burden to society that such care entails.

In 1905, William Osler, the first Professor of Medicine at Johns Hopkins University, gave a farewell address that was much discussed at the time; Osler relied on many of Trollope's arguments to give a widely disseminated speech about mandatory retirement at the age of 60. In addition, in a spirit of provocative argument, he advocated chloroforming everyone over 60 so that society would not have to be burdened by caring for Americans who could no longer be productive employees. The tone of Trollope's novel and Osler's speech reflected the change in societal norms. Whereas previous generations and societies had valued old age and the elderly, newer generations viewed the elderly as a burden.

With rapid industrialization and its incumbent technological changes in the workplace, employers worried about the capabilities of older workers to adapt to the new technology. For example, Graebner highlighted technological changes in the printing industry brought about by Ottmar Mergenthaler's invention of the Linotype machine, which revolutionized the nature of the industry. Older workers were trained to set type by hand, experience that was no longer necessary (Graebner, 1980). Companies refused to hire older workers, including age requirements in job ads, and they even terminated employment of older workers.

In addition to concerns about older workers' capacity to adapt to technological changes, Frederick Taylor's *The Principles of Scientific Management* stressed streamlining production and increasing efficiency by timing work processes and setting standards that employees would be held to. Taylor's writing emphasized the physical nature of work and the need for speed and strength (e.g., Taylor, 1911). Employers were concerned that older workers would not be able to handle the sped-up demands of the faster assembly lines. Given the focus on technological advances and efficiency, organizations viewed older workers as burdens and undesirable. During this period, retirement from work, as before, was infrequent and reserved for individuals with wealth. It would take the economic upheaval of the next period to create the infrastructure and institutions needed for broad-based retirement.

1920s to 1945

The workplaces of the 1920s and early 1930s were characterized by the chaos brought about by aggressive actions of labor unions who wished to exert control in the workplace and the equally aggressive counteractions by organizations who wished to maintain complete control of their employees. Unions used aggressive tactics, including taking over company property through sit-down strikes, boycotts, and even sabotage. Companies hired spies to infiltrate unions, used the racial prejudices of their employees against each other, and forced employees to sign "yellow-dog contracts," which forbade employees from organizing into unions. During this time, employers changed their attitudes toward older workers. Whereas at the beginning of industrialization employers were reluctant to hire older workers because of their perceived physical limitations, in this new era older workers were viewed more positively for a different reason. Employers believed that

older workers would be more conservative and less likely to join militant labor unions.

The Great Depression hit the United States during the fall of 1929. The stock market crash of October 29, 1929, was followed by bank closings, business and housing foreclosures, and an economic depression that circled the globe and lasted until spending due to World War II brought economies into full employment. Between 1932 and 1938, the unemployment within the United States fluctuated from 16.9% to 23.6%. This terrible economic crisis led governments around the world to rethink their roles within their economies and to take significant steps to make sure that such a deep recession would be unlikely to happen in the future.

Franklin Delano Roosevelt (FDR) defeated President Herbert Hoover in the 1932 election, largely due to the public's frustration about President Hoover's hands-off approach to ending the economic crisis as well as Roosevelt's promise of a "New Deal" to resolve the crisis. The New Deal legislation addressed a variety of issues that FDR and his cabinet thought were necessary to produce long-term stability within the U.S. economy. The Fair Labor Standards Act of 1938 set a minimum wage and maximum number of hours for most occupations; the Works Progress Administration created a government agency that employed Americans to build up the infrastructure through the United States, building dams, bridges, and highways among other things; the Wagner Act provided a framework for which labor unions could legally represent employees through collective bargaining. Other legislation dealt with agriculture, banking, and housing. But the most important piece of legislation relevant for this chapter was the Social Security Act passed in 1935.

Although there were pension programs enacted for veterans and government workers, and some individual state programs, it was only during the Great Depression that Congress enacted sweeping legislation that would eventually influence directly or indirectly the retirement experiences of nearly all Americans. Prior to the Great Depression, individual states had begun to enact their own legislation to address old-age economic security. In the 1920s, eight states allowed individual counties to provide old-age pensions, with two states (Minnesota and Wisconsin) providing state assistance to counties that chose to pay these pensions. According to Douglas (1971), the motivations for the passage of the optional pension laws were the increasing percentage of citizens who were elderly plus the increased levels of unemployment of these elderly. Douglas estimated the 1930 level of unemployment among those over 65 to be 41.7% compared to 26.2% in 1890. As the economic depression worsened, individual states passed stronger old-age pension laws. In 1929, California and Wyoming passed mandatory pension legislation that paid old-age pensions to everyone over 65. Additional states soon followed; by the summer of 1934, twenty-eight states had enacted old-age pension laws, with most of those being mandatory. With this swarm of state-level activity, it would have been difficult for the federal government to not consider its own federal law.

In addition to the bevy of state-level legislation, pressure was put on the federal government by heightened grassroots activism in this area. A retired physician, Dr. Francis Townsend, proposed a plan, referred to as the Townsend Plan, that would give all Americans over the age of 60 a stipend of $200 each month. Adjusting for inflation, that amount would translate into roughly $3,200 per month in 2009 U.S. dollars. The plan required those receiving the stipend to not work, thus reducing unemployment for younger employees. In addition, the plan required individuals to spend the money within 30 days, thus providing demand for goods and services to help bolster flagging industries. To pay for the tax, Townsend proposed a national sales tax of 2%. The plan had widespread support among the public, with a reported 20 million people having signed a petition expressing support for the plan. On the other hand, economists were generally not supportive of the plan, and FDR administration officials and congressional officials were disdainful as well.

In the midst of these various pressures, FDR created a Commission on Economic Security in June of 1934 and tasked that committee with coming up with its own federal old-age pension legislation in addition to dealing with unemployment. The commission consisted of cabinet members chaired by the remarkable Secretary of Labor Frances Perkins, who had served with then Governor of New York Roosevelt as his State Industrial Commissioner and in her role of Secretary of Labor was the first female cabinet member. The executive director was Professor Edwin Witte from the University of Wisconsin's Economics Department, a program that was groundbreaking in dealing with progressive employment legislative. In addition, there were a series of business leaders who served as advisors to the commission. The decisions that were made

by this important commission would have a lasting impact on the nature of retirement.

The commission proposed several types of old-age assistance, with the primary type being contributory annuities for which employees would have mandatory deductions taken out of their paychecks and invested into a general retirement fund from which their benefits would then come from. Additional provisions were made for non-contributory payments; these plans would cover those individuals who had not had time to contribute to the trust fund (e.g., they were already over 65 at the time of enactment). These noncontributory payments were proposed to be given only to those individuals who did not have sufficient income to support themselves (determined via a means-test). The commission specifically did not want a means-test enacted for the main portion of the Social Security portion. It was thought that if this pension was given to all individuals, regardless of income, that there would be more broad-based support from the general public.

The Commission on Economic Security chose the age of 65 for retirement, balancing the expense of having a lower age with the desire to gain political support by having the age as low as possible (Costa, 1998). There were several precedents for 65 as the retirement age. The U.S. Army pensions were given to those who were 65 or older unless they were "unusually vigorous." In addition, the 1910 Massachusetts Commission on Old Age and the Post Office used 65 as a cutoff, as did numerous state pension plans and railroad retirements (Costa, 1998). Although this age was chosen based on some precedents, it also created its own precedent that would imprint the age of 65 into the minds of Americans as the age of retirement.

The Social Security Act signed by President Roosevelt on August 14, 1935, was the first comprehensive federal legislation that aimed to cover nearly all American workers. This program was one of the crowning achievements of President Roosevelt's New Deal, which was designed to alleviate poverty and provide long-term security to Americans, which would in turn help alleviate some of the extreme ups and downs of business cycles. As will be noted throughout the rest of the chapter, there have been significant changes to the Social Security program as enacted in 1935. These changes have typically worked to expand the coverage of the program and to tighten up its financial solvency. The first such revision occurred in 1939, during which the program was expanded to include payments for dependent spouses and children, in addition to increasing the amount of payments.

The passage of Social Security was highly controversial, as was its initial assessment. Businesspeople argued that the act would hurt free enterprise and there was, in fact, an initial economic recession that followed the passage of the act, which provided some vindication for some of these critics. In the long term, public support for the Social Security program became quite strong, and it seems indisputable to claim that the original legislation has provided the single most important framework for influencing the retirement behavior of Americans.

Another milestone that occurred during this time was that the first systematic scientific analyses of aging were published. Sir Humphrey Rolleston published *Medical Aspects of Old Age* in 1922 — one of the first medical investigations into aging. Rolleston concluded that genetics played an important role in the aging process but that diet, exercise, and relaxation were likely to have an influence on the effects of aging as well. In the same year, noted psychologist G. Stanley Hall published *Senescence or the Last Half of Life*, which might be the first book-length treatment of the psychological issues faced by growing old. Hall wrote this book after he retired from the presidency of Clark University, a university he helped found in 1889, and was struggling himself with issues of life's meaning and the physical demands of old age. Hall's survey of aging was wide-ranging and included chapters on medical views, historical analysis, the psychology of death, and survey responses of eminent people on their own experiences of aging. One scholar has called Hall's book the first important work in gerontology by an American social scientist (Cole, 1984). These works were important for creating the foundation for a scientific discipline that could investigate the complicated and multidimensional issues related to aging, and especially retirement, that would flourish in the next wave of social science scholars.

In short, this period was perhaps the most important era in the United States in terms of influencing retirement policy and behavior. The first broad-based federal legislation was passed, which created the framework for retirement that exists today, with some important modifications. In addition, the foundation for scientific research into the problems of aging in general, and retirement specifically, was begun during this period. As will be seen, in the next period, the foundation for a broad-based retirement system was expanded through research and legislation.

1945 to 1990

After the initial passage of the Social Security Act and its 1939 revisions, the federal government made significant other modifications to the important act. Revisions in 1950 and throughout the 1970s added additional industries (e.g., hotel workers, agricultural workers, state and federal employees) to the coverage and added regular cost-of-living adjustments to Social Security payouts. Another significant addition to the Social Security legislation was Medicare, which was passed in 1965 by President Lyndon Johnson as part of his Great Society legislation. Medicare was part of the Social Security Act of 1965 and provided for government-funded health insurance for older workers. Medicare is supported by matching contributions by employers and employees through payroll withholding taxes. Later additions to Medicare included a prescription drug benefit, though the initial plan consisted of medical and hospital coverage. The addition of Medicare was useful in providing additional security to seniors. The original Social Security legislation included monthly payments to seniors but did not address health care costs. The Medicare addition provided more assurance that important needs would be provided to most senior Americans.

Although the Social Security Act and its expansions were designed to provide more security and stability for workers in retirement, there were other issues related to older workers unaddressed by that legislation. The Age Discrimination in Employment Act (ADEA) of 1967 prohibited employers from discriminating against employees aged 40 or older. This prohibited employers from refusing to hire workers older than 40 and discriminating against them in layoffs, promotions, or wages. In addition, companies were no longer able to include age requirements in job ads. The opening of the act stated the motivation for it: "in the face of rising productivity and affluence, older workers find themselves disadvantaged in their efforts to retain employment, and especially to regain employment when displaced from jobs." The preamble to the act also mentions that arbitrary age discrimination "burdens commerce and the free flow of goods in commerce."

The ADEA was similar to the Civil Rights Act of 1964, which prohibited discrimination based on race, religion, and other protected classes. Some small differences existed, however. The Civil Rights Act exempted companies with fewer than fifteen employees, whereas the ADEA increased the exempted organizations to those with fewer than twenty employees, thus providing less protection for employees in small businesses. Both acts allowed for organizations to discriminate in the case of bona fide occupational qualifications (BFOQs), where in the case of age it would be "reasonably necessary to the normal operation of the particular business" (Age Discrimination in Employment Act, 1967).

The Mandatory Retirement Act of 1978 eliminated mandatory retirement ages for most federal jobs and most in the private sector. Exceptions were made for defense and law enforcement positions as well as some executive positions. This act radically changed the nature of retirement. Passage of the act recognized that there were significant differences among individuals in terms of the aging process. No single age could meaningfully sort people into effective workers and too-old workers. In addition, retirement now became a voluntary act, allowing employees to work longer if they desired or to retire earlier if that was their fancy. Allowing workers to retire early also stimulated the financial services industry to help develop tools and techniques that were designed to help workers save better so that they could take into account early retirement.

In 1983, the National Commission on Social Security Reform (NCSSR) was constituted by President Reagan, chaired by Alan Greenspan, and tasked with preserving the long-term solvency of the Social Security system. There were some concerns that the Social Security Trust Fund would go bankrupt in less than ten years and needed corrections. The commission considered altering the nature of Social Security by making it voluntary (not mandatory) or that benefits would be paid only to those who needed them financially (means-testing). Those modifications were rejected with the goal of maintaining the basic structure of the legislation while modifying the funding structure to cope with some demographic demands. The fixes to Social Security would make the program solvent well into the twenty-first century, though as will be noted, future politicians proposed changes, small or fundamental, to the nature of Social Security even as the original design of the program remained relatively intact.

In addition to the growth of federal legislation, private industry created their own incentive systems to attract good talent and to encourage older employees to retire at a time that would be beneficial to the organization. The growth of private pensions accelerated during this period, especially as the influence of labor unions increased. Workers in the auto industry collectively bargained for pensions that provided a defined monthly payment to workers after retirement. In 1940, 3.7 million employees were covered by private-sector pensions, whereas that number increased to 19 million private-sector employees covered by pensions in 1958 (Achenbaum, 1983). Employee benefit plans were expanded to include wages but also benefits that helped maintain their old-age security.

In terms of employer attitudes toward older workers, this period might be considered an interesting case study to understand the role of external economic forces on employer attitudes. During the war years, employers turned to a variety of previously neglected sources of labor to cope with the shortage of able-bodied younger males (their typical preferred source of labor). Women, led by Rosie the Riveter, made historic inroads into business, replacing men in a variety of jobs and industries that had previously been shut off from them. Minorities, especially African Americans, made similar gains. In addition, older workers were hired back into the workforce at high rates. After the war, though, as returning soldiers came back and demanded their old jobs back, older workers fell back out of favor.

During this time, migration due to retirement increased dramatically. Retirees began moving to Florida from colder climates in the Midwest and the Northeast. By 1960, 4,000 new residents had moved to Florida, making it disproportionately older. In the period between 1950 and 1960, there was an 80% increase in elderly residents. This rapid influx of retirees created many challenges for the communities in which they chose to live. Many retirees had little other than their monthly Social Security check and hoped to be able to find at least part-time employment, providing challenges to communities that had few jobs. In addition, low-cost housing communities were needed for people with various degrees of mobility. Finally, social services agencies were ill-prepared to deal with the specialized needs that an increased influx of senior citizens entailed.

The communities and government soon adapted to the stresses brought about by the large number of retirees. For example, the city of St. Petersburg, which had once tried to recruit all retirees, worked hard to explain to potential residents that they would need to have at least $250 in fixed income per month and that they could expect few job opportunities. In addition, housing experts worked hard to develop new housing facilities that were designed to meet the needs of the elderly, including suggestions for "wider doorways," "dwelling units on one floor reached by few, if any, stairs," and "handrails for stairs and hand-grips for bathtubs" (Cole, 1957,

p. 23). In addition, high-end retirement communities were being developed throughout the country that provided many amenities and luxuries as well as on-site access to medical care.

Just like in the previous era, when older Americans organized politically (under the Townsend Plan), older Americans organized to better lobby Congress and increase their political clout. Dr. Ethel Percy Andrus, who was a retired high school principal, formed the National Retired Teachers Association (NRTA) in 1947 as a way to provide health insurance to retired teachers, in addition to providing awareness for a more healthy life after retirement. In 1958, the NRTA evolved into the American Association of Retired Persons (AARP) with the following founding principles: "to promote independence, dignity and purpose for older persons; to enhance the quality of life for older persons; to encourage older people 'to serve, not to be served'" (AARP History, accessed 3/17/2011). By the early 1960s, AARP had around 400,000 members, with rapid growth afterward so that by the mid-70s there were 7 million members (Lohmann, 2001). In 1999, the organization changed its name to be represented only by the acronym (and dropped any reference to the American Association of Retired Persons), given that by then they were accepting members who were over the age of 50 but not yet retired. At the current time, AARP is one of the largest nonprofit organizations in the world and one of the country's most powerful lobbying forces.

During this period, research into the general process of aging, and retirement in particular, began to gain its separate identity as a viable research area. In England, the Nuffield Research Unit into the Problems of Ageing was founded at Cambridge University. Researchers in that lab conducted experimental research on the decline in physical and mental performance due to aging (see Macnicol, 2006). The Gerontological Society of America was formed in 1945 and the next year began publishing the *Journal of Gerontology*. During this time, graduate training programs in gerontology started to focus on the needs and challenges of older Americans. The Ethel Percy Andrus Gerontology Center was formed at the University of Southern California (USC) in 1964, with the Leonard Davis School of Gerontology founded at USC in 1975. The Andrus Center is an interdisciplinary research center that promotes research on a variety of issues such as fall prevention and memory loss, whereas the Davis School is a degree-granting entity that was the nation's first doctoral program in gerontology. During this time, the academic community adapted to the needs of aging populations and began research in earnest on the unique and important issues related to aging.

During this time, research specific to the topic of retirement began being conducted in earnest. Some of the first published articles were conducted by industrial sociologists who focused on specific types of jobs (e.g., retirement experiences of ministers; Moore & Hammer, 1948) or focused on helping retired workers adapt to experiences after the war (e.g., Wermel & Gelbaum, 1945). During this time, industrial psychologists (later to be called industrial-organizational psychologists) began to study retirement, though as a whole they were slower to focus on retirement than their sociology counterparts. Some of these early studies focused on attitudes toward retirement (e.g., Saleh & Otis, 1963). Patricia Cain Smith and colleagues created and validated a retirement satisfaction scale that was one of the first attempts to apply the psychometric tools of industrial psychology to retirement (Smith, Kendall, & Hulin, 1969). With these early studies, a foundation of research was being developed that would be expanded upon in future years and by subsequent scholars.

This period consolidated and refined many of the advances made in the previously more revolutionary period. The increase in access to retirement through federal legislation suggested many different areas that individuals, businesses, communities, and governments needed to adapt to the changing realities of more older citizens. As will be demonstrated in the next section, these entities adapted in many significant ways to make retirement and old age more productive, less painful, and more enjoyable for most Americans. Throughout this period, American workers adapted to the new freedom brought about by more prosperous retirement plans and options. Retirement communities redesigned what it meant to live to older ages, and pockets of individuals flocked to mild climates, transforming areas of the country in the Southeast and Southwest.

1990 to 2010 and Onward

Although it may be harder to characterize the recent past, there are several trends that need to be commented on. The population grew older as health care improved. In addition, companies cut back private pension plans as the government encouraged private saving through various tax incentive plans. In addition, older workers were at times welcomed back into the workforce, as they were viewed as fulfilling important work-related roles.

The U.S. government struggled with how to cope with an older population who would have less money available to them through private pension plans. The decline in private pensions began in the 1980s and continued through this period (see Bloom & Freeman, 1992; Even & Macpherson, 1994). As concerns for the federal government's deficit grew, the government considered various revisions to the Social Security Act. President George W. Bush advocated taking a small percentage of their Social Security contributions and investing those dollars into private stock funds. The proposal never gained traction with the Democratic party-controlled legislature and seemed even more unlikely after the crash of the stock market in 2008 and the victory of President Barack Obama.

Meanwhile, the federal government created financial tools that would help workers to save more for retirement and to supplement and replace company pension plans, which were waning in prevalence. Roth individual retirement accounts (IRAs) allowed workers to contribute post-tax income into accounts, which would then not be taxed on withdrawal. 401(k) plans allowed employees to contribute pre-tax dollars to a savings account, thus reducing their taxable income. Many organizations encouraged employee retirement saving by matching contributions up to a certain limit. Increasingly, those matched contributions replaced pension plans as organizations' retirement benefits. These savings plans used incentives in the tax code to increase the savings rate of individual Americans. By nearly all accounts, such programs have been very successful in increasing the savings of Americans to better prepare them for retirement. The federal government significantly increased the amount that individuals could contribute into these accounts, thus making these programs potentially even more significant.

Retirement planning became a big industry within this time. Financial advisors worked hard to attract younger workers and provide them with the planning expertise to help advisees retire with comfort and to retire early if possible. Computer programs were developed to help model the amount of resources that individuals had. Most analysts suggested that typical Americans were not saving as much as they would need to retire at the age and level of luxury that they desired, which distressed lawmakers who worried that these individuals would depend on the government to provide the medical care and living expenses that they were unable to provide for themselves. In addition, the public was wary of the ability of Social Security to provide for future generations, even though most economists viewed the Trust Fund as more solvent than most Americans did.

Social scientists began to study retirement in much more volume than in previous generations, as evidenced by this handbook. Concepts such as *bridge employment* were named even if, as shown in this chapter, these types of employment situations (i.e., gradually reducing the number of hours from full employment to complete retirement) existed long before the concept's name. Complex statistical methodologies, especially those that incorporated longitudinal analyses necessary for studying people over time, were used to answer sophisticated hypotheses about responses to retirement. Research into ageism (i.e., discrimination based on age) proliferated. Even though the notion of discrimination against workers because of their age had existed throughout the period studied in this chapter, systematic research specific to this kind of discrimination did not flourish until this period. In short, retirement research made many advances (see Wang & Shultz, 2010) and began adapting to the demands of the aging population.

Certain business writers advocated that companies consider hiring older workers because older workers were more dedicated and less likely to leave for other companies (e.g., Byham, 2007). In addition, many older workers could be employed at lower salaries and with less training costs. Just like in previous eras, however, older employees had difficulty in areas that required sophisticated technological advances. Given that much of the economic growth of this era was in areas of high-tech computer and internet developments, older employees had difficulties in these important aspects of the economy. One blogger commented that in the renewable energy sector, recruitment materials on websites clearly targeted workers under 30 (Mitchell, 2011). In the economic recession at the end of this period, workers over 45 were more likely to be unemployed for long periods of time (i.e., over six months) compared to younger workers. In addition, age discrimination complaints increased at the beginning of the recession (see Luo, 2009).

Although it is difficult to characterize recent historical phenomena, this period seems characterized by more individual stakes in retirement planning with less reliance on government planning. Older individuals seemed to have more difficulty coping with the economic recession of this time period, as employers were reluctant to hire them given an abundance of workers from which to choose. The social scientists investigating retirement became more sophisticated in their hypotheses and their methodologies.

Lessons Learned

This has been an idiosyncratic review of retirement; I have tried to cover as many of the significant trends over the years as possible to give readers a sense of the transformation of the concept of retirement and how it has changed dramatically throughout the ages of recorded history. Based on my review, I provide a few generalizations that I hope can be "takeaway" messages.

Lesson Learned 1: The experience of retirement is relatively modern. Up until the 1930s, very few people experienced retirement the way that most Americans now experience it (or at least expect to experience it). In prehistoric times, most people simply failed to live to the age that demanded retirement. In ancient times, even as life spans increased, there was little infrastructure or distribution of wealth to support mass retirement. From the Greek and Roman times until the New Deal, only the wealthy had the ability or the means to disengage from the world of work. Most individuals had to work until their deaths, though many were forced to change the nature of their work to accommodate their declining physical capabilities. After the New Deal and the state-level reforms that occurred around the same time, retirement became an increasingly attainable goal for Americans regardless of class or wealth. But the expectations of today's Americans would not even have seemed possible to most Americans 150 years ago.

Lesson Learned 2: The nature of retirement is influenced by economic conditions. The experience of older Americans will always be influenced by the current economic conditions. The desirability of older workers is a good example. In the 1920s, older workers were viewed as undesirable given the fast pace of the assembly lines and the thought that most could not adapt to the quickened pace. And then, in the 1930s, older workers were viewed as desirable given the thought that they were more conservative and less likely to join radical labor unions. During World War II, older workers were again courted to return to the workplace to cope with the labor shortage as younger male workers were sent overseas. Finally, in the current recession, along with the increased technological demands of jobs, older workers are viewed less desirable. Retirement researchers who ignore the importance of the economic context will fail to understand the experience of retirement as it exists in the minds of their participants.

Lesson Learned 3: To understand retirement, you need to know a lot of things! No one discipline has a complete understanding of the concept of retirement. The study of retirement as a serious scientific question arose in the 1920s, about the same time as social science was maturing. Important advances in the understanding of retirement have been made by sociologists, psychologists, economists, health experts, and increasingly by those who identify themselves as gerontologists. Each of these separate disciplines has something to add to the understanding of retirement, but in isolation each discipline misses an important aspect (as mentioned in my first point about economics).

Final Lesson Learned: There is still a lot to learn. The historical study of old age and retirement is relatively recent, with most important works coming out in the last thirty to thirty-five years. There is much to learn about the history of retirement in ancient times as well as the experience of retirement in more recent times. Given how much the concept of retirement has changed, it is important that historians avoid viewing their material through the lens of today's understanding of retirement.

Notes

1. "Too Old to Work" by Joe Glazer on Classic Labor Songs available on Folkways Records.

References

Achenbaum, W. A. (1978). *Old age in the new land: The American experience since 1790.* Baltimore, MD: Johns Hopkins University Press.

Achenbaum, W. A. (1983). *Old age, American values, and federal policies since 1920.* Boston, MA: Little, Brown, and Company.

Administration on Aging. (2010). *Projected future growth of the older population.* Retrieved from http://www.aoa.gov/aoaroot/aging_statistics/future_growth/future_growth.aspx

Age Discrimination in Employment Act. (1967). Retrieved from http://www.eeoc.gov/laws/statutes/adea.cfm.

Arias, E. (2010). *United States life tables, 2006.* (National vital statistics reports, Vol. 58, No. 21). Hyattsville, MD: National Center for Health Statistics.

Bloom, D. E., & Freeman, R. B. (1992). *The fall in private pension coverage in the U.S.* (NBER Working Paper No. 3973). Cambridge, MA: National Bureau of Economic Research.

Byham, W. C. (2007). *70: The new 50.* Bridgeville, PA: DDI Press.

Cole, A. H. (1957, Aug. 4). What the aged need in their homes. *New York Times Magazine,* pp. 23–27.

Cole, T. R. (1984). The prophecy of senescence: G. Stanley Hall and the reconstruction of old age in America. *The Gerontologist, 24,* 360–366.

Cook, S. (1972). Aging of and in populations. In P. Timiras (Ed.), *Developmental physiology and aging* (p. 595). New York, NY: Macmillan.

Costa, D. L. (1998). *The evolution of retirement.* Chicago, IL: University of Chicago Press.

Douglas, P. H. (1971). *Social security in the United States: An analysis and appraisal of the federal Social Security Act.* New York, NY: Da Capo Press.

Even, W. E., & Macpherson, D. A. (1994). Why did male pension coverage decline in the 1980s? *Industrial and Labor Relations Review, 47,* 439–453.

Fischer, D. H. (1978). *Growing old in America.* New York, NY: Oxford University Press.

Graebner, W. (1980). *A history of retirement: The meaning and function of an American institution.* New Haven, CT: Yale University.

Hall, G. S. (1922). *Senescence or the last half of life.* New York, NY: D. Appleton.

Johnson, R. W., & Kaminski, J. (2010). *Older adults' labor force participation since 1993: A decade and a half of growth.* Urban Institute. Retrieved from http://www.urban.org/uploaded-pdf/412011_older_adults_labor_force.pdf.

Lohmann, R. A. (2001). An interview: Hoarce Deets of AARP. *Nonprofit Management and Leadership, 12,* 87–94.

Luo, M. (April 13, 2009). Longer unemployment for those 45 and older. *New York Times,* p. A11.

Macnicol, J. (2006). *Age discrimination: An historical and contemporary analysis.* Cambridge, England: Cambridge University Press.

Mitchell, B. (2011). *Age discrimination in the clean energy workforce?* Retrieved from www.renewableenergyworld.com/rea/blog/post/2011/03/is-your-company-discriminating-and-if-so-how-much-is-it-costing-you.

Moore, E. H., & Hammer, C. (1948). Ministers in retirement. *Sociology & Social Research, 32,* 920–927.

New American Standard Bible. (1995). La Habra, CA: Lockman Foundation.

Paine, T. (1797). *Agrarian Justice.* Retrieved from http://www.ssa.gov/history/tpaine3.html.

Ransom, R. L., & Sutch, R. (1986). The labor of older Americans: Retirement of men on and off the job, 1870–1937. *Journal of Economic History, 46,* 1–30.

Rolleston, H. (1922). *Medical aspects of old age.* London, England: Macmilllan.

Saleh, S. D., & Otis, J. L. (1963). Sources of job satisfaction and their effects on attitudes toward retirement. *Journal of Industrial Psychology, 1,* 101–106.

Shahar, S. (1997). *Growing old in the Middle Ages.* London, England: Routledge.

Smith, P. C., Kendall, L. M., & Hulin, C. L. (1969). *The measurement of satisfaction in work and retirement: A strategy for the study of attitudes.* Chicago, IL: Rand McNally.

Taylor, F. W. (1911). *The principles of scientific management.* New York, NY: Harper and Brothers.

Trollope, A. (1882). *The fixed period.* Leipzig, Germany: Tauchnitz.

Wang, M., & Shultz, K. S. (2010). Employment retirement: A review and recommendations for future investigation. *Journal of Management, 36,* 176–206.

Wermel, M. T., & Gelbaum, S. (1945). Work and retirement in old age. *American Journal of Sociology, 51,* 16–21.

The Demography of Aging and Retirement

Felicia Wheaton *and* Eileen M. Crimmins

Abstract

The United States is both aging and becoming more diverse. To understand the phenomenon of retirement, it is necessary to understand not only the demographic changes that are currently underway but also projections of change in the coming decades. This chapter examines how demography has intersected with public policy, as well as the characteristics of retirees and family dynamics, to shape retirement in the recent past and currently. Combining demographic projections with current knowledge about incentives and disincentives to work or retire allows extrapolation to potential scenarios for the future of retirement.

Key Words: retirement, demographics, population, policy

This chapter is focused on how demographic factors affect retirement patterns and the need for and supply of workers. Changes in population age structure are already well known for the next six to seven decades, which enables us to predict with some certainty the size and composition of the group that will be reaching retirement age. Demographic changes have transformed and will continue to transform both the labor force and the retirement-aged population not only in terms of size but also in terms of gender and racial/ethnic composition.

Demography alone, however, does not determine the destiny of a population; behavioral modifications can reduce or amplify the effect of demographic changes. Such behavioral alterations may occur in response to population change, but they are also affected by policy and economic factors. Long-term changes in the likelihood of working in the formal labor force, rate of pay, and entitlement to retirement income have occurred among women. Among men there have been long-term changes in occupational composition and retirement support options. These transformations mean that men and women

are approaching and entering retirement with novel characteristics and different options that are likely to change the institution of retirement.

What Is Retirement?

Although retirement is now viewed as a normal and expected life course transition in contemporary, industrialized societies, this is a relatively recent phenomenon. Voluntary exit from the workforce was not widespread until the increase in nonagricultural jobs and the creation of government and employer-sponsored pensions in the twentieth century (Thane, 2006). Employment rates of older male workers began to decline in 1880, but rates dramatically fell with the creation and expansion of Social Security retirement benefits and the rise of private pensions in the 1940s and 1950s in the United States (Costa, 1998). By the 1950s, higher retirement incomes, improved health, and the media firmly established the idea of the "golden years," or a period of leisure following a lifetime of work. The concept of retirement had come to signify a unidirectional transition from full-time work to complete withdrawal from the labor force, although this definition was biased toward middle-class males in traditional careers (Han & Moen, 1999).

More recently, retirement appears to be defined by many by receiving retirement benefits from either Social Security or a private pension. Many "retirees" continue to engage in some work for pay even as they collect pensions. So retirement can mean retiring from a long-term job and taking up full-time work while collecting a pension or social security. Because the notion of retirement is socially constructed, its meaning continues to evolve over time with changes in both incentives and disincentives to retire.

Since the 1970s, the definition of retirement has become increasingly heterogeneous due to a variety of factors including greater workforce diversity, labor market shifts away from manufacturing jobs to service jobs, a decline in defined benefit pensions, and institutional incentives that encourage delayed retirement. Early baby boomers (born 1942–1947) appear less likely than members of the GI generation (born 1913–1917) or Silent generation (born 1933–1937) to adhere to the traditional definition of retirement (Johnson, Butrica, & Mommaerts, 2010). Other retirement pathways, such as bridge employment, partial retirement, or continuation of work after claiming retirement benefits, have become more common among younger cohorts and have blurred the retirement transition (Szinovacz & DeViney, 1999). For example, over half of Americans aged 50+ who left full-time career jobs after age 50 first transitioned to bridge employment (Cahill, Giandrea, & Quinn, 2006). Also, nearly a third of those who retire were found to subsequently re-enter the workforce (Warner, Hayward, &

Hardy, 2010). Important differences in retirement are found by gender and race/ethnicity (Brown & Warner, 2008; Flippen & Tienda, 2000).

The heterogeneity of retirement has important implications for research, since the interpretation and comparability of findings are dependent upon how the concept is operationalized. Currently, a number of definitions are used, none of which is dominant (Denton & Spencer, 2009). Gustman and Steimeier (2000) identify five major definitions based on (1) subjective reports, (2) amount of time spent working, (3) transitional or bridge employment, (4) change in work activity, and (5) receipt of retirement benefits. In a study of retiree self-identity, employment status was the most strongly associated with identification as a retiree; however, receipt of a pension or Social Security benefits and being of retirement age were also found to be associated (Szinovacz & DeViney, 1999). Employing multiple definitions may facilitate better understanding of different aspects of retirement behavior and may be necessary for addressing different questions about retirement.

Changing Age Structure

Demographic changes are a major force behind discussions for the need for adjustments in retirement policies and practices. The United States has undergone a major revolution in age composition over the last century, and change will continue through the first part of this century. The U.S. population has aged, with growing numbers of people in the older or "retirement" ages (Figure 3.1). The population aged 65 and older has grown from only 3.1 million in 1900 to about 40.2 million in 2010 (Administration on Aging [AoA], 2010),

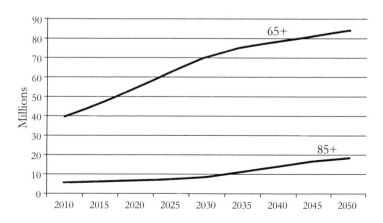

Figure 3.1 Projected Population (2010–2050) Age 65+ and 85+ in the United States
Source: U.S. Census Bureau, U.S. Population Projections: 2009 National Population Projections

but the growth is going to be even more rapid in the upcoming years as the number of people 65+ is projected to more than double to 88.5 million by 2050 (Vincent & Velkoff, 2010). The aged section of the population is also aging as the number and proportion of those 85 years of age and older are growing along with the overall growth in the older population. The population aged 85 and older will more than triple by 2050.

Population aging has occurred because of two factors: long-term decreases in fertility and mortality. Because of century-long declines in mortality at younger ages, more people have survived to older ages. In the last few decades, decreases in mortality at older ages have increased life expectancy beyond the age of retirement and increased the number of people in the older years. The decrease in fertility means that, in general, there are relatively fewer young people in the population as time goes on, increasing the proportion of the population that is older. Past fertility patterns, however, leave an imprint on the population as well. The high fertility during the baby boom, between 1946 and 1964, is going to be a major source of our future aging, as the oldest members of this cohort will turn 65 in 2011. Past, present, and future changes in population age structure are best illustrated by the changes in population pyramids over the six decades from 1980 to 2040 shown in Figure 3.2. The pyramids depict the growing number of people over the age of 65 relative to other age groups. In 1980, baby boomers were young members of the workforce aged 16 to 34; in 2010 they were older members of the workforce, aged 46 to 64 (Figure 3.2). In the coming years, this generation will enter the ranks of retirees. The result will be an increase in the proportion of the population in the retirement ages and at the oldest ages.

The population pyramids indicate the changing relative sizes of the young and old population. In relating age structure trends to potential economic effects, young and old members of society are assumed to be dependent, and those in the middle are assumed to be productive. The productive age groups support the dependent age groups; this is why population aging has important consequences for social policies and programs. The dependency ratio is a measure of the size of the dependent population relative to the working-age population (Figure 3.3). It indicates the number of people under age 20 and over age 65 per 100 working-age adults who are age 20 to 64. A higher dependency ratio signifies that there are fewer working-age adults to support each dependent. This can further be partitioned into old-age and youth dependency ratios. Largely because fertility is not expected to vary much, the youth dependency ratio is projected to remain stable over the next thirty years. On the other hand, the old-age dependency ratio is predicted to almost double from 22 in 2010 to 38 in 2040 (Figure 3.3). This will cause the overall dependency ratio to increase from 67 to 85 dependents per 100 working-age adults. Because most older persons are entitled to Social Security benefits and to Medicare, the size of the elderly population is of great and growing concern for policymakers.

Labor Force Participation

The dependency ratio represents the relative size of age groups, but whether it accurately reflects dependency is contingent upon the extent to which individuals in these age ranges are working and nonworking. Certainly, not all people between the ages of 20 and 64 are in the labor force, nor are all people 65 and over retired. At the young end of the age range, the average age at full-time employment has been rising over time as the length of schooling has increased. At the other end of the age range, the likelihood of working through and beyond age 65 had been falling for decades for men (Mosisa & Hipple, 2006). In fact, for some years, the modal age at retirement has been 62 (Warner, Hayward, & Hardy, 2010; Quinn, 2010). Since the mid-1980s, the trend toward earlier withdrawal from the labor force has stopped and reversed among older men (Quinn, 2010).

In order to understand retirement, it is useful to study the converse—labor force participation. Trends in labor force participation (LFP) rates between 1980 and 2010 differ substantially for men and women, with trends for men being less dramatic. In this time period, the labor force participation of men aged 50–54 and 55–59 declined by 3.9% and 3.2%, respectively (Figure 3.4). The labor force participation of men aged 60–64 increased after the early 90s when the period of decline turned around. The participation of older men rose over the whole period, by 8% for men aged 65–69 and 1.5% for men 70 and older. Among the older age groups, the changes signified a 28.1% increase from 1980 levels among men aged 65–69 and an 11.5% increase among those 70+.

In contrast to trends observed among men, labor force participation rose for women of all ages between 1980 and 2010 (Figure 3.5). In absolute terms, participation rates increased most for women

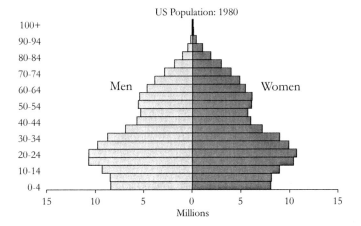

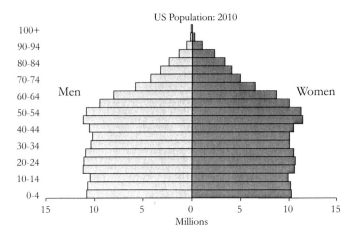

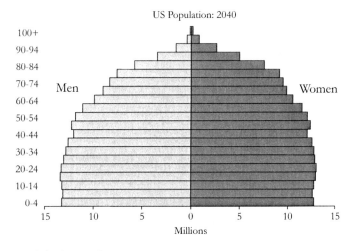

Figure 3.2 Population Pyramids for the United States
Source: U.S. Census Bureau, International Data Base

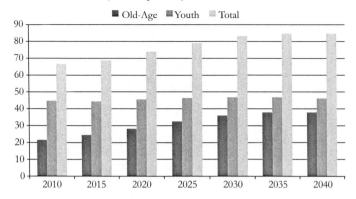

Figure 3.3 Projected Dependency Ratios for the United States, 2010–2040
Source: U.S. Census Bureau, U.S. Population Projections: 2009 National Population Projections,

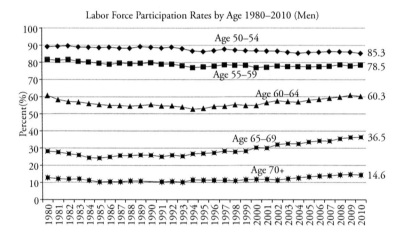

Figure 3.4 Male Labor Force Participation Rates by Age (1980–2010)
Source: U.S. Bureau of Labor Statistics, Labor Force Statistics from the Current Population Survey

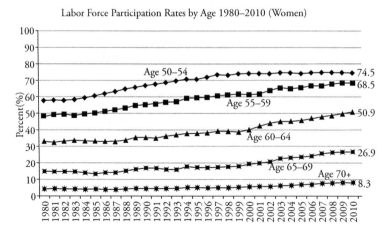

Figure 3.5 Female Labor Force Participation Rates by Age (1980–2010)
Source: U.S. Bureau of Labor Statistics, Labor Force Statistics from the Current Population Survey

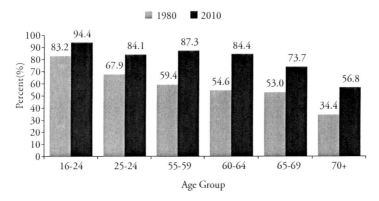

Figure 3.6 Ratio of Women's to Men's Labor Force Participation by Age (1980 vs. 2010)
Source: U.S. Bureau of Labor Statistics, Labor Force Statistics from the Current Population Survey

in the young-old age groups, but in relative terms, the percent increase was greatest for older women. The LFP of women aged 50–54 increased 16.7% from 57.8% to 74.5%, while the LFP of women aged 55–59 rose by 20%. The participation rates of women in the 60–64, 65–69, and 70+ age groups increased by 17.7%, 11.8%, and 3.8%, respectively. However, relative to LFP in 1980, there was a 78.1% and 84.4% increase among women aged 65–69 and 70+.

Because labor force participation at older ages has increased much more dramatically for women compared with relatively stable rates for men, the ratio of women's to men's labor force participation has increased among all age groups between 1980 and 2010, especially for those aged 55–64 (Figure 3.6).

In 2010, the likelihood of men and women being in the labor force is almost the same at age 16–24. Up until age 65, there are about 85 women in the labor force for every 100 men. Older men are still more likely to work relative to older women, although the gap has narrowed in the past thirty years.

While the workforce has become more female, it is also becoming more diverse in terms of racial and ethnic composition (Figure 3.7). In the coming decades, much of the growth of the labor force and the retirement-age population in the United States will come from Hispanic- and Asian-origin workers. These projections reflect past changes in the composition of the working age population.

Overall, these trends indicate that labor force participation has increased over the past thirty

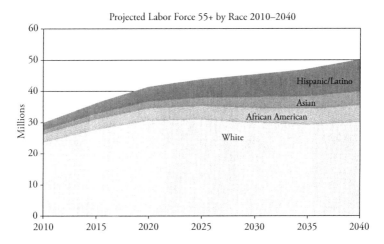

Figure 3.7 Projected Labor Force 55+ by Race 2010–2040
Source: U.S. Bureau of Labor Statistics, Employment Projections

years for both men and women aged 65 and older, though there has been a decline in male labor force participation at ages 50–59. Participation has also increased substantially for women of pre-retirement age (50–64), and the gap between men and women's participation has been greatly reduced. Taken together, it appears that a greater percentage of men and women at or past the traditional retirement age of 65 are remaining in the workforce compared to the past. Many factors may underlie this trend, including increased life expectancy, changing occupational characteristics, amendments to Social Security increasing the eligibility age for full benefits gradually to 67, changes in the economic profiles of workers, shifting patterns of familial demands, and changes in the types of pensions offered by employers.

Changes in the Incentives and Disincentives to Work or Retire

The likelihood of remaining in the labor force versus retiring is a function of competing incentives and disincentives to work. Who retires, when, why, and how depends on public policies, labor market policies, job availability, and worker characteristics including health, financial well-being, and educational attainment.

Public Policy

Social Security eligibility. Not only do public policies create economic incentives to retire or work, but they also contribute to retirement-age norms. Age is explicitly used to define eligibility for Social Security benefits, and laws regulating pensions and age discrimination are age-based. An amendment to Social Security in 1983 has gradually increased the normal retirement age for those born in 1938 and later by two months per year starting in 2000 and increased the penalty for claiming early retirement benefits. By 2027, the retirement age to receive full benefits will have increased from 65 to 67. Although retirement at age 62 is possible, benefits are reduced for early retirement; workers can earn delayed retirement credits by postponing retirement up until age 70. Mastrobuoni (2009) estimated that for individuals born between 1928 and 1941, the average retirement age has risen by about one month per year. Gustman and Steinmeier (2009) indicate that changes to Social Security resulted in a 9% increase in full-time work by men aged 65–67. They also attribute about 1/6 of the increase in labor force participation between 1998 and 2004 to changes in Social Security. On the other hand, 0.6% to 0.9%

more individuals aged 45–64 are estimated to have been enrolled in Social Security disability benefits in 2005 due to a reduction in the generosity of Social Security benefits (Duggan, Singleton, & Song, 2007). While more older workers are remaining in the workforce as a result of increases in the age of full eligibility for Social Security, middle-aged adults appear more likely to claim disability benefits, thus offsetting some of the increase in total labor force participation.

Although there is disagreement about the magnitude of effect of Social Security changes on retirement trends, it is clear that the 1983 amendments have influenced retirement age. This is further illustrated by the observation that Social Security claims now spike at the normal retirement age defined for each birth year under the new rules (e.g., 65 and 2 months for individuals born in 1938), rather than at age 65 (Song & Manchester, 2007b). Finally, since the gradual increase in retirement age will not be complete until 2027, further effects may be seen in the years to come.

Another factor encouraging work at older ages was the passage of the Senior Citizens' Freedom to Work Act in 2000. This eliminated the earnings test for individuals aged 65–70, removing work disincentives among those receiving Social Security benefits. Previously, a proportion of benefits was withheld from workers earning above a certain threshold. The abolishment of the earnings test was associated with both a 0.8% to 2% increase in the work participation rate among those aged 65–69 and an increase in applications for Social Security benefits (Song & Manchester, 2007a). The simultaneous increase in both benefit applications and workforce participation suggests that more individuals are claiming retirement benefits while still working, thus challenging the traditional notion of retirement.

Age Discrimination in Employment Act (ADEA). Legislation pertaining to older workers, such as the Age Discrimination in Employment Act (ADEA) of 1968, may influence the decision to remain in the labor force. Currently, the ADEA protects workers aged 40 and older from age discrimination in hiring, compensation, and termination and prohibits mandatory retirement for most occupations. The impact of the ADEA, however, is dependent upon enforcement by the Equal Employment Opportunity Commission (EEOC), which is responsible for investigating violations filed by employees. Charges related to discharge or layoffs are the most common (40.4%), while hiring discrimination represents only 8.4% of cases (Neumark, 2009). Difficulty in pursuing cases of hiring discrimination may be increasingly consequential for more recent cohorts of older workers who perhaps experience less job stability (Kalleberg, 2009), particularly since older workers have more difficulty finding a new job after becoming unemployed (Lippmann, 2008).

Pensions and Health Insurance

Employers have historically created incentives or disincentives to work/retire, depending on current labor needs, via the provision and characteristics of a pension and/or retiree health benefits. Employer-sponsored pensions can be divided into two major types: defined benefit (DB) and defined contribution (DC). Defined benefit plans provide a specified monthly benefit in retirement using a formula determined by age, job tenure, and earnings history. A worker becomes eligible to receive full benefits after a specified number of years, which is determined by the employer. This encourages long-term employment with one company but creates disincentives to work past attainment of full eligibility, and in some cases those who continue work may even incur a penalty. Defined contribution pensions specify the annual contribution of the employer, which may be matched by the employee, but in contrast to DB plans, benefits are not guaranteed. Instead, retirement benefits are dependent upon investment performance, and the account balance can continue to grow substantially with additional employment. Thus, DC plans lack an age-related incentive to retire and may even encourage work beyond traditional retirement age. In fact, relative to those with a DB pension, workers with a

DC plan retire two years later on average (Friedberg & Webb, 2005). Thus, change in the prevalence of DB versus DC plans is likely to impact labor force participation rates.

In the past thirty years, there has been a steady decline in the number of private-sector workers with defined benefit plans, and a simultaneous increase in those enrolled in a defined contribution pension plan (Figure 3.8). In 1980, 28% of workers were enrolled in DB plans, compared to 8% in DC plans. Yet in 2008, these numbers were essentially reversed: 31% participated in DC plans, and only 3% had a DB plan. The number enrolled in both DB and DC plans was relatively unchanged over this time period, with roughly 11%–12% participating in both types of plans in 1980 and 2008.

In addition to pensions, the availability of employer-sponsored retiree health insurance can influence the decision to either retire or remain in the labor force. Currently, 43% of retired individuals aged 55–64 depend on retiree health insurance from their or their spouses' prior employer (Monk & Munnell, 2009). In general, retiree health benefits are much more likely to be offered to those employed in large firms, unionized occupations, and the public sector (Claxton et al., 2008). Since older adults become eligible for Medicare at age 65 and only after earning sufficient work credits, employer-sponsored retiree health insurance is an important benefit for those who wish to retire prior to age 65. Health insurance premiums in the individual market are often costly for adults at pre-retirement ages because they are at higher risk of age-related diseases, and many already have

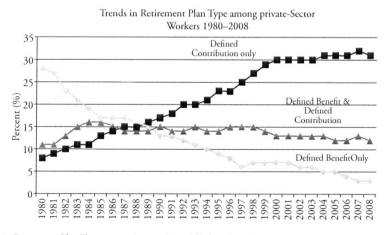

Figure 3.8 Trends in Retirement Plan Type among Private-Sector Workers (1980–2008)
Source: U.S. Department of Labor Form 5500 Summaries for 1979–1998; Current Population Survey data for 1999–2008; Employee Benefit Research Institute estimates for 1999–2008.

pre-existing chronic conditions. Other options, such as forgoing health insurance or enrolling in a spouse's employer-sponsored plan, may be less attractive and more costly (Monk & Munnell, 2009). With retiree health insurance, however, retirees maintain access to group rates. Therefore, the availability of retiree health insurance will tend to encourage early retirement, whereas the lack of retiree health insurance may discourage retirement before age 65 but have little effect on retirement incentives past age 65. Monk and Munnell (2009) find that if retiree health insurance were eliminated, there would be a 7% increase in the workforce aged 55–64, but no effect on retirement decisions among those 65 and older. Conversely, access to retiree health insurance is associated with a 15% to 80% increase in the probability of retirement, depending on the models used by different studies (Monk & Munnell, 2009). The influence of having health insurance available appears to be stronger among those in poor health (Blau & Gilleskie, 2008). Finally, a provision in the recently passed Affordable Care Act called the Early Retiree Reinsurance Program makes insurance available for retirees who are not yet eligible for Medicare. Although this program provides assistance only to employers who maintain health insurance coverage for early retirees age 55 and older until 2014, early retirees will then be able to enroll in health insurance exchanges (Early Retiree Reinsurance Program, http://www.errp.gov).

Over time, there has been a substantial decline in the availability of health insurance to retirees. Of firms with 200+ employees who offered health benefits, two-thirds offered retiree health insurance in 1988, compared to only 33% in 2008, a decline of 50% over the twenty-year span (Claxton et al., 2008). As health care costs continue to escalate, it is likely that this negative trend in coverage will continue and retiree health insurance plans that do survive may become less generous, particularly those offered to early pre-65 retirees (Kaiser/Hewitt, 2006). Several strategies exist for employers who seek to cut spending on current retiree benefits and reduce liability for future retirees. Employers may terminate health plans for new retirees, impose additional eligibility and vesting requirements, or shift a greater share of the costs to retirees in the form of deductibles, copayments, and premiums (Monk & Munnell, 2009). Of 299 large-sized firms surveyed in 2006 that provided coverage to pre-65 retirees, three-quarters increased pre-65 contributions to premiums since 2005, a third increased cost-sharing and out-of-pocket limits, while 11%

eliminated benefits for future pre-retirees and 4% increased eligibility age and/or vesting rules (Kaiser/Hewitt, 2006). Firms also indicated that they were likely to restrict coverage and generosity of retiree insurance plans over the next year from 2006 to 2007. If retiree health insurance continues to erode, the result will be a greater incentive for individuals age 55–64 to remain in the workforce who might have otherwise opted for early retirement.

Worker Characteristics

Health. Older workers approaching retirement today differ in many important ways from earlier generations of retirees. Baby boomers arguably have a greater capacity to work past the traditional retirement age of 65 due to increased life expectancy and decreased disability. Between 1970 and 2006, life expectancy at birth increased from 67.1 to 75.1 years among men (an 8-year increase) and from 74.7 to 80.2 among women, or a 5.5-year gain in life expectancy (National Center for Health Statistics [NCHS], 2010). Over the same period, life expectancy at age 65 increased for men and women by 3.9 and 2.7 years, respectively. This means that the length of time spent in retirement has increased substantially. In order to maintain solvency of the Social Security system and retiree benefits, there is substantial pressure to extend workforce participation to respond to the increased life expectancy.

Trends in the health of older adults near retirement age have been less clear-cut. Findings vary depending on the measure of health and time period examined. In general, the prevalence of many chronic conditions increased in the 1980s and 1990s, while disability and functional limitations declined (Crimmins, 2004; Manton, 2008). Between 1982 and 1993, there was a significant increase in reported ability to work among those in their 60s, which was explained by increases in education, health behaviors, better health over the life course, and a decline in arthritis, cardiovascular, and cerebrovascular diseases (Crimmins, Reynolds, & Saito, 1999). In a more recent study examining trends between 1997 and 2007, small but significant decreases in work disability occurred for both men and women in their 60s and for women in their 50s (Reynolds & Crimmins, 2010).

Poor health often leads to labor force withdrawal among older adults (Bound, Schoenbaum, Stinebrickner, & Waidmann, 1999; Bound, Stinebrickner, & Waidmann, 2010). In a review of eight longitudinal studies, poor health was found to be an important factor in early retirement decision (van den Berg, Elders, & Burdorf, 2010). According to a simulation by Bound and colleagues (2010), older workers with poor physical functioning are ten times more likely than those with average functioning to retire prior to reaching eligibility for pension benefits. In terms of specific health conditions, workers age 47–64 suffering from lung disease and cancer were 13.1 and 4.8 times more likely to retire over an eight-year period (Shultz & Wang, 2007). Those with diabetes were 3.4 times more likely to retire, and those with arthritis 1.9 times more likely to retire than to remain working. Conversely, health is positively associated with labor force participation (Cai, 2010). Despite the importance of health, however, Weir (2007) indicates that major health problems resulting in an inability to work are relatively uncommon as an explanation for labor force exits. For example, he estimates that less than 25% of adults age 70–74 work, although nearly 75% are physically able to do so.

It is somewhat difficult to predict the degree to which health will influence labor force participation among older cohorts in the future due to the uncertainty of future trends in health, potential medical advances, and the physical demands of jobs. Manchester and colleagues (2007) predict that at age 62–67, baby boomers will be 13.7% less likely to be unable to work due to health problems; only 15% of baby boomers are predicted to be unable to work, compared to 17.7% of their parents' generation. Although the exact role health will play in future incentives or disincentives to work is contingent upon future trends, it is clear that good health is positively associated with continued labor force participation.

Income and wealth. Income and wealth are also associated with the timing of retirement. Those with greater financial assets can afford to retire at an earlier age, whereas few pre-retirement assets may encourage workers to remain in the labor force longer (Kim & DeVaney, 2005). Incentives associated with earnings/income differ somewhat. Social Security benefits are progressive, meaning that in retirement low-income workers receive a higher proportion of their pre-retirement income. Therefore, a higher replacement rate of the income earned while working in retirement may encourage low earners to retire early (Butrica, Iams, & Smith, 2007). Indeed, high income is associated with a lower likelihood of claiming early Social Security benefits at age 62, especially if high earnings are concentrated later in an individual's career (Rettenmaier, 2007). On the other hand, workers with limited labor force participation gain relatively more from continued work. When considering both wealth and income simultaneously, Mitchell and Fields (1984) found that base wealth was associated with earlier retirement, while higher income was associated with later retirement.

One of the factors drawing women into the labor force or keeping them there at older ages is the increase in women's wages relative to men's (Figure 3.9). Even since 1980, there have been increases in the ratio of women's to men's wages. Black and Hispanic women make about 90% of male wages, while white and Asian women make almost 80% of male wages (Figure 3.10).

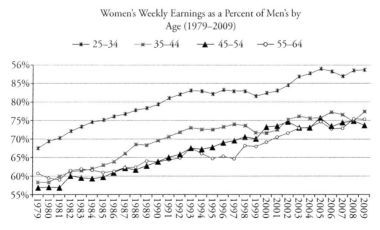

Figure 3.9 Women's Weekly Earnings as a Percent of Men's by Age (1979–2009)
Source: U.S. Bureau of Labor Statistics, Highlights of women's earnings in 2009.

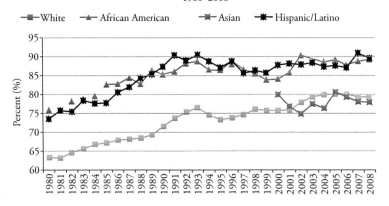

Figure 3.10 Women's Earnings as a Percentage of Men's by Race (1980–2008)
Source: U.S. Bureau of Labor Statistics, Women's earnings as a percent of men's, 2008.

Turning to the economic well-being of baby boomers, it appears that, relative to their parents, members of this cohort have higher per capita income and more accumulated wealth at comparable ages (Congressional Budget Office [CBO], 2004). Reasons for baby boomers' advantage include long-term growth in real wages, increased productivity, and women's greater labor force participation (Shackleton, 2004; Bureau of Labor Statistics [BLS], 2010b). Greater pre-retirement wealth and income may have opposing effects on retirement timing, as discussed above. Currently, wages rise with age and peak around age 55, after which they fall (French, 2005). The decline in worker-firm attachment and instability of the labor market may mean that, in the future, there may be a less curvilinear pattern in earnings relative to previous time periods in which pay was commensurate with years of service. Because older adults who change employers commonly suffer a significant wage reduction (Johnson & Kawachi, 2007), lower pre-retirement incomes may encourage older workers to exit the labor force.

In retirement, many predict that baby boomers will have higher income and wealth and lower rates of poverty vis-à-vis their parents, yet inequality will also increase among certain subgroups (Butrica et al., 2007; Manchester et al., 2007). As retirement becomes a more heterogeneous transition, it is likely that individuals will respond to income and wealth inadequacies in many different ways. How pre-retirement income and wealth influence these divergent pathways of retirement remains to be seen. Financial well-being may create different

incentives for full versus partial retirement (Kim & DeVaney, 2005), bridge employment, or return to the workforce.

Education. In addition to wealth and income, education has been strongly associated with workforce participation at most ages (Toossi, 2009). For instance, the labor force participation rate is 76.6% among those with at least a bachelor's degree versus only 61.0% among high school graduates and 46.3% with less than a high school diploma (Bureau of Labor Statistics, Labor Force Statistics from the Current Population Survey. Education is associated with higher income; on average, workers with a bachelor's degree earn $20,000 more annually relative to high school graduates (Crissey, 2009). Individuals with greater educational attainment also experience better working conditions and job flexibility, both of which encourage a longer working life. Although more education is related to lower workforce participation among teenagers and young adults who appear to delay full-time employment (Mosisa & Hipple, 2006), individuals who have invested substantial time and money into education are probably motivated to recoup their earlier investment at later ages by working at higher rates and working longer. Therefore, more education is associated with a lower probability of retirement (Kim & DeVaney, 2005).

Over time, the average education of the U.S. population has increased markedly. Only 24% of adults age 65 and older had a high school diploma in 1965 compared to 77% in 2008 (Federal Interagency Forum on Aging-Related Statistics, 2010). Although it appears that the rate of increase in educational attainment has stagnated recently (Crissey, 2009), the baby boomers have more education than today's retirees; this will have a positive influence on workforce participation beyond traditional retirement age. In a study by Mermin and colleagues (2007), 15% more of those in the early boomer cohort than the prewar generation received a bachelor's degree. Educational differences explained 28%–33% of the increase in reported probability of working beyond age 62 and 13%–22% of the increase in the reported probability of working beyond age 65.

Joint Retirement

Between 1950 and 2007, the overall labor participation rate of women nearly doubled from 34% to 60%, and in 2007, women comprised 46% of the workforce (Alley & Crimmins, 2007; Lee & Mather, 2008; Toossi, 2002). The labor force participation rate difference between men and women declined from 53% in 1950 to 15% in 2000, and this trend is expected to continue in the future (Toossi, 2002). Participation rates among women aged 55 to 64 rose from 27% in 1950 to 59% in 2008, while the participation rate for women aged 65+ was 13.3% in 2008 (Purcell, 2010). As a result, two retirements are becoming more common within couples, and there is evidence that couples prefer to retire together. For instance, one study found that approximately 20% of spouses retired within one year of each other and 30% more retired within two years of each other (Johnson, 2004).

Yet coordinating joint retirement may be challenging due to differences in age, retirement incentives, health, and a variety of other factors. On average, husbands aged 53 to 64 are four years older than their wives, which may explain why individuals with younger spouses who coordinate retirement tend to retire at older ages (Johnson, 2004). The likelihood of retiring together, however, is significantly lower if a spouse's retirement is due to poor health or job loss (Johnson & Favreault, 2001). Expectations also appear to be important; the likelihood of joint retirement was three times higher among couples in which both partners had such expectations (Ho & Raymo, 2009). Approximately 2 in 5 spouses expected to retire jointly, while both partners expected to do so in 25% of couples.

Overall, it appears that joint retirement is a growing phenomenon among married retirees, although it remains to be seen if the pattern holds for younger cohorts as they approach retirement (Moen, Huang, Plassmann, & Dentinger, 2006). For example,

marital instability, strengthening career attachment and opportunities for women, and greater diversity among baby boomers may alter or reverse this trend (Ho & Raymo, 2009). Yet, the fact that so many dual-worker spouses coordinate retirement highlights the need to consider the retirement transition in context, rather than simply an individual-level decision.

Job Market for Older Adults

The decision of whether to work or retire is influenced by the labor market for older adults. Older workers tend to be concentrated in certain industries and occupations. For example, workers age 55 and older are overrepresented in professional and related occupations (23%); management, business, and financial occupations (19%); and office and administrative support occupations (14%), as shown in Figure 3.11. However, they are underrepresented relative to younger workers in construction and extraction occupations, farming and fishing occupations, or service occupations. The age distribution of workers varies by occupation and industry (Figure 3.12). Farming, fishing, and forestry occupations are dominated by relatively young workers, while a larger proportion of those in professional and management occupations are middle- and older-aged adults. The former occupation is physically demanding, possibly leading to earlier retirement or job change, while the latter may represent workers who have advanced to higher-level positions with experience and who likely have greater education. There is a more bell-shaped age distribution in both the auto and computer industries, albeit for different reasons.

The age structure of an industry/occupation is determined by push and pull factors either encouraging or discouraging work at older ages, the rate of hiring and length of tenure, the time of development of the industry, and older workers' preference for certain job conditions, such as flexible work arrangements and less job-related stress. Industries may age over time if the hiring of young workers does not keep pace with worker aging, or by hiring older workers. Industry job growth is associated with increased hiring of older workers, while higher relative pay among older workers impedes the hiring of older adults (Adler & Hilber, 2009). Workers may age in one job or switch between multiple occupations/industries as they grow older. Job change has actually been quite common among younger baby boomers born between 1957 and 1964; from age 18 to 44, the average member of

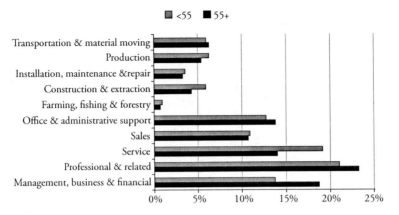

Figure 3.11 Percentage of Younger and Older Workers by Occupation
Source: U.S. Bureau of Labor Statistics, Labor Force Statistics from the Current Population Survey

this cohort held eleven jobs (BLS, 2010b). Job change is also relatively widespread later in life and may involve transition into another occupation or industry. For instance, of workers aged 45 to 75 who left long-term employers for new jobs, only 43% remained in the same broadly defined occupation (Johnson & Kawachi, 2007). Also, 59% of those leaving short-term jobs and 65% of retirees transitioned into different broadly defined occupations. Although new jobs were less stressful and more flexible than previous employment, older adults who

transitioned into a new job experienced a reduction in wages and benefits, especially those who left their previous job involuntarily. The distribution of new jobs across occupations and industries did not differ much among those who changed employers after age 50, yet those in managerial positions tended to move into sales and service occupations. Full-time workers between ages 51 and 55 who changed jobs were particularly likely to leave manufacturing, possibly because the industry has contracted over time, or to seek out more flexible and less physically

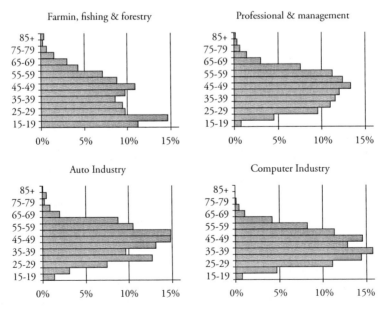

Figure 3.12 Age Distribution of Employees in Selected Industries and Occupations (2010)
Source: U.S. Bureau of Labor Statistics, Labor Force Statistics from the Current Population Survey

demanding work (Johnson, Kawachi, & Lewis, 2009).

Over time, there has been a substantial shift in the labor market, with important implications for workers approaching retirement. Globalization, technological advancements, and deregulation are major forces underlying the private sector's increased demand for a flexible workforce to respond to competition and market fluctuations (Kalleberg, 2009). Privatization of household activities such as cooking and child care has led to growth in the service sector, while there has been a decline in manufacturing. Kalleberg (2009) links these changes to decline in worker-firm attachment; a rise in long-term unemployment; an increase in perceived job insecurity; an increase in nonstandard work including contractual labor arrangements, part-time, and seasonal work; and finally, a shift in risk from employers to workers. These serve to undermine the security of the middle class, increase inequality, and adversely affect job stability.

Financial Crisis

The financial crisis of 2007–2009 has highlighted recent retirement trends, as well as impacted future retirement attitudes and behaviors. A number of underlying factors, such as low interest rates, risky lending practices, and inadequate regulation, led to the burst of the U.S. housing bubble in mid-2007, which triggered a global economic crisis. Nearly all facets of the economy were affected, including the stock market, labor market, and bank solvency, to name a few. The consequences of housing value depreciation, substantial loss of retirement assets, and high unemployment on retirement decisions are far from clear; however, a picture is starting to emerge from recent data.

Many studies on the assets and lifetime earnings of the baby-boom generation seemed to suggest that those currently approaching retirement were much better off financially relative to previous cohorts (Bosworth & Smart, 2009). Yet this may no longer be the case as a result of the financial crisis. For example, between mid-2007 and March 2009, household wealth fell by $13 trillion, or 15%, and home prices have dropped by 10%–15% on average (Bosworth & Smart, 2009). Retirement account assets plummeted from $8.7 trillion in the third quarter of 2007 to $5.9 trillion in the first quarter of 2009, a loss of 32%. Since then, retirement accounts have recovered by 34% to $7.9 trillion in the first quarter of 2010 (Butrica & Issa, 2010).

Despite these worrisome numbers, the financial crisis has disproportionately affected individuals of higher socioeconomic status who had invested more in high-risk markets to begin with. The negative impact of retirement account losses will likely be higher for older individuals, even though at age 67, retirement account assets are predicted to comprise a smaller proportion of retirement assets relative to middle and late boomers (Butrica, Smith, & Toder, 2009; Butrica, Smith, & Toder, 2010). Younger individuals have more time before retirement to contribute to retirement accounts, for stock markets to recover, and to delay drawing on retirement assets. On the other hand, the potential to recoup losses depends on the stock market's future performance and the ability to delay retirement. Butrica and colleagues (2009) used a variety of assumptions to predict income at age 67 if retirement was postponed one year under differing scenarios, taking into account the loss of financial assets during the crisis. Based on their models, younger and lower-income retirees would reap the most benefit in terms of offsetting losses by remaining employed an additional year.

In reality, postponing retirement may be challenging, considering the current labor market and high rates of unemployment. While unemployment among younger adults far surpasses that among those 55 years and older, unemployment rates among men and women 55 to 64 and 65+ are the highest since such data was first recorded in 1948 (Johnson & Mommaerts, 2010b). In addition, older workers spend a greater amount of time looking for work after losing a job. One unique feature of the current recession is the discrepancy in unemployment rates between men and women, since male-dominated sectors such as construction and manufacturing tended to suffer the most. Unemployment was also higher among older minority workers, as well as among those with lower educational attainment. Although it appears that labor force participation among older adults has risen since the financial crisis began, perhaps to offset housing and stock market losses, there is also evidence to suggest that many others are exiting the workforce and opting for early retirement benefits. Coile and Levine (2009) found that those with lower education were more responsive to labor market conditions, while responsiveness to stock markets was greater among the highly educated. They also predict that 50% more older adults will retire than will delay retirement as a result of the economic crisis.

In 2009, a record number of adults aged 62+ were newly awarded Social Security retirement benefits (Johnson & Mommaerts, 2010a). While some of this growth is due to aging of the baby boomer cohort, most of the surge has been attributed to a higher probability of claiming benefits. Older adults who cannot find employment may be involuntarily forced into an early retirement. This idea is supported by a 25% increase in early retirement claims in the 2009 fiscal year compared to the previous year (Dorning, 2009). Thus the recession may jeopardize future economic well-being for those who retire below the age of full eligibility, since monthly Social Security income is reduced and individuals are more likely to deplete personal savings. Another troubling sign was an increase in age discrimination complaints reported to the Equal Employment Opportunity Commission in 2008 and 2009 compared with 2007 (Equal Employment Opportunity Commission [EEOC], 2010).

Future Outlook
Labor Force Diversity

In predicting trends to 2040 and beyond, it is essential to consider not only the aging of the labor force but also the changing composition and growing diversity of the U.S. population. Caucasians comprised 78.9% of the labor force age 55 and older in 2010, but will represent only 60% of the older workforce by 2040 (Figure 3.7). The proportion of African Americans will increase moderately from 8.8% to 10.8%, while the percentage of Asians will grow from 4.2% to 9%. Hispanics as a share of workers 55+ are projected to experience the largest increase, from 8.2% in 2010 to 20.1% of the older labor force in 2040. This is of great importance because minority groups experience quite different patterns of lifetime labor force participation and earnings, and may have different retirement attitudes and expectations.

In terms of employment in later life, Asian males age 55–64 have the highest labor force participation (74.3%), followed by 71.8% among whites and 71.4% among Hispanics. African Americans have the lowest labor force participation of 56.8% at older ages (Figure 3.13). Older white and Asian women age 55–64 have the nearly the same participation rates; 60.8% and 60.2%, respectively, while 54.4% of African American and 52.6% of Hispanic women are in the labor force. In 2009, blacks had the highest unemployment rate (14.8%), followed by Hispanics (12.1%), whites (8.5%), and Asians (7.3%) (Bureau of Labor Statistics, 2010a). In addition to differences in work history among minorities, there are also important disparities in the occupations in which minorities are clustered.

Blacks and Hispanics were underrepresented in management and professional occupations, which was the highest-paying category, but were overrepresented in service occupations (Bureau of Labor Statistics, 2010a). Minorities were observed to cluster in certain occupations, comprising a disproportionate share of workers relative to their representation in the total population. Hispanics made up 14% of the population but represented 42% of housekeepers and maids; 41% of farming, fishing, and forestry occupations; and 44% of construction laborers. African Americans accounted for 29% of security guards, 34% of nursing aides, and a quarter of taxi and bus drivers, while representing 10.7% of the population

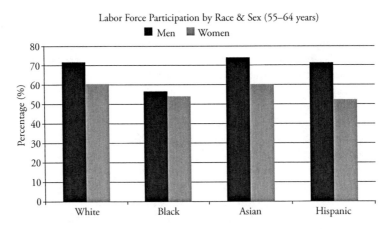

Figure 3.13 Labor Force Participation by Race & Sex (2010)
Source: U.S. Bureau of Labor Statistics, Labor Force Statistics from the Current Population Survey

overall. Meanwhile, Asians comprised only 4.7% of the population but made up 16% of physicians and surgeons and 27% of computer engineers. Such occupational differences are important because Hispanic and black workers tend to be found disproportionately in jobs with low wages and earlier ages of retirement. For example, median weekly earnings are $757 for whites and $880 for Asians, but only $601 and $541 for blacks and Hispanics, respectively (Bureau of Labor Statistics, 2010a). Low-paying jobs are also less likely to offer benefits, including an employer-sponsored pension plan.

Compared to non-Hispanic whites, African Americans and Hispanics are less likely to be offered a retirement plan and are also less likely to participate (Butrica, Johnson, & Council, 2010). Of workers age 25–59, 65% of whites, 56% of blacks, and 38% of Hispanics were offered plans, while 55%, 45%, and 30% were found to participate, respectively. Race/ethnic disparities in pension coverage are partially explained by differences in earnings, occupation, firm size, sector (government versus private), and hours worked. Overall, relative to whites, Hispanics were 14% and blacks 7% less likely to work in a job offering a retirement plan and were 12% and 6% less likely to participate in an employer-sponsored plan. Racial disparities in defined contribution plan availability and participation are further compounded by the fact that to accumulate wealth, workers must make regular and significant contributions. Yet, minorities earn less and are more likely to become unemployed (Bound, Schoenbaum, & Waidmann, 1996; Flippen & Tienda, 2000). Consequently, blacks and Hispanics contribute about a third less to their plans (Smith, Johnson, & Muller, 2004). Hispanics and African Americans also have higher aversion to risk, meaning they may invest conservatively, resulting in lower wealth accumulation; however, this is likely to explain only a small fraction of wealth disparities at retirement (Butrica et al., 2010). Taken together, these observations indicate that minorities are less prepared for the retirement transition, yet they are also more likely to exit the workforce involuntarily.

Relative to whites, black and Hispanic workers nearing retirement are more likely to become unemployed involuntarily, are less likely to become reemployed, and once unemployed are more likely to exit the labor force (Flippen & Tienda, 2000). Although attenuated, significant racial differences persist even after controlling for socioeconomic status, employment characteristics, and health. African Americans approaching retirement experience a steeper decline in labor participation, especially among men, that is mostly explained by their poorer health (Bound et al., 1996). Black men spend a smaller proportion of life in retirement and relatively more time both working and disabled (Hayward, Friedman, & Chen, 1996). Black women would actually have higher labor participation than white women if health was equal (Bound et al., 1996).

Less is known about the retirement patterns of Hispanics. Although Hispanic men have the highest labor force participation overall, this is because the Hispanic population is young relative to other racial and ethnic groups (Toossi, 2006). The picture differs for older Hispanic men and women. Results from the Health and Retirement Survey indicate that, compared to white older adults age 51 to 61 at the first interview, fewer Hispanics of both sexes worked full-time, a greater percentage were employed and disabled/out of the labor force, and fewer were retired at each of four waves from 1992–1998 (Flippen, 2005). Limited pension eligibility may explain the significantly lower rates of retirement among Hispanics. Finally, it is important to note the high degree of heterogeneity in characteristics by citizenship status within the Hispanic population. Of the 8 million Latino baby boomers born between 1946 and 1942, only 43% were born in the United States or a U.S. territory, while 21% are naturalized citizens and 36% are noncitizens (Gassoumis, Wilber, Baker, & Torres-Gil, 2010). Although Latino baby boomers scored poorly relative to non-Latinos on every socioeconomic indicator examined, noncitizens and foreign-born citizens were especially disadvantaged. Hispanic labor force participation was 69.7% among U.S.-born citizens and 66.9% among naturalized citizens, but only 58.2% among Hispanic noncitizens. Among noncitizen Latino baby boomers, low education, income, and wealth coupled with low labor force participation are worrisome, particularly if members of this vulnerable population are ineligible for entitlement programs. On the other hand, demographic characteristics of U.S.-born Latino and non-Latino baby boomers were much more similar (Gassoumis et al., 2010).

Overall, racial and ethnic differences in employment and retirement are much more pronounced for men than women (Flippen, 2005). Also, older Asians do not appear to be disadvantaged with respect to labor force participation and retirement measures discussed, while older Hispanics and African Americans are clearly vulnerable as they approach retirement. Cumulative disadvantage over the life course in work experience, health status, and socioeconomic status explains many of the racial and ethnic disparities in the transition from the labor force into retirement (Brown & Warner, 2008; Flippen & Tienda, 2000; Hayward et al., 1996), although other unmeasured factors such as racism also may play a role. As minority groups will comprise a much larger proportion of the total population by 2040, it is increasingly important to understand ethnic and racial variations in labor force participation and retirement transitions, especially among Hispanics, the fastest growing ethnic group.

Baby Boomer Expectations

Although there is considerable uncertainty about future trends in employment and retirement, it is possible to make tentative projections over the short term by examining baby boomer retirement expectations. The probability of working full-time beyond age 65 self-reported by workers aged 51 to 56 increased from 27% in 1992 to 33% in 2004 (Mermin, Johnson, & Murphy, 2007). Much of this is a result of declines in defined pension retirement plans and employer-sponsored retiree health insurance, as well as greater average education. Certainly there will be a greater need for many baby boomers to remain in the labor force as life expectancy increases and as responsibility for retirement financial well-being shifts from the government and employers to workers.

Employment at older ages also depends on the ability to work. Between 1997 and 2007, modest improvements were observed in work ability. In 2007, work disability and limitation levels at age 67 were comparable to those experienced by individuals at age 64 in 1997 (Reynolds & Crimmins, 2010). Changes have also occurred in the nature of job demands. In the thirty-five-year period from 1971 to 2006, there was a 19% decline in the share of jobs with any general physical demands (Johnson, Mermin, & Resseger, 2007). This is relevant because physically demanding work is associated with earlier retirement (Filer & Petri, 1988). Blue-collar jobs declined by 12% between 1971 and 2006, while the proportion of workers in management and professional occupations increased by 11% (Johnson, Mermin, & Resseger, 2007). Meanwhile, the share of jobs requiring cognitive and interpersonal skills and the proportion involving high stress increased significantly. Together, the shift away from physical job demands to cognitive ones suggests that the majority of older workers will benefit from such

changes. As a result, more baby boomers will be capable of working past age 65.

Retirement preferences and norms may also play a role in baby boomers' higher work expectations for old age. Increases in the normal age to receive full Social Security retirement benefits, hyperbolic depictions of an "old age" crisis, and the recent financial crisis may influence older adults' retirement expectations indirectly. In addition, there is reason to believe that a shift has occurred since the 1970s in which work participation has become a more important component of women's identity (Goldin, 2006). Given the large increase in female labor force participation starting several decades ago, female baby boomers likely have a stronger labor force attachment and greater preference to work past traditional retirement ages than current retirees.

Although more baby boomers expect to remain in the workforce after age 65, there is heterogeneity in expectations and important differences among certain segments of the population. For example, more of those with higher education attainment expect to work longer; 34.5% of college graduates expect to work past age 65, compared to only 29.4% of those with less than a high school diploma (Murphy, Johnson, & Mermin, 2007). Yet it appears that African Americans have lower expectations to delay retirement, and only 28% expect to work past age 65, in contrast to 33% of all other racial groups. Even after adjusting for other factors such as education, pension coverage, and health, African Americans have a 7% lower probability of working beyond age 65 (Murphy, Johnson, & Mermin, 2007). As such, to understand future expectations, researchers need to address variation in expectations, since aggregate statistics can obscure subgroup differences.

Conclusion

Although it is certain that the U.S. population will age, since the future older population has already been born, it is much harder to predict future trends in labor force participation and retirement patterns. If labor force participation rates continue to increase among older adults, the effective size of the older dependent population may actually be lower than projected and the costs of population aging more easily accommodated. At present, just over half of the population aged 60–64, and a third of those aged 65–69, are working. There is considerable potential for an increase in labor force participation among these age groups, as the level of physical inability to work in these age ranges is relatively low. Increasing work at these ages would increase tax revenues and delay or eliminate outlays for Social Security and Medicare. In the future, older adults' participation in the workforce will be an outcome of many changes in the incentives to retire or remain in the workforce discussed previously.

References

Adler, G., & Hilber, D. (2009). Industry hiring patterns of older workers. *Research on Aging, 31*(1), 69–88.

Administration on Aging. (2010). *A profile of older Americans: 2009.* Retrieved from http://www.aoa.gov/AoARoot/Aging_Statistics/Profile/index.aspx

Alley, D., & Crimmins, E. (2007). The demography of aging and work. In K. S. Shultz & G. A. Adams (Eds.), *Aging and work in the 21st century* (pp. 7–23). London, England: Lawrence Erlbaum Associates.

Blau, D. M., & Gilleskie, D. B. (2008). The role of retiree health insurance in the employment behavior of older men. *International Economic Review, 49*(2), 475–514.

Bosworth, B., & Smart, R. (2009). *The wealth of older Americans and the subprime debacle* (Working Paper No. 2009–21). Chestnut Hill, MA: Center for Retirement Research at Boston College.

Bound, J., Schoenbaum, M., Stinebrickner, T. R., & Waidmann, T. (1999). The dynamic effects of health on the labor force transitions of older workers. *Labour Economics, 6*(2), 179–202.

Bound, J., Schoenbaum, M., & Waidmann, T. (1996). Race differences in labor force attachment and disability status. *The Gerontologist, 36*(3), 311–321.

Bound, J., Stinebrickner, T., & Waidmann, T. (2010). Health, economic resources and the work decisions of older men. *Journal of Econometrics, 156*(1), 106–129.

Brown, T. H., & Warner, D. F. (2008). Divergent pathways? Racial/Ethnic differences in older women's labor force withdrawal. *The Journals of Gerontology, Series B: Psychological Sciences and Social Sciences, 63*(3), S122–S134.

Bureau of Labor Statistics. (2010a). *Labor force characteristics by race and ethnicity, 2009* (Report 1026). Washington, DC: U.S. Government Printing Office.

Bureau of Labor Statistics. (2010b). *Number of jobs held, labor market activity, and earnings growth among the youngest baby boomers: Results from a longitudinal survey* (News Release). Retrieved from http://www.bls.gov/news.release/pdf/nlsoy.pdf

Bureau of Labor Statistics. (2010c). *Highlights of women's earnings in 2009* (Report 1025). Washington, DC: U.S. Government Printing Office.

Bureau of Labor Statistics (2009). *The Editor's Desk: Women's earnings as a percentage of men's, 2008.* Retrieved from http://www.bls.gov/opub/ted/2009/ted_20091014.htm.

Bureau of Labor Statistics. (n.d.). *Employment Projections.* Retrieved from http://www.bls.gov/emp/.

Bureau of Labor Statistics. (n.d.). *Labor Force Statistics from the Current Population Survey.* Retrieved from http://www.bls.gov/cps/data.htm.

Butrica, B. A., Iams, H. M., & Smith, K. E. (2007). Understanding baby boomers' retirement prospects. In B. Madrain, O. S. Mitchell, & B. J. Soldo (Eds.), *Redefining retirement* (pp. 70–91). New York, NY: Oxford University Press.

Butrica, B. A., & Issa, P. (2010). *Retirement account balances* (Fact Sheet). Washington, DC: The Urban Institute.

Butrica, B. A., Johnson, R. W., & Council, E. A. (2010). *Racial, ethnic, and gender differentials in employer-sponsored pensions* (Testimony before the ERISA Advisory Council). Washington, DC: The Urban Institute.

Butrica, B. A., Smith, K. E., & Toder, E. J. (2009). *Retirement security and the stock market crash: What are the possible outcomes?* (Discussion Paper 09-05). Washington, DC: The Urban Institute.

Butrica, B. A., Smith, K. E., & Toder, E. J. (2010). *Delaying retirement an additional year could offset stock market losses* (Older Americans' Economic Security No. 23). Washington, DC: The Urban Institute.

Cahill, K. E., Giandrea, M. D., & Quinn, J. F. (2006). Retirement patterns from career employment. *The Gerontologist, 46*(4), 514–523.

Cai, L. (2010). The relationship between health and labour force participation: Evidence from a panel data simultaneous equation model. *Labour Economics, 17*(1), 77–90.

Claxton, G., DiJulio, B., Finder, B., Jarlenski, M., McHugh, M., & Hawkins, S. (2008). *Employer health benefits: 2008 annual survey.* Menlo Park, CA: Kaiser Family Foundation.

Coile, C., & Levine, P. B. (2009). *The market crash and mass layoffs: How the current economic crisis may affect retirement* (Working Paper no. 15395). Cambridge, MA: National Bureau of Economic Research.

Congressional Budget Office. (2004). *The retirement prospects of the baby boomers* (Issue Brief). Washington, DC: U.S. Government Printing Office.

Costa, D. L. (1998). *The evolution of retirement: An American economic history, 1880–1990.* Chicago, IL: University of Chicago Press.

Crimmins, E. M. (2004). Trends in the health of the elderly. *Public Health, 25*(1), 79–98.

Crimmins, E. M., Reynolds, S. L., & Saito, Y. (1999). Trends in health and ability to work among the older working-age population. *The Journals of Gerontology, Series B: Psychological Sciences and Social Sciences, 54*(1), S31–S40.

Crissey, S. R. (2009). *Educational attainment in the United States: 2007* (Current Population Reports P20-560). Washington, DC: U.S. Census Bureau.

Denton, F. T., & Spencer, B. G. (2009). What is retirement? A review and assessment of alternative concepts and measures. *Canadian Journal on Aging, 28*(01), 63–76.

Dorning, M. (2009). Early retirement claims increase dramatically. *New York Times.* Retrieved from: http://articles.latimes.com/2009/may/24/nation/na-retirement24.

Duggan, M., Singleton, P., & Song, J. (2007). Aching to retire? The rise in the full retirement age and its impact on the social security disability rolls. *Journal of Public Economics, 91*(7–8), 1327–1350.

Early Retiree Reinsurance Program. (n.d.). *The Affordable Care Act's Early Retiree Reinsurance Program Fact Sheet.* Retrieved from http://www.errp.gov/about_errp.shtml

Equal Employment Opportunity Commission. (2010). *Age Discrimination in Employment Act FY 1997–2009.* Washington, DC: Author.

Federal Interagency Forum on Aging-Related Statistics. (2010). *Older Americans 2010: Key indicators of well-being.* Washington, DC: U.S. Government Printing Office.

Filer, R. K., & Petri, P. A. (1988). A job-characteristics theory of retirement. *The Review of Economics and Statistics, 70*(1), 123–129.

Flippen, C., & Tienda, M. (2000). Pathways to retirement: Patterns of labor force participation and labor market exit among the pre-retirement population by race, Hispanic origin, and sex. *The Journals of Gerontology, Series B: Psychological Sciences and Social Sciences, 55*(1), S14–S27.

Flippen, C. A. (2005). Minority workers and pathways to retirement. In R. B. Hudson (Ed.), *The new politics of old age policy* (pp. 129–156). Baltimore, MD: Johns Hopkins University Press.

French, E. (2005). The effects of health, wealth, and wages on labour supply and retirement behaviour. *Review of Economic Studies, 72*(2), 395–427.

Friedberg, L., & Webb, A. (2005). Retirement and the evolution of pension structure. *Journal of Human Resources, 40*(2), 281–308.

Gassoumis, Z. D., Wilber, K. H., Baker, L. A., & Torres-Gil, F. M. (2010). Who are the Latino baby boomers? Demographic and economic characteristics of a hidden population. *Journal of Aging & Social Policy, 22*(1), 53–68.

Goldin, C. (2006). The quiet revolution that transformed women's employment, education, and family. *The American Economic Review, 96*(2), 1–21.

Gustman, A. L., & Steimeier, T. L. (2000). Retirement outcomes in the Health and Retirement Study. *Social Security Bulletin, 63*(4), 57–71.

Gustman, A. L., & Steinmeier, T. (2009). How changes in social security affect recent retirement trends. *Research on Aging, 31*(2), 261–290.

Han, S. K., & Moen, P. (1999). Clocking out: Temporal patterning of retirement. *American Journal of Sociology, 105*(1), 191–236.

Hayward, M. D., Friedman, S., & Chen, H. (1996). Race inequities in men's retirement. *The Journals of Gerontology, Series B: Psychological Sciences and Social Sciences, 51*(1), S1–S10.

Ho, J. H., & Raymo, J. M. (2009). Expectations and realization of joint retirement among dual-worker couples. *Research on Aging, 31*(2), 153–179.

Johnson, R. W. (2004). *Do spouses coordinate their retirement decisions?* (Issue Brief No. 19). Chestnut Hill, MA: Center for Retirement Research at Boston College.

Johnson, R. W., Butrica, B. A., & Mommaerts, C. (2010). *Work and retirement patterns for the GI generation, silent generation, and early boomers: Thirty years of change* (Working Paper No. 2010-8). Chestnut Hill, MA: Center for Retirement Research at Boston College.

Johnson, R. W., & Favreault, M. (2001). *Retiring together or working alone: The impact of spousal employment and disability on retirement decisions.* Washington, DC: The Urban Institute.

Johnson, R. W., & Kawachi, J. (2007). *Job changes at older ages: Effects on wages, benefits, and other job attributes* (Working Paper No. 2007-4). Chestnut Hill, MA: Center for Retirement Research at Boston College.

Johnson, R. W., Kawachi, J., & Lewis, E. K. (2009). *Older workers on the move: Recareering in later life.* Washington, DC: AARP Public Policy Institute.

Johnson, R. W., Mermin, G. B. T., & Resseger, M. (2007). *Employment at older ages and the changing nature of work.* Washington, DC: AARP Public Policy Institute.

Johnson, R. W., & Mommaerts, C. (2010a). *Social security retirement benefit awards hit all-time high in 2009* (Fact Sheet). Washington, DC: The Urban Institute.

Johnson, R. W., & Mommaerts, C. (2010b). *How did older workers fare in 2009?* (Research Report). Washington, DC: The Urban Institute.

Kaiser Family Foundation/Hewitt Associates. (2006). *Retiree health benefits examined: Findings from the Kaiser/Hewitt 2006 Survey on Retiree Health Benefits* (No. 7587). Retrieved from http://www.kff.org/medicare/upload/7587.pdf

Kalleberg, A. L. (2009). Precarious work, insecure workers: Employment relations in transition. *American Sociological Review, 74*(1), 1–22.

Kim, H., & DeVaney, S. A. (2005). The selection of partial or full retirement by older workers. *Journal of Family and Economic Issues, 26*(3), 371–394.

Lee, M. A., & Mather, M. (2008). U.S. labor force trends. *Population Bulletin, 63*(2), 1–16.

Lippmann, S. (2008). Rethinking risk in the new economy: Age and cohort effects on unemployment and re-employment. *Human Relations, 61*(9), 1259–1292.

Manchester, J., Weaver, D., & Whitman, K. (2007). Baby boomers versus their parents: Economic well-being and health status. In B. Madrain, O. S. Mitchell, & B. J. Soldo (Eds.), *Redefining retirement* (pp. 112–137). New York, NY: Oxford University Press.

Manton, K. G. (2008). Recent declines in chronic disability in the elderly U.S. population: Risk factors and future dynamics. *Public Health, 29*, 91–113.

Mastrobuoni, G. (2009). Labor supply effects of the recent social security benefit cuts: Empirical estimates using cohort discontinuities. *Journal of Public Economics, 93*(11–12), 1224–1233.

Mermin, G. B. T., Johnson, R. W., & Murphy, D. P. (2007). Why do boomers plan to work longer? *The Journals of Gerontology, Series B: Psychological Sciences and Social Sciences, 62*(5), S286–S294.

Mitchell, O. S., & Fields, G. S. (1984). The economics of retirement behavior. *Journal of Labor Economics, 2*(1), 84–105.

Moen, P., Huang, Q., Plassmann, V., & Dentinger, E. (2006). Deciding the future: Do dual-earner couples plan together for retirement? *American Behavioral Scientist, 49*(10), 1422–1443.

Monk, C., & Munnell, A. H. (2009). *The implications of declining retiree health insurance* (Working Paper No. 2009-15). Chestnut Hill, MA: Center for Retirement Research at Boston College.

Mosisa, A., & Hipple, S. (2006). Trends in labor force participation in the United States. *Monthly Labor Review, 129*(10), 35–57.

Murphy, D., Johnson, R. W., & Mermin, G. B. T. (2007). *Racial differences in baby boomers' retirement expectations* (Older American's Economic Security No. 13). Washington, DC: The Urban Institute.

National Center for Health Statistics. (2010, January). *Health, United States, 2009: With special feature on medical technology* (No. 2010-1232). Washington, DC: U.S. Government Printing Office.

Neumark, D. (2009). The age discrimination in employment act and the challenge of population aging. *Research on Aging, 31*(1), 41–68.

Purcell, P. J. (2010). Older workers: Employment and retirement trends. *Journal of Pension Planning and Compliance, 36*(2), 70–88.

Quinn, J. F. (2010). Work, retirement, and the encore career: Elders and the future of the American workforce. *Generations, 34*(3), 45–55.

Rettenmaier, A. J. (2007). *Earnings dynamics and early retirement.* College Station, TX: Texas A&M University, Private Enterprise Research Center.

Reynolds, S. L., & Crimmins, E. M. (2010). Trends in the ability to work among men and women in the older American population: 1997–2007. *European Journal of Ageing, 7,* 249–256.

Shackleton, R. (2004). The retirement prospects of the Baby Boomers (Economic and Budget Issue Brief). Congressional Budget Office.

Shultz, K. S., & Wang, M. (2007). The influence of specific physical health conditions on retirement decisions. *The International Journal of Aging and Human Development, 65*(2), 149–161.

Smith, K. E., Johnson, R. W., & Muller, L. (2004). *Deferring income in employer-sponsored retirement plans: The dynamics of participant contributions.* Washington, DC: The Urban Institute.

Song, J. G., & Manchester, J. (2007a). Have people delayed claiming retirement benefits? Responses to changes in Social Security rules. *Social Security Bulletin, 67*(2), 1–23.

Song, J. G., & Manchester, J. (2007b). New evidence on earnings and benefit claims following changes in the retirement earnings test in 2000. *Journal of Public Economics, 91*(3–4), 669–700.

Szinovacz, M. E., & DeViney, S. (1999). The retiree identity: Gender and race differences. *The Journals of Gerontology, Series B: Psychological Sciences and Social Sciences, 54*(4), S207–S218.

Thane, P. (2006). The history of retirement. In G. L. Clark, A. H. Munnell, & J. M. Orszag (Eds.), *Oxford handbook of pensions and retirement income* (pp. 33–51). New York, NY: Oxford University Press.

Toossi, M. (2002). A century of change: The U.S. labor force, 1950–2050. *Monthly Labor Review, 125*(5), 15–29.

Toossi, M. (2006). A new look at long-term labor force projections to 2050. *Monthly Labor Review, 129*(11), 19–39.

Toossi, M. (2009). Labor force projections to 2018: Older workers staying more active. *Monthly Labor Review, 132*(11), 30–51.

United States Census Bureau (n.d.). *International Data Base.* Retrieved from http://www.census.gov/population/international/data/idb/informationGateway.php.

United States Census Bureau (2009). *U.S. Population Projections: 2009 National Population Projections.* Retrieved from http://www.census.gov/population/www/projections/2009 projections.html.

van den Berg, T. I. J., Elders, L. A. M., & Burdorf, A. (2010). Influence of health and work on early retirement. *Journal of Occupational and Environmental Medicine, 52*(6), 576–583.

Vincent, G. K., & Velkoff, V. A. (2010). *The next four decades: The older population in the United States: 2010 to 2050* (Current Population Reports P25–1138). Washington, DC: U.S. Census Bureau.

Warner, D. F., Hayward, M. D., & Hardy, M. A. (2010). The retirement life course in America at the dawn of the twenty-first century. *Population Research and Policy Review, 29*(6), 893–919.

Weir, D. R. (2007). Are baby boomers living well longer? In B. Madrain, O. S. Mitchell, & B. J. Soldo (Eds.), *Redefining retirement* (pp. 95–111). New York, NY: Oxford University Press.

Variations on a Retirement Theme: Conceptual and Operational Definitions of Retirement

Terry A. Beehr *and* Nathan A. Bowling

Abstract

Retirement is a complex process. First, it takes place over a period of time that may consist of three phases: older employees simply imagining the possibility of retirement, assessing when it is time to let go of the job, and actually transitioning into retirement (Feldman & Beehr, 2011). Second, research has measured or operationalized retirement in a variety of ways, which partly reflects the fact that there are different types of retirement. Eight ways that research has measured retirement are (1) nonparticipation in the labor force, (2) reduction in hours worked and/or earning, (3) hours worked or earnings below a minimum cutoff, (4) receipt of retirement/pension income, (5) exit from one's main employer, (6) change of career or employment later in life, (7) self-assessed retirement, and (8) some combination of the preceding seven operationalizations (Denton & Spencer, 2009). Some of these retirement measures have been used frequently and others more sparingly, and research is still needed that will determine the degree to which the different forms of retirement matter. That is, to what extent are they predicted by the same causes, and do they predict the same outcomes?

Key Words: retirement, measurement, bridge employment, retirement phases, retirement types

Like many concepts, the meaning of retirement seems simple and clear; that is, knowing who is and who is not retired should be obvious. Careful research on retirement must always measure or operationalize it, however, and while doing so researchers discover that retirement comes in different forms. The present chapter examines eight forms or measures of retirement that have been used in past research, allowing readers to see their similarities and differences, followed by conclusions and recommendation for future research.

At one time retirement was the state the average person entered when he or she (especially males) were no longer physically able to work. Some government and military pensions may have signaled the advent of the concept of paid retirement for older workers (Shultz & Wang, 2011). A traditional view of retirement is that it is the time of one's life starting from the end of paid work and ending with one's death. By that definition (and most others), the years that people spend in retirement have expanded greatly due to people living longer but not necessarily retiring at older ages (e.g., Alley & Crimmins, 2007). Retirement is a difficult concept to define. While it is often generally defined as "withdrawal from paid working life" (e.g., Denton & Spencer, 2009, p. 64), retirement has been operationalized in many different ways. Any study of retirement necessarily must operationalize it, which makes the definition very specific for that study. If retirement is narrowly defined, however, we will miss discovering experiences of older workers and former workers who themselves or someone else would consider retired. For example, the organization might classify people as retired if they are taking retirement pay (e.g., pensions). A clear example is the U.S. military, where people can retire at relatively young ages and subsequently take another full-time job for a decade or more. Their former employer (military) might consider them retired, but for some purposes, U.S. labor statistics might classify them as not retired because they are still active in the paid workforce. Alternatively, the federal government can pay payments to people over a certain age that are usually considered public retirement pay (e.g., monthly Social Security payments in the United States), but those people might be working full-time, even at the same job they have had for most of their lives. The organization for which they work would not consider them to be retired.

Therefore, retirement can be considered as a process rather than a simple, single event (Beehr, 1986; Beehr & Bennett, 2007), one that can evolve over time and can even take a period of years to be resolved (Shultz & Wang, 2011). For example, an older employee can decide to engage in partial retirement (Beehr, 1986), with the employer's agreement, by changing from full-time work to part-time work on the same job. This might go on for two years, for example, at which time the person fully leaves the workforce (full retirement). One could say the *process* of retirement in this case took two years—or probably even more than that, because thinking and planning how to retire probably began well before that period. The retirement process takes place over time, and there can be identifiable phases occurring during that time.

Phases of Retirement and Measuring Retirement

Based on previous research and theory, Feldman and Beehr (2011) have proposed a model of the retirement process that covers three phases: older employees (1) imagining the possibility of retirement (based, e.g., on Beehr, 1986), (2) assessing when it is time to let go of the job (from a career-transition perspective; e.g., Hall & Mirvis, 1996), and (3) actually transitioning into retirement (e.g., as described by Schlossberg, 2003). A variety of theories about retirement can apply to each phase, but some theories are better for describing one phase more than others (Feldman & Beehr, 2011).

During the first phase (imagining retirement), before any concrete plans are made, the idea of retirement can be quite abstract. Some research operationalizes retirement by asking people to predict when they will retire (e.g., how many years from the present, or at what age), and most of the participants in these studies are in this early phase.

In fact, if they have not really thought about retirement before, the researcher's questions might force them to think about or imagine it for the first time. This research approach to retirement also often conceives *expected* retirement time as a criterion or dependent variable. That is, the goal is to determine what predictors will be related to the decision to retire (at a certain time). According to Feldman and Beehr (2011), individual differences, image and continuity theories, and social identity theory can be useful for research examining retirement in this phase. The relatively stable individual differences in age, wealth, and health can help to predict expected time of retirement. That is, older people, wealthier people, and unhealthier people are likely to retire sooner. Much past research has suggested this to be true. Image and continuity theories (e.g., Atchley, 1989) start with an assumption that people strive to have a positive self-image. If older workers view retirees as being "worse" than workers in any way (e.g., less useful), they will not like that self-image and will be less likely to retire soon if their preferred self-image involves being a useful person. Continuity theory of retirement argues that people's basic nature does not change much from before to after retirement. Merging this idea with image theory, one might predict that individuals are more likely to retire if they think they can maintain their current self-image (e.g., I am useful now, and I can continue to be useful after retirement). Social identity theory (e.g., Ashforth, 2001) further argues that our self-image is tied to what other people think of us, especially people who are part of a group with which we identify. If an employee's social identity is tied to working people who do not value retirement very much, he or she is less likely to view retirement positively, for example; but if one's identity is tied to others who have retired and who like retirement (e.g., former coworkers who are now retired), then the image of retirement might be quite positive. It should be noted that actual retirement can be used instead of expected retirement in studies of this first phase (indeed some studies have done that), but that requires either asking retirees retrospectively what they had been thinking when they first imagined retirement or following non-retirees for years into the future until they actually retire. The easy way to do research on this phase is to use a measure of projected retirement time or age.

The second phase of the retirement process is assessing and deciding when it is time to actually retire, and Feldman and Beehr (2011) argue that some of the most pertinent theories for studying this phase of retirement are human stage or development theories, social-normative theories, disengagement theory, approach-avoidance motivation theory, and person-environment fit theory. Stage approaches are forms of adult development theories (e.g., Levinson & Wofford, 2009), and they might argue that retirement is a natural developmental stage people tend to go through at older ages. Although retirement is a natural stage at the end of working and before death, it doesn't necessarily occur at the same age for everyone, but it is characterized by lower engagement in paid work. Social-normative or developmental theories (e.g., Levinson, 1986; Super 1990) propose that retirement timing is determined by what is considered normal or right by other people. The norm, which might come from a group of people as large as a national culture or as small as a workgroup, tells workers when it is the "right" time to retire. Disengagement theory (e.g., Beehr, 1986) projects a somewhat dismal view of retirement, proposing that older workers are encouraged by their society to retire and enter into a marginalized and unimportant role in that society. At a certain age, therefore, the decision to disengage from not only work but from much of society is encouraged. Approach-avoidance motivation theory (Shultz, Morton, & Weckerle, 1998) also can be used to explain decisions at the second phase of the retirement process, focusing on the attraction or repulsion to work in general or to the current job (and implicitly, at least, attraction or repulsion to the concept of retirement). Especially when the motivational forces are conscious and explicitly examined, approach-avoidance theory can be related to self-regulation theory, which has been used to explain choices and actions at other stages of one's career (e.g., see Raabe, Frese, & Beehr, 2007). If the older worker's job has attractive elements, he or she is less likely to retire or more likely to retire to another job (a "bridge" job) that resembles it (e.g., Gobeski & Beehr, 2009); if the job has more aversive or repellant characteristics, however, one is more likely to retire fully or to take a second job that is different from the current one. Person-environment fit theory argues that a good fit between the person's characteristics (e.g., skills and interests) and the job's characteristics (e.g., demands and resources) leads to people remaining in their jobs, but a misfit makes them inclined to leave (e.g., Feldman & Vogel, 2009). For older workers, leaving a job can mean retiring. In this second stage of the retirement process, deciding concretely when it is time to retire, definitions of retirement that include exact timing of retirement acts such as leaving the

job, taking a new (maybe part-time or temporary) job, and accepting pay that is designated for retirees (e.g., pensions) are common operational definitions of retirement.

In the third and final phase, after going through the retirement decision process, the person actually retires and makes a transition to a different life situation (Feldman & Beehr, 2011). During the entire retirement process, the person has been expecting certain situations or outcomes to be present in retirement, and these outcomes may become more concrete at this stage. Two types of related theories can be useful for explaining this phase: rational-economic and motivational-instrumental theories (Feldman & Beehr, 2011). Economic or rational-economic theories of human behavior assume that people are motivated by money and what it can buy, and that older employees' decisions to retire are based on their calculations about whether they can afford to retire. There has been a great deal of economics research on retirement, and one of the basic ideas is that the employees' expected costs and income streams during their retirement are estimated in order to see if retirement would be affordable. These estimates are likely to continue even after people retire, as retirees are concerned about affording to pay for their expenses from the time they retire until they die. Many factors play a role in making these estimates, including projected pension income, inflation rates, real estate values, the availability of bridge jobs, and health care costs. The motivation or motivation-instrumental theories described by Feldman and Beehr (2011) are similar to the economic theories, but with many psychological outcomes and need satisfiers substituted for money. A cost-benefit analysis of present and future situations in work and retirement is undertaken. It can include money and the tangible things money can buy, but it also includes things like status, social relationships, and chances for a satisfying sense of accomplishment. Whichever situation, retirement or continuing to work on the same job, is projected to be more instrumental for achieving desirable outcomes will be chosen. In this phase of retirement, some useful definitions of retirement include economic ones (e.g., accepting a pension) and others that are related to achieving some other desirable outcomes states (e.g., having a satisfying bridge job).

Types of Retirement Definitions

Denton and Spencer (2009) identified eight different conceptualizations of retirement that have appeared in the retirement research literature: (1) nonparticipation in the labor force, (2) reduction in hours worked and/or earning, (3) hours worked or earnings below a minimum cutoff, (4) receipt of retirement/pension income, (5) exit from one's main employer, (6) change of career or employment later in life, (7) self-assessed retirement, and (8) some combination of the preceding seven operationalizations. Given that retirement has been examined in several different disciplines, including industrial and organizational psychology, organizational behavior, economics, sociology, gerontology, and political science, perhaps it should be no surprise that it has been assessed using several different approaches. In the following sections we discuss research on the eight conceptualizations of retirement listed above.

Nonparticipation in the Workforce

Nonparticipation in the workforce, sometimes called full retirement (e.g., Beehr, 1986), is a common, popular, and stereotypic definition of retirement. Some people work most of their adult lives full-time in one or more jobs, and then they drop out of the workforce entirely and permanently when they get older. Their retirement status is a person outside the workforce, not looking for work, and not needing or intending to work again.

Jahoda (1981, 1997) theorized that employment serves one manifest function and five latent functions for workers. The manifest function is financial; it allows people to obtain money. The latent functions are time structure, or planning and organization of one's time on a daily basis; collective purpose, or a feeling of belonging and being useful and needed by other people; social contacts with people outside one's immediate family; social status, or an acknowledged and acceptable role and identity in one's society and culture; and activity, or providing ways to keep busy. Because employment fulfills these latent functions, people who are employed typically have better mental health (Paul & Batinic, 2010). Thus employment does more than provide financial functions because it also fulfills some basic psychological needs that make people happier and better adjusted. Most of the research supporting this theory has compared employed people to unemployed people. A recent study (Paul & Batinic, 2010), however, examined the functions of employment and compared them to both unemployed people who were looking for work and people who were out of the workforce entirely. This second group of people included retirees along with homemakers and students who were not looking for work.

The results showed that retirees who were out of the workforce experienced less of the latent functions of time structure, social contact, collective purpose, and activity than full-time employed people. They did not experience less social status or report lower financial well-being (the manifest function of work) than employed people, nor did they experience less of the latent function of social status. Furthermore, although the latent functions are supposed to result in better mental health, the retirees did not have worse mental health than employed people. Overall, it appears that retirement that is nonparticipation in the workforce may result in some loss of important psychological states, but that the status of retiree is a legitimate societal role, retirement finances may be judged adequate, and there is no need for full retirement to result in declining mental health.

There is quite a lot of research on full retirement or nonparticipation in the workforce (e.g., Dew & Yorgason, 2010; Shannon & Grierson, 2004). So this traditional and popular concept of retirement is common among researchers as well. Research results indicate that people who are older, who are better off financially, who have poorer health, who have less intrinsically attractive jobs, and maybe women more than men are likely to retire fully (e.g., Brougham & Walsh, 2009; Kieran, 2001; Shimizutani & Oshio, 2010; Wang, Zhan, Liu, & Shultz, 2008). Judging by the affiliations of the authors and the titles of the journals for these articles, there has been a tendency for full retirement to be one of the definitions used in the field of economics (e.g., Shannon & Greirson, 2004; Shimizutani & Oshio, 2010) and also in adult development and gerontology (e.g., Price & Joo, 2005; Wanner & McDonald, 1986). It also appeared that many of the studies used secondary data that was obtained in national surveys. We can only speculate, but in such research, operational definitions are often determined by the nature of the measures that are already present in the data and not necessarily ones that are chosen by or would have been preferred by the researchers.

Reduction in Hours Worked and/or Earnings

Some research has operationalized retirement as a significant reduction in hours worked or a reduction in earnings among older workers (e.g., Baker, Gruber, & Milligan, 2003; Blekesaune & Solem, 2005). Using this conceptualization, a person who is currently working would be considered "retired" if he or she presently works fewer hours or earns less than he or she did in the past. Thus, this represents a broad conceptualization of retirement in that it is inclusive of older workers who have completely withdrawn from paid work along with those who are currently working under reduced hours or income. If they have completely withdrawn, they are simultaneously retired by the previous definition above, which is nonparticipation in the workforce. If they are still working, however, and if they will soon leave their current job while leaving employment altogether, this job is considered one possible form of bridge employment by modern retirement researchers. That is, it is a bridge spanning the time between full employment in what might be considered a career-long job and full retirement or nonparticipation in the workforce. Many of the operational definitions of retirement that are not full withdrawal from the workforce are instances of bridge employment, which will become obvious below. An example familiar to many academics is the senior professor who "goes part-time" before fully retiring. This specific example is a phenomenon that has also been called partial retirement (e.g., Beehr, 1986). Indeed, most older workers who become partially retired do fully retire in a few years (e.g., Desmette & Gaillard, 2008).

A few issues concern this particular conceptualization of retirement. First, how large does the reduction in hours worked or earnings have to be before one is considered retired? Should the reduction be assessed in relative or absolute terms? Second, does this conceptualization suggest that retirement exists on a continuum? For example, is a person who has experienced a 50% reduction in hours worked "more retired" than one who has experienced a 25% reduction? Another issue involves whether one experiences a voluntary or involuntary reduction in hours worked and whether that reduction is permanent or temporary. Related to (in)voluntary reduction in hours, an important issue may be whether the reduction in hours worked is coupled with, or due to, the workers' decreased commitment to the workforce participation. The psychological situation (e.g., as may be reflected in self-reported retirement) of workers who are versus are not committed to participation in the workforce is likely to be quite different.

Women who start working part-time in their senior years are more likely than men to define themselves as partially retired (Szinovacz & Deviney, 1999). In a Canadian study that used this conceptualization of retirement, Baker, Gruber, and Milligan (2003) used information from tax returns to assess retirement. Specifically, they inferred that

one was retired when he or she earned zero income after a previous year of positive income. Their results suggested that retirement incentives inherent in the Canadian social security system encourage people to retire. Similarly, Blekesaune and Solem (2005) identified workers as retired when they had an income below $9,000 after earning more than $12,000 in each of the two previous years. Their analyses suggest that lack of work autonomy and the presence of work stressors may contribute to early retirement. However, it is unclear how this type of retirement is related to employees' decisions to retire fully (Gustman & Steinmeir, 1984, 2001). That is, if part-time work is available, it is unclear if that choice is taken more by people who otherwise would have stayed full-time workers or by people who otherwise would have retired fully.

As the concept of bridge employment has become more well recognized, this definition of retirement (partial retirement) has become more common and discussed more frequently. Based on the journals and affiliations of authors, it appears to be a common type of retirement to examine in the adult development or gerontology area and in economics.

Hours Worked or Earnings below a Minimum Cutoff

Another conceptualization of retirement involves working fewer hours or earning less than a prescribed minimum cutoff (Szinovacz & DeViney, 1999; Talaga & Beehr, 1995). Similar to the previous definition, one could be considered "retired" even though he or she is currently working. However, this conceptualization implies that retirement is dichotomous—one is either retired or not retired. Thus the concept of partial retirement does not apply. One issue with this conceptualization of retirement is what standard to use as a minimum cutoff. Norms regarding hours worked and earnings can vary by occupation, geographic region, and era. Thus, it may be difficult to identify a minimum cutoff that can be used across several situations. A government pension plan may implicitly be considered as applying this type of definition of retirement if it has income contingencies for receipt of the government pension. For example, such plans could specify that people over a certain age, who have worked a certain number of years, and *who are currently earning less than a certain amount of money from a job* are eligible for the pension payments. Explicitly or implicitly, this may be done because the person earning over a certain amount of money per year is not considered retired and therefore is not eligible for the pension money.

Hours worked or earnings below a certain cutoff have been used as criteria to identify retirees very often in research. They have been used, however, as criteria to decide who is leaving retirement status and taking up employment after retiring (e.g., in longitudinal studies; Gustman & Steinmeir, 2000). In a study examining gender as a moderator of the relationships between retirement predictors (e.g., number of dependents, occupational level) and retirement, Talaga and Beehr (1995) defined retirement as working fewer than thirty-five hours per week while drawing a pension. Their analyses found that number of dependents was positively related to probability of retirement among women but negatively related to probability of retirement among men. Thirty-five hours of work per week is a relatively large number for defining retirement; at the other extreme, Szinovacz and DeViney (1999) used number of hours worked during the past week to assess retirement, and only participants who reported zero hours worked per week were labeled as being retired. Analyses from that study suggest that although self-identified retirement status is largely a function of workforce participation at a certain level, other factors such as spouse's retirement status, disability, and work history play important roles.

There is no particular pattern regarding which discipline might use this approach more than others. As noted earlier, this criterion is sometimes used for practical purposes, such as to determine who is eligible for government pensions, but overall it has not been used very often in research, and especially not as the sole definition of retirement in a given study.

Receipt of Retirement Income

Some types of income are specifically designated for and expected to be obtained by people defined as retired. This would include the receipt of money from government sources that is intended to aid people financially in retirement, employer or other sources of pensions for retirees, and any other private sources of funds intended for retirees (e.g., in the United States, an Individual Retirement Account into which the individual and the employer may have invested). Most people who can and do access these sources of income are retired by other definitions, too, but not necessarily. That is, some retirees are still working for pay in addition to receiving these funds. Nonetheless, receipt of retirement income has been used as the operational definition of retirement

in research. Thus in the United States, for example, people can start collecting Social Security income from the federal government while still working in the same job or a new one. Their retirement (Social Security) income, however, may be reduced somewhat if they work for pay. A focus on retirement income is especially important in the United States because of the common prediction that an increase in defined contribution over defined benefit pensions will be especially large by the time the final baby boomers retire, and furthermore, the amount of money available to them from government pension sources (Social Security) will be less than for their predecessors (e.g., Butrica, Iams, Smith, & Toder, 2009). The sources, amounts, and types of retirement income therefore might become quite different from a few decades ago. It should be noted, however, that some not entirely predictable circumstances could make their retirement incomes comparable to the previous generation's (e.g., Congress could put more money into the retirement system, investments could begin giving higher returns, the younger generation could put off retirement until they are older and have accumulated more wealth, or families could give more financial support to their retired members).

Receipt of retirement income is one of the most commonly used operational definitions of retirement. It can be used in combination with other indicators of retirement, but sometimes accepting retirement income is the only operational definition used in studies. This may be because some large, preexisting, semi-public datasets have this measure available, making it an easy marker of retirement (e.g., the Health and Retirement Study). Furthermore, research reviews usually conclude that some form of wealth or projected retirement income has been among the most consistent predictors of the decision to retire (e.g., Beehr, 1986; Barnes-Farrell, 2003).

The decision to retire is itself measured variously, and research on the receipt of retirement income illustrates this. For example, having a pension available predicts a lower retirement age, an instance in which age of retirement is used as a measure of the decision to retire (e.g., Arkani & Gough, 2007; Gustman & Steinmeir, 2005). In this case, having pensions available at earlier ages makes it more likely for people to take the pension early (the measure of retirement). Alternatively, in samples of older people, various measures of retirement income are related to people being retired (e.g., Stolzenberg & Lindgren, 2010). The basic principle is consistent and simple—that having better income available in retirement makes people more likely to retire and accept that money. Some variations consistent with this theme of availability of money making people more likely to retire (by accepting retirement money) are that people receiving inherited money are more likely to retire by taking retirement pay (e.g., Brown, Coile, & Weisbrenner, 2010; Coile & Levine, 2007); if years in the workforce is a criterion for receiving pension money, then employees retire later (e.g., Hakola & Uusalito, 2005); and if less money is available for a regular retirement stipend (e.g., Social Security in the United States) and more for a disability pension, fewer people take the regular retirement stipend and more apply for disability retirement pensions (e.g., Duggan, Singleton, & Song, 2007). Related to this last point, it is not necessarily true that these disabilities are not real; an indicator of the validity of disability claims is that people on disability pensions are likely to die sooner than people on regular pensions (e.g., Hult, Stattin, Janlert, & Jarvholm, 2009). Furthermore, money is generally related to health for retirees; analyzing data at both the country level and the individual level, higher pensions are related to better health of retirees (e.g., Esser & Palme, 2010).

Not surprisingly, the operational definition of retirement as the receipt of retirement income is prominent especially in the field of economics, judging by the affiliations of the authors and the titles of the journals for these articles (e.g., Hurd & Panis, 2006; Song & Manchester, 2007). The general finding is that the more money (income or wealth that could generate income) people would have in retirement, the more likely they are to retire.

Exit from One's Main Employer

Some research operationalizes retirement as the act of older employees leaving their main employer (Denton & Spencer, 2009). The concept of a main employer usually refers to an employer where the person has worked for a substantial amount of his or her career. Others have labeled this the career job (e.g., Gobeski & Beehr, 2009; Wang et al., 2008). Of course there are people who might have no clear career job because they have frequently changed jobs or have moved in and out of the workforce so many times during their working years, making a designation of a career job somewhat arbitrary. Nevertheless, this definition of retirement is viable for many people. They may still work in another job even though they are designated as retired from the main employer or career job. For example, someone

who worked as a firefighter for thirty years might retire from that job and start working part-time on his or her own as a chimney repairer.

This operational definition of retirement rarely seems to be used alone in retirement research. It might be used, for example, along with studying receipt of retirement income (e.g., Asch, Heider, & Zissimopoulos, 2005). It is often implicitly or explicitly used in two situations: when the research sample comes from a single employer or when specific topics such as bridge jobs are studied. Thus, a study of people who retired from the U.S. federal civil service (Asch et al., 2005) and a study of people who retired from a single large manufacturing company (Talaga & Beehr, 1995) are examples. Because the samples may have been obtained through contacts with the former employer, one of the definitions is likely to be that the people have retired from that employer (and an unstated assumption is that this was the main employer or career job of the retiree). Often in these studies, however, the sample has been chosen so that everyone in the sample meets this definition. When that happens, the operational definition of retirement as leaving a main employer is a constant rather than a variable. Therefore, such studies cannot tell us much about how this form of retirement is related to any other variable.

Bridge jobs, as noted earlier, have been defined as jobs people take after retiring from a long-term or career job but before completely withdrawing from the workforce (e.g., Feldman, 1994; Sterns & Subich, 2005). By this definition, they are retired, but they are still in the workforce. Some studies of bridge jobs do not operationalize the part of the definition about having retired from a long-term career job, however. They might, for example, simply ask people if they are retired (i.e., they use the self-assessed definition instead). Then they study bridge employment among people who actually have subjectively assessed themselves as being retired, using whatever criteria the participants choose.

Because of these problems (i.e., retirement from the main employer is often a constant instead of a variable, the use of this operationalization of retirement is often combined with other operationalizations, and bridge employment has been operationally defined loosely in some of these studies), there is little research knowledge specifically about leaving one's main employer or career job as a unique definition of retirement, yet it probably represents a prototypical image of retirement. Rau and Adams (2005) for example, operationalized retirement as leaving one's employer (a university system in the midwestern United States). They found that such retirees are attracted to new (i.e., bridge) jobs that had a targeted EEOC statement, offered mentoring opportunities, and allowed flexible scheduling. Even so, research has not used this operational definition of retirement very often in recent years. This might be a result of a new understanding that retirement does not usually fit this prototypical definition anymore. Based on the journals and affiliations of the authors, it appears to be used mostly in economics and gerontology, when it is employed.

Change of Career or Employment Later in Life

Another definition of retirement is that an employee who is in the later stages of the typical working life (determined mostly by age) changes employers or careers. Of course the concept of *later* stages of working life does not have a precise, objective, or stable definition. Over time, the typical age at which people quit working can change based on changes in a variety of variables such as average life span, labor laws, and economic times. According to Denton and Spencer (2009), such a change might be an indicator of the person deciding to do behaviors that eventually place them into one of the other categories of retirement (e.g., might be accompanied by a reduction in working hours and/or an exit from one's main career employer). This type of change might be accompanied by a reduced commitment to work in general. An example would be someone who has been a high school woodshop teacher for most of his or her life and retires to become an independent cabinetmaker (or even to do an unrelated job such as an innkeeper), either full- or part-time. This new occupation would usually be considered bridge employment (Desmette & Gaillard, 2008; Gobeski & Beehr, 2009) because the expectation is that the person will probably retire by withdrawing from the workforce completely in a relatively short time (even though it might be years, it would not be nearly as many years as they had worked previously).

Although a change in career late in life is almost always a case of bridge employment, the employee's new job could be simply a second career job if the change occurred earlier in life. If the second job is one that the person will not occupy for very long before (more) complete retirement, then it would usually be considered a bridge between full career employment and full complete retirement from the workforce. The topic of bridge employment is itself a burgeoning research area. The phenomenon has

been occurring for a long time, but it has increased in recent decades (Wang, Adams, Beehr, & Shultz, 2009), which is likely the reason it has now received a new label (bridge employment) and is the focus of new programs of research. When this operational definition of retirement is used, it usually is in combination with other definitions. For example, Gobeski and Beehr (2009) asked older people for their self-assessed retirement age and what they did (e.g., work in a bridge job) after that retirement age; in general, those who had more positive reactions to their original jobs were more likely to have taken bridge employment that was in the same field than to take another type of bridge job or no bridge job at all. This suggests that the type of bridge job people go into is not necessarily random or due entirely to convenience. Another study (Shultz & Wang, 2007) using this conceptualization of retirement found that, compared with older workers who stayed in the same job, those who changed jobs were more likely to have previously experienced cancer, lung disease, arthritis, or diabetes. Reviews have long concluded that ill health is related to retirement (e.g., Talaga & Beehr, 1989), and it may sometimes be a reason for this particular type of retirement. Wang (2007), looking at people's adjustment to retirement, found that retirees with bridge jobs were more likely to be in a maintaining pattern of adjustment to retirement. That is, their retirement was a stable time of life without too many upsets. People going into a late-life job (bridge employment) probably do so for many reasons (e.g., declining health, ability to find a job they like), and having a job might be good for people's late-life adjustment. This last comment should be considered carefully, however, because there is obvious self-selection occurring. It seems quite likely that people who would not like a bridge job simply do not look for or obtain one.

The research on this type of retirement activity (basically bridge jobs) has come especially from economics and the organizational sciences (organizational psychology and organizational behavior). As noted earlier, there are usually multiple operational definitions used for retirement in these studies, for example, self-reported subjective retirement or accepting retirement income payments.

Self-Assessed Retirement

Some studies have assessed retirement by directly asking participants whether or not they consider themselves to be retired, and household surveys have been recommended as one of the best ways to measure retirement (Bowlby, 2007). This self-assessed retirement is relatively convenient and flexible, and it has been widely used. The researcher can avoid having to define retirement and instead let whatever subjective definition each respondent uses be the standard. A related limitation, however, is that because self-assessed retirement depends upon each respondent's unique definition, the researcher might not know what the retirement definition is in his or her own study, or even if the definition is consistent across people.

This approach can indeed ask the person if, when, why, and how they retired. A frequent technique is to ask current employees when they expect to retire. Many studies have included self-report measures of retirement *intention* (e.g., Desmette & Gaillard, 2008; Gaillard & Desmette, 2010; Jones & McIntosh, 2010; Siegrist et al., 2006) and early retirement (Brougham & Walsh, 2009; Kubicek, Korunka, Hoonnakker, & Raymo, 2010). The assumption is that behavioral intentions will predict the actual behavior (consistent with the theory of planned behavior; e.g., Ajzen, 1985). Researchers can also ask about specific types of employment and retirement events and situations. One study reported that older people who are out of work are more likely to define themselves as retired than younger people (Szinovacz & Deviney, 1999).

The flexibility of the self-report method also means that it can be a way to integrate or compare one type of operational definition of retirement with another. In one example of this approach, Talaga and Beehr (1995) asked participants to self-identify themselves as either (a) unemployed, (b) employed part-time, (c) employed full-time, (d) retired but working full-time, (e) retired but working part-time, or (f) retired and not working. In support of the validity of this measure, they found that self-reported retirement was strongly related (*r*s were greater than 0.75) to other measures of retirement, including pension retirement (i.e., working fewer than thirty-five hours per week while receiving a retirement pension) and degree of retirement (i.e., number of paid hours worked per week). Self-reports also could be used to identify types of bridge employment, as Gobeski and Beehr (2009) did by asking retirees if they worked after retirement and, if so, in what kinds of jobs (career or non-career-related jobs).

Studies that used self-reports of retirement *intention* have found that several personal situations can predict who intends to retire soon or early, including disability or other poor health conditions (Brougham & Walsh, 2009; Desmette & Gaillard, 2008; Harkonmaki et al., 2009) and spouse pressure (van Dam, van der Vorst, & van der Heiden, 2009). Some job conditions such as (lack of) challenging or intrinsically rewarding work (Dam et al., 2009; Siegrist, Wahrendorf, von dem Konesebeck, Jurges, & Borsch-Supan, 2006) or high work stress (Potocnik, Tordera, & Peiro, 2010) are associated with people reporting that they expect to retire sooner. In addition, workers who identify themselves with older workers (Desmette & Gaillard, 2008), who are less committed to their organization (Jones & McIntosh, 2010), and who experience early retirement norms (Potocnik et al., 2010) say they expect to retire sooner. Self-reports of already being retired are related to some of the same general types of variables, such as intrinsically rewarding work (Gobeski & Beehr, 2009), poor health (Pond, Stephens, Alpass, 2010; Shultz & Wang, 2007), and good finances (Coile & Gruber, 2007; Kieran, 2001; Schellenberg & Silver, 2004).

Studies using self-assessed retirement are very common and have appeared in journals or by authors from several different disciplines, including economics (e.g., Maestas, 2010), gerontology or aging (Potocnik et al., 2010; Szinovacz & DeViney, 1999), and organizational psychology (Talaga & Beehr, 1995), among others. It is so common to use surveys in the social sciences that many disciplines readily adopt this measurement approach alone or in combination with others. Indeed, many of the combination measures discussed in the following section combine self-reports with other measures of retirement.

Combinations of Retirement Types

Some studies have operationalized retirement using a combination of two or more of the above seven measures. These combination measures can be useful when researchers fear that any single measure alone does not adequately capture the entire retirement domain. Alternatively, combination measures can be useful when researchers wish to include only participants who are retired and thus want to be highly confident that they are screening out non-retired individuals. In this case, a researcher can be fairly confident, for example, that a participant who is no longer working, who draws a pension, and who self-identifies as being retired is in fact retired. Using any one of these three retirement measures alone affords the researcher less confidence about the participant's retirement status.

Different combinations of measures have varied in which retirement conceptualizations they have combined. For example, Gustman and Steinmeier (2001) used a combination measure of retirement that took into account both self-reported retirement and objective hours worked. They found that individuals who retire early often fail to plan financially for their retirement. In another study, labor force exits or reduced participation in the labor force and receipt of a pension were used together to assess retirement (Haas, Bradley, Longino, Stoller, & Serow, 2006). That study focused on elderly migrants and found that numbers of retirees migrating from one state to another in the United States differed depending on the definition of retirement. There could be public policy implications if a federal government decided to apportion special funding to states based on the idea that retirees are moving there.

One issue concerning this combination approach is whether to combine them and, if so, which conceptualizations to combine and whether or not to weigh them equally. Furthermore, it makes little sense to combine some of the above conceptualizations. For example, nonparticipation in the labor force cannot be combined with change in career or employment later in life because the latter requires that the individual has not yet fully withdrawn from work life.

Conclusion

Much of the world's population is aging, and this includes the workforce. An aging workforce means that the number of retirees is also likely to increase soon. The baby-boomer generation is often cited as the cause of this aging, but there are additional reasons, including decreasing birth rates in much of the world (Wang & Shultz, 2010). With the increase in retirement-aged people, there comes a need to understand who, when, and why people retire, and what they do after they retire. Such information has implications for public policy, employers' decisions and practices, and individuals' decision making and well-being.

Shultz and Henkens (2010) argue that there is a need for interdisciplinary approaches to studying retirement, and we observed that many of the definitions of retirement are used in research in multiple disciplines. Given that retirement is inherently difficult to define (e.g., Beehr, 1986; Ekerdt, 2010) and because it is a topic of study within many different disciplines (e.g., psychology, sociology, economics, political science, gerontology and adult development, and business), it should be no surprise that retirement has been assessed in several different ways. We focused on the eight conceptualizations of retirement discussed by Denton and Spencer (2009). Based on our reading, we suspect that the method used to assess retirement in any given study is sometimes a function of the data that are available to researchers as much as it is a matter of disciplinary preference. This is particularly true when archival data are used, which is somewhat common in studies of retirement.

It is important to note that because different conceptualizations of retirement are not completely redundant with each other, research findings might differ depending on the operationalization that is used. Indeed, a worker who is "retired" according to one operationalization (e.g., receipt of a retirement pension) might not be considered "retired" according to other operationalizations (e.g., nonparticipation in the labor force). Thus, we encourage researchers to think carefully about the potential implications of using one operationalization over another.

Bridge employment is a somewhat new topic of study in retirement research, and its occurrence may be increasing over time. It is a phenomenon that has increased the ambiguity of the meaning and definitions of retirement. A large percentage of older workers no longer enter retirement by leaving a long-term, career job and never working for pay again. That simple, clean definition of retirement often had a specific, clear time at which people stopped working for good. Many of the people who take bridge employment consider themselves both retired and still working, and in this case they fall in Denton and Spencer's (2009) category of a "combination" definition of retirement. Bridge employment, because of its increasing occurrence, because of the relatively little research on it, and because of its interesting but somewhat counter-intuitive nature, is a topic ripe for much more research. We still have much to learn about it.

Future Directions

Given the complexity of retirement, we believe more research is needed to examine its various conceptualizations. First, research should examine whether the antecedents and consequences of retirement differ across operationalizations. It is likely that the psychological consequences of ending participation in the workforce, for example, are not the same as the consequences of receiving retirement income. Second, future studies should examine the relationships between different operationalizations of retirement. Although some studies have reported correlations between certain retirement measures (e.g., Talaga & Beehr, 1995), more work is needed in this area. We observed many instances in the research in which different types of retirement (definitions) co-occurred, which represented Denton and Spencer's (2009) combination category. But to what *extent* do specific types of retirement tend to co-occur? As noted earlier, even research that examines multiple types of retirement at the same time does not necessarily compare them and focus on how they are related to each other. Systematic new research could examine the relationships among the different types of retirement, which might show that a few of them frequently occur together. For example, people who totally withdraw from the workforce as a form of retirement probably consider themselves (and would therefore self-report) as retired. Nevertheless, we do not know how many or which of the definitions normally go together.

Because retirement can best be defined as a process and not a single event (Beehr, 1986; Beehr & Bennett, 2007; Shultz & Wang, 2011), we encourage the use of longitudinal designs aimed at examining within-person changes in retirement status over time. Perhaps a worker who is initially considered retired according to some criteria (e.g., receipt of retirement/pension income) and not another (e.g., nonparticipation in the labor force) will at a later point be considered retired according to all criteria. Such research may further suggest that the threshold for qualifying as retired according to some criteria is higher than it is for others, and also that there might be some common patterns of stages in these definitions of retirement through which many people pass on their way to retirement by all definitions. Many workers who self-label themselves as retired, for example, may not be complete nonparticipants in the workforce. In other words, the threshold for qualifying as a nonparticipant in the workforce may be higher than the threshold for self-assessed retirement.

The presence of multiple operationalizations of retirement also suggests their importance for understanding the role of differences in national cultures. Laws regarding retirement benefits vary from country to country. A few countries have different statutory retirement ages for men versus women. For example, in the United Kingdom and Hungary, women's legal retirement ages are younger than men's (van Dalen, Henkens, Schippers, & Hendrekse, 2010), and in the United States there is no general legal retirement age. Furthermore, the actual ages at which people retired have tended to be younger than the statutory ages, and they vary across European countries and the sexes by as much as six years (van Dalen et al., 2010). Societal differences also exist in regard to personal wealth, health, and attitudes toward retired and older workers. Because of the economic pressure of increasing numbers of retirees on public pensions, one solution is to raise the statutory age of retirement or the age at which people qualify for public pension funds. Although this approach would seem to take care of the problem mathematically, social and political concerns play a role; not everyone is in favor of it. Worker protests in France (BBC, 2010) indicate that workers themselves might believe it is unfair for them to be required to work longer than their parents' generation did. In addition, employers might not like the idea either. A survey of employers in five European countries found that many employers in four of the countries were not in favor of raising the retirement age. Instead, some of them considered older employees to be a burden on their companies (van Dalen et al., 2010). This burden might come in the form of older workers being less productive as they age; this is a common belief, but job performance of older workers does not appear to decline, at least until very old ages; "reviews of field research…have repeatedly concluded that there is little relationship between age and job performance" (Beehr & Bowling, 2002, p. 213; also see meta-analysis by Waldman & Aviolo, 1986). The other issue that might be bothering these European employers is that, because of seniority systems, older workers tend to be paid more than younger workers; we could surmise that their increasing cost is not offset by increasing productivity as they age, a situation that could be perceived as a burden by employers. The cultural and societal factors may differentially impact or be impacted by the various conceptualizations of retirement. For example, some of Denton and Spencer's (2009) definitions of retirement include reduced hours and/or reduced pay. If an employer thought he or she could retain old or hire new older workers without paying them for high seniority, his or her perceptions of older workers as a burden might diminish.

In sum, retirement is a topic that directly impacts many people, as it represents an important career stage and is usually a natural part of aging. As researchers learn more about the complexities of retirement, we hope that older workers will be better able to take full advantage of their retirement years.

References

Ajzen, I. (1985). From intentions to actions: A theory of planned behavior. In J. Kuhl & J. Beckmann (Eds.), *Action-control: From cognition to behavior* (pp. 11–39). Heidelberg, Germany: Springer.

Alley, D., & Crimmins, E. (2007). The demography of aging and work. In K. S. Shultz & G. A. Adams (Eds.), *Aging and work in the 21st century* (pp. 7–24). New York, NY: Psychology Press.

Arkani, S., & Gough O. (2007). The impact of occupational pensions on retirement age. *Journal of Social Policy, 36,* 297–318.

Asch, B., Heider, S. J., & Zissimopoulos, J. (2005). Financial incentives and retirement: Evidence from federal civil service workers. *Journal of Public Economics, 89,* 427–440.

Ashforth, B. (2001). *Role transitions in organizational life: An identity-based perspective.* Mahwah, NJ: Lawrence Erlbaum.

Atchley, R. (1989). A continuity theory of aging. *Gerontologist, 29,* 183–190.

Baker, M., Gruber, J., & Milligan, K. (2003). The retirement incentive effects of Canada's income security programs. *Canadian Journal of Economics, 36,* 261–290.

Barnes-Farrell, J. L. (2003). Beyond health and wealth: Attitudinal and other influences on retirement decision making. In G. A. Adams & T. A. Beehr (Eds.), *Retirement: Reasons, processes, and results* (pp. 159–187). New York, NY: Springer.

BBC. (2010). *France hit by new wave of strikes over pension reforms.* Retrieved from http://www.bbc.co.uk/news/world-europe-11570828.

Beehr, T. A. (1986). The process of retirement: A review and recommendations for future investigation. *Personnel Psychology, 39,* 31–56.

Beehr, T. A., & Bennett, M. M. (2007). Examining retirement from a multi-level perspective. In K. A. Shultz & G. A. Adams (Eds.), *Aging and work in the 21st Century* (pp. 277–302). New York, NY: Psychology Press.

Beehr, T. A., & Bowling, N. A. (2002). Career issues facing older workers. In D. C. Feldman (Ed.), *Work careers: A developmental perspective* (pp. 214–241). San Francisco, CA: Jossey-Bass.

Blekesaune, M., & Solem, P.E. (2005). Working conditions and early retirement: A prospective study of retirement behavior. *Research on Aging, 27,* 1–30.

Bowlby, G. (2007). Defining retirement. *Perspectives on Labor and Income, 8(2),* 15–19.

Brougham, R. R., & Walsh, D. A. (2009). Early and late retirement exits. *International Journal of Aging and Human Development, 69,* 267–286.

Brown, J. R., Coile, C. C., & Weisbrenner, S. J. (2010). The effect of inheritance receipt on retirement. *Review of Economics and Statistics, 92,* 425–434.

Butrica, A. B., Iams, M. I., Smith, K. E., & Toder, E. J. (2009). The disappearing defined benefit pension and its potential impact on the retirement incomes of baby boomers. *Social Security Bulletin, 69,* 1–27.

Coile, C. C., & Gruber, J. (2007). Future social security entitlements and the retirement decision. *The Review of Economics and Statistics, 89,* 234–246.

Coile, C. C., & Levine, P. B. (2007). Labor market shocks and retirement: Do government programs matter? *Journal of Public Economics, 91,* 1902–1919.

Denton, F. T., & Spencer, B. G. (2009). What is retirement? A review and assessment of alternative concepts and measures. *Canadian Journal on Aging, 28,* 63–76.

Desmette, D., & Gaillard, M. (2008). When a "worker" becomes an "older worker": The effects of age-related social identity on attitudes towards retirement and work. *Career Development International, 13,* 168–185.

Dew, J., & Yorgason, J. (2010). Economic pressure and marital conflict in retirement-aged couples. *Journal of Family Issues, 31,* 164–188.

Duggan, M., Singleton, P., & Song, J. (2007). Aching to retire? The rise in full retirement age and its impact on the social security disability rolls. *Journal of Public Economics, 91,* 1327–1350.

Ekerdt, D. J. (2010). Frontiers of research on work and retirement. *Journal of Gerontology: Social Sciences, 65B,* 69–80.

Esser, I., & Palme, J. (2010). Do public pensions matter for health and wellbeing among retired persons? Basic and income security pensions across 13 Western European countries. *International Journal of Social Welfare, 19,* S103–S120.

Feldman, D. C. (1994). The decision to retire early: A review and conceptualization. *Academy of Management Review, 19,* 285–311.

Feldman, D. C., & Beehr, T. A. (2011). A three-phase model of retirement decision-making. *American Psychologist, 66,* 193–203.

Feldman, D. C., & Vogel, R. M. (2009). The aging process and person-environment fit. In S. G. Baugh & S. E. Sullivan (Eds.), *Research in careers* (pp. 1–25). Charlotte, NC: Information Age Press.

Gaillard, M., & Desmette, D. (2010). (In)validating stereotypes about older workers influences their intentions to retire early and to learn and develop. *Basic and Applied Psychology, 32,* 86–98.

Gobeski, K. T., & Beehr, T. A. (2009). How retirees work: Predictors of different types of bridge employment. *Journal of Organizational Behavior, 30,* 401–425.

Gustman, A. L., & Steinmeir, T. L. (1984). Partial retirement and the analysis of retirement behavior. *Industrial and Labor Relations Review, 37,* 403–415.

Gustman, A. L., & Steinmeier, T. L. (2000). Retirement outcomes in health and retirement study. *Social Security Bulletin, 63,* 57–71.

Gustman, A. L., & Steinmeir, T. L. (2001). Retirement and wealth. *Social Security Bulletin, 64,* 66–91.

Gustman, A. L., & Steinmeir, T. L. (2005). The social security early retirement age in a structural model of retirement and wealth. *Journal of Public Economics, 89,* 441–463.

Haas, W. H., III, Bradley, D. E., Longino, C. F., Stoller, E. P., & Serow, W. J. (2006). In retirement migration, who counts? A methodological question with economic policy implications. *The Gerontologist, 46,* 815–820.

Hakola, T., & Uusalito, R. (2005). Not so voluntary retirement decisions? Evidence from a pension reform. *Journal of Public Economics, 89,* 2121–2136.

Hall, D. T., & Mirvis, P. H. (1996). The new protean career: Psychological success and the path with a heart. In D. G. Hall (Ed.), *The career is dead—Long live the career* (pp. 15–45). San Francisco, CA: Jossey-Bass.

Harkonmaki, K., Martikainen, P., Lahelma, E., Pitkaniemi, J., Halmeenmaki, T., Silventoinen, K., & Rahkonen, O. (2009). Intentions to retire, life dissatisfaction and subsequent risk of disability retirement. *Scandinavian Journal of Public Health, 37,* 252–259.

Hult, C., Stattin, M., Janlert, U., & Jarvholm, B. (2009). Timing of retirement and mortality—A cohort study of

Swedish construction workers. *Social Science & Medicine, 70,* 1480–1486.

Hurd, M., & Panis, C. (2006). The choice to cash out pension rights at job change or retirement. *Journal of Public Economics, 90,* 2213–2237.

Jahoda, M. (1981). Work, employment, and unemployment: Values, theories, and approaches in social research. *American Psychologist, 36,* 184–191.

Jahoda, M. (1997). Manifest and latent functions. In N. Nicholson (Ed.), *The Blackwell encyclopedic dictionary of organizational psychology* (pp. 317–318). Oxford, England: Blackwell.

Jones, D. A., & McIntosh, B. R. (2010). Organizational and occupational commitment in relation to bridge employment and retirement intentions. *Journal of Vocational Behavior, 77,* 290–303.

Kieran, P. (2001). Early retirement trends. *Perspectives on Labour and Income, 2*(9), 5–11.

Kubicek, B., Korunka, C., Hoonnakker, P., & Raymo, J. M. (2010). Work and family characteristics as predictors of early retirement in married men and women. *Research on Aging, 32,* 467–498.

Levinson, D. J. (1986). A conception of adult development. *American Psychologist, 41,* 3–13.

Levinson, H., & Wofford, J. C. (2009). *Approaching retirement as the flexibility phase.* Washington, DC: American Psychological Association.

Maestas, N. (2010). Back to work: Expectations and realizations of work after retirement. *Journal of Human Resources, 45,* 718–748.

Paul, K. I., & Batinic, B. (2010). The need for work: Jahoda's latent functions of employment in a representative sample of the German population. *Journal of Organizational Behavior, 31,* 45–64.

Pond, R., Stephens, C., & Alpass, F. (2010). How health affects retirement decisions: Three pathways taken by middle-older aged New Zealanders. *Ageing & Society, 30,* 527–545.

Potocnik, K., Tordera, N., & Peiro, J. M. (2010). The influence of the early retirement process on satisfaction with early retirement and psychological well-being. *International Journal of Aging and Human Development, 70,* 251–273.

Price, C. A., & Joo, E. (2005). Exploring the relationship between marital status and women's retirement satisfaction. *International Journal of Aging and Human Development, 61,* 37–55.

Raabe, B., Frese, M., & Beehr, T. A. (2007). Action regulation theory and career self-management. *Journal of Vocational Behavior, 70,* 297–311.

Rau, B. L., & Adams, G. A. (2005). Attracting retirees to apply: Desired organizational characteristics of bridge employment. *Journal of Organizational Behavior, 26,* 649–660.

Schellenberg, G., & Silver, C. (2004). You can't always get what you want: Retirement preferences and experiences. *Canadian Social Trends, 75*(Winter), 2–7.

Schlossberg, N. K. (2003). *Retire smart, retire happy.* Washington, DC: American Psychological Association.

Shannon, M., & Grierson, D. (2004). Mandatory retirement and older worker employment. *The Canadian Journal of Economics, 37,* 528–551.

Shimizutani, S., & Oshio, T. (2010). New evidence on initial transition from career job to retirement in Japan.

Industrial Relations: A Journal of Economy and Society, 49, 248–274.

Shultz, K. A., & Henkens, K. (2010). Introduction to the changing nature of retirement: An international perspective. *International Journal of Manpower, 31,* 265–270.

Shultz, K. S., Morton, K. R., & Weckerle, J. R. (1998). The influence of push and pull factors on voluntary and involuntary early retirees' retirement decision and adjustment. *Journal of Vocational Behavior, 53,* 45–57.

Shultz, K. S., & Wang, M. (2007). The influence of specific physical health conditions on retirement decisions. *International Journal of Aging and Human Development, 65,* 149–161.

Shultz, K. S., & Wang, M. (2011). Psychological perspectives on the changing nature of retirement. *American Psychologist, 66,* 170–179.

Siegrist, J., Wahrendorf, M., von dem Konesebeck, O., Jurges, H., & Borsch-Supan, A. (2006). Quality of work, well-being, and intended early retirement of older employees: Baseline results from the SHARE study. *European Journal of Public Health, 17,* 62–68.

Song, J. G., & Manchester, J. (2007). New evidence on earnings and benefit claims following changes in the retirement earnings test in 2000. *Journal of Public Economics, 91,* 669–700.

Sterns, H. L., & Subich, L. M. (2005). Counseling for retirement. In S. D. Brown & R. W. Lent (Eds.), *Career development and counseling* (pp. 506–521). Hoboken, NJ: Wiley.

Stolzenberg, R. M., & Lindgren, J. (2010). Retirement and death in office of U.S. Supreme Court justices. *Demography, 47,* 269–298.

Super, D. E. (1990). A life-span, life space approach to career development. In D. Brown (Ed.), *Career choice and development* (2nd ed., pp. 447–486). New York, NY: Wiley.

Szinovacz, M. E., & Deviney, S. (1999). The retiree identity: Gender and race differences. *The Journals of Gerontology, Series B: Psychological Sciences and Social Sciences, 54B,* S207–S218.

Talaga, J. A., & Beehr, T. A. (1989). Retirement: A psychological perspective. In C. L. Cooper & I. Robertson (Eds.), *International review of industrial and organizational psychology, 1989* (pp. 185–211). Chichester, England: Wiley.

Talaga, J. A., & Beehr, T. A. (1995). Are there gender differences in predicting retirement? *Journal of Applied Psychology, 80,* 16–28.

Van Dalen, H. P., Henkens, K., Hendrekse, W., & Schippers, J. (2010). Do European employers support later retirement? *International Journal of Manpower, 31,* 360–373.

van Dam, K., van der Vorst, J. D. M., & van der Heiden, B. I. J. M. (2009). Employees' intentions to retire early: A case of planned behavior and anticipated work conditions. *Journal of Career Development, 35,* 265–289.

Waldman, D. A., & Avolio, B. J. (1986). A meta-analysis of age differences in job performance. *Journal of Applied Psychology, 71,* 33–38.

Wang, M. (2007). Profiling retirees in the retirement transition and adjustment process: Examining the longitudinal change patterns of retirees' psychological well-being. *Journal of Applied Psychology, 92,* 455–474.

Wang, M., Adams, G. A., Beehr, T. A., & Shultz, K. S. (2009). Career issues at the end of one's career: Bridge employment and retirement. In S. B. Baugh & S. E. Sullivan

(Eds.), *Maintaining focus, energy, and options over the life span* (pp. 135–162). Charlotte, NC: Information Age Publishing.

Wang, M., & Shultz, K. S. (2010). Employee retirement: A review and recommendations for future investigation. *Journal of Management, 36,* 172–206.

Wang, M., Zhan, Y., Liu, S., & Shultz, K. (2008). Antecedents of bridge employment: A longitudinal investigation. *Journal of Applied Psychology, 93,* 181–830.

Wanner, R. A., & McDonald, P. L. (1986). The vertical mosaic in later life: Ethnicity and retirement in Canada. *Journal of Gerontology, 41,* 662–671.

PART 2

Retirement Process Theoretical Perspectives

The Life Course Perspective on Life in the Post-retirement Period

Paul Wink *and* Jacquelyn Boone James

Abstract

The conceptualization of the life course is a function of economic, demographic, and sociocultural forces. We use Laslett's (1989) concept of the Third Age as a framework to discuss various influences on life in the post-retirement period among contemporary Americans and consider factors likely to shape patterns of aging among the baby-boom generation. We conclude that Laslett's idyllic dream of the Third Age characterized by an enlightened pursuit of self-fulfillment is unlikely to be fully realized. Instead, the patterns of today will include a proliferation of choices, increasing longevity, and health, but also a growing discrepancy between the haves and have-nots. For most Americans, post-retirement life will be marked by improvements in physical health and fitness if not self-understanding.

Key Words: retirement, Third Age, socioeconomic factors, health

There is nothing sacrosanct about the way social scientists delineate stages of the life course. As documented by Philippe Aries (1965), the emergence of childhood as a distinct stage of development is a product of industrialization and dates back only to the nineteenth century. A systematic study into the psychology of midlife did not begin until the early 1980s and coincided with the aging of the baby-boom generation (Lachman & James, 1997). Similarly, the separation of the young-old from the old-old age is a relatively new phenomenon associated with the graying of industrialized societies and the resulting increased number of individuals experiencing a healthy and prolonged post-retirement period (James & Wink, 2007). In other words, the conceptualization of the life course is a function of the economic, demographic, and sociocultural forces operating within a society at any given point in time. In this chapter we use Laslett's (1989) concept of the Third Age as a framework to discuss the various forces influencing life in the post-retirement

period among contemporary Americans and consider factors likely to shape patterns of aging among the baby-boom generation.

The Concept of the Third Age

For Laslett (1989), a demographer, the emergence of the Third Age coincides with the fact that individuals in the industrialized world live longer, stay in better health, and tend to be more financially secure than they used to be. According to Laslett, the Third Age is possible only when every citizen can be reasonably sure at the onset of the Second Age (early adulthood) that s/he will survive into old age. In the UK and the USA these conditions were met in the early 1950s when the probability of a 25-year-old male reaching the age of 70 exceeded 50% (the likelihood of this happening for women occurred several decades earlier). Additionally, Laslett argues, the Third Age is a collective experience requiring a sizeable proportion of the population (at least 10%) to be currently over the age of 65 (eligible for retirement) and the national wealth as whole to be adequate to finance the necessary standard of living for the elderly. Given all of these requirements and the inevitable structural lag between the emergence of demographic and socioeconomic conditions and changes in attitudes and behavior, Laslett argues that the US, Japan, Australia, UK, and several other industrialized Western European nations met the prerequisites for the Third Age during the early 1980s.

Not surprisingly, given its recent emergence, there are few positive guidelines or maps available for Third Age individuals to follow in crafting a rewarding life. Most contemporary psychological theories of aging deal with how to cope with the inevitable losses in functioning associated with growing old and managing a foreshortened time horizon. For example, Baltes (1997) equates successful aging with the ability to select tasks, optimize performance, and compensate for lost cognitive abilities in a way that enables the individual to maintain a satisfactory level of performance. Others postulate that older adults are able to maintain a high level of life satisfaction despite evident losses in functioning due to an age-related shift in goal orientation from a tenacious pursuit of goals to seeking of alternatives in response to adversity (e.g., Brandtstädter & Greve, 1994; Heckhausen, 2001). Carstensen's (e.g., Carstensen, Isaacowitz, & Charles, 1999) theory of socioemotional selectivity argues that, faced with a limited time to live, older adults place a greater emphasis on close and emotionally satisfying relationships based not on the need to acquire new information but a desire to maintain existing emotional ties. Erikson (1959), the first to fully enunciate the developmental tasks of old age, emphasized the need for older adults to attain ego integrity, a developmental stage that involves reviewing life with the aim of accepting one's life as the only one possible to have been lived. Although life review, as popularized by Robert Butler (1963), plays a significant role in providing meaning for many older adults, the process of reminiscence is ultimately backward-looking and aimed at coming to terms with mortality rather than providing a forward-looking blueprint for the current generation of Third Agers.

According to Laslett (1989), the hallmark of the Third Age is self-fulfillment and self-realization. This is the case, the theory goes, because the post-retirement period is for most adults the first time that they become free from the responsibility of raising children and no longer engage in income-producing labor with its potential for self-alienation. In other words, the Third Age is the only stage in the life cycle where individuals are free to pursue their self-defined goals; as alleged by Vaillant and DiRago (2007), there is something liberating in the knowledge that one is no longer contributing to the GNP. In this regard, the Third Age differs from the First Age, an era of dependence, socialization, immaturity, and education; the Second Age, an era of independence and maturity but also a time when earning and saving and responsibility, especially for children, are emphasized; and the Fourth Age of final dependence, disability, and death. When defined solely in terms of self-fulfillment, the Third Age can coincide with the First Age, as exemplified, for example, by competitive women gymnasts whose crown of life or peak achievement occurs frequently in their teenage years, or the Second Age, as exemplified by professionals such as medical specialists or academics whose work tends to be characterized by a sense of vocation, flexible hours, and freedom from supervision. Despite these areas of overlap, Laslett argues that, for most individuals, the Third Age coincides with the post-retirement period because, adopting a neo-Marxist position, Laslett sees work in a capitalist system as inherently alienating for most individuals who never have a sense of ownership of the product of their labor and in many cases never see the fruit of their labor. "Work may well be justly valued for what it creates … but work in the Second Age is almost wholly imposed by others rather than oneself … it is allied with the loss of personal control over time … [and] what your efforts help to create is never wholly yours to take a proper pride in, to exhibit or dispose of" (Laslett, 1989, p. 149). Similarly, rearing children, while rewarding, places time constraints on individuals and entails physical and emotional labor that detracts from the goal of self-fulfillment, although again, in some instances, caring for a family may be the individual's crown of life and therefore lead to a coalescence of the Second and Third Ages.

In sum, according to Laslett (1989), most individuals can begin to fully realize their dreams and ambitions only in the post-retirement period, a time when they are free to pursue their hobbies and interests relatively free of the "demands of earning a living, of caring for a family, and of the vagaries of patronage" (p. 147). An important feature of the concept of the Third Age is that, unlike the construct of, for example, life review, it is forward-looking, as the desire for self-fulfillment—the defining feature of the Third Age—prods the person to develop his or her abilities and interests and actively engage in life. If taken seriously, the emphasis on self-realization encourages older adults to engage in learning aimed at promoting their interests and dreams. This task, Laslett argues, is best achieved by universities of the Third Age, where older adults engage in collaborative learning, teaching, and research. The new type of learning associated with universities of the Third Age is not aimed at basic socialization but rather at imparting specialized knowledge aimed at helping older adults with such activities as carving, pottery, metalwork, woodwork, and travel. Many of the courses go way beyond hobby-type activities and include, for example, instruction in history, languages, literature, and political science.

Laslett's emphasis on self-fulfillment as the central characteristic of the Third Age is in large part aimed at taking away the stigma of old age, a period in life that is frequently portrayed as a time of indolence. Such negative portrayal of old age is perfectly understandable, Laslett (1989) argues, if we assume that income-producing work and the care for a family are what people find most fulfilling. Based on this premise, relinquishing these activities must mean the end of worthwhile living. The claim that self-fulfillment is more characteristic of activities associated with the Third rather than the Second Age is clearly meant to redress such an imbalance. In other words, Laslett's theory is aimed at imposing parity on all stages of the life cycle by making each of them distinct but, nonetheless, equally valuable. In adolescence and early adulthood we learn the ins and outs of work and intimacy, in middle adulthood we work hard to consolidate the fruits of our labor, and in late adulthood we reap the rewards of our adult strivings by pursuing many of the personally meaningful interests that were of necessity put aside during the earlier stages of the life cycle.

At the same time, by associating old age with personal self-realization, Laslett faces the danger of reinforcing an image of a selfish older adult who is detached from communal responsibilities as he or she embarks on a life of travel and engagement in trivial hobbies. Laslett, however, assumes that responsibility for others is an essential aspect of the process of self-fulfillment. In addition, care for others is a taken-for-granted feature of older adults' responsibility for the consequences of actions undertaken earlier in life. This includes continued responsibility for the well-being of children and civic involvement in the welfare of the country. Indeed, productive aging researchers suggest that older adults continue to contribute to the economy with paid work, volunteer, and caregiving activities (Morrow-Howell, Hinterlong, & Sherraden, 2001). Johnson and Schaner (2005) reported that older adults contributed $160 billion to the U.S. economy in 2005. Laslett's relative de-emphasis of these aspects of the Third Age reflects his emancipatory agenda aimed at de-stigmatizing old age and restoring dignity to its more self-oriented pursuits. In particular, Laslett's stated aim is to redress the negative image of older people associated in the United States with an over-focus on the financial implications of the graying of American society. In other words, the image of an older adult striving actively for self-fulfillment is aimed to counterbalance that of an indolent consumer of precious societal resources dispensed in the form of Social Security, Medicare, and Medicaid. In this regard, Laslett points out that retirement itself can be construed as a generative act because it creates new job opportunities for members of the younger generations.

In painting a decidedly favorable picture of the Third Age, Laslett (1989) is well aware of the danger of scapegoating the Fourth Age as primarily a time of dependency and decrepitude. In response, Laslett points to the increasingly rectangular shape of the survival curve (Fries & Crapo, 1981), meaning that for a growing number of individuals life expectancy approximates the biological limit to the length of life (placed somewhere around the age of 90). This implies, in turn, that for future generations, as the difference between life expectancy and life span narrows, the period of incapacity and terminal illness will be compressed to an ever shorter interlude of the Fourth Age. It should be noted that although it would be erroneous to assume that the Fourth Age is purely a stage of decrepitude, a discussion of the negative and positive aspects of the terminal stage of life falls outside the domain of this chapter.

Having outlined the concept of the Third Age, we will evaluate its merit by first comparing Laslett's blueprint to empirical findings on everyday life among older Americans. In doing so, we will draw on research presented in our edited volume on the dynamics of the early post-retirement period (James & Wink, 2007). We will highlight, in particular, findings from the Institute of Human Development (IHD) longitudinal study consisting of a community-based sample of men and women participants born in the 1920s who were last interviewed in their late 60s/mid-70s (Wink, 2007). We will next discuss the changing patterns of work involvement and retirement among the current generation of Americans. Laslett assumed that the viability of the Third Age as a distinct developmental stage is based on there being a critical mass of individuals experiencing the same need to craft a life free of paid employment. We will probe the social and psychological implications of the increasingly fuzzy boundary surrounding retirement, with some contemporary older adults continuing to give up employment around the age of 65 while others retire from their primary job only to take on other employment on a full-time or part-time basis (Quinn, 2002). We will then discuss cultural factors that are likely to affect everyday life and the nature of self-fulfillment among future generations of Third Agers. In doing so, we will bring into focus current discussions concerning the status of research about emerging adulthood and consider the personal opportunities and dangers associated with softening of social role expectations, a characteristic increasingly shared by both young and older adults. At the beginning of the twenty-first century, there are obvious parallels between the phenomenon known as emerging adulthood (Arnett, 2004) or "youthhood" (Cote, 2000) and the post-retirement period, as both stages increasingly confront individuals with the need to pursue life in an environment that allows for an increasingly diverse pattern of social roles and personal arrangements.

Everyday Life in the Post-retirement Period

Laslett's generally positive vision of the Third Age is strongly supported by research findings on how contemporary American retirees craft their everyday life. Even though the United States, unlike the United Kingdom, does not have, with a few exceptions, a mandatory retirement age, most Americans choose to retire around the age of 65 (we will discuss some recent changes to this pattern in a later section). Although many of the current retirees have benefited from the post–World War II economic boom, largely as a result of Social Security, the poverty rate among older Americans is surprisingly low, with no more than 10% of retirees living below the poverty line. Of course not all older Americans are wealthy. A notable exception is a group of older African Americans, primarily women, who, despite being past the retirement age and unemployed, do not describe themselves as retired. These individuals continue to seek employment because of poverty (Brown, Jackson, & Faison, 2007). In general, Third Age women have fewer economic resources than men (Sorensen, 2007). Thus race and gender clearly play a role in the experience of the Third Age among older Americans and provide vivid demonstration

that the luxury of self-fulfillment and of pursuing interests and hobbies neglected earlier in life is not available to all individuals.

In support of Laslett's contention that the Third Age is the "crown of life," most individuals plan ahead and look forward to retirement (Moen & Altobelli, 2007). Helson and Cate (2007) report, for example, that the majority of women participants in the Mills longitudinal study approaching retirement "became less achievement-oriented and scheduled, and thus become freer to live their own lives" (p. 98). Only a small minority of retirees experience adverse reactions to the relinquishment of the worker role. Contrary to popular belief, the incidence of mental health problems, including anxiety and depression, among Third Age individuals is low, with only 3% of people age 65–79 reporting severe levels of emotional distress (Grafova, McGonagle, & Stafford, 2007). In fact, the vast majority of older Americans report high levels of life satisfaction. Among the men and women in the IHD longitudinal study, 68% indicated that they were satisfied or highly satisfied with life when interviewed in their late 60s/mid-70s. The everyday life of these individuals was characterized by a sense of purpose and engagement in a variety of activities including physical exercise and sports, travel, community service, and personal hobbies. In face-to-face interviews, several of the IHD participants spontaneously commented that they were surprised by the lack of free time since retirement. In support of Carstensen et al.'s (1999) socioemotional theory, many of the IHD participants in their late 60s and 70s emphasized the importance of interactions with relatives and friends. As argued by Vaillant and DiRago (2007), successful retirement is related to having hobbies as well as satisfying relationships with children and grandchildren. Nonetheless, the pattern of involvement in leisure activities shows considerable stability over time (Diehl & Berg, 2007). As a result, it is unlikely that individuals who lack an interest in activities outside of their work will suddenly develop new ones once retired. Rather, as argued by Laslett, the Third Age is a time to pursue and enjoy activities that were put on the back burner during the hectic years of the Second Age.

Although physical health begins to decline at an accelerated rate from the 50s onward (McCullough & Polak, 2007), it is relatively rare for illness and disability to interfere with everyday functioning among individuals in their late 60s to mid-70s. In the IHD study, for example, only a third of the sample experienced illnesses resulting in moderate to severe chronic health problems (Wink, 2007). Despite the fact that intellectual functioning, just like physical health, begins to decline noticeably beginning with late midlife, these losses, once again in support of Laslett's contention, do not impede significantly the daily life and activities of Third Agers. Willis and Schaie (2007), using data from the Seattle longitudinal study, demonstrated that even such seemingly hard-wired aspects of fluid intelligence as spatial orientation and number ability are subject to cohort effects, with the more recent cohorts of older adults showing a higher level of performance and in some instances a less steep gradient of decline. This effect can be attributed to improvements in diet, heightened levels of physical activity, and the tendency among Americans to engage in vigorous mental activities to an older age. Willis and Schaie's findings suggest that the aging baby boomers and successive cohorts will exhibit higher levels of mental functioning to an even older old age.

In sum, the vast majority of older Americans, despite relatively few educational opportunities and less-than-friendly portrayal in the mass media, relish the freedoms offered by retirement and in general possess good enough physical and mental health to take full advantage of the many possibilities and options. Of course even the best laid plans can be thwarted by adverse life events such as health problems and bereavement, the incidence of which, not surprisingly, increases exponentially with old age. The 2000 census data indicate that at age 75–79 close to 50% of women and 16% of ever-married men are widowed. By the age of 85+ these numbers increase to 70% for women and 32% for men (Sorensen, 2007). Findings from the IHD study indicate that depression in old age is predicted by personal physical health, death of a partner, and emotional problems with children (Wink, 2007). Older men are particularly susceptible to the psychologically detrimental effects of bereavement because husbands tend to rely on their spouses for social involvement and performing everyday chores. Even after retirement, women tend to continue doing most of the housework, despite the fact that both partners have equal amounts of free time (Grafova et al., 2007), a fact that would not be surprising to Arlie Hochschild (1990), the author of *The Second Shift*.

It may seem at first glance strange for Laslett to choose as the "crown of life" a stage of the life cycle where individuals are forced to confront the issue of impending mortality. As argued by Neugarten and Datan (1974/1996), and more recently by Carstensen et al. (1999), the second half of the adult life cycle is characterized by a change in time orientation as people begin to mark time by counting years left to live as opposed to those they have lived thus far. This change in time orientation coinciding with the realization of life's limits has important implications for psychosocial and cognitive functioning. It coincides with an increased emphasis on maintaining existing emotionally close relationships rather than pursuing new ones (Carstensen, 2006). The perception of a limited time horizon also leads to changes in goal orientation away from the relentless pursuit of increasingly challenging and ambitious goals to a more flexible adjustment of goals in response to the difficulties encountered in their achievement (Baltes, 1997). Nonetheless, one of the surprising aspects of the aging process is that it is characterized by a decrease rather than an increase in fear of death. Very few Third Agers express a concern about death, although many express anxiety about the death of their partner as well as the process of dying and, in particular, are fearful of pain and loss of dignity and control (Dillon & Wink, 2007; Wink, 2007; Wink & Scott, 2005).

There are two main reasons why older Americans experience low levels of death anxiety. First, normative transitions are rarely a source of trauma. That such transitions are usually made without undue angst is true of midlife, menopause, and empty nest syndrome, and there is every reason to believe that the same is true of timely death in old age. Most older adults are satisfied with life and are accepting of their past (Wink & Schiff, 2002) and therefore experience little personal turmoil and few regrets over lost opportunities. Such maturity is likely to buffer Third Agers from fear of death because death anxiety is particularly characteristic of individuals who perceive their lives as unfulfilled. The second reason why fear of death is not a pervasive feature of older adulthood is due to the uncertainty over how long an individual has to live in post-retirement. As noted by Laslett (1989), the Third Age is characterized by a sense of timelessness or absence of a temporal structure. When we are in our 60s, 70s, and 80s, Laslett writes, "we prepare to die … and yet continue with our plans for ourselves as if the future was entirely open-ended. Since life expectancy varies from individual to individual, a sense of open-endedness is the most appropriate policy" (p. 153). In the IHD study this attitude was evident in the fact that most of the interviewees made definite and specific plans for the near future without giving much attention to the prospect of becoming ill or dying, and yet in response to a more general question were hesitant to speculate what their life might be like in the next five years.

As previously noted, Laslett (1989) suggests that the Third Age is defined by self-fulfillment or self-realization. Yet, what is the exact nature of self-fulfillment in later life? Does it involve new insights and patterns of behavior, or is it characterized by continuity of interests and everyday pursuits, some of which may come to the forefront with the increased availability of time after retirement? Laslett appears to favor the second option by claiming that the Third Age provides individuals with the opportunity to devote their full attention to hobbies that had to be placed on the back burner during the demanding years of the Second Age. Even though Laslett pays little attention to this issue, research evidence confirms his hypothesis that old age is rarely characterized by radical new insight or changes in self-understanding (see, for example, Atchley, 1999). There exists little empirical support, for example, for Erikson's (1959) and Butler's (1963) assertions that most individuals engage in life review aimed at developing a new sense of identity that incorporates the past and present into a smooth and cohesive narrative (e.g., Coleman, 1986; Lieberman & Tobin, 1983). In the IHD study, for example, a solid two-thirds of the participants did not review their life in any formal way, although they might have engaged in sporadic reminiscences. In spite of this, very few of the participants (at most 10%) suffered an adverse effect of not reconciling the past with the present (Wink & Schiff, 2002). Most of the 20% of participants who successfully accomplished a life review were already prone to introspection as young adults and were likely therefore to examine their lives well before old age.

The contention that older adults are not prone to deep levels of self-exploration fits well with the positivity phenomenon, or the tendency to focus on positive stimuli and to avoid negative ones (e.g., Carstensen & Mikels, 2005), as well as the finding that affective complexity tends to decline in old age (Labouvie-Vief, 2003). Labouvie-Vief reports longitudinal and cross-sectional data indicating that older adulthood brings with it a growing tendency for affect optimization (emphasis on positive feelings) but a decline in affective complexity (tendency to acknowledge the presence of competing emotions; Labouvie-Vief & Diehl, 2000; Labouvie-Vief, Diehl, Jain, & Zhang, 2007). This shift away from integration to optimization of affect is interpreted as an adaptive response of older adults

to the need to deal with increased negative experiences and loss with diminished cognitive capacities (Labouvie-Vief, 2003). Mounting evidence in favor of the positivity effect supports the view of older adulthood as characterized by the tendency for mood enhancement at the cost of decreased sensitivity to negative information (Carstensen & Mikels, 2005; Scheibe & Carstensen, 2010). According to socioemotional selectivity theory, the positivity effect is a direct corollary of the awareness by older adults of a limited time perspective (Carstensen, 2006). Further, Carstensen argues that the ability to prioritize emotional goals and focus on positive experiences accounts for the otherwise seemingly puzzling finding that emotional well-being remains intact if not improved well into late adulthood (Carstensen et al., 2010), only to decline close to death (Gerstorf et al., 2010).

Both Labouvie-Vief's dynamic integration theory and Carstensen's socioemotional selectivity theory are supported by personality changes across adulthood. In particular, older adulthood is associated with a decline in neuroticism, extroversion, and openness (McCrae & Costa, 2003) and a concomitant increase in agreeableness and conscientiousness (Mroczek & Spiro, 2003). Thus older adults appear to be more emotionally stable, warm, dependable, and devoid of negative affect, but at the same time less flexible and open to new ideas. The psychologically conservative stance associated with aging is further confirmed by Whitbourne's finding that older adults tend to deal with new identity-salient experiences by assimilating them into pre-established cognitive and affective schemas. In contrast, younger adults are more prone to rely on identity accommodation or the tendency to change identity in response to life experiences (Sneed & Whitbourne, 2003).

Although Labouvie-Vief tends to draw negative implications from her finding that affective complexity declines with age, Helson, Soto, and Cate (2006) point out that the tendency toward emotional simplicity in old age does not necessarily have the same significance as lack of tolerance of ambiguity earlier in life. In the case of older adults, after all, the tendency to avoid affective complexity is likely to reflect lessons learned from earlier stages in life and may signify an acceptance of self and others as they are, a sign of practical wisdom. In his research on age-related changes in creativity, Jaques (1965) found that older artists tended to simplify their works and become less focused on public or external acclaim. Nonetheless, one glance at Donatello's statue of Mary Magdalene, completed when the artist was 69 years of age, provides compelling evidence of the depth of experience and feeling behind the deceptive simplicity of this small and unimposing wooden carving.

In sum, the life of most Third Agers of today is characterized by a continuity of interests and stability of coping strategies that have evolved throughout the course of adulthood (Atchley, 1999; Wink, 2007). As a result, self-realization of Third Aged individuals is devoid, by and large, of new discoveries or radical life changes. This does not necessarily signify undue rigidity or personal foreclosure, but reflects, rather, the cumulative and predictable nature of most human lives. In this regard, it is a folly for middle-aged adults to think that their lives will radically change upon retirement. Time and again, the past has proven to be the best and most robust predictor of the future (see Atchley, 1999; Diehl & Berg, 2007).

Work Patterns among Third Age Individuals

Laslett's view of the Third Age as a time of crafting a life free of employment was formed in the context of the longevity revolution that was in full swing at the time of his writing in the mid- to late 1980s. Indeed, as we have shown, current generations of Third Age adults (or retirees) seem to experience his vision of the Third Age as personally rewarding and satisfying, at least those who are economically in a position to retire. However, Laslett could not have anticipated the "perfect storm" of other economic, social, political, and cultural changes that has been gaining strength over the last few years as the baby-boom generation approaches the Third Age. We have seen changes in the economy; a decreasing supply of younger workers, especially in some sectors; major shifts in both public and private pension systems; and less in the way of personal savings (Munnell & Soto, 2005). Thus, current generations of adults about to enter the Third Age are facing new pressures to continue to work longer, to essentially delay the Third Age. There is some evidence that they are responding.

Some of these Third Age adults who could retire continue to work because they enjoy it and need the meaning, structure, life purpose, and social network that work provides (Moen & Altobelli, 2007). Others continue work in order to maintain costly health benefits and/or to supplement inadequate pensions (Munnell & Sunden, 2004; Smyer & Pitt-Catsouphes, 2007). Some work for both of these reasons (Smyer & Pitt-Catsouphes, 2007).

Some, of course, work because they can ill afford retirement at all (Brown et al., 2007; Sorensen, 2007).

Findings from the National Study of the Changing Workforce revealed that 20% of workers aged 50 and older have already retired from one job but are working in a so-called "retirement job" (Brown, Aumann, Pitt-Catsouphes, Galinsky, & Bond, 2010). The authors state that this will soon become the "new normal"—[as] fully "75% of workers aged 50 and older expect to have retirement jobs in the future" (p. 1). In fact, the trend toward early retirement has been reversed in recent years (Quinn, 2002). Asked why they might want to continue work, workers ages 50–70 say that staying mentally and physically active is a major factor (Cappelli & Novelli, 2010). Current generations of future retirees seem to be viewing retirement with new lenses.

How do these trends fit with Laslett's notion of the Third Age as a time of personal fulfillment? Laslett argued that the Third Age was a time of personal fulfillment and peak satisfaction precisely because people were free of the everyday grind of work. Yet there is some evidence that current generations of Third Agers who continue work fare better in terms of psychological well-being and life satisfaction than those who retire (James & Spiro, 2007; Moen, 2007). We have argued elsewhere that work may be considered as one among many options for realizing the "crown of life," especially during the early retirement years (James & Spiro, 2007). Those who have been throughout their lives almost singularly focused on work and who have not put other dreams on the back burner may find work during retirement even more rewarding as it is freely chosen, just as those (particularly some women) who started careers late may find work during the later years to be fulfilling. Laslett recognized the possibility that for certain people, especially professional people, "work is what they do for themselves, for their own satisfaction, even for pleasure … "; for these individuals, he said, " … the Second Age is generally interfused with the Third Age" (Laslett, 1989, pp. 151–152).

What we are hearing more about, however, is the trend toward easing gradually into retirement. Corporations are responding to such employee demands by creating phased retirement programs (Van Deusen, James, Gill, & McKechnie, 2007; Piktialis, 2007). Such gradual exits from the workforce allow for the development of other pursuits, such as community work or other types of volunteer activities (Morrow-Howell, 2007). Others retire from one job only to find another, which some have referred to as bridge jobs (Giandrea, Cahill, & Quinn 2007); usually these too include less pressure and are less demanding than the career job held prior to retirement. As Moen (2007), citing many studies, has said, "Most workers would like to put in fewer hours on the job, and most retirees, at least those in their 50s, 60s, and 70s, would like to have a job, but not work full time …" (p. 31). Moen refers to the career job as the "Big Job" and says that most retirees are looking for "Not So Big Jobs." "Older workers often seek, not total work or total leisure, but 'some of each'" (Moen, 2007, p. 33).

We must not forget, however, that some people, in fact many people, genuinely want to retire, and that almost everyone does by the age of 80 (Sorensen, 2007). Many look forward to reaping the rewards of a life well lived. Those who say they plan to work cannot anticipate how they will feel when the time comes. Health, negative job experiences, and other life experiences may intervene. Munnell, Soto, and Golub-Sass (2008) in fact say that people generally will not work as long as they think they will. Some people look forward to finding meaningful work in retirement in the form of volunteer activities, special projects, or running for political office (MetLife Foundation/ Civic Ventures, 2005; Freedman, 1999). Many older adults yearn for time with friends and family—especially grandchildren (Vaillant & DiRago, 2007). Some consider giving up their jobs as a generative act, making room for the next generation. Most want greater flexibility and control over how they spend their time no matter what they do (Smyer & Pitt-Castouphes, 2007). We must also not forget that some work out of economic necessity and therefore do not have the luxury of construing their retirement as a personal project (Wink & James, 2007). The timing of retirement varies by social class, race, gender, and personality. Public policy must change to accommodate new views of retirement, but the idea of "retiring retirement" as some have suggested (Dychtwald, Erickson, & Morison, 2004) seems flawed at best, and dangerous thinking after decades of efforts to shore up the last years of the lives of elders. As Sorensen (2007) points out, the reason that so few elders are in poverty is that income from Social Security makes a decent standard of living possible for most people. Retirement, sans work, is here to stay and remains a significant opportunity for realizing Laslett's vision of the Third Age.

Lessons Learned from Emerging Adulthood

The varied patterns of work involvement among Americans in their 60s and 70s reflect a larger trend toward the loosening of social role expectations across the life cycle, including the timing of marriage, parenthood, and entry into the workforce. The nature and implications of these changes are perhaps most starkly exemplified by the recent evolution of early adulthood. In contrast to earlier time periods in American history, the first three-quarters of the twentieth century were marked by a rigid timing of entry into adulthood. A young man graduated from high school or college, obtained a steady job that, in many instances, guaranteed lifetime employment, and married shortly thereafter. A young woman was expected to marry no later than her early 20s and give birth to all of her children by the end of her 20s. Given such a strict regime of social role engagement, the issue of when one became an adult was a moot point, as this transition was assumed to occur naturally with employment and starting a family. However, this pattern of marriage and work was subverted in the post-1960s era by radical social, economic, and technological changes. As argued by Arnett (2004), the widespread availability of the birth control pill decoupled sexual relations from marriage, and the growing national affluence and increased need for graduate education postponed for many Americans the time of entry into the adult world of work. The fact that now not only men but also a growing number of women expect to have a career, in conjunction with the growing fluidity of the work marketplace in the era of globalization, contributes to the postponement of marriage and commitment to a stable career. As a result, Arnett (2004) argues, the majority of American men and women in their 20s are reluctant to define themselves as either adolescents or adults, inhabiting instead a world of emerging adulthood or youthhood (Cote, 2000).

The positive features of emerging adulthood are self-evident, as these new sets of arrangements greatly expand personal freedom of choice, legitimate lifestyles that previously were shunned or ostracized, and, in the case of women, provide a new sense of security and well-being associated with adding the role of worker to the traditional roles of spouse and mother. A prolonged time to establish a career and commit to a long-term romantic relationship increases the chance of making the right, personally fulfilling choice, as evidenced, for example, by the dip in the divorce rate among college-educated Americans (Fischer & Hout,

2006). At the same time, however, the currently evolving pattern of arrangements is seen by many cultural critics as posing a fundamental threat to the fabric of social life and self-identity (e.g., Bellah, Madsen, Sullivan, Swidler, & Tipton, 1985; Lasch, 1979; Rieff, 1966). In particular, as argued by Cote (2000), because modern adulthood "has lost much of its role structure and traditional meaning, it has become much more of a psychological phenomenon (p. 4)," a sentiment expressed as early as the 1960s by Philip Rieff. In other words, whereas in the past self-identity tended to be associated with one's role as worker, spouse, or parent, at present the question of "who am I?" has no clear answer, as identity is no longer firmly constrained by tradition, religion, or any other master narrative. Instead, self-identity needs to be constructed by the individuals based on their personal (psychological) journey of individuation that, contrary to Carl Jung (1953, 1972), is no longer seen as tapping into any commonly shared archetypes. After all, in the world of emerging adults, self-identity is just that—an identity forged by the individual as a self-determining agent that experiences few constraints on the direction of this project and its final outcome. In the postmodern world, self-identity also tends to be increasingly lacking in permanence or stability due to a number of reasons: particularly, changes in our self-definitions in response to the rapidly evolving social conditions, and our adapting to the ever more rapidly changing social reality, including the complex web of interpersonal relations with persons whom we see on a daily basis and those with whom we have only internet contact (e.g., Gergen, 2000).

As suggested by Giddens (1991), under conditions of late modernity it is important for individuals to develop their "agentic" potentials with which to construct reality and act in the world. But turning the self into a "reflexive project" capable of taking full advantage of opportunities offered by the plethora of choices is not an easy task, as it requires the ability to evaluate the available information and know oneself well enough to make decisions that are beneficial for one's long-term welfare and personal growth. In other words, the enterprise of forging an identity in purely psychological terms is a daunting task that, to be successfully achieved, requires a level of cognitive abilities that according to Robert Kegan (1994) are present among no more than a third of American adults. On the one hand, the process of psychological individualization threatens the person who lacks the necessary ego strength with the danger of drowning in

the sea of choices and, on the other hand, is likely to make individuals who have not moved past the conformist stage of ego development vulnerable to external manipulation. The likelihood of the latter scenario is enhanced by saturation of everyday life with mass media messages that conveniently promise to dissipate existential anxiety and identity confusion if one simply purchases the latest Louis Vuitton sunglasses or Jimmy Choo boots, attends a weekend course on transcendental meditation in Aspen, or takes Prozac. According to Cote (2000), "a large number—perhaps majority—[of adults] are not taking advantage of the loosening of traditional constraints but instead passively allow themselves to be manipulated by the profit-based 'mass' structures that have arisen in place of traditional cultural institutions. Because this manipulation is largely based on hedonism and narcissism, there is reason to be concerned about how the future is being planned and how much care is given to generational replacement" (p. 4).

This is not the place to evaluate the claim that our society is becoming more narcissistic and whether this has a detrimental effect on social capital and the ethic of care (see Dillon & Wink, 2007). What is important for our argument is that the relaxation of social roles encountered in emerging adulthood carries with it both positive and negative implications insofar as it allows greater personal freedom and flexibility in shaping one's life but, on the other hand, poses the threat of anomie and pseudo-individualization based on becoming a slave to the ever-present mass media and the increasingly rational and strategic forces of late capitalism that now penetrate our daily lives to an increasing extent (Giddens, 1991). Barry Schwartz (2000) provides empirical support for the hypothesis that "tyranny of choice" has a detrimental effect on psychosocial functioning by demonstrating that individuals who aim to maximize the benefit of their choices tended to report lower levels of mental health than their counterparts who adopted a "satisficing" strategy that resulted in accepting a good enough—rather than perfect—outcome. The predicament of choice and of crafting a purposeful life under conditions of uncertainty and weakening of the hold of tradition is equally applicable to contemporary Third Age individuals as emerging adults. As pointed out by Laslett (1989), the societal insignificance of the non-earners is exemplified by the fact that they are not yet a salesperson's specific target. In other words, the Third Agers may be "a mass but they are not yet a mass market." (p. 142). Nonetheless, the number of commercial messages aimed at older people is steadily growing and likely to increase sharply with the retirement of the baby boomers and the proliferation of lifestyle choices available to elderly Americans.

In sum, we would like to argue that a consideration of "emerging adulthood" provides a useful way of evaluating the opportunities and dangers associated with the changing nature of old age. Just as the current generation of men and women in their 20s is hesitant to embrace the label of adulthood, future generations of individuals in their 60s, 70s, and 80s are likely to be hesitant to call themselves old. Instead, the term "midcourse" will likely span the decades of the 30s to the 70s if not 80s (Moen & Altobelli, 2007) and arguably make the term equally devoid of meaning as the ubiquitous concept of middle class. On the upside, the grouping together of Second and Third Agers is likely to offer more freedom and choice to elderly adults and potentially lessen the stigma associated with being old, since in this scenario the term "older adult" will be presumably reserved for severely incapacitated residents of nursing homes. Because distinctions lead inevitably to "invidious comparisons," the blurring of the boundaries between middle and late adulthood has definite emancipator potential. The downside of a prolonged phase of midcourse is that it will reinforce a culture of youthhood and the tendency among the Third Agers to "prefer to live a considerable physical and psychological distance from [old age]" (Gilleard & Higgs, 2000, p. 45). In other words, "the exhortations to accept old age and mortality, though perhaps still widely preached will represent a type of discourse that is no longer supported by practice" (Gilleard & Higgs, 2000, p. 83). Although it might feel good for older individuals to think of themselves as middle-aged, this realization is unlikely to obviate the fact that most 60- and 70-year-olds lack the body strength, mental agility, and suppleness of skin of individuals in their 30s and 40s. It is important, therefore, to consider the psychological and social pros and cons of grandparents living the lifestyle of their children and perhaps even grandchildren. Although living out the dream of perpetual youth has the clear advantage of facilitating functioning to one's physical and psychological potential, it also surely raises the specter of being an imposter. In addition, although accurate in his portrayal of the decreasing gap between life expectancy and life span, Laslett did not fully grasp the role played by advances in medical knowledge in shaping the self-concept and the everyday life of older adults. Yes, progress in medicine has prolonged lives, but it has also triggered a proliferation of anti-aging techniques resulting in less wrinkled skin, postponement of the signs and signals of menopause, and, in general, delays in the onset of the more visible signs of aging. This, in turn, means that the search for self-fulfillment and self-realization among older adults has increasingly focused on maintaining physical health and prolonging life. On the positive side, the anti-aging trends may enhance the quality of life among older adults; on the negative side, as suggested by Gilleard and Higgs (2000), "age resisting fitness regimes promote a positive image of non-agedness that further reinforces the undesirability and fear of old age" (p. 81). In other words, by reinforcing the link between aging and disease, the anti-aging movement is likely to further stigmatize the aging process, and by holding out the promise of prolonging life indefinitely, it reinforces the tendency to deny mortality. As a result, successful aging is likely to increasingly focus on warding off disease and age-related declines in functioning at the expense of growth in awareness of life's limits and personal mortality. While there is nothing wrong with the aim of staying physically healthy into old-old age, we should not forget that it is the awareness of limits and the finality of life that is conducive to the development of a modicum of wisdom, a heightened concern for the welfare of future generations, an increased propensity to examine one's life, and, as stressed by Laslett, a desire for self-realization. Although individuals with genuine psychological interest in personal growth and self-development have always been in the minority, their numbers and influence in shaping how we think about the goals of human development are likely to decline as human aging becomes increasingly explained in terms of neuropsychology rather than psychological theories emphasizing free will, authenticity, and responsibility. It would be a mistake to over-idealize the past generations of older Americans because, as illustrated in this chapter, a fully fledged life review has always characterized only a small minority of older-aged individuals (Coleman, 1986; Wink & Schiff, 2002), and the same is true of a genuine comprehension of life limits that is associated with higher stages of wisdom or ego development (see, for example, Staudinger & Gluck, 2011). Nonetheless, we would like to argue that from the perspective of psychological growth and development, it makes a difference whether the second half of the life course is conceptualized in terms of a prolonged summer that changes precipitously to winter or whether the vision includes an autumnal interlude.

Conclusion

Laslett's claim that the Third Age is a distinct stage of the life course is based on the observation that individuals in the industrialized world stay healthier and live longer and as a result spend a large portion of their life in the post-retirement period. The growing affluence of the older population in countries such as the United States, Germany, Australia, and Japan means that the Third Agers are in a good position to fulfill some of their interests and desires that had to be postponed because of pressures at work and the demands of parenthood. The merit of Laslett's thesis is that it postulates a rhythm to the life course, with each season characterized by a distinct aim: childhood and early adulthood being a time of learning; middle adulthood a time of maturity and responsibility; and old age, the Crown of Life, providing the individual with well-deserved time for personal fulfillment. Laslett's conceptualization of the life cycle bestows dignity on the aging process and dispels the stigma associated with aging and living a prolonged life that no longer generates economic wealth or contributes to the GNP. But how adequate is Laslett's theory in characterizing the current generation of older Americans and in predicting life in old age of the baby boomers?

Laslett's portrait of the Third Age as a welcome relief from the demands of work and parenting and an opportunity for self-realization applies to many of today's middle-class Americans who do not see their work in terms of a vocation and who retire with enough money to contemplate travel and the pursuit of other interests. At the other end of the economic spectrum are individuals, many of whom are women and racial minorities, who do not have enough income to retire or contemplate leisure activities. As a demographer, Laslett was correct in pointing out the tendency of successive generations of older adults to remain healthier and fitter to an ever older age. The question remains, however, how will the future generations of Third Agers utilize the growing number of years following retirement? As we have argued, the landscape of old age inhabited by the aging baby boomers is likely to differ markedly from that envisioned by Laslett. Laslett's concept of the Third Age is based on the notion of a common experience shared by a substantial number of older adults. In the case of Britain in the 1980s, this involved an increasing number of persons who were forced to retire at the mandatory age of 65 for

men and 60 for women and who could look forward to a number of years of a healthy life. The uniformity of experiences that Laslett thought to be a critical component of the Third Age is, however, increasingly replaced in America by a proliferation of lifestyles, with some older individuals continuing to retire around the age of 65 while others work into their 70s and 80s. While some older persons continue to work full-time, others choose part-time employment or phased retirement or, alternatively, fully retire but have a spouse who continues to be employed. A proliferation of lifestyles and the demise of the Third Age as a uniform stage of adulthood are likely to turn old age into a free market and promote the ideology of survival of the fittest. As documented by Vaillant and DiRago (2007), flexibility of choice regarding work arrangements is most characteristic of affluent professionals who tend to be self-employed and who do not engage in physical labor. According to Giddens (1991), social life in the era of late modernity increasingly places a premium on having a strong sense of agency that allows an individual to fully benefit from the multiplicity of choices in a world characterized by loosened social roles and expectations. A strong sense of agency is also needed to deal with the greater penetration of mass media and consumerism into our daily lives. Confronted with a plethora of messages offering them anti-aging treatments and lifestyle choices geared to "keep up with the Joneses," the Third Agers face the danger of become increasingly other-directed and sensitive to the opinions and approval of others. After all, the chief advertising strategy is to convince consumers that their social image will improve with the purchase of product x or that buying a certain product will make them feel as good as the idealized other. The modern trend toward increased other-directedness and conformity was already foreshadowed by Aldous Huxley in the 1940s in his novel *Brave New World* and subsequently by Richard Sennett (1978) in his book *The Fall of Public Man*.

From a broader social policy perspective, the collapse of the Second and Third Ages into a common midcourse and the concomitant flexibility of work-retirement arrangements are likely to threaten Social Security and Medicare, which, as we know, will become insolvent in the middle of this century unless remedial actions are taken soon. The cache of old-age benefits will surely lose some its shine in a society where no one is old! Modification of the Social Security program to reflect the new proliferation of lifestyles and work patterns is likely to have a particularly negative effect on the poor, the under-privileged, and the vulnerable because they will have the least flexibility and strength to deal with the new environment characterized by "freedom of choice."

In sum, Laslett's dream of the idyllic stage of the Third Age characterized by an enlightened pursuit of self-fulfillment is likely to be never fully realized. Instead, the patterns of today will continue into the future, including a proliferation of choices, increasing longevity, and health, but also a growing discrepancy between the haves and have-nots. For the majority of Americans, life in the 60s, 70s, and 80s will be rewarding and marked by improvements in physical health and fitness if not self-understanding.

References

Aries, P. (1965). *Centuries of childhood: A social history of family life.* New York, NY: Vintage.

Arnett, J. J. (2004). *Emerging adulthood: The winding road from the late teens through the twenties.* New York, NY: Oxford University Press.

Atchley, R. (1999). *Continuity and adaptation in aging: Creating positive experiences.* Baltimore, MD: Johns Hopkins University Press.

Baltes, P. P. (1997). On the incomplete architecture of human ontogeny: Selection, optimization, and compensation as foundation of developmental theory. *American Psychologist, 52,* 366–380.

Bellah, R., Madsen, R., Sullivan, W., Swidler, A., & Tipton, S. (1985). *Habits of the heart: Individualism and commitment in American life.* Berkeley, CA: University of California Press.

Brandtstädter, J., & Greve, W. (1994). The aging self: Stabilizing and protective processes. *Developmental Review, 14,* 52–80.

Brown, E., Jackson, J. S., & Faison, N. A. (2007). The work and retirement experiences of aging black Americans. In J. B. James & P. Wink (Eds.), *The crown of life: Dynamics of the early postretirement period* (pp. 39–60). New York, NY: Springer.

Brown, M., Aumann, K., Pitt-Catsouphes, M., Galinsky, E., & Bond, J. T. (2010). *Working in retirement: A 21st century phenomenon.* New York, NY: Families and Work Institute. Retrieved from http://familiesandwork.org/site/research/reports/workinginretirement.pdf.

Butler, R. (1963). The life review: An interpretation of reminiscence in old age. *Psychiatry: Journal for the Study of Interpersonal Processes, 26,* 65–76.

Cappelli, P., & Novelli, W. D. (2010). *Managing the older worker: How to prepare for the new organizational order.* Boston, MA: Harvard Business Review Press.

Carstensen, L. L. (2006). The influence of a sense of time on human development. *Science, 312,* 1913–1915.

Carstensen, L. L., Isaacowitz, D. M., & Charles, S. T. (1999). Taking time seriously: A theory of socioemotional selectivity. *American Psychologist, 54,* 163–181.

Carstensen, L. L., & Mikels, J. A. (2005). At the intersection of emotion and cognition: Aging and the positivity effect. *Current Directions in Psychological Science, 14,* 117–121.

Carstensen, L. L., Turan, B., Scheibe, S., Ram, N., Ersner-Hershfield, H., Samanez-Larkin, G., ... Nesselroade, J. R. (2011). Emotional experience improves with age: Evidence based on over 10 years of experience sampling. *Psychology and Aging, 26*(1), 21–33.

Coleman, P. (1986). *Aging and reminiscence processes: Social and clinical implications.* Chichester, England: Wiley.

Cote, J. (2000). *Arrested adulthood: The changing nature of maturity and identity.* New York, NY: New York University Press.

Diehl, M., & Berg, K. M. (2007). Personality and involvement in leisure activities during the third age: Findings from the Ohio longitudinal study. In J. B. James & P. Wink (Eds.), *The crown of life: Dynamics of the early postretirement period* (pp. 211–226). New York, NY: Springer .

Dillon, M., & Wink, P. (2007). *In the course of a lifetime: Tracing religious belief, practice, and change.* Berkeley, CA: University of California Press.

Dychtwald, K., Erickson, T., & Morison, B. (2004, March). It's time to retire retirement. *Harvard Business Review,* 48–57.

Erikson, E. E. (1959). *Childhood and society.* New York, NY: Norton.

Fischer, C. S., & Hout, M. (2006). *Century of difference: How America changed in the last one hundred years.* New York, NY: Russell Sage Foundation.

Freedman, M. (1999). *Prime time: How baby boomers will revolutionize retirement and transform America.* New York, NY: Public Affairs.

Fries, J. F., & Crapo, L. M. (1981). *Vitality and aging: Implications of the rectangular curve.* San Francisco, CA: Freeman.

Gergen, K. J. (2000). *The saturated self: Dilemmas of identity in contemporary life.* New York, NY: Basic Books.

Gerstorf, D., Ram, N., Mayraz, G., Hidajat, M., Lindenberger, U., Wagner, G. G., & Schupp, J. (2010). Late-life decline in well-being across adulthood in Germany, the United Kingdom, and the United States: Something is seriously wrong at the end of life. *Psychology and Aging, 25*(2), 477–485.

Giandrea, M. D., Cahill, K. E., & Quinn, J. F. (2007). *An update on bridge jobs: The HRS war babies* (Working Paper No. 407). Washington, DC: Bureau of Labor Statistics. Retrieved from http://www.bls.gov/ore/abstract/ec/ec070060.htm.

Giddens, A. (1991). *Modernity and self-identity: Self and society in the late modern age.* Stanford, CA: Stanford University Press.

Gilleard, C., & Higgs, P. (2000). *Cultures of ageing: Self, citizen and the body.* Harlow, England: Prentice Hall.

Grafova, I., McGonagle, K., & Stafford, F. P. (2007). Functioning and well-being in the Third Age: 1986–2001. In J. B. James & P. Wink (Eds.), *The crown of life: Dynamics of the early postretirement period* (pp. 19–38). New York, NY: Springer.

Heckhausen, J. (2001). Adaptation and resilience in midlife. In M. E. Lachman (Ed.), *Handbook of midlife development* (pp. 345–391). Hoboken, NJ: John Wiley & Sons.

Helson, R., & Cate, R. A. (2007). Late middle age: Transition to the third age. In J. B. James & P. Wink (Eds.), *The crown of life: Dynamics of the early postretirement period* (pp. 83–102). New York, NY: Springer.

Helson, R., Soto, C. J., & Cate, R. A. (2006). From young adulthood through the middle ages. In D. K. Mroczek & T. D. Little (Eds.), *Handbook of personality development* (pp. 337–352). Mahwah, NJ: Lawrence Erlbaum.

Hochschild, A. R. (1990). *The second shift.* New York, NY: Avon Books.

Huxley, A. (1946). *Brave new world*. New York, NY: Harper and Brothers.

James, J. B., & Spiro A. (2007). The impact of work on the psychological health and well-being of older Americans. In J. B. James & P. Wink (Eds.), *The crown of life: Dynamics of the early postretirement period* (pp. 153–173). New York, NY: Springer.

James, J. B., & Wink, P. (Eds.). (2007). *The crown of life: Dynamics of the early postretirement period*. New York, NY: Springer.

Jaques, E. (1965). Death and the mid-life crisis. *International Journal of Psycho-Analysis, 46,* 502–514.

Johnson, R. W., & Schaner, S. G. (2005). *Value of unpaid activities by older Americans tops $160 billion per year* (Perspectives on Productive Aging Brief No. 4). Washington, DC: Urban Institute. Retrieved from http://www.urban.org/UploadedPDF/311227_older_americans.pdf.

Jung, C. G. (1953/1972). *Two essays on analytical psychology*. Princeton, NJ: Princeton University Press.

Kegan, R. (1994). *In over our heads: The mental demands of modern life*. Cambridge, MA: Harvard University Press.

Labouvie-Vief, G. (2003). Dynamic integration: Affect, cognition, and the self in adulthood. *Current Directions in Psychological Science, 12,* 201–206.

Labouvie-Vief, G., & Diehl, M. (2000). Cognitive complexity and cognitive-affective integration: Related or separate domains of adult development? *Psychology and Aging, 15,* 490–504.

Labouvie-Vief, G., Diehl, M., Jain, E., & Zhang, F. (2007). Six-year change in affect optimization and affect complexity across the adult life span: A further examination. *Psychology and Aging, 22,* 738–751.

Lachman, M. E., & James, J. B. (Eds.). (1997). *Multiple paths of midlife development*. Chicago, IL: University of Chicago Press. Studies on successful midlife development: The John D. and Catherine T. MacArthur Foundation series on mental health and development.

Lasch, C. (1979). *The culture of narcissism*. New York, NY: Norton.

Laslett, P. (1989). *A fresh map of life: The emergence of the Third Age*. Cambridge, MA: Harvard University Press.

Lieberman, M. A., & Tobin, S. S. (1983). *The experience of old age: Stress, coping and survival*. New York, NY: Basic Books.

McCrae, R. R., & Costa, P. T., Jr. (2003). *Personality in adulthood: A five-factor theory perspective* (2nd ed.). New York, NY: Guilford.

McCullough, M. E., & Polak, E. L. (2007). Change and stability during the Third Age: Longitudinal investigations of self-rated health and religiousness with the Terman sample. In J. B. James & P. Wink (Eds.), *The crown of life: Dynamics of the early postretirement period* (pp. 175–192). New York, NY: Springer.

MetLife Foundation/Civic Ventures. (2005). *New face of work survey*. San Francisco, CA: Author.

Moen, P. (2007). Not so big jobs and retirements: What workers (and retirees) really want. *Generations: Journal of the American Society on Aging, 31*(1), 31–36.

Moen, P., & Altobelli, J. (2007). Strategic selection as a retirement project: Will Americans develop hybrid arrangements? In J. B. James & P. Wink (Eds.), *The crown of life: Dynamics of the early postretirement period* (pp. 1–18). New York, NY: Springer.

Morrow-Howell, N. (2007). A longer worklife: The new road to volunteering. *Generations, 31*(1), 68–75.

Morrow-Howell, N., Hinterlong, J. E., & Sherraden, M. (Eds.). (2001). *Productive aging: Concepts and controversies*. Baltimore, MD: John Hopkins University Press.

Mroczek, D. K., & Spiro, A., III. (2003). Modeling intraindividual change in personality traits: Findings from the Normative Aging Study. *Journal of Gerontology: Psychological Sciences, 58B,* P153–P165.

Munnell, A. H., & Soto, M. (2005). *What replacement rates do households actually experience in retirement?* (Working Paper No. 2005-10). Chestnut Hill, MA: Center for Retirement Research at Boston College.

Munnell, A. H., Soto, M., & Golub-Sass, A. (2008). *Will people be healthy enough to work longer?* (Working Paper No. 2008-11). Chestnut Hill, MA: Center for Retirement Research at Boston College. Retrieved from http://crr.bc.edu/images/stories/Working_Papers/wp_2008-11.pdf.

Munnell, A. H., & Sunden, A. (2004). *Coming up short: The challenge of 401(k) plans*. Washington, DC: The Brookings Institution.

Neugarten, B., & Datan, N. (1974/1996). The middle years. In D. A. Neugarten (Ed.), *The meaning of age: Selected papers of Bernice L. Neugarten* (pp. 135–159). Chicago, IL: Chicago University Press.

Piktialis, D. (2007). Adaptations to an aging workforce: Innovative responses by the corporate sector. *Generations: Journal of the American Society on Aging, 31*(1), 76–83.

Quinn, J. F. (2002). Changing retirement trends and their impact on elderly entitlement programs. In S. H. Altman & D. Shactman (Eds.), *Policies for an aging society* (pp. 293–314). Baltimore, MD: Johns Hopkins University Press.

Rieff, P. (1966). *The triumph of the therapeutic*. Harmondsworth, England: Penguin.

Scheibe, S., & Carstensen, L. L. (2010). Emotional aging: Recent findings and future trends. *Journal of Gerontology: Psychological Sciences, 65B,* 135–144.

Schwartz, B. (2000). Self-determination: The tyranny of freedom. *American Psychologist, 55,* 79–88.

Sennett, R. (1978). *The fall off public man*. New York, NY: Vintage Books.

Smyer, M. A., & Pitt-Catsouphes, M. (2007). The meanings of work for older workers. *Generations: Journal of the American Society on Aging, 31,* 23–30.

Sneed, J. R., & Whitbourne, S. K. (2003). Identity processing and self-consciousness in middle and later adulthood. *Journal of Gerontology: Psychological Sciences, 58B,* P313–P319.

Sorensen, A. (2007). The demography of the Third Age. In J. B. James & P. Wink (Eds.), *The crown of life: Dynamics of the early postretirement period* (pp. 1–18). New York, NY: Springer.

Staudinger, U. M., & Gluck, J. (2011). Psychological wisdom research; Commonalities and differences in a growing field. *Annual Review of Psychology, 62,* 215–241.

Vaillant, G. E., & DiRago, A. C. (2007). Satisfaction with retirement in men's lives. In J. B. James & P. Wink (Eds.), *The crown of life: Dynamics of the early postretirement period* (pp. 227–242). New York, NY: Springer.

Van Deusen, F. R., James, J. B., Gill, N., & McKechnie, S. P. (2007). *Overcoming the implementation gap: How 20 leading companies are making flexibility work*. Chestnut Hill, MA: Boston College Center for Work & Family.

Willis, S. L., & Schaie, K. W. (2007). Coconstructionist view of the Third Age: The case of cognition. In J. B. James & P. Wink (Eds.), *The crown of life: Dynamics of the early postretirement period* (pp. 131–152). New York, NY: Springer.

Wink, P. (2007). Everyday life in the Third Age. In J. B. James & P. Wink (Eds.), *The crown of life: Dynamics of the early postretirement period* (pp. 242–262). New York, NY: Springer.

Wink, P., & Schiff, B. (2002). To review or not to review? The role of personality and life events in life review and adaptation to older age. In J. D. Webster & B. K. Haight (Eds.), *Critical advances in reminiscence work* (pp. 44–60). New York, NY: Springer.

Wink, P., & Scott, J. (2005). Does religiousness buffer against the fear of death and dying in late adulthood? *Journal of Gerontology: Psychological Sciences, 60B,* P207–P214.

Continuity Theory and Retirement

Monika E. von Bonsdorff *and* Juhani Ilmarinen

Abstract

Continuity theory provides a framework for understanding how adults employ their past concepts, constructs, and experiences to adapt and adjust to the changes brought about by normal aging. The theory assumes that middle-aged and older individuals attempt to preserve existing internal and external continuity when making adaptive choices in their lives. Continuity theory has been used in understanding adjustment to retirement. In addition, work ability, which refers to the balance between employees' resources and job demands, can be understood from a continuity perspective. This perspective is important in light of the recent development in workforce participation of older employees and the trend toward early exit from working life. Work ability varies across time and enables participation in working life at older ages, provided that the job demands are in relation to individuals' resources.

Key Words: internal continuity, external continuity, retirement, adaptation, work ability

Introduction

Continuity theory was developed as a general framework for understanding the adaptation to individual aging (Atchley, 1989). The theory encompasses ways in which adults employ their past concepts, constructs, and experiences to adapt and adjust to the changes brought about by normal aging. A central premise of the theory is that middle-aged and older individuals attempt to preserve existing internal and external continuity when making adaptive choices in their lives. Internal continuity refers to the psychic structure of ideas, temperament, affect, experiences, preferences, dispositions, and skills, whereas external continuity refers to social roles, activities, living arrangements, and relationships.

The continuity theory of normal aging was put forth in late 1980s by Robert Atchley, who had been studying how people adapt to the changes associated with aging. He based a substantial amount of his observations on the Ohio Longitudinal Study of Aging and Adaptation (OLSAA, 1975–1995). According to Atchley,

> Continuity theory was developed to explain a common research finding: Despite significant changes in health, functioning, and social circumstances, a large portion of older adults show considerable consistency over time in their patterns of thinking, activity profiles, living arrangements, and social relationships. (Atchley, 1999, pp. 1)

Continuity theory is one of the most widely used theories in contemporary retirement-related research (Quick & Moen, 1998; Wang, 2007), especially in the context where retirement is seen as an adjustment process (Wang & Shultz, 2010). Together with role theory and the life course perspective, continuity theory has been used to successfully understand retirement-related decision making, the transition to retirement, and the adjustment process. Where some theories view retirement as a disruptive role loss (e.g., role theory), continuity theory sees retirement as an opportunity to maintain a familiar lifestyle and social contacts (Quick & Moen, 1998). Continuity theory has been used to interpret and understand the factors underlying employees' bridge employment intentions and decisions, in addition to early retirement-related decision making (Gobeski & Beehr, 2009; Wang, Zhan, Liu, & Shultz, 2008).

As the workforce in many developed countries ages and the dependency ratio (ratio of population aged 65 and over to population aged 20 to 64) increases, the question of labor force participation is more pressing than ever before (Hardy, 2006; Ilmarinen, 2006). The United Nations World Population Prospects estimations show that the proportion of people over 60 years of age in whole populations in 2050 will be 34.2% in Europe, 27.4% in the United States, 44.2% in Japan, and 31.1% in China (United Nations, 2009). Global aging will impact working life in terms of the possible lack of new workers entering the labor market, labor shortages, and the short-term funding of pensions. Even if statistics show that the employment rate among older men and women has been growing steadily across European countries in the last ten years (Eurostat, 2008), several countries are currently struggling to find competent employees to replace those who are retiring (Hardy, 2006).

Sufficient physical and mental health is a prerequisite for employees' ability to continue working in old age. The mental and physical demands of an individual's job can vary temporarily but should be kept within bounds in the long run. Work ability has been defined as the equilibrium between an employee's perception of the demands of his or her job and his or her ability and resources to cope with those demands (Ilmarinen, 2009). The concept of work ability has gradually evolved from a strictly medical and occupational health idea toward a more holistic and versatile concept (Ilmarinen, 2006; Ilmarinen, Gould, Jarvikoski, & Jarvisalo, 2008), which also takes into consideration factors related to work, work organization, and life outside of work (Ilmarinen, 2006; Ilmarinen & Tuomi, 2004). The Work Ability Index (WAI; Tuomi, Ilmarinen, Jahkola, Katajarinne, & Tulkki, 2002), consisting of seven items concerning subjective assessments of current and future ability, sickness absences, the number of physician-diagnosed illnesses, and psychological resources, can be used to quantify work ability. The WAI has been validated against clinical data (Eskelinen, Kohvakka, Merisalo, Hurri, & Wagar, 1991).

A poor balance between employee resources and job demands may over time have detrimental effects on individuals' health and well-being (Bosma et al., 1997; Kivimaki et al., 2002) and increase the risk of early exit from working life (Ilmarinen & Tuomi, 2004; Krause et al., 1997; Laine et al., 2009; M. E. von Bonsdorff, Huuhtanen, Seitsamo, & Tuomi, 2009a). It has also been found that the work ability of aging employees, especially in the age group 52–58 years old, tends to decline (Ilmarinen & Tuomi, 2004). The maintenance and promotion of work ability, as well as well-being at work, requires cooperation between supervisors and employees (Ilmarinen, 2009). This includes taking work demands, the environment, work organization, and employees' health, functional capacity, and competences into consideration (Tuomi, Huuhtanen, Nykyri, & Ilmarinen, 2001).

In this chapter we will first present an overview of continuity theory and review the existing research on continuity theory and retirement. We will then consider work ability as a continuity construct. To finish the chapter, we will highlight possible future research directions.

Continuity Theory and Retirement
Continuity Theory as a Theoretical Construct

Continuity theory is a general theory that attempts to explain why continuity is a key element in the process of adult development in midlife and later. Unlike some other theories of human development (e.g., the theory of psychosocial development [Erikson, 1963] and the theory of adult personal and social development [Levinson, 1978]), continuity theory was specifically constructed from studies of adaptation in midlife and in older adults (Atchley, 1999).

Much like the other theories on adult development, Atchley (1999) views continuity theory as a feedback systems theory (Buckley, 1967). According to the general form of the feedback systems theory, an initial pattern influences behavioral choices and decisions that in turn influence the nature of life experience. Life experience, in turn, is used to evaluate, refine, or revise the initial pattern and the process of making behavioral choices. Mental frameworks are important in order to organize and interpret prior life events and experiences. In addition to global internal frameworks, such as the self, personal goals, or belief systems, continuity theory focuses on external patterns such as lifestyle, social networks, and activity profiles (Atchley, 1999). Individuals can make effective decisions and obtain a sense of personal agency through their own conception of how the world works and what their personal strengths and weaknesses, capabilities, and preferences are (Buckley, 1967).

Aging requires adaptation, since many physical, psychological, and social changes alter us in ways that require us to make adjustments (Atchley, 1999). There are three general means of adaptation: habituation, conflict management, and continuity (Atchley, 1988). As continuity draws upon past life events and experiences, it is most commonly used as a means of adaptation from midlife onward. Internal pressures toward continuity come from our need for a stable view of ourselves and the surrounding world, whereas external pressures arise from environmental reinforcement and the demands of the roles we occupy (Atchley, 1988).

Even if continuity theory is strongly connected to the individual's past, it is not the opposite of change (Atchley, 1989). In fact, the theory holds that there is a continuous process of development and adaptation in adulthood and old age (Atchley, 1999). Individuals' pasts can be used as a backdrop against which change and evolution can be perceived. In a decision-making situation, an individual might stop to evaluate different alternatives and solutions in the light of past life events and experiences. This is where internal and external continuity frameworks come into play and allow individuals to accommodate high amounts of evolutionary change without experiencing major life crises. According to Atchley (1989), even substantial changes can occur in life without causing serious disruption in individuals' sense of continuity. In terms of adaptation, an individual's goal is not only to adjust to changing circumstances, but also to simultaneously maintain their adaptive capacity.

Individuals encounter change throughout their lives. Change can be caused by intraindividual factors or by external forces, such as the society in which we live. Some of the major changes related to aging are retirement, widowhood, and the onset of functional limitations (Atchley, 1999). As continuity theory deals with change and adaptation in old age, it is important to consider the intraindividual changes brought about by normal aging. Normal aging in individuals is a progressive process that begins before we are born. The aging process slowly impairs our physical and mental capacity and is typically accelerated from midlife onward, with great individual differences. Nevertheless, most individuals cope with these changes and continue on to lead a fully normal life. Only a small proportion must learn to cope with significant, negative changes brought about by aging.

Retirement is a major life change that most individuals face in old age. The timing of retirement is dependent on the employee as well as on the surrounding society and the work organization (Moen, 1996). In the case of a planned transition to retirement, an individual can usually adapt to the changes fairly well, especially when it is seen as a socially valued goal (Atchley, 1999). Transitioning from working life into retirement is increasingly being seen as a dynamic, longitudinal participation process, where the individual makes a flexible transition in and out of retirement (Wang & Shultz, 2010). This line of working life development is aligned with the principles of continuity theory, as it increases the possibilities for both internal and external continuity through longer participation in working life. Longer participation in working life requires that employers are willing to hire older employees and offer them possibilities to continue working. Widowhood is another major life change that we may face during our lives. This devastating event is one of the major causes of discontinuity in, for example, living arrangements (Atchley, 1999). Adaptation to the new life situation brought about by both retirement and widowhood calls for the use of all the individual's available resources, including internal and external continuity.

As noted earlier, the natural age-related decline in physiological and biological properties, such as the decline in muscle strength and mass, starts in midlife (Frontera et al., 2000). Furthermore, for the majority, physical activity declines with older age (Bijnen, Feskens, Caspersen, Mosterd, & Kromhout, 1998), partly due to the aging process, the deterioration of muscle tissue, and an increase in morbidity and the rate of functional decline (Bijnen et al., 1998; Bortz, 2002; Rantanen et al., 1999). In addition, the prevalence of adverse outcomes such as mobility limitations, disability in everyday tasks, and related service use increases with older age (LaCroix, Guralnik, Berkman, Wallace, & Satterfield, 1993; Spillman & Lubitz, 2000). To avoid, retard, or reverse the normal age-related process of decline in functioning (Verbrugge & Jette, 1994), physical as well as mental resources are needed both as compensation and to optimize the remaining resources so as to enable the individual to lead an independent and socially active life in old age (Freund & Baltes, 1998; Jopp & Smith, 2006).

The onset of functional limitations in older age is the third typical change that requires some form of adaptation. According to the OLSAA study, participants exhibited only little difference in activity patterns, but more changes in, for example, personal agency after the onset of functional limitations (Atchley, 1999). This may indicate an association between functional limitations and social structural location via, in particular, personal agency, but also changed personal goals and emotional resiliency. Atchley found several general ways to adapt to functional limitations, including consolidation, decline with continuity, and decline with some offsets (Atchley, 1999).

Internal and External Continuity

Continuity theory divides continuity into two separate types: internal and external (Atchley, 1989). Internal continuity is based on stable mental structures and psychological aspects of consciousness. It also requires that we have memories that link our past to the present. More specifically, internal continuity refers to internal patterns, such as ideas, mental skills, self-concepts, personal goals, worldview, philosophy of life, moral framework, attitudes, values, beliefs, knowledge, skills, temperament, preferences, and coping strategies (Atchley, 1999). Stability in these psychological patterns is vital in terms of psychological security and well-being. Lack of internal continuity is especially noticeable in patients suffering from Alzheimer's disease or amnesia, as they are not able to use memory to present continuity of identity and self.

According to Atchley (1989), individuals are predisposed and motivated toward internal continuity by various pressures and attractions, mainly stemming from the self. First, internal continuity acts as a foundation for day-to-day decision making. It is also closely tied to knowledge, which is vital in interpreting and anticipating events. Second, internal continuity is essential to a sense of ego integrity, which is referred to as the ego's accumulated assurance of its capacity for order and meaning. Third, internal continuity helps meet the need for self-esteem. Individuals use their perceptions of both their success and their expectations to define their self-esteem, bringing about the need for internal continuity. Fourth, the motivation toward internal continuity can stem from the need to meet important basic needs, such as food, housing, income, etc. In addition, individuals exhibiting internal continuity are in general perceived as attractive, comfortable, and predictable to be around (Atchley, 1989).

External continuity refers to consistency over time in social roles, activities, living arrangements, and relationships that make up a distinctive lifestyle (Atchley, 1989, 1999). The external life situations and lifestyles unique to individuals are typically formed in middle age at the latest and tend to be a source of social security. Hence, individuals are inclined to strive to maintain the continuity of these external constructs. Besides the obvious practical advantages of external continuity, continuity theory would lead us to expect psychic payoffs as well (Atchley, 1999) in the actualization of a hoped-for self and avoidance of a feared or disvalued self (Bengtson, Reedy, & Gordon, 1985).

Individuals are also motivated toward external continuity (Atchley, 1989). First, individuals are expected to present themselves in a way that is tied to their past role performances. These roles are formed in the context of working and family life and can vary in their complexity. These roles are subject to change during the life course. Second, the external continuity of relationships is motivated by the desire for predictable social support from the inner circle of close family and friends who travel with us across our lives. These relationships can guard us against the potential need for instrumental dependency. Third, external continuity increases the odds that feedback from others about our self-concept can be accurately anticipated. This way, an individual can concentrate on interacting with those who confirm his or her view of self. Fourth, we see external continuity as an important way to cope with both the physical and mental changes brought about by aging. Both experience and practice are effective preventive and compensatory means to minimize the harmful effects of mental and physical aging. Fifth, external continuity tends to reduce the confusion of personal goals that can accompany life changes, such as widowhood, retirement, or the empty nest. In adjusting to retirement, the most common pattern is to maintain the same set of general personal goals throughout the transition (Atchley, 1989).

Given that gender is an important social structural construction determining people's access to education and community roles, it would be reasonable to expect gender differences in both internal and external continuity (Atchley, 1999). However, only modest gender differences in individuals' internal continuity were found in the OLSAA study. According to Atchley (1999), this may be because the effects that gender has on most of the important constructs of the self have occurred earlier in life. In addition, gender and education can have indirect effects on mental constructs through their relationship to self-rated health or functional capacity (Atchley, 1999). Differences in external continuity in the form of activity level were detected in the OLSAA study. It seemed that, especially among women, aging caused a decline in the activity level among older adults (Atchley, 1999).

Continuity Theory in the Context of Retirement

Although retirement research has been shaped by several theories, none of them were developed specifically as theories of retirement, but rather of the general aging process (Beehr, 1986). To better understand retirement decisions, the retirement transition, and retirement satisfaction at an individual level, researchers have lately turned to two dominant theoretical perspectives in addition to continuity theory, namely role theory (Ashforth, 2001; Carter & Cook, 1995) and the life course perspective (Elder, 1995). Together these three theories have offered means for interpreting, among other things, the antecedents of retirement-related decision making (Gobeski & Beehr, 2009; Kim & Feldman, 2000; Wang et al., 2008), gender and retirement transitions (Moen, 1996; Quick & Moen, 1998), and individual well-being and quality of life during retirement (Beehr, 1986; Kim & Moen, 2002; Moen, 1996; Quick & Moen, 1998; Wang, 2007).

Retirement represents one of the most important changes that occur in later life (Atchley, 1989, 1999). Retirement can be voluntary or involuntary, early or on time, and complete or partial in its nature. The decision to retire early or late often results from the interplay of choice and chance. Life chances in terms of achieving higher socioeconomic status, having better control over work, and having better health typically enable older employees the choice of late retirement (Gould, 2006).

Early retirement is a form of job withdrawal and has been defined as leaving a position or career path of long duration before the age of 65 years (Feldman, 1994; Hanisch & Hulin, 1990, 1991). The decision to retire early is typically preceded by intentions of early retirement (Beehr, 1986). Most of the research to date considers early retirement to be a process that begins with early retirement intentions and ends with adjusting to a new phase in life entailed by the decision to withdraw permanently from working life.

Atchley (1999) viewed retirement on the basis of the OLSAA study by exploring continuity in beliefs about the effects of retirement morale and activity level before and after retirement. He found that most respondents were able to adapt to retirement successfully. Moreover, changes were detected among individuals' beliefs about retirement. Apart from individual changes, these findings indicated that views and stereotypes about retirement are becoming less negative in the general population. Results on the morale of individuals before and after retirement showed that internal continuity of adaptation was high for most of the respondents regardless of their employment/retirement status. For men, retirement seemed to enhance their morale. Stability in the level of activity seemed to be more common than stability in morale in the OLSAA study, as the majority of the still-employed and just-retired men and women had unchanged activity levels over the two-year follow-up (Atchley, 1999).

In the United States, because it has been typical for employees to continue working after retirement (Shultz, 2003), it has also been more difficult to determine the timing of retirement. This phenomenon, termed bridge employment, can involve continuing to work after retirement in a career job or taking up a job in a different field (Feldman, 1994; Shultz, 2003). According to Beehr (1986), defining retirement is rather complex, and there is no reason to expect different types of retirement to be equivalent in their causes or consequences. Instead of conceptualizing retirement as a one-time decision-making event, a dynamic perspective examines bridge employment as a longitudinal workforce participation and retirement transition process (Wang & Shultz, 2010). This view also helps us to capture the adaptation element in the bridge employment process, as bridge employment decisions are often driven by the motivation to adjust to life in retirement (Wang, 2007; Wang et al., 2008).

Adjustment to retirement can be described as the process through which retirees get used to the changes in their life in the transition from work to retirement. It is suggested that individuals who have been deeply involved in their work will try to sustain their daily routines by participating in activities they value highly (Gobeski & Beehr, 2009). Individuals who have been highly committed to their jobs are more likely to seek continuity through some form of participation in working life (Atchley, 1989). The work environment offers a natural way to maintain daily routines and engage in social interaction with colleagues, supervisors, and clients. For some individuals, maintaining these networks and social contacts can influence the decision to continue at work through participating in bridge employment instead of retiring early.

A Continuity Perspective on Retirement-Related Antecedents and Outcomes

Although the retirement process has been widely studied, consensus on the antecedents of early retirement is yet to be reached. Continuity theory is one of the theories that offer both a rationale for selecting a broad set of antecedents of retirement decisions and a comprehensive framework for interpreting employees' behavior (Kim & Feldman, 2000; Wang et al., 2008). When looking closer at the theoretical considerations, continuity theory provides a new perspective that treats retirement as an opportunity to maintain social contacts while avoiding the negative outcomes of retirement (Quick & Moen, 1998; Wang et al., 2008). In their recent study, Gobeski and Beehr (2009) pushed the utility of continuity theory further by interpreting the specific type of bridge employment that people accept. Alternatively, Kim and Feldman (2000) state that aging and retirement can present an opportunity to engage in activities that aging employees value highly outside of work.

Predictors of retirement-related decisions can be classified into micro-level personal factors and meso-level work-related factors (Wang, Adams, Beehr, & Shultz, 2009). Wang and Shultz (2010) point out that the most salient personal predictors of the decision to retire are found at the individual level. Age has been found to have an effect on individuals' ability to continue working. The older the employee becomes, and as health limitations accumulate, the more unlikely s/he is to achieve continuity in life through work (Kim & Feldman, 2000). According to several studies, as employees age, their tendency to retire will increase (Beehr, 1986; Kim & Feldman, 1998; Kim & DeVaney, 2005; Shultz & Wang, 2007; Taylor & Shore, 1995) and at the same time their desire to engage in bridge employment will decrease (Adams & Rau, 2004; Cahill, Giandrea, & Quinn, 2006; Davis, 2003; Kim & Feldman, 2000; Wang et al., 2008). Level of education is associated with employee skills and the ability to perform at work. A low level of education, for example, will often limit the ability to adapt to changes in working life. In contrast, a recent study by Wang et al. (2008) found that a higher level of education was associated with employee desire to engage in bridge employment (see also Gobeski & Beehr, 2009; Kim & DeVaney, 2005; M. E. von Bonsdorff, Shultz, Leskinen, & Tansky, et al., 2009b).

Health is one of the most powerful factors influencing the decision to retire (Beehr, 1986; Feldman, 1994; Karpansalo, Manninen, Kauhanen, Lakka, & Salonen, 2004; Kim & Feldman, 1998; Shultz, Morton, & Weckerle, 1998; Shultz & Wang, 2007; Taylor & Shore, 1995; Topa, Moriano, Depolo, Alcover, & Morales, 2009) and to engage in bridge employment (Kim & Feldman, 2000; Wang et al., 2008). Employees with serious health problems may want to spend the limited time they have left with family and friends, and thus health problems are likely to cause interruptions in employees' lives in terms of continuity (Kim & Feldman, 2000).

Several studies have addressed the role of income in retirement-related decisions. It has been found that people with greater financial resources will be more likely to retire early (Kim & DeVaney, 2005) and that employees are likely to seek financial benefits that help ensure their retirement incomes (Feldman, 1994; Kim & Feldman, 2000; Weckerle & Shultz, 1999). Financial distress often works as a stimulus for retirees to engage in bridge employment (Dendinger, Adams, & Jacobson, 2005; Shultz, 2003). On the other hand, Wang et al. (2008) found that retirees' total wealth did not predict their participation in bridge employment against full retirement. There are several non-work-related constructs, such as personality traits, life satisfaction, family-related concerns, and the physical and cognitive effects of aging, that should be considered in research on retirement decisions (Gobeski & Beehr, 2009). Non-work interests can also be a significant source of continuity for employees who do not experience continuity through their work. As a result, these individuals may be more likely to seek retirement instead of work (M. E. von Bonsdorff et al. 2009b) in order to achieve continuity in their lives (see Atchley, 1989).

At the meso-level, work-related predictors of retirement decisions include characteristics of the job and persons' thoughts and attitudes about work (Wang & Shultz, 2010). A central element in keeping older employees at work is to present them with challenging tasks, opportunities to further develop their skills, and reasonable remuneration in return for their inputs (Adams, 1999; Dendinger, Adams, & Jacobson, 2005; Loi & Shultz, 2007; van Dam, van der Vorst, & van der Heijden, 2009). Nevertheless, research is not unanimous when it comes to occupational goal attainment and retirement decisions.

Adams (1999) found that employees who felt that they had accomplished their goals in working life sensed that they were ready to retire instead of ready to pursue new goals. Thus, researchers have hypothesized that goal attainment is specifically related to career bridge employment (Gobeski & Beehr, 2009).

Low job control, poor work ability, and job dissatisfaction have been identified as some of the most central work-related psychological variables associated with retirement decisions. Both high job demand and low job control independently predicted early retirement, even when adjusted for age, gender, education, and self-rated health (Elovainio et al., 2005; Heponiemi et al., 2008; Sutinen, Kivimaki, Elovainio, & Forma, 2005). Poor work ability has been associated with early retirement intentions (Sell, 2009; Tuomi et al., 2001; M. E. von Bonsdorff et al., 2009a). Individuals who are satisfied with their jobs are less likely to engage in any type of withdrawal behavior, such as turnover or early retirement (Adams & Beehr, 1998). On the other hand, unfavorable psychosocial working conditions and job dissatisfaction can be clearly related to early retirement intentions (Shultz, Morton, & Weckerle, 1998; Wang, 2007), whereas individuals who are satisfied with their current jobs are more likely to want to engage in career bridge employment (Gobeski & Beehr, 2009). Negative work-related affects, such as work stress, have been linked to the decision to seek full retirement instead of bridge employment (Wang et al., 2008; Gobeski & Beehr, 2009).

The results regarding continuity in the retirement transition have thus far been inconsistent (Wang & Shultz, 2010), and Wang (2007) suggested that there are multiple forms of retirement transition and adjustment in the retiree population (see Pinquart & Schindler, 2007). Wang and Bodner (2007), using a nationally representative U.S. sample, demonstrated that some 70% of retirees experienced minimum changes in their well-being during their transition to retirement. The finding was further corroborated by using a nationally representative German sample of retirees (Pinquart & Schindler, 2007). Furthermore, continuity theory has been used to interpret the maintaining and U-shaped recovery patterns of retirees' psychological well-being (Wang, 2007).

The outcomes of retirement decisions, especially regarding bridge employment, have mostly been reported on a micro-level as individual outcomes (Wang & Shultz, 2010). Here, we focus on retirees' adjustment to their retirement life and post-retirement health. In line with continuity theory, health decrements during the retirement transition have been negatively related to the quality of retirement (Kim & Moen, 2002; van Solinge & Henkens, 2008; Wang, 2007). A poor work environment and frequent health complaints have been associated with greater post-retirement improvement in self-perceived health, whereas similar results were not detected among employees who were satisfied with their work (Westerlund et al., 2009).

The findings regarding the reduced financial situation of retirees have been inconclusive, which may in part be due to cultural differences (Wang & Shultz, 2010). Among other variables related to the retirement transition, the voluntariness of retirement (Gall, Evans, & Howard, 1997; van Solinge, 2007; van Solinge & Henkens, 2007) and retirement planning (Reitzes & Mutran, 2004; Wang, 2007) have been found to be positively related to retirees' retirement satisfaction, life satisfaction, and well-being. According to continuity theory, bridge employment (Atchley, 1999; Kim & Feldman, 2000; Quick & Moen, 1998) or volunteer work (Kim & Feldman, 2000; Smith & Moen, 2004) can be an effective way to adjust to retirement and maintain internal and external continuity. Hence, engaging in bridge employment during the retirement process can help individuals experience not only significant changes in psychological well-being but also higher levels of retirement satisfaction later on (Kim & Feldman, 2000; Wang et al., 2009).

The effects of retirement on health outcomes during retirement have been fairly widely reported during the past few years. Recent studies have found that under favorable circumstances retirement can have beneficial health effects (van Solinge, 2007), although opposite (Bosse, Aldwin, Levenson, & Ekerdt, 1987) or neutral (Mein, Martikainen, Hemingway, Stansfeld, & Marmot, 2003; Tuomi, Jarvinen, Eskelinen, Ilmarinen, & Klockars, 1991) findings have also been reported. Westerlund et al. (2010) found that even if retirement did not change the risk of major chronic diseases, it was associated with a reduction in mental and physical fatigue and depressive symptoms among a large French occupational cohort. The effects on health of bridge employment have been studied only recently (Wang et al., 2009). Based on the Health and Retirement Study, Zhan, Wang, Liu, and Shultz (2009) reported on engagement in bridge employment having positive health benefits in terms of fewer major diseases and functional limitations and better mental health (see Wang et al., 2008). These results can partly be interpreted in the context of continuity theory, as engaging in bridge employment helps individuals maintain their habitual level of physical and mental activities.

Work Ability as a Continuity Construct

The concept of work ability is well established in the occupational health field (Ilmarinen, 2009; Ilmarinen et al., 2008), and it has attracted attention in other related fields as well. Work ability has been studied in relation to different occupations and nations (Alavinia, van Duivenbooden, & Burdorf, 2007; Punakallio, Lusa, & Luukkonen, 2004; Sjogren-Ronka, Ojanen, Leskinen, Mustalampi, & Malkia, 2002), socioeconomic inequalities (Aittomaki, Lahdelma, & Roos, 2003), various aspects of work psychology (Feldt, Hyvonen, Makikangas, Kinnunen, & Kokko, 2009), and gerontology (Ilmarinen, 2002; M. B. von Bonsdorff et al., 2011). The broadened concept of work ability presented here in Figure 6.1, which takes into account the surrounding organizational and societal contexts, offers a wide perspective on the relationship between the individual and the work and social environment (Ilmarinen, 2009; Ilmarinen et al., 2008).

Next, we attempt to further extend the concept of work ability to cover the continuity perspective. As individuals live longer and lead healthier lives than ever before, it is important to consider ways in which older employees can remain a part of the active working population (Ilmarinen, 2006). The multidimensional way of looking at work ability has been supported by the goal to lengthen work careers and to prevent work disability (Ilmarinen et al., 2008). In research on late-career participation, an increasing emphasis is being placed on the importance of a dynamic perspective, where participation in working life is seen as a longitudinal process alternating between different bridge employment positions with eventual exit into full retirement (Wang et al., 2009; Wang & Shultz, 2010). In terms of work ability and continuity, it is important to recognize that work ability has a fairly stable structure that from midlife onward predicts several important late-life outcomes. Work ability may vary across time and enable participation in working life at older ages, provided that the job demands match individuals' resources.

We draw on data from the Finnish Longitudinal Study on Municipal Employees (FLAME) to explore work ability from a continuity perspective. The FLAME study, conducted by the Finnish Institute of Occupational Health, has been investigating the work, health, and lifestyle of 6,257 (44.7% men; response rate 85.2%) municipal employees since 1981 (Ilmarinen et al., 1991). The study initially targeted 7,344 municipal employees aged 44–58 years chosen randomly from all persons working in municipal occupations in Finland at baseline. Since the first questionnaire on various work, health, and lifestyle factors was sent out in 1981, four consecutive follow-up data collections have taken place: in 1985 (n = 5,556), 1992 (n = 4,534), 1997 (n = 3,817), and 2009 (n = 3,093). At the last follow-up

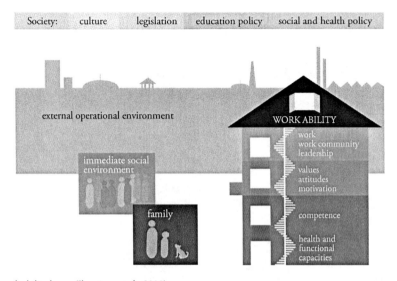

Figure 6.1 The work ability house (Ilmarinen et al., 2008)

in 2009, 3,093 (73.1% of the survivors) completed the questionnaire.

Perceived work ability was measured at each data wave with the first item of the Work Ability Index (Tuomi et al., 1991), where respondents were asked to rate their present work ability to their lifetime best with the question: "*Imagine that if you had been asked to rate your work ability on a scale from 1 to 10, when it was at its best, you would have given it a score of 10. What score would you give your present work ability?*" Considering perceived work ability instead of measured health is relevant in this continuity-related study, as several factors in life besides health factors shape both perceived work ability and continuity. This means that individuals who suffer from illnesses or injuries can still be able to participate in working life and thus preserve continuity.

First, looking at work ability from a continuity perspective shows us that work ability is a fairly stable construct among young and middle-aged employees and is contingent on individuals' past working life experiences. However, from midlife onward an age-related decline in perceived work ability can be observed (Gould, Ilmarinen, Jarvisalo, & Koskinen, 2008), which justifies a focus on this segment of the working population. Work ability is linked to internal and external continuity in that individuals perceive their current resources to some extent relative to their past resources and personal experiences.

The stability of work ability indicates that there is some form of continuity in employee resources with respect to job demands. Research on the development of work ability has shown that 90% of individuals less than 45 years of age consistently report having excellent work ability (Gould et al., 2008). In another study on work ability among managers,

several development trajectories were identified over a ten-year follow-up. According to the results, despite the overall trend toward a decline, the majority of the respondents (88%) were consistently located within the favorable work ability trajectory, and significant changes were detected for only 10% of the respondents during the follow-up (Feldt et al., 2009).

In our FLAME-based study, we aimed at exploring individual work ability trajectories stretching from midlife to life in retirement among 5,357 men and women (mean age at baseline 50.7, SD 3.6). The work ability trajectories were allowed to vary in level and shape. This form of analysis enabled us to explore the longitudinal patterns of changes in perceived work ability over an eleven-year follow-up, as three measurements of work ability (1981, 1985, and 1992) were included in the trajectory analyses.

As can be seen in Figure 6.2, our trajectory analysis revealed that work ability remained fairly stable in groups 1 and 2, which made up nearly 84% of the respondents. This finding is in line with other similar findings on work ability (Feldt et al., 2009; Gould et al., 2008). Work ability followed a distinctive pattern of decline in the other groups. Some of the variation in work ability trajectories can be explained by age differences, since the respondents in group 1 were younger at baseline (50.3 years, SD 3.5) compared to those in groups 4 and 5. All the respondents in group 4, 98% of the respondents in group 5, and 91% of the respondents in group 3 had retired, primarily on disability pension, during the eleven-year follow-up. Out of group 1, 58% were still working in 1992, and those who had retired were receiving an old-age pension (80%).

Second, looking at work ability from a continuity perspective provides a more positive and

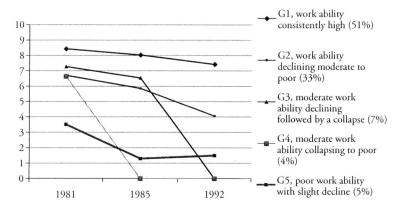

Figure 6.2 Development trajectories of work ability from middle age to retirement age on a scale of 0 to 10

proactive perspective on older employees' involvement in working life. This approach recognizes that the balance between personal resources and job demands can vary in different phases of the individual's working life (Ilmarinen, 2009). Work ability is defined in relation to organizational context (Ilmarinen, 2009; Ilmarinen, Tuomi, & Seitsamo, 2005), which we might have little control over. The fast pace of change in working life can make it difficult to adjust to new circumstances and subsequently maintain continuity through continued participation in working life. Given that work ability (Ilmarinen & Tuomi, 2004) together with individual resources tend to decline with age (Frontera et al., 2000), it is of special importance that work demands, the environment, work organization, and older employees' health, functional capacity, and competences are more closely taken into consideration (Ilmarinen, 2009; Tuomi et al., 2001).

Work ability is related to several late-life transitions and life changes. Poor midlife work ability predicts work disability, retirement, and morbidity (Ilmarinen & Tuomi, 2004). Midlife work ability has far-reaching effects, as poor midlife work ability has been found to predict both early retirement intentions and decisions (Sell, 2009; Tuomi et al., 2001; M. E. von Bonsdorff et al., 2009a) and old age disability among women and mortality among men (M. B. von Bonsdorff et al., 2011). It is especially important to recognize individuals who are at risk of losing their work ability and help them restore and maintain their resources. The focus in the occupational health field is increasingly turning to helping individuals with chronic diseases and partly diminished work ability cope in order to keep them from falling permanently outside of the working force (Gould et al., 2008). According to this view, illnesses or injuries can be overcome, and they do not need to disrupt internal or external continuity. The role of the employer is essential in this process, since the maintenance and promotion of work ability requires fluent cooperation between supervisor and employees (Ilmarinen, 2009).

A recent FLAME study reported on changes in perceived work ability prior to and following retirement according to whether the retiree was receiving an old-age, individual early retirement, or disability pension over a twenty-eight-year time period (M. E. von Bonsdorff et al., 2011). The study showed significant differences in the development of pre- and post-retirement work ability according to different pension benefits. Individuals who exited the workforce due to old age showed a steady decline in their perceived work ability during the follow-up. For persons who exited the workforce due to an individual early retirement pension or a disability pension, a U-shaped curve with a distinctive post-retirement recovery was detected in work ability.

These longitudinal changes in perceived work ability may be due to several age-related and situational factors. The decline in work ability among individuals transitioning to an old-age pension, who represented the majority of the respondents, was probably due to normal aging. The results for the early retirement groups indicate a need to adjust working life to the resources of older employees, as excessively high perceived job demands seem to cause discontinuity in older employees' work ability. This is further indicated by the finding among the early retirement groups of a post-retirement recovery in their vital resources for functioning in later life.

Third, looking at work ability from a continuity perspective is better suited to taking a dynamic perspective on longitudinal participation in the workforce and revealing the potential of older employees. As the trend in late-career participation in working life is evolving with the inclusion of several transitions to and from bridge employment (Wang et al., 2009; Wang & Shultz, 2010), the concept of work ability has to evolve as well. Work ability is the most important asset older employees possess (Ilmarinen, 2009). However, maintaining work ability and employment throughout the life course is not dependent on employees' efforts alone. In order for the process of longitudinal participation in the workforce to succeed in practice, policymakers and, more importantly, employers have to be committed to actively producing employment for older employees. Many older employees have perceived their opportunities to find new employment as weaker than those of younger employees (Mobley, Horner, & Hollingsworth, 1978). Older employees might also be reluctant to change jobs if they have reached a high position in a company and do not have immediate opportunities to attain a similar position elsewhere (Hedge, Borman, & Lammlein, 2006).

Health and work are the most important determinants of work ability (Gould et al., 2008). The work ability of aging employees, especially in the age group 52–58 years, has been found to decline (Ilmarinen & Tuomi, 2004). However, these changes vary according to specific occupational groups and job content (Tuomi, Ilmarinen, Martikainen, Aalto, & Klockars, 1997). It is for these reasons that a more dynamic perspective on

Table 6.1 Odds ratios and 95% confidence intervals for bridge employment intentions in 1992 and 1997 according to work ability between 1981 and 1997[1]

	Work ability in 1981	Work ability in 1985	Work ability in 1992	Work ability in 1997
Bridge employment intentions in 1992, OR (95% CI)	1.09 (1.03–1.14)	1.12 (1.08–1.17)	1.33 (1.27–1.38)	—
Bridge employment intentions in 1997, OR (95% CI)	n.s.	1.07 (1.02–1.12)	1.17 (1.12–1.21)	1.22 (1.18–1.27)

[1] Models adjusted for age, gender, marital status, lifestyle habits, and major diseases.

employment in the late career can be of benefit—if an individual's job demands are not in balance with his or her resources, then a career change could be the solution. Remaining in working life in older age through, for example, bridge employment can help people adjust to life in retirement (Wang, 2007; Wang et al., 2008) and even have a positive effect on health (Zhan et al., 2009).

In the light of the FLAME study, we found that the interest in bridge employment was high among the retired respondents both in 1992 (47% of 3,248 respondents) and 1997 (37% of 3,596 respondents). However, at that time, it would not have been possible for employees to participate in bridge employment due to the existing pension legislation. We found, using logistic regression analysis, that after adjusting for age, gender, marital status, lifestyle habits (smoking, alcohol consumption, physical activity during the previous year), major diseases (musculoskeletal diseases, heart and circulatory diseases, respiratory diseases, metabolic diseases), years spent in retirement, and pension benefit group that work ability predicted bridge employment intentions. More specifically, we found that perceived work ability measured in 1981, 1985, and 1992 predicted bridge employment intentions in 1992, and work ability measured in 1985, 1992, and 1997 predicted bridge employment intentions in 1997 (Table 6.1).

The results of our analyses show that perceived work ability is a consistent predictor of bridge employment intentions even where employees have been retired for several years. Better work ability seems to be an essential factor, as older individuals contemplate their possibilities for continuing in work. It also looks as if the majority of them have managed to retain or even regain their work ability during the aging process. Nevertheless, work ability is an important construct that is linked to most working life transitions. Better work ability helps employees maintain both internal and external continuity through, for example, the social roles, activities, lifestyle, job role, skills, and personal goals to which they have grown accustomed.

Conclusion

This chapter provided an overview of continuity theory from a retirement perspective and reviewed the existing research on retirement-related antecedents and outcomes in terms of continuity theory. In addition, we considered work ability as a continuity construct and presented results from the Finnish Longitudinal Study on Municipal Employees (FLAME) to support our ideas.

Continuity theory, which seeks to understand how adults employ their past concepts, constructs, and experience to adapt and adjust to the changes brought about by normal aging, has been used in understanding retirement-related decision making, the transition to retirement, and the adjustment process. Continuity theory is one of the most widely used theories in retirement-related research (Quick & Moen, 1998; Wang, 2007), especially in the context of retirement as an adjustment process (Wang & Shultz, 2010). In recent studies, continuity theory has helped researchers interpret and understand some of the factors underlying employees' bridge employment intentions and decisions, in addition to early retirement-related decision making (Gobeski & Beehr, 2009; Wang et al., 2008). The utility of continuity theory is best realized in studies related to voluntary retirement decisions, adjustment to retirement, and the process of engagement in bridge employment.

Work ability, which refers to the balance between employees' resources and job demands (Ilmarinen, 2009), can also be looked at from a continuity perspective. This perspective is important in light of the recent development in participation in the workforce of older employees and the trend toward early exit from working life. In terms of work ability and continuity, it is important to recognize that work ability is a fairly stable structure (Gould et al., 2008) that from midlife onward predicts several important late-life outcomes (Sell, 2009; Tuomi et al., 2001; M. B. von Bonsdorff et al., 2011; M. E. von Bonsdorff et al., 2009a).

Based on the FLAME study, we found that perceived work ability from midlife to post-retirement age remained fairly stable for nearly 84% of the respondents. Most of these individuals were able to work until their official pension age. Hence, consistently good work ability was able to support individuals' experience of continuity in that they had sufficient resources to remain in employment until their official retirement age. In addition, we found a U-shaped curve, showing distinct post-retirement recovery, among individuals who had entered early retirement during the twenty-eight-year follow-up. The results indicate that there may be a need to adjust working life to the resources of older employees, as excessively high job demands seem to cause discontinuity in older employees' work ability. As to bridge employment intentions, we found that perceived work ability is a consistent predictor of bridge employment even where employees have been retired for several years. All of the above-mentioned results highlight the importance of shared responsibility between employer and employee in maintaining and promoting work ability and continuity at the same time.

Future Directions

Continuity in the context of retirement and the late career will probably become more important as the age demographics change and the pressure on older employees to participate in working life increases. We hope that researchers will continue to adapt continuity theory in the future in their retirement-related research and that they will continue to find new ways to further extend the utility of continuity theory.

One way to apply continuity theory on the individual level is to look at work ability from a continuity perspective. In this chapter we have outlined how this can be done. Next, we need more research applying continuity theory on the macro-level. As Wang and Shultz (2010) stated, only little is known about the multilevel effects of retirement-related decision making (see Beehr & Bennett, 2007). This means that we do not know what the combined effects of the individual, work, organization, and society are on retirement decisions or outcomes.

Thus far we know little about the effects of employers' attitudes and behavior on individuals' perceptions of internal and external continuity. This line of research would require data covering a broad set of employers combined with a data set on their corresponding employees. Nevertheless, more in-depth knowledge on these issues could be important, as employers typically enable work-related continuity through offering jobs. The possibility of continuity as a collective construct could also be studied on a meso-level (Shultz & Adams, 2007), in this case the company/organizational level.

Working life has changed during the last decades and is becoming more susceptible to changes in the global economy. Yet we do not know whether these changes have an effect on the internal and external continuity that individuals experience. It might be that new technology will make it possible for older individuals to lead independent lives longer. At the same time, major changes in work content and the skills required to do their jobs might cause older individuals to experience discontinuity as they are forced to leave or change their current employment. Public policies, retirement policies included, shape society. This is important when we consider the employment of older individuals. Although culture-related differences clearly exist between the European, American, and Asian countries, the importance of maintaining the work ability of older employees should nevertheless be globally recognized.

Authors' Note

We thank Katja Kokko, PhD, for providing statistical assistance with the development trajectories. The University Alliance Finland, University of Jyvaskyla, and the Academy of Finland (grant n:o 132597) have financially supported the preparation of this manuscript.

References

Adams, G. A. (1999). Career-related variables and planned retirement age: An extension of Beehr's model. *Journal of Vocational Behavior, 55*, 221–235.

Adams, G. A., & Beehr, T. A. (1998). Turnover and retirement: A comparison of their similarities and differences. *Personnel Psychology, 51*, 643–665.

Adams, G. A., & Rau, B. (2004). Job seeking among retirees seeking bridge employment. *Personnel Psychology, 57*, 714–744.

Aittomaki, A., Lahdelma, E., & Roos, E. (2003). Work conditions and socioeconomic inequalities in work ability.

Scandinavian Journal of Work, Environment & Health, 29, 159–165.

Alavinia, S. M., van Duivenbooden, C., & Burdorf, A. (2007). Influence of work-related factors and individual characteristics on work ability among Dutch construction workers. *Scandinavian Journal of Work, Environment & Health, 33,* 351–357.

Ashforth, B. (2001). *Role transitions in organizational life: An identity-based perspective.* Mahwan, NJ: Erlbaum.

Atchley, R. C. (1988). *Social forces and aging* (5th ed.). Belmont, CA: Wadsworth.

Atchley, R. C. (1989). A continuity theory of normal aging. *Gerontologist, 29,* 183–190.

Atchley, R. C. (1999). *Continuity and adaptation in aging. Creating positive experiences.* Baltimore, MD: The Johns Hopkins University Press.

Beehr, T. A. (1986). The process of retirement: A review and recommendations for future investigation. *Personnel Psychology, 39,* 31–55.

Beehr, T. A., & Bennett, M. (2007). Examining retirement from a multi-level perspective. In K. S. Shultz & G. A. Adams (Eds.), *Aging and work in the 21st century* (pp. 303–319). Mahwah, NJ: Lawrence Erlbaum Associates.

Bengtson, V. L., Reedy, M. N., & Gordon, C. (1985). Aging and self-conceptions. Personality processes and social contexts. In J. E. Birren & K. W. Schaie (Eds.), *Handbook of psychology and aging* (2nd ed., pp. 544–593). New York, NY: Academic Press.

Bijnen, F. C., Feskens, E. J., Caspersen, C. J., Mosterd, W. L., & Kromhout, D. (1998). Age, period, and cohort effects on physical activity among elderly men during 10 years of follow-up: The Zutphen Elderly Study. *Journals of Gerontology: Series A, 53,* 235–241.

Bortz, W. M., 2nd. (2002). A conceptual framework of frailty: A review. *Journals of Gerontology: Series A, 57,* 283–288.

Bosma, H., Marmot, M. G., Hemingway, H., Nicholson, A. C., Brunner, E., & Stansfeld, S. A. (1997). Low job control and risk of coronary heart disease in Whitehall II (prospective cohort) study. *British Medical Journal, 314,* 558–565.

Bosse, R., Aldwin, C. M., Levenson, M. R., & Ekert, D. J. (1987). Mental health differences among retirees and workers: Findings from the Normative Aging Study. *Psychology and Aging, 2,* 383–389.

Buckley, W. (1967). *Sociology and modern systems theory.* Englewood Cliffs, NJ: Prentice-Hall.

Cahill, K. E., Giandrea, M. D., & Quinn, J. F. (2006). Retirement patterns from career employment. *The Gerontologist, 46,* 514–523.

Carter, M. A. T., & Cook, K. (1995). Adaptation to retirement: Role changes and psychological resources. *The Career Development Quarterly, 44,* 67–82.

Davis, M. A. (2003). Factors related to bridge employment participation among private sector early retirees. *Journal of Vocational Behavior, 63,* 77–71.

Dendinger, V. M., Adams, G. A., & Jacobson, J. D. (2005). Reasons for working and their relationship to retirement attitudes, job satisfaction and occupational self-efficacy of bridge employment. *International Journal of Aging and Human Development, 61,* 21–35.

Elder, G. H. (1995). The life-course paradigm: Historical, comparative, and developmental perspectives. In P. Moen, G. H. Elder, & K. Lusher (Eds.), *Examining lives in context: Perspectives on the ecology of human development* (pp. 101–140). Washington, DC: American Psychology Press.

Elovainio, M., Forma, P., Kivimaki, M., Sinervo, T., Sutinen, R., & Laine, M. (2005). Job demands and job control as correlates of early retirement thoughts in Finnish social and health care employees. *Work & Stress, 19*(1), 84–92.

Erikson, E. H. (1963). *Childhood and society.* New York, NY: Macmillan.

Eskelinen, L., Kohvakka, A., Merisalo, T., Hurri, H., & Wagar, G. (1991). Relationship between the self-assessment and clinical assessment of health status and work ability. *Scandinavian Journal of Work, Environment & Health, 17* (Suppl. 1), 40–47.

Eurostat. (2008). *Eurostat Yearbook 2008.* Retrieved from http://epp.eurostat.ec.europa.eu/portal/page?_pageid=2693,70381876,2693_70592044&_dad=portal&_schema=PORTAL.

Feldman, D. C. (1994). The decision to retire early: A review and conceptualization. *Academy of Management Review, 19,* 285–311.

Feldt, T., Hyvonen, K., Makikangas, A., Kinnunen, U., & Kokko, K. (2009). Development trajectories of Finnish managers' work ability over a 10-year follow-up period. *Scandinavian Journal of Work, Environment & Health, 35,* 37–47.

Freund, A. M., & Baltes, P. B. (1998). Selection, optimization, and compensation as strategies of life management: Correlations with subjective indicators of successful aging. *Psychology and Aging, 13,* 531–543.

Frontera, W. R, Hughes, V. A., Fielding, R. A., Fiatarone, M. A., Evans, W. J., & Roubenoff, R. (2000). Aging of skeletal muscle: A 12-yr longitudinal study. *Journal of Applied Physiology, 88,* 1321–1326.

Gall, T. L., Evans, D. R., & Howard, J. (1997). The retirement adjustment process: Changes in the well-being of male retirees across time. *The Journal of Gerontology: Psychological Sciences, 52B,* P110–P117.

Gobeski, K. T., & Beehr, T. A. (2009). How retirees work: Predictors of different types of bridge employment. *Journal of Organizational Behavior, 30,* 401–425.

Gould, R. (2006). Choice or chance—Late retirement in Finland. *Social Policy & Society, 5*(4), 519–531.

Gould, R., Ilmarinen, J., Jarvisalo, J., & Koskinen S. (2008). Dimensions of work ability—Summary and conclusions. In R. Gould, J. Ilmarinen, J. Jarvisalo, & S. Koskinen (Eds.), *Dimensions of work ability. Results of the Health 2000 survey.* (pp. 165–176). Helsinki, Finland: Finnish Centre of Pensions, The Social Insurance Institution, National Public Health Institute and Finnish Institute of Occupational Health.

Hanisch, K. A., & Hulin, C. L. (1990). Job attitudes and organizational withdrawal: An examination of retirement and other withdrawal behaviors. *Journal of Vocational Behavior, 37,* 60–78.

Hanisch, K. A., & Hulin, C. L. (1991). General attitudes and organizational withdrawal: An evaluation of a causal model. *Journal of Vocational Behavior, 39,* 110–128.

Hardy, M. (2006). Older workers. In R. H. Birnstock & L. K. George (Eds.), *Aging and the social sciences* (pp. 201–218). London, England: Elsevier.

Hedge, J. W., Borman, W. C., & Lammlein, S. E. (2006). *The aging workforce. Realities, myths and implications for organizations.* Washington, DC: American Psychological Association.

Heponiemi, T., Kouvonen, A., Vanska, J., Halila, H., Sinervo, T., Kivimaki, M., & Elovainio, M. (2008). Health, psychosocial factors and retirement intentions among Finnish physicians. *Occupational Medicine (Lond), 58*(6), 406–412.

Ilmarinen, J. (2002). Physical requirements associated with the work of aging workers in the European Union. *Experimental Aging Research, 28*, 7–23.

Ilmarinen, J. (2006). *Towards a longer worklife—Ageing and the quality of worklife in the European Union.* Helsinki, Finland: Finnish Institute of Occupational Health.

Ilmarinen, J. (2009). Work ability—A comprehensive concept for occupational health research and prevention. *Scandinavian Journal of Work, Environment & Health, 35*, 1–5.

Ilmarinen, J., Gould R., Jarvikoski, A., & Jarvisalo, J. (2008). In R. Gould, J. Ilmarinen, J. Jarvisalo, & S. Koskinen (Eds.), *Dimensions of work ability. Results of the Health 2000 survey* (pp. 13–23). Helsinki, Finland: Finnish Centre of Pensions, The Social Insurance Institution, National Public Health Institute and Finnish Institute of Occupational Health.

Ilmarinen, J., & Tuomi, K. (2004). Past, present and future of work ability. *People and Work, Research Reports 65* (pp. 1–25). Helsinki, Finland: Finnish Institute of Occupational Health.

Ilmarinen, J., Tuomi, K., Eskelinen, L., Nygard, C.-H., Huuhtanen, P., & Klockars, M. (1991). Background and objectives of the Finnish research project on aging workers in municipal occupations. *Scandinavian Journal of Work, Environment & Health, 17* (Suppl. 1), 7–11.

Ilmarinen, J., Tuomi, K., & Seitsamo, J. (2005). New dimensions of work ability. In G. Costa, W. J. A. Goedhard, & J. Ilmarinen (Eds.), *Assessment and promotion of work ability, health and well-being of ageing workers* (pp. 3–8). Amsterdam, The Netherlands: Elsevier International Congress Series No. 1280.

Jopp, D., & Smith, J. (2006). Resources and life management strategies as determinants of successful aging: On the protective effect of selection, optimization, and compensation. *Psychology and Aging, 21*, 253–265.

Karpansalo, M., Manninen, P., Kauhanen, J., Lakka, T. A., & Salonen, J. T. (2004). Perceived health is a strong predictor of early retirement. *Scandinavian Journal of Work, Environment & Health, 30*, 287–292.

Kim, H., & DeVaney, S. A. (2005). The selection of partial or full retirement by older workers. *Journal of Family and Economic Issues, 26*(3), 371–394.

Kim, J. E., & Moen, P. (2002). Retirement transitions, gender, and psychological well-being: A life-course, ecological model. *Journal of Gerontology: Psychological Sciences, 57B*, 212–222.

Kim, S., & Feldman, D. C. (1998). Healthy, wealthy, or wise: Predicting actual acceptances of early retirement incentives at three points in time. *Personnel Psychology, 51*, 623–642.

Kim, S., & Feldman, D. C. (2000). Working in retirement: The antecedents of bridge employment and its consequences for quality of life in retirement. *Academy of Management Journal, 43*, 1195–1210.

Kivimaki, M., Leino-Arjas, P., Luukkonen, R., Riihimaki, H., Vahtera, J., & Kirjonen, J. (2002). Work stress and risk of cardiovascular mortality: Prospective cohort study of industrial employees. *British Medical Journal, 325*, 857–861.

Krause, N., Lynch, J., Kaplan, G. A., Cohen, R. D., Goldberg, D. E., & Salonen, J. T. (1997). Predictors of disability retirement. *Scandinavian Journal of Work, Environment & Health, 23*, 403–413.

LaCroix, A. Z., Guralnik, J. M., Berkman, L. F., Wallace, R. B., & Satterfield, S. (1993). Maintaining mobility in later life. II. Smoking, alcohol consumption, physical activity, and body mass index. *American Journal of Epidemiology, 137*, 858–869.

Laine, S., Gimeno, D., Virtanen, M., Oksanen, T., Vahtera, J., Elovainio, M.,...Kivimaki, M. (2009). Job strain as a predictor of disability pension: The Finnish Public Sector Study. *Journal of Epidemiology & Community Health, 63*, 24–30.

Levinson, D. J. (1978). *Seasons of a man's life.* New York, NY: Knopf.

Loi, J. L. P., & Shultz, K. S. (2007). Why older adults seek employment: Differing motivations among subgroups. *Journal of Applied Gerontology, 26*, 274–289.

Mein, G., Martikainen, P., Hemingway, H., Stansfeld, S., & Marmot, M. (2003). Is retirement good or bad for mental and physical health functioning? Whitehall II Longitudinal Study of Civil Servants. *Journal of Epidemiology and Community Health, 57*, 46–49.

Mobley, W. H., Horner, S. O., & Hollingsworth, A. T. (1978). An evaluation of precursors of hospital employee turnover. *Journal of Applied Psychology, 63*, 408–414.

Moen, P. (1996). A life course perspective on retirement, gender, and well-being. *Journal of Occupational Health Psychology, 1*, 131–144.

Pinquart, M., & Schindler, I. (2007). Changes of life satisfaction in the transition to retirement: A latent-class approach. *Psychology and Aging, 22*, 442–455.

Punakallio, A., Lusa S., & Luukkonen, R. (2004). Functional, postural and perceived balance for predicting the work ability of firefighters. *International Archives of Occupational and Environmental Health, 77*, 482–490.

Quick, H. E., & Moen, P. (1998). Gender, employment and retirement quality: A life course approach to the differential experiences of men and women. *Journal of Occupational Health Psychology, 3*, 44–64.

Rantanen, T., Guralnik, J. M., Sakari-Rantala, R., Leveille, S., Simonsick, E. M., Ling, S., & Fried, L. P. (1999). Disability, physical activity, and muscle strength in older women: The Women's Health and Aging Study. *Archives of Physical Medicine and Rehabilitation, 80*, 130–135.

Reitzes, D. C., & Mutran, E. J. (2004). The transition into retirement: Stages and factors that influence retirement adjustment. *International Journal of Aging and Human Development, 59*, 63–84.

Sell, L. (2009). Predicting long-term sickness absence and early retirement pension from self-reported work ability. *International Archives of Occupational and Environmental Health, 82*, 1133–1138.

Shultz, K. S. (2003). Bridge employment: Work after retirement. In G. A. Adams & T. A. Beehr (Eds.), *Retirement: Reasons, processes and results* (pp. 214–241). New York, NY: Springer.

Shultz, K.S., & Adams, G. A. (2007). In search of a unifying paradigm for understanding aging and work in the 21st century. In K. S. Shultz & G. A. Adams (Eds.), *Aging and work in the 21st century* (pp. 303–319). Mahwah, NJ: Lawrence Erlbaum Associates.

Shultz, K. S., Morton, K. R., & Weckerle, J. R. (1998). The influence of push and pull factors of voluntary and involuntary early retirees' retirement decision and adjustment. *Journal of Vocational Behavior, 53*, 45–57.

Shultz, K. S., & Wang, M. (2007). The influence of specific physical health conditions on retirement decisions. *International Journal of Aging and Human Development, 65*, 149–161.

Sjogren-Ronka, T., Ojanen, M. T., Leskinen, E. K., Mustalampi, S. T., & Malkia, E. A. (2002). Physical and psychological prerequisites of functioning in relation to work ability and general subjective well-being among office workers. *Scandinavian Journal of Work, Environment & Health, 28,* 184–190.

Smith, D. B., & Moen, P. (2004). Retirement satisfaction for retirees and their spouses: Do gender and the decision-making process matter? *Journal of Family Issues, 25,* 262–285.

Spillman, B. C., & Lubitz, J. (2000). The effect of longevity on spending for acute and long-term care. *New England Journal of Medicine, 342,* 1409–1415.

Sutinen, R., Kivimaki, M., Elovainio, M., & Forma, P. (2005). Associations between stress at work and attitudes towards retirement in hospital physicians. *Work & Stress, 19,* 177–185.

Taylor, M. A., & Shore, L. M. (1995). Predictors of planned retirement age: An application of Beehr's model. *Psychology and Aging, 10,* 76–83.

Topa, G., Moriano, A. M., Depolo, M., Alcover, C.-M., & Morales, J. F. (2009). Antecedents and consequences of retirement planning and decision-making: A meta-analysis and model. *Journal of Vocational Behavior, 75,* 38–55.

Tuomi, K., Huuhtanen, P., Nykyri, E., & Ilmarinen, J. (2001). Promotion of work ability, the quality of work and retirement. *Occupational Medicine, 51,* 318–324.

Tuomi, K., Ilmarinen, J., Eskelinen, L., Jarvinen, E., Toikkanen, J., & Klockars, M. (1991). Prevalence and incidence rates of diseases and work ability in different work categories of municipal occupations. *Scandinavian Journal of Work, Environment & Health, 17* (Suppl. 1), 67–74.

Tuomi, K., Ilmarinen, J., Jahkola, A., Katajarinne, L., & Tulkki, A. (2002). *Work Ability Index.* Occupational Health Care No. 19 (2nd revised ed.). Helsinki, Finland: Finnish Institute of Occupational Health.

Tuomi, K., Ilmarinen, J., Martikainen, R., Aalto, L., & Klockars M. (1997). Aging, work, life-style and work ability among Finnish municipal employees. *Scandinavian Journal of Work, Environment & Health, 23* (Suppl. 1), 58–67.

Tuomi, K., Jarvinen, E., Eskelinen, L., Ilmarinen, J., & Klockars, M. (1991). Effect of retirement on health and work ability among municipal employees. *Scandinavian Journal of Work, Environment & Health, 17* (Suppl. 1), 75–81.

United Nations. (2009). *Population Division of the Department of Economic and Social Affairs of the United Nations Secretariat, World Population Prospects: The 2008 Revision.* Retrieved from http://esa.un.org/wpp/unpp/panel_population.htm.

van Dam, K., van der Vorst, J. D. M., & van der Heijden, B. I. J. M. (2009). Employees' intentions to retire early. A case of planned behavior and anticipated work conditions. *Journal of Career Development, 35*(3), 265–289.

van Solinge, H. (2007). Health changes in retirement: A longitudinal study among older workers in the Netherlands. *Research on Aging, 29,* 225–256.

van Solinge, H., & Henkens, K. (2007). Involuntary retirement: The role of restrictive circumstances, timing, and social embeddedness. *Journals of Gerontology: Social Sciences, 62B,* S295–S303.

van Solinge, H., & Henkens, K. (2008). Adjustment to and satisfaction with retirement: Two of a kind? *Psychology and Aging, 23,* 422–434.

Verbrugge, L. M., & Jette, A. M. (1994). The disablement process. *Social Science & Medicine, 38,* 1–14.

von Bonsdorff, M. B., Seitsamo, J., Ilmarinen, J., Nygard, C.-H., von Bonsdorff, M. B., & Rantanen, T. (2011). Work ability in midlife as a predictor of mortality and late-life disability: A 28-year prospective study. *Canadian Medical Association Journal.* doi:10.1503/cmaj.100713.

von Bonsdorff, M. E., Huuhtanen, P., Tuomi, K., & Seitsamo, J. (2009a). Predictors of employees' early retirement intentions: An 11-year longitudinal study. *Occupational Medicine, 60,* 94–100. doi:10.1093/occmed/kqp126.

von Bonsdorff, M. E., Seitsamo, J., Rantanen, T., von Bonsdorff, M. B., Husman, K., Husman, P.,…Ilmarinen, J. (2011). Changes in work ability according to type of pension benefit—A 28-year prospective study. In C.-H. Nygard, M. Savinainen, T. Kirsi, & K. Lumme-Sandt (Eds.), *Age management during the life course.* Proceedings of the 4th Symposium on Work Ability. Tampere, Finland: Tampere University Press. pp. 399–408.

von Bonsdorff, M. E., Shultz, K. S., Leskinen, E., & Tansky, J. (2009b). The choice between retirement and bridge employment: A continuity theory and life course perspective. *International Journal of Aging and Human Development, 69*(2), 79–100.

Wang, M. (2007). Profiling retirees in the retirement transition and adjustment process: Examining the longitudinal change patterns of retirees' psychological well-being. *Journal of Applied Psychology, 92,* 455–474.

Wang, M., Adams, G. A., Beehr, T. A., & Shultz, K. S. (2009). Bridge employment and retirement: Issues and opportunities during the latter part of one's career. In S. G. Baugh & S. E. Sullivan (Eds.), *Maintaining focus, energy, and options through the life span* (pp. 135–162). Charlotte, NC: Information Age Publishing (IAP).

Wang, M., & Bodner, T. F. (2007). Growth mixture modeling: Identifying and predicting unobserved subpopulations with longitudinal data. *Organizational Research Methods, 10,* 635–656.

Wang, M., & Shultz, K. S. (2010). Employee retirement: A review and recommendations for future investigation. *Journal of Management, 36,* 172–206.

Wang, M., Zhan, Y., Liu, S., & Shultz, K. S. (2008). Antecedents of bridge employment: A longitudinal investigation. *Journal of Applied Psychology, 93,* 818–830.

Weckerle, J. R., & Shultz, K. S. (1999). Influences on the bridge employment decision among older USA workers. *Journal of Occupational and Organizational Psychology, 72,* 317–329.

Westerlund, H., Kivimaki, M., Sing-Manoux, A., Melchior, M., Ferrie, J. E., Pentti, J.,… Vahtera, J. (2009). Self-rated health before and after retirement in France (GAZEL): A cohort study. *Lancet, 374,* 1889–1896.

Westerlund, H., Vahtera, J., Ferrie, J. E., Sing-Manoux, A., Pentti, J., Melchior, M.,…Kivimaki, M. (2010). Effect of retirement on major chronic conditions and fatigue: French GAZEL occupational cohort study. *British Medical Journal, 341.* doi:10.1136/bmj.c6149.

Zhan Y., Wang M., Liu S., & Shultz K. (2009). Bridge employment and retiree's health: A longitudinal study. *Journal of Occupational Health Psychology, 14*(4), 374–389.

The Theory of Selection, Optimization, and Compensation

Boris B. Baltes *and* Cort W. Rudolph

Abstract

This chapter reviews research suggesting that behaviors and active coping strategies that are classifiable under the lifespan development meta-theory of Selection, Optimization, and Compensation (SOC) can lead to more successful outcomes for people in both pre- and post-retirement contexts. First, we introduce SOC and define behaviors that are indicative of Selection, Optimization, and Compensation. Then, we explore how SOC can be mapped onto three key processes often associated with retirement: maintenance of job performance, retirement decision making, and positive retirement adjustment. Finally, directions for future research and a call for more careful attention to the developmental processes that underlie retirement phenomena are levied.

Key Words: selection, optimization, and compensation, soc, behavioral coping strategies, delaying retirement, retirement decision making, retirement adjustment

The Theory of Selection, Optimization, and Compensation

The present chapter serves to relate the lifespan development meta-theory of Selection, Optimization, and Compensation (SOC; M. M. Baltes & Carstensen, 1996, 1998; P. B. Baltes, 1997; P. B. Baltes et al., 1984; P. B. Baltes, Staudinger, & Lindenberger, 1999; Freund & P. B. Baltes, 1998) to three basic processes that are associated with retirement. Specifically, this chapter (1) examines the use of SOC strategies for helping older workers maintain their job performance and thus maximize their choices with respect to voluntary retirement, (2) discusses how SOC is related to the process of "successful" retirement in terms of decision making, and (3) examines how the use of SOC strategies is related to positive adjustment once one has retired.

Selection, Compensation, and Optimization

The SOC model provides a framework that aids in understanding successful developmental across the lifespan (M. M. Baltes & Carstensen, 1996; P. B. Baltes, 1997; P. B. Baltes et al., 1984; P. B. Baltes, Staudinger, & Lindenberger, 1999; Freund & P. B. Baltes, 1998). Successful development is broadly defined by the maximization of desirable outcomes and the minimization of undesirable outcomes. The definition of "successful" is of course dynamic, and will be influenced not only by where in the lifecourse a person is, but also by personal and socio-cultural factors (P. B. Baltes et al., 1999 P. B. Baltes, Reese, & Lipsitt, 1980).

The SOC model builds upon the premise that people's resources (e.g., mental, physical, and environmental) are limited at any point in time, and opportunities (e.g., job training) or losses (e.g., physical ability) that arise require choices about the allocation of these limited resources. Furthermore, it is also hypothesized that the more stretched one's resources become, the more effective SOC strategies will be in helping an individual successfully deal with such challenges (Young, B. B. Baltes, & Pratt, 2007). The SOC model suggests that three general behavioral strategies—Selection, Optimization, and Compensation—can be used to successfully manage developmental opportunities or losses. It should be pointed out that the exact operationalization of these three strategies can change depending on the context in which they are used. The following definitions of the key components of this model are taken from Freund and P. B. Baltes (2002); this work also includes a table (p. 643) that identifies the categories of behavior that can serve as guidelines for the classification of observed behaviors within the SOC framework.

Selection

The primary focus of Selection is on the degree to which individuals identify and set goals. Selection thus gives direction to behavior, which is important because resources are often limited to begin with. Because the causal and functional origins of Selection can differ, two basic kinds of Selection can occur: Elective Selection and Loss-Based Selection. Elective Selection occurs when goal selection is guided primarily by preference or external influences, such as social norms, and not imposed by the loss of goal-relevant means. An example of Elective Selection for an employee in a work setting would be choosing to focus on a limited number of work goals after the birth of a child (Young, B. B. Baltes, & Pratt, 2007). Loss-Based Selection occurs when an individual is pressured to change their goals because of the loss of some internal or external resource that is necessary to maintain functioning. Loss-Based Selection often involves the reconstructing of goal hierarchies by redefining one's most important goals, adapting standards, or replacing goals that are no longer achievable. For example, individuals may decide to postpone plans for early retirement when faced with financial hardships or other unexpected losses (e.g., unemployment of a spouse).

Optimization

Optimization refers to the acquisition, refinement, and use of means to achieve goals. General categories of Optimization can include persistence, practice, learning of new skills, and modeling successful others, as well as the scheduling of time and energy. Part of the Optimization process also considers contextualizing the adequacy of means, because the effectiveness of one's means depends on the goals considered and the context in which Optimization is expected to occur. An example of Optimization in the workplace would be an employee attempting to become more sociable with coworkers to increase their social network and, thus, increase their level of social support. Another example of Optimization would be an employee exerting extra effort to achieve higher levels of performance.

Compensation

Compensation entails the processes used to maintain a specified level of functioning when faced with developmental losses. Specifically, Compensation concerns the acquisition and use of alternative means to maintain a desired level of functioning in the face of actual or anticipated decreases in resources. A broad example of Compensation would be employing the help of others (e.g., child care). A more specific example of Compensation in the workplace would be the use of impression management by employees so that losses are less evident or are seen by others as less important (Abraham & Hansson, 1995).

In summary, Elective Selection is defined by behaviors that aid in the process of developing, choosing, and committing oneself to goals or *preferred outcomes*. In contrast, Loss-Based Selection is said to encompass behaviors—such as the reconstruction of one's goal hierarchy or the search for new goals—in response to *non-preferred outcomes*. Optimization and Compensation differ from Selection in that the focus shifts to the processes necessary for future goal attainment. Specifically, while Optimization denotes the various methods of achieving a selected goal or higher levels of functioning in a particular domain, Compensation refers to the processes that are aimed at counteracting losses—be they actual or impending—to maintain progress toward goal attainment.

As an introduction to the SOC model, the definitions given above are purposefully general. To help clarify these definitions, it is helpful to understand how SOC behaviors have been operationalized and measured. For instance, a self-report instrument described in Freund and P. B. Baltes (2002) contains a list of forty-eight items that are presented as a choice between a SOC strategy and a distracter item. An example of an Elective Selection item is: "To achieve a particular goal, I am willing to abandon other goals." For Loss-Based Selection, an example item is: "When I can't do something important the way I did before, I look for a new goal." An example of an Optimization item is: "I keep working on what I have planned until I succeed." Finally, an example of a Compensation item is: "When something in my life isn't working as well as it used to, I ask others for help or advice."

The assessment of SOC behaviors can occur with different methodologies, such as self-report or behavioral observation (for self-report, see Freund & P. B. Baltes, 2002; for behavioral-observational measures of SOC, see Li, Lindenberger, Freund, & P. B. Baltes, 2001 and Gignac, Cott, & Badley, 2002). It is worth mentioning that SOC behaviors have displayed predictive uniqueness when tested against personality factors, intellectual functioning, thinking styles (e.g., Sternberg, 1994), and other models of adaptive coping, such as flexible goal adjustment and tenacious goal pursuit (Freund & P.B. Baltes, 2002).

Research on the SOC model and its efficacy has been conducted with many diverse populations and with many different types of outcomes. Early research on the SOC model focused on older adults and demonstrated that individuals who report—or are observed —using SOC behaviors are generally more successful in their lives in general (e.g., P. B. Baltes & M. M. Baltes, 1997) as well as more successful in mastering situations of overload (e.g., Lang, Rieckman, & M. M. Baltes, 2002). Other research indicates that SOC strategies are not limited to the elderly and may be used by any individual experiencing resource allocation issues, regardless of age. For example, Freund and P. B. Baltes (1998) report that SOC behaviors are used from early adulthood to late adulthood, with middle-aged adults reporting the highest frequency of SOC behaviors. As with earlier studies, these results confirm that individuals reporting higher levels of SOC-related life management strategies have higher scores on various indicators of psychological and emotional well-being.

Research has also examined SOC in relation to work-related outcomes, such as job performance and work-family issues. With respect to job performance, several very pertinent examples can be found in the literature. For example, Abraham and Hansson (1995) examined the use of SOC-related work strategies by older adults, finding that older workers (age 49–69 years) who frequently used SOC strategies reported higher levels of job competence. Similarly, Bajor and Baltes (2003) examined the use of SOC strategies in an age-diverse work sample and found that managers who reported using SOC strategies had higher levels of job performance.

Finally, a recent study by Yeung and Fung (2009) reported that the use of certain SOC strategies was positively related to sales productivity for Chinese insurance salespeople.

With respect to work-family issues, there is evidence for positive outcomes associated with SOC. For example, Wiese, Freund, and P. B. Baltes (2000) applied the SOC model to the often-conflicting goals of career and partnership in young professionals. Their results indicated that participants who reported using more SOC behaviors likewise reported higher levels of global well-being as well as greater satisfaction with their careers and partnerships. Research has also shown that the use of SOC behaviors is related to lower amounts of job and family stressors and subsequently lower amounts of work-family conflict (B. B. Baltes & Heydens-Gahir, 2003; Young, B. B. Baltes, & Pratt, 2007).

In summary, the use of SOC behaviors has been linked to many positive outcomes, both subjective and objective, for both younger and older individuals. In the following sections we will review relevant research and suggest how the use of SOC behaviors may be related to three basic components of the retirement process. First, we discuss how SOC behaviors are related to both job performance and perceptions of job performance, which we argue that older workers need to actively maintain to avoid potentially being forced into retirement. Second, we will discuss how SOC is related to the process of "successful" retirement in terms of decision making and determining the best way and time to retire. Finally, we will examine how the use of SOC behaviors is related to positive adjustment once one has retired.

Age, Job Performance, and SOC

The purpose of this section is to examine how SOC may be related to voluntary retirement decisions. Specifically, we are assuming that a minimum level of job performance needs to be maintained for an individual to have the maximum amount of influence on their choice to retire. That is, if job performance declines below a minimally acceptable level, an employee will likely be involuntarily terminated even if they wish to continue working, regardless of age. Furthermore, we suggest that age-related declines in a variety of areas (e.g., mental and physical) make it more difficult for older workers to maintain an acceptable level of job performance. We argue that the use of SOC strategies may be related to the maintenance of job performance, such that the use of SOC strategies for older workers will allow them to maintain required job performance levels and thus have a greater say in when they choose to retire.

Age-related declines in a variety of areas, including visual acuity, cognitive functioning, psychomotor abilities, and general physical health, are well documented (e.g., Craik & Jennings 1992; Forteza & Prieto, 1994). Research on cognition and aging focuses on fluid intelligence (i.e., intelligence influenced by biological and genetic factors) and crystallized intelligence (i.e., intelligence influenced by experience and culture-based knowledge). Fluid intelligence is the ability to think and reason abstractly and solve problems. Most research confirms the idea that fluid intelligence increases with age, and begins to decrease starting in a person's 30s; however, there are debates on whether this decline actually occurs later in life. Crystallized intelligence refers to the ability to use the knowledge, skills, and experience that one has accumulated over the course of the lifespan, which can be particularly important to older workers. Crystallized intelligence seems to reach its maximum level in the mid-40s, and decline does not appear to occur until the 70s (P. B. Baltes, Freund, & Shu-Chen, 2005). Beyond declines in fluid and crystalized intelligence, there is also evidence for age-related declines in spatial ability and sensory factors (Salthouse, 1982).

More specific to the work arena, studies of workers have found age-related declines in several types of aptitudes (e.g., general intelligence, verbal aptitude, numerical aptitude, spatial aptitude, finger dexterity; see Avolio & Waldman, 1990). Age-related declines have also been found in memory, with older adults having poorer recognition and recall memory than younger adults (e.g., Spencer & Raz, 1995). One study found that the perceptions of younger workers regarding this age-related decline meant that older workers were less likely to be given training, since their memories were not "trusted" (Erber & Danker, 1995). In sum, there are many age-related declines (e.g., mental and physical) with which older workers need to contend.

One would assume that such age-related declines means that there is a negative relationship between age and job performance, but this is not necessarily the case. Most studies of the relationship between age and job performance have examined chronological age and core task performance, and several quantitative reviews have found a variety of results ranging from a positive relationship (Waldman & Avolio, 1986), to no relationship (McEvoy & Cascio, 1989; Ng & Feldman, 2008),

to a curvilinear relationship (i.e., inverted U-shape; Sturman, 2003) between age and job performance. Thus, with respect to the relationship between age and core technical performance, findings have been mixed; however, the majority of reviews have reported a null relationship. This could be because most research in this arena has been cross-sectional in nature, with the observed null relationship being driven by the fact that older workers whose job performance has declined are no longer working. Thus any true relationship between age and job performance is masked by the effects of attrition (Kanfer, Crosby, & Brandt, 1988).

Put another way, there is clearly evidence to suggest that age-related declines – both mental and physical – do occur for older workers, however as suggested here, the relationship between job performance and age does not necessarily reflect this decline. This is likely because older workers who experience developmentally related changes in job performance are those who are let go, and are no longer working. We suggest here that one strategy that older workers may use to maintain their level of job performance when undergoing age-related declines is to engage in active coping strategies that can be classified under the SOC framework.

Several studies have shown that the use of SOC strategies is related to job performance. The basic premise behind this relationship is one that should hold true regardless of the worker's age. That is, all workers are usually in resource-limited situations at work (i.e., time and job resources are limited), and by employing SOC strategies, one can most successfully make use of the limited resources at hand. A study by Bajor and B. B. Baltes (2003) demonstrated this relationship. In this study, Big-5 personality measures, reported use of SOC strategies, and supervisor evaluations of job performance were obtained from 584 bank employees. Results suggested that employees with larger amounts of job autonomy (e.g., managers) who reported higher levels of SOC strategies—most importantly, Loss-Based Selection and Compensation behaviors—had higher levels of job performance. Furthermore, the use of SOC strategies contributed unique variance in predicting workplace performance above and beyond other personality variables (e.g., conscientiousness). Although this study suggests that the use of SOC strategies is related to job performance, regardless of employee age, we know that aging workers may face additional issues above and beyond the common resource challenges facing all workers. Specifically, older workers likely face their own declines in mental and physical resources. Thus, with respect to maintaining job performance, we posit that the use of SOC strategies takes on increasing importance as older adults experience these declines. Indeed, several studies provide support for this argument.

For example, Abraham and Hansson (1995) examined the relationship between the use of SOC and self-reported ability and competence maintenance for 224 older working adults between 40 and 69 years old, sampled broadly from a variety of industries. They also developed a scale of SOC behaviors that included a specific component of Compensation strategies (i.e., impression management) that were hypothesized to be important for older workers. Specifically, impression management may be an effective way to "minimize the impact of unavoidable losses on evaluations of one's performance" (p. 96). A classic example of this technique was provided by P. B. Baltes and M. M. Baltes (1990a), stating that in response to his decreasing ability to play fast movements, the pianist Rubinstein "slows down his speed of playing prior to fast movements, thereby producing a contrast that enhances impression of speed in fast movements" (p. 26). Abraham and Hanson included items in their SOC scale to tap this domain specifically in the workplace (e.g., an example of this strategy would include "Making one's accomplishments of skills highly visible to others," p. 96). The results of this study indicated that the use of SOC behaviors was related to positive workplace outcomes for the entire sample. However, perhaps more interestingly, an interaction between age and SOC behaviors was found, such that as the age of the workers increased, the relationship between SOC and job performance became much stronger. This study also found that older workers reported higher mean levels of SOC behaviors, suggesting that, on average, older workers in the sample were using more SOC strategies.

Yeung and Fung (2009) recently conducted an investigation examining the relationship between SOC and job performance in two studies. The first study was cross-sectional in nature and was intended to study the relationship between the use of SOC strategies and job performance in insurance sales workers. The results indicated that all four SOC components were related to sales productivity for the entire age-diverse sample. Furthermore, they also found an age-by-SOC strategy interaction similar to Abraham and Hansson (1995); Elective Selection and Compensation both interacted with age such that the relationship between these SOC behaviors and job performance was stronger for older workers.

In their second study, Yeung and Fung (2009) used an experience sampling methodology to examine the relationship between momentary measures of SOC strategies and job performance. Again, evidence suggested that for older workers, the use of SOC strategies predicted job performance. This study also found that task difficulty moderated this relationship (i.e., under very high task difficulty, the relationship between SOC and job performance seemed to degrade) and postulated that the relationship between SOC and job performance may be more complex than previously theorized. A possible explanation for the finding above is that high task difficulty situations may also be limited autonomy situations. Prior studies have found that individuals in low autonomy situations have a difficult time making use of SOC strategies, and thus SOC behaviors are limited in range and do not relate to job performance outcomes (Bajor & B. B. Baltes, 2003).

As mentioned, one reason job performance does not demonstrate an intuitive decline with age may be because older workers who cannot keep performance "up to par" are let go via an involuntary attrition process. This effect could also be the reason for the mean-level age differences found in SOC behaviors across all the SOC–job performance studies that have been mentioned herein. Specially, this mean-level age difference could be caused by attrition if older workers who do not use SOC – and thus fail to adequately maintain their required job performance – are let go by their organizations. This would mean that only older workers who engage in more SOC-related behavioral strategies—and consequently demonstrate and maintain higher levels of job performance—remain with their organizations. This attrition effect may mask the relationship between job performance and age that one would theoretically expect to find in an unrestricted (i.e., with respect to SOC) sample of all older employees.

The results of these studies provide support for the notion that the use of SOC strategies may be related to various types of job performance for older workers. Furthermore, it seems that the importance of SOC in maintaining job performance becomes stronger as workers age. Thus, we put forth that the use of SOC strategies by older workers is important if they are to maintain their job performance and have the most flexibility in deciding when they will retire.

SOC and the Action Theoretical Framework

Up until now, we have introduced the SOC model as a developmental meta-theory that explains the adaptability of both cognitive and behavioral processes that facilitate successful aging. We have also introduced the idea that specific applications of SOC may contribute to pre-retirement longevity, particularly as an aid for people who wish to continue working, despite developmental decrements. We will now discuss the application of SOC to the retirement process by focusing on two viewpoints that have been traditionally applied to understanding the retirement process: retirement as a decision-making process and retirement as an adjustment process.

As a means of understanding how SOC strategies may inform both the decision-making and adjustment perspectives of the retirement process, it is helpful to apply the SOC action-theoretical framework developed by P. B. Baltes, M. M. Baltes, Freund, and Lang (1995). This framework presents specific categories of behaviors that are indicative of Selection, Optimization, and Compensation. By conceptualizing SOC in specific, behavioral terms, we will be better able to draw inferences about how SOC may inform retirement decision making and retirement adjustment. As means of understanding this framework, recall that Elective Selection is defined by *preferred outcomes*, whereas Loss-Based Selection is defined by *non-preferred outcomes*. Optimization and Compensation specify the processes necessary for future goal attainment; Optimization denotes the various methods of achieving a selected goal in a particular domain, whereas Compensation refers to the processes that are aimed at counteracting losses to maintain progress toward goal attainment.

Retirement as a Decision-Making Process

Retirement has often been regarded as a decision-making process. That is, retirement has often been conceptualized as some form of rational and motivated choice behavior (Wang & Shulz, 2010). As a freely chosen action, the decision-making perspective of retirement suggests that people actively and consciously decrease their commitment to work and begin to withdraw on terms for which they have planned (e.g., Adams, Prescher, Beehr, & Lepisto, 2002; Feldman, 1994; Shultz & Wang, 2007). However, not all retirement is perceived as freely chosen, and even freely chosen retirement may be perceived as "forced" or restricted under certain conditions (Szinovacz & Davey, 2005). This notion

has been conceptualized previously as the "voluntariness of retirement" (e.g., Beehr, 1986) and refers to the degree to which retirees perceive their decision as being voluntary or involuntary. Research suggests that such perceptions are derived from individuals' choice, motivation, and level of perceived control (i.e., locus of causality) over their retirement decision (e.g., Heckhausen & Schulz, 1995). Indeed, perceptions of forced retirement decisions can be a consequence of internal (e.g., health limitations), external (e.g., family care obligations), or structural forces (e.g., job displacement, benefits considerations). We will now consider these three consequences separately.

One possible internal force that may underscore restricted decision making in retirement is the increasing possibility of health issues with age. Health factors have often been cited as one of the strongest predictors of a person's choice to retire (e.g., Barnes-Farrell, 2003). Indeed, research has consistently demonstrated a link between older workers' health status and planned retirement age (e.g., Farr & Ringseis, 2002; Taylor & Shore, 1995), retirement behaviors (e.g., Hardy & Quadagno, 1995; Herzog, House, & Morgan, 1991; Muller & Boaz, 1988), and retirement satisfaction and adjustment (e.g., Shultz, Morton, & Weckerle, 1998). Furthermore, there is considerable evidence that links abrupt retirement decisions to health limitations (e.g., Bound, Schoenbaum, Stinebrickner, & Waidmann, 1999; Dwyer & Mitchell, 1999; Hayward, Friedman, & Chen, 1998).

Likewise, external forces, such as care obligations, have been shown to relate to perceptions of restricted choice in retirement decisions. Care obligations are often forces largely external to the work environment that represent conditions that may directly conflict with work roles. This conflict may trigger the need to withdraw from work roles, despite a motivated desire to continue working. For example, B. B. Baltes, Rudolph, and Bal (2012) suggest that preexisting structures of dependencies, current or potential future commitments, obligations, or personal factors can have a profound impact on the meanings that older workers construct and attach to work. Such structures may include demands from other roles (e.g., family) that draw one away from work by function of normative pressure (e.g., care obligations). Indeed, research suggests that family care obligations may prompt withdrawal from work roles and can be predictive of retirement decisions (e.g., Hayward, Friedman, & Chen, 1998; Szinovacz & DeViney, 2000; Zimmerman et al., 2000).

Beyond care obligations, there is emerging evidence that one's level of work-family conflict is an important predictor of retirement ideations (Raymo & Sweeney, 2006). Moreover, the decision to retire may serve to buffer work-family conflict for individuals who engage in stressful work roles (Coursolle, Sweeney, Raymo, & Ho, 2010). Interestingly, care obligations may accompany financial obligations, which may require older workers to remain in the workforce (e.g., Szinovacz & Davey, 2005; Blau, 1998; Ruhm, 1996). Note that this case still represents a restricted-choice situation if the individual forced to maintain employment would rather divest themselves of workplace obligations in lieu of care obligations.

Finally, certain structural forces—such as job displacement and benefits considerations—have been shown to relate to perceptions of restricted choice in retirement decisions (e.g., Chan & Stevens, 2002). The notion of job displacement may be particularly damning to older workers' sense of control over their retirement decisions if, by function of developmental declines, they are no longer able to perform within a band of acceptable capacity (e.g., Williamson, Rinehart, & Black, 1992; Zimmerman, Mitchell, Wister, & Gutman, 2000). Interestingly, institutional factors, such as the means by which benefits or pensions are administered, may further contribute to perceptions of restricted choice in retirement decisions (e.g., Gruber & Wise, 1999). For example, in the United States, there is very specific window of opportunity for the collection of retirement benefits via Social Security that may serve to penalize workers who retire past certain thresholds (Social Security Administration, 2010). Within organizations, there is evidence that benefits (e.g., health insurance, early retirement incentives) have a similar effect of restraining retirement choice perceptions (Beehr, Glazer, Nielson, & Farmer, 2000; Blau & Gilleskie, 2003; Fronstin, 1999). Collectively, these structural constraints—ranging from job loss to the policies underlying the administration of benefits—may limit the perception of control over the retirement decision process.

Before turning our attention back to SOC, we must first define the outcomes that we propose SOC to influence, which we will call retirement success. We adopt a multifaceted, psychologically grounded definition of retirement success that can account for both voluntary and involuntary perceptions of this process. Thus we define successful retirement broadly as encompassing (1) the ability to adapt to new and changing conditions that occur as a function of one's withdrawal from work roles, (2) the ability to disengage from such work roles while minimizing the experience of both physical (e.g., poorer physical health and lower activity levels) and psychological (e.g., depression, loneliness, lower life satisfaction and happiness, and a less positive view about retirement) disturbances that may be experienced during the retirement process (e.g., Atchley & Robinson, 1982; Kim & Moen, 2002; Richardson & Kilty, 1991; Ross & Drentea, 1998), and (3) the perception that one has successfully retired. Implicit in this definition is that successful retirement requires flexibility and adaptability to available resources as a means of maximizing gains and minimizing losses throughout the process. It is suggested that one's engagement in SOC behaviors will be predictive of higher levels of successful retirement, both in terms of retirement decision making and in terms of adjustment to retirement.

Under the "ideal" condition in which retirement is perceived as being freely chosen, behaviors that are indicative of Elective Selection may be particularly important predictors of successful retirement. That is, freely chosen decisions to retire are representative of preferred outcomes as defined by SOC. Thus, it is reasonable to posit that individuals with more free choice in retirement decisions are more likely to engage in behaviors that fall under the guise of Elective Selection. Such behaviors could include specifying retirement goals within a hierarchy of other life goals, contextualizing goals to account for personal/social factors, and maintaining commitment toward retirement goals.

However, under the "less ideal" condition where retirement is perceived as occurring under restricted-choice conditions, Loss-Based Selection may be a more important predictor of successful retirement. That is, restricted-choice decisions to retire are representative of non-preferred outcomes as defined by SOC. Thus, as before, it is reasonable to posit that individuals with more restricted choices in retirement decisions are more likely to engage behaviors that fall under the guise of Loss-Based Selection (e.g., focusing on most important goals, reconstruction of goal hierarchy, adaptation of standards, search for new goals, etc.).

Evidence from a variety of domains suggests that strategies for structuring goals may be important in understanding retirement decisions. Applying SOC to this idea, Selection (i.e., either Elective or Loss-Based) may serve as a useful meta-framework for understanding these effects. Indeed, goals have been proposed as an important factor to decision making in a number of domains (e.g., Beach & Mitchell, 1987). Furthermore, goals are central to both Elective and Loss-Based Selection. Goals play an important role in directing and regulating human behavior because they specify desired future states (e.g., Austin & Vancouver, 1996; Bandura, 1986; Pervin, 1989). Goals serve to initiate action by identifying what is valuable, and guide action by specifying a standard for comparison between the present state and the desired state (Austin & Vancouver, 1996; Heckhausen & Kuhl, 1985). Thus, the impact of goals on decision making is threefold: (1) goals provide motivation for action by identifying what is desirable, (2) goals serve as an index of what is possible, and (3) goals help specify what is ultimately acceptable in a particular decision domain.

There is some evidence to suggest that career-related goals are linked to retirement decisions. For example, Beehr (1986) suggests that occupational goal attainment may relate positively to retirement decisions because attaining occupational goals serves to diminish achievement-related reasons for continuing to work. This idea has found partial support in the career commitment literature, where it has been suggested that the degree to which individuals persist in their attempts to achieve occupational goals will depend on their level of career commitment (Colarelli & Bishop, 1990).

With these ideas in mind, Adams (1999) sought to link career commitment and goals to retirement decisions. This research suggests that commitment to one's career and occupational goal attainment play a central role in influencing planned retirement age. Specifically, a positive relationship was demonstrated between career commitment and planned retirement age, which suggests that those who are more committed to their careers are likely to retire later in life than their less-committed counterparts. Similarly, a negative relationship was observed between occupational goal attainment and planned retirement age. This supports the notion that those who believe they have attained their occupational goals may be more likely to say they will retire early because they have accomplished all that they set out to accomplish in their careers. Adams (1999) interpreted these results as evidence that retirement can be viewed as a form of career withdrawal.

Furthermore, evidence suggests that maintaining a stable self-image is important in the retirement process (e.g., Robbins, Lee, & Wan, 1994). Individuals may preserve a sense of well-being and maintain continuity during this transition process through the pursuit of valued goals. Indeed, research suggests that representations of goals that are positive, concrete, and stable are related to late-life satisfaction (Rapkin & Fisher, 1992; Robbins, Payne, & Chartrand, 1990).

Applying these ideas, Brougham and Walsh (2005) investigated the ability of goal assessments to predict retirement intention over and above traditionally studied variables (e.g., health, age, finances). The major finding of this research suggests that goal expectations provide an important source of information for predicting retirement intentions. More specifically, goal expectations predicted large amounts of unique variance in retirement intentions – 17% of the variance in retirement intentions was accounted for by goal expectations, over and above the 25% of the variance predicted by a set of personal and demographic variables.

Taken collectively, there is a great deal of evidence to suggest that strategies for effectively structuring and restructuring goals can effectively aid in the retirement decision-making process. The behaviors that are necessary for structuring goals fit within the SOC framework and map closely onto both Elective and Loss-Based Selection. Next, we focus on retirement as an adjustment process and discuss how SOC may inform our understanding of successful adjustment to retirement.

Retirement as an Adjustment Process

In contrast to conceptualizing retirement as a decision-making process, some have argued that understanding the adjustment process that accompanies retirement is a more comprehensive approach to understanding this phenomenon (e.g., Wang, Adams, Beehr, & Shultz, 2009). Generally, adjustment has been defined as a process through which retirees adapt to changes in various aspects of their lives in the transition from work to retirement (e.g., van Solinge & Henkens, 2008; Wang, 2007). Much like the definition of successful retirement posited earlier, success in adjustment is marked by the achievement of psychological comfort with retirement life. Retirement adjustment is a multi-faceted concept that is often said to encompass both the transition from employment to retirement and facets of post-retirement developmental trajectories (Wang & Shultz, 2010).

Conceptualizing retirement from the adjustment perspective requires one to move beyond the simple decision context and understand the more complex functional mechanisms associated with the retirement process. However, this conceptualization acknowledges that the decision to retire is an important facet of adjustment itself. Indeed, characteristics of the retirement transition process are embedded within the decision to retire and, as such, represent important predictors of success in retirement (e.g., van Solinge & Henkens, 2008). For example, different individuals may make the same decision to retire; however, variables such as the amount of prior planning, decision timing, and available resources may lead to different outcomes across individuals (Wang & Shultz, 2010). Interestingly, evidence suggests that people who perceive their retirement as freely chosen (as opposed to restricted-choice) are more likely to adapt well to retirement (Heidbreder, 1972).

By definition, SOC is an adaptive meta-theory that explains when active engagement in various behavioral strategies can serve to mitigate developmental decrements associated with aging. Thus, it is not surprising that there is evidence from a variety of studies concerning retirement adjustment to suggest that behaviors that are indicative of SOC strategies have been shown to lead to more successful retirement outcomes. For example, goal continuity—a key behavioral strategy as defined by SOC—has been shown to be an important factor in retirement adjustment. In this regard, Robbins, Lee, and Wan (1994) suggest that an important factor in adapting to retirement is the ability to maintain stable and meaningful life goals and purpose (i.e., goal continuity). This is not surprising given evidence that individuals with an orientation toward goal maintenance and loss prevention often have more positive well-being (Ebner, Freund, & P. B. Baltes, 2006)—a factor that has also been shown to influence positive adjustment to retirement (e.g., Gall, Evans, & Howard, 1997).

Applying SOC to this concept, both Elective and Loss-Based Selection specify that maintaining and restructuring one's goal hierarchy is an effective means of managing developmental losses (e.g., P. B. Baltes, M. M. Baltes, Freund & Lang, 1995). In this regard, Atchley (1975) provides a comprehensive treatment of the theoretical importance of maintaining a goal hierarchy to retirement adjustment. Put simply, the more closely one's goals match one's means in retirement, the less adjustment is necessary for successful retirement to occur. On the contrary, unattainable goals can cause distress and make adjustment more difficult. Furthermore, role transitions and (dis)identification processes associated with retirement are said to affect adjustment via the elements contained in one's goal hierarchies. That

is, the position of a person's work role within a goal hierarchy, and one's level of identification with that role, can impact adjustment outcomes.

Atchley (1976) suggests that to the extent that one identifies with their work role, the significance of losing that role is defined by its importance for achieving non-work goals. For some, work roles may be key to achieving non-work goals, and for others there may be only a weak connection. In essence, a person whose job is further down on their hierarchy of goals will have less difficulty adjusting to retirement. For example, if non-work goals (e.g., being a good spouse) or leisure goals (e.g., being a good yachtsman) come before being a good manager, there is less adjustment to make in retirement.

A key factor in the maintenance of a goal hierarchy is goal stability. In terms of SOC, P. B. Baltes, M. M. Baltes, Freund, and Lang (1995) refer to this factor within Selection. Indeed, from a lifespan perspective, goal stability can be viewed as a specific form of continuity, a factor that is important for predicting adaptation across the lifespan (e.g., Datan, Rodeheaver, & Hughes, 1987; Lazarus & Delongis, 1983). From a developmental perspective, continuity refers to an individual's ability to maintain psychological equilibrium by successfully linking past experience to present circumstance, and then to future goals (Robbins, Lee, & Wan, 1994). Research and theory have emphasized the importance that meaningful goals and a clear life purpose have for the achievement of well-being (e.g., Erikson, Erikson, and Kivnick, 1986). Indeed, goal stability is a strong predictor of social adjustment among retirement-age individuals (Smith & Robbins, 1988). One possible explanation for this can be borrowed from psychological theories of the self (Kohut, 1971, 1977), which suggest that continuity maintenance occurs through purposeful, goal-directed behavior. From this perspective, the self is an internal organizing framework, and goals are a structure within this framework that aid in satisfying various needs throughout the lifespan. Kohut (1977) suggests that maintaining an internal sense of one's goals and ideals provides a way of maintaining a sense of equilibrium and meaning across time. In this way, goals serve a stabilizing function that aids in various transitions throughout the lifespan, including retirement.

Beyond processes that approximate Selection, there is a great deal of evidence to suggest that behaviors and strategies that are indicative of Selection and Optimization can greatly impact retirement adjustment. Specifically, within the SOC framework, retirement planning can be thought of as an active Selection and Optimization process that supports retirement adjustment. Indeed, from a theoretical standpoint, retirement represents a major life change that requires planning and preparation. Atchley (1982) argues that successful retirement depends on anticipatory socialization into new roles, and active planning for retirement serves this function because it allows individuals to explore new social and physical environments.

There is preponderance of evidence to suggest that planning for life changes becomes very important to individuals as they approach the end of their careers, and that pre-retirement planning can lead to better adjustment outcomes post-retirement (Ferraro, 1990; Fillenbaum, 1971; Han & Moen, 1999; Kim & Moen, 2001; McKenna, 1988; Perkins, 1995), including increased retirement satisfaction (e.g., Atchley, 1991; Moen, 1996). Consequently, people who plan for retirement have a better sense of their individual needs in retirement, possess favorable attitudes toward retirement, are more confident about the retirement process, and are generally more satisfied during retirement (Mutran, Reitzes, & Fernandez, 1997; Quick & Moen, 1998; Reitzes, Mutran, & Fernandez, 1998). Furthermore, pre-retirement preparation has been linked to better psychological adjustment to retirement, including experiencing lower anxiety and depression during retirement. From the SOC perspective, retirement planning can be viewed as both an Elective Selection process and an Optimization process. From an Elective Selection perspective, retirement planning typically requires individuals to actively set, maintain, and reorganize goals associated with the transition to retirement; from an Optimization perspective, planning behaviors can lead to positive retirement outcomes (e.g., successful adjustment).

Similar research has shown that failure to adequately prepare for retirement can be a barrier to successful retirement adjustment (McPherson & Guppy, 1979; Teak & Johnson, 1983). Individuals who do not plan well for retirement may be more prone to conflicts between work and life identities, and they often retire angry, frustrated, and role-less as compared to individuals who plan for their retirement (e.g., Avery & Jablin, 1988; Dorfman, 1989; Glass, 1995; MacEwen, Barling, Kelloway, & Higginbottom, 1995; Reitzes, Mutran, & Fernandez, 1998; Richardson & Kilty, 1991).

In summary, there is a great deal of evidence from a variety of studies concerning retirement adjustment that suggests that behaviors indicative of SOC strategies lead to more successful retirement outcomes. Indeed, the process of retirement represents a major life change that requires planning and preparation. Strategies for effectively structuring and restructuring goals can effectively aid in the retirement adjustment process. In this regard, retirement planning can be thought of as an active process of Selection and Optimization, which supports retirement adjustment and is of paramount importance when considering adjustment outcomes for retirees. Interestingly, there is little evidence to suggest that Compensation plays a key role in retirement adjustment. This is perhaps not surprising given that Compensation behaviors are typically aimed at counteracting losses that might be mitigated by effective Selection and Optimization.

Conclusion

The preceding sections demonstrate that the SOC model can be used as a meta-framework to understand various processes associated with retirement. With respect to pre-retirement processes, we argue that the use of SOC strategies and behaviors by older workers will allow them to (1) maintain their job performance levels, and (2) effectively make decisions that aid in a "successful" retirement decision-making process. With respect to post-retirement, the use of SOC strategies/behaviors are important in that an individual needs to actively engage in retirement planning (e.g., potential goal restructuring) to ensure that adjustment to retirement is also maximized.

Future Directions

Based upon the existing evidence, it should be clear that individuals who actively engage in SOC-related behaviors have a more positive experience with the retirement process. With this idea in mind, we see three potentially fruitful venues for future investigations into the influence of SOC in retirement. One such venue for applied research involves the development and validation of intervention strategies for training SOC behaviors. Indeed, future research should endeavor to develop interventions aimed at training SOC strategies that may serve to further promote such positive experiences. As such, SOC-based interventions could be designed to, for example, help older workers maintain job performance, maximize perceptions of successful retirement, and perhaps most importantly to the current review, maximize objective indices of successful retirement.

Furthermore, researchers should endeavor to investigate if and how SOC behaviors can demonstrate incremental predictive ability above traditionally studied indices of retirement adjustment. No study to date has directly measured SOC behaviors and linked them to retirement adjustment. Given the strength of the evidence presented here, it would be very helpful to understand how engaging SOC behaviors can account for variation in adjustment above and beyond traditional adjustment indices. Furthermore, there are some potentially interesting interactive relationships that could be probed by this type of study. Indeed, perhaps the influence of SOC on adjustment outcomes is conditional upon other adjustment precursors.

Lastly, to facilitate the ideas suggested herein, research should attempt to document and codify the specific coping behaviors that successful and less successful retirees exhibit, and fit them into the SOC framework. A qualitative methodology may be particularly fruitful in this regard and would go a long way toward building a more complete and comprehensive theory of successful retirement.

References

Abraham, J. D., & Hansson, R. O. (1995). Successful aging at work: An applied study of Selection, Optimization, and Compensation through impression management. *Journal of Gerontology: Psychological Sciences, 50B*(2), 94–103.

Adams, G. A. (1999). Career-related variables and planned retirement age: An extension of Beehr's model. *Journal of Vocational Behavior, 55*, 221–235.

Adams, G. A., Prescher, J., Beehr, T. A., & Lepisto, L. (2002). Applying work-role attachment theory to retirement decision-making. *International Journal of Aging and Human Development, 54*, 125–137.

Atchley, R. C. (1975). Adjustment to loss of job at retirement. *International Journal on Aging and Human Development, 6*, 17–27.

Atchley, R. C. (1976). *The sociology of retirement*. Cambridge, MA: Schenkman.

Atchley, R.C. (1982). The process of retirement: Comparing women and men. In M. Szinovacz (Ed.), *Women's retirement: Policy implications of recent research* (pp. 153–168). Beverly Hills, CA: Sage.

Atchley, R. C. (1991). *Social forces and aging*. Belmont, CA: Wadsworth.

Atchley, R. C., & Robinson, J. L. (1982). Attitudes toward retirement and distance from the event. *Research on Aging, 4*, 299–313.

Austin, J., & Vancouver, J. B. (1996). Goal constructs in psychology: Structure, process and content. *Psychological Bulletin, 120*(3), 338–375.

Avery, C., & Jablin, F. M. (1988). Retirement preparation programs and organization. *Communication Education, 37*, 68–80.

Avolio, B. J., & Waldman, D. A. (1990). An examination of age and cognitive test performance across job complexity and occupational types. *Journal of Applied Psychology, 75*, 43–50.

Bajor, J. K., & Baltes, B. B. (2003). Explicating the relationship between selection optimization with compensation, conscientiousness, motivation, and job performance. *Journal of Vocational Behavior, 63*, 347–367.

Baltes, B. B., & Heydens-Gahir, H. A. (2003). Reduction of work-family conflict through the use of selection, optimization, and compensation behaviors. *Journal of Applied Psychology, 88*, 1005–1018.

Baltes, B. B., Rudolph, C. W., and Bal, A. C. (2012). A Review of aging theories and modern work perspectives. in J.W. Hedge, & W.C. Borman (Eds.) *The Oxford Handbook of Work and Aging* (pp. 117–136). New York, NY: Oxford University Press.

Baltes, M. M., & Carstensen, L. L. (1996). The process of successful aging. *Aging and Society, 16*, 397–422.

Baltes, P. B. (1997). On the incomplete architecture of human ontogeny: Selection, optimization, and compensation as foundation of developmental theory. *American Psychologist, 52*(4), 366–380.

Baltes, P. B., & Baltes, M. M. (1990a). Psychological perspectives on successful aging: The model of selective optimization with compensation. In P. B. Baltes & M. M. Baltes (Eds.), *Successful aging: Perspectives from the behavioral sciences* (pp. 1–34). Cambridge, MA: Cambridge University Press.

Baltes, P. B., & Baltes, M. M. (Eds.). (1990b). *Successful aging: Perspectives from the behavioral sciences*. Cambridge, MA: Cambridge University Press.

Baltes, M. M., & Carstensen, L. L. (1998). Social psychological theories and their application to aging: From individual to collective selective optimization with compensation. In V. L. Bengston & K. W. Schaie (Eds.), *Handbook of theories of aging* (pp. 209–226). New York, NY: Springer.

Baltes, P. B., Baltes, M. M., Freund, A. M., & Lang, F. R. (1995). *Measurement of selective optimization with compensation by questionnaire*. Berlin, Germany: Max Planck Institute for Human Development.

Baltes, P. B., Dittmann-Kohli, F., & Dixon, R. A. (1984). New perspectives on the development of intelligence in adulthood: Toward a dual-process conception and a model of selective optimization with compensation. In P. B. Baltes & O. G. Brim (Eds.), *Life-span development and behavior* (Vol. 6, pp. 33–76). New York, NY: Academic.

Baltes, P. B., Freund, A. M., & Shu-Chen, L. (2005). The psychological science of human ageing. In M. Johnson, V. L. Bengtson, P. G. Coleman, & T. Kirkwood (Eds.), *The Cambridge handbook of age and ageing* (pp. 47–71). Cambridge, UK: Cambridge University Press.

Baltes, P. B., Reese, H. W., & Lipsitt, L. P. (1980). Life-span developmental psychology. *Annual Review of Psychology, 31*, 65–110.

Baltes, P. B., Staudinger, U. M., & Lindenberger, U. (1999). Lifespan psychology: Theory and application to intellectual functioning. *Annual Review of Psychology, 50*, 471–507.

Bandura, A. (1986). *Social foundations of thought and action: A social cognitive theory*. Englewood Cliffs, NJ: Prentice-Hall.

Barnes-Farrell, J. L. (2003). Beyond health and wealth: Attitudinal and other influences on retirement decision-making. In G. A. Adams & T. A. Beehr (Eds.), *Retirement: Reasons, processes, and results* (pp. 159–187). New York, NY: Springer.

Beach, L. R., & Mitchell, T. R. (1987). Image theory: Principals, goals and plans in decision-making. *Acta Psychologica, 66*, 201–220.

Beehr, T. A. (1986). The process of retirement: A review and recommendations for future investigation. *Personnel Psychology, 39,* 31–55.

Beehr, T. A., Glazer, S., Nielson, N. L., & Farmer, S. J. (2000). Work and non-work predictors of employees' retirement ages. *Journal of Vocational Behavior, 57,* 206–255.

Blau, D. M. (1998). Labor force dynamics of older married couples. *Journal of Labor Economics, 16,* 595–629.

Blau, D. M., & Gilleskie, D. B. (2003). *The role of retiree health insurance in the employment behavior of older men* (Working Paper No. 10100). Cambridge, MA: National Bureau of Economic Research.

Bound, J., Schoenbaum, M., Strinebrickner, T. R., & Waidmann, T. (1999). The dynamic effects of health on the labor force transition of older workers. *Labour Economics, 6,* 179–202.

Brougham, R. R., & Walsh, D.A. (2005). Goal expectations as predictors of retirement intentions. *International Journal of Aging and Human Development, 61*(2), 141–160.

Chan, S., & Stevens, A. H. (2002). *How does job loss affect the timing of retirement?* (Working Paper No. 8780). Cambridge, MA: National Bureau of Economic Research.

Colarelli, S. M., & Bishop, R. C. (1990). Career commitment: Functions, correlates, and management. *Group and Organization Studies, 15,* 158–176.

Coursolle, K. M., Sweeney, M. M., Raymo, J. M., & Ho, J. H. (2010). The association between retirement and emotional well-being: Does prior work–family conflict matter? *Journal of Gerontology: Social Sciences, 65B*(5), 609–620. doi:10.1093/geronb/gbp116.

Craik, F. I. M., & Jennings, J. M. (1992). Human memory. In F. I. M. Craik & T. A. Salthouse (Eds.), *Handbook of the psychology of aging* (pp. 51–110). Hillsdale, NJ: Erlbaum.

Datan, N., Rodeheaver, D., & Hughes, F. (1987). Adult development and aging. *Annual Review of Psychology, 38,* 153–180.

Dorfman, L. T. (1989). Retirement preparation and retirement satisfaction in rural elderly. *The Journal of Applied Gerontology, 8,* 432–450.

Dwyer, D. S., & Mitchell, O. S. (1999). Health problems as determinants of retirement: Are self related measures endogenous? *Journal of Health Economics, 18,* 173–193.

Ebner, N. C., Freund, A. M., & Baltes, P. B. (2006). Developmental changes in personal goal orientation from young to late adulthood: From striving for gains to maintenance and prevention of losses. *Psychology and Aging, 21,* 664–678.

Erber, J. T., & Danker, D. C. (1995). Forgetting in the workplace: Attributions and recommendations for young and older employees. *Psychology and Aging, 10,* 565–569.

Erikson, E., Erikson, J., & Kivnick, H. (1986). *Vital involvement in old age.* New York, NY: Norton.

Farr, J. L., & Ringseis, E. L. (2002). The older worker in organizational context: Beyond the individual. In C. L. Cooper & I. T. Robertson (Eds.), *International review of industrial and organizational psychology* (Vol. 17, pp. 31–76). Chichester, England: John Wiley.

Feldman, D. C. (1994). The decision to retire early: A review and conceptualization. *Academy of Management Review, 19,* 285–311.

Ferraro, K. F. (1990). Cohort analysis of retirement preparation, 1974–1981. *Journal of Gerontology, 45,* 521–531.

Fillenbaum, G. G. (1971). Retirement planning programs: At what age, and for whom? *The Gerontologist, 11,* 33–36.

Forteza, J. A., & Prieto, J. M. (1994). Aging and work behavior. In H. Triandis, M. Dunnette, & L. Hough (Eds.), *Handbook of industrial and organizational psychology* (2nd ed., Vol. 4., pp. 447–483). Palo Alto, CA: Consulting Psychologists Press.

Freund, A. M., & Baltes, P. B. (1998). Selection, optimization, and compensation as strategies of life management: Correlations with subjective indicators of successful aging. *Psychology and Aging, 13*(4), 531–543.

Freund, A. M., & Baltes, P. B. (2002). Life-management strategies of selection, optimization, and compensation: Measurement by self-report and construct validity. *Journal of Personality and Social Psychology, 82,* 642–662.

Fronstin, P. (1999). Retirement patterns and employee benefits: Do benefits matter? *The Gerontologist, 39,* 37–48.

Gall T. L., Evans D. R., & Howard J. (1997). The retirement adjustment process: Changes in the well-being of male retirees across time. *The Journals of Gerontology, Series A: Biological Sciences and Medical Sciences, 52A*(3), 110–117.

Gignac, M. A. M., Cott, C., & Badley, E. M. (2002). Adaptation to disability: Applying selective optimization with compensation to the behaviors of older adults with osteoarthritis. *Psychology and Aging, 17,* 520–524.

Glass, J. C. (1995). Retirement planning and clergy: Need and content. *Journal of Religious Gerontology, 9,* 15–33.

Gruber, J., & Wise, D. (1999). *Social security programs and retirement around the world.* Chicago, IL: University of Chicago Press.

Han, S. K., & Moen, P. (1999). Clocking out: Temporal patterning of retirement. *American Journal of Sociology, 105*(1), 191–236.

Hardy, M. A., & Quadagno, J. (1995). Satisfaction with early retirement: Making choices in the auto industry. *Journal of Gerontology: Social Sciences, 50B,* 217–226.

Hayward, M.D., Friedman, S., & Chen, H. (1998). Career trajectories and older men's retirement. *Journal of Gerontology: Social Sciences, 53B,* S91–S103.

Heckhausen, H., & Kuhl, J. (1985). From wishes to action: The dead ends and short cuts on the long way to action. In M. Frese & J. Sabini (Eds.), *Goal-directed behavior: Psychological theory and research on action* (pp. 134–157). Hillsdale, NJ: Erlbaum.

Heckhausen, J., & Schulz, R. (1995). A life-span theory of control. *Psychological Review, 102*(2), 284–304.

Heidbreder, E. (1972). Factors in retirement adjustment: White-collar/blue-collar experience. *Industrial Gerontology, 12,* 61–66.

Herzog, A. R., House, J. S., & Morgan, J. N. (1991). Relation of work and retirement to health and well-being in older age. *Psychology and Aging, 6,* 202–211.

Kanfer, R., Crosby, J. V., & Brandt, D. M. (1988). Investigating behavioral antecedents of turnover at three job levels. *Journal of Applied Psychology, 73,* 331–335.

Kim, J. E., & Moen, P. (2001). Moving into retirement: Preparation and transitions in late midlife. In M. E. Lachman (Ed.), *Handbook of midlife development* (pp. 487–527). New York, NY: John Wiley.

Kim, J. E., & Moen, P. (2002). Retirement transitions, gender, and psychological well-being: A life-course, ecological model. *Journal of Gerontology: Psychological Sciences, 57B,* 212–222.

Kohut, H. (1971). *The analysis of the self.* Madison, CT: International Universities Press.

Kohut, H. (1977). *The restoration of the self.* Madison, CT: International Universities Press.

Lang F. R., Rieckmann, N., & Baltes, M. M. (2002). Adapting to aging losses: Do resources facilitate strategies of Selection, Compensation, and Optimization in everyday functioning? *Journal of Gerontology, 57,* 501–509.

Lazarus, R., & Delongis, A. (1983). Psychological stress and coping in aging. *American Psychologist, 38,* 245–254.

Li, K. Z. H., Lindenberger, U., Freund, A. M., & Baltes, P. B. (2001). Walking while memorizing: Age-related differences in compensatory behavior. *Psychological Science, 12,* 230–237.

MacEwen, K. E., Barling, J., Kelloway, E. K., & Higginbottom, S. F. (1995). Predicting retirement anxiety: The roles of parental socialization and personal planning. *Journal of Social Psychology, 135,* 203–213.

McEvoy, G. M., & Cascio, W. F. (1989). Cumulative evidence of the relationship between employee age and job performance. *Journal of Applied Psychology, 74,* 11–17.

McKenna, J. (1988). Today's opportunity, tomorrow's problem: Retirement planning. In C. N. Fletcher (Ed.), *Selected proceedings, National Family Economics Extension Specialists Workshop* (pp. 113–117). Ames, Iowa: Iowa State University.

McPherson, B., & Guppy, N. (1979). Pre-retirement lifecycle and the degree of planning for retirement. *Journal of Gerontology, 34,* 254–263.

Moen, P. (1996). A lifecourse perspective on retirement, gender and well-being. *Journal of Occupational Health Psychology, 1,* 131–144.

Muller, C. F. & Boaz, R. F. (1988). Health as a reason or a rationalization for being retired? *Research on Aging, 10,* 37–55.

Mutran, E. J., Reitzes, D. C., & Fernandez, M. E. (1997). Factors that influence attitudes toward retirement. *Research on Aging, 19,* 251–273.

Ng, T. W. H., & Feldman, D. C. (2008). The relationship of age to ten dimensions of job performance. *Journal of Applied Psychology, 93,* 392–423.

Perkins, K. (1995). Social insecurity: Retirement planning for women. *Journal of Women and Aging, 7,* 37–53.

Pervin, L. A. (1989). *Goal concepts in personality and social psychology.* Hillsdale, NJ: Lawrence Erlbaum.

Quick, H. E., & Moen, P. (1998). Gender, employment and retirement quality: A lifecourse approach to the differential experiences of men and women. *Journal of Occupational Health Psychology, 3,* 44–64.

Rapkin, B., & Fischer, K. (1992). Personal goals of older adults: Issues in assessment and prediction. *Psychology and Aging, 1,* 127–137.

Raymo, J. M., & Sweeney, M. M. (2006). Work-family conflict and retirement preferences. *Journal of Gerontology: Social Sciences, 61B*(3), 161–169.

Reitzes, D. C., Mutran, E. J., & Fernandez, M. E. (1998). Decision to retire: A career perspective. *Social Science Quarterly, 79*(3), 607–619.

Richardson, V., & Kilty, K. M. (1991). Adjustment to retirement: Continuity vs. discontinuity. *International Journal of Aging and Human Development, 33,* 151–169.

Robbins, S., Payne, C., & Chartrand, J. (1990). Goal instability and later life adjustment. *Psychology and Aging, 5,* 477–480.

Robbins, S. B., Lee, R. M., & Wan, T. T. H. (1994). Goal continuity as a mediator of early retirement adjustment: Testing a multidimensional model. *Journal of Counseling Psychology, 41,* 18–26.

Ross, C. E., & Drentea, P. (1998). Consequences of retirement activities for distress and the sense of personal control. *Journal of Health and Social Behavior, 39,* 317–334.

Ruhm, C. J. (1996). What's the latest? II. Cultural age deadlines for educational and work transition. *The Gerontologist, 36,* 602–613.

Salthouse, T. A. (1982). *Adult cognition: An experimental psychology of human aging.* New York, NY: Springer-Verlag.

Shultz, K. S., Morton, K. R., & Weckerle, J. R. (1998). The influence of push and pull factors on voluntary and involuntary early retirees' retirement decision and adjustment. *Journal of Vocational Behavior, 53,* 45–57.

Shultz, K. S., & Wang, M. (2007). The influence of specific health conditions on retirement decisions. *International Journal of Aging and Human Development, 65,* 149–161.

Smith, L. C., & Robbins, S. B. (1988). Validity of the goal instability scale (modified) as a predictor of adjustment in retirement-age adults. *Journal of Counseling Psychology, 35,* 325–329.

Social Security Administration. (2010). *Fast facts and figures about the Social Security.* Retrieved from http://www.ssa.gov/policy/docs/chartbooks/fast_facts/.

Spencer, W. D., & Raz, N. (1995). Differential effects of aging on memory for content and context: A meta-analysis. *Psychology and Aging, 10,* 527–539.

Sternberg, R. J. (1994). Thinking styles: Theory and assessment at the interface between intelligence and personality. In R. J. Sternberg & P. Ruzgis (Eds.), *Personality and intelligence* (pp. 169–187). New York, NY: Cambridge University Press.

Sturman, M. C. (2003). Searching for the inverted u-shaped relationship between time and performance: Meta-analyses of the experience/performance, tenure/performance, and age/performance relationships. *Journal of Management, 29,* 609–640.

Szinovacz, M. E., & Davey, A. (2005). Predictors of perceptions of involuntary retirement. *The Gerontologist, 45,* 36–47.

Szinovacz, M. E., & DeViney, S. (2000). Marital characteristics and labor force participation. *Research of Aging, 25*(2), 87–121.

Teak, J., & Johnson, D. (1983). Pre-retirement education: A proposed bill for tuition tax credit. *Education Gerontology, 9,* 31–36.

van Solinge, H., & Henkens, K. (2008). Adjustment to and satisfaction with retirement: Two of a kind? *Psychology and Aging, 23,* 422–434.

Waldman, D. A., & Avolio, B. J. (1986). A meta-analysis of age differences in job performance. *Journal of Applied Psychology, 71,* 33–38.

Wang, M. (2007). Profiling retirees in the retirement transition and adjustment process: Examining the longitudinal change patterns of retirees' psychological well-being. *Journal of Applied Psychology, 92,* 455–474.

Wang, M., Adams, G. A., Beehr, T. A., & Shultz, K. S. (2009). Career issues at the end of one's career: Bridge employment and retirement. In S. G. Baugh and S. E. Sullivan (Eds.), *Maintaining focus, energy, and options through the lifespan* (pp. 135–162). Charlotte, NC: Information Age.

Wang, M., & Shultz, K. S. (2010). Employee retirement: A review and recommendations for future investigations. *Journal of Management, 36,* 172–206.

Wiese, B. S., Freund, A. M., & Baltes, P. B. (2000). Selection, Optimization, and Compensation: An action-related approach to work and partnership. *Journal of Vocational Behavior, 57*(3), 273–300.

Williamson, R. C., Rinehart, A. D., & Black, T. O. (1992). *Early retirement: Promises and pitfalls.* New York, NY: Plenum Books.

Yeung, D. Y., & Fung, H. H. (2009). Aging and work: How do SOC strategies contribute to job performance across adulthood? *Psychology and Aging, 24,* 927–940.

Young, L. M., Baltes, B. B., & Pratt, A. (2007). Using Selection, Optimization, and Compensation to reduce job/family stressors: Effective when it matters. *Journal of Business and Psychology, 18,* 1–29.

Zimmerman, L., Mitchell, B., Wister, A., & Gutman, G. (2000). Unanticipated consequences: A comparison of expected and actual retirement timing among older women. *Journal of Women and Aging, 12,* 109–128.

Protean Career Model and Retirement

Najung Kim *and* Douglas T. Hall

Abstract

The classic notion of retirement as the complete withdrawal from the workforce does not adequately describe the current career paths of people who are at the retirement age. Older people are moving away from the traditional career stage model (Super, 1957) and to the career mini-cycle model (Hall, 1993, 2002). Continuous career development and learning will continue well into the later years. Retiring from a job is likely to be the beginning of another career, so retirement from one job is just another type of career transition. Based on this understanding of the protean career over the life span, the concept of career mini-cycles is particularly applicable for older workers, and we explore the unique characteristics of these mini-cycles in the later years of adulthood.

Key Words: Retirement, protean career, career stages, career mini-cycles, learning, late career, older workers

Introduction

In a classic book titled *The Three Boxes of Life, and How to Get Out of Them*, Richard Bolles made the point that most people have three main eras in their lives: one for learning (childhood and formal education), one for work (paid employment), and one for play (retirement). He went on to argue that there is no reason why these activities must necessarily be pursued in this order. He also made the perfectly reasonable point that a person could pursue two or three of these activities during the same life stage.

The Three Boxes of Life was published in 1978, and Bolles's ideas seemed quite radical then. Now, however, changes in economic conditions, human health, and life spans, as well as our quests for meaning and purpose in life, have caused us to rethink the relationships among learning, employment, and retirement. More fundamentally, we are now questioning the nature of and indeed the sheer feasibility of retirement.

Traditionally, retirement has been studied as the permanent exit from the workforce. However, recently, the definition of retirement has changed. There are various routes that individuals can take after the retirement—ranging from a complete withdrawal from the workforce to a start of a new full-time career, with varying forms of bridge employment and transitions in between. Perhaps, because of their financial situations, the way that they relate to work, the desire for continuity, or different life histories affecting the current retirement decision, individuals have a variety of career options in the later stage of their life (Wang, Adams, Beehr, & Shultz, 2009). More and more people change jobs throughout their careers and experience various transitions in and out of the workforce and multiple careers (Denton & Spencer, 2009). Retirement is no longer a definite end to one's working life but can mean many things to different people.

As we have seen in other chapters in the current volume, the boundary between work career and retirement is becoming increasingly blurry (Baltes, 1987; Dannefer, 2003). Many people experiment with partial aspects of retirement while they are still employed (e.g., reduced workloads, leaves of absence, flexible work hours), and others resume some paid employment following formal retirement from another employer. In addition, we are seeing increasing variability in the ages at which people self-define as being retired, with some opting for early retirement (usually aided by employer inducements) and others working into their 70s and 80s.

Even in the 1970s there were indications of these coming changes regarding retirement. As one of the authors of this chapter suggested,

> The difficulty of the transition into retirement may be eased in various ways: part-time work, hobbies, and preparation for retirement. Because we seem to be entering an era of multi-career lives, the person at retirement age (which has been decreasing in recent years) may simply switch to a different employer or a different type of work. Indeed, the greater amount of leisure time people enjoy now, with increased holiday benefits and four-day weeks, is forcing people to plan more creatively the use of leisure time; this could be a good form of preparation for retirement … If multiple careers become more widespread, retirement as we know it today and its concomitant role-removal problems may become a novel experience.
> (Hall, 1976, pp. 88–89)

This process of people moving into a different kind of work later in their career as a transition into full retirement from the workforce is known as bridge employment (Feldman, 2007; Wang et al., 2009; also see chapter 20 in this volume). Bridge employment allows people to find more meaning in the later part of their lives and also experience less difficulty in transitioning into their full withdrawal from the workforce (Feldman & Kim, 2000).

Vaillant (2002), the director of the Harvard Study of Adult Development that has spanned five decades, finds that individual lifestyle choices play a greater role than health, finances, genetics, race, or other factors in predicting how happy and satisfied people will be in their later life and work. Vaillant observes that "Retirement is highly overrated as a major life problem" (Vaillant, 2002, p. 220). He reports that of the men in his study (all of whom had attended Harvard in the World War II era), the ones who "liked working the best at 60 liked retirement the best at 75. In sum, those who liked working liked retirement" (p. 221). Vaillant found that there were four conditions under which retirement is stressful:

- when it is involuntary and unplanned
- if the individual has no other means of support other than salary
- if one's home life is unhappy and work had provided an escape
- if retirement had been caused by poor health

However, these stressful conditions affect only a small group of retirees, and retirement is not as catastrophic as people used to perceive it to be. More and more people continue to work way past the conventional retirement age, and they continue to find joy in work and career, enjoying the later part of their lives.

With this optimistic introduction, we will examine retirement from the perspective of careers. In particular, we will propose that retirement, rather than being the end of a career, can be in fact simply a *transition*, another phase in a career. To do this, we will examine the notion of traditional career stages, and then we will move on to a discussion of how the new global economy has transformed lifelong career cycles into shorter mini-cycles. We explore how the new notion of mini-cycles changes the last stage in the traditional career stages, i.e., "decline stage," into another stage of continuous learning. We will conclude with an in-depth discussion of how these mini-cycles are particularly useful for understanding the learning and transformation that occurs in the later career retirement years.

Our discussions will be informed by the following assumptions that we are making about work and retirement, and it is important to make these assumptions explicit:

- Assumption 1: Individuals have critical learning experiences in the earlier stages of their lives that have long-lasting effects into late career. Particularly important are varied experiences and developmental relationships.
- Assumption 2: In later career people have increased freedom of choice and also have the resources to make personal choices and search for self-fulfillment.
- Assumption 3: People have a "trapeze-like" moment of possibility-with-anxiety when they are trying to explore something new. There is a possibility of radical change or challenge, along with the terror of leaping into the unknown, that sometimes immobilizes the person rather than providing challenge and movement.

The Nature of Career Stages

Let us now consider what we mean by career. A career can be defined as "the individually perceived sequence of work-related experiences and activities over the span of the person's life" (Hall, 2002, p. 12). Just as with the human life cycle, we can think of a person's work career as consisting of a regular series of stages, each with particular developmental tasks, concerns, values, needs, and activities (Hall, 1976, 2002). These stages emerge in a regularized sequence as the person develops.

The person's stage in his or her work career is strongly related to work concerns and attitudes, and the career stage effects could be quite different from those that we might associate with age. For example, a lawyer or a university faculty member who is starting his or her first regular full-time position following graduate or professional training will probably be highly concerned with advancement and establishing a reputation among colleagues, regardless of whether he or she is 27 or 47. Occupational socialization and the role demands related to becoming established have strong personal impacts at any age.

The most widely cited model of career stages is that of Donald Super. Super and his colleagues (1957) found in their research, in the United States in the mid-1950s, that the following career stages emerged in the following age ranges:

- *Growth Stage* (Birth–Age 14). In this stage, thinking about careers starts with fantasy thinking, based on needs and fantasy role-play.
- *Exploration Stage* (Age 15–24). Here the person experiments (15–17) with tentative choices, such as courses, part-time work, and discussion. Next there is a transition period (18–21) when the person enters the labor market or professional training and attempts to enact an occupational identity.
- *Establishment Stage* (Age 26–44). In this stage the person attempts to make a permanent place for him- or herself. There is first a trial period (25–30), which may or may not be successful and which might include job changes before a good fit is found. Then, when the right fit is found, there is a period of stabilization (31–44) as the person settles down in the work and becomes secure.
- *Maintenance Stage* (Age 45–64). Once the person has become established in his or her work, now the focus is on preserving that place.
- *Decline Stage* (Age 65 and on). As physical and mental capabilities decline, the person's work

activities change. New roles must be found. The sub-stages here are deceleration (65–70), when the person may shift from full-time to part-time work or the duties may change, and retirement (71 and on), when the person stops occupational work. However, there is great variability here, with some people stopping completely and easily and others continuing employment until death (Super, Crites, Hummel, Moser, Overstreet, & Warnath, 1957).

According to Super's model, retirement stage falls under the "decline stage," similar to what Bolles (1978) defined as an "era for play." Following this notion, work and career are rarely discussed in the last stage of lifelong career stages. Later, as the global economy was causing fundamental changes in work and career practices, Super revised his view of career stages to include the integration of life stages and work career stages. This revised thinking was illustrated in his "life career rainbow."

The life career rainbow showed how the different life stages, life roles, and career stages unfolded over the span of a person's life (Super, 1980, 1990). The upper bands in the rainbow showed the familiar Super career/life stages (Growth, Exploration, Establishment, Maintenance, Decline) and the typical ages when people are in those stages. The inner nine bands show the life space and the different roles that a person occupies as he or she goes through the life course (child, student, leisurite, citizen, worker, pensioner, spouse, homemaker, parent). Each of these inner bands is drawn like an arc of the rainbow with a different length depending on the life stage that is related to the life space and the role that each arc represents. For instance, individuals start their "worker" life space in mid-20s and are eligible to receive social security and quit working in their 60s. Hence, the "worker arc" starts from mid-20s until the 60s, and the "pensioner arc" falls under the life stage of the 60s and above. Thus, the inner parts of the rainbow are more interior to the person, reflecting the personal determinants of experience, such as psychological and biological factors. The external area beyond the rainbow reflects the larger context, the remote and immediate situational determinants of life and career experience (social structure, historical change, socioeconomic organization and conditions, employment practices, school, community, and family).

Although this notion of a career rainbow emphasizes multiple roles that an individual can have throughout his or her life, it was branched out from Super's (1957) original idea of looking at career development over life span. As Super (1990) commented, there were no new elements in this rainbow model:

> "All the elements used in the figure had been treated in earlier work; it was the graphic representation of a career that was novel." (p. 211)

In addition to the rainbow's conceptual value for research, it has also been used by career counselors as a heuristic device for reflective self-assessment exercises, to help students increase their self-awareness regarding these changing life roles (e.g., University of Oregon, 2004). People are given a copy of the rainbow, and in the arcs for the life roles they write in words to describe how they spent their time and effort, as well as how they feel about each role. By placing themselves in particular roles and in a particular career stage, it helps alert them to what may be coming up next for them in their life and career and gives them a basis for making plans for the future.

One of the demands imposed by the new global economy on both organizations and individuals was the necessity of continuous learning and adaptation. Organizational agility became a core requirement of successful firms, and constant vigilance and environmental scanning were necessities, as Andrew Grove (1999) proclaimed in the title of one of his books, *Only the Paranoid Survive*. At the individual level, Hall (1986) discussed the idea that one effect of the career-long cycles that were the norm in the 1980s was that after the person had settled into the maintenance stage in mid-career, he or she entered into a *career routine*, a period of comfortable, repetitive patterns of everyday behaviors and lifestyle. At this point the person engaged in habitual activities and became relatively immune to change.

In the new economy, however, as Hall (1986) pointed out, there are many external forces that tend to "bust" these career routines. New technologies, markets, and business practices can quickly render one's skills obsolete. Global competition greatly magnifies the number and frequency of these threats to a person's competence. In addition, at the individual level, with longer working lives and increased self-awareness of one's career possibilities, there are increasingly internal psychological drivers of career change.

The result of these and other triggers is that the long maintenance plateau in the lifelong career cycle has been replaced by a series of career changes. These play out as "career mini-cycles" (Hall, 1993,

2002). A new mini-cycle is started when a person begins *exploring* some sort of change—a new way of working, developing new skills, developing new relationships and connections, pursuing some new job opportunities, etc. Then the person engages in some *trial* activity, perhaps doing some part-time "moonlighting" work in a new area or taking on a new project at work that requires learning new skills or concepts. If this trial activity is rewarding and successful, the person might go more deeply into the new area, make a commitment to it, and become *established* in it. This would lead to *mastery* and continued work in this sphere.

These stages in a career mini-cycle are much like the stages in a career-long cycle or a maxi-cycle of career, with the obvious difference that they are shorter and they happen more often. A maxi-cycle of career is composed of various stages and marks that people reach throughout their lives and hence spans for one's lifetime, while a mini-cycle might last 3–5 years and the person might never feel that he or she has truly "settled down." This is a protean career process, which is largely internally driven, guided by the person's values, and it results in ongoing self-reinvention. This model of career mini-cycles is shown in Figure 8.1.

Difference in Mini-cycle Patterns between Early Career and Later Career

Now let us consider how these mini-cycles might begin to look different later in a person's life. Due to the less clear boundary between the institutionalized transitions in the life course compared to transitions in one's career (Baltes, 1987; Elder, Johnson, & Crosnoe, 2004), older workers around retirement age are likely to go through a distinctive set of mini-cycles in this later point in their careers (Hall & Mirvis, 1995). What, then, would be so unique about this set of mini-cycles that people around retirement age experience? What would be the characteristics of this "integrity" (Erikson, 1963) stage that differentiate this later career stage from the other early and mid-careers? We have included a summary of this comparison in Table 8.1, but here we give a detailed explanation for two fundamental differences that determine the degree of protean career orientation in late career mini-cycles.

First, because people in the later stage of the maxi-cycle of their career are more likely to have extensive experiences in work and life, they are likely to have a high degree of self-awareness (Mirvis & Hall, 1994). High self-awareness helps them to be more aware of the mini-cycles that they go through,

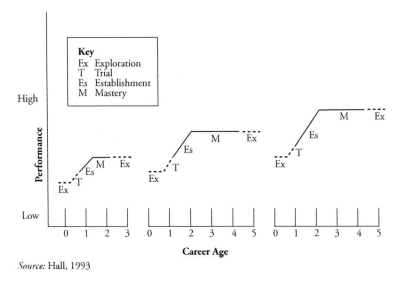

Figure 8.1 A Model of Career Mini-cycles
Source: Hall, 1993

and people in their later career can intentionally select the aspects of learning that they want from that mini-cycle. They may optimize their learning experiences by selecting the skills and tasks that compensate for their weaknesses and emphasize their strengths (Freund & Baltes, 1998). According to the Selection, Optimization, and Compensation (SOC) model, people seek a certain personal goal (e.g., successful aging) by using four strategies: (1) Elective Selection, (2) Optimization, (3) Loss-Based Selection, and (4) Compensation. Furthermore, developmental psychologists have found the positive correlation between age and integrity (Sheldon & Kasser, 2001). In contrast

Table 8.1 Comparing Early/Mid-Career Mini-Cycles and Late Career Mini-Cycles

	Early to mid-career mini-cycles	Late career mini-cycles
Experiences	Less experience	More experience
Self-awareness	Lower self-awareness Less aware of mini-cycles Learning cycles affected by environments/lack of intentionality	Higher self-awareness More aware of mini-cycles Learning cycles affected by one's intention
Type of learning	Various, diverse learning	Focused, selective learning
Perception on the amount of resources (financial, relational, psychological, time)	Less variance across younger people	Greater variance across older people due to cumulative effect of past experiences and paths
Adaptability	Adaptability due to the lack of preexisting paths and experiences	Adaptability due to the abundant resources or inadaptability due to lack of resources Greater variance in the adaptability across older people
Passion for work	With the exception of a few early passion-followers, younger people are in the middle of finding what their passions are or don't have the resources to seek their passion	Older people who haven't discovered their passion in the earlier stage of their life struggle to enjoy the passion that they haven't explored earlier

to their earlier stages of the maxi-cycle, when they had less control over what to learn and what not to absorb as a total newcomer in the workforce, people in their later career stage can be more selective and reflective about the process through which they go. This is all possible due to their high self-awareness or "integrity" in their identity accumulated and developed over time.

Second, because of the cumulative nature of previous experiences and the path-dependency that one's life choices share (Dannefer, 2003), we are more likely to see a greater variance in people's adaptability in the later stage of their careers than in their early and mid-careers. The SOC model also suggests that it is harder for older people to use the four strategies of Selection, Optimization, and Compensation if they lack resources (Freund & Baltes, 2002; Lang, Rieckmann, & Baltes, 2002). The amount of resources that one has may differ based on the cumulative differences that one has built throughout one's life and career, and the amount of resources may affect one's ability to use SOC strategies to be more adaptable and to successfully fulfill one's personal goal at the advanced age.

According to the studies based on cumulative advantage/disadvantage theory (see DiPrete & Eirich, 2006, for review), the cumulative disadvantage process "is capable of magnifying small differences over time and makes it difficult for an individual or group that is behind at a point in time in educational development, income, or other measures to catch up" (DiPrete & Eirich, 2006, p. 273). Here, the types of resources that may cause some variance in this group of people in the retirement age (or later career) are financial/economic resources and social resources (resources that one gets based on his or her socioeconomic status). For instance, the disadvantage that one has as an ethnic minority is experienced at different stages in the life course, and so is the advantage that one is financially well-off. Throughout the life course, this variance gets magnified, and we can find a wider range of variances in resources for people in the later stage of their careers than those in mid-careers or early careers. Hence, adaptability also varies more significantly for older people than younger people.

Third, older people may be more likely to see their work as intrinsically meaningful than younger people. Kasser and Ryan (1993, 1996) argued that the more integrated a person is, the more likely that he or she is pursuing intrinsically meaningful goals rather than extrinsic goals such as approval from others and material gain. Sheldon and Kasser's work

(2001) supported this positive relationship between age and intrinsic values and motivations. However, this positive relationship was constrained by a curvilinear effect. The oldest members (60 and up) showed a slightly lesser tendency for intrinsic values in comparison to middle-aged members.

Wrzesniewski and her colleagues (Wrzesniewski, McCauley, Rozin, & Schwartz, 1997) argued that individuals may find it less compelling to find value and intrinsic purpose in their work if they think they have seen the end of their career. They found that those older people who hold low-status occupations were more likely to have job orientation (i.e., seeing work as means of gaining resources) than career orientation (i.e., seeing work as a stepping stone to advance in one's career) in comparison to their younger counterparts. However, this result was not supported by those people with high-status occupations. Hence, there may be some differences depending on the types of work that one has, but we can expect people in their later career to value intrinsic purpose in their work more than people in their early career. People in their early career may have career orientation toward work and see work as a tool to advance in their career, while people in their later career focus on what is intrinsically meaningful for them and hence tend to seek jobs in which they find personal calling and meaning.

Variations in Mini-cycle Patterns within the Later Career Years

Based on these characteristics of later career, we can think of four different patterns of later career to provide some glimpses of what late-career mini-cycles might look like. These patterns are summarized in Figure 8.2. We can find these four patterns of late career mini-cycles from those people around us. We suggest these patterns based on qualitative evidence, such as our own observations and anecdotes that people have told us.

Model 1: One Career, One Life Seekers

First, there may be a group of individuals that have less adaptability due to the cumulative effect of earlier career experiences in a single career field. Here are two cases of why such an individual might have low adaptability to the later stage of the career. Tom, who followed a one-career-one-life model with all his heart and passion, may have built his life around this one career and therefore may be likely to have a low adaptability in the later stage of his career maxi-cycle. His experience is accumulated in one area, and it is hard for him to switch gears in the

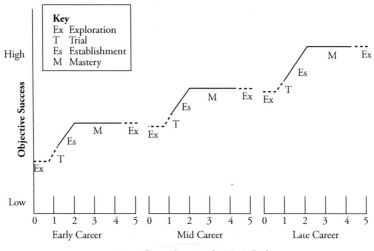

Figure 8.2.a One Career, One Life Seekers

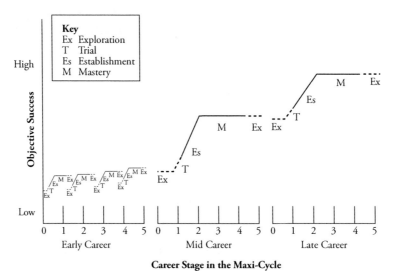

Figure 8.2.b Early-Strugglers Following Path with a Heart

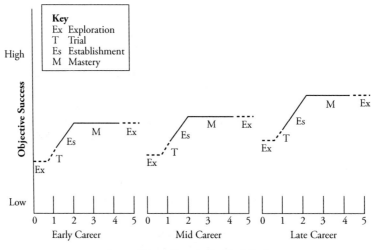

Figure 8.2.c Multi-Careerers

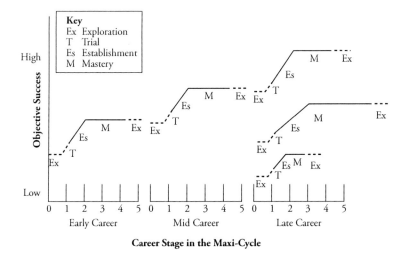

Figure 8.2.d Late Passion-Followers

later stage of his life. Tom does not want to invest in something new since he is getting the most out from his well-developed career where he finds passion. It is also possible that even if one, say Josh, finds little passion in what he has been doing for the last thirty years, he decides not to seek a new job where he may find more passion because of fear that he has about taking that leap. For Josh, who is a security seeker, the resources that he has both financially and relationally do not matter so much and were considered to be not enough to make that shift to another career.

Both Tom and Josh, though due to different reasons, are likely to experience similar late-career mini-cycles, where their late-career path is an extension of their lifelong career. Their exploration stage may branch out from the previous career and is also likely to be shorter. Furthermore, the overall mini-cycle is likely to be shorter since they benefit from the existing resources on the same career and may get adjusted to the new job quicker.

Model 2: Early Strugglers Following Path with a Heart

In contrast to Tom and Josh, John has struggled so much in the early days of his life to figure out where his heart lies. He has a high need for self-awareness, but it took him a while to build his self-awareness and find the career where he found his calling. People like John have a lot of interests in the early stage of their careers and are not sure which profession best fits them. They spend a lot of time exploring the profession where their hearts lie. Therefore, when looking at the late-career

mini-cycles of John, Josh, and Tom, all of these mini-cycles may look alike since all three of them have kept their mid-career in their late career. However, John eventually found a profession after a long struggle in his early career and decided to stick to it for the rest of his life, while Tom and Josh started with one profession and ended with the same one.

Model 3: Multi-Careerers

The third group of individuals accumulated their experiences in transitioning across multiple professions, like the case of Heather. Heather, who has juggled multiple careers, hopping from one profession to another, may find it easy to adapt to a new environment and has a high adaptability. For her, the resources and the experiences that she may lose due to career change may be less than Tom's and Josh's. She has less to lose than Tom or Josh or John, and we expect less cumulative effect of the experiences in one career but more cumulative effect of the transitioning experiences. When you look at the career maxi-cycle of John and that of Heather, they may look alike in the early career stage due to the multiple transitions through which they went. However, Heather continued to try out different careers throughout her life, while John stayed in one profession after finding his heart in one.

Model 4: Late Passion-Followers

Kate, however, considered her job to be a job and did not seek to find passion in her work. As long as her work put the bread on her table, she was happy about it. However, as she entered the later stage of her life, she wanted to seek integrity in what she did and also be a holistic person who brings her passion and her work together. Because her existing skills are appreciated by the field in which she worked for a long time, it is likely that she can earn a decent amount of money from that profession. At the same time, she will start to look for a job that she may have always wanted to do (e.g., painter) and go through a totally new training that she has never done before. This example suggests that multiple mini learning cycles take place spontaneously. While Josh had this exploration phase in the earlier stage of his life, Kate has it in the later stage of her life. Moreover, in comparison to younger workers, people going through mini-cycles in their late career are more likely to pursue a greater number of mini-cycles at a given point. Because older workers tend to prefer part-time jobs over full-time jobs, they are likely to have a portfolio of jobs that they hold in the later part of their career maxi-cycle.

As discussed above, the self-awareness and adaptability that an individual in his or her late career has may differ depending on the maxi-cycle of career that he or she went through. Accordingly, the nature of the mini-cycle that he or she has in the late career is influenced by the previous steps that he or she has taken. When we look at a person's career trajectories in the early and mid-careers and examine the degree of self-awareness and adaptability, we can get a sense of how one's later career may unfold. We suggest that the mechanism via which the previous steps in one's maxi-cycle of career influence the nature of the mini-cycle in the late career is embedded in competence. Specifically, this competence mechanism can influence the mini-cycle in the late career in the following four ways.

First, the past experiences in the earlier part of the career form the way one sees his or her ability to perform the current job. The more experience one has in the same occupational field, the more likely that he or she will have high career self-efficacy that he or she can take into a later career. The outcome that is generated by this degree of self-efficacy is the initial starting point for the mini-cycle in the late career. According to continuity theory (Atchley, 1989), as an individual goes through a transition period, he or she tries to hold onto things that are consistent with his or her past. The individual can organize life around some continuous elements in his or her late career and maintain confidence in those continuous parts in the life. The more relevant one's past experiences are to the current job, the more competent one feels in that job, and the

higher the objective career success level is at the initial stage of the new mini-cycle. Second, the passion that one finds in his or her work increases the competence level. The outcome generated by this competence is the learning cycle itself. The more passionate one is about the new job that he or she starts in the late career, the more likely one is to invest oneself deeply and work hard to be competent about learning new skills (Amabile, 2000; Scarnati, 1998). Thus, a person with a strong passion for that work is more likely to have a steeper learning curve than one who finds the new job hard to be passionate about. Passion accelerates learning of new skills and ultimately increases the person's competence level.

Third, the number of transitions or career crises prior to one's late career can increase one's "adaptability competence." As an individual takes a new job in late career, the person typically worries whether he or she will succeed in adapting to this new setting and this new role. The anxiety is greater if he or she has had no prior transition experiences. However, if the person has had multiple transitions or career crises prior to the late career stage, he or she is more likely to have a high competence in successfully learning this new job. Therefore, the person is more likely to have a steeper learning curve at least in the early phase of the new job in this late career mini-cycle.

Fourth, the reference group that one belongs to (Grote & Hall, 2010) can influence the perceived possibility of exploring a new career, and this perceived possibility may affect one's competence of starting a new job in the late career. For instance, baby boomers who have seen friends around them taking a new job in their late career (e.g., encore careers) would feel comfortable jumping into a new profession. For them, the possibility of exploring a new job in a different occupational field in the late career is higher than their parents' generation or earlier generations. Their peer reference group has a social norm that encourages exploratory behaviors in late career, and this norm increases their adaptability competence.

Universal Characteristics of People in the Retirement Age and Their Effects on Mini-cycles

People in the late career are entering or have entered a different age group and life stage. As they start off their new career or profession, the changes caused by aging may prompt unique mini-cycle learning experiences that apply to this special group of experienced workers. In this section of our chapter, we explore these unique changes and their effects on mini-cycle learning. One of the authors has identified the universal changes through which individuals go as they enter this later stage of their lives—physical, cognitive, emotional, relational, and social perceptual changes (Kim, 2012)—and we borrow from her work to identify those changes that tend to be universal for most older people and are thus less likely to be influenced by the cumulative advantage/disadvantage effect. We will consider the likely impact of each of these universal changes on late career mini-cycles.

Because people in the late stage of their careers used to be in the younger age group in their previous employment and now belong to an older age category, there may be changes that are likely to be new to them, and it may require a certain period of time for them to internalize or cope with these newly developed internal and external characteristics. Gerontologists have identified multiple changes related to aging, and we focus on physical, cognitive, emotional, relational, and social perceptual changes that may prompt both gains and losses (Baltes, 1987; Elder, Johnson, & Crosnoe, 2004; Schulz & Heckhausen, 1996).

First, individuals are likely to experience a decrease in their physical health and condition in the later stage of their life. It may be possible that there are some health disparities across older people depending on their previous health conditions or social environments (Dannefer, 2003; Uhlenberg & Mueller, 2004), but the negative effect of aging on physical health and condition is universally accepted.

Selection, Optimization, and Compensation model (e.g., Baltes & Baltes, 1990) argues that individuals who predominantly experience losses due to this age-related physical change may seek to compensate this loss with the traits and abilities that they select and optimize. For instance, a pianist who continued to perform in his 70s may pick a set of pieces that bring out his emotional maturity while minimizing the need for agile finger movements that were his major strength in his 30s. Therefore, it may be likely that older people tend to avoid starting a new career mini-cycle that requires a significant physical ability. Furthermore, even if their new jobs are physically challenging, they may craft their jobs to better accommodate their physical condition.

Second, in terms of cognitive ability, fluid intelligence—an ability that is required when adapting to

new situations—decreases as people age, but older people have a higher degree of crystallized intelligence, which involves skilled judgment habits that "have become crystallized as the result of earlier learning application of some prior, more fundamental general ability to these fields," in comparison to their younger counterparts (Cattell, 1963, pp. 2–3; Horn & Cattell, 1967; Horn, 1994). The continuous decrease in fluid intelligence affects people in their late career and leads them to perceive declined ability in dealing with new situations. It may also take a longer period of time for them to adjust to a new environment. Due to this cognitive change, finding a component in one's work that is related to what one used to do becomes more important (Atchley, 1989). For older workers, what is inconsistent with their previous experiences may have more impact on their transition experiences than would be the case for younger workers.

Also, due to the increased crystallized intelligence that is buttressed by their past experiences, people in their later career are more likely to make quick connections to their other prior experiences and perceive problems holistically. This aspect of cognitive change is likely to provide people in their later career with an ability to oversee the broader work environment. Thus, designing and searching for jobs that utilize this cognitive ability becomes more significant for older employees than for younger workers. Jobs with high perceived task significance and a high locus of control are likely to be learned more easily by people in their later career than they are for younger people (O'Reilly, Parlette, & Bloom, 1980). Mini learning cycles for the jobs with a high locus of control or that require integrative thinking skills may be shorter and steeper for older people than jobs that require short-term memory and quick responses to new situations.

Third, the ability to recall and recognize negative memories/objects declines as one ages (Charles, Mather, & Carstensen, 2003; Mather & Carstensen, 2003), and people in their later career may be different from younger workers in terms of their emotional experiences at work—older people tend to remember positive things better and forget negative memories better than younger people. Because they perceive less time left in their life, older people want to remember more positive emotions than negative ones (Carstensen, 1995). When people in their later career enter an organization as newcomers, they are likely to have an attention bias toward positive emotions over negative emotions and remember fewer negative emotional experiences than what they actually have experienced.

When comparing their previous experiences to the current one, they may be less likely to use negative experiences as comparison points but rather think of what positive things they currently have or that they are missing in the organization in comparison to their prior work experiences. As they go through a new mini-cycle of career, older people may consciously or unconsciously try to remember positive experiences from this learning opportunity and, after having gone through the new round of mini-cycle, they may remember positive things and forget negative experiences.

Also, people in their later career are likely to be influenced by the collective mood of their coworkers over time (Totterdell, Kellett, Teuchmann, & Briner, 1998). How other people in the workplace feel influences the mood of people in their later career more than that of younger workers, and the emotional component to their transition experiences are more likely to be affected by the collective mood held by coworkers in that new organization. Therefore, how others in their workgroup think of their late career mini-cycles (especially those in a similar age group) may influence older people more than younger people.

Fourth, socioemotional selectivity theory (Carstensen, 1995; Reis, Collins, & Berscheid, 2000), which predicts the effect of age on the quality of emotion, also suggests how older people tend to focus more on close relationships than broadening their network. The theory (Carstensen, 1995; Carstensen, Fung, & Charles, 2003) predicts that different life priorities affect one's social interaction as one ages. Young people focus more on information gathering and hence seek a larger network of people, while older people are more likely to focus on emotional regulation and seek comfort from a close network such as friends and family. In comparison to one's early career experiences where they focused on developing networks with helpful people, people in the later stage of their career are more likely to focus on close relationships such as family, friends, and close coworkers.

Therefore, people in their later career may value what they learn from their close workers more than what they learn from broad organizational training. In order to facilitate the mini learning cycle of older individuals, it may work better to focus on close group learning or mentoring than training sessions with a big group of people. This is also related to how collective mood can influence older people more than younger people. By creating a group learning experience, older people may learn better and are more willing to share their experience and mood with their group members.

Fifth, changes that people experience in their later career come not only from their changed state of physical condition, emotion, cognition, and relationships but also from other people around them. There are a set of prototypical characteristics that people assign to older individuals, and this changed perception of others can influence their mini-cycle learning experiences as well. This change is not only caused by stereotypes associated with older people (Finkelstein & Farrell, 2009; Williams & O'Reilly, 1998) but also due to a self-stereotypical attitude (Levy, 2003)—the outcome of internalizing social perceptions of older age. At the surface level, older people may just enter a new organization (or perhaps a new profession). However, due to the social perception that they may receive from others in the organization and from others outside the organization, older newcomers may perceive their status to be higher or lower in the current organization. They may be likely to experience the same mini learning cycle differently from younger workers due to the change in social perceptions, whether that is negative or positive.

For instance, due to the stereotype of older people being resistant to change, older people may be asked to take jobs that are less dynamic in comparison to what they used to have in previous organizations. They may even internalize this stereotype and try to create a structure that would allow them to minimize the degree of uncertainty at work. A positive cultural image of older people can also influence the way that older people connect with others at work. For instance, in a country where older age is associated with wisdom, others may see an older worker as being wiser in the current organization than how he or she was treated in previous organizations as a younger worker. He or she is respected more, and colleagues may seek his or her advice. That older person may even be perceived to be in a higher position than the younger colleagues.

Future Directions and Research

Our central argument in this chapter has been that retirement does not necessarily represent the end of employment but is rather a *late career transition*, albeit a very important transition. Along with the early adult transition (i.e., when the person is moving into the workforce; Levinson, 1986), this late career transition represents one of the most significant transformations of identity in an individual's life. There is a great need for more empirical work on this late life passage.

Needed Future Research

We know from a considerable body of research what the major factors are that influence a person's decision to retire (e.g., Beehr, Glazer, Nielsen, & Farmer, 2000): financial readiness, health, planned activities, and personal characteristics. However, Beehr et al. (2000) were surprised to find that job characteristics did not predict retirement decisions, after the effects of wealth were removed. They also found that expected retirement activities had less impact than they had expected. They speculate that job stressors may have some impact on some people's decisions to retire.

One implication of the findings of research on retirement decisions is that there is potential value in more *process research* on retirement, as opposed to *variance research*. Variance research focuses on variables that might predict retirement behavior. In process research on retirement, the focus would be on obtaining a clearer understanding of the process of making decisions about retirement, as well as on the process of making late career transitions out of full-time work engagement and into reduced levels of work or into new areas of work.

In particular, we would suggest empirical research that would illuminate the functioning of career mini-cycles in the later career years. Important questions would include how a career mini-cycle in later career is different from one in mid-career. In this chapter, we tried to suggest one of various possibilities of how later career mini-cycles may look different from mini-cycles in early and mid-career. We would speculate that one important difference would be that a later career mini-cycle would entail a greater degree of identity transformation than one in mid-career. Thus, we would expect that the exploration stage of a career mini-cycle may be more difficult and stressful for an older person than for a younger one, even if the older person were passionate about the new late-career activities into which he or she was moving.

Another important research question would be to explore how career mini-cycles map onto the more traditional career-long cycles. Sekaran and Hall (1989) discuss issues in the confluence of different kinds of career and adult life cycle patterns, and their ideas could provide a starting point in focusing research questions and framing hypotheses. Earlier in this chapter we pictured some possible scenarios, based on the superimposition of different kinds of typical mini-cycle patterns on a lifelong career cycle. Would an established professional in an industry who is feeling a bit restless and looking for new opportunities at age 45 experience the exploration phase of a mini-cycle differently than a young person exploring his or her very first job opportunity? Does the exploration phase of a mini-cycle operate differently for a young person exploring his or her first job than for an established professional who is uneasy and seeking new paths at age 45? At that point, if the experienced person is feeling "on top of his or her game" professionally, is it easier to start exploring something else? Or is it harder because the person feels so settled into a successful routine?

Another area to investigate would be what types of earlier career experiences may facilitate better adaptability in later career and, thus, smoother transitions into partial retirement or full retirement. Based upon our earlier discussions, we would predict that people who had experienced more or greater significant career changes in early or mid-career would have developed adaptive capabilities that would serve them well in making retirement transitions.

Search for generational differences. Another question is whether there are generational differences in the experiences of mini-cycles at a given age. For example, how are the retirement transitions of the World War II generation compared with those in the baby-boom cohort? Baby boomers have experienced turbulence in just about every stage of their lives, from the 1960s' and 1970s' social revolution, to the 1980s' and 1990s' economic globalization and restructuring, to the twenty-first century's struggles with terrorism and the Great Recession. The previous generation lived more traditional lives and passed into more traditional retirements. Did these differences make it easier or harder for the World War II generation to navigate their late career passages? We would predict that the retirement transitions are now less difficult for the baby boomers, as they are more experienced with change and are thus more adaptable. But we need some good research on this issue!

Resources to assist late career transitions. Another important factor in a person's adjustment to retirement is the resources available to assist in the transition. Even in an era of tight economic resources in the work settings and in the public sphere, there are probably more resources to help people move into retirement than there were decades ago. For one thing, there is more public awareness of retirement processes and difficulties. Also, specialties such as gerontology, medicine, and social work have advanced and have greater research, conceptual understanding, and tools and techniques to help older people move along into later stages. In employing organizations, however, there are probably fewer resources to assist employees in thinking through and implementing retirement decisions. This is surprising in view of the business need to trim the workforce in many organizations. The prospect of assisting employees in making a satisfying exit from the organization would appear to be a win-win for both parties.

One important question that can be answered with good empirical data is how easy or difficult it is to train new employees in a new job, compared to training older employees moving into a new job. Put another way, what is the difference in the experience of a younger newcomer and an older, long-service "newcomer"? We suggest that employers should prepare to train *older new workers*. Of course, the stereotype is that older workers are more rigid, less amenable to training, but this idea has not really been tested. In fact, there are anecdotal reports of very successful efforts to train and retrain older workers, such as the Vita Needle Company in Newton, Massachusetts, a family-owned manufacturing company that employs twenty senior citizens on the shop floor. Some are in their 80s and 90s. For these employees, the job gives them something meaningful to do, it connects them to other people, and it meets important financial needs. As 98½-year-old Rosa Finnegan reported on the value of the job for her:

> I thought retirement with my husband would be nice. But [he] passed away with a heart attack, so life changed drastically after that. My plans all went astray. I had to make new ones, so this is how I did it. (Shapiro, 2010)

In particular, employees in their late career would appear to be an especially promising group for an organization to practice mass career customization (Benko & Weisberg, 2007). This is a time in life when people are open to new opportunities, which could also entail lateral or even downward moves through the organizational "lattice." The possibilities of reduced involvement, fewer hours, and less pay and responsibility (and stress) could be very attractive. And yet these are employees who possess rich pools of human capital and a wide knowledge of relational resources—networks of customers, coworkers, and suppliers that would not be part of the "package" if older employees are simply replaced by younger ones.

Another spin-off benefit of practicing mass career customization with the older workforce would be that the lessons learned could be easily applied to employee groups in early and middle careers. These younger groups, which may be more career-involved and ambitious (for upward mobility), may be less open to new career practices, but if they can see how well mass career customizations works for older employees, they might be more willing to try for themselves. In general, our opinion is that one of the important ways in which employees gauge what their future in an organization might be like is to observe how longer-service employees are treated. And when younger employees observe older employees being treated with dignity and respect and with ongoing career growth opportunity, this will give them a good feeling about their future treatment by the organization. Thus, career customization for older employees provides not only a benefit for senior groups but also a preview of future career opportunities for younger groups—and thus improved retention.

Conclusion

We would agree with the conclusions of a study by Brookes, Hall, & Smith (1992) of an early retirement incentive program by a large retailer, in which about half of the participants saw their exit as a transition to another job rather than as full retirement from employment. Almost twenty years ago Brooks et al. concluded the following:

> This study suggests that rather than thinking about retirement from an organization as the end of *one's work life, this process of exit might be more usefully thought of as simply another career transition, albeit a critical one. Factors such as planning and pre-retirement expectations, point to the importance of early transition stages such as preparation, encounter, and adjustment as identified by Nicholson (1986).* (Brookes, Hall, & Smith, 1992, pp. 16–17, italics are ours)

In fact, as Brooks et al. observed, there is a need for two separate terms: *organizational retirement* (the exit from a particular employer) and *career retirement* (when the person ceases paid employment). More specifically, we would propose that the late career transition can be thought of as another form of career mini-cycle, with stages of exploration, trial, establishment, mastery, and disengagement, enabled by strong developmental relationships. We see these mini-cycles in all parts of a career, but the transition may be more significant in later career because more of the person's total identity is "in play" at this point. Several different scenarios for how these late career mini-cycles may unfold are presented here, along with ideas and hypotheses for helping to understand the retirement processes. And, finally, we call for more process research on these retirement dynamics.

We conclude with the advice of George Vaillant, who distilled the secrets of aging well down to its essential elements:

Play, create, learn new things and, most especially, make new friends. Do that and getting out of bed in the morning will seem a joy—even if you are no longer "important," even if your joints ache, and even if you no longer enjoy free access to the office Xerox machine. (Vaillant, 2002, p. 248)

References

Amabile, T. M. (2000). Stimulate creativity by fueling passion. In E. Locke (Ed.), *Handbook of principles of organizational behavior* (pp. 331–341). Maiden, MA: Wiley-Blackwell.

Atchley, R. C. (1989). A continuity theory of normal aging. *The Gerontologist, 29*(2), 183–190.

Baltes, P. B. (1987). Theoretical propositions of life-span developmental psychology: On the dynamics between growth and decline. *Developmental Psychology, 23*, 611–626.

Baltes, P. B., & Baltes, M. M. (1990). Psychological perspectives on successful aging: The model of selective optimization with compensation. In P. B. Baltes & M. M. Baltes (Eds.), *Successful aging: Perspectives from the behavioral sciences* (pp. 1–34). New York, NY: Cambridge University Press.

Beehr, T. A., Glazer, S., Nielson, N. L., & Farmer, S. J. (2000). Work and nonwork predictors of employees' retirement ages. *Journal of Vocational Behavior, 57*(2), 206–225.

Benko, C., & Weisberg, A. (2007). *Mass career customization: Aligning the workplace with today's nontraditional workforce.* Cambridge, MA: Harvard Business School Press.

Bolles, R. N. (1978). *The three boxes of life: And how to get out of them: An introduction to life/work planning.* Berkeley, CA: Ten Speed Press.

Brookes, B., Hall, D. T., & Smith, F. (1992). *Retirement as a career transition: A study of the effects of a corporate early retirement incentive program* (Unpublished technical report). Boston University School of Management, Boston, MA.

Carstensen, L. L. (1995). Evidence for a life-span theory of socioemotional selectivity. *Current Directions in Psychological Science, 4*(5), 151–156.

Carstensen, L. L., Fung, H. H., & Charles, S. T. (2003). Socioemotional selectivity theory and the regulation of emotion in the second half of life. *Motivation and Emotion, 27*(2), 103–123.

Cattell, R. B. (1963). Theory of fluid and crystallized intelligence: A critical experiment. *Journal of Educational Psychology, 54*(1), 1–22.

Charles, S. T., Mather, M., & Carstensen, L. L. (2003). Aging and emotional memory: The forgettable nature of negative images for older adults. *Journal of Experimental Psychology: General, 132*(2), 310–324.

Dannefer, D. (2003). Cumulative advantage/disadvantage and the life course: Cross-fertilizing age and social science theory. *Journals of Gerontology, 58B*, S327–S337.

Denton, F. T., & Spencer, B. G. (2009). What is retirement? A review and assessment of alternative concepts and measures. *Canadian Journal on Aging/Revue Canadienne Du Vieillissement, 28*(01), 63–76.

DiPrete, T. A., & Eirich, G. M. (2006). Cumulative advantage as a mechanism for inequality: A review of theoretical and empirical developments. *Sociology, 32*(1), 271–297.

Elder, G. H. J., Johnson, M. K., & Crosnoe, R. (2004). The emergence and development of life course theory. In J. T. Mortimer & M. J. Shanahan (Eds.), *Handbook of the life course* (pp. 3–19). New York, NY: Springer.

Erikson, E. H. (1963). *Childhood and society.* New York, NY: Norton.

Feldman, D. C. (2007). Late career and retirement issues. In H. Gunz & M. Peiperl (Eds.), *Handbook of career studies* (pp. 153–168). Thousand Oaks, CA: Sage.

Feldman, D. C., & Kim, S. (2000). Bridge employment during retirement: A field study of individual and organizational experiences with post-retirement employment. *Human Resource Planning, 23*(1), 14–25.

Finkelstein, L. M., & Farrell, S. K. (2009). An expanded view of age bias in the workplace. In K. S. Shultz & G. A. Adams (Eds.), *Aging and work in the 21st Century* (pp. 73–108). New York, NY: Psychology Press.

Freund, A. M., & Baltes, P. B. (1998). Selection, optimization, and compensation as strategies of life management: Correlations with subjective indicators of successful aging. *Psychology and Aging, 13*(4), 531–543.

Freund, A. M., & Baltes, P. B. (2002). Life-management strategies of selection, optimization, and compensation: Measurement by self-report and construct validity. *Journal of Personality and Social Psychology, 82*(4), 642–662.

Grote, G., & Hall, D. T. (2010). *Reference groups and careers* (Unpublished technical report). Boston University School of Management, Boston, MA.

Grove, A. (1999). *Only the paranoid survive: How to exploit the crisis points that challenge every company.* New York, NY: Crown Business.

Hall, D. T. (1976). *Careers in organizations.* Santa Monica, CA: Goodyear.

Hall, D. T. (1986). Breaking career routines: Midcareer choice and identity development. In D. T. Hall & Associates (Eds.), *Career development in organizations* (pp. 120–159). San Francisco, CA: Jossey Bass.

Hall, D. T. (1993). *The new "career contract": Wrong on both counts* (Technical Report). Executive Development Roundtable, School of Management, Boston University.

Hall, D. T. (2002). *Careers in and out of organizations.* Thousand Oaks, CA: Sage.

Hall, D. T., & Mirvis, P. H. (1995). The new career contract: Developing the whole person at midlife and beyond. *Journal of Vocational Behavior, 47*(3), 269–289.

Horn, J. L. (1994). Theory of fluid and crystallized intelligence. *The Encyclopedia of Human Intelligence, 1*, 443–451.

Horn, J. L., & Cattell, R. B. (1967). Age differences in fluid and crystallized intelligence. *Acta Psychologica, 26*(2), 107–129.

Kasser, T., & Ryan, R. M. (1993). A dark side of the American dream: Correlates of financial success as a central life aspiration. *Journal of Personality and Social Psychology, 65,* 410–422.

Kasser, T., & Ryan, R. M. (1996). Further examining the American dream: Differential correlates of intrinsic and extrinsic goals. *Personality and Social Psychology Bulletin, 22,* 280–287.

Kim, N. (2012). *Work identity change: The role of age* [Work in Progress].

Lang, F. R., Rieckmann, N., & Baltes, M. M. (2002). Adapting to aging losses. *The Journals of Gerontology, Series B: Psychological Sciences and Social Sciences, 57*(6), P501–P509.

Levinson, D. J. (1986). A conception of adult development. *American Psychologist, 41,* 3–13.

Levy, B. R. (2003). Mind matters: Cognitive and physical effects of aging self-stereotypes. *Journals of Gerontology, Series B: Psychological Sciences and Social Sciences, 58*(4), 203.

Mather, M., & Carstensen, L. L. (2003). Aging and attentional biases for emotional faces. *Psychological Science, 14*(5), 409.

Mirvis, P. H., & Hall, D. T. (1994). Psychological success and the boundaryless career. *Journal of Organizational Behavior, 15,* 365–380.

Nicholson, N. (1986). A theory of work role transitions. *Administrative Science Quarterly, 29,* 172–191.

O'Reilly, C. A., III, Parlette, G. N., & Bloom, J. R. (1980). Perceptual measures of task characteristics: The biasing effects of differing frames of reference and job attitudes. *Academy of Management Journal, 23*(1), 118–131.

Reis, H. T., Collins, W. A., & Berscheid, E. (2000). The relationship context of human behavior and development. *Psychological Bulletin, Special Issue: Psychology in the 21st Century, 126*(6), 844–872.

Scarnati, J. T. (1998). Beyond technical competence: A passion for persistence. *Career Development International, 3*(1), 23–25.

Schulz, R., & Heckhausen, J. (1996). A life span model of successful aging. *American Psychologist, 51*(7), 702–714.

Sekaran, U., & Hall, D. T. (1989). Asynchronism in dual-career and family linkages. In M. B. Arthur, D. T. Hall, & B. S. Lawrence (Eds.), *Handbook of career theory* (pp. 159–180). New York, NY: Cambridge University Press.

Shapiro, A. D. (2010). *In their 90s, working for more than just a paycheck.* Retrieved from http://www.npr.org/templates/story/story.php?storyId=130566030

Sheldon, K. M., & Kasser, T. (2001). Getting older, getting better? Personal strivings and psychological maturity across the life span. *Developmental Psychology, 37*(4), 491–501.

Super, D. E. (1980). A life-span, life-space approach to career development. *Journal of Vocational Behavior, 16,* 282–298.

Super, D. E. (1990). A life-span, life-space approach to career development. In D. Brown, L. Brooks, & Associates (Eds.), *Career choice and development* (pp. 197–261). San Francisco, CA: Jossey-Bass.

Super, D. E., Crites, J., Hummel, R., Moser, H., Overstreet, P., & Warnath, C. (1957). *Vocational development: A framework for research.* New York, NY: Teachers College Press.

Totterdell, P., Kellett, S., Teuchmann, K., & Briner, R. B. (1998). Evidence of mood linkage in work groups. *Journal of Personality and Social Psychology, 74*(6), 1504–1515.

Uhlenberg, P., & Mueller, M. (2004). Family context and individual well-being. In J. T. Mortimer & M. J. Shanahan (Eds.), *Handbook of the life course* (pp. 123–148). New York, NY: Springer.

University of Oregon. (2004). *Work, study, and leisure.* Eugene, OR: University of Oregon Career Information System.

Vaillant, G. E. (2002). *Aging well.* Boston, MA: Little, Brown.

Wang, M., Adams, G. A., Beehr, T. A., & Shultz, K. S. (2009) Bridge employment and retirement: Issues and opportunities during the latter part of one's career. In S. G. Baugh & S. E. Sullivan (Eds.), *Maintaining focus, energy, and options over the career* (pp. 135–162). Charlotte, NC: Information Age.

Williams, K. Y., & O'Reilly, C. (1998). Demography and diversity in organizations—A review of 40 years in research. In B. M. Staw & R. I. Sutton (Eds.), *Research in organizational behavior* (pp. 77–140). Stamford, CT: JAI Press.

Wrzesniewski, A., McCauley, C., Rozin, P., & Schwartz, B. (1997). Jobs, careers, and callings: People's relations to their work. *Journal of Research in Personality, 31*(1), 21–33.

Aging, Retirement, and Human Resources Management: A Strategic Approach

Barbara L. Rau *and* Gary A. Adams

Abstract

This chapter introduces the organizational view of retirement by exploring the relationship between organizational strategy and human resource management decisions regarding retirement. The authors begin with an overview of organizational strategy and discuss two methods used to plan for an aging and retiring workforce. Several key human resource decisions related to retirement are then addressed. In the pre-retirement phase, the role of HR in helping employees to prepare for retirement is discussed, focusing primarily on financial planning and other retirement-related benefits. Next, human resource decisions pertaining to managing a retirement-ready workforce are discussed, addressing specifically the issues of knowledge transfer and motivating performance. Finally, interactions with individuals after retirement are discussed by looking at recruitment and bridge employment.

Key Words: aging workforce, human resources strategy, organizational strategy, retirement, strategic human resources management, bridge employment, retirement benefits, succession planning, retirement planning, recruitment, knowledge management

With an aging workforce and increased financial incentives to continue working into one's later years, management of an older workforce and issues surrounding retirement have become increasingly important responsibilities for organizations. Many organizations anticipate that 35%–50% of their workforce will retire over the next five to seven years. For example, the Office of Personnel Management estimated that 45% of its full-time, permanent workforce would be eligible to retire in 2012 (OPM, 2008). The sheer number of retirements, and their subsequent effects on knowledge transfer, culture, innovation, and other key objectives, are forcing organizations to take a more strategic approach to managing the aging workforce. In fact, a national survey by researchers at Boston College found that 75% of employers had done at least some analysis of their workforce demographics in anticipation of

the effects of retirement (Pitt-Catsouphes, Smyer, Matz-Costa, & Kane, 2007).

In the broad sense, an organizational strategy is a plan to gain and retain a competitive advantage in the market (Schuler & Jackson, 1987). For example, a company might focus on being the first to bring new products to the market or sell at the lowest cost. Human resource management practices that support an organization's overall business strategy are thought to play a critical role in sustaining a competitive advantage. This is because a firm's human resources are (1) rare and unique to the organization and (2) difficult to imitate. While a company may be able to copy another's production processes, logistics, or distribution practices, adopting similar HR practices does not guarantee the same results for the simple reason that each firm's human assets differ, and the impact of a given set of policies on any group of individuals is not necessarily the same, particularly when the circumstances or contexts differ.

Retirement can be seen both as a potentially disruptive source of turnover and an opportunity for change. Mass retirements, such as those experienced by companies offering early retirement incentives, can drain an organization of its knowledge and skills base, sometimes leaving less productive (and less desirable) employees. At the same time, these retirements can free up an organization's resources and create opportunities for advancement within an organization. However, even a small number of retirements within a company can send ripple effects throughout the hierarchy, resulting in knowledge loss and straining the culture by disrupting former patterns of work. Strategically managing retirement can help to ensure that the positive effects of retirement are realized while the negative effects are minimized. Further, it can help an organization understand how to time retirements, how to management retirement flow, and how to assess the impact of retirements on the organization as a whole.

From the organization's standpoint, retirement is a phenomenon that must be managed with a strategic perspective, preferably one that is consistent with that of the organization's overall business strategy. Simply put, a company that is looking to cut costs may be interested in encouraging retirement among its highly paid employees, while one that is looking to compete on the basis of quality may be unwilling to part prematurely with the greater knowledge and skills of its older workers. Similarly, a company looking to compete on the basis of innovative product design may benefit from a certain degree of churn or turnover among its employees, while one focused on customer service quality may wish to reduce high turnover rates that interfere with establishing long-term customer relations.

Utilizing the concepts from strategic human resource management, this chapter will explore some key challenges organizations face in managing an aging, retiring, or retired workforce with an eye toward supporting business strategy. We will begin the chapter with an overview of business strategy and implications of retirement for these strategies. We will discuss how organizations plan strategically for retirement through workforce management and succession planning. We will then discuss some key concerns organizations have in managing retirement issues for their pre-retirement workforce, including choice of retirement benefits, managing retirement benefits options, and encouraging employee retirement planning. Next, we discuss the implications of retirement for the current workforce and identify two key concerns of HR managers: knowledge transfer and motivating workers close to retirement. Finally, we discuss the interactions between organizations and retired individuals, including former employees. In particular, we discuss the advantages and challenges of retaining retirees and recruiting them back into the workforce

Managing Retirement Strategically
Strategic Management

The application of human resource management to strategic management has focused on two schools of thought. First, it has been proposed that there is a set of "best practices" that any organization, regardless of its particular situation and context, can benefit from when applied to the management of its human resources. The best practices perspective finds evidence supporting the value of particular HR practices such as pay-for-performance, grievance processes, employee involvement programs, and performance management systems in improving firm profits (Becker & Huselid, 1998; Becker & Huselid, 1999; Huselid, 1995; Pfeffer, 1994). Alternatively, some researchers argue that HR practices must be designed to align with the particular firm strategy and environmental constraints faced by a particular organization (Wood, 1999; Boxall & Purcell, 2008, Schuler & Jackson, 1987).

It is generally accepted that both of these schools of thought have merit. In fact, researchers have begun to acknowledge that a firm's practices need to not only meet the strategy, but to do so in a way that meets the needs of different groups of employees (Lepak & Snell, 2002; Tsui, Pearce, Porter, & Tripoli, 1997). For example, employees with firm-specific knowledge (i.e., knowledge-based employees who are considered both valuable and unique to the organization) will have different needs than job-based employees (i.e., those who are important to the organization but comparatively easy to replace). The term "HR architecture" has been used to refer to the differentiated system of HR practices addressing both the needs of various constituents within the organization and the contingencies posed by the organization's strategy and environment.

Thus, the particular treatment of retirement within an organization depends on the organization's business strategy, its particular environmental constraints and contingencies, and the types of jobs or employment arrangements within the organization. While various typologies of business strategy have been proposed, the following distinctions suggested by Porter (1985) are useful for considering human resource practices: *cost leadership* (competing by providing low-cost product or services)*, innovation/differentiation* (finding ways to set one's products or services apart from competitors), and *quality enhancement* (competing by providing high-quality goods and services).

Schuler and Jackson (1987) discussed the various behaviors that employees would need to exhibit to support three different business strategies. For example, to support an *innovation/differentiation* strategy, employees would need to exhibit high levels of creativity, a long-term focus, a high degree of cooperative and interdependent behaviors, a greater willingness to take risk, and high tolerance for ambiguity and unpredictability. By contrast, to support a *cost leadership* strategy, employees would need to demonstrate predictable and repetitive behaviors, a shorter-term focus, primarily autonomous behaviors, and low risk-taking. Finally, to support a *quality enhancement strategy*, employees would have to exhibit a longer-term focus, high concern for precision and quality, high concern for processes, low risk-taking, and a high degree of commitment to the organization's goals.

Given these distinctions, a different attitude toward employee retirement could be expected by virtue of the organization's strategy and supporting culture of human resources management. Under an innovation/differentiation strategy, the organization may wish to design a retirement plan that will hold the employee to the organization for longer periods of time but also take advantage of their relative willingness to take risks. Under a cost leadership strategy, the organization's culture of stability and low risk-taking might best be supported by a retirement plan that minimizes risk while encouraging an earlier retirement date. Meanwhile, to support quality enhancement, the employer might want to design a benefit plan that minimizes risk while tying the individual to the organization.

The work of the National Council on Compensation Insurance (NCCI), a south Florida-based nonprofit organization, illustrates the value of tailoring a retirement plan to the organization's strategy (Nichols, 2008). In designing its retirement benefits, NCCI first determined its business mission and values and used these to state a philosophy (or objectives) for its retirement plan. NCCI determined that its business strategy required "retention of knowledgeable, long-service employees" and should provide *adequate*

means for employees to retire (Nichols, 2008). After conducting a systematic analysis of options, NCCI decided to make several changes to their retirement plans, including implementation of automatic enrollment and increases to a 401(k), an improved vesting schedule, the addition of a Roth 401(k), implementation of formal retirement education for its employees, and the adoption of a phased retirement option (Nichols, 2008).

This example illustrates one aspect of strategic planning for retirement—matching the business strategy to the specific type of retirement plan. However, organizations must engage in a good deal more than that if they are to be adequately prepared for the effects of retirement. They must also be able to adequately manage their workforce through human resources forecasting and succession planning. Next, we will discuss how organizations plan strategically for retirement through aggregate planning (i.e., looking at the workforce flow as a whole in the organization) and individual succession planning (i.e., looking at how organizations plan for changes in key individual positions).

Methods of Strategic Management
Workforce Management (HR Planning)

A significant component of HR strategy is a clear understanding of the organization's workforce transitions: entry into the organization, movement through the organization, and exiting the organization. HR planning is a term used to describe the process of forecasting and planning for these workforce transitions using a variety of qualitative and quantitative forecasting techniques aimed at predicting an organization's labor supply and demand. It is designed to project the nature and type of jobs that will be needed in the organization, as well as the knowledge, skills, and abilities that will be needed to meet the organization's needs in the future.

HR planning is very proactive in nature. The attempt to specify labor needs three to five years into the future allows organizations to take long-term steps to address anticipated shortfalls or excesses. For example, a sheet-metal manufacturer may project a significant shortfall of skilled welders due to retirements in the next five years. Looking at the labor market and the projected graduation rates of welders from two-year technical colleges, they may also project a shortage of qualified welders in the labor market. This foreknowledge allows them time to establish relationships with area high schools, develop student internships, and/or establish scholarships, all of which would help to increase the supply of welders (and interest in the company as a potential employer) before the projected wave of retirements.

HR planning involves six steps: (1) assessing strategic initiatives and context, (2) forecasting labor demand, (3) forecasting internal and external labor supply, (4) reconciling supply and demand, (5) developing an action plan, and (6) evaluating success. In the first step of strategic planning, the organization needs to assess its strategic initiatives for the next three to five years and conduct a thorough evaluation of the context within which it operates. This will include a review of product or service demands, technological changes, availability of financial resources, absenteeism and turnover trends, projected organizational growth or decline, current productivity levels, and anticipated changes in economic or competitive positioning. This evaluation will help to establish any changes the organization needs to be prepared for in the next three to five years. For example, if the organization anticipates purchasing new technology that will increase worker productivity by 15%, then they may need to prepare to downsize the workforce over the same period.

Once the key changes in the environment are identified, the organization can use either qualitative or quantitative methods to forecast labor demand. Qualitative methods include bottom-up estimates (managerial estimates of the number of employees they will both need and have available to them over the designated time period) and top-down estimates (estimates by top-level management as to the number of employees they are willing to employ). Quantitative estimates include using trend analysis (using past employment trends to project future trends), productivity ratios (using historical ratios between jobs to forecast changes in one job relative to another), and multiple regression to forecast demand using several factors known to predict employment levels within the organization.

There are two primary methods of forecasting labor supply within the organization: skills inventory analysis and Markov analysis. Skills inventory analysis involves tracking (using a human resource information system) the various skills of individuals within the organization. Reports can then be generated to evaluate and estimate the skills that will be available over time. Markov analysis focuses on forecasting movements between jobs within the organization. It uses the organization's past history of job movement (promotion, demotion, lateral moves, and exits) to estimate the probability of various

movements between jobs. These probabilities are then applied to the existing workforce and used to predict labor supply in various positions. Among other things, Markov analysis is useful for anticipating the time employees spend at various positions and levels within an organization (Heneman & Sandver, 1977) and hence can be used to predict both career "slowdown" as one nears retirement and organizational exits due to retirements.

Putting the forecasted demand and forecasted internal supply together, the organization will determine whether there is a predicted shortage or surplus of labor over the next three to five years. A forecasted shortage means the organization will need to hire additional employees, while a surplus may indicate the need for downsizing. Once these needs are determined, an action plan can be developed.

Clearly the implications for retirement are very different in each condition. Shortages will tend to encourage the organization to find ways to retain qualified employees longer (i.e., focus on retention). An organization might, for example, offer older workers an incentive to stay beyond an anticipated retirement age. They may offer flexible work schedules, temporary assignments, consulting contracts, or part-time options such as job-sharing to make working more attractive to older employees (Society for Human Resource Management/American Associations for Retired Persons, 1998). They might also develop bridge employment options (e.g., allowing the individual to take a position with less responsibility or perhaps make a career change). Finally, they might refocus recruitment efforts to bring former retired employees back to the organization or conduct targeted recruitment aimed at attracting retirees back into the workforce.

On the other hand, organizations in retrenchment often focus on employees close to retirement as a way to downsize. An organization may allow vacancies generated through the normal course of retirements to remain unfilled (downsizing through attrition). It may also attempt to generate more vacancies by offering early retirement incentives to encourage voluntary turnover among older workers. Here, too, the organization may consider asking older workers to move to part-time schedules or to take lower-level positions as other vacancies arise (and as a way to reduce compensation levels).

Thus, in either the case of shortage or surplus, employees nearing retirement play a key role in strategic staffing management. The fact that older employees' career trajectories are more predictable than those of younger workers and that some of them may be more open to the possibility of reduced hours or organizational exit makes them an ideal demographic for managing fluctuations in staffing needs. Of course, these strategies often have a cost associated with them. In the case of early retirement programs, for example, the organization will need to wrestle with the effects of knowledge transfer and loss as older, experienced workers retire. We will explore these issues in greater detail below.

Succession Planning

Whereas HR planning is used to forecast an organization's overall labor (and skill) supply and demand, succession planning is used to project staffing changes for an individual position. Succession planning is used primarily for positions, such as key managerial jobs, where it is necessary or desirable to immediately fill a position should it become vacant or where substantial training (both general and firm-specific) may be needed to effectively do the job. Succession planning is both an HR planning tool that allows an organization to maintain smooth transitions and a career planning tool that allows it to identify potential talent and provide the training and experience employees need to progress within the organization. The need for succession planning is increasingly recognized by organizations. According to one study conducted for the Society for Human Resource Management, about 58% of responding companies indicated that their organization had some type of succession planning in place, and about one-quarter had plans to implement succession planning (Fegley, 2006).

Succession planning is generally accomplished by creating a "replacement chart" for key positions. For a given position, the chart indicates which of the current employees are potentially qualified to move into the position and how many years before they would be considered ready to assume the responsibilities. The chart is generally accompanied by an analysis of each potential replacement's knowledge and experience gaps. This allows the organization to (1) identify potential talent, (2) identify any urgent needs for developing a successor pool, and (3) better plan for addressing any gaps that may exist. Organizations vary in the degree of formality used in administering their succession plans. Some use purely subjective assessments of talent, while others send employees to formal assessment centers to identify strengths and weaknesses. Some have formal career development programs that help employees address their knowledge and skill gaps, while others leave employees to figure out how to do

this on their own. More formal programs are generally less subject to problems of favoritism, personal biases, and unequal opportunities for women and minorities.

While historically succession planning has been used for a small subset of key employees, organizations are expanding its use. Some organizations use succession planning throughout their organizations in planning for management and other professional or key technical positions (Rothwell, 2010). Rothwell (2010) described the trend away from succession planning for the purpose of managing promotion to one that meets the need for knowledge transfer. To manage knowledge transfer, organizations are increasingly relying upon retirees, a fact that can and should be planned for in the process of succession planning. Rothwell (2010) referred to this as "technical succession planning" and noted that the key difference is that the focus is on "transferring knowledge from those who possess special knowledge, gained for experience within the organization (institutional memory) and experience doing the work (tacit knowledge)" (p. 52). Such a process requires management commitment, clarification of work processes and technical competencies, a knowledge inventory (identifying who within the organization possesses particular types of knowledge), identification of who is at risk of loss due to retirement, formulation of a plan to address the gap, implementation of the plan, and evaluation of the plan's success (Rothwell, 2010).

Despite the number of companies either implementing or planning to implement succession planning, there is clearly room for improvement. According to Barnett and Davis (2008), most organizational leaders do not feel confident that their succession planning processes will be effective in helping to address impending HR needs such as skills shortages. Further, they argued that data on managerial and CEO performance suggests that many managers (and CEOs) are likely to fail in their positions, suggesting that succession planning is not as effective as it should be. They also argue that this is due in part to poor design and methodology, particularly because the organization focuses too much on specific positions and not more broadly on the organization's talent needs.

These criticisms highlight the need to tie succession planning to the overall staffing plan developed through the staffing planning process as well as the organization's business strategy. Succession planning in an organization that is pursuing a strategy of excellent quality of product or service may find that internal promotion paths that allow for cross-functional experiences and training allow individuals to see the product or service from a variety of perspectives, which, in turn, generates improved quality. As individuals near retirement, they will have gained a variety of experiences that can also make them valuable "rehires" following retirement because they can be placed in many different positions. On the other hand, a company that is focusing on cost containment may conduct succession planning using clear internal promotion paths through one functional area so as to gain efficiencies associated with deep knowledge of a particular area. The narrower job paths and deep knowledge may indicate a need for stronger mentoring and knowledge transfer protocol as these employees near retirement. Succession planning with an eye toward strategy can help the organization to manage career paths more effectively for both the business and its employees. In turn, it is argued that succession planning can aid HR in developing its strategic partnership with the top management team (Barnett & Davis, 2008; Ulrich & Beatty, 2001) as HR begins to demonstrate its ability to fill strategic staffing needs.

Issues for a Pre-Retirement Workforce

From an individual standpoint, retirement is a process that begins long before, and continues well after, one retires. This "temporal view" (Shultz & Wang, in press) of the retirement process is also shared by employers. The key task in the years leading up to the point when a worker officially retires is retirement preparation. Retirement preparation involves planning and taking those actions needed before retirement to help ensure that one has a satisfying lifestyle after retirement. The main way in which organizations help workers with their retirement preparation is through the provision of employee benefits. Although organizations do offer benefits to meet goals for corporate social responsibility, they also offer benefits to attract and retain workers, increase productivity, and foster positive work-related attitudes among employees. As such, employee benefits are an important part of the HR architecture. Employee benefits are expensive for employers. Indeed, employers spend about 30% of their total compensation budgets on employee benefits (BLS, 2010a). This amounts to some 1.5 trillion dollars that is spent annually on employee benefits (EBRI, 2008). Because they are so expensive, it should come as no surprise that organizations must be concerned about costs and cost containment as they develop and administer the types of benefit programs that will help them meet their strategic goals.

Pre-retirement Financial Preparation

One of the most important aspects of retirement preparation is in the area of finances. That is, preparing to replace the stream of income during the time one is retired that had formerly come from work. Traditionally, retirement income has come from three main sources: social security programs, employer-provided retirement benefit programs, and personal savings. Employer-provided retirement income benefit programs have been the main way in which organizations have helped employees fund their retirement years. Retirement income benefit programs are fairly common in the United States, with 71% of private-sector workers having access to such programs and 80% of those having access actually taking part (BLS, 2009a). While there are a variety of specific types of retirement income benefit programs, they are generally divided into two broad categories: (1) defined benefit (DB) plans and (2) defined contribution (DC) plans. Each of these two types of programs has features to consider in the context of an organization's strategy.

As the name implies, DB plans specify a particular benefit payout level (typically in the form of lifetime installments) once the employee retires. The payout level is determined by a formula, which most commonly includes the employee's length of service and earning history with the employer. Employees must work for a specified period of time before becoming eligible (vested) for a payout at retirement. Typically, this vesting period is five years. DB plans are not portable. They cannot be transferred from one employer to another. As a result of these rules the largest payouts accrue to those who have remained with a single employer for a long period of time and have their highest earnings with that employer. The funds used to generate the payout are not under the control of the employees, and the employees do not direct how those funds are invested. In DB plans the organization makes a long-term cost commitment and assumes the market risk (fluctuations in the investment markets). Thus there is considerable uncertainty for the organization. The employee assumes the "service" risk. That is, that they will continue working for the same employer over a long period of time. It is also the case that these plans "penalize" work with that same employer beyond a certain point. This is because the additional benefit amount provided for additional years of work rarely approaches the amount of benefit lost by forfeiting a year of payout. This feature makes it easier to predict when people will retire.

In DC plans the amount of payout upon retirement is not specified, but an amount of investment contribution is. That is, the employer agrees to contribute a certain amount (usually a percent of salary) to a retirement investment account such as a 401(k) or 403(b) account. Oftentimes, both the organization and employee make contributions. The payout at retirement is based on how well the investment account has performed. DC plans are "owned" by the employee, and the employee directs how the contributions are invested across a set of funds (e.g., mutual funds). DC plans are portable. If employees leave an organization they may transfer their account into other retirement accounts. In this type of plan the organization has much greater certainty surrounding the costs of the plan. The amount of contribution is generally known from year to year. Because they are portable, employees do not assume the service risk; however, because they are employee-directed, employees assume the market risk.

At one time DB plans were the more common of the two types of plans. However, over the past twenty years there has been a considerable shift from DB to DC plans, and currently more private-sector workers are covered by DC (56%) than DB plans (31%) (BLS, 2009a). Research suggests that this shift has been driven by several factors, including (1) regulatory changes that make defined benefit plans more difficult and costly to administer; (2) the shift from traditional manufacturing, unionized industries to service (nonunionized) industries, and with it the disappearance of union contracts; and (3) the changing nature of the workforce itself (e.g., increased number of women, dual career couples, education levels, etc.), which has made for an increasingly mobile workforce that needs retirement plans that can "move" with them (e.g., Aaronson & Coronado, 2005; Broadbent, Palumbo, & Woodman, 2006).

In their discussion of pension plans, Westerman and Sundali (2005) use psychological contract theory (Rousseau, 1989, 1995) to describe how the shift from DB to DC plans affects the relationship between the employees and their employers. The term psychological contract refers to an employee's perception of the implicit exchange relationship, or set of mutual obligations, between employee and employer. They can range from being highly relational to highly transactional. Highly relational psychological contracts are based on mutual trust and loyalty and tend to be more long term. Highly transactional psychological contracts are based on the economic exchange of employee effort for employer-provided inducements. They argue that DB plans tend to signal relational psychological contracts between employee and employer whereas, DC plans tend to signal transactional psychological contracts between employee and employer. They also suggest that the shift from DB to DC plans is just one part of a broader movement toward more transactional employment relationships generally. Considering these factors, the shift from DB to DC plans at the aggregate level can be viewed as organizations responding in a strategic manner to align their retirement income benefit offerings to the realities of their production processes and labor markets under a given set of constraints (government regulations and costs).

At the level of the individual organization, these same factors call for designing a retirement income benefit plan that is aligned with the overall strategy of the organization (internal alignment) and the characteristics of labor market (external alignment). Some organizational strategies, such as those that seek to gain competitive advantage through employees who must acquire and use organizational-specific knowledge or customer relationships developed over a long period of time, can be enhanced by benefit strategies that promote long-term relationships between employer and employees. Some organizational strategies can benefit from the predictable exit of employees owing to those workers' preferences or concerns about productivity at older ages (e.g., as might be seen in physically demanding manual labor positions). These types of strategies likely benefit from some of the features of DB plans. On the other hand, some organizational strategies, such as those that seek to leverage technological and other types of innovation among employees, may find that long-term employment relationships do not enhance the organization's ability to compete, nor are they necessarily preferred by a labor market that has grown increasingly concerned with mobility. In these types of scenarios, organizations are likely to benefit from the features of DC plans.

In addition to *offering* retirement income benefits, organizations can also help employees meet retirement income needs by encouraging full participation in those benefit programs as well as by encouraging increased personal savings for retirement. Research data consistently show that many people are woefully unprepared for retirement, and this is especially true in the area of financial preparation (Adams & Rau, in press; Munnell, Webb, & Golub-Sass, 2009; Purcell, 2009a). People optimize neither their participation in plans that are offered through their employer nor their personal savings outside of the workplace. Some of the main reasons for this lack of preparation include a lack of basic financial literacy needed to develop a sound financial plan (Hershey, Mowen, & Jacobs-Lawson, 2003; Hershey, Walsh, Brougham, Carter, & Farrell, 1998; Lusardi & Mitchell, 2007) and the "willpower" needed to implement it (Benartzi & Thaler, 2007). Organizations have begun to address this issue in two ways. The first is by reducing the effort the employee needs to exert to participate in employer-provided retirement income benefit programs such as defined contribution plans. This is accomplished, for example, through automatic enrollments in the plan and escalations that increase the contribution level of the employee over time. Since passage of the Pension Protection Act of 2006, which encouraged automatic enrollments, the number of organizations offering this feature has increased to 19% (BLS, 2010b), with larger organizations more likely to offer it. The research evidence to date would suggest that automatic enrollment increases participation rates in 401(k)-type pension plans (GAO, 2009).

The second way organizations can try to address the issues that prevent employees from optimizing their participation in DC plans, and that may extend into their personal savings outside of the workplace, is by offering financial education and planning benefits to employees. One recent survey found that financial education was provided by 75% of large firms and 51% of small firms and, of those offering financial education, 43% reported providing education focused on retirement and 33% reported providing financial education on topics other than retirement (Miller, 2009). Research on the efficacy of financial education programs suggests that they can produce positive changes in financial knowledge (Hershey et al., 1998), savings behavior (Clark, d'Ambrose, McDermed, & Sawant, 2006; Hershey, Mowen, & Jacobs-Lawson, 2003), and participation in voluntary savings plans (Bayer, Bernheim, & Scholz, 2009). Some evidence also suggests that the most effective way to deliver these types of programs is frequently offered retirement seminars as opposed to written materials (Bayer, Bernheim, & Scholz, 2009).

Both automatic enrollment/escalation and educational programs can have a positive effect on employees' financial preparation for retirement.

However, neither come without costs and other consequences, and a firm's decision about offering them should be a strategic one. This fact was highlighted by several examples given in the GAO report that reviewed automatic enrollment/escalation programs (GAO, 2009). For instance, the GAO report described an employer in a low-wage, high-turnover environment that would tend to incur all of the administrative costs of automatic enrollments for employees who would accumulate only small balances that would likely be taken as lump-sum payouts. Thus, the costs would have been incurred without achieving any of the desired outcomes of the program. It may also be the case in low-wage high-turnover environments that employees would be sensitive to the likelihood of low balances and perceive an automatic contribution as a reduction in salary as opposed to an actual benefit. This may make it more difficult to recruit workers. With regard to offering financial education seminars, there may be situations where they are simply cost prohibitive. This could occur when an organization has adopted a focused low-cost strategy and profit margins are narrow, thus making it difficult to reflect the additional costs of the financial education seminars in the price of its goods and services.

Other Retirement-Related Benefits

In addition to retirement income, an organization can offer many other benefits aimed at protecting employees after they retire. These include retiree health benefits, health savings accounts, and long-term care insurance. Retiree health benefits are health insurance programs that cover workers after they retire. Approximately 23% of private-sector workers over the age of 65 have access to such programs (BLS, 2009b). Changes in government regulations and the downturn in the economy have led some employers to stop offering these benefits or reduce coverage. Unlike some other benefits, unless the organization has made specific promises or surrendered the right to change their plans, these plans can be eliminated or changed by organization. Health savings accounts allow employees and their organizations to contribute to an account to be used to pay the cost of qualified medical expenses if employees are covered by high-deductable health insurance plans. These accounts can be used for retiree health expenses (for those with high-deductible health plans and not enrolled in Medicare) because the balance of the account can be carried forward from year to year and they are portable (the employee retains the account if he or she leaves the employer or the workforce). Approximately 15% of private-sector employees have access to health savings accounts (BLS, 2010c). Long-term care insurance is meant to cover the costs associated with nursing home and certain in-home care. Approximately 16% of private-sector workers have access to this type of insurance.

Like all benefit decisions, the decision by an employer to offer any of these types of benefits, and the manner in which they are offered, should be based on a number of factors. At the most basic level, employers provide benefits to align employee behaviors and attitudes with organizational strategy before they retire and to provide employees with some security after they retire, while being mindful of costs. However, these three goals do not always coincide with one another. For example, in the case of retiree health benefits, an organization may want to foster long-term relationships with employees by demonstrating legitimate concerns for their long-term welfare. Retiree health benefits would seem one mechanism to accomplish this. However, they are costly, and the research suggests that older employees are as much as 21% more likely to leave their current employer if they have access to retiree health benefits (Robinson & Clark, 2010). Thus, rather than encouraging longer tenure, this benefit might be used to encourage employees to retire if its costs can be justified for that purpose. In this case, the organization might be better off considering other benefits that signal organizational support. This example illustrates the need for careful consideration of the utility of each benefit within the package, as well as the way they will interact in affecting employee attitudes and behaviors.

Issues for a Retiring Workforce

As we have just argued, helping employees plan for retirement in a way that is both consistent with, and supportive of, organizational strategy is an important function of human resource management. However, HR is also faced with several strategic decisions regarding the management of a "retirement-ready" or aging workforce. The Bureau of Labor Statistics estimated that the number of workers aged 65 and older increased by 101% between 1977 and 2007 and further projects that between 2006 and 2016 the number of workers aged 65 to 74 will increase an additional 36.5% (BLS, 2008). These numbers have significant implications regarding the management of employees who are close to retirement. We address two key issues here: knowledge transfer, and the

motivation and performance of a retirement-ready workforce.

Knowledge Transfer

One area of particular concern for organizations is the loss of accumulated knowledge that can occur when employees retire (DeLong, 2004). In one recent survey, 71% of employers reported being concerned about the loss of knowledge resulting from the retirement of older employees (MetLife, 2009). Although the sum amount and value of lost knowledge are difficult to quantify, anecdotal evidence suggests that they are considerable. Delong (2008) gives the example of the loss of engineering knowledge critical to maintaining an organization's production process. Another example would be the loss of knowledge regarding customer preferences and idiosyncrasies necessary to make sales. Knowledge itself can be described along a number of dimensions. It can range from explicit, relatively easily expressed knowledge to tacit knowledge that is known by an individual but difficult to express (Polanyi, 1966). Knowledge can also come in several forms ranging from intellectual knowledge focused on information, facts, and concepts to social knowledge focused on interpersonal relationships and access to social networks (Peterson & Spiker, 2005; Nahapiet & Ghoshal, 1998). In order to retain the accumulated knowledge of its retiring employees, organizations need a knowledge management process that is able to identify and transfer valuable knowledge so that it can be used by others to achieve organizational objectives (Argote & Ingram, 2000; Nonaka & Takeauchi, 1995; Slagter, 2007; Wang & Noe, 2010).

The HR manager plays a key role in the knowledge management process. To begin, the HR manager must work with senior managers to determine the size and scope of the knowledge management effort based on an assessment of the organization's strategy, resources, and knowledge base as well as employee demographics and capabilities. These will allow the organization to develop the knowledge management approach most suited to its needs. An important part of this process is being able to locate and identify the type and value of the knowledge to be retained. Once this process is underway, the organization can begin developing the knowledge transfer process.

Key elements of the knowledge transfer process aimed at retiring workers include facilitating an organizational culture that supports knowledge transfer and developing and deploying specific tools needed to achieve knowledge transfer. Important elements of a culture that supports knowledge transfer include (1) valuing employees nearing retirement for what they know, (2) creating mutual respect and trust among the parties to the process, and (3) emphasizing learning and development (Slagter, 2007). Human resources management practices such as reward and recognition programs can facilitate the development of such a culture. The importance of these cultural elements are supported by recent research in the general knowledge management literature linking knowledge management practices to organizational performance (Zack, McKeen, & Singh, 2009). They are especially important in the context of knowledge transfer from retiring employees given that, in most cases, the retiring employee is leaving the organization and transferring their knowledge to a younger generation (Calo, 2008; Stevens, 2010).

In terms of developing and deploying specific knowledge transfer tools, the organization has a wide range of options. Although there are a number of ways to conceptualize them (e.g., Nonaka & Takeuchi, 1995), specific knowledge transfer tools can be seen as falling into two broad overlapping categories: (1) documenting processes and (2) interpersonal processes. Documenting processes focus on knowledge transfer in written (most often in electronic) form to create repositories of knowledge. The tools used to create these involve task-based and cognitive job analysis methods, the development of procedure manuals, expert-system and knowledge-base support tools, and training programs. Interpersonal processes focus on knowledge transfer via interactions with those who have the knowledge. Traditional tools for accomplishing this include succession planning, structured on-the-job training and apprentice programs, job shadowing and developmental job assignments, and coaching/mentoring. Other methods include critical incident and after-action review sessions, communities of practice, story-telling sessions, and internal help desk and consulting teams.

The tools and approaches to knowledge transfer for any particular organization necessarily involve a consideration of all of the issues described above. They must match tools and approaches to strategy and types of knowledge. They must also consider the learning preferences of the knowledge transfer parties (older and younger workers) and tailor their methods accordingly (Piktialis & Greenes, 2008). For instance, we are aware of a large manufacturer of automobile parts with a low-cost strategy achieved through routinization and standardized processes that faced a substantial loss of senior workers through retirement. Although there was a large quantity of knowledge to transfer, much of it was relatively easy to articulate. In this instance, documenting approaches combined with formal and on-the-job training worked well. This organization also recognized differences across the retiring and replacement workforce in terms of age and language (incoming workers were younger and often spoke Spanish as their primary language) and used a technology application with embedded video that included some Spanish language segments. This type of approach would likely not work well in an organization with an innovation/differentiation strategy that needed to transfer a greater amount of tacit knowledge from retiring workers to younger workers. In this instance the organization might consider the more interpersonal knowledge transfer approaches. It would also be important to establish a culture that encourages and values knowledge-seeking on the part of the younger workers and knowledge-sharing on the part of the retiring workers.

Motivation and Performance Management

Another significant challenge for managing a workforce close to retirement is maintaining motivation and work performance. While there is little empirical evidence to suggest that motivation (Forteza & Prieto, 1994; McEvoy & Cascio, 1989; Rhodes, 1983) and performance necessarily decline with age (e.g., McEvoy & Cascio, 1989; Ng & Feldman, 2010; Waldman & Avolio, 1986), there is growing evidence that there is something unique about motivating older workers. Techniques that work on younger workers may not be effective on older workers nearing retirement.

To determine an appropriate strategic response, it is important to consider motivation as it pertains to older workers. While there is not a lot of research on this issue, several theories have been proposed. Kanfer and Ackerman (2004) argued that process-oriented theories of work motivation, such as expectancy theory or goal theory, cannot completely explain differences in work motivation by age. These theories, according to Kanfer and Ackerman (2004), operate in much the same way as for younger workers. Instead, the differences in motivation between younger and older workers can be explained by age-related changes in competencies and motives, including what is needed to protect self-concept.

Research shows that fluid intellectual abilities (Gf) such as abstract reasoning and attention decline as we age. By contrast, crystallized intellectual abilities (Gc) such as experiential knowledge, extent of vocabulary, and verbal comprehension continue to increase even after middle age (Schaie, 1996). Using Kanfer's (1987) model of expectancy theory, Kanfer and Ackerman (2004) proposed that the change in intellectual abilities affects motivation primarily through the effort-performance link. In particular, older workers will begin to lose motivation and interest for high-Gf jobs (e.g., line work, air traffic controller, and engineering) because greater effort is necessary to attain the same level of performance (or, in some cases, performance cannot be maintained even with greater effort). Workers in high-Gf jobs are likely to demonstrate greater interest in jobs that demand high levels of Gc (e.g., supervisory work, teaching). Thus, those who are already in high-Gc jobs are more likely to sustain motivation throughout their careers. This conclusion would appear to be supported by research on career development (Maurer, 2001) that suggests that older workers avoid development opportunities that might put them in a bad light (e.g., technology training) while being drawn to those opportunities that they are more confident they can master (e.g., soft skills training). It is also supported by work by de Lange, Van Yperen, Van der Heijden, and Bal (2010) that concluded that, relative to younger workers, older workers were more likely to indicate their goals were ones of mastery-avoidance (i.e., goals that focused on maintaining performance, memory, skills, and abilities).

Warr (1997, 2001) also suggested that expectancy theory may be useful to understand older workers' motivation but focused primarily on the fact that older workers are motivated by different job characteristics. Older workers' preferences are more likely to include things like security (physical, job, financial) and opportunities to utilize their skills rather than high job demands, job variety, and feedback. Thus, as workers age, organizations may find that they are not motivated by the same things as in the past. This suggests that, as an organization's workforce ages, the reward structure may need to be realigned with worker needs and desires.

Claes and Heymans (2008) conducted focus group sessions with HR managers and identified three motivation theories that might be useful in explaining the work motivation of older workers. First, cognitive evaluation theory (Deci & Ryan, 1991) suggests that feelings of autonomy,

self-efficacy, and relatedness with others influence motivation. HR managers interviewed by Claes and Heymans indicated that older workers attached more importance to having contact with their superiors, a relationship with the owner, and opportunities to take on responsibility and consequently were more motivated when these conditions were met. Second, consistent with Locke and Latham's (1990) goal setting theory, interviews with HR managers suggested that older workers were more motivated when they were given clear goals that were challenging and time-related. Third, the HR managers observed that older workers were highly motivated by the opportunities to mentor others, pass along their knowledge, and gain recognition for their efforts.

Kooij, de Lange, Jansen, and Dikkers (2008) conducted a literature review of age and work motivation using five different conceptualizations of age: chronological, functional, psychosocial, organizational, and life span (de Lange et al., 2006). They concluded that where organizations (or countries) use chronological age as a marker (e.g., to define a "normal" retirement age, offer age-related benefits, or establish a mandatory retirement age), workers are more likely to experience lower job involvement, feelings of work as a burden, and feelings of reduced competence. Further, these organizations are less likely to invest in training and development for older workers. *Chronological age* is therefore argued to have a negative effect on the motivation of older workers. *Functional age*, as determined by cognitive abilities and physical health, was argued to decrease motivation for certain occupations; for example, where Gf demands are high or where reasonable accommodations cannot be made for physical limitations. Healthier older workers are less likely to suffer from motivation declines than those experiencing cognitive or physical decline. *Psychosocial age* refers to the individual's self-concept as it pertains to aging as well as the social perception of age. Kooij et al. (2008) concluded that those who viewed themselves as "old" or who experienced social cues that indicated they were "old" (i.e., limited opportunities for training, lack of performance feedback, assumptions about retirement readiness) were less likely to sustain motivation to work. The impact of *organizational age*, or tenure within an organization, would seem to depend largely on the organization's policies. Kooij et al. (2008) concluded that there was insufficient evidence to determine which was more important: positive motivation effects stemming from steep earnings curves or negative effects stemming from career and earnings plateaus. However, there is considerable research that shows that job attitudes in general are affected by career stage, so it is likely that, regardless of organizational tenure, the stage of one's career will also have an effect on motivation (positive or negative). Finally, Kooij et al. (2008) concluded that there is not strong evidence that *life span age* (early, middle, and late adulthood) has an impact on motivation, although some research indicates that priorities with regard to work and leisure time shift in accordance with life span age.

It is clear that HR managerial laments about the difficulty of motivating older workers nearing retirement are well-founded. This brief summary of the age and motivation literature shows that the research indicates a complexity that is not yet well understood. To match motivation strategy with the organization's strategy, the HR manager must first understand the source of low motivation among older workers. The research summarized here suggests that it could be due to declining physical or cognitive abilities, changing preferences for work-related outcomes, negative social signals, existing organizational policies and practices, life stage pressures, and interactions between the job and the individual.

Still, we can draw some guidance for HR strategy with the understanding that the key question is whether the organization wishes to encourage older workers to retire or wishes to extend older workers' value in the workplace. As with other policies discussed earlier, a company concerned about cost containment may wish to encourage retirement of older, more expensive workers. These organizations could adopt more chronological age policies and practices that establish an implied retirement age. They may want to offer early retirement, create benefits for retired employees, or designate an age for phased retirement eligibility.

On the other hand, an organization that is focused on quality of service, product, or processes may wish to extend the work life of older, knowledgeable workers for as long as possible. HR policies and practices that accommodate older workers' changing physical and cognitive challenges (e.g., job redesign, ergonomic changes, job reassignment, and career development) should increase work motivation for older workers. Accommodating older workers' changing preferences for leisure and work may also encourage them to stay in the workplace longer, albeit with reduced hours but perhaps with sustained motivation.

While complex, the fundamental advice to HR managers is the same whether motivating younger or older workers: to effectively manage motivation, HR managers must understand their business strategy, the current context of work (social, organizational, and demographic), its existing policies and practices, and, of course, the preferences and needs of their workforce.

Issues for Organizational Interactions with Retirees

As noted earlier, for many organizations the relationship between employer and employee does not end when the employment relationship is terminated. Given the projected skill labor shortage, many organizations are taking steps to nurture relationships with former employees and establish relationships with other retirees. In the next section, we discuss the advantages and challenges of retaining retirees and recruiting them back into the workforce.

Retirement Work

While in the past retirement may have been thought of as a one-time exit from full-time work, this is no longer the reality for a sizable portion of older workers (Adams & Beehr, 2003). Indeed, people now engage in a wide range of post-retirement work arrangements (Giandrea, Cahill, & Quinn, 2009; Gobeski & Beehr, 2009; Purcell, 2009b). Much of the research in this area has focused on "bridge employment," with its connotation as a transitional period of gradually stepping down from full-time work to full-time retirement (Feldman, 1994; Shultz, 2003). Even this term, however is becoming a bit of a misnomer. Post-retirement work can take a variety of forms (Wang, Adams, Beehr, & Shultz, 2009). It may be full- or part-time, with one's pre-retirement employer or some other (including self-employment). It may be continuous or include alternating between periods of work and non-work. It can involve the same or different types of work than one did during one's earlier career, and it may be motivated by a variety of reasons (Dendinger, Adams, & Jacobson, 2005; Loi & Shultz, 2007; Wang et al., 2009). Regardless of the form it may take or the reasons for it, many older workers express a desire to continue working after they have formally retired (Bond, Galinsky, Kim, & Brownfield, 2005; Brown, 2005). This desire among older workers and current retirees to continue in paid work has the effect of expanding an employer's internal and external labor markets.

Retention

The key HR issue for the internal labor market (an organization's current employees) is retention. Retention efforts can be aimed at retaining workers in the organization on a full-time basis (delaying retirement altogether) or part-time basis. A study conducted by Hewitt Associates found that 61% of the employers they surveyed indicated that they have or will develop programs to retain targeted employees nearing retirement (Miller, 2008). Owing to the downturn in the economy over the past several years and in response to changes in public pension (e.g., social security) policies, a large number of workers intend to continue working full-time (Agewave, 2010). Retaining employees to work on a part-time basis involves the use of phased retirement and contingent work arrangements. Phased retirement refers to the continuing employment of current employees at a reduced workload. It does not involve a separation from the organization before commencing. Formal phased retirement programs offered to all employees tend to be relatively less common than informal programs. Studies estimate that between 6% and 22% of employing organizations use formal programs, and approximately 50% to 65% offer informal phased retirement on a case-by-case basis (Bond, Galinsky, Kim, & Brownfield, 2005; Hutchens & Grace-Martin, 2006; SHRM, 2008). Contingent work arrangements include approaches such as rehiring retired workers as independent contractors and as "temporary" workers through staffing organizations (Shultz, 2001). These work arrangements do involve employees separating from the organizations before they commence.

An individual's decision to delay retirement and/or pursue post-retirement employment with one's current employer is based on a complex set of factors that include individual differences, contextual factors, and work-related variables (Adams & Beehr, 2003; Beehr & Bennett, 2007; Feldman, 1994). Many of the individual differences such as demographic characteristics and work-related preferences, as well as contextual factors such as the state of the larger economy, are beyond the control of any particular organization. Work-related variables such as working conditions, pay, and benefits are more directly influenced by the organization. These work-related variables can be used to persuade employees who would otherwise retire to continue working for their current employer. As already discussed, workers who have greater accumulated income and have reached pension eligibility are more likely to retire. Thus, the types of benefit plans

offered can have the effect of encouraging continued work with one's current employer.

In addition, workers with positive attitudes about work are more likely to retire later than those with negative attitudes (Adams & Beehr, 1998; Luchak, Pohler & Gellatly, 2008; Madvig & Shultz, 2008; Taylor & Shore, 1995). An organization wanting to retain older workers would need to develop HR practices and policies that contribute to such positive attitudes among older workers. For example, one recent study found that HR practices such as training and development targeting older workers were positively related to perceptions of organizational support, which was, in turn, related to intention to remain with one's employer (Armstrong-Stassen & Ursel, 2009). Of course, organizations can also try to match working conditions to employee preferences. For instance, evidence suggests that workers prefer flexible schedules, which may lead organizations to respond by developing specific flexible work options (Matz-Costa & Pitts-Catsouphes, 2010).

Recruitment

When considering the external labor market (those who do not work for the organization), the key issue is recruitment. Recruitment is the process of attracting potential employees to apply for open positions in an organization. In one national study of 578 organizations, approximately 62% had taken steps to recruit an age-diverse workforce (Pitts-Catsouphes, Smyer, Matz-Costa, & Kane, 2007). Much of the research on applicant attraction suggests that it is based on objective and subjective characteristics of the job (e.g., pay, type of work, etc.) and the organization (e.g., organizational image), the applicants' perceptions of the fit between these characteristics and their own preferences, and the competence and credibility of the recruiter (Chapman, Uggerslev, Carroll, Piasentin, & Jones, 2005; Lievens & Highhouse, 2003).

An organization wishing to engage in the targeted recruitment of retirees can use a number of approaches to attract them. One approach would be to attempt to match the characteristics of the job and organization to those that are generally preferred by older workers. For instance, research shows that there are several main HR practices related to retirees returning to work. These include (1) flexible work options; (2) training and development opportunities; (3) new, challenging, and meaningful work assignments; (4) improved compensation; (5) unbiased feedback and performance evaluation; and (6) recognition and respect (Armstrong-Stassen,

2008a, 2008b; Brown, Aumann, Pitts-Catsouphes, Galinsky, & Bond, 2010). In order to be effective in recruitment, these types of practices have to be communicated in a manner that signals to retirees that the organization values their contributions (Rau & Adams, 2005). Of course, they also have to be communicated via appropriate channels. Organizations have a number of options for targeting retirees who may be active or passive job seekers (Adams & Rau, 2004). Among others, these include (1) direct mail, (2) newspapers/internet, (3) posters in places that retirees frequent, (4) radio, (5) employment agencies, (6) open houses/informational seminars, and (7) networking and referrals (Fyock, 2005).

Like the choice to engage in any other HR activities, the choice to engage in targeted efforts to retain and recruit retirees is based on the strategy of the organization. To begin, it should be recognized that retention and recruitment are only one set of options for ensuring that the work of the organization gets accomplished. There are alternatives that might better fit a particular organization (e.g., job redesign and redistribution, outsourcing, off-shoring, etc.) that can be considered. Organizations choose between retention, recruitment, or some mix of the two based on their advantages and disadvantages. Retention strategies can have the advantages of facilitating knowledge transfer, signaling a long-term commitment to employees, reducing costs for on-boarding, etc. The disadvantages of retention strategies can include a lack of new ideas and approaches, difficulty meeting affirmative action goals, blocked mobility channels for younger workers, etc. Recruitment strategies are just the opposite. They have the advantages of being able to bring in new ideas, helping to meet diversity and affirmative action goals, opening mobility channels, etc. Recruitment strategies have disadvantages in that they can be more costly to implement, they create costs for on-boarding new employees, etc.

Both retention and recruitment can be challenging to implement for organizational reasons as well as legal and regulatory reasons (Hill, 2010; Noble & Harper, 2010). Many of the suggestions for both retention and recruiting rely on the notion of creating part-time work (reduced responsibility, fewer hours per day, fewer days per week, seasonal employment) and creating contingent work arrangements. While these are attractive to retirees, part-time work is not the most optimal configuration for all jobs. In addition, organizations might have legitimate concerns about the job performance of some of its

employees. In this case, certain retirements, like other types of turnover, may be very functional. As a result, these broadly offered retiree retention programs might not make as much sense as limited and focused retention programs.

It is also true that some efforts aimed at retaining older workers can have the opposite effect. That is, rather than retaining workers who would have retired, they may encourage workers who otherwise would have continued working full-time to retire in favor of part-time work (Greller & Stroh, 2003). Indeed, phased retirement and contingent work arrangements have been used as early retirement incentives as opposed to incentives for continued work (Feldman, 2003). There are also legal barriers to phased retirement programs (Hill, 2010; Noble & Harper, 2010). For example, the Pension Protection Act of 2006 relaxed some restrictions on in-service distributions from defined benefit plans while continuing to work for the plan sponsor (e.g., for those 62 and older or who have reached the plan's normal retirement age; Purcell, 2009b). However, there is still little guidance about how to administer these distributions, and some have raised concerns about the legality of targeting older employees for part-time work if that part-time work is at a reduced pay and benefits (Hill, 2010).

Considering the advantages, disadvantages, challenges to implementation, and costs, organizations attempt to choose the mix of retention and recruitment activities that is best aligned with their strategy. Clearly, organizations that are not experiencing or expecting to experience vacancies and those that may be in retrenchment are not likely to be interested in retention or recruitment to any great extent. Organizations adopting a cost leadership strategy with a focus on routine and standardized work processes and/or a workforce concentrated in jobs that require skills that are widely available in the labor market can benefit from broad recruiting approaches (seek to attract large numbers of applicants). In this case, recruiting retirees may be a small part of their broader approach. An organization adopting an innovation strategy where new ideas and approaches are important might be better served by recruitment strategies than retention strategies. An organization adopting a differentiation strategy, which relies on firm-specific knowledge and relationships or requires specialized skills not generally available in the labor market, is likely to benefit from retention strategies and narrowly targeted recruitment efforts.

Conclusion

According to the Government Accountability Office (GAO, 2005), most organizations in the United States have not yet made hiring and retaining older workers a priority. According to AARP's list of "Best Employers for Workers Over 50," some notable exceptions include Cornell University, First Horizon National Corporation, National Institutes of Health, S. C. Johnson & Son, and Massachusetts Institute of Technology (AARP, 2010). These employers engage in a variety of practices, some of which we described in this chapter, to attract, retain, and motivate older workers. However, their practices are not identical. Rather, these organizations design recruitment, training and career development, workplace accommodations, alternative work options such as flexible scheduling, job sharing and phased retirement, employee health, pension, and retiree benefits that are consistent with their overall business strategy. The fact that they give such careful attention to the impact of their policies and practices on older workers sets them apart from most other employers.

From our review of the literature, we can derive several reasons why most employers have yet to fully develop policies and practices pertaining to retirement. First, many employers have not yet felt the pinch of retirements that has been forecasted for several years. While their workforces are aging, employees are choosing to work longer for a variety of social and economic reasons. While these organizations may be feeling some of the effects, such as lower motivation, difficulties with training, and/or increased physical health problems, the effects are still relatively subtle. Until the problems become acute or there is a wave of retirements that creates a crisis of knowledge within the organization, other issues are likely to continue to take priority.

Second, many organizations are new to the concept of strategic HR planning. As such, HR continues to strive to be perceived as a strategic business partner that can add value to an organization. As HR departments increase in sophistication and become strategic business partners, we would expect them to expand their strategic planning efforts and hence become more aware of, and prepared for, issues related to management of an older and retiring workforce.

Third, given the complexity of the issues regarding retirement, organizations may simply be confused as to how to manage the problems they are experiencing. Motivation is a good case in point. While managers struggle with how to motivate older workers or those nearing retirement, they often continue to rely on the same methods of motivation that worked when these individuals were younger. They may, for example, offer carrots in the form of higher pay or sticks in the form of disciplinary action. However, as we have seen, older workers' values, needs, and expectations are different from younger workers', and these tools are not likely to be effective. Hence, what is required is for HR to step back from what has worked in the past, educate themselves on the unique features of an older workforce, and evaluate their current policies and practices against what is needed to support the business strategy.

Fourth, employers cite several barriers to offering more opportunities to older workers. According to the GAO's study (GAO, 2005), these barriers include federal pension regulations prohibiting the distribution of DB pension benefits while an employee is still employed with the organization, older workers' resistance to change and/or new technology, difficulties in rehiring retired workers who are trying to maintain income levels that would still allow them to collect their Social Security and/or Medicare benefits, and societal norms that condition workers to expect retirement by age 65 (or younger).

Finally, we cannot ignore the fact that older workers are still subjected to stereotyping and discrimination. In their review of the age discrimination literature, Wood, Wilkinson, and Harcourt (2008) noted that older workers are underrepresented in the labor market, find it more difficult to re-enter the workforce once they have left it, take significantly longer to find alternative employment, and are less likely to secure a job interview than younger workers. Older workers are stereotyped as being less flexible, resistant to change, less willing to accept new technology, less alert, less reliable (due to health issues), less "trainable," and less productive (Wood et al., 2008). Further, studies on older workers in many countries find that high numbers of them *perceive* that they are discriminated against (e.g., McMullin & Marshall, 2001; Ginn & Arber, 1996).

This list illustrates the challenges associated with bringing retirement into the strategic planning process. To help organizations prepare for the workforce of the future, researchers and educators must work to raise awareness, encourage strategic planning, bring the existing research to bear on older worker issues, and resolve some of the unanswered questions affecting the intersection of HR and older workers. As to this latter point, we offer several suggestions for future research.

Future Directions

To improve the degree to which organizations engage in strategic planning, it would be helpful to identify more clearly (and empirically) the advantages to organizations of engaging in HR planning and succession planning. Research that can establish the extent to which HR planning and succession planning improve HR's strategic value to the organization, as proposed by Ulrich and Beatty (2001), would help to lend these practices credibility and much-needed top management support. In addition, we know that HR planning and succession planning processes can be improved. Research aimed at helping organizations do a better job of both will address the lack of confidence many managers feel with their current planning practices (Barnett & Davis, 2008).

Given the lack of preparedness for retirement by so many workers, there is a great need for research addressing the psychology behind retirement planning and preparation. Adams and Rau (in press) called for additional research exploring why certain demographic groups plan better than others, the role of personality traits in financial planning, and/or psychological barriers to financial planning. This work would allow HR managers to design policies that help to prepare their workforce and/or design interventions (e.g., training) aimed at encouraging financial preparedness.

In the area of motivation, there is a need for more research addressing the relationship between age and motivation, a meta-analysis to estimate age-related effects and identify moderating variables, and, perhaps most importantly, conceptual work that can offer a comprehensive theoretical framework that can incorporate the various perspectives presented/offered by researchers.

In this chapter, we have attempted to highlight some of the key strategic HR decisions that bring the worlds of strategic HR and psychology together. We would be remiss, however, if we failed to mention that there are many other decisions made by organizations regarding the management of older and retirement-age workers that we did not address presently. Each functional area of HR must be considered. In addition to staffing planning, recruitment, benefits, and motivation/performance management, organizations must design training and development programs, compensation structures, employee relations programs, and occupational safety and health programs that meet the needs of an aging workforce. It should be clear by now that the needs of an aging workforce will need to permeate the very culture of the organization.

This cannot be achieved without careful strategic planning. Faced with an aging workforce, most organizations will need to examine their HR policies and practices to ensure that the treatment of older workers is both ethical and legal. But beyond the demands of ethics and legal compliance, anticipated skilled labor shortages mean that organizations need to think more strategically about how they are utilizing the potential of their older workforce. For some organizations, it may mean a focus on retention and seeking labor in unusual places (e.g., among the retired population). For others it may mean retrenchment and downsizing in ways that allow the organization to maintain its knowledge base and manage its key resources more effectively. Today's organizations must resist the temptation to follow the crowd and instead think strategically about which policies and practices make the most sense in their unique competitive situation. In any case, it is clear that HR policies related to retirement will play a key role in meeting the business needs of the future.

References

Aaronson, S., & Coronado, J. (2005). *Are firms or workers behind the shift away from DB pension plan?* Board of Governors of the Federal Reserve System (U.S.), Finance and Economic Discussion Series. Washington, DC: Federal Reserve Board.

AARP. (2010). *AARP best employers for workers over 50.* Washington, DC: Author. Retrieved from http://www.aarp.org/work/employee-benefits/info-09-2009/Best-Employers_Winners_2009.html.

Adams, G. A., & Beehr, T. A. (1998). Turnover and retirement: A comparison of their similarities and differences. *Personnel Psychology, 51,* 643–665.

Adams, G. A., & Beehr, T. A. (2003). *Retirement: Reasons, processes, and results.* New York, NY: Springer.

Adams, G., & Rau, B. L. (2004). Job seeking among retirees seeking bridge employment. *Personnel Psychology, 57*(3), 719–744.

Adams, G. A., & Rau, B. (2011). Putting off tomorrow to do what you want today: Planning for retirement. *American Psychologist, 66,* 180–192.

Agewave. (2010). *Retirement at the tipping point: The year that changed everything.* Conducted by Harris Interactive. Retrieved from http://www.agewave.com/RetirementTippingPoint.pdf

Argote, L., & Ingram, P. (2000). Knowledge transfer: A basis for competitive advantage in firms. *Organizational Behavior & Human Decision Processes, 82*(1), 150–169.

Armstrong-Stassen, M. (2008a). Organisational practices and the post-retirement employment experience of older workers. *Human Resource Management Journal, 18*(1), 36–53.

Armstrong-Stassen, M. (2008b). Human resource practices for mature workers—and why aren't employers using them? *Asia Pacific Journal of Human Resources, 46*(3), 334–352.

Armstrong-Stassen, M., & Ursel, N. (2009). Perceived organizational support, career satisfaction, and the retention of older workers. *Journal of Occupational & Organizational Psychology, 82*(1), 201–220.

Barnett, R., & Davis, S. (2008). Creating greater success in succession planning. *Advances in Developing Human Resources, 10*(5), 721–739.

Bayer, P., Bernheim, B., & Scholz, J. (2009). The effects of financial education in the workplace: Evidence from a survey of employers. *Economic Inquiry, 47*(4), 605–624.

Becker, B. E., & Huselid, M. A. (1998). High performance work systems and firm performance: A synthesis of research and managerial implications. *Research in Personnel and Human Resource Management, 16,* 53–101.

Becker, B. E., & Huselid, M. A. (1999). Strategic human resource management in five leading firms. *Human Resource Management, 38,* 287–301.

Beehr, T. A., & Bennett, M. M. (2007). Examining retirement from a multi-level perspective. In K. S. Shultz & G. A. Adams (Eds.), *Aging and work in the 21st century* (pp. 277–302). Mahwah, NJ: Lawrence Erlbaum.

Benartzi, S., & Thaler, R. (2007). Heuristics and biases in retirement savings behavior. *Journal of Economic Perspectives, 21*(3), 81–104.

Bond, J. T., Galinsky, E., Kim, S. S., & Brownfield, E. (2005). *National study of employers.* New York, NY: Families and Work Institute.

Boxall, P., & Purcell, J. (2008). *Strategy and human resource management* (2nd ed.). Basingsoke, UK: Palgrave Macmillan.

Broadbent, J., Palumbo, M., & Woodman, E. (2006). *The shift from defined benefit to defined contribution pension plans— Implications for asset allocation and risk management.* Report prepared for a Working Group on Institutional Investors, Global Savings and Asset Allocation established by the Committee on the Global Financial System. Retrieved from http://www.bis.org/publ/wgpapers/cgfs27broadbent3.pdf.

Brown, K. S. (2005). *Attitudes of individuals 50 and older toward phased retirement.* Washington, DC: AARP Knowledge Management.

Brown, M., Aumann, K., Pitt-Catsouphes, M. Galinsky, E., & Bond, J. (2010, July). *Working in retirement: A 21st century phenomenon.* Families and Work Institute. Retrieved from http://familiesandwork.org/site/research/reports/workingin-retirement.pdf.

Bureau of Labor Statistics. (2008). *Spotlight on older workers.* Retrieved from http://www.bls.gov/spotlight/2008/older_workers/.

Bureau of Labor Statistics. (2009a, March). Retirement benefits: Access, participation, and take up rates data table. *Employee Benefits Survey.* Retrieved from http://www.bls.gov/ncs/ebs/benefits/2009/ownership/civilian/table02a.htm

Bureau of Labor Statistics. (2009b, March). Health-related benefits: Access data table. *Employee Benefits Survey.* Retrieved from http://www.bls.gov/ncs/ebs/benefits/2009/ownership/civilian/table39a.htm.

Bureau of Labor Statistics. (2010a, June 9). Employer costs for employee compensation news release text. *Economic News Release.* Retrieved from http://www.bls.gov/news.release/ecec.nr0.htm.

Bureau of Labor Statistics. (2010b, August 30). Disparities in automatic enrollment plan availability. *Compensation and Working Conditions.* Retrieved from http://www.bls.gov/opub/cwc/cm20100824ar01p1.htm.

Bureau of Labor Statistics. (2010c, June 9). Financial benefits: Access data table. *Employee Benefits Survey.* Retrieved from http://www.bls.gov/ncs/ebs/benefits/2010/ownership/civilian/table25a.htm.

Calo, T. (2008). Talent management in the era of the aging workforce: The critical role of knowledge transfer. *Public Personnel Management, 37*(4), 403.

Chapman, D., Uggerslev, K., Carroll, S., Piasentin, K., & Jones, D. (2005). Applicant attraction to organizations and job choice: A meta-analytic review of the correlates of recruiting outcomes. *Journal of Applied Psychology, 90*(5), 928–944.

Claes, R., & Heymans, M. (2008). HR professionals' views on work motivation and retention of older workers: A focus group study. *The Career Development International, 13*(2), 95–111.

Clark, R., d'Ambrose, M., McDermed, A., & Sawant, K. (2006). Retirement plans and savings decisions: The role of information and education. *PEF, 5*(1), 45–67.

de Lange, A. H., Taris, T. W., Jansen, P. G. W., Smulders, P., Houtman, I. L. D., & Kompier, M. A. J. (2006). Age as a factor in the relation between work and mental health: Results from the longitudinal TAS study. In J. Houdmont & S. McIntyre (Eds.), *Occupational health psychology: European perspectives on research, education and practice* (Vol. 1, pp. 21–45). Maia, Portugal: ISMAI.

de Lange, A. H., Van Yperen, N., Van der Heijden, B., & Bal, P. (2010). Dominant achievement goals of older workers and their relationship with motivation-related outcomes. *Journal of Vocational Behavior, 77*(1), 118–125.

Deci, E., & Ryan, R. (1991). A motivational approach to self: Integration in personality. *Nebraska Symposium on Motivation, 1990: Perspectives on motivation* (pp. 237–288). Lincoln, NE: University of Nebraska Press.

DeLong, D. (2004). *Lost knowledge: Confronting the threat of an aging workforce.* New York, NY: Oxford University Press.

Delong, D. (2008). Five keys to decisions vis-a-vis an ageing workforce. *Inside Knowledge, 11*(5). Retrieved from http://www.ikmagazine.com/xq/asp/txtSearch.DELONG/exactphrase.1/sid.9B1CAF41-CD0A-4B5D-B168-4480F17D502B/articleid.01D4A543-A588-429C-BB1F-0DFF2693120C/qx/display.htm.

Dendinger, V., Adams, G., & Jacobson, J. (2005). Reasons for working and their relationship to retirement attitudes, job satisfaction and occupational self-efficacy of bridge employees. *The International Journal of Aging & Human Development, 61*(1), 21–35.

EBRI: Employee Benefit Research Institute. (2008). Retirement annuity and employment-based pension income among individuals age 50 and over. *Notes, 29*(11), 2.

Fegley, S. (2006). *2006 succession planning survey report.* Alexandria, VA: The Society for Human Resource Management.

Feldman, D. (2003). Endgame: The design and implementation of early retirement incentive programs. In G. A. Adams & T. A. Beehr (Eds.), *Retirement: Reasons, processes, and results* (pp. 115–135). New York, NY: Springer.

Feldman, D. C. (1994). The decision to retire early: A review and conceptualization. *Academy of Management Review, 19,* 285–311.

Forteza, J. A., & Prieto, J. M. (1994). Aging and work behavior. In H. C. Triandis, M. D. Dunnette, & L. M. Hough (Eds.) *Handbook of industrial and organizational psychology* (2nd ed., Vol. 4, pp. 446–483). Palo Alto, CA: Consulting Psychologist Press.

Fyock, C. (2005, December). Strategies for recruiting workers over 50. *Society for Human Resource Management.* Retrieved from http://www.shrm.org/hrdisciplines/staffingmanagement/Articles/Pages/CMS_014873.aspx.

Government Accountability Office. (2005). *Older workers labor can help employers and employees plan better for the future* (GAO-06-80). Washington, DC: Author.

Giandrea, M., Cahill, K., & Quinn, J. (2009). Bridge jobs: A comparison across cohorts. *Research on Aging, 31*(5), 549–576.

Ginn, J., Arber, S. (1996) Gender, age and attitudes to retirement in mid-life. *Ageing and Society, 16,* 27–55.

Gobeski, K., & Beehr, T. (2009). How retirees work: Predictors of different types of bridge employment. *Journal of Organizational Behavior, 30*(3), 401–425.

Government Accounting Office. (2009). *Automatic enrollment shows promise for some workers, but proposals to broaden retirement savings for other workers could face challenges.* Washington, DC: Author.

Greller, M., & Stroh, L. (2003). Extending work lives: Are current approaches tools or talismans? In G. A. Adams & T. A. Beehr (Eds.), *Retirement: Reasons, processes, and results* (pp. 115–135). New York, NY: Springer.

Heneman, H. G., III, & Sandver, M. G. (1977). Markov analysis in human resource administration: Applications and limitations. *Academy of Management Review, 2*(4), 535–542.

Hershey, D., Mowen, J., & Jacobs-Lawson, J. (2003). An experimental comparison of retirement planning intervention seminars. *Educational Gerontology, 29*(4), 339–359.

Hershey, D., Walsh, D., Brougham, R., Carter, S., & Farrell, A. (1998). Challenges of training pre-retirees to make sound financial planning decisions. *Educational Gerontology, 24*(5), 447.

Hill, T. M. (2010). Why doesn't every employer have a phased retirement program? *Benefits Quarterly, Fourth Quarter,* 29–39.

Huselid, M. A. (1995). The impact of human resource management practices on turnover, productivity, and corporate financial performance. *Academy of Management Journal, 38,* 635–672.

Hutchens, R., & Grace-Martin, K. (2006). Employer willingness to permit phased retirement: Why are some more willing than others? *Industrial & Labor Relations Review, 59*(4), 525–546.

Kanfer, R. (1987). Task-specific motivation: An integrative approach to issues of measurement, mechanisms, processes, and determinants. *Journal of Social and Clinical Psychology, 5,* 237–264.

Kanfer, R., & Ackerman, P. L. (2004). Aging, adult development, and work motivation. *Academy of Management Review, 29*(3), 440–458.

Kooij, D., de Lange, A., Jansen, P., & Dikkers, J. (2008). Older workers' motivation to continue to work: Five meanings of age. *Journal of Managerial Psychology, 23*(4), 364–394.

Lepak, D., & Snell, S. (2002). Examining the human resource architecture: The relationships among human capital, employment, and human resource configurations. *Journal of Management, 28,* 517–543.

Lievens, F., & Highhouse, S. (2003). The relation of instrumental and symbolic attributes to a company's attractiveness as an employer. *Personnel Psychology, 56*(1), 75–102.

Locke, E., & Latham, G. (1990). Work motivation: The high performance cycle. In U. Kleinbeck, -H. Quast, H. Thierry, & H. Hacker (Eds.), *Work motivation* (pp. 3–25). Hillsdale, NJ: Lawrence Erlbaum.

Loi, J., & Shultz, K. (2007). Why older adults seek employment: Differing motivations among subgroups. *Journal of Applied Gerontology, 26*(3), 274–289.

Luchak, A., Pohler, D., & Gellatly, I. (2008). When do committed employees retire? The effects of organizational commitment on retirement plans under a defined-benefit pension plan. *Human Resource Management, 47*(3), 581–599.

Lusardi, A., & Mitchell, O. (2007). Financial literacy and retirement preparedness: Evidence and implications for financial education. *Business Economics, 42*(1), 35.

Madvig, T., & Shultz, K. (2008). Modeling individuals' post-retirement behaviors toward their former organization. *Journal of Workplace Behavioral Health, 23*(1/2), 17–49.

Matz-Costa, C., & Pitt-Catsouphes, M. (2010). Workplace flexibility as an organizational response to the aging of the workforce: A comparison of nonprofit and for-profit organizations. *Journal of Social Service Research, 36*(1), 68–80.

Maurer, T. J. (2001). Career-relevant learning and development, worker age, and beliefs about self-efficacy for development. *Journal of Management, 27,* 123–140.

McEvoy, G. M., & Cascio, W. R. (1989) Cumulative evidence on the relationship between employee age and job performance. *Journal of Applied Psychology, 74*(1), 11–17.

McMullin, J. A., & Marshall, V. W. (2001). Ageism, age relations and garment industry work in Montreal. *The Gerontologist, 41*(1), 111–122.

MetLife. (2009, December). *The emerging retirement model study.* New York, NY: Metropolitan Life Insurance Company.

Miller, S. (2008, August 8). Retiring boomers prompt increase in phased retirement. *Society for Human Resource Management.* Retrieved from http://www.shrm.org/hrdisciplines/ benefits/Articles/Pages/RetiringBoomersPromptPhasedRetirement.aspx.

Miller, S. (2009, November 4). SHRM poll looks at financial education in the workplace. *Society for Human Resource Management.* Retrieved from http://www.shrm.org/hrdisciplines/benefits/Articles/Pages/FinancialEducationPoll.aspx.

Munnell, A., Webb, A., & Golub-Sass, F. (2009). The national retirement risk index: After the crash. *Center for Retirement Research at Boston College,* Issue Brief 9–22.

Nahapiet, J., & Ghoshal, S. (1998). Social Capital, intellectual capital, and the organizational advantage. *Academy of Management Review, 23*(2), 242–266.

Ng, T., & Feldman, D. (2010). The relationships of age with job attitudes: A meta-analysis. *Personnel Psychology, 63*(3), 677–718.

Nichols, G. A. (2008). Reviewing and redesigning retirement plans. *Compensation & Benefits Review, 40,* 40–47.

Noble, F. P., & Harper, E. (2010). Strategy and policy for phased retirement. *Benefits Quarterly, Third Quarter,* 11–14.

Nonaka, I., & Takeuchi, H. (1995). *The knowledge creating company.* New York, NY: Oxford University Press.

Office of Personnel Management. (2008). *An analysis of federal employee retirement data: Predicting future retirements and examining factors relevant to retiring from the federal service.* Washington, DC: Author.

Peterson, S., & Spiker, B. (2005). Establishing the positive contributory value of older workers: A positive psychology perspective. *Organizational Dynamics, 34*(2), 153–167.

Pfeffer, J. (1994). Competitive advantage through people. *California Management Review, 36*(2), 9–28.

Piktialis, D., & Greenes, K. (2008). Bridging the gaps: How to transfer knowledge in today's multigenerational workplace (Report No. 1428-08-RR). New York, NY: The Conference Board.

Pitt-Catsouphes, M., Smyer, M., Matz-Costa, C., & Kane, K. (2007, July). The national study report: Phase II of the national study of business strategy and workforce development. *The Center on Aging & Work/Workplace Flexibility*. Retrieved from http://agingandwork.bc.edu/documents/RH04_NationalStudy_03-07_002.pdf.

Polanyi, M. (1966). *The tacit dimension*. London, England: Routledge & Kegan Paul.

Porter, M. E. (1985). *Competitive strategy*. New York, NY: The Free Press.

Purcell, P. (2009a). *Retirement savings and household wealth in 2007* (Congressional Research Service No. 7-5700). Washington, DC: Congressional Research Service.

Purcell, P. (2009b). Older workers: Employment and retirement trends. *Journal of Pension Planning & Compliance, 36*(2), 70–88.

Rau, B., & Adams, G. (2005). Attracting retirees to apply: Desired organizational characteristics of bridge employment. *Journal of Organizational Behavior, 26*(6), 649–660.

Rhodes, S. R. (1983). Age-related differences in work attitudes and behaviour: A review and conceptual analysis. *Psychological Bulletin, 93*(2), 328–367.

Robinson, C., & Clark, R. (2010). Retiree health insurance and disengagement from a career job. *Journal of Labor Research, 31*(3), 247–262.

Rothwell, W. J. (2010). The future of succession planning. *Training & Development, 64*(9), 51–54.

Rousseau, D. M. (1989) Psychological and implied contracts in organizations. *Employee Rights and Responsibilities Journal, 2*, 121–139.

Rousseau, D. M. (1995). *Promises in action: Psychological contracts in organizations*. Newbury Park, CA: Sage.

Schaie, K. W. (1996). *Intellectual development in adulthood: The Seattle Longitudinal Study*. New York, NY: Cambridge University Press.

Schuler, R. S., & Jackson. S. E. (1987). Linking competitive strategies with human resource management practices. *The Academy of Management Executive, 1*(3), 207–219.

SHRM. (2008). Employee benefits survey. *Society for Human Resource Management*. Alexandria, VA: Author.

Shultz, K. (2001). The new contingent workforce: Examining the bridge employment options of mature workers. *International Journal of Organization Theory & Behavior, 4*(3/4), 247.

Shultz, K. S. (2003). Bridge employment: Work after retirement. In G. A. Adams & T. A. Beehr (Eds.), *Retirement: Reasons, processes, and results* (pp. 215–241). New York, NY: Springer.

Shultz. K. S., & Wang, M. (2011). Psychological perspectives on the changing nature of retirement. *American Psychologist, 66*, 170–179.

Slagter, F. (2007). Knowledge management among the older workforce. *Journal of Knowledge Management, 11*(4), 82–96.

Society for Human Resource Management/AARP. (1998). *Older workers survey*. Alexandria, VA: Author.

Stevens, R. (2010). Managing human capital: How to use knowledge management to transfer knowledge in today's multigenerational workforce. *International Business Research, 3*(3), 77–83.

Taylor, M. A., & Shore, L. M. (1995). Predictors of planned retirement age: An application of Beehr's model. *Psychology and Aging, 10*, 76–83.

Tsui, A., Pearce, J., Porter, L., & Tripoli, A. (1997). Alternative approaches to the employee organization relationship: Does investment in employees pay off? *Academy of Management Journal, 40*, 1089–1121.

Ulrich, D., & Beatty, R. (2001). From partners to players: Extending the HR playing field. *Human Resource Management, 40*, 293–308.

Waldman, D. A., & Avolio, B. J. (1986). A meta-analysis of age difference in job performance. *Journal of Applied Psychology, 71*, 33–38.

Wang, M., Adams, G. A., Beehr, T. A., & Shultz, K. S. (2009) Bridge employment and retirement: Issues and opportunities during the latter part of one's career. In G. S. Baugh & S. E. Sullivan (Eds.), *Maintaining focus, energy, and options over the career* (pp. 135–162). Charlotte, NC: Information Age.

Wang, S., & Noe, R. (2010). Knowledge sharing: A review and directions for future research. *Human Resource Management Review, 20*(2), 115–131.

Warr P. (1997). Age, work, and mental health. In K. W. Schaie & C. Schooler (Eds.), *The impact of work on older adults* (pp. 252–296). New York, NY: Springer.

Warr, P. (2001). Age and work behaviour: Physical attributes, cognitive abilities, knowledge, personality traits, and motives. *International Review of Industrial and Organizational Psychology, 16*, 1–36.

Westerman, J., & Sundali, J. (2005). The transformation of employee pensions in the United States: Through the looking glass of organizational behavior. *Journal of Organizational Behavior, 26*(1), 99–103.

Wood, S. (1999). Human resource management and performance. *International Journal of Management Reviews, 1*, 367–413.

Wood, G., Wilkinson, A., & Harcourt, M. (2008). Age discrimination and working life: perspectives and contestations—a review of the contemporary literature. *International Journal of Management Reviews, 10*(4), 425–442.

Zack, M., McKeen, J., & Singh, S. (2009). Knowledge management and organizational performance: An exploratory analysis. *Journal of Knowledge Management, 13*(6), 392–409.

Economic Theories of Retirement

John Laitner *and* Amanda Sonnega

Abstract

This chapter presents an economist's analysis of how households decide when to retire. It lays out a dynamic model of household behavior in which age of retirement and year-by-year saving/consumption decisions are choice variables. We describe necessary conditions for a solution and suggest interpretations. The model highlights the roles of growth in household consumption expenditures with age, and the age trajectory of earnings, as determinants of the optimal time of retirement. We explain how key parameters might be estimated—and note a set of recent estimates. Then we present two illustrative applications: we derive the model's forecast of the effect of greater longevity on retirement ages, and we examine the consequences for retirement of a stylized Social Security system. Finally, we reference a number of papers that extend and generalize the basic framework that we present.

Key Words: retirement, optimal age of retirement, economic theories of retirement, Social Security and retirement, Social Security, longevity and retirement, compression of morbidity, life-cycle model

This chapter presents an economist's analysis of how households decide when to retire. To do so, it lays out a model of household behavior in which age of retirement is a choice variable. The model is highly stylized. Nevertheless, we argue that it can be extremely useful for studying the determinants of retirement, that its highly structured form facilitates statistical and econometric analysis, and that it has great flexibility for incorporating extensions of specific interest to particular investigations.

The retirement decision is a special case of the general problem of determining how much time a household should allocate to labor as opposed to leisure. We analyze this problem in a life-cycle framework. In the model, a household has two relatively distinct periods of life. In the first, the household participates in the labor market and earns wages. Anticipating a time later in life when it will not be able, or not want, to work, the household saves a portion of its earnings. In its second period, the household draws upon its savings to maintain its consumption despite being retired. In choosing its age of retirement, the household weighs the advantage of more earnings, hence the ability to afford more consumption now and in the future, against the advantage of more leisure.

For the sake of clarity and brevity, this chapter adopts the following conditions and restrictions:

- We study only the behavior of individual households. On the one hand, this means that we do not attempt to model the functioning of the economy as a whole. That is to say, our analysis is "partial equilibrium" in nature.[1] On the other hand, it means that we do not attempt to model employers' strategic behavior vis-à-vis their employees. Conceivably, for example, employers consciously set the age trajectory of their workers' earnings, and/or the parameters of their firms' pension plans, to reduce voluntary departures and to strengthen incentives for productive work effort.[2] Nonetheless, we limit our attention to studying workers' optimal responses to the earnings trajectories that they face. Likewise, we assume that workers search among employers for those with pension arrangements consistent with their own preferences of when to retire.

• We assume that households value leisure time, and, aside from compensation considerations, always prefer leisure time to time at work.

• We study households' planning for retirement and the optimal outcomes emerging from such planning. Our analysis does not feature shocks that catch households totally by surprise.

The organization of this chapter is as follows. The first section develops a static model designed to introduce the basic elements of our analysis. The second section presents a fully dynamic model and analyzes the primary determinants of retirement within it. The third section presents two illustrative applications: we use a calibrated version of the dynamic model to investigate the potential effects of longer life spans (with "compression of morbidity"), and we ask how a stylized Social Security program might affect optimal retirement ages. The fourth section provides references for extensions and generalizations of the dynamic model. The final section concludes.

The Static Model

The retirement decision is a special case of the general problem of determining how much time to allocate to labor as opposed to leisure. We begin with a standard, static model in the latter vein. Section 2 extends the analysis to a more sophisticated framework suitable for a detailed study of retirement (where, however, a number of intuitions from the static model carry over).

Consider a one-person household. The household has L units of time. It must choose the part, say, ℓ, that it will devote to leisure. Its remaining time, $L-\ell$, is left for work. The wage rate is w. The household spends all of its earnings on consumption goods. It purchases c units of goods, each unit having price p.

The standard economic model has three components: (i) a description of household budgetary limitations, which usually depend upon externally given wages and prices; (ii) a description of the household's preferences; and (iii) a description of

any special constraints that the household faces. We have no special constraints in this section (but see section 2).

We begin with the budget. A household's earnings limit the quantity of goods that it can afford to consume. For the household to stay within its budget, we need

$$p \cdot c \leq (L - \ell) \cdot w.$$

Rearranging terms,

$$p \cdot c + w \cdot \ell \leq L \cdot w. \quad (1)$$

The right-hand side is the value of the household's time endowment. The left-hand side is the sum of the household's expenditures on goods, $p \cdot c$, and on leisure, $w \cdot \ell$.

Figure 10.1 graphs the household's "budget line." The budget line is the set of goods/leisure bundles, (c, ℓ), satisfying (1) with equality. In other words, the budget line is the set of bundles each costing the full amount that the household has to spend.

To determine what the household will choose to do, in addition to its budget line, we need to know its preferences over bundles of consumption goods and leisure (c, ℓ). A convenient way of proceeding is to treat the household as if it has a "utility function," say, $u(c, \ell)$. Such a function assigns a number of "utils" to any prospective bundle (c, ℓ) the household might acquire, with a higher number of utils denoting a bundle that is more preferred in the household's eyes. A utility function summarizes the household's underlying preferences: the household prefers (c^1, ℓ^1) to (c^0, ℓ^0) if and only if $u(c^1, \ell^1) > u(c^0, \ell^0)$.[3] A standard modeling assumption, maintained throughout this chapter, is that a household's preferences are fixed—they do not change, for example, if wages and prices do.

Although the elements of a household's budget line are generally directly observable, the household's preferences commonly are not. In practice, economists usually specify a plausible class of utility functions, indexed with one or more parameters, and then seek to estimate or calibrate the latter parameter(s). The parameter-selection process will need to utilize data on the household's past choices—or, if different households' preferences are alike, data on past choices of other households.

To specify a "plausible class" of functions, we identify properties of underlying preferences that we believe are universal. Two are important in this chapter.

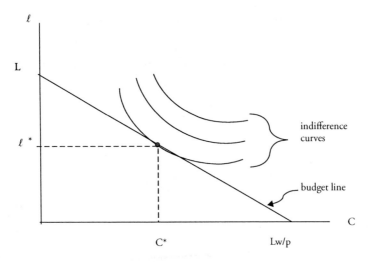

Figure 10.1 A household's budget lines and indifference curves

One property is "monotonicity of preferences": in usual cases, more is preferred to less. A corresponding utility function must be increasing in all arguments. In terms of derivatives,

$$u_c \equiv \frac{\partial u}{\partial c} > 0 \quad \text{and} \quad u_\ell \equiv \frac{\partial u}{\partial \ell} > 0.$$

A second property is "convexity of preferences," which we might think of as a desire for balance rather than extremes. To be more specific, for a given level of satisfaction u_0, graph a household's

indifference curve—the set of all bundles (c,ℓ) such that $u(c,\ell)=u_0$. See Figure 10.2. In the figure, (c_a,ℓ_a) and (c_b,ℓ_b) are alternative choices on the indifference curve—i.e., $u(c_a,\ell_a)=u_0=u(c_b,\ell_b)$.

Suppose we ask: If we take away x units of leisure, how much extra consumption would the household require to maintain the same level of satisfaction as before? Starting from (c_a,ℓ_a), the answer in Figure 10.2 is Δc_a. That is the change in consumption of goods that leaves us on the original indifference curve following a reduction in leisure of x units. Starting from (c_b,ℓ_b), the answer is Δc_b. In Figure 10.2,

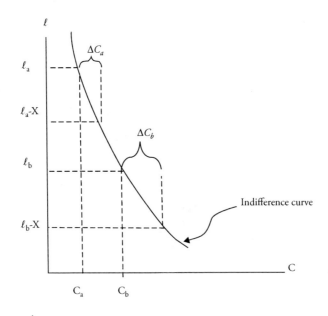

Figure 10.2 Indifference curve shapes

$$\Delta c_a < \Delta c_b \quad (2)$$

This is exactly the outcome we expect, for the following reason. At (c_a, ℓ_a), leisure is relatively abundant and goods are relatively scarce; hence, we expect that only a modest increment in goods will be required to offset an x-unit loss in leisure time. The reverse is true at (ℓ_b, c_b): goods are relatively abundant but leisure is relatively scarce. Thus, at (c_b, ℓ_b) a larger increase in goods will be needed to counterbalance an x-unit loss in leisure. This is the idea of "convexity of preferences." In terms of the picture, it leads to bow-shaped indifference curves.

A convenient way to ensure such an indifference curve shape is to choose a "concave" utility function $u(.,.)$.[4]

Returning to Figure 10.1, our household's choice point is (c^*, ℓ^*). Given a household's utility function $u(.)$, for each level of utility we can draw an indifference curve. Doing this repeatedly for different levels of utility, say, $u_0 < u_1 < u_2$, we can associate a family of indifference curves with the utility function. Figure 10.1 illustrates such a family. With monotonicity of preferences, the curves in the family further northeast correspond to higher satisfaction levels. At (c^*, ℓ^*), the household attains the highest satisfaction feasible within the scope of its budget.

Suppose that we have decided to choose $u(.,.)$ from a class U indexed with a parameter θ. For any given θ, household behavior, i.e., the choice of (c^*, ℓ^*), coincides with solution of

$$\max_{c \geq 0, \ell \geq 0} u(c, \ell; \theta). \quad (3)$$

subject to: $p \cdot c + w \cdot \ell \leq L \cdot w. \quad (4)$

Given a particular θ, we solve (3)–(4) to find (c^*, ℓ^*). The solution will depend upon w and p as well as θ. Think of the maximization as determining functions $\mu^1(.)$ and $\mu^2(.)$ with

$$c^* = \mu^1(w, p; \theta) \text{ and } \ell^* = \mu^2(w, p; \theta). \quad (5)$$

We can use (5) to estimate θ for a given household if we have a history of its behavior. Letting (c_t, ℓ_t) be observations of (c^*, ℓ^*) at time t, and ϵ_t^1 and ϵ_t^2 be measurement errors, we can attempt to estimate θ from regression equations

$$c_t = \mu^1(w_t, p_t; \theta) + \epsilon_t^1,$$

$$\ell_t = \mu^2(w_t, p_t; \theta) + \epsilon_t^2.$$

Provided preferences are immutable, we can use the model for forecasting. For instance, expected leisure and consumption in a future period with $w_t = w$ and $p_t = p$ are $c = \mu^1(w, p; \theta)$ and $\ell = \mu^2(w, p; \theta)$.

Different households may have different utility functions. Frequently, though not always, economists assume that large groups all have the same function. If utility functions differ across households, we might nonetheless be comfortable in assuming that the distribution of utility function parameters applicable to a population remains stable through time. Then, instead of attempting to estimate parameters characterizing preferences, we would attempt to estimate the parameters characterizing the distribution of utility functions.

Finally, consider a change in a given household's environment—say, a reduction in take-home pay due to the imposition of a proportional tax τ on wages. Figure 10.3 shows that one of the budget line's intercepts shifts, and the line rotates.[5] The utility function does not change; we move to a new indifference curve within the original family. The old choice point was (c^*, ℓ^*); the new choice point is (c^{**}, ℓ^{**}).

We can decompose the adjustment into two parts: (i) an adjustment along the old indifference curve to a point at which the slope corresponds to that of the new budget line, i.e., from (c^*, ℓ^*) to $(\overline{c}^*, \overline{\ell}^*)$, and (ii) an adjustment from $(\overline{c}^*, \overline{\ell}^*)$ to the new choice point (c^{**}, ℓ^{**}). The first adjustment

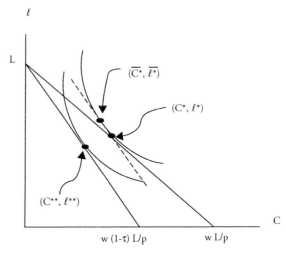

Figure 10.3 The effect of a tax on wages

reflects the fact that with a lower net-of-tax wage, time is less costly for the household. That is to say, the remuneration from an hour's work now buys fewer consumption goods for the household. This tends to cause the household to substitute more leisure, which has become relatively less costly, for consumption goods, which have become relatively more expensive. Economists call this the "substitution effect" of the environmental change. Its direction is unambiguous given the bow shape of the indifference curves.

In part (ii) of the adjustment, the household shifts to a new indifference curve—a lower one in our example. The slope of the old curve at $(\overline{c}^*, \overline{\ell}^*)$, the point before the second adjustment, and at (c^{**}, ℓ^{**}) on the new curve, is, by construction, the same. Hence, we are no longer considering changes in relative valuation. Adjustment (ii), rather, purely reflects a shift in the household's standard of living—in our example, a decline. Economists call this the "income effect" of the environmental change. The shape of the indifference curves does not unambiguously determine how the income effect will influence consumption of goods and of leisure. In the simple context here, however, we expect a negative income effect to cause a decrease in both (as illustrated in Figure 10.3). The reason for this expectation is that both choice items, leisure and goods, are highly desirable—we refer to ℓ and c as "normal" (as opposed to "inferior") options. We expect a household to choose more (less) of both if its budget line shifts outward (inward) in a parallel fashion.

We turn next to a dynamic model.

The Life-Cycle Model

Our second framework is based upon the "life-cycle model" of household behavior due to Modigliani and others.[6] Households live many periods in practice and have decisions to make in each, and Modigliani's model encompasses this. Modigliani's specification stresses decisions of how much to consume at different ages, though subsequent work includes time-allocation choices as well (e.g., Auerbach & Kotlikoff, 1987; Feldstein, 1974). We use a life-cycle model augmented in the latter manner.

For the sake of simplicity, we do not incorporate risk and uncertainty (see below). Thus, at its inception a household knows its life span and earning ability at all future ages. It can, therefore, make a comprehensive plan of what it should do at all future ages.

Dynamic model. Our dynamic model has three elements: a utility function summarizing a household's preferences over leisure-consumption goods outcomes, a description of budgetary accounting, and a description of special restrictions on a household's behavior that limit its latitude for choice. We consider each element in turn. The first two are familiar from section 1.

Begin with preferences. Consider a one-person household that lives through adult ages $s = 0$ to $s = T$. At each age s, the household consumes a flow of goods, c_s, with unit price p_s, and a flow of leisure, ℓ_s. We think of the household as deriving a corresponding flow of utility $u_s = u(c_s, \ell_s)$.

At each moment, the utility function $u{:}R^2 \mapsto R^1$ summarizes the desirability, in the household's eyes, of different current consumption bundles (c_s, ℓ_s).

It will be convenient in this section to decompose the utility function into two parts. We think of a bundle of goods and leisure time (c_s, ℓ_s) as yielding a "flow of services" f to the household. Let the function $f{:}R^2 \mapsto R^1$ determine the latter flow: $f_s = f(c_s, \ell_s)$. Suppose that a household cares about its service flow—not about the flow's components c_s and ℓ_s individually. A second function, $v{:}R^1 \mapsto R^1$, assigns a utility level to each service flow: $u_s = v(f(c_s, \ell_s))$.

We expect more c_s, or more ℓ_s, to yield more services:

$$\frac{\partial f(c_s, \ell_s)}{\partial c_s} > 0 \text{ and } \frac{\partial f(c_s, \ell_s)}{\partial \ell_s} > 0.$$

We also expect more service flow to yield more "utils," so,

$$\frac{\partial v(f_s)}{\partial f} > 0.$$

Since $v(.)$ is itself a utility function, we want it to be concave (see section 1). That requires

$$\frac{\partial^2 v(f)}{\partial f^2} < 0.$$

Figure 10.4 provides a picture. The figure illustrates the implications of concavity in this context. If we increase f by one unit at f_a, the gain in utility is Δv_a. If we increase f by one unit starting at f_b, the increment to utility is Δv_b. Concavity implies that $\Delta v_a > \Delta v_b$.

The idea is that a unit increase in service flow starting from a higher initial level (say, f_b rather than f_a) yields a lower increment to utility.

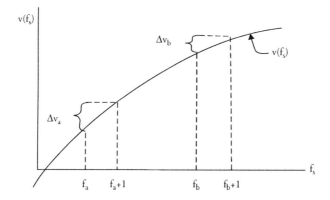

Figure 10.4 Utility as a function of service flow

The actual utility function $u(.,.)$ is increasing because both component functions are. If $f(.,.)$ is increasing and concave, $u(.,.)$ will also be concave. Given the importance of "convexity of preferences," we require that $f(.,.)$ be concave.

Economists often make use of the following functions in their work:

$$v(f) = \begin{cases} \dfrac{f^{\gamma}}{\gamma}, & \gamma \in (0,1) \\ \ln(f), & [\text{``}\gamma = 0\,\text{case''}], \\ \dfrac{f^{\gamma}}{\gamma} & \gamma < 0, \end{cases} \quad (6)$$

$$f(c,\ell) = c^{1-\alpha} \cdot \ell^{\alpha}, \ \alpha \in (0,1). \quad (7)$$

The first is called the "isoelastic utility function," and the second a "Cobb-Douglas" production function for services. These functions have the properties outlined above, and we use them here.

A household ultimately cares about its lifetime utility. Using an integral to sum the flow of utility for different ages, our measure of lifetime utility is

$$\int_0^T e^{-\rho s} \cdot v(f(c_s, \ell_s))\, ds.$$

The new term, $e^{-\rho s}$, where $\rho \geq 0$ is a constant, is a "subjective discount factor," reflecting the household's taste for current over future utility flows. We say that a higher ρ indicates a greater degree of "impatience."

Budgetary accounting must now be dynamic. Let p_s be the price of consumer goods when the household is age s, r_s^N the nominal interest rate, y_s the household's earnings, and A_s its assets (i.e., its net worth) valued in current dollars. We ignore

taxes (at this point). Let w_s be the wage rate (per year) and e_s the "effective" number of work hours per year that the household could potentially supply. "Effective hours" measure variations in earning ability across households. They also measure variations for the same household at different ages. One household might have a higher e_s, $s \in [0,T]$, than another—because it has more education, for instance. On the other hand, for a given household, e_s tends to rise with age in youth, as a household gains more experiential human capital from cumulative time at work, but it may fall late in life, due, for example, to declining health status. We have

$$y_s = (1-\ell_s) \cdot e_s \cdot w_s. \quad (8)$$

The flow growth rate of A_s, which is dA_s/ds, will equal the flow of income minus the flow of consumption expenditures:

$$\frac{dA_s}{ds} = r_s^N \cdot A_s + (1-\ell_s) \cdot e_s \cdot w_s - p_s \cdot c_s.$$

To remove the effects of inflation, divide all terms by p_s. Let $a_s \equiv A_s/p_s$—so that a_s is net worth in constant-dollar terms. The rules of calculus show

$$\frac{da_s}{ds} = \frac{dA_s}{ds} \cdot \frac{1}{p_s} - \frac{A_s}{p_s} \cdot \frac{1}{p_s} \cdot \frac{dp_s}{ds}.$$

The "real interest rate," say, r_s, is the nominal rate minus the rate of inflation:

$$r_s = r_s^N - \frac{dp_s}{ds} \cdot \frac{1}{p_s}.$$

Combining the last three equations,

$$\frac{da_s}{ds} = r_s \cdot a_s + (1 - \ell_s) \cdot e_s \cdot \frac{w_s}{p_s} - c_s.$$

This is our budgetary equation. For simplicity, we assume the real interest rate is constant, $r_s = r$.

The final element of our model is a special constraint: we assume that the economy offers only one type of job: full-time work. A household's time endowment is 1 each period. If the household works full-time, let its leisure be $\overline{\ell} \in (0, 1)$. If it does not work at age s at all, we have $\ell_s = 1$. We discuss this special constraint in more detail below.

Our complete model is as follows:

$$\max_{c_s \geq 0, \ell_s \geq 0} \int_0^T e^{-\rho s} \cdot v(f(c_s, \ell_s)) \, ds, \quad (9)$$

subject to: $\dfrac{da_s}{ds} = r \cdot a_s + (1 - \ell_s) \cdot \dfrac{w_s}{p_s} - c_s,$ (10)

$$a_0 = 0, \ a_T \geq 0, \quad (11)$$

$$\ell_s \in \{\overline{\ell}, 1\}. \quad (12)$$

Condition (9) summarizes household preferences over consumption choices, (10)–(11) summarize budgetary accounting, and (12) is a "special constraint."[7] Notice that the condition $a_0 = 0$ (see (11)) implicitly assumes an absence of inheritances, and $a_T \geq 0$ assumes that households cannot die with unpaid debts. Presumably financial institutions impose the latter restriction by refusing to lend without collateral.

In section 1 we had a calculus problem: we needed to maximize function (3), subject to budget restriction (4). Now we have a calculus of variations—or optimal control theory—problem: we need to find time paths $c_s = c_s^*$, $s \in [0, T]$, and $\ell_s = \ell_s^*$, $s \in [0, T]$, that maximize dynamic criterion (9), subject to constraints (10)–(12).[8]

Discussion. In including special constraint (12), we are assuming that full-time work or full-time retirement are a household's only time allocation options. With full-time work, leisure falls to $\overline{\ell} \in (0,1)$; work hours are $1 - \overline{\ell}$. With full-time retirement, leisure is $\ell_s = 1$, and work is 0. Discretizing household work-choice options is an important modeling assumption.

Possible justifications for (12) are that fixed costs of commuting back and forth to work, needs to keep the same schedule as colleagues and customers, needs on the part of both employers and employees to recoup training costs, etc., make part-time work or highly irregular hours hopelessly inefficient. See, for example, Hurd (1996). Rust and Phelan (1997) write,

The finding that most workers make discontinuous transitions from full-time work to not working, and the finding that the majority of the relatively small number of "gradual retirees" reduce their annual hours of work by taking on a sequence of lower wage partial retirement "bridge jobs" rather than gradually reducing hours of work at their full-time pre-retirement "career job" suggests the existence of explicit or implicit constraints on the individual's choice of hours of work. (p. 786)

Other modeling specifications are certainly feasible. If a household realistically faces a continuous range of options for work time, we would drop (12). We would then need—since negative hours of work are impossible—

$$\ell_s \leq 1 \text{ all } s.$$

Auerbach and Kotlikoff (1987), for instance, follow this second approach.

Yet another possibility would allow a greater range of discrete options than (12). For example, we could allow $\ell_s \in \{\overline{\ell}^1, \overline{\ell}^2, 1\}$, where $\overline{\ell}^1$ represents full-time work, $\overline{\ell}^2$ half-time work, etc. See, for instance, Rust and Phelan (1997).

Solution. Rather than formally deriving the solution to (9)–(12), we refer the reader to Laitner and Silverman (in press). This section presents, and discusses, key elements of the solution.

Retirement is a one-time event for most people, and we proceed under the assumption that that is so. Then for any retirement age R,

$$\ell_s = \begin{cases} \overline{\ell}, & \text{for } s < R, \\ 1, & \text{for } s \geq R. \end{cases}$$

Given an R, first maximize (9)–(12) with respect to c_s. Call the maximized value of criterion (9), conditional on R, $U(R)$. In a second step, maximize $U(.)$ with respect to R.

For any given R, the solution for c_s is

$$c_s = c_0 \cdot e^{\frac{r - \rho}{1 - (1-\alpha)\gamma} s}, \quad s \in [0, R), \quad (13)$$

$$c_s = c_R \cdot e^{\frac{r-\rho}{1-(1-\alpha)\cdot\gamma}(s-R)}, \quad s \in [R,T]. \quad (14)$$

Let c_{R-} be the limiting value on the first segment (i.e., for (13)). That is to say,

$$c_{R-} = \lim_{s \uparrow R} c_s.$$

Then we also need

$$c_R = \kappa \cdot c_{R-},$$

$$\kappa \equiv \kappa(\overline{\ell}, \alpha, \gamma) \equiv [1/\overline{\ell}]^{\frac{\alpha\cdot\gamma}{1-(1-\alpha)\cdot\gamma}}. \quad (15)$$

Given the time-path shapes in (13)–(15), we can set c_0 in (13) from the household's lifetime budget: we pick c_0 so that lifetime consumption expenditures just exhaust lifetime resources.

An intuition for (13)–(14) is as follows. The optimal age profile of c_s reflects two conflicting forces. First, a household's reward for saving money now to spend on consumption later is the interest rate r. Impatience is an offsetting factor. On balance, optimal consumption of goods grows to the extent that $r - \rho$ is positive.

Second, concavity of the utility function favors level consumption. This is clear from Figure 10.4: moving units of service flow from high- to low-flow periods provides a net gain to a household's utility. For $s<R$, we have

$$u_s = \frac{[c_s]^{(1-\alpha)\cdot\gamma} \cdot [\overline{\ell}]^{\alpha\cdot\gamma}}{\gamma}.$$

The closer $(1-\alpha)\cdot\gamma \leq 1$ is to 1, the closer u_s is to being a linear function of c_s. A linear function provides no impulse toward level consumption. Hence, the importance of $r-\rho$ is magnified in (13)–(14) for $(1-\alpha)\cdot\gamma$ near 1—with $r-\rho$ becoming overwhelmingly significant. As we move to small, and then negative, values for $(1-\alpha)\cdot\gamma$, concavity becomes more and more important; hence, a household's urge to keep its service flow f_s nearly constant at different ages rises. That makes $r-\rho$ less important. If $(1-\alpha)\cdot\gamma$ is very negative, the optimal consumption path is virtually level.

Condition (15) emerges because at $s = R$, the household's leisure jumps upward from $\overline{\ell}$ to 1. With our functional form for $f(.)$, leisure time and goods consumption are complementary in production of household utility. That is to say, a post-retirement household is better at producing utility from each unit of c_s. This encourages households to want high

consumption of goods after retirement. The utility function's concavity, on the other hand, favors a level trajectory of service flow f_s. Since more leisure after retirement tends to raise f_s, concavity favors simultaneously dropping c_s to equalize f_s all s. If $(1-\alpha)\cdot\gamma \leq 1$ is near 1, concavity is slight. Complementarity then dominates. In (15), $[1/\overline{\ell}] > 1$ and the exponent $\alpha\cdot\gamma/[1-(1-\alpha)\cdot\gamma]$ will be positive. So, $c_R>c_{R-}$. In other words, optimal consumption of goods will be higher after retirement.

If, however, $\gamma < 0$, concavity is more pronounced. The exponent $\alpha\cdot\gamma/[1-(1-\alpha)\cdot\gamma]$ is then negative, so $c_R<c_{R-}$. In other words, the desire for level consumption overwhelms the desire to take advantage of complementarity. So, consumption of goods after retirement falls. Households enjoy more leisure for $s \geq R$, but their consumption of goods is lower. In a sense, if $\gamma < 0$, households consume more goods prior to retirement to compensate themselves for having so little leisure at that phase of their lives.

Finally, we choose R to maximize (9)–(12). A necessary condition for maximization is

$$\frac{\partial u(c_{R-}, \ell_{R-})}{\partial c} \cdot [y_{R-} - c_{R-} + c_R] = u(c_R, \ell_R)$$
$$- u(c_{R-}, \ell_{R-}). \quad (16)$$

An intuition is as follows. Working a little longer, say, until $R + \Delta R$, yields extra earnings. The flow of earnings is y_R. Any change in goods consumption at retirement is postponed, so the extra resource flow is actually $y_R - (c_{R-} - c_R)$. The gain in utility from the additional resources is then ΔR times the left-hand side of (16).

After retirement, a household enjoys extra leisure. Its flow gain in utility is given on the right-hand side of (16). Postponing retirement yields a total increase in utility of ΔR times this flow. At the optimal retirement age, the gain and loss from postponing R must balance—yielding (16).

With our particular functional forms, (16) is equivalent to

$$\frac{y_{R-}}{c_{R-}} = \begin{cases} [\kappa(\overline{\ell}, \alpha, \gamma) - 1] \cdot \left[\dfrac{1-(1-\alpha)\cdot\gamma}{(1-\alpha)\cdot\gamma}\right], & \text{if } \gamma \neq 0, \\ -\dfrac{\alpha}{1-\alpha} \ln(\overline{\ell}), & \text{if } \gamma = 0. \end{cases}$$

$$(17)$$

Since $\kappa > (<)1$ if $\gamma > (<)0$, in all cases the right-hand side (RHS) is positive.

In the vicinity of the optimizing retirement age, another necessary condition is

$$\frac{y_s}{c_s} \geq (\leq) RHS(17) \quad \text{for} \quad s < (>)R. \quad (18)$$

In words, just prior to retirement, the advantage to continued work must outweigh the benefit of immediate retirement. Conversely, just after age R, the advantage of continued work must be less than the advantage of being retired.[9]

Retirement. In the end, two primary determinants of retirement emerge. One is "positive," and the other is "negative."

Start with the positive inducement to retire. Provided $r>\rho$, optimal consumption expenditure rises with age—recall (13). In our formulation, consumption of goods and leisure are complementary. If consumption of goods rises with age, the desirability of the upward step in leisure that accompanies retirement grows with age. When the desirability reaches a sufficient level, a household retires.

Consider (17)–(18). At early ages,

$$\frac{y_s}{c_s} > RHS(17).$$

Growth in optimal consumption c_s^*, the denominator on the left-hand side, finally leads to equality—and, with it, retirement.

This is a positive inducement for retirement: provided $r>\rho$, one reason that people retire is to take better (i.e., more efficient) advantage of their high late-in-life consumption-of-goods opportunities. Figure 10.5 illustrates.

Figure 10.6 illustrates a negative inducement for retirement. In the figure, efficiency of work hours is constant only through age M. After that, it declines. Deteriorating health status would be one factor.[10] Assuming that employers pay workers according to their productivity, earnings, y_s, trail off for

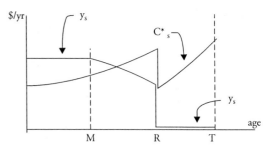

Figure 10.6 Illustration of a negative inducement to retire

$s>M$. After age M the remuneration for work falls lower and lower, making retirement more and more attractive. In terms of (17)–(18), a decline in the numerator of y_s / c_s^* hastens equality in (17).

In a more elaborate specification, declining health status could reduce a household's ability to enjoy both consumption and leisure. This could lead a household in good health to retire to take advantage of its consumption possibilities before poor health could jeopardize the payoff.

Estimated parameter values. Laitner and Silverman (in press) estimate parameters from a model resembling (9)–(12).[11,12] Illustrated estimates are, for example, $\rho = 0.0142$, standard error = 0.0017; $\alpha = 0.6200$, standard error = 0.0367; and $(1 - \alpha) \cdot \gamma = -0.0854$, standard error = 0.0396.

Figures 10.7 and 10.8 illustrate a typical household's life cycle in the Laitner/Silverman sample. Earnings rise rapidly in youth—in the model, due to growth in e_s—and then fall slightly at older ages. Characteristics of the graphs that follow from the specific parameter estimates include:

(i) The optimal time path of consumption expenditure on goods, c_s^*, rises with age. The authors calibrate $r = 0.0375$. With an estimate $\rho = 0.0142$, they have $r-\rho>0$.

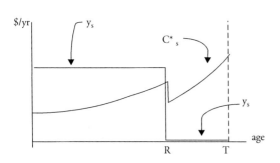

Figure 10.5 Illustration of a positive inducement to retire

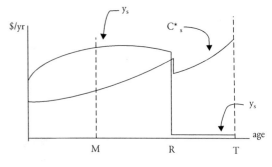

Figure 10.7 Illustrative household earnings and consumption profiles

(ii) Since the estimate of γ is negative, (15) predicts a discontinuous drop in consumption at retirement. The estimated drop is, however, rather modest, namely 8%–10%.

(iii) Leisure is a very important part of household "service flows"—its exponent in $f(c,\ell)$ is larger than the exponent of c.

Figure 10.8 shows the average household's stock of assets. In middle age, when its earnings are at their peak, a household spends less than it earns, and its assets accumulate. After retirement, the household's optimal consumption remains almost as before—a manifestation of "convexity of preferences." The household finances the latter spending through asset decumulation. Using saving and dissaving to uncouple the time paths of consumption expenditure and earnings is a hallmark of Modigliani's life-cycle model.

Both the positive (see Figure 10.5) and negative (see Figure 10.6) inducements for retirement evidently operate in the data.

Digression. Figure 10.7 might seem to suggest that a household might want to delay its start of work until an age S, perhaps substantially later than the date it finishes school. Although our solution algorithm above does not allow this, the logic of (16)–(18) might seem to compel it: y_s / c_s^* might be $< RHS$ (17) for $s<S$ and $\geq RHS$ (17) for $s \geq S$. In other words, it might seem that our two-step solution procedure—which assumes $S = 0$—is likely to be in error.

In fact, a starting age $S> 0$ is highly unlikely to be optimal in practice. We have treated the time profile of e_s as exogenous. This is an oversimplification, however. Suppose a household's effective labor supply rises as a function of cumulative work experience—rather than merely as a function of age. Then a delayed start of work means an equally delayed attainment of maximal earnings. For any given total

career span, an earlier start makes the present value of lifetime earnings higher.

House et al. (2008) provide a detailed analysis. In their formulation,

$$e_s = e(H_s, s),$$
$$\frac{\partial e(H_s, s)}{\partial H_s} \geq 0,$$
$$\frac{dH_s}{ds} = 1 - \ell_s.$$

The idea is that the flow of work hours at age s, $1 - \ell_s$, augments the household's stock of experiential human capital H_s. It is the accumulation of this human capital that causes earnings to rise with age. (Late in life, the second argument of $e(.\,,.)$, the direct effect of age, reduces earning ability as health status declines.) House et al. show that work hours provide two benefits to a young household: take-home pay and enhanced earning ability for the future (through higher H). To determine the optimal starting age for work, say, S, we would need to replace y in (16) with the sum of take-home pay and the investment value of the accompanying increase in H. We would expect such a full accounting to lead to $S^* = 0$.[13]

Applications

This section presents two applications that illustrate the potential usefulness of the dynamic model.

Longevity and retirement. Life expectancy continues to rise (see, for example, Nyce and Schieber, 2005, chapter 2). Increases likely will have important implications for public policy, as well as private planning. We can use our model to investigate the consequences of increasing longevity on future retirement ages.

Most simply, the model would predict that the underlying convexity of preferences will lead households to split increases in longevity between more leisure and more earnings—the latter through more work time. This is easily seen for the static model of section 1. If we increase a household's time endowment L, its budget line shifts northeast in a parallel fashion. The household then moves to an indifference curve corresponding to a higher level of utility. In comparing the new and old choice points, the increase in longevity yields a pure "income effect." Section 1 argues that the consequence will be an increase in both consumption of goods and of leisure.[14] The household can afford to increase its

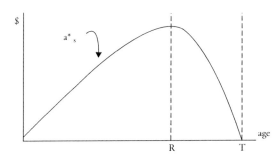

Figure 10.8 The corresponding household asset accumulation profile

consumption of goods only if it works more hours. Since it also takes more leisure, it must be splitting its incremental time endowment between work and leisure.

This intuition carries over to the dynamic model. To provide a quantitative example, use the estimated parameters above: $\alpha = 0.6200$, $\gamma = -0.2247$, and $\rho = 0.0142$. Set $r = 0.0375$. Suppose that a full-time workweek is 40 hours, and that a week has $7 \times 12 = 84$ discretionary hours. Suppose an initial retirement age of 62.5 and life span of 77 years. If full-time leisure is then normalized to $\ell_s = 1$, full-time work leaves $\ell = \bar{\ell} = 44/84 - 0.5238$. So, $\kappa = 0.9204$. Defining $\xi \equiv RHS(17)$, we have $\xi = 1.0124$.

Let

$$\phi(s, s_1) \equiv e^{\frac{r-\rho}{1-(1-\alpha)\cdot\gamma}\cdot(s-s_1)},$$

Conditions (13)–(15) and the lifetime budget constraint imply

$$c_0 \cdot \left[\int_0^R e^{-r\cdot s} \cdot \phi(s, 0)\, ds + \int_R^T e^{-r\cdot s} \cdot \phi(R, 0) \cdot \kappa \cdot \phi(s, R)\, ds \right]$$
$$= \int_0^R e^{-r\cdot s} \cdot y_s\, ds, \quad (19)$$

$$y_R = \xi \cdot c_0 \cdot \phi(R, 0). \quad (20)$$

Following Figure 10.5, suppose that if we increase R, y_R remains unchanged. Then we can differentiate (19)–(20) with respect to T and find dR/dT. Appendix 1 provides details.

We find that

$$\frac{dR}{dT} = 0.2836. \quad (21)$$

This implies that an optimizing household will devote 28% of a change in life span T to additional work, and 72% to additional leisure. In other words, for a change dT in life span, the change in the retirement age dR leaves a fractional gain in lifetime leisure of

$$\frac{dT - dR}{dT} = 1 - \frac{dR}{dT} = 1 - 0.2836 = 0.7164.$$

Figure 10.6 reminds us, however, that y_s may fall as s rises if $s \geq s_0$. If at $s = R$, y_s falls 10% per year of age, then

$$\frac{dR}{dT} = 0.0771. \quad (22)$$

If earnings fall 20 (30) percent per year of age,

$$\frac{dR}{dT} = 0.0446 \ (0.0314).$$

Not surprisingly, in other words, a household allocates less of any increase in longevity to a longer career if its health is deteriorating rapidly.

The public health literature suggests that recent increases in longevity have been accompanied by longer spans of good health. This is the so-called "compression of morbidity." See, for example, Freedman et al. (2002) and Bloom et al. (2007). To the extent that this is the case, the first estimate of dR/dT is, perhaps, the most relevant. Naturally, this issue has very important policy implications for household retirement planning, planning for investments in job-related education and training, business planning, government projections of personal income-tax revenues, etc.

The quantitative results provide a surprise: the optimal increase in work is quite small, even in (21). In other words, the model predicts that households will want to use almost all of an increase in longevity for additional leisure rather than continued work. The reason is that the growth rate of optimal consumption is substantially smaller than the interest rate; hence, the present value of providing one extra year's consumption expenditure is relatively small—and delaying retirement by a small fraction of a year is sufficient to pay for it.

Government programs and the labor supply. The effect on private-sector work incentives of taxes, government transfer payments, and government spending on goods and services is a topic of perennial interest (see section 3). This subsection provides an illustrative example of our model's potential usefulness as a framework for analysis of these topics.

Thinking of the U.S. Social Security system in abstraction, suppose government collects a proportional payroll tax τ on labor earnings and uses the revenues to fund benefit payments to households during their old age. The displacement of private saving for retirement likely to result has been widely studied (Kotlikoff, 1979; Auerbach & Kotlikoff, 1987). We focus on the possible consequences for the average retirement age.

Suppose we add a payroll tax and benefit payment B to the model of section 1. In practice, a household's Social Security benefit depends upon its earnings and number of years of work. However, the relationship is not one-for-one. The benefit formula is progressive, for instance, so that high earners get a smaller incremental return for more work than low earners; benefits depend upon lifetime average earnings, so that one more year's work may make little difference; and, some workers may anticipate less longevity, hence a shorter period of benefits, than others. We make the extreme assumption that B is a constant, independent of individual household actions.

The section 1 budget condition changes to

$$p \cdot c + w \cdot \ell \cdot (1 - \tau) \le L \cdot w \cdot (1 - \tau) + B.$$

Utility is as before. The payroll tax τ causes a substitution effect and an income effect. The tax lowers the value of time from w to $w(1-\tau)$, so the substitution effect leads to more leisure. See the adjustment from (c^*, ℓ^*) to $(\bar{c}^*, \bar{\ell}^*)$ in section 1, Figure 10.3. The income effect of the tax causes a reduction in leisure. See the adjustment from $(\bar{c}^*, \bar{\ell}^*)$ to (c^{**}, ℓ^{**}) in Figure 10.3. The net effect of the tax on leisure, and hence on labor, is ambiguous.

Figure 10.9 shows that introduction of the benefit $B > 0$ has a pure income effect: the household's budget line shifts from $\overline{EF}$ to $\overline{ef}$. (One slight complication is that the household is physically limited by $\ell \le L$; hence, it can access only the bundles on the line segment $\overline{e'f}$.) Since leisure and goods are both "normal," the income effect should increase leisure, hence reduce labor.

With these intuitions in mind, switch to the dynamic model of section 2 and consider corresponding implications for retirement age R. If B_s gives nominal benefits, let their constant-dollar value be

$$b_s \equiv \frac{B_s}{p_s}.$$

For simplicity, assume that a household begins its Social Security benefits at age 65 and that there is no subsequent "earnings test." The U.S. Social Security system indexes benefits to wage growth, using the Consumer Price Index. Note that we have assumed, for this illustrative example, that an individual household's benefits are independent of its actions. (Note also that a household's benefit claiming age need not correspond to its retirement age.)

$$b_s = \begin{cases} 0, & \text{for } s < 65, \\ b \cdot e^{g \cdot (s - 65)} & \text{for } s \ge 65. \end{cases}$$

We change (10) to

$$\frac{da_s}{ds} = r \cdot a_s + (1 - \ell_s) \cdot e_s \cdot \frac{w_s}{p_s} \cdot (1 - \tau) + b_s - c_s.$$

Divide the impact of the Social Security program into (i) the impact through taxes and (ii) the impact from benefits after age 65. Start with (i). As in section 1, taxes have a substitution effect, tending to raise the household's desire for leisure, and an income effect, tending to lower the desire for leisure. With specific functional forms (6)–(7), the substitution and income effects from τ exactly cancel.[15]

Analysis above with the static model implied that effect (ii) would increase leisure and hence, in the dynamic model, would tend to reduce R. To examine this quantitatively, use the same parameter values as in the previous application. Let the Social Security payroll tax be $\tau = 0.10$. Let benefits provide a "replacement rate" of $\theta = 0.46$, with $b = \theta \cdot y_R$.[16] The analogues of (19)–(20) are

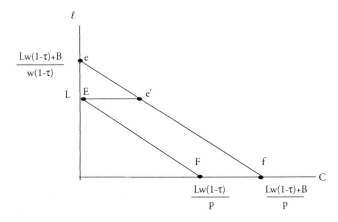

Figure 10.9 A budget line including Social Security benefits B

$$c_0 \cdot \left[\int_0^R e^{-r \cdot s} \cdot \phi(s,0) \, ds + \int_R^T e^{-r \cdot s} \cdot \phi(R,0) \cdot \kappa \cdot \phi(s,R) \, ds \right]$$
$$= \int_0^R e^{-r \cdot s} \cdot (1 - \tau) \cdot y_s \, ds + \int_{65}^T e^{-r \cdot s} \cdot \theta \cdot y_R \, ds,$$

$$(23)$$

$$(1-\tau) \cdot y_R = \xi \cdot c_0 \cdot \phi(R,0). \quad (24)$$

We can show that

$$\frac{dR}{d\theta / \theta} = -1.7343 \quad (25)$$

when y_s is constant at all ages. Appendix2 provides details.

The denominator on the left-hand side of (25) is the percentage change in the replacement rate. If, for example, we raise the replacement rate by 50%, (25) implies that the average U.S. retirement age will fall by almost one year.

As in the previous application, the magnitude of the impact may appear rather modest. Again, note, however, that Social Security benefits arrive late in a household's life. This limits their contribution to the present value of a household's lifetime resources. It is also true that their effect on retirement emerges through c_s^* in the denominator of the left-hand side of (17), yet optimal life-cycle behavior causes a household to distribute any gain in resources quite evenly over all ages.

Extensions and Generalizations

The modeling framework of (9)–(12) admits many generalizations. This section presents a partial list.

• Our model presupposes one-person households. Tobin (1967) shows how to incorporate children and spouses. See also Laitner and Silverman (in press), Scholz and Seshadri (2007), and many others.

• In the current chapter, a household divides its time between labor and leisure. Home production, including care of children, is a third option. See House et al. (2008), McGrattan et al. (1997), Rupert et al. (1995, 2000), Benhabib et al. (1991), Greenwood and Hercowitz (1991), and Aguiar and Hurst (2005).

• We have remarked on the role of experiential human capital above. Ben Porath (1967) studies a model in which agents systematically invest in their own training. See also Ryder et al. (1976), Guvenen (2007), and many others. The model can

be used to study education choices as well (e.g., Becker, 1980; Loury, 1981; Laitner, 2000; and others).

• In addition to the work already cited, the model has been used to study the decision of when to retire (Gustman & Steinmeier, 1986, 2000) and behavior after retirement (Banks et al., 1998; Bernheim et al., 2001; Hurd & Rohwedder, 2003).

• The model of (9)–(12) assumes that households can borrow and lend freely, up to the limit of their lifetime resources. In practice, bankruptcy laws make financial institutions wary of extending loans without collateral. Thus, young households, for example, will not generally be able to borrow against their future earnings. This may restrict their consumption expenditures and lead them to take on extra labor hours. See, for instance, Mariger (1987), Hubbard and Judd (1986), and others.

• We can extend the model to include private intergenerational transfers within family lines, such as bequests and inter vivos gifts (e.g., Laitner, 1992, 2001; Kotlikoff & Spivak, 1981; Friedman & Warshawsky, 1990; and McGarry, 1999).

• The model lends itself, in particular, to analysis of the effects of taxes on labor supply and saving behavior—see, for example, Auerbach and Kotlikoff (1987), Gruber and Wise (1999), Prescott (2004), and many others.

• We can extend the framework to include uncertainty about future earnings and employment (e.g., Gourinchas & Parker, 2002 French, 2005; Low et al., 2010), uncertainty about asset returns (e.g., Samuelson, 1969; Hall, 1978; Campbell & Viceira, 2002), and uncertainty about time of death (e.g., Yaari, 1965; Friedman & Warshawsky, 1990; Mitchell et al., 1999).

• The model has been used to study life-cycle choices on health spending (e.g., Grossman, 1972), uncertainty about disability (e.g., Laitner & Silverman, in press; Low & Pistaferra, 2010), and uncertainty about health expenses (e.g., Hubbard et al., 1994; De Nardi et al., 2010).

• Many variations of utility function have been employed. For example, habit formation may affect consumption and saving behavior (Carroll et al., 2000) or labor supply (Kydland & Prescott, 1982); a household's utility function may be state dependent upon the household's health (see, for example, De Nardi et al., 2010); and risk and uncertainty may be given special treatment (Weil, 1990).

• The model has been used to study long-run growth: interest and wage rates affect household labor supply, savings behavior, and human capital accumulation choices, according to the life-cycle model; the supplies of labor, savings and human capital, in turn, affect interest and wage rates and the prospects for future growth. See, for example, Samuelson (1958), Diamond (1965), and Auerbach and Kotlikoff (1987).

The life-cycle model has proven to be remarkably flexible in terms of admitting new features.

Conclusion

This chapter presents an economist's analysis of household retirement decisions. We describe the essential features of a life-cycle model in which households decide how much to consume and save at each age, and when to retire. The model identifies two paramount determinants of a household's retirement age: the desire to combine maximal leisure with high, late-in-life consumption of goods, and deteriorations of earnings that reduce a household's "cost" of stopping work. To illustrate the model's usefulness, we consider two applications: we investigate the effect of changing longevity on retirement, and we examine the possible impact of Social Security on retirement ages. The section on extensions provides references for extensions and generalizations of the basic model.

Appendix 1

Computational details for the first application of Section 4 are as follows.

From (13)–(15), the left-hand side of (19) is a household's lifetime spending. The right-hand side is the household's total lifetime resources. With monotonicity of preferences, the two must be equal when the household is optimizing. (20) follows from (17).

Use the notation

$$\dot{y}_s \equiv dy/ds.$$

Let

$$\Phi \equiv \int_0^R e^{-r\cdot s} \cdot \phi(s,0)\, ds + \int_R^T e^{-r\cdot s} \cdot \phi(R,0)\; \cdot \kappa\cdot \phi(s,R)\, ds.$$

Differentiating (19)–(20),

$$\Phi\, dc_0 + c_0 \cdot e^{-r\cdot R} \cdot (1-\kappa)\cdot \phi(R,0)\, dR + c_0 \cdot e^{-r\cdot T}$$
$$\cdot \Phi(T,0)\cdot \kappa dT = e^{-r\cdot R}\cdot y_R dR, \qquad (A1)$$

$$\dot{y}_R\, dR = \xi\cdot \phi(R,0)\, dc_0 + \xi\cdot \frac{\partial \phi(R,0)}{\partial R}\cdot c_0 dR. \qquad (A2)$$

Substituting from (A2) into (A1) and collecting terms,

$$\Phi\cdot\left[\frac{\dfrac{y_R}{c_0}\cdot\dfrac{\dot{y}_R}{y_R} - \xi\cdot\dfrac{\partial\phi(R,0)}{\partial R}}{\xi\cdot\phi(R,0)}\right]\frac{dR}{dT}$$
$$+ e^{-r\cdot R}\cdot(1-\kappa)\cdot\phi(R,0)\frac{dR}{dT} \qquad (A3)$$
$$+ e^{-r\cdot T}\cdot\phi(T,0)\cdot\kappa = e^{-r\cdot R}\cdot\frac{y_R}{c_0}\frac{dR}{dT}.$$

Using (20), we can set

$$\frac{y_R}{c_0} = \xi\cdot\phi(R,0).$$

Then (A3) determines dR/dT. (Notice that $\dot{y}_s/y_s$ is the percentage change in y_s with respect to age.)

Appendix 2

In this application, we assume $\dot{y}_R = 0$. Expression (A2) is as above, but we replace (A1) with

$$\Phi\, dc_0 + c_0 \cdot e^{-r\cdot R} \cdot (1-\kappa)\cdot \phi(R,0)\, dR =$$
$$e^{-r\cdot R}\cdot(1-\tau)\cdot y_R\, dR + y_R\cdot\left[\int_{65}^T e^{-r\cdot s}\cdot ds\right]d\theta.$$

We can then proceed as in Appendix 1.

Notes

1. See the references in Section 4 below for examples of "general equilibrium" analysis.

2. On earnings age profiles, see, for example, Lazear (1981) and Akerlof and Katz (1989). On pensions, see Ippolito (1997).

3. See, for example, Varian (1992).

4. The conditions for concavity are $u_{cc} = \partial^2 u/\partial c^2$, $u_{\ell\ell} = \partial^2 u/\partial \ell^2$ < 0, and the determinant of the Jacobian matrix $\begin{pmatrix} u_{cc} & u_{c\ell} \\ u_{\ell c} & u_{\ell\ell} \end{pmatrix}$ positive.

5. The new version of budget condition (1) is $p\cdot c + w\cdot(1-\tau)\cdot \ell \leq L\cdot w\cdot(1-\tau)$.

6. For a summary presentation, see, for example, Modigliani (1986).

7. Note that in the model, multiplication by e_i converts natural hours to "effective hours," with the latter entering budget equation (10). In contrast, it is natural hours that enter the utility function. In practice, people who are efficient at their work may also be efficient at producing a flow of services f_i at home. However, formulation (9) implicitly rules the latter out.

8. See, for example, Kamien and Schwartz (1991).

9. Some households never retire. For such households, the extra revenues from work outweigh the desirability of extra leisure from retirement at all ages—so $y_s/c_s \geq RHS(17)$ all s. For simplicity, we disregard such cases in our exposition.

10. In a more sophisticated model, workers might have the option of spending part of their time investing in job-related skills (e.g., Ben-Porath, 1967). As they neared their likely age of retirement, they might cease such investments. Hence, as their existing skills became obsolete, their earning profile might decline. In other words, changes in optimal investment behavior might be a second factor at work in Figure 10.6.

11. Laitner and Silverman incorporate the chance of disability, and they use married households, with children. Their utility function includes weights for different family sizes (see below)—with different households having potentially different composition, and the same household having potentially different composition at different ages. Laitner and Silverman estimate the weights along with other utility-function parameters.

12. Laitner and Silverman use the U.S. Consumer Expenditure Survey (CEX) 1984–2001, which provides a large cross-section (5,000–7,000 households) annually, and the Health and Retirement Study (HRS) 1992–2002, which provides panel data on a subsample of about 1,000 once-married couples with linked lifetime earning histories. The former provides average consumption by age and time, $\overline{c}_{st}$. Using retirement rates from the March Current Population Surveys, (13)–(15) provide moment conditions to compare with annual changes, $\overline{c}_{s+1,t+1} - \overline{c}_{st}$, from the CEX data. The HRS data provides moment conditions for individual households to compare with (17)–(18).

13. See House et al. (2008). In analysis of R^* this complication makes no difference—once a household retires, H has no future value. Thus, the retirement problem can disregard the investment term.

14. Note that the income effect in Figure 10.3 comes from a southwest shift of the budget line, whereas here we have a northeast shift.

15. This can be seen as follows. Suppose a new proportional tax lowers lifetime earnings by 10%, given the same retirement age as before. Conditions (13)–(15) remain as before; hence, if we lower c_0 by 10%, the household is still exactly solvent. But, with y and c both lower by 10%, condition (17) remains valid with the old retirement age.

16. Given our level earnings trajectories, we take our value of θ from row 2, Table 1, of Biggs and Springstead (2008).

References

Aguiar, M., & Hurst, E. (2005). Consumption versus expenditure. *Journal of Political Economy, 113*, 919–948.

Akerlof, G. A., & Katz, L. F. (1989). Workers' trust funds and the logic of wage profiles. *Quarterly Journal of Economics, 104*, 525–536.

Auerbach, A. J., & Kotlikoff, L. J. (1987). *Dynamic fiscal policy.* Cambridge, England: Cambridge University Press.

Banks, J., Blundell, R., & Tanner, S. (1998). Is there a retirement-savings puzzle? *American Economic Review, 88*(4), 769–788.

Becker, G. S. (1980). *Human capital* (2nd ed.). Chicago, IL: University of Chicago Press.

Ben-Porath, Y. (1967). The production of human capital and the life cycle of earnings. *Journal of Political Economy, 75*, 352–365.

Benhabib, J., Rogerson, R., & Wright, R. (1991). Homework in macroeconomics: Household production and aggregate fluctuations. *Journal of Political Economy, 99*, 1166–1187.

Bernheim, B. D., Skinner, J., & Weinberg, S. (2001). What accounts for the variation in retirement wealth among U.S. households. *American Economic Review, 91*, 832–857.

Biggs, A. G., & Springstead, G. R. (2008). Alternate measures of replacement rates for Social Security benefits and retirement income. *Social Security Bulletin, 68*, 1–19.

Bloom, D. E., Canning, D., Mansfield, R. K., & Moore, M. (2007). Demographic change, Social Security systems, and savings. *Journal of Monetary Economics, 54*, 92–114.

Campbell, J. Y., & Viceira, L. M. (2002). Strategic asset allocation: Portfolio choice for long-term investors. New York: Oxford University Press

Carroll, C. D., Overland, J., & Weil, D. N. (2000). Saving and growth with habit formation. *American Economic Review, 90, 341–355.*

De Nardi, M., French, E., & Jones, J. B. (2010). Why do the elderly save? The role of medical expenses. *Journal of Political Economy, 118*, 39–75.

Diamond, P. A. (1965). National debt in a neoclassical growth model. *American Economic Review, 55,* 1126–1150.

Feldstein, M. (1974). Social Security, induced retirement, and aggregate capital accumulation. *Journal of Political Economy, 82*, 905–926.

Freedman, V. A., Martin, L. G., & Schoeni, R. F. (2002). Recent trends in disability and functioning among older Americans: A critical review of the evidence. *Journal of the American Medical Association, 288*, 3137–3146.

French, E. (2005). The effects of health, wealth, and wages on labour supply and retirement behavior. *Review of Economic Studies, 72*, 395–427.

Friedman, B., & Warshawsky, M. (1990). The cost of annuities: Implications for saving behavior and bequests. *Quarterly Journal of Economics, 105*, 135–154.

Gourinchas, P., & Parker, J. (2002). Consumption over the life cycle. *Econometrica, 70*, 47–89.

Greenwood, J., & Hercowitz, Z. (1991). The allocation of capital and time over the business cycle. *Journal of Political Economy, 99*, 1188–1214.

Grossman, M. (1972). On the concept of health capital and the demand for health. *Journal of Political Economy, 80*, 223–255.

Gruber, J., & Wise, D. A. (1999). *Social security and retirement around the world.* Chicago, IL: University of Chicago Press.

Gustman, A., & Steinmeier, T. (2000). Retirement in dual-career families: A structural model. *Journal of Labor Economics, 18*, 503–545.

Gustman, A. L., & Steinmeier, T. L. (1986). A structural retirement model. *Econometrica, 54*, 555–584.

Guvenen, F. (2007). Learning your earning: Are labor income shocks really very persistent? *American Economic Review, 97*, 687–712.

Hall, R. E. (1978). Stochastic implications of the Life Cycle-Permanent Income hypothesis: Theory and evidence. *Journal of Political Economy, 86*, 971–987.

House, C., Laitner, J., & Stolyarov, D. (2008). Valuing lost home production of dual earner couples. *International Economic Review, 49*, 701–736.

Hubbard, R. G., & Judd, K. (1986). Liquidity constraints, fiscal policy and consumption. *Brookings Papers on Economic Activity, 1*, 1–50.

Hubbard, R. G., Skinner, J., & Zeldes, S. (1994). The importance of precautionary motives in explaining individual and aggregate saving. *Carnegie-Rochester Conference Series on Public Policy, 40*, 59–125.

Hurd, M. (1996). The effect of labor market rigidities on the labor force behavior of older workers. In D. Wise (Ed.),

Advances in the economics of aging (pp. 11–58). Chicago, IL: The University of Chicago Press.

Hurd, M. & Rohwedder, S. (2003). The retirement-consumption puzzle: Anticipated and actual declines in spending at retirement. (NBER Working Paper 9586) Boston, MA: National Bureau of Economic Research.

Ippolito, R. A. (1997). *Pension plans and employee performance: Evidence, analysis, and policy.* Chicago, IL: University of Chicago Press.

Kamien, M. I., & Schwartz, N. L. (1991). *Dynamic optimization: The calculus of variations and optimal control in economics and management.* Amsterdam, The Netherlands: Elsevier.

Kotlikoff, L. J. (1979). Social Security and equilibrium capital intensity. *Quarterly Journal of Economics, 93,* 233–254.

Kotlikoff, L. J., & Spivak, A. (1981). The family as an incomplete annuities market. *Journal of Political Economy, 89,* 372–391.

Kydland, F. E., & Prescott, E. C. (1982). Time to build and aggregate fluctuations. *Econometrica, 50,* 1345–1370.

Laitner, J. (1992). Random earnings differences, lifetime liquidity constraints, and altruistic intergenerational transfers. *Journal of Economic Theory, 58,* 135–170.

Laitner, J. (2000). Earnings within education groups and overall productivity growth. *Journal of Political Economy, 108,* 807–832.

Laitner, J. (2001). Secular changes in wealth inequality and inheritance. *Economic Journal, 111,* 691–721.

Laitner, J., & Silverman, D. (in press). Consumption, retirement, and social security: Evaluating the efficiency of reform that encourages longer careers. *Journal of Public Economics.*

Lazear, E. P. (1981). Agency, earnings profiles, productivity, and hours restrictions. *American Economic Review, 71,* 606–620.

Loury, G. C. (1981). Intergenerational transfers and the distribution of earnings. *Econometrica, 49,* 843–867.

Low, H., Meghir, C., & Pistaferri, L. (2010). Wage risk and employment over the life cycle. *American Economic Review, 100,* 1432–1467.

Low, H., & Pistaferra, L. (2010). *Disability risk, disability insurance and life cycle behavior.* Stanford University. Mimeo.

Mariger, R. P. (1987). A life-cycle consumption model with liquidity constraints: Theory and empirical results. *Econometrica, 55,* 533–557.

McGarry, K. (1999). Inter vivos transfers and intended bequests. *Journal of Public Economics, 73,* 321–351.

McGrattan, E. R., Rogerson, R., & Wright, R. (1997). An equilibrium model of the business cycle with household production and fiscal policy. *International Economic Review, 38,* 267–290.

Mitchell, O. S., Poterba, J. M., Warshawsky, M. J., & Brown, J. R. (1999). New evidence on the money's worth of individual annuities. *American Economic Review, 89,* 1299–1318.

Modigliani, F. (1986). Life cycle, individual thrift, and the wealth of nations. *American Economic Review, 76,* 297–313.

Nyce, S. A., & Schieber, S. J. (2005). *The economic implications of aging societies.* Cambridge, England: Cambridge University Press.

Prescott, E. C. (2004). Why do Americans work so much more than Europeans? *Federal Reserve Bank of Minneapolis Quarterly Review, 28,* 2–13.

Rupert, P., Rogerson, R., & Wright, R. (1995). Estimating substitution elasticities in household production models. *Economic Theory, 6*(1), 179–193.

Rupert, P., Rogerson, R., & Wright, R. (2000). Homework in labor economics: Household production and intertemporal substitution. *Journal of Monetary Economics, 46*(3), 557–579.

Rust, J., & Phelan, C. (1997). How Social Security and Medicare affect retirement behavior in a world of incomplete markets. *Econometrica, 65,* 781–831.

Ryder, H. E., Stafford, F. P., & Stephan, P. E. (1976). Labor, leisure and training over the life cycle. *International Economic Review, 17,* 651–674.

Samuelson, P. A. (1958). An exact consumption-loan model of interest with and without the social contrivance of money. *Journal of Political Economy, 66,* 467–482.

Samuelson, P. A. (1969). Lifetime portfolio selection by dynamic stochastic programming. *Review of Economics and Statistics, 51,* 239–246.

Scholz, J. K., & Seshadri, A. (2007). *Children and household wealth* (Working Paper WP2007–158). Ann Arbor, MI: Retirement Research Center.

Tobin, J. (1967). Life cycle saving and balanced growth. In W. Fellner (Ed.), *Ten economic studies in the tradition of Irving Fisher* (pp. 231–256). New York, NY: Wiley.

Varian, H. R. (1992). *Microeconomic analysis* (3rd ed.). New York, NY: Norton.

Weil, P. (1990). Nonexpected utility in macroeconomics. *Quarterly Journal of Economics, 105,* 29–42.

Yaari, M. E. (1965). Uncertain lifetime, life insurance and the theory of the consumer. *Review of Economic Studies, 32,* 137–150.

A Multilevel Perspective for Retirement Research[1]

Maximiliane E. Szinovacz

Abstract

The aim of this chapter is to show the complexity of retirement processes through a multilevel, contextual approach. First, a conceptual framework for studying retirement as a multilevel phenomenon is presented. The model distinguishes among macro- (e.g., retirement as institution), meso- (organizational retirement policies and cultures), and micro-level (individual retirement) conceptualizations of retirement as well as among macro- (e.g., culture, population structures, labor markets, economy), meso- (e.g., local and regional infrastructures, labor markets, and economies), and micro-level (e.g., families, social networks) structures that impinge on retirement processes. This is followed by a discussion of retirement at each level, its linkages to structural contexts, and the interrelationships among contexts. The chapter concludes with recommendations for future research.

Key Words: multilevel approach, contexts, retirement process, retirement institution, support systems, culture, employers, labor market, family, social networks

Retirement is a complex phenomenon. This complexity is not well captured by theories or research that focus on a single level of inquiry, be it society, employers, or individuals. Yet, as the preceding chapters attest, most research on retirement relies on a single-level approach. Such an approach is particularly problematic in a global and rapidly changing economy where national labor markets are intertwined with each other, policies implemented in one country are precedents for policy development in other nations, and individuals' career and financial prospects are bound to the ups and downs of worldwide financial and labor markets. There are several reasons why most research is anchored in a single-level perspective. Theories, especially those linked to specific disciplines, tend to focus on one level of inquiry. For example, psychologists will emphasize a micro-level perspective pertaining to individuals, or, as in the case of organizational psychology, a meso-level approach targeting

organizations (Barnes-Farrell, 2003; Hershey & Mowen, 2000). Economists have used both macro- and micro-perspectives but rarely tie these two approaches to each other (Hatcher, 2003).

Methodologically, multi-level analyses require specific statistical procedures that can adjust for clustering of responses. Furthermore, because most studies rely on data from single countries and specific time periods, they provide only limited opportunities to assess selected macro-level influences such as culture or economy. Given the paucity of multi-level retirement research, this chapter offers illustrative examples of multilevel influences on retirement. First, a conceptual framework for studying retirement as a multilevel phenomenon is presented. This is followed by a discussion of retirement at each level, its linkages to structural contexts, and interrelationships among contexts. The chapter concludes with recommendations for future research.

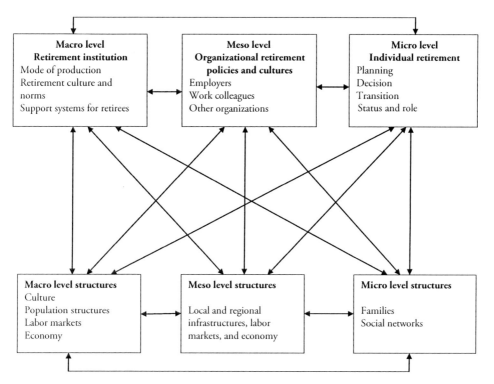

Figure 11.1 A multilevel perspective of retirement
Footnote: Adapted from Szinovacz (2003, p. 23).

Retirement as a Multilevel Phenomenon

Retirement itself is best understood as a multilevel phenomenon (see upper half of Figure 11.1). At the societal or macro-level, retirement can be conceived as an institution, contingent on the mode of production, which reflects cultural norms and values and their manifestation in diverse societal support systems. The meso-level consists of diverse organizations that exert influence on retirement processes, including employers, work colleagues, and other organizations that deal with retirees such as retirement planners or financial institutions. These organizations exert control over the retirement process through specific policies relating to benefits, retirement age, and other supports for older workers and retirees. In addition, organizational cultures can either push older workers toward retirement or promote postponement of retirement as well as post-retirement work. They also influence retirement processes by propagating specific retirement images and expectations. The focus at the micro-level is on individuals' own retirement plans, decisions, and behaviors. Individuals respond to macro- and micro-level influences, but their aggregate attitudes and behaviors also feed back into these larger entities.

Retirement processes cannot be well understood without consideration of the contexts in which they occur. This contextual perspective is implied in several theories, including the life course approach described in an earlier chapter (Bengtson & Allen, 1993; Elder, 1995; Settersten, 2003a). Macro-, meso-, and micro-structures (lower half of Figure 11.1) form the contexts for retirement structures, policies, and behaviors but are also influenced by them (see also Szinovacz, 2003). At the macro-level, these contexts include culture, population structures such as the age composition of the population, fertility and marriage or divorce rates, as well as the economy in general and labor markets in particular. Meso-level structures refer to the local and regional environment, including infrastructure as well as economy and labor markets. Relevant micro-structures consist foremost of families and social networks. It should be noted that the structures noted in Figure 11.1 and discussed in later sections of this chapter are not exhaustive.

Macro-level
Retirement as Institution

The institution of retirement refers to culturally sanctioned structures of late-life withdrawal from the labor force or from sustenance production and of supports for non-working elders. Norms about retirement include expectations about whether or not to retire at all, when to retire, and how the retirement process should occur. They also involve expectations about the economic support of retirees, including whether and how those not engaged in sustenance production or gainful employment should be economically supported and who carries the responsibility for such supports. Both positive (incentives) and negative sanctions (penalties) serve the enforcement of retirement-related norms. Retirement transitions sometimes entail initiation rituals that mark the transition to retirement status as well (Szinovacz, 2003).

Although retirement as we know it today is a relatively new institution, there have always been "retirees"—that is, aged individuals who no longer participate in the labor force. However, well into the early twentieth century, and still today in some developing nations, many people never experienced retirement, nor did they expect a lengthy period of

leisure toward the end of life. Similarly, societal policies and structures were not built around the expectation that individuals would leave the labor market in later life. To better understand the evolvement of retirement as we know it today (for an overview, see also Atchley, 1976), it is important to compare societies along several dimensions that form the basis for the retirement institution (see Table 1). The first three dimensions shown in Table 1 refer to retirement itself: whether it is normative, what triggers the transition into retirement, and whether the transition is planned and voluntary or unplanned and involuntary. The second two dimensions concern the support systems available to retirees, specifically, the normative foundation for supports and who carries responsibility for such support. The last dimension links the institutionalization of retirement (or lack thereof) to the age composition of the labor force. It should be noted that the characterizations presented in Table 1 constitute ideal types in the Weberian sense, that is, they reflect the essence of retirement systems in different societies

Table 11.1 Variations in the institutionalization of retirement (Weberian ideal types)

| Dimensions | Type of society | | | |
	Hunting	Preindustrial	Early industrial	Modern
Normative foundation of retirement	Not normative; group survival; non-workers eliminated	Not normative; non-workers marginal (burden, loss of control)	Partially normative; non-work becomes expected state for selected groups; others remain marginal	Normative; non-work as expected state; deserved leisure
Basis for retirement transition	Disability/death	Disability/death; property transfer	Disability/death; property transfer; age	Age; finances; other obligations; disability; property transfer
Type of retirement transition	Involuntary; unplanned	Involuntary; unplanned	Mixed	Voluntary; planned
Support system	None; community & family	Family; community	Family; self; employers; state	Self; state; employers; family
Normative foundation for support	None	Filial piety; charity	Filial piety; charity; self-sufficiency; retirement as control mechanism	Welfare state; self-sufficiency; filial piety; charity
Labor force	High involvement of elderly	High involvement of elderly	High to moderate involvement of elderly	Low involvement of elderly

and may not correspond to the actual retirement systems in specific societies or among specific population subgroups.

Culture and mode of production. The first dimension refers to cultural variations in norms about retirement, that is, expectations about whether and how individuals should retire. They range from beliefs that individuals no longer capable of work constitute so much of a burden for the social group that their elimination is necessary to acceptance of a period of non-work as an expected and deserved status. In hunting and gathering societies, as well as in other non-industrial and preindustrial societies, the majority did not survive to old age. What then was the fate of the relatively small proportion of those fortunate enough to survive to old age? Their destiny was determined by cultural and economic norms that often reflected the extent of burden that support for such individuals would entail for communities or families. In these societies individuals were essentially expected to work until death. Those unable to work due to illness or disability either had to rely on community or family support or were essentially eliminated through death-hastening strategies, typically on the part of kin (Glascock, 1990). Which of these paths prevailed depended on climate, type of production, and stratification systems. Small hunting-gathering societies in harsh climate zones tended toward death-hastening strategies, whereas larger, socially stratified societies in mild climates and with intensive agriculture leaned toward family and community support (Glascock, 1990, p. 53). Death-hastening techniques ranged from outright killing to abandonment and forsaking of food or all support. Although such practices were mostly restricted to hunting and gathering societies (Glascock, 1990), they have parallels in later preindustrial societies as well. In America, slaves who were no longer "useful" as workers were sometimes abandoned by their owners, although more charitable owners relegated them to light work (Harber & Gratton, 1994). Similarly, servants were often dependent on the goodwill of their employers, as illustrated quite dramatically in the recent British TV series *Downton Abbey*, in which a cook fears she will be dismissed when she starts losing her vision. Community support was also often quite limited. Elders without families could end up in poorhouses where conditions were often so harsh that they may be categorized as death-hastening as well (Evans & Williamson, 1991; Trydegård, 2000). In her children's book *Emil's Pranks*, Astrid

Lindgren provides a vivid description of poorhouses in Sweden:

> Imagine a miserable little tumble-down, two-room cottage, where poor, old, worn-out people live together in a state of dirt, vermin, hunger and wretchedness—then you will know what a poorhouse is, or was.… It was a horrible place to have to live in when poor people grew old and were no longer able to manage for themselves. (Lindgren, 1966, p. 86; cited in Trydegård, 2000, p. 575)

Importantly, these practices were not isolated aberrations but rather culturally founded. They reflected divergent norms about the treatment of elders who could no longer work. Death-hastening in hunting and gathering societies was an expected practice, accepted by both elders and their families (Glascock, 1990). Similarly, the treatment of single, poor elders in preindustrial societies reflected Poor Laws that considered elderly and poor relief as mercy and charity (Evans & Williamson, 1991b; Harber & Gratton, 1994; Trydegård, 2000) and sometimes revoked individuals' civil rights (Williamson & Pampel, 1993). Thus, in these societies retirement is not normative, typically associated with illness or disability, and neither planned nor voluntary.

With increasing urbanization and industrialization in the nineteenth century, and perhaps a cultural shift toward individualism, we see early forms of late-life self-sufficiency that enabled selected groups to leave the labor force without being fully disabled. Farmers began to sell their farms and use the proceeds to support themselves in retirement (Costa, 1998; Haber, 2006). In addition, children's labor was used to build up retirement funds for the household head. This often forced children to delay marriage and to forgo education, thus limiting their prospects for social advancement (Gratton & Rotondo, 1992; Haber & Gratton, 1994). As well, some employers started to offer pensions. Implementation of worker pensions was initially driven by employer concerns about workplace control and efficiency. Pensions allowed firms to manipulate workers, enhance workers' loyalty to the firm, rid themselves of older workers (through mandatory retirement) who were perceived to be inefficient and costly, and create work opportunities for younger individuals. They also helped modernization and depersonalization of the workplace as universal contracts replaced personal accommodations for individual workers (Graebner, 1980; Kohli, 1986; Williamson & Pampel, 1993).

What constitutes the basis for retirement as we know it today in modern societies is, on the one hand, the disassociation between disability and labor force withdrawal, and, on the other hand, and more importantly, the transfer of support structures for retirees from families and communities to the state and the individuals themselves. Although the development of social insurance and pension systems for aging workers and the aged had divergent roots in different countries (Williamson & Pampel, 1993), most, like U.S. Social Security, are contributory systems. Eligibility for benefits is thus tied to work history as well as to age. Individuals now assumed the responsibility of providing for their own old-age security through consistent contributions to the system over a lengthy time period and through individual savings, as social insurance benefits are typically too low to guarantee continuation of one's preretirement lifestyle. Because eligibility was no longer tied to disability, retirement also became a desired period of leisure for still-functional individuals. These developments culminated in the institutionalization of retirement as an expected and desirable life period of deserved leisure. Although recent developments indicate that more individuals postpone retirement (Burtless, 2008; Fast, Dosman, & Moran, 2006; Friedberg, 2007) or engage in some gainful employment after retirement (Cahill, Giandrea, & Quinn, 2006; Giandrea, Cahill, & Quinn, 2007; Quinn, 2000; Shultz, 2003; Ulrich & Brott, 2005), retirement remains normative and an expected life stage in later life. This is evident from individuals' efforts to plan for retirement, some pressure by societal organizations and governments to urge individuals into retirement planning from an early age (Ekerdt, 2004; Ekerdt, Kosloski, & DeViney, 2000), and continued support for Social Security (Cook & Czaplewski, 2008; Rix, 1999). Furthermore, the retirement transition became increasingly voluntary. Most individuals now retire when they wish to do so rather than because they are forced into retirement. Nevertheless, a substantial minority still experiences retirement as a forced transition due to illness, job loss, or mandatory retirement regulations in many countries (Gallo, Bradley, Siegiel, & Kasl, 2000; Gillanders, Buss, Wingard, & Gemmel, 1991; Schultz, Morton, & Weckerle, 1998; Szinovacz & Davey, 2005; Van Solinge & Henkens, 2007).

Supports for retirees. The institutionalization of retirement is closely linked to, and indeed made possible by, developments in the support of retirees. Early hunting and gathering societies often lacked support for non-workers, as such support would have compromised group survival (Glascock, 1990). For example, denial of food to the elderly prevailed during hunger seasons in horticultural societies, and killing or abandonment occurred among nomads such as the Siberian Chukchees (Foner, 1993; Glascock, 1990), a reindeer herding society, or among those exposed to harsh climates like some Eskimo tribes (Atchley, 1976; Glascock, 1990). In preindustrial societies that did provide support to older non-workers, such support was founded on norms of filial piety and charity. Given scarce community resources, care for elders was expected to be primarily a family obligation, whereas charity and public relief constituted secondary sources of support (Evans & Williamson, 1991b). Under tenant farming conditions, landlords also assumed some responsibility for their aging tenant farmers (Held, 1982). Despite filial obligation, often anchored in laws, detailed wills attest that elders did not always trust their children or relatives to provide for them in old age (Held, 1982; Steinmetz, 1988). Indeed, as Steinmetz (1988, p. 43) notes, property transfers to children often suggested "a tug of war over economic control and security between parent and child." Nevertheless, filial obligation constituted the dominant norm for elder support in many preindustrial societies and remains a cultural basis for retirement behaviors, especially in Asian postindustrial societies. For example, norms of filial piety tend to discourage late-life employment in Hong Kong because such employment could signify lack of support on the part of one's children (Ngan, Chiu, & Wong, 1999). Indeed, individuals who co-resided with their children were more prone to retire than those who did not co-reside (Lee, 2005). It is important that these supports essentially cast retirees as dependents on either their families or their communities and thus deprived them of their status and authority.

With industrialization and the separation of workplace and home, support for non-workers started to shift from families and communities to the individuals themselves, employers, and the state. Wages earned by family members allowed household heads to accumulate retirement savings (Gratton & Rotondo, 1992; Haber & Gratton, 1994), and employers offered pensions as a means to control their workforce. A state social insurance program for selected groups of workers was first enacted in nineteenth century Germany, mainly as a means to control laborers and to counteract the socialist movement and potential social unrest, although concerns for the well-being of older individuals played a role as well (Williamson & Pampel, 1993). Because the benefits were quite low and old age insurance eligibility only started at age 70, their contribution to older workers' welfare was limited. In the United States, state-based support for the elderly was first through military pensions. As in the case of Germany, these benefits were initially tied to disability (in the American case due to war-related injuries) and only later expanded to cover all Union Army veterans who served at least 90 days (Williamson & Pampel, 1993). Most Western countries started to implement state social insurance programs for retirees during the first part of the twentieth century, and today most countries, including developing nations, have some sort of social insurance system for aged individuals. Because social insurance and pensions are typically tied to age and work history rather than disability and covered at least partly by workers' contributions, they foster some sense of self-sufficiency and independence in old age and shift dependency from families and communities to the state (Walker, 1983).

Class differences. In preindustrial societies, individuals in the lower and middle socioeconomic status groups essentially worked until they were no longer able to do so and then depended on family support or communal charity. Communities or societies that were not able to support nonproductive elders either resorted to death-hastening measures or relegated these elders to marginal institutions that offered little support, such as poorhouses. In contrast, some form of retirement did exist among the upper echelons of society and more affluent peasant communities. Upper-class families often provided support for aging parents within extended households (Laslett, 1977), whereas among land-owning farmers retirement was mostly founded in transfers of property or land to children, who in turn took economic responsibility for their parents. In some countries (e.g., Bavaria and some parts of Austria), farmhouses sometimes included an *Altenteil, Ausgedinge,* or *Stübl,* i.e., a cottage or room reserved for aging parents after land and farmhouse transfers to the children, based on contractual arrangements involving the exchange of farm property or tenant rights for the retiring farmer's support (Berkner, 1972; Held, 1982). This form of retirement, i.e., transfer of property to heirs with contractual provisions for the aging parents' support, was not restricted to Europe but was also typical for landowners in pre-nineteenth-century America (Haber, 2006). Because marriage often required land ownership, sons sometimes had to postpone marriage until their fathers retired, that is, transferred the property (Goody, 1976). However, co-residence with or close residence of aging parents in attached housing often served the younger generation as well: grandmothers provided child care and older men engaged in some light activities such as making ropes (Goody, 1976; Laslett, 1977).

Class variations in retirement apply to modern societies as well. Because retirement benefits are tied to wages and lower-level jobs often are not covered by pensions, these retirement insurance systems essentially perpetuate existing class differences and wealth distributions among the population. Although Social Security replacement rates are higher for lower-income groups and Social Security led to significant decreases in poverty among the older population in general, the leveling effect of diverse replacement rates remains limited (Engelhardt & Gruber, 2004). Thus, achievement of a financially secured retirement devoted to leisure and characterized by independence from family supports and charity is more characteristic for the upper and middle socioeconomic groups than for those of lower socioeconomic status. Lower socioeconomic status groups may still be somewhat dependent on support by family or have to rely on charity in the form of means-tested income supports for the poor.

Retirement and Social Structures

The institutionalization of retirement and social insurance for retirees is linked to societal structures in several ways. The following sections address three of these linkages. First, the age composition of labor markets reflects the institutionalization of retirement. This can be demonstrated through cross-national comparisons of labor force participation in later life. Second, insurance systems influence and respond to changes in societal structures, including societal age and population structures. Third, cultural beliefs and norms influence specific social insurance regulations. Such influences will be demonstrated in regard to gender and family norms.

Labor force participation in later life. The institutionalization of retirement, that is, the development of welfare states that incorporate some form of social insurance system for the elderly, is evident from comparisons of labor force statistics for developing and developed nations. Variations in the institutionalization of retirement lead to drastic differences in labor force participation rates even within the same continents. Considering Africa, in Niger (2001) the labor force activity rate was 78.7% for men aged 65–69 years and 37.8% for women of the same age group. Similarly, 88.7% of men aged 65–69 and 69.6% of women were in the labor force in Tanzania in 2001, compared to only 25.6% of men and 9.6% of women aged 65 and over in South Africa in 2003. Similarly, in South America, less developed nations like El Salvador have relatively higher activity rates (61.6% for men and 22.3% for women aged 65–69 in 2007) than their more developed counterparts such as Chile (43.6% for men aged 64–69 and 14.4% for women of this age group in 2007). The same trend applies for Asia. For example, in Indonesia, activity rates for 2008 were 69.2% for men and 38.8% for women aged 65–69, much higher than for Japan (49.6% and 26.0%, respectively), which is known for its relatively high late-life labor force participation rate among postindustrial societies. All of these contrast with Western postmodern societies with elaborate welfare systems such as the United States (35.6% activity rate for men and 26.4% for women aged 64–69 in 2008) or Europe. Nevertheless, there are also marked differences among developed nations. For example, activity rates in the United Kingdom were 22.4% for men and 12.4% for women aged 65–69, but only 14.3% and 6%, respectively, for the Netherlands and 5.5% and 1.9%, respectively, for Belgium (International Labour Organization, 2011).

Although reasons for the differences in labor force participation rates among nations of similar development are complex and include economic, cultural, and policy factors, differences in social insurance systems play an important role. Whereas most countries, including developing nations, have some form of social insurance system, they differ widely in regard to the proportion of the population covered by these systems or able to afford contributions to the system. Most social insurance systems cover employees and are thus not applicable to many people in developing countries who work in small self-owned farms or businesses (Barrientos, 2007). Problems for the non-working result especially during transitions between traditional (filial piety, charity) and modern (social insurance) support systems. One good example is rural China. Even though old-age insurance has been offered in rural China for over a decade, many elderly remain unaware of these programs or cannot afford them. On the other hand, traditional support from children is waning despite continuing acknowledgment of filial piety, partly due to outmigration of younger generations into urban areas and partly due to China's one-child policy (Zhang & Goza, 2006), leaving elders economically vulnerable.

Also noteworthy are large gender differences in activity rates across nations, suggesting that gender role ideology plays an important factor. For example, in the more traditional Arabic states such as Iran, labor force participation rates were 31.5% and 3.1% for men and women aged 65 and over compared to 17.5% and 5.5%, respectively, for Israel with its more egalitarian gender roles. However, policy plays a role as well. In European countries that still have different social security eligibility ages for men and women, such as Austria, Italy, and the United Kingdom, labor force participation rates differ markedly for the relevant age groups and then converge after eligibility for both genders is reached, whereas smaller discrepancies exist in countries with the same eligibility ages for men and women, especially where there are no provisions for early retirement such as in Sweden (International Labour Organization, 2011).

Population structures. The institutionalization of retirement and its associated social insurance systems had multiple effects on societal structures. One of these effects concerns age structuring. Because most social insurance systems are age-based, that is, eligibility is defined by age, their development resulted in greater societal age segregation (Henretta, 1992; Kohli, 1986; Riley & Riley, 1994) and what Kohli (1986) calls chronologization of the life course. The life course became divided into distinct age-based stages that are tied to productivity. Children and elders are relegated to nonproductive roles: children on the basis of educational requirements and laws prohibiting child labor and elders based on retirement and its implicit or explicit (e.g., through mandatory retirement rules or earning caps for beneficiaries) discouragement of employment. Similarly, societal institutions became age segregated, attending to specific age groups such as schools for children, workplaces for young and middle-aged adults, and nursing homes for the elderly. Note in contrast that the poorhouses of the past, which housed many destitute elders, were typically not age-segregated and included people of various ages. In addition, eligibility for some social programs other than Social Security is also age-based, most notably Medicare as health insurance exclusively for the elderly. In recent decades the trend toward segmentation of the life course, and especially the sharp age-based division of workers and non-workers in later life, has been partially reversed. More recent policies both in the

United States and in many European countries now encourage later-life employment through increased eligibility ages, higher benefit reductions for early retirement, relaxed earnings tests for social insurance eligibility, and more stringent measures against age discrimination in the workplace (Gustman & Steinmeier, 2008; Hokenstad & Johansson, 2001; Hudson & Gonyea, 2007; OECD, 2005). These policies, together with economic and perhaps attitudinal changes, contributed to rising retirement ages throughout industrialized countries (Burtless, 2008).

Another trend that can be partly attributed to the institutionalization of retirement and social insurance for the elderly is the decline in fertility in most industrialized countries. In the past, old-age support was typically based on transfers from children, thus increasing the utility of high fertility (Boldrin, De Nardi, & Jones, 2005), whereas state-supported social insurance systems do not require high fertility. Recent analyses suggest that the institutionalization of social insurance systems among industrialized countries has indeed contributed to declining fertility rates (Boldrin et al., 2005; Ehrich & Kim, 2007). Because pay-as-you go financing of social security requires a large younger population base to decrease the tax burden on younger workers, the current financing problems of social insurance in Western countries stem partly from the institutionalization of social insurance itself (Ehrich & Kim, 2007).

However, the main reasons for the expected crisis in social security funding (Gonnot, 1995; Munnel, 2007; Social Security Administration, 2010b; Steuerele & Bakija, 1994) are the spike in fertility in the aftermath of World War II (the baby boom) and the extension of the life span. These developments not only contributed to large old-age dependency ratios (Hayward & Zhang, 2001; Serow, 2001) but are also expected to alter the balance between social security contributions (taxes paid) and lifelong benefits as beneficiaries' post-retirement life expectancy increases (Steuerle & Renanne, 2011). These population changes in turn gave rise to policy changes and revisions in social security and pension systems. The new politics of welfare retrenchment are reflected in "a reversal of the previously sacrosanct status of deservingness on the part of older people and the construction of a discourse that ... emphasizes the 'burden' of pensions on the working population" (Walker, 2006, p. 342), a trend further fueled by the current economic depression. To decrease this "burden," many Western nations have altered social security regulations to encourage later retirement, including raises in eligibility ages, increased penalties for early retirement, or reductions in earnings tests for beneficiaries (Hudson & Gonyea, 2007).

These examples demonstrate the mutual influence of social insurance system and population structures on each other. They also offer interesting historical parallels: support for non-working elders or for an expanded period of leisure in later life is tied to the extent of burden such support entails for societies.

Cultural Influences on Social Security

The cultural embeddedness of social insurance systems is perhaps most evident in provisions reflecting specific gender and family norms. The enactment of Social Security in the United States and in most Western nations occurred at a time characterized by traditional gender and family norms. Men were seen as the main providers, and women's primary roles were relegated to the family and home realms (Bernard, 1981). Many women did not work at all or left the labor force for considerable periods of their lives to take care of families and children; they also received lower wages than their male counterparts (Goldin, 1994). A contributory social insurance system based on work history and wages thus offered little protection for women. The United States' Social Security system's response to these norms was the incorporation of a spouse benefit, that is, spouses (typically wives) are entitled to one-half of their spouses' benefits (typically husbands). Calculation of the spouse allowance is based on the benefits of the spouse who is entitled to the higher benefits within the couple. Divorcees are also entitled to a spouse allowance, provided the marriage lasted at least ten years (Social Security Administration, 2010a). As more women entered the labor force and spent more time in the labor force, their dependence on spouse benefits declined. For example, among women aged 62 and over, 57% received benefits as dependents in 1960 compared to only 27% in 2009, whereas the proportion with dual entitlements rose from 5% to 29% (Social Security Administration, 2010a, p. 21). Although this system compensates women for their contributions as homemakers, mothers, and caregivers, it also perpetuates traditional gender and family values by favoring long-lasting marriages over other family arrangements and providing no comparable benefits for same-sex couples (Human Rights Campaign, 2010). Other countries without spouse allowances acknowledge women's family and care contributions through care credits or drop-out years in benefit calculations. However, these credits typically do not account for the full loss of benefits due to family leaves and thus disadvantage women (Favreault, Sammartino, & Steuerle, 2002; Sainsbury, 1996). Yet another approach to compensate women for their dual responsibilities as workers and family caregivers is the provision of different retirement ages for men and women. In several countries, such as Austria, Italy, the United Kingdom, and Poland, women reach eligibility earlier than men (typically at age 60 compared to age 65 for men). However, most of these countries will equalize men's and women's eligibility ages within the next decades (Social Security Administration, 2008), a policy change that has faced considerable opposition in some countries, especially on the part of lower-status women (Steinhilber, 2002).

Meso-level

Whereas retirement at the macro level is reflected in labor force withdrawal patterns of aging individuals and support structures for elderly non-workers, retirement at the meso-level is constituted in specific organizations' retirement policies and programs (see Figure 11.1). Foremost among these are pensions offered by employers, but other policies and programs pertaining to retirement preparation, work adaptations, training, or job search help for older workers are also important. These policies and programs, on the one hand, allow employers to exert control over the retirement transition process and, on the other hand, establish windows of opportunity for individuals' late-life work and retirement. In addition, organizations forge retirement "cultures" that establish either internal or external norms for or on behalf of retirees. Employer policies and programs are subject to various macro- and meso-level influences. Of particular importance are government regulations as well as local, regional, and national economies.

Employer Policies and Programs

As noted earlier, employer pensions go back to the nineteenth century, serving employers as a means to control workers and as a competitive edge in worker recruitment, although considerations for workers' welfare play a role as well (Woodbury, 2001). By setting eligibility criteria that include service years, pensions tie workers to the firm. On the other hand, they can also be used to encourage retirement. Until the enactment of the Age Discrimination in Employment Act in the United States (and still prevalent in many other industrialized nations today), pensions were often tied to mandatory retirement, thus enabling employers to rid themselves of older workers whose productivity may have declined and who are usually more costly than younger workers (Adler & Hilber, 2009; Hatcher, 2003; Munnell, Sass, & Soto, 2006). Nevertheless, workers may be required to leave their jobs once they receive pensions, thus reducing their late-life work opportunities within the firm. However, such control applies mainly to defined benefit policies where eligibility can be tied to service years. In defined contribution plans, workers essentially maintain some control over their retirement exits (Feldman, 2003), although early exits may significantly limit accumulation of retirement savings.

Another mechanism of firms' control over retirement is the provision of early retirement incentives. Such incentives allow workers to leave the firm with pensions or additional employer contributions (e.g., lump-sum payments) before they reach benefit eligibility. They offer firms a means to decrease their workforce in times of labor shortages and to rid themselves of costly and nonproductive workers. However, such programs must be offered to all or specific categories of employees and may thus encourage desirable workers (from the firm's perspective) to retire as well (Feldman, 2003; Kim & Feldman, 1998; Mollica & DeWitt, 2000). Thus, from the workers' perspective, early retirement incentives constitute opportunities to opt for a financially secured early retirement. Nevertheless, workers seem to be reluctant to accept early retirement incentives (Hardy & Hazelrigg, 1999).

Because some older workers desire or need adaptations in work demands to continue in their jobs, employers' willingness to adapt jobs to older workers' needs also constitutes some form of control over retirement. Yet employers in the United States seem rather lukewarm about retaining older workers and reluctant to make adaptations for them (Eschtruth, Sass, & Aubry, 2007; Munnell et al., 2006; Rix, 2002; Timmons, Hall, Fesko, & Migliore, 2011). For example, data from the nationally representative Health and Retirement Study (HRS)[2] indicate that fewer than one-half of workers feel that they could reduce their work hours or move to a less demanding job (see Figure 11.2), although most do not feel that employers give preference to younger workers in promotions (see also Adams, 2002; Charles & Decicca, 2007). Such practices seem to curtail individuals' ability to postpone retirement

(Charles & Decicca, 2007). Similarly, training programs can help older workers remain on their jobs or find new employment. Although training for older workers is offered by diverse organizations, research suggests that on-the-job training seems more effective than other programs in opening work opportunities for older individuals and may help them to postpone retirement when faced with technological change (Bartel & Sicherman, 1993; Gordo & Wolff, 2011).

Thus, employer policies and programs ranging from pensions to work adaptations and training manipulate the desirability and ability of older individuals to continue work and thus their retirement behaviors. The extent to which employers have such control is partially contingent on federal regulations pertaining to older worker retention and hiring, such as age discrimination laws, as well as on the economic environment. Even though some firms have started to implement programs for older workers (Piktialis, 2007; Pitt-Catsouphes, 2007; Timmons et al., 2011), most employers have yet to respond to the prospects of declining labor supply as the baby-boom cohorts enter retirement (Nyce, 2007), a tendency that is only reinforced by the current economic climate.

Retirement Cultures

Retirement cultures at the meso-level reflect firm or local expectations about the retirement process and experience. Such cultures will not only shape workers' and retirees' own expectations about when retirement should occur or what retirees ought to do as well as their inclination to remain with a firm, but they can also function as social control mechanisms by exerting pressure on workers or retirees.

Organizational culture is viewed as an important aspect of retaining or attracting older workers. AARP advises firms: "Retaining older employees must be supported by the organizational culture. If the focus is primarily on retirement rather than on work options, a culture change may be needed" (AARP, 2011). Organizational cultures that foster employment of older workers and, implicitly, postponement of retirement tend to offer universal work options such as hours and job flexibility and a supportive environment (Timmons et al., 2011). They also provide managerial acceptance of late-life work. For example, workers who felt that their supervisors supported older workers were less prone to perceive their retirement as involuntary (Van Solinge & Henkens, 2007).

Organizational culture is not only reflected in managers' approach to older workers but also in pressure by work colleagues. As shown in Figure 11.2, most U.S. workers surveyed in 2008 felt no pressure to retire from work colleagues but still indicated that there was a "usual retirement age for people who work with you or have the same kind of job." Reporting on earlier (1992) data from the HRS, Ekerdt (1998) further found that perceptions of a usual retirement age prevailed in specific work environments, namely, larger and unionized firms, firms with pension coverage, as well as among specific occupational categories. There is also evidence that organizational culture and the extent to which it is shared by workers can influence retirement behaviors. For example, workers offered early retirement incentives were more prone to accept them in high-solidarity (measured by union membership) compared to low-solidarity plants (Hardy & Hazelrigg, 1999; Hardy, Hazelrigg, & Quadagno, 1996). Peer effects on retirement decisions are also evident from a study of Oregon state employees. This study showed that individuals' retirement decisions were influenced by the retirement behaviors of their peers, that is, individuals were more prone to retire if other retirement-eligible employees retired as well (Chalmers, Johnson, & Reuter, 2008). Similar peer effects hold for decisions about participation in specific retirement investment plans (Duflo & Saez, 2002).

In addition to workplace cultures, specific values about retirement and retirees are also promoted by various other organizations and the media. In contrast to earlier emphases on disengagement in retirement and the characterization of retirement as a role-less role (Burgess, 1960; Cumming & Henry, 1961), predominant current values stress engagement, active leisure, and financial planning for retirement (Dennis, 2002; Ekerdt, 1986; Ekerdt, 2004; Ekerdt & Clark, 2001). There are some nuanced variations in themes, depending on the type of organization. For example, although the AARP website (http://www.aarp.org/) provides a mix of advice on divergent post-retirement activities ranging from work to volunteering and leisure activities, the emphasis seems to hover around engagement in work or volunteering. In contrast, financial planning advertisements tend to focus on retirement as "a state of freedom and leisure for personal pursuits" (Ekerdt & Clark, 2001, p. 63), which can be achieved through financial security.

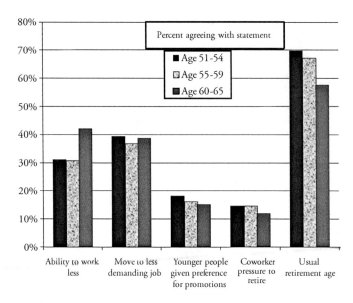

Figure 11.2 Workplace norms for retirement, 2008

Notes:

Based on data from the Health and Retirement Study, 2008, author computation. All data refer to individuals who are currently working, not self-employed, and in the indicated age groups.

The data refer to answers to the following questions:

Could you reduce the number of paid hours in your regular work schedule?

My employer would let older workers move to a less demanding job with less pay if they wanted to.

In decisions about promotion, my employer gives younger people preference over older people.

My coworkers make older workers feel that they ought to retire before age 65.

On your main job, what is the usual retirement age for people who work with you or have the same kind of job?

For the first four questions, the proportions shown reflect the percentage of workers who indicated that they strongly agreed or agreed with the statement; for usual retirement age, the proportion shown reflects the percentage of workers who gave an age rather than indicating that there was no usual age.

Government Regulations

Perhaps the most important macro-level influence on employers' policies and programs for older workers and their retirement are government regulations at both the federal and state level. Because state laws vary considerably, the focus here will be on federal rules.

Age-discriminatory employment practices have been curtailed by passage of the Age Discrimination in Employment Act (ADEA) in 1967 and its amendments in 1978 and 1986. The last amendment outlaws age discrimination and implicitly mandatory retirement for all workers over age 40 except for selected occupations such as police or airline pilots (Hudson & Gonyea, 2007; Neumark, 2003; Neumark, 2009). Studies addressing the specific effects of the ADEA provide somewhat ambiguous evidence. The law seems most effective in preventing dismissal of older workers and thus opening avenues for deferred retirement, whereas its impact on hiring or promotions of older workers is limited (Adams, 2004; Hudson & Gonyea, 2007; Neumark

& Stock, 1999). Indeed, some research suggests that the ADEA may actually undermine hiring of older workers because employers fear they may then not be able to fire these workers (Lahey, 2006). In other countries, compulsory retirement remains acceptable under specific circumstances despite existing age-discrimination legislation. For example, the anti-age-discrimination directive of the European Union allows some compulsory retirement if it can be justified (Connolly, 2008), and Canada, where age discrimination is covered under human rights, explicitly exempts mandatory retirement in some provinces (Gunderson, 2003).

Federal laws further regulate employers' Social Security contributions and pension plans. Of particular interest are pension and tax regulations that restrain employers' ability to retain older workers after benefit receipt or to implement phased retirement, although recent revisions of these federal policies have eased such arrangements considerably (Hudson & Gonyea, 2007). In addition, legislation that increased the costs of defined benefit plans to employers, such as the Employee Retirement Income Security Act of 1974, which required employers to insure pensions, were partially responsible for the shift to defined contribution plans (Munnell & Soto, 2007). Thus, most Western industrialized countries restrain employers' actions in regard to older workers, retirements, and pensions, but there also are significant national differences in the provision of loopholes permitting mandatory retirement or in the ways pensions are regulated.

Economic Influences on Employers

Shifts in the economy are reflected in the hiring and retention of workers, including older workers. One example of these relationships is the auto industry. The downshift in this industry during the late 1980s led to special early retirement programs, especially in plants targeted for closure, and workers in such plants were more prone to accept such incentives, although this may have been partly a function of union membership (Hardy & Hazelrigg, 1999). There is also evidence that hiring and retention of older workers varies by industry. Older workers tend to be hired and retained more in industries where job growth is high, whereas low-growth industries are likely to see more turnover and retirement of older workers (Adler & Hilber, 2009). Similarly, industries with high rates of technological change tend to encourage postponement of retirement, partly through more on-the-job training (Bartel & Sicherman, 1993). Analyses based on the Current Population Survey by the U.S. Census Bureau further indicate considerable variability in older men's labor force participation rates in different states, variations that can be partly attributed to diverse labor market conditions (Munnell, Soto, Triest, & Zhivan, 2008b).

The institutionalization of retirement is typically viewed as a means to provide for the organized succession of workers and to open employment opportunities for young workers (Kohli, 1986). That this argument is widely accepted became clear when proposed raises in retirement age in France led to widespread protests, based mainly on the belief that such raises would reduce job opportunities for younger people (CNN Wire Staff, 2010). Similar views are held by politicians in many Western countries (Gruber, Milligan, & Wise, 2009). It is by no means clear, however, that delayed retirement (or longer retention of older workers) at any one point in time leads to higher unemployment among the young. Indeed, research based on data from twelve OECD countries, including Germany, France,

the United Kingdom, Japan, Canada, and the United States, show that youth and elder employment are both driven by the economy and increase or decrease in tandem (Gruber et al., 2009). The authors conclude that there is "no evidence that increasing the employment of older persons will reduce the employment opportunities of youth and no evidence that increasing the employment of older persons will increase the unemployment of youth" (p. 69).

These examples demonstrate how macro-level as well as meso-level structures impinge on employer behaviors. Both government regulations and economic conditions provide parameters that, on the one hand, curtail what employers can do (e.g., mandatory retirement) and, on the other hand, provide incentives or disincentives for specific actions such as the hiring or retention of older workers or the implementation of specific pension plans.

Micro-level: Individuals' Retirement

Retirement at the micro-level refers to individuals' retirement experiences (see Figure 11.1). In contrast to earlier depictions of retirement as an event (Atchley, 1976c), more recent conceptualizations view retirement as a process that begins with retirement planning and ends with the final transition to the status of full retiree. Although the notion of retirement as a process has permeated the literature for some time (Ekerdt & DeViney, 1993; Gustman & Steinmeier, 1984; Han & Moen, 1999; Kosloski, Ginsburg, & Backman, 1984; Szinovacz, 2003), most research has focused on specific transitions such as withdrawal from the labor market or receipt of benefits (Choi, 2000; Coile, Diamond, Gruber, & Jousten, 2002; Denton & Spencer, 2009; Ekerdt & DeViney, 1990; Szinovacz & DeViney, 1999). The entire retirement process can be divided into three main stages: pre-retirement planning and preparation, which ends with the decision to retire; the retirement transition stage, which begins with the first retirement transition action (e.g., withdrawal from one's career job or from the labor market, receipt of Social Security or pension benefits) and ends with the last action, leading to full retirement (withdrawal from the labor force, receipt of all benefits for which the individual is eligible); and the post-retirement stage, which consists of various adaptation processes to retirement. Although it is conceptually useful to differentiate these three stages, they will often overlap. For example, retirement planning may continue after the first retirement transition, or adaptation processes will occur prior to full retirement. Thus, each of these stages (planning, transitioning, and adaptation) also reflects a process (Han & Moen, 1999; Settersten, 2003b). Because each of these stages has been addressed in detail in other chapters of the handbook, this chapter focuses on how macro-, meso-, and micro-forces impinge on retirement processes.

Macro-level Influences on Retirement Processes

Institutionalization of retirement. The institutionalization of retirement led to the disassociation of retirement and disability and rendered retirement a presumably voluntary and desirable transition (Hardy, 2002). Through its underpinnings by social insurance support systems that linked benefit eligibility to age rather than disability, retirement became an age-structured phenomenon. Indeed, data show that workers' retirement spikes at the ages of early or regular benefit eligibility, e.g., age 62 and age 65/66 for Social Security in the United States, but similar trends apply to other industrialized countries as well (Gruber & Wise, 1999; Kohli, Rein, Guillemard, & Van Gunsteren, 1991). Furthermore, changes in Social Security legislation that increased normal retirement age to 66/67 (depending on year of birth) and removed the earnings test for individuals retiring after reaching full retirement age resulted in increased labor force participation among men aged 65–67 (Gustman & Steinmeier, 2008). Thus, eligibility ages of social insurance systems and regulations pertaining to penalties of early retirement as well as post-retirement work (or the lifting of such sanctions) clearly influence individuals' retirement decisions.

Normative influences. The institutionalization of retirement rendered retirement normative, that is, most individuals expect to retire sometime in their later years and have some notion when this transition should occur (Ekerdt et al., 2000; Joulain, Mullet, Lecomte, & Prevost, 2000; Settersten & Hagestad, 1996). Such timing norms may vary across different work environments and also across different cohorts (Ekerdt, 1998; Mermin, Johnson, & Murphy, 2007). Furthermore, off-time and especially too-early retirement tends to undermine post-retirement well-being (Szinovacz & Davey, 2004b).

Although timing norms tend to be linked to regulatory retirement ages, they can also reflect other norms, such as gender norms. Given the cultural emphasis on the husband's provider role

(Bernard, 1981), many couples (and especially husbands) feel uncomfortable when the husband retires prior to his wife. Thus, many couples aim for joint retirement (Behringer, Perrucci, & Hogan, 2005; Gustman & Steinmeier, 2004; Gustman & Steinmeier, 2002), and retired husbands tend to exert pressure on still-working wives to retire as well (Cahill, Giandrea, & Quinn, 2008; Skirboll & Silverman, 1992; Szinovacz, 1989; Szinovacz & S. DeViney, 2000). As in the case of retiring too early, deviation from the joint retirement norm and especially retirement of husbands prior to their wives tends to undermine well-being as well as marital quality (Davey & Szinovacz, 2004; Kim & Moen, 2002; Myers & Booth, 1996; Szinovacz, 1996; Szinovacz & Schaffer, 2000; Szinovacz & Davey, 2004a).

Traditional gender and family norms embedded in Social Security benefits (spouse allowance, length-of-marriage requirements for divorcees) have dire consequences for the economic well-being of retirees whose life course does not fit these norms. Marriage, and especially long-term marriage, has become increasingly rare among black women (Harrington Meyer, Wolf, & Himes, 2004). Furthermore, many women, and black women in particular, enter their retirement years with low income and low financial assets, including pension prospects (Angel, Jimenénez, & Angel, 2007; Sevak, Weir, & Willis, 2003/4). In combination, these two features result in considerably higher poverty among unattached older black women than among other older population groups. Specifically, in 2009 the percentage below 100% of poverty of individuals aged 65 and over was 3.2% for white men in families and 9.7% for white unrelated men. It was 4.2% for white women in families and 13.7% for white unrelated women. Among blacks aged 65 and over, 10.3% of men in families and 27.0% of unrelated men were below 100% of poverty, compared to 14.0% of women in families and 32.9% of unrelated women (U.S. Bureau of the Census, 2009, Table POV01).[3] Similarly, traditional family norms disadvantage same-sex couples in the United States who have access to neither the spouse allowance nor survivor benefits (Human Rights Campaign, 2010). In contrast, other countries' (e.g., Canada, Denmark) social insurance systems recognize homosexual partnerships. Clearly, the traditional gender and family values embedded in Social Security reinforce lifelong social disadvantage of or discrimination against selected subpopulations.

Meso-influences on Retirement Processes

Among the meso-factors impinging on retirement processes, employer benefit packages are perhaps most important and certainly have received most attention in the literature. However, other meso-factors such as state economies and infrastructures play a role as well.

Employer benefits and retirement transitions. The main benefits offered by employers consist of contributions to their employees' pension and health insurance. The influence of pensions on retirement transitions has been well documented. Of particular interest is whether the trend for employers to offer defined contribution rather than defined benefit plans (Munnell & Soto, 2007) has implications for individuals' retirement decisions. One paper explored this issue by comparing effects of defined contribution and defined benefit coverage on expected retirement age and actual retirement transitions (Munnell, Triest, & Jivan, 2004). The results, based on data from the Health and Retirement Study, indicate that individuals with defined benefit plans expect to retire about one year earlier than their counterparts with defined contribution plans, whereas those with defined contribution plans expect to retire only a fraction of a year earlier than those without pension coverage. Similarly, pension coverage increases the probability of actual retirement, and this effect is more pronounced for individuals with defined benefit than those with defined contribution plans (Munnell et al., 2004). It should be noted that Munnell's data rely on benefit reports by the workers, which are not always accurate, but it is the perceptions of benefits rather than actual benefits that have the strongest influence on workers' behaviors (Chan & Stevens, 2003; Ekerdt & Hackney, 2002).

There is also recent evidence linking retirement transitions to health insurance coverage. For example, individuals whose employers provide health insurance coverage after retirement expect to retire earlier and also do in fact retire earlier than those whose employers cover only current workers (Johnson, Davidoff, & Perese, 2003; Mermin et al., 2007), although the magnitude of these effects remains under debate (Blau & Gilleskie, 2006). Furthermore, estimates indicate that raises in Medicare eligibility age would lead employees without employer health insurance beyond retirement to further delay their retirement transition (French & Jones, 2004).

Taken together, these findings provide clear evidence that shifts in employer retirement policies and programs alter individuals' retirement expectations and behaviors. They also suggest that if employers intend to alter their employees' retirement behaviors through benefit changes, they need to educate workers about their benefit packages.

Regional economies and infrastructures. Because it is often difficult for older workers to move to different locales, their immediate economic contexts can play an important role in retirement decisions. Only a few studies examined whether and how state and local economies influence retirement behaviors. One of these investigations indicated that in cities with declining industries (steel, manufacturing), workers were more prone to retire, whereas the opposite trend held in locations with temporarily expanding industries, such as the coal industry during oil price shocks (Black & Linag, 2005). Similarly, von Wachter (2007) shows that state economic shocks and trends influence retirement behaviors, especially among lower-skilled workers, although comparable though smaller effects of state economies can also be discerned for younger workers. Other studies revealed that state unemployment rates are linked to a lower probability of employment and lower expected retirement age among men aged 55–64 (Munnell, Soto, Triest, & Zhivan, 2008a) and increase involuntary retirement transitions among men but not women (Friedberg, Owyang, & Webb, 2008).

There is very little research on other infrastructures that may affect retirement behaviors or post-retirement lifestyles. Given that some older workers have care responsibilities either for frail spouses or for parents (Szinovacz, 2007; Szinovacz & Davey, 2004b), it would be important to investigate whether the local availability of care agencies, day care centers for the elderly, or even nursing homes influences retirement behaviors. As far as post-retirement lifestyles are concerned, local infrastructures can constrain retirees' leisure pursuits or their involvement in volunteer activities, and such constraints may in turn influence retirees' decisions on whether to remain in the area or move to another location (Golant, 2002; Longino, 2001).

Micro-level Influences on Retirement Processes

The contextual and life course perspectives underlying this chapter point to the importance of individuals' life course trajectories as well as the immediate social and family environment as important micro-level influences on their retirement experiences. Among the most relevant life course experiences are socioeconomic, career, and health trajectories. These trajectories are closely linked.

Cumulative advantage/disadvantage. Research based on cumulative advantage/disadvantage theory indicates that individuals from lower socioeconomic status groups not only accumulate less human capital (e.g., education) early in life but are also more subject to health problems (Ferrero, Shippee, & Schafer, 2009; O'Rand, 2003). Early disadvantage tends to increase risk exposure in adulthood, whereas advantage opens expanded opportunities (O'Rand, 2006). For example, blue-collar jobs tend to be more physically demanding and entail greater health risks than white-collar jobs (Johnson, Mermin, & Resseger, 2011), and physically demanding jobs tend to lead to earlier retirement (Hayward, Friedman, & Chen, 1998). Furthermore, individuals with health problems tend to retire earlier or leave the labor force with disability insurance (Bound, Schoenbaum, Stinebrickner, & Waidmann, 1999; Hayward et al., 1998; Williamson & McNamara, 2003). Similarly, workers experiencing job losses later in life are more prone to retire (Sewin Chan & Stevens, 2002), as are those who experienced more unemployment spells (Hayward et al., 1998). In addition, job loss and unstable work trajectories in later life are stressful and tend to undermine health and life satisfaction (Gallo et al., 2000; Marshall, Clarke, & Ballantyne, 2001). Both job loss and health problems also prompt perceptions of untimely and involuntary retirement (Szinovacz & Davey, 2005; Van Solinge & Henkens, 2007), and such retirement in turn may reduce benefits and preclude work that may be needed to supplement retirement income from social insurance and pensions.

Thus, the assumptions that institutionalized retirement would be voluntary and disassociated from disability do not hold for a noteworthy minority (Szinovacz & Davey, 2005; Van Solinge & Henkens, 2007). As was the case in preindustrial times, involuntary retirement remains linked to class. For example, analyses based on the first four waves of the Health and Retirement Study indicate that perceptions of having been forced to retire are significantly related to human capital and financial assets, although some of these relationships become weaker when health variables are added to the models. This suggests that the socioeconomic status differences in forced retirement are partly due to the association between socioeconomic status and health (Hayward, Friedman, & Chen, 1996; Szinovacz & Davey, 2005).

These examples demonstrate that retirement transition processes are the culmination of individuals' life course trajectories in diverse life realms and can be fully understood only within these contexts. They also indicate that class differences in today's society influence individuals' relative access to the ideal of a desirable, voluntary, and leisure-oriented retirement (see Table 1) as they did in earlier times.

Family and social network contexts. Another assumption of life course theory is that individuals' lives and life course trajectories are closely linked with those of significant others (Settersten, 2003a). Family members and friends may influence individuals' retirement planning, their decisions on when to retire, and their adaptation to retirement. To date, much of the retirement literature has focused on individuals' own characteristics as predictors of these retirement processes, although selected spouse and family characteristics are increasingly viewed as important predictors as well (Szinovacz, 2006; Szinovacz, Ekerdt, Butt, Barton, & Oala, in press). In contrast, there is only scarce information on how other social network members impinge on individuals' retirement processes.

Family and friends may influence individuals' retirement processes in several distinct ways. First, they can play an important part in retirement planning either through involvement in or influence on each other's retirement plans. Such involvement in planning activities is evident from studies showing that spouses often influence each other's retirement decisions (Henkens & van Solinge, 2002; Smith & Moen, 1998) as well as each other's financial preparation for retirement. For example, risk aversion in the allocations in defined contribution plans is related to spouse's risk aversion (Bernasek & Shwiff, 2001). There is also evidence that spouses coordinate their pension decisions and opt for similar rather than diversified investments (Shuey, 2004; Uccello, 2000).

Second, events in families' and friends' lives may serve as anchor points for individuals' retirement decisions. Such anchoring may be voluntary, e.g., when spouses time their retirement in relation to their partner's (Behringer et al., 2005; Blau, 1998; Curl & Townsend, 2008; Gustman & Steinmeier, 2002; Henkens, 1999; Johnson, 2004) or when one spouse's retirement accelerates the retirement transition of the other spouse (Pienta, 2003; Schils, 2008; Szinovacz & DeViney, 2000). Similarly, some parents may postpone retirement until their children are no longer dependent on them, whereas others may retire early to care for dependent children or grandchildren (Brown & Warner, 2008; Cahill et al., 2008; Choi, 2002; Chung, 2010; Hank, 2004; Pienta & Hayward, 2002; Szinovacz & DeViney, 2000; Szinovacz, DeViney, & Davey, 2001). Other family events may spur unplanned, and in some cases involuntary, retirement transitions. For example, illness of spouses or care needs of parents may prompt individuals to retire earlier than planned and to perceive such retirements as forced rather than wanted (Dentinger & Clarkberg, 2002; Johnson & Lo Sasso, 2000; Szinovacz & Davey, 2004b, 2005).

There is also mounting evidence that individuals' retirement can impinge on the quality of their marital and family relationships. Some couples experience upheaval in their marriages following the retirement of one or both spouses, although such problems tend to be short-lived (Davey & Szinovacz, 2004; Szinovacz, 1996; Szinovacz & Davey, 2004a; Szinovacz & Schaffer, 2000; Vinick & Ekerdt, 1991a, 1991b). Others may increase time spent with family members, including adult children and grandchildren (Niederfranke, 1991; Nuttman-Shwartz, 2007; Szinovacz & Davey, 2001), although some adult children have raised concerns that retired parents may become too dependent on them (Remnet, 1987).

Research on retirees' social networks has focused mainly on the question of whether former contacts with work colleagues are supplemented through contacts with kin and other friends. Evidence suggests that contacts with work colleagues decline after retirement (Bossé, Aldwin, Levenson, Workman-Daniels, & Ekerdt, 1990; Francis, 1990), but it remains unclear whether such decline results in reduced network size (Bossé, Aldwin, Levenson, Spiro, & Mroczek, 1993; Van Tilburg, 1992, 2003).

What all of these studies exemplify is that retirement does not occur in a social vacuum. Rather, retirement decisions and adaptations are influenced by family and social contexts and in turn affect the quantity and quality of interactions with kin and friends.

Future Directions

The aim of this chapter was to show the complexity of retirement processes through a multilevel, contextual approach. Such an approach is necessary to understand how the evolvement of retirement as an institution altered the retirement transition processes and the supports and lives of diverse groups of older non-working populations, how changes in employers' benefit schemes manipulate individuals' retirement decisions through shifts in the extent of

supports for older workers and retirees as well as in their investment responsibilities, and how spouses' retirement or health impinges on their partners' retirement transitions and post-retirement adjustment. Such an approach is also needed to understand the heterogeneity among retirees and differential influences of contexts on diverse subgroups. As the privileged classes were protected from the harsh conditions facing many older non-workers in past societies, so it is higher socioeconomic status groups today who are at least partly shielded from the consequences of welfare retrenchment or cuts in employer benefits. Finally, such an approach helps to identify theoretical concepts and dimensions (e.g., control, support norms) that help explain retirement processes across divergent contexts and historical periods. Yet, as noted at the beginning of this chapter, much of retirement research remains founded on a single-level approach. What then are the research questions we have to ask and the research designs we need to implement in order to push retirement research toward a multilevel perspective?

At the most elementary level, multilevel investigations require the inclusion of divergent contexts in their models and analyses. Although microeconomic and sociological models of retirement have started to include family contexts (Gustman & Steinmeier, 1994; Hayward et al., 1998), other contexts are often ignored. For example, studies addressing state-level influences on retirement processes tend to rely exclusively on state-level predictors and rarely integrate individual-level characteristics in their models (Munnell et al., 2008a).

Another shortcoming of current research is that knowledge about the importance of specific contexts on retirement processes remains rather uneven. We have accumulated considerable information about the importance of social insurance and pension systems, as well as individuals' health and finances, and have gained some insights into some work and organizational or regional and national contexts, but we know very little about others, such as normative influences that vary across cultures (e.g., social support or leisure norms) or social networks.

Because a multilevel approach is implicitly comparative, may this be across historical periods, across different nations, across different states or counties, across different employers, or across different socioeconomic status groups, it will be important to develop conceptual models and corresponding operationalizations that allow such multilevel comparisons. For example, rather than comparing later-life labor force participation or retirement ages in specific nations, such models would include theoretical concepts and variables that can capture differences in social insurance and pension coverage such as eligibility ages, the integration between first pillar (social insurance) and second pillar (employer pensions) benefit structures, or the structure of welfare systems (Esping-Andersen, 1996).

Perhaps most importantly, true multilevel approaches require assessment of the linkages among contexts. For example, do retirement behaviors of couples differ in countries that have similar and those that have different social insurance eligibility ages for men and women (Szinovacz, 2002)? Do workplace cultures influence how pensions or retirement incentives affect workers' retirement decisions (Hardy & Hazelrigg, 1999)? Is the influence of individuals' characteristics on retirement transitions similar in states and nations with high and those with low unemployment rates (Munnell et al., 2008b)? Are retirement-age workers with care responsibilities for parents or disabled spouses less prone to retire in countries with expansive support systems for caregivers than in countries that rely mostly on families as support systems for the elderly (Katz, Lowenstein, Prilutzky, & Halperin, 2011; Lowenstein, Katz, & Gur-Yatish, 2008)? Only answers to questions such as these will allow us to grasp the complexity of retirement processes.

Notes

1. This chapter was funded in part by a grant from the National Institutes of Health, R01AG013180, Maximiliane E. Szinovacz, PI. The opinions and conclusions expressed are solely those of the author and do not represent the opinions or policy of the National Institutes of Health.

2. The HRS (Health and Retirement Study) is sponsored by the National Institute on Aging (grant number NIA U01AG009740) and is conducted by the University of Michigan.

3. According to the definition by the US Census Bureau, unrelated individuals are "people of any age who are not members of families or subfamilies". A family "is a group of two people or more (one of whom is the householder) related by birth, marriage, or adoption and residing together; all such people (including related subfamily members) are considered as members of one family" (U.S. Bureau of the Census, 2011).

References

AARP. (2011). *Retaining older workers.* Retrieved from http://www.aarp.org/work/employee-benefits/info-2007/retaining_experienced_workers.html.

Adams, S. (2002). Passed over for promotion because of age: An empirical analysis of the consequences. *Journal of Labor Research, 23*(3), 447–461

Adams, S. (2004). Age discrimination legislation and the employment of older workers. *Journal of Labour Economics, 11*(2), 219–241.

Adler, G., & Hilber, D. (2009). Industry hiring patterns of older workers. *Research on Aging, 31*(1), 69–88.

Angel, J. L., Jimenénez, M. A., & Angel, R. J. (2007). The economic consequences of widowhood for older minority women. *The Gerontologist, 47*, 224–234.

Atchley, R. C. (1976). *The sociology of retirement.* New York, NY: John Wiley.

Barnes-Farrell, J. L. (2003). Beyond health and wealth: Attitudinal and other influences on retirement decision-making. In G. A. Adams & T. A. Beehr (Eds.), *Retirement: Reasons, processes, and results.* New York, NY: Springer.

Barrientos, A. (2007, September 10–15). New strategies for old-age income security in low income countries. *Technical Commission on Old-age, Invalidity, and Survivors' Insurance. World Social Security Forum.* Retrieved from http://www.issa.int/Resursy/Technical-Reports/New-strategies-for-old-age-income-security-in-low-income-countries.

Bartel, A. P., & Sicherman, N. (1993). Technological change and retirement decisions of older workers. *Journal of Labor Economics, 11*, 162–183.

Behringer, A., Perrucci, C. C., & Hogan, R. (2005). Dual-earner couples' expectations for joint retirement: A study of typical and atypical congruent and non-congruent couples. *Gender Realities: Local and Global Advances in Gender Research, 9*, 111–132.

Bengtson, V. L., & Allen, K. R. (1993). The life course perspective applied to families over time. In P. G. Boss, W. J. Doherty, R. LaRossa, W. R. Schumm, & S. K. Steinmetz (Eds.), *Sourcebook of family theories and methods* (pp. 469–498). New York, NY: Plenum.

Berkner, L. K. (1972). The stem family and the developmental cycle of the peasant household: An eighteenth-century Austrian example. *The American Historical Review, 77*(2), 398–418.

Bernard, J. (1981). The good-provider role: Its rise and fall. *American Psychologist, 36*(1), 1–12.

Bernasek, A., & Shwiff, S. (2001). Gender, risk, and retirement. *Journal of Economic Issues, 35*(2), 345–356.

Black, D. A., & Linag, X. (2005). *Local labor market conditions and retirement behavior.* Chestnut Hill, MA: Center for Retirement Research at Boston College.

Blau, D. M. (1998). Labor force dynamics of older married couples. *Journal of Labor Economics, 16*, 595–629.

Blau, D. M., & Gilleskie, D. B. (2006). Health insurance and retirement of married couples. *Journal of Applied Econometrics, 21*, 935–953.

Boldrin, M., De Nardi, M., & Jones, L. E. (2005). *Fertility and Social Security* (Working Paper No. 11146). Cambridge, MA: National Bureau of Economic Research.

Bossé, R., Aldwin, C. M., Levenson, M. R., Spiro, A., & Mroczek, D. K. (1993). Change in social support after retirement: Longitudinal findings from the normative aging study. *Journal of Gerontology: Psychological Sciences, 48*, P210–P217.

Bossé, R., Aldwin, C. M., Levenson, M. R., Workman-Daniels, K., & Ekerdt, D. J. (1990). Differences in social support among retirees and workers: Findings from the Normative Aging Study. *Psychology of Aging, 5*, 41–47.

Bound, J., Schoenbaum, M., Stinebrickner, T. R., & Waidmann, T. (1999). The dynamic effects of health on the labor force transitions of older workers. *Labour Economics, 6*, 179–202.

Brown, T. H., & Warner, D. F. (2008). Divergent pathways? Racial/ethnic differences in older women's labor force withdrawal. *Journal of Gerontology: Social Sciences, 63B*(3), S122–S134.

Burgess, E. W. (1960). *Aging in Western societies*. Chicago, IL: University of Chicago Press.

Burtless, G. (2008). *The rising age at retirement in industrial countries*. Chestnut Hill, MA: Center for Retirement Research at Boston College.

Cahill, K. E., Giandrea, M. D., & Quinn, J. F. (2006). Retirement patterns from career employment. *The Gerontologist, 46*, 514–523.

Cahill, K. E., Giandrea, M. D., & Quinn, J. F. (2008). *A micro-level analysis of recent increases in labor force participation among older workers*. Chestnut Hill, MA: Center for Retirement Research at Boston College.

Chalmers, J. M. R., Johnson, W. T., & Reuter, J. (2008). *Who determines when you retire? Peer effects and retirement*. Retrieved from https://www2.bc.edu/~reuterj/research/cjr_peers_200808.pdf.

Chan, S., & Stevens, A. H. (2002). *How does job loss affect the timing of retirement?* (Working Paper No. 8780). Cambridge, MA: National Bureau of Economic Research.

Chan, S., & Stevens, A. H. (2003). *What you don't know can't help you: Pension knowledge and retirement decision making* (NBER Working Paper No. 10185). Cambridge, MA: National Bureau of Economic Research.

Charles, K. K., & Decicca, P. (2007). Hours flexibility and retirement. *Economic Inquiry, 45*(2), 251–267.

Choi, N. G. (2000). Determinants of engagement in paid work following social security benefit receipt among older women. *Journal of Women and Aging, 12*(3/4), 133–154.

Choi, N. G. (2002). Self-defined retirement status and engagement in paid work among older working-age women: Comparison between childless women and mothers. *Sociological Inquiry, 72*(1), 43–71.

Chung, H. (2010). *The effects of childbearing patterns on the timing of retirement*. (Unpublished doctoral dissertation). University of Massachusetts, Boston, MA.

CNN Wire Staff. (2010). *More than a million protest French retirement change plans*. Retrieved January 6, 2011 from http://www.cnn.com/2010/WORLD/europe/10/19/france.strike/index.html?section=cnn_latest.

Coile, C., Diamond, P., Gruber, J., & Jousten, A. (2002). Delays in claiming Social Security benefits. *Journal of Public Economics, 84*(3), 357–385.

Connolly, M. (2008). Compulsory retirement and age discrimination: A new deference to derogation? *International Journal of Discrimination and Law, 9*, 181–198.

Cook, F. L., & Czaplewski, M. B. (2008). *Public opinion and social insurance: The American experience* (Working Paper Series, WP-08-03). Institute for Policy Research, Northwestern University. Retrieved from http://www.ipr.northwestern.edu/publications/workingpapers/wpabstracts08/wp0803.html.

Costa, D. L. (1998). *The evolution of retirement: An American economic history, 1880–1990*. Chicago, IL: The University of Chicago Press.

Cumming, E., & Henry, W. E. (1961). *Growing old: The process of disengagement*. New York, NY: Basic Books.

Curl, A. L., & Townsend, A. L. (2008). Retirement transitions among married couples. *Journal of Workplace Behavioral Health, 23*(1–2), 89–107.

Davey, A., & Szinovacz, M. E. (2004). Dimensions of marital quality and retirement. *Journal of Family Issues, 25*(4), 431–464.

Dennis, H. (2002). The retirement planning specialty. *Generations, 26*(2), 55–60.

Dentinger, E., & Clarkberg, M. (2002). Informal caregiving and retirement timing among men and women: Gender and caregiving relationships in late midlife. *Journal of Family Issues, 23*(7), 857–879.

Denton, F. T., & Spencer, B. G. (2009). What is retirement? A review and assessment of alternative concepts and measures. *Canadian Journal on Aging, 28*(1), 63–76.

Duflo, E., & Saez, E. (2002). Participation and investment decisions in a retirement plan: the influence of colleagues' choices. *Journal of Public Economics, 85*, 121–148.

Ehrich, I., & Kim, J. (2007). *Has Social Security influenced family formation and fertility in OECD countries? An economic and econometric analysis*. Cambridge, MA: National Bureau of Economic Research.

Ekerdt, D. J. (1986). The busy ethic: Moral continuity between work and retirement. *The Gerontologist, 26*, 239–244.

Ekerdt, D. J. (1998). Workplace norms for the timing of retirement. In K. W. Schaie & C. Schooler (Eds.), *Impact of work on older adults* (pp. 101–123). New York, NY: Springer.

Ekerdt, D. J. (2004). Born to retire: The foreshortened life course. *Gerontologist, 44*(1), 3–9.

Ekerdt, D. J., & Clark, E. (2001). Selling retirement in financial planning advertisements. *Journal of Aging Studies, 15*, 55–68.

Ekerdt, D. J., & DeViney, S. (1990). On defining persons as retired. *Journal of Aging Studies, 4*, 211–229.

Ekerdt, D. J., & DeViney, S. (1993). Evidence for a preretirement process among older male workers. *48*, S35–S43.

Ekerdt, D. J., & Hackney, J. K. (2002). Workers' ignorance of retirement benefits. *Gerontologist, 42*(4), 543–551.

Ekerdt, D. J., Kosloski, K., & DeViney, S. (2000). The normative anticipation of retirement by older workers. *Research on Aging, 22*, 3–22.

Elder, G., Jr. (1995). The life course paradigm: Social change and individual development. In P. Moen, J. G. Elder, & K. Lüscher (Eds.), *Examining lives in context: Perspectives on the ecology of human development* (pp. 101–140). Washington, DC: American Psychological Association.

Engelhardt, G. V., & Gruber, J. (2004). *Social Security and the evolution of elderly poverty* (Working Paper No. 10466). Cambridge, MA: National Bureau of Economic Research.

Eschtruth, A. D., Sass, S. A., & Aubry, J. (2007). *Employers lukewarm about retaining older workers*. Chestnut Hill, MA: Center for Retirement Research at Boston College.

Esping-Andersen, G. (1996). *Welfare states in transition*. London, England: Sage.

Evans, L., & Williamson, J. B. (1991). Old age dependency in historical perspective. In B. B. Hess & E. W. Markson (Eds.), *Growing old in America* (4th ed., pp. 525–530). New Brunswick, NJ: Transaction Books.

Fast, J. E., Dosman, D., & Moran, L. (2006). Productive activity in later life: Stability and change across three decades. *Research on Aging, 28*(6), 691–712.

Favreault, M. M., Sammartino, F. J., & Steuerle, C. E. (Eds.). (2002). *Social Security and the family: Addressing unmet needs in an underfunded system*. Washington, DC: The Urban Institute Press.

Feldman, D. C. (2003). Endgame: The design and implementation of early retirement incentive programs. In G. A. Adams & T. A. Beehr (Eds.), *Retirement: Reasons, processes, and results* (pp. 83–114). New York, NY: Springer.

Ferrero, K. F., Shippee, T. P., & Schafer, M. H. (2009). Cumulative inequality theory for research on aging and the life course. In V. L. Bengtson, M. Silverstein, N. M. Putney, & D. Gans (Eds.), *Handbook of theories of aging* (2nd ed., pp. 413–433). New York, NY: Springer.

Foner, N. (1993). When the contract fails: Care for the elderly in nonindustrial societies. In V. Bengtson & W. A. Achenbaum (Eds.), *The changing contract across generations* (pp. 101–118). Hawthorne, NY: Aldine de Gruyter.

Francis, D. (1990). The significance of work friends in later life. *Journal of Aging Studies, 4,* 405–424.

French, E., & Jones, J. B. (2004). *The effects of health insurance and self-insurance on retirement behavior* (Working Paper No. WP2004-12). Chestnut Hill, MA: Center for Retirement Research at Boston College.

Friedberg, L. (2007). *The recent trend towards later retirement.* Chestnut Hill, MA: Center for Retirement Research at Boston College.

Friedberg, L., Owyang, M., & Webb, A. (2008). *Identifying local differences in retirement patterns.* Chestnut Hill, MA: Center for Retirement Research at Boston College.

Gallo, W. T., Bradley, E. H., Siegiel, M., & Kasl, S. V. (2000). Health effects of involuntary job loss among older workers: Findings form the health and retirement survey. *Journal of Gerontology: Social Sciences, 55B,* S131–S140.

Giandrea, M. D., Cahill, K. E., & Quinn, J. F. (2007). *An update on bridge jobs: The HRS war babies.* Washington, DC: U.S. Department of Labor.

Gillanders, W. R., Buss, T. F., Wingard, E., & Gemmel, D. (1991). Long-term health impacts of forced early retirement among steelworkers. *Journal of Family Practice, 32,* 401–405.

Glascock, A. P. (1990). By any other name, it is still killing: A comparison of the treatment of the elderly in America and other societies. In J. Sokolovsky (Ed.), *The cultural context of aging. Wordlwide perspectives* (pp. 43–56). New York, NY: Bergin & Garvey.

Golant, S. M. (2002). Deciding where to live: The emerging residential settlement patterns of retired Americans. *Generations, 26*(2), 66–73.

Goldin, C. (1994). Understanding the gender gap: An economic history of American women. In P. Burstein (Ed.), *Equal employment opprtunity. Labor market discrimination and public policy* (pp. 17–26). Hawthorne, NY: Aldine De Gruyter.

Gonnot, J. P. (1995). Demographics changes and the pension problem: Evidence from twelve countries. In J. Gonnot, N. Keilman, & C. Prinz (Eds.), *Social security, household, and family dynamics in ageing societies* (pp. 47–110). New York, NY: Kluwer.

Goody, J. (1976). Aging in nonindustrial socieites. In R. H. Binstock & E. Shanas (Eds.), *Handbook of aging and the social sciences* (pp. 117–129). New York, NY: Van Nostrand Reinhold.

Gordo, L. R., & Wolff, J. (2011). Creating employment or keeping them busy? An evaluation of training programmes for older workers in Germany. *Journal of Aging and Social Policy, 23*(2), 198–218.

Graebner, W. (1980). *A history of retirement.* New Haven, CT: Yale University Press.

Gratton, B., & Rotondo, F. M. (1992). The "family fund": Strategies for security in old age in the industrial era. In M. Szinovacz, D. J. Ekerdt, & B. H. Vinick (Eds.), *Families and retirement* (pp. 51–63). Newbury Park, CA: Sage.

Gruber, J., Milligan, K., & Wise, D. A. (2009). *Social security programs and retirement around the world: The relationship to youth employment, introduction and summary.* Cambridge, MA: National Bureau of Economic Research.

Gruber, J., & Wise, D. (1999). *Social security programs and retirement around the world.* Chicago, IL: University of Chicago Press.

Gunderson, M. (2003). Age discrimination in employment in Canada. *Contemporary Economic Policy, 21*(3), 318–328.

Gustman, A. L., & Steinmeier, T. (2004). *Personal accounts and family retirement.* Cambridge, MA: National Bureau of Economic Research.

Gustman, A. L., & Steinmeier, T. (2008). *How changes in Social Security affect recent retirement trends.* Cambridge, MA: National Bureau of Economic Research.

Gustman, A. L., & Steinmeier, T. L. (1984, July). Modeling the retirement process for policy evaluation and research. *Monthly Labor Review, 107*(7), 26–33.

Gustman, A. L., & Steinmeier, T. L. (1994). *Retirement in a family context: A structural model for husbands and wives* (NLS Discussion Paper No. No 94-17). Washington DC: U.S. Bureau of Labor Statistics.

Gustman, A. L., & Steinmeier, T. L. (2002). *Social Security, pensions and retirement behavior within the family* (NBER Working Paper No. 8772). Cambridge, MA: National Bureau of Economic Research.

Haber, C. (2006). Old age through the lens of family history. In R. H. Binstock & L. K. George (Eds.), *Handbook of aging and the social sciences* (6th ed., pp. 59–75). Amsterdam, The Netherlands: Academic Press.

Haber, C., & Gratton, B. (1994). *Old age and the search for security: An American social history.* Bloomington, IN: Indiana University Press.

Han, S., & Moen, P. (1999). Clocking out: Temporal patterning of retirement. *American Journal of Sociology, 105*(1), 191–236.

Hank, K. (2004). Effects of early family life events on women's late life labour market behaviour. *European Sociological Review, 20*(3), 189–198.

Harber, C., & Gratton, B. (1994). *Old age and the search for security: An American social history.* Bloomington, IN: Indiana University Press.

Hardy, M. (2002). The transformation of retirement in twentieth-century America: From discontent to satisfaction. *Generations, 26*(2), 9–16.

Hardy, M. A., & Hazelrigg, L. (1999). A multilevel model of early retirement decisions among autoworkers in plants with different futures. *Research on Aging, 21,* 275–303.

Hardy, M. A., Hazelrigg, L., & Quadagno, J. (1996). *Ending a career in the auto industry: 30 and out.* New York, NY: Plenum Press.

Harrington Meyer, M., Wolf, D. A., & Himes, C. L. (2004). *Linking benefits to marital status: Race and diminishing access to Social Security spouse and widow benefits* (Working Paper No. WP2004-5). Chestnut Hill, MA: Center for Retirement Research at Boston College.

Hatcher, C. B. (2003). The economics of the retirement decision. In G. A. Adams & T. A. Beehr (Eds.), *Retirement: Reasons, processes, and results* (pp. 136–156). New York, NY: Springer.

Hayward, M., Friedman, S., & Chen, H. (1996). Race inequities in men's retirement. *The Journals of Gerontology, Series B: Psychological Sciences and Social Sciences, 51*(1), S1–S10.

Hayward, M. D., Friedman, S., & Chen, H. (1998). Career trajectories and older men's retirement. *Journal of Gerontology: Social Sciences, 53*(2), S91–S103.

Hayward, M. D., & Zhang, Z. (2001). Demography of aging: A century of global change, 1950–2050. In R. H. Binstock & L. K. George (Eds.), *Handbook of aging and the social sciences* (5th ed., pp. 70–85). San Diego, CA: Academic Press.

Held, T. (1982). Rural retirement arrangements in seventeenth-to-nineteenth-century Austria: A cross-community analysis. *Journal of Family History, 7*, 227–254.

Henkens, K. (1999). Retirement intentions and spousal support: A multi-actor approach. *Journal of Gerontology: Social Sciences, 54B*, S63–S74.

Henkens, K., & van Solinge, H. (2002). Spousal influences on the decision to retire. *International Journal of Sociology, 32*(2), 55–74.

Henretta, J. C. (1992). Uniformity and diversity: Life course institutionalization and late-life work exit. *The Sociological Quarterly, 33*, 265–279.

Hershey, D. A., & Mowen, J. C. (2000). Psychological determinants of financial preparedness for retirement. *Gerontologist, 40*(6), 687–697.

Hokenstad, M. C., & Johansson, L. (2001). Retirement patterns and pension policy: An international perspective. *Social Thought, 20*(3/4), 25–32.

Hudson, R. B., & Gonyea, J. G. (2007). The evolving role of public policy in promoting work and retirement. *Generations, 31*(1), 68–75.

Human Rights Campaign. (2010b). *Social Security survival benefits.* Retrieved from http://www.hrc.org/issues/aging/2688.htm.

International Labour Organization. (2011). LABORSTA Internet. Retrieved from http://laborsta.ilo.org/.

Johnson, R. W. (2004). *Do spouses coordinate their retirement decisions?* Chestnut Hill, MA: Center for Retirement Research at Boston College.

Johnson, R. W., Davidoff, A. J., & Perese, K. (2003). Health insurance costs and early retirement decisions. *Industrial and Labor Relations Review, 56*(4), 716–729.

Johnson, R. W., & Lo Sasso, A. T. (2000). *The trade-off between hours of paid employment and time assistance to elderly parents at midlife.* Washington, DC: The Urban Institute.

Johnson, R. W., Mermin, G. B. T., & Resseger, M. (2011). Job demands and work ability at older ages. *Journal of Aging and Social Policy, 23*(2), 101–118.

Joulain, M., Mullet, E., Lecomte, C., & Prevost, R. (2000). Perception of "appropriate" age for retirement among young adults, middle-aged adults, and elderly people. *International Journal of Aging and Human Development, 50*, 73–84.

Katz, R., Lowenstein, A., Prilutzky, D., & Halperin, D. (2011). Employers' knowledge and attitudes regarding organizational policy toward workers caring for aging family members. *Journal of Aging & Social Policy, 23*(2), 159–181.

Kim, J. E., & Moen, P. (2002). Retirement transitions, gender, and psychological well-being: A life-course, ecological model. *Journal of Gerontology: Psychological Sciences, 57*(3), P212–P222.

Kim, S., & Feldman, D. C. (1998). Healthy, wealthy, or wise: Predicting actual acceptances of early retirement incentives at three points in time. *Personnel Psychology, 51*, 623–642.

Kohli, M. (1986). The world we forgot: A historical review of the life course. In V. W. Marshall (Ed.), *Later life* (pp. 271–304). Beverly Hills, CA: Sage.

Kohli, M., Rein, M., Guillemard, A., & Van Gunsteren, H. (1991). *Time for retirement: Comparative studies of early exit from the labor force.* New York, NY: Cambridge University Press.

Kosloski, K., Ginsburg, G., & Backman, C. W. (1984). Retirement as a process of active role transition. In V. L. Allen & E. V. d. Vliert (Eds.), *Role transitions: Explorations and explanations* (pp. 331–341). New York, NY: Plenum Press.

Lahey, J. N. (2006). *How do age discrimination laws affect older workers?* Chestnut Hill, MA: Center for Retirement Research.

Laslett, P. (1977). *Family life and illicit love in earlier generations.* Cambridge, England: Cambridge University Press.

Lee, W. K. M. (2005). Gender differences in retirement decisions in Hong Kong. *Journal of Women and Aging, 17*(4), 59–76.

Longino, C. F. (2001). Geographical distribution and migration. In R. H. Binstock & L. K. George (Eds.), *Handbook of aging and the social sciences* (5th ed., pp. 106–124). New York, NY: Academic Press.

Lowenstein, A., Katz, R., & Gur-Yatish, N. (2008). Cross-national variations in elder care: Antecedents and outcomes. In M. E. Szinovacz & A. Davey (Eds.), *Caregiving contexts: Cultural, familial, and societal implications* (pp. 93–114). New York, NY: Springer.

Marshall, V. W., Clarke, P. J., & Ballantyne, P. J. (2001). Instability in the retirement transition: Effects on health and well-being in a Canadian study. *Research on Aging, 23*(4), 379–409.

Mermin, G. B. T., Johnson, R. W., & Murphy, D. (2007). Why do boomers plan to work longer? *Journal of Gerontology: Social Sciences, 62B*(5), S286–S294.

Mollica, K. A., & DeWitt, R. (2000). When others retire early: What about me? *Academy of Management Journal, 43*(6), 1068–1075.

Munnel, A. H. (2007). *Social Security's financial outlook: The 2007 report in perspective.* Chestnut Hill, MA: Center for Retirement Research at Boston College.

Munnell, A. H., Sass, S. A., & Soto, M. (2006). *Employer attitudes toward older workers: Survey results.* Chestnut Hill, MA: Center for Retirement Research at Boston College.

Munnell, A. H., & Soto, M. (2007). *Why are companies freezing their pensions?* (Working Paper No. CRR WP 2007-22). Chestnut Hill, MA: Center for Retirement Research at Boston College.

Munnell, A. H., Soto, M., Triest, R. K., & Zhivan, N. A. (2008a). *Do state economics or individual characteristics determine whether older men work?* Chestnut Hill, MA: Center for Retirement Research at Boston College.

Munnell, A. H., Soto, M., Triest, R. K., & Zhivan, N. A. (2008b). *How much do state economics and other characteristics affect retirement behavior?* Chestnut Hill, MA: Center for Retirement Research at Boston College.

Munnell, A. H., Triest, R. K., & Jivan, N. A. (2004). *How do pensions affect expected and actual retirement ages?* Chestnut Hill, MA: Center for Retirement Research at Boston College.

Myers, S. M., & Booth, A. (1996). Men's retirement and marital quality. *Journal of Family Issues, 17*, 336–358.

Neumark, D. (2003). Age discrimination legislation in the United States. *Contemporary Economic Policy, 21*(3), 297–317.

Neumark, D. (2009). The Age Discrimination in Employment Act and the challenge of population aging. *Research on Aging, 31*(1), 41–68

Neumark, D., & Stock, W. A. (1999). Age discrimination laws and labor market efficiency. *Journal of Political Economy, 107*(5), 1081–1125.

Ngan, R., Chiu, S., & Wong, W. (1999). Economic security and insecurity of Chinese older people in Hong Kong: A case of treble jeopardy. *Hallym International Journal of Aging, 1,* 35–45.

Niederfranke, A. (1991). Lebensentwürfe von Frauen beim Übergang in den Ruhestand [Life designs of retiring women]. In C. Gather, U. Gerhard, K. Prinz, & M. Veil (Eds.), *Frauen—Alterssicherung* [Women—old age security] (pp. 279–291). Berlin, Germany: Sigma.

Nuttman-Shwartz, O. (2007). Men's perceptions of family during the retirement transition. *Families in Society: The Journal of Contemporary Social Services, 88*(2), 192–202.

Nyce, S. A. (2007). The aging work force: Is demography destiny? *Generations, 31*(1), 9–15.

OECD. (2005). *Ageing and employment policies.* Retrieved from http://www.oecd.org/document/42/0,3343,en_2649_3474 7_36104426_1_1_1_1,00.html.

O'Rand, A. (2006). Stratification and the life course: Life course capital, life course risks, and social inequality. In R. H. Binstock & L. K. Geroge (Eds.), *Handbook of aging and the social sciences* (6th ed., pp. 145–162). Amsterdam, The Netherlands: Elsevier.

O'Rand, A. M. (2003). Cumulative advantage and gerontological theory. *Annual Review of Gerontology and Geriatrics, 22,* 14–30.

Pienta, A. M. (2003). Partners in marriage: An analysis of husbands' and wives' retirement behavior. *Journal of Applied Gerontology, 22*(3), 340–358.

Pienta, A. M., & Hayward, M. D. (2002). Who expects to continue working after age 62? The retirement plans of couples. *Journal of Gerontology: Social Sciences, 57*(4), S199–S208.

Piktialis, D. (2007). Adaptations to an aging work force: Innovative responses by the corporate sector. *Generations, 31*(1), 76–82.

Pitt-Catsouphes, M. (2007). Between a twentieth- and twenty-first-century workforce: Employers at the tipping point. *Generations, 31*(1), 50–56.

Quinn, J. F. (2000). New paths to retirement. In O. S. Mitchell, P. B. Hammond, & A. M. Rappaport (Eds.), *Forecasting retirement needs and retirement wealth* (pp. 13–32). Philadelphia, PA: University of Pennsylvania Press.

Remnet, V. L. (1987). How adult children respond to role transitions in the lives of their aging parents. *Educational Gerontology, 13,* 341–355.

Riley, M., & Riley, J. (1994). Age integration and the lives of older people. *The Gerontologist, 34*(1), 110–115.

Rix, S. E. (1999). The politics of old age in the United States. In A. Walker & G. Naegele (Eds.), *The politics of old age in Europe* (pp. 178–196). Buckingham, United Kingdom: Open University Press.

Rix, S. E. (2002). The labor market for older workers. *Generations, 26*(2), 25–33.

Sainsbury, D. (1996). *Gender equality and welfare states.* Cambridge, England: Cambridge University Press.

Schils, T. (2008). Early retirement in Germany, the Netherlands, and the United Kingdom: A longitudinal analysis of individual factors and institutional regimes. *European Sociological Review, 24*(3), 315–329.

Schultz, K. S., Morton, K. R., & Weckerle, J. R. (1998). The influence of push and pull factors on voluntary and involuntary early retirees' retirement decision and adjustment. *Journal of Vocational Behavior, 53,* 45–57.

Serow, W. J. (2001). Economic and social implications of demographic patterns. In R. H. Binstock & L. K. George (Eds.), *Handbook of aging and the social sciences* (5th ed., pp. 86–102). San Diego, CA: Academic Press.

Settersten, R. A. (2003a). Invitation to the life course: The promise. In R. A. Settersten (Ed.), *Invitation to the life course: Toward new understandings of later life* (pp. 1–12). Amityville, NY: Baywood.

Settersten, R. A. (2003b). Propositions and controversies in life-course scholarship. In R. A. Settersten (Ed.), *Invitation to the life course: Toward new understandings of later life* (pp. 15–48). Amityville, NY: Baywood.

Settersten, R. A., & Hagestad, G. O. (1996). What's the latest? II. Cultural age deadlines for educational and work transition. *The Gerontologist, 36,* 602–613.

Sevak, P., Weir, D. R., & Willis, R. J. (2003/4). The economic consequences of a husband's death: Evidence from the HRS and AHEAD. *Social Security Bulletin, 65*(3), 31–44.

Shuey, K. M. (2004). Worker preferences, spousal coordination, and participation in an employer-sponsored pension plan. *Research on Aging, 26*(3), 287–316.

Shultz, K. S. (2003). Bridge employment: Work after retirement. In G. A. Adams & T. A. Beehr (Eds.), *Retirement: Reasons, processes, and results* (pp. 214–241). New York, NY: Springer.

Skirboll, E., & Silverman, M. (1992). Women's retirement: A case study approach. *Journal of Women and Aging, 4,* 77–90.

Smith, D. B., & Moen, P. (1998). Spousal influence on retirement: His, her, and their perceptions. *Journal of Marriage and the Family, 60,* 734–744.

Social Security Administration. (2008). *Social security programs throughout the world: Europe.* Retrieved from http://www.socialsecurity.gov/policy/docs/progdesc/ssptw/2008-2009/europe/ssptw08euro.pdf.

Social Security Administration. (2010a). *Fast facts & figures about Social Security.* Retrieved from http://www.socialsecurity.gov/policy/docs/chartbooks/fast_facts/.

Social Security Administration. (2010b). *A summary of the 2010 Social Security and Medicare trust fund reports.* Retrieved from http://www.socialsecurity.gov/OACT/TRSUM/tr10summary.pdf.

Steinhilber, S. (2002). *The gender impact of pension reforms: Case studies of the Czech Republic, Hungary, and Poland.* Retrieved from http://www.oecd.org/dataoecd/40/47/2094610.pdf.

Steinmetz, S. K. (1988). *Duty bound. Elder abuse and family care.* Newbury Park, CA: Sage.

Steuerele, C. E., & Bakija, J. M. (1994). *Retooling Social Security for the 21st century: Right and wrong approaches to reform.* Washington, DC: Urban Institute Press.

Steuerle, C. E., & Renanne, S. (2011). *Social Security and Medicare taxes and benefits over a lifetime.* Retrieved from http://www.urban.org/UploadedPDF/social-security-medicare-benefits-over-lifetime.pdf.

Szinovacz, M. (1989). Decision-making on retirement timing. In D. Brinberg & J. Jaccard (Eds.), *Dyadic decision making* (pp. 286–310). New York, NY: Springer.

Szinovacz, M. (1996). Couple's employment/retirement patterns and marital quality. *Research on Aging, 18,* 243–268.

Szinovacz, M., & DeViney, S. (2000). Marital characteristics and retirement decisions. *Research on Aging, 22*, 470–489.

Szinovacz, M., & Schaffer, A. M. (2000). Effects of retirement on marital conflict management. *Journal of Family Issues, 21*, 367–389.

Szinovacz, M. E. (1996). Couples' employment/retirement patterns and marital quality. *Research on Aging, 18*, 243–268.

Szinovacz, M. E. (2002). Couple retirement patterns and retirement age. *International Journal of Sociology, 32*(2), 30–54.

Szinovacz, M. E. (2003). Contexts and pathways: Retirement as institution, process, and experience. In G. E. Adams & T. A. Beehr (Eds.), *Retirement: Reasons, processes, and outcomes* (pp. 6–52). New York, NY: Springer.

Szinovacz, M. E. (2006). Families and retirement. In L. O. Stone (Ed.), *New frontiers of research on retirement* (pp. 165–198). Ottawa, Canada: Statistics Canada.

Szinovacz, M. E. (2007). The future of intergenerational relationships—variability and vulnerabilities (commentary). In K. W. Schaie & P. Uhlenberg (Eds.), *Social structures: Demographic changes and the well-being of older persons* (pp. 262–282). New York, NY: Springer.

Szinovacz, M. E., & Davey, A. (2001). Retirement effects on parent-adult child contacts. *The Gerontologist, 41*(2), 191–200.

Szinovacz, M. E., & Davey, A. (2004a). Honeymoons and joint lunches: Effects of retirement and spouse's employment on depressive symptoms. *Journal of Gerontology: Psychological Sciences, 59B*, P233–P245.

Szinovacz, M. E., & Davey, A. (2004b). Retirement transitions and spouse disability: Effects on depressive symptoms. *Journal of Gerontology: Social Sciences, 59B*(6), S333–S342.

Szinovacz, M. E., & Davey, A. (2005). Predictors of perceptions of involuntary retirement. *The Gerontologist, 45*(1), 36–47.

Szinovacz, M. E., & DeViney, S. (1999). The retiree identity: Gender and race differences. *Journal of Gerontology: Social Sciences, 54B*, S207–S218.

Szinovacz, M. E., & DeViney, S. (2000). Marital characteristics and retirement decisions. *Research on Aging, 22*, 470–489.

Szinovacz, M. E., DeViney, S., & Davey, A. (2001). Influences of family obligations and relationships on retirement: Variations by gender, race, and marital status. *Journal of Gerontology: Social Sciences, 56B*, S20–S27.

Szinovacz, M. E., Ekerdt, D. J., Butt, A., Barton, K., & Oala, C. R. (in press). Families and retirement. In R. Blieszner & V. H. Bedford (Eds.), *Handbook of families and aging* (2nd ed.). Santa Barbara, CA: Praeger (ABC-CLIO).

Szinovacz, M. E., & Schaffer, A. M. (2000). Effects of retirement on marital conflict management. *Journal of Family Issues, 21*, 367–389.

Timmons, J. C., Hall, A. C., Fesko, S. L., & Migliore, A. (2011). Retaining the older workforce: Social policy considerations for the universally designed workplace. *Journal of Aging and Social Policy, 23*(2), 119–140.

Trydegård, G. (2000). From poorhourse overseer to production manager: One hundred years of old-age care in Sweden reflected in the development of an occupation. *Ageing and Society, 20*, 571–597.

U.S. Bureau of the Census. (2009). *Annual social and economic (ASEC) supplement.* Retrieved from http://www.census.gov/hhes/www/cpstables/032010/pov/new01_000.htm.

U.S. Bureau of the Census. (2011). *Current Population Survey (CPS)—Definitions and explanations.* Retrieved http://www.census.gov/population/www/cps/cpsdef.html.

Uccello, C. E. (2000). *Do spouses coordinate their investment decisions in order to share risks?* Chestnut Hill, MA: Center for Retirement Research at Boston College.

Ulrich, L. B., & Brott, P. E. (2005). Older workers and bridge employment: Redefining retirement. *Journal of Employment Counseling, 42*(4), 159–170.

Van Solinge, H., & Henkens, K. (2007). Involuntary retirement: The role of restrictive circumstances, timing, and social embeddedness. *Journal of Gerontology: Social Sciences, 62B*(5), S295–S303.

Van Tilburg, T. (1992). Support networks before and after retirement. *Journal of Social and Personal Relationships, 9*, 433–445.

Van Tilburg, T. (2003). Consequences of men's retirement for the continuation of work-related personal relationships. *Ageing International, 28*(4), 345–358.

Vinick, B. H., & Ekerdt, D. J. (1991a). Retirement: What happens to husband-wife relationships? *Journal of Geriatric Psychiatry, 24*, 23–40.

Vinick, B. H., & Ekerdt, D. J. (1991b). The transition to retirement: Responses of husbands and wives. In B. B. Hess & E. W. Markson (Eds.), *Growing old in America* (4th ed., pp. 305–317). New Brunswick, NJ: Transaction Books.

von Wachter, T. (2007). *The effect of economic conditions on the employment of workers nearing retirement age.* Chestnut Hill, MA: Center for Retirement Research at Boston College.

Walker, A. (1983). Social policy and elderly people in Great Britain: The construction of dependent social and economic status in old age. In A. Guillemard (Ed.), *Old age and the welfare state* (pp. 143–167). London, England: Sage

Walker, A. (2006). Aging and politics: An international perspective. In R. H. Binstock & L. K. George (Eds.), *Handbook of aging and the social sciences* (6th ed., pp. 339–359). Amsterdam, The Netherlands: Elsevier.

Williamson, J. B., & McNamara, T. K. (2003). Interrupted trajectories and labor force participation. *Research on Aging, 25*(2), 87–121.

Williamson, J. B., & Pampel, F. C. (1993). *Old-age security in comparative perspective.* New York, NY: Oxford University Press.

Woodbury, R. (2001). The motivations for business retirement policies. In S. Ogura, T. Tachibanaki, & D. A. Wise (Eds.), *Aging issues in the United States and Japan* (pp. 307–333). Chicago, IL: The University of Chicago Press.

Zhang, Y., & Goza, F. W. (2006). Who will care for the elderly in China?: A review of the problems caused by China's one-child policy and their potential solutions. *Journal of Aging Studies, 20*(2), 151–164.

PART 3

Retirement Research

Research Methods in Retirement Research

Gwenith G. Fisher *and* Robert J. Willis

Abstract

Research on the retirement process has been extensively studied by social science researchers across a variety of disciplines, including economics, sociology, and psychology. The majority of this research has relied on survey research methods, primarily resulting from a huge investment in large public-use datasets of longitudinal surveys. This chapter describes many of the surveys that have been used to study retirement (including the Retirement History Survey, the Health and Retirement Study, the Panel Study of Income Dynamics, the Wisconsin Longitudinal Study, and the Cognitive Economics Study, among others) and key issues in survey research methodology, including sampling design, nonresponse, and treatment of missing data. We also describe the application of experimental methods (including natural experiments) as well as qualitative research to the study of retirement. Finally, this chapter discusses ways in which retirement research methods have evolved and outlines key issues for the future of retirement research.

Key Words: research methodology, survey research, measurement, sample design, quantitative research, longitudinal studies

Introduction

The importance of studying retirement is underscored by the changing demographics of the older population, changes in economic policies related to retirement, and the increasingly varied options regarding the process of retirement. For example, people are living longer, healthier lives than in decades past and working longer. There is a higher proportion of women in the workforce as well as a higher proportion of dual-earner couples. Changes to Social Security policy have been enacted to encourage delayed retirement ages. Fewer employers offer defined benefit pension plans, and defined contribution plans (e.g., 401(k)s) are becoming the norm. The response to these issues is a growing body of research on retirement to answer important questions and guide economic and social policy. Retirement research over the past few decades

has expanded considerably, not only in the United States but globally as well. In recent years, retirement research has become more interdisciplinary and utilizes a variety of data sources and research methods.

Retirement research has covered a wide variety of topics and addressed numerous research questions stemming from multiple theoretical frameworks. Some examples of influential economic theories include life-cycle frameworks (e.g., Ando & Modigliani, 1963; Modigliani, 1986) and behavioral economics (Simon, 1987). In psychology, retirement research has often been framed in terms of a life-course perspective (Elder, 1994; Giele & Elder, 1998), continuity theory (Atchley, 1989), and role theory (Kahn, Wolfe, Quinn, Snoek, & Rosenthal, 1964).

As evidenced by the other chapters in this handbook, retirement is a topic that has been extensively studied by social science researchers across a variety of disciplines, including economics, sociology, and psychology (Topa, Moriano, Depolo, Alcover, & Morales, 2009; Wang & Shultz, 2010). Researchers across multiple disciplines have studied a number of *antecedents* such as wealth (Smith, 1995; Willis, 1999), financial literacy (Lusardi & Mitchell, 2007a), financial planning (Goda, Shoven, & Slavov, 2010), expectations (Bruine de Bruin, Manski, Topa, & van der Klaauw, 2011; Hurd, Reti, & Rohwedder, 2009), health status (McGarry, 2004), family characteristics (Pienta & Hayward, 2002), attitudes (Barnes-Farrell, 2003), and work/family conflict (Raymo & Sweeney, 2006) as well as *outcomes* of retirement, including retirement adjustment (Szinovacz & Davey, 2004), satisfaction (Floyd, Haynes, Doll, Winemiller, Lemsky, et al., 1992; Pinquart & Schindler, 2007), and economic well-being (Smith, 1995, 1997).

The purpose of this chapter is to describe various research methods that have been used to study retirement. Developing a better understanding of retirement research methods is important for many reasons. First, retirement research has been conducted in multiple disciplines (e.g., economics, sociology, psychology, etc.), which may rely on different research methods. Second, it may increase our understanding of the extant body of retirement literature. Third, understanding research methods for studying retirement may guide researchers conducting future studies of retirement.

This chapter is organized as follows: first, we provide various definitions of retirement and an overview of various research centers that facilitate retirement research. The majority of the chapter includes a review of specific research methods, with an emphasis on surveys and survey research methods because the majority of extant retirement research has relied on surveys. We describe additional research methods, including experimental and qualitative research. Then, we describe how retirement research methods have evolved and conclude the chapter with recommendations for future research.

Defining and Measuring Retirement

Retirement research has been primarily conceptualized in two ways: (1) focusing on retirement behavior (e.g., withdrawal from the labor force), including the form and timing with which this behavior takes place, and 2) focusing on outcomes of retirement, including economic, psychosocial, and health experiences post-retirement (Ekerdt, 2010). Indeed, retirement has been defined in many ways in the literature, sometimes making it difficult to compare results across studies. Gustman and Steinmeier (2000) indicated that retirement status can differ depending on the definition of retirement. For example, retirement is frequently defined in terms of withdrawal from the labor force, though this may take many forms, such as full retirement, gradual reduction in work hours, engaging in bridge employment (i.e., moving from one career job to another, often less demanding job), or leaving work due to disability. Particularly in the current economic recession, retirement may consist of forced unemployment among older workers who may desire to continue working but are unable to obtain gainful employment. Retirement has also been conceptualized in terms of filing for pension or Social Security benefits (Gustman, Mitchell, & Steinmeier, 1995), as well as one's "state of mind" rather than a more objective measure of one's labor force or financial status (Lumsdaine & Mitchell, 1999). Some research has also examined retirement in terms of transitions and adjustment to retirement, which is related to but distinct from the act of leaving the workplace. Another issue pertaining to the definition of retirement is that some individuals may change their retirement status over time, such as moving between the status of work and retirement. Some have referred to the notion of working, retiring, and then working again as "unretirement" (Maestas, 2010)—behavior for which NFL quarterback Brett Favre was admonished.

The consequence of having multiple definitions of retirement is that measures of retirement vary across studies. Lumsdaine and Mitchell (1999) provided examples of how varying definitions of retirement yielded different results in terms of workforce participation statistics. Some have examined retirement preferences (e.g., Beehr, 1986; Barnes-Farrell, 2003; Barnes-Farrell et al., 2008; Raymo & Sweeney, 2006). For example, Barnes-Farrell (2003) indicated that individuals' reactions to retirement may depend on the extent to which the timing of and manner by which one retires is consistent with their retirement preferences. However, it is well known that retirement behavior is importantly influenced by wealth, pensions, and other factors (e.g., health status; Wang & Shultz, 2010), which suggests that limiting the definition to retirement preferences omits the consideration or effects of other important factors. Other studies have examined retirement intentions, such as at what age or in what year a person plans to retire (e.g., Barnes-Farrell et al., 2008). Yet still additional studies have measured actual, rather than planned, retirement behavior. In particular, Wang, Zhan, Liu, and Shultz (2008) examined older workers who engage in bridge employment. Rust and Phelan (1997) showed that actual retirement peaked at ages 62 and 65, the ages for early and normal eligibility for Social Security benefits, respectively. Some research has compared retirement preferences or intentions to actual behavior. For example, Hurd, Reti, and Rohwedder (2009) concluded that retirement intentions are generally predictive of actual retirement behavior. However, Barnes-Farrell (2003) indicated that retirement preferences will not always translate to actual retirement behavior, as individuals' circumstances or other constraints may change.

Different conceptualizations of retirement have implications for methods and measures of retirement. The use of longitudinal research methods for studying retirement is critical, because retirement is ultimately a process that unfolds over time. We recommend that researchers continue to examine both retirement behavior as well as retirement outcomes. As social science research becomes more and more interdisciplinary, it is our hope that researchers from multiple disciplines will be able to share a common language and operationalization of what we mean by retirement. Given the dynamic nature of the economy and other factors that may play a role in the timing and form of retirement, we cannot assume that what we know now about retirement will not change in time.

Quantitative Research Methods

In this next section, we will review various quantitative research methods that have been used to conduct retirement research, provide examples from the literature, and identify key strengths and limitations associated with these methods.

Survey Research Methods
PUBLIC-USE DATASETS

The majority of retirement research studies have been largely the result of a major investment in public-use datasets. Such investments include surveys sponsored by the National Institute on Aging (NIA), the National Science Foundation (NSF), the U.S. Department of Labor, and the Social Security Administration, including the Health and Retirement Study (HRS), the Panel Study of Income Dynamics (PSID), and the Wisconsin Longitudinal Study (WLS). (See Table 12.2 for a listing of aging and retirement studies and possible data resources.) This large investment in public-use datasets can

facilitate multi- and interdisciplinary research and guide public policy.

Studies such as the HRS, PSID, and WLS have played a major role in retirement research due to the need for a population perspective. Understanding retirement behavior at the population level is critical for public policy. These surveys provide rich sources of data from nationally representative samples so that research results can be accurately generalized to the population as a whole. Another strength of these public-use datasets is that they have large sample sizes, which facilitates data analyses and provides opportunities for analysis of subgroups. We will discuss more about the issue of sampling later in this chapter.

Retirement History Study (RHS)

The Retirement History Study (RHS) was a dominant source of data for studying retirement in the 1970s and 1980s (Juster & Suzman, 1995). The RHS sample included a cohort of men and unmarried women ages 58–63 surveyed in 1969 and followed longitudinally until 1979. The survey data were strengthened by the linked records of the Social Security quarterly covered earnings file. One of the most widely cited studies conducted using data from the Retirement History Study is by Rust and Phelan (1997), who developed a dynamic programming model that showed that age of retirement peaked at 62 and 65 for the majority of older Americans, coinciding with the early and normal age of eligibility for Social Security benefits.

As described by Juster and Suzman (1995), the RHS became dated by the mid-1980s—a time when significant changes in demographics were taking place, including an increase in the proportion of women in the workforce, increases in longevity due to improved health, and trends toward earlier retirement. It became obvious that women (especially married women) were underrepresented due to the sampling in the RHS, which excluded married women. The RHS did not measure health or cognitive status to aid researchers in understanding the trend toward increasing numbers of people applying for disability insurance. It also lacked good measures of private pensions, which were becoming more prevalent by this point in time. There was some discussion in the federal and academic scientific research community regarding the possibility of re-interviewing the RHS cohort or adding a new cohort to the study, but a decision was made not to do so because of Title 13 of the U.S. Code, outlining the role of the U.S. Census, which could have severely constrained the design of a new retirement survey. This culminated in the decision by the National Institute on Aging to launch a new retirement study, which became the Health and Retirement Study (Juster & Suzman, 1995).

Health and Retirement Study (HRS)

The HRS is a cooperative agreement between the National Institute on Aging and the University of Michigan that began surveying respondents in 1992 (U01 AG009740). It was designed to provide the research community with a rich data source to study the economics, health, and demography of aging. More recently, the HRS has also paid more attention to psychological well-being and other psychosocial issues important in the study of older adults. The HRS is one of the most prominent sources of data for examining labor force participation, pensions, health conditions and health status, economic status, family structure, and financial transfers among family members. According to Juster and Suzman (1995), the HRS is "one of the largest and most ambitious academic social science projects ever undertaken" (p. S7). The National Institute on Aging provided support for the development of the Health and Retirement Study early relative to the scheduled survey data collection, in order to provide ample time for the development of a large, complex interdisciplinary study. One of the unique and powerful features of the HRS is the interdisciplinary collaboration between academic researchers and government agencies (e.g., NIA and SSA), with input from many members of both the academic and federal statistical communities. This differs from other academic research projects that are designed and executed by a principal investigator, small group of researchers, or federal entity.

The original HRS sample in 1992 was a cohort of men and women age 51–61 selected using a multistage, national area-clustered probability sample frame with an oversample of blacks, Hispanics (primarily Mexican Americans), and Florida residents. These individuals were re-interviewed in 1994 and 1996 and then combined with the 1993 AHEAD cohort (i.e., individuals age 70 or older in 1993) and two new cohorts added in 1998 to create a national probability sample of individuals born in 1947 or earlier (i.e., age 51 or older in 1998). The HRS uses a steady-state sampling design with a new cohort of individuals age 51–56 added every six years (e.g., in 1998, 2004, 2010) to prevent the obsolescence that occurred in the Retirement History Survey (Willis, 1999). Another unique characteristic of the

HRS sample design is that age-eligible individuals and their spouses, regardless of age, are interviewed. This approach yields data from both individuals in a couple, gathering more information about the household and creating opportunities for dyadic analyses. At the time this chapter was written, the HRS has conducted ten waves of data between 1992 and 2010 and interviewed more than 33,000 individuals. Response rates are quite high, with the baseline response rate being 81.7% and re-interview response rates ranging from 84% to 93% (Health and Retirement Study, 2008).

The HRS is designed to facilitate the interdisciplinary study of retirement. The HRS includes data on a broad array of topics, including employment and retirement status, occupation, industry, job and work environment characteristics, income, pensions, other retirement plans, housing, assets, estate planning, subjective probabilities (i.e., expectations) of future events, demographic characteristics, heath conditions and health status, health care utilization, cognitive status, physical functioning and disability, family characteristics and intergenerational transfers, health insurance, life insurance, and internet usage. In addition, the HRS has linkages to administrative data, including the Social Security Administration for earnings data, Medicare, and the National Death Index.

To date, more than 2,000 studies (including 1,091 journal articles, 540 reports, 24 books, 125 book chapters, and 240 dissertations) have been conducted using the HRS, with more than one-third of these being related to the study of retirement. Some examples of high-impact studies conducted using data from the HRS include research by Smith (1995, 1997), who demonstrated a strong positive correlation between wealth and health. Willis (1999) expanded upon this finding by relating husband's health status, wife's health status, and household wealth, and illustrated that both husband's and wife's health were strongly correlated with household net worth. Gustman and Steinmeier have published numerous papers on pensions and Social Security, contributing greatly to what we know about various sources of retirement savings and income, as well as retirement trends in relation to pensions and changes in Social Security policy (e.g., Gustman & Steinmeier, 2004, 2009; Gustman, Steinmeier, & Tabatabai, 2010a, 2010b). Bound et al. (1999) examined the dynamic effects of health on labor force transitions, including disability and retirement. Wang and colleagues identified four categories of antecedents of bridge employment in transition to retirement, including individual characteristics, job-related psychological variables, family-related variables, and retirement planning, and found that engaging in bridge employment is associated with better physical and mental health outcomes compared to full retirement (Wang, Zhan, Liu, & Shultz, 2008; Zhan, Wang, Liu, & Shultz, 2009).

For the past decade, international efforts to develop studies like the HRS have grown rapidly. Examples include the English Longitudinal Study of Aging and the Survey of Health, Aging, and Retirement in Europe; the Mexican Health and Aging Study (MHAS); and comparable studies in Ireland, Israel, New Zealand, South Korea, China, Japan, India, and Costa Rica. Table 12.2 presents a list of these studies. New studies in Thailand and Brazil were being developed at the time this chapter was written.

Panel Study of Income Dynamics (PSID)

The PSID is a longitudinal study of aging that has been ongoing since 1968. The study began with two samples in 1968: (1) approximately 3,000 nationally representative families in the United States selected through the University of Michigan Survey Research Center's multistage sampling process (i.e., the "SRC sample"), and (2) an oversample of approximately 2,000 low-income families selected from the Survey of Economic Opportunity (i.e., the "SEO sample"). PSID interviewed individuals from families in these two samples every year from 1968 to 1996 and biennially thereafter—regardless of whether these individuals were living together in the same dwelling. A portion of the low-income (SEO) sample was dropped in 1997 due to budgetary constraints on account of the sample size of the PSID having doubled during its thirty-year history. A third sample of 441 families was added in 1997 and 1999 to increase the generalizability of the sample by including immigrant families who came to the United States since the core panel was selected in 1968. By 2009, the sample size of the post-1968 immigrant families grew to 638 due to split-off families created from the original sample of 441 immigrant families.

A unique feature of the PSID is that sons and daughters of sample members have been interviewed as well, creating an opportunity for researchers to compare economic, social, and health outcomes across up to four generations within the same family as well as among adult siblings. In the 2007 wave of PSID, there were 4,383 parent-child pairs in which both the parent and the adult child completed a core interview. This sample facilitates research regarding how one (or more) generations concurrently affect one another, such as how current parental or grandparental circumstances affect adult children's outcomes (and vice versa). Another analytic opportunity with data in the PSID is to examine outcomes of succeeding generations at the same age. For example, Lee and Solon (2009) and Gouskova, Chiteji, and Stafford (2010) have used PSID data to study intergenerational income mobility using information on father-son pairs at the same age (e.g., earnings at 40 years of age for both fathers and sons).

The PSID is similar to the HRS in terms of being a panel study and providing a rich source of interdisciplinary data. Topics covered by the PSID include employment and retirement, income, wealth, pensions, health, health insurance, health expenditures, demographics, as well as a disability and use of time supplement. The PSID is primarily funded by the National Institute on Aging and the National Science Foundation, with additional support from other government agencies and organizations, including the Eunice Kennedy Shriver National Institute of Child Health and Human Development, the Economic Research Service of the U.S. Department of Agriculture, the U.S. Department of Health and Human Services, the U.S. Department of Housing and Urban Development, and the Indiana University Purdue University Center on Philanthropy. To date, more than 3,000 journal articles, books, book chapters, and dissertations have been written using data from the PSID.

The PSID is an excellent complement to the HRS because it gathers important data about savings and consumption behavior throughout individuals' working lives, rather than beginning in their early 50s. This is important because the economic status of individuals nearing or at retirement is strongly influenced by savings and consumption behaviors throughout one's working life (Hurd, 1997). Examples of key findings from the PSID regarding retirement include Juster et al.'s (2006) explanation of the decline in savings rates in the United States that began in the early 1980s. Using data in the PSID, they determined that large improvements in capital gains of corporate equities explain this decline in savings rates. Altonji and Doraszelski (2005) examined racial disparities in wealth and found that large differences in wealth accumulations observed between blacks and whites at older ages can be explained to some degree by differences in savings and investment choices earlier in life.

Cognitive Economics Study (CogEcon)

The Cognitive Economics Project (CogEcon) was launched in 2007 by Robert Willis at the University of Michigan's Survey Research Center as part of a data innovation program project to study economic behavior using survey research methods (P01-AG026571). The CogEcon project was designed by a team of economists to help understand the cognitive bases of economic decision making. CogEcon data are linked to an additional dataset containing a large battery of cognitive ability measures from the Cognition in the USA or CogUSA Study (McArdle, Fisher, & Rodgers, 2007). The combined CogEcon/CogUSA study provides an unprecedented opportunity for psychologists and economists to link cognitive ability with economic knowledge and behavior.

Data were collected via internet and mail surveys, with responses from a national sample of approximately 1,000 respondents. The first wave of the CogEcon study included measures of work status, financial sophistication, income, wealth, asset allocation, consumption, and risk tolerance. The second wave of the survey occurred after the economic decline that began in late 2008, resulting in a valuable opportunity to assess economic outcomes before and after the recent economic decline.

The recent economic downturn that began in 2008 further changed the retirement picture for many older Americans, as many people who had planned to retire at about that time could no longer afford to do so. One of the key findings from the CogEcon study was that individuals who had planned to retire in 2008 or 2009 delayed their retirement an average of 1.6 years (McFall, 2011). One of the first papers from this study examined the relationship between fluid intelligence and individuals' ability to answer financial literacy questions correctly, controlling for effort (Delavande, Rohwedder, & Willis, 2008). In addition, these researchers found that personality variables were significantly related to the amount of effort that respondents put into answering financial literacy questions. Shapiro (2010) found that individuals with a higher cognitive ability are more risk tolerant and that those who are more risk tolerant hold a higher fraction of their wealth in stocks (a relatively risky asset). This finding accords with findings in an emerging literature. For example, Dohmen, Falk, Huffman, and Sunde (2010; using German data) found that more intelligent individuals are both more risk tolerant and more patient (i.e., put more weight on future vs. present outcomes). Further, Hudomiet, Kezdi, and Willis (2011) found that individuals with higher levels of cognitive ability view the stock market as having higher returns with less risk, and that their beliefs about returns reacted more strongly in response to the financial crisis.

RAND American Life Panel (ALP)

The American Life Panel, conducted by Kapteyn and colleagues at the RAND Corporation, is an internet survey conducted among participants of the Reuters/University of Michigan Survey of Consumers (which is based on a random digit dialing (RDD) sample frame). Recognizing that not all of the targeted ALP respondents use the internet, the ALP investigators reduce sampling bias by providing individuals who do not have internet access with a device that connects to their TV (i.e., web TV). The ALP allows for experimental exploration of new topics not covered by established surveys such as the HRS. For example, ALP modules provided data for an early exploration of the role of financial literacy in retirement planning (Lusardi & Mitchell, 2007b) and research on subjective judgments about the adequacy of retirement income (Binswanger & Schunk, 2009). The capacity to design, field, and analyze data from online surveys quickly allowed the ALP to create a monthly high-frequency panel survey that tracks employment, consumption and expenditures, and expectations. The ALP began collecting data in November 2009, only two months after the fall of Lehman Brothers set off the financial crisis and Great Recession (Hurd & Rohwedder, 2010).

Wisconsin Longitudinal Study

The Wisconsin Longitudinal Study (WLS) is a publicly available longitudinal study of 10,317 men and women randomly sampled among those who graduated from a Wisconsin high school in 1957 (i.e., born around 1939). The original wave of data was collected in 1957 from sampled individuals or their parents. Follow-up surveys were conducted among original participants in 1964, 1975, 1992, and 2004. Additional data have been collected from selected siblings, spouses of the original respondents, spouses of the selected siblings, and widow(er)s of the graduates and siblings in 2006. Topics covered by the WLS include demographic characteristics, labor market experiences, military experience, retirement, family characteristics and functioning, intergenerational transfers and relationships, psychological characteristics, social participation, physical and mental health and well-being, and morbidity and mortality from late adolescence through 2008.

One of the most notable studies of retirement based on data from the WLS examined the relationship between work/family conflict and retirement preferences (Raymo & Sweeney, 2006). In particular, these researchers found that individuals who experienced higher levels of work demands interfering with family demands and family demands interfering with work demands were significantly more likely to want to retire in the next ten years compared to those who experienced lower levels of work-to-family and family-to-work conflict.

Americans' Changing Lives Study

The Americans' Changing Lives (ACL) is a national longitudinal panel study conducted by House and colleagues (House, 2002) with oversamples of blacks/African Americans studied between 1986 and 2002. It was designed to gather data on sociological, psychological, mental, and physical health issues in middle and later adulthood. Data from the ACL are available from the Inter-university Consortium for Political and Social Research (ICPSR). Herzog, House, and Morgan (1991) used data from the Americans' Changing Lives study to examine the role of work and retirement on health and well-being in later life. Specifically, they studied patterns of labor force participation (including nonparticipation) and found, as hypothesized, that individuals whose work status was consistent with their preferences had higher levels of physical health and psychological well-being compared to those whose work status was constrained by other factors.

CROSS-NATIONAL STUDIES

Although the majority of this chapter focuses on retirement research in the United States, it is important to note that many other countries around the world have developed studies modeled after the HRS. This creates excellent opportunities for cross-national studies of retirement patterns and trends, which present rich opportunities for the study of retirement. Table 12.2 presents a list of such studies.

Gruber and Wise (1999) compared the retirement income system (e.g., Social Security in the United States) among eleven industrialized nations to examine the role of policies and the retirement income system on retirement timing. They concluded that (1) social security eligibility ages are important predictors of early labor force withdrawal, (2) many countries have unemployment and disability programs that play an important role in early retirement, and (3) implicit tax rates on social security programs have an important effect on the early retirement age. Rohwedder and Willis (2010) used data from the HRS, the English Longitudinal Study of Ageing (ELSA), and the Survey of Health, Aging, and Retirement in Europe (SHARE, a study of eleven European countries) in 2004 to determine whether retirement leads to cognitive decline. By examining comparable measures of episodic memory in relation to labor force participation among people in their 50s and 60s cross-nationally at a country-aggregate level, they concluded that early retirement has a significant negative impact on cognitive functioning.

GOVERNMENT DATASETS

Government databases have played a crucial role in retirement research in the United States for many decades. Examples of data sources include the Social Security Administration, the Bureau of Labor Statistics, and the Census Bureau. The Social Security Administration's administrative records and earnings files have been used to provide objective sources of employment earnings and Social Security income data. The Bureau of Labor Statistics (BLS) provides valuable information concerning labor force statistics (e.g., employment, hours, and earnings), which is helpful for understanding and documenting trends in labor force patterns for the U.S. population as a whole, as well as by characteristics such as age, gender, and occupational sector. Every month, the BLS Current Employment Statistics program surveys approximately 140,000 businesses and government agencies, representing approximately 440,000 individual worksites.

The Census Bureau conducts a number of surveys and provides a wide array of economic data (e.g., employment, housing prices, and income), some of which may be useful to researchers studying retirement. For example, the Current Population Survey (CPS) gathers data concerning work experience, income, household composition, migration, health insurance coverage, and receipt of noncash benefits. CPS data are useful for specific analyses, as well as for the post-stratification of population-based survey sample weights, which will be explained later in the chapter.

The retirement literature also includes studies based on some lesser-known government or federal surveys. For example, von Bonsdorff, Shultz, Leskinen, and Tansky (2009) used data from the Merit Principle Survey that was conducted by the U.S. Merit Systems Protection Board (MSPB) to examine the choice between full retirement and bridge employment. This survey was conducted among more than 17,000 federal employees.

OTHERS SURVEYS

Not all survey-based retirement research has been conducted using large-scale public-use or government datasets. Many studies have been done using smaller samples from a particular organization or occupational sector. One distinct advantage of these other, smaller surveys on retirement is that researchers who conduct these surveys have a great deal of flexibility over the design and content compared to the use of archival datasets.

There are many examples of retirement research using smaller surveys. One study by Talaga and Beehr (1995) published in the *Journal of Applied Psychology* sought to determine whether there are gender differences in predicting retirement decisions. They gathered data from older working employees and retirees of a large Midwestern manufacturing organization. Their results indicated that there were gender differences in retirement decisions primarily in specific situations, such as when individuals had dependents living in their household, when one's spouse was in poor health, and when one's spouse had already retired. Adams (1999) conducted a survey among non-faculty employees of two Midwestern state universities and analyzed data from $n = 172$ individuals age 45 or older to determine the role of career-related variables (career commitment, career growth opportunity, and occupational goal attainment) on planned retirement age. He found that career commitment and occupational goal attainment significantly predicted retirement age after controlling for personal and work-related variables (including age, gender, marital status, income, and job satisfaction). Although studies like these have contributed to our understanding of the retirement process, smaller studies in a single organization or small number of organizations may not be generalizable to the population as a whole.

Survey Methods

In this next section, we describe a variety of research methods specific to the conduct of surveys. This includes an overview of various sampling techniques and examples of how various survey samples have been selected for large-scale surveys used to study retirement. We also discuss sample design issues, survey nonresponse, data collection mode, and measurement issues, including measurement error and reliability and innovations in survey measurement techniques.

Survey Sampling

As mentioned previously, one of the critical elements in retirement research is the population perspective. That is, in order to make meaningful conclusions about a population's retirement behavior, it is necessary that data be generalizable to a population as a whole. The target population for a study refers to the group about which a researcher wants to generalize. Once a researcher identifies the target population, the next step is to specify the sample frame for the study. The sample frame includes the methods by which all elements of the target population will be obtained. A key part of the survey process is to select the elements of the sample frame to be included in a particular study. The goal is to obtain as much coverage of the target population as possible within a particular sample frame (Groves et al., 2009; Groves & Couper, 2002). Sampling error occurs when not all elements of a sampling frame are measured. Maximizing the response rate of a survey may not minimize bias. It is possible that even when the response rate is high, nonresponse may occur disproportionately in relation to key characteristics of sample members.

The HRS provides one example of how a sample frame has been implemented in retirement research. The original HRS design traded off between (a) sampling individuals young enough not to be retired (e.g., age 51) to allow an unbiased longitudinal study of the retirement process and (b) observing actual retirements in the near future following the launch of the study in 1992 (i.e., age 56). In other words, it is important to observe people at a young enough age such that few have experienced retirement. Beginning observation of the retirement process after some have already retired is problematic because those still working at later ages are likely to be healthier, in better jobs, and earning higher wages than those who have already retired. Failing to observe the initial conditions can lead to bias.

A probability sample refers to the concept that elements of a sample frame are selected using chance methods. Elements in the sample frame have a nonzero probability of being selected. A probability sample is quite useful when making statistical inferences from a sample about a population because the probability of selection from the population is known. A simple random sample is when all individuals in the sample frame have an equal probability of being selected. A stratified sample is when the population is classified into subpopulations based on supplementary information (e.g., geographical location or individuals' demographic characteristics, such as age, race, or gender), and then the sample is selected separately for each stratum. Proportionate stratification takes place when units (e.g., individuals or households) are selected from each stratum in proportion to the stratum's frequency in the population. Disproportionate sampling occurs when units are selected from the population at a different rate than they occur in the population. Disproportionate sampling is typically used to "maximize the precision of the estimator of the population mean within available resources" (Kalton, 1983, p. 24).

Clustered sampling refers to a sampling technique in which frame elements are selected jointly rather than selecting sample frame elements individually (Groves et al., 2009). Geographical area clustering is probably the most common type of sample clustering. Clustered geographical sampling is frequently used to reduce survey costs because the cost involved in conducting a simple random sample across a large geographical area is usually prohibitive. For example, when conducting a survey in a wide area (e.g., across the nation), it is often significantly more cost-effective to cluster interviewing in particular geographical areas rather than to select a simple random sample across the wide geographical area.

Sample Designs

Next we describe how these sample design principles are applied to common retirement research studies. The HRS is a multistage area-clustered national probability sample (Health and Retirement Study, 2008). The first step in selecting the sample was to identify geographical area clusters representative of the nation as a whole. The sample was stratified by age and race to ensure enough participants within a particular birth cohort and racial/ethnic group. Interviews were conducted with eligible and willing participants. Survey interviewers conducted a face-to-face household screening by approaching households in these areas and determining whether any age-eligible individuals resided in the dwelling.

The sample design for the PSID was similar to HRS in that it also involved a multistage area-clustered probability sample. The Wisconsin Longitudinal Study, on the other hand, was based on a simple random sample of individuals who graduated from Wisconsin high schools during a particular year (i.e., 1957). The limited geographical area of the WLS (i.e., constrained to one state rather than trying to represent the U.S. population across the contiguous 48 states) made it feasible to conduct a simple random sample for this study. Smaller surveys in retirement research (e.g., Adams, 1999; Davis, 2007; Talaga & Beehr, 1995) have not been aimed toward population-based research and therefore have used simple random samples or convenience samples among participants located in specific regions.

Sample Characteristics

Prior retirement research has varied in terms of the extent to which a study's sample generalizes to the U.S. population as a whole. For example, the Retirement History Survey sample consisted of a cohort of men and unmarried women ages 58–63 in 1969. As a result, this sample did not adequately sample women because it did not include married women as part of the sample frame. The demographic trend toward an increasing proportion of women in the workforce (i.e., currently about 60%, which is up from 44% in 1970; U.S. Bureau of Labor Statistics, 2010) indicates that an adequate survey sample for retirement research should include both women and men in order to obtain a clearer and more accurate picture of retirement behavior at the population level. Some research has intentionally focused on specific organizations, industries, or occupations (e.g., the financial sector; Helppie, Kapinos, & Willis, 2010). However, research that is designed to assess retirement trends and behavior at the population level should be conducted in a manner that is generalizable across a variety of occupations.

Samples in retirement research have typically been defined in terms of individuals. One particular strength of the HRS is that it includes spouses (regardless of the spouse's age). Although the PSID interviews only one respondent per household (and gathers data about other household members via proxy), other households (e.g., adult siblings and children) are linked via the "PSID gene." As the chapter by Matthews and Fisher in this handbook illustrates, many studies have underscored the importance of family in the retirement process (Szinovacz, 2003; Wang & Shultz, 2010). As a result, it is necessary to include family members as part of the sample in order to evaluate the role of family in the retirement planning, decision, and adjustment processes.

The majority of retirement research to date has examined retirement from the perspective of workers or retirees. Another perspective important for understanding the complete retirement landscape pertains to employers (Lumsdaine & Mitchell, 1999). Therefore, sampling work organizations, rather than individuals, is another approach. For example, Mitchell, Utkus, and Yang (2005) analyzed data from more than 500 employer pension plans covering nearly 740,000 workers to measure the effect of employer incentives on employees' retirement savings behavior. The National Employer Survey, conducted by the U.S. Census Bureau, is another data source that may facilitate retirement research. Also, the HRS gathered employer pension plan summary documents as an additional source of data concerning the types of pension plans offered to employees.

Survey Nonresponse

Survey nonresponse can affect results and inferences made about the population. There are two primary types of nonresponse: (1) unit nonresponse, which refers to missing a person, household, employer, or pension plan in a survey, and (2) item nonresponse, which pertains to a respondent not answering a particular question in a survey. Unit nonresponse can be problematic for three primary reasons: (1) it may lead to biases in population point estimates, (2) it may inflate the variance of point estimates, and (3) it may result in biases of estimators of precision (Dillman, Eltinge, Groves, & Little, 2002).

Dillman et al. (2002) described reasons for survey unit nonresponse, including failure to deliver the survey request, many influences on survey participation, and survey design factors (e.g., call scheduling, length of data collection period, respondent incentives, and follow-up procedures). Item nonresponse factors include survey mode (e.g., item nonresponse being more prevalent with a self-administered questionnaire), interviewers and interviewer training (e.g., the extent to which the interviewer probes for an answer, or the degree of rapport between an interviewer and respondent), respondent attributes, question topics, and question characteristics, including question structures (e.g., open vs. close-ended questions and skip patterns) and question difficulty.

The HRS employs a variety of survey techniques to minimize survey unit nonresponse. Study interviewers are carefully selected and highly trained, respondents are mailed materials about the survey and a monetary incentive in advance of being specifically asked to participate in the survey, interviewers call respondents at multiple times during the day or evening to schedule interviews, interviews are conducted in multiple languages (e.g., English and Spanish), extensive tracking methods are used to locate respondents who may have moved or changed telephone numbers, and participants are formally thanked for their participation in the study. To minimize item nonresponse, great care is taken to develop questions that can be easily understood by respondents, and interviewers are carefully trained regarding how to establish rapport with respondents, reassure respondents regarding the privacy of the confidential information they provide, and probe for responses. In spite of these efforts, nonresponse will still occur to some degree. Missing data resulting from nonresponse and various strategies for dealing with missing data will be discussed later in this chapter.

Survey Data Collection Mode

Prior retirement research has been conducted using a variety of survey modes, including paper-and-pencil surveys, computer-assisted telephone and in-person interviews (i.e., CATI and CAPI), and internet or web-based surveys. These modes differ from one another along various dimensions, including the degree of interviewer involvement (e.g., the need for the interviewer to probe responses or motivate respondents to participate or provide responses, the degree of respondent privacy, channels of communication, technology usage, availability, cost, and possible sources of survey error). For example, the HRS is primarily conducted using face-to-face and telephone interviews, although some supplemental data are collected via self-administered questionnaires sent via mail, and recently the HRS has explored the viability of collecting HRS data via the internet. The RAND American Life Panel (ALP) and the Cognitive Economics projects rely primarily on internet surveys. Because internet access and usage is strongly correlated with cognitive ability and age, the ALP supplies internet access devices to those without internet access. The CogEcon project supplements internet survey data collection via mail surveys (Hsu, Fisher, & Willis, 2008).

There are strengths and limitations associated with each of these modes. We highlight a few of these here, though for a more detailed review of various survey modes, please see Groves et al. (2009). Face-to-face interviews are very expensive but can be quite useful for encouraging participation, establishing rapport with respondents, and reducing item-level missing data by probing responses and encouraging respondents to answer questions. Telephone interviews offer many of the same strengths as face-to-face interviews with regard to the interviewer/respondent dynamic, although telephone surveys can be much more cost-effective than in-person interviews. The increased usage of cell phones and canceling of landline service has posed challenges and reduced coverage rates for telephone survey interviewing (Brick et al., 2007; Peytchev, Carley-Baxter, & Black, 2010). Web surveys have become significantly more common within the past fifteen years. Internet surveys are significantly less expensive to administer than telephone interviews because they are self- rather than interviewer-administered and can be completed at a respondent's convenience at virtually any time of day or night. With internet surveys, one major concern is a sampling or response bias because respondents who regularly use the internet differ from those who do not in important ways. This is especially true among older adults, who are often the target sample for studies of retirement. In general, older adults who use the internet are more highly educated and wealthier than those who do not use the internet (Hsu et al., 2008), which can lead to sampling bias.

MIXED-MODE DESIGNS

There are a number of benefits to using a mixed-mode strategy, which is why studies (e.g., HRS) often rely on such techniques. The use of multiple modes may reduce survey costs and increase participation and response rates (Groves et al., 2009). The Cognitive Economics (CogEcon) Survey recognized the potential sampling bias that would be created by conducting only an internet survey (Hsu et al., 2008). As a result, the co-investigators on this study developed a mixed-mode survey design in which some respondents were mailed a paper-and-pencil version of the questionnaire. Results of this data collection effort proved to be quite successful, with the overall response rate for the first wave being 87%, and 4.5% higher than it would have been without the addition of the mail surveys sent to respondents who did not complete the web survey.

Measurement Issues
MEASUREMENT ERROR AND RELIABILITY

One of the most complete treatments of the issue of measurement error in the economics literature is a chapter in the *Handbook of Econometrics* by Bound, Brown, and Mathiowetz (2001). In this chapter the authors thoroughly discuss the issue of measurement error in surveys, describing the ways in which various types of measurement error can affect variable estimates. They illustrate multiple ways to estimate measurement error in survey data. One approach is to use multiple indicators of the key variables of interest to estimate measurement reliability. The challenge of this approach is that the indicators that one might use to estimate reliability may be tainted with measurement error as well. For example, using Social Security earnings data as a validation of self-report measures of earnings assumes that the Social Security Administration records are accurate. Another method is to validate measures against other, ideally more accurate, sources of data (e.g., comparing self-reports of financial information to administrative or employer records). The advantage of the validation approach is that the more objective source data can be used to adjust or "correct" survey data. Nevertheless, it is important to note that what many consider to be objective sources of data are not necessarily a measurement panacea and are subject to measurement error themselves, as almost anyone who has worked with administrative, payroll, or other such datasets can attest. These data may contain errors and may not measure precisely the same construct as the subjective or survey measures under consideration (Bound et al., 2001).

Although we will discuss the issue of missing data later in this chapter, Bound et al. (2001) suggested that one way a researcher can adjust for measurement error is to treat the error as missing data, because in essence a researcher is missing valid data in cases where there is measurement error. However, this approach presumes that the measurement error can be identified and adjusted.

Differences between individuals with regard to how respondents interpret survey questions may affect the reliability of retirement measures. Bruine de Bruin and colleagues have conducted a number of studies in which they have assessed and improved the measurement of expectations. For example, they have sought to determine how research participants interpret expectation questions as well as respond to questions with a focal point response (e.g., 50%), when in fact the respondent does not know the answer and is merely guessing. One method of measuring expectations is to present respondents with questions asking about the subjective probability that various events will happen (e.g., the probability that they will work until the age of 62, or live to a certain age). Bruine de Bruin and Carman (2012) evaluated responses of 50% to these types of questions. Their results indicated that the 50% response to probability questions is more likely to be explained by respondents not knowing the answer than by other reasons. Secondly, Bruine de Bruin, Parker, and Mauer (2011) showed that a two-step response procedure improved the measurement of individuals' perceptions of low-probability risks. First, participants provided responses from 0%–100% regarding an expected degree of risk. Respondents who initially provided a response of 0%–100% were asked a second, follow-up question with six categorical response options (between 0% and 100%) to obtain more specificity.

Another example of a study aimed toward improving the measurement of retirement-related constructs using evaluations of psychometric quality was conducted by Davis (2007), who examined the construct of psychological planning for retirement. In particular, Davis methodically developed a twenty-three-item scale composed of four dimensions of psychological retirement planning: anticipation of loss, developing a structure, spousal/partner relationships, and identity.

INNOVATIONS IN SURVEY MEASUREMENT TECHNIQUES

Adaptive Testing

One recent advancement in survey measurement that is relevant to the retirement literature is the use of adaptive measures. With the use of computer-assisted telephone or in-person interviews (i.e., CATI or CAPI) as well as the rapidly increasing use of web surveys, computer adaptive testing technology can be applied to survey research measures. This approach aims to match the precision of the question being asked to other, previously known characteristics about the respondent. Based on the respondent's answer to the first question, the "difficulty level" of the subsequent question is adjusted. In other words, if a respondent answers the initial question correctly, a more difficult question will follow. If the initial question is answered incorrectly, an easier question will follow. This method has frequently been used to measure various cognitive abilities but has also been successfully used for other constructs (e.g., personality; Waller & Reise, 1989). This represents a methodological advantage by shortening the length of test or survey measures while measuring the construct with more precision than a shorter version of a scale without adaptation. For respondents at the extreme low and high ends

of the distribution, an adaptive test may be able to measure the construct more precisely (Thissen & Mislevy, 2000). In other words, the adaptive version of the measure may be shortened by up to 50% while maintaining a comparable level of precision compared to the full-length version of the measure (Weiss & Kingsbury, 1984). Researchers using this approach sacrifice some measurement precision (reliability) because the adaptive measure uses fewer items, but they are able to assess a wider range of abilities or a broader construct domain while reducing test or survey administration time. One of the disadvantages and practical constraints of this approach is that the development of the adaptive test relies on a large item pool for calibrating the difficulty level of the items.

The HRS successfully adopted adaptive testing methodology beginning in the 2004 wave to improve upon existing HRS measures of cognitive ability and assess fluid intelligence with a block adaptive measure of quantitative reasoning ability (McArdle, Fisher, Rodgers, Woodcock, & Horn, 2011; Fisher, McArdle, Rodgers, Weir, & Willis, 2011). McArdle, Smith, and Willis (2009) and Smith, McArdle, and Willis (2010) used these data to examine the correlation between wealth and cognitive ability. Their results indicated that numerical ability is positively associated with family wealth, particularly for the financial decision maker in the family.

Bracketing Technique

In order to reduce the amount of missing data on economic questions, the HRS has employed a simple bracketing technique (Juster & Suzman, 1995). If a respondent answers "don't know" or "refuses" to answer a question pertaining to an economic question, such as the amount of income one received or current value of a 401k account, the respondent will be asked a follow-up question regarding whether the income amount (or account value) was more than or less than a particular bracket amount (e.g., $25,000). If the respondent says more than that amount, then he or she is asked if the amount is more than a larger amount (e.g., $50,000). If the respondent says no, then a previously missing response is known to be some value between the two brackets (e.g., $25,000 and $50,000 in this example). This technique has been quite effective for reducing the proportion of item nonresponse as well as improving the quality of imputations for nonresponses. For example, Juster and Suzman (1995) indicated that 90% of individuals who answered "don't know" were willing to answer with a bracket amount, and 50% of respondents who "refused" to give an answer were willing to give a bracket amount. The success of this technique has led the HRS to use the bracketing technique for nearly all income, wealth, and other financial questions, using bracket values that have been optimized to maximize their explanatory power (Heeringa, Hill, & Howell, 1995). This bracketing technique is believed to elicit quantitative responses from respondents who may be uncertain about the precise value or concerned about privacy and unwilling to provide such personal information to a stranger (Hauser & Willis, 2005).

Data Analysis Issues
Missing Data

Missing data is a common issue and potential challenge in any type of research. Survey unit and item-level nonresponse is probably the most likely type of missing data encountered in retirement research. The social science literature is replete with discussions regarding the issue and treatment of missing data (e.g., Rubin & Little, 2002; McArdle & Hamagami, 1992). The extent to which missing data is problematic and what can be done about it depends on the assumptions regarding the reason for the missing data.

Rubin (1976) described four types of missing data assumptions. Assuming that data are missing on variable Y, missing completely at random (MCAR) occurs when the probability of data missing on Y is completely unrelated to Y or any other variable in the dataset. A significantly weaker assumption than MCAR is missing at random (MAR), which is the probability that data missing on Y is unrelated to Y after controlling for other variables in the analysis. Data may be considered to be "ignorable" when the data are MAR and the parameters governing the missing data process are unrelated to the parameters to be estimated. Data are considered "non-ignorable" when data are missing in a systematic manner and failing to treat these missing data will produce results that are not representative of the population. It is necessary to model non-ignorable missing data to obtain good estimates of the variables of interest. A common approach is to use Heckman's (1976, 1979) approach for regression models with selection bias on the dependent variable. His initial application concerned models of female labor supply. Economic theory suggests that labor force participation and hours of work depend (among other things) on the market wage that a woman could receive. While the market wage of working women can be observed, the potential wage of nonparticipants cannot be observed. Moreover, since labor force participation is a self-selected status and labor force participants are a non-random sample of the population of women, it may not be appropriate to impute the "missing" wages of nonparticipants using the MAR assumption. Heckman's selection model offers a method for handling selection bias by jointly modeling the labor force participation and hours of work decisions under the assumption that the logarithm of hourly wages is normally distributed and correlated with error term in the labor supply equation. An important limitation of the model is that if identification solely by functional form is to be avoided, an exclusion restriction is required so that at least one variable with a nonzero coefficient in the selection equation does not appear in the equation of interest (Sartori, 2003).

TREATMENT OF MISSING DATA

The best solution to unwanted missing data is prevention. As we described previously, large surveys (e.g., the HRS and PSID) take many costly steps to minimize missing data from the outset. For example, the HRS uses a variety of survey research methods (e.g., mailing pre-contact letters, offering incentives, establishing rapport with respondents, maintaining contact with respondents via newsletters) and survey design techniques (e.g., careful design and review of survey questions, use of the bracketing technique described earlier to obtain valid estimates of financial information when a survey respondent's response is "don't know" or the respondent is otherwise unwilling to provide a precise estimate). However, an inherent challenge in survey research is that not all sample members participate, and not all participants answer all questions. Therefore, analysts must determine the most appropriate method for dealing with missing data.

Listwise and Pairwise Deletion

The simplest method for handling missing data is to use listwise deletion. Listwise deletion can be used for virtually any type of statistical analysis (not counting, of course, the fact that this method may reduce the sample size below a necessary or desirable threshold for a particular analytic method), and no special or complicated computation methods are needed (Allison, 2002). However, listwise deletion may bias results if respondents who are omitted from analysis are systematically different from respondents with complete case data. This is likely to be the case if the assumption underlying the missing data is anything except MCAR. Another method for treating missing data is pairwise deletion, or available case analysis. Whereas listwise deletion analyzes only data available on complete cases, pairwise deletion computes statistics using all of the data available on the variables in the model. This is an appropriate technique when data are MCAR, but the derived estimates may be quite biased if data are only MAR. The two primary limitations of pairwise deletion are that parameter estimates (including test statistics and estimated standard errors) are biased when produced using conventional statistical software, and covariance or correlation matrices in smaller samples may not be "positive definite," which means that regression models cannot be computed (Allison, 2002). A third approach to missing data is to impute the missing values, which we describe in the next section.

Imputations

There are many different computational methods that fall under the heading of imputations. Simply put, imputation refers to a process in which missing data values are filled in with estimates of what the actual values might be if the data were not missing. Some methods are more complex than others. A basic method is to substitute the mean or median value on a particular variable. Another approach is to use a hot deck method in which a missing value is filled in using data from a randomly selected similar case. There are also a variety of complex regression modeling techniques for estimating missing values. For a more detailed description of imputation methods and applications, see Groves et al. (2009) and Rubin (1987). The use of imputed data has been somewhat controversial and is generally accepted in some disciplines (e.g., economics, sociology) more than others (e.g., psychology). There are multiple software packages available to perform imputations, including the "mi" command in Stata 11 (StataCorp, 2011) and Imputation and Variance Estimation software (IVEware; Raghunathan, Solenberger, & Van Hoewyk, 2002), to name a few.

The HRS has imputed values for economic questions to derive summary values of wealth measures. Heeringa, Little, and Raghunathan (2002) described a Bayesian approach to multiple imputation of the HRS data collected using the bracketing response format. Results of this approach were found to be superior to complete case analysis, mean or median substitution, as well as the hot deck method. Fisher, Hassan, Rodgers, and Weir (2009) used a multiple-step, regression-based approach using IVEware to impute missing data on cognitive ability measures in the HRS.

Other Approaches

Unit-level nonresponse can be adjusted via Heckman selection models, as mentioned earlier. Sample weights can also be adjusted for nonresponse. For example, researchers can develop propensity models using logistic regression analysis to model the probability of whether an individual responds to a survey. By understanding factors related to nonresponse, propensity scores can then be used to make a nonresponse adjustment to survey weights. However, these methods depend on the assumption that error, conditioned on measured variables, is "ignorable" (Rubin & Little, 2002).

Sample Weights

Sample weights are used to adjust sample design characteristics so that statistical computation of point estimates and variances in point estimates accurately represent the population. Sample weights are critical for the analysis of complex sample survey data found in many large, population-based public-use datasets (which have been used for hundreds of studies on retirement across multiple disciplines). The HRS is intentionally geographically stratified and clustered (because this increases the fieldwork efficiency while still obtaining a nationally representative sample). In addition, the HRS sample includes oversamples of blacks, Hispanics, and Florida residents. Failure to use sample weights in the analysis would result in these oversampled individuals' responses being overemphasized relative to non-blacks, non-Hispanics, and non-Florida residents. In other words, sample weights adjust the proportion to which these responses count based on the probability with which these individuals represent others in the population as a whole. Failure to include the clustering and stratification variables in an analysis would result in underestimated variance estimates (e.g., estimated standard errors that are lower than what they should be with the sample clustering and stratification taken into account).

Typically sample weights are derived by taking the inverse probability with which each individual was selected into the sample. Additional adjustments can be made to sample weights to account for unit nonresponse. One approach is to replace the sample mean with a new estimator (Bethlehem, 2002). Weighting adjustments are made on the basis of auxiliary data, which is information that has been measured in the survey but is also known about the distribution of the population. This corrects for known differences between the sample and the population (Gelman & Carlin, 2002).

Post-stratification is a frequently used technique in developing survey weights (Bethlehem, 2002; Little, 1986). The goal of post-stratification is to reduce differences between a sample and the population by using "stratified sample estimators for unstratified designs" (Gelman & Carlin, 2002, p. 290). Post-stratification uses an outside data source as a reference. If the sample distribution is different from the population distribution on known demographic variables, estimates for each demographic category are combined with known population post-stratum totals. For example, the HRS sample weights have been post-stratified using data from the Current Population Study (CPS) survey, which is conducted annually by the U.S. Census Bureau. The first step in the post-stratification of the HRS is to create a table with dimensions defined by correlates of non-response (e.g., age, sex, race, and ethnicity). The second step is to obtain weighted counts for each cell (stratum) for both the HRS and the CPS. Then each weight in the HRS is adjusted in a manner that yields the same cell-specific totals as in the CPS.

Practically speaking, some statistical software packages are better equipped to handle complex sample survey design variables (sample weights, stratification, and cluster variables) than others. Stata has a set of "svy" commands and SAS has a series of "PROC SURVEY" commands that incorporate cluster, stratification, and sample weight variables in the analysis. Only recently has SPSS developed such procedures; it has a new complex samples module that is currently available as an add-on to the base SPSS program.

Analytic Strategies

REGRESSION ANALYSIS

Regression analysis is the predominant analytic technique utilized in retirement research. This is because the majority of retirement research involves the examination of many factors in predicting retirement behavior (i.e., where some aspect of retirement behavior is the criterion or dependent variable) or in examining predictors of retirement-related outcome variables. Commonly used models include linear and logistic regression. In short, linear regression is used when the dependent or criterion variable is continuous, whereas logistic regression is used for a binary dependent variable (e.g., retired vs. not retired) and predicts the probability of whether an event (e.g., retirement) occurs. Further, multinomial logistic regression allows examining discrete outcomes with more than two categorical values. Wang et al. (2008) and von Bonsdorff et al. (2009)

used multinomial logistic regression to study bridge employment decisions.

STRUCTURAL EQUATION MODELING

Structural equation modeling (SEM) is a useful analytic strategy that has been widely used in retirement research, particularly for longitudinal research and modeling the retirement process. The model-testing capabilities of SEM techniques have allowed researchers to test models and advance theories of retirement behavior, particularly because SEM can be used to test models in confirmatory as well as exploratory ways. Although SEM is considered a causal modeling technique, it is important for researchers to appropriately use longitudinal data and exercise caution when making causal assumptions. Causal assumptions will not hold when testing a model with cross-sectional data, even if results suggest that the model fits the data well.

A couple of recent examples of SEM in the retirement literature have examined early retirement and retirement planning. Specifically, Kubicek, Korunka, Hoonakker, and Raymo (2010) used data from the Wisconsin Longitudinal Study to examine work and family characteristics (including work-family conflict) as predictors of early retirement. Noone, Alpass, and Stephens (2010) used data from the New Zealand Health, Work and Retirement Survey to test a model of retirement planning and preparedness to determine whether there were any gender differences. Their results showed that women were somewhat economically disadvantaged compared to men, which had a negative impact on women's financial readiness for retirement.

MULTILEVEL MODELING

The use of multilevel modeling (also referred to as hierarchical linear modeling, mixed modeling, random coefficients modeling, random effects modeling, or nested modeling) in retirement research has been on the rise in recent years. Such models are useful for estimating parameters that vary at more than one level and have been useful for measuring change over time. Wang (2007) used data from the HRS and growth mixture modeling (a special type of multilevel modeling that considers longitudinal change trajectories) to determine whether there are multiple longitudinal patterns of retirees' psychological well-being and, if so, to what extent individual and contextual variables predict those patterns. His results identified three unobserved subgroups of retirees and found support for both individual factors (e.g., bridge employment) and contextual factors (the work status of one's spouse) in predicting those longitudinal change patterns. Similarly, Pinquart and Schindler (2007) used growth mixture modeling to examine the retirement adjustment process by modeling changes in life satisfaction among three unobserved subgroups of retirees. In addition to growth mixture modeling, multilevel modeling is also useful when considering effects among dyads (e.g., husband and wife) or social units (e.g., family, organizations). We think that this is one direction in which future retirement research will expand in the coming years.

Experimental Research Methods
True Experiments

Although the majority of retirement research is based on survey research data, important retirement research has also been conducted in lab and field experiments, in which researchers have been able to manipulate key independent variables to observe the effect on dependent variables of interest. In economics, one of the primary assumptions is that individuals will maximize utility subject to constraints. Experimental settings give researchers the opportunity to modify the framework to allow for constraints. In a laboratory setting, the researcher has the opportunity to manipulate and control variables of interest that cannot be controlled in an observational study or survey. Laibson and colleagues have conducted numerous lab and field experimental studies to improve our understanding of retirement behavior. For example, Choi, Laibson, and Madrian (2010) examined portfolio choice in a hypothetical experiment to determine why individuals invest in high-fee mutual funds.

In addition, experiments and vignettes have been built into surveys. For example, Barsky, Juster, Kimball, and Shapiro (1997) used a vignette in the HRS to measure risk aversion. This set of questions presented respondents with hypothetical scenarios of gambles over lifetime income. Responses to these questions separated respondents into four categories of risk preferences. Another example of the use of vignettes to make a cross-national comparison of perceived work disability in the United States was conducted using the ALP data discussed earlier and in the Netherlands using the similarly designed Center Data internet panel (Kapteyn, Smith, & van Soest, 2007).

Natural or Quasi-experiments

Both private- and public-sector institutions have developed policies that can have a large impact on whether individuals continue working or leave, as well as whether and how employees financially plan for retirement by saving in defined contribution benefit plans (e.g., 401(k) plans). These policies can change, and an important aspect of retirement research involves careful examination of the policy implications. Variations in policies create quasi- (or natural) experimental conditions that can then be examined to determine the effect of policies on behavior. For example, research in the 1990s examined "window plans," referring to employer-provided defined benefit pension plans in which benefits would be highest if an employee retired during a particular "window." Because employers did not necessarily anticipate the rise in defined contribution pension plans, research on these window plans constituted a natural experiment (Lumsdaine & Mitchell, 1999). Choi, Laibson, Madrian, and Metrick (2002) studied employees' savings behavior using retirement savings plan administrative data from employees in several large corporations that implemented changes to the design of their 401(k) plans. These researchers concluded that employer pension plan administrators can have a powerful influence on employee savings and investment behavior based on 401(k) plan features. Beshears, Choi, Laibson, and Madrian (2010) examined the impact of automatic enrollment in employer-sponsored retirement savings plans, including an analysis of employee participation in a firm that switched from an employer match to a non-contingent employer contribution.

Natural experiments have also been exploited by using natural cross-national variation in laws and policies to examine retirement behavior. For example, Rohwedder and Willis (2010) conducted a cross-national study in which they examined the existence of national policies as instrumental variables to determine their effect on disability and retirement behavior. Gruber and Wise (1999) evaluated the effects of changes in employment laws on retirement patterns in the United States, Japan, and Western Europe and concluded that changes in laws had a large effect on retirement behavior.

Qualitative Research Methods

The vast majority of retirement research is theoretical or quantitative. Most of the qualitative research conducted in retirement research is performed as part of the quantitative research development process regarding how to improve survey methods and measurement rather than as an end in itself. Some studies have made important contributions to the retirement literature by employing qualitative research designs. Qualitative research involves open-ended data collection techniques in interviews, surveys, and focus groups. For example, Bruine de Bruin et al. (2008) conducted structured qualitative interviews and utilized cognitive interviewing techniques to examine expectations of survival, the probability that respondents would work full-time after ages 62 and 65, and expectations of stock market returns.

Cognitive interviews were conducted as part of the development of the Cognitive Economics survey. During these interviews, respondents described what they were thinking as they approached each question in the survey and thought through their responses to each of the questions. Researchers also obtained valuable feedback regarding the usability and screen design on the internet survey. Collectively, data from this qualitative study were used to make significant improvements to the final survey design.

New research on financial literacy is being conducted to better articulate what people know and don't know regarding various aspects of finance. This is useful for the development of survey measures that minimize the use of words or phrases that are not common or well-understood in vernacular among lay individuals. For example, an individual may understand and practice the principle of diversification by investing money in retirement accounts across a variety of asset types, but may not be familiar with the word "diversification." Experience with the HRS has shown that many older working Americans do not understand the difference between "defined benefit" vs. "defined contribution" pension plans, so survey questions have been modified to explain these types of pension plans when asking respondents about the type of retirement plans that they have (Gustman et al., 2010b).

There are certainly a few limitations to qualitative research. First, qualitative research is quite labor-intensive. Secondly, it is often difficult to code open-ended responses in a manner that will be useful for making empirical comparisons. Nonetheless, qualitative research can be a valuable tool for helping us describe and understand retirement phenomena.

Evolution of Retirement Research Methods

During the past two decades, retirement research has evolved in many ways. This includes a movement toward the sampling and study of more women in relation to retirement, the conduct of more longitudinal research, and a heavier emphasis

on interdisciplinary research. We will discuss each of these issues next.

Study of Women and Retirement

Historically, early studies of retirement focused on men rather than women, reflecting the fact that men used to comprise the majority of the labor force. Szinovacz (1991) clearly highlighted an earlier gender role bias such that retirement research focused either on men's retirement behavior or the effects of husbands' retirement on their wives. Along the same lines, the sampling of the Retirement History Survey included only a sample of men and unmarried women. Beginning in the mid-1980s, retirement research began to focus more on studies of gender differences as well as women's issues in retirement (Honig, 1998; Hsu, 2011; Noone et al., 2010; Quick & Moen, 1998). This trend reflects the increase in the proportion of women in the workforce, as well as the importance of understanding the retirement process for women. Financial security in retirement is a particularly important issue for women. Not only do women typically live longer than men, but historically lower wages, interrupted work histories, and roles as caregivers put women at a higher risk for old-age poverty compared to men (Munnell & Jivan, 2005). The National Center for Women and Retirement Research in New York was the outgrowth of a federally funded project in 1986 entitled Pre-Retirement Education Planning (PREP) and further highlights an emphasis on the study of women and retirement.

Longitudinal Research

Although cross-sectional research holds some merit for understanding retirement behavior, longitudinal data are critical for the study of a process that unfolds over time. Longitudinal data permit the examination of factors in temporal relation to retirement, such as a health shock that precedes a decision to stop working (Bound & Waidmann, 2002), health outcomes following retirement (Zhan et al., 2009), or an analysis of how the recent economic decline affects retirement and related behavior (McFall, 2011; Hudomiet, Kezdi, & Willis, 2011; Shapiro, 2010). In addition, longitudinal data can serve to increase the generalizability of the sample. For example, Lumsdaine and Mitchell (1999) suggested that cross-sectional research is more likely to omit important individuals from study, such as those who retire early or die at younger ages. Secondly, longitudinal research allows researchers to examine the effects of policy changes on retirement behavior and outcomes. For example, the longitudinal nature of the HRS permits the examination of changes to Social Security policy (e.g., changes in normal ages of eligibility for benefits) on withdrawal from the workforce.

Developments in statistical modeling techniques and software, such as structural equation modeling (SEM), multilevel modeling, and latent growth/decline curve modeling, have also facilitated longitudinal data analysis in retirement research. We believe that future research will rely even more heavily upon the use of longitudinal designs and further our understanding of retirement as a process.

Interdisciplinary Research
ORGANIZATION OF RETIREMENT RESEARCH

A major source of research support for retirement research in the United States comes from the National Institute on Aging, which funds research directly through a variety of grant mechanisms, supports fourteen research centers on the economics and demography of aging,[1] and is the major funder of the Health and Retirement Study and other data sets used by retirement researchers.

A significant amount of retirement research is conducted through the Retirement Research Consortium (RRC), which is funded by the United States Social Security Administration via cooperative agreements. The RRC consists of three retirement research centers: the Center for Retirement Research at Boston College, the Michigan Retirement Research Center at the Institute for Social Research at the University of Michigan, and the National Bureau of Economic Research (NBER) in Cambridge, Massachusetts (see Table 12.1). According to the Social Security Administration, the purpose of these centers is to (1) conduct research and evaluation on a wide array of topics related to Social Security and retirement

policy; (2) disseminate information on Social Security and retirement issues relevant to policy makers, researchers, and the general public; and (3) train scholars and practitioners in research areas relevant to Social Security and retirement issues. (Davies & Fisher, 2009), These centers also facilitate access to valuable data sources for the study of retirement. Collectively, these centers play a significant role in promoting and facilitating research on retirement by providing researchers with funding and disseminating working papers so that researchers and policy makers better understand key issues regarding retirement and relevant issues among the aging population. For links to these research centers, please refer to Table 12.1.

In addition to the three retirement research centers supported by the Social Security Administration, some support has been provided by the SSA for financial literacy centers at the RAND Corporation, Boston College, and the University of Wisconsin. Prior research has indicated that many adults have low levels of financial literacy, demonstrated by their having difficulty understanding interest rates, compound interest calculations, the effect of inflation, and other important aspects of personal finances (Lusardi, 2008; Lusardi & Mitchell, 2007a, 2009). The goal of these financial literacy centers has been to develop and test programs aimed toward improving financial literacy, financial planning, and financial decision making to help Americans plan for a financially secure retirement. A few examples of interdisciplinary research conducted by researchers affiliated with these centers include (1) examining the role of cognition (e.g., financial knowledge) in relation to retirement planning (Laibson, Madrian, Beshears, Choi, & Zeldes, in progress), (2) how learning from one's peers can affect retirement savings decisions (Beshears, Choi, Laibson, Madrian,

Table 12.1 Retirement Research Centers

Center	Location	Website
Center for Retirement Research at Boston College	Boston College, Boston, MA	http://crr.bc.edu/
Michigan Retirement Research Center	Institute for Social Research University of Michigan, Ann Arbor, MI	http://www.mrrc.isr.umich.edu/
National Bureau of Economic Research	Cambridge, MA	http://www.nber.org/

& Milkman, 2010), and (3) work by Wallace and Lusardi (in progress) to target K–8 education to improve financial literacy. At the time this chapter was written, future funding for these financial literacy centers was uncertain.

EXAMPLES OF INTERDISCIPLINARY RETIREMENT RESEARCH

Retirement research has benefitted from an increasing number of collaborations across disciplines. For instance, Willis, Shapiro, and colleagues' Cognitive Economics project has studied the relationship between a wide variety of cognitive ability measures, portfolio choice, and economic status in a national sample of older adults (Delavande et al., 2008; Hudomiet et al., 2011; Shapiro, 2010). In their paper entitled "Mental Retirement," Rohwedder and Willis (2010) conducted a cross-national study of retirement and cognitive functioning and concluded that retirement is significantly and causally related to cognitive decline among older adults in their early 60s. Duckworth and Weir (2010) recently completed a paper using data from the HRS that examined the relationship between personality, lifetime earnings, and retirement wealth. They reported that conscientiousness and emotional stability were related to objective measures of lifetime earnings after controlling for education and cognitive ability.

Many of the large survey datasets that have greatly contributed to the retirement literature (e.g., the Health and Retirement Study, the Panel Study of Income Dynamics, the Wisconsin Longitudinal Study, etc.) have been particularly valuable due to having data across a broad array of topics relevant to the retirement process. The number of cross-disciplinary collaborations (e.g., McArdle et al., 2009; Shapiro, 2010) also appears to be on the rise. We both expect and recommend that this trend continues in order to increase our knowledge about and understanding of retirement.

Future Directions

We expect that future retirement research will be interdisciplinary and longitudinal, and will continue to shed light on retirement issues facing women as well as men. Next we describe some additional issues regarding future retirement research, such as measurement and other research needs, including the need to balance measurement consistency and innovation, a need to study multiple cohorts, and a need for more cross-national research.

Measurement

There appear to be disciplinary differences in the extent to which and how measurement properties of constructs are reported in the literature. For example, it is much more common for psychological researchers to report indices of measurement reliability, such as coefficient alpha as an index of internal consistency reliability (Cortina, 1993). This difference is most likely due to disciplinary differences in the training and focus on measurement and assessment, as social science disciplines do not place equal emphasis on the importance of psychometrics and micro-level measurement issues. To some extent, the focus in psychology is based on the notion that the "true" construct is a latent variable, which in principle cannot be measured directly. In economics and demography, the desired variables are treated as observed, rather than latent, variables, though possibly subject to some degree of measurement error. However, some important constructs really are latent variables (e.g., "permanent income"; Friedman, 1957).

The lack of measurement focus in some disciplines may be exacerbated to some extent by the reliance on data from large-scale surveys. As we described earlier, the majority of the empirical retirement literature is based on survey research and often archival datasets (e.g., the HRS and PSID). Such studies often focus their efforts on having a broad array of questions measured by a single or very few items, rather than measuring a few constructs with multiple indicators of the construct. This represents a methodological tradeoff of breadth vs. depth of measurement, occasionally leaving researchers with fewer or suboptimal measures for their study. For further discussion regarding the opportunities and challenges associated with using archival datasets, see Fisher and Barnes-Farrell (in press).

It has been well documented that health plays a key role in the retirement process (McGarry, 2004). Although a full description of how health status is measured in the retirement literature is beyond the scope of this chapter, we would like to note that significantly more attention has been paid to the issue of how to measure health than retirement. For example, McGarry (2004) indicated that understanding the role of health in relation to financial status in the retirement process has been hampered by challenges associated with measuring health status.

In general, we recommend that researchers aim to strike a balance by recognizing the need for good measurement while not assuming that less-than-ideal measures completely lack utility. We advocate that retirement researchers should pay careful attention to the measurement properties of key variables in their research. This is particularly the case when using single-item indicators.

Need to Balance Consistency in Measurement and Scientific Innovation

One important goal for successful retirement research in longitudinal surveys is to balance consistency of measurement over time with the need for scientific innovation. This includes having consistent measures of topics longitudinally, to be able to study trends like labor force participation, while being willing to incorporate new measures or measures of new topics to be closer to the cutting edge of science (e.g., the incorporation of new measures of fluid cognitive abilities in the HRS in order to examine the role that cognitive abilities [e.g., quantitative reasoning] play in retirement planning and decision making). Other examples of scientific innovation in survey research include collection of genetic material and genetic analysis, and biomarkers. Scientific innovation also includes developing new data collections as the world changes. We have seen this with the worldwide development of aging studies to examine health and retirement issues in other countries, much like the HRS in the United States. Another example includes surveys to evaluate the impact of the economic crisis in that began in 2008. The Cognitive Economics project launched an additional survey to gather important data regarding the effect that the recent financial crisis had on retirement behavior. Using data from the Cognitive Economics survey and the HRS, McFall (2011) found that, on average, individuals who planned to retire in 2008 or 2009 delayed their retirement an average of 1.6 years. This survey illustrates the importance of a flexible data collection strategy that allows researchers to study the effects of unexpected changes in the world.

Need for Multiple Cohorts

Extant research has illustrated that retirement behavior is importantly influenced by public policy and the economy (e.g., Ekerdt, 2010; McFall, 2011; Rohwedder & Willis, 2010; Shapiro, 2010), which is readily apparent in the wake of the recent economic decline. Because the economic climate is dynamic and ever-changing, we cannot assume that current patterns will hold true for the future. Prior research illustrated trends toward early retirement (Lumsdaine & Mitchell, 1999), to retirement in the 1990s peaking at ages 62 and 65 (Rust & Phelan,

1997), and recent evidence that individuals plan to work longer (McFall, 2011; Shapiro, 2010). Future research will need to examine additional cohorts to determine how current policies and economic and workplace conditions affect future retirement behavior. Secondly, successive cohorts may differ from older cohorts in important ways that may impact retirement behavior and adjustment. Additional research should study young people to obtain early measures of retirement preferences, intentions, and planning and follow them over time. The topic of financial planning for retirement, particularly among younger people, is growing in importance with a shift from defined benefit to defined contribution pension plans.

Global and Cross-National Research

The growing number of aging and retirement studies across the world (see Table 12.2) creates excellent opportunities to understand retirement behavior on a global level and compare the retirement process across countries. The important role of the influence of pension, disability, and tax policies on retirement was convincingly demonstrated in a groundbreaking study by Gruber and Wise (1999). They showed that almost all of the differences in retirement rates across high-income OECD countries were attributable to incentives created by these policies. A recent paper by Rohwedder and Willis (2010) found that retirement has a negative effect on cognition, measured by comparable measures of word recall in the HRS, ELSA, and SHARE data, as well as national policies as instruments to correct for possible endogeneity of individual retirement status. In another influential study, Banks, Marmot, Oldfield, and Smith (2006), using data from HRS (supplemented by NHANES) and ELSA, found that while older Americans say that they are in better health than comparable people from Britain, the British are in better health than Americans when objective measures are used. Comparative research using the HRS and its sister surveys from around the world is just beginning, but future cross-national research promises to shed new light on the effects of economic and social policies on health and retirement.

Concluding Remarks

Retirement research covers a vast array of topics. The majority of retirement research has been quantitative and based on surveys. Publicly available data from large, national longitudinal panel surveys like the Health and Retirement Study (HRS)

Table 12.2 Retirement Research Data Sources

Source	Website
Government Resources	
U.S. Census Bureau	http://www.census.gov/
Current Population Survey (CPS)	http://www.census.gov/cps/
Bureau of Labor Statistics	http://www.bls.gov/
U.S. Academic Data Resources	
Inter-university Consortium for Political and Social Research (ICPSR)	http://www.icpsr.umich.edu/icpsrweb/ICPSR/
Michigan Center for the Demography of Aging (MiCDA)	http://micda.psc.isr.umich.edu/
Health and Retirement Study (HRS)	http://hrsonline.isr.umich.edu/
Panel Study of Income Dynamics (PSID)	http://psidonline.isr.umich.edu/
Wisconsin Longitudinal Study (WLS)	http://www.ssc.wisc.edu/wlsresearch/
Americans Changing Lives (ACL)	http://www.icpsr.umich.edu/icpsrweb/ICPSR/ studies/4690
International Retirement Studies	
English Longitudinal Study of Ageing (ELSA)	http://www.ifs.org.uk/elsa/
International Survey of Health, Ageing, and Retirement in Europe (SHARE)	http://www.share-project.org/
SHARE-Israel	http://igdc.huji.ac.il/Home/Home.aspx
The Irish Longitudinal Study on Aging	http://www.tcd.ie/tilda/
Mexican Health and Aging Study (MHAS)	http://www.mhas.pop.upenn.edu/english/home. htm
Health, Work and Retirement (New Zealand)	http://hwr.massey.ac.nz
Chinese Health Aging and Retirement Longitudinal Study (CHARLS)	http://charls.ccer.edu.cn/charls/
Korean Longitudinal Study of Aging (KLoSA)	http://www.kli.re.kr/klosa/en/about/introduce.jsp
Japanese Study of Aging and Retirement (JSTAR)	http://www.rieti.go.jp/en/projects/jstar/index.html
Longitudinal Aging Study in India (LASI)	http://www.hsph.harvard.edu/pgda/lasi.html
Costa Rica Longevity and Healthy Aging Study (CRELES)	http://www.ccp.ucr.ac.cr/creles/index.htm
Thailand and Brazil—in early development at the time this chapter was written	

and the Panel Study of Income Dynamics (PSID) have played a key role in the retirement research arena. Although these large datasets have provided a valuable resource for the study of retirement, other important research has been conducted using smaller studies in which researchers can more easily control the design and measures of the study. In addition to survey research, retirement research consists of a blend of survey and experimental methods. Manipulating independent variables in a laboratory setting as well as observing naturally occurring differences have played a key role in developing our understanding of causal relations in retirement behavior.

The economic climate is dynamic and ever-changing. We have already observed that some previous trends in retirement behavior (e.g., a tendency toward early retirement) are no longer the norm. Tumultuous economic changes can affect retirement behavior (e.g., McFall, 2011; Hurd & Rohwedder, 2010; Shapiro, 2010). Additional research is needed to determine the extent to which demographic and economic changes affect or alter what we already know about retirement. Future research should continue to examine the retirement process longitudinally and with an interdisciplinary lens. We particularly encourage specific attention to measurement issues, multiple (and younger) cohorts, and the need to study retirement cross-nationally.

Acknowledgements

We gratefully acknowledge Charlie Brown, Kate McGonagle, Heather Hewett, and Ruth Shamraj for their help and suggestions.

Notes

1. A list of the NIA Aging Centers and additional information can be found at http://agingmeta.psc.isr.umich.edu/.

References

Adams, G. A. (1999). Career-related variables and planned retirement age: An extension of Beehr's model. *Journal of Vocational Behavior, 55*, 221–235.

Allison, P. D. (2002). *Missing data.* Thousand Oaks, CA: Sage.

Altonji, J. G., & Doraszelski, U. (2005). The role of permanent income and demographics in black/white differences in wealth. *The Journal of Human Resources, 40*, 1–30.

Ando, A., & Modigliani, F. (1963). The "life cycle" hypothesis of saving: Aggregate implications and tests. *American Economic Review, 53*, 55–84.

Atchley, R. (1989). A continuity theory of normal aging. *The Gerontologist, 29*, 183–190.

Banks, J., Marmot, M., Oldfield, Z., & Smith, J. P. (2006). Disease and disadvantage in the United States and England. *Journal of the American Medical Association, 295*, 2037–2045.

Barnes-Farrell, J. L. (2003). Beyond health and wealth: Attitudinal and other influences on retirement decision-making. In G. A. Adams & T. A. Beehr (Eds.), *Retirement: Reasons, processes, and results* (pp. 159–187). New York, NY: Springer.

Barnes-Farrell, J. L., Dove-Steinkamp, M., Golay, L., Johnson, N. C., & McGonagle, A. (2008, November). How does the nature of the work-family interface influence planned retirement age of men and women? In G. G. Fisher (Chair), *The graying of the American workforce: Implications for occupational health psychology.* Symposium presented at the European Academy of Occupational Health Psychology, Valencia, Spain.

Barsky, R. B., Juster, F. T., Kimball, M., & Shapiro, M. (1997). Preference parameters and behavioral heterogeneity: An experimental approach in the Health and Retirement Study. *Quarterly Journal of Economics, 112*, 537–579.

Beshears, J., Choi, J., Laibson, D., Madrian, B. C. (2010). The impact of employer matching on savings plan participation under automatic enrollment. In D. A. Wise (Ed.), *Research findings in the economics of aging* (pp. 311–327). Chicago, IL: University of Chicago Press.

Beshears, J., Choi, J., Laibson, D., Madrian, B. C., & Milkman, K. L. (2010). *The effect of providing peer information on retirement savings decisions* (Working Paper). Santa Monica, CA: RAND Financial Literacy Center.

Beehr, T. A. (1986). The process of retirement: A review and recommendations for future investigation. *Personnel Psychology, 39*, 31–56.

Bethlehem, J. G. (2002). Weighting nonresponse adjustments based on auxiliary information. In R. M. Groves, D. A. Dillman, J. L. Eltinge, & R. J. A. Little, (Eds.), *Survey nonresponse* (pp. 275–287). New York, NY: Wiley.

Binswanger, J., & Schunk, D. (2009). *What is an adequate standard of living during retirement?* (CESifo Working Paper No. 2893). Munich, Germany: Center for Economic Studies.

Bound, J., Brown, C., & Mathiowetz, N. (2001). Measurement error in survey data. In J. J. Heckman & E. Learner (Eds.), *Handbook of econometrics* (Vol. 5, pp. 3705–3843). North Holland: Elsevier.

Bound, J., Schoenbaum, M., Stinebrickner, T. R., & Waidmann, T. (1999). The dynamic effects of health on the labor force transitions of older workers. *Labour Economics, 6*, 179–202.

Bound, J., & Waidmann, T. A. (2002). Accounting for recent declines in employment rates among the working-aged disabled. *Journal of Human Resources, 37*, 231–250.

Brick, J. M., Brick, P. D., Dipko, S., Presser, S., Tucker, C., & Yuan, Y. (2007). Cell phone survey feasibility in the U.S.: Sampling and calling cell numbers versus landline numbers. *Public Opinion Quarterly, 71*, 23–39.

Bruine de Bruin, W., & Carman, K. G. (2012). Measuring risk perceptions: What does the excessive use of 50% mean? *Medical Decision Making, 32*, 232–236.

Bruine de Bruin, W., Manski, C. F., Topa, G., & van der Klaauw, W. (2011). Measuring consumer uncertainty about future inflation. *Journal of Applied Economics, 26*, 454–478.

Bruine de Bruin, W., Parker, A. M., & Mauer, J. (2011). Assessing small non-zero perceptions of chance: The case of H1N1 (swine) flu risks. *Journal of Risk and Uncertainty, 42*, 145–159.

Bruine de Bruin, W., van der Klaauw, W., Downs, J. S., Fischhoff, B., Topa, G. & Armantier, O. (2008, September). *Lay interpretations of questions about inflation expectations.* Paper presented at the University of Michigan Conference on Understanding Economic Decision Making, Jackson Hole, WY.

Choi, J. J., Laibson, D., & Madrian, B. C. (2010). Why does the law of one price fail? An experiment on index mutual funds. *Review of Financial Studies, 23*, 1404–1432.

Choi, J. J., Laibson, D., Madrian, B. C., & Metrick, A. (2002). Defined contribution pensions: Plan rules, participant decisions, and the path of least resistance. *Tax Policy and the Economy, 16*, 67–114.

Cortina, J. M. (1993). What is coefficient alpha? An examination of theory and applications. *Journal of Applied Psychology, 78*, 98–104.

Davies, P. S., & Fisher, T. L. (2009). The retirement research consortium: Past, present, and future. *Social Security Bulletin, 69(4),* 27–33. Available online at http://www.ssa.gov/policy/docs/ssb/v69n4/v69n4p27.html.

Davis, G. (2007). *From worker to retiree: A validation study of a psychological retirement planning measure* (Unpublished doctoral dissertation). Bowling Green State University, Bowling Green, OH.

Delavande, A., Rohwedder,. S., & Willis, R. J. (2008). *Preparation for retirement, financial literacy, and cognitive resources* (Working Paper No. 2008-190). Ann Arbor, MI: Michigan Retirement Research Center, University of Michigan.

Dillman, D. A., Eltinge, J. L., Groves, R. M., and Little, R. J. A. (2002). Survey nonresponse in design, data collection, and analysis. In R. M. Groves, D. A. Dillman, J. L. Eltinge, & R. J. A. Little (Eds.), *Survey nonresponse* (pp. 3–26). New York, NY: Wiley.

Dohmen, T., Falk, A., Huffman, D., & Sunde, U. (2010). Are risk aversion and impatience related to cognitive ability? *American Economic Review, 100,* 1238–1260.

Duckworth, A., & Weir, D. R. (2010). *Personality, lifetime earnings, and retirement wealth.* (Working Paper No. 2010-235). Ann Arbor, MI: Michigan Retirement Research Center, University of Michigan.

Ekerdt, D. (2010). Frontiers of research on work and retirement. *Journal of Gerontology: Social Sciences, 65B,* 69–80.

Elder, G. H. (1994). Time, human agency, and social change: Perspectives on the life course. *Social Psychology Quarterly, 57,* 4–15.

Fisher, G. G., & Barnes-Farrell, J. L. (in press). Use of archival data in occupational health psychology research. In M. Wang, R. R. Sinclair, & L. E. Tetrick (Eds.), *Research methods in occupational health psychology: State of the art in measurement, design, and data analysis.* New York, NY: Routledge.

Fisher, G. G., Hassan, H., Rodgers, W. L., & Weir, D. R. (2009). *Health and Retirement Study imputation of cognitive functioning measures: 1992–2006* (HRS Documentation Report). Ann Arbor, MI: Survey Research Center, University of Michigan.

Fisher, G. G., McArdle, J. J., Rodgers, W. L., Weir, D. R., & Willis, R. J. (2011). *Documentation of fluid intelligence measures in the Health and Retirement Study: 2010 and beyond* (Report in progress).

Floyd, F. J., Haynes, S. N., Doll, E. R., Winemiller, D., Lemsky, C., Burgy, T. M., … Heilman, N. (1992). Assessing retirement satisfaction and perceptions of retirement experiences. *Psychology and Aging, 7,* 609–621.

Friedman, M. (1957). *A theory of the consumption function.* Princeton, NJ: Princeton University Press.

Gelman, A., & Carlin, J. B. (2002). Post-stratification and weighting adjustments. In R. M. Groves, D. A. Dillman, J. L. Eltinge, & R. J. A. Little (Eds.), *Survey nonresponse* (pp. 289–302). New York, NY: Wiley.

Giele, J. Z., & Elder, G. H. (Eds.) (1998). *Methods of life course research: Qualitative and quantitative approaches.* London, England: Sage Publications.

Goda, G. S., Shoven, J. B., & Slavov, S. N. (2010, August). *How do long-run financial planning expectations and decisions respond to short-run fluctuations in financial markets?* Paper presented at the 12th Annual Joint Conference of the Retirement Research Consortium, Washington, DC.

Gouskova, E., Chiteji, N., & Stafford, F. (2010) Estimating the intergenerational persistence of lifetime earnings with life course matching: Evidence from the PSID. *Labour Economics, 17,* 592–597.

Groves, R. M., & Couper, M. P. (2002). Designing surveys acknowledging nonresponse. In M. Ver Ploeg, R. A. Moffitt, & C. F. Citro (Eds.), *Studies of welfare populations: Data collection and research issues* (pp. 13–48). Washington, DC: National Academy Press.

Groves, R. M., Fowler, F. J., Couper, M. P., Lepkowski, J. M., Singer, E., & Tourangeau, R. (2009). *Survey Methodology* (2nd ed.). New York, NY: Wiley.

Gruber, J., & Wise, D. A. (1999). *Social security and retirement around the world.* Chicago, IL: University of Chicago Press.

Gustman, A. L., Mitchell, O. S., & Steinmeier, T. L. (1995). Retirement measures in the Health and Retirement Survey. *The Journal of Human Resources, 30* (Suppl.), S57–S83.

Gustman, A. L., & Steinmeier, T. L. (2000). Retirement outcomes in the Health and Retirement Study. *Social Security Bulletin, 63,* S57–S83.

Gustman, A. L., & Steinmeier, T. L. (2004). Social security, pensions and retirement behavior within the family. *Journal of Applied Econometrics, 19,* 723–737.

Gustman, A. L., & Steinmeier, T. L. (2009). How changes in social security affect retirement trends. *Research on Aging, 31,* 261–290.

Gustman, A. L., Steinmeier, T. L., & Tabatabai, N. (2010a). What the stock market decline means for the financial security and retirement choices of the near-retirement population. *Journal of Economic Perspectives, 24,* 161–182.

Gustman, A. L., Steinmeier, T. L., & Tabatabai, N. (2010b). *Pensions in the Health and Retirement Study.* Cambridge, MA: Harvard University Press.

Hauser, R., & Willis, R. J. (2005). Survey design and methodology in the Health and Retirement Study and the Wisconsin Longitudinal Study. In L. Waite (Ed.), *Aging, health and public policy: Demographic and Economic perspectives. Supplement to population and development review* (Vol. 30, pp. 209–235). New York, NY: Population Council.

Health and Retirement Study. (2008). *Sample sizes and response rates.* Ann Arbor, MI: Institute for Social Research, University of Michigan.

Heckman, J. J. (1976). The common structure of statistical models of truncation, sample selection and limited dependent variables and a simple estimator for such models. *Annals of Economic and Social Measurement, 5,* 120–137. Cambridge, MA: National Bureau of Economic Research.

Heckman, J. J. (1979). "Sample selection bias as a specification error." *Econometrica, 47,* 153–161.

Heeringa, S. G., Hill, D. H., & Howell, D. A. (1995). *Unfolding brackets for reducing item nonresponse in economic surveys* (HRS Working Paper No. 94-029). Ann Arbor, MI: Institute for Social Research, University of Michigan.

Heeringa, S. G., Little, R. J. A., & Raghunathan, T. E. (2002). Multivariate imputation of coarsened survey data on household wealth. In R. M. Groves, D. A. Dillman, J. L. Eltinge, & R. J. A. Little (Eds.), *Survey nonresponse* (pp. 357–372). New York, NY: Wiley.

Helppie, B., Kapinos, K., & Willis, R. J. (2010). *Occupational learning, financial knowledge, and the accumulation of retirement wealth* (Working Paper No. 2010-237). Ann Arbor, MI: Michigan Retirement Research Center, University of Michigan.

Herzog, A. R., House, J. S., & Morgan, J. N. (1991). Relation of work and retirement to health and well-being in older age. *Psychology and Aging, 6,* 202–211.

Honig, M. (1998). Married women's retirement expectations: Do pensions and Social Security matter? *The American Economic Review, 88,* 202–206.

House, J. S. (2002). *Americans' Changing Lives: Waves I, II, III, and IV, 1986, 1989, 1994, and 2002* (ICPSR Study No. 4690). Ann Arbor, MI: Inter-university Consortium for Political and Social Research, University of Michigan.

Hsu, J. W. (2011). *Aging and strategic learning: the impact of spousal incentives on financial literacy.* Essays on the acquisition of human capital (Unpublished doctoral dissertation). Department of Economics, University of Michigan.

Hsu, J. W., Fisher, G. G., & Willis, R. J. (2008, August). *Internet access and cognitive ability: Analysis of selectivity of internet interviews in the Cognitive Economics Survey.* Paper for Conference on "Measurement and Experimentation with Internet Panels: Innovative features of Internet Interviewing," Zeist, Netherlands.

Hudomiet, P., Kezdi, G., & Willis, R. J. (2011). Stock market crash and expectations of American households. *Journal of Applied Econometrics, 26*(3), 393–415.

Hurd, M. D. (1997). The economics of individual aging. In M. R. Rosenzweig & O. Stark (Eds.), *Handbook of population and family economics* (Vol. 1, Pt. 2, pp. 891–966). North Holland: Elsevier.

Hurd, M. D., Reti, M., & Rohwedder, S. (2009). The effect of large capital gains or losses on retirement. In D. A. Wise (Ed.), *Developments in the economics of aging* (pp. 127–163). Chicago, IL: University of Chicago Press.

Hurd, M. D., & Rohwedder, S. (2010). *The effects of the economic crisis on the older population* (Working Paper No. 2010-231). Ann Arbor, MI: Michigan Retirement Research Center, University of Michigan.

Juster, F. T., Lupton, J. P., Smith, J. P., and Stafford, F. P. (2006). The decline in household saving and the wealth effect. *The Review of Economics and Statistics, 88,* 20–27.

Juster, F. T., & Suzman, R. (1995). An overview of the Health and Retirement Study. *Journal of Human Resources, 30,* S7–S56.

Kahn, R. L., Wolfe, D. M., Quinn, R., Snoek, J. D., & Rosenthal, R.A. (1964). *Organizational stress.* New York, NY: Wiley.

Kalton, G. (1983). *Introduction to survey sampling.* Newbury Park, CA: Sage.

Kapteyn, A., Smith, J. P., & van Soest, A. (2007). Vignettes and self-reports of work disability in the United States and the Netherlands. *The American Economic Review, 97,* 461–473.

Kubicek, B., Korunka, C., Hoonakker, P., & Raymo, J. M. (2010). Work and family characteristics as predictors of early retirement in married men and women. *Research on Aging, 32,* 467–498.

Laibson, D., Madrian, B., Beshears, J., Choi, J., & Zeldes, S. P. (in progress). *Optimal knowledge and saving for retirement.* Santa Monica, CA: RAND Financial Literacy Center.

Lee, C., & Solon, G. (2009). Trends in intergenerational income mobility. *The Review of Economics and Statistics, 91,* 766–772.

Little, R. J. A. (1986). Survey nonresponse adjustments for estimates of means. *International Statistical Review, 54,* 139–157.

Lumsdaine, R. L., & Mitchell, O. S. (1999). New developments in the economic analysis of retirement. In O. Ashenfelter & D. Card (Eds.), *Handbook of labor economics* (Vol. 3, pp. 3261–3307). North Holland: Elsevier.

Lusardi, A, (2008). Household saving behavior: *The role of financial literacy, information, and financial education programs* (Working Paper). Available at SSRN: http://ssrn.com/abstract=1094102.

Lusardi, A., & Mitchell, O. S. (2007a). Baby boomer retirement security: The roles of planning, financial literacy, and housing wealth. *Journal of Monetary Economics, 54,* 205–224.

Lusardi, A., & Mitchell, O. S. (2007b). *Financial literacy and retirement planning: New evidence from the Rand American Life Panel* (Working Paper No. WP2007-157). Ann Arbor, MI: Michigan Retirement Research Center, University of Michigan.

Lusardi, A., & Mitchell, O. S. (2009). *How ordinary consumers make complex economic decisions: Financial literacy and retirement readiness* (Working Paper No. 15350). Cambridge, MA: National Bureau of Economic Research.

Maestas, N. (2010). Back to work: Expectations and realizations of work after retirement. *Journal of Human Resources, 45,* 718–748.

McArdle, J. J., Fisher, G. G., & Rodgers, W. L. (2007). *Cognition and aging in the USA. Documentation of study methodology.* Ann Arbor, MI: Institute for Social Research, University of Michigan.

McArdle, J. J., Fisher, G. G., Rodgers, W. L., Woodcock, R., & Horn, J. L. (2011). *An experiment in measuring fluid intelligence over the telephone in the Health and Retirement Study (HRS).* Manuscript in preparation.

McArdle, J. J., & Hamagami, F. (1992). Modeling incomplete longitudinal and cross-sectional curves using latent growth structural models. *Experimental Aging Research, 18,* 145–166.

McArdle, J.J., Smith, J.P., & Willis, R. J. (2009). *Cognition and economic outcomes in the Health and Retirement Study* (Working Paper No. 15266). Cambridge, MA: National Bureau of Economic Research.

McFall, B. (2011) *Crash and wait? The impact of the great recession on the retirement planning of older Americans* (Unpublished doctoral dissertation). Department of Economics, University of Michigan, Ann Arbor, MI.

McGarry, K. (2004). Health and retirement: Do changes in health affect retirement expectations? *Journal of Human Resources, 39,* 624–648.

Mitchell, O. S., Utkus, S. P., Yang, T. (2005). *Turning workers into savers? Incentives, liquidity, and choice in 401(k) plan design* (Working Paper No. 11726). Cambridge, MA: National Bureau of Economic Research.

Modigliani, F. (1986). Life cycle, individual thrift, and the wealth of nations. *American Economic Review, 76,* 297–313.

Munnell, A. H., & Jivan, N. (2005). *What makes older women work?* (Brief WOB#1). Chestnut Hill, MA: Center for Retirement Research at Boston College.

Noone, J., Alpass, F., & Stephens, C. (2010). Do men and women differ in their retirement planning? Testing a theoretical model of gendered pathways to retirement preparation. *Research on Aging, 32,* 715–738.

Peytchev, A., Carley-Baxter, L. R., & Black, M. C. (2010). Coverage bias in variances, associations, and total error from exclusion of the cell phone-only population in the United States. *Social Science Computer Review, 28,* 287–302.

Pienta, A. M., & Hayward, M. D. (2002). Who expects to continue working after age 62? The retirement plans of couples. *Journal of Gerontology, 57B,* S119–S208.

Pinquart, M., & Schindler, I. (2007). Changes in life satisfaction in the transition to retirement: A latent-class approach. *Psychology and Aging, 22,* 442–455.

Quick, H. E., & Moen, P. (1998). Gender, employment, and retirement quality: A life course approach to the differential experiences of men and women. *Journal of Occupational Health Psychology, 3,* 44–64.

Raghunathan, T. E., Solenberger, P. W., & Van Hoewyk, J. (2002*). IVEware: Imputation and variance estimation software user guide.* Ann Arbor, MI: Survey Research Center, Institute for Social Research, University of Michigan.

Raymo, J. M., & Sweeney, M. M. (2006). Work–family conflict and retirement preferences. *Journals of Gerontology: Social Sciences, 61B,* S161–S169.

Rohwedder, S., & Willis, R. J. (2010). Mental retirement. *Journal of Economic Perspectives, 24,* 119–138.

Rubin, D. B. (1976). Inference and missing data. *Biometrika, 63,* 581–592.

Rubin, D. B. (1987). *Multiple imputation for nonresponse in surveys.* New York, NY: Wiley.

Rubin, D. B., & Little, R. J. A. (2002). *Statistical analysis with missing data* (2nd ed.). New York, NY: Wiley.

Rust, J., & Phelan, C. (1997). How Social Security and Medicare affect retirement behavior in a world of incomplete markets. *Econometrica, 65,* 781–831.

Sartori, A. E. (2003). An estimator for some binary-outcome selection models without exclusion restrictions. *Political Analysis, 11,* 111–138.

Shapiro, M. D. (2010). *The effect of the financial crisis on the well-being of older Americans: Evidence from the Cognitive Economics Study* (Working Paper No. 2010-228). Ann Arbor, MI: Michigan Retirement Research Center, University of Michigan.

Simon, H. (1987). Behavioral economics. *The New Palgrave: A Dictionary of Economics, 1,* 221–224.

Smith, J. P. (1995). Racial and ethnic differences in wealth in the Health and Retirement Study. *Journal of Human Resources, 30,* S158–S183.

Smith, J. P. (1997). Wealth inequality among older Americans. *Journal of Gerontology, 52B,* 74–81.

Smith, J. P., McArdle, J. J., & Willis, R. J. (2010). Financial decision making and cognition in a family context. *The Economic Journal, 120,* F363–F380.

StataCorp. (2011). *Multiple imputation for missing data.* Retrieved from http://www.stata.com/stata11/mi.html.

Szinovacz, M. (1991). Women and retirement. In B. B. Hess & E. W. Markson (Eds.), *Growing old in America* (4th ed, pp. 293–303). New Brunswick, NJ: Transaction Publishers.

Szinovacz, M. E. (2003). Contexts and pathways: Retirement as institution, process, and experience. In G. A. Adams & T. A. Beehr (Eds.), *Retirement: Reasons, processes, and results* (pp. 6–52). New York, NY: Springer.

Szinovacz, M. E., & Davey, A. (2004). Honeymoons and joint lunches: Effects of retirement and spouse's employment on depressive symptoms. *Journal of Gerontology: Psychological Sciences, 59B,* P233–P245.

Talaga J. A., & Beehr, T. A. (1995). Are there gender differences in predicting retirement decisions? *Journal of Applied Psychology, 80,* 16–28.

Thissen, D., & Mislevy, R. J. (2000). Testing algorithms. In H. Wainer (Ed.), *Computerized adaptive testing: A primer* (pp. 101–133). Mahwah, NJ: Lawrence Erlbaum Associates.

Topa, G., Moriano, J. A., Depolo, M., Alcover, C. M., & Morales, J. F. (2009). Antecedents and consequences of retirement planning and decision-making: A meta-analysis and model. *Journal of Vocational Behaviour, 75, 38–55.*

U.S. Bureau of Labor Statistics. (2010). *Employment status of the civilian noninstitutional population 16 years and over by sex, 1973 to date.* Retrieved from ftp://ftp.bls.gov/pub/special.requests/lf/aat2.txt

von Bonsdorff, M. E., Shultz, K. S., Leskinen, E., & Tansky, J. (2009). The choice between retirement and bridge employment: A continuity and life course perspective. *International Journal of Aging and Human Development, 69,* 79–100.

Wallace, D., & Lusardi, A. (in progress). *Building financial literacy for K-8 pre-service teachers and adult learners.* Santa Monica, CA: RAND Financial Literacy Center.

Waller, N. G., & Reise, S. P. (1989). Computerized adaptive personality assessment: An illustration with the Absorption scale. *Journal of Personality and Social Psychology, 57,* 1051–1058.

Wang, M. (2007). Profiling retirees in the retirement transition and adjustment process: Examining the longitudinal change patterns of retirees' psychological well-being. *Journal of Applied Psychology, 92,* 455–474.

Wang, M., & Shultz, K. S. (2010). Employee retirement: A review and recommendations for future investigation. *Journal of Management, 36,* 172–206

Wang, M., Zhan, Y., Liu, S., & Shultz, K. (2008). Antecedents of bridge employment: A longitudinal investigation. *Journal of Applied Psychology, 93,* 818–830.

Weiss, D. J., & Kingsbury, G. G. (1984). Application of computerized adaptive testing to educational problems. *Journal of Educational Measurement, 21,* 361–375.

Willis, R. J. (1999). Theory confronts data: How the HRS is shaped by the economics of aging and how the economics of aging will be shaped by the HRS. *Labor Economics, 6,* 119–145.

Zhan, Y., Wang, M., Liu, S., & Shultz, K. S. (2009). Bridge employment and retirees' health: A longitudinal investigation. *Journal of Occupational Health Psychology, 14,* 374–389.

Age, Gender, and the Retirement Process

Barbara Griffin, Vanessa Loh, *and* Beryl Hesketh

Abstract

This chapter considers the complex role of age and gender in the retirement process. Although typically used as control variables in research, we discuss relevant theories that might explain why both age and gender need to be considered as key drivers of the process, then review empirical findings related to their effect on retirement timing, on the various patterns of work and non-work that people choose when transitioning to full retirement, on the extent that people plan for retirement, and on their level of adjustment in retirement.

Key Words: retirement, age, gender, retirement planning, subjective life expectancy, older workers, bridge employment, phased retirement

Retirement research has frequently examined demographic factors, particularly age and gender, albeit often as control variables rather than as the main focus of study. As a result, there is substantial evidence indicating that age and gender influence the retirement process from financial planning, choices regarding timing, adjustment to the retirement role, and preference for types of activity in retirement. However, less attention has been given to identifying the underlying reasons as to why these two demographic variables play a significant role. This is an important issue because the career patterns of both women and older workers are evolving quite rapidly, creating the possibility that established relationships of age and gender with retirement may not be relevant for the upcoming generation of retirees.

Age

Retirement has traditionally been regarded as being synonymous with old age and the rest period or stage of life that begins after stopping full-time work up until death. Although more current conceptions of retirement recognize that the timing and process will vary for individuals in an increasingly diverse workforce, the timing of the retirement process is strongly tied to age.

Age is becoming an increasingly important issue for organizations, with commentators (e.g., Alley & Crimmins, 2007; Wang & Shultz, 2010) noting that in the majority of developed countries the workforce is aging, largely due to factors such as increasing life expectancies, decreasing birth rates, and the aging of the relatively large baby-boomer generation (defined as those born between 1946 and 1964). For example, although the proportion of the U.S. workforce aged 55 and over increased from 12.4% to only 12.9% between 1998 and 2000 (Fullerton, 1999; Fullerton & Toossi, 2001), it rose to 14.3% in 2002, 18.1% in 2008, and is projected to comprise almost 25% of the U.S. workforce by 2018 (Toossi, 2004, 2009). Furthermore, the only group for whom workforce participation rates rose significantly between 1998 and 2008, and are projected to be higher in 2018, were those aged 55 years and over (Toossi, 2009).

The aging workforce and impending retirement of such a large cohort of workers has many implications for policymakers around the world (OECD, 2006). One major concern is how governments will be able to provide adequate pension and health care support for such a large cohort when they retire and the overall labor participation rate significantly decreases. Therefore, despite a trend during the late twentieth century toward earlier retirements by workers in many developed countries (Hardy, 2006), a more recent focus has been on the development of strategies to encourage workers to retire later rather than earlier. Henkens and Van Dalen (2003, p. 242) summarize the widespread response to the changing demographic landscape with the comment, "the goal of raising retirement ages seems to have obtained in almost every western society the status of a mantra in public policy circles." Strategies have included increasing the age of eligibility for pension and superannuation benefits, and encouraging organizations to better support and value older workers with the introduction of legislation aimed at removing age discrimination at work. For example, Szinovacz (2003) reported that in the United States most retirements now occur at around ages 62 and 65, which corresponds with the ages at which individuals become eligible for Social Security benefits.

This increased predominance of older workers and the need to retain them for longer means that issues relating to retirement are likely to become more salient, not only for governments but also for organizations and for a greater proportion of the employed workforce.

Challenges Faced by Older Workers

The most obvious reason for the link between age and retirement is the slow or sudden decline in health that occurs more frequently with age. Age-related declines in physical and cognitive abilities, which may result from biological or genetic factors, work or environmental factors, or a combination of both, have traditionally placed a natural upper limit on how long a person will continue to be effective in his or her job. Although mandatory retirement ages have largely been outlawed as a form of age discrimination in many developed countries, upper age limits may still exist for certain jobs that require particularly high levels of physical, motor, and/or cognitive skills such as air traffic controllers, commercial airline pilots, and high court judges (Hedge, Borman, & Lammlein, 2006; Wang & Shultz, 2010).

However as Hedge et al. (2006) argued, average age-related declines in physical and cognitive abilities do not necessarily mean that an older worker will perform more poorly than a younger worker because there are often greater differences in the extent and rate of decline over time between individuals than within individuals. Furthermore, as Hansson, DeKoekkoek, Neece, and Patterson (1997) highlight, individual differences in ability become more prominent with age, so that among older workers there will be considerable variation in the level of adjustment required for them to continue working productively.

In addition, the changing nature of work and advent of technology have greatly reduced the physical demands of work, and the trend toward increasing health and longevity for later generations suggests that average age-related declines are likely to slow down or be less marked in more recent birth cohorts (Hedge et al., 2006; McArdle, Fisher, & Kadlee, 2007). With continued advances in medicine, science, and technology, individuals are likely to become more able to adapt to and compensate for certain age-related changes by using aids to correct for these changes, drawing on prior experience, receiving relevant training and education, or changing work strategies and job designs (Hedge et al., 2006), thus delaying the need for retirement.

Nevertheless, despite the above and attempts to reduce age discrimination in workplaces, research suggests that robust age norms and social expectations still exist about the appropriate times at which individuals should begin transitioning to retirement (van Solinge & Henkens, 2007), and the extent of organizational support for older workers remains mixed (Hardy, 2006). Adams (2004) provided evidence that age discrimination laws in the United States may have improved employment rates and reduced retirement rates of older workers, but they did not improve recruitment rates of older workers, who are still likely to find it more difficult than younger workers to find a job. Even in countries with age discrimination laws, older workers tend not to be hired for positions that provide employee training and skill development, generous pension benefits, or those that require high numerical skills or extensive computer use (Garen, Berger, & Scott, 1996; Heywood, Ho, & Wei, 2000; Heywood, Jirjahn, & Tsertsvardze, 2010; Hirsch, Macpherson, & Hardy, 2000).

In general, workers are likely to have fewer employment options the older they get, which may in turn impact their transitions to retirement and uptake of bridge employment. As Hardy (2006) noted, educating employers about the strengths and limitations of older workers might help to remove some of the challenges they face by reducing the negative effects of age stereotyping and discrimination in the workplace. It is important for employers to recognize that age accounts for only a fraction of the between-person variability in work performance, work-related needs, and retirement transition patterns, and relatively large differences exist between individuals of the same age. Employers could better support older workers by redesigning jobs to enable them to work longer, providing more flexible work arrangements to support caregiving responsibilities and transitions into retirement, providing training, and encouraging lifelong learning and skill development for continued worker effectiveness.

Theoretical Explanations of the Link between Retirement and Age

Although a number of theories on aging have been related to the retirement process in the literature, three key theories are frequently associated with the more comprehensive conceptualization of retirement as a process in which individuals are transitioning from work to retirement (Wang & Shultz, 2010). The first is social identity or role theory (Burr, 1972; Cottrell, 1942), which describes how people transition in and out of different roles throughout life, often holding multiple roles simultaneously. Contrary to the view that it is normal and appropriate for people to disengage from active roles in society as they age, role theory posits that difficulties adjusting to the processes of aging and retirement are likely to occur because of *role loss* (e.g., losing the role of being an employee), or *role strain*, which arises when role expectations are not being sufficiently met (Goode, 1960). Optimal adjustment is thought to occur when the role transition fits the individual's values, goals, and needs and when role balance is achieved (Marks & MacDermid, 1996). For example, in a study of Swiss workers and retirees aged 58 to 70, Teuscher (2010) found that, consistent with role theory, the profession or career domain was important for both workers' and retirees' self-description, but that retirees rated other domains, including family roles and personal values, as being more important than did workers. This suggests that retirees do not lose their identification with their pre-retirement profession, but rather gain greater diversity in their personal identities.

Similar to the role theory focus on older people continuing to engage in active roles in society,

Atchley's (1989) continuity theory presents retirement as a process whereby retirees strive to maintain the same social relationships and lifestyle patterns they had prior to retirement. Essentially, an individual's adjustment to aging and well-being later in life depends on the extent to which he or she can continuously and consistently carry out preferred habits, activities, roles, and other lifestyle patterns as he or she ages. This theory suggests that when work has high centrality and importance, older people will either delay retirement or attempt to continue some form of work activity in retirement.

The third theoretical approach taken by retirement researchers is based on a contemporary developmental life-course perspective (e.g., Elder, 1995), where a person's life course or developmental trajectory is thought to be age-graded through existing social structures and institutions. Social interactions within a particular cultural context help to shape age norms and expectations, which are likely to influence both the timing and process of retirement (Hershey, Henkens, & van Dalen, 2010). For example, the expectation that most workers will cease work and retire at some time before death has become a cultural norm in developed countries only in the last century, and is yet to be institutionalized in many developing countries where people typically work until they are no longer able to do so (Beehr & Bennett, 2007; Szinovacz, 2003; Thane, 2006). The significant role of social context in life-course perspectives suggests that different social groups and generational cohorts are likely to exhibit different developmental trajectories in their transitions to retirement.

Although these theories provide some understanding of the relationship between age and retirement, two recent studies on retirement adjustment (Wang, 2007; Pinquart & Ines, 2007) illustrated how people follow different trajectories of adjustment that could not be explained by any one theory. This problem indicates that perhaps a new theory of aging and the retirement process is required.

Griffin and Hesketh (2010b) are currently undertaking longitudinal research on retirement decision making and adjustment within a person-environment (P-E) fit framework (Dawis & Lofquist, 1984; Hesketh & Dawis, 1991) that provides a more comprehensive basis for charting changes in individual interests, needs, and values, as well as capabilities, and examining how these "fit" with the rewards and demands in evolving work, retirement, and post-work environments.

Empirical Results

Timing of retirement. It is not surprising that in terms of retirement timing and decision making, studies (e.g., Bidewell, Griffin, & Hesketh, 2006; Taylor & Shore, 1995) consistently show that older workers generally nominate older preferred retirement ages than younger workers. Furthermore, we suggest that the concept of "norms" for retirement age may be stronger for younger people compared to older people. In an examination of intended retirement age (Griffin & Hesketh, 2006), 77% of those aged less than 40 years and 82% of those aged 40 to 49 years nominated 55, 60, or 65 years as their likely retirement age. In contrast, only 56% of those aged 50 or over nominated these "traditional" retirement ages, suggesting that older people are "chunking" years together to a lesser extent than younger people and are making more fine-grained decisions about their intended retirement age.

Not only is age positively correlated with intended or actual retirement age, but some research suggests that other factors known to predict retirement age are moderated by chronological age. Griffin and Hesketh (2006), for example, reported that attitudes to and expectations about retirement had more impact on planned retirement age for younger participants who had not reached the age of being eligible for retirement than they had on those who were older and had entered the age period of eligibility for retirement. In contrast, attitudes and feelings about current work were more influential in predicting planned retirement age for older people than for younger people. These data provide a picture of shifting attention and focus given to retirement as one ages. It is possible that for those for whom retirement is a current option (i.e., older participants), current circumstances are more salient in the decision about when to leave work, whereas when it is only an option for the future (as for younger participants), "future" variables, such as expectations about retirement, are the most predictive.

The fact that retirement is considered as a decision-making process enacted over an extended period of time (Ekerdt, Kosloski, & DeViney, 2000; Sterns & Gray, 1999) suggests a complex interplay of multiple factors. Models of retirement timing therefore need to incorporate the possibility that younger workers and older workers think about retirement timing in different ways and that the impact of certain factors changes over the decision-making period.

Mode of retirement, including post-retirement work. As noted by many authors (e.g. Hardy, 2002; Pleau,

2010; Quinn & Kozy, 1996), the "traditional" pattern of retirement—where a person is engaged in steady employment till a set point in time, after which they withdraw completely from the workforce—is becoming less normative and replaced by a more complex transition from work. For example, Griffin, Hesketh, and Loh (2010b) asked older public-sector employees in Australia about their expected pattern of retirement, finding that only 30.3% intended to take the traditional route, 42.5% planned to "officially retire" from their regular place of work and then engage in some form of post-retirement or bridge employment, and 27.2% intended to transition into retirement by gradually reducing the number of hours or days spent at their regular place of work before officially retiring. The latter pattern of transition is often referred to as "phased retirement" (Pleau, 2010). Not surprisingly, older workers were more likely to indicate that they would be following the traditional pattern of retirement and younger workers more likely to be planning to transition by way of bridge employment or phased retirement. However, this difference in choice may represent different opportunities or perceptions of opportunity to pursue one's preferred pattern of transition, given that employers have reportedly been selective in granting older workers flexible transitional employment arrangements (Hutchens, 2010).

Planning for retirement. As discussed elsewhere (see chapters by Yao and Peng and by Hershey, Jacobs-Lawson, and Austin, this volume), the shift away from government- and work-sponsored retirement funds toward individuals assuming greater responsibility for their financial needs in retirement has resulted in individual retirement planning becoming an increasingly important part of the retirement process (Glass & Kilpatrick, 1998a). Age is a key variable when it comes to life planning in general (Prenda & Lachman, 2001) and retirement preparation in particular. Consistent with socially reinforced age norms and the normative view of retirement as a later life event, older workers typically engage in more retirement planning than younger workers (e.g., Employee Benefit Research Institute, 2006; Hershey et al., 2010; Petkoska & Earl, 2009). However, this relationship may hold only for personal financial planning and saving for retirement, as Petkoska and Earl (2009) found that the extent to which people engaged in leisure planning and the coordination of post-employment activities was unrelated to age when education, gender, and income were controlled for.

Retirement adjustment. Research on the effect of age on retirement adjustment has been mixed. While some studies have found that older retirees adjust better than younger retirees (e.g., Bacharach, Bamberger, Biron, & Horowitz-Rozen, 2008; Joukamaa, Saarijarvi, & Salokangas, 1993), others have found age to be a nonsignificant predictor of retirement adjustment (Donaldson, Earl, & Muratore, 2010; Wong & Earl, 2009)

Recent longitudinal analyses have extended the existing research on adjustment to account for change over time. Wang (2007) and Pinquart and Ines (2007) both identified multiple trajectories of changing retirement adjustment, although the effect of age on these adjustment patterns was somewhat different. Pinquart and Ines (2007) used data from Germany and found that age at retirement predicted which trajectory a retiree was likely to follow. Those who were older at retirement tended to show an initial decline in satisfaction but thereafter continued on a trajectory of stable or increasing satisfaction with retirement. In contrast, younger retirees tended to experience a sharp rise in satisfaction at the time of retirement followed by decreasing satisfaction over time. These results could suggest that those who retire at older ages are more attached to their work role, delaying retirement either because of the intrinsic fulfillment gained from work or because of the income, and therefore are more likely to have a drop in life satisfaction when leaving work. However, Wang's (2007) results from an American sample indicated that an initial decline in satisfaction at retirement occurred only for those who retired earlier than they had expected.

Life Expectancy

The discussion to date considers chronological age as the variable of interest. Another age-related, but rarely considered, construct is subjective life expectancy or expected age at death. Death is not a subject that is generally spoken about openly, yet it would be surprising if a prospective retiree did not give thought to how many years of life he had left, what his health and financial status might be during those years, and where he might live in his later years. Although not often studied in psychological research on retirement, life expectancy, albeit actuarial estimates rather than self-rated estimates, are commonly used by financial planners as a guide for people in determining how to allocate and invest their retirement savings.

Self-estimates of likely age at death predict actual mortality (Prem & Debats, 2006; Siegel, Bradley, & Kasl, 2003), and recent research indicates that factors influencing the self-estimates of pre-retirees include demographic variables such as parents' age at death, income, health, gender and education, personality variables such as optimism, and environmental variables such as social support (e.g., Griffin, Hesketh, & Loh, 2010a; Ross & Mirowsky, 2002; van Solinge & Henkens, 2010).

Hesketh and Griffin (2007) highlighted the importance of subjective life expectancy by showing that it was a stronger predictor of preferred retirement age than current income, expected retirement income, or self-reported health. Those who expected to live longer planned to retire later. O'Brien, Fenn, and Diacon (2005) also showed that those who thought they would live to an older age were more likely to buy retirement pensions, while Mirowsky (1997) suggested they also had a greater sense of control over their lives. More recently, Griffin, Hesketh, and Loh (in press) found that longevity predicted later preferred retirement, actual retirement, and even return to paid work by those who had already retired.

We think that self-estimates of longevity provide "mental" blocks of time within which individuals apportion work, transitioning, and retirement, as well as considerations of how to distribute their finances and activities. As workers age and begin to transition into retirement, thoughts of life expectancy may also be a trigger for changing values. According to socioemotional selectivity theory (Carstensen, Fung, & Charles, 2003; Carstensen, Isaacowitz, & Charles, 1999), individuals who realize that their time is not infinite experience a change in goals, with increasing value placed on experiencing meaningful social connections and less value on knowledge-relevant goals. This sort of change parallels the shift in focus that can occur as people transition from work to retirement.

Further research is needed to examine the link between self-estimates of the amount of time left in life and retirement financial planning. In particular, a more extensive examination is needed of the way in which health or mood might affect estimates of the "block of time" left and how this could alter the value placed on finance, activity, and other factors contributing to a retirement decision. Also interesting would be an investigation into how overly optimistic or pessimistic estimates, given one's context, could adversely affect retirement decision making.

Gender

Whereas many early studies on retirement were conducted with male-only or predominantly male samples, some of the more recent research has examined gender as a key variable that can impact the retirement process. This shift in focus was predicated on the acknowledgement that males and females have often had different work and background experiences, including job type, pay, career progression, and longevity, which are likely to have relevance for retirement decision making and adjustment (Glass & Kilpatrick, 1998b; Rosenman & Scott, 2009). This concept fits with the life-course perspective of retirement (Elder, 1995) in which retirement is conceptualized as a transition on a trajectory influenced by early life events. As detailed below, research over the last decade, while not always consistent, indicates that gender has played a complex role in retirement. Exactly how and why this might be so is still not clearly understood (Beehr & Bennett, 2007). Furthermore, even the more recently published research tends to be based on older cohorts, so little is known as to whether the ongoing changes in women's workforce participation and the increasing similarity between women and men's life patterns (Moen & Spencer, 2006) will affect the upcoming generation of retirees and if the retirement experiences of these still-employed men and women will actually become more similar.

Historically, men and women have been "products of past age- and gender-graded institutions and norms … producing asymmetries in power, resources, needs and preferences" (Moen & Spencer, 2006, p. 144). A number of these asymmetries are related to factors known to be key issues affecting the retirement process. Before reviewing the empirical literature on gender differences in retirement, we discuss possible explanations as to why there may be an observed difference.

Accounting for Differences

Finance. Women tend to have more discontinuous or interrupted work histories than men (Calasanti, 1996; DeViney & Solomon, 1995; Jacobs-Lawson, Hershey, & Neukam, 2004), with both financial and career progression consequences. Obviously less time spent at work means that, on average, women are more likely to have earned less and accumulated less savings (Glass & Kilpatrick,

1998b; Quick & Moen, 1998; Rosenman & Scott, 2009). For example, in 2009 in Australia the average superannuation payout to women was $73,000 compared to an average of $155,000 for men (Association of Super Funds of Australia, 2009).

This lack of work continuity is also a factor in limiting women's career progression to more senior and highly paid roles. However, actual participation rates of women in the workforce have increased considerably in the last 50 years—38% of adult women in America were employed in 1960 compared to 60% in 2000 (Alley & Crimmins, 2007)—suggesting that in the future female retirees may be better financially prepared. Nevertheless, the effect of increased participation could be tempered by the rise in part-time work, casual arrangements, and temporary jobs, which are more often filled by women (Yerkes, 2010).

DeViney and Solomon (1995) added that women are also more likely to have an interrupted marital career (i.e., being widowed, divorced, or remarried at some point), especially in older age groups (Glass & Kilpatrick, 1998b), resulting in significantly lower monthly retirement incomes than men.

There was also a difference in average level of education between men and women in previous generations (Yerkes, 2010). Given the relationship of education with career success and financial advantage (Judge, Klinger, & Simon, 2010), education may also account for observed gender differences in current retirees. However, the previous disparity appears to be disappearing, at least in most Western societies, with the proportion of women with a university education even exceeding that of men in some countries. This change could well alter the retirement experiences of women compared to men in future cohorts.

Another factor that has acted to reduce women's retirement incomes is the gender difference in life expectancy in most Western countries. According to the Australian Bureau of Statistics (2009), average life expectancy at age 65 is a further 18.54 years for males compared to 21.62 years for females. This means that not only have women accumulated less finance to fund their retirement, but the money they do have has to be spread across a greater number of years.

Health. Health status has been identified as a key variable affecting the retirement process. A study by Liang et al. (2008) analyzed data from the Health and Retirement Study to show how gender affected the level of functional impairment as well as the rate of decline in impairment in older adults.

Despite the fact that women live longer on average (Crimmins & Saito, 2001), they not only had lower levels of health than men, but they declined in functional status at a faster rate after the age of 50. Interestingly, there was a greater gender gap for older people than younger people, which the authors posited may be due to relative improvements in the socioeconomic status of younger women. However, others (e.g., Orel, Ford, & Brock, 2004) have noted that in midlife women are also more involved than men in elder care, which can take a toll on their physical and psychological health. Nevertheless, the cohort for the Liang et al. (2008) study was born prior to 1947, and it remains to be seen if the health gap between men and women will continue as the baby-boom generation ages and transitions through retirement.

Socialization. The social role theory perspective (Eagly, 1987) also offers an explanation for the variance in workforce participation. It outlines how women, at least from the current generation of retirees, were expected to take on responsibilities for family caregiving to a greater extent than men, while men more generally took on a "breadwinner" role. Furthermore, childbearing and childrearing responsibilities were likely to lead to women having a lower emotional attachment to work, which in turn promoted broader role identification with reduced centrality of work and career in the attitudes of women (Isaksson & Johansson, 2000). These social differences may affect attitudes to pre-retirement planning and account for the variation in retirement transition and post-retirement activity. For example, women are more likely to transition through phased retirement (Griffin et al., 2010b) and to engage in volunteer work in retirement (Griffin & Hesketh, 2008), possibly to accommodate their family and caregiving orientation.

Empirical Results

Timing of retirement. In terms of when and why people retire, there are mixed results regarding gender, which suggests that more complex contextual and social factors also have an effect. Using longitudinal data from the U.S. Health and Retirement Study, Hogan and Perrucci (2007) showed that women, regardless of race and age, were less likely to retire over time than men. In contrast, a survey from Hong Kong (Lee, 2005) found that men worked to older ages than women, and in Australia the average retirement age for people aged 45 and over was 47 for women, compared to 58 for men (Australian Bureau of Statistics, 2009). This

difference continued for those not yet retired, with women's intended retirement age being approximately two years younger than men's intended retirement age.

Despite the results above, studies examining the predictors of retirement age have shown a number of similarities between the factors that influence men's and women's thinking about when to retire, although some differences have been found in the strength of relationships between these factors and retirement age. Much of the more recent research has been conducted on Scandinavian workers, which has highlighted a differential impact of health, finance, and work factors on the retirement timing of men and women. In Finland, men appeared to be more influenced by health, whereas women were somewhat more affected by work-related psychological factors (von Bonsdorff, Huuhtanen, Tuomi, & Seitsamo, 2010). In Denmark, salary had a greater impact on intended retirement age for men, and men were also more influenced than women to stay longer at work in the presence of high job control and job security (Larsen, 2008). Likewise in Sweden (Soidre, 2005), positive work conditions acted to retain males in the workforce, while job demands tended to push women out of the job market. Somewhat differently, Pienta and Hayward (2002) analyzed American data to show that work factors affected males' and females' retirement plans equally, but age and health were predictive of only men's early retirement. An earlier study in America (Talaga & Beehr, 1995) also found gender differences when there were dependents still living at home and when one's spouse was ill or retired. In contrast, another study of American workers (Reitzes, Mutran, & Fernandez, 1998) found that gender did not interact with predictors of retirement, except that men were less likely to retire early if they had depression or a non-repetitive job.

Mode of retirement, including post-retirement work. In the same way that pre-retirement work patterns have been significantly different for men and women, post-retirement work and the way in which individuals choose to transition from work to non-work has also been different. In Griffin et al.'s (2010b) recent study, men showed a preference for taking post-retirement bridge employment, whereas women showed a preference for phased retirement, easing slowly out of their current work. One underlying cause of this preference difference could be due to greater opportunity for men to engage in bridge employment on the basis of education and finance (Wang, Zhan, Liu, & Shultz, 2008) and higher participation by women in lower-status jobs that offer more opportunity to reduce to part-time and casual appointments.

Given the diverse patterns of work and non-work that people are choosing as they transition to a state of full and permanent non-work, retirement is becoming increasingly difficult to define, both for researchers and for older workers themselves (Pleau, 2010). It is therefore somewhat surprising that individuals' self-categorization or identification with the retiree role has received so little research attention. Szinovacz and DeViney (1999) suggest that the timing and extent to which a person assumes the retiree identity could well have important consequences for his or her behavior, attitudes, and well-being. In Szinovacz and DeViney's (1999) study using data collected during the late 1980s for the National Survey of Families and Households, men's retiree identity was more strongly tied to their career and work history, while women's appeared to be more flexible and influenced by a variety of life circumstances.

In contrast to the lack of research on retiree identity, there is a growing body of literature focused on the various forms of bridge employment or post-retirement work undertaken by retirees (see chapter by Cahill, Giandrea, and Quinn in this volume). In light of the educational, work, and social differences discussed above, it is not surprising that this research has found gender differences in the work-related roles in which people engage during retirement. Not only have male retirees generally been more likely than females to engage in bridge employment (Griffin & Hesketh, 2008; Singh & Verma, 2003), but also the type of bridge employment that men and women engage in is different. Davis (2003), for example, found that men more than women engaged in career bridge employment (related to their pre-retirement career). In contrast, and perhaps as a result of socialized roles, Griffin and Hesketh (2008) found that female retirees engaged in more volunteer work than male retirees, despite having lower incomes, and this gender difference was also reflected in a sample of non-retired people regarding their intentions for volunteering when in retirement. Furthermore, a recent study (Pleau, 2010) identified interesting interactions between gender and finance in predicting engagement in bridge employment. High salary was associated with greater odds of bridge employment for women but lower odds for men, whereas high accumulated wealth had the opposite effect, being associated with lower odds of taking bridge employment by women but higher odds by men.

Planning for retirement. The issues discussed above would suggest that women are likely to be disadvantaged when it comes to retirement planning, but as the studies reviewed below indicate, the relationship between gender and planning is not straightforward.

While most people are likely to engage in at least some form of retirement planning, men are significantly more likely to begin retirement planning earlier than women, discuss retirement more than women, and view retirement planning as more important (Kragie, Gerstein, & Lichtman, 1989; Larsen, 2008; Taylor & Doverspike, 2003). Moreover, men appear to do more financial planning than women and are more likely to use employer-sponsored retirement plans. Quick and Moen (1998) found, for example, that 53% of men, compared to only 37% of women, had spent a significant amount of time planning for retirement. Contrary to expectations, financial self-efficacy does not appear to account for these gender differences (Dietz, Carrozza, & Ritchey, 2003), but they may arise because those with less money tend to engage in less financial planning (Jacobs-Lawson et al., 2004), or be due to traditional gender roles of women as caregivers and men as breadwinners (Moen, 1996; Talaga & Beehr, 1995). The relative lack of planning by women found in older cohorts is also reflected in those women's anticipation of greater difficulties in financing their retirement (Jacobs-Lawson & Hershey, 2003).

However, in a recent Australian study of employees over age 50, Petkoska and Earl (2009) did not find gender differences in the amount of financial preparation late-career employees were undertaking. As Neukam and Hershey (2003) noted, more women are now engaging in retirement planning than ever before, in part because of their increased workforce participation and the strong shift toward worker contributions-based retirement savings.

In contrast to the results on financial planning, it seems that women are generally engaged in more planning than men in the domains of health and interpersonal relationships (Petkoska & Earl, 2009). Petkoska and Earl (2009) also found that the number of goals listed in each of the four domains of finances, health, interpersonal relationships, and work was a positive predictor of retirement planning in that particular domain. Evidence for gender differences in retirement goals is provided by Hershey, Jacobs-Lawson, and Neukam (2002), who showed that men tended to have more leisure goals than women, while women had more goals than men that related to contact with others. Consistent with this research, in their study of Australian public-sector employees, Onyx and Baker (2006) found that women planned to spend significantly more time doing volunteer work and socializing with friends following retirement than men.

There has been less research investigating factors beyond demographics that might promote retirement planning. One study (Jacobs-Lawson et al., 2004) indicated that there are apparent gender differences in what motivates people to engage in retirement planning. For women, age, income, future time perspective, and level of worry about retirement determined the amount of time spent planning, whereas for men the effect of these variables depended on how worried they were about achieving their retirement goals. The authors argue that unless such differences are taken into account when developing intervention programs, such programs will be largely ineffective.

Understanding why some people engage in little or no retirement planning is important in light of the presumed benefits of planning, which include more positive views of retirement, greater post-retirement satisfaction, and better post-retirement adjustment (Taylor & Doverspike, 2003). This relationship holds regardless of gender (Quick & Moen, 1998) and therefore suggests that women could be at an inherent disadvantage in terms of retirement adjustment.

Retirement adjustment. Despite the above, research on the role of gender in adjustment to retirement has revealed somewhat inconsistent findings. Some studies have found that retired women have lower levels of life satisfaction than retired men (Quick & Moen, 1998; Seccombe & Lee, 1986) and experience more problems adjusting to retirement (van Solinge & Henkens, 2008), which could be a result of their greater financial stress (Kim & Moen, 2001). Others find the opposite relationship, arguing that women may adapt more easily because their retirement activities are more closely aligned to gender-typical roles (Barnes & Parry, 2004). In contrast, other research has failed to find gender differences in retirement adjustment (Kim & Feldman, 2000; Wong & Earl, 2009; Wu, Tang, & Yan, 2005). Likewise, there are apparently few differences in the factors that predict life satisfaction in older people (Waddell & Jacobs-Lawson, 2010).

As discussed earlier, recent evidence indicates that retirees can follow a number of different trajectories in terms of adjusting to retirement (Pinquart & Ines, 2007; Wang, 2007). Pinquart and Ines (2007) found that gender was one of the key variables that differentiated those on the different trajectories of retirement adjustment. There was a greater proportion of women in the group that had a temporary decline in satisfaction after retirement, but more men in the group that had a temporary increase in satisfaction (despite overall declining satisfaction over the final period at work and ongoing throughout retirement).

Couples

A small but growing literature (e.g., Ho & Raymo, 2009; Pienta & Hayward, 2002; Smith & Moen, 2004) acknowledges the interconnectedness of couples in terms of retirement planning and the theoretical importance of household decision making. Retirement research has typically examined retirement at the individual level, focusing on factors such as an individual's age, gender, health, income, and work conditions. More recently, however, with the rise of dual-income families, the number of households experiencing two retirements, oftentimes simultaneously, is also increasing. This highlights the need for more research aimed at examining the process of retirement at the family level, and raises interesting questions about the effects of synchronous and asynchronous patterns and expectations of retirement within couples on retirement planning, decision making, and outcomes.

Related to this research have been investigations as to how marital status interacts with gender in determining work and retirement-related activities. For example, married women (but not men) are less likely than their single counterparts to be employed in old age (O'Rand & Farkas, 2002), potentially because they derive some economic protection from their husband's income (Pleau, 2010).

Husbands and wives may respond differently to factors at work and home in terms of what influences them to retire. Pienta (2003) found that wives were more likely to retire in response to family factors, economic resources, and the personal characteristics of both themselves and their spouse. In contrast, family and spouse characteristics were less influential on the husband's retirement decision. A further example of how a retirement predictor can be uniquely shaped by gender and marital status was provided in a study of the effect of caregiving on exit from the workforce into retirement (Dentinger & Clarkberg, 2002). The authors found that caring for a spouse had a significant impact on retirement timing, but in opposite ways for men and women. Social role theory was used as an explanation of the results, which showed that when women had an ill husband to care for they were five times more likely to retire, whereas men with a sick wife were more than 50% *slower* to retire. Similarly, Talaga and Beehr (1995) reported that women were more likely to be retired than men when they had a spouse in ill health or a greater number of dependent children. In contrast, work-family conflict had a similar effect on the desire to remain at work for both husbands and wives (Raymo & Sweeney, 2006).

A spouse's role has also been shown to impact retirement adjustment. For example, Moen, Kim, and Hofmeister (2001) found that both men and women who retired while their spouse was still employed reported the most marital conflict, but it appeared that once a couple had "settled into retirement" (i.e., retired for more than two years), there was actually an increase in marital satisfaction. Furthermore, the highest level of marital conflict occurred in situations where the wife was employed and the husband retired. Szinovacz (2003) suggested three reasons for why men retiring earlier than their spouses is often most problematic, particularly for couples that hold traditional gender role attitudes. First, this type of retirement transition contradicts dominant gender role norms and expectations. Second, it typically results from adverse circumstances that prevent couples from preferred joint retirement. Lastly, because their spouse is still working, it prevents men from reorienting to the marital relationship. Barnes and Parry (2004) added that although the majority of men and women they interviewed held traditional gendered assumptions, those who were less fixed in their gender roles and assumptions appeared to be the most successful in adjusting to the process of retirement.

The complexity of relationships between adjustment, marriage, and gender is further illustrated by Smith and Moen (2004), who report that only about half (59%) of couples are jointly satisfied with retirement. In their study, joint satisfaction occurred when wives felt that their husbands were not unduly influential in their retirement decision. Moen's later research (e.g., Moen, Huang, Plassmann, & Dentinger, 2006) highlights the changing context in terms of gender and retirement, showing that in older cohorts, wives' planning for retirement tended to be shaped by their husband's planning, but in younger cohorts couples were making plans independently.

Future Research

Aside from some unavoidable biological effects of age and gender on the retirement process, the extant research suggests that these two demographic variables have a complex impact that needs to be more clearly understood. Longitudinal investigations examining the effect of age and gender are an obvious gap in the literature. As Taylor and Shore (1995) noted, longitudinal research is required to separate developmental or age-linked effects from time-linked or cohort-specific factors (e.g., current social and economic conditions) in order to further our understanding of how these factors impact the change in retirement decisions over time. New data analytic methods such as hierarchical linear modeling and latent growth curve analysis can allow researchers to compare age-based models in which the developmental trajectories of within-person or intra-individual change are modeled over time and across cohorts, while occasion-based models can be used to examine these trajectories as separately modeled for each cohort to examine cohort-specific effects (Settersten, 2006). Given the changing social and environmental contexts, ongoing research must determine if current findings regarding the impact of age and gender hold for future cohorts of retirees.

References

Adams, S. J. (2004). Age discrimination legislation and the employment of older workers. *Labour Economics, 11*, 219–241.

Alley, D., & Crimmins, E. (2007). The demography of aging and work. In K. S. Shultz & G. A. Adams (Eds.), *Aging and work in the 21st century* (pp. 7–23). Mahwah, NJ: Lawrence Erlbaum Associates.

Association of Super Funds of Australia Limited. (2009). *Super design for women* [Media Release August 31, 2009]. Retrieved from http://www.superannuation.asn.au/mr090831/default.aspx.

Atchley, R. C. (1989). A continuity theory of normal aging. *The Gerontologist, 29*, 183–190.

Australian Bureau of Statistics. (2009). *Employment arrangements, retirement and superannuation, Australia* (Catalogue No. 6361.0). Retrieved from http://www.ausstats.abs.gov.au/Ausstats/subscriber.nsf/0/1A653F883363040DCA2575C8001ECB4E/$File/63610_apr%20to%20jul%202007%20(re-issue).pdf.

Bacharach, S., Bamberger, P., Biron, M., & Horowitz-Rozen, M. (2008). Perceived agency in retirement and retiree drinking behavior: Job satisfaction as a moderator. *Journal of Vocational Behavior, 73*(3), 376–386.

Barnes, H., & Parry, J. (2004). Renegotiating identity and relationships: Men and women's adjustments to retirement. *Ageing and Society, 24*(2), 213–233.

Beehr, T.A., & Bennett, M. M. (2007). Examining retirement from a multi-level perspective. In K. S. Shultz & G. A. Adams (Eds.), *Aging and work in the 21st century* (pp. 277–302). Mahwah, N J: Lawrence Erlbaum Associates.

Bidewell, J., Griffin, B., & Hesketh, B. (2006). Timing of retirement: Including a delay discounting perspective in retirement models. *Journal of Vocational Behavior, 68*, 368–387.

Burr, W. R. (1972). Role transitions: A reformulation of theory. *Journal of Marriage and the Family, 34,* 407–416.

Calasanti, T. (1996). Gender and life satisfaction in retirement: An assessment of the male model. *Journal of Gerontology, 51B,* S18–S29.

Carstensen, L. L., Fung, H. H., & Charles, S. T. (2003). Socioemotional selectivity theory and the regulation of emotion in the second half of life. *Motivation and Emotion, 27,* 103–123.

Carstensen, L. L., Isaacowitz, D. M., & Charles, S. T. (1999). Taking time seriously: A theory of socioemotional selectivity. *American Psychologist, 54,* 165–181.

Cottrell, L. S. (1942). The adjustment of the individual to his age and sex roles. *American Sociological Review, 7,* 617–620.

Crimmins, E., & Saito, Y.(2001). Trends in health life expectancy in the United States, 1970–1990: Gender, racial, and educational differences. *Social Science and Medicine, 52,* 1629–1641.

Davis, M. A. (2003). Factors related to bridge employment participation among private sector early retirees. *Journal of Vocational Behavior, 63*(1), 55–71.

Dawis, R. V., & Lofquist, L. H. (1984). *A psychological theory of work adjustment: An individual-differences model and its applications.* Minneapolis, MN: University of Minnesota Press.

Dentinger, E., & Clarkberg, M. (2002). Informal caregiving and retirement timing among men and women: Gender and caregiving relationships in late midlife. *Journal of Family Issues, 23*(7), 857–879.

DeViney, S., & Solomon, J. C. (1995). Gender differences in retirement income: A comparison of theoretical explanations. *Journal of Women and Aging, 7*(4), 83–100.

Dietz, B. E., Carrozza, M., & Ritchey, N. (2003). Does financial self-efficacy explain gender differences in retirement saving strategies? *Journal of Women and Aging, 15*(4), 83–96.

Donaldson, T., Earl, J. K., & Muratore, A. M. (2010). Extending the integrated model of retirement adjustment: Incorporating mastery and retirement planning. *Journal of Vocational Behavior, 77*(2), 279–289.

Eagly, A. H. (1987). *Sex differences in social behavior: A social-role interpretation.* Hillsdale, NJ: Erlbaum.

Ekerdt, D. J., Kosloski, K., & DeViney, S. (2000). The normative anticipation of retirement by older workers. *Research on Aging, 22,* 3–22.

Elder, G. H. (1995). The life-course paradigm: Social change and individual development. In P. Moen, G. H. Elder, & K. Lusher (Eds.), *Examining lives in context: Perspectives on the ecology of human development* (pp. 101–139). Washington, DC: American Psychological Press.

Employee Benefit Research Institute. (2006, April). *Will more of us work forever? The 2006 Retirement Confidence Survey* (Issue Brief No. 292). Washington, DC: Author.

Fullerton, H. N. (1999). Labor force projections to 2008: Steady growth and changing composition. *Monthly Labor Review, 122,* 19–32.

Fullerton, H. N., & Toossi, M. (2001). Labor force projections to 2010: Steady growth and changing composition. *Monthly Labor Review, 124,* 21–38.

Garen, J., Berger, M., & Scott, F. (1996). Pensions, non-discrimination policies, and the employment of older workers. *Quarterly Review of Economics and Finance, 36,* 417–429.

Glass, J. C., & Kilpatrick, B. B. (1998a). Financial planning for retirement: An imperative for baby boomer women. *Educational Gerontology, 24*(6), 595–617.

Glass, J. C., & Kilpatrick, B. B. (1998b). Gender comparisons of baby boomers and financial preparation for retirement. *Educational Gerontology, 24*(8), 719–715.

Goode, W. (1960). Theory of role strain. *American Sociological Review, 25,* 483–496.

Griffin, B., & Hesketh, B. (2006). *Evolving mental models for retirement.* Paper presented at the 21st Annual Conference of the Society for Industrial and Organizational Psychology, Dallas, TX.

Griffin, B., & Hesketh, B. (2008). Post-retirement work: The individual determinants of paid and volunteer work. *Journal of Occupational and Organizational Psychology, 81,* 101–121.

Griffin, B., Hesketh, B., & Loh, V. (2010a, October). *How long will I live? Predictors of subjective life expectancy.* Paper presented at the 7th Annual Collaborators' Meeting of the 45 and Up Study, Sydney, Australia.

Griffin, B., Hesketh, B., & Loh, V. (2010b, July). Predictors and anticipated outcomes of planned retirement transition patterns. In B. Hesketh (Chair), *Retirement transition and adjustment: Time perspective and patterns of change.* Symposium conducted at the 27th International Congress of Applied Psychology, Melbourne, Australia.

Griffin, B., Hesketh, B. & Loh, V. (in press). The influence of subjective life expectancy on retirement transition and planning: A longitudinal study. *Journal of Vocational Behavior.*

Hansson, R. O., DeKoekkoek, P. D., Neece, W. M., & Patterson, D. W. (1997). Successful aging at work: Annual review, 1992–1996: The older worker and transition to retirement. *Journal of Vocational Behavior, 51,* 202–233.

Hardy, M. (2006). Older workers. In R. H. Binstock & L. K. George (Eds.), *Handbook of aging and the social sciences* (6th ed., pp. 201–218). Amsterdam, The Netherlands: Elsevier.

Hardy, M. A. (2002). The transformation of retirement in twentieth-century America: From discontent to satisfaction. *Generations, 26*(2), 9–16.

Hedge, J. W., Borman, W. C., & Lammlein, S. E. (2006). *The aging workforce: Realities, myths, and implications for organizations.* Washington, DC: American Psychological Association.

Henkens, K., & Van Dalen, H. P. (2003). Early retirement systems and behavior in an international perspective. In G. A. Adams & T. A. Beehr (Eds.), *Retirement: Reasons, processes, and results* (pp. 242–263). New York, NY: Springer.

Hershey, D. A., Henkens, K., & van Dalen, H. P. (2010). Aging and financial planning for retirement: Interdisciplinary influences viewed through a cross-cultural lens. *The International Journal of Aging and Human Development, 73,* 1–38.

Hershey, D. A., Jacobs-Lawson, J. M., & Neukam, K. A. (2002). The influence of aging and gender on workers goals for retirement. *International Journal of Aging and Human Development, 55,* 163–179.

Hesketh, B., & Dawis, R. V. (1991). The Minnesota Theory of Work Adjustment: A conceptual framework. In B. Hesketh & A. Adams (Eds.), *Psychological perspective on occupational health and rehabilitation* (pp. 1–16). Sydney: Harcourt Brace Javanovich.

Hesketh, B., & Griffin, B. (2007). Self-estimates of life expectancy as an influence on intended retirement age. In G. G. Fisher (Chair), *International perspectives on older worker:*

Work and the retirement process. Symposium conducted at the 22nd Annual Conference of the Society for Industrial and Organizational Psychology, New York, NY.

Heywood, J. S., Ho, L. S., & Wei, X. (2000). The determinants of hiring older workers: Evidence from Hong Kong. *Industrial and Labor Relations Review, 52*, 444–459.

Heywood, J. S., Jirjahn, U., & Tsertsvardze, G. (2010). Hiring older workers and employing older workers: German evidence. *Journal of Population Economics, 23*, 595–615.

Hirsch, B. T., Macpherson, D. A., & Hardy, M. A. (2000). Occupational age structure and access for older workers. *Industrial and Labor Relations Review, 53*(3), 401–418.

Ho, J., & Raymo, J. M. (2009). Expectations and realization of joint retirement among dual-worker couples. *Research on Aging, 31*, 153–179.

Hogan, R., & Perrucci, C. C. (2007). Black women: Truly disadvantaged in the transition from employment to retirement income. *Social Science Research, 36*, 1184–1199.

Hutchens, R. (2010). Worker characteristics, job characteristics, and opportunities for phased retirement. *Labour Economics, 17*, 1010–1021.

Isaksson, K., & Johansson, G. (2000). Adaptation to continued work and early retirement following downsizing: Long-term effects and gender differences. *Journal of Occupational and Organizational Psychology, 73*, 241–256.

Jacobs-Lawson, J. M., & Hershey, D. A. (2003). Perceptions of financial stability in retirement: Do Americans really know what to expect? In S. P. Shohov (Ed.), *Advances in psychology research* (pp. 123–136). New York, NY: Nova Science Publishers.

Jacobs-Lawson, J. M., Hershey, D. A., & Neukam, K. A. (2004). Gender differences in factors that influence time spent planning for retirement. *Journal of Women and Aging, 16*(3), 55–69.

Joukamaa, M., Saarijarvi, S., & Salokangas, R. K. (1993). The TURVA project: Retirement and adaptation in old age. *Zeitschrift fur Gerontologie, 26*(3), 170–175.

Judge, T. A., Klinger, R. L., & Simon, L. S. (2010). Time is on my side: Time, general mental ability, human capital, and extrinsic career success. *Journal of Applied Psychology, 95*(1), 92–107.

Kim, J. E., & Moen, P. (2001). Is retirement good or bad for subjective well-being? *Current Directions in Psychological Science, 10*, 83–86.

Kim, S., & Feldman, D. C. (2000). Working in retirement: The antecedents of bridge employment and its consequences for the quality of life in retirement. *Academy of Management Journal, 43*, 1195–1210.

Kragie, E. R., Gerstein, M., & Lichtman, M. (1989). Do Americans plan for retirement? Some recent trends. *Career Development Quarterly, 37*, 232–239.

Larsen, M. (2008). Does quality of work life affect men and women's retirement planning differently? *Applied Research in Quality of Life, 3*, 23–42.

Lee, W. K. M. (2005). Gender differences in retirement decision in Hong Kong. *Journal of Women & Aging, 17*, 59–76.

Liang, J., Bennett, J. M., Shaw, B. A., Quiñones, A. R., Ye, W., Xu, X., & Ofstedal, M. B. (2008). Gender differences in functional status in middle and older age: Are there any age variations? *Journal of Gerontology: Social Sciences, 63*, S282–S292.

Marks, S. R., & MacDermid, S. (1996). Multiple roles and the self: A theory of role balance. *Journal of Marriage and the Family, 58*, 417–432.

McArdle, J. J., Fisher, G. G., & Kadlee, K. M. (2007). Latent variable analyses of age trends of cognition in the health and retirement study, 1992–2004. *Psychology and Aging, 22*(3), 525–545.

Mirowsky, J. (1997). Age, subjective life expectancy, and the sense of control: The horizon hypothesis. *Journal of Gerontology: Social Sciences, 52B*(3), S125–S134.

Moen, P. (1996). A life course perspective on retirement, gender and well-being. *Journal of Occupational Health Psychology, 1*(2), 131–144.

Moen, P., Huang, Q., Plassmann, V., & Dentinger, E. (2006). Deciding the future: Do dual-earner couples plan together for retirement? *American Behavioral Scientist, 49*(10), 1422–1443.

Moen, P., Kim, J. E., & Hofmeister, H. (2001). Couples' work/retirement transitions, gender, and marital quality. *Social Psychology Quarterly, 64*, 55–71.

Moen, P., & Spencer, D. (2006) Converging divergences in age, gender, health, and well-being: Strategic selection in the third age. In R. H. Binstock & L. K. George (Eds), *Handbook of aging and the social sciences* (6th ed., pp. 129–144). Amsterdam, The Netherlands: Elsevier.

Neukam, K. A., & Hershey, D. A. (2003). Financial inhibition, financial activation, and saving for retirement. *Financial Services Review, 12*, 19–37.

O'Brien, C., Fenn, P., & Diacon, S. (2005). *How long do people expect to live? Results and implications* (CRIS Research Report 2005-1). Retrieved from Nottingham University Business School, Centre for Risk and Insurance Studies website: http://www.nottingham.ac.uk/business/cris/papers/crisresearchreport2005-1.pdf.

Onyx, J., & Baker, E. (2006). Retirement expectations: Gender differences and partner effects in an Australian employer-funded sample. *Australasian Journal of Aging, 25*(2), 80–83.

O'Rand, A. M., & Farkas, J. I. (2002). Couples' retirement timing in the United States in the 1990s. *International Journal of Sociology, 32*, 11–29.

Orel, N. A., Ford, R. A., & Brock, C. (2004). Women's financial planning for retirement: The impact of disruptive life. *Journal of Women and Aging, 16*, 39–53.

Organisation for Economic Cooperation, Development. (2006). *Live longer, work longer*. Paris, France: OECD Publishing.

Petkoska, J., & Earl, J. K. (2009). Understanding the influence of demographic and psychological variables on retirement planning. *Psychology and Aging, 24*, 245–251.

Pienta, A. M. (2003). Partners in marriage: An analysis of husbands' and wives' retirement behavior. *Journal of Applied Gerontology, 22*, 340–358.

Pienta, A. M., & Hayward, M. D. (2002). Who expects to continue working after age 62? The retirement plans of couples. *The Journals of Gerontology, Series B: Psychological Sciences and Social Sciences, 57B*(4), S199–S208.

Pinquart, M., & Ines, S. (2007). Changes of life satisfaction in the transition to retirement: A latent-class approach. *Psychology and Aging, 22*(4), 442–455.

Pleau, R. L. (2010). Gender differences in postretirement employment. *Research on Aging, 32*(3), 267–303.

Prenda, K., & Lachman, M. (2001). Planning for the future: A life management strategy for increasing control and life satisfaction in adulthood. *Psychology and Aging, 16*, 206–216

Prem, F., & Debats, D.L. (2006). Sources of life strengths as predictors of late-life mortality and survivorship. *International Journal of Aging & Human Development, 62*(4), 303–334.

Quick, H. E., & Moen, P. (1998). Gender, employment, and retirement quality: A life course approach to the differential experiences of men and women. *Journal of Occupational Health Psychology, 3*(1), 44–64.

Quinn, J. F., & Kozy, M. (1996). The role of bridge jobs in the retirement transition: Gender, race and ethnicity. *The Gerontologist, 36*, 363–372.

Raymo, J. M., & Sweeney, M. M. (2006). Work-family conflict and retirement preferences. *Journal of Gerontology: Social Sciences, 61B*, S161–S169.

Reitzes, D. C., Mutran, E. J., & Fernandez, M. E. (1998). The decision to retire: A career perspective. *Social Science Quarterly, 79*(3), 607–619.

Rosenman, L., & Scott, W. (2009). Financing old age: Why is there still gender inequality? *Australian Social Work, 62*(2), 287–298.

Ross C. E., & Mirowsky, J. (2002). Source family relationships, social support and subjective life expectancy. *Journal of Health and Social Behavior, 43*(4), 469–489.

Seccombe, K., & Lee, G. R. (1986). Gender differences in retirement satisfaction and its antecedents. *Research on Aging, 8*, 426–440.

Settersten, R. A. (2006). Aging and the life course. In R. H. Binstock & L. K. George (Eds.), *Handbook of aging and the social sciences* (6th ed., pp. 3–39). Amsterdam, The Netherlands: Elsevier.

Siegel, M., Bradley, E. H, & Kasl, S. (2003). Self-rated life expectancy as a predictor of mortality: Evidence from the HRS and AHEAD surveys. *Gerontology, 49*(4), 265–271.

Singh, G., & Verma, A. (2003). Work history and later-life labor force participation: Evidence from a large telecommunications firm. *Industrial and Labor Relations Review, 56*, 699–715.

Smith, D. B., & Moen, P. (2004). Retirement satisfaction for retirees and their spouses: Do gender and the retirement decision-making process matter? *Journal of Family Issues, 25*(2), 262–285.

Soidre, T. (2005). Retirement-age preferences of women and men aged 55–64 years in Sweden. *Ageing and Society, 25*(6), 943–963.

Sterns, H. L., & Gray, J. H. (1999). Work, leisure, and retirement. In J. C. Cavanaugh & S. K. Whitbourne (Eds.), *Gerontology: An interdisciplinary perspective* (pp. 355–390). New York, NY: Oxford University Press.

Szinovacz, M. E. (2003). Contexts and pathways: Retirement as institution, process, and experience. In G. Adams & T. Beehr (Eds.), *Retirement: Reasons, processes, and results* (pp. 6–52). New York, NY: Springer.

Szinovacz, M. E., & DeViney, S. (1999). The retiree identity: Gender and race differences. *Journal of Gerontology: Social Sciences, 54B*, S207–S218.

Talaga, J. A., & Beehr, T. A. (1995). Are there gender differences in predicting retirement decisions? *Journal of Applied Psychology, 80*, 16–28.

Taylor, M., & Doverspike, D. (2003). Retirement planning and preparation. In G. Adams, & T. Beehr (Eds.), *Retirement:* *Reasons, processes, and results* (pp. 53–82). New York, NY: Springer.

Taylor, M., & Shore, L. M. (1995). Predictors of planned retirement age: An application of Beehr's model. *Psychology and Aging, 10*, 76–83.

Teuscher, U. (2010). Change and persistence of personal identities after the transition to retirement. *The International Journal of Aging and Human Development, 70*, 89–106.

Thane, P. (2006). The history of retirement. In G. L. Clark, A. H. Munnell, & J. M. Orszag (Eds.), *The Oxford handbook of pension and retirement income* (pp. 33–51). Oxford, England; New York, NY: Oxford University Press.

Toossi, M. (2004). Labor force projections to 2012: The graying of the U.S. workforce. *Monthly Labor Review, 127*, 3–22.

Toossi, M. (2009). Labor force projections to 2018: Older workers staying more active. *Monthly Labor Review, 132*, 30–51.

Van Solinge, H., & Henkens, K. (2007). Involuntary retirement: The role of restrictive circumstances, timing, and social embeddedness. *Journals of Gerontology: Social Sciences, 62B*, S295–S303.

van Solinge, H., & Henkens, K. (2008). Adjustment to and satisfaction with retirement: Two of a kind? *Psychology and Aging, 23*, 422–434.

Van Solinge, H., & Kenkens, K. (2010). Living longer, working longer? The impact of subjective life expectancy on retirement intentions and behavior. *European Journal of Public Health, 20*, 47–51.

von Bonsdorff, M. E., Huuhtanen, P., Tujomi, K., & Seitsamo, J. (2010). Predictors of employees' early retirement intentions: An 11-year longitudinal study. *Occupational Medicine, 60*, 94–100.

Waddell, E. L., & Jacobs-Lawson, J. M. (2010). Predicting positive well-being in older men and women. *The International Journal of Aging and Human Development, 70*(3), 181–197.

Wang, M. (2007). Profiling retirees in the retirement transition and adjustment process: Examining the longitudinal change patterns of retirees' psychological well-being. *Journal of Applied Psychology, 92*, 455–474.

Wang, M., & Shultz, K. S. (2010). Employee retirement: A review and recommendations for future investigation. *Journal of Management, 36*, 172–206.

Wang, M., Zhan, Y., Liu, S., & Shultz, K. (2008). Antecedents of bridge employment: A longitudinal investigation. *Journal of Applied Psychology, 93*, 818–830.

Wong, J. Y., & Earl, J. K. (2009). Towards an integrated model of individual, psychosocial, and organizational predictors of retirement adjustment. *Journal of Vocational Behavior, 75*, 1–13.

Wu, A. S., Tang, C. S., & Yan, E. C. (2005). Post-retirement voluntary work and psychological functioning among older Chinese in Hong Kong. *Journal of Cross-Cultural Gerontology, 20*, 27–45.

Yerkes, M. (2010). Diversity in work: The heterogeneity of women's employment patterns. *Gender, Work and Organization, 17*(6), 696–720.

The Employer's Perspective on Retirement

Kène Henkens *and* Hendrik P. van Dalen

Abstract

In this chapter we discuss the literature with respect to the role of employers in retirement processes of older workers and provide suggestions for future research. In the first part of this chapter we will review existing theoretical insights regarding the employers' actions and attitudes toward older workers and retirement. In the next section we will discuss empirical findings with regard to age-related stereotypes in the workplace and age norms with respect to retirement and present some results from an international comparative employer study. We conclude with a section on the management of retirement processes, focusing on the exit and hiring of older workers.

Key Words: stereotypes, older workers, age norms, employers, firms, retirement, hiring, recruitment, productivity, aging

Introduction

Extending people's working life is seen as a key element in curtailing the rising costs associated with an aging population. In the countries of the OECD and of the European Union, a host of initiatives has been taken that aim to delay retirement and support the labor force participation of older workers (OECD, 2006b). At the government level, these initiatives vary from pension reforms that limit opportunities for an early exit from the workforce to legislation against age discrimination to public campaigns that combat negative stereotyping in the workplace. At the organizational level, employers are urged to develop policies geared toward increasing the employability of older workers, for instance by means of lifelong learning. However, these government initiatives may not achieve their goals if proposals and targets for extending the working life of older workers are not actively supported by employers. Vickerstaff, Cox, and Keen (2003) state that any significant change in retirement behavior will come primarily from changes in employer policies. In this chapter we argue that for a better understanding

of older workers' career decisions, we need to incorporate the driving forces of retirement processes at the demand side of the labor market. Employers are key players in defining the opportunities for retirement as well as the opportunities for working longer. As a result, the success of policies aimed at delaying retirement depends to a large extent on the actions and attitudes of employers.

Although retirement has traditionally been thought of as a discrete and abrupt discontinuation of work, today's "retirement" can be characterized as a process that can take multiple forms, offering the option of a gradual transition from full-time work to "full-time" retirement. While some older workers are affected by processes of disengagement from work and mental withdrawal from their jobs even years before they actually retire (Ekerdt & DeViney, 1993), others of the same generation continue to work and sometimes take on a second career. Increasing numbers of older workers continue to extend their working lives through continued career or bridge employment (Von Bonsdorff, Shultz, Leskinen, &

Tansky, 2009). Many others are in some type of hybrid employment or phased retirement situation, and increasingly fewer older workers appear to be opting for full retirement. How retirement processes evolve is to a large extent determined by employers' decisions regarding exit and re-entry of workers at the end of their career. Yet how employers view the changing nature of retirement is largely unknown (Wang, Zhan, Liu, & Shultz, 2008).

In this chapter we discuss the relevant literature with respect to the role of employers in the retirement processes of older workers. In the first part of this chapter we will review existing theoretical insights regarding the employers' actions and attitudes toward older workers and retirement. In the next section we will discuss empirical findings from the literature. Much of what we know about employers and retirement comes from studies designed from the supervisor's (Henkens, 2000; Henkens, Van Solinge, & Cozijnsen, 2009; Rosen & Jerdee, 1982) or employer's (Taylor & Walker, 1998; Van Dalen, Henkens, Hendrikse, & Schippers, 2010) point of view. These studies, using samples of employers or supervisors, reveal a huge variety in organizations' age-management policies, which is reflected in considerable differences in the extent to which organizations support delaying labor force exit of their older workers, are willing to hire older workers, and employ the policies to maintain and enhance the productivity of their workers. In the final paragraph we discuss the main findings and present suggestions for future research.

Aging, Productivity, Wages, and Retirement: Theoretical Perspectives

In understanding the employer's perspective, it is instructive to start from very basic principles capturing the most essential elements with which an employer has to deal in his or her organization. Standard economic theory predicts that the demand for labor depends crucially on the relative prices of labor and capital, as well as the technology employed to produce goods and services (Hamermesh, 1996). For matters of brevity we will not discuss the influence of changes in the price of capital. Static neoclassical theory predicts that the price of labor is in line with the labor productivity of the individual worker. This so-called spot market view of the labor market is bound to give a false impression because the declining age-wage profile, as predicted by human capital theory, rarely occurs (OECD, 2006a). A more realistic model of labor demand can be traced to theories that cover the life cycle of workers. Thurow (1975) was one of the first to suggest that while labor income and productivity are related, they are not necessarily related at every single moment in a worker's career. He explained that employers have an understanding—an *implicit contract*—with their employees regarding the relationship between productivity and earnings during the course of their careers. This understanding, Thurow stated, is based on the seniority principle, such that during the first phase of workers' careers their earnings are *lower* than their productivity, and during the second phase their earnings are *higher* than their productivity. He explained that the prospect of a gradual rise in their incomes acts as an incentive for employees to continue working for "their" employer, where their investments yield the highest returns. Moreover, the prospect of an increasing age-income profile may serve as an incentive for older workers to transfer their skills and knowledge to younger colleagues without the risk of losing their competitive advantage.

Lazear (1979) stressed that this implicit contract is bound to be unsustainable if workers work beyond the age at which the net present value of wages exceeds that of the productivity profile. If people can keep working until their time of death, such a deal will clearly be unsustainable. Therefore, employers will opt for either mandatory retirement schedules or the use of private pension schemes that penalize continued employment beyond a certain age. The trouble with these types of implicit contracts is that the sustainability of the contract is negatively affected by the aging of the population (Lazear, 1979). Seniority wages imply a heavy wage burden for employers. Whereas firms in some countries in the past could thrive because of a relatively young population age structure enjoying "a demographic dividend" (Bloom & Williamson, 1998), now firms will have to face an aging population structure and bear the costs of a "demographic hangover" if nothing changes and labor force aging takes its course. In that respect, one can understand the changes in pension design and retirement over time. The option of using private pension systems as an instrument of retirement policy has been used in Western European countries, where early retirement plans have been designed in such a manner that retiring early is an offer one cannot refuse (Venti & Wise, 1998). The issue of mandatory retirement was a moot problem in these welfare states. However, this situation has changed with the aging of populations. In the past decade, governments in most European countries have implemented or announced radical pension reforms that have phased out the option of early retirement and have stimulated working longer, and the credit crunch has put a serious dent in the nest eggs of most older workers. As a consequence, the issue of mandatory retirement has increased in prominence. Aligning wage and productivity over the life course, thereby changing the implicit contract, will be the focus of attention in most firms.

Additional factors make an aging population an even more serious liability. First of all, there are taxes, social security premiums, and pension premiums that increase the price of labor. This is a relevant factor, as an aging population increases the fiscal burden due to age-related pension and health care costs. For the United States, Munnell and Sass (2008) state that whereas pension reforms make the costs of providing retirement benefits more age-neutral, health insurance has taken its place as a major factor that drives up compensation costs as workers age.[1] An aging population thus increases the gap between net and gross wages, making it either increasingly difficult to survive as a firm, vis-à-vis firms in other countries that are not so hard hit by aging populations, or necessary to shift the aging burden toward employees, thereby decreasing the incentive to supply labor.

Age and Discrimination

According to human capital theory, productivity depends on initial education and experience acquired over the life course. However, the older workers become, the more divergent experiences they accumulate. Labor supply is heterogeneous, and employers can never be sure about the future productivity of an individual employee. This applies to employees currently enrolled, but even more so to new employees still to be hired. Employers are well aware of their employees' track records within their organization, and they have information about employee productivity. However, employers do not know how workers' health may change as they age and whether they will be able to keep up with new technological developments. Employers have access to what Phelps (1972) called "previous statistical experiences": information on how certain categories of employees tend to behave and develop. In particular when hiring, many employers use these statistical experiences to formulate expectations regarding the future productivity of employees who belong to a particular category (the uncertainty surrounding the productivity of the existing workforce is assumed to be less pronounced). In an earlier

study, Becker (1957) pointed out that employers may have "a taste for discrimination" against some groups, and that this may—under certain circumstances—result in these groups not being employed by them at all.

Employers and Retirement: Empirical Results

This short overview of the theory on the relationship between age and productivity brings a number of issues to the foreground. The first question is to what extent age and productivity are related in everyday practice, how employers perceive this relationship, and to what extent employers expect that an aging workforce increases the gap between pay and productivity. In the next section, we discuss the existing stereotypes about the timing of retirement. The second issue deals with the question of how employers manage their aging workforce and the retirement processes. Later, we discuss employer support for workers working longer and whether employers opt for additional training to enhance the productivity of workers over the course of their career. In addition, we also discuss whether employers consider the option of demotion of older workers so as to bring pay and productivity in line for the incumbent workers. In the section of this chapter titled "Hiring Older Workers," we look at employers' preferences and practices when it comes to hiring older workers.

Relationship Age-Productivity between Facts and Stereotypes

Research on the relationship between age and productivity takes place within various disciplines and with various methods and various units of measurement (for an overview, see Skirbekk, 2004, 2008). For instance, macroeconomic studies tend to focus on isolating the effect of population age structure on labor productivity, and the general consensus seems to be that an aging population is associated with a negative effect on labor productivity (Davis, 2005; Feyrer, 2008; Tang & MacLeod, 2006) or economic growth (Bloom & Williamson, 1998; Headey & Hodge, 2009). Studies with a focus at the micro-level of firms or employees have produced mixed results. For instance, an early meta-analysis performed by Waldman and Avolio (1986) showed that age was positively related to productivity measures of job performance, but somewhat negatively related to supervisors' ratings of performance. McEvoy and Cascio (1989) showed on the basis of sixty-five empirical studies that the relationship between age and performance was virtually absent. Later on, Sturman (2003) refined the previous insights by performing a meta-analysis of 115 empirical studies. By making use of three age-related variables (chronological age, job experience, and organizational tenure), he showed that the relationship follows an inverted U-shape: a positive relationship between age and performance at young ages and a negative job performance relationship when age is high (49 years or older). Finally, in a meta-analysis, Ng and Feldman (2008) evaluated the relationship between age and ten dimensions of job performance on the basis of 380 empirical studies. They suggest that the reason for mixed findings is that previous studies have focused rather narrowly on core task activities and neglected the activities that affect the environment in which core tasks take place, such as "organizational citizenship behavior" (Borman, Penner, Allen, & Motowidlo, 2001; LePine, Erez, & Johnson, 2002). The literature shows that the relationship between age and productivity is difficult to measure on the basis of empirical data. For instance, productivity assessments are often based on perceptions that might by biased by ageism attitudes, a stereotypical and often negative bias against older adults.

It is well documented in the psychological literature that many stereotypes prevail regarding older adults. Stereotypes may be partly accurate representations of reality, or at least of the local reality to which the perceiver is exposed (Judd & Park, 1993). Stereotypes may, however, also lead to social exclusion, not only because one may judge people on the basis of average and inaccurate representations of the category, but also because stereotypes may lead to self-fulfilling prophecies, when those who are subject to negative stereotypes behave accordingly (Hilton & Von Hippel, 1996).

Although gradually more and more information is cumulated in the literature on the aging labor market (cf. Munnell & Sass, 2008), research on perceptions of productivity by employers and employees is still rather limited. One early study carried out by Kirchner and Durnette (1954) asked workers and supervisors about the problems of older employees. Kirchner and Durnette (1954) and Bird and Fishers' (1986) replication of this study led to the conclusion that supervisors had less positive attitudes toward older workers than did workers. Several other studies have shown that biases against older workers are quite pervasive (Chui, Chan, Snape, & Redman, 2001; Finkelstein & Burke, 1998; Finkelstein, Burke, & Raju, 1995; Hassell & Perrewe, 1995;

Henkens, 2000; Loretto, Duncan, & White, 2000; McGregor & Gray, 2002; Remery, Henkens, Schippers, & Ekamper, 2003). Most of the studies are, however, highly descriptive. For example, Finkelstein et al. (2000) carried out a study in which managers were asked to give written justifications of employment-related ratings. This study showed that the age of rated employees mattered to most managers. The analysis of employers' attitudes stresses the importance of distinguishing stereotypes regarding various dimensions of productivity. This body of research has shown that attitudes and stereotypes about older workers are mixed, that is, older persons are viewed as having both positive and negative attributes. Positive characteristics attributed to older employees include experience, loyalty to the organization, reliability, and interpersonal skills. Qualities such as the acceptance of and the ability to use new technologies and the adjustment to organizational changes are attributed primarily to younger workforce members. The first large-scale survey among European employers has been carried out within the framework of the ASPA (Activating Senior Potential in Ageing Europe), in which approximately 6,000 employers in eight European countries participated (Henkens & Schippers, 2012). The survey underscored the wide existence of age-related stereotypes among employers (see Figure 14.1). Employers report large differences between younger and older workers in terms of the productivity dimensions of each presented to them. In short, on abilities for which younger workers scored high points, older workers scored low points, and vice versa. Older workers are considered to have better social skills and to be more reliable, more accurate, and more committed to their work. Younger employees, on the other hand, score much better on qualities such as new technology skills, mental and physical capacity, willingness to learn, and flexibility. A recent study by Van Dalen et al. (2010b) comparing stereotypes among employers and employees indicated that the patterns found among the answers given by employers and employees are remarkably similar. Both employers and employees share most of the prevailing stereotype views, though employers rate the productivity of older workers generally lower than younger employees.

The study revealed that two dimensions were found to underlie perceptions of productivity: stereotypes about hard qualities and stereotypes about soft qualities. Hard qualities refer to qualities such as flexibility, physical and mental capacity, the willingness to learn, and new technology skills. Soft qualities

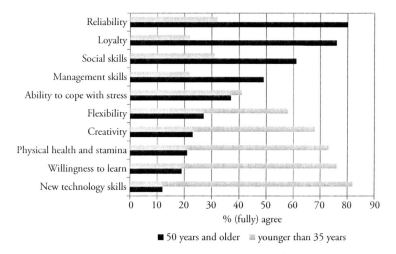

Figure 14.1 Employer ratings of dimensions of the productivity of younger and older workers. Percentage of employers that consider the dimension a "strong" point.

refer to qualities such as commitment to the organization, reliability, and social skills. The comparative advantage of older workers (50 years and older) lies primarily in their soft skills, whereas the comparative advantage of younger workers lies primarily in their hard abilities. However, the weights attached to the hard and soft qualities of productivity differ substantially. Hard qualities carry a much greater weight in the evaluation of the productivity of workers than soft qualities. This holds for the evaluation of the productivity of older and younger workers alike. For both employees as well as employers, the results indicate that younger raters have a significantly poorer opinion of older workers than older raters. It is unclear whether these differences reflect prejudice against older workers by younger raters or prejudice in favor of older workers by older raters. But it does indicate that non-economic factors affect evaluations of older workers. Employers often draw on seemingly neutral justifications pertaining to market and corporate financial well-being to justify ageist stereotypes and discrimination toward older workers (Roscigno, Mong, Byron, & Tester, 2007).

Besides issues that have to do with the accuracy of images and stereotypes toward older workers, there are several other research questions that have received relatively limited attention in the scientific literature. The first has to do with the origins of employers' perceptions of older workers. To what extent are these perceptions tied to a specific context? How stable are these perceptions? The literature suggests that stereotypical beliefs and discriminatory attitudes are at least to some extent related to the frequency of contact with older workers,

suggesting that familiarity with older workers may reduce negative stereotypes and discrimination. More contact with older workers is related to less negative age stereotypes and more support for older workers working longer (Henkens, 2005). Many questions remain with respect to the importance of type and intensity of the interaction in reducing negative stereotyping and the possible mediating effects of employers' age. The second issue has to do with the consequences of employers' perceptions of older workers. Redman and Snape (2006) show that age discrimination acts as a stressor, with adverse psychological consequences for job and life satisfaction as well as for commitment and withdrawal cognitions at work. The question of whether (and if so which) stereotypes have an impact on organizations' retirement policies has received little attention to date. A study carried out by Chui et al. (2001), using part-time management students as respondents, showed that age stereotypes influence discriminatory attitudes at work in terms of decisions on training, promotion, and retention.

Stereotype View on the Timing of Retirement

Whereas negative stereotypes about older workers' productivity may be related to a low level of support for extending working lives, opinions about retirement are subject to existing age norms, inside and outside the organization. The importance of age norms is emphasized among life-course scholars interested in aging. Life transitions, including retirement, are subject to social norms about appropriate timing. Age norms are woven into the fabric of many social institutions in both formal and informal ways (Settersten, 1998). Formal age norms are codified in diverse laws and rules; norms about the "right time" to retire are formally expressed in age boundaries established by public and private pension schemes. Scholars believe that informal age norms, defined as shared judgments or expectations regarding age-appropriate behaviors, exert significant influence on behaviors of group members (Settersten & Hagestad, 1996). Like other social groups, work organizations have shared expectations about ages at which particular transitions ought to occur (Lawrence, 1996). Organizational or workplace norms regarding retirement will signal older employees when they should move out of the workplace (e.g., Feldman & Beehr, 2011; Henkens, 2005; Potocnik, Tordera, & Peiró, 2009; Van Dam, Van der Vorst, & Van der Heijden, 2009). One of the more pervasive beliefs in today's workplace is that older workers should retire somewhere in their mid-50s or early 60s (Joulain & Mullet, 2001; McCann & Giles, 2003). At this point in life one should reap the rewards of years of hard work and enjoy one's "golden years." On the one hand, these views may be well intended and reflect positive attitudes toward older workers: a well-earned retirement at the end of a long career of hard work. On the other hand, as McCann and Giles (2003) indicate, the support of retirement may also reflect underlying attitudes that younger workers have more to offer to an organization than older workers. A belief among employers that older workers want to retire as soon as possible will hamper efforts to extend the working life. To date, only limited information about the existing age

norms and their impact on organizations' policies and practice is available. Data from the European ASPA project about age norms among employers suggest that these norms are widespread and provide little support for those workers willing to work into their late 60s. Specifically, employers in the ASPA survey were asked the following two questions: First, at what age would you say a person is too old to be working twenty hours or more per week? Second, at what age would you say a person is generally too young to retire permanently? The results (see Figure 14.2) indicate that employers in most countries have explicit ideas about the appropriate timing of retirement. In most countries the public pension age serves as a point of reference, and workers are perceived as too old to work much longer beyond that age. The results also indicate that the exiting norms provide limited support for the EU policy target of a progressive increase of about five years in the effective average age at which people stop working in the European Union, to be realized in 2010.

Some particularly relevant aspects of the organizational context are the opinions and attitudes held by the older worker's supervisor. A large-scale survey among recently retired older workers in the Netherlands (Henkens & Van Solinge, 2003) made clear that one-third of the retirees would have remained in the workforce for an extra year if they had been asked to do so by their supervisors. There is, however, also evidence that supervisors prefer not to interfere with retirement decision making, which they consider to be a private affair, and that they are hesitant to raise a discussion on extending working life (Henkens et al., 2009).

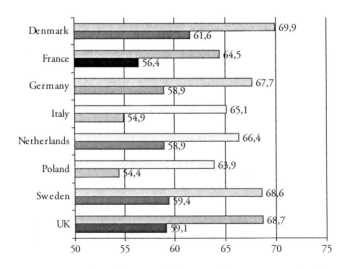

Figure 14.2 Existing age norms among employers: The age at which a person is too young to retire. The age at which a person is too old to work 20 hours per week.

Managing the Retirement Process
Keeping or Dismissing Older Workers?

Prior to the 1970s, retirement was mainly conceptualized as resulting from factors beyond individual control, like health problems or employers' considerations (Hurd, 1990). Later research frames retirement as mainly a matter of individual choice. Ekerdt, Kosloski, and DeViney (2000) stated that, around the turn of the century, retirement is a formalized transition within the life course, but one that grants workers agency in directing that transition. The shift from retirement as a transition beyond individual control to retirement as a matter of individual choice is reflected in the retirement literature. Retirement is mainly viewed as a voluntary and employee-driven transition (e.g., Hanisch & Hulin, 1990; Hardy, 2002). Early retirement arrangements, however, are often tied to labor market conditions. The practice of offering employees early retirement incentives as a way of reducing the company's workforce is forcing many older people to withdraw from the labor force involuntarily (Armstrong-Stassen, 2001). Moreover, empirical studies consistently indicate that a substantial proportion of retirees (20%–30%) perceive their retirement as forced or involuntary (see Isaksson & Johansson, 2000; Shultz, Morton, & Weckerle, 1998). Many studies acknowledge that retirement may occur under conditions that leave the individual limited choice over the transition, such as poor health or job loss (e.g., Gallo, Bradley, Siegel, & Kasl, 2000; Herzog, House, & Morgan, 1991; Isaksson & Johansson, 2000). As such, retirement may be less a matter of individual choice and agency and much more externally structured and constrained than previously assumed. Dorn and Sousa-Poza (2010) analyzed data for nineteen countries, and their results suggest that generous social security programs trigger not only more voluntary early retirement, but also more involuntary retirement, suggesting that generous social security benefits also make it more attractive for firms to push older workers into retirement. In many countries social security and pension reforms make it increasingly difficult for employers to lay off older workers via social security prior to the retirement age. To what extent these reforms are supported by employers eager to retain their older employees is not well documented. Research in several European countries suggests that employers' support for delaying retirement in their country as a whole may be modest, but their support for delaying retirement in their own organizations is still low (Van Dalen, Henkens, & Schippers, 2009). This is a remarkable finding given the characteristics of current generations of older workers, who are generally healthier, better educated, and working in jobs and sectors that place less emphasis on physical capacity. The lack of support for delaying retirement may to a certain extent be traced back to the labor market circumstances that are characterized by an excess of workers and high unemployment rates.

Lack of support for delaying retirement cannot be seen in isolation of employers' personnel policies toward their aging workforce. A central question in that respect is whether employers succeed in reducing the wage productivity gap at later ages. Reasoning from a human capital perspective, one might expect that policies to make older workers more attractive to employers emphasize measures to enhance productivity (by means of training programs) or bring wages in line with productivity (by means of demotion). Neither policy seems to play a major role in the policies of most employers.

On-the-job training is often reserved for younger workers who are viewed as cheaper and more worthy of the long-term investment (Taylor, Brooke, & di Biase, 2010; Taylor & Urwin, 2001). It may seem like older workers are caught in a catch-22: to remain attractive to employers they should be trained, but they are not trained because they are expected to retire soon. As the expected retirement age rises, so should investments in training, which would allow workers to remain productive longer.

Lazear's theory of implicit contracts contends that it is not necessarily a decline in productivity that is behind the lack of support for working longer and application of mandatory retirement rules. It is in the nature of the contract that workers are paid more than they are worth at older ages, even when productivity remains the same. From the perspective of the employer, a reduction of wages might therefore be an alternative to retirement. While wage policies are frequently discussed as a solution among policymakers, employers generally avoid cutting wages as a means to rebalance the costs and productivity of older workers (Munnell & Sass, 2008; Van Dalen, Henkens, & Schippers, 2010a). Employers point out first that employees are little inclined to move down the ladder. And those employees who *are* prepared to take a step down in terms of their position and duties tend not to be willing to do so in terms of their employment conditions. So, in the end, demotion may lead to resignations by the firm's better workers and a reduced effort from those who remain. Another reason why employers might be reluctant to apply wage declines at a prescribed age is the probability that this would be branded as a violation of age discrimination laws (Hatcher, 2003).

In many countries in Europe, the most widely implemented measures tend to be the ones that "spare" the older workers, such as additional leave, increased holiday entitlements, workload reductions, age limits for working overtime, or irregular work. These policies are based on insights that stressful working conditions, heavy workloads, and physical demands promote early retirement (Hayward, 1986; Henkens & Tazelaar, 1997; Kubicek, Korunka, Hoonakker, & Raymo, 2010).[2] These policies, however, do not address the other side of the coin. Older workers' retirement preferences have to do not only with the degree to which workers find work mentally or physically demanding, but also with the extent to which the job is intrinsically rewarding in terms of job challenge (Adams, 1999; Zappalà, Depolo, Fraccaroli, Guglielmi, & Sarchielli, 2008) and autonomy (Blekesaune & Solem, 2005) and socially rewarding in terms of social support from colleagues and supervisors (Armstrong-Stassen, 1994; Vecchio, 1993). Many policy initiatives are aimed at reducing the workload, but few are aimed at making work more attractive. One of the elements in organizational policies that may provide opportunities to rebalance costs and productivity at the end of workers' careers is the option of phased retirement. Workers gradually reduce their working hours to adapt to a post-retirement lifestyle, whereas employers may still benefit from the skills and benefits of these workers. Results of a study by Hutchens and Grace-Martin (2006) carried out among U.S. employers shows that employers are often willing to provide this opportunity, but primarily as part of an informal arrangement. These arrangements imply employers' control over the question of whether phased retirement is possible and feasible given the specific job and business conditions.

The limited support for retention of older workers put a question mark behind the notion that employers cannot afford to lose their current generations of highly skilled older-aged employees, who are seen as the repositories of institutional intelligence. In that notion it is assumed that organizations will simply refuse to lose so much of this precious asset. Munnell and Sass (2008) state that there may be some logic in this claim, but due to the aging of their workforce most employers will have an abundance, not a shortage, of institutional intelligence in their organizations. Employers may therefore have some interest in retaining their most valuable older workers but are not very likely to support workers to delay their retirement across the board as long as they perceive alternative options to fill their vacancies.

Hiring Older Workers

Accumulated evidence suggests that retirement transitions are not only being delayed as a result of pension reforms, but are also becoming considerably more dynamic (Hardy, 1991; Herz, 1995; Singh & Verma, 2003; Szinovacz, 2003). Retirement increasingly constitutes a series of decisions regarding the structure of the late career that can span a period of twenty years and can include multiple transitions. The literature indicates that there is an increasing diversity in the pathways that older workers take into their full-time retirement. On the one hand, many older workers prefer some kind of phased retirement from their main career job, remaining in the same occupation and organization where they used to be. On the other hand, bridge employment offers possibilities to pursuit new challenges on the labor market, by means of a different job and organization. While post-career transitions into self-employment are increasingly common (Giandrea, Cahill, & Quinn, 2008), most older adults seeking bridge employment are dependent on employers' decisions to hire them. An important question is for what jobs and under what conditions?

How employees' preferences with respect to the types of bridge employment between their career jobs and full retirement match with employers' hiring practices is an important area of inquiry. The increasing phenomenon of post-career job self-employment might reflect workers' preferences, but it might also reflect the restrictions workers experience from employers who are not willing to hire them. Workers might want to work in a different field or occupation, but how likely are employers to recruit them for these vacancies? Most studies on re-employment consistently show that older jobseekers have difficulty finding a suitable job, and the new jobs they are able to find come with lower pay and benefits (Johnson & Park, 2011). Older workers often indicate that they are subjected to age-related discrimination (Berger, 2009). Specifically, older workers, particularly those approaching 50 years old and those approaching retirement age, are most likely to experience workplace age discrimination (Roscigno et al., 2007).

An important question is which employee characteristics do fit the employers' preferences. For employers, finding a right match between supply and demand of labor is a costly process, and employers are likely to not only compare older and younger workers but also to rank older workers on the basis of expected returns. Research into the selection practices of employers who use candidate profiles, so-called "vignettes," has shown that the selection criteria used tend to relate to characteristics of the applicants that cannot be changed, such as sex, age, and social background (Van Beek, Koopmans, & Van Praag, 1997). In addition, a study by Karpinska et al. (2011) using a vignette design shows that employers tend to have a narrow focus when it comes to the question of whether or not to re-employ an older worker retired from his or her career job. Besides favoring younger retirees over older retirees, employers emphasize the continuity in the career. A short absence from the labor force is permitted; a longer absence brings risk of punishment. Early retirees who are not able to regain employment soon after leaving their career job are at a much higher risk of a permanent exclusion from the labor force. In addition, there seems to be a discrepancy between employees' preferences for bridge employment in a different field and employers' willingness to hire them. Contrary to the existing stereotype that older workers have difficulty adapting to organizational changes, retirees often seem to be keen on acquiring new experiences outside their original career field. However, the opportunity structure provided by employers appears to be highly contingent on earlier work experience, and access to other occupations is often limited.

The aging of the population in Western countries will also affect the labor market. The outflow of large baby-boom cohorts reaching retirement age in the coming years will presumably lead to a situation that differs fundamentally from what organizations experienced in the final quarter of the twentieth century, when the labor market was chiefly characterized by excess supply. The labor market is expected to change from a "demand-driven market," in which employers are in a dominant position, to a "supply-driven market," in which employees assume a dominant position. It is unclear how employers will respond to this change. To predict the future labor market for older workers is a difficult endeavor, but too much optimism about the future prospects for older workers should be toned down. Munnell and Sass (2008) state that the notion that employers will increase their demand for older workers as a result of structural labor shortages are overblown at best. The authors argue that first of all, it is questionable to believe that the economy (and demand for workers) will grow at a historic rate. Second, employers increasingly operate in a global economy and respond to changes in the global supply of labor, instead of changes in the domestic supply of labor. Third, older workers are often working in sectors and occupations that were expanding fast when they were young and are now expanding slowly or contracting. Expanding sectors seek primarily younger workers with the latest skills and knowledge, and younger workers seek employment in fast-growing sectors.

While it is difficult to predict the demand for older workers in the future, current research strongly suggests that re-employment comes into the picture only when organizations have recruitment problems and few alternatives available. Though it may be true that labor-force shortages may be beneficial to early retirees' employment prospects, their chances for re-employment are low when labor force supply is sufficient and positions could be filled by younger applicants (Conen, Henkens, & Schippers, 2011). Johnson and Park (2011) show that in the United States, workers age 50 to 61 who lost their jobs between mid-2008 and the end of 2009 were a third less likely than those age 25 to 34 to find work within twelve months, and those age 62 or older were only half as likely. Re-employment was low among all age groups, however. The likelihood of finding a job within a year was only 36% at age 25 to 34, 24% at age 50 to 61, and 18% at age 62 and older.

Conclusions and Discussion

Retirement is an increasingly complicated process of labor force withdrawal. The decision to retire transcends considerations about the pros and cons of retirement at the individual or the household level for the older worker. To achieve a better understanding of older workers' career decisions, we need to incorporate the driving forces of retirement processes at the demand side of the labor market. Employers are key players in defining the opportunities for retirement as well as the opportunities for working longer. As a result, the success of policies aimed at delaying retirement is to a large extent dependent on the actions and attitudes of employers. Thus, to fully understand the process of retirement, one should delineate the role that employers play in the late career employment-retirement nexus. In this chapter we make several observations that may guide future research questions.

Our first observation is that there is a rich literature about the age-productivity nexus and the difficulties in measuring this relationship. However, we lack studies that confront employers' perceptions about declining productivity with information on actual productivity. Future studies might also look at the origins of the stereotypes on productivity and retirement timing, and study their consequences. The consequences may relate to hiring and firing decisions, but also to the HRM policies focused on older workers in organizations that might bridge a perceived wage-productivity gap. Designing policies that enhance the employability and productivity of older workers is one of the challenges personnel managers will face in the near future. It is not clear whether existing biases toward older workers hamper or stimulate the development of these types of policies.

Our second observation is connected to the management of the retirement process by employers. Although retirement has been frequently used to lay off older workers when they threaten the profitability of the firm or when market forces more or less dictate firms to downsize the workforce (Wang & Shultz, 2010), management of retirement processes by employers that also address the preferences and needs of employees is mostly absent. This is, however, increasingly relevant, since pension and social security reforms will make it more difficult to lay off older workers. The management of retirement requires that the issue is discussed by the employee and his or her supervisor. Few studies have looked at employee-employer communication practices with respect to retirement. One study carried out in the Netherlands showed that a large majority of employees in their 50s discuss retirement with their spouse and colleagues (Henkens & Van Solinge, 2003). A small minority discuss the issue with their supervisor. Many managers see retirement as a private affair. However, employees see retirement as an occupational career transition in which firms and supervisors play a key role. Future studies might take a closer look at the interaction processes that take place between employees and supervisors, with respect to retirement. It would be particularly interesting to study the misperceptions about the opinions and behaviors of each other. The co-orientation model as advanced by McLeod and Chaffee (1973) can be used to understand the role of communication in perceptions of others' opinions as well as their accuracy. At this point it seems that the Thomas theorem is applicable here: "If men define situations as real, they are real in their consequences." (Merton, 1995) This may be very relevant for workers who perceive their employer as supporting early retirement and employers who perceive older workers are unwilling to be trained and looking forward to a life without work, without asking. Although many co-orientation studies have been carried out to identify the accuracy of individuals' perceptions of others, co-orientation has not been explored in the context of retirement. To facilitate effective retirement planning on the part of the employer and employee, more insight is needed into communicating the preferences and restrictions that both actors face.

More insight in the social processes that take place in the years before retirement may also provide additional answers to the question of why many employers are only lukewarm to retain or hire older workers. Are economic considerations the real driving forces behind the difficulties that older workers experience in extending their career? Or are psychological processes, with misperceptions, stereotypes, and prejudice, the major impediments for a match between employers and their employees at the end of their career?

Notes

1. To bare the increasing costs of health insurance for employers are inclined to cut the health benefits and shift costs to retirees. Mermin et al., (2007) conclude that the erosion of employer retiree health benefits is the most important factor explaining the US babyboomers' expectations to work longer than people born a decade earlier.

2. Another explanation of the existence of this type of older worker friendly personnel policies may have to do with the unions distributional preferences: unions pay more attention to older workers preferences than younger workers preferences because older workers are more likely to be member of a union.

References

Adams, G. A. (1999). Career-related variables and planned retirement age. An extension of Beehr's model. *Journal of Vocational Behavior, 55,* 221–235.

Armstrong-Stassen, M. (1994).Coping with transition: A study of layoff survivors. *Journal of Organizational Behavior, 15,* 597–621.

Armstrong-Stassen, M. (2001). Reactions of older employees to organizational downsizing. The role of gender, job level and time. *Journal of Gerontology: Psychological Sciences, 56B*(4), P234–P243.

Becker, G. S. (1957). *The economics of discrimination.* Chicago, IL: University of Chicago Press.

Berger, E. D. (2009). Managing age discrimination: An examination of the techniques used when seeking employment. *The Gerontologist, 49*(3), 317–332.

Bird, C. P., & Fisher, T. D. (1986). Thirty years later: Attitudes toward the employment of older workers. *Journal of Applied Psychology, 71,* 515–517.

Blekesaune, M., & Solem, P. E. (2005). Working conditions and early retirement: A prospective study of retirement behavior. *Research on Aging, 27*(1), 3–30.

Bloom, D. E., & Williamson, J. G. (1998).Demographic transitions and economic miracles in emerging Asia. *World Bank Economic Review, 12*(3), 419–455.

Borman, W. C., Penner, L. A., Allen, T. D., & Motowidlo, S. J. (2001). Personality predictors of citizenship performance. *International Journal of Selection and Assessment, 9*(1–2), 52–69.

Chui, W. C. K., Chan, A. W., Snape, E., & Redman, T. (2001). Age, stereotypes and discriminatory attitudes towards older workers. An east-west comparison. *Human Relations, 54*(5), 629–661.

Conen, W., Henkens, K., & Schippers, J. (2011). Are employers changing their behavior toward older workers? An analysis of employers' surveys 2000–2009. *Journal of Aging and Social Policy, 23*, 141–158.

Davis, E. P. (2005). Challenges posed by ageing to financial and monetary stability. *Geneva Papers on Risk and Insurance-Issues and Practice, 30*(4), 542–564.

Dorn, D., & Sousa-Poza, A. (2010). "Voluntary" and "involuntary" early retirement: An international analysis. *Applied Economics, 42*(4), 427–438.

Ekerdt, D. J., & DeViney, S. (1993). Evidence for a preretirement process among older male workers. *Journal of Gerontology: Social Sciences, 48B*(2), S35–S43.

Ekerdt, D. J., Kosloski, K., & DeViney, S. (2000). The normative anticipation of retirement by older workers. *Research on Aging, 22*(1), 3–22.

Feldman, D. C., & Beehr, T. A. (2011, April). A three-phase model of retirement decision making. *American Psychologist, 66*(3), 193–203.

Feyrer, J. (2008). Aggregate evidence on the link between age structure and productivity. *Population and Development Review, 34*, 78–99.

Finkelstein, L. L., Higgins, K. D., & Clancy, M. (2000). Justifications for ratings of old and young job applicants: An exploratory content analysis. *Experimental Aging Research, 26*(3), 263–283.

Finkelstein, L. M., & Burke, M. J. (1998). Age stereotyping at work: The role of rater and contextual factors on evaluations of job applicants. *Journal of General Psychology, 125*(4), 317–345.

Finkelstein, L. M., Burke, M. J., & Raju, N. S. (1995). Age discrimination in simulated employment contexts. An integrative analysis. *Journal of Applied Psychology, 80*(6), 652–663.

Gallo, W. T., Bradley, E. H., Siegel, M., & Kasl, S. (2000). Health effects of involuntary job loss among older workers: Findings from the Health and Retirement Survey. *Journal of Gerontology: Social Sciences, 55B*(3), S131–S140.

Giandrea, M. D., Cahill, K. E., & Quinn, J. F. (2008). *Self-employment transitions among older American workers with career jobs.* Washington, DC: U.S. Dept. of Labor, U.S. Bureau of Labor Statistics, Office of Productivity and Technology.

Hamermesh, D. S. (1996). *Labor demand.* Princeton, NJ: Princeton University Press.

Hanisch, K. A., & Hulin, C., L. (1990). Job attitudes and organizational withdrawal: An examination of retirement and other voluntary withdrawal behaviors. *Journal of Vocational Behavior, 37*, 60–78.

Hardy, M. A. (1991). Employment after retirement. Who gets back in? *Research on Aging, 13*(3), 267–288.

Hardy, M. A. (2002). The transformation of retirement in twentieth century America: From discontent to satisfaction. *Generations, 26*(2), 9–16.

Hassell, B. L., & Perrewe, P. L. (1995). An examination of beliefs about older workers: Do stereotypes still exist? *Journal of Organizational Behavior, 16*(5), 457–468.

Hatcher, C. B. (2003).The economics of the retirement decision. In G. A. Adams & T. A. Beehr (Eds.), *Retirement: Reasons, processes, and results* (pp. 136–158). New York, NY: Springer.

Hayward, M. D. (1986). The influence of occupational characteristics on men's early retirement. *Social Forces, 64*, 1032–1045.

Headey, D. D., & Hodge, A. (2009). The effect of population growth on economic growth: A meta-regression analysis of the macroeconomic literature. *Population and Development Review, 35*(2), 221–248.

Henkens, K. (2000). Supervisors' attitudes about early retirement of subordinates. *Journal of Applied Social Psychology, 30*(4), 833–852.

Henkens, K. (2005). Stereotyping older workers and retirement: The manager's point of view. *Canadian Journal on Aging, 24*(4), 353–366.

Henkens, K., & Schippers, J. (Eds.) (2012). Active ageing in Europe, special issue of *International Journal of Manpower*, forthcoming.

Henkens, K., & Tazelaar, F. (1997). Explaining retirement decisions of civil servants in the Netherlands. *Research on Aging, 19*, 139–173.

Henkens, K., & Van Solinge, H. (2003). *Het eindspel: Werknemers, hun partners en leidinggevenden over uittreding uit het arbeidsproces* [The endgame: Workers, spouses and supervisors about retirement from the labor force]. Assen: Van Gorcum/Stichting Management Studies.

Henkens, K., Van Solinge, H., & Cozijnsen, R. (2009). Let go or retain? A comparative study of the attitudes of business students and managers about the retirement of older workers. *Journal of Applied Social Psychology, 39*(7), 1562–1588.

Herz, D. E. (1995, April). Work after early retirement: An increasing trend among men. *Monthly Labor Review*, 13–20.

Herzog, A. R., House, J. S., & Morgan, J. N. (1991).Relation of work and retirement to health and well-being in older age. *Psychology and Aging, 6*(2), 202–211.

Hilton, J. L., & Von Hippel, W. (1996). Stereotypes. *Annual Review of Psychology, 47*, 237–271.

Hurd, M. D. (1990). Research on the elderly: Economic status, retirement, and consumption and saving. *Journal of Economic Literature, 18*, 565–637.

Hutchens, R., & Grace-Martin, K. (2006). Employer willingness to permit phased retirement: Why are some more willing than others? *Industrial & Labor Relations Review, 59*(4), 525–546.

Isaksson, K., & Johansson, G. (2000). Adaptation to continued work and early retirement following downsizing: Long-term effects and gender differences. *Journal of Occupational and Organizational Psychology, 73*(2), 241–256.

Johnson, R. W., & Park, J. S. (2011, January). *Can unemployed older workers find work?* (Older Americans' Economic Security Report No. 25). Washington, DC: Urban Institute.

Joulain, M., & Mullet, E. (2001). Estimating the "appropriate" age for retirement as a function of perceived occupational characteristics. *Work and Stress, 15*, 357–365.

Judd, C. M., & Park, B. (1993). Definition and assessment of accuracy in social stereotypes. *Psychological Review, 100*(1), 109–128.

Karpinska, K., Henkens, K., & Schippers, J. (2011). The recruitment of early retirees: A vignette study of the factors that affect managers' decisions. *Ageing & Society, 31*(4), 570–589.

Kirchner, W. K., & Durnette, M. D. (1954). Attitudes towards older workers. *Personnel Psychology, 7*, 257–265.

Kubicek, B., Korunka, C., Hoonakker, P., & Raymo, J. M. (2010). Work and family characteristics as predictors of early retirement in married men and women. *Research on Aging, 32*(4), 467–498.

Lawrence, B. S. (1996). Organizational age norms: Why is it so hard to know one when you see one? *The Gerontologist, 36*(2), 209–220.

Lazear, E. P. (1979). Why is there mandatory retirement. *Journal of Political Economy, 87*(6), 1261–1284.

LePine, J. A., Erez, A., & Johnson, D. E. (2002). The nature and dimensionality of organizational citizenship behavior: A critical review and meta-analysis. *Journal of Applied Psychology, 87*(1), 52–65.

Loretto, W., Duncan, C., & White, P. J. (2000).Ageism and employment. Controversies, ambiguities and younger people's perceptions. *Ageing & Society, 20*(3), 279–302.

McCann, R., & Giles, H. (2003).Ageism and the workplace. A communication perspective. In T. D. Nelson (Ed.), *Ageism, stereotyping and prejudice against older persons* (pp. 163–199). Cambridge, MA: MIT Press.

McEvoy, G. M., & Cascio, W. F. (1989).Cumulative evidence of the relationship between employee age and job-performance. *Journal of Applied Psychology, 74*(1), 11–17.

McGregor, J., & Gray, L. (2002). Stereotypes of older workers: The New Zealand experience. *Social Policy Journal of New Zealand, 18*, 163–177.

McLeod, J. M., & Chaffee, S. H. (1973). Interpersonal approaches to communications research. *American Behavioral Scientist, 16*(4), 483–488.

Mermin, G. B. T., Johnson, R. W., & Murphy, D. P. (2007). Why do boomers plan to work longer? *The Journals of Gerontology, Series B: Psychological Sciences and Social Sciences, 62*(5), S286–S294.

Merton, R. K. (1995). The Thomas Theorem and the Matthew Effect, *Social Forces, 74*(2), 379–422.

Munnell, A. H., & Sass, S. A. (2008). *Working longer: The solution to the retirement income challenge*: Washington, DC: The Brookings Institution.

Ng, T. W. H., & Feldman, D. C. (2008). The relationship of age to ten dimensions of job performance. *Journal of Applied Psychology, 93*(2), 392–423.

OECD. (2006a). *Live longer, work longer. A synthesis report*. Paris, France: Organisation for Economic Cooperation and Development.

OECD. (2006b). *Live longer, work longer. Ageing and employment policies*. Paris, France: Organisation for Economic Cooperation and Development.

Phelps, E. S. (1972). The statistical theory of racism and sexism. *The American Economic Review, 62*(4), 659–661.

Potocnik, K., Tordera, N., & Peiró, J. M. (2009).The role of human resource practices and group norms in the retirement process. *European Psychologist, 14*(3), 193–206.

Redman, T., & Snape, E. (2006). The consequences of perceived age discrimination amongst older police officers: Is social support a buffer? *British Journal of Management, 17*(2), 167–175.

Remery, C., Henkens, K., Schippers, J., & Ekamper, P. (2003). Managing an aging workforce and a tight labor market: Views held by Dutch employers. *Population Research and Policy Review, 22*(1), 21–40.

Roscigno, V. J., Mong, S., Byron, R., & Tester, G. (2007). Age discrimination, social closure and employment. *Social Forces, 86*(1), 313–334.

Rosen, B., & Jerdee, T. H. (1982). Effects of employee financial status and social adjustment on employers' retention/retirement recommendations. *Ageing and Work, 5*, 111–118.

Settersten, R. A. (1998). Time, age, and the transition to retirement: New evidence on life course flexibility? *International Journal of Aging and Human Development, 47*(3), 177–203.

Settersten, R. A., & Hagestad, G. O. (1996). What the latest? II. Cultural age deadlines for educational and work transitions. *The Gerontologist, 36*(5), 602–613.

Shultz, K. S., Morton, K. R., & Weckerle, J. R. (1998). The influence of push and pull factors on voluntary and involuntary early retirees' retirement decision and adjustment. *Journal of Vocational Behavior, 53*(1), 45–57.

Singh, G., & Verma, A. (2003). Work history and later life labor force participation: Evidence from a large telecommunications firm. *Industrial and Labor Relations Review, 56*(4), 669–715.

Skirbekk, V. (2004). Age and individual productivity: A literature survey. *Vienna Yearbook of Population Research, 133*–153.

Skirbekk, V. (2008). Age and productivity potential: A new approach based on ability levels and industry-wide task demand. *Population and Development Review, 34*, 191–207.

Sturman, M. C. (2003). Searching for the inverted U-shaped relationship between time and performance: Meta-analyses of the experience/performance, tenure/performance, and age/performance relationships. *Journal of Management, 29*(5), 609–640.

Szinovacz, M. E. (2003). Contexts and pathways: Retirement as institution, process, and experience. In G. A. Adams & T. A. Beehr (Eds.), *Retirement: Reasons, processes, and results* (pp. 6–52). New York, NY: Springer.

Tang, H. M., & MacLeod, C. (2006). Labour force ageing and productivity performance in Canada. *Canadian Journal of Economics-Revue Canadienne D Economique, 39*(2), 582–603.

Taylor, P. E., Brooke, L., & di Biase, T. (2010).European employer policies concerning career management and learning from a life-span perspective. In G. Naegele (Ed.), *Soziale Lebenslauf Politik* [Social life course politics] (pp. 474–497). Wiesbaden, Germany: VS Verlag.

Taylor, P. E., & Urwin, P. (2001). Age and participation in vocational education and training. *Work, Employment & Society, 15*(4), 763–779.

Taylor, P. E., & Walker, A. (1998). Employers and older workers. Attitudes and employment practices. *Ageing & Society, 18*(6), 641–658.

Thurow, L. C. (1975). *Generational inequality*. New York, NY: Basic Books.

Van Beek, K. W. H., Koopmans, C. C., & Van Praag, B. M. S. (1997). Shopping at the labour market: A real tale of fiction. *European Economic Review, 41*(2), 295–317.

Van Dalen, H. P., Henkens, K., Hendrikse, W., & Schippers, J. J. (2010). Do European employers support later retirement? *International Journal of Manpower, 31*(3), 360–373.

Van Dalen, H. P., Henkens, K., & Schippers, J. (2009). Dealing with older workers in Europe: A comparative survey of employers' attitudes and actions. *Journal of European Social Policy, 19*(1), 47–60.

Van Dalen, H. P., Henkens, K., & Schippers, J. (2010a). How do employers cope with an ageing workforce? Views from employers and employees. *Demographic Research, 22*, 1015–1036.

Van Dalen, H. P., Henkens, K., & Schippers, J. (2010b). Productivity of older workers: Perceptions of employers and employees. *Population and Development Review, 36*(2), 309–330.

Van Dam, K., Van der Vorst, J. D. M., & Van der Heijden, B. I. J. M. (2009). Employees' intentions to retire early: A case of planned behavior and anticipated work conditions. *Journal of Career Development, 35*(3), 265–289.

Vecchio, R. P. (1993). The impact of differences in subordinate and supervisor age on attitudes and performance. *Psychology and Aging, 8*(1), 112–119.

Venti, S. F., & Wise, D. A. (1998). The cause of wealth dispersion at retirement: Choice or chance? *American Economic Review, 88*(2), 185–191.

Vickerstaff, S., Cox, J., & Keen, L. (2003). Employers and the management of retirement. *Social Policy & Administration, 37*(3), 271–287.

Von Bonsdorff, M. E., Shultz, K. S., Leskinen, E., & Tansky, J. (2009). The choice between retirement and bridge employment: A continuity theory and life course perspective. *International Journal of Aging & Human Development, 69*(2), 79–100.

Waldman, D. A., & Avolio, B. J. (1986). A meta-analysis of age-differences in job performance. *Journal of Applied Psychology, 71*(1), 33–38.

Wang, M., & Shultz, K. S. (2010). Employee retirement: A review and recommendations for future investigation. *Journal of Management, 36*(1), 172–206

Wang, M., Zhan, Y., Liu, S., & Shultz, K. S. (2008). Antecedents of bridge employment: A longitudinal investigation. *Journal of Applied Psychology, 93*(4), 818–830.

Zappalà, S., Depolo, M., Fraccaroli, F., Guglielmi, D., & Sarchielli, G. (2008). Postponing job retirement? Psychosocial influences on the preference for early or late retirement. *Career Development International, 13*(2), 150–167.

Retirement Attitudes: Considering Etiology, Measurement, Attitude-Behavior Relationships, and Attitudinal Ambivalence

Daniel A. Newman, Gahyun Jeon *and* Charles L. Hulin

Abstract

Attitudes—overall positive or negative evaluations of an object—have played a prominent role in classic models of retirement from work. This chapter attempts to make four contributions to the study of attitudes toward retirement. First, we extend the Cornell model of role evaluations (Smith, Kendall, & Hulin, 1969) to specify the origins of retirement attitudes. Second, we review the major instruments designed to measure retirement attitudes. This review reveals nine distinct categories of scientific constructs: (a) attitudes toward *retirement* (the role state of being retired), (b) attitudes toward *retiring* (the role transition decision), (c) attitudes toward *retirees* (including stereotypes about retired persons), (d) beliefs and expectations about retirement (attributes of retirement; what it is like), (e) retirement preferences/desires (e.g., "if I had a choice, I would retire at age 55…"), (f) behavioral intentions (e.g., "I intend to retire at age 55…"), (g) planning/preparation activities (e.g., saving money), (h) retirement efficacy or perceived control (ability to retire), and (i) retirement entitlement (e.g., the belief that a person who works hard does or does not deserve to be able to retire). Third, we discuss retirement in light of two models of the attitude-behavior relationship. We begin by integrating retirement attitudes and related behavioral constructs into an extended theory of planned behavior (Ajzen, 1991) model of retirement, which also includes social identity and anticipated affect as antecedents of the behavioral desire to retire; we then specify the retirement implications of the attitude-engagement model (Harrison, Newman, & Roth, 2006; Hanisch & Hulin, 1991). Fourth, we propose a future research focus on retirement ambivalence—simultaneously holding positive and negative views toward retirement.

Key Words: attitudes, retirement, job satisfaction, withdrawal, behavioral engagement, ambivalence

Who will take care of you,
How'll you get by,
When you're too old to work
and you're too young to die?
—From "Social Security Song (Too Old to Work)" by *Joe Glazer*

The Unique Meaning of Retirement

In some regards, the choice of a job or an occupation is the most important decision an individual makes. Our work influences us throughout our lives

as few other activities do. For many, work is as much about the search for daily meaning as it is about the search for our daily bread (Terkel, 1974). From our late teens until retirement we spend more time at work than at any other activity. Our early work roles influence our values and even our personalities (Roberts, 2006; Roberts, Caspi, & Moffitt, 2003; Roberts & Wood, 2006). *Retirement* represents a behavioral choice to give up one's work role, and the outcomes that work provides, for a much different role. The choice to retire is a choice between one set of activities (work) and a different set of activities (e.g., leisure activities or bridge employment done in retirement). This is a choice between two sets of activities and two social settings, as well as a choice that carries with it a significant change in individuals' self-images and feelings of "mattering." Individuals are likely to make their choice about retirement based on a comparison between the utility (anticipated satisfaction) of retirement and the experienced satisfaction from their work. Their satisfactions with their work roles are empirically related to their retirement desires and intentions (Hanisch & Hulin, 1991). This decision carries with it changes in many life outcomes that may not be fully appreciated by those approaching an age when retirement is feasible. The anticipated effects of retirement on their personal and social identities are also a likely factor in retirement decision making.

In the United States, and indeed in many countries and cultures of the world, you are what you do…to do nothing is to be nothing. Work and its quotidian tasks give our lives coherence. A lack of work denies our basic humanity (Green, 1993). One of the first questions we ask of a new acquaintance is "What do you do?" Their occupation tells us much about them. If their answer is "I am retired," we have learned something, but it is probably much less than if we knew what they did before retirement. For individuals, their identity, self-worth, and imputed self-meaning may undergo significant changes following retirement. This may surface when they try to identify themselves. Are they *retired?…a retired school teacher?…a part-time volunteer?…a part-time worker?…somebody who putters around the house?* What is their new identity?

Work roles provide a sense of identity, a source of relationships outside the family, a set of obligatory activities that structure time, a source of autonomy, a continuing chance to develop skills and knowledge, a purpose in life, feelings of self-worth and self-esteem, income and security, and proscribed activities that give meaning to leisure time. Some of the outcomes provided by a work role are provided by retirement (e.g., income and security, autonomy), but others are lacking in retirement. Given the importance of work and the changes resulting from a lack of work in the lives of individuals (due to retirement), it is essential that we study retirement using the best theoretical frameworks, methods, and measurement scales available.

We conceptualize retiring as a choice between two roles and the two sets of activities that the two roles comprise. Individuals make a decision to continue working or to retire; this decision is not made in the abstract. A choice to retire is made within the framework of one's job. Studies of retirement and retirement decisions that ignore that retiring is a choice to give up one social/organizational role for a different role may ignore half of the important variance of the variables and constructs influencing the decision. Variance in retirement decisions contributed by the satisfactions one experiences in his/her work role may be as important as the utility of retirement itself.

It is equally important that our approach to retirement recognizes the extremes of work and retirement. Some of us have known a 75- or 80-year-old worker who refuses to retire even though she or he might be better off financially in retirement; the work role for such an individual, as compared to the role of a retiree, must offer satisfactions beyond what the person can conceive of in the role of a retiree. Some individuals, even when embedded in a dissatisfying and demotivating job, report that they "…can't quit, I wouldn't be anybody if I did," (Hulin, in press). Other individuals can make a transition from working in a job they find greatly satisfying to being retired without apparently experiencing any feelings of loss. In this chapter, we explore retirement within the broad limits of the framework of these life-changing decisions.

Origins of Retirement Attitudes: The Comparison-Level and Extended Cornell Models

To formalize the notion of role comparison in our decision-theoretic perspective on retirement attitudes (i.e., to describe how attitudes relate to the choice between remaining in the current role vs. transitioning into the retired role), we first invoke Thibaut and Kelley's (1959) comparison level model. This model (and adaptations of it; see Hulin, 1991) specifies three sets of role outcomes: (a) the outcomes currently experienced in one's focal role or job, (b) CL—the *comparison level*, or the set of outcomes experienced (directly or vicariously) in past roles, and (c) CL_{Alt} (or CL_{Retire})—the comparison level for an alternative role, capturing the

Table 15.1 Adapted from Thibaut-Kelley (1959) Comparison-Level Model of Relations between CL, CL$_{Retired}$, Satisfaction, and Behavior

	CL	CL$_{Retired}$	Job/Role Satisfaction	Behavior
Current role outcomes				
Situation A	>	>	Satisfied	Not retire
Situation B	>	<	Satisfied	Retire
Situation C	<	>	Dissatisfied	Not retire
Situation D	<	<	Dissatisfied	Retire

Notes: Adapted from Hulin (1991). CL = Comparison Level. CL$_{Retired}$ = Comparison Level for Retirement Role. The ">" inequality implies that a person's focal role outcomes are comparatively "greater than" the CL outcomes.

counterfactual outcomes that would accrue to a person if she or he were willing and able to switch into another, available role (e.g., to move into the role of retiree). The key predictions of the comparison-level model are (a) satisfaction with the current role is a function of comparing one's current outcomes against CL, whereas (b) the behavioral decision to switch roles (e.g., to retire) is a function of comparing one's current outcomes against CL$_{Alt}$ (or CL$_{Retire}$; see Table 15.1). As such, our adaptation of Thibaut and Kelley's (1959) model says that individuals are predicted to retire when their anticipated outcomes and satisfactions in retirement exceed their current job outcomes and satisfactions.

Another model of work-related attitudes that can be used for understanding retirement attitudes is the Cornell model, originally developed by Patricia Cain Smith and colleagues (Smith, Kendall, & Hulin, 1969; Hulin, 1991) to describe the origins of job satisfaction (as measured via the Job Descriptive Index, or JDI) and of retirement attitudes (as measured via the Retirement Descriptive Index, or RDI). A modified version of the Cornell model appears in Figure 15.1 (see Judge, Hulin, & Dalal, 2012). The modified Cornell model, like the Thibaut-Kelley (1959) comparison-level model, emphasizes a set of comparison processes in the determination of job/role attitudes. First, one's *work role contributions* (e.g., time, effort, talent) are evaluated in reference to the relevant *opportunity costs* (i.e., other roles one could occupy given the same level of time, effort, and talent) in determining job/role satisfaction. Second, one's *work role outcomes* (e.g., rewards, salary, job characteristics, prestige, interpersonal treatment) are evaluated in reference to the relevant *frames of reference* (i.e., rewards and outcomes from other jobs/roles one

could occupy) in determining job/role satisfaction. For example, among individuals who hold identical jobs, those who live in a community with poor economic conditions and substandard housing will report higher levels of job satisfaction (Hulin, 1966). This is attributed to a frame of reference effect—one's work role conditions and outcomes are perceived more positively when compared to a lower frame of reference.

Judge et al. (2012) further modified the Cornell model by incorporating personality (Figure 15.1; see also Judge, Heller, & Mount, 2002). Personality is proposed to have at least three effects on role satisfaction (see Judge & Larsen, 2001): (a) among individuals who experience the same job stimuli, those with higher neuroticism/negative affectivity will experience these stimuli as more negative (Larsen & Ketelaar, 1991); (b) individuals with higher *core self-evaluations* (a broad personality trait) will select into more complex and satisfying jobs (Judge, Bono, & Locke, 2000); and (c) individuals with low neuroticism have better emotion regulation ability (Joseph & Newman, 2010). In Judge et al.'s (2012) integrated model of job attitudes (Figure 15.1), personality operates by influencing the perceived costs of work inputs (time, effort, stress), as well as by influencing the frames of reference against which work outputs (salary, working conditions, prestige) are interpreted.

For the current discussion of retirement attitudes, the implication of the extended Cornell model (Smith et al., 1969; Judge et al., 2012; Hulin, 1991) is that we can explicitly modify the model to specify the precursors of *attitudes toward retirement* (see Figure 15.2). Specifically, Figure 15.2 is parallel to Figure 15.1, except that (a) the outcome variable in Figure 15.2 is *retirement* attitudes,

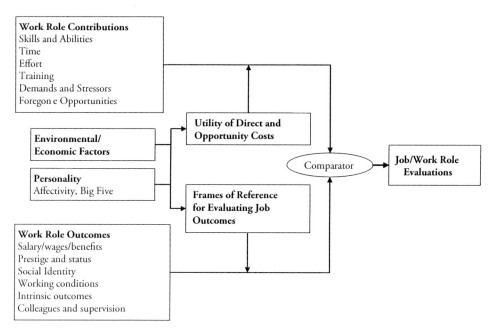

Figure 15.1 Extended Cornell Model (originally Smith, Kendall, & Hulin, 1969; adapted by Judge, Hulin, & Dalal, 2012)
Note: We have altered Judge et al.'s (2012) extended Cornell model by adding social identity as a work role outcome.

(b) the *retirement outcomes* in Figure 15.2 represent the benefits of being retired, and (c) the *role contributions* ("what is given up") in the Figure 15.2 retirement attitude model are the same as the *role outcomes* (what is received) from the Figure 15.1 job attitude model. That is, many of the outcomes of the job role are the very same things that are given up in retirement (retirement contributions = work role outcomes; e.g., salary, status, job conditions, colleagues). According to Figure 15.2,

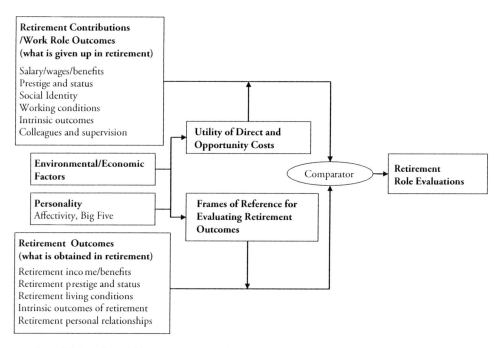

Figure 15.2 Extended Cornell Model for Retirement Attitudes

retirement attitudes derive from a comparison of what was given up (job/work outcomes) against the outcomes associated with the newer, retirement role. As in Judge et al.'s (2012) extended Cornell model, personality and economic factors still play a role in retirement attitudes in Figure 15.2 by virtue of their effects on frames of reference (including perceptions of peers' retirement conditions) and the opportunity costs of not retiring.

A comparison of Figure 15.1 with Figure 15.2 can yield a variety of insights about the likely relationship between job attitudes (job satisfaction) and retirement attitudes (retirement satisfaction). First, we note that because "Work Role Outcomes" (Figure 15.1) are equivalent to "Retirement Contributions" (i.e., work role outcomes = what is given up in retirement; Figure 15.2), some readers might interpret Figures 15.1 and 15.2 together as implying a *negative* association between job satisfaction and retirement satisfaction. That is, if one's job has great benefits, status, working conditions, and colleagues, then job satisfaction should be heightened and retirement satisfaction should be curbed, according to the *comparison processes* depicted in Figures 15.1 and 15.2. Those who leave a more satisfying job role should experience less satisfaction directed toward the retirement role, because they have given up a lot. On the other hand, both Figure 15.1 and Figure 15.2 specify that *personality* may be an important factor in how one perceives role outcomes/benefits. The role of personality in Figures 15.1 and 15.2 could potentially produce a *positive* correlation between job satisfaction and retirement satisfaction. This is because some individuals may be disposed to select particular frames of reference (e.g., upward social comparison), enabling them to perceive similar levels of satisfaction across roles (from the job role to the retirement role). In other words, some individuals are predisposed to dissatisfaction, regardless of whether they occupy a job role or a retirement role. Indirect evidence for this sort of process comes from Hanisch and Hulin (1991), who report a correlation between job satisfaction and retirement valence (anticipated future retirement satisfaction) of positive $r = 0.18$. People who are satisfied with their jobs tend to expect to be satisfied with retirement.

In light of the above paragraph, an interesting question is: What is the actual correlation between job satisfaction and later retirement satisfaction? That is, the role *comparison process* implies a negative association between job and retirement satisfactions, whereas the *dispositional process* implies a positive association between job and retirement satisfactions. In one large sample cited by Topa, Moriano, Depolo, Alcover, and Morales (2009), the correlation between job satisfaction and retirement satisfaction was $r = -0.07$ ($N = 794$). This empirical evidence supports the relative roles of work outcomes/benefits in Figures 15.1 and 15.2—i.e., work outcomes/benefits that contribute positively to job satisfaction would contribute negatively to retirement satisfaction, according to the comparison process. However, the small magnitude of the observed correlation ($r = -0.07$) could imply that personality factors tend to produce similar satisfactions across roles (positive correlation), which offsets an otherwise large negative correlation that might be obtained from the comparison process. Thus the reported small negative observed correlation between job satisfaction and retirement satisfaction (Topa et al., 2009) may represent a combination of two, countervailing processes (a comparison process and a personality process). We need more studies that attempt to measure all of the constructs in Figures 15.1 and 15.2, to enable a multivariate test of these fully specified models.

Review of Retirement Attitude Measures

Attitude has been defined as "a psychological tendency that is expressed by evaluating a particular entity with some degree of favor or disfavor" (Eagly & Chaiken, 1993, p. 1; cf. Campbell, 1950). In the study of retirement attitudes, there has been surprisingly little consensus in how these attitudes should be measured. In an attempt to summarize retirement attitude measures in the social sciences, we searched databases including PsycInfo, EBSCO, Social Science Citation Index, ProQuest digital dissertations, ERIC, and Medline. Our literature review of retirement attitude scales over the past fifty years (described below) returned over two dozen separate instruments designed to measure retirement attitudes. A list of these retirement attitude measures is given in Table 15.2. After compiling these various instruments, we content-analyzed them with the goal of determining the consensus content among the various retirement attitude scales. Indeed, some of the item content of so-called "retirement attitude" scales does not appear to strictly measure *attitudes*, at least according to the above definition for what an attitude is. Results of this content analysis appear in Table 15.3.

In short, the above list of retirement attitude measures runs the gamut of cognitive/evaluative

Table 15.2 Retirement Attitude Measures

Author(s)	Year	Journal/Book	Measure	# of items
Van Dam, van der Vorst, & van der Heijden[a]	2009	Journal of Career Development	Attitude toward early retirement	5
Zappala et al.[b]	2008	Career Development International	Preference for early or late retirement index	2
Elovainio et al.[c]	2005	Work & Stress	Early retirement thoughts	2
Lim[d]	2003	Employee Relations	Attitudes towards retirement	34
Joo & Grable[e]	2001	Family and Consumer Sciences Research Journal	Retirement attitudes (within the 1998 Retirement Confidence Survey (RCS))	3
Adams & Beehr[f]	1988	Personnel Psychology	Retirement intentions	4
Taylor & Shore[g]	1995	Psychology and Aging	Health, financial readiness, retirement attitudes, and fulfillment of retirement needs by the organization	
			—Psychological factors	14
			—Personal factors	4
			—Job and organizational factors	4
			—Planned and preferred retirement age	2
Gordon[h]	1994	Affilia	Attitude toward retirement	7
			—6 items from Greene et al. (1969)	
Turner, Bailey, & Scott[i]	1994	Journal of Applied Gerontology	Attitudes toward retirement	1
Hatch[j]	1992	Gender & Society	Attitude toward older workers' retirement	2
			Attitude toward life in retirement	1
			Subjective retirement	1
Hanisch[k]	1990	Dissertation—University of Illinois Urbana-Champaign	Desire to retire	1
Erdner & Guy[l]	1990	Aging and Human Development	Attitude toward retirement	1
Anson, Antonovsky, & Sagy[m]	1989	Sex Roles	Gains and losses in retirement scale	
			—Losses in retirement	11
			—Gains in entering retirement	5
			—Gains in leaving work	4
Staples[n]	1988	Dissertation—The George Washington University	The Attitude toward Retirement and Lifelong Career Development Survey (ARLCDS)	27
Matthews & Brown[o]	1987	Research on Aging	Attitude toward retirement	1

(Continued)

Table 15.2 (Continued)

Author(s)	Year	Journal/Book	Measure	# of items
Atchley & Robinson[p]	1982	Research on Aging	Attitude toward retirement	14
Johnson & Higgins (commissioned)[q]	1979	American Attitudes toward Pensions and Retirement	Quality of retired life compared to quality of working life	N/A
McGee, Hall, & Lutes-Dunckley[r]	1979	The Journal of Psychology	Attitude toward retirement	1
Skoglund[s]	1979	Research on Aging	Experiences and perceptions of the personal work and retirement situation	10
Eden & Jacobson[t]	1976	Journal of Vocational Behavior	Attitude toward retirement	3
Glamser[u]	1976	Journal of Gerontology	Attitude toward retirement	5
Boyak & Tiberi[v]	1975	Paper presented at 28th Annual Gerontological Society meeting	Retirement attitude "L" scale	19
			How people feel about aging and retirement	6
			Retirement attitude "S-D" scale	12
Goudy, Powers, & Keith[w]	1975	Journal of Gerontology	Attitude toward retirement	
			—Anticipated enjoyment in Retirement	4
			—Avoid retirement	4
			—Suggested retirement age	1
Parnes & Nestel[x]	1974	The Preretirement Years	Attitude toward retirement index	4
Jacobson[y]	1972	Occupational Psychology	Pre-retirement attitudes	6
Miljus[z]	1970	The Preretirement Years	Propensity to retire	8
Greene et al.[aa]	1969	Preretirement Counseling: Retirement adjustment and the older worker	Resistance to retirement scale	6
Smith, Kendall, & Hulin[ab]	1969	The Measurement of Satisfaction in Work and Retirement: A Strategy for the Study of Attitudes	Retirement descriptive index	
			—Activities and work	18
			—Financial situation	18
			—Health	9
			—People with whom you associate	18
Thompson & Streib[ac]	1958	Journal of Social Issues	Satisfaction with Retirement Scale	4
Thompson[ad]	1956	Dissertation	Attitude toward retirement	3

Table 15.3 Retirement Attitude Constructs and Example Items

Construct Categories

I. Attitudes (valenced reactions—like vs. dislike)

A. ***Attitude toward retirement*** (includes anticipated satisfaction/valenced reactions as well as actual satisfaction of those who have already retired; attitudes toward the role *state*, *not* the abstract concept/social policy of retirement; includes retirement outcomes)

Examples:

I expect to enjoy retirement.[g]

When I imagine what retirement will be like, I feel depressed.[g]

I look forward to having more leisure time after retirement.[g]

Evaluate the degree to which retirement is a pleasant time of life.[j]

All things considered, how do you really feel about the prospects of retirement?[l]

In general, what is your overall feeling toward retirement?[k]

I expect life to be satisfying after I retire.[n]

Your life in retirement: (sad/happy; active/inactive; meaningful/meaningless; idle/busy; bad/good; sick/healthy; tense/relaxed)[p]

I think that things will go well for me in retirement.[u]

My retirement: (good/bad; rough/smooth; active/passive; worthless/valuable; rewarding/painful; boring/exciting)[v]

Activities and work (during retirement): tiresome, exciting, hard, boring, limited, same thing every day, relaxing, gives sense of accomplishment[ab]

Financial situation (during retirement): barely live on income, insecure, well off, steady, bad, need outside help, worry about it, have to make do[ab]

Health (during retirement): have a lot of minor ailments, need little or no medical care, failing, never felt better, poor[ab]

People with whom you associate (during retirement): worried, boring, active, too quiet, complaining, too slow, intelligent, hard to meet, healthy, interested in doing things[ab]

How often do you miss the feeling of doing a good job?[ac]

How often do you feel that you want to go back to work?[ac]

How often do you miss being with the other people at work?[ac]

B. **Attitude toward retiring**

Examples:

There is nothing worse I can think of than having to retire.[d]

In general, how do you feel about eventually retiring?[h]

Do you personally look forward to retiring, or not?[q]

C. **Attitude toward retirees**

Examples:

Older workers who don't retire when they can afford to are foolish.[j]

Older people should be forced to retire at some age so as to open up jobs and promotions for younger people.[q]

Retirees are a burden on society.[s]

Older people are valuable because of their experience.[v]

II. ***Beliefs & Expectations*** (attributes of retirement) if expectations are heavily valenced, they become attitudes

Examples:

Retirement leads to premature death.[d]

Retirement causes people to suffer from mental problems.[d]

When people retire, they lose touch with who they are.[d]

It will be hard to replace my friends from work.[d]

I will probably be sitting around alone after I retire.[d]

I feel that retirement will allow me to enjoy more leisure activities.[g]

Retirement means that one is no longer contributing to society.[m]

Retirement gives people a chance to reestablish relations with old friends and meet new people.[m]

In the first three years after retirement, the health of the retiree may improve.[m]

Retirement is an opportunity to pursue interests and new work options.[n]

When I retire, I won't worry about money because I can always work part-time.[n]

I don't need to plan for retirement because it won't be there anyway.[n]

(Continued)

Table 15.3 (Continued)

Construct Categories

III. *Preferences/Desires for Retirement Age or Type* (If I had my choice..., [may/may not be realistic]; partial vs. complete retirement; on-time vs. early retirement)

Examples:

At what age would you like to retire?[b]

If it were possible to choose between work and retirement, what would you choose?[c]

I would like to retire in the near future.[f]

When would you prefer to retire?[g]

Here is a list of things that people do about work when they get on in years. Assuming you would have an adequate amount of retirement income, which one of the things on this list would you prefer to do?[q]

—Retire when I reach the normal retirement age for my employment

—Retire before I reach the normal retirement age for my employment

—Retire at a normal or early retirement age for my employment and take a job with another employer

—Instead of retiring, continue to work full-time as long as I can at the same job and the same pay

—Instead of retiring, continue to work full-time as long as I can at a less demanding job with less pay

—Instead of retiring, continue to work part-time as long as I can

—Other

—Not sure

And at what age would you prefer to (retire/retire before normal retirement/take a less demanding job)?[q]

If for some reason you were permanently to lose your present job tomorrow, what would you do? If "other," specify here _____.[z]

If by some chance you were to get enough money to live comfortably without working, do you think that you would work anyway?[z]

IV. *Intentions* (what one intends to actually do)

Examples:

I plan to retire in the near future.[f]

When do you plan to retire?[g]

Now which one of the things on this list are you actually most likely to do?[q]

—Retire when I reach the normal retirement age for my employment

—Retire before I reach the normal retirement age for my employment

—Retire at a normal or early retirement age for my employment and take a job with another employer

—Instead of retiring, continue to work full-time as long as I can at the same job and the same pay

—Instead of retiring, continue to work full-time as long as I can at a less demanding job with less pay

—Instead of retiring, continue to work part-time as long as I can

—Other

—Not sure

And at what age are you most likely to (retire/take a less demanding job)?[q]

V. *Planning/Preparation Activities* (e.g., saving money, investing in retirement account, etc.; includes having retirement goals, maintaining human capital/skills)

Examples:

Have you considered applying for a disability pension, private disability pension, or any other pension?[c]

I have already made plans for what I am going to do as soon as I retire.[d]

I feel it is pointless to plan for retirement because it is too far away to know what I will need.[e]

I think preparing for retirement takes too much time and effort.[e]

VI. *Efficacy, or Perceived Control* (ability to retire, if I wanted to; includes belief that pension, social security, etc., will exist)

Examples:

At what age do you expect you could realistically retire?[b]

I expect to begin collecting a pension in the near future.[f]

My pension will be adequate to meet my financial needs after retirement.[g]

Is there a compulsory retirement plan where you work; that is, do you have to stop working at your present job at a certain age? At what age?[z]

Table 15.3 (Continued)

Construct Categories

VII. ***Entitlement*** (a person who works hard deserves to be able to retire…)
Examples:
I think that people should have the opportunity to retire early.[a]
After a lifetime of work, a person should be entitled to some years of leisure.[m]

Note: Superscripts indicate references for the items, which correspond to the reference superscripts listed in Table 2; e.g., [a] = Van Dam et al., 2009; [b] = Zappala et al., 2008; etc.

retirement constructs. The nine categories of retirement constructs measured by retirement attitude scales are (a) attitudes toward *retirement* (the role state of being retired), (b) attitudes toward *retiring* (the role transition decision), (c) attitudes toward *retirees* (including stereotypes about retired persons), (d) beliefs and expectations about retirement (attributes of retirement; what it is like), (e) retirement preferences/desires (e.g., "if I had a choice, I would retire at age 55…"), (f) behavioral intentions (what one intends to do), (g) planning/preparation activities (e.g., saving money), (h) retirement efficacy or perceived control (ability to retire), and (i) retirement entitlement (e.g., the belief that a person who works hard does or does not deserve to be able to retire). Whether these nine conceptually distinct content areas are empirically distinct remains an open question. Given that many established retirement attitude instruments combine content across these domains, we expect that these nine categories of retirement constructs might strongly overlap in practice. In theory, however, these retirement construct categories play specific roles in the retirement attitude-behavior system.

Next, we review models of retirement attitudes that attempt to clarify the relative nomological positions of the above sets of constructs. These models will draw functional distinctions, for instance, between attitudes toward retirement (i.e., the role state) versus efficacy/perceived control over retiring, versus attitudes toward retiring (i.e., the role transition decision).

Retirement Attitude-Behavior Relationships

One of the presumed reasons researchers and practitioners have been interested in retirement attitudes is the theorized association between retirement attitudes and behavior. This attitude-behavior connection has been emphasized in models of the retirement process (see Feldman, 1994; Wang & Shultz, 2010; cf. Beehr, 1986), which have generally specified the role of attitudes (both retirement attitudes and job attitudes) in voluntary retirement behavior. In the current chapter, we discuss retirement attitudes in light of two general models of the attitude-behavior relationship: (a) the theory of planned behavior (Ajzen, 1991) and (b) the attitude-engagement model (Harrison, Newman, & Roth, 2006). These two models are generically compared in Table 15.4, where it is shown that the theory of planned behavior focuses on specific attitudes toward a specific behavior enacted in a particular context and timeframe (e.g., the behavioral retiring decision; see Ajzen & Fishbein, 1977), whereas the attitude-engagement model focuses on general attitudes toward one's role (e.g., job satisfaction) and general behavioral syndromes (e.g., organizational withdrawal, behavioral engagement). The two models are described in more detail below, and we attempt to apply both models to the phenomenon of retirement.

The Theory of Planned Behavior

The theory of planned behavior (TPB; Ajzen, 1991; 1988) is an extension of Fishbein and Ajzen's (1975) theory of reasoned action. In the TPB (see Figure 15.3), attitudes are related to behavior by way of behavioral intentions. [As an aside, we note that whereas Ajzen (1991) defines behavioral intentions broadly as "the motivational factors that influence a behavior" (p. 181), the section below describes more fine-grained distinctions between behavioral intentions, behavioral self-predictions, and behavioral desires]. Ajzen's (1991) theory focuses on attitudes toward the behavior (e.g., attitudes toward *retiring*) rather than attitudes toward the role (e.g., attitudes toward *retirement*). *Attitudes toward retiring* can be conceptualized under the expectancy-value model as a sum of the products of behavioral beliefs (i.e., associations between a behavior and an attribute or outcome; e.g., "retirement leads to premature death") and the evaluation of that attribute

Table 15.4 Models of the Attitude-Behavior Relationship

Theoretical Model	References	Attitudinal Construct	Behavioral Construct	Other Related Constructs
Theory of Planned Behavior	Ajzen (1991, 1988, 2002); Fishbein & Ajzen (1975)	Attitude toward the potential future behavior (retiring)	Specific behavior (e.g., "retiring from this job at age 65")	Behavioral beliefs, subjective norm, perceived behavioral control, behavioral intentions
Attitude-Engagement Model	Harrison, Newman, & Roth (2006); Newman, Joseph, & Hulin (2010) [see Fishbein & Ajzen (1974); Fisher (1980); Hanisch & Hulin (1991); March & Simon (1958)]	Attitude toward the current role state (job satisfaction)	General behavioral syndrome (e.g., the *behavioral engagement* construct)	Absence, lateness, turnover, organizational citizenship, job performance

or outcome (e.g., "death is bad"). That is, attitude toward retiring would be indexed as the product of "retirement leads to premature death" × "death is bad" (see Ajzen & Fishbein, 2008). Alternatively, attitudes toward the behavior (retiring) can be measured via direct measures [e.g., "Retiring from work at age 65 is (extremely good/extremely bad)"].

In the TPB model, behavioral intentions are additionally predicted by subjective norms and perceived behavioral control (Figure 15.3). Subjective norms are the summed product of descriptive normative beliefs ("Most of my friends retired when they were 65 years old") weighted by identification with the referent ("When it comes to retirement, how much do you want to be like your friends?"). Subjective norms can alternatively be measured as

injunctive normative beliefs (e.g., "My children think that I should retire when I am 65 years old") weighted by the motivation to comply (e.g., "When it comes to retirement, I want to do what my children think I should do") and summed across beliefs (cf. Manning, 2009, who suggests that descriptive norms predict behavior better than do injunctive norms). As yet another measurement alternative, subjective norms can be measured directly (e.g., "Most people who are important to me think that I should retire when I am 65 years old").

Intentions are also predicted by perceived behavioral control (Figure 15.3). The notion of perceived behavioral control is the key construct that distinguishes TPB from its precursor theory of reasoned action (Fishbein & Ajzen, 1975), and it captures

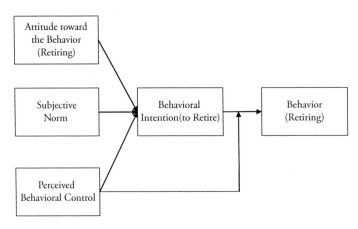

Figure 15.3 Theory of Planned Behavior for Retiring from Work

the extent to which, for example, the retiring behavior is voluntary/under volitional control and can thus be predicted by intentions alone (Ajzen, 2002). Perceived behavioral control can be indexed as the summed product of control belief strength ("I expect that I will have built up a retirement benefit of 50% of my current annual income when I am 65") with power of control ("Having a retirement benefit of 50% of my current annual income would enable me to retire when I am 65"). Perceived behavioral control can also be measured directly (e.g., "Whether or not I retire when I am 65 is completely up to me"). Finally, the link between intentions and the actual behavior is moderated by perceived behavioral control (see Figure 15.3), such that intentions are more likely to manifest in behavior when one perceives high behavioral control.

Meta-analytic evidence supports several contentions from the TPB (Figure 15.3). Armitage and Conner (2001) showed via large-scale meta-analysis that attitude, subjective norm, and perceived behavioral control each accounted for unique variance in behavioral intentions (together accounting for 39% of the variance in behavioral intentions, $R_{TPB,\text{int}ent} = 0.63$; $r_{attitude,\text{int}ent} = 0.49$; $r_{norm,\text{int}ent} = 0.34$; $r_{control,\text{int}ent} = 0.43$). The three predictors also accounted for 20% of the variance in observed behavior ($R_{TPB,behav} = 0.44$) and 31% of the variance in self-reported behavior ($R_{TPB,behav} = 0.55$). Behavioral intentions correlated $r_{\text{int}ent,behav} = 0.47$ with behavior, on average.

Armitage and Conner (2001) further drew distinctions between behavioral intentions (e.g., "I intend to perform behavior X"), behavioral self-predictions (e.g., "I am likely to perform behavior X"), and behavioral desires (e.g., "I want to perform behavior X"). Perhaps not surprisingly, the three TPB variables predicted behavioral desires more strongly ($R_{TPB,desires} = 0.73$) than they predicted behavioral intentions and self-predictions ($R_{TPB,strict\_\text{int}ent} = 0.57$; $R_{TPB,self\_predictions} = 0.58$). Also, perceived behavioral control captured meaningful incremental variance for predicting behavioral intentions ($\Delta R^2 = 0.08$) and self-predictions ($\Delta R^2 = 0.07$), but perceived behavioral control was less relevant when predicting desires ($\Delta R^2 = 0.02$). Finally, intentions and self-predictions predicted behavior better than desires did, although zero-order correlations for these effects were not reported. In short, the data from TPB studies indicate that attitudes toward behavior and subjective norms very strongly predict behavioral desires; that attitudes, norms, and perceived behavioral control together strongly predict behavioral intentions; and

that behavioral intentions predict behavior better than desires do. Thus empirical effect sizes indicate that the TPB (Ajzen, 1991; Figure 15.3) is strongly supported, on average.

More recent research has suggested possible extensions to the TPB. For example, Ajzen, Czasch, and Flood (2009) suggested that the intention-behavior relationship is stronger for individuals with conscientious personalities. Further, Rise, Sheeran, and Hukkelberg (2010) conducted a meta-analysis to support the inclusion of *self-identity* as a unique predictor alongside the other three TPB antecedents of behavioral intentions (unique $\Delta R^2 = 0.06$ for self-identity). Self-identity involves the use of socially meaningful categories to describe oneself [e.g., "I think of myself as a…" (professor, plumber, father, blood donor)]. Rise et al.'s (2010) meta-analytic results suggested that self-identity and attitudes toward the behavior were the two strongest unique predictors of behavioral intentions ($\beta = 0.28$ & 0.29, respectively), whereas subjective norms and perceived behavioral control were less strong, albeit still meaningful unique predictors of behavioral intentions (both βs = 0.18). These results have particularly major implications for TPB models of the relationship between attitudes toward retiring and retiring behavior (Figure 15.3) because they suggest that TPB models of retirement attitudes should be supplemented with notions of self-identity and the salient social roles that are served by one's job.

As another extension of TPB, Rivis, Sheeran, and Armitage (2009) showed meta-analytically that anticipated affect (e.g., anticipated joy, anticipated regret) after performing the behavior was also a meaningful unique predictor of behavioral intentions, controlling for the three TPB antecedents ($\beta = 0.26$; unique $\Delta R^2 = 0.05$ for anticipated affect). Thus the anticipation of emotion (regret, happiness) following retirement is an area that likely merits further investigation when developing retirement attitude-behavior models that extend the specifications in Figure 15.3.

We now note that the above results regarding the theory of planned behavior align nicely with several of the categories of attitude measures identified in the above review of instruments used to assess retirement attitudes (Table 15.3). First, the TPB model (Figure 15.3) explicitly specifies four of the construct categories reviewed: attitude toward retiring, beliefs and expectations about retirement (as antecedents and components of attitudes toward retiring), perceived control/efficacy, and retiring behavioral intentions. Further, the recent extensions of TPB (reviewed above) suggest the importance of all five additional construct categories: preferences/desire for retirement age or type [Armitage and Conner's (2001) results, if generalizable, imply desire for retiring would be strongly predicted by attitude toward retiring and by subjective norm but would predict retiring behavior less strongly than would retirement intentions], attitudes toward retirement (including anticipated affect, regret), attitudes toward retirees (which influence the degree to which one's social identity affects the desire to retire—if the attitudes toward retirees are negative or inconsistent with one's social identity, then desire to retire should be low; retirement entitlement beliefs also fit in here, as they are beliefs about whether retirees are deserving), and planning/preparation activities (as antecedents of perceived control/efficacy). Thus, all nine of the categories of retirement attitude constructs (see Table 15.3) can be incorporated into an extended TPB model of retirement attitude-behavior relations. Figure 15.4 illustrates how the sets of constructs identified in the retirement instruments reviewed above can be incorporated into our extended TPB model for retirement. One major attitude construct conspicuously missing from the Figure 15.4 [extended TPB] model is job satisfaction (i.e., attitude toward the current work role). These attitudes are considered in the attitude-engagement model, reviewed next.

The Attitude-Engagement Model

The attitude-engagement model (Harrison, Newman, & Roth, 2006) deals with relationships between attitudes toward one's current role (e.g., job satisfaction) and behavioral outcomes. This model is depicted in Figure 15.5. The attitude-engagement model was developed from earlier ideas articulated by Fishbein and Ajzen (1974); Fisher (1980); Hanisch, Hulin, and Roznowski (1998); and March and Simon (1958). In particular, Harrison et al.'s (2006) attitude-engagement model attempts to resolve a longstanding puzzle about the meager observed relationships between job satisfaction and work behavior (Brayfield & Crockett, 1955; Iaffaldano & Muchinsky, 1985; Judge, Thoresen, Bono, & Patton, 2001) by noting that *a broad attitude predicts a broad behavioral criterion* (see Fishbein & Ajzen, 1974). The attitude-engagement model conceptualizes a broad behavioral criterion—labeled *behavioral engagement* (see Figure 15.5; Newman & Harrison, 2008)—which (a) is specified as the latent behavioral factor that mutually underlies job performance, organizational citizenship behavior, and withdrawal behaviors including lateness, absenteeism, and turnover, and (b) is defined as the general "tendency to contribute desirable inputs toward one's work role" (Harrison et al., 2006, p. 309). Since the introduction of Harrison et al.'s (2006) model, Newman, Joseph, and Hulin (2010) have expanded the model to include job involvement as an attitude measure and to subsume Hanisch's (1995) organizational withdrawal construct (see Hulin, 1991; Hanisch & Hulin, 1990, 1991). The version of the model shown in Figure 15.5 also lists *retirement* as a behavioral indicator of withdrawal, along with turnover (cf. Newman et al., 2010; see Hanisch, 1995).

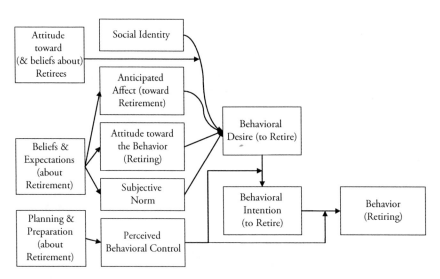

Figure 15.4 Extended Theory of Planned Behavior Model for Retiring from Work

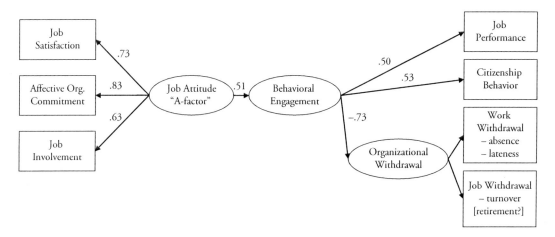

Figure 15.5 The Attitude-Engagement Model (Harrison, Newman, & Roth, 2006; updated by Newman, Joseph, & Hulin, 2010, to include organizational withdrawal construct and job involvement)

Note: Parameter estimates are from Newman, Joseph, & Hulin's (2010) meta-analysis (RMSEA = 0.067; CFI = 0.96; harmonic mean N = 2,231), although Newman et al.'s (2010) analysis did not include measures of retirement behavior.

Empirical evidence from meta-analysis has supported the attitude-engagement model (Harrison et al., 2006). For the model in Figure 15.5, Newman et al. (2010) reported adequate goodness of fit to meta-analytic correlational data (RMSEA = 0.067; CFI = 0.96; harmonic mean N = 2,231). The key finding from the attitude-engagement model is that the latent attitude-behavior correlation is greater than 0.5 (i.e., job attitudes strongly predict work behavior when both attitude and behavior are conceptualized at a broad level of abstraction; Harrison et al., 2006; Newman et al., 2010). Also, work behavior concepts (job performance, citizenship behavior, and withdrawal) exhibit adequate factor loadings onto the broad behavioral engagement construct (Figure 15.5; all input correlations were based upon non-common-source measures, which are not inflated by percept-percept bias), while job attitude constructs (job satisfaction, organizational commitment, and job involvement) load onto the higher-order attitude "A-factor" (Figure 15.5; Newman et al., 2010). In short, the attitude-engagement model seems to fit the available data well, and all the theorized parameter estimates are adequate or large. Broad attitudes (i.e., the "A-factor") predict broad behaviors (i.e., "behavioral engagement").

What implications does the attitude-engagement model have for the study of retirement attitudes? First, the model suggests that retirement behavior is a reflection of a more general *withdrawal construct*, which can also be manifested through other withdrawal behaviors, such as absence and turnover (Figure 15.5). Similarly, the withdrawal construct

itself is a reflection of a more general behavioral engagement construct that also manifests through job performance and organizational citizenship behavior (Figure 15.5). Second, unlike the theory of planned behavior (Ajzen, 1991), which focuses on specific attitudes toward the behavior, the attitude-engagement model directly involves attitudes toward one's current job role; i.e., job satisfaction (cf. Thibaut & Kelley, 1959). Individuals who experience negative job attitudes (low job satisfaction) are likely to have a tendency to withhold desirable behavioral inputs from their work roles, and *retirement* is one of several possible courses of action through which work inputs/behavioral engagement can be reduced. The implication for job attitudes research is that job attitudes are very strongly related to the broad, behavioral engagement construct (correlation >0.5; Harrison et al., 2006). However, bivariate correlations between job satisfaction and retirement behavior are likely to be much smaller in magnitude (i.e., meta-analytic r = –0.02; k = 11; N = 9,764; Topa et al., 2009) because job satisfaction and retirement are each an imperfect indicator of the corresponding latent construct (see Figure 15.5). There are likely to be many important predictors of one's retirement decision other than job satisfaction (Johns, 1998; Topa et al., 2009; Wang & Shultz, 2010).

One final, albeit major implication of the attitude-engagement model depicted in Figure 15.5 is that retirement can be thought of as a form of job withdrawal (Hanisch & Hulin, 1991) similar to turnover. In fact, *voluntary retirement* (e.g., in countries that do not have a mandatory retirement age, or among individuals who have the discretion and capability to choose when they will retire) *is explicitly a form of turnover*. As such, dominant models of turnover may be informative when attempting to characterize the relationship between attitudes and retirement. Two of these models are Mobley's (1977) model of turnover and Lee and Mitchell's (1994) unfolding model of voluntary turnover. In Mobley's (1977) model, job (dis)satisfaction leads to turnover by way of a series of mediators, including (in causal order): thinking of quitting, evaluation of expected utility of search and cost of quitting, intention to search for alternatives, search for alternatives, evaluation of alternatives, comparison of alternatives vs. present job, intention to quit/stay, and finally decision to quit/stay. A similar sequence may link job satisfaction to retirement. The fact that there are so many intermediate steps may help explain why the satisfaction-retirement correlation is so low: because a causal bottleneck may occur at any step in the long sequence. In Lee and Mitchell's (1994) unfolding model, there are four proposed paths by which individuals decide to quit their jobs. These paths variously involve (or do not involve) *a shock* or jarring event (e.g., a financial incentive offered for retiring, a health problem, company layoffs); the engagement of a *script* or pre-existing plan of action; an *image violation* in which the individual's values and goals are perceived to not fit with the employing organization's; *lowered satisfaction*, which comes from loss of intellectual, emotional, or other job benefits; and, finally, *search for alternatives* and anticipated *likelihood of another offer*. The key insight is that leaving one's job can sometimes stem from two paths that are causally independent of job satisfaction levels: (a) a shock that engages a preexisting script to leave (e.g., an unanticipated retirement opportunity, an episode of abusive supervision, a negative health event, health problem of a spouse), or (b) a shock that produces an image violation that in turn causes one to leave (e.g., perception that one's values/ethics are violated by the organization, or that one's goals cannot be achieved in the organization; see Lee, Mitchell, Holtom, McDaniel, & Hill, 1999). If the unfolding model were generalized to the retirement decision, then the idea that people can decide to leave their jobs for reasons totally unrelated to job satisfaction may also help explain the small correlation between satisfaction and retirement. Given the close conceptual link between turnover and retirement in the attitude-engagement model, it seems the application

of Mobley's (1977) intermediate linkages model or of Lee and Mitchell's (1994) unfolding model to the retirement process may prove informative.

In the above section we reviewed two models of the attitude-behavior relationship that pertain to retirement. The extended theory of planned behavior for retiring from work (Figure 15.4) dealt with attitudes toward the retiring behavior itself (attitudes toward the role transition decision), whereas the attitude-engagement model dealt with broad attitudes toward the current job role (job satisfaction) and the broad behavioral syndrome of behavioral engagement—of which retirement is simply a specific, lower-order instantiation. The use of these two models reinforces the point that a specific attitude predicts a specific behavior, whereas a broad attitude predicts a broad behavioral construct (Ajzen & Fishbein, 1977).

Retirement Ambivalence

The dominant viewpoint on attitude research within the field of organizational psychology has involved treating attitudes as a directional, bipolar continuum of evaluation that ranges from positive to negative. When discussing retirement attitudes, we assert that it might be useful to consider the notion of attitudinal ambivalence (Kaplan, 1972; Scott, 1969). Attitudinal ambivalence involves conditions where "an individual has the opportunity to simultaneously indicate both a favorable and an unfavorable attitude toward a given stimulus object" (Kaplan, 1972, p. 362)—that is, experiencing a positive evaluation and a negative evaluation at the same time. Two types of ambivalence have been distinguished (see reviews by Fabrigar, MacDonald, & Wegener, 2005, and Kruglanski & Stroebe, 2005): (a) within-dimension ambivalence—when an attitude object is associated with both positive and negative beliefs, or both positive and negative emotions, and (b) between-dimension ambivalence—when an attitude object is subject to affective-cognitive inconsistency, or to evaluative-affective inconsistency. We deal here with the former type of ambivalence only. The measurement of attitudinal ambivalence generally follows one of two strategies: (a) direct measurement of ambivalence—subjective reports of experienced tension, conflict, mixed feelings, and indecision, or (b) indirect measurement of ambivalence—based on elicitation of both positive and negative reactions (thoughts and feelings) toward an attitude object, after which the more numerous reactions (e.g., positive reactions) are categorized as *dominant reactions*, while the minority/

less numerous reactions (e.g., negative reactions) are categorized as *conflicting reactions*; these two quantities—the integer number of dominant reactions and the number of conflicting reactions—are then combined numerically using one of a half-dozen available formulas to index the level of ambivalence toward the object (see summary by Priester & Petty, 1996). [As an aside, we note that in contrast to this common measurement strategy, it is also conceptually possible to consider the *stronger* type of reaction (e.g., negative reaction) or *more salient* type of reaction as dominant, even if this type of reaction is *less numerous* when reactions are elicited.] Generally, ambivalence is thought to be high under two conditions: when the positive and negative reaction components are similar in magnitude, and when both components have at least moderate intensity (Thompson, Zanna, & Griffin, 1995).

One thought-provoking representation of attitudes (and of attitudinal ambivalence) comes from the associative network metaphor (Fazio, 1995). In this representation, an *attitude* is thought of as a link or association between two nodes: an attitude object node and an evaluative node (positive or negative evaluation). For example, attitude toward retirement is a link between the retirement node (i.e., the attitude object) and the positive evaluation node (i.e., the evaluation node). In this framework, *ambivalence* can be depicted as the simultaneous association of an attitude object with both the positive evaluation node and the negative evaluation node. To add to this, a *belief* can be represented as an association between an attitude object and an attribute (Fishbein & Ajzen, 1975). One example of such a belief is the association between the attitude object *retirement* and the attribute *boredom/idleness*. This belief could be stated as such: "Retirement is a period of idleness when one has little to occupy his or her time." An example of a network representation of retirement ambivalence is shown in Figure 15.6.

On the left-hand side of Figure 15.6, we see the attitude object nodes *retirement* and *work*—each representing a particular role state about which an individual might have attitudinal evaluations or beliefs. In the center of Figure 15.6, we see a column of attribute nodes (e.g., money, loss of identity, leisure, health, death/mortality, family time) that might each be associated with the attitude object node *retirement*. These links (e.g., between retirement and leisure) represent beliefs. Lastly, we see connections between the attributes in the center of Figure 15.6 and the positive and negative

evaluative nodes on the right-hand side of Figure 15.6. In the example shown in Figure 15.6, money, health, and leisure attributes are linked to the positive evaluation node, whereas death, boredom, and loneliness attributes are linked to the negative evaluation node. The point of Figure 15.6 is to convey that a simple measure of the association between retirement and the positive evaluation (i.e., *attitude toward retirement*) masks a much more elaborate system of beliefs about the attributes of retirement, which can be evaluated as simultaneously both positive and negative. Given the likelihood that this sort of schema can exist in the mind of an employee, we here posit that retirement attitude research should consider the notion of *retirement ambivalence*—the simultaneous possession of both positive and negative evaluations of retirement, which are similar in magnitude and at least moderate in strength.

What are the consequences of attitudinal ambivalence? We note past researchers have suggested that ambivalence is related to lower accessibility of the overall attitudinal evaluation (longer response latency—likely due to indecision or to the extra effort required to resolve conflicting reactions; see review by Jonas, Bromer, & Diehl, 2000). In other words, ambivalent individuals should take longer to formulate or express their retirement attitudes. Also, initial ambivalence may lead to greater consistency between the final attitude toward behavior and behavioral intentions (likely due to the role of ambivalence in eliciting more systematic processing of relevant information; see Jonas, Diehl, & Bromer, 1997; Maio, Esses, & Bell, 2000). Thus individuals with retirement ambivalence may exhibit behavioral intentions more consistent with their retirement attitudes, once those attitudes have been formed.

Where does ambivalence come from? In terms of personality, individuals who have chronic concerns about making errors tend to be more ambivalent, whereas those with high need for cognition exhibit lower levels of ambivalence (Thompson & Zanna, 1995; see Kruglanski & Stroebe, 2005). Ambivalence may also be rooted in conflicting value systems that an individual may hold simultaneously (Katz & Hass, 1988). Another theoretical viewpoint emphasizes the role of attitude change over time in the origins of ambivalence. Specifically, the PAST model (Past Attitudes are Still There) of attitude change is a metacognitive perspective of persuasion, which states that when prior attitudes are no longer considered appropriate, the rejected attitude does not disappear but stays with a different label ("wrong idea"). The prior attitude will influence

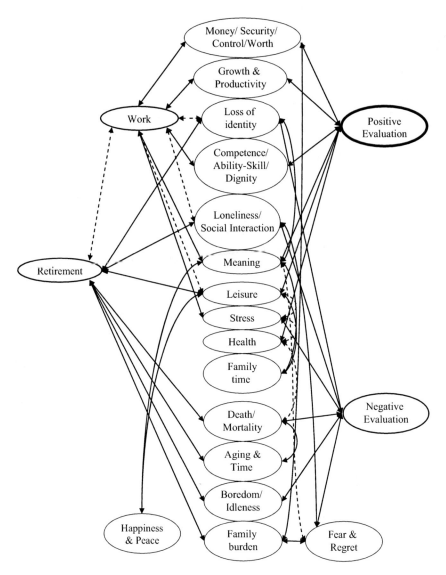

Figure 15.6 Retirement Ambivalence Schema (dotted line = negative association)

the new attitude, and the transition from the prior attitude to the new attitude may seem like attitudinal ambivalence (Petty, Tormala, Brinol, & Jarvis, 2006). More importantly, when prior and current attitudes conflict, they can lead to a state of implicit ambivalence and together influence the current response. This model may explain the implicit attitudes of those who do not hold an explicit attitude toward retirement. Although one does not seem to have a strong attitude toward the idea of retirement at the moment, one may be influenced by her or his own prior attitudes toward any aspect of retirement. Finally, ambivalence may arise because both work and retirement are very complex situations/roles containing both positive and negative attributes and

outcomes. Ambivalence results from having to consider both the positive and negative outcomes that will be associated with whichever of the roles one chooses. Given the life-changing importance of the retirement decision and its centrality to one's identity and values (described in the opening paragraphs of this chapter), the length of time over which individuals consider this major decision, and the number of stakeholders usually involved in retirement outcomes, it is our position that retirement is an attitude object particularly prone to ambivalence. Predictions of behaviors enacted as a result of retirement ambivalence are likely to be influenced by multiple sources of variance yet to be explored. This area awaits future research.

Conclusions

In this chapter, we have attempted to accomplish five objectives. First, we developed a model of the origins of retirement attitudes based upon an extension of the Cornell model (Judge et al., in press; Smith et al., 1969). This model emphasized a role comparison process (i.e., work role versus retirement role), in light of individual personality processes (e.g., individual differences in the choice of frames of reference). Second, we reviewed the major measures of retirement attitudes, to identify nine categories of scientific constructs that these retirement measures reflect. Third, we integrated all nine categories of retirement attitude constructs into an extended theory of planned behavior model for retirement from work (Figure 15.4). This model adapts the original theory of planned behavior (Ajzen, 1988) by considering social identity, attitudes (and anticipated affect) toward retirement, attitudes toward retirees, planning and preparation activities, and desire/preference for retirement. This extended theory of planned behavior model should be tested in future research, with the goal of predicting and explaining the specific, narrow behavior of individual retirement decisions. Fourth, we described the attitude-engagement model as a way of connecting work role evaluations (e.g., job satisfaction) with behavioral outcomes conceptualized at a very broad level of abstraction (e.g., retirement is a lower-order reflection of job withdrawal, which in turn is a reflection of organizational withdrawal, which is a reflection of the broad behavioral engagement construct, which is strongly correlated with the broad job attitude construct; Figure 15.5). The attitude-engagement model also highlights the conceptual similarity between retirement and turnover, implying that established attitude-turnover models might generalize as attitude-retirement models, at least in some circumstances. Fifth and finally, we introduced the notion of retirement ambivalence, which stems from simultaneously associating retirement with both positive and negative attributes. Retirement ambivalence, and the attempted resolution of ambivalence that occurs prior to making a decision of whether to retire or not, may result in a set of retirement attitudes that defy simple explanations.

In all, we have discussed where retirement attitudes come from, how they are measured, how different elements of the retirement attitude construct space combine in the prediction of retirement behavior, and the novel idea that retirement attitudes may mask a complex system of both positive and negative evaluations concurrently held. Throughout the chapter, our goal was to introduce provocative models and ideas for future research on retirement attitudes, rather than simply to review past findings on the topic. We hope that eventual tests of these ideas and models will offer new insights for retirement researchers.

References

Adams, G. A., & Beehr, T. A. (1988). Turnover and retirement: A comparison of their similarities and differences. *Personnel Psychology, 51,* 643–664.

Ajzen, I. (1988). *Attitudes, personality, and behavior.* Homewood, IL: Dorsey Press.

Ajzen, I. (1991). The theory of planned behavior. *Organizational Behavior and Human Decision Processes. Special Issue: Theories of Cognitive Self-Regulation, 50*(2), 179–211.

Ajzen, I. (2002). Perceived behavioral control, self-efficacy, locus of control, and the theory of planned behavior. *Journal of Applied Social Psychology, 32*(4), 665–683.

Ajzen, I., Czasch, C., & Flood, M. G. (2009). From intentions to behavior: Implementation intention, commitment, and conscientiousness. *Journal of Applied Social Psychology, 39*(6), 1356–1372.

Ajzen, I., & Fishbein, M. (1977). Attitude-behavior relations: A theoretical analysis and review of empirical research. *Psychological Bulletin, 84*(5), 888–918.

Ajzen, I., & Fishbein, M. (2008). Scaling and testing multiplicative combinations in the expectancy-value model of attitudes. *Journal of Applied Social Psychology, 38*(9), 2222–2247.

American attitudes toward pensions and retirement: Hearing before the Select Committee on Aging, House of Representatives, 96th Cong. 1 (1979).

Anson, O., Antonovsky, A., & Sagy, S. (1989). Family, gender, and attitudes toward retirement. *Sex Roles, 20,* 355–369.

Armitage, C. J., & Conner, M. (2001). Efficacy of the theory of planned behaviour: A meta-analytic review. *British Journal of Social Psychology, 40*(4), 471–499.

Atchley, R. C., & Robinson, J. L. (1982). Attitudes toward retirement and distance from the event. *Research on Aging, 4,* 299–313.

Beehr, T. A. (1986). The process of retirement: A review and recommendations for future investigation. *Personnel Psychology, 39,* 31–56.

Brayfield, A. H., & Crockett, W. H. (1955). Employee attitudes and employee performance. *Psychological Bulletin, 52,* 396–424.

Boyak, V. L., & Tiberi, D. M. (1975). *A study of pre-retirement education.* Paper presented at 28th Annual Gerontological Society meeting, Louisville, Kentucky.

Campbell, D. T. (1950). The indirect assessment of social attitudes. *Psychological Bulletin, 47,* 15–38.

Eagly, A. H., & Chaiken, S. (1993). *The psychology of attitudes.* Fort Worth, TX: Harcourt Brace Jovanovich.

Eden, D., & Jacobson, D. (1976). Propensity to retire among older executives. *Journal of Vocational Behavior, 8,* 145–154.

Elovainio, M., Forma, P., Kivimaki, M., Sinervo, T., Sutinen, R., & Laine, M. (2005). Job demands and job control as correlates of early retirement thoughts in Finnish social and health care employees. *Work & Stress, 19*(1), 84–92.

Erdner, R. A., & Guy, R. F. (1990). Career identification and women's attitudes toward retirement. *Aging and Human Development, 30*(2), 129–139.

Fabrigar, L. R., MacDonald, T. K., & Wegener, D. T. (2005). The origin and structure of attitudes. In D. Albarracín, B. T. Johnson, & M. P. Zanna (Eds.), *The handbook of attitudes and attitude change* (pp.79–124). Mahwah, NJ: Erlbaum.

Fazio, R. H. (1995). Attitudes as object-evaluation associations: Determinants, consequences, and correlates of attitude accessibility. In R. E. Petty & J. A. Krosnick (Eds.), *Attitude strength: Antecedents and consequences* (pp. 247–282). Mahwah, NJ: Lawrence Erlbaum Associates.

Feldman, D. C. (1994). The decision to retire early: A review and conceptualization. *Academy of Management Review, 19,* 285–311.

Fishbein, M., & Ajzen, I. (1974). Attitudes towards objects as predictors of single and multiple behavioral criteria. *Psychological Review, 81*(1), 59–74.

Fishbein, M., & Ajzen, I. (1975). *Belief, attitude, intention, and behavior: An introduction to theory and research.* Reading, MA: AddisonWesley.

Fisher, C. D. (1980). On the dubious wisdom of expecting job satisfaction to correlate with performance. *Academy of Management Review, 5,* 607–612.

Glamser, F. D. (1976). Determinants of a positive attitude toward retirement. *Journal of Gerontology, 31*(1), 104–107.

Glazer, J. (1981). Social Security Song (Too Old to Work). In: album *Jellybean Blues,* Collector Records, Silver Spring, MD.

Gordon, E. B. (1994). The relationship of attitudes toward work and toward retirement: A female perspective. *Affilia, 9,* 269–287.

Goudy, W. J., Powers, E. A., & Keith P. (1975). Work and retirement: A test of attitudinal relationships. *Journal of Gerontology, 30*(2), 193–198.

Green, A. (1993). *Wobblies, pilebutts, and other heroes.* Urbana, IL: University of Illinois Press.

Greene, M. R., Pyron, H. C., Manion, U. V, & Winklevos, H. (1969). *Preretirement counseling, retirement adjustment, and the older employee.* Eugene, OR: University of Oregon, Graduate School of Management and Business, College of Business Administration.

Hanisch, K. A. (1990). *A causal model of general attitudes, work withdrawal, and job withdrawal, including retirement* (Doctoral dissertation). Retrieved from ProQuest Dissertations and Theses Database. (AAT9114258)

Hanisch, K. A. (1995). Behavioral families and multiple causes: Matching the complexity of responses to the complexity of antecedents. *Current Directions in Psychological Science, 4*(5), 156–162.

Hanisch, K. A., & Hulin, C. L. (1990). Job attitudes and organizational withdrawal: An examination of retirement and other voluntary withdrawal behaviors. *Journal of Vocational Behavior, 37,* 60–78.

Hanisch, K. A., & Hulin, C. L. (1991). General attitudes and organizational withdrawal: An evaluation of a causal model. *Journal of Vocational Behavior, 39*(1), 110–128.

Hanisch, K. A., Hulin, C. L., & Roznowski, M. (1998). The importance of individuals' repertoires of behaviors: The scientific appropriateness of studying multiple behaviors and general attitudes. *Journal of Organizational Behavior, 19,* 463–480.

Harrison, D. A., Newman, D. A., & Roth, P. L. (2006). How important are job attitudes? Meta-analytic comparisons of integrative behavioral outcomes and time sequences. *Academy of Management Journal, 49*(2), 305–325.

Hatch, L. R. (1992). Gender differences in orientation toward retirement from paid labor. *Gender & Society, 6,* 66–85.

Hulin, C. (1991). Adaptation, persistence, and commitment in organizations. In M. D. Dunnette & L. M. Hough (Eds.), *Handbook of industrial and organizational psychology* (Vol. 2, 2nd ed., pp. 445–505). Palo Alto, CA: Consulting Psychologists Press.

Hulin, C. L. (1966). Effects of community characteristics on measures of job satisfaction. *Journal of Applied Psychology, 50*(2), 185–192.

Hulin, C.L. (in press). Work and being: The meanings of work in contemporary society. Festschrift for Dan Ilgen and Neil Schmidt.

Iaffaldano, M. T., & Muchinsky, P. M. (1985). Job satisfaction and job performance: A meta-analysis. *Psychological Bulletin, 97,* 25–273.

Jacobson, D. (1972). Fatigue-producing factors in industrial work and pre-retirement attitudes. *Occupational Psychology, 46,* 193–200.

Johns, G. (1998). Aggregation or aggravation: The relative merits of a broad withdrawal construct. *Journal of Organizational Behavior, 19,* 453–462.

Jonas, K., Bromer, P., & Diehl, M. (2000). Attitudinal ambivalence. In W. Stroebe & M. Hewstone (Eds.), *European review of social psychology* (Vol. 11, pp. 35–74). Chichester, United Kingdom: Wiley.

Jonas, K., Diehl, M., & Bromer, P. (1997). Effects of attitudinal ambivalence on information processing and attitude-intention consistency. *Journal of Experimental Social Psychology, 33,* 190–210.

Joo, S., & Grable, J. E. (2001). Factors associated with seeking and using professional retirement-planning help. *Family and Consumer Sciences Research Journal, 30,* 37–63.

Joseph, D. L., & Newman, D. A. (2010). Emotional intelligence: An integrative meta-analysis and cascading model. *Journal of Applied Psychology, 95*(1), 54–78.

Judge, T. A., Bono, J. E., & Locke, E. A. (2000). Personality and job satisfaction: The mediating role of job characteristics. *Journal of Applied Psychology, 85*(2), 237–249.

Judge, T. A. Heller, D., & Mount, M. K. (2002). Five-factor model of personality and job satisfaction: A meta-analysis. *Journal of Applied Psychology, 87*(3), 530–541.

Judge, T. A., & Larsen, R. J. (2001). Dispositional affect and job satisfaction: A review and theoretical extension. *Organizational Behavior and Human Decision Processes. Special Issue: Affect at Work: Collaborations of Basic and Organizational Research, 86*(1), 67–98.

Judge, T. A., Thoresen, C. J., Bono, J. E., & Patton, G. K. (2001). The job satisfaction–job performance relationship: A qualitative and quantitative review. *Psychological Bulletin, 127*(3), 376–407.

Judge, T. R., Hulin, C. L., & Dalal, R. (2012). Job satisfaction and job affect. In S. W. J. Kozlowski (Ed.), *The Oxford handbook of industrial and organizational psychology.* (pp. 496–525) New York, NY: Oxford University Press.

Kaplan, K. J. (1972). On the ambivalence-indifference problem in attitude theory and measurement: A suggested modification of the semantic differential technique. *Psychological Bulletin, 77,* 361–372.

Katz, I., & Hass, R. G. (1988). Racial ambivalence and American value conflict: Correlational and priming studies of dual cognitive structures. *Journal of Personality and Social Psychology, 55*, 893–905.

Kruglanski, A. W., & Stroebe, W. (2005). The influence of beliefs and goals on attitudes: Issues of structure, function, and dynamics. In D. Albarracín, B. T. Johnson, & M. P. Zanna (Eds.), *The handbook of attitudes* (pp. 323–368). Mahwah, NJ: Lawrence Erlbaum Associates.

Larsen, R. J., & Ketelaar, T. (1991). Personality and susceptibility to positive and negative emotional states. *Journal of Personality and Social Psychology, 61*, 132–140.

Lee, T. W., & Mitchell, T. R. (1994). An alternative approach: The unfolding model of voluntary employee turnover. *Academy of Management Review, 19*(1), 51–89.

Lee, T. W., Mitchell, T. R., Holtom, B. C., McDaniel, L. S., & Hill, J. W. (1999). The unfolding model of voluntary turnover: A replication and extension. *Academy of Management Journal, 42*, 450–462.

Lim V. K. (2003). An empirical study of older workers' attitudes towards the retirement experience. *Employee Relations, 25*(4), 330–346.

Maio, G. R., Esses, V. M., & Bell, D. W. (2000). Examining conflict between components of attitudes: Ambivalence and inconsistency are distinct constructs. *Canadian Journal of Behavioural Science, 32*(1), 58–70.

Manning, M. (2009). The effects of subjective norms on behaviour in the theory of planned behaviour: A meta-analysis. *British Journal of Social Psychology, 48*(4), 649–705.

March, J. G., & Simon, H. A. (1958). *Organizations* (3rd ed.). New York, NY: Wiley.

Matthews, A. M., & Brown, K. H. (1987). Retirement as a critical life event: The differential experiences of women and men. *Research on Aging, 9*, 548–571.

McGee, M. G., Hall, J., & Lutes-Dunckley, C. J. (1979). Factors influencing attitude towards retirement. *The Journal of Psychology, 101*, 15–18.

Miljus, R. (1970). The propensity to retire. In H. Parnes, B. Fleisher, R. Miljus, and R. Spiu (Eds.), *The preretirement years* (Vol. 1, pp. 169–202). Washington, DC: U.S. Department of Labor.

Mobley, W. H. (1977). Intermediate linkages in the relationship between job satisfaction and employee turnover. *Journal of Applied Psychology, 62*(2), 237–240.

Newman, D. A., & Harrison, D. A. (2008). Been there, bottled that: Are state and behavioral work engagement new and useful construct "wines"? *Industrial and Organizational Psychology: Perspectives on Science and Practice, 1*(1), 31–35.

Newman, D. A., Joseph, D. L., & Hulin, C. L. (2010). Job attitudes and employee engagement: Considering the attitude "A-factor." In S. Albrecht (Ed.), *The handbook of employee engagement: Perspectives, issues, research and practice* (pp. 43–61). Cheltenham, United Kingdom: Edward Elgar.

Parnes, M. S., & Nestel, G. (1974). *The pre-retirement years* (Vol. 4). Columbus, Ohio: Center for Human Resource Research, Ohio State University.

Petty, R. E., Tormala, Z. L., Brinol, P., & Jarvis, W. B. G. (2006). Implicit ambivalence from attitude change: An exploration of the PAST model. *Journal of Personality and Social Psychology, 90*, 21–41.

Priester, J. R., & Petty, R. E. (1996). The gradual threshold model of ambivalence: Relating the positive and negative bases of attitudes to subjective ambivalence. *Journal of Personality and Social Psychology, 77*, 431–449.

Rise, J., Sheeran, P., & Hukkelberg, S. (2010). The role of self-identity in the theory of planned behavior: A meta-analysis. *Journal of Applied Social Psychology, 40*(5), 1085–1105.

Rivis, A., Sheeran, P., & Armitage, C. J. (2009). Expanding the affective and normative components of the theory of planned behavior: A meta-analysis of anticipated affect and moral norms. *Journal of Applied Social Psychology, 39*(12), 2985–3019.

Roberts, B. W. (2006). Personality development and organizational behavior. *Research in Organizational Behavior, 27*, 1–40.

Roberts, B. W., Caspi, A., & Moffitt, T. (2003). The kids are alright: Growth and stability in personality developments from adolescence to adulthood. *Journal of Personality and Social Psychology, 81*, 670–683.

Roberts, B. W., & Wood, D. (2006). Personality development in the context of the neo-socioanalytic model of personality. In D. Mroczek & T. Little (Eds.), *Handbook of personality development* (pp. 11–30). Mahwah, NJ: Erlbaum.

Scott, W. A. (1969). Structure of natural cognitions. *Journal of personality and social psychology, 12*, 261–278.

Skoglund, J. (1979). Job deprivation in retirement: Anticipated and experienced feelings. *Research on Aging, 1*, 481–493.

Smith, P. C., Kendall, L. M., & Hulin, C. L. (1969). *The measurement of satisfaction in work and retirement: A strategy for the study of attitudes*. Oxford, England: Rand McNally.

Staples, P. A. (1998). *Attitudes toward retirement and lifelong career development among adolescents, young adults, and midlife adults* (Doctoral dissertation). Retrieved from ProQuest Dissertations and Theses Database. (AAT9840698)

Taylor, M. A., & Shore, L. M. (1995). Predictors of planned retirement age: An application of Beehr's model. *Psychology and Aging, 10*(1), 76–83.

Terkel, S. (1974). *Working: People talk about what they do all day and how they feel about what they do*. New York, NY: Pantheon.

Thibaut, J. W., & Kelley, H. H. (1959). *The social psychology of groups*. New York, NY: Wiley.

Thompson, M. M., & Zanna, M. P. (1995). The conflicted individual: Personality-based and domain-specific antecedents of ambivalent social attitudes. *Journal of Personality, 63*, 259–288.

Thompson, M. M., Zanna, M. P., & Griffin, D. W. (1995). Let's not be indifferent about attitudinal ambivalence. In R. E. Petty & J. A. Krosnick (Eds.), *Attitude strength: Antecedents and consequences* (pp. 361–386). Mahwah, NJ: Lawrence Erlbaum.

Thompson, W. E. (1956). *The impact of retirement* (Doctoral dissertation). Retrieved from ProQuest Dissertations and Theses Database. (AAT0017012)

Thompson, W. E., & Streib, G. F. (1958). Situational determinants: Health and economic deprivation in retirement. *Journal of Social Issues, 14*, 18–34.

Topa, G., Moriano, J. A., Depolo, M., Alcover, C., & Morales, J. F. (2009). Antecedents and consequences of retirement planning and decision-making: A meta-analysis and model. *Journal of Vocational Behavior, 75*(1), 38–55.

Turner, M. J., Bailey, W. C., & Scott, J. P. (1994). Factors influencing attitude toward retirement and retirement planning among midlife university employees. *Journal of Applied Gerontology, 13*, 143–156.

Van Dam, K., van der Vorst, J. D. M., & van der Heijden, B. 1. J. M. (2009). Employees' intentions to retire early. *Journal of Career Development, 35*, 265–289.

Wang, M., & Shultz, K. S. (2010). Employee retirement: A review and recommendations for future investigation. *Journal of Management, 36*(1), 172–206.

Zappala, S., Depolo, M., Fraccaroli, F., Guglielmi, D., & Sarchielli, G. (2008). Postponing job retirement? Psychosocial influences on the preference for early or late retirement. *The Career Development International, 13*(2), 150–167.

Planning and Adaptation to Retirement: The Post-retirement Environment, Change Management Resources, and Need-Oriented Factors as Moderators

Mary Anne Taylor *and* Meline Schaffer

Abstract

We propose that the relationship between retirement planning and subsequent adaptation is moderated by two types of fit between personal characteristics and the retirement environment. The first type is the fit between the change in the post-retirement environment and the change management resources of the individual. Dimensions of environmental change include work content, organizational context, work/leisure balance, and conditions of organizational exit. Change management resources include health, motivational/cognitive belief systems related to mastery and control of the environment, personality factors associated with adaptation, social resources, and marketable job skills. The second type of fit is the match between an individual's financial, social, generative, and work-oriented needs and the extent to which these are addressed in retirement planning and satisfied in the post-retirement environment (Wang & Shultz, 2010). Throughout the chapter, we discuss the importance of modifying change management resources and addressing individual needs through planning as a means to maximize the planning-adaptation relationship.

Key Words: retirement planning, retirement adaptation, needs in retirement

Retirement planning has a logical relationship to a variety of facets of retirement adjustment and post-retirement satisfaction, given its potential to shape realistic expectations regarding retirement and its ability to facilitate further specific preparatory behaviors (Taylor & Doverspike, 2003; Taylor, Shultz, Spiegel, Morrison, & Greene, 2007; Topa, Moriano, Depolo, Alcover, & Morales, 2009; Wang & Shultz, 2010). Planning may facilitate adjustment and affective reactions to retirement immediately after the workforce transition and may, to some extent, shape the retirement experience in the longer term.

Planning may positively impact outcomes related to post-retirement well-being ranging from psychosocial satisfaction to financial satisfaction (Noone, Stephens, & Alpass, 2009; Rosenkoetter & Garris, 2001). While one might expect a robust effect of planning on these affectively oriented variables, a comprehensive meta-analysis reports only a modest empirical relationship between retirement planning and most outcomes (Topa et al., 2009). Depending on the content of planning, the nature of the sample, and the dimension of post-retirement adjustment or satisfaction under investigation, researchers report findings ranging from significant effects of planning on well-being (Noone et al., 2009) to no effects of pre-retirement planning on well-being, absent the consideration of moderating variables (Donaldson, Earl, & Muratore, 2010). This suggests a need to investigate potential moderators of the planning-adaptation relationship.

Empirical support for potential moderators of the relationship between retirement planning and affective responses to retirement was provided by Topa et al. (2009), whose meta-analysis revealed a remarkable amount of variability in the relationship between planning and affective outcomes. While these researchers tested for the significance of some moderators of this relationship, a lack of specificity in many studies made it difficult to fully explore the potential impact of intervening or interactive variables. The results of the meta-analysis and the inconsistent findings between planning and adjustment suggests that it may benefit researchers and practitioners to carefully consider how planning may interact with characteristics of research participants and the post-retirement environment to determine subsequent adjustment. In this chapter, we suggest that the effects of planning on affective reactions to retirement and post-retirement adjustment are moderated by a number of factors, including the personal resources and needs of the individual and the interaction between the retirement environment and these characteristics. Our emphasis on both the post-retirement environment and the individual's characteristics as determinants of adjustment is drawn from Wang and Shultz (2010). In their recent review of employee retirement, the authors emphasize the fit between these personal and environmental factors (P-E fit) as an important framework for understanding satisfaction in retirement. Extending their proposition to planning, we believe that the role of retirement planning in subsequent well-being cannot be fully understood without reference to the content of planning, the post-retirement environment of the individual, and the resources and needs that the individual brings to the retirement process. Consideration of potential interactions between variables within these three dimensions (planning content, environment, individual characteristics) may help us extend our understanding of the impact of planning on subsequent well-being.

In our current models, we consider two major aspects of P-E fit in our discussion of the role of planning in adjustment and satisfaction. The first aspect involves the "fit" between the amount of post-retirement environmental change and the level of personal change management resources as a moderator of planning effectiveness (see Figure 16.1). Basically, we propose that knowledge and skills gained in any form of retirement planning are more effectively implemented by those who have stronger change management skills, that the change itself is more positive for those who are physically and psychologically well-armed for the transition, and that this adaptive advantage will be most apparent when the individual's retirement environment is dissimilar to the pre-retirement environment. In

this discussion, the environmental change, or "E" side of the equation encompasses shifts in the nature of work, the organizational context, change in the work/leisure balance experienced upon retiring, and conditions of organizational exit. We then turn to a discussion of the "P," or personal side, involving change management resources, and review literature supporting the importance of physical, motivational, personality, and social and work-oriented factors as significant influences on adjustment. We also believe there is a reciprocal relationship between planning and change management resources. As noted, they may influence planning effectiveness, and certain change management resources may also be impacted by planning. Thus, as part of this discussion, we also explore the potential of planning as a device for enhancing change management resources.

The second major aspect of "P-E fit" and its interface with planning involves the "fit" between need-based aspects of the post-retirement environment and the need-related resources of the individual, and draws on the work of Wang and Shultz (2010) noted earlier (see Figure 16.2). In this second segment, we focus on the congruence between the needs of the individual and selected facets of the content of the retirement environment as another major moderator of the effects of planning. Past research tells us that financial, social, generative, and work-oriented needs of the individual are important determinants of post-retirement adjustment (Dendinger, Adams, & Jacobson, 2005). As in our model of change resources, we believe there may be a reciprocal relationship between needs and retirement planning. Existing levels of needs may moderate the effectiveness of planning in related domains, and planning may be used to influence the level of needs as well. The extent to which planning can address the somewhat unique needs of an individual may determine adjustment to challenges in related life domains post-retirement. Thus, as in the change management segment, we examine the fit between the needs, planning, and retirement environment, and we also include a consideration of how to enhance knowledge relevant to needs through planning.

In sum, a consideration of both individual change management resources and needs in conjunction with an examination of the post-retirement environment may help us improve our models of the role of retirement planning in adjustment. Joint consideration of personal and contextual factors is necessary to understand retirement dynamics and to maximize prediction of behaviors in the retirement domain (Adams & Rau, 2004). We also seek to incorporate variables at a number of levels: personal, work-oriented, and organizational. This is in keeping with the suggestion that retirement research can benefit from multilevel models (Beehr & Bennett, 2007). Although not explicit in the model, we would expect that the change-oriented aspect of P-E fit would be most relevant and predictive of adjustment early in retirement, when change is maximized, and the need-oriented aspect of P-E fit would have an ongoing impact. This presumes that retirement is dynamic and is a changing, fluid process, with the relevance of predictors and the very nature of adjustment shifting over time.

From our perspective, there is no simple relationship between planning and adjustment, and no "one best" type of planning program. Rather, one would expect that the relationship between planning and adjustment is moderated by both post-retirement environmental and personal factors Thus, we argue for a consideration of individual needs and resources as well as the post-retirement environment when designing planning programs or when assessing the effectiveness of planning. This is consistent with the view that retirement adaptation may depend on clusters of personal characteristics and the interaction of these characteristics with contextual variables (Wang, 2007).

We do realize that this perspective would often lead to anticipated three-way interactions between planning, personal characteristics, and retirement environment characteristics. Furthermore, it is possible to develop more complex models that recognize the potential interaction of sub-factors within these three major categories. While these may be difficult to test empirically, the main purpose of this chapter is to simply suggest that we consider both personal factors (change management resources and needs) and environmental factors (changes in the job content, job setting, work/leisure balance, and conditions of exit) when constructing hypotheses regarding the effects of planning on post-retirement adaptation. Our overall concept that there are two different processes in retirement, one related to the changes associated with retirement and the other associated with finding an environment that supplies resources, has been noted in a different but conceptually related framework. Van Solinge and Henkins (2008) suggest that characteristics of the retirement transition and access to resources in retirement may comprise two different dimensions of the retirement environment that are differentially related to

satisfaction and adjustment. They also acknowledged the importance of coping mechanisms and psychological resources as moderating variables in shaping a satisfying post-retirement experience. In this chapter, we seek to expand this work by incorporating a comprehensive range of change-related resources as well as personal needs into the model and examining the interaction of planning with these and environmental variables in order to understand the planning-adjustment relationship.

Managing Change: P-E Fit and Effects of Planning

In this first segment, we examine the P-E fit relevant to change and begin with an examination of shifts in the post-retirement environment. Past work on continuity theory postulates that individuals are highly motivated to avoid disruption in activities or roles that are central in their life and value the predictability offered by continuity in these activities (Atchley, 1999). In the retirement literature, the theory has been successfully utilized to predict post-retirement behaviors such as bridge employment (Wang et al., 2008), the nature of post-retirement work chosen by individuals (Gobeski & Beehr, 2009), and post-retirement mental and physical health (Zhan, Wang, Liu, & Shultz, 2009). It should be noted that even positive change carries the potential for some stress given that it carries a degree of uncertainty (Nelson et al., 2011). A summary of the proposed model is supplied by Figure 16.1.

Dimensions of Environmental Change

We address three structural dimensions and one perceptual dimension of the retirement work environment that characterize the potential *change* experienced by retirees as they move from their regular job into a retirement option (Shultz, 2003; Wang et al., 2008). The amount of change in the work environment post-retirement may be associated with more stress and higher demands on personal resources. The three structural dimensions are (a) the same or different type of work, (b) working in same or different organizations, and (c) balance of work and non-work in retirement (no work/part-time work/full-time work). The fourth dimension relates to perceived conditions of organizational exit, which have been shown to relate to retirement adjustment (Donaldson, Earl, & Muratore, 2010; Wong & Earl, 2009). This variable, as defined in the Healthy Retirement Project by Wells and colleagues, encompasses factors such as gradual versus

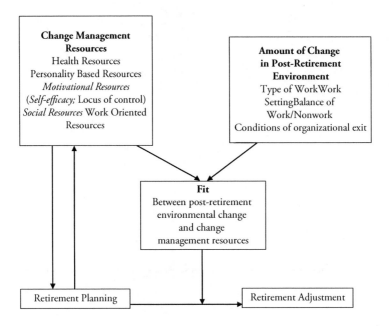

Figure 16.1 Hypothesized relationship between change management resources, amount of change in the post-retirement environment, and the planning-adjustment relationship. Italicized change management resources represent those resources that are most likely to be impacted by retirement planning.

abrupt entry into retirement and perceived choice in the retirement decision and timing of retirement (Wells, DeVaus, Kendig, Quine, & Petralia, 2006.)

In general, the more *change* involved in each of the four dimensions, the greater the potential for stress and the more important the individual change management resources in moderating the potentially positive effects of planning on subsequent adjustment and satisfaction. This suggests that investigations of the planning-adjustment relationship should include an assessment of the change involved as one moves from the pre-retirement to the post-retirement setting. As the change in each of these structural dimensions increases, personal resources relevant to change management become more critical. Similarly, as the conditions of organizational exit become more negative, or less under the control of the individual, change management resources are more critical in moderating the relationship between planning and adjustment.

We also acknowledge that change associated with one of the dimensions (e.g., change in work content) may be more stressful than another (e.g., change in the amount of leisure versus work). Furthermore, it is certain that affective reactions to the nature of the change may determine how an individual manages the transition (e.g., shifting from a more stressful full-time job to a less stressful part-time job involves change associated with positive affect). In addition, future research may find that simultaneous shifts on the four dimensions interact to produce perceptions of greater change than that predicted by a simpler additive model. The amount of perceived change in each dimension and associated affect could certainly be assessed in future research and may refine the effects of change suggested by our model.

In our next segment, we examine the personal side of the "P-E" dynamic in change management. We believe that the same general individual attributes that predict adjustment to other life changes will predict how well individuals manage the transition to a new retirement environment, and that these factors will interact with planning in the prediction of adjustment and affective reactions to retirement. In this segment, we summarize the potential role of change management resources in determining adjustment to retirement and in moderating the effects of planning on retirement adjustment. We also discuss whether the levels of these moderators can be shifted through targeted planning.

Personal Change Management Resources

Physical, motivational, personality-based, social, and work-oriented variables related to change management may impact the effectiveness of retirement planning on adaptation. While we base our selection of these categories on the work of Wang and Shultz (2010), our categories differ in some respects. First, while we acknowledge the potential impact of emotions on adjustment noted in their work, we believe that emotional states such as moods may have only transient effects on the impact of planning. We also add personality as a resource relevant to adaptation and include social support and leisure interests as indicators of the social context variable identified in their research.

As noted, these change management resources are viewed as potential moderators of the impact of planning on affective outcomes post-retirement. The possibility of shifting these resources through planning is also discussed when appropriate. While some of the resources (e.g., health, personality) may be resistant to change through planning, they are still important to consider from a research perspective since they may have a significant influence on the impact of planning and on subsequent adjustment. Considering personal moderators of planning effectiveness may also inform retirement planning specialists, since knowledge of individual standing on these resources may help one tailor planning interventions to the needs of the client.

Health resources. Physical status or health is one of the most consistent and powerful influences on the retirement experience as a whole, with positive relationships reported between health and the ability to plan (Topa et al., 2009), the probability of engaging in post-retirement bridge employment (Wang et al., 2008; Zhan, Wang, Liu, & Shultz, 2009), the timing of retirement (van Solinge & Henkins, 2009), attitudes toward retirement (Reitzes & Mutran, 2004), and retirement satisfaction and adjustment (Donaldson, Earl, & Muratore, 2010; Price & Balaswamy, 2009). The pervasive influence of this factor on retirement affect and behavior suggests that it should be incorporated into any model of planning, and that positive health status is likely to enhance the effects of planning, while poor health is likely to decrease one's ability to put information and skills acquired in planning to good use. Furthermore, the importance of health in virtually every aspect of retirement argues for its importance in retirement planning. We first discuss the role of health as a potential moderator of the relationship between planning and post-retirement adjustment and affect, and then consider whether it may also be changed by planning.

We believe that health has a significant impact on the effectiveness of planning, in that poor health may impede the ability to apply information learned in planning or to implement goals formulated during planning. While this has not been examined empirically, there is clear evidence that poor health is associated with involuntary workforce exit and the poorer subsequent adjustment associated with this variable (Ho & Raymo, 2009; Noone, Stephens, & Alpass, 2009; Wong & Earl, 2009). The lack of ability to make plans for the changes associated with workforce exit may exacerbate the stress experienced by individuals in poor health. Indeed, health concerns and their effect on overall well-being may be so severe that they overshadow the impact of traditional planning programs on workforce exit and adjustment and may curtail the ability to plan. For example, Shultz and Wang (2007) found that very severe health concerns are associated with full retirement, and more minor health concerns are associated with changing jobs and retiring within a longer time frame (within eight years). Thus, health may be viewed as a moderator of the effectiveness of retirement planning, with planning having a stronger impact for those with more positive levels of health. One would expect that this effect would be strongest when the change from the pre-retirement to the post-retirement environment was most dramatic. In other words:

Proposition 1: The positive relationship between planning and adjustment is expected to be stronger for those with positive levels of health than for those who are less healthy. This effect should be pronounced when the retirement environment involves greater rather than less change. For those in poor health, the positive planning-adjustment relationship would be weaker, particularly when the individual faces great change in the post-retirement environment.

This suggests a simple moderating effect of health on the planning-adjustment relationship that is strongest in situations where the post-retirement environment demands a greater degree of adaptation. Whether this effect is due to the inability of those in poor health to engage in detailed planning, their inability to implement planning information, or the overwhelming effects of poor health on other aspects of life more central to adaptation is an important question for future research.

What is clear at this point is that health is a critical variable in the retirement experience. While it is helpful to include it in research as a potential moderator of the planning-adjustment relationship, we also view health as a potential resource that should be incorporated into retirement planning interventions. The persistent effect of this variable on a range of retirement-related outcomes suggests that we should try to integrate information on the importance of health into both long- and short-term planning in the way of informational seminars and wellness training. While health may not be as malleable as other change management resources and thus is depicted as not easily changed in our model, particularly when health problems are severe, this does not mean that the variable is rigid or fixed. Instruments for assessing employee health behaviors are available, and feedback based on such measures may encourage changes related to health (c.f. Fowles, Terry, Xi, Hibbard, Bloom, & Harvey, 2009). More involved, longer-term interventions have been shown to enhance some aspects of health even for chronically ill individuals in the short term and long term and thus increase the level of this individual resource that is so critical in negotiating the changes in retirement (Rybarczyk, DeMarco, DeLaCruz, Lapidos, & Fortner, 2001). Organizational investments in employee wellness as part of retirement planning may be returned in the form of lowered future health costs (Maynard, 2008). Thus, organizations have ethical and economic incentives for health planning interventions.

Motivational resources. These are also important influences on retirement and may moderate the impact of planning on post-retirement adaptation. The reciprocal relationship with planning shown in our model suggests that they may also be modified through planning interventions. These motivational resources include cognitive belief systems such as retirement self-efficacy, or the belief that one can negotiate the retirement process, and locus of control, or a more generalized belief system about one's ability to impact environmental factors (Rotter, 1966).

These cognitive belief systems, related to perceptions of mastery and control over the environment, have been shown to predict adjustment to change in a variety of settings. A general sense of mastery may be related to subsequent satisfaction in retirement and more positive effects of retirement planning (Donaldson et al., 2010; Price & Balaswamy, 2009). One form of mastery discussed below, self-efficacy, may encompass one's confidence in the ability to reach retirement goals and one's perceived ability to apply planning information in order to overcome obstacles. A second related construct, locus of control, is a more general construct involving beliefs

about one's ability to control life events. Clearly, we would expect information gained in planning to be utilized more effectively by those with high confidence and a sense of mastery over life events, and we explore those relationships in the following discussion.

A specific conception of mastery tailored to the retirement experience is self-efficacy. Self-efficacy as defined by the ability to successfully negotiate the retirement transition has been shown to have a positive impact on one's anticipated retirement age and retirement adjustment (Taylor & Shore, 1995; van Solinge & Henkins, 2005). This mastery-oriented construct is also anticipated to moderate the relationship between planning and later adaptation, with more positive levels of self-efficacy related to higher effectiveness of planning. Again, we would expect the strongest effects in high-change environments, which demand more resources from the individual in order to adapt successfully.

As a methodological note, the utility of self-efficacy may be moderated by both the status of the individual (retired versus still employed) as well as the type of post-retirement experience that is desired (Adams & Rau, 2004). For example, a "ceiling effect" for self-efficacy exists in that it may not predict job seeking when the retiree desires a very high-status, difficult-to-attain job. In the current setting, this would suggest that self-efficacy would moderate the effectiveness of planning on adjustment when the individual has realistic rather than unrealistic post-retirement expectations and goals. In situations where it is reasonable to assume that individuals would be realistic in their choice of retirement options, self-efficacy should enhance the effects of planning and may have the greatest effects under conditions of the greatest job change.

Proposition 2: Positive levels of retirement self-efficacy will enhance the positive effects of retirement planning on general adaptation to retirement. This effect should be strongest when the post-retirement environment involves a great degree of change.

As noted, while self-efficacy may moderate the impact of planning, it may also be changed through planning interventions that are designed to identify areas where individuals lack confidence and supplying needed information to them (Taylor-Carter & Cook, 1995). While it does not appear that this cognitive factor is directly addressed in many planning programs, enhancing this belief system and clarifying retirement goals during retirement planning could amplify the positive consequences of planning (Bandura & Locke, 2003; Petkoska

& Earl, 2009). Classic techniques for improving self-efficacy, such as providing information on how to reach retirement goals and using satisfied individuals from different retirement settings (part-time employees in the same and different employment; full-time retirees) as models to convey information on their experience, may be practical ways to raise self-efficacy (Bandura, 1999).

Our second motivational construct, locus of control, is a general sense of mastery over the environment. Control over the retirement transition is related to later affective reactions to retirement (Calvo, Haverstick, & Sass, 2009). Perceived control over the specific timing of retirement and the retirement process may emerge as an important moderator of the planning-adjustment relationship (Potocnik, Tordera, & Peiro, 2010). While control over the retirement process and the timing of the decision may be heavily influenced by external variables such as organizational norms and health, we believe that these internalized beliefs regarding ones' ability to overcome external hurdles may still moderate the planning-adjustment relationship.

Proposition 3: Locus of control will moderate the positive relationship between planning and adjustment. The positive planning-adjustment relationship will be strongest for those with internal locus of control. This effect should be pronounced when post-retirement work environments involve a great degree of change.

While some long-term investigations of locus of control have found that it shifts as a function of environmental and social influences, it seems unlikely that general locus of control could be shifted as a result of retirement planning and thus is viewed as more difficult to shift through planning in our model (Legerski, Cornwall, & O'Neil, 2006). Thus, we view locus of control as a moderator of planning and adjustment to retirement rather than as a factor that can realistically be changed through short-term retirement planning programs.

Personality-based resources. While research in this domain is new and evolving, available studies suggest that personality factors have the potential to predict life satisfaction and retirement satisfaction of retirees, and they may serve as a significant moderator of the planning-adaptation relationship. One promising area of research in this domain involves the Big Five personality traits (McCrae & Costa, 2008). Extroversion, conscientiousness, openness to experience, and agreeableness may be positively related to different indices of affective reactions to retirement such as life satisfaction and retirement satisfaction, while neuroticism is associated with more negative affect (Bye & Pushkar, 2009; Robinson, Demetre, & Corney, 2010; Stephan, 2009). While research is quite limited, there are logical reasons for believing that personality may have an impact on the planning-adjustment relationship. Extroversion may enhance effects of information gained in planning through its facilitative effects on post-retirement activities (Lockenhoff et al., 2009). Given the centrality of post-retirement activities and social activities in retirement well-being, we would expect that extroverts would show more benefits from planning, particularly from socially oriented aspects of planning, than those who are more introverted. Extroverts may also be more likely to interact with others and may have greater opportunity to apply information and discuss options learned in planning. Thus, extroversion may enhance the effects of planning given that these individuals may be more likely to engage in more activities and continued planning behaviors central to adjustment.

Conscientiousness may exert a positive effect on adjustment through its impact on increasing constructive behaviors and the fact that highly conscientious individuals may be more likely to apply useful information gained in planning in the post-retirement environment (Robinson et al., 2010). Again, we have no direct evidence that this will moderate the effects of planning on adjustment, but the general positive relationship between this factor and adaptation, and the likelihood that highly conscientious individuals may be more likely to use the information gained in planning, argues that it may be a significant moderator.

Openness to experience is related to a higher need for cognition, which may lead to more openness to planning and to pursuing additional information after planning (Bye & Pushkar, 2009). Openness to experience may make the retirement transition less threatening and, again, may help strengthen the relationship between planning and subsequent adjustment.

It may be the case that agreeableness is associated with a more positive retirement transition given its negative association with resistance to change (Saksvik & Hetland, 2009). While agreeableness is positively associated with post-retirement satisfaction and positive life experiences, it appears unrelated to pre-retirement satisfaction (Robinson, Demetre, & Corney, 2010). Research on the predictive power of this personality trait is mixed, and further work is needed to clarify the relationship between agreeableness, planning, and adjustment (Lockenhoff et al., 2009).

In contrast to the more beneficial relationship between the personality factors previously discussed and adaptation, we would expect that the general increase in anxiety associated with neuroticism could potentially interfere with the ability to use planning information effectively. The effects of neuroticism may be linked to feelings that retirement is unexpected and to the general negative relationship between the anxiety inherent in neuroticism and adaptation (Lockenhoff et al., 2009).

One would expect that this personality characteristic may impede the potentially beneficial effect of planning, particularly in high-change post-retirement environments. In general, neuroticism is associated with more negative reactions to life change and lower levels of life satisfaction (Luhmann & Eid, 2009). The limited research on this factor in the retirement literature has also revealed a significant negative relationship between neuroticism and post-retirement satisfaction (Lockenhoff et al., 2009; Robinson et al., 2010). Neuroticism may increase anxiety about the transition and may be associated with a lack of control over the process.

While work in the area of personality and retirement adaptation is limited, based on the pattern of results noted above, we propose the following:

Proposition 4: Those who are more outgoing, conscientious, agreeable, and open to experience would profit more from planning, particularly in high-change post-retirement environments. Those who are more neurotic may show fewer benefits from planning, particularly in high-change post-retirement environments.

While these personality characteristics may be viewed as important resources that impact the individual's ability to utilize planning information in order to negotiate the changes in retirement, they are likely to be stable and best viewed as a relatively inflexible moderator of the impact of planning on adjustment (McCrae, Terracciano, & Khoury, 2007). Those with positive levels of those traits associated with successful adaptation would be expected to respond favorably to retirement planning interventions. While it may be difficult to shift neuroticism through planning, one-on-one retirement counseling may provide greater structure and support for those who are more threatened by the retirement process.

An additional personality characteristic outside the domain of the Big Five that holds great promise in the area of planning and adjustment is future time perspective. Hershey and Mowen (2000) found that conscientiousness and emotional stability were positively related to an individual's future time perspective, or the tendency to take a long-term perspective toward life planning. This future time perspective was in turn related to financial preparedness for retirement. Other researchers report a positive relationship between future time perspective, financial and lifestyle preparation, and developmental fulfillment (Bal, Jansen, van der Velde, de Lange, & Rousseau, 2010; Noone, Stephens, & Alpass, 2010). This suggests that future time perspective may enhance the effects of planning in that those with more future-oriented perspectives may be more likely to engage in planning and seek out additional constructive information as a result of planning. Future time perspective may also influence the extent to which older employees experience and seek out developmental opportunities at work and experience satisfaction in this domain (Bal et al., 2010). This may be related to later adjustment after leaving the workforce. Therefore, we expect:

Proposition 5: Future time perspective will moderate the planning-adjustment relationship in that the planning-adjustment relationship should be stronger for those with a future-oriented perspective. Again, we expect the strongest positive effects in post-retirement environments involving high change.

An important methodological issue was raised by Petkoska and Earl (2009). While they did not find a significant relationship between future time perspective and planning, they suggested that the time frame tapped by their perspective scale may not have incorporated the long time span typical of planning. They note that research incorporating future time perspective needs to match the time scope of the measure to the phenomenon under investigation.

Given the stability of personality variables over the life span noted by researchers in this area, it is depicted in our model as a factor that would not be easily changed through planning. Thus, we regard it as a moderator of planning effectiveness but not a variable that may be amenable to planning interventions.

Social resources. As noted by Wang and Shultz (2010), the social context may serve as a critical determinant of the nature of the retirement experience and is viewed as an internal resource. We focus on the specific variables of leisure and social support as indicators of the social context. In this discussion, we examine the role of leisure interests and activities as one social resource that may amplify the benefits of planning on adjustment. In keeping with the reciprocal relationship between this variable and planning, we discuss the possibility of shifting an individual's leisure interests through planning. A second social consideration is social support, a factor that is external to the individual but one that may moderate the benefits of planning and its effect on subsequent adjustment. Consistent with our discussion of leisure, we incorporate possible ways to increase the standing of individuals on this factor through planning.

Leisure. Engaging in leisure activities is beneficial for retirees, resulting in increased social contact and structure for free time. Leisure may be related to increases in overall satisfaction and adjustment in retirement and may be most important for those who are interested in full retirement or options that greatly increase the amount of leisure time relative to work. Thus, we would expect leisure to moderate the relationship between planning and adjustment and have the strongest impact when leisure time is increased post-retirement.

While engaging in leisure activities may be important for retirees, most retirees do not report developing new leisure activities once they retire (Long, 1987; Vinick & Ekerdt, 1991). Instead, they tend to pursue the interests they had pre-retirement and are simply able to devote more time to these activities. In interviews with retirees before and after retirement, Vinick and Ekerdt (1991) found that those without leisure activities they wished to pursue reported being bored once they had retired and had problems with a lack of structure in their retirement.

Further research supports the importance of leisure in successful post-retirement adaptation. Heo, Lee, McCormick, and Pederson (2010) found that older adults who were very committed to a leisure activity reported more positive affect and higher levels of subjective well-being than those who did not. Similarly, Silverstein and Parker (2002) found that retirees who increased the amount of leisure activities they engaged in perceived an improvement in their quality of life. Dropping leisure activities, in contrast, was related to a perceived decrease in quality of life. Thus, there is ample evidence of the simple effect of leisure on adaptation.

Long (1987) reports many potential reasons that engaging in leisure activities in retirement may be so beneficial. Retirees reported that leisure activities kept them mentally active, gave them a sense of purpose, provided them with social interaction, and helped to provide structure for their time. For individuals who have fully retired, these benefits that result from engaging in leisure activities may be particularly important because these retirees may

not be getting this same sense of purpose and interaction from other aspects of their lives.

Given these effects of leisure on adaptation and resistance to developing new leisure skills, those who have high levels of existing leisure interests may be more likely to benefit from planning. The initial level of interest in leisure skills may lead them to seek out more information about the social aspects of retirement, and they may be more likely to apply advice regarding leisure opportunities from retirement counselors. They may also be more likely to find appealing leisure activities among the range of options presented in retirement planning seminars. As noted, research suggests that those who lack leisure interests or skills may not be as likely to seek out new opportunities, and it may be the case that information provided in planning is less likely to be utilized. Thus, while research investigating potential interactions between leisure interests and planning is lacking, we believe that positive levels of leisure skills and interests may amplify the beneficial effects of planning. We also expect that this effect would be greatest when the retiree enters a retirement environment that has more potential time for leisure activities.

Proposition 6: The positive planning-adjustment relationship is expected to be stronger for those who have leisure skills and interests than for those who lack these interests. The effect should be strongest in retirement environments where the amount of leisure time relative to work is increased.

While leisure skills may not be easily modified, leisure planning is an emerging aspect of preparation for the retirement transition (Petkoska & Earl, 2009). Activities such as reading about leisure options and joining groups or teams based on one's non-work interests may be simple ways to encourage leisure activities post-retirement. Given that research finds that individuals may not easily acquire leisure skills, such simple, low-investment activities may hold promise for shifting levels of leisure interests.

As a methodological note, leisure activities may be particularly beneficial for certain groups of potential retirees. Silverstein and Parker (2002) report that increasing leisure activities is most important for those who have less contact with family members, are less healthy, or were widowed. Similarly, Long (1987) reports that leisure activities are a valuable means for filling time for those who are less healthy or are more isolated.

Social support. Social support is an important determinant of a number of endeavors associated with a positive retirement experience, including seeking post-retirement work (Adams & Rau, 2004), satisfaction experienced in retirement (Price & Balaswamy, 2009), and later retirement adjustment (Taylor, Goldberg, Shore, & Lipka, 2008). It may have its positive impact by serving as a psychological buffer against stress and allowing individuals to feel more supported in managing the changes associated with retirement and applying the knowledge from planning to overcome challenges. It may also influence planning in that others serve as a source of information relevant to retirement. A recent, unique study on the role of social support in financial planning suggests that support from work peers and friends may increase clarity of retirement goals, which encourages and facilitates planning (Hershey, Henkens, & Van Dalen, 2010). The same study found that social support from the spouse/partner had positive effects on planning through encouraging a more future-oriented time perspective in the future retiree, which is associated with planning. While this research involved financial planning, certainly the dynamics of social support and the benefits reported are relevant to other aspects of retirement planning. It appears that social support may provide psychological support, motivation for planning, and information relevant to planning amplifying the positive effects of planning on adjustment. Social support may have a pervasive positive influence on adaptation in new retirement environments, particularly high-change ones.

Proposition 7: Higher levels of social support would be associated with more positive effects of planning on adaptation, particularly in post-retirement environments that involve great change.

As a methodological note, researchers have found that the type of employment an individual is engaged in pre-retirement (professional, paraprofessional, or nonprofessional) but not the extent of employment (full- or part-time) is linked to post-retirement social support and satisfaction (Price & Dean, 2009), with higher-paying professional jobs yielding more positive levels of satisfaction. It appeared that those in professional jobs were more likely to have the opportunity to remain socially engaged post-retirement.

While many individuals may view social support as relatively inflexible, it is logical to expect that it can shift in the same way that leisure interests can shift. While both factors would be viewed as more challenging to change through planning than some others, they may be shifted through more intensive interventions. They also may shift in tandem.

Engaging in more non-work activities may allow individuals to expand their social network and enhance social support. While simply continuing social relationships that one has developed during work may be an important source of support, this is more common for those who are retiring out of higher-paying professional jobs (Price & Dean, 2009).

Work-related resources: Job skills. Within this category, we consider the job skills possessed by the individual as a potential moderator of the planning-adjustment relationship, in that those with more marketable skills and those with skills compatible with the desired post-retirement environment may benefit more from planning. The impact of job skills on post-retirement adjustment may be strongest in post-retirement environments where the work-to-leisure ratio is higher and when the retiree has job skills relevant to the desired type of post-retirement employment. In terms of reciprocal effects with planning, job skills may be difficult to shift and are not typically incorporated into planning programs. However, assessment of existing job skills and feedback to participants may help them realize more benefits from planning.

At present, there is very limited research on this topic. Existing work on a military sample revealed that those who have transferable knowledge, skills, and abilities (KSAs) showed greater adjustment levels post-retirement (Spiegel & Shultz, 2003). Similarly, those who have job skills relevant to bridge employment are likely to choose that path of post-retirement employment rather than bridge employment in a different field (Gobeski & Beehr, 2009). In terms of planning, we would expect that an investigation of the compatibility between one's current KSAs and the KSAs in the desired post-retirement job would be an important component of the planning-adjustment relationship. Given that intensive skills training is not incorporated in most retirement planning interventions, we would expect that those with incompatible or less-marketable job skills would benefit less from a typical retirement planning program.

Proposition 8: The positive planning-adjustment relationship will be stronger for those with job skills that are more marketable and compatible with their desired retirement environment. Those with incompatible or less-marketable skills will show fewer benefits of planning, particularly in conditions where the post-retirement job content differs from that of the pre-retirement environment and the work-to-leisure ratio is higher.

Again, job skills may be modifiable within limits and could be incorporated into long-term career and retirement planning for individuals. Researchers have noted that this type of training and planning is often absent for late-career employees, who could greatly benefit from role models and other interventions designed to enhance later career development (Gibson & Barron, 2003). Realistically, changes to one's standing on this variable would take greater investment than found in a typical planning seminar. Thus, it is designated as a factor that is not readily shifted through planning in our model.

Summary

In sum, we view the health-oriented, cognitive, personality, social, and work-oriented resources as important potential moderators of the planning-adjustment relationship in that they impact the individual's ability to utilize planning information in order to manage the change inherent in retirement environments. The greater the environmental changes as one moves from the pre-retirement environment to the post-retirement environment, the more powerful and relevant are these resources as moderators of the effects of planning on adaptation. In addition, we view these change management resources as differentially amenable to change through planning interventions, as depicted in Figure 16.1. Thus, while including both personal and environmental factors as potential moderators of the planning-adjustment relationship is important, research on ways to shift change management resources through various types, degrees, and intensity of planning interventions is needed as well.

Need-Related Aspects of the P-E Fit and Effects of Planning

The change management resources reviewed may moderate the planning-adaptation relationship through their influence on the ability to effectively utilize planning information as a means to cope with the *changes* in retirement, particularly in early stages of the process. Needs may also impact the significance of planning as a factor in adaptation and may have an ongoing influence on the *congruence* of the new retirement environment with retiree goals and desires. Researchers have found that a number of different needs may interact with post-retirement work environments to drive retirement adjustment and that salient needs may be significant factors in the choice of post-retirement options (Brougham

& Walsh, 2009; Dendinger, Adams, & Jacobson, 2005; Wang et al., 2008; Winston & Barnes, 2007; Wong & Earl, 2009). According to Wang and Shultz (2010), these needs may determine the fit of a person with the post-retirement environment and thus shape affective reactions in retirement. Need-relevant planning may actually be more effective when individuals have lower levels of some needs (e.g., financial planning may be more effective for those with lower financial needs) and less effective or relevant when individuals have lower levels of other needs (e.g., social planning may be less relevant or effective for those with lower social needs). Thus, a consideration of the existing level of a given need and the type of planning offered is critical in understanding the relationship between needs, planning, the post-retirement environment, and adaptation. As in the change management segment, we also focus on ways to try to enhance post-retirement need satisfaction through planning. Aspects of the retirement environment and of the individual relevant to this discussion focus on the following needs: (a) financial, (b) social, (c) generative, and (d) work-oriented needs. A summary of our proposed relationships is supplied by Figure 16.2.

Financial needs. Clearly, financial needs and resources influence a variety of affective post-retirement outcomes, including well-being (Noone et al., 2009; Petroska & Earl, 2009; van Solinge & Henkins, 2008). High incomes may facilitate the congruence of the post-retirement environment with retirees' expectations and desires (Hira, Rock, & Loibl, 2009). Furthermore, it may be the case that those with greater financial resources will experience greater benefits from financial planning. Those with higher incomes simply have more resources to invest, and it is likely that they would have more freedom to explore different financial need-fulfilling options discovered through planning.

We expect that those with greater financial needs are less likely to be able to engage in planning that enhances the post-retirement adjustment experience, and less likely to have the financial resources available to allow them to profit from planning information. We also anticipate that lower-income individuals are less likely to be able to find post-retirement employment that offers a financially satisfying existence. All of these factors—the inability to engage in financial planning and implement financial planning information and limitations on the ability to find post-retirement work that satisfies financial needs—may attenuate the

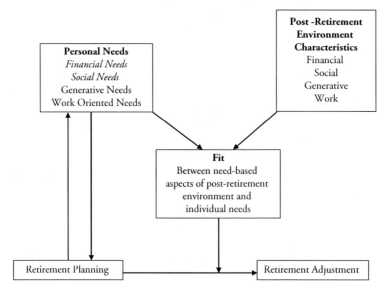

Figure 16.2 Hypothesized relationship between personal needs, post-retirement environmental characteristics, and the planning-adjustment relationship. Italicized personal needs represent those needs that are most likely to be impacted by retirement planning.

planning-adjustment relationship in low-income groups. Thus, we expect that:

Proposition 9: The positive financial planning–financial adjustment relationship is stronger for those with lower levels of financial need than for those with higher levels of financial need. This effect would be strongest in retirement environments that are financially challenging.

Future research that explores ways to facilitate the financial planning of low-income groups and their ability to locate post-retirement employment that satisfies their needs is sorely needed. There is relatively less research on these issues facing low-income groups in the I/O literature than on more financially satisfied individuals. While financial needs are viewed as changeable through planning in our model, the impact of planning may not be as simple as depicted. It may be easier to shift the financial need level of one with moderate existing financial resources than for those who are very financially challenged (Taylor & Geldhauser, 2007).

Social needs. The extent to which the post-retirement environment provides satisfaction of social needs and the level of existing social needs of the retiree may also impact the planning-adjustment relationship. Satisfaction of social needs can take place through a variety of mechanisms post-retirement. Research suggests that a consideration of social networks and roles should be central in investigations of successful aging (Cornwell, Schumm, & Laumann, 2008). Continuing social

relationships from the pre-retirement environment into the post-retirement environment is one means of enhancing adjustment, and for those who engage in this type of behavior and other socially engaged behaviors, retirement of any kind is unlikely to be disruptive in terms of the social aspect of life (Cozijinsen, Stevens, & van Tilburg, 2010). Thus, those with low levels of social needs (those with high social resources) may not particularly need planning in order to adjust to social aspects of post-retirement life, even though they may benefit somewhat from this type of planning.

Unlike financial needs, social needs in and of themselves are not likely to impose barriers on access to or utility of planning information. And unlike leisure skills, social connectedness can come from a variety of interpersonal contacts and is not constrained by the interest or motivation to learn new activities. Thus, those who have the highest levels of social needs could reap the greatest benefits from social planning.

One might argue that those with high levels of social needs may be more likely to lack the skills to develop satisfying interpersonal relationships and may be less likely to benefit from planning. However, if "successful" retirement planning is defined as an increase in post-planning social satisfaction as compared to pre-planning levels of social satisfaction, then the greatest increments in social satisfaction may be seen in those with higher social needs. Since we are primarily interested in the ability of planning to cause a change in social satisfaction, we argue that those with lower initial levels of social satisfaction (higher social needs) may show the greatest benefits from planning. Planning should facilitate the development of socially oriented behaviors that satisfy this need and may make the individual more aware of the importance of considering social aspects of the post-retirement environment. Thus, we expect effects of planning to be amplified for those with high social needs.

Proposition 10: The positive social planning–social adjustment relationship will be stronger for those who have high social needs than for those who have low social needs. This effect would be stronger in retirement environments that are socially challenging.

In terms of the reciprocal relationship between planning and social needs, social planning is not generally included in retirement planning, so the degree to which these needs can be shifted is difficult to determine. As we noted in our segment on social support and leisure planning, there is no reason why social planning cannot gain status as an important factor in retirement preparation. Researchers have started to recognize and emphasize the espoused importance of interpersonal planning in adjustment and the impact of social factors on well-being (Adejumo, 2010; Herero & Extremera, 2010; Petkoska & Earl, 2009). Simple interventions such as teaching potential retirees how to use e-mail and related technology as a means to connect with others may have an impact on social need satisfaction and a sense of connectedness (Hogeboom, McDermontt, Perrin, Osman, & Bell-Ellison, 2010). This may particularly facilitate the development of new connections for those who lack the ability or interest to explore other sources of social need satisfaction in retirement (Dunning, 2009).

Generativity needs. Erikson (1950) initially coined the term *generativity* to refer to the seventh stage of human development, which occurs during middle adulthood. According to McAdams and de St. Aubin (1992), generativity is not just a goal of the individual; it is also a goal of society as a whole. Generativity is associated with such positive outcomes as increased life satisfaction (Huta & Zuroff, 2007; McAdams, de St. Aubin, & Logan, 1993), self-esteem, and positive affect (Ackerman, Zuroff, & Moscowitz, 2000) and negatively associated with depression (Stewart & Vandewater, 1998). Generativity is often framed as a part of productive aging by older individuals in that a sense of giving to others is an important aspect of being engaged in life (Reichstadt, Sengupta, Depp, Palinkas, & Jeste, 2010).

Generativity may be expressed through involvement in the community through political involvement (Hart, McAdams, Hirsch, & Bauer, 2001) or volunteering (Kleiber & Nimrod, 2008; Narushima, 2005). It can also be expressed in the workplace through mentoring others or by passing along knowledge to others (Parise & Forret, 2008). Like social needs, there are many different, accessible avenues for satisfying this particular need outside work (Brougham & Walsh, 2009). While not typically framed as "generativity planning," we argue that planning advice that incorporates information about ways to give back to the community, to the profession, or to society in general would be valuable to many potential retirees, and particularly beneficial for those with higher generativity needs. Those with high generativity needs may be more likely to utilize this information to explore experiences that enhance this aspect of adaptation.

Proposition 11: The generativity planning–generativity adjustment relationship will be stronger for those who have high generativity needs than for those who have low generativity needs. This effect would be stronger in retirement environments that are challenging in terms of generative options.

Given that generativity appears to function somewhat like a personality trait, being stable over time, it does not appear that one's standing on this variable would be amenable to planning. Furthermore, unlike social and financial needs, it seems to be important only for a segment of the population. Thus, while planning may be tailored to meet the needs of those who are highly generative, there is no reason to think we could shift this trait through planning.

Work-related needs. In this segment, we consider the role of stereotypes and norms within the post-retirement environment and their fit with individuals' need to be valued at work as a potential moderator of the planning-adjustment relationship. For those who find work central to their self-esteem, and for those who wish to achieve work-oriented developmental goals, finding a post-retirement environment in which they feel valued may be an important moderator of the effectiveness of work-related planning on adjustment. It is important to acknowledge that in the general population, commitment to work and work centrality may not be strongly and consistently related to adjustment, but may have more moderate effects on well-being (Topa et al., 2009; Wong & Earl, 2009). Many individuals may disengage from work and find satisfying substitutes for the needs supplied from the activity of working.

For those individuals who have lower-stress, more satisfying jobs, continuing work such as in the form of bridge employment is more likely (Wang et al., 2008), and thus relevant planning could prove to be important in adjustment. Planning may help enhance the ability to locate new work or facilitate continuing bridge employment with the same organization (Jones & McIntosh, 2010). We would expect that the positive effects of such employment planning on work-related adjustment would be maximized when the organization has a climate conducive to an employee's work-related needs, such as the need to feel valued by the firm.

Stereotypes and norms that are an integral part of work climates for older workers are relevant to this discussion. A meta-analysis of stereotypes relevant to older employees suggested that increased age is associated with decreased perceived attractiveness of employees and, in some situations, decreased perceived competence (Kite, Stockdale, Whitley, & Johnson, 2005). However, positive stereotypes such as the idea that older employees are reliable and productive can coexist with negative beliefs, and the positive aspects of the stereotype can have a facilitative effect on developmental aspirations of older workers (Gaillard & Desmette, 2010; Henkens, 2005). Negative stereotypes about older individuals have a predictably disabling impact on older workers and are inversely associated with managers' interest in retaining older employees. Thus, negative stereotypes are likely to attenuate the potentially positive effects of employment planning on work-related adjustment, while positive ones may accentuate these effects.

Organizational norms supporting continued employment may serve as another aspect of climate that moderates the planning-adjustment relationship. Findings in this area mirror those of the stereotyping research. Norms that pressure individuals to retire are associated with stronger intentions to retire early and younger actual retirement ages (Potocnik, Tordera, & Peiro, 2009). It is likely that this organizational factor produces effects similar to those of stereotypes, in that it creates a climate that is not conducive to the need to feel valued at work. Note that the dynamic of the environment is quite different in this proposition than in the other need-oriented propositions. Negative or challenging work environments in terms of stereotypes may well have a very personalized, debilitating impact on the individual. Rather than amplifying the potential benefits of planning, negative environments are expected to weaken them, even for those who are high in the need for work.

Proposition 12: The positive employment planning–employment adjustment relationship will be stronger for those who have high work-oriented needs than for those who have low work-oriented needs. This planning is expected to have the strongest effect on adjustment when the individual is in a pre-retirement and post-retirement environment with a positive climate (positive stereotypes, supportive employment norms) for older employees.

Similar to generativity, purely work-oriented needs, excluding the part of the need associated with finances or social contact, seem to be relevant to just a segment of the population. The need per se may not be shifted through planning, although planning may certainly provide information for those who seek and desire employment. Thus, we do not focus on whether we may shift levels of work-oriented needs in our model.

As a final consideration in our discussion of the relevance of needs as a moderator of the planning-adjustment relationship, we propose that spiritual needs of potential retirees may also be important. Although not included in our formal model, these are emerging as an additional consideration in post-retirement satisfaction and well-being (McFarland, 2010). While planning for spiritual needs is not traditionally a part of retirement planning, the criticality of meeting these needs should not be overlooked, and researchers have called for active planning in this arena (Koepke & Ellor, 2005). Available research suggests that the relationship between a given form of spirituality or religion is complex, with effects on well-being influenced in part by social satisfaction and existential belief systems (Cohen & Hall, 2009). While firms are very likely to be highly sensitive to providing any information related to religion to employees, more informal planning sources might provide potential retirees with locations of religious organizations or with information on how to locate these organizations.

Summary. As noted throughout this segment, needs may interact with planning. Planning is more likely to enhance adjustment when the individual is able to apply planning information in order to gravitate into or shape a post-retirement environment that fulfills central needs.

Planning that is tailored to individual needs, while labor-intensive and impractical in some settings, is needed to optimize the P-E fit of the retiree with his or her post-retirement environment. Incorporating comprehensive financial, social, generative, and work-oriented information into seminars may be much more beneficial than focusing on only one aspect. Even group-oriented seminars can incorporate discussions of financial and social needs, since these are likely to be relevant to a number of individuals involved in planning.

Conclusion

The current model suggests that the planning-adjustment relationship is moderated by two types of P-E fit. The first type consists of the fit between personal (physical, motivational, personality-based, social, and work-oriented) change management resources and the aspects of change in the post-retirement environment (type of work, same/different employer, work/non-work balance, conditions of organizational exit) that may facilitate the positive impact of planning on subsequent retirement adaptation. The second type of fit consists of financial, social, generative, and work-oriented needs and the challenge posed to each need by the post-retirement environment. Both types of fit may influence the ability of planning to impact adjustment.

Future Directions

The current model assumes that retirement adjustment is dynamic, which argues for longitudinal studies that assess shifts in the importance of predictors of adaptation over time. The change management resources may have their strongest impact early in adjustment, when the transition period is most demanding, while needs may have a continuing impact on retirement well-being. Planning tailored to the point of adjustment of the retiree is therefore an important consideration in maximizing its potentially positive effects on well-being.

In addition to these methodological changes, measuring adjustment and related affective measures before and after planning may allow us to gain a better understanding of the impact of planning on well-being. Simply examining overall levels of adjustment post-planning masks the increments in well-being over baseline that may be gained by planning. Continuing to expand the nature and content of retirement planning in order to identify the types of planning most conducive to the change management resources and need satisfaction is an important goal.

Thus, change management P-E fit, need-based P-E fit, the type and nature of retirement planning, the nature of the adjustment measure under consideration, and the point at which adjustment is being assessed post-retirement may be important for researchers and practitioners to consider when evaluating and designing research or applied interventions. Past research in this area provides the foundation needed for building and extending our theories regarding the complex relationship between the personal characteristics, environmental characteristics, and planning as determinants of retirement well-being.

References

Ackerman, S., Zuroff, D., & Moscowitz, D. S. (2000). Generativity in midlife and young adults: Links to agency, communion, and well-being. *International Journal of Aging and Human Development, 50,* 17–41.

Adams, G., & Rau, B. (2004). Job seeking among retirees seeking bridge employment. *Personnel Psychology, 57,* 719–744.

Adejumo, A. (2010). Influences of social support, self-efficacy and personality on the general health of retirees in Lago, Nigeria. *Educational Gerontology, 36,* 907–918.

Atchley, R. C. (1999). *Continuity and adaptation in aging: Creating positive experiences.* Baltimore, MD: Johns Hopkins University Press.

Bal, P. M., Jansen, P. G. W., van der Velde, M. E. G., de Lange, A. H., & Rousseau, D. M. (2010). The role of future time perspective in psychological contracts: A study among older workers. *Journal of Vocational Behavior, 76,* 474–486.

Bandura, A. (1999). Self-efficacy: Toward a unifying theory of behavioral change. In R. F. Baumeister (Ed.), *The self in social psychology* (pp. 285–298). New York, NY: Psychology Press.

Bandura, A., & Locke, E. A. (2003). Negative self-efficacy and goal effects revisited. *Journal of Applied Psychology, 88,* 87–99.

Beehr, T. A., & Bennett, M. M. (2007). Examining retirement from a multi-level perspective. In K. S. Shultz & G. A. Adams (Eds.), *Aging and work in the 21st century* (pp. 277–302). New York, NY: Psychology Press.

Brougham, R. R., & Walsh, D. A. (2009). Early and late retirement exits. *The International Journal of Aging and Human Development, 69,* 267–286.

Bye, D., & Pushkar, D. (2009). How need for cognition and perceived control are differentially linked to emotional outcomes in the transition to retirement. *Motivation and Emotion, 33,* 320–332.

Calvo, E., Haverstick, K., & Sass, S. (2009). Gradual retirement, sense of control, and retirees' happiness. *Research on Aging, 31,* 112–135.

Cohen, A. B., & Hall, D. E. (2009). Existential beliefs, social satisfaction, and well-being among Catholic, Jewish, and Protestant older adults. *International Journal for the Psychology of Religion, 19,* 39–54.

Cornwell, B., Schumm, L. P., & Laumann, E. O. (2008). The social connectedness of older adults: A national profile. *American Sociological Review, 73,* 185–203.

Cozijinsen, R., Stevens, N. L., & van Tilburg, T. G. (2010). Maintaining work-related personal ties following retirement. *Personal Relationships, 17,* 345–356.

Dendinger, V. M., Adams, G. A., & Jacobson, J. D. (2005). Reasons for working and their relationship to retirement attitudes, job satisfaction and occupational self-efficacy of bridge employees. *The International Journal of Aging and Human Development*, *61*, 21–35.

Donaldson, C., Earl, J. K., & Muratore, A. M. (2010). Extending the integrated model of retirement adjustment: Incorporating mastery and retirement planning. *Journal of Vocational Behavior*. doi:10.1016/j.jvb.2010.03.003.

Dunning, T. (2009). Aging, activities, and the internet: Online communities and aging. *Activities, Adaptation, and Aging*, *33*, 263–264.

Erikson, E. H. (1950). Eight stages of man. In D. C. Funder & D. J. Ozer (Eds.), *Pieces of the personality puzzle* (pp. 201–209). New York, NY: Norton.

Fowles, J. B., Terry, P., Xi, M., Hibbard, J., Bloom, C. T., & Harvey, L. (2009). Measuring self-management of patients' and employees' health: Further validation of the Patient Activation Measure (PAM) based on its relation to employee characteristics. *Patient Education and Counseling*, *77*, 116–122.

Gaillard, M., & Desmette, D. (2010). Invalidating stereotypes about older workers influences their intentions to retire early and to learn and develop. *Basic and Applied Social Psychology*, *32*, 86–98.

Gibson, D. E., & Barron, L. A. (2003). Exploring the impact of role models on older employees. *Career Development International*, *8*, 198–209.

Gobeski, K. T., & Beehr, T. A. (2009). How retirees work: Different predictors of bridge employment. *Journal of Organizational Behavior*, *30*, 401–425.

Hart, H. M., McAdams, D. P., Hirsch, B. J., & Bauer, J. J. (2001). Generativity and social involvement among African Americans and white adults. *Journal of Research in Personality*, *35*, 208–230.

Henkens, K. (2005). Stereotyping older workers and retirement: The managers' point of view. *Canadian Journal on Aging*, *24*, 353–366.

Heo, J., Lee, Y., McCormick, B. P., & Pedersen, P. M. (2010). Daily experience of serious leisure, flow and subjective well-being of older adults. *Leisure Studies*, *29*, 207–225.

Herero, V. G., & Extremera, N. (2010). Daily life activities as mediators of the relationship between personality variables and subjective well-being among older adults. *Personality and Individual Differences*, *49*, 124–129.

Hershey, D. A., Henkens, K., & Van Dalen, H. P. (2010). Aging and financial planning for retirement: Interdisciplinary influences viewed through a cross cultural lens. *International Journal of Aging and Human Development*, *70*, 1–38.

Hershey, D. A., & Mowen, J. C. (2000). Psychological determinants of financial preparedness for retirement. *The Gerontologist*, *40*, 687–697.

Hira, T., K., Rock, W. L, & Loibl, C. (2009). Determinants of retirement planning behavior and differences by age. *International Journal of Consumer Studies*, *33*, 293–301.

Ho, J.-H., & Raymo, J. M. (2009). Expectations and realization of joint retirement among dual-worker couples. *Research on Aging*, *31*, 153–179

Hogeboom, D. L., McDermott, R. J., Perrin, K. M., Osman, H., & Bell-Ellison, B. A. (2010). Internet use and social networking among middle aged and older adults. *Educational Gerontology*, *36*, 93–111.

Huta, V., & Zuroff, D. C. (2007). Examining mediators of the link between generativity and well-being. *Journal of Adult Development*, *14*, 47–52.

Jones, D. A., & McIntosh, B. R. (2010). Organizational and occupational commitment in relation to bridge employment and retirement intentions. *Journal of Vocational Behavior*. doi:10.1016/j.jvb.2010.04.004.

Kite, M. E., Stockdale, G. D., Whitley, B. E., & Johnson, B. T. (2005). Attitudes toward younger and older adults: An updated meta-analytic review. *Journal of Social Issues*, *61*, 241–266.

Kleiber, D., & Nimrod, G. (2008). Expressions of generativity and civic engagement in a "learning in retirement" group. *Journal of Adult Development 15*, 76–86.

Koepke, D. R., & Ellor, J. (2005). Spiritual need four: Opportunities to be served and to share with others. *Journal of Religion, Spirituality and Aging*, *17*, 97–119.

Legerski, E. M., Cornwall, M., & O'Neil, B. (2006). Changing locus of control: Steelworkers adjusting to forced unemployment. *Social Forces*, *84*, 1521–1537.

Lockenhoff, C. E., Terracciano, A., & Costa, P. T. (2009). Five-factor model personality traits and the retirement transition: Longitudinal and cross-sectional associations. *Psychology and Aging*, *24*, 722–728.

Long, J. (1987). Continuity as a basis for change: Leisure and male retirement. *Leisure Studies*, *6*, 55–70.

Luhmann, M., & Eid, M. (2009). Does it really feel the same? Changes in life satisfaction following repeated life events. *Journal of Personality and Social Psychology*, *97*, 363–381.

Maynard, L. J. (2008). Short term impact of a voluntary health intervention on overall vs. preventive healthcare consumption. *International Journal of Consumer Studies*, *32*, 296–302.

McAdams, D. P., & de St. Aubin, E. (1992). A theory of generativity and its assessment through self-report, behavioral acts, and narrative themes in autobiography. *Journal of Personality and Social Psychology*, *62*, 1003–1015.

McAdams, D. P., de St. Aubin, E., & Logan, R. L. (1993). Generativity among young, midlife, and older adults. *Psychology and Aging*, *8*, 221–230.

McCrae, R. R., & Costa, P. T. (2008). The five-factor theory of personality. In O. P. John, R. W. Robbins, & L. A. Pervin (Eds.), *Handbook of personality psychology: Theory and research* (pp. 159–181). New York, NY: Guilford.

McCrae, R. R., Terracciano, A., & Khoury, B. (2007). Dolce far niente: The positive psychology of personality stability and invariance. In A. D. Ong & M. H. M. van Dulman (Eds.), *Oxford handbook of methods in positive psychology* (pp. 176–188). New York, NY: Oxford University Press.

McFarland, M. J. (2010). Religion and mental health among older adults: Do the effects of religious involvement vary by gender? *The Journals of Gerontology, Series B: Psychological Sciences and Social Sciences*, *65B*, 621–630.

Narushima, M. (2005). "Payback time": Community volunteering among older adults as a transformative mechanism. *Ageing & Society*, *25*, 567–584.

Nelson, D. L., & Simmons, B. L. (2011). Savoring eustress while coping with distress: The holistic model of distress. In J. C. Campbell & L. E. Tetrick (Eds.), *Handbook of occupational health psychology* (2nd ed., pp. 55–74). Washington, DC: American Psychological Association.

Noone, J. H., Stephens, C., & Alpass, F. (2010). The process of retirement planning scale (PRePS): Development and validation. *Psychological Assessment*, *22*, 520–531.

Noone, J. H., Stephens, C., & Alpass, F. M. (2009). Preretirement planning and well-being in later life: A prospective study. *Research on Aging, 31*, 295–317.

Parise, M. R., & Forret, M. L. (2008). Formal mentoring programs: The relationship of program design and support to mentors' perceptions of benefits and costs. *Journal of Vocational Behavior, 72*, 225–240.

Petkoska, J., & Earl, J. K. (2009). Understanding the influence of demographic and psychological variables on retirement planning. *Psychology and Aging, 24*, 245–251.

Potocnik, K., Tordera, N., & Peiro, J. M. (2009). The role of human resource practices and group norms in the retirement process. *European Psychologist, 14*, 193–206.

Potocnik, K., Tordera, N., & Peiro, J. M. (2010). The influence of the early retirement process on satisfaction with early retirement and psychological well-being. *International Journal of Aging and Human Development, 70*, 251–273.

Price, C. A., & Balaswamy, S. (2009). Beyond health and wealth: Predictors of women's retirement satisfaction. *International Journal of Aging and Human Development, 68*, 195–214.

Price, C. A., & Dean, K. J. (2009). Exploring the relationship between employment history and retired women's social relationships. *Journal of Women and Aging, 21*, 85–98.

Reichstadt, J., Sengupta, G., Depp, C., Palinkas, L. A., & Jeste, D. V. (2010). Older adults' perspectives on successful aging: Qualitative interviews. *The American Journal of Geriatric Psychiatry, 18*, 567–575.

Reitzes, D. C., & Mutran, E. J. (2004). The transition to retirement: Stages and factors that influence retirement adjustment. *The International Journal of Aging and Human Development, 59*, 63–84.

Robinson, O. C., Demetre, J. D., & Corney, R. (2010). Personality and retirement: Exploring the links between the Big Five personality traits, reasons for retirement and the experience of being retired. *Personality and Individual Differences, 48*, 792–797.

Rosenkoetter, M. M., & Garris, J. M. (2001). Retirement planning, use of time, and psychosocial adjustment. *Issues in Mental Health Nursing, 22*, 703–722.

Rotter, J. B. (1966). Generalized expectancies for internal versus external control of reinforcement. *Psychological Monographs, 80*(1), 1–28.

Rybarczyk, B., DeMarco, G., DeLaCruz, M., Lapidos, S., & Fortner, B. (2001). A classroom mind/body wellness intervention for older adults with chronic illness: Comparing immediate and 1-year benefits. *Behavioral Medicine, 27*, 15–27.

Saksvik, I. B., & Hetland, H. (2009). Exploring dispositional resistance to change. *Journal of Leadership and Organizational Studies, 16*, 175–183.

Shultz, K. S. (2003). Bridge employment: Work after retirement. In G. A. Adams & T. A. Beehr (Eds.), *Retirement: Reasons, processes, and results* (pp. 215–241). Mahwah, NJ: Erlbaum.

Shultz, K., & Wang, M. (2007). The influence of specific health conditions on retirement decisions. *The International Journal of Aging and Human Development, 65*, 149–161.

Silverstein, M., & Parker, M. G. (2002). Leisure activities and quality of life among the oldest old in Sweden. *Research on Aging, 24*, 528–547.

Spiegel, P. E., & Shultz, K. S. (2003). The influence of preretirement planning and transferability of skills on Naval officers' retirement satisfaction and adjustment. *Military Psychology, 15*, 284–306.

Stephan, Y. (2009). Openness to experience and active older adults' life satisfaction: A trait and facet level analysis. *Personality and Individual Differences, 47*, 637–641.

Stewart, A. J., & Vandewater, E. A. (1998). The course of generativity. In D. P. McAdams & E. de St. Aubin (Eds.), *Generativity and adult development: How and why we care for the next generation* (pp. 75–100). Washington, DC: American Psychological Association.

Taylor, M. A., & Doverspike, D. (2003). Retirement planning and preparation. In G. Adams & T. Beehr (Eds.), *Retirement: Reasons, processes, and results* (pp. 53–82). New York, NY: Springer.

Taylor, M. A., & Geldhauser, H. (2007). Low-income older workers. In K. E. Shultz & G. A. Adams (Eds.), *Aging and work in the 21st century* (pp. 25–49). Mahwah, NJ: Lawrence Erlbaum Associates.

Taylor, M. A., Goldberg, C., Shore, L. M., & Lipka, P. (2008). The effects of retirement expectations and social support on post-retirement adjustment: A longitudinal analysis. *Journal of Managerial Psychology, 23*, 458–470.

Taylor, M. A., & Shore, L. M. (1995). Predictors of planned retirement age: An application of Beehr's model. *Psychology and Aging, 10*, 76–83.

Taylor, M. A., Shultz, K., Spiegel, P., Morrison, B., & Greene, J. (2007). Predicting the retirement adjustment of military retirees: The central role of expectations. *Journal of Applied Social Psychology, 37*, 1697–1725.

Taylor-Carter, M. A., & Cook, K. (1995). Adaptation to retirement: Role changes and psychological resources. *Career Development Quarterly, 44*, 67–82.

Topa, G., Moriano, J. A., Depolo, M., Alcover, C.-M., & Morales, J. F. (2009). Antecedents and consequences of retirement planning and decision-making: A meta-analysis and model. *Journal of Vocational Behavior, 75*, 38–55.

van Solinge, H., & Henkens, K. (2005). Couples' adjustment to retirement: A multi-actor panel study. *The Journals of Gerontology, Series B: Psychological Sciences and Social Sciences, 60B*, S11–S20.

van Solinge, H., & Henkens, K. (2008). Adjustment to and satisfaction with retirement: Two of a kind? *Psychology and Aging, 23*, 422–434.

van Solinge, H., & Henkens, K. (2009). Living longer, working longer? The impact of subjective life expectancy on retirement intentions and behavior. *European Journal of Public Health, 20*, 47–51.

Vinick, B. H., & Ekerdt, D. J. (1991). Retirement: What happens to husband-wife relationships. *Journal of Geriatric Psychiatry, 24*, 23–40.

Wang, M. (2007). Profiling retirees in the retirement transition and adjustment process: Examining the longitudinal change patterns of retirees' psychological well-being. *Journal of Applied Psychology, 92*, 455–474.

Wang, M., & Shultz, K. S. (2010). Employee retirement: A review and recommendations for future investigation. *Journal of Management, 36*, 172–206.

Wang, M., Zhan, Y., Liu, S., & Shultz, K. S. (2008). Antecedents of bridge employment: A longitudinal investigation. *Journal of Applied Psychology, 93*, 818–830.

Wells, Y., DeVaus, D., Kendig, H., Quine, S., & Petralia, W. (2006). *Healthy Retirement Project* (Technical Report). Melbourne, Australia: Lincoln Centre for Ageing and Community Care Research, La Trobe University.

Winston, N. A., & Barnes, J. (2007). Anticipation of retirement among baby boomers. *Journal of Women and Aging, 19*, 137–159.

Wong, J. Y., & Earl, J. K. (2009). Toward an integrated model of individual, psychosocial, and organizational predictors of retirement adjustment. *Journal of Vocational Behavior, 75*, 1–13.

Zhan, Y., Wang, M., Liu, S., & Shultz, K. S. (2009). Bridge employment and retirees' health: A longitudinal investigation. *Journal of Occupational Health Psychology, 14*, 374–389.

Retirement Decision Making

Steve M. Jex *and* James Grosch

Abstract

Due to the aging of the workforce, combined with increased life expectancy, interest in retirement among researchers has increased dramatically. One area in particular that has attracted a large portion of this interest is retirement decision making. The primary objective of this chapter is to review the extant literature on retirement decision making, organized according to three major "decision points" in the retirement process. In addition to reviewing this literature, we identify a number of gaps in both research and theory underlying retirement decision-making research. The chapter concludes with a number of suggestions for applying what we know about retirement decision making to influence retirement-related decisions, for the benefit of both individuals and organizations.

Key Words: retirement, retirement planning, decision making, bridge employment

As most readers undoubtedly know, and as many chapters in this volume will point out, the workforce around the world is aging. Specifically, between 2002 and 2012 it is estimated that the number of employees in the United States close to retirement age (55 and older) will increase by 49.3%, or at a rate almost four times greater than that of the overall labor force (Toossi, 2004). In addition to the general aging of the workforce, we also know that overall life expectancy in many countries (e.g., Japan, Italy, Norway, Canada) is increasing into the 80s. This first trend obviously means that a significant and growing portion of the active workforce will at least be contemplating retirement. When combined with the second trend, however, it is evident that the choices one makes about retirement will become increasingly important because people will have to live with the consequences of these decisions much longer.

Largely due to these demographic shifts and their implications for society in general, the study of retirement has grown considerably in the past decade, and a good portion of this research has examined the decision-making process leading up to retirement. One obvious reason for studying retirement decision making is that a greater understanding of this process is helpful to organizations that are trying to influence this decision. Since one of the consequences of an aging workforce might be shortages of younger employees, organizations might want to entice older employees to stay on the job longer. Another important reason for studying retirement decision making is that it may provide us with clues as to the factors that tend to maximize or detract from happiness and well-being in retirement. While this obviously has implications for individuals, it is also an important issue for society as a whole because happiness and well-being in retirement might be related to health and, as a result, may be related to health care costs.

The purpose of this chapter is to review the current empirical literature on retirement decision making. Given the amount of research conducted on this topic, we make no claim to be comprehensive in that review, although we do attempt to discern general conclusions and trends that have emerged in this area. In addition to summarizing the current state of the literature, we will also suggest future research that is needed on retirement decision making. This is important because changes in health care legislation, government funding of social insurance programs, economic conditions, and general societal trends may impact the process of retirement, and thus what we currently know may be outdated twenty years from now.

The chapter will begin with a broad overview of the process of retirement. This is important to cover because retirement can take many forms, and there are now several theoretical models that describe the process of retirement. After covering the process of retirement at a general level, we then discuss each of the major "decision points" in the retirement process, and what is known about specific factors that predict these decision points. This will be followed by a discussion of major gaps in the retirement decision-making literature. The chapter concludes with a discussion of ways that organizations can use retirement research to impact actual retirement decision making by workers, as well as suggestions for future research.

Retirement: An Overview

According to Feldman (1994), retirement is defined as the "withdrawal from an organizational position or career path of considerable duration … taken with the intention of reduced psychological commitment to work thereafter" (p. 287). This definition assumes that retirement represents withdrawal from *both* a career and a particular work setting. Another important implication of this definition, and empirical data support this, is that retirement takes many different forms; that is, there is not a "one size fits all" model of retirement that applies to everyone. Specifically, some people retire by withdrawing completely from the workforce, while others hold part-time, seasonal, or even full-time jobs and still consider themselves "retired."

Given the amount that has been written about retirement in recent years (e.g., Wang & Shultz, 2010), it is easy to forget that retirement is a relatively recent phenomenon, simply because in the past people did not live long enough for retirement to really matter. However, since today the life expectancy in most industrialized countries is approaching or slightly beyond 80 years of age, retirement represents a significant portion of most people's lives, and thus interest in retirement as a topic of research has grown considerably in a relatively short period of time.

Another factor that has generated research interest in retirement is that most industrialized countries do not have a mandatory retirement age. Thus, for most people today retirement represents a *lifestyle choice* rather than a forced transition. Given this element of choice, there is considerable variability in the ages at which people retire, as well as the factors that ultimately determine retirement. Furthermore, the choices that people make about retirement (e.g., whether or not to retire early, or to work part-time after retiring) have consequences for organizations, as well as for the solvency of social insurance funds. Thus, there are ultimately a number of reasons why a greater understanding of the retirement process is of interest to organizations as well as to governments.

As a topic of interest to psychologists, the study of retirement has been a very recent phenomenon. Beehr's review article published in 1986 (Beehr, 1986) is generally seen as the beginning of extensive research on retirement among industrial-organizational (I-O) psychologists, although this was certainly not the first examination of retirement in the I-O literature (see Smith, Kendall, & Hulin, 1969, for example). In addition to generating interest in retirement research, Beehr's review was also significant because it was the first to propose a model of the retirement process. In this model it was proposed that the most direct predictor of the actual *act* of retirement is one's *intent to retire*. Furthermore, one's intent to retire is predicted by one's preference to retire or the extent to which one is thinking about retirement. Finally, one's preference to retire is impacted by both environment and personal factors. Environmental factors would include aspects about one's job as well as one's personal life, while personal factors would include characteristics of the individual. We will have more to say about each of these categories throughout this chapter.

In addition to providing researchers with a much-needed theoretical framework from which to study retirement, Beehr's model also highlights the fact that retirement is a *process* that plays out over a long period of time. Thus, although most workers retire in their early to mid-60s, the decision of when to actually retire is impacted by experiences and decisions that occurred much earlier in life. Perhaps the best example of this is in the area of financial planning. Despite what is known about the importance of financial planning, empirical data have shown a great deal of variability in the degree to which people begin planning for retirement, and the extent to which they do so (Ekerdt, Hackney,

Kosloski, & DeViney, 2001). Such decisions, which are made many years prior to retirement itself, obviously have major implications for the timing of the retirement decision as well as the form that retirement will take.

The Criterion: Retirement "Decision Points"

As Beehr (1986) and many subsequent retirement researchers have pointed out, retirement decision making actually encompasses a number of decisions made over time. In order to study retirement decision making, however, it is important to isolate the most important decisions in that process. We believe there are three key sequential decision points in the retirement process, which are summarized in Figure 17.1. As can be seen, these key decision points include (1) the decision to begin planning for retirement, (2) the actual decision to retire, and (3) choosing the actual form that retirement takes. Each of these will be discussed below.

Planning for Retirement

Despite considerable evidence suggesting that financial resources are positively associated with retirement satisfaction (Elder & Rudolph, 1999), there is also evidence of considerable variability in financial planning for retirement (Ekerdt et al., 2001). That is, some people begin saving very early in life for retirement, while others wait until they are much closer to retirement age before they begin any type of financial planning associated with retirement (Hira, Rock, & Loibl, 2009). Given what is known about college saving and the fact that many people do not save for college or do so when it is late (Kane, 1999), this should not necessarily be a surprise. Fortunately, there has been an attempt by researchers to examine the factors that impact one's decision to engage in some form of financial planning for retirement.

Perhaps the most obvious factor that predicts the decision to financially plan for retirement is a person's financial resources (e.g., income level, financial assets, etc.). Since retirement savings represents a form of deferred income, it stands to reason that individuals who are paid very little or who have very few financial assets would be unlikely to plan for retirement (Hira et al., 2009). Such individuals probably live "paycheck to paycheck" and therefore would be unable to financially plan for retirement even if they had the desire to do so.

In contrast, individuals who have substantial incomes and have accumulated a significant amount of wealth will have the discretionary income to set aside for retirement (DeVaney & Zhang, 2001). Individuals with such financial resources in many cases work for organizations that provide generous pension programs and access to other financial planning tools (e.g., 401(k) plans, retirement counseling).

Despite the impact of financial resources, it has been shown that financial resources do not tell the whole story. It has been shown, for example, that in some cases people do not engage in financial planning for retirement even though, at least on the surface, they have the financial resources to do so. One reason for this, according to Jacobs-Lawson and Hershey (2005), is that people simply differ in the extent to which they plan for the future. Some people carefully plan for the future, while others simply "live for the moment"; as one might expect, people with a more future orientation are more likely to engage in financial planning for retirement than those who simply live for the moment.

In order to plan for retirement, it is typically necessary to seek out the services of a financial planning professional or seek out information about investing on one's own. Furthermore, because of their occupation or simply because of interest, some people feel very comfortable discussing financial planning options with a professional or making investment decisions on their own. In other cases, however, people do not feel comfortable in this arena. It is not surprising, then, that Jacobs-Lawson and Hershey (2005) found that comfort with investments was a significant predictor of financial planning for retirement.

A final predictor of the decision to plan for retirement, at least in terms of finances, is the goals that one sets for retirement. According to Schulz

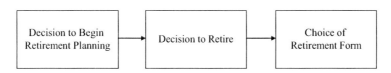

Figure 17.1 Summary of the major decision points in the retirement process

(2002), people differ widely in terms of what they want their retirement to be like. Some people hope to travel extensively, others want to start a new business, and some want to relocate to a warmer climate. Whatever a person's goals for retirement might be, any goal that one might aspire to has some financial cost. Thus, it is not surprising that individuals who have clearly stated goals are more likely to engage in financial planning for retirement.

To this point we have covered only one form of retirement planning—financial planning. While certainly important, there are other ways that people plan for retirement. One of the most important nonfinancial forms of planning for retirement is maintaining one's health. One can engage in extensive financial planning for retirement, but if one's health fails, such financial planning is likely to have little impact. While an extensive coverage of health maintenance is beyond the scope of this chapter, there are some findings that are directly relevant to the prediction of health-related planning for retirement. It has been clearly found, for example, that gender impacts health maintenance—women are generally more diligent about maintaining their health compared to men (Bertakis, Azari, Helms, Callahan, & Robbins, 2000). It has also been shown that people who have substantial financial resources (these people are already more likely to plan financially) are more likely to take steps to maintain their health as they head toward retirement (Smith & Kingston, 1999).

Another variable that likely impacts health-related planning is health locus of control, or the extent to which people believe they have control over the state of their health (Wallston & Wallston, 1978). We know that people who have an *internal* health locus of control take more active steps to improve their health (e.g., regular exercise), compared to those with an external health locus of control (Wallston, Wallston, Smith, & Dobbins, 1984). Given this and other findings, it stands to reason that individuals with an internal health locus of control would probably be more likely to take positive steps to ensure that they are healthy upon retirement.

A final way that we see people planning for retirement is *socially*. Since for most people retirement represents a period in one's life where there is a good deal more discretionary time available, people need to fill this time through any number of ways such as hobbies, volunteer work, leisure pursuits (e.g., golf), or travel, to name a few. Again, as in the case with health planning, there is not a great deal of research that has addressed this issue. We

suspect, however, that a key variable in determining this form of planning is *work centrality*. According to Paullay, Alliger, and Stone-Romero (1994), work centrality represents the extent to which one's life revolves around one's work and work activities. For those who have a high degree of work centrality, we would assume that much less effort would be made to develop non-work interests and social relationships. Conversely, for those with low work centrality, we would assume that it is much more likely that such individuals would develop both interests and social relationships outside of the workplace and, as a result, would be better prepared for the transition into retirement.

In summary, then, we view retirement planning as occurring in three major areas: financial, health, and social. Furthermore, each of these forms of retirement planning is predicted by different variables, so it is very likely that many people are not prepared in all three. That is, some people may be prepared financially but may have neglected their health and/or may have only a vague idea what they are going to do after they retire. In other cases, people may be healthy, and have a good idea of what they want to do during retirement, but may have neglected to plan financially.

Despite this variability in retirement planning profiles, we do believe that in general it is possible to develop a description of the type of individual who is most likely to engage in retirement planning activities. Specifically, individuals who have at least above-average incomes, who do not feel intimidated about seeking investment information, who have a future orientation, who have a set of concrete goals associated with retirement, who have an internal health locus of control, and who have developed interests and social relationships outside of work are most likely going to be the best prepared for retirement.

The Decision to Retire

For many years in the United States, as well as in other countries, it was legal for most organizations to establish a mandatory retirement age for their workers. As a result, deciding when to leave the workforce was a pretty straightforward process. In 1978, however, the mandatory retirement age of 65 in the United States was abolished, although there are some occupations (e.g., military officers, air traffic controllers, FBI agents) where a mandatory retirement age still exists. Given the absence of a mandatory retirement age for most workers, the actual decision to retire is now a more complex matter. In this section we summarize research on the factors that drive this decision.

Perhaps the most obvious predictor of the decision to retire is age. As would be expected, the older people are the more likely they are to decide to retire (Adams & Rau, 2004). It has also been shown that, like retirement planning, the actual retirement decision is also driven by financial considerations. Generally speaking, individuals who have large incomes and who have engaged in considerable investment and financial planning have been shown to retire earlier than those with lower incomes and fewer financial assets (Gruber & Wise, 1999). This relationship, however, is more complex than one might think because it depends to some degree on what one's financial needs will be in retirement. According to continuity theory (Atchley, 1989), most people want to maintain their pre-retirement lifestyle after they retire. Therefore, it stands to reason that individuals who have large incomes and substantial investments will also need more money after they retire in order to continue their pre-retirement lifestyle. Conversely, individuals with lower incomes may very well need less income in retirement because their post-retirement financial needs are more modest.

Somewhat related to financial assets are the nature of the pension plan of the organization for which a person is working and the provisions of the government policy concerning retirement. Pension plans vary widely, but in most cases the amount of one's pension is determined by some combination of (a) years of service with the organization and (b) salary level prior to retirement. Given these considerations, it is very likely that individuals who begin their careers relatively young and remain in the same organization their entire career are likely to retire at earlier ages than those who delay the start of their career or who make many job changes. Related to the general provisions of pension programs, there is also fairly clear evidence that early retirement incentives do influence retirement behavior (Stock & Wise, 1990).

Government policies regarding pension benefits vary widely, and a complete examination of such policies around the world is well beyond the scope of this chapter (interested readers can refer to the chapter by Yao and Peng in this volume). Suffice it to say, however, that such policies do influence retirement choices. For many decades in the United States, for example, the normal retirement age (NRA) at which one could obtain full pension benefits from the Social Security system was 65. In

1983, however, due in large part to concerns about the financial solvency of the Social Security system, Congress enacted legislation that gradually increases the NRA over time until it reaches 67 for workers born in 1967 or later. Furthermore, despite the fact that most people do not rely on Social Security benefits as their sole source of retirement income, Social Security eligibility does impact choice of retirement age. For example, if someone were considering retiring at the age of 65, it is certainly possible that such a person would consider delaying his or her retirement two years in order to receive full retirement benefits from the federal government. We should also note that the minimum age that a person can begin to receive pension benefits (which are reduced) is 62, and this too may impact choice of retirement age. For example, an individual who is considering retiring at the age of 60 may strongly consider delaying retirement for two years in order to supplement his or her retirement income with Social Security benefits (albeit with a reduced amount).

Despite the impact that the Social Security system may have on retirement behavior in the United States, in many other countries the impact of the government-sponsored pension system is much greater. In Western Europe and Scandinavian countries, for example, government pensions are quite generous and typically represent a larger portion of post-retirement income than is the case in the United States (Blondal & Scarpetta, 1997). A recent illustration of this is the upheaval in France surrounding the decision of the government to raise the retirement age from 60 to 62, largely due to concern over funding these benefits. While raising the retirement age two years does not appear to be a major change, the reaction to it attests to the fact that the age of 60 has become highly ingrained as the "anchoring point" for the proper age of retirement in that country.

Health is another variable that impacts multiple decision points in the retirement process, and retirement age is no exception. For example, in some cases people are forced to retire at a fairly young age because of health problems (Barnes-Farrell, 2003), particularly in physically demanding or dangerous jobs (e.g., law enforcement, fire services); healthier people can obviously work until they are older. However, as with financial resources, the relationship between health and choice of retirement age is complex. For example, in some cases, healthy individuals who have well-defined and long-standing retirement goals (e.g., travel extensively) may choose to retire relatively early because achieving those retirement goals is contingent on maintaining one's health. In effect, some people may decide to "quit while they're ahead" and pursue their retirement goals while they are healthy enough to do so even if they still could work longer.

Another complicating factor in the relation between health and choice of retirement age is that it is not only an individual's health that matters—health of one's spouse also comes into play in many cases (Talaga & Beehr, 1995). In some cases, otherwise healthy individuals may be forced to retire in order to care for a spouse who is ill. This is particularly the case for chronic and debilitating illnesses such as Alzheimer's disease, since the healthy spouse must often assume responsibility for caregiving (Dentinger & Clarkberg, 2002).

Up to this point we have discussed predictors of retirement age that are of a personal nature—finances and health, and to a lesser extent one's goals in retirement. We also know, however, that a number of work-related variables also play a role in one's choice of retirement age as well. Perhaps the most obvious work-related predictor of retirement age is the extent to which people enjoy their work and find it fulfilling (Beehr & Bennett, 2007). If people enjoy their work, and it is a major part of their life, one would assume that such individuals would opt for a later retirement age. This certainly makes intuitive sense and is also consistent with theories of aging that stress maintaining continuity in one's life during the later years (Atchley, 1989).

One feature of an enjoyable job that seems to be particularly important for older employees who decide to remain in the workplace is job flexibility. For example, allowing employees to have a say in how many hours they work per week, or permitting workers to shift to less demanding jobs as they get older, are employer accommodations that are associated with an increase in the age of expected retirement (Hurd & McGarry, 1993).

If enjoyment of work and job flexibility may cause people to postpone retirement, what work characteristics might lead people to opt for an earlier retirement age? As stated earlier, one factor that often comes into play is the physical demands of a job. Despite considerable variability within age cohorts, older people generally have more difficulty keeping up and are more likely to experience adverse health outcomes (e.g., musculoskeletal disorders) in physically demanding jobs or those in which the pace of work is very fast (Jex, Wang, & Zarubin, 2007; Grosch & Pransky, 2009) or repetitive (Filer & Petri, 1988). Thus, retirement might be a way of getting rid of such job requirements even if there is not a mandatory retirement age. Another characteristic of work that may facilitate the decision to retire is a change in technology (Bartel & Sicherman, 1993). Again, there is undoubtedly difference among older workers with respect to adjusting to new technology; however, older workers generally have a harder time adjusting to technological changes compared to younger workers (Friedberg, 2003). Thus, in some cases retirement may be a way for some older workers to cope with the demands imposed by technological changes.

In addition to the demands of a job, the social environment of the workplace may contribute to one's decision to retire at a given age. Although certainly not true of all work environments, there is considerable evidence that age discrimination does exist. While a complete explanation of the reasons for age discrimination is beyond the scope of this chapter, the most general reason for this occurring in organizations is that it is a reflection of a somewhat "youth centered" culture overall. Thus, it is often the case that older employees feel discriminated against in terms of promotion opportunities, layoffs, and work assignments (Johnson & Neumark, 1997). Furthermore, one way to cope with perceived age discrimination at work is to simply withdraw from the work environment through retirement. In fact, there is evidence that perceived age-related discrimination is one factor that does contribute to one's decision to retire (Johnson & Neurmark, 1997).

Finally, in addition to the factors that have already been discussed, we believe that there are likely to be a number of other factors contributing to one's choice of retirement age that are somewhat idiosyncratic or that defy categorization. For example, in a study predicting retirement choices among a sample of public-sector employees, Beehr, Glazer, Nielson, and Farmer (2000) found that one of the best predictors of the timing of retirement was simply whether the study participants were "tired of work." This is obviously a rather vague variable, and we know of no systematic effort to define it precisely. Nevertheless, the predictive power of this variable suggests that in many cases the decision to retire may not be driven by any one factor in particular, but by whether a worker simply desires a change in life and sees retirement as a way to achieve this change.

Form of Retirement

In the retirement literature, it is generally acknowledged that people can retire in one of two ways. First, for some people, retirement marks a complete break from the workforce. An individual who chooses this form of retirement might spend his or her time pursuing leisure activities, doing volunteer work, or perhaps out of necessity devoting his or her time to caregiving activities. It is also possible that some people retire completely simply because they are too ill to hold any type of employment.

The second form of retirement acknowledged in the literature is a more partial withdrawal from the workforce. The term "bridge employment" is used to describe any form of employment that a person might hold after formally retiring (Feldman, 1994). Furthermore, within the bridge employment literature, the distinction is often made between bridge employment in one's professional field and bridge employment that is unrelated (Wang, Zhan, Liu, & Shultz, 2008). A retired college professor teaching part-time would be an example of the former, while a retired nurse working in a bookstore would be an example of the latter.

Having defined what is meant by "form" of retirement, we now turn our attention to predictors of one's choice of retirement form. As with the other decision points in the retirement process, one's financial situation plays a major role in the form of retirement that one chooses. In general, those who have larger post-retirement income are more likely to retire fully. In contrast, those with lower levels of post-retirement income are more likely to engage in some form of bridge employment; stated differently, some people engage in bridge employment simply because they need to supplement their post-retirement income (Feldman, 1994; Wang et al., 2008).

Post-retirement income, however, is certainly not a perfect predictor of one's propensity to engage in bridge employment. For example, there are people with relatively large post-retirement incomes who do engage in bridge employment, while there are others with relatively modest incomes who do not. One factor that explains such discrepancies is the differences in work attachment (Beehr et al., 2000). For those with high work attachment, completely disengaging from work is understandably a very difficult adjustment. Thus, for such individuals one way to cope with the loss of one's regular work role is to engage in some form of bridge employment, even if the individual really does not need the money.

For many people, work is also a domain where they can fulfill their social needs. Thus, another reason that some people engage in bridge employment is for social interaction or to provide a way to structure their time. Such individuals, one would assume, do not feel that they can obtain enough social interaction or structure of their time without some involvement in the workforce. In other cases, some people might fulfill social needs or find time structure through leisure activities or perhaps through volunteering.

In addition to investigating the decision to seek bridge employment overall, there has also been research on the type of bridge employment that people seek in retirement. Feldman (1994) proposed that people who hold professional jobs are more likely to seek bridge employment in that same profession, and empirical research has supported that (Gobeski & Beehr, 2009). One important qualifier to this, however, is job satisfaction. That is, those who hold professional jobs that they *liked* are more likely to seek bridge employment in that same profession. Professionals who did not like their jobs, on the other hand, tend not to seek employment in the same profession.

Another factor that may impact choice of bridge employment in the same profession is an individual's perception of the factors driving his or her retirement decision-making process. Retirement researchers (e.g., Beehr & Adams, 2003; Beehr, 1986) have long distinguished between "push" and "pull" factors driving retirement. Push factors would be things such as heavy work demands, perceived age-related discrimination, and perhaps an inability to adapt to new technology. Pull factors, on the other hand, would be things such as the opportunity to spend more time with one's spouse, opportunity for pursuit of leisure activities, and simply having the opportunity to reduce the pace of life. Research has shown not only that retirement due to "push" factors is negatively associated with retirement satisfaction, but also that it is negatively associated with engaging in bridge employment in the same profession (Gobeski & Beehr, 2009).

Summary. In examining the major decision points in the retirement process, it is quite obvious that there are a number of recurring themes. The first is that every step in this decision-making process is impacted by financial considerations. It is difficult, for example, to plan financially for retirement if one lives "paycheck to paycheck." It is also the case that one's choice of retirement age as well as the form that retirement will take are both impacted by financial considerations—those who have greater financial resources will likely retire earlier and are less likely to engage in bridge employment.

The other variable that impacts every step in the retirement decision-making process is health, both one's own and that of one's spouse. Generally speaking, people who are healthier will be more likely to engage in retirement planning simply because they can foresee having a future, whereas those in poor health may not be able to. It is also the case that poor health (their own or their spouses') may force them to retire earlier than they really want to, either because they cannot work or because they have caregiving responsibilities.

Despite the importance of wealth and health in the retirement decision-making process, there are clearly numerous other things that enter into the process. While we see no need to repeat these for the reader, we do believe it is worth highlighting two of the most important of these: attachment to work and retirement goals.

We see people's psychological investment in work, typically captured by variables such as work centrality, job involvement, or work attachment, as a key driving force in the retirement decision-making process. Although this may not strongly impact retirement planning, it is likely to strongly impact the actual decision to retire as well as the form of retirement. Those who are highly psychologically invested in work will probably hold on to their work as long as they can, and in some cases may never retire at all.

We see retirement goals as also being very important and in fact impacting all decision points in the retirement decision-making process. This is because one's goals in retirement typically have an economic cost and require certain lifestyle choices. For example, a person whose goal is to travel extensively in retirement would certainly need to begin planning financially much earlier than someone whose goals are more modest. Such an individual would also need to prepare by maintaining one's health, because traveling extensively would be difficult if one were in poor health.

Gaps in the Retirement Decision-Making Literature

As is evident from the preceding section, considerable progress has been made in understanding the retirement decision-making process. Despite this progress, however, there are still significant gaps in the retirement decision-making literature, and unfortunately between research findings (e.g., what is known about factors that predict retirement satisfaction) and the retirement behavior of individuals. In this section we discuss those gaps; specifically, we

discuss what we perceive as gaps in (1) theoretical foundations of retirement research, (2) research findings, and (3) research findings and retirement behavior, particularly with respect to retirement planning.

Theoretical Foundations

Since retirement research is a relatively new endeavor, it is understandable that there is not a great deal of theory driving this research (see Beehr, 1986, for a notable exception). Of course there are theories that address the aging process in a more general sense (e.g., Erikson, 1950), but there are few theories that address retirement decision making specifically. Thus, one major need in the retirement decision-making literature is simply for more theoretical efforts such as Beehr's (1986).

In addition to formulating more theories of the retirement decision-making process, we also believe that it is time that retirement researchers take a critical look at some of the theories that form the basis of retirement research in general (Wang & Shultz, 2010). The most dominant theory guiding retirement research is Atchley's (1989) continuity theory. The basic premise of continuity theory is that when people age they try to do so in a way that allows them to maintain their preferred lifestyle. Applied specifically to retirement decision making, this theory implies that retirement decisions will be made in such a way that the person will be able to maintain his or her pre-retirement lifestyle.

While this theory certainly does have empirical support, and there is undoubtedly anecdotal evidence of its validity, it does not capture the process of retirement for everyone. For example, for people who hold relatively stressful jobs where perhaps they are faced with high levels of job demands and low decisional control (Karasek & Theorell, 1990), retirement would provide an opportunity to reverse those conditions and thus continuity would *not* be desired. Similarly, for many people retirement may provide the opportunity to pursue interests and hobbies that they were unable to pursue when they were full-time members of the workforce. Thus, while we are certainly not dismissing continuity theory, we do not believe that it represents the driving force in retirement in a substantial portion of people.

We propose that rather than providing the opportunity for *continuity*, retirement for many provides the opportunity for *compensation*. That is, for many people retirement represents a time when they are able to structure their lives or participate in activities that they were unable to do when they were working. For example, during a person's work life, exercise and fitness activities might have been squeezed in prior to or after work. Thus, in retirement such a person might have a goal of engaging in considerable fitness activities. It is also possible that some people may see retirement as a time in their lives when they can compensate for some of the perceived deficiencies in their pre-retirement job. For example, a person who works for a number of years may see retirement as an opportunity to engage in more stimulating, creative activities. Conversely, a person who has worked in a highly complex job for many years may see retirement as an opportunity to engage in relatively mundane activities such as simple home maintenance activities or lawn care.

While both of these examples make intuitive sense, and in fact have been acknowledged in the retirement literature (Beehr & Adams, 2003), most retirement research has proceeded with the underlying notion that the driving force behind retirement decisions is to maintain continuity. Retirement researchers need to examine the factors that might lead a person to view retirement in a compensatory fashion—job satisfaction would be a logical one— rather than simply assume that continuity drives everything.

As far as theories applied specifically to retirement decision making, Wang and Shultz (2010) propose five: (1) rational choice theory, (2) image theory, (3) role theory, (4) theory of planned behavior, and (5) expectancy theory. While we will not provide an extensive review of these theories, we will discuss some of the assumptions common to most of them and examine the impact on retirement decision-making research.

Although there is one exception—that being image theory—the other four theories view decision makers as *highly rational,* which is not surprising since some of these theories have their roots in economics. What does rational mean in the context of retirement decision making? Simply put, we believe it means that people will attempt to make decisions in such a way that they will maximize their long-term outcomes while minimizing their costs. As an example, many people (though certainly not all) save regularly for retirement through pension contributions, IRAs, and 401(k)s. The amount they save, however, is not so great that it causes them significant financial hardship in the present.

What, then, is the limitation of rationality as an underlying assumption of retirement decision-making research? We believe that the primary limitation stems from the simple fact that considerable evidence exists that many of the decisions that people make are simply *not* rational, at least when viewed from the outside. Consider, for example, the decision to engage in financial planning for retirement. As stated earlier in this chapter, nearly half of people make very little effort to save for retirement, despite what is known about the critical role of financial planning. In some cases income levels are so low that people have little, if any, discretionary income to save for retirement planning.

In many cases, however, people would appear to have enough discretionary income to save for retirement but choose not to. Some people may choose to have the maximum amount possible financed on a home, or choose to spend a large portion of their discretionary income on vacations or other leisure pursuits (e.g., skiing). People who make such choices would not appear to be "rational," at least in an economic sense, but they are in fact making theses choice based on *something.* We suspect that what might be at play here is the previously mentioned variable *future orientation,* or the inclination to consider the future implication of the decisions one makes in the present, but obviously this is purely conjecture.

Another example of apparent irrationality in retirement decision making is the fact that many people ignore the health planning aspect of retirement. Compared to the failure to plan financially, this behavior (to us, at least) is *highly* irrational because the failure to take care of one's health essentially nullifies all other forms of retirement planning. That is, a person may have considerable retirement savings, clear retirement goals, and a social network to participate in upon retirement. However, if one is in very poor health upon retirement, or dies shortly after retirement due to poor health, all of those other forms of planning are meaningless.

While we are not saying that all retirement decision making is irrational, we do believe that there is enough irrationality to warrant the attention of researchers. Furthermore, to the extent that we can understand what appear to be irrational decisions that people often make on the road to retirement (e.g., engaging in financial planning but not taking care of their health), it may be possible to intervene in a way that alters those decisions and makes them more rational. Considerable research exists on cognitive biases in decision making (see Sanderson, 2010, for a summary), and this research would be helpful in identifying how these biases may impact retirement decision making.

A second general assumption of the theories underlying retirement decision making is that retirement occurs in a *social context*. This is evident, for example, in the theory of planned behavior, where the subjective norms of others contribute to the relationship between attitudes and behavior (Ajzen, 1991). In the context of retirement research, this implies that people look to others, such as their spouse and perhaps children, in making retirement decisions—in fact, this has been supported in retirement research (Beehr et al., 2000).

We feel, however, that one potentially important aspect of the social environment in which retirement occurs has been largely ignored in retirement research; namely, the experiences of those close to the person who have retired. In particular, we believe that the retirement-related experiences of one's parents or other significant persons in one's life (e.g., spouse's parents, other relatives) may have a major impact a person's retirement decision making. Social learning theory (Bandura, 1977) proposes that humans learn not only from the direct consequences of their own behavior but also by observing the consequences of others' behavior as well. This principle, we believe, is certainly relevant to the decisions one makes concerning retirement.

As an example, suppose that someone's father retires at the age of 67 and ends up dying of a massive heart attack six months later. This could potentially impact that person's retirement decision making in two ways. First, this may motivate the person to pay much more attention to health-related planning for retirement. Secondly, it may potentially motivate a person to retire at an earlier age because of the desire to have more enjoyable post-retirement years. It is also possible that such an experience could cause a person to avoid retirement due to the association between retiring and death. Obviously this represents a purely hypothetical situation, but in our opinion it is an influence on retirement decision making that has largely been ignored in the research literature.

A third and final assumption of theories underlying retirement decision making is that the process of retirement is *analogous to changing jobs* (Adams & Beehr, 1998). While there are some similarities between retirement and job changing, we believe that these are two fundamentally different processes. When one changes jobs, more often than not it is to obtain more of something (e.g., pay, status, etc.) or perhaps to live in a more desirable geographical location. Retirement, on the other hand, represents a more fundamental transition in one's lifestyle.

Retirement also represents a realization (either explicitly or implicitly) that one is coming close to the end of life. We believe that retirement researchers have not given enough attention to the impact of people's attitudes toward death on the retirement process. Those who are highly anxious about death may put off planning for retirement, or may decide not to retire at all, in order to avoid facing this reality. On the other hand, those who accept death as a normal part of life may embrace retirement as an enjoyable stage of life and, as a result, plan carefully for it. These examples are again conjecture, but we feel that retirement research should take this into account.

Research to Practice

In many areas of the social sciences there is a gap between research and practice—that is, what we know does not always get applied in "real world" situations. In retirement research, there are two primary areas where we see major gaps between research and practice: (1) retirement planning and (2) the actual decision to retire. Each of these will be discussed below.

Thinking back to the discussion of retirement planning earlier in this chapter, it is fairly obvious that the decision to plan (or not to plan) for retirement is a key variable impacting other decision points and ultimately satisfaction with retirement. Specifically, individuals who engage in financial planning for retirement, who take care of their health, and who have specific plans for their post-retirement years may approach other retirement-related decisions (e.g., when to retire, the form that retirement takes) differently than those who do not engage in such planning activities. Furthermore, these choices may ultimately impact satisfaction with retirement. Despite the importance of retirement planning, empirical data suggest that many people do not engage in a great deal of retirement planning, particularly that of a financial nature (Lusardi & Mitchell, 2005).

From a societal perspective, this is a very serious situation given the dire financial state of many government-funded pension programs both in the United States and in other countries. To the extent that people do not plan financially, there will be more dependence on government pensions programs and ultimately greater crises in such programs.

While we do not have concrete suggestions as to how to facilitate higher levels of financial planning, we strongly suspect that the key to influencing such behaviors lies with both employers and the federal government. As far as employers, providing employees with more opportunities for deferred savings programs would likely help. Simply offering such programs, however, is not enough. Employers also need to make sure that such programs are *clearly explained* to employees so that they can make informed decisions as to whether or not they will participate. As was pointed out earlier in this chapter, one of the reasons some people do not engage in financial planning for retirement is simply because they are uncomfortable with financial matters. Taking the mystery out of investing for retirement would probably go a long way toward facilitating earlier financial planning for retirement.

The other form of retirement planning behavior that organizations may be able to influence is that related to health. While there are obviously some exceptions, there is also considerable empirical evidence that health promotion efforts in the workplace can facilitate healthier behavior among employees (Parks & Steelman, 2008). Thus, to the extent that organizations do facilitate the health of their employees, such efforts will not only reduce short-term health care costs but also pay more long-term benefits by facilitating health among retirees. In addition, by facilitating employee health, organizations would make it possible for those who want to work longer to actually be able to do so. This is important for society as a whole, since government-funded pension programs in many countries are strapped financially. It is also important for individuals' satisfaction in retirement, since those in better health will probably view the decision to retire as more of a matter of free choice compared to those who feel forced into retirement due to poor health.

In addition to helping employees with more effective retirement planning, organizations can also take steps to help employees with the actual decision to retire. As stated earlier in this chapter, the actual decision to retire is impacted by what might be described as both "pull" and "push" factors (Beehr, 1986). Pull factors would include things such as the opportunity for more leisure time and travel; push factors, on the other hand, would include things such as heavy job demands, conflict with coworkers, and age-related discrimination. As might be expected, those who retire because they feel pulled toward the positive aspects of retirement tend to be much happier than those who feel they have been pushed into retirement due to negative aspects of the pre-retirement job situation (Barnes-Farrell, 2003).

While some the factors that may push older employees toward retirement are obviously somewhat subjective (e.g., feeling "tired of work"), we believe that others can be impacted by organizations. For example, age-related discrimination is a reality in many organizations, although it is often measured subjectively (Finkelstein & Farrell, 2007). Thus, it would seem to us that if organizations want older employees to work longer, one way to facilitate this would be to identify potential instances of age-related discrimination and rectify them. In a more general sense, organizations might also be wise to create an age-friendly atmosphere where older employees are seen as a valuable resource and treated with dignity by those within the organization.

In addition to preventing age-related discrimination, organizations also need to look at the content of the work that older employees perform. As has been pointed out earlier (Jex et al., 2007), older employees may have difficulty performing certain types of work, particularly when it is very physically demanding or requires that one works very quickly. Recognizing this, it would seem that organizations wishing to keep older employers on the job longer could take steps to redesign jobs to make them more compatible with older employees' ability levels (Krause et al., 1997). It may also be possible to create roles whereby older employees can serve as mentors to younger, more inexperienced colleagues.

Summary and Conclusions

Our major goals in this chapter were twofold: (1) to summarize the extant literature on retirement decision making and (2) to offer suggestions for future research on retirement decision making, as well as suggestions for applying what is known in order to influence the retirement decisions of employees.

As far as the first goal, it is quite evident that there are key variables that impact all steps in the retirement decision-making process. These include not only variables that are more objective in nature (e.g., wealth, health, pension plan, etc.) but also a number of variables that are highly subjective (e.g., work centrality, retirement goals, future orientation, feeling pushed out of work, feeling tired of work, etc.). Given this mixture of both objective and subjective predictors, it is not surprising that predicting any of the steps in the retirement process is challenging. Furthermore, this probably explains why people may at times make somewhat illogical choices during the retirement process. For example, a person may have considerable financial resources (which is associated with earlier retirement) yet choose to keep working well beyond the traditional retirement age because work is highly central to his or her identity. Conversely, a person may be lacking in financial resources yet retire fairly early because work is viewed as a burden and he or she wants to pursue other activities that are not possible with a full-time job.

The major point we are making is that retirement decision making is the result of complex interactions among a number of variables, and that it can be a highly idiosyncratic process. Thus, in future research on retirement decision making, we would like to see researchers examine *interactions* between important predictors rather than simply focusing on the main effects. We suspect, for example, that a high level of work centrality would attenuate the relationship between most variables and the decision to retire; that is, individuals with a high level of work centrality probably tend to stay in the workforce longer regardless of whether they have the financial resources to retire.

Another emphasis in future research should be to develop a greater understanding of some of the psychological variables that have been shown to impact retirement decision making. Perhaps the best example of this is the feeling that one is simply "tired of working" (Beehr et al., 2000). While this appears to be an important variable, it is also very vague. Thus, in future research we need to develop a greater understanding of the factors that might lead a person to feel this way, which would perhaps enable organizations to influence it. Another variable that appears to be important, particularly with regard to retirement planning, is *future orientation,* yet we also know very little about it. The key issue is whether this is a relatively stable trait or whether it is something that can be changed; if it can be changed, this might be a way to increase retirement planning behaviors.

Another suggestion for future research is to incorporate qualitative research methods (e.g., interviews) with more traditional surveys. This is important, we believe, due to the highly idiosyncratic nature of retirement decision making. It would also give researchers a better indication of the tradeoffs that people may make in the process of making retirement-related decisions. For example, a person may have considerable financial resources and low work centrality but choose to keep working because of the desire to pass on his or her wealth to children and grandchildren.

A final suggestion for future research is to conduct more intervention studies on efforts to influence different decision points in the retirement process. While there has been research examining the impact of early retirement incentives (Feldman, 2003), more work is needed on interventions designed to influence retirement planning and the decision to pursue bridge employment. In the case of retirement planning, interventions are important because they have the potential to positively impact the quality of life in retirement. In the case of bridge employment, this is an important behavior to impact as organizations are faced with labor shortages in the years to come.

References

Adams, G. A., & Beehr, T. A. (1998). Turnover and retirement: A comparison of their similarities and differences. *Personnel Psychology, 51,* 643–665.

Adams, G. A., & Rau, B. (2004). Job seeking among retirees seeking bridge employment. *Personnel Psychology, 57,* 719–744.

Ajzen, I. (1991). The theory of planned behavior. *Organizational Behavior and Human Decision Processes, 50,* 179–211.

Atchley, R. C. (1989). A continuity theory of normal aging. *The Gerontologist, 29,* 183–190.

Bandura, A. (1977). *Social learning theory.* Englewood Cliffs, NJ: Prentice-Hall.

Barnes-Farrell, J. L. (2003). Beyond health and wealth: Attitudinal and other influences on retirement decision making. In G. A. Adams & T. A. Beehr (Eds.), *Retirement: Reasons, processes, and results* (pp. 159–187). New York, NY: Springer.

Bartel, A., & Sicherman, N. (1993). Technological change and retirement decisions of older workers. *Journal of Labor Economics, 11,* 162–183.

Beehr, T. A. (1986). The process of retirement: A review and recommendations for future investigation. *Personnel Psychology, 39,* 31–56.

Beehr, T. A., & Adams, G. A. (2003). Introduction and overview of current research and thinking on retirement. In G. A. Adams & T. A. Beehr (Eds.), *Retirement: Reasons, processes, and results* (pp. 1–15). New York, NY: Springer.

Beehr, T. A., & Bennett, M. M. (2007). Examining retirement from a multi-level perspective. In K. S. Schultz & G. A. Adams (Eds.), *Aging and work in the 21st century* (pp. 277–302). New York, NY: Psychology Press.

Beehr, T. A., Glazer, S., Nielson, N. L., & Farmer, S. J. (2000). Work and non-work predictors of employees' retirement ages. *Journal of Vocational Behavior, 57,* 206–225.

Bertakis, K. D., Azari, R., Helms, L. J., Callahan, E. J., & Robbins, J. A. (2000). Gender differences in the utilization of health care services. *Journal of Family Practice, 49,* 147–152.

Blondal, S., & Scarpetta, S. (1997). Early retirement in OECD countries: The role of social security systems. *OECD Economic Studies, 29,* 7–49. Dentinger, E., & Clarkberg, M. (2002). Informal caregiving and retirement timing among men and women. *Journal of Family Issues, 23,* 857–879.

DeVaney, S. A., & Zhang, T. C. (2001). A cohort analysis of the amount in defined contribution and individual retirement savings. *Financial Counseling and Planning, 12,* 89–104.

Ekerdt, D. J., Hackney, J., Kosloski, K., & DeViney, S. (2001). Eddies in the stream: The prevalence of uncertain plans for retirement. *Journal of Gerontology: Social Sciences, 56B*, S162–S170.

Elder, H. W., & Rudolph, P. M. (1999). Does retirement planning affect the level of retirement satisfaction? *Financial Service Review, 8*, 117–127.

Erikson, E. H. (1950). *Childhood and society*. New York, NY: W. H. Norton.

Feldman, D. C. (1994). The decision to retire early: A review and conceptualization. *Academy of Management Review, 19*, 285–311.

Feldman, D. C. (2003). Endgame: The design and implementation of early retirement incentive programs. In G. A. Adams & T. A. Beehr (Eds.), *Retirement: Reasons, processes, and results* (pp. 83–114). New York: Springer.

Filer, R. K., & Petri, P. A. (1988). A job-characteristics theory of retirement. *The Review of Economics and Statistics, 70*, 123–128.

Finkelstein, L. M., & Farrell, S. K. (2007). An expanded view of age bias in the workplace. In G. A. Adams & T. A. Beehr (Eds.), *Retirement: Reasons, processes, and results* (pp. 73–108). New York, NY: Springer.

Friedberg, L. (2003). The impact of technological change on older workers: Evidence from data on computer use. *Industrial and Labor Relations Review, 56*, 511–529.

Gobeski, K. T., & Beehr, T. A. (2009). How retirees work: Predictors of different types of bridge employment. *Journal of Organizational Behavior, 37*, 401–425.

Grosch, J. W., & Pransky, G. S. (2009). Safety and health issues for an aging workforce. In S. J. Czaja and J. Sharit (Eds.), *Aging and work: Issues and implications in a changing landscape* (pp. 334–358). Baltimore, MD: The Johns Hopkins University.

Gruber, J., & Wise, D. A. (1999). Social security and retirement around the world. *Research in Labor Economics, 18*, 1–40.

Hira, T. K., Rock, W. L., & Loibl, C. (2009). Determinants of retirement planning behaviour and differences by age. *International Journal of Consumer Studies, 33*, 293–301.

Hurd, M., & McGarry, K. (1993). *The relationship between job characteristics and retirement* (Working Paper No. 4558). Cambridge, MA: National Bureau of Economic Research.

Jacobs-Lawson, J. M., & Hershey, D. A. (2005). Influence of future time perspective, financial knowledge, and financial risk tolerance on retirement savings behaviors. *Financial Services Review, 14*, 331–344.

Jex, S., Wang, M., & Zarubin, A. (2007). Aging and occupational health. In K. S. Schultz & G. A. Adams (Eds.), *Aging and work in the 21st century* (pp. 199–224). New York, NY: Psychology Press.

Johnson, R. W., & Neumark, D. (1997). Age discrimination, job separations, and employment status of older workers. *Journal of Human Resources, 32*, 779–811.

Kane, T. (1999). *The price of admission: Rethinking how Americans pay for college*. New York, NY: Brookings Institution Press.

Karasek, R. A., & Theorell, T. (1990). *Healthy work: Stress, productivity, and the reconstruction of life*. New York, NY: Basic Books.

Krause, N., Lynch, J., Kaplan, G. A., Cohen, R. D., Goldberg, D. E., & Salonen, J. T. (1997). Predictors of disability retirement. *Scandinavian Journal of Work Environment and Health, 23*, 403–414.

Lusardi, A., & Mitchell, O. S. (2005). *Financial literacy and planning: Implications for retirement well-being* (Michigan Retirement Research Center Research Paper No. WP 2005-108). Retrieved from http://ssrn.com/abstract=881847.

Parks, K. M., & Steelman, L. A. (2008). Organizational wellness programs: A meta-analysis. *Journal of Occupational Health Psychology, 13*, 58–68.

Paullay, I. M., Alliger, G. M., & Stone-Romero, E. F. (1994). Construct validation of two instruments designed to measure job involvement and work centrality. *Journal of Applied Psychology, 79*, 224–228.

Sanderson, C. A. (2010). *Social psychology*. New York, NY: John Wiley & Sons.

Schulz, J. H. (2002). The evolving concept of "retirement": Looking forward to the year 2050. *International Social Security Review, 55*, 85–115.

Smith, J. P., & Kingston, J. P. (1999). Demographic and economic correlates of health in old age. *Demography, 34*, 159–170.

Smith, P. C., Kendall, L. M., & Hulin, C. L. (1969). *The measurement of satisfaction in work and retirement*. Chicago, IL: Rand McNally.

Stock, J. H., & Wise, D. A. (1990). Pensions, the option value of work, and retirement. *Econometrica, 58*, 1151–1180.

Talaga, J. A., & Beehr, T. A. (1995). Are there gender differences in predicting retirement decisions? *Journal of Applied Psychology, 80*, 16–28.

Toossi, M. (2004). Labor force projections to 2012: The graying of the U.S. workforce. *Monthly Labor Review, 127*, 3–22.

Wallston, B. S., & Wallston, K. A. (1978). Locus of control and health: A review of the literature. *Health Education Monographs, 6*, 107–117.

Wallston, K. A., Wallston, B. S., Smith, S., & Dobbins, C. J. (1987). Perceived control and health. *Current Psychological Research and Reviews, 6*, 5–25.

Wang, M., & Shultz, K. S. (2010). Employee retirement: A review and recommendations for future investigation. *Journal of Management, 36*, 172–206.

Wang, M., Zhan, Y., Liu, S., & Shultz, K. (2008). Antecedents of bridge employment: A longitudinal investigation. *Journal of Applied Psychology, 93*, 818–830.

Feeling Like It's Time to Retire: A Fit Perspective on Early Retirement Decisions

Daniel C. Feldman

Abstract

This chapter examines early retirement decision making from the perspective of person-environment (P-E) fit theory. First, we suggest that changes in workplace environments as well as in workers' values and skills are likely to lead to declines in fit as individuals approach retirement. Second, perceptions of employee fit held by coworkers and supervisors also have a strong influence on self-perceptions of P-E fit; others' perceptions of fit are likely to become more negative as employees reach retirement age, too. Third, changes in the nature of occupations and organizations have cascading effects on how older workers perceive fit with their jobs and work groups. These signals of declining fit, in turn, lead to increased motivation to retire early. The chapter concludes with avenues for future research on the relationship between P-E fit and early retirement decisions.

Key Words: person-environment fit, person-job fit, person-organization fit, person-vocation fit, older workers, early retirement, retirement, retirement decisions

Most previous research on the topic of early retirement has defined it as "retirement before age 65" or "retirement before eligibility for full pension." In this chapter, we reconsider how older workers perceive "early" retirement, why person-organization (P-O) fit is likely to decline as individuals approach retirement age, and how colleagues' perceptions of an individual's fit colors his or her own self-perceptions about when it is time to retire.

The first goal of the paper is to look beyond objective criteria for "early retirement" and "older worker" and to consider alternative definitions as well. Whether employees perceive they are retiring "early" is a more complex phenomenon than simply determining whether they are eligible for full pension benefits and have reached age 65 (Feldman, 1994). Drawing from the gerontology and psychology literatures on aging, we suggest that retirement decisions are also influenced by how old workers feel, their age relative to other people in the same firm or

occupation, the typical age at which other people in the firm or occupation retire, and how old they are perceived to be by others (Cleveland & Shore, 1992; Lawrence, 1988). Drawing from the economics literature, we suggest that more and more workers are now participants in fixed-contribution plans rather than fixed-benefit pension plans and, as such, the timing of their retirement decisions is less tied to chronological age and years of service (Blau, 1998; Papke, 2003). Drawing from the organizational sciences literature, we suggest that retirement does not mean the end of work. Indeed, many early retirees continue to work part-time or start new careers before leaving the workforce altogether (Doeringer, 1990; Kim & Feldman, 1998, 2000).

The second goal of the chapter is to examine early retirement decision making from a person-environment (P-E) fit perspective (Edwards, Cable, Williamson, Lambert, & Shipp, 2006; Kristof-Brown, 1996). This literature suggests that individuals try to achieve congruence of their abilities and interests with an organization's demands and values. At the time of entry, that fit is achieved through the organization's recruitment, selection, and socialization practices (Cable & Judge, 1997; Cable & Parsons, 2001).

What has received less attention in the literature, though, is the decline of fit that occurs with aging and greater years of service to an organization or a profession (Feldman & Vogel, 2009; Vogel & Feldman, 2009). Fit is dynamic rather than static in nature (Ostroff, Shin, & Feinberg, 2002). Over the course of a life span or career span, the skills, interests, and values of individuals may change substantially. By the same token, over the course of thirty to forty years, the work demands of occupations and the cultures of organizations may change dramatically, too. Thus, what might have been a good initial fit at age 25 might later be a poor fit at age 65. In this chapter, we explore why perceptions of fit may decline over time and how these signposts of poor fit lead older employees to decide it is time for them to retire early. Further, while Schneider, Smith, and Goldstein's (2000) attraction-selection-attrition (ASA) paradigm has mainly been used to examine the early attrition of early-career new hires, the ASA paradigm may also be helpful in explaining early retirement decisions as well.

In the third and final section of the chapter, we consider important avenues for future research on early retirement decisions. Here we focus on: differential rates of decline in skill-, value-, and interest-fit (Kanfer & Ackerman, 2004; Stephan, Fouquereau, & Fernandez, 2008); the role of personality traits in the early retirement decision-making process (Bradley, Brief, & George, 2002; Kahneman & Tversky, 1973; Tokar & Subich, 1997); the ways in which family and friends influence perceptions of fit (Henkens, 1999; van Dam, van der Vorst, & Heijden, 2009); how poor fit leads to the process of disengagement (Moen, Huang, Plassman, & Dentinger, 2006; Nimrod & Kleiber, 2007); and how job and community embeddedness interact with declining fit in determining early retirement decisions (Mitchell & Lee, 2001).

Objective vs. Subjective Definitions of "Early" Retirement

Objective Definitions of Early Retirement

As noted above, three objective criteria have typically been used in previous research to define early retirement: age, years of service, and eligibility for full pension benefits. There are a variety of reasons why these three criteria have historically been so important in the early retirement literature (Doerpinghaus & Feldman, 2001; Hira, Rock, & Loibl, 2009).

At a very basic level, the decision to retire involves an assessment of whether an individual can afford to live without working full-time or at all. Up until thirty years ago or so, the majority of employees in the United States had "fixed-benefit" pension plans in which employees received monthly pension benefits. These annual pension benefits were usually calculated as a multiplicative function of years of service and percentage of salary. (A common computational formula was one in which employees earned 2% of their last year of salary per year of service, typically capped at 30–35 years of service.) An employee who was making $100,000 would therefore be able to receive an annual pension benefit of $60,000 after thirty years of service. At the same time, organizations imposed penalties on employees who retired early (e.g., 4% per year before age 65 or 30 years of service) since, from an actuarial standpoint, those employees could be expected to collect pension benefits for a longer period of time.

While these objective criteria still play a major role in understanding early retirement decisions, exclusive reliance on these criteria may no longer be warranted. First, more and more employees are now participating in "fixed-contribution" pension plans. In these pension plans, employees receive a set amount of money from their employers each month to invest as they best see fit. In fixed-contribution plans, then, the ability of employees to retire early relies on their skill in managing their investments as well as on their age and years of service (DeVaney & Zhang, 2001; Schiamberg & McKinney, 2003). Second, more and more employees are not planning on retiring without ever working again, but rather plan on "working in retirement" instead (Feldman, 1994). Thus, the notion of needing enough money to retire without working is shifting, since retirement no longer signals lack of future earning capacity (Ruhm, 1990; Shultz, 2003). Third, the majority of workers in the United States have spouses who also work, and many individuals try to time their retirements to coincide with those of their spouses (Moen, Huang, Plassmann, & Dentinger, 2006). Therefore, treating the retirement decision as one made solely by the individual employee on the basis of his or her own earnings may miss a considerable amount of the variance in the decision-making process (Pienta, 2003; Feldman & Kim, 1998, 2000).

Subjective Definitions of Early Retirement

Beyond the financial ability to retire, older workers also develop global perceptions and feelings about whether it is time to retire. These perceptions and feelings emerge not only from self-reflection but also from the broader social environment as well.

In some important research on aging, Lawrence (1988) and Cleveland and Shore (1992) argue that the definition of age should encompass more than just chronological age. In thinking about their age, older workers also compare themselves to others around them and try to infer how others see them. For example, older workers consider the "normative age" at which people retire in their occupations or organizations. If people typically retire at age 70, individuals who think about retiring at age 60 might think of it as "retiring early"; if people typically retire at age 55, individuals who think about retiring at age 60 might think of themselves as hanging on too long. Older workers also consider their "relative" age that is, how old they are relative to others in the same occupation. Thus, a 60-year-old patrol cop might perceive himself as too old to still be working, while a 60-year-old physician might perceive herself as too young to retire.

In addition, workers make assessments about how unusual it is for someone their age to still be in the workforce full-time. For instance, being a 60-year-old public school teacher is relatively uncommon, since many people enter teaching right from college and accrue thirty years of service in middle age. In contrast, being a 60-year-old professor is relatively common, since many people entering academe do so in their 30s, and there are few physical demands that impinge upon their ability to keep on working full-time. Being demographically dissimilar, then, creates additional incentives, beyond chronological age, for individuals to consider retiring early (Desmette & Gaillard, 2008; Zappala, Depolo, Fraccaroli, Guglielmi, & Sarchielli, 2008).

Second, the research on image theory (Beach & Frederickson, 1989) and continuity theory (Atchley, 1989) also suggests that individuals' definitions of early retirement are subjective in nature. These theoretical approaches suggest that individuals have rather global ideas about how they see their futures and, in most cases, workers see themselves as being quite similar in retirement as they are at present. Thus, older individuals who are relatively disengaged from their work do not envision themselves as laboring forever, while older workers who have been deeply involved in their professions simply cannot see themselves as retirees at any age

(Elfenbein & O'Reilly, 2007; Szinovacz, DeViney, & Davey, 2001).

Third, major transitions in career stages and life stages also prompt individuals to think about retiring early, independent of age and years of service (Hall & Mirvis, 1996; Super, 1990). As individuals mature, they develop more realistic ideas of how far they can go in their careers—or if they can go any further at all. If older workers feel they have accomplished as much as they are going to accomplish—particularly if they have fallen short of their "dream"—they may be more willing to retire early (Levinson, 1986). There is also considerable evidence that workers in later life stages identify more heavily with non-work roles than with work roles. Thus, as adult children leave home, move to different cities, and become parents themselves, older workers might choose to spend more time devoted to family roles rather than to work roles (Barnes-Farrell, 2003; Spokane, 1985; Stephens & Feldman, 1997; Stryker, 1968).

Last here, when the average life expectancy for most U.S. citizens was lower (ages 68–72) and most people worked until eligibility for Social Security (ages 62–65), retirement usually meant the end of participation in the labor force. However, today there are increasing opportunities for older workers to engage in bridge employment, namely, self-employment, part-time employment, or full-time employment after leaving long-held positions but before total withdrawal from the labor force. Consequently, the decision to retire early is not necessarily the same as the decision to leave work. Indeed, in many cases, the decision to retire early can open up opportunities for older workers to enter jobs that they might find more enjoyable, more challenging, less stressful, and/or less time-consuming (Feldman, 1994; Gobeski & Beehr, 2009).

In sum, then, what it means to "retire early" has changed substantially over the past thirty years. As a consequence, there is still a great deal of variance in early retirement decisions that is not accounted for by chronological age, years of service, and the individual's own salary.

Person-Environment Fit and the Decision to Retire Early

Over the past two decades, person-environment fit has re-emerged as a major theoretical construct in the organizational sciences. Person-environment fit (P-E fit) theory suggests that when individuals achieve congruence with their work environments, they are more likely to remain in those environments longer, experience greater satisfaction at work, and perform more effectively on their jobs (Edwards et al., 2006; Kristof-Brown, 1996). Conversely, when older individuals begin viewing themselves as less productive at work and more disaffected from the organization's values, they are more likely to view early retirement as an attractive option (Herrbach, Mignonac, Vandenberghe, & Negrini, 2009). Below, we consider the different ways person-environment fit has been conceptualized in the literature, why P-E fit is likely to decline over time, and how declining P-E fit is likely to lead to early retirement.

Dimensions of Fit

Person-environment fit research has examined the different areas in which individuals can achieve fit (e.g., skills, interests, and values). Moreover, researchers have examined P-E fit at one point in time (static fit) and across time (dynamic fit) (Edwards et al., 2006; Kristof-Brown, 1996). Beyond these distinctions among *fit content* and *time frames*, researchers have utilized several other ways of assessing P-E fit. Below, we discuss various operationalizations of the construct. In addition, we highlight how differences in the way that fit is conceptualized can lead researchers to draw very different conclusions about its impact on early retirement.

Several researchers have made a distinction between *global* and *facet-specific* measures of fit. Researchers exploring global fit look at how overall perceptions of fit emerge and how those perceptions affect employees' work attitudes and job behaviors. In contrast, researchers looking at facet-specific measures of fit have a priori ideas about the most important content elements of fit (e.g., skills, knowledge, values, interests, etc.) and combine scores on those specific facets to measure fit (Edwards & Shipp, 2007; Jansen & Kristof-Brown, 2006).

Fit has also been conceptualized in terms of *levels of the environment* (Kristof-Brown, Jansen, & Colbert, 2002; Spokane, Meir, & Catalano, 2000; Vogel & Feldman, 2009). At the most macro-level, person-environment fit can be conceptualized as the degree of congruence between an individual and his/her profession or occupation, that is, how well the individual's skills and values match the demands and culture of the vocation (known as *person-vocation fit*). At successively lower levels, person-environment fit can be conceptualized as the degree of congruence between an individual and his or her organization (*person-organization fit*), the degree of congruence between an individual and his

or her work group (*person-group fit*), and the degree of congruence between an individual and his or her tasks (*person-job fit*).

Other researchers have drawn a distinction between *supplementary* and *complementary fit*. Supplementary fit occurs when individuals bring skills and values that are similar to those of others in the workplace. In contrast, complementary fit occurs when individuals bring unique skills, values, or perspectives to their work environments (Muchinsky & Monahan, 1987).

Last here, fit has been differentiated in terms of *source of perceptions*. The vast majority of research studies on P-E fit have used *self-perceptions* (Vazire, 2010); that is, researchers rely on employees themselves to self-report the degree of fit they experience with their environments. To a lesser extent, researchers have also explored *managers' and coworkers' perceptions of fit*. However, given that individuals' perceptions of themselves are highly influenced by the cues they receive from their environments, others' perceptions of employee fit warrant additional attention as well (Cable & Judge, 1996; Piasentin & Chapman, 2006).

We expect that how fit is operationalized will significantly influence the extent to which older workers are found to experience declining P-E fit. Because organizations typically put more energy into achieving fit at time of entry than in renegotiating P-E fit over time (Schneider et al., 2000), we expect that longitudinal studies will find stronger effects for age than cross-sectional studies do. We also expect that studies use global measures of fit will show that older workers have lower P-E fit than studies that use facet-specific measures (Edwards et al., 2006; Kristof-Brown, 1996). Here, the rationale is that global measures can be unduly influenced by negative perceptions of one particular dimension of a work situation (e.g., low value fit). However, if four content dimensions of fit are equally weighted and combined into an index of P-E fit, the maximum variance any one content factor could account for would be only 25%.

In general, it is also our expectation that perceptions of poor fit in the immediate work environment will have the strongest impact on early retirement decisions (Feldman & Vogel, 2009; Vogel & Feldman, 2009). That is, we expect that older workers' global perceptions of P-E fit will be most negative when individuals perceive that they have poor person-job or poor person-group fit (compared to their perceptions of person-organization or person-occupation fit). The rationale here is that older workers will be more sensitive to immediate social cues than to distal social cues. Further, social norms about the age-appropriate time to retire are stronger locally than distally (Barnes-Farrell, 2003; Cleveland & Shore, 1992).

While we believe that the effects of poor fit will be more evident locally than distally, the evidence also suggests that poor person-occupation fit does have cascading negative consequences for person-organization and person-job fit (Shultz, Morton, & Weckerle, 1998). Thus, an individual who perceives poor fit with his or her occupation as a physician is unlikely to find an oasis of good fit in any organization. The basic lack of fit on some important dimension(s) of an occupation (e.g., skills) makes it hard to find a comfortable professional home anywhere (Vogel & Feldman, 2009).

We also predict that older workers who have achieved complementary fit will experience greater declines in P-E fit than those who have achieved supplementary fit. The positive premium people in organizations put on similarity is high (Muchinsky et al., 1987; Strauss, Barrick, & Connerley, 2001). Groups often tolerate individuals who bring something different to the table (supplementary fit) because it is to their business advantage to do so. However, as workers age, relational demography differences may strengthen the sense of distance that older workers with complementary fit already feel from their colleagues (Dunning, Johnson, Ehrlinger, & Kruger, 2003; Tsui, Porter, & Egan, 2002).

Last here, older workers' self-reports of fit are likely to be more powerful predictors of job attitudes and intentions to retire, while managers' and colleagues' perceptions of employee fit may be better predictors of job performance (Bernardin, 1979; Hoffman & Woehr, 2006). Individuals respond affectively and emotionally at work on the basis of their own perceptions. Not surprisingly, then, employee perceptions of fit are excellent predictors of job attitudes and decisions to turnover. However, individuals do not necessarily process others' perceptions of fit accurately; individuals can distort their perceptions of others' views to be consistent with their own (Bretz & Judge, 1994; Hoobler, Wayne, & Lemmon, 2009). Since individuals have a tendency to see themselves in a positive light, supervisors' perceptions of fit may be more negative, but more accurate, reflections of actual performance on the job (Beauregard & Dunning, 1998; Fiske & Taylor, 1991).

Time-Related Changes in Person-Environment Fit

For a variety of reasons, there can be declines in P-E fit over time. As the attraction-selection-attrition (ASA) model (Schneider et al., 2000) suggests, in the early part of one's tenure in an occupation or organization, individuals who have poor fit are likely to self-select out or be forced out of those positions by their employers. However, individuals who initially achieve a high level of fit early in their careers can experience substantial decline in that fit, both because the work environment changes and because individuals' skills, abilities, and values change over time. We highlight the most salient of these changes and illustrate how they might motivate middle-aged and older workers to consider early retirement.

Changes in the Environment

The underlying argument here is that changes in the environment can decrease the degree of fit for older workers because older workers might find their altered environments less compatible with their skills, interests, and values. These environmental changes could occur in the occupation, the organization, the work group, or the job itself.

Changes in the occupation. Across a period of years, the skill demands of an occupation can change dramatically (Feldman & Vogel, 2009). To be sure, some elements of occupational environments improve over time. Some occupations, like nursing, have seen their salaries and professional status surge well beyond what might have been expected forty years ago. However, in terms of the work itself, the initial degree of fit is likely to slip as individuals grow older.

One salient example of this dynamic can be seen in medicine. Over the past forty years, more and more of physicians' time has been taken up with billing and insurance issues, computerizing medical records, and office management. At the same time, the degree of autonomy that physicians have in prescribing a course of treatment has declined, the amount of litigation they face has increased, and risk management is more exacting and more onerous. As these environmental changes accumulate, the degree of fit between older workers and their occupations may decline and make early retirement look more attractive.

Cascading effects of occupational fit on organizational fit and job fit. As noted earlier, it is conceptually possible to distinguish among occupational fit, organizational fit, job fit, and group fit

(Kristof-Brown et al., 2002). However, as a practical matter, changes in occupational fit have cascading effects on the degree of organizational fit and job fit (Feldman & Vogel, 2009). As fit with the occupation declines, individuals find it harder and harder to identify organizations that are congruent with their current (and/or long-held) skill sets (Vogel & Feldman, 2009). Using the example of medicine again, with the dramatic changes in the delivery of health care today, it would be virtually impossible to find any health care facility or medical practice that would be immune from the demands of insurance carriers and malpractice lawyers.

Since the decision to retire is made in the context of a specific organization, the cascading effects of occupational fit do influence early retirement decisions (Mishel, Bernstein, & Schmitt, 2001). If older workers perceive that they could find work environments that would better suit their needs, the obvious alternative to early retirement would be turnover and changing organizations (Dalton & Todor, 1993; Mitchell & Lee, 2001). However, if the major problem is lack of fit at the occupational level, individuals will despair of finding another organization that would be much better.

Social-normative expectations. Feldman and Beehr (2011) highlight how important social-normative influences are on the decision to retire. The norms that supervisors, colleagues, family members, and friends hold about the appropriate retirement age also influence early retirement decisions.

A recent empirical study suggests that the norms or expectations other people hold about whether a specific individual should retire were strongly related to that individual's intentions to retire in the near future (van Dam, van der Vorst, & Heijden, 2009). Another series of studies on relational demography come to much the same conclusion, but from a different perspective (Cleveland & Shore, 1992; Lawrence, 1988; Tsui et al., 2002). When workers view themselves as old relative to others in their work group, they are more likely to conclude that it is time to retire (Feldman & Beehr, 2011). Thus, as an individual begins to feel old relative to others in the workplace and in similar jobs—and as more and more friends and colleagues start to retire—the individual feels greater external pressure to retire as well.

Age discrimination in the workplace. Unfortunately, normative beliefs about the appropriate retirement age can also result in more than just subtle social cues suggesting that older workers retire. Indeed, age discrimination against older workers still exists in the workforce (Desmette & Gaillard, 2008), although the extent and intensity of that discrimination may not be as great as it was a generation ago (Posthuma & Campion, 2009). Older workers are often stereotyped as less motivated to excel, less energetic, more resistant to change, and more difficult to train (Ng & Feldman, 2008; Wang, Adams, Beehr, & Shultz, 2009).

Due to this age discrimination, older workers are more reluctant to enter the job market again and are more pessimistic that they could find suitable positions elsewhere (Farr & Ringseis, 2002). As the workplace is perceived as increasingly hostile in nature, then, older workers are more likely to consider early retirement rather than changing jobs (Barnes-Farrell, 2003). In addition, although the use of early retirement incentives should be non-coercive (Feldman & Beehr, 2011), in practice older workers often perceive that their real choice is between accepting early retirement incentives or being laid off in the near future (Dosman, Fast, Chapman, & Keating, 2006). Thus, many of the early retirements we see today are not taken voluntarily but rather to avoid potentially more dire personnel actions ahead.

Generational and group composition differences. As the attraction-selection-attrition (ASA) paradigm suggests, individuals tend to select themselves into organizations and work groups where they have values similar to those of their colleagues (Schneider et al., 2000). As time passes, the degree of person-group (P-G) fit might decline for two reasons: (1) generational changes in values and social mores, and (2) changes in the composition of the work group.

Norms about social interactions (e.g., social distance, frequency, and formality) inevitably change over time. Depression-era adults were once dismayed by the informality and lack of respect shown by their baby-boomer offspring; today, baby boomers are frequently put off by the short bursts of abbreviated communications they receive electronically from their offspring. When individuals become relatively older than their colleagues, they may find themselves out of sync with the social mores of their colleagues and feel more isolated from them.

At the same time, the group into which the individual was originally hired is almost assuredly no longer intact. Over time, people leave, get promoted, or go into different functional areas. Consequently, what might have been very high person-group fit at the time of hiring may no longer be a good fit thirty years later (Feldman & Vogel, 2009; Mishel et al., 2001). As just one example of this change, in the 1970s people used to joke about IBM meaning "I've been moved" because the corporation was noted for moving people from location to location and building a strong sense of community among its employees. Today, over 50% of IBM employees have no fixed office and work "virtually"; now its employees joke that IBM means "I'm by myself." For those older workers who are experiencing poor P-G fit, then, retiring early may seem like a more feasible solution than looking for a greater sense of community elsewhere.

Job alternatives to full-time employment and full-time retirement. While there are certainly other changes in the environment that could be examined here, the last one we will consider is that older workers no longer face a choice between working full-time for their current employers and being fully retired. With more opportunities for bridge employment (Doeringer, 1990; Feldman, 1994), older workers may be able to find better fit in part-time positions, self-employment, and starting new careers altogether (Wang et al., 2008).

Older workers may be more willing to retire early because they no longer face as much uncertainty about what life after retirement would be like. At least in the short run, retirement would not necessarily mean no work, no structure to the day, and less social contact. Instead, bridge employment represents an attractive alternative to "hanging in there" for more years simply to avoid the uncertainty associated with full retirement (Gobeski & Beehr, 2009; Wang et al., 2008). Equally importantly, bridge employment provides an additional financial safety net for those older employees who are on the bubble regarding whether they can afford to retire or not (Herrbach et al., 2009; Ruhm, 1990).

Changes in the Person

Just as there are changes in the environment that may contribute to poorer fit over time, so, too, are there changes within the person that can contribute to poorer P-E fit. These within-person changes—due to changing abilities, values, emotions, and family roles—may lead older workers to consider scaling back from full-time work, making late-career changes, or exiting the workforce altogether at an earlier age. Depending upon the extent of these within-person changes, individuals may be less motivated to try to change their current work environments or to find other work environments that would be more congruent with their profiles.

Changes in cognitive ability. Some recent advances in cognitive psychology have highlighted the ways in which cognitive abilities change with age. These include slower reaction times (Ratcliff, Thapar, & McKoon, 2001), smaller working memory capacity (Spencer & Raz, 1995), poorer dual-task (multitasking) performance (Verhaeghen, Steitz, Sliwinski, & Cerella, 2003), and shorter verbal memory span (Bopp & Verhaeghen, 2005). Taken together, these studies suggest that cognitive abilities decline somewhat with age, with the declines more noticeable after middle age (Feldman & Vogel, 2009). Depending upon the type of job, these declines in cognitive ability may lead older workers to become more aware of "slowing down" and to consider early retirement as an alternative (Bunce & Sisa, 2002).

Fortunately, these declines in cognitive ability may not lead to commensurate drops in job performance (Ng & Feldman, 2008). As Kanfer and Ackerman (2004) note, older workers may rely more on "crystallized intelligence" (knowledge and experience accumulated over time) to compensate for declines in "fluid intelligence" (ability to process large amounts of new information quickly). Further, as older workers become more aware of declining cognitive abilities, they may compensate for them by performing their jobs more conscientiously (Farr & Ringseis, 2002; Feldman & Vogel, 2009).

Changes in physical health and ability. As a general finding, workers in poorer health are more likely to retire early (Feldman, 1994). While relatively small declines in physical health may lead older workers to seek out special accommodations with current employers, major illnesses make it more difficult for individuals to find any work environments that would be suitable given their energy levels (Feldman & Vogel, 2009; Kim & Feldman, 1998, 2000). It is also important to note here that early retirement decisions are also driven by health problems experienced by the spouses and elderly parents of older workers (Brougham & Walsh, 2005; Hira, Rock, & Loibl, 2009).

As white-collar jobs constitute an increasingly large proportion of the labor force in industrialized economies, declines in physical abilities that occur with aging may not be as systematically related to early retirement decisions as they once were. For those workers whose jobs do rely on physical abilities, however, the age-related declines that have been most systematically documented are lower muscle strength (Khalil & Merhi, 2000), slower recovery times from injuries and illnesses (McArdle, Vasilaki, & Jackson, 2002; Thomson, Griffiths, & Davison, 2000), and greater bone density loss (Currey, Brear, & Ziopos, 1996).

Changes in values and emotions. Independent of any specific workplace environment, there are changes in values and emotions that individuals experience as they age. These changes in values and emotions, in turn, can lead to perceptions of poorer fit and a greater propensity to retire early.

In terms of values, the change most germane to P-E fit is the shift in emphasis from accumulating extrinsic rewards to experiencing intrinsic rewards (Borg, 1990; van der Velde, Feij, & van Emmerik, 1998). Older workers tend to derive greater psychic benefit from feelings of "generativity," that is, making a contribution (Levinson, 1986) rather than obtaining additional badges of accomplishment (e.g., pay raises and promotions). While this change in values does not lead to the decline of P-E fit per se, it does lead older workers who have been attached to their jobs for purely financial reasons to consider early retirement instead. Further, for those older workers for whom the need to make a contribution or "give back" is particularly strong, early retirement hastens the time at which they can start their new endeavors.

There are two changes in emotions that also impact perceptions of P-E fit over time. The first is that older workers have a greater need for emotionally gratifying experiences and a lower tolerance for emotionally negative experiences (Feldman & Vogel, 2009; Vogel & Feldman, 2009). As Carstensen's (1995) "socioemotional selectivity theory" suggests, older workers are less willing to put up with unpleasant situations; they are more aware that they have limited time left in their lives and do not want to waste it unproductively. As a result, older workers are likely to be more sensitive to declines in P-E fit and choose early retirement over staying in unsatisfying work environments (Carstensen, Isaacowitz, & Charles, 1999). Second, there are changes in workers' preferences for social interaction across the life span. While younger employees tend to focus their efforts on expanding business networks, older employees want to spend more time with close friends and family and reduce the amount of energy they invest in peripheral relationships (Carstensen, Pasupathi, Mayr, & Nesselroade, 2000). Particularly if the quality of P-G fit declines, older workers are more likely to choose early retirement over remaining in a socially unsatisfying work environment.

Career and life stage theories make several of the same observations as the research cited above does (Mirvis & Hall, 1996; Super, 1990). These theories do not typically articulate the specific age at which an individual is considered "old" or the specific age at which an individual is considered "late-career" (Feldman & Beehr, 2011). However, this research does describe the ways in which older individuals start disengaging from the workforce (Barnes-Farrell, 2003; Levinson & Wofford, 2009). And, once this process begins and individuals start ramping up preparations for retirement, the actual decision to retire is made more quickly (Feldman & Beehr, 2011; Freund & Baltes, 2002; Hedge, Borman, & Lammlein, 2006).

Directions for Future Research

In this final section, we highlight some important directions for future research on the relationship between person-environment fit and early retirement decisions. We have chosen these topics not only for their potential to improve our theoretical understanding of the issue but also for their potential to improve the management of older workers and their transition into retirement.

One theme that runs through all the directions for future research below is that declines in person-environment fit are neither inevitable nor linearly negative. For instance, older workers often craft their jobs to highlight their competitive strengths and lessen the importance of their relative weaknesses. Thus, older workers may increase their citizenship behavior to compensate for declining in-role performance. There are also individual differences that may soften declines in P-E fit. For example, older workers vary in their levels of positive affect, their openness to change, and their adaptability. These personality traits, in turn, help older workers adjust more readily to changing workplace demands. Indeed, there may even be changes in work environments that mitigate declines in P-E fit over time. As older workers become an increasingly large segment of the labor force, discrimination against older workers may decline and opportunities for older workers to obtain additional training may become more numerous. Therefore, as future research on P-E fit unfolds, it is important to consider not only the mean differences between older and younger workers but also the variance among older workers as well.

Differential Rates of Decline

While overall P-E fit is likely to decline as workers approach retirement, it appears that not all aspects of individuals' performance decline at the same rate of speed (Ng & Feldman, 2008). For instance, while older workers' heightened preference for fulfilling social relationships and socially meaningful work seems quite consistent across individuals, the rate of decline in skills varies tremendously depending on the kind of jobs individuals perform. In many jobs, such as sales, older workers' performance may not decline at all; in other jobs, where quick decision making under time pressure is involved, there may more drop-off in performance (Feldman & Vogel, 2009). Further, even if the core task performance of older workers declines with age, increased performance in organizational citizenship behaviors and decreased involvement in counterproductive work behaviors often compensate for that drop-off (Ng et al., 2011). In general, though, there has been little research on the differential rates of decline of skill fit, interest fit, and goal fit, nor much comparative research on declines in person-vocation, organization, job, and group fit (Vogel et al., 2009). To understand which older workers will choose to retire early and when, greater attention to these questions is warranted.

Moreover, such research would give us a better handle on whether early retirees will seek bridge employment at all and, if so, whether they will seek bridge employment in the same general vocation or in another field altogether (Feldman & Beehr, 2011). For instance, we might expect decline in skill fit to be associated with bridge employment outside the current vocation, while decline in goal fit might be associated with fewer work hours but in the same organization. Along the same lines, we might expect that older workers with high person-vocation fit but low person-organization fit would seek full-time employment in the same profession elsewhere, but older workers with both low person-vocation fit and low person-group fit would be more likely to retire altogether.

Disengagement and Re-engagement
There is increasing evidence that declining fit is associated with early retirement. However, the psychological processes by which perceptions of declining fit lead to early retirement decisions are less frequently addressed in the literature. One possible mechanism that is worth studying in this regard is the process of psychological disengagement (Feldman & Beehr, 2011).

Between initial recognition of declining fit and actual retirement, there is likely to be a period during which employees psychologically disengage from work (Nimrod & Kleiber, 2007). Loss of work is not the only loss that occurs with retirement; unfortunately, retirement is also associated with loss of status, loss of structure to the day, and loss of

companionship. Consequently, older workers who are thinking about retiring have to go through a process in which they disconnect from long-held roles. Surprisingly little research has been done on the period between announcement of retirement plans and actual exit. A particularly relevant setting for such research would be organizations in which there are formal and/or phased-in early retirement programs, where the disengagement process can be studied longitudinally.

At the same time, though, early retirees in particular have to develop new "scripts" for their lives because they potentially have many more years ahead of them (Moen et al., 2006). While researchers have documented the fact that many early retirees are engaged in bridge employment, much less research has been done on the process of deciding whether and where such bridge employment would take place (Kim & Feldman, 1998, 2000). Only fairly recently have researchers focused greater attention on how older workers imagine their futures without work and identify with the "retiree" role (Brougham & Walsh, 2005; Hira, Rock, & Loibl, 2009). Much more research is needed, then, on how older workers re-engage at work as bridge employees and how they reinvest energy that used to go into work into other roles in their lives (Feldman & Kim, 1998, 2000; Greller & Simpson, 1999).

Fit, Early Retirement, and Embeddedness
Mitchell, Holtom, Lee, Sablynski, and Erez (2001) define embeddedness as the accumulated forces that keep an individual in his or her job. Embeddedness emerges not only from the degree of fit individuals have with their jobs but also from the social links they have established with coworkers and the sacrifices they would have to make (e.g., loss of income) in order to leave. Moreover, individuals become embedded in their jobs at least in part because they are embedded in the communities in which they live. That is, many workers (and their families) become established in a particular community, and it is the attachment to that community that compensates for less-than-ideal jobs in employees' cost-benefit calculations.

Previous research suggests that thinking about early retirement emerges either as dissatisfaction with the current work environment heightens or as enthusiasm for new pursuits grows. However, the decision to leave a job is not made in isolation. Jobs and organizations are embedded in communities, and individuals often have ties within those communities that keep them working at their jobs despite some inclination to retire. Therefore, we suggest that the relationship between declining fit and early retirement intentions will be moderated by community embeddedness. That is, the relationship will be stronger when community embeddedness is low and weaker when community embeddedness is high.

There are several rationales for this hypothesis. First, as noted earlier, individuals tend to time their retirements to coincide with those of their partners. As a result, early retirement intentions may not be put into action until the spouse is ready to retire as well, particularly if the couple wishes to travel or relocate upon retirement (Feldman, 1994). Second, as embeddedness research suggests, fit is not the only element that determines whether older workers choose to exit their jobs or not (Mitchell et al., 2001). Rather, in some cases, a large number of satisfying social ties can partially compensate for declining fit. In still other cases, large perceived sacrifices associated with leaving can hold people back from retiring despite declining fit. Third, while job embeddedness and community embeddedness are separate theoretical constructs, in practice they are positively related (O'Driscoll, Ilgen, & Hildreth, 1992). That is, individuals who are embedded in their communities might exert greater effort to turn around declining person-job fit because they recognize that loss of their jobs might necessitate relocation from their communities. Moving forward, then, the early retirement literature might benefit from greater attention to how the broader life environment mitigates (or exacerbates) the connection between P-E fit and early retirement.

Personality, P-E Fit, and Early Retirement

The role of personality has been studied in the research on adjustment to new roles, including adjustment to retirement (Bradley, Brief, & George, 2002; Tokar & Subich, 1997). However, relatively little attention has been given to the role of personality in the retirement decision-making process itself (Feldman & Beehr, 2011). This is an important avenue for future research.

There are a variety of reasons why we might expect personality to influence both perceptions of person-environment fit and decisions about early retirement. First, traits like self-esteem and positive affectivity may help older workers buffer negative feedback from the immediate environment (Cohn, 1978; Payne & Hartley, 1987). As noted earlier, older workers may receive more negative signals from managers that their performance is poor or that

it is time for them to retire. However, older workers who have positive dispositions are less likely to view their current situations as poor fits and would therefore be less likely to retire early. Second, personality traits associated with mastery, control, and perseverance—such as locus of control, hardiness, and conscientiousness—may also influence older workers to delay retirement. In the face of declining fit, older workers with traits related to mastery and control are more likely to exert effort to re-establish fit or to find alternative ways of performing satisfactorily (Layton, 1987; Ng & Feldman, 2010). Third, even if older workers are pushed into early retirement involuntarily, positive affect and mastery might help them adjust more readily to their new roles as retirees (Bailey & Hansson, 1995).

In sum, then, personality traits may influence perceptions of fit directly, may influence the decision to retire directly, or may moderate the relationship between perceptions of fit and early retirement. That is, the relationship between perceptions of declining fit and early retirement decisions may be weaker for those older workers who are high on positive affect and sense of mastery. In addition, further research on personality traits in the context of retirement would nicely complement the growing field of research that examines the effects of aging on emotions (Carstensen et al., 1999, 2000).

Relative Fit and Early Retirement

Last here, much more research is needed on the topic of relative fit. In most of the research we discussed above, P-E fit has been used as a predictor of individuals' decisions to leave their jobs, either via turnover or retirement. The underlying assumption in this research area has been that perceptions of declining fit lead to decisions to leave jobs and that those decisions are based on assessments of poor fit in current positions.

However, as decision theorists point out, all decisions are made in the context of available alternatives (Kahneman & Tversky, 1973). Consequently, even if P-E fit is declining, it does not necessarily mean that individuals will retire in the near future. While we would expect the relationship between declining P-E fit and early retirement to be significant, declining P-E fit would not in and of itself be the only major predictor of early retirement. If older workers with poor P-E fit perceive that fit with the bridge employee role or full retiree role would be even worse, they will not choose to retire voluntarily.

In some sense, then, we need an unfolding model of retirement that parallels Mitchell and

Lee's (2001) unfolding model of turnover. There are a variety of ways that older workers withdraw from the workforce—via early retirement, retirement "on time," movement into part-time bridge employment within the same firm, bridge employment in a different firm, self-employment, and so forth. Declines in different types of P-E fit would lead to different types of exit strategies, depending upon the various opportunities open to older workers and the constraints under which they operate. In constructing such a model, relative fit into different roles—along with absolute declines in P-E fit in the current job—must surely be taken into account as well.

References

Atchley, R. (1989). A continuity theory of aging. *Gerontologist, 29*, 183–190.

Barnes-Farrell, J. L. (2003). Beyond health and wealth: Attitudinal and other influences on retirement decision-making. In G. A. Adams & T. A. Beehr (Eds.), *Retirement: Reasons, processes, and results* (pp. 159–187). New York, NY: Springer.

Bailey, L. L., & Hansson, R. O. (1995). Psychological obstacles to job or career change in late life. *Journal of Gerontology: Psychological Sciences, 50*, 250–288.

Beach, L. R., & Frederickson, J. R. (1989). Image theory: An alternative description of audit decisions. *Accounting, Organizations, and Society, 14*, 101–112.

Beauregard, K. S., & Dunning, D. (1998). Turning up the contrast: Self-enhancement motives prompt egocentric contrast effects in social judgments. *Journal of Personality and Social Psychology, 74*, 606–621.

Bernardin, H. J. (1979). The predictability of discrepancy measures of role constructs. *Personnel Psychology, 32*, 139–153.

Blau, D. M. (1998). Labor force dynamics of older married couples. *Journal of Labor Economics, 16*, 595–629.

Bopp, K. L., & Verhaeghen, P. (2005). Aging and verbal memory span: A meta-analysis. *The Journals of Gerontology: Psychological Sciences and Social Sciences, 60*, 223–233.

Borg, I. (1990). Multiple facetisations of work values. *Applied Psychology: An International Review, 39*, 401–412.

Bradley, J. C., Brief, A. P., & George, J. M. (2002). More than the Big Five: Personality and careers. In D. C. Feldman (Ed.), *Work careers: A developmental perspective* (pp. 27–62). San Francisco, CA: Jossey-Bass.

Bretz, R. D., & Judge, T. A. (1994). Person-organization fit and the theory of work adjustment: Implications for satisfaction, tenure, and career success. *Journal of Vocational Behavior, 44*, 32–54.

Brougham, R. R., & Walsh, D. A. (2005). Goal expectations as predictors of retirement intentions. *International Journal of Aging and Human Development, 61*, 141–160.

Bunce, D., & Sisa, L. (2002). Age differences in perceived workload across a short vigil. *Ergonomics, 45*, 949–960.

Cable, D. M., & Judge, T. A. (1996). Person–organization fit, job choice decisions, and organizational entry. *Organizational Behavior and Human Decision Processes, 67*, 294–311.

Cable, D. M., & Judge, T. A. (1997). Interviewers' perceptions of person-organization fit and organizational selection decisions. *Journal of Applied Psychology, 82*, 546–561.

Cable, D. M., & Parsons, C. K. (2001). Socialization tactics and person-organization fit. *Personnel Psychology, 54*, 1–23.

Carstensen, L. L. (1995). Evidence for a life-span theory of socioemotional selectivity. *Current Directions in Psychological Science, 4*, 151–156.

Carstensen, L. L., Isaacowitz, D. M., & Charles, S. T. (1999). Taking time seriously. A theory of socioemotional selectivity. *American Psychologist, 54*, 165–181.

Carstensen, L. L., Pasupathi, M., Mayr, U., & Nesselroade, J. R. (2000). Emotional experience in everyday life across the adult life span. *Journal of Personality and Social Psychology, 79*, 644–655.

Cleveland, J. N., & Shore, L. M. (1992). Self- and supervisory perspectives on age and work attitudes and performance. *Journal of Applied Psychology, 77*, 469–484.

Cohn, R. M. (1978). The effect of employment status change on self attitudes. *Social Psychology, 41*, 81–93.

Currey, J. D., Brear, K., & Zioupos, P. (1996). The effects of ageing and changes in mineral content in degrading the toughness of human femora. *Journal of Biomechanics, 29*, 257–260.

Dalton, D. R., & Todor, W. D. (1993). Turnover, transfer, absenteeism: An interdependent perspective. *Journal of Management, 19*, 193–219.

Desmette, D., & Gaillard, M. (2008). When a "worker" becomes an "older worker": The effects of age-related social identity on attitudes toward retirement and work. *Career Development International, 13*, 168–185.

DeVaney, S. A., & Zhang, J. C. (2001). A cohort analysis of the amount in defined contribution and individual retirement savings. *Financial Counseling and Planning, 12*, 89–104.

Doeringer, P. B. (1990). Economic security, labor market flexibility, and bridges to retirement. In P. B. Doeringer (Ed.), *Bridges to retirement* (pp. 3–22). Ithaca, NY: Cornell ILR Press.

Doerpinghaus, H. I., & Feldman, D. C. (2001). Early retirement penalties in defined benefit pensions. *Journal of Managerial Issues, 13*, 273–287.

Dosman, D., Fast, J., Chapman, S. A., & Keating, N. (2006). Retirement and productive activity in later life. *Journal of Family Economic Issues, 27*, 401–419.

Dunning, D., Johnson, K., Ehrlinger, J., & Kruger, J. (2003). Why people fail to recognize their own incompetence. *Current Directions in Psychological Science, 12*, 83–87.

Edwards, J. R., Cable, D. M., Williamson, I. O., Lambert, L. S., & Shipp, A. J. (2006). The phenomenology of fit: Linking the person and environment to the subjective experience of person-environment fit. *Journal of Applied Psychology, 91*, 802–827.

Edwards, J. R., & Shipp, A. J. (2007). The relationship between person-environment fit and outcomes: An integrative theoretical framework. In C. Ostroff & T. A. Judge (Eds.), *Perspectives on organizational fit* (pp. 209–258). San Francisco, CA: Jossey Bass.

Elfenbein, H. A., & O'Reilly, C. A. (2007). Fitting in: The effects of relational demography and person-culture fit on group process and performance. *Group & Organization Management, 32*, 109–142.

Farr, J. L., & Ringseis, E. L. (2002). The older worker in organizational context: Beyond the individual. *International Review of Industrial and Organizational Psychology, 17*, 31–75.

Feldman, D. C. (1994). The decision to retire early: A review and conceptualization. *Academy of Management Review, 19*, 285–311.

Feldman, D. C., & Beehr, T. A. (2011). A three-phase model of retirement decision-making. *American Psychologist, 66*(3), 193–203.

Feldman, D. C., & Kim, S. (1998). Early buyout offers in the context of downsizing: Empirical evidence from the Korean electronics industry. *International Journal of Human Resource Management, 9,* 1008–1025.

Feldman, D. C., & Kim, S. (2000). Bridge employment during retirement: A field study of individual and organizational experiences with post-retirement employment. *Human Resource Planning, 23,* 14–25.

Feldman, D. C., & Vogel, R. M. (2009). The aging process and person-environment fit. In S. G. Baugh & S. E. Sullivan (Eds.), *Research in careers* (pp. 1–25). Charlotte, NC: Information Age Press.

Fiske, S. T., & Taylor, S. E. (1991). *Social cognition* (2nd ed.). New York, NY: McGraw-Hill.

Freund, A. M., & Baltes, P. B. (2002). Life-management strategies of selection, optimization, and compensation: Measurement by self-report and construct validity. *Journal of Personality and Social Psychology, 82,* 642–662.

Gobeski, K. T., & Beehr, T. A. (2009). How retirees work: Predictors of different types of bridge employment. *Journal of Organizational Behavior, 30,* 401–425.

Greller, M. M., & Simpson, P. (1999). In search of late career: A review of contemporary social science research applicable to the understanding of late career. *Human Resource Management Review, 9,* 309–347.

Hall, D. T., & Mirvis, P. H. (1996). The new protean career: Psychological success and the path with a heart. In D. T. Hall (Ed.), *The career is dead: Long live the career* (pp. 15–45). San Francisco, CA: Jossey-Bass.

Hedge, J. W., Borman, W. C., & Lammlein, S. E. (2006). *The aging workforce: Realities, myths, and implications for organizations.* Washington, DC: American Psychological Association.

Henkens, K. (1999). Early retirement intentions and spousal support: A multi-actor approach. *The Journals of Gerontology: Psychological Sciences and Social Sciences, 54,* 63–73.

Herrbach, O., Mignonac, K., Vandenberghe, C., & Negrini, A. (2009). Perceived HRM practices, organizational commitment, and voluntary early retirement among late-career managers. *Human Resource Management, 48,* 895–915.

Hira, T. K., Rock, W. L., & Loibl, C. (2009). Determinants of retirement planning behaviors and differences by age. *International Journal of Consumer Studies, 33,* 293–301.

Hoffman, B. J., & Woehr, D. J. (2006). A quantitative review of the relationship between person–organization fit and behavioral outcomes. *Journal of Vocational Behavior, 68,* 389–399.

Hoobler, J. M., Wayne, S. J., & Lemmon, G. (2009). Bosses' perceptions of family-work conflict and women's promotability: Glass ceiling effects. *Academy of Management Journal, 52,* 939–957.

Jansen, K. J., & Kristof-Brown, A. L. (2006). Toward a multidimensional theory of person-environment fit. *Journal of Managerial Issues, 18,* 193–212.

Kahneman, D., & Tversky, A. (1973). On the psychology of prediction. *Psychological Review, 80,* 251–273.

Kanfer, R., & Ackerman, P. L. (2004). Aging, adult development, and work motivation. *Academy of Management Review, 29,* 440–458.

Khalil, Z., & Merhi, M. (2000). Effects of aging on neurogenic vasodilator responses evoked by transcutaneous electrical nerve stimulation relevance to wound healing. *The Journals of Gerontology: Biological and Medical Sciences, 55,* 257–263.

Kim, S., & Feldman, D. C. (1998). Healthy, wealthy, or wise: Predicting actual acceptances of early retirement incentives at three points in time. *Personnel Psychology, 51,* 623–642.

Kim, S., & Feldman, D. C. (2000). Working in retirement: The antecedents and consequences of bridge employment and its consequences for quality of life in retirement. *Academy of Management Journal, 43,* 1195–1210.

Kristof, A. L. (1996). Person-organization fit: An integrative review of its conceptualizations, measurement, and implications. *Personnel Psychology, 49,* 1–49.

Kristof-Brown, A. L., Jansen, K. J., & Colbert, A. E. (2002). A policy-capturing study of the simultaneous effects of fit with jobs, groups, and organizations. *Journal of Applied Psychology, 87,* 985–993.

Lawrence, B. S. (1988). New wrinkles in the theory of age: Demography, norms, and performance ratings. *Academy of Management Journal, 31,* 309–337.

Layton, C. (1987). Externality and unemployment: Change score analyses on Rotter's Locus of Control Scale for male school-leavers and men facing redundancy. *Personality and Individual Differences, 8,* 149–152.

Levinson, D. (1986). A conception of adult development. *American Psychologist, 41,* 3–13.

Levinson, H., & Wofford, J. C. (2009). *Approaching retirement as the flexibility phase.* Washington, DC: American Psychological Association.

McArdle, A., Vasilaki, A., & Jackson, M. (2002). Exercise and skeletal muscle ageing: cellular and molecular mechanisms. *Ageing Research Reviews, 1,* 79–93.

Mishel, L., Bernstein, J., & Schmitt, J. (2001). *The state of working America: 2000–2001.* Ithaca, NY: Cornell University Press. OK

Mitchell, T. R., Holtom, B. C., Lee, T. W., Sablynski, C. J., & Erez, M. (2001). Why people stay: Using embeddedness to predict voluntary turnover. *Academy of Management Journal, 44,* 1102–1121.

Mitchell, T. R., & Lee, T. W. (2001). The unfolding model of voluntary turnover and job embeddedness. *Research in Organizational Behavior, 23,* 189–246.

Moen, P., Huang, Q., Plassmann, V., & Dentinger, E. (2006). Deciding the future: Do dual-earner couples plan together for retirement? *American Behavioral Scientist, 49,* 1422–1443.

Muchinsky, P. M., & Monahan, C. J. (1987). What is person-environment congruence? Supplementary versus complementary models of fit. *Journal of Vocational Behavior, 31,* 268–277.

Ng, T. W. H., & Feldman, D. C. (2008). The relationship of age to ten dimensions of job performance. *Journal of Applied Psychology, 93,* 392–423.

Ng, T. W. H., & Feldman, D. C. (2010). The effects of locus of control on career embeddedness. *Journal of Organizational and Occupational Psychology, 84,* 173–190.

Ng, T. W. H., & Feldman, D. C. (2010). Organizational tenure and job performance. *Journal of Management, 36,* 1220–1250.

Nimrod, G., & Kleiber, D. A. (2007). Reconsidering change and continuity in later life: Toward an innovation theory of successful aging. *International Journal of Aging and Human Development, 65,* 1–22.

O'Driscoll, M. P., Ilgen, D. R., & Hildreth, K. (1992). Time devoted to job and off-job activities, interrole conflict, and affective experiences. *Journal of Applied Psychology, 77,* 272–279.

Ostroff, C., Shin, Y., & Feinberg, B. (2002). Skill acquisition and person-environment fit. In D.C. Feldman (Ed.), *Work careers: A developmental perspective* (pp. 63–90). San Francisco: Jossey-Bass.

Papke, L. E. (2003). Individual financial decisions in retirement savings plans: The role of participant direction. *Journal of Public Economics, 88,* 39–61.

Payne, R., & Hartley, J. (1987). A test of a model for explaining the affective experience of unemployed men. *Journal of Occupational Psychology, 60,* 31–47.

Piasentin, K. A., & Chapman, D. S. (2006). Subjective person–organization fit: Bridging the gap between conceptualization and measurement. *Journal of Vocational Behavior, 69,* 202–221.

Pienta, A. M. (2003). Partners in marriage: An analysis of husbands' and wives' retirement behavior. *Journal of Applied Gerontology, 22,* 340–358.

Posthuma, R. A., & Campion, M. A. (2009). Age stereotypes in the workplace: Common stereotypes, moderators, and future research directions. *Journal of Management, 35,* 158–188.

Ratcliff, R., Thapar, A., & McKoon, G. (2001). The effects of aging on reaction time in a signal detection task. *Psychology and Aging, 16,* 323–341.

Ruhm, C. J. (1990). Bridge jobs and partial retirement. *Journal of Labor Economics, 8,* 482–501.

Schiamberg, L. B., & McKinney, K. G. (2003). Factors influencing expectations to move or age in place at retirement among 40- to 65-year-olds. *Journal of Applied Gerontology, 22,* 19–41.

Schneider, B., Smith, D. B., & Goldstein, H. W. (2000). Attraction-selection-attrition: Toward a person-environment psychology of organizations. In W. B. Walsh, K. H. Craik, & R. H. Price (Eds.), *Person-environment psychology* (pp. 61–86). Mahwah, NJ: Erlbaum.

Shultz, K. S. (2003). Bridge employment: Work after retirement. In G. A. Adams & T. A. Beehr (Eds.), *Retirement: Reasons, processes, and results* (pp. 214–241). New York, NY: Springer.

Shultz, K. S., Morton, K. R., & Weckerle, J. R. (1998). The influence of push and pull factors on voluntary and involuntary early retirees' retirement decision and adjustment. *Journal of Vocational Behavior, 53,* 45–57.

Spencer, W. D., & Raz, N. (1995). Differential effects of aging on memory for content and context: A meta-analysis. *Psychology and Aging, 10,* 527–539.

Spokane, A. R. (1985). A review of research on person-environment congruence in Holland's theory of careers. *Journal of Vocational Behavior, 26,* 306–343.

Spokane, A. R., Meir, E. I., & Catalano, M. (2000). Person-environment congruence and Holland's theory: A review and reconsideration. *Journal of Vocational Behavior, 57,* 137–187.

Stephan, Y., Fouquereau, E., & Fernandez, A. (2008). The relation between self-determination and retirement satisfaction among active retired individuals. *International Journal of Aging and Human Development, 66,* 329–345.

Stephens, G. K., & Feldman, D. C. (1997). A motivational approach for understanding work versus personal life investments. *Research in Personnel and Human Resources Management, 15,* 333–378.

Strauss, J. P., Barrick, M. R., & Connerley, M. L. (2001). An investigation of personality similarity effects (relational and perceived) on peer and supervisor ratings and the role of familiarity and liking. *Journal of Occupational and Organizational Psychology, 74,* 637–657.

Stryker, S. (1968). Identity salience and role performance: The relevance of symbolic interaction theory for family research. *Journal of Marriage and the Family, 30,* 558–564.

Super, D. E. (1990). A lifespan-life-space approach to career development. In D. Brown & L. Brooks (Eds.), *Career choice and development* (2nd ed., pp. 197–261). San Francisco, CA: Jossey-Bass.

Szinovacz, M. E., DeViney, S., & Davey, A. (2001). Influences of family obligations and relationships on retirement: Variations by gender, race, and marital status. *Journal of Gerontology: Social Sciences, 56B,* S20–S27.

Thomson, L., Griffiths, A., & Davison, S. (2000). Employee absence, age and tenure: A study of nonlinear effects and trivariate models. *Work & Stress, 14,* 16–34.

Tokar, D. M., & Subich, L. M. (1997). Relative contributions of congruence and personality dimensions to job satisfaction. *Journal of Vocational Behavior, 50,* 482–491.

Tsui, A. S., Porter, L. W., & Egan, T. D. (2002). When both similarities and dissimilarities matter: Extending the concept of relational demography. *Human Relations, 55,* 899–929.

van Dam, K., van der Vorst, J. D. M., & Heijden, B. I. J. M. (2009). Employees' intentions to retire early. A case of planned behavior and anticipated work conditions. *Journal of Career Development, 35,* 265–289.

van der Velde, M. E. G., Feij, J. A., & van Emmerik, H. (1998). Change in work values and norms among Dutch young adults: Ageing or societal trends? *International Journal of Behavioral Development, 22,* 55–76.

Vazire, S. (2010). Who knows what about a person? The self-other knowledge asymmetry (SOKA) model. *Journal of Personality and Social Psychology, 98,* 281–300.

Verhaeghen, P., Steitz, D. W., Sliwinski, M. J., & Cerella, J. (2003). Aging and dual-task performance: A meta-analysis. *Psychology and Aging, 18,* 443–460.

Vogel, R. M., & Feldman, D. C. (2009). Integrating the levels of person-environment fit: The roles of vocational fit and group fit. *Journal of Vocational Behavior, 75,* 68–81.

Wang, M., Adams, G. A., Beehr, T. A., & Shultz, K. S. (2009). Career issues at the end of one's career: Bridge employment and retirement. In S. G. Baugh & S. E. Sullivan (Eds.), *Maintaining focus, energy, and options over the life span* (pp. 135–162). Charlotte, NC: Information Age Publishing.

Wang, M., Zhan, Y., Liu, S., & Shultz, K. (2008). Antecedents of bridge employment: A longitudinal investigation. *Journal of Applied Psychology, 93,* 818–830.

Zappala, S., Depolo, M., Fraccaroli, F., Guglielmi, D., & Sarchielli, G. (2008). Postponing job retirement? Psychosocial influences on the preferences for early or late retirement. *Career Development International, 13,* 150–167.

Bridge Employment

Kevin E. Cahill, Michael D. Giandrea, *and* Joseph F. Quinn

Abstract

This chapter focuses on the prevalence, determinants, and outcomes of bridge jobs that follow full-time career employment and precede labor force withdrawal. Since the mid-1980s, the labor force participation rates of older Americans have been rising, reversing a century-long trend toward earlier and earlier retirement among men. A majority of older Americans now stay in the labor force when they leave their career jobs. They retire gradually, in stages. For them, retirement is not a one-time permanent event, but a process. For some, bridge jobs are a quality-of-life choice, a way to remain active and productive, often in a new line of work. For others, they are a financial necessity to augment inadequate retirement resources. We argue that bridge jobs are largely a positive phenomenon for individuals, employers, and the country as a whole. For individuals, continued work increases financial stability in old age and can provide non-pecuniary benefits as well. Employers are able to hire from a larger pool of experienced workers. Finally, the nation benefits from the additional goods and services produced, which somewhat alleviate the economic challenges of an aging population.

Key Words: bridge jobs, economics of aging, retirement trends, partial retirement, gradual retirement

Introduction and Overview

The retirement trends and patterns of older Americans—when and how older workers leave the labor force—have changed substantially over the past several decades. Most notable is the end of a century-long decline in the labor force participation rates of older men that occurred in the mid-1980s (Purcell, 2009; Quinn, 2010; Shultz & Wang, 2011). In 1910, the average age of retirement for men, defined here as the youngest age at which more than one-half of the population is out of the labor force, was 74 years. By 1940 it had declined to 70, by 1971 to 65, and by the early 1980s it was 63, where it remained essentially unchanged for more than two decades (Burtless & Quinn, 2002).[1] Evidence now suggests that this long-term trend

toward earlier and earlier retirement has not only stopped but reversed, with an increase in the average retirement age of men to 64 by 2004 and back to age 65 by 2009 (Quinn, Cahill, & Giandrea, 2011). For older women, labor force participation rates were almost unchanged between the mid-1960s and the mid-1980s, with earlier retirements largely offset by a contemporaneous increase in labor force participation among married women. But since the mid-1980s, older women displayed a break from trend similar to that of older men (Quinn, 2010). Many more older men and women are working today than prior trends would have predicted.

One reason for the dramatic change in retirement trends is that the retirement environment in the United States looks very different today than it did in the past. During the twentieth century, Americans grew more prosperous and accumulated wealth, many firms provided pension benefits, and the nation launched and significantly expanded the Social Security program. The increased wealth and the availability of public and, for many, employer pension benefits meant that individuals could afford more leisure, one form of which was early retirement.

Beginning in the 1980s, however, a number of important changes in the retirement landscape occurred, and a gradual shift began to take place toward a "do-it-yourself" approach to labor force withdrawal (Munnell, 2007; Munnell, Cahill, Eschtruth, & Sass, 2004). Many of these changes are now well established, and in some cases further changes are likely to occur. Mandatory retirement, which once covered about one-half of the American workforce, was first delayed from age 65 to age 70 in 1978, and then eliminated for the vast majority of American workers in 1986 (Quinn et al., 2011; von Wachter, 2002). Changes to Social Security regulations legislated in 1983 slowly increased the normal retirement age (NRA) from 65 to 66 and will eventually raise it to 67 for individuals born after 1959 (Congressional Budget Office, 2001). Despite this increase in the NRA, which is equivalent to an across-the-board benefit cut, Social Security faces long-run financial shortfalls, which will necessitate further reduced benefits or increases in the revenues (primarily the FICA payroll tax at present) that fund the program (Board of Trustees of OASDI, 2010; Congressional Budget Office, 2002, 2009; Lavery, 2009). In addition, Social Security increased the delayed retirement credit (from 3% to 8% per year of delay) for those postponing receipt of Social Security benefits until after age 65, eliminating what had been a strong retirement incentive (or work disincentive) for the average worker at age 65.

In the employer pension world, traditional defined benefit (DB) plans, which typically guaranteed monthly payments based on tenure with the firm and some measure of average salary, had similar age-specific work disincentives, usually at the earliest age of pension eligibility. But these traditional DB plans have largely been supplanted by defined contribution (DC) plans, like 401(k)s, which operate more like tax-deferred individual savings accounts that individuals draw down in retirement. They are age-neutral by nature and contain no age-specific work disincentives or retirement incentives (Munnell, 2006; Quinn, 2010). In addition to the substantial investment and

longevity risks associated with DC pensions, these pensions are often less generous to retirees than DB pensions (Munnell & Sunden, 2004). Finally in the past decade private savings rates reached their lowest level since the Great Depression (U.S. Department of Commerce, Bureau of Economic Analysis, 2010). With these changes, and potential cutbacks in Medicare and Medicaid eligibility and coverage, many older Americans face a choice between lower living standards in retirement or working longer.

Increasingly, older Americans have stabilized the traditional three-legged retirement income stool (Social Security, employer pensions, and accumulated savings) by adding a fourth leg—labor market earnings. As we will see, Americans are now working longer than prior cohorts did. In addition, many are retiring gradually, in stages. For these individuals, retirement is not a one-time permanent event. It is a process, a blend of work and leisure that depends on many factors including age, health, job satisfaction, and the state of an individual's financial well-being. Older Americans are showing flexibility with respect to the timing of complete labor force withdrawal, the number of hours worked, and the possibility of re-entering the labor force after an initial exit. The concept of work and retirement as dichotomous states among older Americans—one is either working or retired—hides much of the interesting reality behind labor force withdrawal late in life today.

After some brief background on when older Americans leave the labor force, this chapter will focus on *how* they do so, with an emphasis on bridge jobs that follow career employment and precede complete labor force withdrawal. We begin by documenting the prevalence of bridge job employment, and how its prevalence compares to that of other forms of transitional retirement, such as "phased retirement," which does not involve a change in employer, and "re-entry," which involves a return to work after an initial exit (sometimes described as an "unretirement").[2] We then focus on the correlates of bridge job activity. Financial incentives within Social Security and employer pensions are important, as are many other factors, such as age, health, and health insurance status. Finally, we discuss several outcomes related to the bridge job phenomenon: the financial and psychological benefits of continued work for individuals, the opportunities to hire from an experienced labor pool for employers, and the benefits of increased production for the nation as a whole.

We conclude with a discussion of retirement trends and bridge jobs in the future. Most of the components of the new retirement landscape are permanent. We do not anticipate a return of mandatory retirement provisions, a resurgence of defined benefit pension plans, or more generous or earlier Social Security benefits. In addition, Americans are living healthier and longer lives, working at less physically demanding occupations, and enjoying technological advances that permit more flexibility concerning when and where one works. Finally, the recent economic recession and expectations that slow growth, high unemployment, and lower asset prices might persist for years to come have given Americans pause about severing ties with the labor force. The combination of permanent changes in the retirement environment and a cyclical downturn that may have long-lasting effects suggests that we have entered a new era of retirement in the United States.

Trends in Labor Force Participation and the Prevalence of Bridge Jobs

As noted above, older Americans, on average, are working longer than pre-1985 trends would have predicted. Tables 19.1 and 19.2 show labor force participation rates for individual ages of men (since 1950) and women (since 1970), to 1985 and then beyond, through 2011. Declines among men between 1950 and 1985 are significant, on the order of 60% for men aged 65 and over. For those aged 62, there is little change between 1950 and 1960 (when men were still ineligible for Social Security benefits before age 65), and then a decline over twenty-five

years of nearly 40% once age 62 eligibility was legislated for men in 1961. From the mid-1980s through 2011, however, the labor force participation trends among these older men are all positive—increases on the order of 60% (on a smaller base) for those aged 68, 50% at age 65 and 72, and 16% at age 62.

For women, the percentage declines were more modest before 1985 (even when compared to the men's declines just since 1970), but the subsequent break from trend in the mid-1980s is even more dramatic. At age 62, a decline of 13% (over fifteen years) turns into an increase of 55% (over twenty-six years). At ages 65, 68, and 70, analogous declines in the 20% to 30% range turn into labor force participation increases near 100%.

An interesting question is the impact of the recession on these trends. The data since 2007 do not suggest a turnaround—see the bottom row in Tables 19.1 and 19.2. Older women's participation rates continued to increase after 2007, although there are small declines in 2011 at ages 60, 62, and 65. Participation rates for older men also continued to increase during the recession, with a few small declines noted in the past two years. Survey data on the expected retirement age of workers strongly suggest that continued work is on the horizon. As seen in Table 19.3, the percentage of current workers expecting to retire at age 66 or later, or never, rose slowly and steadily, by 24 points over seventeen years (from 11% in 1991 to 35% in 2008, prior to the October crash). From early 2008 to early 2009, however, that percentage jumped by six points and then by three more points, to 44%, by 2012. A survey of about 1,300

Table 19.1 Labor Force Participation Rates: Men, By Age, 1950–2011

	55	60	62	65	68	70	72
Year							
1950	90.6	84.7	81.2	71.7	57.7	49.8	39.3
1960	92.8	85.9	79.8	56.8	42.0	37.2	28.0
1970	91.8	83.9	73.8	49.9	39.4	30.1	24.8
1975	87.6	76.9	64.4	39.4	23.7	23.7	22.6
1980	84.9	74.0	56.8	35.2	24.1	21.3	17.0
1985	83.7	71.0	50.9	30.5	20.5	15.9	14.9
% Change 1950–1985	–8%	–16%	–37%	–57%	–64%	–68%	–62%

(Continued)

Table 19.1 (Continued)

	55	60	62	65	68	70	72
Year							
1985	83.7	71.0	50.9	30.5	20.5	15.9	14.9
1990	85.3	70.5	52.5	31.9	23.4	17.1	16.4
1995	81.1	68.9	51.3	33.5	22.4	20.6	16.0
2000	79.8	66.2	53.0	35.9	28.1	20.2	18.5
2005	80.6	67.7	57.7	39.7	32.2	23.8	21.6
2007	81.7	70.4	57.5	43.6	28.9	23.6	22.1
2008	83.8	68.9	56.6	43.7	29.8	24.1	22.0
2009	83.4	69.4	60.6	42.5	33.3	26.1	24.3
2010	82.2	69.0	59.0	42.7	33.4	24.7	23.9
2011	81.6	69.2	58.8	45.5	32.4	28.1	22.3
% Change 1985–2011	–3%	–3%	16%	49%	58%	77%	50%
% Change 2007–2011	0%	–2%	2%	4%	12%	19%	1%

Source: U.S. Bureau of Labor Statistics

Table 19.2 Labor Force Participation Rates: Women, By Age, 1970–2011

	55	60	62	65	68	70	72
Year							
1970	52.6	44.0	36.1	22.1	15.0	12.2	8.6
1975	51.6	41.0	32.9	19.5	12.3	9.0	7.8
1980	52.8	41.3	31.8	20.8	10.8	9.0	7.3
1985	55.5	41.9	31.5	16.2	12.1	9.0	8.2
% Change 1970–1985	6%	–5%	–13%	–27%	–19%	–26%	–5%
	55	60	62	65	68	70	72
Year							
1985	55.5	41.9	31.5	16.2	12.1	9.0	8.2
1990	59.8	44.8	34.9	20.6	15.2	11.7	8.0
1995	62.2	47.8	34.8	21.5	14.8	10.2	9.5
2000	65.2	51.5	38.7	23.2	16.6	10.9	10.8

Table 19.2 (Continued)

	55	60	62	65	68	70	72
Year							
2005	69.8	55.7	44.6	28.3	20.6	16.7	11.8
2007	70.3	56.7	46.4	32.1	22.5	16.3	13.2
2008	71.3	59.4	48.0	32.6	22.3	17.1	14.6
2009	73.2	58.3	48.9	33.4	23.0	20.2	15.8
2010	72.8	61.0	49.7	33.7	23.7	17.3	14.6
2011	71.9	60.7	48.7	33.6	25.2	17.8	15.8
% Change 1985–2011	30%	45%	55%	107%	108%	98%	93%
% Change 2007–2011	2%	7%	5%	5%	12%	9%	20%

Source: U.S. Bureau of Labor Statistics.

Table 19.3 Worker's Expected Retirement Age, 1991–2012

	< 60	60–64	65	66–69	70+	Never	66+ and Never
Year							
1991	19	31	34	2	9	0	11
1995	21	24	35	3	11	0	14
2000	22	22	28	6	13	4	23
2005	16	19	26	7	17	6	30
2008	11	21	24	9	20	6	35
2009	9	17	23	10	21	10	41
2010	9	19	24	9	24	9	42
2011	7	16	26	11	25	8	44
2012	8	16	26	11	26	7	44

Source: Helman, Copeland, & VanDerhei (2012; see Figure 30).

full-time employees conducted by MetLife in 2009 found that 59% said they plan to retire after age 65 (MetLife, 2010). Further, the percentage of young baby boomers (the subset born between 1955 and 1964) expecting to retire after age 65 increased from 49% to 60% between the 2008 and 2009 surveys.

Labor force participation is dichotomous. One is either in or out of the labor force, and one can be in by remaining full-time in a career job or by retiring from that job and working a few hours per week in a sunnier climate—or anything in between. These are very different labor supply decisions, but participation rates do not distinguish among them. We must look behind the participation numbers to discern what is happening, and this is what the bridge job literature does. As we will see, not only are older Americans remaining in the labor force longer, they are also leaving it in very diverse ways. For some, retirement remains a one-time, permanent exit from a career job and from the labor market all at once—the traditional, stereotypical retirement. More common among older Americans, however, are gradual retirements, occasionally reduced hours for the same employer ("phased retirement"), but more often a job change from a career job to a new full-time or part-time position ("partial retirement"; Kantarci & van Soest, 2008). As we discuss in more detail below, bridge jobs are an important form of gradual retirement that involve a change in employer and sometimes a switch between wage-and-salary work and self-employment.

The term "retirement" can be misleading because it means different things to different people and to different researchers. For some, retirement means leaving a particular career (e.g., "retired" from the legal profession) and may not be indicative of one's current labor force status. Others may classify themselves as retired once they begin receiving Social Security benefits or an employer pension, regardless of work status. Still others may not consider themselves retired until they cease all paid work or even all volunteer work. The concept of retirement is subjective and may seem unrelated to one's prior work history, current work status, or expectations for future employment. The term obfuscates as much as it illuminates. In this chapter, therefore, we concentrate on the transition from full-time career employment through bridge jobs to eventual labor force withdrawal. Where along the way one is defined as "retired" is somewhat arbitrary and not very important. To keep things simple and unambiguous, we define "retirement" as complete labor force withdrawal.

A main conclusion from the literature on retirement transitions is that the majority of individuals with career jobs move to another job before exiting the labor force—they leave in stages. Therefore, the minority of retirements from career jobs are of the stereotypical type—an abrupt and permanent move from full-time career employment to complete labor force withdrawal (Cahill, Giandrea, & Quinn, 2006; Quinn, 1999; Ruhm, 1990).

Bridge jobs are an important part of the retirement process. By our definition, a bridge job follows career employment. What constitutes a career job is debatable. Our definition requires full-time and long duration; in particular, 1,600 or more hours per year with tenure of ten years or more. A job after career employment, therefore, is a bridge job if it is part-time, regardless of tenure, or full-time but less than ten years' duration.[3]

Using this definition of full-time career (FTC) employment, Quinn (1999) estimated that, at a minimum, between one-third and one-half of older Americans with career jobs would utilize bridge jobs before exiting the labor force completely. This early analysis was based on a sample of individuals aged 51 to 61 in 1992 from the Health and Retirement Study (HRS), a large nationally representative longitudinal survey of older Americans (Karp, 2007). It examined retirement transitions observed during the first three biennial waves of HRS data—surveys conducted in 1992, 1994, and 1996—and based the estimate on only those who had left a career job by 1996. Cahill et al. (2006) performed a similar analysis with three additional waves of HRS data, through 2002. The authors observed more transitions from career employment with the extended dataset and found that about 60% of men and women who made a job transition moved to a bridge job before exiting the labor force completely. In a further follow-up, Giandrea, Cahill, and Quinn (2009) examined bridge job prevalence among a cohort of younger (by six years) retirees from the HRS, aged 51 to 56 in 1998, known as the "war babies." With data from 1998 through 2006, the authors found that, among the war babies who transitioned from career employment by 2006, 64% moved to a bridge job prior to exiting the labor force completely. The younger cohort of retirees utilized bridge jobs as much as their slightly older peers did, and perhaps a little more.

To what extent do these estimates of bridge job prevalence depend upon the definition of career employment? The shorter the job tenure required, the more jobs will be defined as new "careers" and the fewer will be designated "bridge jobs." Cahill et al. (2006) examined the sensitivity of their results to changes in the definition of a full-time career job. Reducing the tenure requirement to eight years resulted in a slight (3%) increase in the number of men with a career job; reducing the tenure requirement to five years resulted in a 6% increase. The corresponding changes for women were slightly higher. The number of women designated with a career job increased by 5% with the eight-year tenure requirement and by 11% with the five-year requirement. The authors concluded that the qualitative results are robust; the definitional changes for career employment have some impact on the career-versus-bridge job classification, but for any reasonable definition of career and bridge jobs the latter are a very important part of the retirement process in the United States.

Other studies yielded similar results about the prevalence of bridge job activity. For example, Kim and DeVaney (2005) modeled the choice among continued full-time work, partial retirement, and complete retirement, using a reduction of fifteen or more hours per week worked and self-reported retirement status to determine work status. They based their definition of retirement on Gustman and Steinmeier (2000), who considered multiple definitions in their analysis of retirement outcomes and recommended a hybrid definition that accounted for both a reduction in hours worked and self-reported retirement status. Ruhm (1990, 1991) used the longest job held as a reference point for analyzing bridge job employment, while Maestas (2010) used a combination of hours worked and self-assessed retirement status to differentiate among partial retirement, complete retirement, unemployment, and absence from the labor force. The prevalence of gradual retirement in these studies ranged from about one-third of those who were no longer working full-time in Kim and DeVaney (2005) to about 50% in Maestas (2010) to more than 50% in Ruhm (1990).

Likewise, Mutchler, Burr, Pienta, and Massagli (1997) analyzed older men in the Survey of Income and Program Participation (SIPP) to assess blurred versus crisp exits from the labor force. A blurred retirement comprised multiple transitions between employment and non-employment; a crisp retirement was a single transition from being employed to being out of the labor force. While only one-quarter of their sample experienced a transition over a twenty-eight-month observation period, 60% of these had blurred transitions, qualitatively consistent with the results described above.

Bridge jobs are not a new phenomenon. Studies based on the Retirement History Study (RHS), a longitudinal dataset that followed American men and unmarried women aged 58 to 63 in 1969 through 1979, reveal considerable bridge job activity.[4] Gustman and Steinmeier (1984) examined the labor force behavior of white men in the RHS relative to the main job that was held at age 55. They found that about one-quarter of the youngest respondents and over one-third of the oldest respondents self-reported that they were partially retired at some point between 1969 and 1975. The authors concluded that binary measures of retirement status miss the important phenomenon of partial retirement. Ruhm (1990) used the RHS to examine bridge jobs and found that well over one-half of RHS respondents with career jobs did not retire directly but rather exited through at least one other job. Ruhm, who defined a "career" job

as the longest spell of employment with a single firm, demonstrated an important alternative to the traditional one-time permanent retirement. As far back as the 1970s, many older American men with career jobs were not choosing one-time exits from the labor force, but rather were leaving career jobs for partial retirement at some point in their working lives (Quinn, Burkhauser, & Myers, 1990).

Bridge jobs are one route by which older workers can leave the labor force. Kantarci and van Soest (2008) summarized the research on phased retirement (cutting back on labor force intensity at one's current employer) and partial retirement (changing employers). They highlighted some of the subjective and objective measures of gradual retirement, including a reduction in working hours, a lower wage rate, a reduction in earnings (through hours worked or the wage rate), and pension receipt. Regardless of the measure, they found that the flexible U.S. labor market was conducive to job and employer changes later in life, and therefore to bridge job activity. They note that phased retirement (with the same employer) might be more of an option in European countries where the job market is less flexible than in the United States.

Evidence suggests that many older American workers would prefer reduced hours on a career job to continued full-time work; however, such arrangements are often not available. For example, in a 2001–2002 survey of employers, Hutchens and Chen (2007) found that less than 10% of establishments would permit phased retirement among white-collar workers if certain conditions, such as continued health insurance benefits, were required. When facing such constraints, older workers have to choose among remaining full-time on a current job, switching jobs, or leaving the labor force. Employers also have a choice, between retaining valuable older workers by providing flexible work arrangements or losing these workers, who may opt for reduced hours with another firm. In a survey of 950 employers, Hutchens and Grace-Martin (2006) found that only 14% reported no option for phased retirement. Importantly, while most did not have established rules for who would be eligible for this program, older workers considered valuable by the employer and who wanted phased retirement (reduced hours, flexible starting times, job sharing arrangements) were often able to work out informal agreements with their employers.

Van Soest, Kapteyn, and Zissimopoulos (2007) asked Dutch workers whether they were eligible to work reduced hours with their existing employer before complete labor force exit. Approximately one-third of the sample of Dutch workers said that they had the opportunity to reduce hours before complete retirement, with women and those with higher levels of education most likely to have the option. Many respondents also expressed reluctance about full-time employment after the normal retirement age; instead, they favored part-time employment prior to complete labor force withdrawal.

Charles and Decicca (2007) investigated work hours flexibility before retirement in the United States using the HRS and found that those who were unable to reduce work hours were more likely to leave the labor force by a stated date than those with some work hours flexibility. Moreover, rather than pushing workers into bridge job employment, these constraints resulted in earlier labor force departure, possibly because of the transition costs associated with switching employers or changing occupations. Gielen (2009) found that British men working more than full-time were able to cut back on hours before retirement, unlike those who worked less than full-time. The author concluded that labor force participation rates, particularly of women, might be higher among older individuals if there were more opportunities to reduce hours among those working full-time. Aaronson and French (2004) point out that, among men in the United States, a reduction in hours is typically associated with a decline in hourly wage, especially for those who changed employers. Whether workers would be as willing to cut back hours if wages and hours are determined jointly is an interesting research question.

Re-entry into the labor force, or "unretirement," is another nontraditional exit route. Evidence suggests that approximately 15% of older workers who leave the labor force directly from career employment end up back in the labor force at some point before complete retirement (Cahill, Giandrea, & Quinn, 2011).[5] Maestas (2010) found that almost one-half of older workers experienced partial retirement or re-entry after an initial exit, and reported that labor force re-entry was frequently anticipated prior to retirement. Many older workers rely on the possibility of re-entry as a way to supplement retirement income or maintain a social network if retirement proves unsatisfactory. This finding suggests that there is much more to work later in life than just receiving a paycheck. For example, Griffin and Hesketh (2008) found that those who were tired of their jobs in their pre-retirement years were less likely to re-enter the labor force or do volunteer work after leaving those positions.

Much of the evidence described above pertains to workers with career employment. How do older workers who never had a career job leave the labor market? A recent paper by Cahill, Giandrea, and Quinn (2012) explored the timing and types of job switches of those without career employment. They found that the prevalence and frequency of job switches among these older workers were similar to those with career jobs. Further, job switches from wage-and-salary employment to self-employment and between white-collar and blue-collar work were also similar by career job status. The authors concluded that the labor force withdrawal patterns of workers without career jobs are also diverse.

The retirement literature has clearly established that older Americans leave the labor market in a very interesting variety of ways. Bridge jobs, phased retirement, and re-entry are all common among today's older workers, to the point that traditional one-time, permanent retirements are the exception rather than the rule. For most, retirement is indeed a process, a reflection of the flexibility of the American workforce and labor market.

Determinants of Work after Retirement

Why are older Americans working longer and exiting the labor force gradually? There are economic incentives for doing so. Social Security and employer pensions have changed in recent years in ways that are now less likely to discourage work later in life. These changes have been described as shifting retirement planning to a "do-it-yourself" approach, in which individuals plan their own retirement benefits and bear the responsibility to provide adequate financial resources for themselves, especially in the fortuitous case of a longer-than-expected life span (Munnell et al., 2004; Munnell & Sunden, 2004). This is a fundamental shift from the second half of the last century, when the combination of Social Security and employer pensions (both defined benefit plans) ensured many Americans predictable benefits throughout retirement, however long that might last.

Perhaps the most significant change in retirement income began in the early 1980s with the advent of 401(k) plans. These defined contribution plans were rare prior to 1980 but, within the span of thirty years, they have largely supplanted, in the private sector, the defined benefit plans that dominated previously (Munnell, 2006; Papke, 1999). Among the almost one-half of workers who participated in an employment-based retirement plan in 1992, 42% had a DB plan only, 41% had

DC only, and 17% had both. By 2004, the analogous numbers were 26, 56, and 18%; over 70% had a DC plan, and well over one-half had only a DC plan (Copeland, 2009). Further, many DB plans in the private sector today are actually hybrids, such as cash balance plans, so the traditional DB plans that remain are now mostly found in the public sector (Cahill & Soto, 2003; Munnell, 2006; Munnell & Perun, 2006). The reasons for the switch to DC plans are many, and include longer retiree life spans, changes in funding and reporting requirements that made DB plans more expensive for employers, and declines in the occupations and industries (often unionized) in which DB plans were common (Gale, Papke, & VanDerhei, 2005; Munnell & Perun, 2006; Munnell & Sunden, 2004).

The shift from DB to DC plans is significant because their economic incentives are very different. DB plans usually contain financial incentives that encourage employees to remain with the firm until a certain age, while future benefits accrue, but then discourage continued tenure with the firm after that age. Typically, and usually at the earliest age of benefit eligibility, the increase in future monthly benefits the worker would enjoy for delaying benefit receipt does not fully compensate for the benefits forgone (i.e., the monthly benefit checks that the worker could have received but chose to decline). These adjustments to monthly benefits are typically less than actuarially fair, and therefore the lifetime (present discounted) value of the expected benefit stream declines with continued work after the age of pension eligibility. In essence, this is equivalent to a pay cut (one earns a paycheck but loses lifetime pension wealth during an additional year of work) or an implicit tax on work, and can be a strong financial incentive to leave the career job at a specific age.

DC plans contain no such age-specific financial incentives to leave the firm. They operate like savings accounts and do not decline in value if the employee chooses to work an additional year. Therefore, individuals with DC pensions might be expected to retire later than those with DB plans, all else equal, and some evidence suggests that this is indeed the case. Friedberg and Webb (2005) found that those with DC pensions left the labor force about two years later than those with DB plans, other things equal. Munnell, Cahill, and Jivan (2003) found that individuals with DC plans expected to retire about one year later than otherwise similar individuals with DB plans. DC plans also contain other attributes that can influence work decisions. Unlike in DB plans, individuals assume the investment risk of their DC funds. If the market declines substantially just prior to retirement, retirement income could be substantially less than expected. Coile and Levine (2006) found, however, that the labor market behavior of older workers as a group was not particularly responsive to stock market shocks of the 1990s and early 2000s, mostly because so few held a substantial amount of stocks.

One option for workers to reduce their vulnerability to market fluctuations is to re-balance their portfolios toward safer assets as they approach retirement. Rebalancing is not a cure-all, however, and individuals with DC plans may still have to adjust (reduce retirement consumption or work longer) if their DC assets decline prior to retirement. Individuals with DC plans who choose not to annuitize their assets are also exposed to longevity risk (outliving their assets) and may choose to work longer to hedge against this risk.

Several studies from the 1990s investigated the relationship between pensions and retirement behavior. Stock and Wise (1990) developed the concept of the "option value" of work that gauges the differences in an individual's utility from either exiting the labor force or remaining employed until the normal retirement age of a defined benefit pension. Their simulations showed that increases in the normal retirement age for a DB pension or a switch from a DB to a DC pension both reduce the retirement rate of workers. It is worth noting, however, that these two changes may have different effects on the likelihood of workers taking bridge jobs. Samwick (1998) refined some of the conclusions of Stock and Wise (1990) using a dataset that combined household demographic and economic information from the Survey of Consumer Finances with household pension information from the Pension Provider Survey. He demonstrated that it is *changes* to retirement wealth (and in particular, to pension wealth), as opposed to the level of retirement wealth per se, that have a substantial effect on the decision to retire. Regarding pensions and bridge jobs, Cahill et al. (2006) found that career workers with DB pensions were less likely to transition to bridge jobs before complete labor force withdrawal than those with DC pensions or no pensions. Those with DC pensions were no more or less likely to transition to a bridge job than those with no pension at all.

Changes to Social Security, both legislated and proposed, also encourage work later in life. The most obvious one is the gradual increase in the normal retirement age from 65 to 67 that began with individuals born in 1938 (age 62 in 2000) and later.

The NRA is now 66 for individuals born between 1943 and 1954, and is scheduled to start increasing again (two months per year) for those born in 1955 and later, reaching 67 for individuals born after 1959 (Congressional Budget Office, 2001; U.S. Social Security Administration, 2010a). Another change to Social Security pertains to the earnings test, the earnings threshold above which Social Security benefits are reduced. In 2000, the earnings test was eliminated for individuals older than their NRA, while those who claim Social Security benefits while younger than their NRA lose one dollar of benefits for every two dollars of earned income above $14,160 (in 2010) (U.S. Social Security Administration, 2010b).[6] Even though the benefit reduction due to the earnings test is eventually returned to the recipient, on average, in the form of higher monthly benefits later, the elimination of the earnings test after the NRA provided an additional incentive to remain working (Gruber & Orszag, 2003). Interestingly, Gruber and Orszag (2003) found that the elimination of the earnings test resulted in no discernable effect on labor supply among men 65 and older.

Finally, over a twenty-year period, legislation slowly increased the delayed retirement credit after the NRA (the reward for delaying Social Security benefit receipt) from 3% to 8% per year of delay. The 3% reward was less than actuarially fair, resulting in a loss of Social Security wealth with continued work—a subtle pay cut. The current 8% figure (about what it always was between ages 62 and 65) is close to actuarially fair, eliminating this important work disincentive for the average worker.

Anderson, Gustman, and Steinmeier (1999) estimated that approximately one-quarter of the reduction in labor force participation among older men from the late 1960s to the early 1980s was attributable to changes in private pensions and more generous Social Security benefits. Coile and Gruber (2007) showed that Social Security incentives were significant determinants of the retirement decisions of older men but that substantial spikes in retirement hazards at the early retirement age of 62 and the normal retirement age of 65 remained even after controlling for Social Security regulations. Liebman, Luttmer, and Seif (2009) found that older Americans responded as expected to effective marginal tax rates and benefit regulations. In particular, workers are more likely to retire when effective marginal tax rates are high and less likely to retire when marginal benefits from additional work are substantial. In a study of 12 OECD nations, Gruber and Wise (2004) identified a very strong relationship between the implicit tax on work through the nation's retirement program regulations and labor force participation among its older workers. The more the system "taxed" the earnings of older employees, by reducing their lifetime retirement benefits, the larger the proportion of men aged 55 to 64 who were out of the labor force. Finally, Coile (2004), using the HRS, considered how couples make joint decisions based on each spouse's pension and Social Security incentives. She found that men tend to be responsive to their spouse's financial incentives but that women are not. Using the older RHS, Blau (1998) found that, more generally, the labor force status of a spouse influences the probability of the other spouse entering or exiting the labor force, i.e., that there exists a preference for shared leisure between spouses.

One way that older Americans might be able to retire early is to rely on their own savings to offset some of the income decline that accompanies labor force withdrawal. This does not appear to be an option for most Americans, however. Data from the National Income and Product Accounts show that savings rates in the past decade reached their lowest levels since the Great Depression (U.S. Department of Commerce, Bureau of Economic Analysis, 2010). Further, estimates of wealth holdings reveal that 56% of American retirees and 54% of American workers had less than $25,000 in savings and investments in 2010 excluding home value and any defined benefit pension wealth (Helman, Copeland, & VanDerhei, 2010).[7]

Other factors, such as health insurance, also play an important role in the work decisions of older individuals. Johnson, Davidoff, and Perese (2003) investigated how health insurance premiums affect retirement rates. For those younger than the Medicare eligibility age of 65, health insurance premiums can become one of the most significant retirement costs. The authors found that provision of retiree health insurance by employers substantially increased retirement rates and that increases in the premiums paid by retirees reduced retirement rates.

Gustman and Steinmeier (1994) also investigated the role of employer-provided health insurance and its impact on the labor force behavior of older individuals. Using data from the 1970s and 1980s, they found that the provision of retiree health insurance increased retirement rates modestly. The benefits acted to reduce retirement before the age of pension eligibility and then increased retirement among eligible workers. Blau and Gilleskie (2001) also considered the role of employer-provided health insurance on the retirement decisions of men under two scenarios. When the individual shared the cost of insurance with the employer, the retirement rate increased by two percentage points; when the employer paid the entire cost, the rate increased by six percentage points.

Using data sets such as the National Medical Expenditure Survey, the Survey of Income and Program Participation, and the Health and Retirement Study, Karoly and Rogowski (1994), Madrian (1994), and Rogowski and Karoly (2000) also found that the presence of employer-provided retiree health insurance increased the likelihood of retiring before age 65. Finally, Robinson and Clark (2010) used data from the Health and Retirement Study and estimated that those with employer-provided retiree health insurance were about 20% more likely to exit their career job than those without. These transitions from full-time career positions, defined by the authors as jobs of at least thirty hours per week that last at least ten years, included both bridge job employment and direct exits from the labor force.

As one might expect, age and health status are also important determinants of retirement transitions. Cahill et al. (2006) found that, even after controlling for other economic and demographic characteristics, age had a significant impact on the likelihood of continued career work or bridge employment. As they aged, individuals were less likely to remain on a career job and less likely to transfer to a bridge job after leaving career employment.

Likewise, health status is an important determinant of the retirement transition. Maestas (2010) found that those with fair or poor self-assessed health were less likely to return to the labor force after retiring and that a negative health shock reduced the probability of bridge employment or re-entry. Cahill et al. (2006) found that among those with full-time career jobs in their work history (typically a relatively healthy subsample of all older Americans), those men and women who reported being in fair or poor health were much less likely to take bridge jobs following career employment than otherwise similar individuals.

McGarry (2004) found that changes in self-assessed health status were strongly correlated with changes in a worker's subjective estimate of how long he or she would continue to work and concluded that health status was even more important than financial variables in determining the probability of working at a specified future age. Other studies have also focused on the nonfinancial determinants of retirement. For example, Han and Moen (1999) examined actual transitions and expected work-life trajectories of older workers at six upstate New York firms and found that the timing of retirement depended on three dimensions: "historical context" (external trends), "biographical pacing" (career path), and "social heterogeneity" (gender and social variations).

Improvements in health and longevity, combined with the shift toward "do-it-yourself" retirement planning, imply that individuals will need to finance more years of retirement on their own. Working longer eases this burden by increasing lifetime earnings and by reducing the number of years during which assets are depleted. As discussed in the next section, one way to make this pro-work choice more attractive to older individuals is for policymakers to focus on removing barriers to employment, which could open the door to a variety of work arrangements. For example, Chen and Scott (2003) explored several forms of gradual retirement that may be available to older workers at their existing firms, such as job sharing, work schedule reductions, and re-entry as temporary employees.

The "do-it-yourself" approach to retirement could lead to a business cycle effect with respect to the timing of retirement (Cahill, Giandrea, & Quinn, 2008). Workers' expectations and plans in a defined contribution pension world are likely to be updated in response to the changing state of their finances. In an economic downturn, many older workers will want to postpone retirement to make up for lost asset values and might be expected to retire earlier in a boom if the value of their investments is higher than expected. This is a fundamental shift from the past. In a defined benefit environment, retirement incomes are less sensitive to market conditions, as investment risk is borne by the employer. The existence and size of this effect are important empirical questions.

To this point, the focus of this chapter has been on labor supply—the decisions of workers. However, retirement transitions are also dependent on labor demand by employers. A strong labor market, as in the 1990s and mid-2000s, provided older workers and others with job opportunities. The jobs available were generally less physically demanding than in the past, as the economy shifted away from manufacturing toward service occupations. An important question is whether these same opportunities will exist in the future, in the face of the recent recession and persistently high unemployment.

Outcomes of Continued Work in Retirement

In the future, to help maintain their standard of living in retirement, many older Americans will rely on earnings to supplement Social Security benefits, employer pensions, and savings. Bridge jobs will be an important part of this strategy, as individuals seek ways to remain in the labor force following career employment. What does this mean for individuals, employers, and the country as a whole?

In many ways, continued work is a positive development, as individuals accumulate more wealth and, as a result, have more financial stability later in life. A study by the Congressional Budget Office (2004) shows that for a representative household earning median pre-tax income and expecting Social Security benefits, delaying retirement (defined here as labor force withdrawal) from age 62 to 66 reduces by more than 50% the amount of assets needed at age 62 to maintain 80% of pre-retirement after-tax income (from about $510,000 to less than $250,000). The reduction is so large because each additional year of work both provides additional income and displaces a year of retirement, during which assets would have been depleted. The affect is cumulative, so that if retirement is delayed by eight years, from age 62 to age 70, the amount of resources needed in retirement is reduced by nearly 90%, from about $510,000 to about $52,000. Munnell and Sass (2008) have made the same point, noting the impact of a few more years of work on the ratio of years of work to years of retirement. An individual who works forty years, from age 20 to 60, and then is retired for twenty years, until age 80, has a ratio of 2:1. Working just another five years, until age 65, changes the ratio to 3:1.

Research has also shown that continued work later in life is associated with social and psychological benefits as people remain active and productive in later years (Committee for Economic Development, 1999). Part of this research is based on responses to questions about why people work late in life. While retirees widely report that earnings are important—90% of retirees cite at least one financial reason for continued work—other factors are important as well (Helman et al., 2010). For example, according to the 2010 EBRI Retirement Confidence Survey, 92% of retirees said they worked for pay because they wanted to stay active, and 86%

said they worked for pay because they enjoyed working.[8] Citing Brown (2003), Pitt-Catsouphes and Smyer (2005) report that two-thirds of workers 45 years and older work because it makes them feel useful, 68% work because they like being productive and helping others, and 76% work because they enjoy the job. Beyond a paycheck, work provides a sense of accomplishment and is an important social outlet.

Kim and Feldman (2000) applied the continuity theory of aging to analyze other benefits to older workers. Continuity theory states that older individuals try to maintain familiar behavioral patterns and activities as they age. In this context, as workers approach retirement they may attempt to maintain a presence in the labor force, even if a reduced one, as a method of adjusting to changing life situations. Other research has shown that the desire to pass along skills and knowledge to younger generations (the "generative" reason for work) is a positive predictor of bridge job satisfaction (Dendinger, Adams, & Jacobson, 2005). Dendinger et al. (2005) also found that the financial reason for work was not a significant determinant of job satisfaction or attitudes toward retirement. Finally, Lim and Feldman (2003) reported that the relationship between retirement anxiety and willingness to take bridge employment was not statistically significant and, further, that bridge jobs were viewed positively by some workers because they provided meaningful and structured work activity. This structure may provide continuity and reduce the anxiety of workers who were moving from one life stage to another.

Research has also shown that continued work later in life can have a positive impact on an individual's health. Wang, Adams, Beehr, and Shultz (2009) summarized the existing literature on health and retirement and concluded that those who transitioned to bridge jobs were healthier than those who did not, even after controlling for pre-retirement health status. Moreover, those who participated in phased retirement, or continued work in the same field but at a reduced intensity, had superior mental health outcomes than others. In another study, Wang (2007) found that HRS workers who transitioned to bridge jobs before complete retirement were more likely than those who retired directly from career employment to maintain their psychological well-being through the retirement process. Likewise, Zhan, Wang, Liu, and Shultz (2009), using HRS data from 1992 through 1998, concluded that those who transitioned to bridge jobs reported fewer major illnesses than those who left the labor force completely. Moreover, they found that those who took bridge jobs in the same field in which they had their career also reported better mental health outcomes than those who exited the labor force. Dave, Rashad, and Spasojevic (2008) used the HRS to assess the impact of retirement on health as well and found that full labor force exit resulted in a deterioration of mental and physical health, but the negative impacts of retirement on health were reduced if the individual held a bridge job rather than completely left the labor force. They suggested that lifestyle changes brought about by labor force exit could be partially offset by social and physical activity and that bridge employment may meet some of these needs.

The relationship between continued work and positive health outcomes is not definitive, however. Neuman (2008) used the HRS to assess changes in health after retiring or reducing hours below 1,200 hours per year. After correcting for the endogeneity of retirement, he found no evidence that self-perceived health deteriorated as a result of exiting the labor force.

Of course, additional work later in life is not good news for everyone. While continued work and bridge jobs can provide a more financially secure retirement and non-pecuniary benefits for many, for others, especially those at the lower end of the socioeconomic spectrum, additional work may impose significant hardship. Individuals might not want to remain in physically demanding jobs, and some older Americans may be in such poor health that paid work of any kind is difficult or impossible. If additional work is a solution for a shortfall in public and private retirement income, these vulnerable individuals run the risk of being left behind.

For employers, more individuals working later in life means a larger labor pool, many of whom have a lifetime of experience. Older workers may become an increasingly attractive option for employers because slow growth in the under-age-55 workforce is unlikely to be offset by other alternatives, such as increasing capital or immigration (Munnell et al., 2004). Munnell et al. (2004) also highlighted other reasons why older workers may be more attractive to employers in the future: older people today are healthier and have more education than prior cohorts, and jobs are less physically demanding than in the past. On the other hand, there are impediments to hiring older workers. Older workers are more expensive than younger workers and may need training to develop necessary skills, and employers might not want to or be able to offer

the flexible work schedules that many older workers desire. The key for employers is to understand how to best harness older workers' desire to continue working beyond traditional retirement ages in light of the benefits and impediments that are the reality behind hiring older workers (James, Swanberg, & McKechnie, 2007; Munnell et al., 2004; Pitt-Catsouphes & Matz-Costa, 2009).

From a national perspective, increased work late in life is also good news, as fewer individuals are dependent on public programs. While Social Security benefits are age-neutral on average—that is, expected lifetime benefits are independent of the timing of initial benefit receipt because of a now actuarially fair delayed retirement credit—individuals who work longer continue to contribute payroll taxes to the system. And most important, with additional productive work, the nation has more goods and services to distribute among the aged and non-aged populations. In the end, citizens consume goods and services, not Social Security or employer pension checks, and the more there is to distribute, the easier are the trade-offs faced by an aging society.

The end result is that continued work late in life, including bridge job employment, can be advantageous to many older Americans, to employers, and to the nation as a whole. In today's high-unemployment climate, however, many employers are reluctant to hire. In the future, this may be one of the biggest challenges to continued work later in life: even if older Americans prefer to remain in the labor force, will there be enough appropriate jobs to keep them employed?

The topic of labor demand has received relatively little attention in the academic literature on retirement (Hutchens & Grace-Martin, 2006). One reason is that aggregate unemployment has not been a primary issue in recent decades. The overall unemployment rate, which was near 10% in 1982 and 1983, declined to under 5.0% by 1997, and then to 4.0% in 2000—the lowest level since the late 1960s (U.S. Bureau of Labor Statistics, 2010). In fact, during the recession in 2001, when the aggregate rate jumped to 6.0% (in 2003), older Americans actually experienced an *increase* in labor force participation, unlike workers in all other age groups (Eschtruth & Gemus, 2002). Older Americans needed to keep working in order to supplement their resources in retirement, so they did. Labor demand was not a significant barrier.

But times have changed and, with high unemployment lingering, labor demand may be a barrier to work in the years ahead. In light of this possible scenario, researchers should focus more attention on the demand side of the labor market for older workers and on employer preferences in order to determine how older workers can best fit their needs. The research could be combined with outreach programs to educate employers about the benefits and costs of hiring older workers.

Another option for older Americans, especially in the face of weak labor demand, is to adjust their standards of living downward to match what is available from Social Security benefits, private pensions, and savings, or rely on their children to help support them in retirement. This view of retirement and old age would undo some of the gains of the past fifty years, returning to a world in which old age was more often associated with financial distress. Prior to 1974, for example, individuals age 65 and older had an official poverty rate that was higher than that of people 18 to 64 and children (under 18). In 1974 the elderly rate dipped below the children's rate, and in 1994 it fell below that of working-age individuals (18 to 64) (DeNavas-Walt, Proctor, & Smith, 2010). Since the early 1990s, official poverty among older Americans has continued to decline to the point where, in 2010, those age 65 and over had a much lower rate of poverty (9.0%) than either children (22.0%) or those age 18 to 64 (13.7%).[9] Barriers to work later in life and insufficient labor demand may reverse this trend. Therefore, a potentially fruitful avenue of research is the topic of consumption in retirement; e.g., to what extent would cutting back in the face of a shortfall of retirement income impact the living standards of older Americans?

Another topic that might resurface during recessionary times is age discrimination. With a high unemployment rate, there may be more room for discrimination against older workers, either through termination or failure to hire. Establishing that age discrimination is on the rise is difficult, but researchers could utilize large micro-level datasets that ask about older workers' labor market experiences to see if responses to age-discrimination questions correlate with the business cycle. Slack in the labor market may also make employers less willing to accommodate requests for flexible work schedules that older workers may prefer. Requests for reduced hours that might have been accommodated in the past might not be with many other workers willing to step in to fill a job. So far, early indications are that the recent increases in elderly labor force participation rates

have not turned around during the current recession and its wake, but we have only three full years (2009–2011) of relevant data. Continued analysis of labor force participation, phased retirements, and bridge jobs—when, how, and why older Americans retire—remains a fruitful avenue for research.

Conclusion

For most older Americans, retirement is a process, not a single event. The majority of career workers exit the workforce gradually, occasionally by reducing hours worked on a current job but much more often by switching to a new bridge job after career employment, often in a new line of work. This flexibility of the American workforce is one component of the shift toward a "do-it-yourself" approach to retirement that began more than thirty years ago. For many, income from earnings is an important fourth leg to the traditional three-legged retirement income stool, as many retirees are unable or unwilling to rely on only Social Security benefits, private pensions, and savings during a potentially lengthy retirement.

Continued work later in life, however, is not a panacea when it comes to shortfalls in retirement income. For many, such as those in poor health, with outdated skills, in physically demanding jobs, or in slack labor markets, continued work may not be a realistic option. For others, when faced with the choice between maintaining one's living standard by working longer or retiring as planned with a lower standard of living, the better (or only) option may be increased leisure and lower consumption over more work and more income. Also important is the role of labor demand. Even if older Americans would like to remain working, will there be appropriate and sufficient job opportunities for them to do so? Policymakers should keep these issues in mind when considering policies that encourage more work late in life.

While much is known about the retirement patterns of older Americans, many questions remain. As noted often in this chapter, a major concern is whether labor demand for older workers, with their skill sets, will provide opportunities for them to remain active members of the labor force. The topic of labor demand was less pressing when unemployment was low; it becomes a more serious concern with unemployment hovering near double digits.

Another key topic concerns workers' plans and preferences. From 1998 through 2010, 56% to 72% of workers in the annual Retirement Confidence Survey indicated that they plan to work after retirement or after age 65. During the same period, the percentage of retirees who actually reported working in retirement averaged only 27% (Helman et al., 2010). When faced with the choice of continued work or lower living standards, what will older Americans do in the future? A related topic is how younger cohorts will behave when they approach traditional retirement ages. An analysis of two cohorts of older workers suggests that younger retirees are following in the footsteps of (slightly) older ones, but the age difference in this study was only six years (Giandrea et al., 2009). It will be worthwhile to continue this research by examining the retirement expectations and eventual behavior of the younger cohorts in the Health and Retirement Study.

Retirement income security is another very important topic for further research. To what extent will the "do-it-yourself" approach to retirement leave older Americans vulnerable, especially given likely changes in Social Security benefits and/or eligibility ages, and responses to anticipated Medicare and Medicaid deficits? How might other public policy initiatives make retirement years more secure?

For many older Americans, continued work late in life will improve their standards of living in retirement and their financial stability. Employers will also benefit because they can draw from a larger pool of older workers with a lifetime of labor market experience. The country as a whole will benefit as well, as more individuals remain economically productive and more goods and services are produced, alleviating the economic challenges faced by an aging society. Bridge job employment has been and will continue to be an important component of labor market departure, allowing many older Americans to move gradually from full-time career employment to complete retirement, while improving their economic well-being along the way.

Author Note

All views expressed in this paper are those of the authors and do not necessarily reflect the views or policies of the U.S. Bureau of Labor Statistics.

Notes

1. The one exception is a one-year decline to age 62 in 1994. The early retirement trend dates back to the 1800s. According to Costa (1998), the labor force participation rate of American men 65 and older declined from 84% in 1870 (based on the gainful employment definition of the labor force) to 47% in 1948 and to 16% in 1985; for men aged 55 to 64, the labor force participation rate declined from 90% in 1948 to 68% in 1985 (Costa, 1998, 1999).

2. Kantarci and van Soest (2008) note that the literature is inconsistent with respect to the terminology of phased retirement versus partial retirement. In this chapter, we use the terminology identified by Kantarci and van Soest in which "phased retirement" refers to a reduction in hours with the same employer and "partial retirement" refers to a job change late in life, often to a position with fewer demands (see Johnson, Kawachi, & Lewis, 2009).

3. The definition of full-time (1,600 hours) has not been controversial, but some analysts consider ten years too long and would consider, for example, a nine-year full-time job late in life as another career job, not a bridge job. We have experimented with tenure definitions of eight and five years; . As discussed in the text, the quantitative results change, but not much; the qualitative conclusions remain the same.

4. The RHS was the predecessor of the HRS. The RHS started in 1969, with interviews every two years until 1979. The HRS began in 1992, also with interviews every two years, and is still underway today, having added additional cohorts over time, the "war babies" in 1998, the "early boomers" in 2004, and the "mid-boomers" in 2010. See Irelan (1988) for a description of the Retirement History Study and Karp (2007) for a description of the Health and Retirement Study.

5. Cahill et al. (2011) used a relatively restrictive definition of absence from the labor force. To classify as having re-entered the labor force, they required individuals to have left a job and then remain out of the labor force for at least two years before beginning the next job.

6. The Social Security earnings test exempt amount was $10,080 in 2000 and increased every year to $14,160 in 2009. The threshold remained at $14,160 through 2011, and increased to $14,640 in 2012. For the calendar year in which an individual attains his or her NRA, the exempt amount for earnings in the months prior to reaching the NRA is $37,680 (in 2010), and the amount that is withheld is one dollar in benefits for every three dollars of earnings above the threshold (U.S. Social Security Administration, 2010b).

7. The term "retiree" in the Retirement Confidence Survey is defined as an individual who is retired (self-defined) or an individual who is age 65 or older and not working full-time. The term "worker" is defined as anyone who is not a "retiree."

8. As noted above, the term "retiree" in the Retirement Confidence Survey is defined as an individual who is retired (self-defined) or an individual who is age 65 or older and not working full-time. The term "worker" is defined as anyone who is not a "retiree."

9. For official poverty rates by age over time, see U. S. Census Bureau, http://www.census.gov/hhes/www/poverty/data/historical/people.html, accessed May 16, 2012. These poverty rates are based on consumption patterns in the mid-1950s, and poverty thresholds are updated only because of changes in the cost of living. Analysts have calculated new experimental poverty rates based on more sophisticated measures of both the poverty thresholds and the definition of household income to be compared to the appropriate threshold. These new measures suggest that poverty among people aged 65 and older could actually be more than double the official rate (18.7% in 2008, compared to the official rate of 9.7%), slightly higher than the experimental rate for children (17.9%) and much higher than the rate for those 18 to 64 (14.3%). See Wu (2010), Table 2. The primary reason for the dramatic increase in elderly poverty in the new measure is the treatment of out-of-pocket medical costs for the elderly.

References

Aaronson, D., & French, E. (2004). The effect of part-time work on wages: Evidence from the social security rules. *Journal of Labor Economics, 22*, 329–352.

Anderson, P. M., Gustman, A. L., & Steinmeier, T. L. (1999). Trends in male labor force participation and retirement: Some evidence on the role of pensions and social security in the 1970s and 1980s. *Journal of Labor Economics, 17*, 757–783.

Blau, D. M. (1998). Labor force dynamics of older married couples. *Journal of Labor Economics, 16*, 595–629.

Blau, D. M., & Gilleskie, D. B. (2001). Retiree health insurance and the labor force behavior of older men in the 1990s. *Review of Economics and Statistics, 83*, 64–80.

Board of Trustees of OASDI. (2010). *The 2010 annual report of the board of trustees of the federal old-age and survivors insurance and federal disability insurance trust funds.* Washington, DC: U.S. Government Printing Office.

Brown, S. K. (2003). *Staying ahead of the curve 2003: The AARP working in retirement study.* Washington, DC: AARP.

Burtless, G., & Quinn, J. F. (2002). *Is working longer the answer for an aging workforce?* (Issue Brief No. 11). Chestnut Hill, MA: The Center for Retirement Research at Boston College.

Cahill, K. E., Giandrea, M. D., & Quinn, J. F. (2006). Retirement patterns from career employment. *The Gerontologist, 46*, 514–523.

Cahill, K. E., Giandrea, M. D., & Quinn, J. F. (2008). *A micro-level analysis of recent increases in labor force participation among older workers* (Working Paper No. 8). Chestnut Hill, MA: The Center for Retirement Research at Boston College.

Cahill, K. E., Giandrea, M. D., & Quinn, J. F. (2011). Reentering the labor force after retirement. *Monthly Labor Review, 134*(6), 34–42.

Cahill, K. E., Giandrea, M. D., & Quinn, J. F. (2012). Older workers and short-term jobs: patterns and determinants. *Monthly Labor Review, 135*(5), 19–32.

Cahill, K. E., & Soto, M. (2003). *How do cash balance plans affect the pension landscape?* (Issue Brief No. 14). Chestnut Hill, MA: The Center for Retirement Research at Boston College.

Charles, K. K., & Decicca, P. (2007). Hours flexibility and retirement. *Economic Inquiry, 45*, 251–267.

Chen, Y. P., & Scott, J. C. (2003). Gradual retirement: An additional option in work and retirement. *North American Actuarial Journal, 7*, 62–74.

Coile, C. (2004). Retirement incentives and couples' retirement decisions. *Topics in Economic Analysis and Policy, 4*, 1–28.

Coile, C., & Gruber, J. (2007). Future social security entitlements and the retirement decision. *The Review of Economics and Statistics, 89*, 234–246.

Coile, C., & Levine, P. B. (2006). Bulls, bears, and retirement behavior. *Industrial and Labor Relations Review, 59*, 408–429.

Committee for Economic Development. (1999). *New opportunities for older workers.* New York, NY: Research and Policy Committee of the Committee for Economic Development.

Congressional Budget Office. (2001). *Social security: A primer.* Washington, DC: U.S. Government Printing Office.

Congressional Budget Office. (2002). *The looming budgetary impact of society's aging.* Washington, DC: U.S. Government Printing Office.

Congressional Budget Office. (2004). *Retirement age and the need for saving.* Washington, DC: U.S. Government Printing Office.

Congressional Budget Office. (2009). *CBO's long-term projections for social security.* Washington, DC: U.S. Government Printing Office.

Copeland, C. (2009). Retirement plan participation and asset allocation, 2007. *Employee Benefit Research Institute Notes, 30*, 13–23.

Costa, D. (1998). *The evolution of retirement: An American economic history, 1880–1990.* Chicago, IL: University of Chicago Press.

Costa, D. (1999). *Has the trend toward early retirement reversed?* Paper presented at the First Annual Joint Conference for the Retirement Research Consortium, Washington, DC.

Dave, D., Rashad, I., & Spasojevic, J. (2008). The effects of retirement on physical and mental health outcomes. *Southern Economic Journal, 75*, 497–523.

DeNavas-Walt, C., Proctor, B. D., & Smith, J. C. (2010). *Income, poverty, and health insurance coverage in the United States: 2009.* Washington, DC: U.S. Census Bureau.

Dendinger, V. M., Adams, G. A., & Jacobson, J. D. (2005). Reasons for working and their relationship to retirement attitudes, job satisfaction and occupational self-efficacy of bridge employees. *International Journal of Aging and Human Development, 61*, 21–35.

Eschtruth, A., & Gemus, J. (2002). *Are older workers responding to the bear market?* (Just the Facts No. 5). Chestnut Hill, MA: The Center for Retirement Research at Boston College.

Friedberg, L., & Webb, A. (2005). Retirement and the evolution of pension structure. *Journal of Human Resources, 40*, 281–308.

Gale, W. G., Papke, L. E., & VanDerhei, J. (2005). The shifting structure of private pensions. In W. G. Gale, J. B. Shoven, & M. J. Warshawsky (Eds.), *The evolving pension system: Trends, effects and proposals for reform* (pp. 51–76). Washington, DC: Brookings Institute Press.

Giandrea, M. D., Cahill, K. E., & Quinn, J. F. (2009). Bridge jobs: A comparison across cohorts. *Research on Aging, 31*, 549–576.

Gielen, A. C. (2009). Working hours flexibility and older workers' labor supply. *Oxford Economic Papers, 61*, 240–274.

Griffin, B., & Hesketh, B. (2008). Post-retirement work: The individual determinants of paid and volunteer work. *Journal of Occupational and Organizational Psychology, 81*, 101–121.

Gruber, J., & Orszag, P. (2003). Does the social security earnings test affect labor supply and benefit receipt? *National Tax Journal, 56*, 755–773.

Gruber, J., & Wise, D. A. (2004). *Social security programs and retirement around the world.* Chicago, IL: University of Chicago Press.

Gustman, A. L., & Steinmeier, T. L. (1984). Partial retirement and the analysis of retirement behavior. *Industrial and Labor Relations Review, 37*, 403–415.

Gustman, A. L., & Steinmeier, T. L. (1994). Employer provided health insurance and retirement behavior. *Industrial and Labor Relations Review, 48*, 124–140.

Gustman, A. L., & Steinmeier, T. L. (2000). Retirement outcomes in the health and retirement study. *Social Security Bulletin, 63*, 57–71.

Han, S. K., & Moen, P. (1999). Clocking out: Temporal patterning of retirement. *The American Journal of Sociology, 105,* 191–236.

Helman, R., Copeland, C., & VanDerhei, J. (2010). *The 2010 retirement confidence survey: Confidence stabilizing, but preparations continue to erode* (Issue Brief No. 340). Washington, DC: Employee Benefit Research Institute.

Helman, R., Copeland, C., & VanDerhei, J. (2012). *The 2012 retirement confidence survey: Job insecurity, debt weigh on retirement confidence, savings* (Issue Brief No. 369). Washington, DC: Employee Benefit Research Institute.

Hutchens, R., & Grace-Martin, K. (2006). Employer willingness to permit phased retirement: Why are some more willing than others? *Industrial and Labor Relations Review, 59,* 525–546.

Hutchens, R. M., & Chen, J. (2007). The role of employers in phased retirement: Opportunities for phased retirement among white-collar workers. In T. Ghilarducci & J. Turner (Eds.), *Work options for older Americans* (pp. 95–118). Notre Dame, IN: University of Notre Dame Press.

Irelan, L. M. (1988). Retirement history study: Introduction. *Social Security Bulletin, 51,* 32–37.

James, J. B., Swanberg, J. E., & McKechnie, S. P. (2007). *Responsive workplaces for older workers: Job quality, flexibility and employee engagement* (Issue Brief No. 11). Chestnut Hill, MA: The Sloan Center on Aging and Work at Boston College.

Johnson, R. W., Davidoff, A. J., & Perese, K. (2003). Health insurance costs and early retirement decisions. *Industrial and Labor Relations Review, 56,* 716–729.

Johnson, R. W., Kawachi, J., & Lewis, E. K. (2009). *Older workers on the move: Recareering in later life* (Research Report No. 2009-08). Washington, DC: AARP Public Policy Institute.

Kantarci, T., & van Soest, A. (2008). Gradual retirement: Preferences and limitations. *De Economist, 156,* 113–144.

Karoly, L. A., & Rogowski, J. A. (1994). The effect of access to post-retirement health insurance on the decision to retire early. *Industrial and Labor Relations Review, 48,* 103–123.

Karp, F. (2007). *Growing older in America: The health and retirement study.* Washington, DC: U.S. Department of Health and Human Services.

Kim, H., & DeVaney, S. A. (2005). The selection of partial or full retirement by older workers. *Journal of Family and Economic Issues, 26,* 371–394.

Kim, S., & Feldman, D. C. (2000). Working in retirement: The antecedents of bridge employment and its consequences for quality of life in retirement. *The Academy of Management Journal, 43,* 1195–1210.

Lavery, J. (2009). *Social security finances: Findings of the 2009 Trustees Report* (Social Security Brief No. 30). Washington, DC: National Academy of Social Insurance.

Liebman, J. B., Luttmer, E. F., & Seif, D. G. (2009). Labor supply responses to marginal social security benefits: Evidence from discontinuities. *Journal of Public Economics, 93,* 11–12.

Lim, V. K., & Feldman, D. (2003). The impact of time structure and time usage on willingness to retire and accept bridge employment. *International Journal of Human Resources Management, 14,* 1178–1191.

Madrian, B. (1994). Employment-based health insurance and job mobility: Is there evidence of job-lock? *Quarterly Journal of Economics, 109,* 27–54.

Maestas, N. (2010). Back to work: Expectations and realizations of work after retirement. *Journal of Human Resources, 45,* 719–748.

McGarry, K. (2004). Do changes in health affect retirement expectations. *Journal of Human Resources, 39,* 624–648.

MetLife. (2010). *Study of employee benefits trends: Findings from the 8th annual national survey of employers and employees.* New York, NY: Metropolitan Life Insurance Company.

Munnell, A. H. (2006). Employer sponsored plans: The shift from defined benefit to defined contribution. In G. L. Clark, A. H. Munnell, & M. Orszag (Eds.), *The Oxford handbook of pensions and retirement income* (pp. 359–380). Oxford, England: Oxford University Press.

Munnell, A. H. (2007). Working longer: A potential win-win proposition. In T. Ghilarducci & J. Turner (Eds.), *Work options for older Americans* (pp. 11–43). Notre Dame, IN: University of Notre Dame Press.

Munnell, A. H., Cahill, K. E., Eschtruth, A., & Sass, S. A. (2004). *The graying of Massachusetts: Aging, the new rules of retirement, and the changing workforce.* Boston, MA: The Massachusetts Institute for a New Commonwealth.

Munnell, A. H., Cahill, K. E., & Jivan, N. A. (2003). *How has the shift to 401(k)s affected the retirement age?* (Issue Brief No. 13). Chestnut Hill, MA: The Center for Retirement Research at Boston College.

Munnell, A. H., & Perun, P. (2006). *An update on private pensions* (Issue Brief No. 50). Chestnut Hill, MA: The Center for Retirement Research at Boston College.

Munnell, A. H., & Sass, S. A. (2008). *Working longer: The solution to the retirement income challenge.* Washington, DC: Brookings Institution Press.

Munnell, A. H., & Sunden, A. (2004). *Coming up short: The challenge of 401(k) plans.* Washington, DC: Brookings Institution Press.

Mutchler, J. E., Burr, J. A., Pienta, A. M., & Massagli, M. P. (1997). Pathways to labor force exit: Work transitions and work instability. *Journal of Gerontology: Social Sciences, 52B,* S4–S12.

Neuman, K. (2008). Quit your job and get healthier? The effect of retirement on health. *Journal of Labor Research, 29,* 177–201.

Papke, L. E. (1999). Are 401(k) plans replacing other employer-provided pensions? Evidence from Panel Data. *Journal of Human Resources, 34,* 346–368.

Pitt-Catsouphes, M., & Matz-Costa, C. (2009). *Engaging the 21st century multi-generational workforce: Findings from the age & generations study* (Issue Brief No. 20). Chestnut Hill, MA: The Sloan Center on Aging and Work at Boston College.

Pitt-Catsouphes, M., & Smyer, M. A. (2005). *Older workers: What keeps them working?* (Issue Brief No. 1). Chestnut Hill, MA: The Sloan Center on Aging and Work at Boston College.

Purcell, P. (2009). *Older workers: Employment and retirement trends.* Washington, DC: Congressional Research Service.

Quinn, J. F. (1999). *Retirement patterns and bridge jobs in the 1990s* (Issue Brief No. 206). Washington, DC: Employee Benefit Research Institute, 1–23.

Quinn, J. F. (2010). Work, retirement, and the encore career: Elders and the future of the American workforce. *Generations, 34,* 45–55.

Quinn, J. F., Burkhauser, R. V., & Myers, D. A. (1990). *Passing the torch: The influence of economic incentives on work and retirement.* Kalamazoo, MI: W.E. Upjohn Institute for Employment Research.

Quinn, J. F., Cahill, K. E., & Giandrea, M. D. (2011). *Early Retirement: The Dawn of a New Era?* (Policy Brief). New York, NY: TIAA-CREF Institute.

Robinson, C., & Clark, R. (2010). Retiree health insurance and disengagement from a career job. *Journal of Labor Research, 31*, 247–262.

Rogowski, J., & Karoly, L. (2000). Health insurance and retirement behavior: Evidence from the Health and Retirement Survey. *Journal of Health Economics, 19*, 529–539.

Ruhm, C. J. (1990). Bridge jobs and partial retirement. *Journal of Labor Economics, 8*, 482–501.

Ruhm, C. J. (1991). Career employment. *Industrial Relations, 30*, 193–208.

Samwick, A. A. (1998). New evidence on pensions, social security, and the timing of retirement. *Journal of Public Economics, 70*, 207–236.

Shultz, K. S., & Wang, M. (2011). Psychological perspectives on the changing nature of retirement. *American Psychologist, 66*, 170–179.

Stock, J. H., & Wise, D. (1990). Pensions, the option value of work, and retirement. *Econometrica, 58*, 1151–1180.

U.S. Bureau of Labor Statistics. (2010). *Labor force statistics from the Current Population Survey*. Retrieved from U.S. Bureau of Labor Statistics: http://www.bls.gov/cps/prev_yrs.htm.

U.S. Census Bureau. (2010). *Historical poverty tables—People*. Retrieved from U.S. Census Bureau: http://www.census.gov/hhes/www/poverty/data/historical/people.html.

U.S. Department of Commerce, Bureau of Economic Analysis. (2010). *National income and product accounts, Table 5.1*. Retrieved from http://www.bea.gov/national/nipaweb/Index.asp.

U.S. Social Security Administration. (2010a). *Social Security Benefits*. Retrieved from Social Security Online: http://www.ssa.gov/OACT/ProgData/nra.html.

U.S. Social Security Administration. (2010b). *Exempt amounts under the earnings test*. Retrieved from Social Security Online: http://www.ssa.gov/oact/cola/rtea.html.

van Soest, A., Kapteyn, A., & Zissimopoulos, J. (2007). *Using stated preferences data to analyze preferences for full and partial retirement* (Discussion Paper No. 2785). Bonn, Germany: Institute for the Study of Labor.

von Wachter, T. (2002). The end of mandatory retirement in the US: Effects on retirement and implicit contracts (Working Paper No. 49). Berkeley, CA: Center for Labor Economics, University of California Berkeley.

Wang, M. (2007). Profiling retirees in the retirement transition and adjustment process: Examining the longitudinal change patterns of retirees' psychological well-being. *Journal of Applied Psychology, 92*, 455–474.

Wang, M., Adams, G. A., Beehr, T., & Shultz, K. S. (2009). Bridge employment and retirement: Issues and opportunities during the latter part of one's career. In S. Baugh & S. Sullivan (Eds.), *Maintaining focus, energy, and options over the career* (pp. 135–162). Charlotte, NC: Information Age.

Wu, K. B. (2010). *Impact of modernizing the American poverty measure on the poverty status of older persons* (Fact Sheet No. 205). Washington, DC: AARP Public Policy Institute.

Zhan, Y., Wang, M., Liu, S., & Shultz, K. S. (2009). Bridge employment and retirees' health: A longitudinal investigation. *Journal of Occupational Health Psychology, 14*, 374–389.

Adjustment to Retirement

Hanna van Solinge

Abstract

This chapter provides a summary of developments in retirement adjustment research. The chapter starts with a review of the major theoretical approaches to adjustment to life events in general, and retirement in particular. The second part provides a summary of empirical findings. To organize these findings, a distinction is made between research focusing on the descriptive question regarding the general impact of retirement on the individual, and research posing the explanatory question of why adjustment is more difficult in some cases than in others. The last part highlights future directions that may be fruitful for researchers in this area. Both methodological issues and empirical gaps in the literature are adressed. This chapter seeks to contribute to the understanding of how the loss of work affects successful aging and hopes to offer more insight into the circumstances under which retirement jeopardizes the well-being of older adults.

Key Words: adjustment to retirement, retirement satisfaction, determinants, adjustment process, well-being, empirical findings, life events, retirement transition

Introduction

Retirement is a major life transition in late adult life that may profoundly affect one's patterns of everyday activity, social networks, and economic resources, requiring adjustment for both the retiree and other members of the household. In this chapter, retirement is conceptualized as a process through which retirees get used to the changed aspects of life that result from the work-retirement transition and seek to achieve psychological comfort with their retirement life (Van Solinge & Henkens, 2008). This chapter seeks to contribute to our understanding of how work and the loss of work affects successful aging, and hopes to offer more insight into the circumstances under which retirement jeopardizes the well-being and psychological comfort of older workers.

How well individuals adjust to retirement, as well as the threats and challenges associated with this major life transition, have been the focus of interest to researchers and counselers, as well as the lay public. The latter is best reflected in the vast amount of self-help books dealing with the retirement transition that have been published in recent years. In the media and commercials, (early) retirement is depicted as an attractive and tempting option, which every worker will opt for if financially feasible (Ekerdt & Clark, 2001). This representation suggests that retirement is a transition that can be made smoothly and that the adjustment is quick and easy. Little is known, however, about the actual process of adjusting to retirement and the heterogeneity in this process.

The central purpose of this chapter is to provide a summary of developments in retirement adjustment research. The first part of this chapter includes a review of the major theoretical approaches to adjustment to life events in general, and retirement in particular. The second part provides a summary of empirical findings. To organize these findings, a distinction is made between (1) research focusing on the descriptive question regarding the general impact of retirement on the individual, and (2) posing the explanatory question of why adjustment is more difficult in some cases than in others. The last part highlights future directions that may be fruitful for researchers in this area. Both methodological issues and empirical gaps in the literature are adressed.

Theoretical Approaches of Adjustment to Life Events, Retirement in Particular

The transition from work to retirement is a major life event in late adult life. How well individuals adjust to retirement has been a focus of interest to researchers from various scientific disciplines, such as epidemiology, psychology, and sociology. Underlying these diverse approaches are distinct theoretical frameworks for the study of human adaptation to life events in general or retirement in particular.

The nature of retirement has changed tremendously over the past decades. Until the 1960s retirement was typically viewed as a "crisis" event, creating a challenge to personal well-being. Nowadays, retirement is commonly seen as a new life stage—between the years of career building and old age—that offers opportunities for the development of new identities, roles, and lifestyles (Blaikie, 1999; Moen, 2003). This frame switch is clearly reflected in the research focus, questions, and theoretical approaches that have been adopted in studies on retirement adjustment in the past fifty years.

The older studies, in particular those conducted before 1985, predominantly started from the assumption that retirement is an inherently stressful life-changing event that has similar effects on all who experience it. Much of the literature in this period was grounded in the stressful life event approach (e.g., Pearlin, Menaghan, Lieberman, & Mullan, 1981). Retirement research within the *stress tradition* concentrates on the outcomes of the transition process. The central question is whether or not retirement affects physical or mental health (e.g., Barron, Strein, & Suchman, 1952; Vallery-Masson, Poitrenaud, Burnat, & Lion, 1981). The influence of retirement on health or well-being is studied by comparing retirees with employees who remained in the labor force. Stress models are relatively simple and straightforward and usually concentrate on sociodemographic background variables and key resources (e.g., age, gender, marital status, income). This approach is still common in epidemiological studies into the impact of retirement on health or health behavior (e.g., Gallo, Bradley, Siegel, & Kasl, 2000, 2001; Mein, Martikainen, Hemingway, Stansfeld, & Marmot, 2003). The emphasis is on the prediction of illness or poor well-being, rather than on the explanation of the mechanism or conditions by which the transition affects physical or mental health. Further, stress models presuppose that live events entail readjustment, but this process of adjustment is considered as a black box. This is a limitation of this approach.

So-called *stage models* have long dominated the psychological literature on the responses to life changes or loss (Wortman, Cohen Silver, & Kessler, 1993) and are very popular among practitioners and the broader public. Adjustment is portrayed as a progression of orderly transformations or stages over time. For example, following a loss, individuals have to go through several stages, moving from distress to adaptation to recovery (e.g., Bowlby, 1980; Kübler-Ross, 1969; Williams, 1999). Stage models have also been applied to responses to the loss of employment. Atchley (1976) proposed a five-stage model for retirement adaptation: honeymoon, disenchantment, reorientation, stability, and termination. So far, stage theory has received little direct support from empirical studies. Stage models usually fail to define number, sequence, content, and length of phases or stages, so that no verifiable hypotheses can be derived (see Fryer, 1985, for an evaluation of this literature). The strength of this approach—its explicit consideration of the dynamic nature of retirement adjustment—is also its weakness due to the stringent pattern it predicts.

Although researchers still view retirement as a potentially challenging life-changing event, more recent studies have acknowledged that retirement may also have beneficial effects (e.g., Mein, Martikainen, Hemingway, Stansfeld, & Marmot, 2003; Wang, 2007). Moreover, there is a growing recognition of the fact that the impact of retirement may vary across individuals, and also within individuals over time (Wang, 2007). The major theoretical perspectives that have been applied as frameworks to study this heterogeneity in retirement adjustment include role theory, continuity theory, and the life course perspective. These approaches stem from various scientific traditions, and some of them are typically rather robust, others more complex. The *role theoretical approach* emphasizes the importance of roles that individuals perform or enact. Throughout the life course, people enter and exit social roles; that is, they become parents, widowers, retirees, etc. Role entries and exits are by definition transitions (Ebaugh, 1988). Role theory assumes that individuals vary in the extent to which they are committed to or identify with their different roles, and this has consequences in terms of adjustment to life transitions. Leaving a role that is vital to an individual's self-identity puts risk on one's well-being. Much of the retirement adjustment literature from the 1950s onward is based on the role theoretical approach, or at least includes references to this theoretical framework (for an overview see Ferraro, 2001). Early studies, in particular, focused on the loss of the work role occasioned by retirement and suggested that this loss would cause people to feel anxious or depressed, leading to difficult adjustment and low levels of well-being in retirement. Others suggested that retirement may not have such negative consequences provided that the retiree could replace his or her former work role with other meaningful activities. Role theory is very popular in retirement research, maybe partially because of its initial self-evident nature. A clear revenue of the role-based theoretical approach is its emphasis on the heterogeneity in the retirement experience and the recognition of the importance of the work context. A closer look at the theory and its empirical applications, however, reveals that the operationalization of the key theoretical notion—centrality of a role to one's self identity—is not straightforward. Often this notion is conceptualized as simply role occupancy, and operationalized through asking respondents to indicate whether or not they occupy specific roles (e.g., involvement in leisure activities or volunteer work). Role involvement has also been conceptualized as an individual's behavioral commitment to a role in terms of the number of hours spent in role participation. Psychological commitment has been operationalized as work attachment (Drentea, 2002) or the salience of the role in relation to other activities (Coursolle, Sweeney, Raymo, & Ho, 2010). Although empirical studies may disclose associations between work role attachment and succeeding adjustment or well-being in retirement, they usually do not succeed to unravel the underlying mechanism. For example, it remains unclear which aspects of the role loss (e.g., loss of status, social contacts, or income) particularly challenge retirees' well-being.

The role loss argument has been frequently countered with a reference to *continuity theory*. This theory originates in the observation that a large proportion of older adults show consistency in their activities and relationships despite their changing physical, mental, and social statuses. Unlike the stress approach and role theory, continuity theory presupposes that life events are not stressful by definition and that individuals try to maintain a continuity of lifestyle by adapting strategies that are connected to their past experiences (Maddox, 1968). Atchley (1971) has expanded continuity theory to explain older adults' response to retirement. Atchley stated that satisfactory adjustment is associated with integration between stages of the life cycle. He stressed the value of continuing activities in old age (or in retirement) that were of value in middle age (or before retirement). Many retirement studies refer to continuity theory as a general framework for analyzing retirement adjustment (e.g., Nuttman-Shwartz, 2008; Richardson & Kilty, 1991; Robbins, Lee, & Wan, 1994; Von Bonsdorff, Shultz, Leskinen, & Tansky, 2009). Continuity theory predicts that there should not be a significant drop in well-being when people transition from work into retirement life, unless severe difficulty in maintaining social relationship and lifestyle patterns is experienced. The theory, however, offers few concrete definitions of continuity and how this variable impacts retirement adjustment. For example, it is not clear which type, quality, or quantity of activities is most important. Nonetheless, continuity theory may provide some relevant guidance for practice, as it may offer individuals as well as retirement counselors useful directions for strategies to ease adjustment to retirement. Continuity theory has some correspondence with *psychological adjustment research*, which also concentrates on adaptive reactions to life changes (i.e., coping). Coping refers to the cognitive and behavioral efforts people make to reduce, master, or tolerate stressful life events. The central question guiding this type of research is whether certain ways of coping are more effective in promoting well-being than others (Schroevers, Kraaij, & Garnefski, 2007).

A more complex view of retirement adjustment derives from the *life course perspective*. The central premise of the life course perspective is that individuals construct their own life course through the choices and actions they take within the opportunities and constraints of history and social circumstances. The life course perspective draws attention to five concepts that seem crucial for understanding adjustment to retirement and postretirement well-being: (a) contextual embeddedness of life transitions, (b) interdependence of life spheres, (c) timing of life transitions, (d) trajectories and pathways, and (e) agency (Elder & Johnson, 2003; Hagestad, 1990). Contextual embeddedness implies that the experience of life transitions will be contingent on the specific circumstances under which the transition occurs, including past statuses and roles, and societal context. It is further assumed that life spheres are interdependent, so that experiences in one sphere (e.g., work life) are influenced by experiences in other spheres (e.g., marital life). Further, the experience of life transitions is contingent on their timing in terms of personal expectations and cultural age norms. The notion of trajectories and pathways points to the historical context of life experiences and their development over time. The life course principle of "human agency within structure" implies that individuals have plans, make choices, and undertake actions within the opportunities and constraints of their social worlds, which are shaped by history and social circumstances (Elder and Johnson, 2003; Settersten, 2003). Much of the more recent research on the impact of retirement is grounded in the life course perspective. In retirement research, contextual embeddedness is generally interpreted in terms of the characteristics of the retirement transition, such as involuntary retirement (e.g., Van Solinge & Henkens, 2008), gradual retirement (Calvo, Haverstick, & Sass, 2009; De Vaus, Wells, Kendig, & Quine, 2007), or bridge employment (Von Bonsdorff et al., 2009). Studies that investigated the interdependency of lives and life spheres in the retirement process have, for example, examined the effect of spouses' employment status (Kim & Moen, 2002), spousal adjustment (Van Solinge & Henkens, 2005), or synchronization of work and retirement within couples (Ekerdt & Vinick, 1991; Henretta, O'Rand, & Chan, 1993b) on post-retirement well-being or adjustment. In retirement research, the recognition of the importance of human agency in how the transition is experienced is relatively new (e.g., Taylor & Cook, 1995; Van Solinge & Henkens, 2005). This in contrast to, for example, the self-help literature that underscores that the experience of surviving previous transitions is a resource in retirement adjustment (e.g., Hinden, 2010; Schlossberg, 2004).

The life course perspective explicitly locates life transitions in the social contexts of other roles, relations, developmental processes, and history. As such, it provides a promising general framework for the study of the heterogeneity in the retirement experience. It offers, however, few concrete hypotheses as to how the various contexts affect adjustment to retirement. An example with regard to timing may

illustrate this. Individuals tend to have an awareness of their own position in the social timetable and describe themselves as "off time" or "on time" (Hagestad & Neugarten, 1985). When the retirement transition occurs off time, individuals may not have had the chance to go through anticipatory socialization or may be financially unprepared, or the individual may lack peers with whom he or she shares transition experiences and who can provide social support. Off-time retirement may thus induce difficult adjustment and reduced well-being as a result of changes in resource levels (e.g., support and income).

Wang, Henkens, and Van Solinge (2011) have argued that retirement adjustment research needs an integrated theoretical framework that, on the one hand, accounts for the complex nature of retirement adjustment, and on the other hand allows the formulation of concrete and testable hypotheses. They proposed to apply a resource-based dynamic perspective to further the theoretical development of retirement adjustment. They argue that retirement adjustment is a longitudinal process. How this process is experienced is contingent on the individual's access to economic, social, and psychological resources and changes in these resources during the retirement transition.

Empirical Findings

Key questions addressed in the empirical literature on retirement adjustment can be summarized as follows: (1) What is the general impact of retirement on the individual (i.e., how well people may get used to the retirement life)? (2) What are the factors that account for interindividual differences in adjustment to retirement? These questions are used to structure the evaluation of the literature. In interpreting the results, however, the reader should be aware that studies differ considerably in their conceptualization of adjustment, as well as in their methodology. Since these differences may impede the comparability of results across studies, this section elaborates on these two issues before reviewing the literature.

The conceptualization of retirement adjustment varies greatly. The majority of studies evaluate adjustment of retirees by their post-retirement well-being or some other measure of psychological comfort. These studies have in common that they infer adjustment indirectly via outcome measures. The underlying assumption is that these outcome measures are valid indicators of the difficulties retirees experience in making the transition to retirement. Low levels of well-being, in particular, are assumed to indicate poor adjustment (Braithwaite & Gibson, 1987). The number of studies that focus on adjustment as the process of getting used to the changed circumstances of life, and how this process develops over time, is much more limited. Among the examples are a few qualitative studies, such as Savishinsky (2000), Nuttman-Shwartz (2004), and Weiss (2005). These studies provide phenomenological descriptions of the retirement experience based on interviews with a restricted number of older adults who undergo the transition from work to retirement. An example of a quantitative study that examined adjustment to retirement in a more direct way is Van Solinge and Henkens (2005). They investigated adjustment on the basis of the older worker's and partner's own evaluation of the difficulties they had in adjusting to retirement.

Studies differ also with regard to their research methodology. Two issues are particularly relevant. The first issue concerns the study design. Retirement research increasingly benefits from the availability of longitudinal studies that start before the event of retirement and follow retirees over a longer time period. Still, many studies on retirement adjustment rely on cross-sectional designs and examine adjustment on the basis of retrospective evidence (e.g., Guerriero Austrom, Perkins, Damush, & Hendry, 2003; Isaksson & Johansson, 2000; Martin Matthews & Brown, 1987; Wong & Earl, 2009) or by comparing differences in psychological comfort between workers and retirees (e.g., Bossé, Aldwin, Levenson, & Ekerdt, 1987; Drentea, 2002; Herzog, House, & Morgan, 1991; Midanik, Soghikian, Ransom, & Tekawa, 1995). Cross-sectional designs, however, seriously limit the possibilities for studying causal relationships, since they do not allow controlling for selection into retirement or for pre-retirement levels of the explanatory variable at hand. A second issue concerns the data collection strategy. Sample strategies vary considerably across studies. Three types prevail: convenience samples, national representative samples, and cluster samples. Despite the clear disadvantages, many retirement studies rely on non-probability or convenience samples (Fouquereau, Fernandez, & Mullet, 2001; Potocnik, Tordera, & Peiró, 2009). The problem with convenience samples is that they are subject to unknown selectivity. In other words, it is not known how the sample differs from a sample that was randomly selected, and whether people who were left out might behave differently than the people in the convenience sample. A growing number of retirement studies make use of national representative samples of older adults. Examples are the English Longitudinal Study on Ageing (ELSA); the Health and Retirement Survey (HRS) in the United States; and the Survey of Health, Ageing and Retirement in Europe (SHARE). These studies have the clear advantage that they cover a broad array of old-age related issues and that the results can be generalized to the total population of older adults in the age range at hand. A disadvantage, however, is that the actual number of retirement transitions that can be observed is often relatively limited (e.g., Cozijnsen, Stevens, & Van Tilburg, 2010; Pinquart & Schindler, 2007). To address this drawback, retirement studies may instead opt for cluster or "two-stage sampling": in the first stage a specific firm or organization is chosen; in the second stage a sample *within* that organization is selected. Examples of studies that recruited participants from the near-retirement workforce in specific companies, work settings, or occupational groups are Hardy and Hazelrigg (1999); Dorfman (2002); Taylor, Shultz, Morrison, Spiegel, and Greene (2007); and Van Solinge and Henkens (2005). Given their main focus on the retirement transition, these studies generally include rich information on a variety of retirement-related issues. This benefit greatly compensates for the potential limitations with regard to the generalizability of the results.

The Impact of Retirement on the Individual

Studies that concentrate on the impact of retirement on individuals generally have a descriptive nature. The central research question is whether or not retirement has implications for psychological comfort. An evaluation of the literature reveals that many studies lack an explicit theoretical foundation but *do* include general references to theoretical frameworks for the study of human adaptation to life events, such as the stress approach, role theory, or continuity theory. The general underlying assumption in this type of work is that the loss of the work role will cause reduced well-being. Researchers typically characterize retirees relative to workers or to themselves while still working along many dimensions of psychological comfort. Indicators of this psychological comfort include happiness (Beck, 1982), emotional well-being (Herzog et al., 1991; Richardson & Kilty, 1991), retirement satisfaction (Gall, Evans, & Howard, 1997; Quick & Moen, 1998), life satisfaction (Calasanti, 1996), and mental health and depression (Midanik et al., 1995; Tuomi, Järvinen, Eskelinen, Ilmarinen, & Klockars,

1991). The literature has demonstrated a noticeable heterogeneity of findings. Cross-sectional research has found that retirees in comparison with workers tend to report higher life satisfaction (Isaksson & Johansson, 2000), whereas other studies did not find differences (Herzog et al., 1991; Warr, Butcher, Robertson, & Callinan, 2004) or found slightly lower levels of well-being among retired persons (Alpass et al., 2007). Longitudinal studies yield heterogeneous findings as well. For example, in a study by Gall, Evans, and Howard (1997) among 224 Canadian males, several aspects of the retirees' well-being were found to change from pre- to one year post-retirement. The data reveal an average increase in psychological health (less distress), energy level, and financial and interpersonal satisfaction, but no change could be observed in general life satisfaction. Richardson and Kilty (1991) found significant declines in well-being and satisfaction with relationships from pre- to six months post-retirement in a study of 250 American men and women, but an increase from six to twelve months. Another indicator of well-being, namely morale, however, continuously decreased over time. Kim and Moen (2002) found increases in morale among newly retired men, but not women. Mayring (2000), in a study of 329 German older adults, observed no significant changes in global life satisfaction between six months before and eighteen months after retirement. To reconcile these inconsistent findings, Wang (2007) and Pinquart and Schindler (2007) have argued that multiple forms of retirement adjustment coexist in the retiree population. Using longitudinal data from two nationally representative samples, these researchers found empirically different adjustment profiles in terms of life satisfaction change. In both studies the majority of older adults experienced minimum psychological well-being changes during the retirement transition. Smaller proportions (9% in the German data vs. 25% in the U.S. data) experienced negative changes in psychological well-being during the initial transition stage, but then showed improvements afterward. About 15% of German retirees (5% in the United States) experienced positive changes in psychological well-being. This diversity in the retirement experience has been corroborated in quantitative studies that used more direct measures of adjustment. A longitudinal study on retirement in the Netherlands (Van Solinge & Henkens, 2008) revealed that for almost half of the workers adjustment was fairly rapid: they became accustomed to a non-working life within a month; over

three-quarters within a year. One in every five older workers stated that retirement took quite some getting used to, whereas two-thirds disagreed with this statement. The vast majority of respondents (86%) said that they were satisfied with retirement. More than 40% of older workers stated that the years since retirement had been better than the two years preceding retirement.

Determinants of Retirement Adjustment

A large number of studies, from various scientific traditions, have investigated the hetereogeneity in the retirement experience, posing the explanatory questions of why adjustment to retirement is more difficult in some cases and has more negative consequences in terms of psychological comfort than in others, and which factors account for these differences. An evaluation of this literature reveals four major issues. First, almost all studies evaluate adjustment of retirees by their post-retirement well-being or some other measure of psychological comfort. Few studies examine the process of adjustment in a more direct way, e.g., on the basis of the individual's own evaluation of the retirement experience. Second, the theoretical foundation of many studies is rather implicit. Although the majortity of studies include references to general theoretical frameworks, such as role theory, continuity theory, or the life course perspective, or to all of them, most lack elaborated theoretical models as well as concrete hypotheses. Third, adjustment studies have largely adopted an individualistic approach. Few studies model the impact of other actors on the older worker's retirement adjustment. Fourth, across studies there is an enormous variety in the predictors of retirement adjustment that are considered. These predictors can be summarized in four broader categories and are used to structure the current evaluation of the literature: (1) individual attributes; (2) access to resources, and changes in these resources upon retirement; (3) situational characteristics; and (4) psychological attributes.

Individual attributes (e.g., age and gender) are usually considered as control variables in studying retirement adjustment. Several authors (Calasanti, 1996; Moen, 1996; Price, 2003), however, have stressed that this does not do justice to the large and structural gender differences in the labor market, which may translate to differences in the retirement experience. Women are overrepresented in secondary labor market positions and work arrangements that allow them to combine work and care obligations. They are more likely to work in part-time jobs or to work fewer years in pension-covered employment because of interruptions in their careers (Laczko & Phillipson, 1991). On the one hand, many retirement studies are guided by the assumption that women, given their greater experience with role transitions and interrupted careers, as well as their inclination to see the family role as their primary identity, are psychologically better prepared for adjusting to retirement (e.g., Gratton & Haug, 1983; Price, 2003; Talaga & Beehr, 1995). On the other hand, it has been argued that women, given their understandably more discontinuous work trajectories and their clustering in industries and occupations that are more prone to cutbacks, have greater risk to experience financial vulnerability, resulting in lower retirement satisfaction (for an overview see Slevin & Wingrove, 1995). There is, however, little empirical evidence for the assumption that adjustment to retirement is easier for women than for men, and the evidence with regard to retirement satisfaction is mixed (Szinovacz, 2003).

Resources are means or assets (material, social, or psychological) that can be used to cope with a difficult situation or to accomplish a goal. The individual's access to resources greatly "defines" the conditions of retirement and influences the opportunities and quality of the retirement experience (Kim & Moen, 2002; Reitzes & Mutran, 2004). Resources shape what people can do (physically) and what they can afford (financially) in retirement. The assumption is thus that retirees who have more access to resources (e.g., higher incomes, better health) have fewer adjustment problems and are more satisfied in retirement. It has been argued that it is not only the availability of or access to resources that produces distress, but rather the change (e.g., a loss) in the level of resources one possesses that influence the adjustment outcomes (cf. Hobfoll, 1989). This may particularly be the case where the loss cannot otherwise be compensated for (Steverink, Lindenberg, & Ormel, 1998).

Financial resources may constrain the maintenance of the pre-retirement lifestyle. Health problems restrict the possibilities of taking up new activities and may thus disrupt the individual's leisure plans after retirement. There is indeed evidence that limited financial resources and poor health hamper adjustment and result in lower levels of satisfaction with retirement (e.g., Calasanti, 1996; Fouquereau, Fernandez, Paul, Fonseca, & Uotinen, 2005; Hardy & Quadagno, 1995; Seccombe & Lee, 1986).

Retirement also requires a reorganization of activities and leisure time. According to continuity theory, post-retirement participation in activities can be considered as a type of resource (Atchley, 1989). It helps to provide time structure and continuity in the daily context and may as such contribute to retirement adjustment and retirement satisfaction (Butrica & Schaner, 2005). Involvement in volunteer work is distinct from other leisure activities, such as sports, traveling, or family visits, in the sense that it may provide more opportunities for the maintenance of self-esteem and social status (Van Willigen, 2000). Further, social participation through membership in and attendance of voluntary associations creates social capital. Through these networks and links, individuals have access to support systems, which can be utilized to contribute to positive outcomes for the individual (Granovetter, 1973; Lin, 1999). Bridge employment is a special form of productive activity that may help retirees to maintain continuity during the retirement process, thus enhancing well-being (Shultz, 2003). Empirical studies support the hypothesis that participation in post-retirement activities such as volunteer work (Dorfman & Douglas, 2005; Kim & Feldman, 2000; Smith & Moen, 2004; Van Solinge & Henkens, 2008), leisure activities (Dorfman & Douglas, 2005; Kim & Feldman, 2000; Nimrod, 2008; Pushkar et al., 2009; Reeves & Darville, 1994), and bridge employment (Kim & Feldman, 2000; Von Bonsdorff et al., 2009; Wang, 2007; Zhan, Wang, Liu, & Shultz, 2009) are associated with higher life satisfaction.

Partners are considered important resources in the process of adjustment to stressful life events, such as illness or disability (Northouse, Dorris, & Charron-Moore, 1995; Ross, Mirowsky, & Goldsteen, 1990), international relocation (Harvey & Miller, 1998), and retirement (Van Solinge & Henkens, 2005). Partners can provide resources, such as companionship and social support, which make adjustment easier. Marital status as well as marital quality have been shown to relate to retirement adjustment. Specifically, married retirees tend to adjust more easily than single or widowed retirees (Pinquart & Schindler, 2007). Retirees with happier marriages are more likely to be satisfied with retirement (Calasanti, 1996; Szinovacz & Davey, 2004; Wang, 2007).

There is evidence that change in the level of resources (especially loss) challenges adjustment to and well-being in retirement. Health decline during the retirement transition has a negative impact on retirement satisfaction (Van Solinge & Henkens, 2008), or well-being in retirement (Kim & Moen, 2002; Wang, 2007). The findings regarding retirees' financial decline have been mixed. The negative impact of financial decline on retirement satisfaction was found for a recent Dutch sample (Van Solinge & Henkens, 2008), but not in American samples of persons who retired in the 1990s (Kim & Moen, 2002; Wang, 2007). Finally, van Solinge and Henkens (2008) showed that losing a partner during the retirement transition had a negative impact on retirement satisfaction.

Situational characteristics are deemed important in adjusting to the retirement transition as well. In retirement research, three types of situational characteristics can be distinghuised: pre-retirement job characteristics, social and psychological job commitment, and circumstances under which individuals leave their job.

Retirement may bring both loss and gain. Effects likely depend on the particular job and its characteristics, such as physical demands, workload, and intrinsic value carried. There is evidence for the assumption that stopping work may have positive effects on well-being to the extent that it allows older workers to disassociate themselves from demanding and stressful work, and negative effects to the extent that it implies the cessation of stimulating and challenging work. Work stress (e.g., Wang, 2007), psychological and physical job demands (e.g., Quick & Moen, 1998), job dissatisfaction (e.g., Wang, 2007), and unemployment before retirement (e.g., Marshall, Clarke, & Ballantyne, 2001; Pinquart & Schindler, 2007) are positively related to various adjustment outcomes, whereas job challenge (Van Solinge & Henkens, 2008) is negatively associated with retirement adjustment and retirement satisfaction.

In addition to objective characteristics of the older worker's job, their social and psychological job commitment may also account for significant variation in retirement outcomes. Studies applying the role theory argue that the impact of retirement likely depends on the worker's work role identity (Shultz, Morton, & Weckerle, 1998; Wheaton, 1990). Supporting role theory, individuals who have a strong attachment to their work feel less positive about leaving their jobs (Taylor & Shore, 1995). Other studies suggest that work role identity is negatively related to a variety of adjustment outcomes, such as morale (Martin Matthews & Brown, 1987), retirement satisfaction (Quick & Moen, 1998), and self-esteem (Reitzes & Mutran, 2006).

The particular circumstances in which retirement takes place are considered important as well. The general idea is that expected and/or gradual changes are more easily adapted than are unanticipated and abrupt events (Moen, 1996; Thoits, 1983). This may be attributed to the fact that individuals may not have had the chance to go through anticipatory socialization. Unexpected transitions may also give rise to unfavorable social comparisons with one's peers who are not experiencing the event (Hagestad & Neugarten, 1985). Moreover, the lack of personal control impedes adjustment (Wrosch & Freund, 2001). Many workers are "forced" to leave the labor force long before the usual retirement age (Van Solinge & Henkens, 2007). Empirical studies reveal that involuntary retirement has negative effects on health (Gallo et al., 2000; He & Marshall, 2003; Herzog et al., 1991; Van Solinge & Henkens, 2005) and well-being (Gall et al., 1997; Isaksson & Johansson, 2000). Older workers who perceive retirement as forced tend to have more adjustment problems (Van Solinge & Henkens, 2005) and are at risk of experiencing long-lasting negative effects on post-retirement well-being (Calvo et al., 2009; Hardy & Quadagno, 1995; Quick & Moen, 1998) and health (Gallo et al., 2006; Hyde, Ferrie, Higgs, Mein, & Nazroo, 2004; Van Solinge & Henkens, 2008). Workers who feel they had to retire "too early" are less satisfied (Floyd, Haynes, & Rogers Doll, 1992; Hardy & Hazelrigg, 1999).

Although it is widely recognized that the life course and life transitions are products of social structure and human agency (e.g., Settersten, 2003), *psychological correlates* of retirement are not often taken into account in retirement research (e.g., Barnes-Farrell, 2003). Personality or psychological dispositions are thought to influence life events, such as retirement, via their association with emotional appraisals, motivational priorities, and coping strategies (Löckenhoff, Terracciano, & Costa, 2009). Indeed, studies that examined psychological predispositions in the retirement adjustment process suggest that psychological factors have an impact on adjustment. Bye and Pushkar (2009), in a study of 351 adults who were experiencing the transition to retirement, found that two dispositional traits—motivation for effortful cognitive activity and perceived control—led to greater psychological well-being through problem-focused coping and greater engagement with voluntary activities. Other psychological resources that have been studied in relation to retirement adjustment are personality traits (Löckenhoff et al., 2009), goal directedness

(Robbins et al., 1994), retirement expectations (Taylor, Goldberg, Shore, & Lipka, 2008), and self-efficacy (Van Solinge & Henkens, 2005). Results suggest that psychological resources influence the individual's responses to the change accompanied with retirement, stressing the importance of agency in the retirement process.

Conclusion

In the past decades, retirement has evolved from an abrupt transition from a working to a non-working life into a process that spans a much longer period. Retirement increasingly constitutes a series of decisions regarding the structure of the late career that can span a period of twenty years and can include multiple transitions into and out of the labor force. Retirement is thus a multistage process, involving the preparation (planning), the actual process of labor force exit (retirement transition), the post-retirement adjustment to the loss of the work role and the social ties associated with work, and the development of a satisfactory post-retirement lifestyle. This chapter concentrated on post-retirement adjustment.

The central purpose of this chapter was to provide a summary of developments in retirement adjustment research. The review of the literature on retirement adjustment has shown a huge variety in conceptualizations, conceptual frameworks, and methodologies. Although this diversity complicates a comparison of results across studies, some general conclusions can be drawn. With respect to the first key question—How well do individuals adjust to retirement?—taken as a whole, survey data suggest that retirement is typically a satisfactory experience. A significant proportion (10%–25%) of older workers, however, experience difficulties in adjusting to retirement. With regard to the second key question—Why is adjustment much more difficult and why does it have more negative implications in some cases than in others?—empirical findings suggest that resources, situational characteristics, and psychological factors contribute to the understanding of the heterogeneity in retirement adjustment, and that a lack of control over the retirement transition is among the most powerful predictors of the development of adjustment problems.

Future Directions

Retirement adjustment is increasingly viewed as a multidimensional and dynamic process that is actively shaped by the individual within the opportunities and constraints of history and social circumstances and influenced by social relationships within the household and the workplace. This has consequences for research in terms of study design and conceptual framework.

First, the increasingly dynamic character of the retirement transition (people may retire gradually, or utilize bridge jobs before complete withdrawal from the labor force), and adjustment to retirement in particular, requires a longitudinal design that follows a group of older workers over a longer period of time. Although longitudinal surveys on retirement are gradually more available, much research on adjustment is still founded on cross-sectional data. Cross-sectional designs, however, cannot disentangle causation vs. selection interpretations (Kasl & Jones, 2000) of low levels of well-being in retirement. Moreover, cross-sectional designs do not account for the dynamic nature of retirement adjustment. Conceptualizing retirement and retirement adjustment as a dynamic process not only provides opportunities for studying temporal fluctuations in well-being during the retirement process (e.g., Pinquart & Schindler, 2007; Wang, 2007; Wang et al., in press) but also allows for the investigation of the interrelatedness of post-retirement employment choices (e.g., second careers, bridge employment) in relation to retirement adjustment, as is suggested in research by Wang, Zhan, Liu, and Shultz (2008). Further, Von Bonsdorff, Shultz, Leskinen, and Tansky (2009) indicate that bridge employment may help retirees to maintain their psychological well-being during the retirement transition process. As such, studying the dynamic patterns of older adults' employment choices provides another way for us to understand the retirement transition and adjustment process.

Second, social embeddedness of the retirement transition implies that the retirement process is shaped by social relationships within the family and with colleagues and supervisors. In studies on decision making on retirement, this social embeddedness has been variously acknowledged, e.g., by including spousal or marital relationship (Haug, Belgrave, & Jones, 1992; Henretta, O'Rand, & Chan, 1993a; Smith & Moen, 1998; Szinovacz & DeViney, 2000) or supervisor characteristics (Vecchio, 1993), or by incorporating (perceived) spousal attitudes or behavior (e.g., Davey & Szinovacz, 2004; Henkens & Van Solinge, 2002; Pienta & Hayward, 2002) into the models. Studies that examine the influences of the spouse or other actors in the retirement adjustment process are much rarer. Among the few examples are studies by Smith and Moen (2004) and Van Solinge and Henkens (2005), which used multi-actor data from both retirees and their spouses. This research suggests the importance of examining adjustment to and satisfaction with retirement for retirees and their spouses individually as well as jointly. Social interdependency in the retirement process may become even more relevant in the future as a growing proportion of older adults approaches retirement as part of a dual-earner couple, requiring tuning of and adjustment to two retirements. In order to further the investigation of social interdependency of the retirement adjustment process, researchers may consider adopting a multi-actor design, which allows the direct assessment of attitudes and behavior of relevant actors in the retirement adjustment process.

Third, retirement is a multidimensional transition that affects several life domains. The multidimensional nature of this transition is clearly reflected in the research literature, where the consequences of retirement for finances (Whiting, 1998), health (e.g., Mein et al., 2003), social networks (e.g., Van Tilburg, 2003), leisure (e.g., Huovinen & Piekkola, 2002), and marriage (e.g., Davey & Szinovacz, 2004) have received considerable attention. The review of the empirical literature in this chapter has shown that the retirement process is multidimensional as well, requiring older adults to make efforts along various tracks, such as adjustment to the loss of the work role, the social ties associated with work, changes in material resources, and the development of a satisfactory post-retirement lifestyle. This multidimensional character of retirement has consequences for the conceptualization of retirement adjustment. In most studies, adjustment is studied via general measures of psychological comfort or well-being. The underlying assumption that these measures are valid indicators of the difficulties retirees experience in making the transition to retirement is, however, debatable. Although measures for psychological comfort may be empirically correlated with adjustment, their relationship may be more complex. For example, it is possible to adjust to a new situation (e.g., a chronic illness) without enjoying it, and the fact that an outcome is positive does not necessarily imply that adjustment was easy. As such, outcomes cannot be considered simply as a function of the ease of adjustment. Moreover, the pace and ease of adjustment may vary across these various dimensions. Financial adjustment may, for example, be much easier than the adjustment to new roles within the household or to the lack of time

structure. This may be difficult to trace with general measures of well-being. Key to advancing research in this area is the development of a comprehensive model of retirement adjustment that explicitly recognizes the multidimensional character of the transition. In this respect, additional measures could be developed, such as more direct evaluations of the difficulties retirees (and their spouses) experience in adjusting to the various aspects of retirement, as well as the individual's assessment regarding whether or not retirement has been integrated into his or her life, and how long this process has taken (see Van Solinge & Henkens, 2008).

Fourth, the conceptualization of retirement adjustment as a process that is shaped by the choices and actions that individuals take within the opportunities and constraints of history and social circumstances, and that is embedded in social relationships, has consequences in terms of the conceptual framework. Taking an interdisciplinary approach will enhance our understanding of how retirement adjustment is influenced by these various forces. Empirical findings indeed suggest that not only the availability of financial and other resources and health but also the situational characteristics and psychological factors account for heterogeneity in the retirement adjustment process. Typically, however, most studies concentrate in their models on one group of factors. Research on the impact of retirement could benefit from an integration of these factors into one single model.

Fifth, research should pay more attention to two important determinants of heterogeneity that have been relatively neglected in retirement adjustment research: psychological attributes and personality variables, and the wider societal context. Despite the fact that psychological variables have proved to be good predictors of adjustment in other types of life transitions, such as relocation transition (Kling, Ryff, Love, & Essex, 2003), cross-cultural adjustment (Wang & Takeuchi, 2007), and transition to parenthood (Levy-Shiff, 1994), very few empirical studies have linked them as predictors of retirement adjustment. Given that personality variables have important impact on individuals' coping style and social behaviors, more research should focus on explicating how these variables may act as a resource in the retirement transition and subsequent adjustment. Further, there is substantial international variation in retirement contexts and processes. The rules and regulations restricting the options for retirement or continued employment as well as the generosity of old-age pensions differ across nations and cultures, and this may significantly affect retirement adjustment. As such, there is a need for additional cross-national research that examines the impact that national contexts have on older workers' adjustment to retirement as well as their post-retirement well-being.

Finally, the research on individual differences in retirement adjustment also has practical applications. For those involved in counseling, the research findings suggest that to help clients to manage the retirement transition, counselors should consider not only financial but also social and psychological preparation for retirement. Research findings consistently show that a lack of choice in the retirement transition jeopardizes well-being. Improving self-management skills may thus help older adults realize a positive retirement experience and contribute to their well-being.

References

Alpass, F., Towers, A., Stephens, C., Fitzgerald, E., Stevenson, B., & Davey, J. (2007). Independence, well-being, and social participation in an aging population. *Annals of the New York Academy of Sciences, 114,* 241–250.

Atchley, R. C. (1971). Retirement and leisure participation: Continuity or crisis? *Gerontologist, 11*(1), 13–17.

Atchley, R. C. (1976). *The sociology of retirement.* New York, NY: John Wiley and Sons.

Atchley, R. C. (1989). A continuity theory of normal aging. *The Gerontologist, 29*(2), 183–190.

Barnes-Farrell, J. L. (2003). Beyond health and wealth: Attitudinal and other influences on retirement decision-making. In G. A. Adams & T. A. Beehr (Eds.), *Retirement: Reasons, processes, and results* (pp. 159–187). New York, NY: Springer.

Barron, M. L., Strein, G., & Suchman, E. A. (1952). Research on the social disorganization of retirement. *American Sociological Review, 17*(4), 479–482.

Beck, S. H. (1982). Adjustment to and satisfaction with retirement. *Journal of Gerontology, 37*(5), 616–624.

Blaikie, A. (1999). *Ageing & popular culture.* Cambridge, England: Cambridge University Press.

Bossé, R., Aldwin, C. M., Levenson, R., & Ekerdt, D. J. (1987). Mental health differences among retirees and workers: Findings from the Normative Aging Study. *Psychology and Aging, 2*(4), 383–389.

Bowlby, J. (1980). *Loss.* New York, NY: Basic Books.

Braithwaite, V. A., & Gibson, D. M. (1987). Adjustment to retirement: What we know and what we need to know. *Ageing & Society, 7*(1), 1–18.

Butrica, B. A., & Schaner, S. G. (2005). *Satisfaction and engagement in retirement.* Washington, DC: Urban Institute.

Bye, D., & Pushkar, D. (2009). How need for cognition and perceived control are differentially linked to emotional outcomes in the transition to retirement. *Motivation and Emotion, 33*(3), 320–332.

Calasanti, T. (1996). Gender and life satisfaction in retirement: An assessment of the male model. *Journal of Gerontology: Social Sciences, 51B*(1), S18–S29.

Calvo, E., Haverstick, K., & Sass, S. A. (2009). Gradual retirement, sense of control, and retirees' happiness. *Research on Aging, 31*(1), 112–135.

Coursolle, K. M., Sweeney, M. M., Raymo, J. M., & Ho, J.-H. (2010). The association between retirement and emotional well-being: Does prior work-family conflict matter? *The Journals of Gerontology, Series B: Psychological Sciences and Social Sciences, 65B*(5), 609–620.

Cozijnsen, R., Stevens, N. L., & Van Tilburg, T. G. (2010). Maintaining work-related personal ties following retirement. *Personal Relationships, 17*(3), 345–356.

Davey, A., & Szinovacz, M. E. (2004). Dimensions of marital quality and retirement. *Journal of Family Issues, 25*(4), 431–464.

De Vaus, D., Wells, Y., Kendig, H., & Quine, S. (2007). Does gradual retirement have better outcomes than abrupt retirement? Results from an Australian panel study. *Ageing & Society, 27,* 667–682.

Dorfman, L. T. (2002). Stayers and leavers: Professors in an era of no mandatory retirement. *Educational Gerontology, 28,* 15–33.

Dorfman, L. T., & Douglas, K. (2005). Leisure and the retired professor. Occupation matters. *Educational Gerontology, 18,* 343–363.

Drentea, P. (2002). Retirement and mental health. *Journal of Aging and Health, 14*(2), 167–194.

Ebaugh, H. R. F. (1988). *Becoming an ex: The process of role exit.* Chicago, IL: University of Chicago Press.

Ekerdt, D. J., & Clark, E. (2001). Selling retirement in financial planning advertisements. *Journal of Aging Studies, 15*(1), 55–68.

Ekerdt, D. J., & Vinick, B. H. (1991). Marital complaints in husband-working and husband-retired couples. *Research on Aging, 13*(3), 364–382.

Elder, G. H., & Johnson, M. K. (2003). The life course and aging. Challenges, lessons, and new directions. In R. A. Settersten (Ed.), *Invitation to the life course. Towards new understandings of later life* (pp. 49–81). New York, NY: Baywood.

Ferraro, K. (2001). Aging and role transitions. In R. H. Binstock & L. K. George (Eds.), *Handbook of aging and the social sciences* (Vol. 5, pp. 313–330). New York, NY: Academic Press.

Floyd, F. J., Haynes, S. N., & Rogers Doll, E. (1992). Assessing retirement satisfaction and perceptions of retirement experiences. *Psychology and Aging, 7*(4), 609–621.

Fouquereau, E., Fernandez, A., & Mullet, E. (2001). Evaluation of determinants of retirement satisfaction among workers and retired people. *Social Behavior and Personality, 29*(8), 777–785.

Fouquereau, E., Fernandez, A., Paul, M. C., Fonseca, A. M., & Uotinen, V. (2005). Perceptions of satisfaction with retirement: A comparison of six European Union countries. *Psychology and Aging, 20*(3), 524–528.

Fryer, D. (1985). Stages in the psychological response to unemployment: A (dis)integrative review. *Current Psychological Research & Review, Fall,* 257–273.

Gall, T. L., Evans, D. R., & Howard, J. H. (1997). The retirement adjustment process: Changes in well-being of male retirees across time. *Journal of Gerontology: Social Sciences, 52B*(3), S110–S117.

Gallo, W. T., Bradley, E. H., Siegel, M., & Kasl, S. (2000). Health effects of involuntary job loss among older workers: Findings from the Health and Retirement Survey. *Journal of Gerontology: Social Sciences, 55B*(3), S131–S140.

Gallo, W. T., Bradley, E. H., Siegel, M., & Kasl, S. V. (2001). The impact of involuntary job loss on subsequent alcohol consumption by older workers: Findings from the Health and Retirement Survey. *Journal of Gerontology: Social Science, 56B*(1), S3–S9.

Gallo, W. T., Teng, H. M., Falba, T. A., Kasl, S. V., Krumholz, H. M., & Bradley, E. H. (2006). The impact of late career job loss on myocardial infarction and stroke: A 10 year follow up using the health and retirement survey. *Occupational and Environmental Medicine, 63*(10), 683–687.

Granovetter, M. S. (1973). The strength of weak ties. *American Journal of Sociology, 78*(6), 1360–1380.

Gratton, B., & Haug, M. R. (1983). Decision and adaptation. Research on female retirement. *Research on Aging, 5*(1), 59–76.

Guerriero Austrom, M., Perkins, A. J., Damush, T. M., & Hendry, H. C. (2003). Predictors of life satisfaction in retired physicians and spouses. *Social Psychiatry and Psychiatric Epidemiology, 38*, 134–141.

Hagestad, G. O. (1990). Social perspectives on the life course. In R. H. Binstock & L. K. George (Eds.), *Handbook of aging and the social sciences* (Vol. 5, pp. 151–168). New York, NY: Academic Press.

Hagestad, G. O., & Neugarten, B. L. (1985). Age and the life course. In R. H. Binstock & E. Shanas (Eds.), *Handbook of aging and the social sciences* (Vol. 2, pp. 35–61). New York, NY: Van Nostrand Reinhold.

Hardy, M. A., & Hazelrigg, L. (1999). A multilevel model of early retirement decisions among autoworkers in plants with different futures. *Research on Aging, 21*(2), 275–303.

Hardy, M. A., & Quadagno, J. (1995). Satisfaction with early retirement: Making choices in the auto industry. *Journal of Gerontology: Social Sciences, 50B*(4), S217–S228.

Harvey, J. H., & Miller, E. D. (1998). Toward a psychology of loss. *Psychological Science, 9*(6), 429–434.

Haug, M. R., Belgrave, L. L., & Jones, S. (1992). Partners' health and retirement adaptation of women and their husbands. *Journal of Women and Aging, 4*(3), 5–29.

He, Y. E., & Marshall, V. W. (2003). Later-life career disruption and self-rated health. An analysis of General Social Survey data. *Canadian Journal of Aging, 22*(1), 45–57.

Henkens, K., & Van Solinge, H. (2002). Spousal influence on the decision to retire. *International Journal of Sociology, 32*(2), 55–73.

Henretta, J. C., O'Rand, A. M., & Chan, C. G. (1993a). Gender differences in employment after spouse's retirement. *Research on Aging, 15*(2), 148–169.

Henretta, J. C., O'Rand, A. M., & Chan, C. G. (1993b). Joint role investments and synchronization of retirement. A sequential approach to couples' retirement timing. *Social Forces, 71*(4), 981–1000.

Herzog, A. R., House, J. S., & Morgan, J. N. (1991). Relation of work and retirement to health and well-being in older age. *Psychology and Aging, 6*(2), 202–211.

Hinden, S. (2010). *How to retire happy: The 12 most important decisions you must make before you retire.* New York, NY: McGraw-Hill.

Hobfoll, S. E. (1989). Conservation of resources. A new attempt of conceptualizing stress. *American Psychologist, 44*(3), 513–524.

Huovinen, P., & Piekkola, H. (2002). *Early retirement and the use of time by older Finns* (787). Helsinki, Finland: ETLA.

Hyde, M., Ferrie, J. E., Higgs, P., Mein, G., & Nazroo, J. (2004). The effect of pre-retirement factors and retirement route on circumstances in retirement: Findings from the Whitehall II study. *Ageing & Society, 24*(2), 279–296.

Isaksson, K., & Johansson, G. (2000). Adaptation to continued work and early retirement following downsizing: Long-term effects and gender differences. *Journal of Occupational and Organizational Psychology, 73*(2), 241–256.

Kasl, S. V., & Jones, B. A. (2000). The impact of job loss and retirement on health. In L. F. Berkman & I. Kawachi (Eds.), *Social epidemiology* (pp. 118–136). Oxford, England: Oxford University Press.

Kim, J. E., & Moen, P. (2002). Retirement transitions, gender and psychological well-being: A life-course ecological model. *Journal of Gerontology: Psychological Science, 57B*(3), P212–P222.

Kim, S., & Feldman, D. C. (2000). Working in retirement: The antecedents of bridge employment and its consequences for quality of life in retirement. *Academy of Management Journal 43*(6), 1195–1210.

Kling, K. C., Ryff, C. D., Love, G., & Essex, M. (2003). Exploring the influence of personality on depressive symptoms and self-esteem across a significant life transition. *Journal of Personality and Social Psychology, 85*, 922–932.

Kübler-Ross, E. (1969). *On death and dying.* London, England: Tavistock.

Laczko, F., & Phillipson, C. (1991). *Changing work and retirement. Social policy and the older worker.* Philadelphia, PA: Milton Keynes.

Levy-Shiff, R. (1994). Individual and contextual correlates of marital change cross the transition to parenthood to education. *Developmental Psychology, 30*, 591–601.

Lin, N. (1999). Building a network theory of social capital. *Connections, 22*(1), 28–51.

Löckenhoff, C. E., Terracciano, A., & Costa, P. T., Jr. (2009). Five-factor model personality traits and the retirement transition: Longitudinal and cross-sectional associations. *Psychology and Aging, 24*(3), 722–728.

Maddox, G. L. (1968). Persistence of life style among the elderly: A longitudinal study of patterns of social activity in relation to life satisfaction. In B. L. Neugarten (Ed.), *Middle age and aging: A reader in social psychology* (pp. 181–183). Chicago, IL: University of Chicago Press.

Marshall, V. W., Clarke, P. J., & Ballantyne, P. J. (2001). Instability in the retirement transition: Effects on health and well-being in a Canadian Study. *Research on Aging, 23*(4), 379–409.

Martin Matthews, A., & Brown, K. H. (1987). Retirement as a critical life event. The differential experiences of men and women. *Research on Aging, 9*(4), 548–571.

Mayring, P. (2000). Pensionierung als Krise oder Glücksgewinn? Ergebnisse aus einer quantitativ-qualitativen Längsschnittuntersuchung. [Retirement as crisis or gain of happiness? Results of a qualitative/ quantitative longitudinal study.] *Zeitschrift für Gerontologie, 33*(2), 124–133.

Mein, G., Martikainen, P., Hemingway, H., Stansfeld, S. A., & Marmot, M. G. (2003). Is retirement good or bad for mental and physical health functioning? Whitehall II longitudinal study of civil servants. *Journal of Epidemiology and Community Health, 57*(1), 46–49.

Midanik, L. T., Soghikian, K., Ransom, L. J., & Tekawa, I. S. (1995). The effect of retirement on health and health behaviors: The Kaiser Permanente Retirement Study. *Journal of Gerontology: Social Sciences, 50B*(1), S59–S61.

Moen, P. (1996). A life course perspective on retirement, gender and well-being. *Journal of Occupational Health Psychology, 1*(2), 131–144.

Moen, P. (2003). Midcourse. Navigating retirement and a new life stage. In J. T. Mortimer & M. J. Shanahan (Eds.), *Handbook of the life course* (pp. 269–291). New York, NY: Kluwer.

Nimrod, G. (2008). In support of innovation theory: Innovation in activity patterns and life satisfaction among recently retired individuals. *Ageing & Society, 28*(6), 831–846.

Northouse, L. L., Dorris, G., & Charron-Moore, C. (1995). Factors affecting couples' adjustment to recurrent breast cancer. *Social Science Medicine, 41*(1), 69–76.

Nuttman-Schwartz, O. (2004). Like a high wave: Adjustment to retirement. *The Gerontologist, 44*(2), 229–236.

Nuttman-Schwartz, O. (2008). Bridging the gap: The creation of continuity by men on the verge of retirement. *Ageing & Society, 28*, 185–202.

Pearlin, L. I., Menaghan, E. G., Lieberman, M. A., & Mullan, J. T. (1981). The stress process. *Journal of Health and Social Behavior, 22*(4), 337–356.

Pienta, A. M., & Hayward, M. D. (2002). Who expects to continue working after age 62? The retirement plans of couples. *Journal of Gerontology: Social Sciences, 57B*(4), S119–S208.

Pinquart, M., & Schindler, I. (2007). Changes of life satisfaction in the transition to retirement. A latent-class approach. *Psychology and Aging, 22*(3), 442–455.

Potocnik, K., Tordera, N., & Peiró, J. M. (2009). The role of human resource practices and group norms in the retirement process. *European Psychologist, 14*(3), 193–206.

Price, C. A. (2003). Professional women's retirement adjustment: The experience of reestablishing order. *Journal of Aging Studies, 17*(3), 341–355.

Pushkar, D., Chaikelson, J., Conway, M., Etezadi, J., Giannopoulus, C., Li, K., & Wrosch, C. (2009). Testing continuity and activity variables as predictors of positive and negative affect in retirement. *Journal of Gerontology: Psychological Sciences, 65B*(1), 42–49.

Quick, H. E., & Moen, P. (1998). Gender, employment, and retirement quality: A life course approach to the differential experiences of men and women. *Journal of Occupational Health Psychology, 3*(1), 44–64.

Reeves, J. B., & Darville, R. L. (1994). Social contact patterns and satisfaction with retirement of women in dual-career/earner families. *International Journal of Aging & Human Development, 39*, 163–175.

Reitzes, D. C., & Mutran, E. J. (2004). The transition into retirement: Stages and factors that influence retirement adjustment. *International Journal of Aging and Human Development, 59*(1), 63–84.

Reitzes, D. C., & Mutran, E. J. (2006). Lingering identities in retirement. *The Sociological Quarterly, 47*, 333–359.

Richardson, V., & Kilty, K. M. (1991). Adjustment to retirement: Continuity vs. discontinuity. *International Journal of Aging and Human Development, 32*(2), 151–169.

Robbins, S. B., Lee, R. M., & Wan, T. T. H. (1994). Goal continuity as a mediator in early retirement adjustment: Testing a multidimensional model. *Journal of Counseling Psychology, 41*(1), 18–26.

Ross, C. E., Mirowsky, J., & Goldsteen, K. (1990). The impact of family on health. The decade review. *Journal of Marriage and the Family, 52*(4), 1059–1078.

Savishinsky, J. (2000). *Breaking the watch. The meaning of retirement in America*. Ithaca, NY: Cornell University Press.

Schlossberg, N. K. (2004). *Retire smart, retire happy*. Washington, DC: American Psychological Association.

Schroevers, M., Kraaij, V., & Garnefski, N. (2007). Goal disturbance, cognitive coping strategies, and psychological adjustment to different types of stressful life event. *Personality and Individual Differences, 43*(2), 413–423.

Seccombe, K., & Lee, G. R. (1986). Gender differences in retirement satisfaction and its antecedents. *Research on Aging, 8*(3), 426–440.

Settersten, R. A. (2003). Propositions and controversies in life-course scholarship. In R. A. Settersten (Ed.), *Invitation to the life course. Toward new understandings of later life* (pp. 15–48). New York, NY: Baywood.

Shultz, K. S. (2003). Bridge employment. Work after retirement. In G. A. Adams & T. A. Beehr (Eds.), *Retirement: Reasons, processes, and results* (pp. 214–241). New York, NY: Springer.

Shultz, K. S., Morton, K. R., & Weckerle, J. R. (1998). The influence of push and pull factors on voluntary and involuntary early retirees' retirement decision and adjustment. *Journal of Vocational Behavior, 53*(1), 45–57.

Slevin, K. F., & Wingrove, C. R. (1995). Women in retirement: A review and critique of empirical research since 1976. *Social Inquiry, 65*(1), 1–21.

Smith, D. B., & Moen, P. (1998). Spousal influence on retirement: His, her and their perception. *Journal of Marriage and the Family, 60*(3), 734–744.

Smith, D. B., & Moen, P. (2004). Retirement satisfaction for retirees and their spouses. *Journal of Family Issues, 25*(2), 262–285.

Steverink, N., Lindenberg, S., & Ormel, J. (1998). Towards understanding successful ageing: Patterned change in resources and goals. *Ageing & Society, 18*(4), 441–467.

Szinovacz, M. E. (2003). Contexts and pathways. Retirement as institution, process and experience. In G. A. Adams & T. A. Beehr (Eds.), *Retirement: Reasons, processes, and results* (pp. 6–52). New York, NY: Springer.

Szinovacz, M. E., & Davey, A. (2004). Honeymoons and joint lunches. Effects of retirement and spouse's employment on depressive symptoms. *Journal of Gerontology: Psychological Sciences, 59B*(5), P233–P245.

Szinovacz, M. E., & DeViney, S. (2000). Marital characteristics and retirement decisions. *Research on Aging, 22*(5), 470–498.

Talaga, J. T., & Beehr, T. A. (1995). Are there gender differences in predicting retirement decisions? *Journal of Applied Psychology, 80*(1), 16–28.

Taylor, M. A., & Cook, K. (1995). Adaptation to retirement: Role changes and psychological resources. *The Career Development Quarterly, 44*(1), 67–82.

Taylor, M. A., Goldberg, C., Shore, L. M., & Lipka, P. (2008). The effects of retirement expectations and social support on post-retirement adjustment: A longitudinal analysis. *Journal of Managerial Psychology, 23*(4), 458–470.

Taylor, M. A., & Shore, L. M. (1995). Predictors of planned retirement age: An application of Beehr's model. *Psychology and Aging, 10*(1), 76–83.

Taylor, M. A., Shultz, K. S., Morrison, R. F., Spiegel, P. E., & Greene, J. (2007). Occupational attachment and met expectations as predictors of retirement adjustment of naval officers. *Journal of Applied Social Psychology, 37*(8), 1697–1725.

Thoits, P. A. (1983). Dimensions of life events that influence psychological distress. An evaluation and synthesis of the literature. In H. B. Kaplan (Ed.), *Psychosocial stress. Trends in theory and research* (pp. 33–103). New York, NY: Academic Press.

Tuomi, K., Järvinen, E., Eskelinen, L., Ilmarinen, J., & Klockars, M. (1991). Effect of retirement on health and work ability among municipal employees. *Scandinavian Journal of Work Environment and Health, 17*(Suppl. 1), 75–81.

Vallery-Masson, J., Poitrenaud, J., Burnat, G., & Lion, M.-R. (1981). Retirement and morbidity: A three year longitudinal study of a French managerial population. *Age and Ageing, 10*(4), 271–276.

Van Solinge, H., & Henkens, K. (2005). Couples' adjustment to retirement: A multi-actor panel study. *Journal of Gerontology: Social Sciences, 60B*(1), S11–S20.

Van Solinge, H., & Henkens, K. (2007). Involuntary retirement. The role of restrictive circumstances, timing and social embeddedness. *Journal of Gerontology: Social Science, 62B*(5), 295–303.

Van Solinge, H., & Henkens, K. (2008). Adjustment to and satisfaction with retirement: Two of a kind? *Psychology and Aging, 23*(2), 422–434.

Van Tilburg, T. G. (2003). Consequences of men's retirement for the continuation of work-related personal relationships. *Ageing International, 28*(4), 345–358.

Van Willigen, M. (2000). Differential benefits of volunteering across the life course. *Journal of Gerontology: Social Science, 55B*(5), S308–S318.

Vecchio, R. P. (1993). The impact of differences in subordinate and supervisor age on attitudes and performance. *Psychology and Aging, 8*(1), 112–119.

Von Bonsdorff, M. E., Shultz, K. S., Leskinen, E., & Tansky, J. (2009). The choice between retirement and bridge employment: A continuity theory and life course perspective. *International Journal of Aging & Human Development, 69*(2), 79–100.

Wang, M. (2007). Profiling retirees in the retirement transition and adjustment process. Examining the longitudinal change patterns of retiree's psychological well-being. *Journal of Applied Psychology, 92*(2), 455–474.

Wang, M., Henkens, K., & Van Solinge, H. (2011). Retirement adjustment: A review of theoretical and empirical advancements. *American Psychologist, 66*(3), 204–213.

Wang, M., & Takeuchi, R. (2007). The role of goal orientation during expatriation: A cross-sectional and longitudinal investigation. *Journal of Applied Psychology, 92*, 1437–1445.

Wang, M., Zhan, Y., Liu, S., & Shultz, K. S. (2008). Antecedents of bridge employment: A longitudinal investigation. *Journal of Applied Psychology, 93*(4), 818–830.

Warr, P., Butcher, V., Robertson, I., & Callinan, M. (2004). Older people's well-being as a function of employment, retirement, environmental characteristics and role preference. *British Journal of Psychology, 95*(3), 297–324.

Weiss, R. S. (2005). *The experience of retirement*. Ithaca, NY: Cornell University Press.

Wheaton, B. (1990). Life transitions, role histories and mental health. *American Sociological Review, 55*(April), 209–223.

Whiting, K. (1998, November). *Divergent paths: Women's experiences of the retirement process*. Paper presented at the AIFS Conference on Changing Families, Challenging Futures, Melbourne, Australia.

Williams, D. (1999). Human responses to change. *Futures, 31*(6), 609–616.

Wong, J. Y., & Earl, J. K. (2009). Towards an integrated model of individual, psychosocial, and organizational predictors of retirement adjustment. *Journal of Vocational Behavior, 75*(1), 1–13.

Wortman, C. B., Cohen Silver, R., & Kessler, R. C. (1993). The meaning of loss and adjustment to bereavement. In M. Stroebe, W. Stroebe, & R. O. Hansson (Eds.), *Handbook of bereavement: Theory, research and intervention* (pp. 349–366). Cambridge, England: Cambridge University Press.

Wrosch, C., & Freund, A. M. (2001). Self-regulation of normative and non-normative developmental challenges. *Human Development, 44*(5), 264–287.

Zhan, Y., Wang, M., Liu, S., & Shultz, K. S. (2009). Bridge employment and retirees' health: A longitudinal investigation. *Journal of Occupational Health Psychology, 14*(4), 374–389.

The Association of Retirement with Physical and Behavioral Health

William T. Gallo

Abstract

Retirement is a variable, often complex process whose impact on somatic and behavioral well-being likely involves such factors as the linearity and quality of the transition, its desirability, and attributes of the former job and retiree, particularly recent health trends. Yet studies have only begun to capture the intricacies of this critical life transition. This chapter surveys the scientific literature on the association between retirement and physical health and health behaviors. The section on physical health describes studies of self-assessed health, functional status, chronic conditions, biological markers of disease, and mortality, while the behavioral research section covers investigations of physical activity, alcohol use, smoking, and body weight. Research in these areas has produced a set of largely inconsistent results, owing to differences in design, measurement, and statistical methodology. Isolation of an average, population-level effect of retirement may not be achievable, given that variation in the retirement experience and its antecedents produces dissimilar health and behavioral outcomes. Future studies should therefore focus on identifying factors that distinguish groups of individuals who are most detrimentally affected by retirement.

Key Words: retirement, physical health, health behaviors

Retirement is a complicated life transition. The culmination of a decades-long period of involvement with the labor market, retirement can prescribe a tremendous alteration of daily schedule, social relationships, personal meaning, and identity. Conventional wisdom suggests that in many societies, work is venerated. In the United States, for example, it is extremely common to ask about the nature of work ("What do you do for a living?") immediately upon making acquaintance with someone. In fact, it is rather likely that the question of work will precede questions of family and avocation in many circles, and can establish the relative tenor of dialogue (e.g., replying that "I am a university professor" can either abruptly end a conversation or occasion an engaging one, depending on who has asked this question of me, and how he or she views

his or her status in relation to mine). In any case, employment designates role, workplace and societal identities, and social relationships. Depending on its features, it may encourage physical and mental health, as well as elements of cognitive well-being. If all of this is so, then one might surmise that retirement is bad for health. That is, if work defines, to a greater or lesser degree, who we are, what our relative status is, with whom we interact, and whether or not we are well, then its elimination upon retirement would surely precipitate health decline. Or would it?

Recall that the first sentence of this chapter argues that retirement is complicated. So perhaps the answer is not so clear. Indeed, while the early studies that examined the association between retirement and health were based on the idea that retirement was necessarily stressful—in which the stress was provoked by losses of status, opportunity to demonstrate mastery, work role, etc.—and therefore anticipated negative effects, contemporary research in this field considers in much greater detail the context in which the retirement takes place. Just think about all of the factors that might lead one group of individuals to exhibit good health after retirement and another to present with poor health. Was the job stressful? Did the employee feel valued? Was there pressure to retire? Are the retiree's personal savings, pension, and annuities sufficient to maintain his or her living standards and quality of life? Will he or she continue to work in some capacity, easing into retirement? Will he or she enjoy spending more time with family members? What expectations will they have of him or her? How does he or she feel? What will he or she do with the additional free time? These are just a few of the ideas that you might have.

While your list is probably more extensive than mine, I would assume that most, if not all, of the factors that one could conjure would fit into the following categories: the type and quality of the transition; elements of the former job; the perception of retirement as a desirable or unwelcome change; personal characteristics of the retiree; and, perhaps most importantly, health status and the general direction of its recent trajectory. These are, for certain, many of the criteria that inform the models by which researchers evaluate the relationship between retirement and subsequent well-being (Wang & Shultz, 2010).

The purpose of this chapter is to review the scientific literature on the association between retirement and two outcome groups: physical health and health behaviors. The section on physical health summarizes studies of self-assessed health, functional status, chronic conditions, biological markers of disease, and mortality. The behavioral research section covers investigations of physical activity, alcohol use, smoking, and body weight. It is important to note that the direction of the relationship of retirement to both groups of outcomes is ambiguous. Methodological treatment of context, along with data quality, therefore brings about wide variation in findings across studies.

Each segment begins with a brief overview—highlighting the major empirical or conceptual challenges—which is followed by a critical synopsis of relevant evidence. In some cases, the literature is presented in a fairly chronological manner, which mirrors the methodological development of the

science. However, where explication benefits from contrapuntal presentation of studies from different periods, or where groups of studies are linked by a common measure, setting, or result, chronological presentation is discharged. The final section of the chapter reflects on the realities of research on physical health and health behaviors, and offers some suggestions for moving forward the field.

Physical Health

The question of whether retirement affects physical health remains fundamentally unanswered. Older research in this area reported either null or modest adverse effects of retirement, while more recent studies have found both negative and positive effects. A small literature that investigates the relationship of retirement to survival is similarly opaque.

Several critical matters, yet unresolved, hinder progress on obtaining clearer evidence related to this question. First, the overwhelming majority of studies have not been designed to invalidate the wholly plausible idea that ill health in retirement simply represents continuation of pre-retirement trajectories of health (Ekerdt, 1987; Kasl & Jones, 2000). To view retirement as a potentially health-altering exposure, studies would minimally require health data for multiple adjacent periods prior and subsequent to retirement (Jokela et al., 2010; Westerlund et al., 2009). This has generally not been the case; instead, retrospective cross-sectional and two-period longitudinal studies have comprised the dominant designs. Second, the lines of inquiry that have addressed the role of health in the retirement decision and the impact of retirement on health have effectively developed in parallel. The consequence of this is potentially selection-biased inference in the bulk of research on this topic. In fact, two major studies that have accounted for health selection in analyzing the impact of retirement on physical health (Dave, Rashad, & Spasojevic, 2008; Neuman, 2008) have drawn opposite conclusions with the same data source. Third, studies have infrequently modeled involuntary (also known as "forced" or "off-time") retirement, which must be disaggregated from voluntary (i.e., "normative" or "on-time") retirement if researchers are to isolate the component that best conforms to the characterization of retirement as a stressful life transition, which is one major, though dated, paradigm in retirement research. This is despite consistent evidence of its negative association with post-retirement health in the few studies that have isolated involuntary retirements (Dave et al., 2008; Swan, Dame, & Carmelli, 1991; van Solinge, 2007). Finally, much research has ignored important sample heterogeneity (Moen, 1996), particularly perceptions of the work environment (e.g., work stress, job satisfaction, collegial relations, etc.). In doing so, studies have obscured group-level differences that may prescribe varying health outcomes after retirement.

The greater part of the early research on the physical health impact of retirement did not suggest a convincing link. Three analyses of data from the Veterans Administration Normative Aging Study (Ekerdt, Baden, Bosse, & Dibbs, 1983; Ekerdt, Bosse, & Goldie, 1983; Ekerdt, Sparrow, Glynn, & Bosse, 1984), set in Boston, initiated contemporary research on the association between retirement and physical health. Assessing changes in somatic complaints (Ekerdt, Bosse, et al., 1983), health status based on medical examinations (Ekerdt, Baden, et al., 1983), and blood pressure and serum cholesterol (Ekerdt et al., 1984) within the context of a two-period longitudinal design, Ekerdt and colleagues found no compelling evidence that retirement led to adverse variations in health when compared to continuing to work. Among the three outcomes investigated, only blood pressure and serum cholesterol were modestly, adversely, responsive to retirement. Nevertheless, the changes observed in that study were judged to be clinically insignificant (Ekerdt et al., 1984).

Investigations of Israeli and British data from the same period (Kremer, 1985; Mein, Martikainen, Hemingway, Stansfeld, & Marmot, 2003) produced similar conclusions to those generated by the Normative Aging Study reports. In the Israeli study, pre-/post-retirement analyses of health status and physician visits on 310 individuals who retired from industrial and services jobs suggested a moderate negative change. Supplementary analysis nonetheless ruled out definitive attribution of such changes to retirement. The British research, a single follow-up analysis of 1,010 civil servants who participated in the Whitehall II study, found that decrements in physical functioning for individuals who retired at age 60 were not statistically different from those reported by members of the employed comparison group (Mein et al., 2003).

Alongside the research that suggests a null association between retirement and physical health are several studies that have indicated a detrimental effect. Cautious interpretation of the findings from these studies is, however, merited, chiefly because of differences across studies in the referent group to which retirement is compared. For example, two investigations with quite persuasive results (Swan et al., 1991; van Solinge, 2007) compared involuntary to normative retirement, whereas two others, which reported substantially more tepid findings (Behncke, 2009; Dave et al., 2008), compared retirement to continuing employment. An additional point worth noting is that the latter studies employed more rigorous statistical methods to reduce bias stemming from health selection into retirement. It is therefore not certain whether the more modest findings derive from the alternative comparison group or methodological modifications. The remaining report in this class (Tuomi, Jarvinen, Eskelinen, Ilmarinen, & Klockars, 1991) was hybrid of sorts, wherein work content (e.g., physical work, mental work) and work status (e.g., actively working, age-qualified retirement, disability retirement) were combined in such a way that retirement's effect must be evaluated within given content strata. The results appear, moreover, to be dominantly framed in intra-class (i.e., pre-/post-) comparisons.

Swan and colleagues (1991) investigated chronic disease outcomes in 1,103 participants of the Western Collaborative Group Study, a 27-year longitudinal assessment of men, between 39 and 59 years of age, drawn from ten California companies in 1960–1961. The authors reported that involuntary retirement was associated with a higher number of chronic conditions, poorer physical functioning, and lower self-assessed health than voluntary retirement (Swan et al., 1991). A report based on data from 778 older individuals enrolled in the Dutch NIDI study (van Solinge, 2007), a six-year follow-up study, also compared involuntary to voluntary retirements. In a quite unique way, the NIDI research categorized involuntary retirements along a continuum, from "a bit" to "very," where three reasons for the nature of the involuntary exit (health, organizational, other) were separately parameterized. This study found that involuntary retirements were negatively linked to changes in self-assessed health, where both health and organizationally motivated retirements were significant correlates.

Thirteen years (1992–2005) of national data from the U.S. Health and Retirement Survey (HRS) were analyzed in a rather exhaustive assessment of physical functioning and chronic disease outcomes (Dave et al., 2008). Among other elements, the authors' empirical approach segregated complete from partial retirements and involuntary from voluntary retirements; attempted to circumscribe health selection by exclusion of participants who were most likely to retire due to ill health and instrumental variable (IV) estimation; and used sample stratification to investigate differential effects resulting from variation in personal characteristics and those of the former job. Translating regression estimates to "marginal effects," the authors reported that complete retirement led to a 5% to 14% decline in mobility and ADL function and a 4% to 6% increase in chronic disease, with involuntary retirement producing estimates at the high end of these ranges. Buffering effects were observed for retirees who were married, held bridge jobs, or were physically active in retirement. A fairly comparable approach to analyzing three waves of the English Longitudinal Study of Ageing (ELSA) yielded rather consistent conclusions (Behncke, 2009) to those of the HRS study. Exploiting information on the relative timing of retirement and chronic disease diagnosis to establish temporal precedence of retirement, the authors of the ELSA report found that retirement was, on average, associated with a 9% increase in the likelihood of reporting any chronic condition. Among individual conditions, retirement raised the probability of cardiovascular diseases and cancer by 3%. Tests for heterogeneity suggested that male retirees had higher likelihood of reporting cardiovascular diseases and lower likelihood of arthritis and cancer than women.

A Finish examination (Tuomi et al., 1991) that was undertaken among 6,258 workers in 1985, 870 of whom retired in the four-year observation period, generated two notable findings. First, men who retired from mental work had significant increases in musculoskeletal disorders after disability retirement. And second, male retirees whose former jobs involved mixed (i.e., mental/physical) content had significant increases in the prevalence of cardiovascular diseases after age-related retirements. Speculating on the motivation for their findings, the authors suggested that the observed post-retirement changes may be an artifact of "devoted" workers' underacknowledging the existence of the health conditions in the pre-retirement period. Indirectly supporting this argument, they point out that musculoskeletal problems are more likely to occur in workers whose jobs exact high mental demands. However, the authors concede other potential pathways. For example, they conjectured that the cardiovascular disease finding may trace itself to discontinuation of stimulating, health-beneficial work, which may somehow be protective.

In contrast to the above studies, positive health effects of retirement have been demonstrated in four studies that were set in four different countries. Swiss research (Mojon-Azzi, Sousa-Poza, & Widmer, 2007) used five waves of Swiss Household Panel data ($N = 523$) to explore whether retirement influenced several domains of well-being, among them self-rated health (calculated change) and perceived changes in self-rated health. Estimates of the likelihood of positive inter-panel change indicated a protective effect of retirement. Indeed, retirement almost doubled the log odds of a lower-to-higher assessment of health, and increased the log odds of reporting better follow-up health by 20%. In contrast to earlier findings that were produced by a single follow-up assessment (Mein et al., 2003), results from a six-wave Whitehall II study (Jokela et al., 2010), covering fifteen years, suggested initial improvement in physical functioning associated with statutory and voluntary early retirement. Longitudinal plots of physical functioning indicated, however, that short-term improvements in health diminished over time.

A prospective analysis of data ($N = 14,714$) from the French national Gas and Electric Company (GAZEL) also supported the thesis of retirement as a salutary life transition (Westerlund et al., 2009). Considering fifteen years of data—arrayed so that seven self-rated health assessments, pre- and post-retirement, could be studied—the authors found that the likelihood of suboptimum self-rated health (a binary variable based on an 8-point Likert-scaled assessment) increased in the pre-retirement period but declined sharply immediately after retirement, remaining below its pre-retirement level throughout the entire post-retirement observation period (Westerlund et al., 2009). The persuasiveness of the GAZEL study's findings is enhanced by the broad set of health and chronic disease variables controlled in the analyses.

The final study to suggest a protective effect of retirement is a recent U.S. investigation of HRS data (Neuman, 2008) that in many ways mirrored the other recent HRS analysis (Dave et al., 2008), which found adverse effects of retirement. One major difference, which likely motivates the studies' inconsistent conclusions, appears to be a greater emphasis on results derived from IV estimation in Neuman's assessment. More specifically, Neuman (2008) used IV estimation to account for health selection into retirement, whereas Dave and colleagues (2008) primarily relied on sample selection (i.e., omitting participants who reported health problems prior to retirement) and pseudo-regression techniques (i.e., regressing the exposure, retirement, on pre-retirement health status to demonstrate a null relationship) to limit the potential endogeneity of retirement. Arguing that the sample-selection approach taken by Dave et al. permits bias to be introduced by health declines that take place between the pre-retirement health assessment and the actual retirement, Neuman instrumented respondents' retirement markers with related variables—notably spousal retirement eligibility—that were uncorrelated with respondents' health status. Finding positive effects of retirement on self-ratings of health and a null relationship with the objective health measures that were found to be adversely affected by retirement in Dave and colleague's analysis, Neuman concluded that health selection likely biases the results of analyses that do not instrument retirement.

Mortality following retirement has been assessed in a relatively small collection of studies, which may be differentiated primarily according to whether or not they explicitly address the related matters of retirement "scheme" (i.e., early vs. normative retirement) and retirement age. Early retirement and retirement age have stimulated many of the contemporary reports, which have evaluated the potential consequences of raising the minimum retirement age in light of the critical fissures in many national pension plans. As a rule, retirement has been associated with some excess risk of mortality. However, negative health selection into retirement and inadequate controls for health status at retirement have likely biased mortality risk upward. Two reports have, conversely, suggested reduced mortality risk.

Coronary mortality was considered in a match-paired, case-control study of 1,136 married white men (age 30–75) who died of coronary heart disease in the U.S. state of Florida (Casscells et al., 1980). From interviews with wives of the deceased, investigators determined employment status at the time of death and obtained data on history of myocardial infarction (MI). Controlling for age and MI hospitalization, this study found an 80% increased risk of coronary mortality for those who were retired. Morris et al. (1994) uncovered a comparable association in a five-year follow-up investigation of data from the British Regional Heart Study, reporting an 86% elevation of all-cause mortality associated with non-health-related retirement (Morris, Cook, & Shaper, 1994). Nevertheless, the validity of this finding has been questioned (Kasl & Jones, 2000), as Morris et al. report, in the same study, a lesser effect of unemployment (than retirement) on mortality, an implausible result given the uniformity

of evidence regarding the association between job loss and adverse health and the contradictory results of many retirement studies (Kasl & Jones, 2000). Specifically, Kasl and Jones contend that better baseline health adjustments and/or updates to such adjustments over the observation period would conceivably reduce the magnitude of the mortality estimate. The results of analysis of Greek data from the European Investigation into Cancer and Nutrition (EPIC) (Bamia, Trichopoulou, & Trichopoulos, 2008) generally appear to support the Kasl and Jones argument. With a large sample size ($N = 16,827$) and controls for a broad array of confounders, including substantial health markers, Bamia et al. (2008) found only a 51% elevation in five-year all-cause mortality risk associated with retirement.

There is some ambiguity regarding the impact on survival of early retirement and retirement age. Studying 3,971 rubber tire workers in the United States, a report by Haynes and colleagues found approximately 40% increased risk of mortality four to five years after early retirement, but not normal retirement (Haynes, McMichael, & Tyroler, 1978). Even so, a sub-study indicated significantly higher morbidity among the early retirees than normative retirees, which suggests some influence of health selection. Results from the Greek EPIC study (Bamia et al., 2008) indicated a more modest effect on survival of early retirement, in which a five-year decrease in retirement age raised mortality risk by 10%. A prospective cohort study of former U.S. employees of the Shell Oil Company who retired between 1973 and 2003 (Tsai, Wendt, Donnelly, de Jong, & Ahmed, 2005) reported 21% to 58% higher mortality risk associated with retiring at 55 than with retiring at 60 or 65, with variation in risk across socioeconomic strata.

In contrast, a seven-year follow-up study of 2,397 older Israeli adults (Litwin, 2007), which linked household survey data to death registry records, found no survival differential between early and on-time retirees. Interestingly, this study found reduced risk of mortality among early retirees prior to adjusting for baseline health status and other covariates. Somewhat consistent evidence was indicated by sex-stratified analysis of administrative data ($N = 129,675$) from a German health insurance fund (Brockmann, Muller, & Helmert, 2009). After adjustment for the duration of hospital stays in the two-year period prior to retirement, the authors found reduced risk of mortality of 12% for retired men and 23% for retired women.

Health Behaviors
Physical Activity

Physical activity has been more intensively studied in the context of retirement than alcohol use, smoking, or weight changes. In addition, numerous studies have suggested that retirement-related modifications in physical activity lie beneath observed changes in other dimensions of health. Nevertheless, the investigation of this particular behavior in relation to retirement is complex. Indeed, this complexity is prominently reflected by a wide variation in measurement across the few published studies, which have used such disparate measures as self-reports of leisure-time exercise, post-retirement television viewing, and physiologic signals of movement recorded by body-borne instruments.

The foundation of the assessment problem in physical activity is that, for many individuals, the set of tasks that define activity during employment are eliminated upon retirement. For this reason, there exists no credible post-employment corollary for the physical demands of work. Researchers are therefore presented a task whose best approach yields an incomplete picture; in other words, comparing physical activity before and after retirement is a suboptimal endeavor. To illustrate, take the case of the stevedore, who, while working, is required to perform strenuous lifting in the normal course of a given workday. Though the retired stevedore may devote some of his retirement time to lifting heavy objects—for example, rearranging the household furniture or cleaning out a long-neglected storage area—he is unlikely to do so as intensively as he would while employed. How then can researchers reasonably expect to assess global changes in the stevedore's physical activity? Clearly, they cannot. The stevedore example does not, of course, hold for all workers. A literary editor or agent who prefers to spend his retirement days translating the writings of Elias Canetti may subject himself to the very same physical conditions and demands of the former job. The point is that, on balance, the nature of physical activity is apt to change as workers transition to retirement.

Actual measurement obfuscates the matter further. Customary work-related activity is often measured by broad occupational classifications, which are poor proxies for pre-retirement physical activity. Even given more acceptable measures of manual occupational demands, comparison with retirement activity is untenable. Let us return to the stevedore example for illustration. Assume now that the researcher has pre-retirement data on the prevalence and frequency of "pulling, pushing, or lifting heavy objects," as is more often obtainable from national surveys. Of what value are such data to studying the stevedore's *change* in engaging these activities, which is the presumed catalyst for variations in well-being? Relief from such demands is implied by the transition to retirement, but a presumption of relief is hardly equivalent to actual measurement of change.

Faced with these constraints, the researcher has several options, each of which has unmistakable drawbacks. One is to ignore direct measurement of pre-retirement activity—relying on retirement to *imply* the termination of physical activity, which, as previously described, may be grossly represented by occupational classification or similar markers of the pre-retirement job. An alternative option is to examine leisure-time physical activity, which can be equivalently measured pre- and post-retirement but strongly discounts the elimination of employment-related activity. This approach is essentially a quasi-natural experiment of the impact of eliminating the time constraints imposed by employment. Yet another option is to rely on self-reported changes, provided in the post-retirement period. This final option places the responsibility on the respondent to define the scope of the physical activity (e.g., will the assessment include employment-based activity or not?), which can result in a great deal of heterogeneity in responses.

The scientific literature, which comprises two rather dated studies separated from a small assemblage of recent studies by nearly a decade, quite clearly exhibits these challenges. This low volume, coupled with wide diversity in measurement and methodology, makes it difficult to draw any definitive conclusions on whether and how retirement affects physical activity. Even so, an interesting, and fairly nuanced, literature has developed, with the balance of the findings suggesting increased physical activity post-retirement.

The earliest study in this area, an investigation of steel and factory workers in England (Patrick, Bassey, Irving, Blecher, & Fentem, 1986), may be the most comprehensive, despite several serious limitations including a small sample ($n = 64$) and no comparison group. This study, which was designed to assess retirement-related changes in the duration and intensity of physical activity, used body-borne miniature magnetic tape recorders to track heart rate elevation and footfall signals at two time points, approximately one year apart. Data on a subsample were taken at several additional follow-up periods.

The working and retirement measurement interval covered two discrete day-long periods—separated by several days—during which investigators gathered data on walking (time and intensity) and heart rate. Pre-retirement activity recordings were established during work shifts; post-retirement measurements were meant to capture routine movement and exertion. While the findings did not suggest variations in heart rate across the retirement transition, they did indicate significantly reduced walking among women factory workers.

The other early study (Midanik, Soghikian, Ransom, & Tekawa, 1995) assessed the effect of retirement on self-reports of regular exercise, using two periods of data ($N = 595$) sampled from a California health maintenance organization, Kaiser Permanente. Employing a residualized change methodology in which exercise at follow-up was covaried with its corresponding baseline measure, the authors found significantly increased risk of engaging in regular exercise associated with retirement. In fact, retired workers were nearly three times as likely to report regular exercise as similar individuals who did not retire over the two-year study frame, an effect that was inflated by an exceptionally strong effect (adjusted risk ratio = 3.5) among men. This finding, coupled with lower stress levels among participants who retired, led the authors to conclude that retirement was generally associated with increased well-being.

Of the four recent studies (Evenson, Rosamond, Cai, Diez-Roux, & Brancati, 2002; Henkens, van Solinge, & Gallo, 2008; Mein, Shipley, Hillsdon, Ellison, & Marmot, 2005; Slingerland et al., 2007), two have been performed in the Netherlands (Henkens et al., 2008; Slingerland et al., 2007). Assessing changes in health-enhancing physical activity among 684 retirees and a comparison group of 287 non-retirees in the Eindhoven area (the GLOBE study), Slingerland and colleagues reported that retirement reduced work-related transport activity but had no bearing on sports and non-sports-related leisure-time activity (Slingerland et al., 2007). Several methodological flaws in this study were nonetheless highlighted in a subsequent letter (Henkens, van Solinge, & Gallo, 2007) to the journal in which the GLOBE study was published. Foremost was the impetus for the seemingly patent finding regarding the decline in work-related transportation activity. Henkens et al. (2007) argued that time expended walking or bicycling *to work* was almost certain to decrease with retirement, even in the case that bridge employment was embedded in

the measure. The letter furthermore critiqued the GLOBE study's categorizing of the physical activity measures ("hardly ever," "<1 hour/week," "1–2 hours/week," and ">2 hours/week"), which created an artificial upper boundary at >2 hours/week. This truncation, or ceiling, precluded comprehensive evaluation of changes in physical activity between time points, as membership in this top-most category at the initial period ruled out inference of physical activity increase (Henkens et al., 2007).

Motivated by the recent evidence of more prevalent perceptions of forced retirement, the other Dutch report, part of the NIDI study (Henkens et al., 2008) analyzed panel data ($N = 1,064$) from 2001 and 2007 to test whether the perceived voluntariness of retirement provoked differences in self-reported change in physical activity. Reporting that both voluntary and involuntary retirements led to increases in physical activity, compared with remaining employed, the authors speculated that separate mechanisms could have motivated the findings. Whereas health investment, or the welcome introduction of leisure time, may have provoked more exercise or other related activity among the voluntarily retired, the imposition of unanticipated financial harm may have prompted the increase among the involuntarily retired. In other words, the authors suggested that the involuntarily retired may have had to substitute bicycling, walking, or other manual activities for car travel, public transport, and other activities that were within their financial means while working (Henkens et al., 2008).

The lone U.S. investigation analyzed 7,782 white and African American participants of the Atherosclerosis Risk in Communities (ARIC) Study (Evenson et al., 2002). Evaluating data on physical activity derived from the Baecke questionnaire (Baecke, Burema, & Frijters, 1982), which disaggregates sport, leisure, and work dimensions, this study found that participants who retired over the six-year observation period were more likely to increase their sports participation than non-retirees, with additional analyses suggesting a strong maintenance effect across the retirement boundary. Nevertheless, the authors also reported that retirees were more likely to increase their television viewing, obscuring the total effect of retirement on physical activity.

Data from the Whitehall II project were used to model physical activity in the context of phased retirement from civil service (Mein et al., 2005). In this study, information on quantity and frequency of a range of physical activities was used to classify retirees into those who met or exceeded United

Kingdom Department of Health recommendations and those who did not; sex-specific analyses were then conducted to assess whether there were differences in meeting the recommended physical activity standard by retirement status. The authors reported a graded effect, where both men and women who were completely retired (working hours = 0) had the highest likelihood of meeting the recommended standard, and those who were partially retired (< 30 hours) and who worked full-time in retirement (≥30 hours) demonstrating increasingly lower likelihood. While these findings do suggest that physical activity is enhanced by reducing work-related time constraints, its cross-sectional design limits any inference of causality that might be implied if observation of the retirement transition and measurement of pre-retirement activity were possible.

Alcohol Use

Evidence on the effects of retirement on alcohol use is inconclusive. In general, research in this area has been spotty, limited to a small assemblage of studies diverging in target samples and measurement. Several investigations have suggested that retirement leads to increased drinking or problem drinking, while others have found declines or no retirement-related change. Reasonable theoretical arguments for both positive and negative changes in alcohol consumption exist alongside these contradictory findings. The line of reasoning that supports increased drinking after retirement evolves from two general themes (Ekerdt, De Labry, Glynn, & Davis, 1989). First is the idea that retirement is associated with loss—for example, loss of status, professional position, identity, role, or employment-based social support. As such loss is assumed to be stressful (Rosow, 1974), from this perspective, retirement would naturally lead to increased or harmful drinking as a means of coping. Second is the notion that retirement introduces leisure time and wider social liberties. In this case, more unstructured time or reduced consequences for alcohol use would encourage greater alcohol use. Conceptual arguments for expecting decreased alcohol use following retirement, on the other hand, principally relate to the severance of social ties with colleagues who encourage drinking, and to relief from work-related stress (Ekerdt et al., 1989).

The scientific literature in this field dates back to a study by Ekerdt and colleagues in which drinking behavior was assessed over a two-year period among 416 community-dwelling men in a 1989 Veterans Administration Normative Aging Study in Boston (Ekerdt et al., 1989). Regularity of alcohol consumption and markers of problem drinking were compared at two time points by retirement status among 100 retirees and 316 men who remained employed. The results suggested that retired participants were more likely to report the onset of periodic heavy episodic drinking and problem drinking at follow-up than non-retirees. Ekerdt and colleagues attributed the findings to loss of status and esteem, and expanded opportunities for drinking.

Problem drinkers were the focus of two studies (Bacharach, Bamberger, Cohen, & Doveh, 2007; Neve, Lemmens, & Drop, 2000) that generated somewhat consistent results. A 2000 cohort study of residents of the Dutch Limburg province (Neve et al., 2000) found a decrease in alcohol-related problems associated with retirement. Analyzing data from two time points separated by nine years (1980–1989), this study assessed alcohol-related effects of several significant life transitions, including retirement, using Cahalan's summary measure of problem drinking (Cahalan & Cisin, 1968). The authors highlighted the fact that their results were inconsistent with Ekerdt's conceptual argument (Ekerdt et al., 1989) that the elimination of work as a life-structuring factor would tend to yield increased alcohol use. Similarly, a 2007 investigation of U.S. men (Bacharach et al., 2007) reported a decline in problem drinking after retirement. Analyzing workers selected from blue-collar occupations, selected because of the apparent permissive culture of drinking in blue-collar jobs, this longitudinal investigation focused on the effect of retirement on problem drinking in a group of 71 men with a history of problem drinking. A control sample of 236 without such a history was also studied. A secondary aim was to test whether changes in social support mediated the retirement–problem drinking relationship. The findings of this study indicated that retirement was related to a net decline in the severity of drinking problems among problem drinkers, a decline that was partially mediated by changes in the breadth of social support.

Somewhat mixed findings were implied by the Kaiser Permanente study (Midanik et al., 1995), which examined a range of alcohol measures, including heavy drinking, alcohol problems, and frequency of drunkenness. Whereas no changes in alcohol consumption and frequency of drunkenness were suggested by retirement status in the full analytic sample, a nearly threefold increase in alcohol problems was revealed for retirement among women, but not men. Quite in contrast, the sole

HRS study (Perreira & Sloan, 2001), which analyzed four waves of data (N = 3,907), found a considerably robust effect of retirement on alcohol use among men. Three related findings were reported. First, retirement elevated the risk of increased drinking by 60%. Second, among men with a history of problem drinking, retirement lowered the risk of reduced drinking by 30%. And finally, the retirement-related increases in alcohol use persisted up to four years after the transition. Similar results were suggested by the Dutch NIDI study (Henkens et al., 2008), which reported that retirement lowered by 53% the risk of reducing alcohol consumption.

Smoking

To our knowledge, only three studies have analyzed the impact of retirement on smoking, producing ambiguous results. As part of their broader study of behavioral consequences of retirement, Henkens and colleagues (Henkens et al., 2008) found that participants who perceived their retirements as involuntary had significantly higher risk of increased smoking and lower risk of decreased smoking than study members who continued to work. In contrast, a population-based cohort study in the United Kingdom (Lang, Rice, Wallace, Guralnik, & Melzer, 2007) used data from two waves of the ELSA to examine whether the transition to retirement was associated with increased risk of smoking cessation among 1,712 smokers aged 50 and above. Results suggested that retirees were more than twice as likely to quit smoking as those who were still employed at follow-up. Finally, the Kaiser Permanente study (Midanik et al., 1995) reported no changes in current smoking associated with retirement.

Weight Change

The potential impact of retirement on body weight has received moderate attention from researchers, stimulated by obesity's epidemic proportions in the United States, the imminent retirement of the baby-boom generation, and the related solvency of public health insurance programs for the elderly. The public costs of obesity-related health complications in an aging population are considerable, as obesity has been associated with increased morbidity and mortality from such major chronic diseases as stroke, diabetes, heart disease, and cancer (Finkelstein, Fiebelkorn, & Wang, 2003).

Researchers have been clear in pointing out that the path from retirement to weight change is not direct, where such factors as diet, physical activity, and sedentary behavior (Matthews et al., 2008) likely mediate the effect. Attributes of the pre-retirement job, notably physical demands, have been identified as important effect modifiers, and several have been studied. The introduction of leisure time, which may be used for health-promoting or health-harming activities that may influence weight, is also often discussed. As is the case with retirement research on other health behaviors, investigations of body weight have been helped by the introduction of the HRS, whose data have been analyzed in at least four recent studies.

The early research on body mass and weight change relied on anthropometric measurements to determine potential effects of retirement. These studies (Patrick, Bassey, & Fentem, 1982; Patrick et al., 1986), which were conducted on individuals retiring from manual work in the United Kingdom, assessed the impact of retirement on body fat and muscle mass. The initial investigation (Patrick et al., 1982) took measurements of body fat and muscle from a small sample (n = 73) of male steelworkers during the participants' last year of employment and a year after they retired. Standardized methods were used to assess body mass, percent body fat, fat mass, and fat-free mass. Five additional annual measurements of lateral soft-tissue radiographs of the thigh were taken from a subsample of 26 men to provide a more direct measure of fat and muscle width, and an accompanying questionnaire was used to provide a subjective assessment of whether participants noticed a change in physical activity one year after retirement. Significant changes in body fat and limb muscle were found, as body fat increased by 3% and limb muscle decreased by 1% one year post-retirement.

The follow-up study to the 1982 research (Patrick et al., 1986) assessed body weight and composition changes among three groups of retired steel and factory workers: 25 male steelworkers and 39 factory workers of both sexes. Its results demonstrated increases in thigh fat (5%) and body weight (2%) for female factory workers one year following retirement, a finding consistent with related decreases in physical activity (described above in the Physical Activity section), as well as a 5% decrease in thigh muscle mass among male factory workers. Changes in body weight and composition were not, however, observed among male steelworkers.

More recent research (Chung, Domino, & Stearns, 2009; Chung, Popkin, Domino, & Stearns, 2007; Forman-Hoffman et al., 2008; Gueorguieva, Sindelar, Wu, & Gallo, 2010) has examined secondary data from the HRS to examine variation in weight and body mass around the retirement transition. A 2007 report by Chung and colleagues (Chung et al., 2007) used five waves (1992–2002) of the HRS to determine whether retirement influenced household food consumption patterns, and, in turn, whether food consumption changes affected BMI. Its findings indicated that whereas retirement gave rise to less food consumption outside the home, at-home consumption patterns remained unaltered. Moreover, the decrease in food consumption outside the home resulted in an increase, albeit a rather small one, in BMI, a counterintuitive result that appears to have been caused by negative confounding with one or more adjustment variables. A follow-up study (Chung et al., 2009), which analyzed the same data set, investigated changes in BMI associated with retirement. Using an IV approach that was designed to account for the health-related endogeneity of retirement, the authors found a modest increase (1.45 lbs. for the average person) in BMI for the full sample. Stratified regressions furthermore demonstrated particularly strong effects (nearly four times the magnitude of the effect in the total sample) among participants with lower wealth and those previously employed in physically demanding occupations.

The remaining HRS studies (Forman-Hoffman et al., 2008; Gueorguieva et al., 2010) have analyzed weight changes with HRS data. Using the six waves (1994–2002) of the HRS, Forman-Hoffman and colleagues employed sex-stratified repeated measures analysis to determine whether retirement was associated with a 5% increase or decrease in BMI (relative to no change) over any two-wave period, reporting 24% increased odds of weight gain among women retirees. This effect was magnified among normal-weight women and those previously employed in blue-collar professions. No effect was found for men. A similar HRS investigation (Gueorguieva et al., 2010) explored trajectories of BMI up to six years after retirement by occupation type, its results suggesting that retirement precipitated a significant, consistent upward trend in BMI for blue-collar workers following a modest pre-retirement increase. The authors concluded that the observed BMI slope-change is likely attributable to the elimination of physically demanding work-related activity.

Only one recent investigation (Nooyens et al., 2005) has been performed outside of the United States. Nevertheless, its findings are quite consistent with those of the HRS studies. This Dutch analysis, undertaken in the rural region of Doetinchem, examined weight change and waist circumference among 288 males who retired from jobs in varying occupational classes, finding that individuals retired from physically active jobs had greater weight change and waist circumference than those who were previously employed in sedentary jobs.

Future Directions

Research on somatic health and behavioral effects of retirement has produced a set of conflicting, and sometimes confusing, results, which is hardly startling given that the meaning and experience of this significant life transition are extraordinarily variable. If one were to ask a layperson (i.e., non-scientist) whether retirement is good or bad for health, one could almost bet that in most cases the response would be "it depends." And surely this is an accurate rejoinder. A health or behavioral effect of retirement, if such a thing exists, should depend on many different factors, both perceptible and perceived, from life spheres starting with work (e.g., physical demands of the former job) and ending at home (e.g., perceived marital quality). "It depends" also extends to the cognitive framing of retirement. Limiting our example to variation in the former employment environment, it is conceivable that the "relief" experienced by retirees who endured poor decision latitude or excessive physical labor while employed could precipitate improvements in well-being, whereas the "loss" dealt to retirees whose positions afforded control, or apposite cognitive requirements that engendered occupational esteem, could be health damaging in some way. Yet obviously this is not the whole story. That is, even among the subgroups, health in retirement will be differentiated. There is no reason, for example, to think that all manual laborers will benefit from the discontinuation of their daily physical work regimen. Whereas many former manual workers will use their expanded leisure time as an opportunity to invest in their well-being—perhaps exercising more or performing more targeted (i.e., less routine) physical effort—others will become sedentary, drawing down the health benefits of manual labor. While this type of argument can be extended to the level of case study, there is really no need to do so. Its essence should now be clear. Retirement is in no way a classic health exposure (such as, for example, smoking), and empirical attempts to treat it as such will only add to the confusion about its association with health.

This is not to suggest, of course, that researchers strongly discount the evidence from observational studies, whose findings for the average retiree in a given sample comprise the basis of our knowledge on this topic. It is rather to encourage that a reasonable skepticism be applied to evaluating the results, given the following realities: (a) there exist legitimate theoretical models that support the notion of retirement as health promoting and health harming; (b) studies have not so adequately accounted for pre-retirement well-being as to dampen the notion that post-retirement health is merely a continuation of health prior to retirement; and (c) research on physical health and health behaviors has thus far taken a naive view of an exceptionally complex process, insufficiently treating sample heterogeneity and largely ignoring the intricacies of the retirement transition.

Of these three realities, the first is virtually immutable. Within each of the major paradigms of retirement research (namely, stressful life events, life course, role, and continuity theories), situational determinants—in conjunction with how they are appraised, dealt with, and adjusted to—may dictate either positive or negative health outcomes. To have a sense of how different retirement is from a classic exposure, such as cigarette smoking, imagine suggesting that the perceived importance, or centrality, of smoking leads one group of smokers to develop lung cancer and another to increase breathing capacity or lung volume. This would be a ludicrous claim in the context of smoking. However, it is not at all out of place in retirement theory. Indeed, two groups of workers who offer dissimilar assessments of the importance of their occupational roles, but are otherwise quite comparable, might well be hypothesized to exhibit opposite health or behavioral effects after retirement. If there is an exception to this reality, it is the designation of forced retirement. Non-normative retirements carry an explicitly negative "charge" that distinguishes them from on-time retirements, the result of which is considerably less ambiguity in application of a particular retirement theory. Data from the Dutch NIDI study (van Solinge, 2007), which scales this "charge" according to *how* forced, or involuntary, the retirement is perceived to be, is an exciting advance and should be replicated in other aging and retirement studies.

The second reality, though perhaps less absolute than the first, remains a thorny point in the literature and should therefore be kept in mind while reading the scientific studies on retirement. It concedes that it is very difficult to attribute health changes

to retirement when researchers who perform observational studies normally know quite little about retirees' long-term health trajectories prior to initial observation. A glimmer of hope is provided by the large national retirement surveys, administered in many countries now, which first survey participants approximately a decade before normal retirement age, the point at which common chronic diseases typically first emerge. Nonetheless, critical information on well-being and behavior prior to midlife, which is necessary to obtain a more complete rendering of the relevant trajectory, remains missing.

The final reality is the least absolute, and therefore the most vulnerable to advances in methodology. Two issues are subsumed within this reality: individual heterogeneity and heterogeneity of retirement transition. Take a look at the first issue. It could be reasonably argued that much of retirement research has essentially looked upon all retirees as a uniform set of economic actors, while this is plainly not the case. Whereas sex stratification, which is meant to account for differences in labor force attachment and occupation class (Kasl, 1980), has often been applied to retirement studies of physical health and health behaviors, few other attempts to differentiate retirees have been made. Yet examples of differentiation abound. Behavioral norms, which may involve attitudes toward body weight or use of tobacco, imaginably vary by occupational category, as do various forms of work stress. These are just two examples of many. The point is that, in the subfield of retirement research reviewed in this chapter, there is a pressing need to separately assess strata of retirees whose health and/or behavior are distinctly intertwined with their personal attributes, occupational characteristics, labor force participation, or retirement likelihood.

Now consider the second issue: differences in the path to retirement. Indirect retirement transitions persist despite what appears to be the end of the decades-long trend toward earlier labor force withdrawal, at least in the United States (Toosi, 2004). Yet although considerable time has passed since the first attempts to model retirement's complexity (Moen, 1996; Mutchler, Burr, Pienta, & Massagli, 1997), relatively little progress has been made in the outcomes addressed in this chapter. Bridge employment, forced retirement, and late-career layoff remain increasingly common pathways to permanent labor force withdrawal and must be accounted for in future research on these particular outcomes.

The bad news is that empirical analysis of pathways to retirement is no simple matter. Nearly prohibitive data requirements—necessary for inferring the effects of individual differences and reasonably distinct paths from work to retirement—make necessary complex modeling of indirect retirement. The good news is, however, that an enormous head start has been provided by work on mental health effects of retirement (Wang, 2007) and late-career job loss (Deb, Gallo, Ayyagari, Fletcher, & Sindelar, 2011), which have used latent variable methods to confront many of these data limitations. Finite mixture modeling (FMM) and growth mixture modeling (GMM), two of the latent modeling techniques, have the potential to unmask sample heterogeneity and identify complex pathways to retirement and beyond. Mixture models have yielded critical differences in retirement transitions (Wang, 2007). Their application to physical health and behavioral impacts of retirement, in which numerous additive and competing variables are simultaneously at play, will very likely lead to additional important findings.

Mixture models have specific appeal for retirement research. First, while the allure of such models is enhanced when there is conceptual support for the classification and differential behavior of the latent groups, a firm theoretical basis is not necessary. Thus, mixtures may simply prove a means of parsimoniously partitioning the sample (Deb et al., 2011). This is important for retirement research, in which there exist equally plausible conceptual arguments for health-promoting and health-harming impacts, as has been repeatedly suggested. Second, mixture models permit the relationship of retirement to the outcomes of interest to be performed within subpopulations that include small percentages of participants, whereas definitive (i.e. manual) classification naturally leads to statistical power problems. Finally, mixture models capture sample heterogeneity that is based on complex configurations of factors, which are generally not apparent from observed data. In a practical way, what this means is that uncommon groups that demonstrate particular health vulnerability to the experience of retirement can be identified for intervention. So, for example, if it is professional workers with low-stress jobs but poor marital quality who exhibit clinically significant increases in alcohol use after retirement, mixture models can isolate this group, while traditional statistical techniques would exhaust most samples in the process of multiple stratification. Similarly, mixture models can help researchers determine whether the health of retirees who suffered late-career job loss, in particular those who experienced multiple employment transitions post–job loss, would differ from those who followed a linear path to retirement.

Scientific investigation of the relationship between retirement and physical health and health behaviors has evolved somewhat slowly, largely leaving unknown whether and how retirement affects these particular dimensions of well-being. Moreover, while it is commonly accepted that retirement will not affect all groups of workers equally, few legitimate attempts have been made to identify which groups are susceptible to negative (or positive) effects of retirement. If retirement is to be accepted as so significant a life transition as to affect health, then future studies must combine longitudinal data with state-of-the-art statistical methods to isolate workers whose physical health and health behaviors are affected by retirement. Only then will conclusions regarding the impact of retirement on physical health and health behaviors be possible.

Author Note

I would like to acknowledge Huei-wern Shen, Dana Friedman, Lauren Evans, and Xu Wang for their assistance on earlier versions of this chapter.

References

Bacharach, S., Bamberger, P., Cohen, A., & Doveh, E. (2007). Retirement, social support and drinking behavior: A cohort analysis of males with a baseline history of problem drinking. *Journal of Drug Issues, 37*, 525–549.

Baecke, J. A., Burema, J., & Frijters, J. E. (1982). A short questionnaire for the measurement of habitual physical activity in epidemiological studies. *American Journal of Clinical Nutrition, 36*, 936–942.

Bamia, C., Trichopoulou, A., & Trichopoulos, D. (2008). Age at retirement and mortality in a general population sample: The Greek EPIC study. *American Journal of Epidemiology, 167*, 561–569. doi: kwm337 [pii] 10.1093/aje/kwm337.

Behncke, S. (2009). *How does retirement affect health?* Bonn, Germany: Institute for the Study of Labor (IZA).

Brockmann, H., Muller, R., & Helmert, U. (2009). Time to retire—time to die? A prospective cohort study of the effects of early retirement on long-term survival. *Social Science & Medicine, 69*, 160–164. doi: S0277-9536(09)00237-8 [pii] 10.1016/j.socscimed.2009.04.009.

Cahalan, D., & Cisin, I. H. (1968). American drinking practices: Summary of findings from a national probability sample. *Quarterly Journal of Studies on Alcohol, 29*, 130–151.

Casscells, W., Hennekens, C. H., Evans, D., Rosener, B., De Silva, R. A., Lown, B., . . . Jesse, M. J.(1980). Retirement and coronary mortality. *Lancet, 1*(8181), 1288–1289.

Chung, S., Domino, M. E., & Stearns, S. C. (2009). The effect of retirement on weight. *Journal of Gerontology: Social Sciences, 64B*, 656–665. doi:10.1093/geronb/gbn044.

Chung, S., Popkin, B. M., Domino, M. E., & Stearns, S. C. (2007). Effect of retirement on eating out and weight change:

An analysis of gender differences. *Obesity, 15,* 1053–1060. doi:10.1038/oby.2007.538.

Dave, D., Rashad, I., & Spasojevic, J. (2008). The effects of retirement on physical and mental health outcomes. *Southern Economic Journal, 75,* 497–523.

Deb, P., Gallo, W. T., Ayyagari, P., Fletcher, J. M., & Sindelar, J. S. (2011). The effect of job loss on overweight and drinking. *Journal of Health Economics, 30,* 317–327.

Ekerdt, D. J. (1987). Why the notion persists that retirement harms health. *The Gerontologist, 27,* 454–457. doi: 10.1093/geront/27.4.454.

Ekerdt, D. J., Baden, L., Bosse, R., & Dibbs, E. (1983). The effect of retirement on physical health. *American Journal of Public Health, 73,* 779–783.

Ekerdt, D. J., Bosse, R., & Goldie, C. (1983). The effect of retirement on somatic complaints. *Journal of Psychosomatic Research, 27,* 61–67.

Ekerdt, D. J., De Labry, L., Glynn, R., & Davis, R. (1989). Change in drinking behaviors with retirement: Findings from the normative aging study. *Journal of Studies on Alcohol, 50,* 347–353.

Ekerdt, D. J., Sparrow, D., Glynn, R. J., & Bosse, R. (1984). Change in blood pressure and total cholesterol with retirement. *American Journal of Epidemiology, 120,* 64–71.

Evenson, K. R., Rosamond, W. D., Cai, J., Diez-Roux, A. V., & Brancati, F. L. (2002). Influence of retirement on leisure-time physical activity. The Atherosclerosis Risk in Communities Study. *American Journal of Epidemiology, 155,* 692–699. doi: 10.1093/aje/155.8.692.

Finkelstein, E. A., Fiebelkorn, I. C., & Wang, G. (2003). National medical spending attributable to overweight and obesity: How much, and who's paying? *Health Affairs (Millwood), Supplemental Web Exclusives,* W3-219-W3-226.

Forman-Hoffman, V. L., Richardson, K. K., Yankey, J. W., Hillis, S. L., Wallace, R. B., & Wolinsky, F. D. (2008). Retirement and weight changes among men and women in the Health and Retirement Study. *Journal of Gerontology: Social Sciences, 63,* S146–S153.

Gueorguieva, R., Sindelar, J. L., Wu, R., & Gallo, W. T. (2010). Differential changes in body mass index after retirement by occupation: Hierarchical models. *International Journal of Public Health, 56,* 111–116. doi: 10.1007/s00038-010-0166-z.

Haynes, S. G., McMichael, A. J., & Tyroler, H. A. (1978). Survival after early and normal retirement. *Journal of Gerontology, 33,* 269–278.

Henkens, K., van Solinge, H., & Gallo, W. (2007). RE: "Aging, retirement, and changes in physical activity: Prospective cohort findings from the globe study." *American Journal of Epidemiology, 166,* 2. doi:10.1093/aje/kwm208.

Henkens, K., van Solinge, H., & Gallo, W. T. (2008). Effects of retirement voluntariness on changes in smoking, drinking and physical activity among Dutch older workers. *European Journal of Public Health, 18,* 644–649. doi:10.1093/eurpub/ckn095.

Jokela, M., Ferrie, J. E., Gimeno, D., Chandola, T., Shipley, M. J., Head, J.,…Kivimaki, M. (2010). From midlife to early old age: Health trajectories associated with retirement. *Epidemiology, 21,* 284–290. doi: 10.1097/EDE.0b013e3181d61f53.

Kasl, S. V. (1980). The impact of retirement. In C. L. Cooper & R. Payne (Eds.), *Current concerns in occupational stress* (pp. 137–186). New York, NY: John Wiley.

Kasl, S. V., & Jones, B. A. (2000). The impact of job loss and retirement on health. In L. F. Berkman & I. Kawachi (Eds.), *Social epidemiology* (pp. 118–136). New York, NY: Oxford University Press.

Kremer, Y. (1985). The association between health and retirement: Self-health assessment of Israeli retirees. *Social Science & Medicine, 20,* 61–66.

Lang, I. A., Rice, N. E., Wallace, R. B., Guralnik, J. M., & Melzer, D. (2007). Smoking cessation and transition into retirement: Analyses from the English Longitudinal Study of Ageing. *Age and Ageing, 36,* 638–643. doi: 10.1093/ageing/afm119.

Litwin, H. (2007). Does early retirement lead to longer life? *Ageing and Society, 27,* 739–754.

Matthews, C. E., Chen, K. Y., Freedson, P. S., Buchowski, M. S., Beech, B. M., Pate, R. R., & Troiano, R. P.(2008). Amount of time spent in sedentary behaviors in the United States, 2003–2004. *American Journal of Epidemiology, 167,* 875–881. doi: kwm390 [pii] 10.1093/aje/kwm390.

Mein, G. K., Martikainen, P., Hemingway, H., Stansfeld, S., & Marmot, M. G. (2003). Is retirement good or bad for mental and physical health functioning? Whitehall II longitudinal study of civil servants. *Journal of Epidemiology and Community Health, 57,* 46–49.

Mein, G. K., Shipley, M. J., Hillsdon, M., Ellison, G. T., & Marmot, M. G. (2005). Work, retirement and physical activity: Cross-sectional analyses from the Whitehall II study. *European Journal of Public Health, 15,* 317–322. doi: 10.1093/eurpub/cki087.

Midanik, L. T., Soghikian, K., Ransom, L. J., & Tekawa, I. S. (1995). The effect of retirement on mental health and health behaviors: The Kaiser Permanente Retirement Study. *Journal of Gerontology: Social Sciences, 50B,* S59–S61. doi: 10.1093/geronb/50B.1.S59.

Moen, P. (1996). A life course perspective on retirement, gender, and well-being. *Journal of Occupational Health Psychology, 1,* 131–144.

Mojon-Azzi, S., Sousa-Poza, A., & Widmer, R. (2007). The effect of retirement on health: A panel analysis using data from the Swiss Household Panel. *Swiss Medical Weekly, 137,* 581–585. doi: smw-11841 [pii] 2007/41/smw-11841.

Morris, J. K., Cook, D. G., & Shaper, A. G. (1994). Loss of employment and mortality. *BMJ, 308,* 1135–1139.

Mutchler, J. E., Burr, J. A., Pienta, A. M., & Massagli, M. P. (1997). Pathways to labor force exit: Work transitions and work instability. *Journal of Gerontology: Social Sciences, 52,* S4–S12.

Neuman, K. (2008). Quit your job and get healthier? The effect of retirement on health. *Journal of Labor Research, 29,* 177–201.

Neve, R. J. M., Lemmens, P. H., & Drop, M. J. (2000). Changes in alcohol use and drinking problems in relation to role transitions in different stages of the life course. *Substance Abuse, 21,* 163–178.

Nooyens, A. C., Visscher, T. L., Schuit, A. J., van Rossum, C. T., Verschuren, W. M., van Mechelen, W., & Seidell, J. C. (2005). Effects of retirement on lifestyle in relation to changes in weight and waist circumference in Dutch men: A prospective study. *Public Health Nutrition, 8,* 1266–1274. doi: S1368980005001527 [pii].

Patrick, J. M., Bassey, E. J., & Fentem, P. H. (1982). Changes in body fat and muscle in manual workers at and after retirement. *European Journal of Applied Physiology and Occupational Physiology, 49,* 187–196. doi: 10.1007/bf02334067.

Patrick, J. M., Bassey, E. J., Irving, J. M., Blecher, A., & Fentem, P. H. (1986). Objective measurements of customary physical activity in elderly men and women before and after retirement. *Experimental Physiology, 71*, 47–58.

Perreira, K. M., & Sloan, F. A. (2001). Life events and alcohol consumption among mature adults: A longitudinal analysis. *Journal of Studies on Alcohol, 62,* 501–508.

Rosow, J. M. (1974). Work requirements, work incentives: Their role in public assistance. *The Social and Rehabilitation Record, 1*, 27–31.

Slingerland, A. S., van Lenthe, F. J., Jukema, J. W., Kamphuis, C. B. M., Looman, C., Giskes, K., ... Brug, J. (2007). Aging, retirement, and changes in physical activity: Prospective cohort findings from the GLOBE study. *American Journal of Epidemiology, 165*, 1356–1363. doi: 10.1093/aje/kwm053.

Swan, G. E., Dame, A., & Carmelli, D. (1991). Involuntary retirement, Type A behavior, and current functioning in elderly men: 27-year follow-up of the Western Collaborative Group Study. *Psychology and Aging, 6*, 384–391.

Toosi, M. (2004). Labor force projections in 2012: The graying of the U.S. workforce. *Monthly Labor Review, 127*, 37–57.

Tsai, S. P., Wendt, J. K., Donnelly, R. P., de Jong, G., & Ahmed, F. S. (2005). Age at retirement and long term survival of an industrial population: Prospective cohort study. *BMJ, 331*, 995. doi: bmj.38586.448704.E0 [pii] 10.1136/bmj.38586.448704.E0.

Tuomi, K., Jarvinen, E., Eskelinen, L., Ilmarinen, J., & Klockars, M. (1991). Effect of retirement on health and work ability among municipal employees. *Scandinavian Journal of Work, Environonment, and Health, 17* (Suppl. 1), 75–81.

van Solinge, H. (2007). Health change in retirement: A longitudinal study among older workers in the Netherlands. *Research on Aging, 29*, 225–256.

Wang, M. (2007). Profiling retirees in the retirement transition and adjustment process: Examining the longitudinal change patterns of retirees' psychological well-being. *Journal of Applied Psychology, 92*, 455–474.

Wang, M., & Shultz, K. (2010). Employee retirement: A review and recommendations for future investigation. *Journal of Management, 36*, 172–206.

Westerlund, H., Kivimaki, M., Singh-Manoux, A., Melchior, M., Ferrie, J. E., Pentti, J., ... Vahtera, J. (2009). Self-rated health before and after retirement in France (GAZEL): A cohort study. *Lancet, 374*, 1889–1896. doi: S0140-6736(09)61570-1 [pii] 10.1016/S0140-6736(09)61570-1.

Leisure Activities in Retirement

Lorraine T. Dorfman

Abstract

The literature reviewed in this chapter points to a number of conclusions regarding leisure activity in retirement. Retirees participate in many different kinds of activities including informal activities with friends and family; formal social participation in clubs, organizations, and volunteering; and individual solitary activities. These activities provide meaning through relaxation, personal growth, feelings of achievement, and giving back to the community. Retirees continue pre-retirement leisure activities and also engage in new leisure activities after retiring, thus supporting major theoretical perspectives in gerontology and adult development. Personal characteristics—in particular gender, health, and socioeconomic status—are correlated with leisure activity in retirement. Participation in leisure activities is associated with psychosocial and physical well-being in retirement, although the direction of causality is not clearly established. Future directions for research are identified.

Key Words: formal activity, gender, health, informal activity, leisure meaning, socioeconomic status, solitary activity, well-being

Many people look forward to retirement as a long-awaited opportunity to spend time in personally satisfying, meaningful pursuits that may have been postponed because of the demands of labor force participation. When retirement occurs, retirees have the choice of engaging in any number of activities that promise to be rewarding for them. A common way of spending time in retirement is in some kind of leisure activity, which has been defined by Kelly (1982) as "something that is done for its own sake that provides intrinsic satisfaction and freedom of choice" (p. 32). What constitutes leisure activity, however, is rather subjective, with retired individuals defining for themselves the activities that they view as "leisure." To illustrate, gardening might be viewed as a necessary chore by one retiree, whereas for another it is a pleasurable leisure activity. Likewise, volunteer work or even paid work may be viewed as "leisure" activity by one retiree

but as "work" by another. What is common in both these cases is that the activities involve choice and self-determination.

Hendricks and Cutler (1990) suggest that after withdrawing from the labor force, leisure activities can become a central focus of the retiree's life. They also point out that leisure may become even more important in the lives of older people in the future because of increasing life expectancy, improvements in health, changes in the broader economy, and a complex retirement picture that includes early retirement for some individuals and movement in and out of the labor force for others (Hendricks & Cutler, 2003). Additionally, the unprecedented number of baby boomers now moving into their retirement years can be expected to increase the salience of leisure activity for older individuals and for society as a whole.

This chapter begins with a discussion of the various meanings of leisure and reviews major theoretical perspectives that are relevant to leisure activity in retirement. It goes on to describe leisure activities that retirees participate in most frequently and the correlates of leisure participation. The chapter then examines the relationship between leisure activity and various measures of well-being in retirement, and concludes by offering some directions for the future.

Meanings of Leisure

The meanings of leisure are numerous and reflect an individual's life history, opportunities, choices, and values. Often the same leisure activity can have several meanings for a given individual. The various meanings of leisure discussed below appear frequently in the research literature; however, no rank ordering of their importance is implied.

Relaxation/Play

Retirement, of course, holds the promise of freedom from work commitments and free time to do as one wishes. Retirees have reported "freedoms from ..." as an important aspect of retirement; for some retirees, retirement is seen as a new beginning, a new phase of life with the opportunity to leave behind the structure and responsibilities of work and to relax and enjoy newfound free time (Gibson, Ashton-Shaeffer, Green, & Corbin, 2002; Wang & Shultz, 2010). Lawton (1993) describes this reaction as an experiential dimension of retirement, with intrinsic satisfaction gained from time for diversion and relaxation. In a longitudinal study of Harvard men over a fifty-year time period, Vaillant (2002) found that the activities that helped make retirement rewarding for the men included ones that helped them rediscover how to play, which may have been forgotten or postponed in their busy lives. Vaillant described play in retirement as "learning how to maintain self-respect while letting go of self-importance" (p. 229).

Provide Meaning/Direction and Personal Growth

One of the challenges of retirement is to find activities that can provide the personal meaning, direction, and satisfaction that the work role had previously provided (Hendricks & Cutler, 2003). These activities may contribute to the individual's feelings of self-actualization, identity, and self-concept (Hendricks & Cutler, 1990, 2003; Kelly, 1982; Lawton, 1993; McGuire, Boyd, & Tedrick, 2009; O'Brien, 1988; Wang, 2007). Hendricks and Cutler (1990) note that if leisure becomes the functional equivalent of work, it may help to maintain feelings of identity and self-concept that were once provided by work. That work role will probably have spanned many decades and become a central part of the individual's identity and self-concept. The challenge for the retiree is to find those specific leisure activities that can provide some of the rewards and personal gratifications that were once provided by the work role. For some retired individuals, this may mean experimenting with completely new roles after they retire.

In their study of women who had retired mainly from professional careers, Gibson et al. (2002) found that meaning and direction in retirement were expressed in volunteering, an activity that often utilizes some of the same professional skills that were garnered and expressed in the work role. Meaning can likewise be found in leisure activities such as taking classes or seminars where retirees learn new things (Thang, 2005; Wang & Shultz, 2010). Although common retirement activities such as volunteering and taking classes can provide these rewards, more unusual activities have also been found to provide personal gratification and opportunities for growth. This was the case for a group of retirees in North Carolina who participated in shag dancing, a form of "serious leisure" that contributed to feelings of identity (as shaggers) and provided a means of self-expression (Brown, McGuire, & Voelkl, 2008).

Feelings of Achievement

Leisure activities can contribute to feelings of achievement in retirement by giving the retiree the opportunity to demonstrate mastery or a sense of accomplishment (Brown et al., 2008; Kelly, 1982) as well as providing opportunities for creativity (McGuire et al., 2009; Vaillant, 2002) and providing the environment in which such activities can take place and are enhanced (Thang, 2005). Lifelong learning, creative hobbies, attending book clubs, artistic activities, and applying a particular skill that may have been developed in the workplace are all examples of activities that can result in feelings of achievement. At the same time, retirees may be demonstrating a "busy ethic" (Ekerdt, 1986) that replaces the feelings of achievement formerly provided by participation in the workforce by engaging in a number of activities that utilize their mental and physical skills and that demonstrate continued engagement and productivity during the retirement years. In this way, they may be as "busy" as during their working years.

Being Useful/Giving Back

In terms of adult psychosocial development, retirement may be a time of life when people can both demonstrate continued generativity, in terms of helping others and contributing to society through productive activity, and at the same time achieve a sense of integrity in old age by feeling that they are doing something meaningful with their lives (Erikson, Erikson, & Kivnick, 1986). Many retirees feel that retirement is a phase of life when they finally have the time and opportunity to give back to their communities and to the larger society (Gibson et al., 2002; Kelly, 1982). Kelly (1982) describes this motivation as a desire to build community, whereas McGuire et al. (2009) note that such leisure activities may also reflect a need to be needed. Whatever their motivation, however, retirees can be useful in many different ways: by engaging in a multitude of volunteer roles; by providing informal help to family, friends, and neighbors; and by being a mentor and role model for younger people.

Social Interaction

Among other things, the work role provides opportunities for social interaction with colleagues who frequently also become friends. Consequently, many retirees look for social interaction and a sense of belongingness in leisure activities to replace the lost social contacts at work. In the long-term Harvard Study of Adult Development, Vaillant (2002) found that one of the things that made retirement rewarding for the men was being able to replace their workmates with other social network contacts after they retired. Many different settings ranging from socially oriented clubs to formal organizational participation can provide opportunities for such companionship. Likewise, opportunities for social interaction and forming new friendships may be found in regularly performed group physical activities (Brown et al., 2008).

Health/Keeping Fit

Lastly, students of leisure have noted the importance of health and keeping fit as one of the meanings and rewards of leisure (Kelly, 1982; McGuire et al., 2009; Zhan, Wang, Liu, & Shultz, 2009). This is obviously a concern of older people as they face or expect to face declines in energy and health over time. Consequently, "working out" and regular activities such as walking, swimming, and working around the house and garden can play an important role in the activity repertoire of retired people.

Theoretical Perspectives
Activity Theory

An early theory in social gerontology suggested that in order to age successfully, retired people need to maintain high activity levels, which in turn contribute to social integration and life satisfaction (Havighurst & Albrecht, 1953). Essentially, activity theory posits a positive relationship between activity and late-life satisfaction and suggests that the greater the role loss, the lower the satisfaction (Lemon, Bengston, & Peterson, 1972). The theory further argues that positive aging is related to maintaining the activity levels of middle age and that it is important to replace lost roles with new ones (McGuire et al., 2009; Zhan et al., 2009). This, however, may not always be feasible given the health issues and declining energy that can accompany advancing age. Activity theory can be applied to a wide variety of activities: to informal activities such as visiting with and/or helping family, friends, and neighbors; to formal participation in volunteering or as a member of clubs and organizations; and to solitary activities such as listening to the radio or watching television, reading, or engaging in a hobby on one's own. Activity theory shares some similar concepts with role theory in that it proposes a relationship between the social roles that individuals play and outcomes such as a sense of identity and self-concept (McGuire et al., 2009; Wang, 2007).

There is more evidence to support the activity theory of aging than another early theory, disengagement theory, which holds that in order to age successfully, it is adaptive for older people to withdraw from work and other social roles (Cumming & Henry, 1961). According to disengagement theory, this withdrawal is mutual, with society withdrawing social roles from the individual as he or she ages and the individual withdrawing from society. Research such as the MacArthur Studies of Successful Aging (Rowe & Kahn, 1997), a long-term, multidisciplinary effort involving data from several nations, refute this premise by documenting that successful aging is characterized by continued active engagement in life. Applied to leisure activity in retirement, the MacArthur studies suggest a positive relationship between leisure participation and positive adjustment to retirement. Other studies also provide support for tenets of activity theory by pointing to increased leisure participation in retirement (Agahi & Parker, 2005; Iwasaki & Smale, 1998; Nimrod, 2008a; Nimrod & Kleiber, 2007). Agahi and Parker (2005), for example, reported an increase in leisure participation in all four clusters of activities under investigation (social/cultural, physical, intellectual, and expressive) in two samples of Swedish respondents aged 77+ that were collected in 1992 and 2002. Interestingly, in that study the overall level of leisure participation was higher among the 2002 respondents, even though reported mobility of the 2002 respondents was poorer. Retirees may also be adding completely new leisure activities to their leisure repertoire that may substitute for the lost work role; for example, Nimrod and Kleiber (2007) found that 19 of the 20 individuals enrolled in a Learning in Retirement class had added at least one new activity since retiring, and the average number of activities added was 4.68. Agahi, Ahacic, and Parker (2006) also reported that some individuals added new leisure activities during retirement, such as restaurant visits, dancing, and study circles.

Selective Optimization with Compensation

In some ways related to activity theory is the model of selective optimization with compensation (SOC) (Baltes & Baltes, 1990; Baltes & Carstensen, 1996). Elements of this model include *selection*, in which the older individual concentrates on fewer activities and life domains that have most priority; *optimization*, in which the individual engages in particular activities or behaviors that enrich his or her life; and *compensation*, in which certain behavioral capacities are lost but are compensated for by other perhaps less strenuous or demanding activities. The model of selective optimization with compensation may help explain how retired people adjust their activity levels over time to adapt to decrements in health and energy, and how they choose particular activities that are more appropriate to their current abilities while still being able to attain their goals. For example, a retiree may not be able to leave home to attend meetings of a club or organization but may be able to socialize with friends and family who come to visit, which results in some restructuring of the person's social world.

Baltes and Baltes (1990) observe that socioemotional selectivity theory is a variant of the selective optimization with compensation model. According to socioemotional selectivity theory, people select emotionally meaningful interactions and activities and therefore have the option of reducing or eliminating certain social contacts as they grow older if they choose (Baltes & Carstensen, 1996). It should be noted that the socioemotional selectivity theory is operating on the basis of time perspective change during the aging process, whereas the SOC model operates more on the basis of aging-related reduction in physical and cognitive capacity. These two theoretical perspectives complement each other in understanding retirees' motivation and participation in activities. Hendricks and Cutler (2004), in a test of volunteerism and socioemotional selectivity theory, suggest that the theory attempts to find a middle ground between the assumption that people withdraw from social involvements in later life and the belief that they continue the level of social involvement of earlier phases of the life course.

Continuity Theory

Continuity theory (Atchley, 1993, 1999, 2003) has received considerable support in gerontology and includes a number of concepts that can be usefully applied to leisure activity and retirement. Essentially, continuity theory is a theory of adult development and posits that it is adaptive for older adults to continue activities and behavioral patterns that were established earlier in life (Atchley, 1993). Additionally, continuity theory proposes that two types of continuity, values and personality ("internal continuity") and activities and lifestyle ("external continuity"), are important in the continuing process of adult development in later life. Atchley (1993) claims that external continuity can help older people cope with the changes that occur in later life; it is reasonable to expect that this will hold for such later-life transitions as retirement. Atchley noted earlier (1971) that leisure activity in retirement can also provide identity continuity because many people have skills that they can carry over into retirement activities.

Continuity theory presumes that "most people continuously learn from their life experiences and intentionally continue to grow and evolve in directions of their own choosing" (Atchley, 2003, p. 125). Continuity is seen as a general pattern that allows also for adaptive change to new circumstances to occur. It is important to point out, however, that although change can and does occur in the continuity theory perspective, the theory suggests that most people will prefer continuity to the extent that it is possible (Atchley, 1993).

Research in both the United States and other countries has provided empirical support for continuity theory. Recently, Pushkar et al. (2010), in an investigation of seventeen optional activities that included social, leisure, exercise, creative, and volunteer activities in retirement, found that only 13% and 12% of activity frequency scores either increased or decreased over time. The authors concluded that continuity of these "voluntary" activities was dominant. Earlier, Bossé and Ekerdt (1981) tracked self-perception of leisure activities of men in a Veterans Administration sample over a three-year period from pre- to post-retirement. Contrary to both hypothesis and retirees' pre-retirement expectations, the authors found continuity in retirees' perception of leisure activities over that time period. Also in a study of retirees over time, Atchley (1999) reported stability in activity levels in retired men and women over a two-year period. In a nationally representative sample of the Swedish population and a study of the oldest old in Sweden, Agahi et al. (2006) found continuity in leisure activities for all nine leisure activities investigated over three waves of data collection, although some individuals also started new activities. And in a Scottish sample of men studied within six months prior to retirement and again 12–18 months post-retirement, the most common pattern was not to take up new activities, but to spend more time in things they had done earlier (Long, 1987).

Life Course Theory

Although several theoretical approaches had contributed earlier to what became known as the life course perspective, its concepts were systematized and integrated by Elder and his colleagues (Elder & Johnson, 2003; Elder, Johnson, & Crosnoe, 2003). Life course theory has five major principles: (1) human development and aging are processes that continue throughout life; (2) individuals have agency—that is, people have the ability to construct their own life course through their own choices and actions (within the parameters of the time and place they live); (3) the life course of individuals is shaped by the historical times and places they experience; (4) timing of events is important in a person's life; and (5) lives are linked and lived interdependently (Elder & Johnson, 2003; Elder, Johnson, & Crosnoe, 2003). The first and second principles of life course theory are particularly applicable to the study of leisure activity and retirement. First, leisure activities are developmental and often reflect interests and activities developed earlier in an individual's life course. For example, an artist may enjoy teaching children in volunteer art projects during retirement, thus both continuing a lifelong commitment to artistic endeavors and helping transmit that interest and commitment to younger generations. Likewise, highly educated professionals may decide to take Learning in Retirement classes that reflect their intellectual interests, or use their professional skills to serve others, such as a lawyer who helps staff

a free legal clinic. Second, retired individuals have agency or choice in selecting and continuing leisure activities that they consider personally meaningful and worthwhile. This may vary over the course of retirement, so that a retiree may decide early in retirement to learn a new foreign language in order to facilitate travel plans, and later when travel is less feasible decide to take some adult education classes. Retirees choose leisure activities based on the alternatives they perceive are available to them within the social context in which they happen to live. Consequently, an urban-dwelling retiree may have many more leisure choices available to her or him (say at a senior center that offers many educational and social activities) than does a retiree living in a remote rural community with few leisure options.

Types of Leisure Activity

In a study conducted by Weiss (2005), one-fifth of the respondents followed from pre-retirement into retirement said they wanted to retire in order to gain the leisure time that retirement promised, highlighting the desire for leisure among recent retirees. As mentioned earlier, some research does show an increase in leisure activity participation after retirement (e.g., Agahi & Parker, 2005; Iwasaki & Smale; 1998; Rosenkoetter, Garris, & Engdahl, 2001). Rosenkoetter et al. (2001) observed an increase in frequency of participation in a variety of leisure activities from pre- to post-retirement. The seven activities they investigated included hobbies, watching television, reading, seeing relatives, seeing friends, religious activities, and travel. Additionally, some retirees may be exposed to and decide to add completely new types of activities to their activity repertoire after retiring. Because there is such an array of leisure choices from which to choose in retirement, the discussion below focuses on the most frequent leisure activities that have been reported by retirees.

Solitary Activities

Some retired persons prefer individual, solitary activities to activities that involve social interaction. These activities include, but are not limited to, listening to radio and watching television, leisure reading, and creative activities such as painting, photography, or playing music. Data from several countries as well as from the United States indicate that watching television, DVDs, and videos is common among retired people cross-nationally. For example, in a study of five European nations, Gagliardi et al. (2007) found that watching television or listening to radio were by far the most frequent leisure activities that were reported across nations (88%); similar results were observed in a study in Taiwan, with 81.9% of respondents reporting watching television, DVDs, or videos each day (Chen & Fu, 2008). However, among Swedish respondents aged 75+, reading was found to be the most popular leisure activity (Paillard-Borg, Wang, Winblad, & Fratiglioni, 2009).

Since unstructured leisure time is what many retirees especially appreciate about retirement, they may also enjoy the relaxation of what Weiss (2005) refers to as "puttering." Putterers may relish finally having the freedom to spend a few hours a day in activities such as reading the morning newspaper while enjoying several leisurely cups of coffee, working crossword puzzles, or doing things around the house or garden. In essence, they have the choice of participating or not participating in any kind of more organized leisure activity on any given day.

Informal Social Activities with Friends and Family

In contrast to individuals who prefer mainly solitary activities, many retirees look for retirement activities that will help keep them socially engaged and help ward off the social isolation that sometimes can occur with increasing age. In their comparative European study, Gagliardi et al. (2007) observed that although activities such as watching television were most common among older people, the next most common activity was visiting relatives and friends (68%–70% of respondents reported such activities). It appears that although other forms of leisure participation may be common, social activities may provide the most personal enjoyment for retirees (Chen & Fu, 2008). Some of the activities described below, such as volunteering, travel, and educational activities, also provide opportunities for substantial social interaction.

Volunteer Activities

About one-fourth of people of retirement age (65+) participate in unpaid volunteer work (Morrow-Howell, 2010; U.S. Bureau of Labor Statistics, 2009). The rate of volunteering is increasing, and older people spend more time in volunteering than do their younger counterparts (Chambré, 1993; Hendricks & Cutler, 2004; Morrow-Howell, 2010; Musick & Wilson, 2008), at least until ages 75 or 80, when volunteer activity begins to decline. Some of the motivations for volunteering include the desire to help others or to "give back"

to the community, to remain active, and to gain new knowledge or experiences (Chambré, 1993; Morrow-Howell, 2010; Okun & Eisenberg, 1992; Weiss, 2005). Volunteering therefore confers benefits to the volunteer as well as to the recipient of volunteer services. Barriers to older persons' volunteering include lack of transportation, inadequate training, boring or "make work" jobs, volunteer opportunities that do not include older people, few volunteer opportunities available in their geographical area, lack of awareness of volunteer opportunities, and, importantly, not being asked to volunteer (James, Besen, Matz-Costa, & Pitt-Catsouphes, 2010).

Retirees are most likely to volunteer in religious organizations, health care settings, and community service agencies (Chambré, 1993; Morrow-Howell, 2010). Using data from the American Changing Lives Survey, Herzog and Morgan (1993) found that among persons aged 55+, those who were working part-time were more likely to volunteer than those who were not working at all; however, when those who were not working did volunteer, they spent as much time volunteering as did part-time workers. Mutchler, Burr, and Caro (2003) and Musick and Wilson (2008), also analyzing data from the American Changing Lives Survey, later reported that people who were fully retired were the ones who volunteered the most hours.

Hobbies, Games, and Sports

Research on time use in retirement that was conducted by Weiss (2005) includes a category of hobbies, games, and sports participation. In that study, the respondents, most of whom were retired from middle-class occupations, said they participated in hobbies such as sewing, making furniture, photography, music, and investing. They also spent time playing games, particularly bridge. In a study of older people in five European countries, hobbies were also found to be significant in leisure activity participation (Gagliardi et al., 2007). Weiss (2005) points out that hobbies that are satisfying for retirees tend to have certain characteristics: providing relaxation, being absorbing, requiring skills, and providing recognition.

With respect to sports activities, which often reflects a desire to keep fit, Chen and Fu (2008) found that nearly half (48.5%) of their respondents aged 60+ reported participating in physical activities; these activities represented the second most frequently reported activity category in the study. Sports and exercise were also reported by a smaller, but not negligible, percentage (26%) of retirees in a study by Dorfman and Kolarik (2005). Frequent sports engaged in by retirees include golf and tennis (Weiss, 2005).

Travel

Travel is a frequently stated goal of many retirees (Staats & Pierfelice, 2003), yet Blazey (1992) found that travel did not increase (or decrease) with retirement. That said, when retirees were asked in the Staats and Pierfelice study (2003) what they wanted to do in the next five years, travel was by far the most frequent response (31.7%). In addition, Staats and Pierfelice found that travel was the most frequently mentioned activity immediately after respondents retired and continued to be a frequent response for what respondents said they did in the first five years after retirement. In the Dorfman and Kolarik (2005) retirement study, travel was the second most frequently mentioned leisure activity (32%). It has been observed that retirees travel differently from persons who have not yet retired; for example, Blazey (1992) reported that retirees were more likely to take package tours, travel longer and with more people, and visit friends and family than were pre-retirees. Retirees generally express very positive views on the benefits of travel (Nimrod, 2008b; Weiss, 2005). In the research conducted by Weiss (2005), respondents saw travel as offering complete freedom; they wanted to be able to go when and where they chose before being limited by poor health or illness and expressed a need to travel now while they still could. Likewise, Nimrod's (2008b) respondents felt that retirement offered the opportunity to travel when, where, and for as long as they wished. Travel can serve to preserve old interests by visiting places that were related in some way to the former work role as well as to express new interests; it can also provide the opportunity to spend quality time with loved ones who are not geographically proximate.

Educational Activities

James et al. (2010) observed that there are multiple benefits of lifelong learning: it can provide intellectual stimulation, improve old skills and help people learn new ones, and open the doors to part-time work, if desired. Learning in Retirement classes are offered in many different settings, including senior centers, public libraries, other community centers, and retirement communities, and can include many different kinds of course offerings (Streib & Folts, 2003). In Sun City, Florida, for example, an educational program started in 1976 now offers about forty different courses to its residents (Streib & Folts, 2003). Such Learning in Retirement classes tend to be focused on a common interest and help to structure a retiree's time (Weiss, 2005). Formal learning opportunities are also appearing in other countries, such as Sweden; for example, Paillard-Borg et al. (2009) recently observed that "mental activities," which included taking courses as well as reading and political and cultural interests, were the most prevalent leisure activities reported by elders aged 75+ in Stockholm.

Work as Leisure

For some retirees, work activity in retirement is considered as time spent in leisure; "leisure" and "work" become intertwined and inseparable activities. Some respondents in Weiss's (2005) mostly middle-class Boston area sample viewed work as an attractive way to spend their leisure time in retirement; the same was true for professors in the study by Dorfman and Kolarik (2005). Weiss (2005) suggests that although the meaning of work is likely to change from pre- to post-retirement, working in retirement can provide benefits to the retiree such as feelings of achievement, continued social contacts, and a continued sense of identity as well as providing income. Work in retirement is often part-time, so as to allow time for non-work activities, and is particularly common among retired professionals such as physicians, attorneys, and professors. To illustrate, although retirees interviewed by Dorfman and Kolarik (2005) reported volunteer, travel, work around the house and garden, and sports/exercise activities, a full 70% continued paid or unpaid professional work. For such professionals, there appears to be continuity in the core of engagement and in the meaning of activity throughout the life course (Kelly, 1982; Wang, Zhan, Liu, & Shultz, 2008).

Factors Related to Leisure Participation
Gender

McGuire (1982), in his review of earlier studies revealing gender differences in leisure participation (e.g., more home-based activities for women; more sports and formal organizational participation for men), concluded that "… it is evident that there are marked differences in the activity patterns of older men and women. Rather than being an age-related phenomenon, these differences are a carryover from sex role socialization throughout life" (p. 139). McGuire and his colleagues came to essentially the same conclusion in work published more recently (McGuire et al., 2009). Other researchers have also provided evidence that leisure activities are often gendered among individuals of retirement age. For example, Weiss (2005) observed that men were somewhat more likely to participate in administrative roles in voluntary associations, whereas women were more likely to seek activities where they could be with people or take on the role of helper. Armstrong and Morgan (1998) reported that British men were more likely to engage in outdoor, walking, and strength activities, and women were more likely to engage in home-based activities. Janke, Davey, and Kleiber (2006) found that women participated significantly more in informal activities and significantly less in physical activities than did men. Stanley and Freysinger (1995) reported that men in the Ohio Longitudinal Study participated more in sports over time than did women. Additionally, in a study of retirement satisfaction, Floyd et al. (1992) found that women rated social activities as a source of enjoyment in retirement more highly than did men. Taken together, the above results, although also possibly reflecting cohort and socialization differences, converge in suggesting that currently retired women are more likely to engage in activities that involve informal social interaction, home, and helping, whereas currently retired men are more likely to engage in physical and formal organizational activities.

Somewhat inconsistent findings are reported in regard to gender differences in overall amount of leisure participation (e.g., Lefrançois, Leclerc, & Poulin, 1998; Rosenkoetter et al., 2001; Stanley & Freysinger, 1995). Rosenkoetter et al. (2001), using the 72-item Retirement Assessment Questionnaire, reported that men were more likely to increase participation in hobbies after retiring than were women. However, Stanley and Freysinger (1995) found in a 16- year longitudinal study of aging that men's participation in a variety of activity clusters (sports, home activities, social activities, volunteerism, and hobbies and crafts) declined over time, whereas women's participation tended to be more constant. Different findings were observed by Lefrançois et al. (1998), who found that women over age 65 were less involved in a variety of leisure activities (exercise and sport, travel, social activities, and outdoor recreation) than were men. There are a number of potential explanations for these inconsistent findings, including differences in the samples (e.g., one study included only retirees from an international corporation living in the southeastern U.S., whereas others included broader occupational representation), cultural differences affecting activity selection because data were collected in different countries, and variation in the length of time that respondents were followed after their retirement.

Age and Health

Research is consistent in pointing out that both participation in leisure activity and frequency of leisure participation are affected by health status (Chen & Fu, 2008; Gagliardi et al., 2007; Garfein & Herzog, 1995; Lefrançois et al., 1998; Mutchler, Burr, & Caro, 2003; Searle & Isa-Ahola, 1988; Stanley & Freysinger, 1995; Strain, Grabusic, Searle, & Dunn, 2002). This conclusion is based on health as measured by self-reports as well as by functional measures such as ADL/IADL limitations. With respect to the latter measures, Garfein and Herzog (1995) reported that functional status of elders aged 60–96 was related to productive involvement in a number of activities, ranging from housework to volunteering to helping family and friends. Lefrançois et al. (1998) found that poor health was the most important predictor of inactivity in persons aged 65 and older, concluding that it was not age per se that predicted activity in later life but rather that age and health tend to be correlated. Similarly, Searle and Isa-Ahola (1988) reported that better health was second only to leisure attitude in predicting leisure participation in a Canadian sample. It has been observed that there is an interaction between health and gender in regard to leisure participation, with men's frequency of leisure participation more likely to be affected by their health status than women's (Stanley & Freysinger, 1995), suggesting the need to investigate important interaction effects in leisure participation.

Socioeconomic Status

Among major indicators of socioeconomic status, education and occupation are both related to participation in leisure activities and frequency of leisure participation. Research suggests that leisure participation is likely to reflect differences in human and social capital among older persons with different educational and occupational levels (Morrow-Howell, 2010; Mutchler et al., 2003). Volunteerism is an example of how human and social capital can affect leisure participation; both Morrow-Howell (2010) and Mutchler et al. (2003) point out that today's older people with substantial human and social capital and a wealth of experience are more likely to volunteer than those who do not have such accumulated capital.

Education. Higher educational level is often found to be associated with participation in leisure activities (Chen & Fu, 2008; Lefrançois et al., 1998; Morrow-Howell, 2010; Mutchler et al., 2003; Paillard-Borg et al., 2009; Strain et al., 2002). In fact, Lefrançois et al. (1998) reported in a study conducted in the Montreal, Canada, area that lower educational level was the second strongest predictor of inactivity in individuals aged 65+, as measured by participation in exercise and sports activities, travel, social activities, and outdoor recreation. Furthermore, data from Taiwan revealed that higher educational level was correlated not only with activity participation among people aged 60 and older but also with enjoyment of the leisure (Chen & Fu, 2008).

Occupational level. Osgood and Mizruchi (1982) point out that the type of occupation affects both the kind and amount of leisure participation, with some jobs, especially professional and managerial ones, involving leisure-like activities that in some respects seem more like play than work. This blurring of work and play appears to carry over into retirement so that professionals and highly skilled white-collar workers choose equivalent leisure activities that Stebbins (2000) refers to as "serious leisure," or the systematic pursuit of an absorbing and substantial leisure activity. Retired professionals, for example, might engage in a "liberal arts hobby" such as taking classes, reading, or volunteer work (Stebbins, 2000, p. 2). This was the case in a study of retired professors, where the most frequent leisure activity reported was volunteering (Dorfman & Kolarik, 2005). Likewise, Herzog and Morgan (1993), using data from the American Changing Lives survey, found that occupation was related to participation in volunteer activity, with professional and clerical/sales workers most likely to volunteer; the researchers speculated that professionals in particular may be attracted to work-like leisure activities because they tend to have enjoyed their work. Rosenkoetter et al. (2001) also observed occupational differences in leisure participation, with managerial and professional retirees reading more, traveling more, and participating in more social activities than did skilled and administrative clerical workers. Another study that considered occupational differences revealed that white-collar occupation retirees, particularly professional ones, demonstrated a higher level of skill utilization in leisure activities and also participated in more leisure activities than did retirees from blue-collar occupations (O'Brien, 1981).

Leisure Activities and Well-Being in Retirement
Psychosocial Well-Being

One caveat in considering research on leisure activity and psychosocial well-being in retirement is that well-being has been operationalized by investigators in a number of different ways: these include life satisfaction, depression, morale, retirement satisfaction, happiness, self-concept, and stress. This inconsistency of measures is one reason that findings on psychosocial well-being in retirement are not always comparable. A second caveat is that leisure activity and well-being are likely to have reciprocal effects, so that leisure activity can be either a cause or effect of psychological well-being in retirement (Iwasaki & Smale, 1998). With these limitations in mind, the literature review below first turns to research on leisure activity and life satisfaction in retirement, life satisfaction being the most commonly utilized measure of psychosocial well-being.

Life satisfaction. Floyd et al. (1992) sums up a prevailing view that life satisfaction in retirement is associated with activities that can replace the rewards that were previously obtained from work. Although replacement of the rewards of the workplace may or may not be the primary motivation for choice of leisure activities among retirees, the preponderance of evidence is that participation in leisure activities in retirement is associated with life satisfaction (Austrom, Perkins, Damush, & Hendrie, 2003; Kelly & Ross, 1989; Longino & Kart, 1982; Mishra, 1992; Moen, Fields, Quick, & Hofmeister, 2000; Nimrod, 2007b, 2008a; O'Brien, 1981; Peppers, 1976; Riddick & Daniel, 1984). It is not entirely clear, however, whether involvement in just a few or a larger number of leisure activities is more conducive to life satisfaction of retirees. On the one hand, Kelly (1982) suggests that involvement in a few activities may be more satisfying than involvement in a greater variety of activities, with people selecting those activities that they find most personally rewarding. On the other hand, a number of empirical studies have documented that both participation in a larger number of leisure activities and more frequent leisure participation are related to life satisfaction in retirement (Bevil, O'Connor, & Mattoon, 1993; Moen et al., 2000; Nimrod, 2007a; Peppers, 1976). Some studies also find that adding new leisure activities in retirement and increasing the number of leisure activities are conducive to life satisfaction (Nimrod, 2007a, 2008a; Peppers, 1976). Nimrod's (2008a) Israeli data indicate that "innovators," the 50% of her sample who added at least one new activity in retirement, had significantly higher levels of life satisfaction than did other retirees.

Researchers have also investigated the relationship between specific leisure activities and life satisfaction in retirement. Peppers (1976) found that participation in social and physical activities had the most positive effect on life satisfaction among male retirees, even when controlling for health and income. Social activities including visits with children and grandchildren have also been reported as conducive to life satisfaction in samples of Australian (O'Brien, 1981) and Israeli (Nimrod, 2007b) retirees. Lemon et al. (1972), however, found that only informal social activity with friends was related to life satisfaction among in-movers to a California retirement community, and that effect was not strong. But a replication of that study found a positive relationship in general between informal social activity, including social activity with relatives, and life satisfaction (Longino & Kart, 1982). Results for formal organizational participation are also somewhat equivocal. Some studies have shown a positive relationship between participation in either clubs and organizations or volunteer work and life satisfaction in retirement (Kelly & Ross, 1989; Mishra, 1992; Moen et al., 2000; Morrow-Howell, 2010). However, Cutler and Danigelis (1993) reported that formal organizational participation does not necessarily result in psychological well-being, with participation in religious activities being the only exception.

Other measures. Researchers have also investigated leisure activities in relation to depression, retirement satisfaction, morale, happiness, self-concept, and stress. With respect to depression, Morrow-Howell, Hinterlong, Rozario, and Tang (2003) found that hours spent volunteering among older adults were related negatively to depression; however, a ceiling effect of 100 hours volunteering per year was noted. Both volunteering and participation in clubs and organizations were associated with lower levels of depression and also with higher levels of self-esteem, retirement satisfaction, and life satisfaction in the Cornell Retirement and Well-Being Study (Moen et al., 2000). Janke et al. (2006), using three waves of the American Changing Lives Survey, observed a negative relationship between a broad range of activities, including informal, formal, and physical activities, and depression; Herzog, Franks, Markus, and Holmberg (1998) likewise reported a range of leisure activities ranging from volunteer work to attending classes

to traveling to be negatively related to depression. Additionally, Herzog et al. (1998) observed that the relationship between leisure activities and well-being was mediated by self-concept. Concerning morale, Freysinger, Alessio, and Mehdizadeh (1993) found in the Ohio Longitudinal Study that overall level of activity influenced women's morale over time even more than did their health. Overall activity level was likewise reported to influence happiness in elders aged 67–95 in another longitudinal study (Menec, 2003). There is also some evidence that a particular kind of leisure activity, physically active leisure, may reduce stress among retirees (Zuzanek, Robinson, & Iwasaki, 1998).

Physical Well-Being

As previously noted, there is a relationship between health status and leisure participation in retirement, with better health positively associated with activity participation. Janke et al. (2006) investigated change in leisure activities over an eight-year period (mean age of respondents at first wave was 66.6 years) and observed that an increase in functional limitations was negatively related to activity participation. Likewise, Menec (2003) documented that functional status among respondents aged 67–95 was related to overall activity over a six-year period. In the Menec study, functional status affected particular activities differentially: participation in both social and productive activities was reported to be related to functional status, whereas more solitary activities were not. Morrow-Howell et al. (2003), focusing attention specifically on volunteer activity, found that volunteering was associated with both better functional and better self-perceived health.

Some investigators have also examined the relationship between leisure activity and mortality. In a prospective study of men and women aged 65+, Glass, Mendes de Leon, Maratolli, and Berkman (1999), after controlling for other factors related to survival, reported that all three types of activity under investigation (social, productive, and fitness) were associated with survival. Research from Sweden provides findings consistent with these (Agahi & Parker, 2010; Lennartson & Silverstein, 2001). In the Lennartson and Silverstein (2001) study, which used the Swedish Panel Study of Living Conditions of the Oldest Old (SWEOLD), individuals aged 77 and older were investigated for mortality risk over a five-year period. Findings revealed a lower mortality risk for individuals engaged in activities such as hobbies and gardening. The study conducted by Agahi and Parker (2010), also using Swedish national data, examined gender differences in the effect of leisure participation on the survival of men and women aged 65+. Results indicated that participation in cultural activities was related to survival in both sexes; however, participation in organizations and study groups predicted survival for women, while participation in hobbies and gardening predicted survival for men.

Quality of Activities

Increasingly, investigators are turning not only to frequency of leisure participation but also to the quality of that participation in assessing the relationship between leisure participation and well-being of retirees. Pinquart and Schindler (2009) observed that "given that free time increases after retirement and that many workers are retiring at an earlier age, leisure *satisfaction* [italics added] is an important aspect of older adults' subjective well-being" (p. 311). Guinn (1999) investigated quality of leisure participation in a retired Texas sample and found that intrinsic motivation for activities, including challenge, competence, self-determination, and commitment, were associated with life satisfaction. Intrinsic motivation for activities (e.g., curiosity, interest) was also a trigger for new activities in retirement for retirees enrolled in a Learning in Retirement class (Nimrod & Kleiber, 2007).

Results from several other nations converge in suggesting a relationship between quality of activity participation and well-being in retirement. In a longitudinal Canadian study, Iwasaki and Smale (1998) found little effect of actual leisure participation on retirees; results of that study suggested that it may be more important to focus on how people feel and think about their leisure activities—in other words, the meaning of those activities—in understanding the relation between activity and psychological well-being. In another study of Canadian retirees, activities that reflected belongingness and self-esteem had the strongest effect on quality of life, as assessed by the Bradburn Affect Balance Scale (Romsa, Bondy, & Blenman, 1985). In Israel, Litwin and Shiovitz-Ezra (2006) examined informal, formal, and solitary activities of retirees and found only a weak or nonexistent relationship between participation in those activities and well-being; however, a strong relationship between social relationship quality and well-being was observed when a social relationship quality variable was entered into the model along with the three activity variables. The researchers concluded that it is not so much what people *do* that matters as it is their interaction with the people with whom they do the activity, and their feelings about the people with whom they interact. In a Turkish sample, Şener, Terzioğlu, and Karabulut (2007) reported that satisfaction with leisure activities was a strong predictor of life satisfaction among retired men, second only to frequency of participation. And finally, in a study that examined why French retirees engaged in retirement activities, intrinsic motivation for knowledge and stimulation were significant predictors of retirement satisfaction (Stephan, Fouquereau, & Fernandez, 2008).

Conclusion

The literature reviewed above supports a number of conclusions regarding leisure activity in retirement. Many of these conclusions are reported in studies in both the United States and other industrialized nations. First, retirees participate in many different kinds of retirement activities, including informal social activities with friends and family, formal social participation in clubs and organizations and through volunteering, and solitary activities such as reading, watching television, and individual hobbies. All of these activities can provide meaning to the retired individual through relaxation, personal growth, feelings of achievement, and a sense of giving back to the community. Second, retirees continue pre-retirement leisure activities and also engage in new activities after retiring, thus providing support for major concepts of both activity and continuity theories of aging. Since participation in these activities is a developmental process involving individual choice and agency, there is also support for life course theory and the model of selective optimization with compensation. Third, personal characteristics including gender, health, and socioeconomic status are associated with participation in leisure activity in general and sometimes with specific leisure activities. For example, with respect to gender, currently retired females appear more likely to participate in informal, social, and home-based activities, whereas currently retired males appear more likely to participate in physical and some organizational activities. These patterns, however, may change as new cohorts of older people reach retirement age, reflecting changes in gender socialization and the opportunity structure. Finally, leisure activity is associated with psychosocial and physical well-being in retirement, although the direction of causality is not clearly established. A substantial body of research shows a positive relationship between activity and psychosocial well-being, as measured by constructs such as life satisfaction, morale, happiness, and positive self-concept. Research likewise shows a relationship between retirement activity and both health and survival.

Future Directions

Although substantial progress has been made in our understanding of leisure activity in retirement, leisure among retired persons continues to receive considerably less attention in the literature than do other issues such as financial well-being and health. However, as more people live not only to experience retirement, but to live a longer portion of their lives in the retirement years, it is imperative that we investigate more fully lifestyle factors such as how individuals spend their leisure time and the kinds of activities they believe provide meaning and fulfillment in their lives. The following directions, although not all-inclusive, are suggested for future research on leisure activity in retirement.

• More longitudinal studies are clearly called for given steadily increasing life expectancy, with many retirees experiencing retirements that last several decades or even longer. Retirees' choice of leisure activities is likely to change over the course of retirement due to changing interests, advancing age, and the likelihood of health limitations developing. Although there is some longitudinal research available, frequently this research follows retirees for only a short period of months or years after they retire. It is necessary to systematically study retirees over the entire course of their retirement in order to understand changes in activity patterns and the correlates of such changes.

• Cohort analysis is needed to elucidate the leisure activity patterns of different cohorts of retirees. Different birth cohorts will have experienced different life events and lived through different historical times and social changes that can markedly affect their choice of leisure activities, both before and after retirement. It would be valuable for future researchers to compare the activities of younger and older retired cohorts, as well as to compare the activities of individuals just as they enter their retirement years with those who have already been retired.

• Interaction effects should be examined more fully in order to explicate the joint effects of such phenomena as health, age, gender, socioeconomic status, and residential location on leisure participation. In some cases, older individuals may suffer double or triple jeopardy in access to leisure activities, as in the circumstance of an older, low-income, rural female who may lack the financial and transportation means to participate in activities.

• Both qualitative and quantitative research methods are necessary to gain a more comprehensive understanding of the leisure activity of retirees. The two kinds of research serve to inform and complement each other, with qualitative studies providing insights into the personal meaning of leisure activity, while quantitative studies further our understanding of the correlates and consequences of leisure participation (Hendricks & Cutler, 2003).

• A considerable body of research examines overall leisure participation of retirees, with a smaller amount focusing on specific kinds of leisure activities and their relation to specific retirement outcomes. Future research can inform the field by providing greater specificity and by addressing such questions as the relationship between particular leisure activities and life satisfaction.

• Much more information is needed on the leisure activities of major subpopulations of retirees, especially those of different races, ethnic groups, and cultures. This emphasis will be increasingly important as our older population becomes ever more diverse. McGuire et al. (2009) point out that there are some important challenges to be addressed in studying phenomena such as racial and ethnic differences in leisure activity of older people; these include the diversity that exists within as well as between groups, size and representativeness of samples, clear definition of terms such as "race" and "ethnicity," and interaction effects.

• We know little about how leisure activity in retirement varies by residential settings, especially with respect to urban-rural differences and size of community. Opportunities to participate in leisure activities can vary substantially in different residential settings, particularly because limitations imposed by population size and density may result in the inability of a community to support many activities. It would also be valuable to have more information about leisure activities of retirees who live in different kinds of housing arrangements. For example, it would be useful to know if the activities of retirees who live in various kinds of congregate settings differ substantially from those who live in single-family dwellings or apartments.

• The changing role and status of women in society and their varying life courses raise the question of how leisure activities of women now entering retirement differ from those of preceding cohorts of women. Another interesting question is whether leisure patterns in retirement differ for retired women who participated in the labor force all or most of their adult lives, for women who re-entered the labor force in midlife, and for women who were intermittent workers.

• A final issue deserving investigation is whether retired individuals who are involved in planning, implementing, and evaluating leisure activities—in other words, given a sense of control over the activities that they are being offered—are more satisfied with those activities than individuals who are not given the opportunity for involvement (Purcell & Keller, 1989; Wang & Shultz, 2010). Information on this issue could be particularly helpful for activity planning in settings such as senior centers and other community organizations that provide programming for retirees.

References

Agahi, N., Ahacic, K., & Parker, M. G. (2006). Continuity of leisure participation from middle to old age. *Journal of Gerontology: Social Sciences, 61B*, S340–S346.

Agahi, N., & Parker, M. G. (2005). Are today's older people more active than their predecessors? Participation in leisure-time activities in Sweden in 1992 and 2002. *Ageing and Society, 25*, 925–941.

Agahi, N., & Parker, M. G. (2010). Leisure activities and mortality: Does gender matter? *Journal of Aging and Health, 20*, 855–871.

Armstrong, G. K., & Morgan, K. (1998). Stability and change in levels of habitual physical activity in later life. *Age and Ageing, 27*(S3), 17–23.

Atchley, R. C. (1971). Retirement and leisure participation: Continuity or crisis? *The Gerontologist, 11*, 13–17.

Atchley, R. C. (1993). Continuity theory and the evolution of activity in later adulthood. In J. R. Kelly (Ed.), *Activity and aging* (pp. 5–16). Newbury Park, CA: Sage.

Atchley, R. C. (1999). *Continuity and adaptation in aging.* Baltimore, MD: Johns Hopkins University Press.

Atchley, R. C. (2003). Why most people cope well with retirement. In J. R. Ronch & J. A. Goldfield (Eds.), *Mental wellness in aging: Strengths-based approaches* (pp. 123–138). Baltimore, MD: Health Professions Press.

Austrom, M. G., Perkins, A. J., Damush, T. M., & Hendrie, H. C. (2003). Predictors of life satisfaction in retired physicians and spouses. *Social Psychiatry and Psychiatric Epidemiology, 38*, 134–141.

Baltes, M. M., & Carstensen, L. L. (1996). The process of successful aging. *Ageing and Society, 16*, 397–422.

Baltes, P. B., & Baltes, M. M. (1990). Selective optimization and compensation. In P. B. Baltes & M. M. Baltes (Eds.), *Successful aging: Perspectives from the behavioral sciences* (pp. 1–34). New York, NY: Cambridge University Press.

Bevil, C. A., O'Connor, P. C., & Mattoon, P. M. (1993). Leisure activity, life satisfaction, and perceived health status in older adults. *Gerontology & Geriatrics Education, 14,* 3–19.

Blazey, M. (1992). Travel and retirement status. *Annals of Tourism Research, 19*, 771–783.

Bossé, R., & Ekerdt, D. J. (1981). Changes in self-perception of leisure activities with retirement. *The Gerontologist, 21*, 650–654.

Brown, C. A., McGuire, F. A., & Voelkl, J. (2008). The link between successful aging and serious leisure. *International Journal of Aging and Human Development, 66*, 73–95.

Chambré, S. M. (1993). Volunteerism by elders: Past trends and future projects. *The Gerontologist, 33*, 221–228.

Chen, S., & Fu, Y. (2008). Leisure participation and enjoyment among the elderly: Individual characteristics and sociability. *Educational Gerontology, 34*, 871–889.

Cumming, E., & Henry, W. E. (1961). *Growing old: The process of disengagement.* New York, NY: Basic Books.

Cutler, S. J., & Danigelis, N. L. (1993). Organized contexts of activity. In J. R. Kelly (Ed.), *Activity and aging* (pp. 146–163). Newbury Park, CA: Sage.

Dorfman, L. T., & Kolarik, D. C. (2005). Leisure and the retired professor: Occupation matters. *Educational Gerontology, 31*, 343–361.

Ekerdt, D. J. (1986). The busy ethic: Moral continuity between work and retirement. *The Gerontologist, 26*, 239–244.

Elder, G. H., Jr., & Johnson, M. K. (2003). The life course and human development: Challenges, lessons, and new directions. In R. A. Settersten, Jr. (Ed.), *Invitation to the life course: Toward new understandings of later life* (pp. 49–81). Amityville, NY: Baywood.

Elder, G. H., Jr., Johnson, M. K., & Crosnoe, R. (2003). The emergence and development of life course theory. In J. Mortimer & J. Shanahan (Eds.), *Handbook of the life course* (pp. 3–19). New York, NY: Kluwer Academic/Plenum.

Erikson, E., Erikson, J., & Kivnick, H. (1986). *Vital involvement in old age.* New York, NY: W. W. Norton.

Floyd, F. J., Haynes, S. N., Doll, E. R., Winemiller, D., Lemsky, C., Burgy, T. M.… Heilman, N. (1992). Assessing retirement satisfaction and perceptions of retirement experiences. *Psychology and Aging, 7*, 609–621.

Freysinger, V., Alessio, H., & Mehdizadeh, S. (1993). Re-examining the morale-physical health-activity relationship: A longitudinal study of time changes and gender differences. *Activities, Adaptation, & Aging, 17*, 25–41.

Gagliardi, C., Spazzafumo, L., Marcellini, F., Mollenkopf, H., Ruoppila, I., Tacken, M., & Szemann, Z. (2007). The outdoor mobility and leisure activities of older people in five European countries. *Ageing and Society, 27*, 683–700.

Garfein, A. J., & Herzog, A. R. (1995). Robust aging and the young-old, old-old, and oldest old. *Journal of Gerontology: Social Sciences, 50B*, S77–S87.

Gibson, H., Ashton-Shaeffer, C., Green, J., & Corbin, J. (2002). Leisure and retirement: Women's stories. *Society and Leisure, 25*, 257–284.

Glass, T., Mendes de Leon, C., Marottoli, R. A., & Berkman, L. (1999). Population based study of social and productive activities as predictors of survival among elderly Americans. *British Medical Journal, 319*, 478–483.

Guinn, B. (1999). Leisure behavior motivation and the life satisfaction of retired persons. *Activities, Adaptation & Aging, 23*, 13–20.

Havighurst, R. J., & Albrecht, R. (1953). *Older people.* New York, NY: Longman, Green & Co.

Hendricks, J., & Cutler, S. (2004). Volunteerism and socio-emotional selectivity in later life. *Journal of Gerontology: Social Sciences, 59B*, 251–257.

Hendricks, J., & Cutler, S. J. (1990). Leisure and the structure of our life worlds. *Ageing and Society, 10*, 85–94.

Hendricks, J., & Cutler, S. J. (2003). Leisure in life-course perspective. In R. Settersten, Jr. (Ed.), *Invitation to the life course: Toward new understandings of later life* (pp. 107–134). Amityville, NY: Baywood.

Herzog, A. R., & Morgan, J. N. (1993). Formal volunteer work among older Americans. In S. A. Bass, F. G. Caro, & Y. Chen (Eds.), *Achieving a productive aging society* (pp. 119–142). Westport, CT: Auburn House.

Herzog, R. A., Franks, M. M., Markus, H. R., & Holmberg, D. (1998). Activities and well being in older age: Effects of self-concept and educational attainment. *Psychology and Aging, 13*, 179–185.

Iwasaki, Y., & Smale, B. J. A. (1998). Longitudinal analyses of the relationships among life transitions, chronic health problems, leisure and psychological well-being. *Leisure Sciences, 20*, 25–52.

James, J. B., Besen, E., Matz-Costa, C., & Pitt-Catsouphes, M. (2010). *Engaged as we are: The end of retirement as we know it?* The Sloan Center on Aging & Work at Boston College. Retrieved from http://aging and work.bc.edu/documents/1824 Engaged As We Age.pdf.

Janke, M., Davey, A., & Kleiber, D. (2006). Modeling change in older adults' leisure activities. *Leisure Sciences, 28*, 285–303.

Kelly, J. R. (1982). *Leisure.* Englewood Cliffs, NJ: Prentice-Hall.

Kelly, J. R., & Ross, J. (1989). Later-life leisure: Beginning a new agenda. *Leisure Sciences, 11*, 47–59.

Lawton, M. P. (1993). Meanings of activity. In J. R. Kelly (Ed.), *Activity and aging* (pp. 25–41). Newbury Park, CA: Sage.

Lefrançois, R., Leclerc, G., & Poulin, N. (1998). Predictors of activity involvement among older adults. *Activities, Adaptation, and Aging, 22*, 15–29.

Lemon, B. W., Bengston, V. L., & Peterson, J. A. (1972). An exploration of the activity theory of aging: Activity types and life satisfaction among in-movers to a retirement community. *Journal of Gerontology, 27*, 511–523.

Lennartson, C., & Silverstein, M. (2001). Does engagement with life enhance survival of elderly people in Sweden? The role of social and leisure activities. *Journal of Gerontology: Social Sciences, 56B*, S335–S342.

Litwin, H., & Shiovitz-Ezra, S. (2006). The association between activity and wellbeing in later life: What really matters? *Ageing & Society, 26*, 225–242.

Long, J. (1987). Continuity as a basis for change: Leisure and male retirement. *Leisure Studies, 6*, 55–70.

Longino, C. F., & Kart, C. S. (1982). Explicating activity theory: A formal replication. *Journal of Gerontology, 37*, 713–722.

McGuire, F. A. (1982). Leisure time, activities, and meanings: A comparison of men and women in late life. In N. J. Osgood (Ed.), *Life after work: Retirement, leisure, recreation, and the elderly* (pp. 133–147). New York, NY: Praeger.

McGuire, F. A., Boyd, R. K., & Tedrick, R. E. (2009). *Leisure and aging* (4th ed.). Champaign, IL: Sagamore Publishing.

Menec, V. H. (2003). The relation between everyday activities and successful aging: A 6-year longitudinal study. *Journal of Gerontology: Social Sciences, 58B*, S74–S82.

Mishra, S. (1992). Leisure activities and life satisfaction in old age: A case study of retired government employees living in urban areas. *Activities, Adaptation & Aging, 16*, 7–26.

Moen, P., Fields, V., Quick, H. E., & Hofmeister, H. (2000). A life-course approach to retirement and social integration. In K. Pillemer, P. Moen, E. Wetherington, & N. Glasgow (Eds.), *Social integration in the second half of life* (pp. 76–107). Baltimore: MD: Johns Hopkins University Press.

Morrow-Howell, N. (2010). Volunteering in later life: Research frontiers. *Journal of Gerontology: Social Sciences, 65B*, 461–469.

Morrow-Howell, N., Hinterlong, J., Rozario, P., & Tang, F. (2003). Effects of volunteering on well-being of older adults. *Journal of Gerontology: Social Sciences, 58B*, S137–S145.

Musick, M. A., & Wilson, J. (2008). *Volunteers: A social profile.* Bloomington, IN: Indiana University Press.

Mutchler, J. E., Burr, J. A., & Caro, F. G. (2003). From paid worker to volunteer: Leaving the paid workforce and volunteering in later life. *Social Forces, 81*, 1267–1293.

Nimrod, G. (2007a). Expanding, concentrating and diffusing: Post retirement leisure behavior and life satisfaction. *Leisure Sciences, 29*, 91–111.

Nimrod, G. (2007b). Retirees' leisure activities, benefits, and their contribution to life satisfaction. *Leisure Studies, 26*, 65–80.

Nimrod, G. (2008a). In support of innovation theory: Innovation and activity patterns and life satisfaction among recently retired individuals. *Ageing & Society, 28*, 831–846.

Nimrod, G. (2008b). Retirement and tourism: Themes in retirees' narratives. *Annals of Tourism Research, 35*, 859–878.

Nimrod, G., & Kleiber, D. A. (2007). Reconsidering change and continuity in later life: Toward an innovation theory of successful aging. *International Journal of Aging and Human Development, 65*, 1–22.

O'Brien, G. E. (1981). Leisure attributes and retirement satisfaction. *Journal of Applied Psychology, 66*, 371–384.

O'Brien, G. E. (1988). Work and leisure. In W. F. VanRaaij, G. M. VanVeldhoven, & K. E. Warneryd (Eds.), *Handbook of economic psychology* (pp. 538–568). Dordrecht, The Netherlands: Kluwer Academic Publishers.

Okun, M. A., & Eisenberg, N. (1992). Motives and intent to continue organizational volunteering among residents of a retirement community area. *Journal of Community Psychology, 20*, 183–187.

Osgood, N. J., & Mizruchi, E. H. (1982). Participation in work, retirement, and leisure: A comparison of blue collar, white collar, and professional workers. In N. J. Osgood (Ed.), *Life after work: Retirement, leisure, recreation, and the elderly* (pp. 221–248). New York, NY: Praeger.

Paillard-Borg, S., Wang, H., Winblad, B., & Fratiglioni, L. (2009). Pattern of participation in leisure activities among older people in relation to their health conditions and contextual factors: A survey in a Swedish urban area. *Ageing & Society, 29*, 803–821.

Peppers, L. G. (1976). Patterns of leisure and adjustment to retirement. *The Gerontologist, 16*, 441–446.

Pinquart, M., & Schindler, I. (2009). Change of leisure satisfaction in the transition to retirement: A latent-class analysis. *Leisure Sciences, 31*, 311–329.

Purcell, R. Z., & Keller, M. J. (1989). Characteristics of leisure activities which may lead to leisure satisfaction among older adults. *Activities, Adaptation, & Aging, 13*, 17–29.

Pushkar, D., Chaikelson, J., Conway, M., Etezadi, J., Giannopoulus, C., Li, K.... Wrosch, C. (2010). Testing continuity and activity variables as predictors of positive and negative affect in retirement. *Journal of Gerontology: Psychological Sciences, 65B*, 42–49.

Riddick, C. C., & Daniel, S. N. (1984). The relative contribution of leisure activities and other factors to the mental health of older women. *Journal of Leisure Research, 16*, 136–148.

Romsa, G., Bondy, P., & Blenman, M. (1985). Modeling retirees' life satisfaction levels: The role of recreational, life cycle, and socio-enivronmental elements. *Journal of Leisure Research, 17,* 29–39.

Rosenkoetter, M., Garris, J., & Engdahl, R. (2001). Postretirement use of time: Implications for preretirement planning and postretirement management. *Activities, Adaptation, & Aging, 25,* 1–17.

Rowe, J. W., & Kahn, R. L. (1997). Successful aging. *The Gerontologist, 37,* 433–440.

Searle, M. S., & Iso-Ahola, S. E. (1988). Determinants of leisure behavior among retired adults. *Therapeutic Recreation Journal, 22,* 38–46.

Şener, A., Terzioğlu, R. G., & Karabulut, E. (2007). Life satisfaction and leisure activities during men's retirement: A Turkish sample. *Aging & Mental Health, 11,* 30–36.

Staats, S., & Pierfelice, L. (2003). Travel: A long-range goal of retired women. *The Journal of Psychology, 137,* 483–494.

Stanley, D., & Freysinger, V. J. (1995). The impact of age, health, and sex on the frequency of older adults' leisure activity participation: A longitudinal study. *Activities, Adaptation, & Aging, 19,* 31–42.

Stebbins, R. A. (2000). The extraprofessional life: Leisure, retirement and unemployment. *Current Sociology, 48,* 1–18.

Stephan, Y., Fouquereau, E., & Fernandez, A. (2008). The relation between self-determination and retirement satisfaction among active retired individuals. *International Journal of Aging and Human Development, 66,* 329–345.

Strain, L. A., Grabusic, C. C., Searle, M. S., & Dunn, N. J. (2002). Continuing and ceasing leisure activities in later life: A longitudinal study. *The Gerontologist, 42,* 217–223.

Streib, G. F., & Folts, W. E. (2003). A college in a retirement community. *Educational Gerontology, 29,* 801–808.

Thang, L. L. (2005). Experiencing leisure in later life: A study of retirees and activity in Singapore. *Journal of Cross Cultural Gerontology, 20,* 307–318.

U.S. Bureau of Labor Statistics. (2009). *Volunteering in the United States 2008.* Washington, DC: Bureau of Labor Statistics, United States Department of Labor.

Vaillant, G. E. (2002). *Aging well.* Boston, MA: Little, Brown, & Co.

Wang, M. (2007). Profiling retirees in the retirement transition and adjustment process: Examining the longitudinal change patterns of retirees' psychological well-being. *Journal of Applied Psychology, 92,* 455–474.

Wang, M., & Shultz, K. (2010). Employee retirement: A review and recommendations for future investigation. *Journal of Management, 36,* 172–206.

Wang, M., Zhan, Y., Liu, S., & Shultz, K. (2008). Antecedents of bridge employment: A longitudinal investigation. *Journal of Applied Psychology, 93,* 818–830.

Weiss, R. S. (2005). *The experience of retirement.* Ithaca, NY: Cornell University Press.

Zhan, Y., Wang, M., Liu, S., & Shultz, K. (2009). Bridge employment and retirees' health: A longitudinal investigation. *Journal of Occupational Health Psychology, 14,* 374–389.

Zuzanek, J., Robinson, J. P., & Iwasaki, Y. (1998). The relationship between stress, health, and physically active leisure as a function of life-cycle. *Leisure Sciences, 20,* 253–275.

Family, Work, and the Retirement Process: A Review and New Directions

Russell A. Matthews *and* Gwenith G. Fisher

Abstract

Changes in the demographic characteristics of the older workforce amidst an increasingly complex retirement landscape underscore the need to examine the role of family in relation to the retirement process. Family is an important part of life, and for many the most salient role in life. The decision regarding whether and when to retire is often not an individual decision, but rather one that unfolds within a larger family context. This chapter reviews prior research on the relationship between family-related factors (e.g., marital status, spousal influence and social support, and family caregiving responsibilities) and retirement. We also review relevant prior research on the intersection of work and family domains in relation to retirement. We follow this with a summary as well as recommendations for future directions of research examining family factors related to retirement research.

Key Words: family and retirement, family roles, work-family conflict, work-family enrichment, work-family enhancement, work-family and retirement

To date, several reviews have sought to summarize past research examining the retirement process (e.g., Beehr, 1986; Kanfer & Ackerman, 2004; Wang & Shultz, 2010). Perhaps one of the most fundamental developments of the past thirty years of retirement research is the conclusion that retirement is not necessarily a single event. Rather, it is a decision-making and behavioral process that unfolds over time (Beehr, 1986; Kim & Moen, 2001; Szinovacz, 2003; Wang & Shultz, 2010). Furthermore, retirement decision making is a process that is influenced by individual characteristics, internal attributes and attitudes, as well as by external factors.

In their recent review of the retirement literature, Wang and Shultz (2010) presented a thorough model of issues and relationships that have been considered in retirement research. In their model, they described four family factors as inputs to the

retirement process: marital and dependent care status, spouse's working status, marital quality, and family support. However, as discussed by Szinovacz (2006), the dynamic relationship between family and retirement is still poorly understood. The objective of this chapter is to review the role of family as well as the intersection between work and family in the retirement process in more detail. To achieve this goal, we first provide a primer on why the family context is so important with regard to the retirement process. We then turn our attention to reviewing past research that has sought to link family-related factors to the retirement process. These factors can generally be categorized in terms of family characteristics, such as marital status, spousal influence and social support, and dependent care status (e.g., children and elder care responsibilities). In addition, we review a small but impactful set of studies that explicitly examine retirement decision making and adjustment process in terms of the intersection between work and family domains. We follow this with a summary and a discussion of basic conclusions from the research as well as future directions regarding family factors related to retirement research.

The Importance of Family

Family plays an important role in peoples' lives, and for many, family is the most salient role in life (Cinamon & Rich, 2002). Many social science disciplines study family and have used a variety of different terms to describe the importance of family. Common examples include family role salience (Greenhaus & Beutell, 1985), family role expectations (Amatea, Cross, Clark, & Bobby, 1986), and family centrality (Carr, Boyar, & Gregory, 2008). In addition, there has been a significant amount of research conducted over the last thirty years to examine the intersection between work and family, such as the extent to which work conflicts with or interferes with family (or vice versa) as well as the extent to which work enhances or facilitates one's family life (or vice versa; Bellavia & Frone, 2005; Greenhaus & Powell, 2006; Voydanoff, 2006). As we discuss in more detail later in the chapter, to the extent that work affects family and family affects work, this intersection between work and family has implications for the retirement process (Baltes & Young, 2007; Barnes-Farrell, 2003).

Research on how family-related characteristics might affect the retirement process is generally grounded within a life course perspective (Szinovacz, 2003; Wang, 2007; Wang & Shultz, 2010). In particular, life course theorists purport that attitudes and behaviors are influenced by past events and actions such that any decision made in the present is influenced by social and historical events from an individual's past (Elder, 1994; Giele & Elder, 1998). As such, retirement itself is conceptualized as one of several different life transitions an individual will experience over the course of his or her life and is embedded in the context of the larger dynamic family system in which decisions are made (Moen & Sweet, 2004). Taken together, it is not the least bit surprising that family factors can and do influence the retirement process.

Family Demographics Relevant to Retirement

As other chapters in this handbook have clearly articulated, there are many demographic characteristics and trends relevant to the study of retirement

and the aging workforce. For brevity we will not repeat them all here, but we would like to highlight some of the key family characteristics among the older workforce because they have implications for the retirement process. Drawing on data from the 2005–2009 American Community Survey, it is estimated that 59.8% of individuals age 55 or older are married. According to the 2010 Current Population Survey, among married couples where at least one individual is age 55 or older, the majority of couples have at least one person in the couple who is still working. For example, 16.7% are couples where only the husband is working. Another 12.4% include couples where only the wife is working. Interestingly, almost a third (30.8%) of all married couples age 55 or older are dual-earner couples (i.e., both individuals in the couple are still working). In addition, the workforce today includes many more women compared to a few decades ago. In 1970, 44% of married women between ages 45 and 64 were in the workforce; in 2003 the percentage was 67.4% (U.S. Census Bureau, 2004–2005), which constitutes a 53% increase during the last three decades.

Statistics regarding the family status of individuals in the workforce should also be considered in the larger context of the changing demographics of today's workforce. For example, recent data from the U.S. Bureau of Labor Statistics (2010) suggests that across all married couples, only 18% are ones in which only the husband works (down from 36% in 1967). Furthermore, the labor force participation rate of mothers with children under age 18 rose from 47.4% in 1975 to 71.6% in 2009. Not surprising, unmarried mothers are more likely to participate in the labor force than married women (75.8% versus 69.8%, respectively). Also, in married couples in 2008, women contributed 35% of the families' income, a 9% increase from 1970. And in 2008, in 27% of dual-earner couples, wives earned more than their husbands (compared to 18% in 1987).

It has also been estimated that in 2008 approximately 2.6 million older adults had one or more grandchildren who lived with them for whom they were responsible for the majority of the children's basic needs (e.g., food, shelter, clothing; U.S. Census Bureau, 2010). Among these grandparents who have primary responsibility for these children, 61.5% were still employed. Taken together, these statistics have important implications for understanding the role of family characteristics in the retirement process, which we explain next.

Family Characteristics and the Retirement Process

Family can be conceptualized in multiple ways, including one's marital status and dependent care status, such as the number of children and grandchildren one has and/or whether an individual has elder care responsibilities. We will review several of these aspects of family in turn in relation to the retirement process.

Spousal Relationships

MARITAL STATUS

By far, marital status is the family-related characteristic that has received the most attention in the retirement literature. Marital status is a salient indicator of how one may define "family." For example, Baltes and Young (2007) indicated that in terms of family, older workers tend to focus on their marital relationships, whereas younger workers are oriented more toward their children. This viewpoint is often grounded within the life course perspective (Moen & Sweet, 2004). For example, when individuals remove themselves from work (i.e., retire), or reduce their involvement in the work domain (e.g., transitions from full-time to part-time work), they may invest more time and energy in the family domain (e.g., Shultz, Morton, & Weckerle, 1998; Wang, Zhan, Liu, & Shultz, 2008). Thus, the family domain conveys not only additional demands and resources that influence the retirement process, but also external expectations (i.e., from spouses) that can influence the process (Pienta & Hayward, 2002).

Prior research has demonstrated that individuals who have a retired spouse are more likely to retire compared to those with a working spouse (Blau, 1998; Pienta, 2003; Szinovacz, 1989; Szinovacz & DeViney, 2000). Related to this, past research has shown that married adults hold more positive attitudes about retirement compared to unmarried individuals, even after controlling for other factors strongly related to retirement, including income, health, and retirement planning (Mutran, Reitzes, & Fernandez, 1997). The tendency for early retirement is higher for both men and women when household wealth is greater (Pienta & Hayward, 2002). Although marital status and having children were not predictive of early retirement, Kim and Feldman (1998) demonstrated that individuals with an employed spouse are less likely to take early retirement incentives. It has also been shown that individuals who have spouses who are about to retire are more likely to feel like they have

voluntarily been "pulled" into retirement (Shultz et al., 1998).

Another line of research has sought to examine preference for and actual behavioral patterns for joint retirement within married couples. Gustman and Steinmeier (2000) examined this issue in terms of dual-earner couples versus only male-earner couples. They note that husbands of working wives are more likely to retire sooner than husbands with non-working spouses. In particular, the authors suggest that retirement rates (i.e., percentage of men) increase substantially after age 60 for husbands with employed spouses, whereas for husbands with non-working spouses, they appear to be more likely to delay retirement until age 65. As we will discuss later in the chapter, it is possible that the trends observed as recently as in the last five to ten years may have changed very recently as part of the recent economic downturn. Furthermore, it is important to keep in mind that Social Security policy has a large impact on the timing of retirement. Thus, although a significant amount of research suggests that spouses may try to plan their retirement together, the timing of retirement for spouses who are not the same age may be influenced by Social Security and/or Medicare eligibility (for a recent discussion of these issues see Vere, 2011).

Specific to dual-earner couples, several studies have demonstrated a trend toward married couples reporting a preference toward joint retirement (Blau, 1998; Henkens, 1999; Szinovacz & Schaffer, 2000). Furthermore, growing evidence suggests that within married couples, joint retirement is a planned action that is a shared decision (An, Christensen, & Gupta 2004; Henkens, 1999; Smith & Moen, 1998). Ho and Raymo (2009) noted that approximately 40% of men and women expect to retire around the same time as their partner. However, Ho and Raymo presented several interesting additional findings. First, only 24% of couples actually retired within the same year. For couples where both members expected to retire jointly, these couples were more than three times more likely to actually retire jointly compared to couples who did not expect to retire jointly. As such, Ho and Raymo argued that expectations for and discussions of joint retirement are important antecedents of joint retirement actually taking place. The issue of joint retirement, disjointed retirement, and the effects on post-retirement adjustment is something we will return to later in this chapter.

However, the issue of joint retirement becomes more complicated when taking the health of one's partner into account (Lumsdaine & Mitchell, 1999).

For example, Dentinger and Clarkberg (2002) have illustrated the critical effect of a spouse's health status on shaping early retirement decisions. These researchers found that when women were required to provide physical care to a disabled husband, these women were significantly more likely to retire early. Conversely, though, men who were required to provide physical care to a disabled wife responded by delaying their retirement. Dentinger and Clarkberg indicated that these results are not particularly surprising if interpreted from a sex-role perspective wherein men perceive a need to shoulder the financial burden of having an ill spouse, whereas women more frequently assume the caregiving role.

SPOUSAL INFLUENCE

Another line of research has sought to examine the degree to which individuals influence their partner's decision to retire based on the premise that retirement decision making is grounded within the family (Benitez-Silva & Dwyer, 2006; Henkens, 1999; Henkens & van Solinge, 2002; Moen, 1998; Pienta & Hayward, 2002; Shuey, 2004; Szinovacz & DeViney, 2000). Past research has suggested that individuals who report more frequent discussions with their spouse about retirement are more likely to perceive that they retired voluntarily rather than involuntarily (Shultz et al., 1998). Beyond this relatively straightforward finding, one of the most interesting findings within this research is that individuals generally see their spouses as being more influential in their personal retirement decision-making process than the spouses themselves (Smith & Moen, 1998).

The degree to which spouses influence one another appears to be a complex process. First, Benitez-Silva and Dwyer (2006) have argued, based on data collected as part of the Health and Retirement Study, that men form expectations about retirement more independently than women (i.e., men are less influenced by their spouse). Alternatively, Gustman and Steinmeier (2000) have suggested, based on data from the National Longitudinal Survey of Mature Women, that the retirement decision for women is not strongly influenced by their husbands, whereas wives' influences on their husbands' decisions to retire is stronger.

Another interesting finding in relation to the asymmetrical effects that partners have on one another is provided by Pienta and Hayward (2002). In their study, they note that women are more likely to take into account their partner's health status when formulating a decision to retire than they are to consider their own health status. In fact, personal health status was not a significant predictor of retirement decisions for women, but was for men (Pienta & Hayward, 2002). Pienta and Hayward have noted that this finding may be a result of women having fewer health issues at the time of the study, reducing the potential impact of their personal health status on retirement decisions.

In light of these seemingly conflicting results, as discussed by Smith and Moen (1998), the degree of influence partners have over one another may be moderated by other factors. Specifically, Smith and Moen (1998) found that proximity to retirement for the husband affected the degree to which husbands influenced their wives' retirement decision. Alternatively, men who held frequent discussions about retirement with their wives were more likely to see their wives as having a great impact on their retirement decisions. This finding is similar to that found by Pienta and Hayward (2002), who showed that frequent discussions of retirement between spouses was associated with a lower rate of planning to work until the age of 62, and that this effect was stronger for men than it was for women.

SPOUSAL SOCIAL SUPPORT

Closely tied to the role of spousal influences on retirement decisions, Henkens and Tazelaar (1997) examined the effect of perceived spousal support for retirement. First, these authors determined that individuals who perceived their partner to have a negative attitude toward retirement were less likely to report being interested in retiring. Alternatively, individuals who reported feeling their spouse was positive toward retirement reported a great willingness to retire. Furthermore, using their longitudinal data, Henkens and Tazelaar found that for those who initially stated they planned to retire, the probability that they actually did so was lower if the perceived level of social support from their partner was low. For individuals who did not indicate a plan to retire, but who eventually did retire, perceived spousal social support was stronger than for those who did not retire. However, as discussed by the authors, this study does not delve into the pathways through which spousal social support influences the retirement process, and only hints at the possible influences the perceptions of family-based social support may have on the retirement process.

Similar results to those reported by Henkens and Tazelaar (1997) have been shown in terms of predicting plans for early retirement. In their study, van Dam, van der Vorst, and van der Heijden (2009) examined how perceived pressure from spouses (e.g., the antithesis of support) impacted individuals' intentions to retire early. In fact, within their model, which used the theory of planned behavior to predict intentions toward early retirement, perceived spousal pressure for early retirement was the strongest predictor.

Kin Relationships

In addition to the role of marital status, researchers have sought to examine the role that other kin relationships have on the retirement process. Of this research, the majority has focused particularly on the role of children. For instance, Reitzes, Mutran, and Fernandez (1998) examined the effect that the number of children one has on the decision to retire. The authors found that having more children was related to greater delays in retirement. Furthermore, although this effect was found for both men and women, it was stronger for women. Reitzes et al. (1998) suggested that one reason women may enter the workforce in the first place is due to the need to financially support their children. As such, continued economic pressure may encourage women to retain a full-time job longer to ensure that the children are supported.

Szinovacz, DeViney, and Davey (2001) have also shown that individuals who are financially responsible for children are less likely to retire. Szinovacz et al. (2001) also provide evidence that women who have less frequent contact with their children are more likely to delay retirement. Szinovacz et al. (2001) suggest that systematic barriers (i.e., geographical distance) may prevent frequent contact. As such, these women have less of a "pull" on them to leave the workforce for family-related reasons. However, based on their full set of analyses, Szinovacz et al. (2001) noted that the presence of kin relationships and the interaction between such factors as gender and race, frequency of contact with children, and financial dependency of children on respondents produces an extremely complex picture that requires further examination.

The complexity of the retirement and children issue is highlighted by Pienta and Hayward's (2002) results in which they found that the presence of dependent children resulted in a delay in retirement for men, but not women. This is in contradiction to results by Reitzes et al. (1998) and Szinovacz et al. (2001). However, regardless of the complexity of potential interactions, perhaps the most important point made by Szinovacz et al. is that the addition of the family variables included in the predictive

model do not impact the explanatory influence of other traditional variables (e.g., socioeconomic status, health, job dissatisfaction) included in the various models. Rather, the inclusion of the family characteristics examined in their study allowed for further refinement of their predictive models, and models that fail to include family characteristics are incomplete (Szinovacz et al., 2001).

Although retirement research has not exclusively focused on retirement among older adults with primary responsibility for raising grandchildren, the issue is certainly relevant to this discussion of kin relationships. We would expect to find similar patterns of relationships for grandchildren as we do for children, such as delayed retirement among people with financial responsibility for grandchildren.

Research on Bridge Employment

Since the early 1990s, a growing body of literature has sought to examine predictors of bridge employment (Wang & Shultz, 2010). Bridge employment refers to a labor force participation pattern in which older workers exit their career-focused jobs and begin to move toward fully withdrawing from the labor force (Shultz, 2003; Wang et al., 2008). Thus far, this research has found predictors of bridge employment to include age (Adams & Rau, 2004; Loi & Shultz, 2007), health (Kim & Feldman, 2000), financial pressure (Weckerle & Shultz, 1999), and retirement anxiety (Lim & Feldman, 2003).

Several studies have explicitly sought to examine family-related factors that may encourage or discourage engagement in bridge employment. For example, Adams and Rau (2004) found that retirees who perceived a sense of social support from family and friends were more likely to engage in job search behaviors. Adams and Rau also noted that their findings are consistent with past research that has examined the role of social support from family and friends and job-seeking behaviors in unemployed individuals (cf. Vinokur & Caplan, 1987).

Somewhat surprising is the consistent finding across prior research that marital status is not related to bridge employment decisions. This is inconsistent with research that has shown marital status being related to other retirement behaviors, such as full retirement (e.g., Blau, 1998; Pienta, 2003; Szinovacz, 1989; Szinovacz & DeViney, 2000). However, Kim and Feldman (2000) determined that unmarried individuals were no more likely to engage in bridge employment than married individuals. Other researchers have also shown that marital status is not predictive of full retirement, partial retirement, or continued full-time employment (Davis, 2003; Gobeski & Beehr, 2009; Kim & DeVaney, 2005). Furthermore, Wang et al. (2008) demonstrated that neither marital status nor marital quality is related to bridge employment decisions. Interestingly though, Davis (2003) found no support for the argument that family-related pull factors (e.g., the desire to spend more time with spouse and family) actually reduced the attractiveness of bridge employment opportunities for individuals in the private sector.

Two factors that do predict bridge employment include (1) if an individual's partner is still employed and (2) having dependent children (e.g., Kim & Feldman, 2000). These results are consistent with research by Szinovacz et al. (2001) in their examination of factors associated with delayed retirement. In sum, the various results suggest that the role of family-related factors in predicting bridge employment is still very poorly understood (Wang & Shultz, 2010). Therefore, additional research is needed to further examine the role of family in relation to bridge employment.

Retirement from a Work-Family Perspective

As the previous research we have summarized has shown, family variables play an important role in the retirement process. Since the early 1980s (i.e., a time when the proportion of women joining the workforce began to increase substantially; U.S. Bureau of Labor Statistics, 2010), a vast amount of research has been conducted to examine the interface between work and family. Work-family research has traditionally been conceptualized in the area of work stress, as the process of managing work and other roles (e.g., family) may be a stressor (Greenhaus, Allen, & Spector, 2006). According to role theory, individuals juggle multiple roles, such as work and family. Role conflict occurs when two or more sets of pressures occur at the same time such that compliance with one set makes it more difficult to comply with the other set (Kahn, Wolfe, Quinn, Snoek, & Rosenthal, 1964). Greenhaus and Beutell (1985) identified three specific sources of work-family role conflict: time-based conflict, strain-based conflict, and behavior-based conflict. Time-based conflict refers to the notion that time spent in one role is time that is not available to meet the demands of an additional role. For example, time spent at work conflicts with the time one can spend with family. Strain-based conflict occurs when strain experienced in one role affects performance in another role, such as depression, anxiety,

or irritability at work affecting one's relationship with his or her family. Behavior-based conflict occurs when the manner in which one behaves in one role is carried over but incompatible with another role. An example of behavior-based conflict would be a parent closely supervising a young child at home and then supervising individuals at work very closely to the point where the employees may perceive they are being micromanaged.

Hobfoll's (1989) conservation of resources model has also been applied to understanding the work-family interface (Fisher, Bulger, & Smith, 2009; Grandey & Cropanzano, 1999). The conservation of resources model suggests that individuals are motivated to conserve or seek resources that are necessary for meeting the demands of various roles. Conflict or interference may emerge when resources are lost or threatened. This model also implies that work-family enrichment may take place when resources obtained in one domain can facilitate or enhance one's experience in another domain. Time and energy are frequently mentioned as resources relevant to the work-family interface. Consistent with both role theory and the conservation of resources model, Voydanoff (2006) developed a more recent conceptualization of the work-family interface. In particular, she proposed that work-family outcomes stem from work-family demands on individuals and the resources needed to meet them.

Work-Family Conflict

Work-family conflict is one of the most frequently studied constructs within the work-family literature (Casper, Eby, Bordeaux, Lockwood, & Lambert, 2007; Eby, Casper, Lockwood, Bordeaux, & Brinley, 2005). Interest in work-family conflict has been driven in part by the myriad of individual and organizational outcomes it has been found to predict. Work-family conflict has been shown to negatively relate to family satisfaction (e.g., Ford, Heinen, & Langkamer, 2007), job satisfaction (e.g., Allen, Herst, Bruck, & Sutton, 2000), life satisfaction (e.g., Kossek & Ozeki, 1998), depression, anxiety disorders, mood disorders, physical health complaints, hypertension, and alcohol consumption (e.g., Frone, 2000; Frone, Yardley, & Markel, 1997; Greenhaus et al., 2006).

Work-family conflict is bidirectional; work can interfere with family responsibilities, and family can interfere with work demands (Frone, 2003). Antecedents of work-family conflict include role-specific involvement and stressors (e.g., job involvement, time pressure, lack of autonomy, and role ambiguity as antecedents of work-to-family conflict; family involvement, parental stressors, and marital stressors as antecedents of family-to-work conflict; Frone, Russell, & Cooper, 1992), and personality (e.g., conscientiousness, which is associated with lower levels of conflict, and neuroticism, which is associated with higher levels of conflict; Wayne, Musica, & Fleeson, 2004). Additional research has shown crossover effects in which work stress and work-family conflict may affect other family members (Westman & Etzion, 2005).

WORK-FAMILY CONFLICT AND RETIREMENT

There are many ways work-family conflict may relate to retirement. First, the life course perspective takes into account various life stages and transitions one encounters as well as influences of family members and intersections of various roles during one's lifetime (Bengston & Allen, 1993; Raymo & Sweeney, 2006). Baltes and Young (2007) referred to various life-cycle stages derived from a constellation of factors (e.g., family size, developmental age of older child, and breadwinner work status) and how these stages relate to work and family demands.

Some research on retirement has examined the role of work stress in relation to retirement (e.g., Elovainio et al., 2005). Individuals may seek retirement as a way to minimize or avoid work stress. For example, Barnes-Farrell (2003) described retirement as a means of escape among older workers responding to "push" forces from the workplace. An obvious issue regarding retirement and work-family conflict is time (e.g., time-based conflict). Time is a limited resource, and time spent working is time not available for other roles, such as family, community activities, or leisure. One way to minimize time-based conflict is to spend less time at work. This may take the form of full retirement or reducing one's work hours. Some research (e.g., Staines & O'Connor, 1980) has suggested that work-family conflict should decrease as the age of one's youngest child increases. This indirectly suggests that older workers should experience less work-family conflict, a trend that has received only limited attention in the work-family literature (Matthews, Bulger, & Barnes-Farrell, 2010). However, as noted previously, some older workers may care for or have custody of grandchildren. Secondly, children are not the only potential source of work-family conflict. Older workers may be faced with elder-care responsibilities, including caring for a parent or other relative, or an ill spouse.

As noted by Yeandle (2005), the stress associated with additional family care demands can be confounded by the suddenness with which these demands can develop. Data from the 2010 EBRI Retirement Confidence Survey (Helman, Greenwald, Copeland, & VanDerhei, 2010) suggest that approximately 41% of retirees left the workforce earlier than they planned. This seemingly large proportion is likely to have been driven by the economic recession that began in late 2008. Of those respondents who left the workforce early, 19% of respondents indicated that they retired early in order to care for a spouse or other family member. Addressing these care demands is complicated by the fact that, although most organizations have work-life benefits in place related to child care, the majority of organizations provide only limited support (i.e., have limited benefits and policies in place) to help workers manage the caregiving role (Dikkers, Geurts, den Dulk, & Peper, 2005). For example, the Society for Human Resource Management estimates that only 11% of employers allow for elder-care leave above federal requirements (i.e., FMLA) and that only 3% of employers subsidize the cost of elder care (Society for Human Resource Management, 2010).

Some prior research suggests that older workers are more oriented toward their family lives and leisure activities (e.g., Evans & Bartolomé, 1984). As a result, these individuals may be more likely to experience work-family conflict. To date, only a few studies have systematically examined the retirement process in relation to work-family conflict. In one such study, Raymo and Sweeney (2006) examined the relationship between work-family conflict and preferences toward retirement.

Raymo and Sweeney (2006) argued that given what is known about the predictive power of experiences of work-family conflict, perceptions of work-family conflict should be important in terms of the development, maintenance, and alterations to retirement preferences and planning. Within their sample of individuals aged 52–54, Raymo and Sweeney (2006) found that individuals who experienced higher levels of both work-to-family and family-to-work conflict were significantly more likely to want to retire in the next ten years. These effects were found even after controlling for other variables, such as gender, education, income, pension status, health, and whether one's spouse was working. Although these authors hypothesized that the relationship between work-family conflict and preference to retire would be stronger for women than for men, they did not find this gender difference. Raymo and Sweeney also noted that the antecedents of work-family conflict may be different for older adults compared to younger adults. For example, older workers may experience pressure to retire from their spouse, which younger workers would not experience.

In a related study, Desmette and Gaillard (2008) examined the role of work/non-work conflict, which they defined as work-to-private life conflict. Although similar to the concept of work-to-family conflict, Desmette and Gaillard described work-to-private life conflict, which is a broader construct than work-family conflict and incorporates aspects of life outside of work beyond just the family domain. Among a sample of workers aged 50–59, Desmette and Gaillard found that experiences of conflict between work and non-work domains influence retirement decisions, at least to some degree. Although work-to-private life conflict did not statistically predict desire for early retirement, it did predict individuals' desire for bridge employment, after controlling for age, health, and wealth. Individuals who felt like their work life was conflicting with their private life reported a greater desire to engage in bridge employment activities (i.e., reducing the number of hours they work). Thus, results by Desmette and Gaillard are somewhat inconsistent with those reported by Raymo and Sweeney (2006). However, these inconsistent results are themselves informative.

In examining work-to-private life conflict, Desmette and Gaillard (2008) asked respondents to consider their non-work life more broadly compared to Raymo and Sweeney (2006), who asked respondents specifically about the extent to which their work life interferes with their family life. Given that past research has consistently demonstrated that the family domain plays an important role in the retirement process (Szinovacz, 2003), these results appear to reinforce the need to ask respondents about conflict between work and family specifically, as well as work and other non-work roles.

In a more recent study, Kubicek, Korunka, Hoonakker, and Raymo (2010) examined the role perceptions of work-family conflict within a larger conceptual model seeking to predict early retirement. As part of the development of their conceptual model, the authors argued that organizations, in an effort to retain older workers who contribute significant knowledge, skills, and abilities, can modify early retirement decisions by re-engineering aspects of the work environment (e.g., through flexible work arrangements). In turn, by positively re-engineering the work domain, these changes may positively influence family-based characteristics in terms of reducing perceived demands and increasing the perceptions of available resources. Related to this, Kubicek et al. suggested that if an individual perceives his or her family life to be particularly stressful, this may encourage the individual to delay retirement in order to use the work domain as an "escape" from the pressure of the family domain.

Within their model, Kubicek et al. (2010) position job and marital satisfaction as mediators of the effects of work-to-family and family-to-work conflict, respectively, on early retirement decisions. Although not empirically tested, job satisfaction and marital satisfaction seemed to equally relate to early retirement decisions, albeit in the opposite direction. Interestingly, the indirect effect of work-to-family conflict on early retirement (via job satisfaction) decisions was over twice as large as that of family-to-work conflict (via marital satisfaction). As such, these results suggest that experiences of work-to-family conflict encouraged early retirement, whereas experiences of family-to-work conflict resulted in delayed retirement decisions. In turn, these results provide support for the argument that demands in the family domain might encourage one to remain employed longer as a potential coping mechanism (Kubicek et al., 2010). Again, consistent with other work-family studies, these effects were found after controlling for traditional predictors of early retirement decisions (e.g., health insurance, income, pension, education). Furthermore, both family demands (i.e., in terms of spouse's health) and family resources (i.e., social support) demonstrated small but significant indirect effects on early retirement in their final empirical model.

Work-Family Enhancement and Retirement

During the last ten years, work-family researchers have been looking beyond conflict at the intersection of work and family and have begun to investigate the extent to which engagement in multiple roles such as work, family, and/or community may enrich or enhance workers' lives (Voydanoff, 2005; Carlson, Kacmar, Wayne, & Grzywacz, 2006). Work-family enhancement or enrichment refers to the notion that participation in one role (e.g., work) may lead to additional resources or benefits in another role (e.g., family). For example, work can enrich one's family life by providing esteem, skills, income, positive mood, and other benefits that make it easier to perform family-related roles. Carlson et al. (2006)

conducted pioneering work in this area by developing measures to assess work-family enrichment and demonstrating that enrichment is empirically distinct from conflict. Work-family enhancement has been shown to be positively related to important affective and behavioral outcomes, including job, life, and family satisfaction (Carlson et al., 2006; Fisher et al., 2009); job performance; family performance (Carlson, Grzywacz, & Kacmar, 2010); and turnover intentions (McNall, Masuda, & Nicklin, 2009). Barnes-Farrell, Dove-Steinkamp, Golay, Johnson, and McGonagle (2008) suggested that work-family enhancement is related to the planned timing of retirement such that individuals with higher perceptions of enhancement intended to remain in the workforce longer. This finding seems intuitive, as those whose family life benefits from their work (i.e., perceive higher levels of work-to-family enhancement) would be more likely to continue working (i.e., delay retirement), whereas individuals who experience lower levels of work-to-family enrichment would not have the same incentive to continue working. This is consistent with Barnes-Farrell's (2003) conceptualization of "push" and "pull" forces of retirement.

Additional research to examine the role of work-family conflict as well as work-family enhancement in relation to the retirement decision-making process is certainly needed. We need to clearly identify the work-family needs of older workers. For example, older workers may have heterogeneous caregiving responsibilities, including more elder-care responsibilities, needs to care for a spouse, and in some cases the care of grandchildren (Lumsdaine & Mitchell, 1999). A higher proportion of older workers may fall into the sandwiched generation of those caring for both younger and older family members concurrently (Hammer & Neal, 2008). This may contrast with the needs of younger working parents who may be more focused on caregiving for younger children.

Family Characteristics and Retirement Transition and Adjustment

A considerable amount of research has sought to examine how individuals transition and adjust to retirement. The majority of this research has been based on either continuity theory (Atchley, 1989) or a life course perspective (Wang, 2007). The use of these two paradigms has allowed researchers to take a longitudinal perspective when conceptualizing relationships between constructs (Wang & Shultz, 2010). In terms of operationalizing adjustment, a

myriad of different constructs has been examined. Some of these include physical health (Ekerdt, Baden, Bossé, & Dibbs, 1983), satisfaction with retirement (Smith & Moen, 2004), and a variety of outcomes related to family and couple functioning. However, as noted by Wang and Shultz (2010), results from this body of research are mixed at best. Put simply, individuals can take different pathways to retirement, and their post-retirement experiences may differ dramatically as a result (Han & Moen 1999; Wang, 2007; Wang & Shultz, 2010).

A significant portion of past research on retirement transition and adjustment has taken a dyadic perspective based on the premise that just as retirement decisions are grounded in the family system, so are post-retirement experiences. Within the following sections we review past research on retirement transition and adjustment research with an explicit attempt to incorporate aspects of the family domain. The majority of this research can be conceptualized as focusing on three general sets of outcomes: retirement satisfaction, post-retirement marital quality and conflict, and post-retirement depression.

Retirement Satisfaction

At a general level, a body of previous research has sought to examine differences in retirement satisfaction for married versus unmarried individuals. To this end, it has been shown that married individuals report higher retirement satisfaction than unmarried individuals (Price & Joo, 2005). This finding is consistent with past research that suggests that married individuals report generally greater well-being than unmarried individuals (Bierman, Fazio, & Milkie, 2006; van Solinge & Henkens, 2008). Furthermore, the loss of one's spouse during retirement can also dramatically affect perceptions of retirement satisfaction (van Solinge & Henkens, 2008).

Although past research has shown that personal health impacts retirement satisfaction (e.g., van Solinge & Henkens, 2008), past research has also shown that partner health may also impact perceptions of retirement satisfaction (Myers & Booth, 1996). For example, poor health for one's partner may increase care demands as well as reduce opportunities for joint activities in retirement (Haug, Belgrave, & Jones, 1992; Myers & Booth, 1996; Smith & Moen, 2004).

A series of studies has sought to examine how joint retirement is related to retirement satisfaction. The general finding is that couples who coordinate their retirements, and thus retire within a relatively short period of one another, report greater retirement satisfaction compared to couples in which one retires long before the other (Gustman & Steinmeier, 2000; Henretta, O'Rand, & Chan, 1993; Moen, Kim, & Hofmeister, 2001; Smith & Moen, 2004; Szinovacz, 1996). However, in terms of examining the degree to which partners are perceived as influencing one another's decision to retire, Smith and Moen (2004) yielded some interesting results. Specifically, Smith and Moen determined that women were significantly more satisfied with their retirement when they did not feel like their husbands were influential in their retirement decision-making process. On the other hand, men were more likely to report higher levels of retirement satisfaction if they felt like their partners were involved in their retirement decision-making processes.

Past research has also sought to examine changes in household activities upon retirement. For example, as might be expected, men do engage in more household-related activities post-retirement (e.g., Fitzpatrick, Vinick, & Bushfield, 2005). What is interesting to note is that changes in division of labor are not as drastic as might be expected. Fitzpatrick et al. (2005) noted that men do increase their participation in household activities, but not as much as their partners had expected. What is even more interesting to note is that the incongruence between expectations and reality does not appear to negatively impact retirement satisfaction.

Marital Quality & Conflict

With regard to prior research that has sought to examine issues of marital quality and conflict, it is important to note that past research has shown that perceptions of marital quality are related to gender, such that men tend to report higher levels of martial quality than women (e.g., Veroff, Douvan, Orbuch, & Acitelli, 1999). To this end, several studies within the retirement literature have examined life after retirement for couples in terms of experienced quality and conflict. Specifically, Moen et al. (2001) have demonstrated that couples that retire congruently report greater marital quality than couples in which partners do not retire at the same time.

An interesting set of studies consistent with continuity theory (Atchley, 1992) has demonstrated that the retirement process reinforces pre-retirement experiences. For example, marriages with better quality prior to retirement got even better after retirement, whereas marriages with poor quality got worse after retirement (Davey & Szinovacz, 2004; Dew & Yorgason, 2010; Myers & Booth, 1996).

Specifically related to marital conflict, Davey and Szinovacz (2004) have shown that when women remained employed, it further amplifies pre-existing interaction patterns (i.e., good marriages got better, and poor marriages got even worse). In general, continued employment for women after their partners have retired appears to be associated with increases in marital conflict (Davey & Szinovacz, 2004). This reinforcement effect may be a function of the fact that couples generally maintain similar behavioral patterns after retirement as they do before retirement. Again, for example, as discussed by Fitzpatrick et al. (2005), although more than three-quarters of partners expected to engage in more activities together with their spouse/partner after retirement, less than half actually did experience an increase. However, Fitzpatrick et al. suggested that the incongruence between expectations and reality did not appear to negatively impact retirement satisfaction. For marriages that improve post-retirement, Davey and Szinovacz note that several factors may be at play. For example, these couples may be the ones who do actually experience an increase in joint activities (Fitzpatrick et al., 2005).

Depression

A relatively consistent finding in past research is that retired husbands who have wives who are still working report higher levels of depression compared to retired husbands with retired wives (Szinovacz, 1996; Moen et al., 2001; Myers & Booth, 1996). In a more detailed examination of this issue, Szinovacz and Davey (2004) sought to examine how depressive symptoms in retired men may vary in terms of how long these men have been employed. Szinovacz and Davey determined that compared to newly retired husbands with continuously working wives, husbands who had been retired for longer periods of time but still had employed spouses reported lower levels of depression. However, these men still reported significant levels of depression. Thus, although some adjustment took place (e.g., a reduction in depressive symptoms), these men still reported higher levels of depression in relation to their family situation.

In a related study, Kim and Moen (2001) also found that men who have been retired for an extended period of time report fewer depressive symptoms if their wives are not employed. However, somewhat counter to Szinovacz and Davey (2004), Kim and Moen (2001) found that men who have recently retired tend to show lower levels of depressive symptoms if their wives have remained employed.

Collectively, this research illustrates that family-related characteristics, and in particular marital status and couple dynamics, are related to retirement transition and adjustment. This research has focused on marital relationships, and little has been done regarding the role of other family members (e.g., children) with regard to psychological retirement outcomes. Additional research is needed to develop a more complete picture of the role of family in terms of adjusting to retirement. For example, do family factors moderate the relationship between the type of retirement (e.g., full retirement vs. bridge employment) and retirement satisfaction?

Summary and Conclusions

Demographic trends have underscored the need to simultaneously consider family, work, and the retirement process. For example, there is a higher proportion of women in the workforce as well as a higher proportion of dual-earner couples who will have to navigate the retirement process compared to decades ago, when men were the dominant and sole breadwinners. Marital status and spouse's work status, influence, and support have all been shown to be related to the retirement process. In addition, research has demonstrated the interdependence of retirement decision making between members of a couple. Although research on the role of marital relationships in the retirement decision-making, transition, and adjustment process has dominated the body of family-related retirement research, children also play a role in retirement planning and behavior. For example, characteristics of children (e.g., number and ages of children) as well as the notion of having financial responsibility for children and the frequency of contact with children have also been demonstrated to play a role in the retirement process.

Taken together, research that has included family variables in models predicting retirement behavior does not negate the effects of other variables known to be important determinants of retirement (e.g., health, wealth, and job satisfaction; Barnes-Farrell, 2003), but improves overall model prediction.

Future Directions
Recent Economic Changes

The retirement landscape is changing as a result of shifts in demographic trends, such as having more women in the workforce and people remaining in the workforce until later ages (due to many factors, including increased longevity, changes in social security policies that encourage individuals to remain in the workforce longer, and a shift away from defined benefit pension plans and toward defined contribution plans). In addition, there are many paths to retirement, including full retirement, gradually reducing one's work hours, and bridge employment. The recent economic downturn that began in 2008 further complicates the retirement picture, as many people who had planned to retire at about that time could no longer afford to. Recent research by McFall (2011) has found that individuals who had planned to retire in 2008 or 2009 delayed their retirement an average of 1.6 years. Unmarried individuals were more likely to delay their retirement compared to their married counterparts (McFall, personal communication, January 12, 2011).

Additional research is needed to examine the role of family in relation to retirement in the current economic climate. For example, how have retirement preferences, intentions, and financial planning behaviors changed as a result of the recent economic declines? To what extent do family-related factors moderate those relationships?

Cohort Effects

Closely related to the need to examine family-related factors in the current economy is whether the research results obtained over the last decade or two will generalize to future cohorts. It remains an empirical question as to whether retirement patterns differ by cohorts, and the extent to which relationships among family-related variables and the retirement process will still hold. Although researchers should continue to study older workers at or nearing retirement, additional attention should be paid to understanding the retirement preferences, intentions, and behaviors among younger cohorts as well. For example, there is evidence to suggest that cultural shifts are taking place, resulting in more gender equality in industrialized nations like the United States (Inglehart & Norris, 2003). Taking this trend into account, future research is needed to examine how retirement planning and decisions take place in younger cohorts, particularly in terms of understanding the role of spousal influence.

Work-Family and Retirement

To date, very little research has been conducted regarding the relationship between work-family conflict and retirement. Much more research is needed on work-family conflict in relation to retirement, such as how it is related to plans, retirement timing, bridge employment, and adjustment. Based on prior research, which has shown that work-family conflict does predict retirement (e.g., Raymo & Sweeney, 2006), future research should examine specific sources of this conflict. Additionally, given that older workers may not experience conflict between work and family demands at the same levels as younger workers (Matthews et al., 2010)—because they are in a different life stage and no longer have young children or any children at home, or because they have adjusted to these demands and therefore do not experience much strain while trying to balance work and family roles—work-family enrichment seems promising as a stronger predictor of retirement behavior (Barnes-Farrell et al., 2008). Future research should further examine the role of work-family enrichment in relation to retirement decisions, including bridge employment, as well as with regard to retirement transitions and adjustment.

In addition, the work-family literature would be strengthened by a closer examination of work-family benefits offerings and participation in these benefits plans, particularly among benefits relevant to older workers. By increasing our understanding of work-family benefits, we can determine the extent to which such programs add any incentive for or facilitate older workers remaining in the workforce. For example, if workers have access to flexible work arrangements or elder-care resources, they may be able to or prefer to delay retirement rather than retire in order to fulfill the caregiving role. This research may have a larger practical impact for work-family research in general, something sorely missing within the literature (Kossek, Baltes, & Matthews, 2011).

Retirement Financial Planning

The economic literature has recently focused more attention on the issue of financial literacy, recognizing that financial literacy is related to financial decision making and outcomes, as well as retirement planning (e.g., Lusardi, 2008; Lusardi & Mitchell, 2007). This research has found that in general older Americans are fairly financially illiterate, which was also illustrated by the high rates of foreclosures and debt problems that arose during the recent housing and financial crisis. In older-couple households, men typically have primary responsibility for household finances (Hsu, 2011). For example, Hsu's recent analysis from the Cognitive Economics Survey, using a national sample of individuals age 51 or older, found that only

16% of women reported being the most knowledgeable about household finances, and less than half of women indicated that they were equally knowledgeable about finances (relative to their husbands). However, more research is needed to investigate the role of family dynamics (e.g., marital status, marital quality, and spousal influence) in the retirement planning process. It will also be important to examine these issues across multiple cohorts, based on the previous argument that the extent to which patterns across cohorts are consistent is an empirical question that remains to be answered.

Methodological Issues
LONGITUDINAL RESEARCH

Retirement is a process that unfolds over time, rather than a discrete event. As such, longitudinal research should be conducted to accurately depict this process (Wang & Shultz, 2010). The purpose of longitudinal designs is to better understand the underlying causal mechanisms behind these dynamic processes as well as how these processes may evolve over time (Menard, 2002). The application of longitudinal methods is nothing new in the retirement literature (e.g., Henkens & Tazelaar, 1997) and is gaining importance within the work-family literature as well (Casper et al., 2007).

One outstanding issue within each of these literatures is the failure to conceptually incorporate time into theoretically derived models. Put another way, although data may be collected longitudinally, some researchers have failed to develop sound hypotheses regarding why the data should be collected longitudinally, and at which points in time (i.e., length of time lags between assessments) it is most critical to make repeated assessments. Without theoretical guidance about how relationships of interest develop and change over time, researchers are left to make critical decisions about appropriate lags between assessments based on "intuition, chance, convenience, or tradition," all of which are prone to error and invite criticism (Mitchell & James, 2001, p. 533). Without a clearer understanding of the role of temporal lags, researchers run the continued risk of reporting underestimated predictor-outcome relationships, or potentially more seriously, reporting inappropriate causal inferences (Menard, 2002). This issue takes on added importance in light of the fact that most work-family literature is grounded within a stressor-strain paradigm, given that very little is known about the temporal process through which stressors affect strains.

In terms of research that focuses on retirement-related processes and examines the work-family interface regarding the retirement process, more attention needs to be given to when and how frequently assessments are made. Providing a justification for why data were collected at particular intervals is critical to help clarify the role of time in the retirement stressor-strain process.

MEASUREMENT ISSUES

As mentioned elsewhere in this handbook by Fisher and Willis, there are variety of ways to define retirement, including retirement preferences, intentions, and actual retirement behavior. Such different definitions of retirement may influence the interpretation of study results. In addition, this is an issue of concern for work-family scholars interested in the retirement process. For example, retirement researchers are well equipped at collecting or using data on health and economic status (e.g., income and wealth). What work-family scholars have to contribute is their expertise in collecting data that can be used to describe the workplace (e.g., organizational stressors), particularly psychological attitudes (e.g., organizational commitment, job satisfaction). The use of valid measures of psychological constructs is common practice to work-family scholars. That said, many of the existing measures that might be used were not developed with older workers in mind. As we have attempted to document in this chapter, experiences of older workers nearing retirement are often substantially different from individuals in younger cohorts (in part because they are at different points of their life course). As such, measures that have been developed based on individuals in the middle of their life course (i.e., individuals with children) need to be validated for individuals who are further along in their life course (i.e., older individuals considering retirement).

Although the emphasis of this chapter is on the role of work, family, and the retirement process, and much of the work–non-work research has focused on family in the non-work domain, it is important to mention that there may be other roles outside of work that may play a role in the retirement process. In particular, it may be advantageous to consider the work–non-work interface more broadly than simply work-family (Fisher et al., 2009).

Concluding Remarks

We have sought to present a chapter that is accessible to both established retirement researchers interested in understanding the role of family in the retirement process, as well as work-family scholars who may be interested in the relation between work-family issues and the retirement process. Family is a very important aspect of life for the majority of older adults. With the majority of older adults at or nearing retirement being married or partnered, the spousal relationship is the most salient aspect of family, particularly in relation to the retirement process. As we described, children and grandchildren are additional factors that can affect retirement.

Retirement is a decision-making process, rather than a single decision, and one in which family plays a key and pivotal role. The decision regarding whether and when to retire is often not an individual decision, but rather one that unfolds within a larger family context. Specifically, marital status, spousal influence and social support, family caregiving responsibilities, and work-family conflict can affect retirement decisions and the process in which one retires (e.g., full retirement, gradual retirement, or bridge employment). Family is also a significant factor in the retirement transition process. Future research should more clearly identify the needs of older workers, further evaluate the role of family in retirement (e.g., bridge employment and retirement planning), explore cohort effects, and attend to methodological issues by continuing to use longitudinal research designs and attend to measurement issues. We also suggest that work-family or work-life enrichment or enhancement holds promise for furthering our understanding of work, family, and retirement.

References

Adams, G., & Rau, B. (2004). Job seeking among retirees seeking bridge employment. *Personnel Psychology, 57,* 719–744.

Allen, T. D., Herst, D. E. L., Bruck, C. S., & Sutton, M. (2000). Consequences associated with work-to-family conflict: A review and agenda for future research. *Journal of Occupational Health Psychology, 5,* 278–308.

Amatea, E. S., Cross, E. G., Clark, J. E., & Bobby, C. L. (1986). Assessing the work and family role expectations of career-oriented men and women: The life role salience scales. *Journal of Marriage and Family, 48,* 831–838.

American Community Survey. (2005–2009). Statistical abstract of the United States. Table S1201: Marital Status. Retrieved from http://factfinder.census.gov.

An, M. Y., Christensen, B. J., & Gupta, N. D. (2004). Multivariate mixed proportional hazard modeling of the joint retirement of married couples. *Journal of Applied Econometrics, 19*(6), 687–704.

Atchley, R. (1989). A continuity theory of normal aging. *The Gerontologist, 29*, 183–190.

Atchley, R. C. (1992). Retirement and marital satisfaction. In M. Szinovacz, D. Ekerdt, & B. H. Vinick (Eds.), *Families and retirement* (pp. 145–158). Newbury Park, CA: Sage.

Baltes, B. B., & Young, L. M. (2007). Aging and work/family issues. In G. Adams & K. Shultz (Eds.), *Aging and work in the 21st century* (pp. 251–275). Lawrence Erlbaum Associates Applied Psychology Series.

Barnes-Farrell, J. L. (2003). Beyond health and wealth: Attitudinal and other influences on retirement decisionmaking. In G. A. Adams & T. A. Beehr (Eds.), *Retirement: Reasons, processes, and results* (pp. 159–187). New York, NY: Springer.

Barnes-Farrell, J. L., Dove-Steinkamp, M., Golay, L., Johnson, N., & McGonagle, A. (2008, November). How does the nature of the work-family interface influence planned retirement age of men and women? In G. G. Fisher (Chair), *The graying of the American workforce: Implications for occupational health psychology*. Symposium presented at the 8th conference of the European Association of Occupational Health Psychology, Valencia, Spain.

Beehr, T. A. (1986). The process of retirement: A review and recommendations for future investigation. *Personnel Psychology, 39*, 31–56.

Bellavia, G. M., & Frone, M. R. (2005). Work-family conflict. In J. Barling, E. K. Kelloway, & M. R. Frone (Eds.), *Handbook of work stress* (pp. 113–148). Thousand Oaks, CA: Sage.

Bengston, V. L., & Allen, K. R. (1993). The life course perspective applied to families over time. In P. G. Boss, W. J. Doherty, R. LaRossa, W. R. Scham, & S. K. Steinmetz (Eds.), *Sourcebook of families, theories and methods: A contextual approach* (pp. 469–499). New York, NY: Plenum.

Benitez-Silva, H., & Dwyer, D. S. (2006). Expectation formation of older married couples and the rational expectations hypothesis. *Labour Economics 13*(2), 191–218.

Bierman, A., Fazio, E. M., & Milkie, M. A. (2006). A multifaceted approach to the mental health advantage of the married: Assessing how explanations vary by outcome measure and unmarried group. *Journal of Family Issues, 27*, 554–582.

Blau, D. M. (1998). Labor force dynamics of older married couples. *Journal of Labor Economics, 16*, 595–629.

Carlson, D. S., Grzywacz, J. G., & Kacmar, K. M. (2010). The relationship of schedule flexibility and outcomes via the work-family interface. *Journal of Managerial Psychology, 25*, 330–355.

Carlson, D. S., Kacmar, K. M., Wayne, J. H., & Grzywacz, J. G. (2006). Measuring the positive side of the work-family interface: Development and validation of a work-family enrichment scale. *Journal of Vocational Behavior, 68*, 131–164.

Carr, J. C., Boyar, S. L., & Gregory, B. T., (2008). The moderating effect of work-family centrality on work-family conflict, organizational attitudes, and turnover behavior. *Journal of Management, 34*, 244–262.

Casper, W. J., Eby, L. T., Bordeaux, C., Lockwood, A., & Lambert, D. (2007). A review of research methods in IO/OB work-family research. *Journal of Applied Psychology, 92*, 28–43.

Cinamon, R. G., & Rich, Y. (2002). Gender differences in the importance of work and family roles: Implications for work-family conflict. *Sex Roles, 47*, 531–541.

Current Population Survey. (2010). *America's families and living arrangements: 2010* [Data File]. Retrieved from U.S. Census Bureau website: http://www.census.gov/population/www/socdemo/hh-fam/cps2010.html.

Davey, A., & Szinovacz, M. E. (2004). Dimensions of marital quality and retirement. *Journal of Family Issues, 25*, 431–464.

Davis, M. A. (2003). Factors related to bridge employment participation among private sector early retirees. *Journal of Vocational Behavior, 63*, 55–71.

Dentinger, E., & Clarkberg, M. (2002). Informal caregiving and retirement timing among men and women. *Journal of Family Issues, 23*, 857–879.

Desmette, D., & Gaillard, M. (2008). When a "worker" becomes an "older worker": The effects of age-related social identity on attitudes towards retirement and work. *Career Development International, 13*, 168–185.

Dew, J., & Yorgason, J. (2010). Economic pressure and marital conflict in retirement-aged couples. *Journal of Family Issues, 31*, 164–188.

Dikkers, J. S. E., Geurts, S. A. E., den Dulk, L., & Peper, B. (2005). Work-nonwork culture, utilization of work-nonwork arrangements, and employee-related outcomes in two Dutch organizations. In S. A. Y Poelmans (Ed.), *Work and family: An international research perspective* (pp. 147–172). Mahwah, NJ: Lawrence Erlbaum Associates.

Eby, L. T., Casper, W. J., Lockwood, A., Bordeaux, C., & Brinley, A. (2005). Work and family research in IOOB: Content analysis and review of the literature (1980–2002). *Journal of Vocational Behavior, 66*, 124–197.

Ekerdt, D. J., Baden, L., Bossé, R., & Dibbs, E. (1983). The effect of retirement on physical health. *American Journal of Public Health, 73*, 779–783.

Elder, G. H. (1994). Time, human agency, and social change: Perspectives on the life course. *Social Psychology Quarterly, 57*, 4–15.

Elovainio, M., Forma, P., Kivimaki, M., Sinervo, T., Sutinen, R., & Laine, M. (2005). Job demands and job control as correlates of early retirement thoughts in Finnish social and health care employees. *Work & Stress, 19*, 84–92.

Evans, P., & Bartolomé, F. (1984). The changing pictures of the relationship between career and family. *Journal of Occupational Behavior, 5*, 9–21.

Fisher, G. G., Bulger, C. A., & Smith, C. S. (2009). Beyond work and family: A measure of work/nonwork interference and enhancement. *Journal of Occupational Health Psychology, 14*, 441–456.

Fitzpatrick, T. R., Vinick, B. H., & Bushfield, S. (2005). Anticipated and experienced changes in activities after husbands retire. *Journal of Gerontological Social Work, 46*, 69–84.

Ford, M. T., Heinen, B. A., & Langkamer, K. L. (2007). Work and family satisfaction and conflict: A meta-analysis of cross-domain relations. *Journal of Applied Psychology, 92*, 57–80.

Frone, M. R. (2000). Interpersonal conflict at work and psychological outcomes: Testing a model among young workers. *Journal of Occupational Health Psychology, 5*, 246–255.

Frone, M. R. (2003). Work-family balance. In J. C. Quick & L. E. Tetrick (Eds.), *Handbook of occupational health psychology* (pp. 143–162). Washington, DC: American Psychological Association.

Frone, M. R., Russell, M., & Cooper, M. L. (1992). Antecedents and outcomes of work-family conflict: Testing a model of the work-family interface. *Journal of Applied Psychology, 77,* 65–78.

Frone, M. R., Yardley, J. K., & Markel, K. S. (1997). Developing and testing an integrative model of the work-family interface. *Journal of Vocational Behaviors, 50,* 145–167.

Giele, J. Z., & Elder, G. H. (Eds.). (1998). *Methods of life course research: Qualitative and quantitative approaches.* London, England: Sage.

Gobeski, K. T., & Beehr, T. A. (2009). How retirees work: Predictors of different types of bridge employment. *Journal of Organizational Behavior, 37,* 401–425.

Grandey, A. A., & Cropanzano, R. (1999). The conservation of resources model applied to work-family conflict and strain. *Journal of Vocational Behavior, 54,* 350–370.

Greenhaus, J. H., Allen, T. D., & Spector, P. E. (2006). Health consequences of work-family conflict: The dark side of the work-family interface. In P. L. Perrewe & D. C. Ganster (Eds.), *Research in occupational stress and well-being* (Vol. 5, pp. 61–98). Amsterdam, The Netherlands: JAI Press/Elsevier.

Greenhaus, J. H., & Beutell, N. J. (1985). Sources of conflict between work and family roles. *Academy of Management Review, 10,* 76–88.

Greenhaus, J. H., & Powell, G. N. (2006). When work and family are allies: A theory of work-family enrichment. *Academy of Management Review, 31,* 72–92.

Gustman, A. L., & Steinmeier, T. L. (2000). Retirement in dual-career families: A structural model. *Journal of Labor Economics, 18,* 503–545.

Hammer, L. B., & Neal, M. B. (2008). Sandwiched generation caregivers: Prevalence, characteristics, and outcomes. *The Psychologist-Manager Journal, 11,* 93–112.

Han, S., & Moen, P. (1999). Clocking out: Temporal patterning of retirement. *American Journal of Sociology, 105,* 191–236.

Haug, M. R., Belgrave, L. L., & Jones, S. (1992). Partners' health and retirement: Adaptation of women and their husbands. *Journal of Women and Aging, 4,* 5–29.

Helman, R., Greenwald, M., Copeland, C., & VanDerhei, J., (2010). *The 2010 Retirement Confidence Survey: Confidence stabilizing, but preparations continue to erode* (Issue Brief No. 340). Washington, DC: Employee Benefit Research Institute. Retrieved from http://www.ebri.org/pdf/briefspdf/EBRI_IB_03-2010_No340_RCS.pdf.

Henkens, K. (1999). Retirement intentions and spousal support: A multifactor approach. *Journal of Gerontology: Social Sciences, 54B,* S63–S73.

Henkens, K., & Tazelaar, F. (1997). Explaining early retirement decisions of civil servants in the Netherlands: Intentions, behavior and the discrepancy between the two. *Research on Aging, 19,* 129–173.

Henkens, K., & van Solinge, H. (2002). Spousal influences on the decision to retire. *International Journal of Sociology, 32,* 55–74.

Henretta, J. C., O'Rand, A. M., & Chan, C. G. (1993). Joint role investment and synchronization of retirement: A sequential approach to couples' retirement timing. *Social Forces, 71,* 981–1000.

Ho, J., & Raymo, J. (2009). Expectations and realization of joint retirement among dual-worker couples. *Research on Aging, 31,* 153–179.

Hobfoll, S. E. (1989). Conservation of resources: A new attempt at conceptualizing stress. *American Psychologist, 44,* 513–524.

Hsu, J. W. (2011). *Aging and strategic learning: The impact of spousal incentives on financial literacy. Essays on the acquisition of human capital* (Unpublished doctoral dissertation). Department of Economics, University of Michigan, Ann Arbor, MI.

Inglehart, R., & Norris, P. (2003). *Rising tide: Gender equality and cultural change around the world.* Cambridge, United Kingdom: Cambridge University Press.

Kahn, R. L., Wolfe, D. M., Quinn, R., Snoek, J. D., & Rosenthal, R. A. (1964). *Organizational stress.* New York, NY: Wiley.

Kanfer, R., & Ackerman, P. L. (2004). Aging, adult development, and work motivation. *Academy of Management Review, 29,* 440–458.

Kim, H., & DeVaney, S.A. (2005). The selection of partial or full retirement by older workers. *Journal of Family and Economic Issues, 26,* 371–394.

Kim, J. E., & Moen, P. (2001). Is retirement good or bad for subjective well-being? *Current Directions in Psychological Science, 10,* 83–86.

Kim, S., & Feldman, D. C. (1998). Healthy, wealthy, or wise: Predicting actual acceptances of early retirement incentives at three points in time. *Personnel Psychology, 51,* 623–642.

Kim, S., & Feldman, D. C. (2000). Working in retirement: The antecedents of bridge employment and its consequences for quality of life in retirement. *Academy of Management Journal, 43,* 1195–1210.

Kossek, E. E., Baltes, B. B., & Matthews, R. A. (2011). How work-family research can finally have an impact in the workplace. *Industrial and Organizational Psychology: Perspectives on Science and Practice, 4*(3), 352–369.

Kossek, E. E., Ozeki, C. (1998). Work-family conflict, policies, and the job-life satisfaction relationship: A review and directions for organizational behavior/human resources research. *Journal of Applied Psychology, 83,* 139–149.

Kubicek, B., Korunka, C., Hoonakker, P., & Raymo, J. M. (2010). Work and family characteristics as predictors of early retirement in married men and women. *Research on Aging, 32,* 467–498.

Lim, V., & Feldman, D. (2003). The impact of time structure and time usage on willingness to retire and accept bridge employment. *International Journal of Human Resource Management, 14,* 1178–1191.

Loi, J., & Shultz, K. (2007). Why older adults seek employment: Differing motivations among subgroups. *Journal of Applied Gerontology, 26,* 274–289.

Lumsdaine, R., L., & Mitchell, O. S. (1999). New developments in the economic analysis of retirement. In O. Ashenfelter & D. Card (Eds.), *Handbook of labor economics* (Vol. 3, pp. 3261–3307). New York, NY: Elsevier.

Lusardi, A. (2008). *Household saving behavior: The role of financial literacy, information, and financial education programs* (Working Paper). Retrieved from SSRN: http://ssrn.com/abstract=1094102.

Lusardi, A., & Mitchell, O. S. (2007). Baby boomer retirement security: The roles of planning, financial literacy, and housing wealth. *Journal of Monetary Economics, 54,* 205–224.

Matthews, R. A., Bulger, C. A., & Barnes-Farrell, J. L. (2010). Work social supports, role stressors, and work-family conflict: The moderating effect of age. *Journal of Vocational Behavior, 76,* 78–90.

McFall, B. H. (2011). *Crash and wait? The impact of the great recession on the retirement planning of older Americans* (Unpublished doctoral dissertation). Department of Economics, University of Michigan, Ann Arbor, MI.

McNall, L. A., Masuda, A. D., & Nicklin, J. M. (2009). Flexible work arrangements, job satisfaction, and turnover intentions: The mediating role of work-to-family enrichment. *The Journal of Psychology: Interdisciplinary and Applied, 144,* 61–81.

Menard, S. (2002). *Longitudinal research* (2nd edition). Thousand Oaks, CA: Sage.

Mitchell, T. R., & James, L. R. (2001). Building better theory: Time and the specification of when things happen. *Academy of Management Review, 26,* 530–547.

Moen, P. (1998). Recasting careers: Changing reference groups, risks and realities. *Generations, 22,* 40–45.

Moen, P., Kim., J. E., & Hofmeister, H. (2001). Couples' work/ retirement transitions, gender, and marital quality. *Social Psychology Quarterly, 64,* 55–71.

Moen, P., & Sweet, S. (2004). From "work-family" to "flexible careers": A life course reframing. *Community, Work & Family, 7,* 209–226.

Mutran, E. J., Reitzes, D. C., & Fernandez, M. E. (1997). Factors that influence attitudes toward retirement. *Research on Aging, 19,* 251–273.

Myers, S., & Booth, A. (1996). Men's retirement and marital quality. *Journal of Family Issues, 17,* 336–357.

Pienta, A. M. (2003). Partners in marriage: An analysis of husbands' and wives' retirement behavior. *Journal of Applied Gerontology, 22,* 340–358.

Pienta, A. M., & Hayward, M. D. (2002). Who expects to continue working after age 62? The retirement plans of couples. *Journal of Gerontology, 57B,* S119–S208.

Price, K. P., & Joo, F. (2005). Exploring the relationship between marital status and women's retirement satisfaction. *International Journal of Aging and Human Development, 61,* 37–55.

Raymo, J. M., & Sweeney, M. M. (2006). Work-family conflict and retirement preferences. *Journal of Gerontology: Social Sciences, 61B,* S161–S69.

Reitzes, D. C., Mutran, E. J., & Fernandez, M. E. (1998). The decision to retire early: A career perspective. *Social Science Quarterly, 79,* 607–619.

Shuey, K. M. (2004). Worker preferences, spousal coordination, and participation in an employer-sponsored pension plan. *Research on Aging, 26,* 287–316.

Shultz, K. S. (2003). Bridge employment: Work after retirement. In G. A. Adams and T. A. Beehr (Eds.), *Retirement: Reasons, processes, and results* (pp. 214–241). New York, NY: Springer.

Shultz, K. S., Morton, K. R., & Weckerle, J. R. (1998). The influence of push and pull factors on voluntary and involuntary early retirees' retirement decision and adjustment. *Journal of Vocational Behavior, 53,* 45–57.

Smith, D. B., & Moen, P. (1998). Spousal influence on retirement: His, her, and their perceptions. *Journal of Marriage and the Family, 60,* 734–744.

Smith, D. B., & Moen, P. (2004). Retirement satisfaction for retirees and their spouses: Do gender and the retirement decision-making process matter? *Journal of Family Issues, 25,* 262–285.

Society for Human Resource Management. (2010). *2010 employee benefits: Examining employee benefits in the midst of a recovering economy.* Alexandria, VA: Author.

Staines, G. L., and O'Connor, P. (1980). Conflicts among work, leisure, and family roles. *Monthly Labor Review, 103,* 36–39.

Szinovacz, M. (1996). Couples' employment/retirement patterns and perceptions of marital quality. *Research of Aging, 18,* 243–268.

Szinovacz, M. E. (1989). Decision-making on retirement timing. In D. Brinberg & J. Jaccard (Eds.), *Dyadic decision making* (pp. 286–310). New York, NY: Springer.

Szinovacz, M. E. (2003). Contexts and pathways: Retirement as institution, process, and experience. In G. A. Adams & T. A. Beehr (Eds), *Retirement: Reasons, processes, and results* (pp. 6–52). New York, NY: Springer.

Szinovacz, M. E. (2006). Families and retirement. In L. O. Stone (Ed.), *New frontiers of retirement research* (pp. 165–198). Ottawa, Canada: Statistics Canada.

Szinovacz, M. E., & Davey, A. (2004). Honeymoons and joint lunches: Effects of retirement and spouse's employment on depressive symptoms. *Journal of Gerontology: Psychological Sciences, 59B,* P233–P245.

Szinovacz, M. E., & DeViney, S. (2000). Marital characteristics and retirement decisions. *Research on Aging, 22,* 470–498.

Szinovacz, M. E., DeViney, S., & Davey, A. (2001). Influences of family obligations and relationships on retirement: Variations by gender, race, and marital status. *Journal of Gerontology: Social Sciences, 56B,* S20–S27.

Szinovacz, M., & Schaffer, A. M. (2000). Effects of retirement on marital conflict management. *Journal of Family Issues, 21,* 367–389.

U.S. Bureau of Labor Statistics. (2010). *Women in the labor force: A databook (2010 edition)* (Report 1026). Washington, DC: Author.

U.S. Census Bureau. (2004–2005). *Statistical abstract of the United States. Table no. 577: Labor force participation rates by marital status, sex, & age: 1970 to 2003.* Retrieved from http://www.census.gov/prod/2004pubs/04statab/labor.pdf.

U.S. Census Bureau. (2010). *Facts for features—Grandparents Day 2010: Sept. 12* (CB10-FF. 16). Washington, DC: Author.

van Dam, K., van der Vorst, J. D. M., & van der Heijden, B. I. J. M. (2009). Employees' intentions to retire early: A case of planned behavior and anticipated work conditions. *Journal of Career Development, 35,* 265–289.

van Solinge, H., & Henkens, K. (2008). Adjustment to and satisfaction with retirement: Two of a kind? *Psychology and Aging, 23,* 422–434.

Vere, J.P. (2011). Social Security and elderly labor supply: Evidence from the Health and Retirement Study. *Labour Economics, 18*(5), 676–686.

Veroff, J., Douvan, E., Orbuch, T., & Acitelli, L. (1999). Happiness in stable marriages: The early years. In T. N. Bradbury (Ed.), *The developmental course of marital dysfunction* (pp. 152–179). New York, NY: Cambridge University Press.

Vinokur, A., & Caplan R. D. (1987). Attitudes & social support: Determinants of job-seeking behavior & well-being among the unemployed. *Journal of Applied Social Psychology, 17,* 1007–1024.

Voydanoff, P. (2005). Social integration, work-family conflict and facilitation, and job and marital quality. *Journal of Marriage and Family, 67,* 666–679.

Voydanoff, P. (2006). *Work, family, and community: Exploring interconnections.* Mahwah, NJ: Erlbaum.

Wang, M. (2007). Profiling retirees in the retirement transition and adjustment process: Examining the longitudinal change

patterns of retirees' psychological well-being. *Journal of Applied Psychology, 92*, 455–474.

Wang, M., & Shultz, K. S. (2010). Employee retirement: A review and recommendations for future investigation. *Journal of Management, 36*, 172–206.

Wang, M., Zhan, Y., Liu, S., & Shultz, K. (2008). Antecedents of bridge employment: A longitudinal investigation. *Journal of Applied Psychology, 93*, 818–830.

Wayne, J. H., Musisca, N., & Fleeson, W. (2004). Considering the role of personality in the work-family experience: Relationships of the big five to work-family conflict and facilitation. *Journal of Vocational Behavior, 64*, 108–130.

Weckerle, J. R., & Shultz, K. S. (1999). Influences on the bridge employment decision among older USA workers. *Journal of Occupational and Organizational Psychology, 72*, 317–330.

Westman, M., & Etzion, D. (2005). The crossover of work-family conflict from one spouse to the other. *Journal of Applied Social Psychology, 35*, 1936–1957.

Yeandle, S. (2005). *Older workers and work-life balance*. York, United Kingdom: Joseph Rowntree Foundation.

PART 4

Retirement Practice

Social Security, Pension Systems, and Retirement Savings

Xiang Yao *and* Haoran Peng

Abstract

Under the pressure of an aging society, establishing a sustainable old-age security system (i.e., social security, pensions, and retirement saving systems) and providing adequate pension benefits for older people become critically important. Before initiating reform, it is necessary for us to understand the current status of old-age security systems. Due to differences in history, population structure, and socioeconomic environment, most countries have a wide variety of old-age security systems. This chapter selects four countries (i.e., the United States, Germany, China, and India) and introduces each of their old-age security systems, then analyzes the major issues and challenges for these countries. In the end, this chapter makes a conclusion based on comparisons among these countries and recommends directions of reform for the future.

Key Words: social security, pension system, retirement saving

Introduction

How to provide adequate retirement benefits for each citizen is a huge task faced by many countries, especially those experiencing severe aging and financial crises. In order to solve this problem, most countries have established an old-age security system. The main objectives of old-age security systems are to replace some fraction of pre-retirement earnings, to ensure adequate living conditions for people after retirement, and to prevent destitution in old age.

There is a tendency to share the obligation to provide retirement benefits among country, employer, and individual. In most countries, the old-age security system mainly comprises social security, pension systems, and retirement saving, which is called a three-pillar system[1] (World Bank, 1994). Considering the fact that each country has different definitions of social security, pension system, and retirement saving, in order to avoid misunderstanding, we define each component in this chapter as

follows: (1) social security refers to schemes that are public-managed and tax- or contribution-financed; (2) pension system refers to all kinds of occupational pension schemes, which usually have tax advantages; and (3) retirement saving refers to voluntary saving by individuals via private saving plans, which are typically encouraged by tax incentive as well.

Because each country has a different population structure, economic development status, and culture and traditions, the specific institutional arrangements vary greatly among different countries. The purpose of this chapter is to introduce several different kinds of old-age security systems in the world. We select four countries—the United States, Germany, China, and India—for the following reasons. China and India are developing countries and have the largest populations in the world. Therefore, it is greatly significant to investigate the old-age security systems of these two countries. While the United States and Germany are both industrialized and developed countries, the United States is the most influential and powerful country in the world, and Germany is a traditional European country and a major member of the European Union. The four countries cover almost half of the population of the world and can reflect the typical old-age security systems of countries with different socioeconomic backgrounds. Based on many previous literatures, we will analyze the characteristics and problems of old-age security systems in the four countries in the following sections.

The United States
Background

The United States is the third most populous nation in the world, with an overall population of 310 million. In 2009, the fertility rate was 2.05 children per mother, or 13.82 births per 1,000 inhabitants, which was 30% below the world average. Nevertheless, together with millions of legal and illegal immigrants per year, the population growth rate is higher than most other industrialized nations, such as Germany and Japan. In 2007, over one-eighth of the U.S. population reached aged 65. Compared with other industrialized nations, the United States has suffered less from population aging. However, population growth is the fastest among minorities such as Hispanics. This tendency is changing the country's population structure continually.

The economy of the United States is the most powerful in the world. Although it dropped from the peak due to the 2008 global financial crisis, its nominal GDP was still estimated to be $14.3 trillion in 2009. As a result of the bad economy, the U.S. unemployment rate has maintained at over 9% since 2008's recession, and a broader measure of unemployment (called U-6) has been over 16% since the beginning of 2010 (Bureau of Labor Statistics, 2010). The unemployment particularly affected teenagers, especially African Americans and Hispanics, the fastest growing populations in the United States. On the other hand, the baby-boomer generation (76 million people who were born between 1945 and 1964) has begun to retire since the beginning of the recession. These two facts will jointly influence the United States' economy in the future.

The Old-Age Security System in the United States: An Overview
SOCIAL SECURITY

In the United States, the old-age security system consists of three main pillars: Social Security,

private pensions, and voluntary saving arrangements. Social Security is a social insurance program officially titled "Old-Age, Survivors, and Disability Insurance" (OASDI) in reference to its three portions. It is funded through dedicated payroll taxes called FICA (Federal Insurance Contributions Act) tax. This program is the single greatest expenditure in the U.S. federal budget. During 2009, $891 billion were earned as income (taxes and interest) versus $708 billion paid out as benefits, with a $183 billion annual surplus. An estimated 162 million people paid for the program, and 51 million retired or disabled workers, survivors, and their families received benefits—roughly 3.2 workers per beneficiary. Social Security system is a pay-as-you-go (PAYGO) system because it is paid by using revenue from the FICA tax, to which employers and employees contribute jointly. OASDI, the largest component of FICA tax, is the retirement portion of the Social Security system (the other portion is Medicare). Currently, the entire FICA tax is 15.3% of annual gross compensation; the employee's share of the tax for the OASDI benefit is 6.2% of wages up to a limit[2] of $106,800 in 2010 (the employee's share was temporarily reduced to 4.2% in 2011). This limit, known as the Social Security Wage Base (SSWB), goes up annually in line with real wage growth and inflation. Employers will match the tax for a total of 15.3%. Self-employed individuals are responsible for the entire 15.3%. The proceeds of this tax are deposited separately into different trust funds and withdrawn separately from the appropriate fund. Of the total 15.3% tax, 12.4% is for OASDI to pay all retirement benefits.

Per the current policy, eligibility for retirement benefits depends on the number of years in which contributions are made before retirement, with a minimum requirement of ten years of contributions. Reduced benefits can be paid as early as when the individual is 62, while full retirement benefits depend on the normal retirement age (NRA), of which the calculation depends on a retiree's year of birth. For current retirees, the normal retirement age is 66 for retirees who were born before 1954, between 66 and 67 for retirees who were born between 1954 and 1960 (increased by two months for each year), and 67 for retirees who were born after 1960.

The Social Security Administration keeps track of an employee's covered earnings throughout his or her career. When the employee decides to retire from work, his or her retirement benefit depends on his or her Primary Insurance Amount (PIA), which is based on the age when the person starts to receive benefits and his or her earnings record. The Average Indexed Monthly Earnings (AIME) is used to calculate the PIA, which is the monthly average earning of beneficiaries from their workforce entry to retirement. The retiree's record of nominal earnings for the highest 35 years is used as computation earnings. Earlier years' earnings are revalued up to the year when the employee reaches age 62 by Social Security's average wage index (AWI). Since there are many employees who have worked fewer than 35 years, in order to make the total number of years reach 35, the incomes of the years during which the employee did not work would be counted as zero and put in the calculation formula. If the employee works beyond age 62 and earns more than any of the amounts in his or her AIME, this amount replaces the lower amount and the AIME is recalculated. But there is no further revaluation of earnings by the AWI after age 60. The PIA is decided by two bend points of the AIME, through which an employee can calculate the amount of money he or she can get. According to the 2011 PIA formula, these two bend points are $753 and $4,542. Consequently, for AIME below the previous score ($753), PIA is calculated as 90% of AIME. For the parts over $753 and less then 4542, 32% of AIME is counted; for those over then the scond bend point, the PIA is calculated as 15% of AIME over the scond bend point. According to the 2011 PIA formula, these two bend points are $753 and $4,542 sequentially, which are adjusted annually for inflation. If the employee retires at his or her normal retirement age, the basic monthly retirement benefit is the PIA. An employee will get more or less than the PIA separately when he or she retires after or before the normal retirement age. For example, according to the current policy, for someone born after 1960 who retires at age 62 (the earliest possible age for retiring), his or her pension will be only 70% of his or her PIA. Also administered by the Social Security Administration, Supplemental Security Income (SSI) as a means-tested scheme is another element of publicly provided pensions that is dedicated to provide an income "safety net" for low-income individuals with limited resources.

401(K) PLAN AND IRA

The second pillar of the U.S. old-age security system, the pension system, is the employer-sponsored defined contribution (DC) pension program, such as a 401(k). Some form of defined benefit (DB) pension program used to be the main form of employer pension plan, and currently many companies still do have DB pension programs. However, because the cost rate is fixed in a DC pension program and cannot be influenced by dependency ratio (retirees/employees) change, the DC pension programs have been growing rapidly, either as replacements for or supplements to the traditional DB pension program.

There are two main kinds of 401(k) plan available now: the traditional 401(k) and the Roth 401(k) (named after its chief legislative sponsor, the late Senator William Roth of Delaware). The traditional 401(k) plans were first introduced as compensation arrangement programs under which an employee can choose to have a portion of his or her compensation contributed to a qualified retirement plan as a pre-tax reduction in salary. Since 1998, legislation has imposed a mandatory 401(k) plan contribution on employers for their employees unless the employees expressly select not to contribute. Until the end of 2003, it was said that 401(k) had included 42.4 million active participants (Employee Benefit Research Institute, 2005).

The traditional 401(k) and Roth 401(k) are the same in that contributions are paid into an individual account for each member, and the contributions are invested. The most remarkable feature of the traditional 401(k) is that it can defer current income taxes on savings until withdrawals. The Roth 401(k) was carried out in 2006. In this program, people can allocate some or all of their contributions to a Roth account, in which contributions are post-tax and no taxes are paid under normal distributions. Compared with the Roth 401(k), the traditional 401(k) allows participants to borrow from their accounts for expenses such as residence, education, and medical care. If participants are likely to be in a higher tax bracket in the future, then the Roth plan is better for them. Similar to 401(k), there are other corresponding plans for nonprofit organizations (403(b) plan) and government (457(b) plan) employees.

According to its contribution source, an Individual Retirement Arrangement (IRA) can be regarded as a voluntary saving arrangement and a retirement plan account set up by employees themselves if certain eligibility criteria are met. Both 401(k) and IRA plans have similar contribution and distribution rules, and under certain criteria a 401(k) plan can be rolled into an IRA plan. Like the 401(k) plan, there are two main types of IRA: the traditional IRA and the Roth IRA. They are the same in that contributions are tax-deductible and all transactions within the IRA have no tax impact. However, in a traditional IRA, withdrawals at retirement are often taxed as income, whereas Roth IRA withdrawals are usually tax-free.

Issues and Challenges

EFFECT OF BABY-BOOM GENERATION RETIREMENT

The post–World War II baby boomers have made significant contributions to the U.S. economy. However, as we mentioned before, most of them will retire in the coming years. Their retirement will pose great challenges for the nation's Social Security system. This is because PAYGO social security systems will face financial unbalance when there is a decline in the working population (Browning, 2008). Specifically, the cost rate (pension cost/covered wages) will rise when the dependency ratio (retirees/works) increases in the PAYGO system, while the contribution rate (contribution/covered wages) stays the same; eventually, the cost rate will exceed the contribution rate. Then the social security system will hardly be able to make ends meet. In fact, with baby boomers on the verge of retirement, increased longevity, and lower birth rates, the ratio of workers to retirees continues to decline, from 16 to 1 in 1950 to about 3 to 1 now; by 2030, the ration will be 2 to 1 (Giandrea, 2008). Accordingly, the system will start tapping into the Social Security Trust under the prediction that payroll tax revenue cannot cover the Social Security benefits by 2017. Solutions like raising the FICA contribution and benefit base limit for some taxpayers or cutting benefits are still under debate.

TREND FOR LATER RETIREMENT AND ITS INFLUENCE ON THE LABOR MARKET

Baby boomers' retirement saving accounts also lost heavily during the 2008 economic crisis—their 401(k)s/IRAs lost about 30% of their asset value in 2008 (Munnell, 2009). Unlike younger workers who have more time to rebuild their provision for old age once the economy recovers, the baby boomers who are near retirement were greatly affected by the economic crisis (OECD, 2009). The only real option for them to reduce lost savings is to keep working. Besides the effect of the economic crisis, there is a trend toward delaying retirement since the late 1990s, after the trend for many decades was toward early retirement (Blau & Goodstein, 2010; Wang & Shultz, 2010). No matter what the reasons are, this trend will benefit the current Social Security system, because if the rising of the

retirement age is faster than the increase of the life expectancy, the current trend of late retirement will reduce the total financial burden caused by population aging. Nevertheless, since job vacancies are limited during rough times, delaying retirement does not help to reverse the trend of a high unemployment rate. In addition, the unemployment rate is particularly higher among African Americans and Latino Americans, which may cause serious social problems, such as a high crime rate. Finally, more difficult times may be ahead—the current retirement system may no longer have the ability to support younger workers with the same level of benefits their parents enjoyed. Future research is needed for considering the problems caused by late retirement.

PROBLEMS WITH THE SOCIAL SAFETY NET FUNCTION FOR POOR ELDERLY

The fundamental purpose of a social security system is to ensure a base level of support for retirees. From this perspective, social security programs are playing a crucial role in improving the well-being of older people who are poor. However, there are some researchers criticizing the current Social Security program, which makes the rich richer and the poor poorer (Friedman, 1972). For example, there is no payroll tax on compensation above Social Security Wage Base (SSWB), thus low-income earners need to pay a higher percentage of their total income than high-income earners. In addition, it can be expected that wealthier individuals, who generally have higher life expectancies, would receive more benefits than poorer taxpayers over a longer period. Other researchers have supported different points of view by arguing that Social Security benefits are calculated by a progressive benefit formula that provides larger relative benefits for lower-paid workers (Fagnoni, 1999). Hence more analyses are needed to figure out the net redistributive effect of the program. Moreover, minorities who tend to have relatively shorter life expectancies, such as blacks and Hispanics, are more likely to benefit from disability and survivor benefits that help protect against lost earnings (Hendley & Bilimoria, 1999). In addition to the debate on distribution between the rich and poor, some empirical findings suggest that the redistributions are not always well targeted to those most in need; the redistributive effects change over time and depend on the definition of income (Brown, Lyn, & Fullerton, 2009). Income significantly and negatively correlates with mortality, but the effect of income-adjusted mortality rates is relatively small on redistribution benefits (Duggan, Gillingham, & Greenlees, 1995). Therefore, future research is needed to examine the function of the Social Security system on redistribution benefits.

Germany
Background

Germany is the most powerful player in the EU because it is not only the most populous country but also the largest national economy in Europe. The German population has been estimated to be 81.8 million in January 2010, with an overall life expectancy at birth of 79.9 years. Germany has the lowest fertility rate in the world: in 2009 the fertility rate was 1.38 children per mother, or 7.9 births per 1,000 inhabitants. Because the death rates are continuously exceeding the birth rates, the rate of natural increase in the population of Germany continues to be below zero. Although Germany has the second largest immigrant population in Europe, the German population has continuously declined since 2002, which is straining the country's social welfare structure.

Since the country reunified in 1989, the German government has made much effort to reconcile the economic system of the two former republics, and especially to modernize the former East German states. This is a long-term process, scheduled to last until the year 2019. Reunification brings benefits to German economy not only because of the economic restructure itself but also because of the achievement of a bigger market and lower labor price. But this drastic change also results in some social problems: in 2008 the unemployment rate in the former East Germany (12.7%) was twice as high as in the former West Germany (6.2%).

During the reunifying process, the German economy met some troubles in the beginning of the 2000s. Between the years 2002 and 2004, the economic growth practically stagnated. Together with Germany's aging population, the economic problems led the German government to push through a wide-ranging program, named Agenda 2010, to improve economic growth and thus reduce unemployment. In the latter part of the first decade of the 2000s, the world economy experienced high growth, from which Germany also profited as a leading exporter. Just before the recession in 2008–2009, Germany was the largest national economy in Europe, the fourth-largest by nominal GDP in the world, and the world's second largest exporter.

The Old-Age Security System in Germany: An Overview

As the original cradle of social insurance, the German old-age insurance system (GOAIS) has a long history. Chancellor Otto von Bismarck established Germany's public pension system, which was the first formal pension system in the world, in 1889. After World War II, the German social security system espoused the principles of equivalence (a relatively strict link between contributions and benefits) and income maintenance based on the male breadwinner model (in which men should be the main earner while their wives should mainly shoulder housework and child raising). As the number of retirees was relatively small and the number of workers was growing steadily, the poverty rates among older people were quite low. The German retirement benefit system successfully provided a high and reliable level of retirement income and became a model for many social security systems around the world.

However, after the German reunification, the financial burden of the federal government caused a reform of the social security system. Specifically, the income maintenance principle for stable contribution rates was replaced by a more flexible and contribution-oriented expenditure pension policy. In order to reduce public pension liability to maintain financial sustainability of public finances, the German retirement benefit system had slowly transformed to a multi-pillar pension system. Some occupational and personal pension schemes, called "Riester pensions" (named after the minister of labor and social affairs at the time, Walter Riester), have been introduced to meet the shortfalls in public benefits after 2000.

Regarding the three-pillar classification of the old-age security system in Germany, the first pillar is the public pension (Borsch-Supan & Wilke, 2006). Most working populations are covered by the German Public Pension Insurance (Gesetzliche Rentenversicherung, GRV), not only for all types of employees in the private and public sectors but also for some groups of self-employed and some other parts of the labor force-related population (around 90% of the labor force). Civil servants' public pension system covers about 7% of the labor force, and the other 3% of the labor force (most of them self-employed) are self-insured. In Germany, GRV is the main source of pensions for the majority of retirees.

Like the U.S. government, the German government decided to postpone the statutory retirement age via the Rürup Commission in 2003. This commission proposed increasing the normal retirement age stepwise (one month per year until 2024 and two months per year afterward) between 2012 and 2029 from 65 to 67 for both men and women. The pension is payable from age 67 with five years of contributions and from age 63 with thirty-five years of contributions for those born in 1964 and later. The minimum qualifying period is five years; fewer than five years of contributions earn no benefit. Early retirement implies permanent benefit decrements amounting to 0.3% per month compared to the statutory retirement age, up to a 14.4% maximum. Later retirement after 67 earns a 0.5% increment for each month of additional work.

The GRV is mainly contribution-financed with a contribution rate of 19.9% of gross income in 2009, which was equally shared by employee and employer. The Riester reform in 2001 states that the total contribution rates to GRV must stay below 20% until 2020 and 22% until 2030. The insured employee usually contributes 9.95% of monthly earnings. If monthly earnings are less than EUR 400 (mini-jobs), then there are no mandatory contributions for the employee (voluntary contributions can be made). If monthly earnings are in the range of EUR 401–800 (midi-jobs), the employee pays a reduced contribution. The annual ceiling for the contribution is EUR 66,000 (EUR 55,800 in the former East states) in 2010. The self-employed labor force also contributes 19.9% of monthly income. The minimum monthly contribution is EUR 79.60 and the maximum is EUR 1,054.70 (EUR 895.50 in the former East states). Compared with the GRV contributors, civil servants do not pay explicit contributions for their pensions, but their gross wages are lower than other employees with a comparable education. Consequently, civil servants get more a generous pension benefit (about 75% of gross earnings) and are protected from any benefit reform.

The most important characteristic of the GRV system is the "earnings point" (*Entgeltpunkte*) scheme. In this scheme, workers earn pension points based on their individual earnings for each year of contribution. A year's contribution reaching the national average wage of contributors earns one pension point. Contributions based on lower or higher income earn proportionately less or more pension points. The ceiling is equivalent to 214% of the relevant average earnings. At retirement, regular pension payments from the GRV system are strictly contribution-related and free from redistribution. Benefits are the products of retirees' earning points,

their years of service life, current pension-point value, and other adjustment factors. Pension-point value is indexed to gross wages, which are updated annually (it was EUR 326.4 in 2009).

In 2009, contribution payments of the total public pension system accounted for about 72.4% of total funds. The remaining 27.6% were derived from the state budget. Since the public subsidy accounts for a considerable part of pension payments, the public pension financing has to be characterized as a mix of contributions and taxes. Because these public pensions are roughly proportional to the labor income average over the entire working life, this system is more like "retirement insurance" rather than "social security" as in the United States.

The second (voluntary and privately managed) pillar consists of occupationally funded schemes. The objective for the German pension reform in 2001 was to reduce the public pension payments for participants and to improve pensioners' entitlements to occupational and personal pensions, which are broadly defined as supplementary pensions. The employer and the employee finance most occupational pension plans jointly. In principle, the program design is very similar to the pension system in the U.S., such as 401(k). According to the reform, a certain percentage of gross earnings (the maximum contribution is 4% of gross earnings since 2008) should be voluntarily invested into occupational and personal pension schemes that are publicly supported by tax reductions. Employees have the right to convert up to 4% of their pre-tax earnings (up to a certain contribution limit) into an occupational pension scheme. Usually the schemes provide a direct subsidy that is generous, especially for low-income households with children.

Finally, the third pillar consists of voluntary, subsidized individual plans. Personal pension schemes are funded schemes and take the form of pension insurance or a savings plan with a bank or an investment firm. The government recommends that employees invest in these pension plans. However, these plans are not mandated. Before the German pension reform in 2001, the most popular means of personal old-age insurance was "life insurance" (i.e., *Lebensversicherung*), which does not always contain pension insurance. Although this insurance covers a previously defined person in the case of death of the insured, it can also be transformed into a lump-sum payment or annuity when an agreed age is reached. In 2005, about 42.9% of households owned some kind of supplementary pension plans (Borsch-Supan, Reil-Held, & Schunk, 2008).

Issues and Challenges

THE IMBALANCE BETWEEN REVENUE AND EXPENDITURE OF THE PENSION SYSTEM

The sustainability of the German retirement benefit system depends upon stable contribution rates as a guarantee. As mentioned before, Germany has one of the lowest fertility rates in the world. Death rates are exceeding low-level birth rates continuously, which caused a particularly dynamic change pattern in the age structure of the population. Consequently, a smaller working population will have to support a greatly expanded aging population in the foreseeable future, and the German government will face enormous pressure on public pension budgets. In fact, Germany has already struggled to make up the deficits of their PAYGO system. The introduction of the Riester Reform in 2001 and Rürup Commission in 2003 aimed to achieve less intergenerational burden through partly replacing PAYGO by funded pensions. Although the retirement age has been increased and private pension plans have been introduced, whether the public pension gap can be fulfilled in the long run still needs further observation.

THE ECONOMIC CRISIS AND ITS INFLUENCE ON RETIREMENT BENEFITS

Most countries are influenced by the recent financial crisis, and pension funds, especially private old-age security funds, have shrunk. With investments losing an average of 23% of their value during 2008, the financial crisis has hit pension funds in OECD countries especially hard. In 2008, the pension funds' real investment return for Germany was about –8% (Organisation for Economic Co-operation and Development [OECD], 2009). The consequences of the global financial crisis also threatened the core success factors of the German pension reform, such as cutting the pension level and raising the mandatory retirement age (Bonin, 2009). Unemployment and lower earnings reduced the contribution revenue of the public pension systems, making it more difficult for them to deliver pension benefits. Although compared to other developed countries German pension funds suffered less in this financial crisis due to the fund investment strategy (German pension funds tend to be invested mainly in bonds, especially government bonds, instead of in equities), how to prevent the pension account from losing values, not only in the economic recession but also in the subsequence inflation, is still a serious problem for Germany.

THE IMPACT OF GLOBALIZATION ON RETIREMENT POLICY

Globalization creates great economic chance for developing countries to improve their economy, which also benefits developed countries with opportunities for purchasing cheaper goods and services. However, globalization is a double-edged sword in that capital flows more freely to those regions that offer lower production costs, which causes the industrial structure imbalance within well-developed countries, such as Germany. In order to maintain economic vitality, the German government has undertaken a greater effort to relax labor laws and policies, including reducing the labor cost per person and increasing temporary and part-time jobs, which could be detrimental to the operation of the social security system. Furthermore, in order to create a business-friendly environment to meet the needs of globalization, some OECD countries choose to reduce employer social security contribution rates, which increases the savings burden of employees and poses a risk of declining coverage and benefit adequacy for old-age security systems. For Germany, such reforms need to be treated with caution.

China
Background

Since 1978, China has made the transition from a planned economy to a market economy, and kept an amazingly fast economic growth rate. Accordingly, the living conditions of Chinese people have greatly improved. Accompanying these achievements, China is experiencing a dramatic demographic transition, from a high birth rate and high mortality to low birth rate and low mortality, and is thus facing severe population aging problems. According to the 2010 National Census in China, the percentage of people over 60 has reached 13.26%. This population structure has been attributed to longer life expectancy and lower fertility rates, which are mainly the result of the one-child family planning policy in China. Compared with many developed countries, the Chinese are becoming older too quickly, while China's per-capita income is still relatively low. In addition, due to the traditional idea that boys are more important than girls, China is expected to face a severe sex imbalance. For example, in the year 2000, the birth rates were 116.86 males to 100 females (Sin, 2005). If the one-child policy continues, the burden of old-age security for China will become unbearable. Although the trend of population aging is severe in China, the current mandatory retirement age is 60 for male workers, 50 for common female workers, and 55 for females in managerial positions. In fact, the effective retirement age is far below these standards.

During a period of fast economic growth, China also experienced one of the most rapid increases in income inequality. According to an estimate by the OECD (2004), China's Gini coefficient (commonly used as a measure of inequality of income, it can range from 0 to 1; higher Gini coefficients usually indicate more unequal distribution) has reached 0.46. The severe income disparities in China may easily cause social unrest if they cannot be handled properly in the future. In this situation, the redistribution of old-age security systems naturally needs more attention.

Another important issue in China is the urban-rural separation. In the early 1950s, China established the household registration system (i.e., *hukou*). Under this system, the Chinese population was not allowed to move freely between urban and rural areas. On the one hand, the urban residents are covered by complete social welfare systems. When they reach the retirement age, they begin to receive social security benefits provided by the government. On the other hand, rural residents have to depend on the support of their offspring and personal savings for retirement. With the process of urbanization, the barrier between urban and rural areas started to break. Since the 1980s, millions of peasants from inland provinces, called *peasant workers*, have flooded into industrial cities in East China. However, it is impossible for China to reduce the huge differences between urban and rural areas in a short time. Until now, it was very difficult for rural residents to enjoy the same benefits as urban residents, such as old-age benefits, health care service, and education. Nevertheless, most recently the Chinese government has decided to provide social security to all Chinese citizens, as written in China's Social Security Act that was issued on July 1, 2011.

The Old-Age Security System in China: An Overview

Generally speaking, the current old-age security system in China also includes three pillars: mandatory social security, enterprise supplementary pension, and voluntary personal savings. In the first mandatory pillar, there is still no unified national social security system in China. The Chinese government provides different social security schemes for different kinds of people. There are three types of mandatory social security schemes currently operating in China—a budget-financed pension scheme for civil servants and employees of public institutions, a basic pension scheme for urban workers, and a newly developed rural social pension scheme for rural residents.

In China, civil servants and employees of public institutions enjoy generous pension benefits that amount to 88%–90% of their salary at retirement (assuming full career length of 35 years or longer) (Sin, 2005). Generally, the amount of pension benefits is related to the seniority of the worker and the length of work. These expenditures are paid directly through general budget allocations. Recently, in order to alleviate the financial burden, the Chinese central government has launched pilot reforms of the pension scheme for employees of public institutions in several provinces. However, this effort has encountered resistance from various interest groups.

The urban worker basic pension scheme originated in the labor insurance, which was established at the beginning of the foundation of the People's Republic of China. It acted as an enterprise-based PAYGO system until the mid-1990s. After China made the transition to a market-based economy, some state-owned companies began to feel the heavy burden of social security expenditures. In order to create a fair market environment, and partly influenced by the pension reform in Latin America, the Chinese government decided to establish a new pension scheme for urban workers. According to State Council Document No. 26 in 1997, the urban worker basic pension scheme is composed of two tiers, the social pool and the individual account. The first tier, the social pool, continues on a PAYGO basis and is financed by employers. The second tier, the individual account, is a defined contribution scheme that is financed by employees and employers. The 1997 reform is typically described as *structural reform*, from a pure PAYGO system to a mixed pension system. However, in practice, the mixed pension system faces great challenges, one of which is the problem of the "empty individual account." This is mainly caused by the failure of China to resolve the transition cost. The Chinese government intended to absorb the transition cost through the current contributions of employers, but this did not succeed. In order to guarantee the payment of pension benefits, local governments have to "borrow" money from individual accounts to cover the deficit in the funds of the social pool, which leads to the problem of "empty individual accounts." If this problem cannot be resolved, China's pension reform will be doomed to failure. Based on several pilot projects in Liaoning, Jilin, and Heilongjiang provinces, China finally promulgated State Council Document No. 38 in 2005. According to this document, the framework of the urban worker basic pension scheme is not changed, and the social pool and individual account remain. Some revisions have been made to the contributions and benefits criteria. This 2005 reform is known as the *parametric reform*, which aims to downsize the individual account and strengthen the linkage between contributions and benefits. More details about the 1997 reform and 2005 reform are shown in Table 24.1.

Unlike civil servants and urban workers, there has not been a unified pension scheme for rural residents for a long time. Some regions with good economic conditions created some small-scale pilot schemes, but the majority of rural residents rely on their land and family for support when they become older. However, the situation has changed rapidly. During the process of urbanization, many rural residents lost their land, and young people flooded into the cities. The family ties have become weakened,

and in order to avoid old-age poverty in rural areas, it is urgent for China to establish a formal rural pension scheme. In 2009, the Chinese government promulgated a new rural pension scheme that will be gradually introduced throughout the country. The financing of the new rural pension scheme comprises individual contribution, government subsidy, and collective assistance at the village level. Individual accounts are established for rural residents and are mainly financed through individual contributions and collective assistance. Local governments with good economic conditions can also provide allowances. Rural residents over 60 years old are entitled to receive pension benefits. The total pension benefits consist of a basic pension and a pension from an individual account. The basic pension is funded by government subsidy, and a monthly pension from an individual account is equal to the accumulated account balance at retirement divided by 139 if rural residents reach 60 years of age.

The second pillar in the old-age security system in China, which is officially called the "enterprise annuity," was first piloted in the 1990s and formally

Table 24.1 The Basic Content of 1997 Reform and 2005 Reform of China Urban Worker Basic Pension Scheme

	The 1997 Reform	The 2005 Reform
Contributions	Total contributions to individual accounts are equal to 11% of the contributory wage[1] and are shared by employees and employers. The contribution rate of employees gradually increases from 4% to 8%, and the rest is paid by employers. Total contributions by employers are not supposed to exceed 20% of the contributory wage. Except the part put into an individual account, the remainder of the contribution enters into social pool.	Total contributions to individual accounts are equal to 8% of the contributory wage and paid by employees only. Total contributions by employers are not supposed to exceed 20% of the contributory wage and are put into the social pool completely.
Benefits	The pension benefits consist of two parts: (1) a monthly basic pension from the social pool equal to 20% of the last year's local average monthly wage, and (2) a monthly pension from the individual account equal to the accumulated account balance at retirement divided by 120.	The pension benefits consist of two parts: (1) a monthly basic pension from the social pool is calculated by a formula and closely related to the contributory wage and the length of contribution.[2] (2) a monthly pension from the individual account equal to the accumulated account balance at retirement divided by a number, which is linked to retirement age, life expectancy, etc.

Note: 1. The contributory wage is subject to a minimum of 60% and a maximum of 300% of the local average monthly wage. 2. The formula is $0.5 * A * (Q + 1) * n\%$, where A = average monthly wage for the year prior to retirement; n = the length of contribution calculated by year; Q = the average of the contribution index. The contribution index is the ratio of the individual contributory wage to the average local monthly wage.

started in 2004. It covered 33,000 enterprises, encompassed 10.38 million people, and accumulated CNY 191.10 billion by the end of 2008 (Zhu, 2009). The enterprise annuity plans are mostly in the form of defined contributions and run on a voluntary basis. Enterprises that want to build enterprise annuity plans must fulfill some prerequisites, such as having already participated in the urban worker basic pension scheme without contribution delay, being in good financial status, etc. The contribution to the enterprise annuity plan is shared by the employee and employer up to a maximum of 1/6 of the last year's wages, with employer contribution no more than 1/12. In order to encourage the development of enterprise annuities, up to 5% of the wage in the employer contribution is deductible before corporate tax (OECD, 2010). In practice, the enterprise annuity schemes are set up mainly by the large profitable state-owned enterprises. For many small and private enterprises, the contribution for the first pillar is already hard to bear, not to mention for the second pillar.

In addition to the first and second pillars, if people wish to pursue a higher-quality post-retirement life, the third pillar—voluntary personal savings—needs to be considered. It is well known that the Chinese household savings ratio is very high. For example, Modigliani and Cao (2004) estimated that the household savings-to-income ratio in China was close to 34% in 1994. They pointed out that one possible reason would be the lack of social security in China. Although the Chinese government has made great efforts to expand social security coverage in recent years, there are still many people not covered by social security, such as migrant workers, peasants, and low-income people. They still depend mostly on personal savings or children for old-age support.

Issues and Challenges

EXTENDING COVERAGE OF THE OLD-AGE SECURITY SYSTEM

The government has the obligation to provide old-age security for each citizen. However, China has a long way to go to fulfill this duty. For example, the urban worker basic pension scheme covered 218.91 million people by the end of 2008, including 165.87 million active employees and 53.04 million retirees (Zhu, 2009). The majority of rural residents were not included in the new rural pension scheme until 2010. One of the important tasks that China faces in the near future is to extend coverage of the old-age security system to all citizens.

Rural residents and those people who are in informal sectors or have flexible employment should be paid great attention in this process. China can accomplish this task by implementing various pension schemes and making them more attractive to low-income people, through actions such as lowering the contribution rate and increasing the government subsidy.

UNIFYING THE CURRENT FRAGMENTED OLD-AGE SECURITY SYSTEM

China has a highly fragmented old-age security system. Not only are there huge differences between urban and rural citizens, but there also exists great variation across regions. Consider the urban worker basic pension scheme as an example. In practice, most of these schemes are organized at the provincial level as well as county or city level, which directly results in great variations in contribution rates and pension entitlements. This fragmented system is harmful to free labor mobility because pension entitlements are difficult to continue when people change jobs from one region to another. Many people have no choice but to opt out of the scheme, especially peasant workers. A fundamental solution to this problem is to unify the urban worker basic pension scheme at the country level, which may inevitably influence the regional interests. Additionally, gradually diminishing the gap between urban and rural residents and finally establishing a unified urban-rural social security system is a major challenge that China will face in the future.

IMPROVING THE EQUITY OF THE OLD-AGE SECURITY SYSTEM

Due to the lack of a unified national social security system, the equity of China's old-age security system needs to be greatly improved. A majority of people are dissatisfied with the fact that pension benefits for civil servants are too generous and have urged the government to improve pension benefits and reduce the difference of pension benefits among different social sectors. It is also imperative for China to strengthen the protection of rural residents and low-income people in urban areas, who are more vulnerable to various risks. One way to accomplish this task is to establish the minimum pension institution as soon as possible. In addition, China should pay more attention to intergenerational equity when conducting pension reform. For example, it is unfair to impose the burden of the transition cost of urban worker basic pension reform to the next generation by imposing high contribution rates among current workers. This is one of the reasons why many young people are not willing to join the scheme. In fact, high contribution rates have become an important impediment to the extension of coverage to the old-age security system.

IMPROVING THE PERFORMANCE OF THE PENSION FUND INVESTMENT

Poor performance of the pension fund investment has plagued the Chinese government. Funds from the first pillar are currently invested in government bonds and bank deposits with very low average real yields. For example, in years with high inflation, such as 2009 and 2010, the average real yields may be negative. For the second pillar, the enterprise annuity has broader investment channels than the first pillar, but the amount of investing stocks is limited. Immature domestic financial markets and narrow investment channels are two major obstacles to pension funds achieving good investment performance. Jackson and Howe (2004) emphasized the mutual importance of a funded pension system and evolving financial markets, which have great significance for China now. With the rapid increase in the size of pension funds, it is vital for China to manage them well and get higher returns under conditions of absolute safety.

KEEPING THE FINANCIAL SUSTAINABILITY OF THE OLD-AGE SECURITY SYSTEM

The financial sustainability of the old-age security system is crucial for any government. In China, the problem of empty accounts in the first pillar is the greatest threat to the operation of the urban worker basic pension scheme. During the economic transition period, the Chinese government should take more responsibility to absorb the transition cost. Effective ways may include selling state assets and increasing the government subsidy. Besides this, in order to keep old-age security systems in balance, it is necessary for China to consider adjusting the one-child policy and increasing the normal retirement age gradually. The impacts of these measures on both the labor market and the old-age security system need be fully considered.

India
Background

As one of the most populous countries in the world, India has seen great economic growth since it implemented an "open-society, open-economy" policy in 1991. Financial reforms have made great progress in India, which has created a favorable basis for reform in the old-age security system.

However, there are still many problems plaguing India's pension reform, especially population aging and the employment structure. India has a large population base and is experiencing a demographic transition from high fertility and high mortality to low fertility and low mortality, which lead to longer life expectancy and a greater amount of the aged population. During the period from 2005–2010, life expectancy at birth was 63.2 years for males and 66.7 years for females; life expectancy at age 60 was 16 years for males and 18 years for females (Asher, 2007). The rising number of the older population will inevitably pose great challenges to the long-term financial sustainability of India's public pension system.

In the employment market, the share of organized (formal) sector and unorganized (informal) sector in 2003 were 9.9% and 91.1%, respectively, and the share of public-sector employment in total employment in 2001 was 3.3% (Asher, 2007). This means that the majority of employees work in the private, unorganized sector. However, most of these people are not covered by any formal social security or pension schemes. It has been argued that providing old-age security for informal sector employees is a big challenge to most developing countries. For India, due to its unique employment structure, the situation seems to be more stressful. Accompanied by the shrinkage of family size, like many other countries, India's traditional old-age family support mechanisms are gradually collapsing, which underlines the need for establishing a formal mechanism for providing old-age security.

The Old-Age Security System in India: An Overview

The old-age security system is rather complicated in India. It mainly comprises the following seven components: civil service schemes, the Employees Provident Fund Organization (EPFO) schemes, public-sector enterprise pension schemes, occupational pension schemes, voluntary tax-advantaged saving schemes, social assistance schemes, and micro-pension schemes.

CIVIL SERVICE SCHEMES

In India, civil servants at the central, state, and local government levels have a similar structure of retirement schemes. Civil servants can mainly rely on an unfunded, non-contributory, defined benefit pension scheme, which has fairly generous benefits.

Besides this, civil servants are entitled to receive benefits from the General Provident Fund (GPF) scheme, to which they are mandated to contribute 6% of their salary. At retirement, civil servants can receive a lump-sum gratuity with a ceiling based on their length of service and salary level before retirement.

These civil service schemes are subject to great reform pressure because of fiscal unsustainability. According to Asher (2007), while civil servants at all levels of government constitute only about 3% of the total labor force, their retirement benefits are already equivalent to nearly 2% of the GDP. In order to deal with this situation, the central government introduced a newly defined contribution scheme called the New Pension Scheme (NPS), which requires new civil servants entering after January 1, 2004, to participate. The government also decided to allow the unorganized sector workers to join the NPS, which is very helpful to expand the coverage.

EMPLOYEES PROVIDENT FUND
ORGANIZATION (EPFO) SCHEMES

The Indian government established the EPFO in 1952, and it administers various mandatory schemes including a defined contribution scheme, the Employees' Provident Fund (EPF), a defined benefit Employees' Pension Scheme (EPS), and an Employees' Deposit Linked Insurance (EDLI) scheme. EPFO schemes are set up for private-sector workers in organizations with more than twenty employees in 181 types of industries.

In 1952, the EPF scheme was first established. The employee and employer contributed 12% and 3.67% of monthly wages, respectively, which was credited into the employee's EPF account. At the time of retirement, employees receive a lump-sum benefit, which cannot truly cover the longevity and inflation risk.

The EPS was not set up until 1995, running on the basis of a PAYGO system. Total contribute rate of the EPS is 9.49% of the covered wage—8.33% contributed by the employer, 1.16% by the government. The benefits, including family pensions to survivors, are paid monthly and are increased at the trustees' discretion. Compared with the EPF, the EPS is more likely to help deal with the longevity risk, though it is widely believed that the EPS is underfunded (Palacios, 2001).

The EDLI scheme, which was established in 1976, requires the employer to contribute at a rate of 0.5%. So, the total combined contribution rate of EPFO schemes is rather high, reaching 25.66%.

Besides this, additional administrative charges are levied by the EPFO. The EPFO funds are not permitted to be invested in equities, but are invested only in low-risk fixed-income securities issued by the government and public sector.

OCCUPATIONAL PENSION SCHEMES

In addition to the statutory EPFO schemes, some private-sector companies provide supplemental retirement income for employees by establishing occupational pension schemes. Most of these schemes have defined benefits, but recently there is a tendency to switch from defined benefits to defined contributions. The schemes are either self-managed or managed by the life insurance companies. The pension funds are allowed to be invested in equities and can be invested only domestically. Unlike the investment of the EPFO funds, the investment of the pension funds is much closer in terms of following modern portfolio principles.

PUBLIC-SECTOR ENTERPRISE
PENSION SCHEMES

The public-sector enterprises mainly include Reserve Bank of India, state-owned banks and insurance companies, electricity boards, state oil companies, those listed on the stock exchanges, etc. These public-sector enterprises have their own pension schemes, which usually adopt the type of defined benefits. Due to lack of transparency, many details about these pension schemes are unknown to the public, such as the design, administration, and supervision of these schemes, as well as their financial conditions.

VOLUNTARY TAX-ADVANTAGED
SAVING SCHEMES

The voluntary tax-advantaged saving schemes comprise various small saving schemes administered by individual and group annuity schemes provided by private and public life insurance companies. These schemes can be subscribed to by any individual. In order to encourage private saving for retirement, some of these funds enjoy tax benefits, and interest rates on small saving schemes have previously been set higher than market rates. These benefits may be subject to reconsideration in the future for distorting allocation of savings.

SOCIAL ASSISTANCE SCHEMES

Before 1995, the government of India did not provide any social assistance program for the poor. The National Social Assistance Scheme (NSAS), targeted at covering the destitute and elderly, was first introduced on August 15, 1995. NSAS has three components, one of which is the National Old Age Pension Scheme (NOAPS), which aims to support the poor elderly. NOAPS has strict eligibility criteria and offers low levels of benefit, which lead to limited coverage. In addition, these schemes are usually underfunded, poorly targeted, and suffer from significant leakages (Rajan, Mishra, & Sarma, 1999). In 1999, another program for the elderly destitute who have nothing to depend on, called Annapurna, was announced by the Indian government. But the progress for implementing this scheme has been very slow (Rajan, 2007).

MICRO-PENSION SCHEMES

Micro-pension schemes are specifically designed for workers in the unorganized sector. These schemes are typically designed as a defined contribution plan and are based on voluntary savings. Generally, in the accumulation phase, the contribution is accumulated over a long period of time and made in increments through investment in financial and capital markets by professional fund managers. In the payout phase, when participants reach an predetermined age (usually 58 or 60 years), the accumulated balances can be withdrawn in the form of a lump-sum annuity, a phased withdrawal, or a combination of these payment methods. The first and most well-known micro-pension scheme for the unorganized sector in India was launched by UTI Asset Management Company and SEWA (Self Employed Women's Association) in 2006. Until now, micro-pension schemes have played a limited role in protecting unorganized sector workers from old-age poverty.

Issues and Challenges

As we described above, India has a very complex old-age security system, targeted at different sectors of the labor force. The reform of pension and insurance schemes is now a priority on the agenda of the Indian government, but India still faces a great challenge to push the reform forward.

KEEPING A BALANCE BETWEEN ORGANIZED AND UNORGANIZED SECTORS

Although most of India's labor force is employed in the unorganized sector, there are few pension schemes covering them. As such, with the tendency of increasing employment in the unorganized sector, most Indian workers are excluded from access to formal pension schemes, keeping the coverage

rate very low. In order to address the unbalanced coverage between the organized and unorganized sectors, it is imperative for the Indian government to design appropriate pension schemes for workers in the unorganized sector, fully considering their demands and characteristics.

PROBLEMS WITH SOCIAL ASSISTANCE SCHEMES

There is no doubt that the social assistance schemes contribute to elderly poverty reduction. However, the effectiveness of these means-tested schemes is highly questionable for their low levels of coverage, poorly defined target population, meager benefits level, and inefficient delivery. The Indian government is clearly in a dilemma over how to solve these problems. On the one hand, the fiscal capacity of the central and state governments is limited. On the other hand, the task of eliminating poverty is urgent. The potential solution critically depends on the decisions of governments at all levels.

THE FISCAL UNSUSTAINABILITY OF PUBLIC PENSION SCHEMES

As mentioned above, the civil service schemes and EPS are facing the problem of fiscal unsustainability due to their generous benefits. However, most unorganized workers severely lack retirement provision even if they join the micro-pension scheme or receive benefits from some social assistance schemes. The manifested gap between different social groups has an adverse effect on social cohesion and stability. Cutting some expenditures on civil servants and transferring saved money to social assistance schemes may be a feasible solution. Meanwhile, the Indian government should strengthen the actuarial basis of various pension schemes.

COORDINATING DIFFERENT REGULATORY AGENCIES

It is obvious that India has not established any coordination between the different regulatory agencies that supervise different kinds of pension schemes. For example, the NPS is now under the supervision of the Provident Fund Regulatory and Development Authority (PFRDA), which helps to improve the compliance and invest in funds with low transaction costs. It is clearly conflictive for EPFO to act as both the administrator and the supervisor of funds at the same time. The insurance and annuity products are provided by the life insurance companies, which are regulated by the Insurance Regulatory and Development Authority (IRDA).

The investment behavior of various pension funds on financial and capital markets is monitored by the Securities and Exchange Board of India (SEBI). As such, in order to increase transparency, reduce management costs, and enhance information sharing, close coordination among these regulators is critical.

ACCELERATING THE DEVELOPMENT OF A PRIVATE ANNUITY MARKET

With the role of government and family in providing old-age security gradually weakening, the importance of a private annuity market will be highlighted in the near future. However, India's private annuity market is still underdeveloped. It is essential for India to break the monopoly status of the Life Insurance Corporation (LIC) of India and introduce competition in the private annuity market. Though the Indian government has moved in the right direction in recent years, it still has a long way to go to fulfill its policy goal in this area.

Conclusions

In this chapter, we reviewed different socioeconomic backgrounds and old-age security systems in four important countries—the United States, Germany, China, and India. Each country's old-age security system suffers from some issues that need to be fixed. The common problem facing all the countries is the financial sustainability of the old-age security system, especially the public-managed social security system. For developed countries, longevity and low birth rates may be the key causes for this issue. For developing countries, institution transition costs and too generous benefits are the main reasons.

In addition, developing countries have many specific problems, such as issues regarding low coverage, poor equity, and limited investment tools. It is typical in developing countries that highly fragmented old-age security systems and limited coverage lead to severe inequality between rural and urban citizens, as well as between workers in organized and unorganized sectors. This situation must be changed in the future in order to expand coverage and maintain social stability. What's more, after expanding coverage, how to integrate various schemes is still a huge challenge for many developing countries. At the same time, a lack of proper and reliable investment channels and tools limits the capacity to manage pension funds for developing countries. Promoting the development of a capital market will be helpful to establish a sustainable old-age security system.

Notes

1. A possible 4th pillar is family support, although the extent varies across countries.

2. This limit is only for OASDI and there is no limit for HI. The individual tax rate for HI of 1.45% is applied to gross compensation

References

Asher, M. (2007, August). *Pension reform in India*. Paper presented at the conference on "The Indian Economy at 60: Performance and Prospects," A Conference to Mark 60 Years of Indian Independence organized by Australia South Asia Research Centre, The Australian National University.

Blau, D. M., & Goodstein R. (2010). Can social security explain trends in labor force participation of older men in the United States? *Journal of Human Resources, 45*, 328–363.

Bonin, H. (2009). 15 Years of pension reform in Germany: Old successes and new threats. *The Geneva Papers, 34*, 548–560.

Borsch-Supan, A. H., & Wilke, C. B. (2006). The German public pension system: How it will become an NDC system look-alike. In R. Holzmann and E. Palmer (Eds.), *Pension reform: Issues and prospects for non-financial defined contribution (NDC) schemes* (pp. 589–626). Washington, DC: World Bank.

Borsch-Supan, A., Reil-Held, A., & Schunk, D. (2008). Saving incentives, old-age provision and displacement effects: Evidence from the recent German pension reform. *Journal of Pension Economics and Finance, 7*, 295–319.

Brown, J. R., Lynn, J., & Fullerton, D. (2009). *Is social security part of the social safety net?* (NBER Working Paper). Chicago, IL: University of Chicago Press.

Browning, E. K. (2008). The anatomy of Social Security and Medicare. *The Independent Review, 13*(1), 5–27.

Bureau of Labor Statistics (BLS). (2010). *The employment situation—October 2010*. Economic News Release of United States Department of Labor. Retrieved from http://www.bls.gov/news.release/pdf/empsit.pdf.

Duggan, J. E., Gillingham, R., & Greenlees, J. S. (1995). *Progressive returns to Social Security? An answer from Social Security records* (Research Paper No. 9501). Office of Economic Policy, Treasury Department, Washington, DC.

Employee Benefit Research Institute. (2005). *History of 401(k) plans: An update*. Washington, DC: Employee Benefit Research Institute. Retrieved from http://www.ebri.org/pdf/publications/facts/0205fact.a.pdf.

Fagnoni, C. M. (1999). *Social Security and minorities: Current benefits and implications of reform*. Testimony before the Subcommittee on Social Security, Committee on Ways and Means, House of Representatives, Washington, DC.

Friedman, M. (1972). Second lecture. In W. Cohen and M. Friedman (Eds.), *Social Security: Universal or selective?* (p. 35). Washington, DC: American Enterprise Institute.

Giandrea, M. D., Cahill, K. E., & Quinn, J. F. (2008). *Self-employment transitions among older American workers with career jobs* (Working Paper). Washington, DC: U.S. Bureau of Labor Statistics.

Hendley, A. A., & Bilimoria, N. F. (1999). Minorities and Social Security: An analysis of racial and ethnic differences in the current program. *Social Security Bulletin, 62*(2), 59–64.

Jackson, R., & Howe, N. (2004). *The graying of the Middle Kingdom: The demographics and economics of retirement policy in China*. Center for Strategic and International Studies. Newark, NJ: Prudential Foundation.

Modigliani, F., & Cao, S. (2004). The Chinese saving puzzle and the life cycle hypothesis. *Journal of Economic Literature, 42*(1), 145–170.

Munnell, A. (2009). *The financial crisis and restoring retirement security*. Testimony before the Committee on Education and Labor, U.S. House of Representatives. Available at http://i457.com/Documents/educomm/aliciamunnelltestimony.

Organisation for Economic Co-operation and Development. (2004). *Income disparities in China: An OECD perspective*. Paris, France: Author.

Organisation for Economic Co-operation and Development. (2009). Pension systems at a glance: Retirement-income systems in OECD countries. Paris, France: Author.

Organisation for Economic Co-operation and Development. (2010). *OECD economic surveys: China 2010*. Paris, France: Author.

Palacios, R. (2001). India: The old age income security (Report No. 22034-IN). Washington, DC: World Bank.

Rajan S. I. (2007). Population aging, health and social security in India (Discussion Paper No.3), CREI Discussion Paper Series. Osaka, Osaka City University, Centre for Research on Economic Inequality.

Rajan S. I., Mishra, U. S., & Sarma, P. S. (1999). *India's elderly: Burden or challenge*. New Delhi, India: Sage.

Sin, Y. (2005). *China: Pension liabilities and reform options for old age insurance* (Working Paper, No. 2005-1). Washington, DC: World Bank.

Wang, M., & Shultz, K. (2010). Employee retirement: A review and recommendations for future investigation. *Journal of Management, 36*, 172–206.

World Bank. (1994). *Averting the old age crisis: Policies to protect the old and promote growth*. Oxford, England: Oxford University Press.

Zhu, Y. (2009). *A case study on social security coverage extension in China* (Working Paper No.7). Geneva, Switzerland: International Social Security Association.

Employment Law and Retirement

Christina L. Causey *and* Joanna N. Lahey

Abstract

Employment law can have a profound effect on retirement decisions and outcomes for older workers. This chapter explores the effects of three types of government regulation on retirement outcomes: direct regulation of retirement and pensions, employment protection laws, and government transfer programs. This chapter discusses employment laws that encourage and discourage work at later ages and how they affect well-being during retirement.

Key Words: retirement, regulation, pensions, older workers, ERISA, ADEA, ADA, disability

Government regulation affects labor supply outcomes and retirement for older workers through several channels. This chapter discusses how different employment laws in the United States affect retirement, in terms of both the decision to retire and the characteristics of retirement itself. Some laws prevent work at later ages, while others either push workers into retirement or pull workers into the labor force. Government regulation can make it easier or harder to work, to find new work, or to leave the labor force. The first type of law discussed in this chapter is federal laws that directly regulate retirement and pensions. One such law is the federal Employee Retirement Income Security Act (ERISA), which sets minimum standards for pension and health plans in private industry. In addition to ERISA, other pension acts have contributed to the variable nature of retirement.

The second type of law discussed here is employment protection laws, specifically anti-discrimination laws. These laws also directly affect employment for older workers by discouraging employers from removing covered employees from the workforce. However, they may also create perverse incentives that discourage employers from

hiring these employees. This chapter discusses the Age Discrimination in Employment Act (ADEA) and the Americans with Disabilities Act (ADA) in depth.

The third type of government regulation, mentioned briefly in this chapter but discussed in depth throughout this handbook, is government transfer programs. The rules on take-up for these programs can provide an implicit tax on hours worked or labor force participation. The transfers themselves can make retirement more attractive for people on the margin of work. Examples include Social Security, Medicare and other retirement insurance, Social Security Disability Insurance (SSDI), and Supplemental Security Income (SSI).

Pensions and Retirement Regulation

Although Social Security is a major source of income for most retirees in the United States, benefits are considered inadequate to maintain quality of life in retirement for many (Diamond, 2004). As the private savings rate in the United States has declined over the years, pension plans have comprised an increasing percentage of retirement income for workers and have become a large factor in retirement decisions. Though estimates vary, most studies agree that fewer than half of the workers in the United States have an employer-provided pension plan, and workers who are female, Hispanic, low-wage, or part-time are more likely to lack plans (Befort, 2006). Because pensions serve as retirement income security and provide a variety of tax benefits, they are used as an incentive in labor contracts and thus impact employer-employee relationships, helping employers attract and retain workers.

Most private employee benefit plans are subject to the regulations of the Employee Retirement Income Security Act (ERISA). IRAs and public-sector pension plans that do not fall under ERISA are subject to similar rules in the Internal Revenue Code and associated regulations because they receive special tax benefits. Because the preferential treatment of a growing number of pension plans leads to forgone tax revenues, this favored treatment has become one of the largest tax expenditures of the federal government (Zhang, 2003).

Some believe that the traditional legal apparatus that regulated employee benefit programs was motivated by a need to encourage the departure of older workers from the workforce to make room for younger individuals seeking to enter the workforce (Penner, Perun, & Steuerle, 2002). However, Lazear (1979) suggests that mechanisms such as vested pensions and mandatory retirement increase labor market efficiency and benefit both employers and employees by increasing the present value of worker productivity (Neumark & Stock, 1999; Jolls, 1996). In Lazear's contract theory, workers are paid less than their marginal product early in their career and are rewarded by receiving more than their marginal product late in their career (Lazear, 1979). This payment mechanism discourages shirking and encourages company loyalty when there is imperfect supervision and there are gains to firm-specific human capital.

ERISA

Overview. ERISA is federal legislation enacted in 1974 with the primary goal of protecting and ensuring delivery of employee retirement benefits promised by employer-sponsored plans. Nothing in ERISA requires that employers establish qualified plans; it simply regulates those that choose to do so. The legislation sets up standards for plan design, delivery of benefits, and disclosures (Employee Retirement Income Security Act of 1974). Subsequent pension laws operate within or modify this initial framework.

Most employer-sponsored benefit plans must have assets placed in trusts and meet certain funding requirements, and there are required reports to the regulating agency as well as mandatory disclosures to plan participants. Additionally, benefit plans must have a provision for vesting after a certain number of years—this means that the employee has exclusive rights to the portion of his or her retirement fund that has "vested," and an employer or creditor cannot acquire the benefits or otherwise reach the funds. ERISA generally requires plans to be uniform in participation and coverage rules, as well as to apply to a large portion of the employees by satisfying a non-discrimination test that prevents the plans from solely benefiting higher-paid employees. However, plans that pay welfare benefits, such as health or life insurance, are subject to fewer regulations and are given more flexibility (Penner et al., 2002).

There are also a variety of tax incentives that are incorporated into ERISA, many of which have aspects that can favor both employers and employees. For employers, the use of benefit plans allows for income tax deductions on contributions and for tax-free accumulation of assets in tax-sheltered trusts. Employees also benefit from the deferred income tax liability on contributions and tax-sheltered earnings on investments. Any violations or disputes can be pursued in federal court (Employee Retirement Income Security Act of 1974).

Congress intended the regulations of ERISA to be supplemented by extensive federal common law, but federal courts have been largely inconsistent in their interpretation of provisions, making cohesion difficult (Carr & Liebross, 1992). Because ERISA preempts state laws, it is intended to provide a uniform federal employee benefit regime that is still subject to federal law relating to taxation, labor relations, employment discrimination, Social Security, and similar provisions. Courts have displayed a great deal of disagreement about the scope of the preemption of ERISA, although they generally find that certain aspects of state laws regarding insurance, banking, and securities that implement or are compliant with ERISA still apply (Lawrence & Taylor, 1996). This uncertainty over the scope of preemption, and the corresponding struggle between state and federal pension laws, makes it difficult for firms to ensure that they are in compliance with regulations and leaves employers vulnerable to lawsuits.

Types of plans. Under ERISA, qualified plans are divided into defined contribution and defined benefit plans. Defined benefit plans use a formula based on pre-retirement earnings to set the benefits for an employee, usually in the form of a life annuity. Employees are generally not required to contribute, and contributions for all participants are held in one trust (Befort, 2006). A defined benefit plan's investment performance does not impact the employee's entitlement, insulating the employee from market risk (Tweel, 2010). Additionally, if an employer cannot meet its obligations to defined benefit plans, a federal agency, the Pension Benefit Guaranty Corporation (PBGC), provides additional protection by ensuring that pension benefits at normal retirement age are paid up to a maximum monthly guarantee set each year.

In defined contribution plans, employers only promise a contribution rate to an individual employee's account, and both employers and employees typically contribute. Benefits accumulate over time, and the employee gets the investment earnings and usually bears the market risk (Tweel, 2010). Employee stock ownership plans (ESOPs), 401(k) and 403(b) plans, and profit-sharing plans are all types of defined contribution plans. Defined contribution plans are becoming increasingly popular; as of 2005, twice the number of workers had defined contribution plans as those who had defined benefit plans (Befort, 2006). However, defined contribution plans are not covered by the PBGC because contributions legally belong to the plan participant, rather than the employer, and cannot be lost due to changes in company profitability.

There has also been growth in the provision of hybrid plans, such as cash balance plans, as a replacement for defined benefit plans (Zhang, 2003). In a cash balance plan, the account is credited annually by an established formula that generally includes a fixed rate of compensation from the employer and an accumulating interest rate, which insulates the pension from market risk. These trends away from defined benefit plans require lower overall benefits to be paid by the employer and allow employers to avoid certain excise taxes that generally must be paid if they want to recover assets from a terminated defined benefit plan (Befort, 2006). The decrease in defined benefit plans may also be attributed to the greater potential for fiduciary liability of employers that is associated with these plans (Zhang, 2003).

Impact on retirement. Some of the ERISA provisions may force older workers into retirement or part-time employment. For example, ERISA requires that employers who have qualified pension or retirement benefit plans provide an opportunity for participation to those who work at least 1,000 hours a year. Employers may be less likely to hire older workers who want to work full-time so that the employer can avoid providing retirement benefits. As a result, older workers may be forced into early retirement (Forman, 2000). Vesting rules in ERISA, which allow employers to require minimum years of service before employees have access to benefits, can also make work less appealing for older workers who do not plan to stay with an employer long enough to satisfy these requirements (Forman, 2000). As vesting requirements have decreased in recent years, however, this has become less of an issue.

The type of pension plan an employee has may also affect retirement decisions. Burtless and Quinn (2002) argue that a primary factor in the trend of early male retirement until the mid-1980s was the increase in wealth from the expansion of employer-sponsored pension plans, specifically defined benefit plans. However, Ruhm (1996) questions this conclusion. Most defined benefit plans are structured to encourage workers to remain employed until they have completed a minimal term of years or have reached a critical age; in general, they encourage workers to stay employed longer, since the monthly pension increases the longer they work under the plan (Burtless & Quinn, 2000). However, under a defined benefit plan, if an employee works too long, the value of his or her lifetime pension accumulation may decrease if the plan offers benefits starting at a certain age but does not increase benefits for workers who delay retirement. This would essentially constitute a pay cut that circumvents age discrimination laws because it does not reflect a direct cut in wages (Burtless & Quinn, 2000; Burtless & Quinn, 2002). Employers may use these age-specific retirement incentives to encourage early retirement (Clark & Quinn, 1999).

Defined contribution plans, conversely, are age-neutral and do not encourage early retirement or cause the other age-specific consequences of defined benefit plans. Additionally, it is easier for employees with defined contribution plans to switch employers without facing as many reductions in accrued benefits (Zhang, 2003). Because these types of plans are increasingly popular among employers, workers should have less pressure to leave their jobs to avoid a decrease in pension benefits (Burtless & Quinn, 2000). Some consider this trend of a growing number of workers reaching retirement under an age-neutral defined contribution plan to be a factor in the decrease in early retirement among male workers (Burtless & Quinn, 2002). Additionally, using data from the Health and Retirement Study (HRS), Munnell et al. (2004) found that those with defined contribution plans tend to retire around a year later on average than those with defined benefit plans. Manchester (2010) reached the same result when examining the retirement decisions of college and university faculty. Friedberg and Webb (2000), using HRS data, estimated that those with defined contribution plans would retire around two years later than those with defined benefit plans.

However, because defined contribution plans give individual employees more control over investment decisions, and are thus not as protected by ERISA's fiduciary standards, these plans may actually provide less retirement security (Zhang, 2003). These self-directed plans also appear to have a disparate impact on different demographics. Brown and Weisbenner (2007) found that, even when it is not the best financial decision in terms of investment risk, married men who are well-educated and high earners are more likely to choose a self-managed plan. Conversely, Zanglein (2001) argued that women and minorities, who tend to be more conservative investors, are more severely impacted by these self-directed plans.

ERISA has also affected the nature of retirement and the possibility of phased, or partial, retirement and part-time employment. For example, the coverage and participation requirements discussed above that mandate pension benefits to workers who work at least 1,000 hours a year may lead to employers hiring only workers willing to agree to part-time employment. This may force older workers who would prefer to be working normal hours into accepting part-time employment that falls below the 1,000 hours a year, eliminating the possibility of pension benefits. For workers whose employment options are limited and who need the additional income, part-time work may seem a better alternative to full retirement.

The ERISA requirement that plans have a minimum benefit accrual formula, which is the rate of individual pension entitlement, ensures that long-time employees receive adequate benefits even if they switch employers toward the end of their careers. It may also encourage phased retirement or a shift to part-time work with another employer. As a result, older workers are not forced to remain with a long-time employer to receive retirement benefits and can change employers if necessary before they reach normal retirement age.

However, aspects of ERISA that limit the availability of benefits until workers fully retire may discourage partial retirement. For instance, the limitation on in-service distributions in ERISA, which prohibits most distributions to active employees, discourages phased retirement (Forman, 2000). This effect has been somewhat ameliorated by later pension laws, which have expanded access to certain benefits before retirement. Vesting rules requiring that workers remain employed for a certain number of years before receiving pension benefits may also discourage re-entry into the workforce after an interruption in work or temporary retirement, especially if it is difficult for older workers to find new employment (Lahey, 2008a; Diamond & Hausman, 1984).

Other Pension Laws

Overview. Pension laws passed after ERISA have modified the original framework of retirement plan regulation. The Revenue Act of 1978 established 401(k) plans and simplified employee pensions (SEPs), both types of defined contribution plans. A 401(k) plan generally allows an employee to contribute some of his or her wages to the plan, often with the employer "matching" the contribution. Employees benefit from 401(k) plans because of the ability to avoid current income taxes on contributions and tax-sheltered earnings on the investments; employers benefit from these plans because their contributions are deductible and they can avoid taxes on payroll (Polk, 2009). The tax treatment of a 401(k) plan is similar to that of a 403(b) plan, which is available only to public school employers, tax-exempt nonprofit organizations, and qualified ministers. An SEP is a type of Individual Retirement Arrangement (IRA) that is simple to set up, has low administrative costs, is funded only by employer contributions, and is always fully vested. Eligibility for IRAs and employee stock ownership plans (ESOPs) was expanded in the Economic Recovery Tax Act of 1981. An ESOP is a type of plan whereby the employer makes tax-deductible contributions to a trust that mainly invests in the employer's stock, with the stock allocated to employees based on certain variables such as salary, years of service, or position in the company.

Older women, who have been less likely to stay in the workforce or with the same employer as consistently as men, have traditionally been less likely to have private pension income. However, in 1984, the Retirement Equity Act addressed these issues by setting up survivor protections and eligibility changes that made it easier for younger workers to get pension credits (Morris, 1987). The greater protection for spouses of participants provided by the Tax Reform Act of 1986, which increased access to joint and survivor annuities, also improved things for older women who are dependent on a spouse's retirement income. Additionally, the Senior Citizens Freedom to Work Act of 2000 provided that the spouse and children of someone of normal retirement age could receive benefits even if the worker delayed retirement. It also modified the limitation on outside income that would reduce Social Security benefits.

The Unemployment Compensation Amendments of 1992 encouraged turning lump-sum distributions into IRAs or qualified pension accounts by providing that a certain percentage of lump sums would be treated as tax revenue. In 1996, the Small Business Job Protection Act increased access to retirement plans by modifying distribution rules, and it established simplified retirement plans (SIMPLE plans) for small businesses that required that employers match elective employee contributions of up to $6,000 a year. The Economic Growth and Tax Relief Reconciliation Act of 2001 (EGTRRA) simplified rules for plans such as pension and retirement plans by, for example, allowing more elective contributions to 401(k) and 403(b) plans and providing more access to tax-free rollovers between plans. This legislation was set to expire at the end of 2010, but the Tax Relief, Unemployment Insurance Reauthorization, and Job Creation Act of 2010 granted a two-year extension to EGTRRA.

More recently, the Pension Protection Act (2006) established new rules affecting both defined benefit and defined contribution plans, expanding the eligibility of tax-free rollovers between plans and changing vesting rules. Instead of mandating, as EGTRRA did, that only matching contributions had to vest under either a three-year cliff or a six-year graded schedule, the Pension Protection Act requires that *all* employer contributions to qualified defined contribution plans be subject to those same rules. The Pension Protection Act also established minimum funding requirements for defined benefit plans to discourage default and contained provisions to encourage diversification in defined contribution plans (Martin & Rafsky, 2006). As was shown by the Enron scandal, forgoing diversification by concentrating plan assets in corporate stock may be beneficial for the employer in terms of stock value increases and tax benefits, but it can devastate employees' retirement plans if the company's stock value declines rapidly (Kaplan, 2004).

Goals of pension reform. Smaller employers, who have traditionally had less pension plan coverage, have been the focus of much of the pension reform legislation. Many of the new types of plans developed by Congress, such as simplified employee pensions (SEPs), were created with the hope of improving small employers' pension plan participation rates by providing less complicated forms of coverage (Zhang, 2003). This goal seems to be largely unrealized, as a recent Small Employer Retirement Survey found that almost half (47%) of smaller employers who did not provide retirement plans had never even heard of SEPs, and a similar percentage (43%) were not likely to start providing pension plans in the next two years (Small Employer Retirement Survey, 2003).

Pension reform proposals have generally claimed to improve retirement security for all workers. However, in a study of proposed reforms that formed the basis of EGTRRA, Perun (2001) found that the proposals primarily benefited those who were in a position to save a substantial portion of their incomes to make the maximum contributions. This indicates that most pension reforms maintain the status quo by benefiting highly paid executives over low-income workers.

Impact on retirement. Expansion of pension coverage may have, in general, contributed to a decline in labor force participation, particularly among older men (Samwick, 1998). However, employers use pension plans as a means of establishing retirement incentives or disincentives based on employment needs. These plans can impact workers' retirement decisions by either encouraging or discouraging retirement at certain ages (Clark & Quinn, 1999).

In particular, Ruhm (1996) finds that pension plans increase the likelihood of older workers leaving the labor supply at some ages and decrease it at others, suggesting that the effects of pension plan incentives are complex. Lumsdaine et al. (1994) argue that changes in an employer's defined benefit plan policy, such as an increase in the early retirement age, have a much greater impact on retirement decisions than changes in Social Security policy. In a study of the low quit rates among workers in the federal government, Ippolito (1987) finds that retirement behavior closely follows the incentives of pension plans. If, for example, the pension plan is constructed to maximize total lifetime pension entitlement given that the employee retired within a particular age window, the worker is less likely to leave employment before that retirement age. Kotlikoff and Wise (1984) examined the retirement incentives of those with defined benefit plans, finding that most plans provide an incentive for retirement after the normal plan retirement age, while some provide an incentive for retirement after the early retirement age. Using data from a *Fortune* 500 company, Kotlikoff and Wise (1989) also found that when the employer's pension policy had financial incentives through benefit accrual for workers to retire at age 55, employee departure rates closely track these incentives and increase after age 55.

There has been a recent trend in pension laws toward encouraging delayed retirement through federal regulations of benefit plans. For example, the Small Business Protection Act of 1996 modified minimum distribution rules so that older workers could postpone distributions until age 70 ½, at which time workers must begin taking required minimum distributions from qualified retirement plans and IRAs (Forman, 2000). The Senior Citizens Freedom to Work Act of 2000, which allowed dependents to receive benefits even if the worker had delayed retirement, also provided relief for spouses and children of workers who had reached normal retirement age. It also repealed the limitation on outside income that may be earned before Social Security benefits are reduced. Additionally, EGTRRA contains a catch-up contribution provision that allows employees over 50 to make additional contributions to their plans, as long as contributions do not exceed earnings. This type of provision that allows additional accrual of benefits may encourage delayed retirement (Zhang, 2003).

Tax provisions also encourage continued employment. For instance, the Internal Revenue Code places a limit on annual benefits that can be paid to plan participants, which is determined according to retirement age (Internal Revenue Code of 1986, § 415(b)). Employees who are older have a higher dollar limit on benefits, which may lead to older workers delaying retirement. Other federal tax provisions for individuals over age 65, including an increased standard income tax deduction and the exclusion of some capital gains from home sales, may also impact the timing and nature of retirement (Conway & Rork, 2008).

However, there remain some aspects of pension plan design that may encourage retirement at the normal retirement age. For example, some plans will begin distributing benefits at the normal retirement age, such that there is no financial incentive beyond salary to continue working (Chen & Scott, 2003). Tax provisions that increase wealth and eligibility

for lump-sum payments from benefit plans may actually encourage early retirement. However, the tendency to dissipate lump sums may require that workers work longer to accrue sufficient retirement savings (Forman, 2000).

Although phased retirement has become more common as an alternative to full retirement, the pension system was not originally designed to accommodate this trend (Scahill & Forman, 2002). For example, the Tax Reform Act penalizes withdrawal of funds from plans before age 59 ½ with an additional 10% excise tax, discouraging early or partial retirement (Penner et al., 2002). Vesting rules under the pension laws, which generally allow employers to require up to six years of service before benefit accruals fully vest, could discourage older workers from re-entering the workforce after a gap in employment.

Anti-Discrimination Laws

Anti-discrimination laws are a type of employment protection law that protects workers specifically from discrimination. An early example of this kind of law is the Civil Rights Act of 1964 that protects against discrimination based on race, gender, or religion. In general, when enforced, these employment protection laws are effective at protecting people from discrimination that can be detected, such as unfair dismissal or discrimination on the job. However, firms may compensate for the inability to remove workers by increasing differential treatment on margins that cannot be detected, such as hiring. In general, this process may result in decreased firing but also decreased hiring of the protected group. Employment protection laws may also decrease overt discrimination through forcing changes in social norms or the cultural environment, for example, by outlawing negative advertisements or inappropriate treatment on the job.

Age Discrimination Law

What is U.S. age discrimination law? Age discrimination laws protect older people from employment-based discrimination. The first age discrimination laws were state laws, beginning in 1903 in Colorado. Some laws are more restrictive than others, and many of these laws have changed over time. The federal Age Discrimination in Employment Act (1967) protects people over the age of 40 from discrimination in hiring (including prohibiting age-related advertisements), firing, promotion, layoff, compensation, benefits, job assignments, and training. The law affects firms that regularly employ twenty or more employees. The current law also protects against mandatory retirement for most occupations (Lahey, 2008b).

If a state has its own age discrimination statutes, the ADEA allows the claimant to file with the state Fair Employment Practices (FEP) office within 300 days of the occurrence of the incident. In the few states that do not have statutes, the claimant must file with the EEOC within 180 days. The EEOC can then dismiss the claim, at which point the claimant may pursue a civil action in court, or the EEOC can seek to settle or mediate. If the settlement or mediation is unsuccessful, the EEOC can then sue, or, if it chooses not to sue, the claimant may sue (Neumark, 2001).

Exemptions to the ADEA include a "bona fide occupational qualification," or BFOQ, that is directly related to age, for example, in an acting position. In practice, the courts have also allowed age to be considered a BFOQ in cases where public safety may be affected, including occupations such as pilots, air traffic controllers, or bus drivers. The federal law also exempts high-salaried policymaking positions from age discrimination law.

Unlike the case of the Civil Rights Act (CRA), the ADEA does not allow damages for emotional pain and suffering or for punitive damages. Damages are limited to "make whole" damages and lawyer fees. These awards can include hiring, reinstating, promoting, back pay, and restoring benefits. Lawyer fees often make up the majority of the award to ADEA recipients. Additional damages are awarded only in rare cases in which the defendant has willfully violated the law, and these damages are limited to twice the amount of actual damages (O'Meara, 1989; Lindemann & Kadue, 2003). Because of these limits to damages, the majority of plaintiffs under the ADEA have been white male middle managers in their 50s who have lost sizeable salaries and benefits (Schuster & Miller, 1984; O'Meara, 1989). In 2002, ADEA suits averaged $69,500 in relief per suit at a total of $1.39 million dollars. By comparison, discrimination suits under Title VII of the CRA averaged $117,206 in relief per suit.[1] Recently, the average amount awarded per ADEA suit has increased and is closer in size to awards for Title VII.[2]

A strict interpretation of employment protection law allows only for disparate treatment cases, requiring proof of intentional discrimination. However, another interpretation of employment law allows for disparate impact cases, in which a policy indirectly impacts a protected group differently than the unprotected group. Minimum height requirements are a common example in which there is a disparate impact on women, who are shorter than men on average. In ADEA cases, disparate impact generally involves decisions based on seniority or wages, such as the decision to fire those who have the highest salaries or who have been with the firm the longest. In *Smith v. City of Jackson* (2005), the United States Supreme Court held that the ADEA authorizes recovery for disparate impact claims of discrimination. The Court also held that the "reasonable factors other than age" (RFOA) test, rather than a "business necessity" test, is the appropriate standard for determining the legality of practices that disproportionately affect older individuals. This ruling differed from the EEOC's earlier position that an employment practice that had a disparate impact on individuals within the protected age group could not be a reasonable factor other than age unless it was justified as a business necessity. The recent *Ricci v. DeStefano* (2009) decision may have made it more difficult for plaintiffs to win disparate impact cases by making the case that disparate treatment can arise when plaintiffs try to avoid disparate impact. Because younger people are not a protected class in most states, *Ricci v. DeStefano* will probably not have as large an effect for ADEA cases as for cases involving race, gender, or religion.

Burden of proof in disparate impact cases can also affect court interpretation of employment protection cases. If the plaintiff bears the burden of proof, then he or she must prove that the policy is intentionally discriminatory. Conversely, if the defendant bears this burden of proof, then he or she must prove that the policy had a bona fide business rationale. This burden of proof has shifted from defendant to plaintiff and back in age cases since the 1970s. Currently, the 2005 *Smith v. City of Jackson* ruling is that "it is not enough to simply allege that there is a disparate impact on workers, or point to a generalized policy that leads to such an impact. Rather, the employee is 'responsible for isolating and identifying the specific employment practices that are allegedly responsible for any observed statistical disparities'" (*Smith v. City of Jackson*, 2005, citing *Wards Cove Packing Co. v. Atonio*, 1989). The recent 2009 *Gross v. FBL Financial Services* ruled that unlike Title VII legislation, burden of proof would not shift from the plaintiff to the defendant in a "mixed-motive" case in which age is one of many factors resulting in an adverse decision. Instead, the plaintiff must show "but-for" causation, in which age was the factor resulting in that decision (*Gross v. FBL Financial Services*, 2009).

Enforcement. Between 1967 and 1978, the ADEA was publicized, but there was no formal enforcement mechanism at the federal level for violations of the law. The original 1967 federal law protected workers aged 40 to 65 and allowed for mandatory retirement and other discriminatory behavior after age 65. In 1978, the law expanded to cover those aged 40 to 70, and in 1986 it removed the upper age limit entirely, with mandatory retirement phased out in professions with tenure until 1994. In 1978, the law was changed to allow the right to a jury trial in ADEA cases, and in 1979 the Department of Labor moved enforcement to the Equal Employment Opportunity Commission (EEOC), both of which strengthened the enforcement of the ADEA (Hersch & Viscusi, 2004; Neumark, 2001). In practice, over 95% of employment discrimination cases are brought by private attorneys, not the EEOC; of the cases filed in federal court for employment discrimination, 92% are never brought to trial (Gregory, 2001).

The theoretical effects of the ADEA could increase employment, decrease employment, or have no effect on employment. We would expect that firms would decrease potentially illegal activities in areas in which they are likely to be caught if the sanctions are both strong and enforced. In practice, we would expect that removal of employees would be more likely to bring claims of discrimination than would failure to hire. First, current employees have more information about their performance and their removal than they do on why they were not hired. Second, current employees have more to lose from their removal than do potential employees who may not have been hired even in the absence of discrimination. Therefore, we would expect to see a decrease in firing of protected workers combined with a decrease in hiring of those workers. The size of these competing effects will determine the overall effect of the laws on employment for protected workers.

As the enforcement and strength of the law changed over time, we would expect the empirical effects of the law to change over time. In theory, the enforcement of the law was weaker between 1967 and 1978 than it was after 1978, and therefore firms may not have taken it into account when making hiring decisions. Adams (2004) finds a positive effect of the law, which could have been caused by a decrease in age-related advertisements or a change in social norms influenced by the law.

There may also have been a decrease in firing caused by the increased threat of individual lawsuits. These individual lawsuits may not have been widespread enough for firms to take them into account during the hiring decision, but could still have increased employment overall.

During the later period, when there was much stronger enforcement, Lahey (2008b) shows that hiring decreased by 0.2 percentage points among men most likely to be affected by the law in states and years in which more time was given to file a suit. Employment also decreased—weeks worked dropped by 0.8 to 1.3 weeks per year and 1.6 to 3 percentage points to claim that they were not employed compared to men in states and years in which less time was given to sue. The hiring of women and minorities did not seem to be affected by the ADEA, and those groups were extremely unlikely to bring lawsuits during the 1978–1991 time period studied. Only white men over 50, the group that brought the majority of age discrimination lawsuits (Schuster & Miller, 1984; O'Meara, 1989), seem to have been affected by the law; they were less likely to be hired or fired.

Mandatory retirement. Mandatory retirement provisions have been studied separately under the ADEA, and different effects are predicted under different circumstances. One reason that mandatory retirement has been studied differently is that employers who keep their workers over a long period of time may use mandatory retirement as a tool when monitoring employees is difficult. The type of contract system they use is called a *Lazear contract* in economics terminology, in which the worker is paid less than his or her marginal product early in his or her career and more than his or her marginal product later in his or her career. Neumark and Stock (1999) and Jolls (1996) suggest that the ADEA improves efficiency during this time period in companies with long-term Lazear-type contracts; the ADEA provides a commitment device that the company will not renege on its implicit promise. The ADEA thus improves employee willingness to be compensated at lower wages when first entering a firm on the promise of higher wages later.

Additional work on the effects of ADEA and the end of mandatory retirement finds an increase in labor force participation for some industries. Mitchell and Luzadis (1988) find that prior to age discrimination laws in 1960, pension plans rewarded delayed retirement, but by the 1980s union plans actively encouraged early retirement, while non-union plans encouraged delayed retirement. Von Wachter (2002) examines the shift of mandatory retirement to age 70 in 1978 and its end in 1986 using imputed probability of being covered by mandated retirement, and finds that the labor force participation of workers age 65 and older increases by 10% to 20% in 1986 in specific industries. Ashenfelter and Card (2002) show that the abolition of retirement for college professors in 1994 (when mandatory retirement was phased out for industries with tenure) reduced retirement for those aged 70 and 71.

Discrimination still exists. Age discrimination still exists in the U.S. labor force, despite ADEA legislation, and thus may still discourage or prevent older people from staying in the labor force. From 1992 to 2008, on average 15.79% of ADEA cases, for a total of 44,624 cases, were described as "merit resolutions," or successful claims, by the EEOC (author's calculations).[3] These numbers give a lower bound on discrimination because many instances of age discrimination are never litigated, and cases of hiring discrimination often go undetected. Experimental evidence also shows the existence of age discrimination. A 2002–2003 labor market experiment in Boston, MA, and St. Petersburg, FL, sent out thousands of résumés and measured the response rate based on date of high school graduation. Because of the need to make treatment and control groups similar except for age, the study was limited to entry-level women with work histories of ten years or less. Among this group, applicants under age 50 were 40% more likely to be called back for an interview than were those over age 50 (Lahey, 2008a).

European Age Discrimination Law: Framework Directive 2000/78/EC

The majority of Europe has only recently implemented age protection guidelines based on the European Union's Framework Directive 2000/78. Article 13 of the 1998 EC Treaty allowed for future employment protection legislation by permitting "appropriate action to combat discrimination based on sex, racial or ethnic origin, religion or belief, disability, age or sexual orientation" (*Lisa Jacqueline Grant v. South-West Trains Ltd*, 1998, I-621, 651; Riesenhuber, 2009). Member states adopted Directive 2000/78 in 2000, and it was slated to be implemented through national laws by December 2003, allowing for an additional three years to formulate age and disability legislation (Adnett & Hardy, 2007; Bell, 2002; Riesenhuber, 2009). However, the Directive covers only employment discrimination and specifically excludes state social security and social protection programs.

Most countries used at least one extension before completely implementing or changing their laws to conform to the Framework Directive, implementing their laws between 2003 and 2006. The Framework Directive is similar to the U.S. ADEA law in its ban on age-based advertisements, but differs in many respects from the federal U.S. law. Most member states disallow discrimination based on age generally and do not just protect a class of older workers. This difference is similar to some U.S. state laws. Unlike the modern ADEA, most member states still allow mandatory retirement or upper ages at which these laws no longer apply. The Directive allows for an exception that is similar to the U.S. BFOQ, called "legitimate aims" but is much broader in scope for exceptions and, as an example, may include positive hiring for younger workers as a legitimate aim. Enforcement, penalties for breaking the law, and prosecution differ dramatically across countries. For more information on age protection law in Europe, see Lahey (2010) and Ten Bokum et al. (2009).

Americans with Disabilities Act

Another employment protection program that may have strong effects on older workers is the Americans with Disabilities Act (ADA). The ADA, enacted in 1990, is meant to protect the disabled from discrimination. The employment portion of this act protects persons with disabilities who are qualified for a specific employment position "with or without reasonable accommodation" (Americans with Disabilities Act of 1990). The definition of disabled in the ADA includes those who have a "physical or mental impairment that substantially limits one or more major life activities," have a record of such an impairment, or are regarded as disabled (Americans with Disabilities Act of 1990). This definition is more generous than that for Social Security Disability Insurance or Supplemental Security Insurance, both of which require that the disability be work-limiting (Burkhauser & Daly, 2002). Although this law does not specifically target older workers, the likelihood of being disabled increases with age (U.S. Department of Commerce, 1997), and almost 60% of charges of ADA violations between 1993 and 2007 were filed by individuals over 40 years old (Bjelland et al., 2010).

Similar to the ADEA, ADA employment discrimination complaints are filed with the local EEOC office, which then provides a right-to-sue letter. The first state law preventing disability discrimination was implemented in 1969 in Idaho and covered state employees (Hotchkiss, 2003). In 1992 all employers with 25 or more employees were subject to the ADA. In 1994 this number was changed to all employers with 15 or more employees. In 2008, an amendment to the act broadened the definition of "disability" further in order to offset Supreme Court rulings that limited those protected by the ADA (ADA Amendment Act of 2008). Specifically, it made the following changes to the definition and interpretation of disability:

1. Directs EEOC to revise the portion of its regulations that defines the term "substantially limits"

2. Expands the definition of "major life activities" by including two non-exhaustive lists:

   a. The first list includes many activities that the EEOC has recognized (e.g., walking) as well as activities that the EEOC has not specifically recognized (e.g., reading, bending, and communicating).

   b. The second list includes major bodily functions (e.g., "functions of the immune system, normal cell growth, digestive, bowel, bladder, respiratory, neurological, brain, circulatory, endocrine, and reproductive functions").

3. States that mitigating measures other than "ordinary eyeglasses or contact lenses" shall not be considered in assessing whether an individual has a disability

4. Clarifies that an impairment that is episodic or in remission is a disability if it would substantially limit a major life activity when active

5. Provides that an individual subjected to an action prohibited by the ADA (e.g., failure to hire) because of an actual or perceived impairment will meet the "regarded as" definition of disability, unless the impairment is transitory and minor

6. Provides that individuals covered only under the "regarded as" prong are not entitled to reasonable accommodation

7. Emphasizes that the definition of "disability" should be interpreted broadly.

There is no general consensus on the effects of ADA legislation on employment. Employment for disabled people has decreased, or at least did not increase, since 1990 (Stapleton & Burkauser, 2003). Acemoglu and Angrist (2001) argue that the ADA decreases employment for all disabled men and for disabled women under the age of 40. They find a decrease in hiring of the disabled but no change in job separations. Similarly, DeLeire (2000) finds a drop in employment that is stronger for men in manufacturing, managerial, or blue-collar positions. He finds very little effect on wages. Hotchkiss (2003) also finds that wages do not change for the majority of disabled, but that wages for workers with musculoskeletal disabilities declined 4% more than for workers without disabilities, suggesting that they value the benefit of accommodation. Jolls and Prescott (2004) also find a negative effect on employment and suggest that the pathway is through the cost of "reasonable accommodations" legislation rather than increased hiring costs.

However, Hotchkiss and Rovba (2003) argue that the findings in Acemoglu and Angrist (2001) and DeLeire (2000) are not the result of employer decisions but of a reclassification of who is termed disabled after ADA reforms and that employment actually improved for the disabled. As Stapleton and Burkhauser (2003) explain, the Current Population Survey asks about work-limiting disabilities, a definition that is sensitive to the interaction between physical disability and the cultural, legislative, and employment environment the worker faces. Still, Stapleton and Burkhauser (2003) argue that it is valid to use these data for analysis, although interpretations differ across different studies. In general, studies that define disability as having a work-limiting disability find negative effects of the ADA on employment for the disabled (Acemoglu & Angrist, 2001; DeLeire, 2000, 2003), and studies that limit the definition to people who say that they are "able to work at all" find positive effects (Hotchkiss & Rovba, 2003; Kruse & Schur, 2003a, 2003b). Blanck, Schur, Kruse, Schwochau, and Song (2003) argue that neither of these definitions of disabled cover the population targeted by the ADA, and thus the true impact of the ADA on the population targeted is still an open research question.

Although the definitions of disability are different for the ADA than for transfer programs targeting those with disabilities, it was hoped that the ADA would decrease the need for SSI and SSDI by enabling the disabled to work. However, that does not seem to be the case. Burkhauser and Daly (2002) find that the disabled are much more sensitive to government transfer program rules than they are to the ADA, which suggests that proposals targeting such transfer programs may provide maximal impact on the labor force participation of older disabled people.

Government Transfer Programs

Government transfer programs to older people can have strong labor market disincentive effects, or in some cases incentive effects, on these potential workers. The majority of these programs penalize work in some way, disallowing full receipt of benefits if the recipient earns over a certain amount. A key tension in program and regulation design for transfer programs is covering those who genuinely need the benefit while not discouraging those who do not need the benefit from working. Many of these programs are covered in more detail in other chapters, so they will be touched upon only briefly here.

Social Security

Social Security is a government program that has had strong effects on labor supply and the well-being of older people. The years set for early retirement age (ERA) and normal retirement age (NRA) have strong effects on the retirement hazard for older workers. It is likely that, moving forward, the ERA will remain at 62 while the NRA moves to older ages, perhaps eventually being pegged to life expectancy. These changes, along with changes to earnings rules, may have profound effects on labor market participation of older workers in the future. In this handbook, Yao and Peng (chapter 24) discuss the effects of Social Security in more detail. The 1999 *Handbook of Labor Economics* chapter by Lumsdaine and Mitchell contains an earlier review of the effects of Social Security.

Medicare and Retirement Insurance

Health care is an important determinant of the labor supply of older workers. Because health insurance is often unaffordable on the private market for older people, access to group insurance is a strong reason to keep working. Government provision and regulation of health insurance in retirement will have strong effects on workers working full-time jobs in order to remain insured. With the new health care bill, it will be interesting to see if the ties between labor market supply and health insurance access are loosened. Recent research suggests that increasing access to health insurance will decrease the labor supply of older workers under the age of 65. However, educated older workers will be more likely to move to self-employment, less educated workers will be more likely to leave the labor force entirely, and particularly vulnerable older men will be more likely to move into the labor force upon receipt of health insurance (Boyle & Lahey, 2010).

In this handbook, Mortensen and Villani (chapter 29) discuss Medicare and retirement insurance in more detail. An earlier review on health insurance and the labor market by Janet Currie and Bridget Madrian can be found in the 1999 *Handbook of Labor Economics*.

Social Security Disability Insurance (SSDI)

For those whose working lives are cut short by a disability, SSDI provides an important source of income and health insurance prior to Social Security and Medicare receipt. SSDI was created in 1956 through Title II of the Social Security Act (Burkhauser & Daly, 2002). It is financed by a payroll tax and is not means-tested. In 1984, SSDI was liberalized and the labor force drop out rate of displaced high school dropouts doubled (Autor & Duggan, 2003). Bound and Waidmann (2002) attribute the relative decline in employment for individuals with disabilities in the 1990s to increases in SSDI. In 1999, the government attempted to encourage labor force entry among participants through the "Ticket to Work and Work Incentive Improvement Act," which provides job-related training and placement services for those with disabilities and allows states to provide Medicaid coverage to disabled individuals who work. An early literature review of the labor market effects of SSDI can be found in the 1999 *Handbook of Labor Economics* chapter by Bound and Burkauser. The labor market and other effects of SSDI have become a thriving area of recent research, some of which is summarized in Autor and Duggan's (2006) paper in the *Journal of Economic Perspectives*.

Supplemental Security Income (SSI)

SSI is a means-tested cash transfer program for low-income people age 65 or older, blind, or disabled. Recipients must be unable to do any work for which they are qualified by age, education and experience. There is a five-month waiting period for permanent benefits. Both the percentage of people over age 65 claiming SSI and the actual number of those claiming SSI have diminished since the mid-1970s, as the numbers of blind and disabled adults and children now make the majority of recipients. Participation among those eligible for SSI is also relatively low among those over age 65; researchers estimate this participation rate between 45% and 60% (Daly and Burkhauser, 2003).

Burkhauser and Smeeding (1981) and Daly and Burkhauser (2003) discuss the theory of the work disincentives in this program, which are complicated by the interaction between SSI and Social Security, with SSI acting as a tax on Social Security income as well as providing an incentive to take early Social Security benefits. Empirically, Duggan (1984) finds SSI work disincentives for people over the age of 54. Similarly, Powers and Neumark (2003) and Neumark and Powers (2005) also find work disincentives; for those most likely to participate, the implied elasticity of employment and hours with respect to benefits is generally between −0.2 and −0.3. Additionally, as with any asset-tested program, there is also concern that SSI may decrease savings. Neumark and Powers (1998) find evidence that it does reduce savings among people nearing retirement age who are likely to participate in the program.

Conclusion

Pension and retirement regulation can act as a lever changing the timing of retirement for older workers. Provisions from these laws also affect the income, savings, and ability to find additional employment during retirement from a primary job. Employment protection laws discourage worker dismissals but may make it difficult for unemployed older workers to find work, thus encouraging retirement. Finally, government transfer programs may discourage work at older ages while allowing those who have difficulty working to enjoy a minimum standard of quality of life.

Author Note

Corresponding author. Contact TAMU Mailstop 4220, College Station, TX, or jlahey@nber.org. Thanks to Stephen F. Befort, Susanne Bruyere, Melissa Causey, Christine Jolls, Olivia Mitchell, John C. Scott, Andrew Segna, and Mo Wang for insightful comments and discussion. Thanks also to Jillian Boles for excellent research assistance.

Notes

1. http://www.eeoc.gov/eeoc/litigation/reports/02annrpt.html.

2. Authors' calculations from http://www.eeoc.gov/eeoc/statistics/enforcement/litigation.cfm.

3. http://archive.eeoc.gov/stats/adea-a.html.

References

Acemoglu, D., & Angrist, J. D. (2001). Consequences of employment protection? The case of the Americans with Disabilities Act. *Journal of Political Economy, 109*(5), 915–957.

ADA Amendments Act of 2008, Pub. L. No. 110–325 (2008).

Adams, S. J. (2004). Age discrimination legislation and the employment of older workers. *Labour Economics, 11*(2), 219–241.

Adnett, N., & Hardy, S. (2007). The peculiar case of age discrimination: Americanising the European social model? *European Journal of Law and Economics, 23*, 29–41.

Age Discrimination in Employment Act of 1967, Pub. L. No. 90-202, 81 Stat. 602.

Americans with Disabilities Act of 1990, 42 U.S.C. § 12111 (2009).

Ashenfelter, O., & Card, D. (2002). Did the elimination of mandatory retirement affect faculty retirement. *American Economic Review, 92*(4), 957–980.

Autor, D. H., & Duggan, M. G. (2003). The rise in the disability rolls and the decline in unemployment. *Quarterly Journal of Economics, 118*(1), 157–206.

Autor, D. H., & Duggan, M. G. (2006). The growth in the social security disability rolls: A fiscal crisis unfolding. *Journal of Economic Perspectives, 20*(3), 71–96.

Befort, S. F. (2006). The perfect storm of retirement insecurity: Fixing the three-legged stool of Social Security, pensions, and personal savings. *Minnesota Law Review, 91*, 938–988.

Bell, M. (2002). *Anti-discrimination law and the European Union.* New York, NY: Oxford University Press.

Bjelland, M., Bruyère, S., von Schrader, S., Houtenville, A., Ruiz-Quintanilla, A., & Webber, D. (2010). Age and disability employment discrimination: Occupational rehabilitation implications. *Journal of Occupational Rehabilitation, 20*(4), 456–471.

Blanck, P. D., Schur, L., Kruse, D., Schwochau, S., & Song, C. (2003). Calibrating the impact of the ADA's employment provisions. *Stanford Law & Policy Review, 14*(2), 267–290.

Bound, J., & Burkhauser, R. V. (1999). Economic analysis of transfer programs targeted on people with disabilities. In O. C. Ashenfelter & D. Card (Eds.), *Handbook of labor economics* (pp. 3417–3528). Amsterdam, The Netherlands: Elsevier Science.

Bound, J., & Waidmann, T. (2002). Accounting for recent declines in employment rates among the working-aged disabled. *Journal of Human Resources, 37*(2), 231–250.

Boyle, M., & Lahey, J. (2010). Labor market effects of public health insurance: Evidence from a US department of veterans affairs expansion. *Journal of Public Economics, 94*(7–8), 467–478.

Brown, J. R., & Weisbenner, S. J. (2007). *Who chooses defined contribution plans?* (NBER Working Paper No. 12842). Cambridge, MA: National Bureau of Economic Research. Retrieved from http://www.nber.org/papers/w12842.

Burkhauser, R. V., & Daly, M. C. (2002). U.S. disability policy in a changing environment. *Journal of Economic Perspectives, 16*(1), 213–224.

Burkhauser, R. V., & Smeeding, T. M. (1981). The net impact of the social security system on the poor. *Public Policy, 29*(2), 159–178.

Burtless, G., & Quinn, J. F. (2000). *Retirement trends and policies to encourage work among older Americans* (Working Paper No. 175). Boston College, Department of Economics. Retrieved from http://fmwww.bc.edu/EC-P/WP436.pdf.

Burtless, G., & Quinn, J. F. (2002). *Is working longer the answer for an aging workforce?* (Issue Brief No. 11). Boston, MA: Center for Retirement Research.

Carr, W. K., & Liebross, R. L. (1992). Wrongs without rights: The need for a strong federal common law of ERISA. *Stanford Law & Policy Review, 4*, 221–232.

Chen, Y. P., & Scott, J. C. (2003). Gradual retirement: An additional option in work and retirement. *North American Actuarial Journal, 7*(3), 62–74.

Clark, R. L., & Quinn, J. F. (1999). *Effects of pensions on labor markets and retirement* (Working Paper No. 194). Boston College, Department of Economics. Retrieved from http://fmwww.bc.edu/ec-p/wp431.pdf.

Conway, K. S., & Rork, J. C. (2008). Income tax preferences for the elderly. *Public Finance Review, 36*(5), 523–562.

Currie, J., & Madrian, B. C. (1999). Health, health insurance and the labor market. In O. C. Ashenfelter & D. Card (Eds.), *The handbook of labor economics* (pp. 3309–3407). Amsterdam, The Netherlands: North- Holland.

Daly, M. C., & Burkhauser, R. V. (2003). The supplemental security income program. In R. Moffitt (Ed.), *Means tested transfer programs in the United States* (pp. 79–140). Chicago, IL: University of Chicago Press for the NBER.

DeLeire, T. (2000). The wage and employment effects of the Americans with Disabilities Act. *Journal of Human Resources, 35*(4), 693–715.

DeLeire, T. (2003). The Americans with Disabilities Act and the employment of people with disabilities. In D. C. Stapleton & R. V. Burkhauser (Eds.), *The decline in employment of people with disabilities: A policy puzzle* (pp. 259–278). Kalamazoo, MI: W. E. Upjohn Institute for Employment Research.

Diamond, P. A. (2004). Social security. *The American Economic Review, 94*(1), 1–24.

Diamond, P. A., & Hausman, J. A. (1984). Individual retirement and savings behavior. *Journal of Public Economics, 23*(1–2), 81–114.

Duggan, J. (1984). The labor-force participation of older workers. *Industrial and Labor Relations Review, 37*(3), 416–430.

Employee Retirement Income Security Act of 1974, Pub. L. No. 93-406, 88 Stat. 829.

European Council Directive 2000/78/EC. (2000). Employment Framework Directive.

European Court of Justice. (1998). *Lisa Jacqueline Grant v. South-West Trains Ltd*, Case C-249/96, *European Court Reports*, I-621, 651.

Forman, J. B. (2000). How federal pension laws influence individual work and retirement decisions. *Tax Lawyer, 54*(1), 143–184.

Friedberg, L., & Webb, A. (2000). *The impact of 401(k) plans on retirement* (Economics Working Paper Series 545849). University of California at San Diego, Department of Economics.

Gregory, R. F. (2001). *Age discrimination in the American workplace: Old at a young age.* New Brunswick, NJ: Rutgers University Press.

Gross v. FBL Financial Services Inc. 557 U.S. (2009).

Hersch, J., & Viscusi, W. K. (2004). Punitive damages: How judges and juries perform. *Journal of Legal Studies, 33*, 1–36.

Hotchkiss, J. L. (2003). *Labor market experience of workers with disabilities: The ADA and beyond.* Kalamazoo, MI: W. E. Upjohn Institute for Employment Research.

Hotchkiss, J. L., & Rovba, L. (2003). Employment outcomes. In *Labor market experiences of workers with disabilities: The ADA and beyond* (pp. 21–48). Kalamazoo, MI: W. E. Upjohn Institute for Employment Research.

Internal Revenue Code of 1986, 26 U.S.C. § 415(b) (2007).

Ippolito, R. A. (1987). The implicit pension contract: Developments and new directions. *The Journal of Human Resources, 22*, 441–467.

Jolls, C. (1996). Hands-tying and the Age Discrimination in Employment Act. *Texas Law Review, 74*, 1813–1846.

Jolls, C., & Prescott, J. J. (2004). *Disaggregating employment protection: The case of disability discrimination* (NBER Working Paper No. 10740). Cambridge, MA: National Bureau of Economic Research.

Kaplan, R. L. (2004). Enron, pension policy, and Social Security privatization. *Arizona Law Review, 46*(53), 53–90.

Kotlikoff, L. J., & Wise, D. A. (1984). *The incentive effects of private pension plans* (NBER Working Paper No. 1510). Cambridge, MA: National Bureau of Economic Research.

Kotlikoff, L. J., & Wise, D. A. (1989). *The wage carrot and pension stick: Retirement benefits and labor force participation.* Kalamazoo, MI: W. E. Upjohn Institute for Employment Research.

Kruse, D., & Schur, L. (2003a). Employment of people with disabilities following the ADA. *Industrial Relations, 42*(1), 31–66.

Kruse, D., & Schur, L. (2003b). Does the definition affect the outcome? In D. C. Stapleton & R. V. Burkhauser (Eds.), *The decline in employment of people with disabilities: A policy puzzle* (pp. 279–300). Kalamazoo, MI: W.E. Upjohn Institute for Employment Research.

Lahey, J. (2008a). Age, women, and hiring: An experimental study. *Journal of Human Resources, 43*(1), 30–56.

Lahey, J. (2008b). State age discrimination laws and the age discrimination in employment act. *Journal of Law and Economics, 51*(3), 433–460.

Lahey, J. (2010). International comparison of age discrimination laws. *Research on Aging, 32*(6), 679–697.

Lawrence, T. H., & Taylor, R. M. (1996). Traversing the preemption triangle: ERISA, ADA, and state disability discrimination laws. *The Labor Lawyer, 12*, 57–67.

Lazear, E. P. (1979). Why is there mandatory retirement? *Journal of Political Economy, 87*(6), 1261–1284.

Lindemann, B. T., & Kadue, D. D. (2003). *Age discrimination in employment law.* Portland, OR: BNA Books.

Lumsdaine, R. L., & Mitchell, O. S. (1999). New developments in the economic analysis of retirement. In O. C. Ashenfelter & D. Card (Eds.), *The handbook of labor economics* (pp. 3261–3307). Amsterdam, The Netherlands: North-Holland.

Lumsdaine, R. L., Stock, J. H., & Wise, D. A. (1994). *Retirement incentives: The interaction between employer-provided pensions, social security, and retiree health benefits* (NBER Working Paper No. 4613). Cambridge, MA: National Bureau of Economic Research.

Manchester, C. F. (2010). The effect of pension plan type on retirement age: Distinguishing plan incentives from career length preferences. *Southern Economic Journal, 77*(1), 104–125.

Martin, C. C., & Rafsky, J. (2006). The Pension Protection Act of 2006: An overview of sweeping changes in the law governing retirement plans. *The John Marshall Law Review, 40*, 843–866.

Mitchell, O. S., & Luzadis, R. A. (1988). Changes in pension incentives through time. *Industrial and Labor Relations Review, 42*(1), 100–108.

Morris, S. J. (1987). Overview of pension law. *Journal of the American Academy of Matrimonial Lawyers, 3*, 1–11.

Munnell, A. H., Triest, R. K., & Zhivan, N. A. (2004). *How do pensions affect expected and actual retirement ages?* (Working Paper No. 2004-27). Boston, MA: Center for Retirement Research. Retrieved from http://crr.bc.edu/working-papers/how-do-pensions-affect-expected-and-actual-retirement-ages/.

Neumark, D. (2001). Age discrimination in the U.S.: Assessment of the evidence. In Z. Hornstein (Ed.), *Outlawing age discrimination* (pp. 43–62). Bristol, United Kingdom: Joseph Rowntree Foundation.

Neumark, D., & Powers, E. (1998). The effect of means-tested income support for the elderly on pre-retirement saving: Evidence from the SSI program in the U.S. *Journal of Public Economics, 68*(2), 181–206.

Neumark, D., & Powers, E. (2005). The effects of changes in state SSI supplements on pre-retirement labor supply. *Public Finance Review, 33*(1), 3–35.

Neumark, D., & Stock, W. A. (1999). Age discrimination laws and labor market efficiency. *Journal of Political Economy, 107*(5), 1081–1125.

O'Meara, D. P. (1989). *Protecting the growing number of older workers: The age discrimination in employment act.* Philadelphia, PA: University of Pennsylvania.

Penner, R. G., Perun, P., & Steuerle, E. (2002). *Legal and institutional impediments to partial retirement and part-time work by older workers.* Washington, DC: The Urban Institute.

Perun, P. (2001). *The limits of saving* (Retirement Project Occasional Paper No. 7). Washington, DC: The Urban Institute. Retrieved from http://www.urban.org/pdfs/retire_7.pdf.

Polk, L. T. (2009). *ERISA practice and litigation.* St. Paul, MN: Thomson Reuters.

Powers, E. T., & Neumark, D. (2003). The interaction of public retirement income programs in the U.S. *American Economic Review Papers and Proceedings, 93*(2), 261–265.

Ricci v. Stefano, 557 U.S. (2009).

Riesenhuber, K. (2009). The EC anti-discrimination Framework Directive 2000/78. In N. ten Bokum, T. Flanagan, R. Sands, & R. von Steinau-Steinruck (Eds.), *Age discrimination law in Europe* (pp. xxvii–xlvi). The Netherlands: Kluwer Law International.

Ruhm, C. (1996). Do pensions increase the labor supply of older men? *Journal of Public Economics, 59*(2), 157–175.

Samwick, A. A. (1998). New evidence on pensions, social security, and the timing of retirement. *Journal of Public Economics, 70*, 207–236.

Scahill, P. L., & Forman, J. B. (2002, June). *Protecting participants and beneficiaries in a phased retirement world.* Paper presented at the Society of Actuaries Retirement Implications of Demographic and Family Change Symposium, San Francisco, CA.

Schuster, M., & Miller, C. S. (1984). An empirical assessment of the age discrimination in employment act. *Industrial and Labor Relations Review, 38*(1), 64–74.

Small Employer Retirement Survey. (2003). *The 2003 Small Employer Retirement Survey (SERS) summary of findings.* Washington, DC: Employee Benefit Research Institute. Retrieved from http://www.ebri.org/pdf/surveys/sers/2003/03sersof.pdf.

Smith v. City of Jackson, 544 U.S. 228, 241 (2005).

Smith v. City of Jackson, 544 U.S. 228, 241 (2005) citing Wards Cove Packing Co. v. Atonio, 490 U.S. 656 (1989).

Stapleton, D. C., & Burkhauser, R. V. (Eds.). (2003). *The decline in employment of people with disabilities: A policy puzzle.* Kalamazoo, MI: W. E. Upjohn Institute for Employment Research.

ten Bokum, N., Flanagan, T., Sands, R., & von Steinau-Steinruck, R. (Eds.). (2009). *Age discrimination law in Europe.* The Netherlands: Kluwer Law International.

Tweel, C. A. (2010). Retirement savings in the face of increasing longevity: The advantages of deferring retirement. *North Carolina Banking Institute, 14*, 103–138.

U.S. Department of Commerce. (1997). *Census brief: Disabilities affect one-fifth of all Americans* (Census Bureau Publication No. CENBR/97-5). Washington, DC: Author. Retrieved from http://www.census.gov/prod/3/97pubs/cenbr975.pdf.

Von Wachter, T. (2002). *The end of mandatory retirement in the US: Effects on retirement and implicit contracts* (The Center for Labor Economics Working Paper No. 49). Retrieved from http://www.columbia.edu/~vw2112/papers/vonwa_mr_2009.pdf.

Zanglein, J. E. (2001). Investment without education: The disparate impact on women and minorities in self-directed defined contribution plans. *Employee Rights & Employment Policy Journal, 5*(1), 223–272.

Zhang, Y. (2003). The economic growth and Tax Relief Reconciliation Act of 2001 and private pension system. *University of Pennsylvania Journal of Labor and Employment Law, 5*(3), 629–653.

Effective Financial Planning for Retirement

Douglas A. Hershey, Joy M. Jacobs-Lawson, *and* James T. Austin

Abstract

In industrialized nations around the world, effective financial planning for retirement has become a cornerstone of the successful aging process. A financially secure retirement is one in which the retiree is unconstrained by money-related concerns, and all key options remain open (Mottern & Mottern, 2006). The implications of such a lifestyle are broad and far reaching—but relatively few future retirees can realistically expect to experience this level of financial freedom. Our objective in this chapter is to critically examine the factors that differentiate the quality of individuals' retirement-related financial planning efforts. In doing so, we examine not only the characteristics of effective retirement planners and savers, but also the underlying dimensions that help to explain their success. This is accomplished by synthesizing empirical and theoretical work on retirement preparedness, exploring global trends related to *financial planning for retirement* (FPR), and presenting a tripartite conceptual model of the financial planning process. Our broad goals in developing this review are to shed light on emerging trends, identify key unresolved issues, and point out limitations and profitable directions for future research.

Key Words: retirement, financial planning, aging, planning, investing, finance, psychology

Introduction

For industrialized nations around the globe, financial planning for retirement in the twenty-first century presents a host of challenges to individuals, financial professionals, and institutions. For individuals, the task has become a full-time job just to stay abreast of the range of financial products and services that are offered. That, combined with the computational complexities associated with the task, has left many overwhelmed and effectively marginalized when it comes to managing their own late-life savings. Financial professionals also face challenges in terms of staying abreast of the changing marketplace. Perhaps a greater challenge for those in the industry, however, involves finding ways to get investors to trust their advice at a time in which the average investor has become jaded and distrustful. Institutions, such as large pension funds

and governments, are confronted with the challenge of designing pension financing systems that are on the one hand equitable and supportive, but at the same time sustainable in the face of the onslaught of baby boomers who each day creep closer to retirement. When it comes to *financial planning for retirement* (FPR), these are indeed challenging times.

So just how effective are individuals at FPR? Unfortunately, a definitive answer is difficult to formulate, as perspectives tend to be as wide ranging as the variety of measures used to assess planning competence. Economists rely on econometric indicators (such as household saving rates and wealth accumulations) as the gold standard when it comes to measuring future financial security (Sabelhaus, 1997). Sociologists, in turn, often use normative data to determine how aggressively individuals are planning relative to peers, or performance relative to some form of life course timeline (Ekerdt, Kosloski, & DeViney, 2000). Psychologists, in contrast, frequently use self-report indicators to tap the quality of individuals' saving efforts (e.g., Stawski, Hershey, & Jacobs-Lawson, 2007). And finance researchers often rely on industry archival data (cf. Croy, Gerrans, & Speelman, 2010a). An adequate multidisciplinary definition of FPR is not currently available, which also limits the conclusions that can be drawn regarding planning effectiveness. But methodological differences aside, the clear takeaway message from each of these disciplines is that when it comes to individual patterns of saving for retirement, there exists much room for improvement.

Scope of the Review

In this chapter we endeavor to summarize what is known about the factors associated with effective FPR from the individual's perspective. In other words, we strive to capture the key psychological, social, and economic dimensions that make some people better financial planners than others. However, given the breadth of the topic, we acknowledge at the outset that any such attempt will in some ways be biased and incomplete. A second goal of this chapter will be to explore the varied cultural contexts in which financial planning and saving take place. Finally, a conceptual model is presented that is designed to capture three important dimensions that underlie the task of saving for the future: (1) the capacity to plan and save, (2) the willingness to plan and save, and (3) opportunities to plan and save for the future. These three dimensions were adapted from an organizational research model published by Blumberg and Pringle (1982). More will be said about this model in a subsequent section of the chapter.

We do not attempt to address the literature on retirement transitions, nor how one should go about planning and saving for old age. Other excellent books and reviews have been penned on these topics. Instead, our focus is on empirical and theoretical articles on planning competence that have appeared in the primary literature. Whereas some review articles tend to be literature driven (e.g., all papers on a topic during some set period of time), the present review will be issue driven in that we strive to address the key set of topics that bear on financial planning competence. In selecting articles for consideration, we found it beneficial to draw upon journals from a diverse set of fields including psychology, sociology, economics, financial counseling, and finance, rather than limiting the scope of the chapter to a single discipline. This breadth reflects the multidisciplinary nature of the topic. In addition, although our focus is on work published since the early 1990s, in certain instances we found it useful to include other, more seminal works that first appeared in the literature prior to that date.

In addition to capturing intrapersonal dimensions of the financial planning task that bear on effectiveness, we explore, when possible, how the planning and saving process is shaped by cultural constraints. In light of important systemic differences across countries, one of the goals of this chapter is to describe the factors that characterize effective financial planning for retirement in relation to broad geographic and/or geopolitical contexts. With those overarching goals and limitations in mind, we now proceed to examine the range of forces that shape investor behaviors.

Global Perspectives

There are a common set of issues related to retirement preparedness that can be identified across most industrialized nations. But in most societies there are unique elements associated with the planning process that lead to culture-specific idiosyncrasies. For example, employer pension provisions are particularly strong in many countries in Western Europe (Askins, 2010; Hughes & Stewart, 2004) and notably so in the Netherlands (Alessie & Kapteyn, 2001; van Dalen, Henkens, & Hershey, 2010), which has implications for how much individual workers will need to accumulate in personal retirement savings. The emphasis on individual saving is particularly important in the U.S. and the U.K. (Waine, 2006), which highlights the need for workers to be well informed when deciding how to invest their retirement savings. In South Africa, the collapse of apartheid led to the extension of universal basic pension benefits to South Africans (Asher, 2006), which has done much to improve the overall quality of life in old age. And in Brazil, relatively few high-quality work-related pension opportunities exist outside the civil service system, and income inequality levels tend to be high (Queiroz, 2007). This lack of occupational pensions means that many lower-income Brazilian workers are heavily reliant on state-based pension support in old age (Barrientos, 2002), despite the fact that fewer than half formally contribute to the social welfare system.

Old-age support systems also vary widely across East Asia and the Pacific Rim, with population aging, urbanization, patterns of rapid economic development, and the effects of globalization all driving systemic changes in pension support systems (Holtzmann, MacArthur, & Sin, 2000; Phang, 2006). But, that said, the availability of retirement investment products has bourgeoned in recent years across Asia, where investors are increasingly taking advantage of new saving opportunities (Lai, 2010). In Hong Kong, few working adults plan for retirement, which is complicated by the fact that many Chinese workers feel the ability to count on family members for support is eroding (Lee & Law, 2004). In Australia and New Zealand, government policies have put in place employer-mandated superannuation guarantee programs (Barrett & Tseng, 2007; St. John, 2007; Worthington, 2008), which on the one hand has reduced the need for personal savings among workers, but on the other hand has increased workers' responsibility for the management of their own retirement resources (Gerrans, Clark-Murphy, & Speelman, 2006).

A recent survey of retirees living in twenty-seven countries across five continents revealed that fewer than half of the respondents (48%) enjoyed sufficient retirement income (AXA, 2008). That same investigation found that 54% of working adults expected a similar shortfall once they retire. A sufficient income was reported by two-thirds of retirees in only four of the twenty-seven countries surveyed: Switzerland, New Zealand, China, and Canada. Data from the 2010 and 2011 Retirement Confidence Surveys indicate that although a majority of American workers are confident that they are saving enough for retirement, fewer than half have carried out some of the most basic tasks associated with the financial planning process, such as computing how much retirement income will be needed or setting appropriate financial goals (Helman, Copeland, & VanDerhei, 2010, 2011; see also Millar & Devonish, 2009). In fact, Lusardi (1999) found that among individuals over the age of 51, as many as one-third of respondents had not thought about retirement at all. According to one industry report, failing to calculate how much in the way of savings will be needed is equivalent to "driving while blindfolded" (Wells Fargo, 2009).

Data examining the adequacy of savings in Europe are not much more encouraging (Fornero, Lusardi, & Monticone, 2009), despite the fact that household saving rates are significantly higher in E.U. countries than they are in the United States (Eurostat, 2009). Findings from the European Employee Benefits Benchmark investigation reveal that over one-third of Europeans have concerns about their pension savings, a number that jumps

to over one-half for citizens in the United Kingdom and Ireland (AON, 2010). Similar findings have been reported based on a twelve-country investigation carried out by Litwin and Sapir (2009). But that said, there is substantial heterogeneity across European nations, and future financial worry levels (as well as retirement saving rates) tend to vary appreciably (Hershey, Henkens, & van Dalen, 2010a).

In sum, the global pension panorama is a complex one in which the adequacy of different channels of support varies widely across nations (AXA, 2008; Whitehouse, 2007); accordingly, we also see vast differences in the need for individuals to save that tend to covary with different forms of structural and institutional support. Next, we turn our attention to the three foundations of financial support upon which most pensioners in industrialized nations rely.

The Three-Pillar System

In light of key structural differences in retirement systems around the globe, it would be useful to describe some of the major sources of income for retirees. We begin with a description of the "three-pillar" system, which includes state-based pensions, occupational (employer) pensions, and individual savings. These three different sources of retirement income, taken together, account for the bulk of financial support received by pensioners in more-developed nations.

First-pillar public retirement plans—sometimes referred to as state-based old-age pension programs—are either redistributive or mandatory funding schemes that seek to guarantee for the retiree a basic standard of living in old age. These social security systems serve an insurance function—they are a financial safety net for retirees—which is particularly important for those at the lower end of the socioeconomic spectrum. Although the financing mechanisms that underlie state-based plans differ from one country to the next, many are based on a "pay as you go" approach, in which employer contributions and the payroll taxes of workers are used to provide benefits for pensioners.

According to McGillivray (2006), public schemes are designed to replace from 40%–45% of wages in countries with strong occupational pensions (e.g., Canada, the United States), and substantially more (up to 70% or more) in certain Western European countries, the former Soviet Union and its satellites, and other parts of the developing world. These plans tend to be contributory in nature, and the defined benefit (DB) amount one can expect to receive is typically calculated on the basis of one's final income at the time of retirement and the number of years the worker contributed to the system. In a study of pensions in 53 countries, Whitehouse (2007) found that 32 countries had public defined benefit (DB) arrangements, and 19 of the 53 had defined contribution (DC) arrangements, in which employer contributions are actively managed by the individual worker. DB plans are the only type found in the Middle East and North Africa; they are found in half of the countries in Eastern Europe and Central Asia, and in more than half of the high-income Organisation for Economic Co-operation and Development (OECD) countries including Canada, France, Japan, and Spain (Whitehouse, 2007). First-tier support has not been universally embraced throughout much of East Asia and the Pacific Rim (Asher, 2010), where in many countries the absence of state-based support for the elderly reflects the deeply ingrained view that "handouts" would serve to threaten the family and its informal support system (Holzmann, MacArthur, & Sin, 2000). In light of shifting population and work patterns that are expected to take place during the first quarter of the twenty-first century, many existing first-pillar systems will require radical structural reforms in an attempt to remain sustainable in the decades to come (Clark, 2003).

For many retirees, occupational pensions—which are typically managed by either one's employer or labor union—make up a significant second pillar of financial support in old age. This is particularly true in countries with modest state-based support systems such as the United Kingdom and United States (Munnell, 2006). But that said, some continental European countries and industrialized nations throughout the rest of the world have signaled an interest in moving in the direction of funded private plans (Organisation for Economic Co-operation and Development, 2009). In the United States, occupational pensions have dramatically increased in popularity over the past seventy years, with somewhat fewer than 10% of workers covered by them in 1940, to more than 40% of workers in 2010. A phenomenal growth in employer pensions has also been witnessed in the United Kingdom over the past century, with some 83% of workers receiving second-tier coverage as of 2001 (UKDWP, 2003). In the United States, occupational pensions were once dominated by a defined benefit (DB) approach, but over the past two decades they have shifted in the direction of DC arrangements (Munnell, Webb, & Golub-Sass, 2009). These employer plans are often referred to as 401(k) or 403(b) plans, which refer to the sections of the U.S. tax code under which they were established. With DC plans, the employee invests a portion of his or her earnings in a tax-deferred savings vehicle, and the employer typically matches a portion of those contributions. Under this type of arrangement, the employee is largely responsible for managing his or her own retirement savings. A comparable shift away from DB plans in the direction of DC plans has not been witnessed in other countries that support voluntary employer pensions, such as Canada and the Netherlands (Munnell, 2006).

Individual savings and voluntary retirement plans make up the third pillar of retirement income support. It is clearly within this dimension of the three-pillar system that individuals have the most direct control over their own financial future. To stimulate voluntary private savings, many countries offer generous tax advantages for workers who invest their resources in certain savings accounts, individual retirement accounts, supplemental employer saving arrangements, and investment opportunities for the self-employed. Despite the myriad of investment vehicles available, there is clear evidence that many households—even those with substantial resources—fail to save enough for retirement (Venti, 2006). Data from the 2010 Retirement Confidence Survey indicated that 27% of American workers surveyed had total accumulated savings of less than $1,000, and 43% had set aside less than $10,000 (Employee Benefit Research Institute [EBRI], 2010). The picture is indeed more heterogeneous in Europe, with a recent investigation (Hershey, Henkens, & van Dalen, 2010a) finding that saving behavior is quite common among workers in Denmark, Austria, and Slovakia, where over 80% of the population set aside discretionary resources for old age. Saving rates were much lower in former Eastern Bloc countries such as the Ukraine, Russian Federation, and Bulgaria, where only 25%–35% of the population indicated that they had saved for retirement.

As members of the baby-boom generation continue to leave the workforce, public support systems will become increasingly strained, and the relative significance of the third pillar of retirement income—personal savings—will take on additional importance. To that end, high-quality financial saving and investment decisions will become one of the keys to successful aging in contemporary society. This is true not only in more developed countries such as Canada, Germany, France, and the United States, but also in developing nations throughout Latin America, Eastern Europe, Central Asia, and the Middle East.

It is important to point out that there are other sources of retirement income support in addition to the three pillars outlined above. Although these tend not to be primary sources of support, they do nonetheless contribute to the overall financial picture for many retirees. These sources include financial gifts from children and family members, inheritances, early retirement incentives and buyouts, income from savings and investments, equity withdrawals from one's house (i.e., reverse mortgages), and the decision to take on some form of bridge employment during retirement. It is worth noting, however, that opportunities for these secondary support mechanisms differ markedly as a function of occupation, socioeconomic status, family situation, and country of origin. In developing countries, informal sources of support (e.g., support from one's children; land ownership) tend to take on added importance. In fact, Velladics, Henkens, and van Dalen (2006) found evidence that individuals in former Eastern European countries rely more on their children for old-age care relative to other European countries. In that respect, children can be viewed as a capital good (Nerlove, Razin, & Sadka, 1987; Schultz, 1974).

In sum, the three types of retirement income outlined above—state-based support, occupational pensions, and private savings—make up the lion's share of income for most retirees. The latter of the three has received the majority of attention from retirement finance researchers in recent years, due to the range of issues that have bearing on the quality of individuals' financial and investment decisions.

The Challenge of Financial Planning for Retirement

The task of planning and saving for retirement, on a very basic level, involves effectively balancing one's post-employment resource needs against one's future income streams. The challenge lies not only in the dynamic nature of the task but also among certain uncertainties inherent in the planning process. In terms of the task, both the life course perspective (Elder, Johnson, & Crosnoe, 2003) and the life cycle model (Modigliani & Brumberg, 1954)—drawn from the sociology and economics literatures, respectively—suggest that an individual's level of motivation to plan and save should differ at different points in the adult life span (see also van

Dalen & Verbon, 1999). Moreover, planning and saving practices have been shown to vary with one's work situation and career stage (Berger & Denton, 2004), thereby contributing further evidence to the existence of a normative life span developmental pattern. One of the keys to effective planning, therefore, is to find ways to maximize personal savings contributions when one's overall motivational level to do so is attenuated.

To complicate matters, shifting state-based pension priorities and the dynamic environment in which savings and investments grow and change over time adds a layer of uncertainty and challenge to the task of effective financial planning. Consider, for example, the impact that the 2007–2008 global financial shock had on investors. Although most individuals failed to change their basic saving and investment strategy in response to the crisis (Gerrans, 2010), in the time span from mid-2007 to mid-2008, retirement savings in OECD countries fell by $4 trillion dollars (Whitehouse, 2009). Equally troubling was the fact that pension fund assets plummeted by up to 35% (Boersch, 2009). Although clearly an aberration, this riotous market volatility serves to underscore the uncertainty associated with the personal retirement planning process. Accordingly, market volatility spawns declines in investor confidence (Dailami & Masson, 2009), and, presumably, financial worry ensues. In light of these external dynamics, a degree of flexibility on the part of the investor and a willingness to adapt are essential when it comes to effectively managing one's personal finances (Butrica, Smith, & Toder, 2010).

Taking into consideration the cognitive and motivational complexities faced by individuals when it comes to planning and saving, it is reasonable to pose the question: Who should ultimately be responsible for the management of one's retirement finances—the individual, the employer, or the state? On the one hand, there is a longstanding tradition in countries such as the United Kingdom, Canada, and the United States of allowing workers to manage their own financial affairs. This "libertarian" approach to saving clearly highlights the importance of individual responsibility, with each worker being accountable for the quality of his or her own decisions. The "paternalistic" view of saving, in contrast, stresses the role of the employer or the state (or both) when it comes to ensuring individuals' late-life financial security—a perspective adopted by many countries throughout Western Europe (the Netherlands as a case in point). Middle ground in this debate can be found among emerging "libertarian paternalistic" perspectives, which highlight the role of public and private institutions when it comes to shaping saving behaviors, while at the same time still respecting individual freedom of choice. One example of this approach can be found in the choice architecture model of saving advanced by Sunstein and Thaler (2008).

FPR: Process and Implications

At the individual level, FPR is best thought of as an ongoing process as opposed to a discrete task or event. According to McCarthy, FPR involves six stages: "(1) collecting data to identify where you are [financially], (2) defining personal and financial goals, (3) identifying problems and constraints, (4) charting a course of action, (5) implementing the plan, and (6) periodically reviewing, revising and monitoring the plan" (1996, p. 2). However, being effective at each of these six stages clearly requires different types of capacities, motives, and opportunities, which makes the overall task of financial planning for late life simple and straightforward for a select few, a significant challenge for most, and seemingly impossible for others (EBRI, 2002).

It is well worth mentioning that those who are effective retirement planners and savers can arguably expect to achieve a higher standard of living and quality of life than those who are less attentive to the task. Across a series of investigations, retirement planning and/or saving for the post-employment period has been shown to be related to the quality of health care one can expect to receive (Jurges, 2010), the quality of one's housing and possessions (Gibler & Taltavull, 2010), happiness and life satisfaction (Bender & Jivan, 2005; Price & Balaswamy, 2009; Taylor & Doverspike, 2003; Spiegel & Shultz, 2003; Wang & Shultz, 2010), a sense of "ownership" of one's retirement (Olson & Wiley, 2006), enhanced leisure and recreational opportunities (Chung, Domino, Stearns, & Popkin, 2009; Scherger, Nazroo, & Higgs, 2011), a sense of financial security and independence (Miron-Shatz, 2009), and a feeling of financial freedom (Neukam & Hershey, 2003). Last but certainly not least, households with a propensity to plan have been found to acquire more wealth (Ameriks, Caplin, & Leahy, 2003). Given the clear benefits of engaging in a conscientious pattern of personal financial planning over one's working life, it is surprising just how many individuals fail to adequately save for old age. This lack of action begs the question: What are the dimensions that

distinguish savers from non-savers? We address this question below.

Conceptual Model of Investor Behavior

In this section of the chapter we develop a conceptual framework for understanding the array of factors that contribute to the ability to plan and save effectively for old age. As a foundation for our conceptual model, we have adapted a model of work performance advanced by Blumberg and Pringle (1982). In that model, the authors contend that the quality of an individual's work performance is determined by three primary dimensions: the capacity to perform the work, the willingness to perform the work, and the opportunity to perform. The first dimension, capacity, includes various cognitive and individual difference factors that distinguish the worker from others, such as one's ability, knowledge, skills, intelligence, and level of training and education. It is clear how these factors would likely contribute to differences in the ability to effectively plan and save for retirement. The second dimension, willingness, is a motivational force defined by the psychological and emotional characteristics that determine the likelihood of carrying out a task. Examples of factors that make up this dimension include the clarity and nature of one's financial and retirement goals, degree of retirement anxiety, attitude, personality makeup, perception of social norms, and one's self-image and values. Like the first dimension, it is clear how factors linked to willingness would have an important impact on the tendency of individuals to plan and save. The third dimension in the model—opportunity—comprises influences that are external to the individual. According to Blumberg and Pringle, these are environmental opportunities or constraints that are related to task performance. In the retirement planning context, opportunities include such factors as the availability of a voluntary workplace retirement savings program, tax incentives to save, reasonable access to knowledgeable financial advisors, and the requisite discretionary income with which to invest.

Figure 26.1 graphically represents the three dimensions of the Blumberg and Pringle model as they relate to FPR. Unlike the originators of the model, who conceived of the dimensions as being additive, in this configuration we acknowledge the potential for inter-dimensional interactions. Accordingly, the "crossed" factors in the model are sketched in such a way as to represent seven of the eight uniquely different types of planners (or

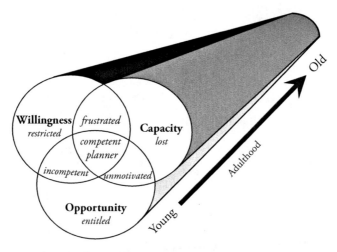

Figure 26.1 Conceptual Model of the Three Dimensions that Underlie the Tendency to Plan and Save.

non-planners, as the case may be). The "competent planner" is at high levels on all three dimensions—a clear *willingness* to plan and save, the cognitive and intellectual *capacity* to do so, and sufficient *opportunities* to effectively invest. Relative to the competent planner, each of the other types of individuals is in some way lacking. That does not mean that the other subtypes would not be likely to plan and save; it means only that if they were to do so, they would have to overcome certain obstacles to effective performance. A description of each of the eight types of financial planners, developed on the basis of high and low levels on each of the three dimensions, can be found in Table 26.1. The one subtype not shown in the figure is individuals who are low on all three dimensions. We have identified this type as "non-planners" on the basis of three negative (i.e., low) predispositions. This subtype may provide particularly fertile opportunities for intervention.

One important aspect of the conceptual model is the representation of continuity (and thus strengthening) of predispositions over the course of adulthood, as illustrated by the conical shape of each of the three factors. This developmental aspect of the model is designed to convey the notion that for most individuals, a predisposition early in adulthood—say, a positive attitude toward planning—would be expected to be maintained over time. That is, one may think of the entrenchment of willingness, capacity, and opportunity as developmentally stable, with individuals proceeding along an established trajectory. Theoretical and empirical support for this proposition can be found in the work of economists and decision researchers, who have

identified a cognitive decision-making bias in which people favor the status quo. This "status quo bias" (Kahneman, Knetsch, & Thaler, 1991) suggests that individuals are predisposed to maintain an established pattern of behavior unless the incentive to change is compelling. The influential power of the status quo has been borne out in both laboratory and field experiments involving the choice of financial investments (Samuelson & Zeckhauser, 1988) and consumer preference decisions (Hartman, Doane, & Woo, 1991; Johnson, Hershey, Meszaros, & Kenreuther, 2000).

Other support for the notion of continuity over change can be found among the tenets of image theory (Beach & Mitchell, 1987; Beach, 1998). According to the theory, individuals adopt a set of concrete behavioral tactics that are designed to achieve a favored goal state (e.g., saving to ensure financial security in old age; spending freely to maximize hedonic experience). In making ongoing decisions about behavior, tactics will be reviewed for the possibility of revision only when one mentally "forecasts" that those tactics will fail to lead to the desired goal state (Beach, 1993). Thus, the absence of a negative discrepancy in one's forecast, or a lack of change in the environmental circumstances that support one's tactics, should result in continuity of the established pattern of behavior.

The theoretical propositions cited above are not the only reasons why one would expect to see a general pattern of life span continuity when it comes to financial planning. Indeed, many of the individual difference and situational constituents of the tripartite model center around stability rather than change. Examples of this include the stability of

Table 26.1 Eight Types of Financial Planners Obtained by Crossing the Three Dimensions that Make up the Capacity-Opportunity-Willingness Model.

Competent Planner	Characteristics: HW, HC, HO. This is the best case scenario when it comes to FPR. The competent planner is not only willing and capable to engage in adaptive planning and saving behaviors, but also has optimal opportunities to do so. Likely to exhibit very high FPR performance.
Restricted Planner	Characteristics: HW, LC, LO. Although this individual is willing to plan and save for the future, he or she lacks not only the capacity to do so competently, but also good opportunities to save. Lacking in opportunity and capacity, this individual is effectively restricted from producing high levels of performance. Likely to exhibit low to moderate FPR performance.
Lost Planner	Characteristics: LW, HC, LO. This individual has the capacity to plan and save but, lacking in willingness and opportunity, he or she is effectively "lost" when it comes to having sufficient motivation and mechanisms through which to demonstrate effective FPR performance. Likely to exhibit low to moderate FPR performance.
Entitled Planner	Characteristics: LW, LC, HO. In this scenario the individual has optimal opportunities to plan and save (thereby making him or her "entitled"), but he or she falls short when it comes to the two internal dimensions necessary to be a good financial planner. Likely to exhibit low FPR performance.
Frustrated Planner	Characteristics: HW, HC, LO. This individual has both the willingness and capacity to plan and save, but lacks good opportunities to invest. Despite the latter, given high levels of motivation this person is likely to find some mechanism(s) to fulfill the desire to set aside resources for the future. Likely to exhibit high FPR performance.
Incompetent Planner	Characteristics: HW, LC, HO. The incompetent planner is one who is willing to save and who has the opportunity to invest, but who lacks the cognitive and intellectual capacity to effectively carry out the task. This individual is likely to be engaged by the task but, based on cognitive or knowledge deficits relative to others, would be the most likely to make suboptimal investment decisions. Likely to exhibit moderate FPR performance.
Unmotivated Planner	Characteristics: LW, HC, HO. This individual has the capacity and opportunity to plan and save but, due to some internal factor(s) (e.g., negative attitude toward finances; poor personality predisposition), lacks the level of motivation required to perform at a high level. Likely to exhibit moderate FPR performance.
Non-planner	Characteristics: LW, LC, LO. This is the worst case scenario. The non-planner has little interest in planning and saving and lacks the cognitive and intellectual wherewithal to do so effectively. To compound matters, he or she lacks reasonable opportunities to save. Likely to exhibit very low FPR performance, or avoid retirement planning and saving activities altogether.

Note 1: LW = low willingness, LC = low capacity, LO = low opportunity, HW = high willingness, HC = high capacity, HO = high opportunity.
Note 2: Predictions regarding FPR performance levels were adapted on the basis of Blumberg and Pringle (1982, Table 2).

personality traits and intellectual abilities throughout adulthood, the tendency to engage in employment within particular occupational spheres (the vocational personalities defined by John Holland), and the likelihood of enmeshment in social milieus that are differentially supportive (or not) of FPR. Recognition of the importance of these stabilizing forces when it comes to planning and saving, and the resulting pattern of continuity these forces are likely to promote, brings to mind the old adage that "leopards don't change their spots." Within a range of limits, highly engaged planners *tend to* remain engaged in the planning process, and non-planners *tend to* remain disengaged.

It is also recognized, however, that an age-linked pattern of continuity when it comes to planning and saving is not immutable. Baltes, Reese, and Lipsitt (1980) point to three classes of developmental influences that *can* lead to changes in behavior: (a) normative age-graded influences, (b) normative history-graded influences, and (c) non-normative life events. An example of a normative age-graded influence would be the social force dimensions that lead many workers to become interested in financial planning around the age of 50. History-graded influences are exemplified by the 2007–2008 global financial crisis and the resulting increase in societal discussions about the importance and vulnerability of retirement savings. And non-normative events involve significant life experiences that would affect the ability to meet one's saving goals—such as the financial impact of an appreciable health shock, or receiving a sizeable unanticipated inheritance. All three classes of influences can alter one's behavioral propensities; however, their effect on the willingness to save will naturally be constrained by existing individual differences in capacity and opportunity.

We also acknowledge the potential for overlap between one dimension of the model and another. Orthogonal dimensions are not claimed. For instance, it is easy to see how an effective information campaign by an employer—what would be considered part of the opportunity dimension—could motivate an increased willingness to save. Another example would be the way in which an increase in the willingness to plan for the long term (for whatever reasons) could lead one to meet with a financial advisor to seek out new and different investment opportunities. A third example involves the individual with superior knowledge, skills, and abilities (elements of the capacity dimension) who on the basis of his or her KSAs is more likely to land a good job and, therefore, have superior opportunities to plan financially.

Empirical Research on Financial Planning for Retirement

In this section of the chapter we use the tripartite model outlined above to organize key empirical research findings on the factors that influence the tendency to plan and save. In doing so, our goal is to provide a framework for understanding the broad field of forces (Lewin, 1951) that impinge on the worker as he or she makes (or fails to make) key investment decisions.

Capacity to Plan and Save

Financial literacy. Of the numerous factors that influence planning and saving behaviors, perhaps none has received as much attention as the quality of individuals' financial knowledge (Lusardi, 2011). Indeed, the twenty-first-century thrust of financial literacy education is in some ways equivalent to educational initiatives launched during the second half of the twentieth century, designed to increase levels of digital literacy and health literacy in the population. Dozens of investigations have been carried out on financial literacy during the past three decades, which have revealed that the extent and veracity of one's domain-specific knowledge is related to the tendency to plan for the post-employment period (Ekerdt, Hackney, Kosloski, & DeViney, 2001; Hershey, Jacobs-Lawson, McArdle, & Hamagami, 2007; Lusardi & Mitchell, 2006), the likelihood of saving (or having positive intentions to save) (Croy et al., 2010a; Grable & Lytton, 1999; Hershey & Mowen, 2000; Lusardi & Mitchell, 2007), and the nature of one's information search and investment strategies (Kimball & Shumway, 2010; Moore, Kurtzberg, Fox, & Bazerman, 1999; Qihua & Jinkook, 2004; Van Rooij, Lusardi, & Alesie, 2011).

An unsettling finding from a study by Lusardi and Mitchell (2006) revealed that only about half of Americans had sufficient financial knowledge to compute interest rates over a five-year period; similarly, few knew the difference between nominal and real interest rates (see also Hilgert, Hogarth, & Beverly, 2003; and Volpe, Chen, & Liu, 2006). Lack of financial sophistication is not limited to American workers, but it extends to individuals living in Europe and other parts of the world (Christelis, Jappelli, & Padula, 2010; Lusardi & Mitchell, 2011; Smith & Stewart, 2008). When workers with weak domain-specific knowledge are confronted by the complexities of modern-day investing, it is no wonder so many people fail to carry out even the most basic financial planning activities, such as determining how much will need to be saved for old age (Pension Research Council, 2010).

Decision-making skills and abilities. There is a growing literature that points to the fact that cognitive and intellectual abilities have a direct bearing on the capacity to make sound financial planning decisions. A study by Ackerman and Beier (2006) found that both crystallized and fluid intelligence are implicated in the ability to acquire domain-specific financial knowledge, with crystallized intellect being the stronger predictor of the two. This is not an inconsequential finding in light of numerous published studies that have shown fluid intelligence declines over much of adulthood (Horn & Hofer, 1992).

Another investigation (Hershey, Jacobs-Lawson, & Walsh, 2003) revealed that the ability to formulate an efficient "decision script" for solving retirement investment problems covaried with both age and domain-specific knowledge, which led the authors to conclude that the observed developmental differences stem from age-linked declines in fluid abilities. And in a study carried out on over 11,000 English adults beyond the age of 50, Banks and Oldfield (2007) observed that low levels of numerical ability were associated with low levels of retirement savings, even when controlling for other dimensions of cognitive ability and educational attainment.

In addition to intellectual influences on investment capabilities, cognitive factors have been implicated in the quality of individuals' financial decisions (Agarwal, Driscoll, Gabaix, & Laibson, 2009). A large number of studies, in fact, have shown that a variety of perceptual biases and illusions lead to suboptimal financial judgments and investment decisions (Nofsinger, 2001; Pronin, 2011). Some of these biases lead individuals to make over-investments, others lead to under-investments, and still others lead the individual to postpone taking action when doing so is clearly counter-indicated. While a complete description of biases and effects goes beyond the scope of this review, a partial list of cognitive biases drawn from the literature is shown in Table 26.2. What is perhaps most troubling is the fact that by definition these cognitive biases occur without awareness, which means that it is nearly impossible to prevent them unless the decision maker is well aware of their existence and how they operate (Charupat & Deaves, 2004).

Willingness to Plan and Save

If one thinks of the capacity to plan for retirement as placing limits on the ability to plan effectively, then one might think of the willingness dimension as psychological factors that constrain performance within that range of limits. Collectively, the willingness factors (e.g., goals, personality traits, attitudes, and affect) initiate a degree of motivational inertia that drives individuals to act, or fail to act, as the case may be.

Importance of goals. In the retirement planning context, financial goals may be thought of as either residing at the meta-level (e.g., have the goal of sufficient income adequacy throughout retirement), the meso-level (e.g., meeting with a professional financial advisor once a year), or the micro-level (e.g., contributing $400 to a Roth Individual Retirement Account [IRA] plan from the next paycheck). Having goals at all three levels is important, given the hierarchically organized nature of individuals' psychological goal structures (Austin & Vancouver, 1996; Klein, Austin, & Cooper, 2008). A key to success when it comes to FPR involves the self-monitoring of micro-level goals to ensure that they are being accomplished so as to fulfill meso- and macro-level goals. The theoretical propositions outlined in image theory (Beach, 1998; Beach & Mitchell, 1987) suggest that this form of monitoring is a natural part of individuals' "progress decisions," in which one attempts to identify whether an ongoing pattern of behavior (e.g., regular savings contributions of $400/month) will lead to desired long-range outcomes (e.g., personal savings that will result in a 70% retirement income replacement

Table 26.2 Partial list of Cognitive and Decisional Biases Shown to Affect Financial Reasoning and Investing for Retirement.

Attachment bias	Fast thinking bias	Positive outcome bias
Attentional bias	Future self effect	Projection bias
Availability cascade	Halo effect	Pseudo-certainty effect
Bandwagon effect	Herd instinct	Restraint bias
Bias blind spot	Hindsight bias	Representativeness heuristic
Break-even effect	Illusion of control	Risk aversion effect
Choice-supportive bias	Interloper effect	Rosy retrospection
Confirmation bias	Money illusion	Selective perception
Delay discounting	Negativity bias	Status quo bias
Disposition effect	Neglect of probability	System justification
Egocentric bias	Never happen to me effect	Telescoping effect
Endowment effect	Optimism bias	Wishful thinking
Exponential growth bias	Ostrich effect	
False consensus effect	Overconfidence effect	

rate). If, through the process of action control, one perceives that higher-order goals are unlikely to be met, then either superordinate goal expectancies are revised (i.e., downgraded), or strategic changes in micro-level goal striving are enacted in an effort to bring planning and saving behaviors in line with pre-existing aspirations (Bagozzi & Dholakia, 1999; Hershey & Jacobs-Lawson, 2009).

The breadth of goals related to financial planning for retirement is indeed extensive, but the picture becomes infinitely more complex when one considers the range of goals (beyond finances) that surrounds broader aspects of the retirement preparation process (e.g., maintaining sound psychosocial adjustment; ensuring high levels of social and interpersonal engagement; selective engagement in lifestyle-appropriate recreational activities). Moreover, many retirement goals can be considered "deadline goals," that is, goals that need to be achieved within specified time frames. Multiple deadline goals can be tricky to master inasmuch as they require the individual (i) to allocate sustained time and effort to achieving individual goals, while at the same time (ii) simultaneously and strategically allocating resources across different goal domains. Work by Mitchell and his colleagues (Mitchell, Harman, Lee, & Lee, 2008; Mitchell, Lee, Lee, & Harman, 2004) have referred to these two dimensions as the "pacing" and "spacing" of one's personal resources, respectively. These authors go on to point out that individual differences in resource allocation priorities can be understood on the basis of attributions individuals make regarding the perceived importance of different goals, how difficult they are to achieve, their temporal range, the degree of urgency in meeting goal deadlines, and the extent to which individuals are accountable for their goal accomplishments. Thus, the study of attributions surrounding retirement goals could provide a particularly fruitful avenue for future research.

A dearth of goal-based retirement planning investigations have appeared in the literature, but of those that have, most have focused on the role that goal clarity plays in determining the likelihood of exhibiting adaptive planning and saving behaviors. A recent investigation of nearly 1,500 New Zealanders revealed that the clarity of one's financial goals was moderately correlated with perceived financial preparedness (Noone, Stephens, & Alpass, 2010). Similarly, Stawski et al. (2007) found retirement goal clarity to be predictive of financial planning activities, which in turn were predictive of saving behaviors. In a methodologically

sophisticated investigation of Australian workers by Petkoska and Earl (2009), goals were found to be a positive and consistent predictor of planning across multiple retirement domains (e.g., financial, health, interpersonal/leisure). Moreover, a longitudinal intervention study by Hershey, Mowen, and Jacobs-Lawson (2003) revealed that the addition of a goal-setting module to an information-based financial information seminar resulted in increased planning activities at a one-year follow-up. Taken together, the findings from these investigations and others suggest that having clear and specific financial planning goals serves an important motivational function when it comes to the retirement preparation process.

Impact of personality on FPR. Of the various theoretical approaches to personality that have been advanced, only one—trait theory—has been empirically studied in relation to retirement planning practices. Of these investigations, most have focused on only one or two traits in relation to saving or financial preparedness, sometimes examined in combination with other psychological or demographic indicators.

An investigation by Noone et al. (2010) revealed that among New Zealanders, both an internal locus of control and a long future time perspective were positively related to financial preparedness, and an investigation by Davis and Chen (2008) demonstrated that an internal locus of control was associated with high levels of financial knowledge. In a different study that used the Theory of Planned Behavior (Ajzen & Fishbein, 2004) as a theoretical backdrop, Croy et al. (2010a) found that perceptions of behavioral control had significant positive effects on the intention to save among a sample of 2,300 Australian savings fund members. Furthermore, in a series of studies on the relationship between personality and FPR, Hershey and colleagues (Hershey & Mowen, 2000; Hershey et al., 2007; Jacobs-Lawson & Hershey, 2005) found that conscientiousness, future time perspective, and risk tolerance were all related to either the tendency to save or the nature of one's saving and investment decisions. However, a study of Australian workers by Petkoska and Earl (2009) failed to reveal a relationship between future orientation and late-life financial planning practices.

An investigation by Loix, Pepermans, Mentens, Goedee, and Jegers (2005) identified an individual difference dimension they referred to as "orientation to finances," which was found to covary with financial information seeking and personal financial planning practices. Neymotin (2010) demonstrated a link between self-esteem and financial planning, in which those who earned high scores on the construct were more likely to engage in planning activities relative to their low-self-esteem counterparts. And finally, a report by Ferrari, Barnes, and Steel (2009) revealed that relative to non-procrastinators, procrastinators were failing at financial planning for retirement and, accordingly, had more regret over their financial decisions. On a related note, O'Donoghue and Rabin (1998) put forth a theoretical model of procrastination designed to illustrate how delayed retirement savings practices could best be conceived of as a problem of self-control.

Continuing with the topic of personality, it seems that more studies have focused on financial risk tolerance than any other single trait. An investigation by Jacobs-Lawson (2004) found that risk tolerance was positively related to financial allocations among women who made hypothetical contributions to a DC plan. Bajtelsmit, Bemasek, and Jianakoplos (1999) also found risk tolerance levels to be linked to retirement investment strategies, as did Hariharan, Chapman, and Domian (2000) and Sunden and Surette (1998). Furthermore, using data drawn from six waves of the Survey of Consumer Finances, Yao, Gutter, and Hanna (2005) found that blacks and Hispanics were less likely to take financial risks than whites. Interestingly, in an investigation that used data from the Retirement Confidence Survey, Joo and Grable (2001) identified financial risk tolerance as being positively related to the likelihood of seeking advice from financial professionals. Turning to research on financial planning among couples, an investigation by Roszkowski, Delaney, and Cordell (2004) suggests that an open pattern of communication between husbands and wives can bring dyadic financial risk tolerance levels into equilibrium (see also Gilliam, Dass, Durband, & Hampton, 2010).

An investigation by Gilliam, Goetz, and Hampton (2008) indicates that dyadic risk tolerance relationships can be complex, inasmuch as certain demographic factors (notably gender and wives' level of education) interact to determine risk tolerance levels among members of the dyad. Specifically, Gilliam and colleagues reported that wives with advanced levels of educational attainment (i.e., a university degree) were found to have higher levels of financial risk tolerance, but the risk tolerance scores of husbands married to university-educated women were lower than those of men married to women with a high school education. By way of explanation, the authors suggest that dyads that include a highly educated woman could be expected to have a higher household income, thereby reducing the need for the husband to assume high levels of risk in order to accomplish their long-range financial goals.

Attitudinal investigations of FPR. Relative to other areas of research, investigations into the relationship between attitudes and FPR are lacking. One exception can be found in the work of Croy and his colleagues (2010a), who found that the perceived importance of saving had strong positive effects on the perceived future likelihood of saving. In a different investigation, Grable and Joo (2001) found that positive and proactive attitudes toward retirement were associated with the seeking of advice from financial professionals. Furthermore, an investigation by Glass and Kilpatrick (1998) suggested that the perceived importance of financial planning was positively related to one's existing level of retirement savings.

In the wake of the global financial crisis, investor trust in institutions is an attitudinal variable that has taken on added significance (Jordan & Treisch, 2010; Salisbury, 2008). Garling, Kirchler, Lewis, and Van Raaij (2009) identified seven factors that have implications for trust in financial institutions. These factors include an institution's competence, stability, integrity, benevolence, transparency, value congruence, and reputation. Institutional trust is important in the age of increasing DC pension programs because it serves to determine the types of institutions with which workers will choose to invest, the strategies they use to manage their resources, and their level of financial worry. Unfortunately, by seemingly all accounts, confidence in institutions is seriously lacking (Zinn, 2006). Singh and Sirdeshmukh (2000) define "cognitive trust" as the belief that institutions will act responsibly and not behave in a potentially injurious fashion.

With regard to the developments to pension programs in the twenty-first century, a critical question is which type of institution will be able to provide workers with the security they desire: employers, a financial intermediary (e.g., banks, insurance companies), or the state? A recent survey carried out by Helman et al. (2010) found that among American workers, only 23% reported being "very confident" in the ability of private employers to meet this need, 19% expressed high levels of confidence in banks, 13% indicated being very confident in insurance companies, and only 11% of respondents indicated high levels of confidence in the government. Moreover, it has been reported that institutional trust is systematically lower among members of minority groups relative to Caucasians (SPRY Foundation, 2000).

Affective considerations. Only a handful of investigations have explored the role of emotions when it comes to retirement planning and saving (Zinn, 2006), and of those that have, nearly all have focused on some form of negative affect. Data from the 2010 Retirement Confidence Survey revealed that 40% of American respondents endorsed the statement "[I] worry about being financially dependent on others during [my] retirement/later years" (Helman et al., 2010). Similarly, in countries throughout Europe, retirement-related affect is equally problematic, with respondents from about half of the twenty-three countries surveyed in a study by Hershey et al. (2010a) reporting moderate to high levels of savings-related worry. In that investigation, worry was reportedly higher in countries with high levels of income inequality and a high future old-age dependence ratio (i.e., few workers relative to many retirees). In a psychometric investigation of FPR, Neukam and Hershey (2003) found evidence for two separate affect-related constructs: financial worry (i.e., concerns about insufficient income adequacy in retirement) and planning worry (i.e., worry about the inability to plan effectively), with the latter being negatively related to financial saving practices.

In addition to worry, researchers have looked at linkages between the anticipation of retirement and anxiety. Hayslip, Bezerlein, and Nichols (1997) found indisputable evidence of anticipatory retirement anxiety among a sample of university faculty members, and in a study of Canadian workers, retirement anxiety levels were found to be negatively related to expectations of (future) satisfaction with retirement finances (MacEwen, Barling, Kelloway, & Higginbottom, 1995). In related work, Gutierrez, Hershey, and Gerrans (2011) argued that the prospect of anxiety brought on by meeting with a financial professional can be a hindrance when it comes to seeking financial advice.

In one of the only studies that could be located on positive affect in relation to financial planning, Grable and Roszkowski (2008) found that being in a happy mood (a transient emotional state) was associated with higher levels of financial risk tolerance when answering hypothetical financial investing questions. Those not in a happy mood showed a reduced willingness to accept risk, which the authors concluded was consistent with tenets of the Affect Infusion Model (AIM; Forgas, 1995). According to the AIM, differing mood states can cause decision makers to construe subjective probabilities differently, with good moods leading individuals to focus on positive cues from the environment and bad moods leading individuals to attend to negative features of the financial decision-making situation.

Consumer segmentation research. Consumer attitudinal segmentation studies have been carried out that have sought to develop typologies of financial planners. A 2004 investigation by MacFarland, Marconi, and Utkus found evidence of five qualitatively different types of retirement planners based on survey-based attitudinal responses from over 1,100 individuals. The first segment—"successful planners"—made up 21% of the sample. These were individuals with a strong, goal-oriented vision of a successful retirement. The "up and coming planners" (26%) were those individuals who possessed the characteristics of successful planners but who lacked confidence in the quality of their plans. The "secure doers" (20%) had a high level of interest in planning but were security-conscious to a fault—unwilling to take on an appropriate level of market risk. "Stressed avoiders" (19%) were those respondents who found financial matters to be stressful, anxiety provoking, and confusing. Finally, the "live-for-today avoiders" (14%) were not particularly stressed by the prospect of financial planning, but instead were found to be uninterested in the future whatsoever. MacFarland and colleagues found that participant direction in a workplace retirement saving plan covaried with these five different consumer segments. A different typology was developed on the basis of data drawn from the Retirement Confidence Survey, which found evidence of six distinct types of retirement planners: retiring savers, planners, cautious savers, impulsives, strugglers, and deniers (EBRI, 1998).

The research cited in this section of the chapter clearly indicates that a variety of psychological individual difference dimensions impact not only the willingness to plan and save but also the ability of individuals to carry out the task. Next, we turn our attention to the last of the three dimensions in the conceptual model; specifically, the way in which opportunities affect retirement planning practices.

Opportunity to Plan and Save

The opportunity dimension of the conceptual model refers to facilitators and constraints associated with planning and saving that are external to the individual. Sociologists often refer to these opportunity elements as contextual factors, and psychologists describe them as situational variables. In the context of financial planning for retirement, these external forces can be generally broken down into three major categories: social forces, institutional opportunities, and economic dynamics and incentives. Each is discussed separately below.

Social forces. Both perceived social norms and social support mechanisms have been implicated in the likelihood and quality of planning and saving for retirement (Bailey, Nofsinger, & O'Neill, 2003), although a relatively small number of investigations have been published on either topic. Social norms are important because they provide pre-retirees with reference information on the normative behavior of peers (Liefbroer & Billari, 2010), thereby shaping individuals' behavioral predispositions (Etzioni, 2000). Such a mechanism would seem to be particularly important in helping to guide the complex behavioral repertoire involved in saving for the future. Social norms dictate, in part, the financial goals one is likely to set, whether or not resources are set aside for the post-retirement period, the specific investment strategies one is likely to adopt, and the age at which one begins to save.

In an investigation of Australian savings fund members, Croy and colleagues (2010b) demonstrated that injunctive social norms (what is commonly approved or disapproved of) exert a greater force on saving intentions than disjunctive social norms (what is commonly done). Although economists have sounded the alarm when it comes to delaying the age at which one should start saving for retirement (Byrne, Blake, Cairns, & Dowd, 2006), psychologists have identified a bimodal distribution among American retirees when it comes to the perceived age at which one should begin saving (Hershey, Brown, Jacobs-Lawson, and Jackson, 2001). In that study, some indicated that workers should begin saving for retirement upon entering the workforce, whereas others believed individuals should wait until their 40s, when children are more likely to have left the household. In an intriguing investigation of workplace saving patterns, Duflo and Saez (2002) studied university librarians working in a large, eleven-building university library system. They found that the likelihood of worker contributions to a tax-deferred savings account (TDSA) was dependent on the specific library in which one worked, which suggests that savings behaviors are partially governed by local norms operating in one's immediate workplace. This workplace savings effect may, in part, be due to different norms governing the gathering and sharing of financial information in specific workplace settings (Loibl & Hira, 2006). More large-scale studies are clearly needed on this topic in an attempt to establish an empirically based normative savings timetable.

Relative to research on social norms, there is more in the way of literature that addresses the role of social support mechanisms in relation to financial planning. However, studies in this area are also sparse. In an empirical extension of social learning theory, MacEwen et al. (2001) found that Canadian parents' financial and activity planning for retirement had an effect on their adult children's expectations of retirement well-being. This indicated a parent-to-child mechanism through which retirement anxiety is transmitted (see also Lusardi, 2001, on this point). However, Dan (2004) failed to find a link between parental financial planning for retirement and the planning practices of their adult children. Perhaps it is the case that lessons learned as a child are too distal in nature to have an impact on money management behaviors some twenty to forty years in the future.

Having a partner, friends, or colleagues who are supportive of sound financial planning practices has, in contrast, unequivocally been shown to have a positive impact on FPR. A study of over 3,000 households by DeVaney and Chiremba (2005) revealed that financial planning was positively related to being married, and an investigation by Hershey, Henkens, and van Dalen (2010b) found that a partner's support of pre-retirement planning had a positive impact on planning activities, which was mediated by one's future time perspective. That same study demonstrated that friends and colleagues who were supportive of saving also had a positive effect on financial planning tendencies, an effect mediated by retirement goal clarity.

For many, financial professionals also play an important role when it comes to social support for the financial planning process. The phrase "financial professional" is a broad one that implies one who provides financial advice on a professional basis. This subsumes a number of different occupations including financial planners, financial counselors, and financial advisors, each of whom may have earned different forms of accreditation or professional credentials (e.g., CFP, CSA, AFC, and CPA). Some financial professionals work in a sales capacity offering products to investors, whereas others strictly serve in an advisory capacity. Some charge a fee for their services, and others do not.

The good news is that financial professionals have been identified as being more analytical than members of the general population when they were in "reasoning mode." This was the finding from a study by Nofsinger and Varma (2007), which was based on respondents' performance on the Cognitive Reflection Test (a test designed to assess general reasoning abilities). Moreover, in that same investigation, highly analytical planners scored higher on a measure of financial patience than those who were less analytical, and they performed better on inter-temporal choice problems. These are all promising findings for pre-retirees who seek competent professional advice. The bad news, however, is that at least one recent study calls into question the competence of financial professionals. An investigation based on the accounts of over 32,000 clients of a German discount brokerage firm revealed that working with a financial professional was associated with lower total returns (relative to self-managed accounts), higher portfolio risk levels, a higher likelihood of loss, and a greater frequency of trades (Hackethal, Haliassos, & Jappeli, 2009). This study also found that clients of professional advisors tended to be older and have more in the way of wealth. Joo and Grable (2001; see also Grable & Joo, 2001) identified wealth to be a predictor of professional advice-seeking, but they also found that clients were more likely to exhibit better financial behaviors when they had better attitudes toward retirement and higher levels of financial risk tolerance. On the whole, more research is warranted on the effectiveness of financial planning professionals and financial educators, as well as their ability to tailor professional interactions to the needs of individual clients (Glass & Kilpatrick, 1998).

Although more in the realm of technological support than social support, scholars have found convincing evidence that a variety of electronic tools and decision support systems contribute to financial literacy, planning competence, and patterns of saving. Particularly notable information and support systems include the internet and media sources (Glass & Kilpatrick, 1998; Harrison, Waite, & Hunter, 2006; Koonce, Mimura, Mauldin, Rupured, & Johnson, 2008) and computerized financial planning programs such as the *Quicken Financial Planner* and *Torrid Technology's Retirement Savings Planner* (Lusardi, 2008), and on the horizon there exists the commercial prospect of intelligent agent-assisted decision support systems (i.e., computer bots) that can aid individuals with the task of personal financial planning (Gao, Wang, Xu, & Wang, 2007).

Institutional opportunities. Institutions are uniquely poised to serve as a catalyst for encouraging employees to plan and save for the future.

Forward-thinking policies, programs, financial literacy seminars, and planning guidance have all been shown to have a beneficial impact on the financial behaviors of pre-retirees. One study by Kim, Kwon, and Anderson (2005) found that employees who attended a workplace financial education program had higher levels of retirement confidence than their peers. Kim, Garman, and Quach (2005) reported a similar finding, but in addition found that attendance at a financial education workshop was related to both employees' and spouses' contributions to retirement plans. In a similar vein, Joo and Grable (2005) found that employer educational programs were related to the likelihood of having an established retirement savings plan. Clearly, this line of research on workplace retirement programs has important implications not only for the employees who benefit from them but also for the employers who administer the programs, retirement educators, and policymakers.

Work from the fields of behavioral economics (which has been described as the application of psychology to finance; Charupat, Deaves, & Luders, 2005) and behavioral finance has also contributed in important ways to our understanding of investor behavior. Moreover, findings from these fields have implications for institutions that offer retirement savings and investment products. According to Charupat et al. (2005), behavioral researchers have found that not only are individuals prone to cognitive biases that lead to suboptimal investment decisions, but they also rely on their emotions when investing, which can adversely cloud their judgments. To make matters worse, Charupat and colleagues point out that investors are predictably overconfident in the quality of their investment decisions, even when those decisions are flawed.

In order to combat these rational shortcomings, a variety of paternalistic approaches have been introduced as of late, including auto-enrollment retirement savings programs (in which employees automatically participate in a payroll deduction savings program unless they opt out; John, 2011), target date investment funds (in which the investor simply chooses the planned date at which to retire and his or her resources are managed based on an appropriate level of risk; Basu, Byrne, & Drew, 2011), and programs such as Save More Tomorrow (which allows employees to postpone initial savings payroll deductions for a number of months, after which deductions periodically increase at a specified rate; Thaler & Benartzi, 2007). Taken together, behaviorally inspired approaches such as the ones outlined above help to combat a lack of employee inertia when it comes to initiating investments, they protect the worker from excessive risk when managing assets, and they direct attention to important ongoing investment decisions when warranted (Clark & Knox-Hayes, 2009). Other institutions that offer financial products such as banks, insurance companies, and pension funds could benefit from taking into account principles from behavioral finance and behavioral economics by designing user-friendly investment vehicles that consumers find attractive.

Economic dynamics and incentives. There is little doubt that elements of the external economic environment are linked to individuals' financially based retirement saving and investment decisions (Adams & Rau, 2011; Hatcher, 2003). As pointed out above, in countries around the world, significant economic shocks, bank closures, and market upheavals do much to erode investor trust and confidence in financial systems and institutions. Moreover, trends in funding levels for first-pillar social security systems and the perceived adequacy of public pensions also presumably have an impact on workers' expectations of the need to save. Other factors that affect the need for personal savings during retirement include the rate of inflation (both prior to and following employment), the availability of occupational pensions, their income replacement value, and whether second-pillar sources are associated with cost of living adjustments. Indeed, there is no shortage of economic forces to give the individual investor pause as he or she navigates the rocky road to a financially secure retirement.

One class of incentives that are generally believed to have a positive effect on pre-retirement worker savings are TDSAs (Venti & Wise, 1991). TDSAs are savings accounts that provide tax incentives for contributions up to some allowable annual limit. Examples of TDSAs include IRA and 401(k) plans in the United States, Registered Retirement Savings Plans (RRSPs) in Canada, and Self-Invested Personal Pensions and Group Personal Pension Plans (SIPPs and GPPPs) in the United Kingdom. These types of accounts have become increasingly popular among individual investors over the past three decades, in part due to the shift from DB to DC accounts in many countries. In general, participation rates in TDSAs have been shown to increase among workers as a function of age and level of income (Springstead & Wilson, 2000).

A different form of incentivized saving has been proposed by social workers Shobe and Sturm (2007). They have suggested an extension to the idea of youth Individual Development Accounts (IDAs; Giuffrida, 2001) to promote retirement saving behaviors. "Retirement IDAs" are designed to cultivate savings habits among children living in the United States by creating a savings account for each child upon birth. The account would be funded to the tune of $1,500 per child, or some economically feasible amount at the time the accounts are legislated. Additional deposits could be made by the child either from wages, scholarships, or monetary gifts, or they may be made by friends or family members on behalf of the child. Contributions would be subject to a matching amount for children whose families live below the federal poverty level, in an effort to cultivate a habit of saving among those who are at a greater risk of living in poverty after leaving the workforce. According to Shobe and Sturm (2007), the accounts would teach children important lessons about money management and investing, while at the same time cultivating a lifelong pattern of saving.

Demographic Indicators

In addition to the various psychological, social, and situational factors related to planning and saving outlined above, a host of demographic indicators has been shown to be related to FPR. Many of these findings have come from research carried out by economists, who seem predisposed to focus on the predictive value of demographic and structural variables. These effects, while interesting, have limited implications for the development of theory. This is because demographic indicators are, in and of themselves, not explanatory variables, but instead proxies that covary with other indicators that are explanatory in nature. Take gender as an example. There is nothing inherent in being male or female that leads individuals to be good planners and savers. Rather, gender is related to other variables (e.g., financial knowledge, availability of workplace pensions, income level) that are related to financial preparedness.

With that limitation in mind, it is worth pointing out that demographic indicators can serve an important function when it comes to interventions, by allowing counselors and educators to target those who are most at risk of experiencing poverty in old age. Furthermore, knowledge gained from demographic investigations can be useful in the development of public policy initiatives aimed at encouraging individuals to save. Finally, understanding the extent to which demographic markers are associated with planning and saving has relevance to basic research, inasmuch as they can be used as control variables in models as a way of reducing error variance.

Of the various demographic indicators that have been investigated, perhaps none has received as much attention as age. In study after study, older pre-retirees have been shown to be more engaged in the financial planning process than their younger counterparts (DeVaney, 1995; Fernandez-Lopez, Otero, Vivel, & Rodeiro, 2010; Glass & Kilpatrick, 1998; Hershey et al., 2007; Hira, Rock, & Loibol, 2009; Phua & McNally, 2008). There are many good reasons why age is significantly related to planning. Among them is the fact that older adults have higher incomes (and thus potentially more discretionary income to invest); they are nearer to retirement age and the reality of the post-employment period is likely in sharper focus; and, relative to younger adults, older adults tend to be more knowledgeable about financial matters. Moreover, increases in age have been shown to be inversely related to one's willingness to take on investment risk (Dulebohn, 2002). And although age is not synonymous with the concept of saving horizon, they are positively correlated with one another, and the latter has been observed to be highly related to the likelihood of making regular savings contributions (Fisher & Montalto, 2010).

Gender has also been shown to be linked to financial planning processes, with men generally outperforming women in terms of planning, saving, and financial accumulations (Glass & Kilpatrick, 1998; Moen, Erickson, Agarwal, Fields, & Todd, 2000; Noone et al., 2010). This is in part due to the fact that men have higher incomes than women (and thus more resources to invest, which means increased opportunity; Jefferson & Preston, 2005), women tend to have more discontinuous work patterns than men (thereby affecting their pension eligibility; Schultz, Rosenman, & Rix, 1999), and among older cohorts of individuals, traditional sex-role patterns dictate that men be responsible for family financial planning activities (Glass & Kilpatrick, 1998). This latter gender difference seems to be less pronounced among younger individuals, with women in contemporary society taking on greater responsibility for their own financial futures (Adams & Rao, 2011; Jefferson, 2009). Furthermore, Helman et al. (2011) found that perceptions of a comfortable future retirement are higher among men compared to women.

Despite the corpus of studies that have found gender effects in FPR, a handful of investigations have revealed either small or nonexistent findings between the sexes. According to Noone and colleagues (Noone et al., 2010), studies that report limited gender effects tend to be historically more recent. These authors contend that shrinking sex differences are the result of (a) women's more positive perceptions of retirement that have occurred over the past two decades, (b) a trend toward higher levels of socioeconomic status among women during that same time period, and (c) more continuous patterns of workforce involvement among women that stem from trends toward educational and occupational equality. Indeed, these rapidly shifting trends and their impact on FPR are a cogent reminder that retirement, as a social institution, is dynamically changing, as are the strategies that different subgroups of individuals use to prepare for the post-employment period.

For understandable reasons, household income has been found to covary not only with financial planning activities but also with retirement savings contributions (Fernandez-Lopez et al., 2010; Hira et al., 2009; Lee, 2003; Schellenberg, Turcotte, & Ram, 2005). This is because high-income individuals often have more discretionary resources to invest, they tend to be more knowledgeable about financial matters, they are likely to have clearer financial goals, and they are more likely to engage the services of a financial professional. All of these factors have previously been shown to be associated with either high levels of involvement in FPR or savings accumulations. Accordingly, worker confidence in having sufficient resources for a comfortable retirement is positively related to income (Helman et al., 2011; Kim et al., 2005). Taylor and Geldhauser (2007) point out that low-income workers, who are overrepresented by women and minority group members, are less likely to engage in both formal (e.g., financial) and informal (e.g., psychological; attitudinal) forms of retirement planning, and Gruber and Wise (1999) report that one's financial status is a predictor of the timing of one's departure from the workforce. Finally, in an information processing study of investors, high-income, highly educated males were the most likely to carry out a thorough search of relevant information when making investment decisions (Loibl & Hira, 2009).

Partnership status is yet another demographic indicator that has shown to be predictive of planning and saving, with individuals in a dyadic relationship shown to plan and save more than their single counterparts (EBRI, 2009; Glass & Kilpatrick, 1998). One apparent reason for this is because dual-earner households typically have higher combined incomes than single households, and therefore more discretionary resources to invest. Other possible reasons why working couples typically "outperform" single workers have to do with a desire to ensure financial security for one's partner, and the potentially higher levels of social support for planning and saving that one may experience when in a committed relationship. In general, findings from research on same-sex couples mirror the findings from studies on different-sex dyads, suggesting a planning benefit of partnership (Mock, Tayor, & Savin-Williams, 2006). However, Mock and Cornelius (2007) present empirical evidence to indicate that the interdependence of retirement planning is particularly strong among lesbian couples.

One's health status, and among couples the health status of one's partner, has also shown to be linked to retirement planning and saving (Fisher & Montalto, 2010). Using data from the Health and Retirement Study (HRS), Lum and Lightfoot (2003) found that healthy individuals nearing retirement were more likely to have an IRA and were likely to have more money invested in same. The authors speculate that this is due to the fact that those in ill health experience more in the way of out-of-pocket expenditures for health care. These authors went on to speculate that those with poor health may foresee a shorter life span for themselves, thereby limiting the amount they are willing to set aside for old age. In that same study, Lum and Lightfoot found that having a partner in ill health was associated with a decreased likelihood of working in a job that provided a pension plan. Along related lines, Gupta and Larson (2010) suggest that pre-retirement health shocks can be expected to have a larger economic effect on individuals living in countries such as the United States relative to those living in welfare states such as Denmark or Sweden (where health care services are subsidized), due to the sheer magnitude of expenditures in countries where the patient bears the burden of the cost.

Taken together, the demographic findings presented above perhaps raise more questions than they answer. Inasmuch as demographic indicators are not explanatory constructs in and of themselves, it leaves open to question as to why these variables (e.g., age, gender, income, partnership status) covary with planning and saving practices. For some markers—such as income—the answer to this question is fairly clear. Higher incomes are important

because they increase the availability of discretionary resources to invest. But a full understanding of the mechanisms that underlie associations of planning and saving with age, gender, and partnership status is lacking. A number of interesting investigations have systematically explored the impact of demographic factors on FPR (e.g., Petkoska & Earl, 2009), but future research is needed to flesh out the causal mechanisms that covary with these indicators. At present, we have only speculative evidence as to the nature of the linkages between FPR, demographic indicators, and key underlying psychosocial-economic constructs.

Limitations and Future Directions

In this section of the chapter we begin by describing the limitations of research on FPR. In doing so, we will comment on (a) disciplinary shortcomings of existing empirical work; (b) the lack of integrative approaches designed to explain financial planning practices, as well as the need for closer collaborations among stakeholders; (c) insufficiencies associated with methodologies and research designs; and (d) cultivating ways to motivate children and adolescents to think about their future financial needs. These limitations will be followed by a future directions section, which outlines a series of significant questions, issues, and challenges related to effective financial planning. These questions are designed to encourage the reader to think deeply about innovative directions the field might take, as well as their implications.

Limitations of Existing Research

Disciplinary shortcomings. Each discipline can be credited with making unique contributions to our understanding of the financial planning process. But at the same time, each has exhibited certain weaknesses or shortcomings when it comes to conceptualizing, designing, and implementing their work. Take research from the field of economics as an example. In an effort to develop robust predictive models, economists have relied almost exclusively on econometric predictors of saving behavior. Their hesitance to employ psychosocial constructs leaves their models in some respects incomplete (Elster, 1989). Particularly valuable at this point in time would be the inclusion of empirically validated perceptual and self-report predictors of saving (e.g., personality constructs; perceived financial goals; indices of social support) in ongoing longitudinal investigations, such as the HRS.

Turning to psychology, in some respects the Achilles' heel in that field is the opposite of the fault exhibited by economists. In developing their models of financial planning competence, psychologists have demonstrated a reluctance to adopt clear, objective, and verifiable measures of key outcome variables (e.g., household saving rates; wealth accumulations). Instead, they have shown a reliance on perceptual and self-report outcome measures that call into question the accuracy and veracity of respondents' claims. Another shortcoming is that psychologists rely heavily on cross-sectional research designs and convenience sampling, which can tell only part of the story when it comes to understanding retirement planning as a process and generalizing the findings. More will be said below about the role that commonly used research designs play in advancing our understanding of FPR.

One of the clear strengths of work by sociologists has been their ability to conceptualize broad theoretical frameworks (such as the life course perspective; Elder & Johnson, 2002) that explain the ways in which agency and contextual factors shape individuals' behaviors (Hitlin & Elder, 2007). But that said, attempts to empirically test propositions regarding the interaction between human agency and context have not been forthcoming (see van Solinge & Henkens, 2005, 2007, for notable exceptions). Thinking on the topic of FPR would truly be advanced if sociologists could transform elements of theory into clear, testable hypotheses. Identification of a normative timetable for the financial planning process (and individuals' perceptions of same) would be a particularly valuable contribution, as would identification of the mechanisms through which social forces and contexts shape saving predispositions.

Next, we turn our attention to the field of finance, which as a discipline has developed some very attractive lifetime savings models (e.g., the life-cycle savings model; the permanent income hypothesis). Despite the existence of these models, the field of finance seems to lack consensus when it comes to predictions regarding the timing of saving behavior and the form it should take. For example, strategies for reducing equity in favor of cash for the individual who is approaching retirement are poorly specified, as are propositions about how to manage longevity risk. Like sociologists, in the coming years those in finance could advance the field by transforming key elements of dominant theories into empirically testable propositions. Further progress would be made by testing the limits of those propositions in relation to particular subgroups of workers and retirees who exhibit special needs.

Integrative approaches. The field of forces that motivate individuals to plan and save for old age is extensive, and the nature of the interrelationships between intra-psychic, economic, and contextual variables is indeed complex. With that being the case, it is clear that holistic and interdisciplinary approaches to the study of financial planning are needed (Adams & Rau, 2011; Altfest, 2004). Relatively few scholars have pursued work in that direction (see Dan, 2004; Dulebohn, 2002; and Hershey, 2004, for notable exceptions). But among those who have, the results have been generally fruitful. It is only by stepping outside traditional disciplinary boundaries that retirement researchers will take meaningful strides toward constructing a comprehensive theoretical framework from which to conceptualize the determinants of investor behavior. Toward that end, future interdisciplinary collaborations among empiricists will be an important key to success.

In addition to the need for increased collaborations among disciplines, opportunities also exist for closer collaborations among key stakeholders in the financial and retirement planning arena. Examples of stakeholders who might benefit from interacting with one another include:

1. governmental institutions (such as the Social Security Administration, which funds a network of financial literacy centers that include retirement as part of their mandate)

2. non-governmental organizations (e.g., the European Financial Planning Organization) that provide advice to individuals through web-based computational tools and resources, as well as other forms of modern networks

3. financial firms that profit from wealth creation and management (e.g., AXA Equitable; JP Morgan Chase, MassMutual, Wells Fargo)

4. researchers who are interested in building and testing models of savings practices and investor behavior

5. practitioners who are interested in the development and evaluation of educational, training, and intervention programs

Methodology and design. Near the beginning of this chapter we noted a takeaway message across contributing disciplines—when it comes to individual patterns of saving for retirement, there is much room for improvement. One way to improve knowledge of FPR, in addition to conceptualization, is through careful attention to measurement, design, and analysis. Our approach in this brief section is to describe selected prototypical studies and to then offer observations on the study of FPR from the perspective of research strategy.

Consider measurement first. An exemplary approach is represented in work by Noone and colleagues (Noone et al., 2010). Their careful investigation resulted in a validated instrument, the Process of Retirement Planning Scale (PRePS). This instrument was justified through review of research constructs defined using either single or few indicators. Instrument development (across financial, health, psychosocial, and lifestyle domains) used a general model of planning (Friedman & Scholnick, 1997) as well as data from several pilot studies to identify subscales that focus on retirement representation, the decision to retire, and the preparedness stages of planning. A sample of 3,000 persons aged 49–60 from the New Zealand electoral roll comprised the intended respondents, and a response rate of 53% was achieved before data cleaning. Variables measured in a single questionnaire included the PRePS, the HRS retirement planning measure, future time perspective, locus of control, age and time to retirement, the Economic Living Standards Index to capture socioeconomic status, educational attainment, and the Social Functioning Scale to assess self-reported health. The analysis showed appropriate use of confirmatory factor analysis (cf. MacCallum & Austin, 2000). A similar study reported by Muratore and Earl (2010) but conducted in Australia with a smaller sample produced the 27-item Retirement Planning Questionnaire II. Both of these studies point to strategies that improve measurement of constructs in FPR.

Design refers to structuring data collection in terms of units (usually persons, but sometimes dyads, families, or other groups), manipulations and measures, and occasions/sequencing. The majority of the research we reviewed and cited is quantitative in nature. A qualitative tradition offers understanding through a different approach. An exemplary study was reported by Kemp and colleagues (Kemp, Rosenthal, & Denton, 2005). These authors worked from the quantitative literature to identify themes that were assembled into life-history interviews with 51 mid- to later-life Canadians. The interviews were used to understand catalysts and constraints associated with planning in financial, personal, and familial domains. The authors oversampled females to understand gendered pathways to retirement planning. An important finding was that constraints and catalysts varied between individuals and over time, which suggests the need for longitudinal research, whether it be qualitative or quantitative

in nature. Working from quantitative findings to design a qualitative study is also an attractive reversal that, if repeated, could result in a back-and-forth cycle that improves understanding and enriches knowledge.

Most studies in the domain of FPR are cross-sectional, but Wang and Shultz (2010) advocated longitudinal approaches to the study of retirement adjustment and later advanced a resource dynamics approach (Wang, Henkens, & van Solinge, 2011). Temporal aspects fit well with the perspective taken by Noone et al. (2010) in which a chain of cognitive representations precedes the process of planning for retirement, although measurement at earlier developmental points (adolescence, early career, mid-career) would give a better vantage point on group or individual trajectories. Temporal dynamics of resources could be useful linking concepts between different aspects of retirement. In particular, this framework could link FPR as addressed in this chapter to actual adjustment levels during retirement. Event history models with multiple spells might also be useful as individuals retire (occasionally through "bridge employment") and then return to work (sometimes cycling between the two).

We have mentioned the AXA (2008) Retirement Scope survey, which spanned multiple continents and twenty-six nations. This large-scale project provided a snapshot of retirement perceptions for a firm whose business model is assisting individuals in wealth creation and management. Such surveys have smaller numbers of items (sometimes anchor and rotating) and are designed to provide useful information to the firm for strategic planning, but they also serve a secondary purpose of dissemination to individuals and researchers. They are not generally peer-reviewed but can provide useful information nonetheless. The HRS, operated by the University of Michigan Institute for Social Research on behalf of several federal agencies since 1992, surveys more than 22,000 Americans over the age of 50 every two years. This large-scale survey supports archival research to a greater extent than industry efforts such as the AXA Retirement Scope survey.

Experimental research is uncommon in FPR, but two studies illustrate the range. Hershey, Mowen, and Jacobs-Lawson (2003) conducted a study that compared retirement planning seminars structured using information, motivation (goal-setting), information plus motivation, and a control seminar on memory. Results for a sample of 118 individuals showed that the information and motivation seminar had the greatest effects on goal clarity, planning practices, and saving practices. Beshears and colleagues at the NBER reported a field experiment to investigate the effects of social marketing norms (Beshears, Choi, Laibson, Madrian, & Milkman, 2010). Specifically, separate letters promoting quick enrollment in a savings plan and easy escalation of savings were mailed to members of three groups at a manufacturing firm. Two of the groups were created by providing relative information about peers' savings in five- and ten-year age ranges, while the third was a no-information control condition. The results indicated effects for quick enrollment in a savings plan, but not for the easy escalation letters.

We advise consideration of a classic article by Cronbach (1984). He discussed what Raymond Cattell called a "treasure chest" in describing for researchers a set of facets for studying phenomena proposed in 1946. Cattell's initial facets were persons (P), tests or situations (J), and occasions (O), but extensions provide additional potential for systematic research on FPR. When developmental considerations are added to permit separation of age, cohort, and time of measurement (cf. Adam, 1978), the study of the relationship of FPR to other constructs and domains addressed in this handbook is enhanced. Indeed, designs informed by the data box and cross-sequential strategies should assist in robust knowledge creation and honor a commitment to longitudinal research advocated by Wang and Shultz (2010; also see Shultz & Wang, 2011).

Analysis refers to how researchers investigate obtained data, and typical categories for grouping statistics include descriptive, inferential, and exploratory. Primary analysis of single studies and secondary analysis of archival data are the most prevalent analyses we found in reviewing literature for this chapter. Both strategies are valuable in their own right. Meta-analysis of primary studies (Cooper, Hedges, & Valentine, 2009) would also help to support within- and cross-discipline integration. However, this will occur only if common measures can be specified in exogenous and endogenous domains, and if primary researchers provide a minimum set of statistics in their publications.

A chapter on the topic of analysis by Zickar and Gibby (2003) presents strategies for the general study of retirement. These authors focus on longitudinal techniques in a section that presents hierarchical linear models and latent growth models. They then touch on discontinuous change (e.g., spline regression fit to different sections of a temporally ordered variable using theoretical points of expected discontinuity), and they also present other techniques including logistic regression, item response theory (which, for example, could be used to analyze the scale data collected by Noone et al. [2010]), missing data, and computational models (i.e., simulations). Taken together, the recommendations found in the Zickar and Gibby chapter provide good food for thought when it comes to analytic approaches that investigators might adopt.

Cultivating financial literacy among children and adolescents. Many scholars have written about the need for financial literacy training early in life in order to stimulate successful patterns of personal money management and life span saving, but few have taken meaningful steps in that direction. Findings from a 2008 survey of high school students carried out by the Jump$tart Coalition (Mandell, 2008) revealed that American teenagers' level of financial knowledge is woefully inadequate.

Of the financial literacy programs that have been developed, few have been subject to empirical scrutiny (Varcoe, Martin, Devitto, & Go, 2005). Those that have been evaluated have been shown to improve not only literacy rates but also money management skills and financial confidence (Danes, Huddleston-Casas, & Boyce, 1999; Varcoe et al., 2005). Moreover, a paper published in 2001 by Bernheim, Garrett, and Maki reached the conclusion that high school curriculum mandates that stress household financial decision making are beneficial, although the effects of these programs tend to be gradual. The importance of early and continual inculcation of financial literacy training is that educators can positively exploit supra- and subconscious implementation intentions and goal intentions (Dijksterhuis & Aarts, 2010; Klein et al., 2008), as well as increase future time orientation, as suggested by Shobe and Sturm (2007).

Despite the development of national standards for youth financial education in the United States some years ago (Jump$tart Coalition, 2007), crosswalks to national and state standards provided by the National Endowment for Financial Education ([NEFE], 2007a), and parallel standards for adults (Institute for Financial Literacy, 2007), a comprehensive and integrated approach to financial education from childhood to adulthood remains lacking. One of the closer approximations, although limited to secondary educational settings, is the High School Financial Planning Program (HSFPP) produced by NEFE (2007b). Adding retirement considerations to early education (such as how to use retirement calculators, and understanding the way in which interest compounds over time) could help youth to initiate individual savings accounts earmarked for retirement. Program evaluations, based on logic models, are needed to document outputs, outcomes, and impact along those lines.

One key to the success of educational interventions at the K–12 level will be to ensure that program content is both engaging and lifestyle relevant (Zollo, 2003). If not, the intervention will stand the risk of being disregarded. Toward that end, games aimed at enhancing personal financial literacy seem to be one fruitful applied direction, such as the game "Get Rich Slow," which is available from the Center for Retirement Research at Boston College ([CRRBC], 2011). A different player-friendly intervention entitled "Save! The Game," which is designed to be played on iPhones by younger children, has as its goal to motivate long-term saving behaviors (Massachusetts Mutual Life Insurance Company, 2010). Developing games and ensuring that core FPR concepts are front and center when it comes to financial literacy instruction are just two practical strategies for improving financial competence among youth. Certainly, more in the way of motivational interventions will also be needed in the coming years if we are to be successful at cultivating future cohorts of savers. Ideally, all such programs will be designed to take into account age levels, individual differences in interests, and pre-existing propensities to plan and save.

Future Directions

In this section, we outline a number of issues and questions designed to identify gaps and limitations in the current literature. Our hope is that these questions will stimulate meaningful discussions of ways to design and implement forward-thinking theoretical investigations, and how those investigations, in turn, can inform efforts aimed at intervention and application.

1. There has been much discussion in recent years about designing "libertarian paternalist" approaches to public and private pension systems. As part of this approach, control over policies and saving practices are largely managed by the employer or the state. Within these systems, however, individuals are still responsible for certain key financial investment decisions. When it comes to the development of personal savings initiatives, under what circumstances should "libertarian paternalist" policies be enacted? How far-reaching should these initiatives be when it comes to taking control out of the hands of investors and placing the responsibility for pension planning and saving in the hands of institutions?

2. What is the best way to encourage individuals to make regular retirement savings contributions? What are the barriers to stimulating a successful pattern of saving in terms of individuals' capacity to effectively plan and save, their willingness to take on financial management tasks, and their opportunities to save for the future?

3. In what way could social influence forces be harnessed to encourage individuals to plan and save effectively for old age?

4. What meaningful steps could be taken to educate children to grow up to be forward-thinking planners and savers? In raising children to become fiscally responsible adults, what are the respective roles of parents, employers, and the state?

5. How can technology be harnessed to support effective planning and saving practices? What types of computational tools and decision support systems would be most useful for advanced investors? How would these tools be different from the ones that would be most useful to novices?

6. How can findings from market segmentation studies be used to develop "tailored" saving intervention programs that meet the psychological needs and predispositions of workers with different planning orientations (e.g., successful planners, secure doers, stressed avoiders, live-for-today avoiders)?

7. What measurement, design, and analysis strategies will support research and evaluation efforts across the disciplines that examine FPR? A predominant quantitative tradition yields many studies that feature limited measurement using self-report perceptions, cross-sectional designs, and regression-based analyses. In what ways can investigators develop and deploy improved measures, add to their models' consideration of temporal factors, and be creative in their analytical strategies?

8. How could Bayesian concepts be incorporated into the development of personal financial planning strategies? More specifically, how could individuals' perceptions of prior probabilities associated with health, longevity, and quality of life be meaningfully integrated into individuals' long-range financial plans so as to custom-tailor appropriate goal-striving activities.

9. Would it be possible to develop a generally agreed upon definition of "FPR"? In what ways

would having such a definition help to advance research in the field? Could a definition of financial planning for retirement serve as the basis for developing benchmark accomplishments, which in turn could help to establish developmentally appropriate performance levels associated with the planning process?

Conclusion

In this chapter we have attempted to sketch a portrait, in broad form, of the factors that are associated with effective FPR. The relative importance of these factors is, of course, largely contingent on the country in which the pre-retiree resides, as it dictates not only the types and availability of institutional support but also the social norms that govern behavior. Moreover, the picture becomes more complex upon recognition of the fact that a catalyst for one person may be a constraint for another (Kemp et al., 2005). A centerpiece of the chapter involved presenting a theoretical model of effective FPR, which posited the existence of three major sets of forces that shape individual behavior. This model, which acknowledges forces of capacity, willingness, and motivation, served as the basis for defining eight different types of planning predispositions, as well as an organizational framework from which to characterize existing empirical findings. The chapter closed with a set of discussion questions aimed at encouraging the reader to think about future directions for the field.

References

Ackerman, P. L., & Beier, M. E. (2006). Determinants of domain knowledge and independent study learning in an adult sample. *Journal of Educational Psychology, 98*, 366–381.

Adam, J. (1978). Sequential strategies and the separation of age, cohort, and time of measurement contributions to developmental data. *Psychological Bulletin, 85*, 1309–1316.

Adams, G. A., & Rau, B. L. (2011). Putting off tomorrow to do what you want today. *American Psychologist, 66*, 180–192.

Agarwal, S., Driscoll, J. C., Gabaix, X., & Laibson, D. (2009). The age of reason: Financial decisions over the life-cycle with implications for regulation. *Brookings Papers on Economic Activity* (Fall 2009). Available: http://www.brookings.edu/~/media/Files/ Programs/ES/BPEA/ 2009_fall_bpea_papers/2009_fall_bpea_agarwal.pdf

Ajzen, I., & Fishbein, M. (2004). *Attitudes and the attitude–behavior relation: Reasoned and automatic processes*. New York, NY: John Wiley & Sons.

Alessie, R., & Kapteyn, A. (2001). Savings and pensions in the Netherlands. *Research in Economics, 55*, 61–82.

Altfest, L. (2004). Personal financial planning: Origins, developments and a plan for future direction. *American Economist, 48*, 53–60.

Ameriks, J., Caplin, A., & Leahy, J. (2003). Wealth accumulation and the propensity to plan. *The Quarterly Journal of Economics, 118*, 1007–1047.

AON. (2010). *Expectations vs. reality: Meeting Europe's retirement challenge*. London, England: AON Consulting.

Asher, A. (2006). Pensions in Africa. In G. L. Clark and A. H. Munnell (Eds.), *Pensions and retirement income* (pp. 816–836). Oxford, United Kingdom: Oxford University Press.

Asher, M. G. (2010). *The global economic crisis: An opportunity for strengthening Asia's social protection systems?* (Asian Development Bank Institute (ADBI) Working Paper No. 198). Tokyo, Japan: ADBI.

Askins, P. (2010). The future of pensions policy in Europe. *Pensions: An International Journal, 15*, 245–248.

Austin, J. T., & Vancouver, J. B. (1996). Goal constructs in psychology: Structure, process, and content. *Psychological Bulletin, 120*, 338–375.

AXA. (2008). *AXA Retirement Scope 2008: New dynamics*. Retrieved from http://www.axa.com/en/press/research/retirementscope/

Bagozzi, R. P., & Dholakia, U. (1999). Goal setting and goal striving in consumer behavior. *Journal of Marketing, 63*, 19–32.

Bajtelsmit, V. L., Bermasek, A., & Jianakoplos, N. A. (1999). Gender differences in defined contribution pension decisions. *Financial Services Review, 8*, 1–10.

Bailey, J. J., Nofsinger, J. R., & O'Neill, M. (2003). A review of major influences on employee retirement investment decisions. *Journal of Financial Services Research, 23*, 149–165.

Baltes, P. B., Reese, H., & Lipsett, L. (1980). Lifespan developmental psychology. *Annual Review of Psychology, 31*, 65–110.

Banks, J., & Oldfield, Z. (2007). Understanding pensions: Cognitive function, numerical ability and retirement saving. *Fiscal Studies, 28*, 143–170.

Barrett, G., & Tseng, Y. (2007). *Retirement saving in Australia* (Social and Economic Dimensions of an Aging Population Research Paper No. 177). Ontario, Canada: SEDAP.

Barrientos, A. (2002). *Comparing pension schemes in Chile, Singapore, Brazil and South Africa* (IDM Dicussion Paper No. 67). Manchester, United Kingdom: Institute for Development Policy and Management.

Basu, A. K., Byrne, A., & Drew, M. E. (2011). Dynamic lifecycle strategies for target date retirement funds. *Journal of Portfolio Management, 37*, 83–96.

Beach, L. R. (1993). Image theory: An alternative to normative decision theory. *Advances in Consumer Research, 20*, 235–238.

Beach, L. R. (1998). *Image theory: Theoretical and empirical foundations*. Mahwah, NJ: Erlbaum.

Beach, L. R., & Mitchell, T. R. (1987). Image theory: Principles, goals and plans in decision-making. *Acta Psychologia, 66*, 201–220.

Bender, K. A., & Jivan, N. A. (2005). *What makes retirees happy?* (Issue Brief No. 28). Boston, MA: Center for Retirement Research at Boston College.

Berger, E. D., & Denton, M. A. (2004). The interplay between women's life course work patterns and financial planning for later life. *Canadian Journal on Aging, 23*, S99–S113.

Bernheim, B. D., Garrett, D. M., & Maki, D. M. (2001). Education and saving: The long-term effects of high school financial curriculum mandates. *Journal of Public Economics, 80*, 435–465.

Beshears, J., Choi, J. J., Liabson, D., Madrian, B. C., & Milkman, K. L. (2010). *The effect of providing peer information on retirement savings decisions* (Financial Literacy Center Working Paper Series). Retrieved from http://www.financialliteracyfocus.org/academics/proj/ppy1/docs/B4-E.pdf.

Blumberg, M., & Pringle, C. D. (1982). The missing opportunity in organizational research: Some implications for a theory of work performance. *Academy of Management Review, 7,* 560–569.

Boersch, A. (2009). Pension funds and the financial crisis. *International Pension Issues 4/09.* Munich: Allianz Global Investors.

Butrica, B. A., Smith, K. E., & Toder, E. J. (2010). What the 2008 stock market crash means for retirement security. *Journal of Aging & Social Policy, 22,* 339–359.

Byrne, A., Blake, D., Cairns, A., & Dowd, K. (2006). There's no time like the present: The cost of delaying retirement saving. *Financial Services Review, 15,* 213–231.

Center for Retirement Research at Boston College (CRRBC). (2011). *Retirement game: "Get Rich Slow."* Boston: Author. Retrieved from http://crr.bc.edu/special_projects/retirement_game.html

Charupat, N., & Deaves, C. (2004). How behavioral finance can assist financial professionals. *Journal of Personal Finance, 3,* 41–51.

Charupat, N., Deaves, C., & Luders, E. (2005). Knowledge vs. knowledge perception: Implications for financial professionals. *Journal of Personal Finance, 4,* 50–61.

Christelis, D., Jappelli, T., & Padula, M. (2010). Cognitive abilities and portfolio choice. *European Economic Review, 54,* 18–38.

Chung, S., Domino, M. E., Stearns, S. C., & Popkin, B. M. (2009). Retirement and physical activity: Analyses by occupation and wealth. *American Journal of Preventive Medicine, 36,* 422–428.

Clark, G. L. (2003). *European pensions & global finance.* New York, NY: Oxford University Press.

Clark, G. L., & Knox-Hayes, J. (2009). The "new" paternalism, consultation and consent: Expectations of UK participants in defined contribution and self-directed retirement savings schemes. *Pensions, 14,* 58–74.

Cooper, H. M., Hedges, L. V., & Valentine, J. (2009). *Handbook of research synthesis and meta-analysis* (2nd ed.). New York, NY: Russell Sage Foundation.

Cronbach, L. J. (1984). A research worker's treasure chest. *Multivariate Behavioral Research, 19,* 223–240.

Croy, G., Gerrans, P., & Speelman, C. (2010a). The role and relevance of domain knowledge, perceptions of planning importance, and risk tolerance in predicting savings intentions. *Journal of Economic Psychology, 31,* 860–871.

Croy, G., Gerrans, P., & Speelman, C. (2010b). Injunctive social norms primacy over descriptive social norms in retirement savings decisions. *International Journal of Aging and Human Development, 71,* 259–282.

Dailami, M., & Masson, P. (2009). *Measures of investor and consumer confidence and policy actions in the current crisis.* (The World Bank Policy Research Working Paper Series No. 5007). Washington, DC: The World Bank.

Dan, A. A. (2004). *What are people doing to prepare for retirement? Structural, personal, work, and family predictors of planning* (Doctoral dissertation). DAI-A 65/01, 251. Retrieved from http://etd.ohiolink.edu/view.cgi/ Dan%20Amy %20Anne. pdf?case1079241195

Danes, S. M., Huddleston-Casas, C., & Boyce, L. (1999). Financial planning curriculum for teens: Impact evaluation. *Financial Counseling and Planning, 10,* 26–39.

Davis, G. D., & Chen, Y. (2008). Age differences in demographic predictors of retirement investment decisions. *Educational Gerontology, 34,* 225–246.

DeVaney, S. A. (1995). Retirement preparation of older and younger baby boomers. *Financial Counseling and Planning, 6,* 25–34.

DeVaney, S. A., & Chiremba, S. T. (2005). Comparing the retirement savings of the baby boomers and other cohorts. *Compensation and Working Conditions Online.* Retrieved from http://www.bls.gov/opub/cwc/cm20050114ar01p1.htm

Dijksterhuis, A., & Aarts, H. (2010). Goals, attention, and (un) consciousness. *Annual Review of Psychology, 61,* 467–490.

Dulebohn, J. H. (2002). An investigation of the determinants of investment risk behavior in employer-sponsored retirement plans. *Journal of Management, 28,* 3–26.

Duflo, E., & Saez, E. (2002). Participation and investment decisions in a retirement plan: The influence of colleagues' choices. *Journal of Public Economics, 85,* 121–148.

Employee Benefit Research Institute. (1998). *Retirement planning personalities: From deniers to planners.* Washington, DC: Author. Retrieved from http://www.ebri.org/pdf/surveys/rcs/1998/rcs-personalities.pdf

Employee Benefit Research Institute. (2002). *The 2002 Retirement Confidence Survey summary of findings.* Washington, DC: Author. Retrieved from http://www.ebri.org/pdf/surveys/rcs/2002/02rcssof.pdf

Employee Benefit Research Institute. (2009). *Retirement Confidence Survey: 2009 RCS Fact Sheet.* Washington, DC: Author. Retrieved from http://www.ebri.org/files/FS-03_RCS-09_Saving.FINAL.pdf

Employee Benefit Research Institute. (2010). *Trends in savings and investments among workers* (Issue Brief No. 158). Washington, DC: Author.

Ekerdt, D. J., Hackney, J., Kosloski, K., & DeViney, S. (2001). Eddies in the stream: The prevalence of uncertain plans for retirement. *Journal of Gerontology, 56B,* S162–S170.

Ekerdt, D. J., Kosloski, K., & DeViney, S. (2000). The normative anticipation of retirement by older workers. *Research on Aging, 22,* 3–22.

Elder, G. H., Jr., & Johnson, M. K. (2002). Perspectives on human development in context. In C. von Hofsten & L. Bergman (Eds.), *Psychology at the turn of the millennium* (Vol. 2, pp. 153–175). East Sussex, United Kingdom: Psychology Press.

Elder, G. H., Jr., Johnson, M. K., & Crosnoe, R. (2003). The emergence and development of life course theory. In J. T. Mortimer & M. J. Shanahan (Eds.), *Handbook of the life course* (pp. 3–19). New York, NY: Springer.

Elster, J. (1989). Social norms and economic theory. *Journal of Economic Perspectives, 3,* 99–117.

Etzioni, A. (2000). Social norms: Internalization, persuasion, and history. *Law & Society Review, 34,* 157–178.

Fernandez-Lopez, S., Otero, L., Vivel, M., & Rodeiro, D. (2010). What are the driving forces of individuals' retirement savings? *Czech Journal of Economics and Finance, 60,* 226–251.

Ferrari, J. R., Barnes, K. L., & Steel, P. (2009). Life regrets by avoidant and arousal procrastinators: Why put off today what you will regret tomorrow? *Journal of Individual Differences, 30,* 163–168.

Fisher, P. J., & Montalto, C. P. (2010). Effect of saving motives and horizon on saving behaviors. *Journal of Economic Psychology, 31,* 92–105.

Forgas, J. P. (1995). Mood and judgment: The Affect Infusion Model (AIM). *Psychological Bulletin, 117,* 39–66.

Fornero, E., Lusardi, A., & Monticone, C. (2009). *Adequacy of saving for old age in Europe* (Center for Research on Pensions and Welfare Policies Working Paper No. 87/09). Moncalieri, Italy: CeRP.

Friedman, S. L., & Scholnick, E. K. (1997). *The developmental psychology of planning: Why, how, and when do we plan?* Mahwah, NJ: Erlbaum.

Gao, S., Wang, H., Xu, D., & Wang, Y. (2007). An intelligent agent-assisted decision support system for family financial planning. *Decision Support Systems, 44,* 60–78.

Garling, T., Kirchler, E., Lewis, A., & Van Raaij, F. (2009). Psychology, financial decision making, and financial crises. *Psychological Science in the Public Interest, 10,* 1–47.

Gerrans, P. (2010). Retirement savings investment choices in response to the global financial crisis: Australian evidence. *Social Science Research Network* (posted June 12, 2010). Retrieved from http://papers.ssrn.com/sol3/papers.cfm?abstract_id=1623549

Gerrans, P., Clark-Murphy, M., & Speelman, C. (2006). How much investment choice is enough for members? *Australian Accounting Review, 16,* 14–22.

Gibler, K. M., & Taltavull, P. (2010). Using preferences for international retiree housing market segmentation. *Journal of Property Research, 27,* 221–237

Gilliam, J., Dass, M., Durband, D. B., & Hampton, V. (2010). The role of assertiveness in portfolio risk and financial risk tolerance among married couples. *Journal of Financial Counseling and Planning, 21,* 53–67.

Gilliam, J. E., Goetz, J. W., & Hampton, V. L. (2008). Spousal differences in financial risk tolerance. *Financial Counseling and Planning, 19,* 3–11.

Giuffrida, I. (2001). *Individual development accounts for youth: Lessons from an emerging field.* Washington, DC: Corporation for Enterprise Development. Retrieved from http://cfed.org/assets/pdfs/idas_for_youth.pdf

Glass, J. C., & Kilpatrick, B. B. (1998). Gender comparisons of baby boomers and financial preparation for retirement. *Educational Gerontology, 24,* 719–745.

Grable, J. E., & Joo, S. (2001). A further examination of financial help-seeking behaviour. *Financial Counselling and Planning, 12,* 55–73.

Grable, J. E., & Lytton, R. H. (1999). Financial risk tolerance revisited: The development of a risk assessment instrument. *Financial Services Review, 8,* 163–181.

Grable, J. E., & Roszkowski, M. J. (2008). The influence of mood on the willingness to take financial risks. *Journal of Risk Research, 11,* 905–923.

Gruber, J., & Wise, D. A. (1999). Introduction and summary. In J. Gruber & D. A. Wise (Eds.), *Social security and retirement around the world* (pp. 1–35). Chicago, IL: University of Chicago Press.

Gupta, N. D., & Larsen, M. (2010). The impact of health on individual retirement plans: Self-reported versus diagnostic measures. *Health Economics, 19,* 792–813.

Gutierrez, H. C., Hershey, D. A., & Gerrans, P. (2011). What to do when clients are reluctant to share. *CSA: Certified Senior Advisor, 49,* 39–44.

Hackethal, A., Haliassos, M., & Jappelli, T. (2009). *Financial advisors: A case of babysitters?* (Center for Economic Policy Research Research Paper DP7235). Retrieved from http://www.cepr.org/pubs/new-dps/dplist.asp?dpno=7235

Hariharan, O., Chapman, K. S., & Domian, D. L. (2000). Risk tolerance and asset allocation for investors nearing retirement. *Financial Services Review, 9,* 159–170.

Harrison, T., Waite, K. W., & Hunter, G. L. (2006). The internet, information and empowerment. *European Journal of Marketing, 40,* 972–993.

Hartman, R. S., Doane, M. J., & Woo, C. (1991). Consumer rationality and the status quo. *The Quarterly Journal of Economics, 106,* 141–162.

Hatcher, C. B. (2003). The economics of the retirement decision. In G. A. Adams & T. A. Beehr (Eds.), *Retirement: Reasons, processes, and results* (pp. 136–158). New York, NY: Springer.

Hayslip, B., Bezerlein, M., & Nichols, S. (1997). Assessing anxiety about retirement: The case of academicians. *International Journal of Aging and Human Development, 44,* 15–36.

Helman, R., Copeland, C., & VanDerhei, J. (2010). *The 2010 Retirement Confidence Survey: Confidence stabilizing, but preparations continue to erode* (Issue Brief No. 340). Washington, DC: EBRI.

Helman, R., Copeland, C., & VanDerhei, J. (2011). *The 2011 Retirement Confidence Survey: Confidence Drops to Record Lows, Reflecting "the New Normal"* (Issue Brief No. 355). Washington, DC: EBRI.

Hershey, D. A. (2004). Psychological influences on the retirement investor. *CSA: Certified Senior Advisor, 22,* 31–39.

Hershey, D. A., Brown, C. E., Jacobs-Lawson, J. M., & Jackson, J. (2001). Retirees' perceptions of important retirement planning decisions. *The Southwest Journal on Aging, 16,* 91–100.

Hershey, D. A., Henkens, K., & van Dalen, H. (2010a). What drives retirement income worry in Europe: A multilevel analysis. *European Journal of Aging, 7,* 301–311.

Hershey, D. A., Henkens, K., & van Dalen, H. K. (2010b). Aging and financial planning for retirement: Interdisciplinary influences viewed through a cross-cultural lens. *International Journal of Aging and Human Development, 70,* 1–38.

Hershey, D. A., & Jacobs-Lawson, J. M. (2009). Goals for retirement: Content, structure and process. In R. R. Brougham (Ed.), *New directions in aging research* (pp. 167–186). Hauppauge, NY: Nova Science.

Hershey, D. A., Jacobs-Lawson, J. M., McArdle, J. J., & Hamagami, F. (2007). Psychological foundations of financial planning for retirement. *Journal of Adult Development, 14,* 26–36.

Hershey, D. A., Jacobs-Lawson, J. M., & Walsh, D. A. (2003). Influences of age and training on script development. *Aging, Neuropsychology, and Cognition, 10,* 1–19.

Hershey, D. A., & Mowen, J.C. (2000). Psychological determinants of financial preparedness for retirement. *The Gerontologist, 40,* 687–697.

Hershey, D. A., Mowen, J. C., & Jacobs-Lawson, J. M. (2003). An experimental comparison of retirement planning intervention seminars. *Educational Gerontology, 29,* 339–359.

Hilgert, M., Hogarth, J., & Beverly, S. (2003). Household financial management: The connection between knowledge and behavior. *Federal Reserve Bulletin, 89,* 309–322.

Hira, T. K., Rock, W. L., & Loibl, C. (2009). Determinants of retirement planning behavior and differences by age. *International Journal of Consumer Studies, 33,* 293–301.

Hitlin, S., & Elder, G. H. (2006). Agency: An empirical model of an abstract concept. In F. C. Billari (Ed.), *Advances in life course research* (pp. 33–67). Kidlington Oxford, United Kingdom: Elsevier Science.

Holzmann, R., MacArthur, I. W., & Sin, Y. (2000). *Pension systems in East Asia and the Pacific: Challenges and opportunities.* Washington, DC: The World Bank.

Horn, J. L., & Hofer, S. M. (1992). Major abilities and development in the adult period. In R. J. Sternberg & C. A. Berg (Eds.), *Intellectual development* (pp. 44–99). New York, NY: Cambridge University Press.

Hughes, G., & Stewart, J. (2004). *Reforming pensions in Europe: Evolution of pension financing and sources of retirement income.* Cheltenham, United Kingdom: Elgar.

Institute for Financial Literacy. (2007). *National standards for adult financial literacy education* (2nd ed.). Retrieved from www.financiallit.org/resources/pdf/21.2.1_NationalStandards&Benchmarks_SecondEdFinal.pdf

Jacobs-Lawson, J. M. (2004). Influences of age and investor characteristics on women's retirement investment decisions. *Dissertation Abstracts International: Section B: Sciences and Engineering, 64 (9B),* 4654.

Jacobs-Lawson, J. M., & Hershey, D. A. (2005). Influence of future time perspective, financial knowledge, and financial risk tolerance on retirement savings behaviors. *Financial Services Review, 14,* 331–344.

Jefferson, T. (2009). Women and retirement pensions: A research review. *Feminist Economics, 15,* 115–145.

Jefferson, T., & Preston, A. (2005). Australia's "other" gender wage gap: Baby boomers and compulsory superannuation accounts. *Feminist Economics, 11,* 79–101.

John, D. C. (2011). *The business case for 401(k) automatic enrollment.* Retrieved from http://www.retirementmadesimpler.org/ResourcesAndResearch/BusinessCaseForAuto401ks.shtml

Johnson, E. J., Hershey, J., Meszaros, J., & Kenreuther, H. (2000). Framing, probability distortions, and insurance decisions. In D. Kahaneman & A. Tversky (Eds.), *Choices, values and frames* (pp. 224–240). New York, NY: Cambridge University Press.

Joo, S., & Grable, J. E. (2001). Factors associated with seeking and using professional retirement-planning help. *Family and Consumer Sciences Research Journal, 30,* 37–63.

Joo, S., & Grable, J. E. (2005). Employee education and the likelihood of having a retirement savings program. *Journal of Financial Counseling and Planning, 16,* 37–49.

Jordan, S., & Treisch, C. (2010). The perception of tax concessions in retirement savings decisions. *Qualitative Research in Financial Markets, 2,* 158–184.

Jump$tart Coalition. (2007). *National standards for K-12 personal finance education.* Washington DC: Author.

Jurges, H. (2010). Health inequalities by education, income and wealth: A comparison of 11 European countries and the US. *Applied Economics Letters, 17,* 87–91.

Kahneman, D., Knetsch, J. L. & Thaler, R. H. (1991). Anomalies: The endowment effect, loss aversion, and status quo bias. *Journal of Economic Perspectives, 5,* 193–206.

Kemp, C., Rosenthal, C., & Denton, M. (2005). Planning for later life: Catalysts and constraints. *Journal of Aging Research, 19,* 273–290.

Kim, J., Garman, E. T., & Quach, A. (2005). Workplace financial education participation and retirement savings by employees and their spouses. *Journal of Personal Finance, 4,* 92–108.

Kim, J., Kwon, J., & Anderson, E. A. (2005). Factors related to retirement confidence: Retirement preparation and workplace financial education. *Financial Counseling and Planning, 16,* 77–89.

Kimball, M. S., & Shumway, T. (2010). *Investor sophistication and the home bias, diversification, and employer stock puzzles* (Social Science Research Network Working Paper Series). Retrieved from http://ssrn.com/abstract=1572866

Klein, H. K., Austin, J. T., & Cooper, J. T. (2008). Goal choice and decision processes. In R. Kanfer, G. Chen, & R. Pritchard (Eds.), *Work motivation: Past, present, and future* (pp. 101–150). Abingdon, England: Routledge Academic.

Koonce, J. C., Mimura, Y., Mauldin, T. A., Rupured, A. M., & Jordan, J. (2008). Financial information: Is it related to savings and investing knowledge and financial behavior of teenagers? *Financial Counseling and Planning, 19,* 19–28.

Lai, I. (2010). Leaving it for tomorrow: Retirement products vary widely across Asia, where market demand is especially strong. *Best's Review,* Dec. 1, 2010. Retrieved from http://www.thefreelibrary.com/_/print/PrintArticle.aspx?id=244949309

Lee, W. K. M. (2003). Women and retirement planning: Towards the "feminization of poverty" in an aging Hong Kong. *Journal of Women and Aging, 15,* 31–53.

Lee, W. K. M., & Law, K. W. (2004). Retirement planning and retirement satisfaction: The need for a national retirement program and policy in Hong Kong. *The Journal of Applied Gerontology, 23,* 212–233.

Leetmaa, P., Rennie, H., & Thiry, B. (2009). *Household saving rate higher in the EU than in the USA despite lower income.* Statistics in Focus, 29/2009. Luxembourg: Eurostat.

Lewin, K. (1951/1976). *Field theory in social science: Selected theoretical papers.* Chicago, IL: University of Chicago Press.

Liefbroer, A. C., & Billari, F. C. (2010). Bringing norms back in: A theoretical and empirical discussion of their importance for understanding demographic behaviour. *Population, Space and Place, 16,* 287–305.

Litwin, H., & Sapir, E. V. (2009). Perceived income adequacy among older adults in 12 countries: Findings from the Survey of Health, Ageing, and Retirement in Europe. *The Gerontologist, 49,* 397–406.

Loibl, C., & Hira, T. K. (2006). A workplace and gender-related perspective on financial planning information sources and knowledge outcomes. *Financial Services Review, 15,* 21–42.

Loibl, C., & Hira, T. K. (2009). Investor information search. *Journal of Economic Psychology, 20,* 24–41.

Loix, E., Pepermans, R., Mentens, C., Goedee, M., & Jegers, M. (2005). Orientation toward finances: Development of a measurement scale. *The Journal of Behavioral Finance, 6,* 192–201.

Lum, Y., & Lightfoot, E. (2003). The effect of health on retirement saving among older workers. *Social Work Research, 27,* 31–44.

Lusardi, A. (1999). Information, expectations, and savings for retirement. In H. Aaron (Ed.), *Behavioral dimensions of retirement economics* (pp. 81–115). Washington, DC: Brookings Institution and Russell Sage Foundation.

Lusardi, A. (2001). *Explaining why so many people do not save* (CRR Working Paper Series No. 2001-05). Boston: Center for Retirement Research.

Lusardi, A. (2008). *Household saving behaviour: The role of financial literacy, information, and financial education programs*

(NBER Working Paper No. 13824). Retrieved from http://www.nber.org/papers/w13824

Lusardi, A. (2011). *Americans' financial capability* (Pension Research Council Working Paper No. 2011-02). Retrieved from http://www.pensionresearchcouncil.org/publications/document.php?file=936

Lusardi, A., & Mitchell, O. S. (2006). *Financial literacy and planning: implications for retirement well being* (Working Paper No. WP2006-01). Pension Research Council, The Wharton School. Retrieved from http://www.pensionresearchcouncil.org/publications/document.php?file=6

Lusardi, A., & Mitchell, O. S. (2007). Baby boomer retirement security: The roles of planning, financial literacy, and housing wealth. *Journal of Monetary Economics, 54,* 205–224.

Lusardi, A., & Mitchell, O. S. (2011). *Financial literacy around the world: An overview.* Retrieved from http://www.financialliteracyfocus.org/files/FLatDocs/Lusardi_Mitchell_Overview.pdf

MacCallum, R. A., & Austin, J. T. (2000). Applications of structural equation modeling in psychological research. *Annual Review of Psychology, 51,* 201–226.

MacEwen, K. E., Barling, J., Kelloway, E. K., & Higginbottom, S. F. (1995). Predicting retirement anxiety: The roles of parental socialization and personal planning. *Journal of Social Psychology, 135,* 203–213.

MacFarland, D. M., Marconi, C. D., & Utkus, S. P. (2004). Money attitudes and retirement plan design: One size does not fit all. In O. S. Mitchell & S. P. Utkus (Eds.), *Pension design and structure: New lessons from behavioral finance* (pp. 97–120). Oxford, United Kingdom: Oxford University Press.

Mandell, L. (2008). *The financial literacy of young American adults.* Washington, DC: Jump$tart Coalition.

Massachusetts Mutual Life Insurance Company. (2010). *Save! The game.* Springfield, MA: Author. Available from http://itunes.apple.com/us/app/save-the-game/id360805496?mt=8

McCarthy, J. T. (1996). *Financial planning for a secure retirement* (2nd ed.). Brookfield, WI: International Foundation of Employee Benefit Plans.

McGillivray, W. (2006). Structure and performance of defined benefit schemes. In G. L. Clark, A. H. Munnell, & J. M. Orszag (Eds.), *Pensions and retirement income* (pp. 223–240). New York, NY: Oxford University Press.

Millar, M., & Devonish, D. (2009). Attitudes, savings choices, level of knowledge and investment preferences of employees toward pensions and retirement planning: Survey evidence from Barbados. *Pensions: An International Journal, 14,* 299–317.

Miron-Shatz, T. (2009). "Am I going to be happy and financially stable?": How American women feel when they think about financial security. *Judgment and Decision Making, 4,* 102–112.

Mitchell, T. R., Harman, W. S., Lee, T. W., & Lee, D. Y. (2008). Self regulation and multiple deadline goals. In R. Kanfer, G. Chen, & R. D. Pritchard (Eds.), *Work motivation: Past, present, and future* (pp. 199–232). Mahwah, NJ: CRC Press, for the Society for Industrial and Organizational Psychology.

Mitchell, T. R, Lee, T. W., Lee, D. Y., & Harman, W. S. (2004). Attributions and the action cycle of work. In M. Martinko (Ed.), *,Attribution Theory in the Organizational Sciences: Theoretical and Empirical Contributions* (pp. 25–47). Greenwich, CT: Information Age.

Mock, S. E., & Cornelius, S. W. (2007). Profiles of interdependence: The retirement planning of married, cohabiting, and lesbian couples. *Sex Roles, 56,* 793–800.

Mock, S. E., Taylor, C. J., & Savin-Williams, R. C. (2006). Aging together: The retirement plans of same-sex couples. In D. Kimmel, T. Rose, & D. Steven (Eds.), *Lesbian, gay, bisexual and transgender aging: Research and clinical perspectives* (pp. 152–174). New York, NY: Columbia University Press.

Modigliani, F., & Brumberg R. (1954). Utility analysis and the consumption function: An interpretation of cross-section data. In K. K. Kurihara (Ed.), *Post-Keynesian economics* (pp. 388–436). Piscataway, NJ: Rutgers University Press.

Moen, P., Erickson, W. A., Agarwal, M., Fields, V., & Todd, L. (2000). *The Cornell retirement and well-being study.* Ithaca, NY: Gerontology Research Institute.

Moore, D. A., Kurtzberg, T. R., Fox, C. R., & Bazerman, M. H. (1999). Positive illusions and forecasting errors in mutual fund investment decisions. *Organizational Behavior and Human Decision Processes, 79,* 95–114.

Mottern, A., & Mottern, R. (2006). Choo$e wealth: A choice theory based financial management program. *International Journal of Reality Therapy, 25,* 16–22.

Munnell, A. H. (2006). Employer-sponsored plans: The shift from defined benefit to defined contribution. In G. L. Clark, A. H. Munnell, & J. M. Orszag (Eds.), *Pensions and retirement income* (pp. 359–380). New York, NY: Oxford University Press.

Munnell, A. H., Webb, A., & Golub-Sass, F. (2009). *The national retirement risk index: After the crash.* Chestnut Hill, MA: Center for Retirement Research at Boston College. Retrieved from http://crr.bc.edu/images/stories/Briefs/IB_9–22.pdf

Muratore, A. M., & Earl, J. K. (2010). Predicting retirement preparation through the design of a new measure. *Australian Psychologist, 45,* 98–111.

National Endowment for Financial Education. (2007a). *What's a cross-walk and why is it so important?* Retrieved from http://hsfpp.nefe.org/channels.cfm?chid=64&tid =1&deptid=14

National Endowment for Financial Education. (2007b). *NEFE high school financial planning program.* Retrieved from http://hsfpp.nefe.org/

Nerlove, M., Razin, A., & Sadka, E. (1987). *Household and economy—Welfare economics of endogenous fertility.* New York, NY: Academic Press.

Neukam, K. A., & Hershey, D. A. (2003). Financial inhibition, financial activation, and saving for retirement. *Financial Services Review, 12,* 19–37.

Neymotin, F. (2010). Linking self-esteem with the tendency to engage in financial planning. *Journal of Economic Psychology, 31,* 996–1107.

Nofsinger, J. R. (2001). *Investment madness: How psychology affects your investing … and what to do about it.* Upper Saddle River, NJ: Pearson Education.

Nofsinger, J. R., & Varma, A. (2007). How analytical is your financial advisor? *Financial Services Review, 16,* 245–260.

Noone, J. H., Stephens, C., & Alpass, F. (2010). The process of retirement planning scale (PRePS): Development and validation. *Psychological Assessment, 22,* 520–531.

O'Donoghue, T., & Rabin, M. (1998). Procrastination in preparing for retirement. In H. Arron (Ed.), *Behavioral dimensions of retirement economics* (pp. 125–156). Washington, DC: Brookings Institution Press.

Olson, D. L., & Wiley, P. (2006). Benefits, consumerism, and an "ownership" society. *Benefits Quarterly, 22,* 7–14.

Organisation for Economic Co-operation and Development. (2009). *Pensions at a glance 2009: Retirement income systems in OECD countries*. Paris, France: Author.

Pension Research Council. (2010). *Financial literacy: Implications for retirement security and the financial marketplace* (Working Paper No. 2010–11). Author. Retrieved from http://www.pensionresearchcouncil.org/publications/document.php?file=882

Petkoska, J., & Earl, J. K. (2009). Understanding the influence of demographic and psychological variables on retirement planning. *Psychology and Aging, 24,* 245–251.

Phang, H. S. (2006). Retirement income systems in Asia. In G. L. Clark, A. H. Munnell, & J. M. Orszag (Eds.), *Pensions and retirement income* (pp. 799–815). Oxford, United Kingdom: Oxford University Press.

Phua, V. C., & McNally, J. W. (2008). Men planning for retirement. *Journal of Applied Gerontology, 27,* 588–608.

Price, C. A., & Balaswamy, S. (2009). Beyond health and wealth: Predictors of women's retirement satisfaction. *International Journal of Aging and Human Development, 68,* 195–214.

Pronin, E. (2011). *Overcoming biases to wise investing.* FINRA Investor Education Foundation. Retrieved from http://www.finrafoundation.org/web/groups/foundation/@foundation/documents/foundation/p118416.pdf

Qihua, L., & Jinkook, L. (2004). Consumer information search when making investment decisions. *Financial Services Review, 13,* 319–32.

Queiroz, B. L. (2007). The determinants of male retirement in urban Brazil. *Nova Economia Belo Horizonte, 17,* 11–36.

Roszkowski, M. J., Delaney, M. M., & Cordell, D. M. (2004). The comparability of husbands and wives on financial risk tolerance. *Journal of Personal Finance, 3,* 129–144.

Sabelhaus, J. (1997). Public policy and saving in the United States and Canada. *Canadian Journal of Economics, 30,* 253–275.

Salisbury, D. L. (2008, April 23). Benefit trends: Change is now constant. *The Wall Street Journal,* pp. A11–A12.

Samuelson, W., & Zeckhauser, R. (1988). Status quo bias in decision making. *Journal of Risk and Uncertainty, 1,* 7–59.

Schellenberg, G., Turcotte, M., & Ram, B. (2005). Preparing for retirement. *Canadian Social Trends, 78,* 8–11.

Scherger, S., Nazroo, J., & Higgs, P. (2011). Leisure activities and retirement: Do structures of inequality change in old age? *Ageing and Society, 31,* 146–172.

Schultz, J. H., Rosenman, L., & Rix, S. E. (1999). International developments in social security privatization: What risk to women? *Journal of Cross-Cultural Gerontology, 14,* 25–42.

Shobe, M. A., & Sturm, S. L. (2007). Youth individual development accounts: Retirement planning initiatives. *Children & Schools, 29,* 172–181.

Shultz, K., & Wang, M. (2011). Psychological perspectives on the changing nature of retirement. *American Psychologist, 66,* 170–179.

Schultz, T. W. (1974). Fertility and economic values. In T. W. Schultz (Ed.), *Economics of the family: Marriage, children, and human capital* (pp. 3–22). Cambridge, MA: National Bureau for Economic Research. Retrieved from http://www.nber.org/books/schu74–1

Singh, J., & Sirdeshmukh, D. (2000). Agency and trust mechanisms in consumer satisfaction and loyalty judgments. *Journal of the Academy of Marketing Science, 28,* 150–167.

Smith, B., & Stewart, F. (2008). Learning from the experience of OECD countries: Lessons for policy, programs and evaluations. In A. Lusardi (Ed.), *Overcoming the saving slump: How to increase the effectiveness of financial education and saving programs* (pp. 345–367). Chicago, IL: University of Chicago Press.

Spiegel, P., & Shultz, K. (2003). The influence of preretirement planning and transferability of skills on naval officers' retirement satisfaction and adjustment. *Military Psychology, 15,* 285–307.

Springstead, G. R., & Wilson, T. M. (2000). Participation in voluntary individual savings accounts: An analysis of IRAs, 401(k)s, and the TSP. *Social Security Bulletin, 63,* 34–39.

SPRY Foundation. (2000). *Redefining retirement: Research directions for successful aging among America's diverse seniors.* Washington, DC: Author.

Stawski, R. S., Hershey, D. A., & Jacobs-Lawson, J. M. (2007). Goal clarity and financial planning activities as determinants of retirement savings contributions. *International Journal of Aging and Human Development, 64,* 13–32.

St. John, S. (2007). KiwiSaver and the tax treatment of retirement saving in NZ. *New Zealand Economic Papers, 41,* 251–267.

Sunden, A. B., & Surette, B. J. (1998). Gender differences in the allocation of assets in retirement savings plans. *The American Economic Review, 88,* 207–211.

Sunstein, C., & Thaler, R. (2008). *Nudge: Improving decisions about health, wealth, and happiness.* London, England: Yale University Press.

Taylor, M. A., & Doverspike, D. (2003). Retirement planning and preparation. In G. A. Adams & T. A. Beehr (Eds.), *Retirement: Reasons, processes, and results* (pp. 53–82). New York, NY: Springer.

Taylor, M. A., & Geldhauser, H. A. (2007). Low-income older workers. In K. S. Shultz & G. A. Adams (Eds.), *Aging and work in the 21st century* (pp. 25–49). Mahwah, NJ: Lawrence Erlbaum.

Thaler, R. H., & Benartzi, S. (2007). Save more tomorrow: Using behavioral economics to increase employee saving. In S. Maital (Ed.), *Recent developments in behavioral economics* (pp. 131–154). Cheltenham, United Kingdom: Elgar.

United Kingdom Department for Work and Pensions (UKDWP). (2006). *Second tier pension provision: 1978/79 to 2003/04.* Retrieved from http://www.gov-news.org/gov/uk/news/second_tier_pension_provision_197879_to_200304/50069.html

van Dalen, H. P., Henkens, K., & Hershey, D. A. (2010). Perceptions and expectations of pension savings adequacy: A comparative study of Dutch and American workers. *Ageing & Society, 30,* 731–754.

van Dalen, H. P., & Verbon, H. A. A. (1999). In L. J.G. van Wissen & P. A. Dykstra (Eds.), *Population issues—An interdisciplinary focus* (pp. 123–157). New York, NY: Kluwer Academic/Plenum.

Van Rooij, M., Lusardi, A., & Alessie, R. (2011). Financial literacy and stock market participation. *Journal of Financial Economics, 101,* 449–472.van Solinge, H., & Henkens, K. (2005). Couples' adjustment to retirement: A multi-actor panel study. *The Journals of Gerontology: Psychological Sciences and Social Sciences, 60B,* S11–S20.

van Solinge, H., & Henkens, K. (2007). Involuntary retirement: The role of restrictive circumstances, timing, and social embeddedness. *The Journals of Gerontology: Psychological Sciences and Social Sciences, 62B,* S295–S303.

Varcoe, K. P., Martin, A., Devitto, Z., & Go, C. (2005). Using a financial education curriculum for teens. *Financial Counseling and Planning, 16,* 63–71.

Velladics, K., Henkens, K., & van Dalen, H. P. (2006). Do different welfare states engender different policy preferences? Opinions on pension reforms in Eastern and Western Europe. *Ageing & Society, 26,* 475–495.

Venti, S. F. (2006). Choice, behavior, and retirement saving. In G. L. Clark, A. H. Munnell, & J. M. Orszag (Eds.), *Pensions and retirement income* (pp. 603–617). New York, NY: Oxford University Press.

Venti, S. F., & Wise, D. A. (1991). The saving effect of tax-deferred retirement accounts: Evidence from SIPP. In B. D. Bernheim & J. B. Shoven (Eds.), *National saving and economic performance* (pp. 103–130). Chicago, IL: University of Chicago Press.

Volpe, R. P., Chen, H., & Liu, S. (2006). An analysis of the importance of personal finance topics and the level of knowledge possessed by working adults. *Financial Services Review, 15,* 81–98.

Waine, B. (2006). Ownership and security: Individualised pensions and pension policy in the United Kingdom and the United States. *Competition and Change, 10,* 321–337.

Wang, M., Henkens, K., & van Solinge, H. (2011). Retirement adjustment: A review of theoretical and empirical advancements. *American Psychologist, 66,* 204–213.

Wang, M., & Shultz, K. (2010). Employee retirement: A review and recommendations for future investigation. *Journal of Management, 36,* 172–206.

Wells Fargo. (2009). *Workers fail to save enough for expected retirement lifestyle.* Retrieved from https://www.wellsfargo.com/press/2009/20091105_Retirement

Whitehouse, E. (2007). *Pensions panorama: Retirement-income systems in 53 countries.* Washington, DC: The World Bank.

Whitehouse, E. (2009). Pensions during the crisis: Impact on retirement income systems and policy responses. *The Geneva Papers on Risk and Insurance—Issues and Practice, 34,* 536–547.

Worthington, A. C. (2008). Knowledge and perceptions of superannuation in Australia. *Journal of Consumer Policy, 31,* 349–368.

Yao, R. Gutter, M. S., & Hanna, S. D. (2005). The financial risk tolerance of blacks, Hispanics and whites. *Financial Counseling and Planning, 16,* 51–62.

Zickar, M. J., & Gibby, R. E. (2003). Data analytic techniques for retirement research. In G. A. Adams & T. A. Beehr (Eds), *Retirement: Reasons, processes, and results* (pp. 264–292). New York, NY: Springer.

Zinn, J. O. (2006). Risk, affect, and emotion. *FQS: Forum Qualitative Sozialforschung* [Forum Social Research], *7,* Art. 29. Retrieved from http://www.qualitative-research.net/index.php/fqs/article /view/67/137

Zollo, P. (2003). *Getting wiser to teens: More insights into marketing to teenagers.* Ithaca, NY: New Strategist Publications.

List of Abbreviations

AIM	Affect Infusion Model
DB	Defined Benefit
DC	Defined Contribution
CRRBC	Center for Retirement Research at Boston College
EBRI	Employee Benefits Research Institute
E.U.	European Union
FPR	Financial Planning for Retirement
HC	High Capacity
HRS	Health and Retirement Study
HO	High Opportunity
HW	High Willingness
IDA	Individual Development Accounts
IRA	Individual Retirement Account
LC	Low Capacity
LO	Low Opportunity
LW	Low Willingness
NEFE	National Endowment for Financial Education
OECD	Organisation for Economic Co-operation and Development
TDSA	Tax-Deferred Saving Accounts
U.K.	United Kingdom
U.S.	United States

Recruitment and Retention Strategies for Mature Workers

Jeanette N. Cleveland *and* Sarina M. Maneotis

Abstract

This chapter discusses reasons and methods for retaining older individuals in the workplace and recruiting those who have retired back to the workplace. Characteristics of older workers that organizations should retain and recruit are described. Factors associated with a healthy workplace for older individuals, including generational concerns and organizational culture, are also presented. After the case is made for retaining and recruiting older workers, several example scenarios are presented to make our retention and recruitment strategy implementation concrete. Finally, recommended methods for retention and recruitment are suggested.

Key Words: mature workers, intergenerational recruitment and retention, work flexibility, multi-generational support

To retire or not to retire? Is this the question? Given the conflicting messages that boomers are receiving today, retirement decisions no longer reflect a dichotomous decision: yes or no. Rather, voluntary retirement is becoming an increasingly gradual and varied process. Importantly, the term itself, "retirement," soon may be "retired." Organizations today continue to provide incentives for employees to retire early. Women and men have responded by retiring earlier than they ever have during the last century (women at 63 in the late 1990s versus 65 in the 1960s; men at 74 in 1910 versus 63 in the 1990s) (Committee for Economic Development, 1999). On the other hand, with the combination of increased life expectancy, larger-than-expected expenses, and smaller savings (Alley & Crimmins, 2007), there is a trend, albeit NOT a consistent one, reflecting employed boomers who intend to continue working or, if retired, who are returning or who want to return to work.

There are a number of individual and organizational reasons for retirees to stay in the workplace longer than average or to return to the workplace after retirement. As such, it is of interest to organizations to attract these retirees back to work or, importantly, to be more proactive in retaining mature employees as a valuable human resource. In this chapter, we will first discuss factors associated with retirement versus continued employment. We will then describe the characteristics of retirees that organizations would do well to recruit back into the workforce. Relatedly, we will discuss characteristics of older workers that organizations may want to retain in the workforce (prevent from retiring), if possible. Next, we will summarize the strategies that organizations can use to retain older workers, or recruit those that are already retired. Finally, to make our recommendations more concrete, we will provide several scenarios involving strategies for managing retirement decisions.

Why Do Individuals Retire?

Not all older people want to or are able to continue to work. There are several factors associated with the decision to retire early, including, health, financial and economic situation, work conditions, and personal/family reasons. Each is discussed in depth below.

Health factors. As is well established in the literature, poor health is associated with earlier retirement (e.g., Shultz & Wang, 2007; Taylor & Shore, 1995; Wang & Shultz, 2010); young retirees are much less healthy than their cohorts who decide to remain in the workforce. For example, over half (55%) of retirees age 51–59 indicate that health or impairment limits the amount or type of paid work they can do (National Academy on an Aging Society, 2000). Young retirees are three times more likely to report being in fair to poor health than their working counterparts; workers age 60 and older are twice as likely to report that they are in very good to excellent health (National Academy on an Aging Society, 2000). Over 20% of workers age 55–61 and over 10% of workers age 62–63 left the workforce due to disability or poor health (Uccello, 1998). Although the estimated proportion of Americans with chronic disability has declined to 20%, the actual number of older people living with chronic disabilities has increased. There is considerable racial and ethnic variability in the experience of good health, and population figures describing the incidence of chronic disabilities may not apply equally to all groups (Federal Interagency Forum on Aging-Related Statistics, November, 2004).

Financial and economic factors. Individuals who retire at an earlier age have family income nearly half that of their working counterparts (National Academy on an Aging Society, 2000). They are less satisfied with their financial status than workers the same age and less secure about their financial position in the future. One reason that individuals choosing to retire, and retiring at an earlier age, may be less well-off financially is that retirement may not be a choice at all. That is, there is a portion of workers who are involuntarily forced to leave work before they choose to. Nearly 14% of workers age 55–61 and 10% of workers age 62–63 have been laid off or forced to leave because their business closed. Older workers are often encouraged to leave through financial incentives associated with some pension structures. Approximately 62% of men and 40% of women cited financial incentives as retirement reason.

Workplace factors. Aspects of the work itself can influence the age at which individuals retire. Limited opportunity for growth activities (Beehr, Glazer, Nielson, & Farmer, 2000) and high stress and high workload positions (Wang & Shultz, 2010) are associated with retiring at an earlier age, whereas opportunity for growth activities (Beehr et al., 2000) is associated with staying in the workforce longer. In addition, attitudes about the work can influence retirement decisions. That is, employees who are more committed and satisfied with their work are likely to stay in the workforce (Adams, Prescher, Beehr, & Lepisto, 2002; Taylor & Shore, 1995).

In addition to employees' perspective of the work environment, employers' attitudes matter as well. Some employers perceive (and experience) higher costs for retaining older workers. That is, seniority and other factors may be associated with a higher average total compensation package for older employees. Cost of health insurance for workers age 55–59 can be almost double that of those aged 20–44. Further, some employers have negative perceptions and stereotypes regarding older workers. Indeed, two-thirds of workers age 45–75 report that they have observed or experienced age bias on the job.

While negative attitudes toward older workers exist, some employers simply do not actively consider older workers' recruitment and retention needs as part of their business planning and thus are less likely to maintain an older employee pool. Thus, organizational policy is an additional work factor associated with retirement decisions. Providing health insurance can keep employees from retiring (Beehr et al., 2000) as can the use of performance-enhancing HR policies (Potocnik, Tordera, & Peiro, 2009). Retirement-enhancing policies, on the other hand, are understandably related to earlier retirement (Potocnik et al., 2009). Retirement-enhancing policies will be less effective, however, if there are strong group norms to remain in the organization (Potocnik et al., 2009).

Personal and family factors. Caring for dependents is associated with the timing of retirement (Beehr et al., 2000). Spousal health also impacts retirement, but this varies by gender. Women are more likely to retire if their spouse is in poor health, whereas men are more likely to retire if their spouse is in good health (Talaga & Beehr, 1995). Caregiving responsibilities can interfere with work—among workers age 50 or older, 23% care for a parent, 22% care for a spouse, 21% care for a school-age child, and 8% care for another family member (Parkinson, 2002). As with spousal health, the trends for dependents and retirement decisions differ between men and women. The more dependents men have, the less likely they are to retire, whereas women are more likely to retire as the number of dependents increases

(Talaga & Beehr, 1995). It appears then that as their family's need for care increases (poor spousal health, large number of dependents), women are more likely to retire to help provide such care. Men, on the other hand, are more likely to stay in the workplace under similar conditions. Presumably, they choose to provide financially instead.

Trends. Overall then, factors associated with earlier retirement tend to be negative. Compared to the general population, those who retire between ages 51 and 59 are more likely to be female, white, married, in poorer health, less well-off financially, and less educated (National Academy on an Aging Society, 2000). Workers who retire at age 60 or older, on the other hand, tend to be male, white, married, in better health, better off financially, and possess more education (National Academy on an Aging Society, 2000). As such, early retirees tend to be less healthy, less wealthy, less educated, female, and from jobs with lower skill levels. The population of early retirees includes individuals who have health-related issues and can no longer work, individuals whose families need more care and/or attention, and individuals who want to work a bit longer but either are "right-sized" involuntarily or are out of work in their early to mid-/late 60s and cannot find re-employment. Also, they may be in jobs or occupations where younger talent is less expensive both in terms of salary and benefits/medical expenses or in jobs that have changed or are changing in the way they are performed—often increasing the use of integration of technology like Twitter, Facebook, and instant messaging.

According to retirementjob.com, the number of people who were retired and are now back seeking employment has generally doubled in the last year. There is also a growing number of out-of-work 50+-year-old job seekers who do not consider themselves retired yet are unemployed. A recent MetLife study reported that current workers between 55 and 70 expect to keep working until they are 70, while workers over age 66 expect to work until they are 76. By 2020, the trend is that older people (over 45 years) will account for 36% of the population, with the percentage of Americans 65 years and older tripling since 1900. Importantly, older workers' (over 55 years) participation in the workforce will increase to 20% by 2015 (or 1 in 5) compared to 1 in 6 workers in 2008 (Workplace Flexibilty, 2010).

The Benefits of Retaining Older Workers

There are several reasons for retaining older individuals in the workforce. Broadly, we will classify these reasons into three groups: organizational, individual (employee), and societal. We also discuss barriers preventing older workers from staying in or returning to the workplace.

Organizational benefits. There is an apparent, pending labor force shortage that may create both interest in and pressures on older workers to remain in workplace. The rate of the civilian workforce growth is projected to decline by approximately 50% in the first half of this century. Retiring baby boomers may lead to a labor shortage of approximately 10 million workers by the end of this decade. Also, older workers make up an increasing proportion of managers, supervisors, and executives with vital experience and knowledge (U.S. General Accounting Office, 2001).

Employee benefits. Many older individuals want or need to continue working. Work has a positive influence on quality of life, providing a sense of continued usefulness and promoting a sense of better physical and mental well-being (Diener, Sug, Lucas, & Smith, 1999). Employees should not be forced to retire if they wish to remain in the workforce. Forced retirement is negatively related to retirement satisfaction (van Solinge & Henkins, 2008), as is retiring earlier than expected (Quick & Moen, 1998). However, working post-retirement is positively associated with retirement satisfaction (Quick & Moen, 1998) and psychological well-being (Wang, 2007). Additionally, retiring early is negatively associated with psychological well-being shortly following retirement; however, this negative trend does seem to reverse itself over time (van Solinge & Henkins, 2008). Continuity explains why remaining in the workforce has a positive impact on employees. Having a stable environment, physically and socially, is important to maintaining physical and psychological health (Atchley, 1989).

Economically, most people over age 45 know (or indicate) that they need to work at least part-time in retirement for financial reasons. Declines in benefit pension plans and overall pension rates slowdowns, as well as market uncertainty with defined contribution plans, increase economic uncertainty. Importantly, over one-third of workers aged 45–54 and 25% of workers age 55–64 indicate that they have not saved money for retirement on a regular basis (Workplace Flexibility, 2010).

Societal. It has been suggested that retaining older workers in United States will help to ease pressures on Social Security, finance health care, and assuage the projected labor shortage (Walker, 2007). Further, older workers have experience (Jex,

Wang, & Zarubin, 2007) and skills from which society can benefit (Brandon, 2009). Older workers also serve critically important mentoring functions in organizations, helping newer (and typically younger) workers to adjust to the demands and the realities of the workplace.

Barriers. Despite the fact that older workers display a number of more desirable work behaviors, such as organizational citizenship behaviors, safety behaviors, and fewer counterproductive behaviors than younger workers (Ng & Feldman, 2008), there are often persistent stereotypes that older workers are less desirable employees and colleagues. Referred to as ageism, some individuals and organizations systematically stereotype and discriminate against older workers. Dennis and Thomas (2007) report 16,585 age-bias complaints to the EEOC in 2005. These beliefs in turn impact behavior. Indeed, a selection study by Bendick and colleagues (Bendick, Brown, & Wall, 1999) found that, all things equal, an older applicant (age 57 compared to age 32) received lower ratings from study participants. Negative attitudes toward older workers can also foster a negative climate such that older workers may feel pressured to leave the workplace (Potocnik et al., 2009).

In addition to negative attitudes, older workers may also have other personal and health factors that younger workers do not. For example, older workers may have an ailing spouse to tend to while not at work. Younger workers may have no spouse at all. This not only puts a financial and psychological strain on an older worker, but also makes health care packages more important than they might be for a younger worker. Further, due to demands such as spousal illness, flextime may also be more important to an older worker. As such, organizations that do not offer health care packages and flexible working options may make for a difficult place for an older worker to remain and could turn off an older applicant from applying.

In summary, then, there are competing forces to facilitate organizations to both encourage mature workers to exit the workforce as well as to recruit and retain them. The basis for encouraging older workers to retire early is largely financial (e.g., older workers tend to make more money and have high health care costs) and based on mostly inaccurate age stereotypes (e.g., that older workers are lower performers, do not keep up to date, and so forth). However, the basis for older worker retention and recruitment are multifaceted and varied, reflecting individual employee, organizational and societal benefits.

Recruitment and Retention of Mature Workers

Do organizations really value the knowledge and experience of mature workers? A number of studies by the Society for Human Resource Management, the National Older Worker Career Center, and the Committee for Economic Development indicate that 59% of employers do not recruit older workers, 65% of employers have no retention practices, and 71% of employers have no specific provisions or benefits for older workers (SHRM Survey Program, 2003). Nevertheless, demographic realities suggest that organizations will increasingly be asked to consider mature applicants when filling key jobs. One question is how to best attract and retain these applicants. Table 27.1 lists a number of strategies that have been identified as potential methods for attracting and retaining high-quality older workers.

In this section, we discuss recruitment and retention practices and policies and the organizational support for these programs that is needed to enhance mature worker participation. The formal human resources (HR) practices of recruitment and retention (e.g., job sharing, flexible work hours and schedules, training, and so forth) are critical yet not sufficient for successful recruitment and retention of mature workers. That is, these important practices must be in place and available to mature workers (and those recently retired), yet the mere presence does not guarantee that employees/potential employees will know or utilize them. Drawing from the work and family literature (e.g., Allen, 2001), there must be broader and informal support

Table 27.1 Recruitment and Retention Strategies for Older Workers

Recruitment	Retention
Employee referrals	Comprehensive benefits packages
Collaboration with community peers	Phased or modified retirement
Recruitment from volunteer jobs	Job flexibility
Formal recruitment programs	Other workplace accommodations
Tapping into retiree associations	Professional growth and development among businesses
Placement agencies focused on seniors	

within the organization for these programs, including supervisor (leader) and coworker support as well as a mature or age-friendly organizational culture. Therefore, in this section, we also address the importance of both informal micro- and macro-support in the form of supervisor/coworker support and age-friendly organizational culture. Table 27.2 identifies a number of characteristics of organizations that, when paired with formal programs for increasing the recruitment and retention of older workers, can serve to support these organizational efforts.

Recruiting

The organizations that have been successful in recruitment/retention of older workers state that the emphasis on older workers is sometimes informal or even unintended. The major goal of recruitment, in general, is to broaden and increase the pool of qualified applicants and employees, and increasing attention to older applicants can be a side effect of broader efforts to improve the breadth and depth of the pools. The employee referral or word-of-mouth appears to be an especially effective way that companies recruit older workers. Satisfied current employees often pass on their positive experiences to their personal connections, and this often results in good matches between new employees and the organizational culture. More formal recruiting methods may target community organizations that comprise a higher proportion of the older population, including AARP, Offices on Aging in local cities, volunteer agencies, retirement agencies, and placement agencies specializing on older workers. These recruitment strategies, although emphasizing older workers, are similar to strategies used to recruit many other diverse groups, e.g., women, specific ethnic groups, new graduates, and so forth. The effectiveness of any of these strategies is likely to depend on the extent to which organizations are open to and interested in attracting older applicants. That is, organizations that fail to provide visible support for hiring older applicants are unlikely to succeed in the end in attracting high-quality older applicants.

Retention

The good news for employers who want to BEGIN to actively retain and develop their older workforce is that many strategies used by organizations to retain older workers are universal in nature—available and useful for all employees or potential employees. Virtually all structured

Table 27.2 Components of a Worker-Supportive Cultural Context

Component	Description
Strong values	Values that provided framework for developing/implementing practices that fully support worker
Multilevel decision and loyalty	Sense of partnership among employees within the organization
A sense that employees were valued	Respect, caring, and recognition for performance
Open communication	Employees can communicate with managers and leadership to express views/positions and ensure they were heard.
Independence and autonomy	Provided freedom and autonomy to perform work roles, leading to high job satisfaction among older workers
Opportunities for socialization and community involvement	Informal social time to allow relationships to develop that lead to enhanced teamwork, productively, and morale
Teamwork	Organizational respondents referred to being part of a larger team with superordinate or comment goals or business-related problems.
A low-pressure and relaxed atmosphere	Organizational respondents described this type as being a good fit and matching needs/desires of older workers.
Multigenerational issues	Employers were aware of and just starting to understand age stereotypes among older and younger works and to consider generational diversity when older and younger employees work together.

retention initiatives or practices revolve around increasing the perception that targeted employees are employed in "good jobs." However, precisely defining a "good job" is not an easy task (Schmitt, 2005). Financially, good jobs offer decent pay, employer-paid health insurance, and a pension. Yet in 2004, only 25.2% of American workers had a job that met each of these three criteria. Arguably, our economy has not created or maintained large numbers of "good jobs" in thirty years. After controlling for improvement in the "human capital" of the U.S. workforce (e.g., workers today are on average older and much better educated than they were in the late 1970s), the economy today appears to create 25%–30% FEWER good jobs than it did 25–30 years ago. Even this may be an overly positive statement: declines in both the quality of many employer-provided health insurance plans and the quality of pension plans are not reflected in these numbers. It may seem obvious or trite, but organizations that care about attracting and retaining good workers will be more likely to succeed if they offer good jobs.

Job and work flexibility. A retention practice that continually emerges as important for all workers is job flexibility. Indeed, flexibility is one of the ways an organization can concretely indicate its willingness to support and accommodate the needs of older workers. This can mean adjustment in employees' work schedule and responsibilities to meet worker needs and encourage older workers to remain on the job. There are many methods to enhance flexibility and retention through telecommuting, compressed schedules, job-sharing situations, and part-time and seasonal employment. Further, allowing workers to retrain into other positions or modify their roles to address changing needs and preferences is motivating. These job flex modifications result in a more specific retention strategy use—that of professional growth and development opportunities.

According to Feldblum, co-director of Workplace Flexibility 2010, in testimony to the Special Committee on Aging (2008), workplace flexibility should be a national priority. Flexible work arrangement is defined as having three categories: (1) flexibility in the scheduling of hours worked, such as alternative work schedules (e.g., flextime, compressed workweeks, and nontraditional start and end times); (2) flexibility in the number of hours worked, such as part-time, job shares, and phased retirement or part-year work; and (3) flexibility in the place of work, such as working at home, at a satellite location, or at different locations. Each of

these are intended to change the time and/or place that work is conducted in such a way that makes it as manageable and predictable as possible for both employees and employers. By demonstrating a willingness to move beyond rigid employment schedules and arrangements, organizations can give credible and concrete evidence of their support for older workers.

Organizational factors that impact retired job seekers include flexible scheduling, opportunities to mentor, and including an EEO policy in job ads (Rau & Adams, 2005). Opportunities to mentor and EEO policy seem slightly less important but, taken with flexible opportunities, produce the most appeal to older workers in one study (Rau & Adams, 2005). Indeed, most older workers do not find the traditional 8–5, five-days-a-week job to be ideal and prefer flexible options (Sloan Center, 2009). Older workers juggle many roles, and it is important for these roles to be considered by the organization not only during recruitment, but also throughout the employment process as well (Wickham & Parker, 2007). That is, organizations must not forget about older workers' (or any worker for that matter) other obligations once hired.

Workplace flexibility is not new, and older workers indicate that it would help them remain in the workplace. In fact, flexible worker arrangement and other nonmonetary characteristics of work may be more important than wages to many older workers. Mature workers indicate a desire for alternative schedules, shorter hours, and longer vacations. More than one-third of mature workers indicated reduced working hours as the most attractive feature of a phased retirement option. Some innovation in the workplace is slowly evolving—public employers have developed innovative phased retirement plans, and public employers have more across-the-board flexible work options that can benefit older workers. AARP and others have identified private business innovations focused on flexibility for older workers, including re-training, job transition support, career path redesign, and part-time and job-sharing opportunities. However, many of these innovations are implemented informally, as few organizations have formal written policies (Hutchens, 2003).

Many older individuals are either continuing to work or seeking employment to continue/supplement their income, access health insurance (or other employer-sponsored benefits), or engage in meaningful work. Strategies that businesses in some states (e.g., Minnesota) have implemented to increase the retention and productivity of experienced workers include flexible work arrangement (both in terms of hours and work location), continuing skill development (updating skills or learning new ones), health and safety measures to accommodate changes in the physical ability of older workers (ergonomics), support for caregiver workers (because half of all workers will be caring for an older relative by 2010), customized compensation and benefits for all generations in the workplace, and an organizational climate to bridge among generations so the vital organizational knowledge is transmitted. In Minnesota, for example, effective recruiting strategies include hosting open houses targeted especially to older workers in the community, presenting at senior centers, or co-sponsoring career fairs for older workers in other community organizations (Knatterud, 2007).

Training. According to Spokus (2008), training is vital. Seven basic prerequisites for training older workers include motivation, structure, familiarity, organization, time, active participation, and learning strategies (Sterns & Doverspike, 1989). In addition, it is important to examine the job and work areas for possible design modifications. These may include redesigning the workstation to facilitate the physical needs and strengths of older workers; installing adjustable light sources to enhance selected areas; providing lift aids; providing rest periods; avoiding rapid, awkward, and repetitive actions; and providing foot traction. As you will notice, all of these suggestions are beneficial for the safety of older workers and for the well-being of all employees (Rothwell, Sterns, Spokus, & Reaser, 2008).

Bridge employment. Given that an organization recognizes the value of older workers and wishes to recruit them to the company, there are certain populations that can be focused on with more success than recruitment based on age alone. For example, retirees who are more likely to accept bridge employment are healthy, have job satisfaction, and are more educated (Wang, Zhan, Liu, & Shultz, 2008). Therefore, resources would be best directed at older workers who also possess these qualities. The older the retiree is, the less likely he or she will be to accept work. Also less likely are those with a higher degree of wealth or job stress, and those who had more retirement planning prior to retirement (Wang et al., 2008). Further, those who had a longer organizational tenure are more likely to accept bridge employment (Kim & Feldman, 2000). Retirees with working spouses and dependents have also been shown to be more likely to return to work (Kim & Feldman, 2000).

Beyond general tendencies to return to work, some retirees will be more inclined to return to the same field of work than others. Those more amenable to returning to the same field tend to be wealthier, have less job stress and more job satisfaction (Wang et al., 2008), have more job skills, and are retired from careers that are high in motivating job characteristics (Gobeski & Beehr, 2009). Labor-intensive fields can expect their retirees to return to work in different fields (Gobeski & Beehr, 2009).

Context for Best Practices in Recruitment and Retention: Develop and Multi-source Support for Mature Workers

The National Center on Workforce Development/Adult (NCWD/A), funded by the U.S. Department of Labor's Office of Disability Employment Policy (ODEP), examined practices and strategies by U.S. companies seeking to recruit and retain older workers. A number of themes emerged from phone conversations with employees at 18 companies across 13 states that reflect the motivational factors that contributed to companies targeting older workers, the cultural context of businesses that implement these practices, and the range of recruitment and retention practices and initiatives that they utilized.

First, several themes emerged that provided the impetus for these organizations to develop recruitment and retention strategies. These organizations actively examined both internal and external demographics. That is, in addition to overall labor force changes, the organizations tracked and were responsive to the demographics within their organization. These organizations developed initiatives targeting older workers yet implemented them as part of wider initiative around diversity and inclusion with the goal of improved work lives for all employees. Second, these employers perceived older workers as better workers. The organizations valued and included reliability, long-term commitment to the company, and strong work ethic as traits held by older workers. Relatedly, these employers emphasized a multigenerational workforce. Such diversity reflected variations and complementary strengths, creating potential for mutual learning and ultimately greater understanding across age groups. Organizations that valued older workers for their expertise and knowledge devised innovative approaches to retaining that knowledge base with attractive accommodations or by luring mature experts back into a working relationship.

Organizational Culture

As with the family-friendly organizational culture, the organizational climate of the companies provided the context for the recruitment and retention strategies in these organizations for older workers. These organizations found that older workers were well suited for positions because of the company's atmosphere, the type of jobs available, or the skills and attributes being sought. There was a "good fit" with the job and the organizational culture. The employers believed that hiring and retaining older workers made good business sense, noting that it solved a corporate problem (such as high turnover or low commitment) or broadened the company's market potential. These organizations were less inclined to state that they recruited older workers only because "it was the morally right thing to do."

Many of the characteristics of these organizations as listed in Table 27.2 reflect a productive and healthy organizational culture that is positive for ALL employees and not only older workers, including, for example, open communication, valuing independence and autonomy, teamwork, and low-pressure and relaxed atmosphere (as opposed to highly competitive and individualistic). The key feature throughout the context was that these organizations held strong values to fully support workers or their human capital.

Multi-age Generational Supportive Work Environments: Availability of Recruitment/Retention Programs and Managerial Support

Organizational climate is defined as the shared perception of formal and informal organizational policies, practices, and procedures (Reichers & Schneider, 1990; Schneider, 2000). It is what people see and report happening to them in organizations, and thus its focus is on the situation and its link to perceptions, feelings, and behaviors, or behavioral patterns of the employees. Organizational climate is more behaviorally oriented than organizational culture such that climates for creativity, safety, work-family, multi-age, or generational support may be found in the workplace (Schneider, 2000). These climates represent the specific patterns of interactions and behaviors that support multigenerational understanding and support in the organization.

There is evidence that supportive work environments affect many employee outcomes, including work, family, and health (Allen, 2001; Berg, Kalleberg, & Applebaum, 2003; Breaugh & Frye, 2007; Wang & Walumbwa, 2007). Supportive environments are characterized by the existence of a range and choice of human resource programs (Thomas & Ganster, 1995; Frye & Breaugh, 2004; Wang & Walumbwa, 2007) and managers who are supportive of employees' concerns (Breaugh & Frye, 2008; Lapierre et al., 2008; Thomas & Ganster, 1995; Thompson, Jahn, Kopelman, & Prottas, 2004). Such practices—for example, family-friendly or age-friendly programs—are designed to decrease the conflict that employees experience within work and non-work demands. With less conflict, it is expected that employees will report improved work attitudes and behaviors on the job and the organization will be more successful in the recruitment and retention of qualified employees (Allen, 2001; Kossek & Ozek, 1998).

Employee perceptions regarding the supportiveness of their organization are related to intentions to leave the organization (Anderson et al., 2002; Allen, 2001; Thompson, Beauvais, & Lyness, 1999). Employees who perceive their organization to be more supportive report greater job satisfaction (Anderson et al., 2002; Thomas & Ganster, 1995) and organizational commitment (Bragger, Rodriguez-Srednicki, Kutcher, Indovino, & Rosner, 2005) than those who see their organization as less supportive. Employee perceptions of organizational support for life off the job contribute to the positive effect of family-friendly benefits offered by the organization. Supportive supervisors directly and indirectly influence employee job attitudes, job satisfaction, and organizational commitment (Allen, 2001). Anderson et al. (2002) reported that managerial support directly affected job satisfaction and absenteeism.

Although recent research indicates that the mere presence or availability of human resource policies and programs is related to higher perceptions of organizational performance (Perry-Smith & Blum, 2000) and greater market values for these organizations (Arthur, 2003), empirical research on employees' actual use of such programs (e.g., work-life programs) is limited (Hammer, Cullen, & Shafiro, 2006). The little research available on the utilization or uptake suggests conflicting findings (e.g., Hammer et al., 2005). The conflicting findings regarding utilization suggest that there are probably many moderator and mediator variables that influence the actual effectiveness of such formal organization-sponsored supports (Hammer et al., 2006). One such moderator or mediator of the relationship between the number of age-supportive programs available and employee perceptions of acceptance and respect within the workplace is the multifaceted construct of organizational climate as it relates to multiage generation supportiveness. For example, even when formal policies and programs are in place, "corporate culture may either enhance or thwart development and effectiveness of the practice" (Starrels, 1992, p. 261). Just as other aspects of the organization's culture have been shown to influence employees' attitudes about the organization (e.g., Trice & Beyer, 1993), employee perceptions about age-friendly climates may influence their beliefs and decisions about whether or not to engage in multiage generational recruitment and retention programs.

Managerial or leader support. Leaders play a strong role in the experiences of followers, especially in helping to shape their work attitudes. The influence of leaders on follower job attitudes is well documented. For example, transformational leadership affects followers' commitment through a shared vision, identification with the leader, and meaning-making (Bass, 1995). Similarly, meta-analytic evidence supports the relationship between leader-member exchange and organizational commitment and turnover intentions (Gerstner & Day, 1997). This work focuses on behaviors of the leader in the work role, but non-work aspects of leaders may also play a role in shaping follower attitudes. To date, the effect of leaders' personal experiences on followers has received little empirical investigation. There are several reasons why leaders' family experiences, such as being a parent or their perceptions of how work positively or negatively affects their own family life, may affect followers' job attitudes.

First, leaders play a significant role in the development of organizational climate, including work-family climate and potentially, by extension, multiage friendly climate. Schein (1983, 1990) suggests that leaders are critical in the emergence, development, and ongoing management of organizational climate. Leaders send cues or messages to employees about the climate of the organization by what they pay attention to, how they react to critical incidents, their style as role models and coaches, and the criteria with which they reward performance. A leader may support employees' balance of work and life, reward healthy behaviors, and model a balanced lifestyle. A leader who models related behavior will likely be more successful at promoting a certain climate because his or her actions have high symbolic value. For example, a leader who has children, cares for elderly parents, and demonstrates a strong personal value for family may promote a work-family

supportive climate. Alternatively, a leader for whom work has detrimental influences on his or her own family situation may see this situation as normative and not be inclined to facilitate the work-family interface for others.

As noted by Allen (2001), widely used measures of work-family culture (e.g., Thompson et al., 1999) do not always distinguish manager support from organizational support (see, however, Allen, 2001), although there is evidence that support from managers is related to but not identical to support from the organization. The extent to which employees perceive the organization to be supportive of their work and non-work needs and demands is an important factor in how employees experience work-life balance (Hammer, Neal, Newson, Brockwood, & Colton, 2005). Recent research suggests that a supportive work climate is one means by which organizations can make it easier for employees to balance diverse age generation interactions, work, and family demands (Allen, 2001; Thomas & Ganster, 1995; Thompson et al., 1999; Thompson et al., 2004). Allen (2001) found it was important to disentangle employee perceptions of managerial or leader support from perceptions of organizational support or generally a climate where employees are encouraged to utilize retention policies and programs (Allen, 2001; Carr, Schmidt, Ford, & DeShon, 2003; Thompson et al., 1999; Warren & Johnson, 1995; Wise, 2005). Specifically, both supervisors and members of key organizational units (e.g., HR department/manager) may subvert or enhance them by, for example, refusing to encourage or allow employees to participate in them or by implementing them inconsistently (Starrels, 1992).

Intergenerational Considerations: Supportive Coworkers and Mentoring

Social support is of general psychological and sociological interest because its absence can erode well-being and its presence can help people avoid or manage stress (Cohen & Wills, 1985). Social support has particular relevance to industrial/organizational behavior research as a variable affecting employee well-being in the workplace. Social support can be defined as "an interpersonal transaction that involves emotional concern, instrumental aid, information or appraisal" (Carlson & Perrewé, 1999, p. 514). Karasek and Theorell (1990, p. 69) make specific reference to the role of coworkers and supervisors when they define social support in the work context as "overall levels of helpful interaction available on the job from both coworkers and supervisors." The social support and work-family literature has tended to explore either global family-supportive culture dimensions or supervisory support. Wallace (2005) warns of the danger of employing global measures because they may mask the effects of alternative sources of support. Specifically, one neglected dimension of social support is coworker support.

Wills and Shinar's (2000) review of the social support literature generated five dimensions of social support, including social comparison support (information about the appropriateness of behavior); companionship support (friendship and affiliation); informational support (advice regarding resources and courses of action); instrumental support (various types of tangible support others can provide); and emotional or affective support (raising perceptions of self-worth and self-esteem). It is instrumental support as a form of social support that is of interest in the current situation since it refers to assistance with meeting role demands that solves practical problems (Semmer, Elfering, Jacobshagen, Perrot, Beehr, & Boos, 2008).

Support from the work (and family) domains can be formal and informal (Behson, 2005). Formal work supports include temporal and locational flexibility as well as access to various aging-oriented policies and programs. Informal support from work includes supervisory support, coworker support, and the age (or multigeneration) friendliness of the organizational culture (Thompson & Pottras, 2005). Highlighting the importance of informal support for employees (for example, balancing work and family), Thompson et al. (2004, p. 558) report that "it is not tangible policies or practices, per se, that affect an employee's attitudes and intentions. Instead, the more intangible aspects of an organization's culture, including support from the employee's supervisor and the organization's ability to communicate respect for employees' non-work lives [affect work-family outcomes]." Coworker support then is an important intangible and informal dimension of an organization's culture impacting the employee experience of work.

Enhanced social support likely results in employees being better able to perform and feeling more satisfied with all aspects of their life (Marcinkus, Whelan-Berry, & Gordon, 2007). A number of studies report the positive influence of coworker support on various individual well-being variables in the workplace. Research exploring stress among police officers generally reports that peer and coworker support buffers the effects of stress related to police work (He, Zhao, & Archbold, 2002; Morris, Shinn, & DuMont, 1999). Marcinkus et al. (2007) argue that peers and colleagues are sources of social support that help relieve occupational stress and reduce turnover. Ducharme and Martin (2000) report that the social support received from colleagues enhances employee job satisfaction. According to Berman, West, and Richter (2002, p. 217), supportive coworker relationships can also "reduce workplace stress, increase communication, help employees and managers accomplish their tasks, and assist in the process of accepting organizational change." Wallace's (2005) study of lawyers' job stress reports that coworker support functions as a moderator of lawyers' job demands and has both buffering and amplifying effects.

Given the evidence that coworker support influences a broad array of individual well-being outcomes, it is important to explore the impact that coworker support has on work and family outcomes among older workers. In the work and family research arena, for example, there is evidence that support from work colleagues influences the utilization of certain work-family arrangements. Yap and Tng (1990) report that employees who perceived their supervisors and work colleagues as supportive were more likely to use telecommuting. Lingard and Francis (2006), in their study of construction workers, report that social support from one's coworkers and supervisor is also very important in the prevention of job burnout. They go on to report that practical support from both coworkers and supervisors moderated the relationship between work-to-family conflict (WFC) and emotional exhaustion. Thus, when employees experience practical support from their coworkers and/or their supervisors, the relationship between WFC and emotional exhaustion is significantly weaker than when practical support is lacking.

Cleveland, McCarty, and Jones (2006) found that support from colleagues is important for employees, regardless of the level of managerial support, regardless of marital status (married/partnered or single), and particularly in jobs with high demands and with lower levels of managerial support. Employees who reported more coworker support indicated less work-to-family conflict, higher satisfaction with their jobs, and less intent to leave their positions. Perhaps most important is the finding that such support also led to higher overall family satisfaction, especially for those employees experiencing the highest job demands. Therefore, while the majority of research on the effects of support in the workplace concentrate on that of one's manager/supervisor, McCarthy et al.'s findings underscore the importance of examining the support received from one's colleague(s) when it comes to both work and life outcomes, indicating importance to both individuals and their organizations.

Hammer, Saksvik, Nytro, Torvatn, and Bayazit (2004) review the importance of workplace norms and emphasize the importance of unwritten, informal, and taken-for-granted beliefs about how people should think and behave for determining and governing acceptable behavior in the workplace. It is common that these norms and habits develop over time without attention from management. Over time, these norms and attitudes can become quite influential in informal employee behavior. The norms, attitudes, and habits that are developed around coworker support for work and family are, therefore, imperative in managing work and age issues. Organizations should take stock of the prevailing age attitudes among coworkers. If these norms are contrary to organizational policy or counterproductive in enabling employees to balance work and age domains, action should be taken to address this situation. Ensuring that a diversity policy exists would be useful in the first instance. An intervention that might be appropriate for changing attitudes would include offering training programs aimed at increasing awareness of an age policy (where it exists), developing productive and constructive communication skills, and highlighting the inevitable and positive influence of diversity at work, which includes age and generational diversity.

Intergenerational coworker support: Age fabric of support. Different generations of workers have different needs, interests, skills, and resources. The type of organizational support optimal for recruiting and retaining valued workers is likely to vary as a function of both who is receiving this support and who is offering it. In order to attract and retain the best and most qualified employees, an organization must develop a healthy organizational climate for all its members, especially for employees as they age. To maximize the effectiveness of HR practices described previously, employees must perceive that they will continue to be rewarded and valued should they choose to explore alternative work arrangements like job sharing, reduced hours, job redesign, or phased retirement. Central features of an age-generation friendly organizational climate are both supervisory and coworker support; the latter, in our view, is critical. For many seniors or mature people, updating, learning, and performing most effectively require positive peer understanding, interactions, and support. Coworkers provide both the context and the fabric of the workplace. It is important to understand, then, the characteristics, needs, and motivations of the multiple generations of employees in the workplace in order to develop and shape an age-generation supportive organizational climate.

There are four generations of American employees currently in the workplace, presenting more age diversity than ever before (Erickson, 2008). Much of this chapter has targeted boomers in terms of the recruitment and retention strategies because this group is a very large proportion of the workforce, and they are entering retirement eligibility. However, to maximize the effectiveness of these practices, organizations should address not only the needs of older workers themselves but the links among older workers, middle-age workers (Gen X), and the youngest of workers (Gen Y).

Traditionalists (born between 1928 and 1945), known as the WWII generation, spent their teens in the hustle/bustle of post-war and continue to work in organizations. Many are the parents of the baby boomers. They shaped the policies and procedures that govern organizations today. Understanding the traditionalists can show how corporate life is based on traditional preferences rather than on any operational constraint—and therefore is able to be modified or changed. Traditionalists likely believed that world was going in the right direction. Many were high in optimism and likely to see the world as filled with much personal opportunity. The traditionalists' views of world would most likely result in them wanting to join in and be active contributors (Erickson, 2008).

Baby Boomers, or simply boomers, (born between 1946 and 1964) are the largest proportion of the current population and workplace. Boomers have not really influenced how the corporate world is run (Erickson, 2008). To boomers, traditionalists look rule-bound and likely motivated by security and financial reward (that leads to security). Boomers are idealistic, with a commitment to contributing to goals beyond oneself and one's family. They perceived that the world was not working well and were skeptical and mistrustful of authority. Boomers believed that to change this, the world required one to get personally involved.

They want to make a difference in world and are motivated to do something meaningful. Boomers are also competitive and continue to work more hours than any other working age group, with an average of 45.1 hours per week compared to 44.8 hours among Gen Xers, 43.5 among traditionalists, and 41.1 among Gen Yers. Boomers prefer the world to perform on a merit-based system and use money and position as markers of success (similar to traditionalists). Boomers like financial reward because it signals winning or competitiveness (rather than success). Because it is still run in ways consistent with traditionalists' view, the corporate world may not be well suited to meet the needs of boomers or the generations to follow (X and Y).

Generation Xers (born between 1965 and 1980) are much smaller in population size than boomers. They likely will have lots of influence in shaping the work and social policies that affect boomers' lives, and they may not be overly eager to step into boomer roles in the same way. Gen Xers' assumptions about the world reflect a need for self-reliance and the ability to take care of oneself. They are reluctant to relocate away from their "tribe"/family. As employees, they question whether their current job is still the best opportunity. Gen Xers must be convinced or "re-recruited" every day to feel more secure and possibly committed to an organization that potentially may decide to downsize at any time. They may look less committed to work and may look like they work less. This perception could be a source of frustration to boomer coworkers. To boomers, Gen Xers may appear cynical, disloyal, and unwilling to accept challenge and responsibility, reflecting a slacker image. However, this may reflect the Gen Xers' need to keep as many work options open as possible.

Gen Xers grew up with Internet, so keeping up with changes in technology is more comfortable, and they are able to access a wide variety of information. They have caused boomers to change their style of interacting/communicating to nonwritten form via the internet (e.g., Facebook, etc.). Boomers and Gen Xers may conflict, as the latter see rules as interesting but not set in stone and are accustomed to changing them, especially if they do not make sense. Holding on to outdated or inapplicable rules because it might set bad precedence does not make sense to Gen Xers. They expect to be treated individually, for example, by organizations allowing flexible schedules or other reasonable accommodations to meet their individual needs. Gen Xers do not equate physical appearance (particularly work-appropriate appearance) with competence or motivation, as do the boomers.

To Gen Xers, boomers represent a continual dilemma or obstacle, as boomers hold the vast majority of the "good jobs" and appear to limit Gen Xers' economic opportunities or flexibility. Further, Gen Xers may somewhat resent boomers' custodial role of environment or national debt. This may result in conflict over entitlement benefits (as in Gen Xers paying boomers' pensions or social security) and less talent across Gen Xers.

As teens, many Generation Xers lived in single-parent homes and observed an increase in unemployment and the disappearance of the notion of "lifetime employment." Gen Xers may perceive that the adults in their lives were being abandoned by organizations upon which they depended. This is the single most widely shared experience of this generation.

Generation Yers, or the millennials (born after 1980), will be the largest consumer and employee group in the history of the United States—70 million. Gen Yers are the children of boomers, and many are the upbeat siblings of Gen Xers. They will influence the options of boomers just by their sheer size. However, they are not a fully formed generation, as their behaviors, especially in the workplace, are not well known or tracked yet. A sense of impatience and immediacy is the single most salient characteristic of Gen Yers, reflected in the belief in living life to its fullest now. They are multitaskers with the simultaneous use of cell phones, text messaging, music downloads, instant messaging, and gaming. Gen Yers are not stressed by technology as are many boomers. A number of Gen Yers are considered "nonlinear thinkers," where most corporate processes seem inefficient to them.

Global warming and natural disasters are prominent influences shaping Gen Yers' environmental concerns. Technology is influential, especially as a communication tool, because Gen Yers have never known a world that is not wired. Gen Yers have always had working mothers, whereas Gen Xers experienced more upheaval with previously stay-at-home moms shifting to working moms. Gen Yers' attitudes toward women working are both more relaxed and more choice-oriented than any generation before. As a group, they are used to a very pro-child life with doting boomer parents.

In relation to the workplace, women in Generation Y believe they are free to determine and choose the life path that is best for them and their families. Thus they typically are not supporting a cause or a social injustice, as were boomer women. Further, the need to prove one's competence and abilities at work does not rest on their shoulders as success can be defined beyond the career for these individuals. However, this sense of choice among Gen Y women may be a threat to organizations, as it may reflect a major potential drain of talent. Therefore, it is important to restructure the work environment such that it will attract and retain women.

Intergenerational coworker support: Potential points of conflicts and implications for employee retention and recruitment of talent. One of the most significant areas for intervention to retain and recruit mature and emerging employee talent is to create and provide an informal, supportive organizational culture. Both informed and supportive leaders/managers and coworkers are critical in shaping and providing the basis for a supportive organizational climate. One way an organization can do this is to understand the varying needs underlying the diversity among the age generations. There are a number of areas where there is potential for conflict between traditionalists and boomers, boomers and Gen Xers, and possibly Gen Yers. For example, although boomers want to have an impact on the world and at work, they have not been influential on how work is structured. They value the meaning of work and are idealists. They work hard and long hours, as do traditionalists, but the reason for doing so differs; boomers like competition, while traditionalists like symbols of success—e.g., large paycheck, high-status jobs, and so forth. Although boomers and Gen Xers share the characteristics of low trust, they have the potential for conflict because low trust manifests itself in very different ways between the two generations. Among boomers, it is the belief that the workplace can be working differently and that one must be involved and work hard to change the workplace. On the other hand, Gen Xers do not emulate boomers, and the lack of trust is reflected in their belief that one needs to be self-reliant and take care to look after oneself at work (because the workplace will not). Therefore, boomers and Gen Xers may clash over work involvement and the role of investing one's time and energy at work. Gen Xers need to be reassured that the organization will reward them and is a good place to work. It is not clear, given their youth, how Gen Yers and boomers (or Gen Xers) will support each other. However, there is potential among Gen Yers to take the lead in shaping a positive team and social fabric for both boomers and Gen Xers. They are upbeat and more team-oriented, and have more positive affect toward boomer parents and Gen Xers. They are both multitaskers and

nonlinear thinkers, so it is possible that they will be influential translators among traditionalists, boomers, and Gen Xers and provide a constructive and conciliatory social support environment at work. Importantly, the ultimate success of formal recruitment and retention strategies will be contingent on informal interactions and support among the multiple generations within the workplace.

Organizational Scenarios

Based on the research reviewed above, we give several recommendations for how to recruit and retain a broad variety of older workers. Specifically, we highlight several key differences, such as gender and job field, in the following scenarios to demonstrate the techniques that are best suited to individuals. Our goal is that by making our recommendations more concrete, it will increase the ease of applying the available research to our current workplaces.

Scenario 1. The first scenario will depict a white male in his mid-50s (54–56) who is no longer working due to layoffs caused by the recent economic downturn and because he has a chronic health condition (e.g., diabetes). He has some college education, although he largely worked in semi-skilled or skilled manufacturing jobs. He is personable and has solid knowledge of home construction and improvement equipment and tools. However, his chronic condition(s) prevent him from standing on his feet for more than about an hour at a time and from climbing ladders.

There are several things we can glean from this brief description of this gentleman. The first is that his leaving his job was not optional. As it was a forced decision, he is likely to be less happy if he were to choose to retire at this point than someone who made the decision under his or her own volition. Additionally, because his health prevents him from continue a physically demanding job, he will likely need to explore a new field of employment. As he is out of work, he will need to be recruited, rather than retained in the workforce.

To recruit this individual, organizations should be mindful of the health benefits it has to offer. With several health ailments, our gentleman will likely be looking to work for an organization with reasonable health care benefits. Even though he has some education and a good deal of knowledge about the field of construction, a recruiting organization should be mindful that on-boarding and training will still be required for this individual. For older workers, Beier (2008) recommends training programs be more structured than self-guided, allow more time for learning, and point out how new knowledge links to that which the older worker already possesses.

Scenario 2. Our second example is a female, approximately 62 years old, who is recently retired from a highly skilled and highly knowledge-based organization. She is in excellent health, although her husband, who is 65, has advanced metastatic prostate cancer. Although her husband continues to work reduced hours (for health insurance), she is considering returning to work, as she does not have a significant retirement portfolio. They have three children who are still in public schools—middle school and high school—so college education is still ahead of them.

As the woman in our second example did not retire from a physically demanding job, it is likely that she can return to work in the same field. As with scenario 1, some (re)training may be necessary to update her skill set. Unlike the first scenario, our example probably will not weigh health care packages significantly in her job search decisions, but flextime may be important to allow her the ability to care for her husband. Especially given that women often retire if their spouse is in poor health (Talaga & Beehr, 1995), an organization looking to recruit the woman in this scenario should emphasize its flextime policy to her. Additionally, even though she is returning to work to supplement the family income, many older workers place higher value on flextime than they do wages (Feldblum, 2008).

Scenario 3. Next, we have a healthy male who retired at 67 and is now 69. He is highly educated in medicine, enjoys the flexibility of retirement, stays physically active, and loves to travel with his spouse to visit family and friends overseas. However, he realizes that even though he has about $500,000 in retirement savings, it will likely run out before he and/or spouse dies.

Here again we have an individual looking to return to work for financial reasons. Unlike the previous two scenarios, the gentleman in scenario 3 does not have any personal or spousal health issues. As such, health care packages will likely not do much in the way of enticing him. Given that the type of job he qualifies for is well paid, what may make or break the case for this individual is again flexible working options. Whereas the woman in scenario 2 will probably be more focused on policies that allow her to set her own hours around her husband's care schedule, the man in scenario 3 may value vacation time and short workweeks more. This will allow

him to continue to enjoy traveling and to take long weekends to camp, bike, hike, etc.

Scenario 4. Finally, we present a woman who is 63 and recently widowed. Her husband had a great pension, but this did not pass on in full to her; she receives a very modest amount. Although she has worked all her life, she held mostly part-time jobs with few benefits and no retirement plans.

For the woman in this scenario, flexible working options and benefits will be less important. She does not have an ailing spouse to care for and does not list traveling among her hobbies. She is more interested in working to supplement her current income and build a reserve for the future. Additionally, with the loss of her spouse, work can serve as a means to create a stable environment and maintain social ties (Atchley, 1989). Given her past experience in part-time work, customer service may be a good choice for this woman. In addition, customer service jobs provide social interaction, and some companies, such as Starbucks, provide benefits even for part-time employees, which would help her with her future plans.

Conclusions and Recommendations

As with many human resource practices, the goals of recruitment and retention practices include enhancing the productivity of the organization and the performance and success of its members. Individual performance and success at their simplest level are functions of the workers' ability and motivation. Our current HR systems emphasize and focus on recruiting, selecting, and retaining applicants and employees based largely on individual differences in ability. As this chapter (and others in the handbook) indicate, older or mature employees who remain in the workplace have demonstrated their competence. There are few differences in typical performance among older and younger employees across a wide range of occupations. Additionally, an employee's motivation is linked to a greater degree to typical performance, whereas ability is more strongly linked with maximum performance (Sackett, Zedeck, & Fogli, 1988). To maximize the effectiveness of recruitment and retention practices devoted to attracting older individuals back to work or retaining older employees, it is essential that organizations shift the focus of HR systems from ability-based practices to practices designed to address the motivators and needs of its aging (and diverse) employees. Concretely, the work context—including the availability of age-relevant practices (e.g., phased retirement benefits), the design of the job, the quality of older employee-supervisor-coworker interactions, and an age friendly organizational climate—may be more important to older workers than the assessment of ability and/or performance differences.

There are at least three areas where we can benefit from greater research. First, we can examine recruitment and retention of mature workers within the framework of career development or management theory. Numerous theories of career development exist, yet all past models have either been based on men or assumed that all workers follow the same general (and linear) career path. Current career models do recognize the likelihood of multiple career transitions, including Super's states model, which indicates that career stages occur multiple times during the life span, and the Stern-Pachett model, which is non-age-specific (Sterns & Subich, 2002). However, future career theories must integrate expanded conceps of middle age, especially employees from 55 to 75 years old.

Second, one important feature of attracting high-quality mature applicants is that the organization is perceived or branded as an age-friendly organization. This "branding" cannot be solely cosmetic; word-of-mouth practices are particularly valuable beyond more traditional advertising, especially when the realities of the organization do not correspond to the image that the it is attempting to cultivate (Van Hoye & Lievens, 2009).

Finally, treating applicants with respect and utilizing personable recruiters favorably influence applicant attraction and intent to pursue the available position (Chapman et al., 2005). One way to induce feelings of respect among job applicants is to provide information on organizations (Boezeman & Ellemers, 2008). Further, by providing information on available task and emotional support within the organization, applicants feel as though they are respected (Boezeman & Ellemeers, 2008). Also, using mature workers to recruit retirees can produce a larger pool of older applicants, as job seekers respond favorably to recruiters who are similar to themselves (Barber, 1998).

The availability of HR practices for recruitment and retention of an age-diverse workplace is a necessary but insufficent initial step. Drawing from the stress literature and work-family research, organizations must develop an age-supportive organizational climate. Formal HR practices are only one aspect of support. A positive and productive work climate also requires intergenerational support provided by supervisors and coworkers as distinct yet critical ingredients to the development of such a climate.

References

Adams, G. A., Prescher, J., Beehr, T. A., & Lepisto, L. (2002). Applying work-role attachment theory to retirement decision-making. *International Journal of Aging and Human Development, 54*(2), 125–137.

Allen, T. D. (2001). Family-supportive work environments: The role of organizational perceptions. *Journal of Vocational Behavior, 58*, 414–435.

Alley, D., & Crimmins, E. (2007). The demography of aging and work. In K. S. Shultz & G. A. Adams (Eds.), *Aging and work in the 21st century* (pp. 7–24). Mahwah, NJ: Lawrence Erlbaum.

Anderson, S. E., Coffey, B. S., & Byerly, R. T. (2002). Formal organizational initiatives and informal workplace practices: Links to work-family conflict and job-related outcomes. *Journal of Management, 28*(6), 787–810.

Arthur, M. M. (2003). Share price reactions to work-family human resource decisions: An institutional perspective. *Academy of Management Journal, 46*, 497–505.

Atchley, R. C. (1989). A continuity theory of normal aging. *The Gerontologist, 29*(2), 183–190.

Barber, A. E. (1998). *Recruiting employees: Individual and organizational perspectives.* Thousand Oaks, CA: Sage.

Bass, S. A. (1995). *Older and active: How Americans over 55 are contributing to society.* New Haven, CT: Yale University Press.

Beehr, T. A., Glazer, S., Nielson, N. L., & Farmer, S. J. (2000). Work and nonwork predictors of employees' retirement ages. *Journal of Vocational Behavior, 57*, 206–225.

Beier, M. E. (2008). Age and learning in organizations. In G. P. Hodgkinson & J. K. Ford (Eds.), *International review of industrial & organizational psychology* (Vol. 23, pp. 83–105). Hoboken, NJ: John Wiley & Sons, Ltd.

Bendick, M., Brown, L. E., & Wall, K. (1999). No foot in the door: An experimental study of employment discrimination against older workers. *Journal of Aging & Social Policy, 10*, 5–23.

Behson, S. J. (2005). The relative contribution of formal and informal organizational work-family support. *Journal of Vocaional Behavior, 66*, 487–500.

Berg, P., Kalleberg, A. L., & Appelbaum, E. (2003). Balancing work and family: The role of high-commitment environments. *Industrial Relations: A Journal of Economy & Society, 42*, 168–188.

Berman, E. M., West, J. P., & Richter, M. N., Jr. (2002). Workplace relations: Friendship patterns and consequnces (according to managers). *Public Administration Review, 62*, 217–230.

Boezeman, E. J., & Ellemers, N. (2008). Volunteer recruitment: The role of organizational support and anticipated respect in non-volunteers' attraction to charitable volunteer organizations. *Journal of Applied Psychology, 93*, 1013–1026.

Bragger, J. D., Rodriguez-Srednicki, O., Dutcher, E. J., Indovino, L., & Rosner, E. (2005). Work-family conflict, work-family climate, and organizational citizenship behavior among teachers. *Journal of Business and Psychology, 20*(2), 303.

Brandon, E. (2009, August). Boomers take a step back down the career ladder. *US News and World Report.* Retrieved from http://money.usnews.com/money/retireent/articles/2009/08/31/boomers-take-a-step-back-down-the-career-ladder.

Breaugh, J. A., & Frye, K. (2007). An examination of the antecedents and consequences of the use of family-friendly benefits. *Journal of Managerial Issues, 19*, 35–52.

Breaugh, J. A., & Frye, K. (2008). Work-family conflict: The importance of family-friendly employment practices and family-supportive supervisors. *Journal of Business Psychology, 22*, 345–353.

Carlson, D. S., & Perrewé, P. L. (1999). The role of social support in the stressor-strain relationship: An examination of work-family conflict. *Journal of Management, 25*, 513–540.

Carr, J. Z., Schmidt, A. M., Ford, K., & DeShon, R. P. (2003). Climate perceptions matter: A meta-analytic path analysis relating molar climate, cognitive and affective states and individual level work outcomes. *Journal of Applied Psychology, 88*(4), 605–619.

Chapman, D. S., Uggerslev, K. L., Carroll, S. A., Piasentin, K. A., & Jones, D. A. (2005). Applicant attraction to organizations and job choice: A meta-analytic review of the correlates of recruiting outcomes. *Journal of Applied Psychology, 90*(5), 928–944.

Cleveland, J. N., McCarthy, A., & Jones, A. (2006, September). The influence of managerial support and family structure on work-family outcomes. Presented at the Irish Academy of Management Conference. Cork, Ireland.

Cohen, S., & Wills, T. A. (1985). Stress, social support, and the buffering hypothesis. *Psychological Bulletin, 98*, 310–357.

Committee for Economic Development. (1999). *New opportunities for older workers*. Washington, DC: Author.

Dennis, H., & Thomas, K. (2007). Ageism in the workplace. *Aging Workforce, 31*, 84–89.

Diener, E., Suh, E. M., Lucas, R. E., Smith, H. L. (1999). Subjective well-being: Three decades of progress. *Psychological Bulletin, 125*, 276–302.

Ducharme, L. J., & Martin, J. K. (2000). Unrewarding work, coworker support, and job satisfaction: A test of the buffering hypothesis. *Work and Occupations, 27*, 22–243.

Erickson, T. (2008). *Retire retirement*. Boston, MA: Harvard Business Press.

Federal Interagency Forum on Aging-Related Statistics. (2004, November). *Older Americans 2004: Key indicators of well-being*. Washington, DC: U.S. Government Printing Office. Retrieved from http://www.agingstats.gov/agingstatsdotnet/Main_Site/Data/2004_Documents/entire_report.pdf.

Feldblum, C. R. (2008, April). *Leading by example: Making government a model for hiring and retaining older workers*: Hearing before the S. Special Committee on Aging, 110th Congress (Statement of Chai R. Feldblum, Geo. U.L. Center). Retrieved from http://scholarship.law.georgetown.edu/cong/68.

Frye, K., & Breaugh, J. A. (2004). Family-friendly policies, supervisor support, work-family conflict, family-work conflict, and satisfaction. *Journal of Business and Psychology, 19*, 197–220.

Gerstner, C. R., & Day, D. V. (1997). Meta-analytic review of leader-member exchange theory: Correlates and construct issues. *Journal of Applied Psychology, 82*, 827–844.

Gobeski, K. T., & Beehr, T. A. (2009). How retirees work: Predictors of different types of bridge employment. *Journal of Organizational Behavior, 30*, 401–425.

Hammer, L. B., Cullen, J. C. & Shafiro, M. (2006). Work-family best practices. In F. Jones, R. Burke, & M. Westman (Eds.),

Work-life balance: A psychological perspective (pp. 261–275). East Sussex, England: Psychology Press.

Hammer, L. B., Neal, M. B., Newsom, J. T., Brockwood, K., & Colton, C. L. (2005). A longitudinal study of the effects of dual-earner couples' utilization of family-friendly workplace supports on work and family outcomes. *Journal of Applied Psychology, 90*, 799–810.

Hammer, T. H., Saksvik, P. Ø., Nytrø, K., Torvatn, H., & Bayazit, M. (2004). Expanding the psychosocial work environment: Workplace norms and work-family conflict as correlates of stress and health. *Journal of Occupational Health Psychology, 9*, 83–97.

He, N., Zhao, J., & Archbold, C. A. (2002). Gender and police stress: The convergent and divergent impact of work environment, work-family conflict, and stress coping mechanisms of female and male police officers. *Policing: An International Journal of Police Strategies & Management, 25*, 687– 708

Hutchens, R. M. (2003). *The Cornell study of employer phased retirement policies: A report on key findings*. Ithaca, NY: School of Industrial and Labor Relations, Cornell University. Retrieved from http://digitalcommons.ilr.cornell.edu/lepubs/1/.

Jex, S., Wang, M., & Zarubin, A. (2007). Aging and occupational health. In K. S. Shultz & G. A. Adams (Eds.), *Aging and work in the 21st century* (pp. 199–224). New York, NY: Psychology Press.

Karasek, R., & Theorell, T. (1990). *Healthy work: Stress, productivity, and the reconstruction of working life*. New York: Basic Books.

Kim, S., & Feldman, D. C. (2000). Working in retirement: The antecedents of bridge employment and its consequences for quality of life in retirement. *Academy of Management Journal, 43*(6), 1195–1210.

Knatterud, L. (2007) Director of Aging Transformation for the MN Department of Human Services.Summary: A Blueprint for Preparing Minnesota for the Age Wave. http://www.dhs.state.mn.us/2010.

Kossek, E. E., & Ozeki, C. (1998). Work-family conflict, policies, and the job-life satisfaction relationship: A review and directions for organizational behavior-human resources research. *Journal of Applied Psychology, 83*, 139–149.

Lapierre, L. M., Spector, P. E., Allen, T. D., Poelmans, S., Cooper, C. L., O'Driscoll, M. P., ... Kinnunen, U. (2008). Family-supportive organization perceptions, multiple dimensions of work–family conflict, and employee satisfaction: A test of model across five samples. *Journal of Vocational Behavior, 73*, 92–106.

Lingard, H., & Francis, V. (2006). Does a supportive work environment moderate the relationship between work-family conflict and burnout among construction professionals? *Construction Management and Economics, 24*, 185–196.

Marcinkus, W. C., Whelan-Berry, K. S., & Gordon, J. R. (2007). The relationship of social support to the work-family balance and work outcomes of midlife women. *Women In Management Review, 22*, 86–111.

Morris, A., Shinn, M., & DuMont, K. (1999). Contextual factors affecting the organizational commitment of police officers: A levels of analysis perspective. *American Journal of Community Psychology, 27*, 75–105.

National Academy on an Aging Society. (2000). *Who are young retirees and older workers?* Retrieved from www.agingsociety.org

Ng. T. W. H., & Feldman, D. C. (2008). The relationship of age to ten dimensions of job performance. *Journal of Applied Psychology, 93*(2), 392–423.

Older workers and the need for workplace flexibility. (2010). Retrieved from www.workplaceflexibility2010.org

Parkinson, D. (2002). *Research report, voices of experience: Mature workers in the future workforce.* New York, NY: The Conference Board.

Perry-Smith, J. E., & Blum, T. C. (2000). Work-family human resource bundles and perceived organizational performance. *The Academy of Management Journal, 43*, 1107–1117.

Potocnik, K., Tordera, N., & Peiro, J. M. (2009). The role of human resource practices and group norms in the retirement process. *European Psychologist, 14*(3), 193–206.

Quick, H. E., & Moen, P. (1998). Gender, employment, and retirement quality: A life course approach to the differential experiences of men and women. *Journal of Occupational Health Psychology, 3*(1), 44–64.

Rau, B. L., & Adams, G. A. (2005). Attracting retirees to apply: Desired organizational characteristics of bridge employment. *Journal of Organization Behavior, 26*, 649–660.

Reichers, A. E., & Schneider, B. (1990). Climate and culture: An evolution of constructs. In B. Schneider (Ed.), *Organizational climate and culture* (pp. 5–39). San Francisco, CA: Jossey-Bass.

Rothwell, W. J., Sterns, H. L., Spokus, D., & Reaser, J. M. (2008). *Working longer: New strategies for managing, training, and retaining older employees.* New York, NY: AMACOM: American Management Association.

Sackett, P. R., Zedeck, S., and Fogli, L. (1988). Relations between measures of typical and maximum performance. *Journal of Applied Psychology, 73*, 482–486.

Schein, E. (1990). *Organizational culture and leadership.* San Francisco, CA: Jossey-Bass.

Schein, E. H. (1983). The role of the founder in creating organizational culture. *Organizational Dynamics, 12*, 13–28.

Schmitt, J. (2005, October). How good is the economy at creating good jobs? Report for the Center of Economic and Policy Research. Retreived from http://www.cepr.net/documents/publications/labor_markets_2005_10.pdf.

Schneider, B. (2000). The psychological life of organizations. In N. M. Ashkanasy, C. P. M. Wilderom, & M. F. Peterson (Eds.), *Handbook of organizational culture and climate* (pp. 225–244). Thousand Oaks, CA: Sage.

Semmer, N. K., Elfering, A., Jacobshagen, N., Perrot, T., Beehr, T. A., & Boos, N.(2008). The emotional meaning of instrumental social support. *International Journal of Stress Management, 15*, 235–251.

SHRM Survey Program. (2003). *SHRM/NOWCC/CED Older workers survey.* Alexandria, VA: SHRM Research.

Shultz, K. S., & Wang, M. (2007). The influence of specific physical health conditions on retirement decisions. *International Journal of Aging and Human Development, 65*(2), 149–161.

Sloan Center on Aging and Work. (2009). *Recruitment and retention of older workers* (Fact Sheet No. 21). Retrieved from http://www.bc.edu/agingandwork.

Special Committee on Aging. (2008, April). *Leading by example: making government a model for hiring and retaining older workers.* (Serial No. 110-27). Washington, DC: U.S. Government Printing Office.

Spokus, D. (2008). Succession practices in New York state government. In W. Rothwell, J. Alexander, & M. Bernhard (Eds.), *Cases in government succession planning: Action-oriented strategies for public-sector human capital management, workforce planning, succession planning, and talent management* (pp. 177–184). Amherst, MA: HRD Press.

Starrels, M. E. (1992). The evolution of workplace family policy research. *Journal of Family Issues, 13*, 259–278.

Sterns, H., & Doverspike, D. (1989). Aging and the training and learning process. In I. I. Goldstein (Ed.), *Training and development in organizations* (pp. 299–329). San Francisco, CA: Jossey-Bass.

Sterns, H. L., & Subich, L. M. (2002). Career development in mid-career. In D. C. Feldman (Ed.), *Work careers* (pp. 186–213). San Francisco, CA: Jossey-Bass.

Talaga, J. A., & Beehr, T. A. (1995). Are there gender differences in predicting retirement decisions? *Journal of Applied Psychology, 80*(1), 16–28.

Taylor, M. A. & Shore, L. M. (1995). Predictors of planned retirement age: An application of Beehr's model. *Psychology and Aging, 10*(1), 76–83.

Thomas, L., & Ganster, D. C. (1995). Impact of family-supportive work variables on work-family conflict and strain: A control perspective. *Journal of Applied Psychology, 80*, 6–15.

Thompson, C. A., Beauvais, L. L., & Lyness, K. S. (1999). When work-family benefits are not enough: The influence of work-family culture on benefit utilization, organizational attachment, and work-family conflict. *Journal of Vocational Behavior, 54*, 392–415.

Thompson, C. A., Jahn, E., Kopelman, R., & Prottas, D. (2004). The impact of perceived organizational and supervisory family support on affective commitment: A longitudinal and multilevel analysis. *Journal of Managerial Issues, 16*, 545–565.

Thompson, C. A., & Pottras, D. J. (2005). Relationships among organizational family support, job autonomy, perceived control, and employee well-being. *Journal of Occupational Healthy Psychology, 10*, 100–118.

Trice, H. M., & Beyer, J. M. (1993). *The cultures of work organizations.* Englewood Cliffs, NJ: Prentice Hall.

Uccello, C. E. (1998). *Factors influencing retirement: Their implications for raising retirement age.* Washington, DC: AARP.

U.S. General Accounting Office (2001). *A report to the ranking minority member, Subcommittee on Employer-Employee Relations, Committee on Education and the Workforce, House of Representatives, Older Workers: Demographic Trends Pose Challenges for Employers and Workers (GAO-02-85).* Washington, DC: U.S. Government Printing Office.

Van Hoye, G., & Lievens, F. (2009). Tapping the grapevine: A closer look at word-of-mouth as a recruitment source. *Journal of Applied Psychology, 94*(2), 341–352.

van Solinge, H., & Henkins, K. (2008). Adjustment to and satisfaction with retirement: Two of a kind? *Psychology and Aging, 23*(2), 422–434.

Walker, D. (2007, February). *Some best practices and strategies for engaging and retaining older workers.* Retrieved from www.gao.gov/cgi-bin/getrpt?GAO-07-433T

Wallace, J. E. (2005). Job stress, depression and work-to-family conflict: A test of the strain and buffer hypotheses. *Industrial Relations, 60*, 510–537.

Wang, M. (2007). Profiling retirees in the retirement transition and adjustment process: Examining the longitudinal change

patterns of retirees' psychological well-being. *Journal of Applied Psychology, 92*(2), 455–474.

Wang, M., & Shultz, K. S. (2010). Employee retirement: A review and recommendations for future investigation. *Journal of Management, 36,* 172–206.

Wang, M., Zhan, Y., Liu, S., & Shultz, K. S. (2008). Antecedents of bridge employment: A longitudinal investigation. *Journal of Applied Psychology, 93*(4), 818–830.

Wang, P., & Walumbwa, F. (2007). Family-friendly programs, organizational commitment, and work withdrawal: The role of transformational leadership. *Personnel Psychology, 60*(2), 397–427.

Warren, J. A., & Johnson, P. J. (1995). The impact of workplace support on work-family role strain. *Family Relations, 44,* 163–169.

Wickham, M., & Parker, M. (2007). Reconceptualising organizational role theory for contemporary organizational contexts. *Journal of Managerial Psychology, 22,* 440–464.

Wills, T. A., & Shinar, O. (2000). Measuring perceived and received social support. In S. Cohen, L. G. Underwood & B. H. Gottlieb (Eds.), *Social support measurement and intervention: A guide for health and social scientists* (pp. 86–135). New York: Oxford University Press.

Wise, S. (2005). The right to time off for dependents. *Employee Relations, 27*(2), 126–140.

Yap, C. S., & Tng, H. (2002). Factors associated with attitudes towards telecommuting. *Information & Management, 19,* 227–235.

Designing Early Retirement Incentive Programs

Yujie Zhan

Abstract

As a result of the aging trend of the population, contemporary organizations are undergoing a major revolution in the age composition of their workforce. Offering early retirement incentive programs to a specific group of employees has been introduced as one way to downsize and restructure workforce composition for organizations. This chapter describes the nature of early retirement incentive programs from both employers' and employees' perspectives, specifically, why employers want to offer and why employees want to accept early retirement incentives. Then, this chapter details how to design an effective early retirement incentive program to satisfy the organization's strategic goal in human resource management, taking consideration of who to offer, what to offer, and how to implement. Future research directions are discussed.

Key Words: early retirement incentive program, eligibility, content of early retirement incentive program, process of early retirement incentive program

Introduction

Today, many countries have been experiencing a trend of population aging as life expectancy increases and birth rates decrease (Tyers & Shi, 2007). At the same time, the average age of retirement has been decreasing in many developed countries since the 1970s (Ebbinghaus, 2006). For example, as of June 2007 in the United States, 70.7% of men and 75.6% of women claimed Social Security benefits before the normal retirement age (i.e., full retirement age, the age at which retirement benefits are equal to the primary insurance amount; varying from age 65 to age 67 by year of birth; U.S. Social Security Administration) compared to 36% and 59% in 1970, respectively (Benítez-Silva & Heiland, 2008). In Europe, recent estimates of the average age of retirement range from 58 to 63 years old (Hagan, Jones, & Rice, 2009). This trend could be a result of individual preferences, organizations' retirement-related human resource management policies and practices,

and macro-level labor demands and economic challenges. From the organizational perspective, early retirement incentive programs function as financial inducements that organizations offer older workers to attract them toward retirement in the near future (Feldman, 2003). Such programs play an increasingly important role for organizations with aging workforces and during tough economic times.

As a result of the aging trend of population, contemporary organizations are undergoing a major revolution in the age composition of their workforces, with a growing percentage of older employees approaching retirement (see chapter 3 by Wheaton & Crimmins in this handbook). Although the average age retirement age is decreasing, the workforce participation rates of older Americans have been rising since the mid-1980s (Quinn, 2010). By 2012, the number of workers over 55 is projected to grow at nearly four times the rate of the overall workforce (Alley & Crimmins, 2007). Such age composition may bring some problems to organizations. For example, because of seniority in the organizational ladder, older employees are generally more costly than younger employees for organizations (Cleveland & Lim, 2007; Ng & Feldman, 2008). Facing harsh economic conditions, organizations may want to not only downsize their workforce but also replace older employees with lower-salaried younger ones. Furthermore, given the incredibly rapid technology revolution, younger workers' skill and knowledge sets are often viewed as more suitable to organizations entering new ventures. Therefore, in order to maintain good personnel structure, achieve optimal skill and knowledge combinations, and keep labor costs acceptable, many organizations may have to establish retirement-related human resource management programs to restructure their human resources (Wang & Shultz, 2010).

In the United States, the Social Security system provides complex incentives that can affect the labor supply behavior of workers between early and normal retirement age because an individual's Social Security retirement benefit is partly based on the age they start to receive the benefit (the closer they are to age 67 when they retire, the more benefit they will receive). In addition, at the organizational level, employers can also influence the employee headcount by introducing and crafting their early retirement incentive programs to encourage early retirement decisions. This chapter first discusses the nature of early retirement incentive programs, focusing on the reasons why employers establish such programs as well as the determinants influencing employees' acceptance of them. Moreover, the chapter introduces how to design an early retirement incentive package to satisfy the organization's strategic goal in human resource management in a way that enhances rather than threatens the employee-organization relationship. Finally, this chapter discusses future directions for research on early retirement incentive programs.

Nature of Early Retirement Incentive Programs

The end of mandatory retirement provides employees with control over the timing of retirement. Although employees are able to choose to retire at an earlier age than the normal retirement age, they could lose their eligibility for maximum Social Security benefits due to early exit. Thus, early retirement incentive programs constitute one type of practice that facilitates voluntary retirement and provides employees with the opportunity to retire

early with compensation for the potential financial loss. Although early retirement incentive programs appear to offer older workers more flexibility in deciding when to retire, the offer of early retirement incentives is frequently implemented to serve organizational goals such as attempting to reduce employment or restructure the workforce composition (Hardy & Quadagno, 1995). Therefore, the opportunity for early retirement may be accompanied by downsizing goals that place older workers' continued employment in question.

Due to the combination of inducement and coercion involved in an early retirement incentive program, individual decisions regarding whether to accept an early retirement incentive package could be a risky choice for employees. Specifically, when provided with an opportunity to receive an early retirement incentive package by an organization under economic pressure, employees eligible for this package need to compare the results of accepting versus not accepting the package. Accepting this package indicates a certain outcome, including early exit, incentives based on early exit, and lost maximum Social Security benefit, while not accepting the package might bring individuals to a risky position with a chance of being laid off before reaching normal retirement age. Therefore, strategically implemented early retirement incentive programs may indicate different meanings for employers and employees.

Employer Motivation to Implement an Early Retirement Incentive Program

Wang and Shultz (2010) have conceptualized retirement as a part of human resource management that helps organizations to reach their goals. At different times in the life of an organization, managers may find themselves in the position of having to reduce their workforce or adjust the age composition of their workforce for different reasons, such as a major change of technology, economic shocks, or a projected increase in the number of older workers (Hayden & Pfadenhauer, 2005; Kim & Feldman, 1998). In retirement literature in the 1990s, early retirement incentive programs have been extensively studied because "many organizations were seeking to improve their competitiveness through global manufacturing relocation or outsourcing peripheral services" (Wang & Shultz, 2010, p. 180). In the current business environment, employers considering reducing and/or restructuring their workforce need to establish a program that would support not just the organizational goal but also its employees' welfare. The use of voluntary early retirement programs is one such approach (Hayden & Pfadenhauer, 2005). Given the strategic meaning and the voluntary nature of early retirement incentive programs, there may be strong incentives for employers to offer such programs to older employees.

First and foremost, for organizations, an early retirement incentive program supports financial and personnel goals. As noted by Wheaton and Crimmins in chapter 3 of this handbook, "workers age 55 and older are overrepresented in professional and related occupations; management, business, and financial occupations; and office and administrative support occupations" (pp. 22–41). A workforce overrepresented by older workers could be problematic in terms of an organization's financial budget and organizational development. Specifically, research has suggested that older workers may be more costly in terms of receiving higher wages and having above-average likelihood of sickness absenteeism (e.g., Ng & Feldman, 2008). In terms of organizational development, for organizations that go through structural changes and/or attempt to create a new or different organizational culture, longtime older employees tend to be more resistant (Posthuma & Campion, 2009). Therefore, given the constraints of employment law protections for older workers and/or collective agreements with seniority rules, early retirement incentive programs are one major socially acceptable way that helps organizations realize financial savings and balance age composition by replacing older employees with younger employees (Ebbinghaus, 2006; Feldman, 2003; Hallberg & Eklof, 2010).

Second, due to their voluntary nature, early retirement incentive programs deliver a positive message to employees. For employees considering moving to retirement, such programs give a feeling of control over their future decisions. Employees may view the early retirement incentives as organizations' investment to recognize long service and investment in the exchange relationship, which potentially increases employee reception and satisfaction with such programs and their commitment to their organizations (Wang & Zhan, 2012). A survey conducted in universities has found that both faculty and administrators support well-designed, noncoercive retirement incentive programs that increase certainty choice while preserving individual rights (Clark & Hammond, 2001). Therefore, a voluntary early retirement incentive program serves as a cooperative method for organizations that is less likely to raise legal disputes and conflicts and more likely to improve the employee-organization relationship, especially if the program is structured properly (Ebbinghaus, 2006).

In addition to the reception of employees desiring to retire, early retirement incentive programs may also deliver a supportive message to employees who stay with the organization by emphasizing the recognition of long service and investment in employee welfare. Also, given that early retirement incentives are provided as a downsizing strategy, they to some extent reduce the need for involuntary layoffs, which would help support positive employee morale. Research is consistent in the finding that early retirement incentives increase early retirement intentions and decisions of older employees (Clark & Hammond, 2001); however, much less is known about the potential impacts of such programs on remaining employees.

Determinants of Employee Participation in Early Retirement Incentive Programs

The decision to retire early has been discussed in theoretical work (Feldman, 1994) and explored in many studies of different groups of workers (e.g., Blekesaune & Solem, 2005; Kim & Feldman, 1998). Wang and Shultz (2010) conceptualize retirement as a decision-making process in which older employees rationally choose between work and leisure. In general, employee decisions regarding whether to participate in early retirement incentive programs result from the comparison between the prospective value of certain consequences of an early exit versus the consequences of staying with an organization until the normal or desired retirement age with the probability of being laid off (Keefe, 2001). The results of such comparison could be driven by both push factors, which are negative considerations that force older workers to retire, and pull factors, which are positive considerations that attract older workers toward retirement (Shultz, Morton, & Weckerle, 1998). Specifically, on the one hand, push factors, such as high work stress and the perception of not being valued at work, reduce the value of working or staying in the workplace. Poor health and disability also lead to the perception of being not productive and reduce older workers' capability of working. On the other hand, pull factors usually facilitate retirement decisions by increasing the attractiveness of retirement. Typical examples of pull factors include relaxation, pursuit of hobbies, spouse retirement, and time with families. It should be pointed out that early retirement incentives can be perceived as either pull or push factors toward retirement (Hanks, 1990; Shultz et al., 1998). Given that early retirement incentive programs offer cash incentives to provide some compensation for anticipated losses resulting from early termination of salaries and saving plans, for older workers who have already planned to retire early under some condition, early retirement incentives function as a pull factor that attracts older workers toward retirement. However, as a corporate initiative, early retirement incentives also serve as a downsizing strategy and necessitate decision making under pressure. Some older workers may feel pushed out with no acceptable alternative to retirement (Hanks, 1990).

The push and pull factors that determine one's participation in early retirement incentive programs can be grouped into three main categories. First are individual attributes, including demographic characteristics, financial considerations, health condition and disability, and anticipation of the benefits from retirement such as opportunities for self-fulfillment and leisure. In general, employees who have sufficient financial savings, are less healthy or have disabilities, and anticipate more benefits of retirement are more likely to accept early retirement incentive packages (e.g., Blakeley & Ribeiro, 2008). Among these factors, financial considerations have been viewed as one of the most important factors that influence older workers' acceptance of early retirement packages. Financial considerations may broadly include having attained financial security (Baillargeon, 1982), expecting stable post-retirement income such as having a pension plan or having been guaranteed a higher paid position (Mein et al., 2000), and taking advantage of financial inducements offered by employers (Higgs et al., 2003).

The second category includes family-related factors, such as marital status, spouse employment status, dependent children and older parents, and sickness and disabilities of family members (Feldman, 2003). As an important life sphere, family life may push or pull individuals to early retirement. From the negative aspects (i.e., push factors), individuals may have to quit early in order to take care of dependent older parents or disabled family members, which is likely to result in the perception of involuntary retirement. From the positive aspects (i.e., pull factors), enjoying family time is one of the most attractive benefits provided by retirement. For example, by studying a sample of nurses, an occupation that observes high early retirement percentages, Blakeley and Ribeiro (2008) identified free time to enjoy family as a top reason for wanting

to take early retirement. Given this reason, spouse employment status and retirement plan matter a lot in influencing one's participation in an early retirement program. In the same study, Blakeley and Ribeiro found that people listed "I want to retire at the same time as my spouse/partner" as an important consideration in early retirement. Thus, joint retirement serves as an attractive factor pulling older workers to retirement.

The third category of early retirement reasons relates to organizational or work-related factors that usually function as push factors for older workers. This category includes high levels of work stress and general job dissatisfaction due to a disliked supervisor and/or coworkers (Avery, McKay, & Wilson, 2007; Shultz et al., 1998), excessive job demands, and limited control (Elovainio et al., 2005). In addition, comparing to younger workers, older workers are more likely to view some work- and organization-related factors as aversive, such as excessive and rapid technological, managerial, and cultural changes (Robertson, 2000) in the work setting as well as an ageism climate that expresses negative stereotypes toward older workers (Posthuma & Campion, 2009).

In spite of the lack of consistent findings, it is particularly important to explore the impacts of job performance on employees' acceptance of early retirement incentive offers. Given the legal and social policy reasons, early retirement incentives are usually offered to groups of potential retirees based on objective criteria such as age, years of service, positions, or functional departments/areas. Although organizations may want to retain good performers while encouraging poor performers to leave, they have little control on the performance level of employees who are eligible for early retirement incentive offers. Feldman (2003) has proposed a curvilinear relationship between performance and acceptance of an early retirement incentive package. Specifically, on the one hand, the best performers are likely to accept such a package because they are more likely to have accumulated a good amount of retirement savings due to their higher salaries, and they have greater opportunities for future employment. On the other hand, the poorest performers are likely to accept early retirement incentive offers because they have less hope of getting significant pay increases and lower expectations of gaining any further intrinsic satisfaction if they remain on the job (Kim & Feldman, 1998). Given the potential impacts of various determinants of early retirement program participation, organizations need to take serious consideration in designing and implementing these programs.

Designing an Early Retirement Incentive Program (ERIP)
Who to Offer: Eligibility

The eligible group is the set of individuals that will be offered the opportunity to participate in the early retirement incentive program. The criteria for eligibility vary across different organizations depending on the organizations' staffing objectives. Basically, it needs to be decided whether the early retirement incentive program will be offered to all employees or a subset of employees. Several issues may be considered in this process. First, employers usually choose to set a minimum age and/or minimum number of years of service to participate. It is recommended that employers look over their applicable benefit plan documents, such as pension and/or health insurance plans, to see if there is any criterion that may influence their decision regarding the eligibility group (Hayden & Pfadenhauer, 2005). For example, if the pension plan has a statement allowing those who are at least 60 years of age with at least five years of service to begin collecting their pension, the organization may want to incorporate such requirements into the eligibility of the early retirement incentive program. Second, the early retirement incentive program may target only employees on certain organizational hierarchies or in certain functional areas. When setting the eligibility criteria, for example, employers need to consider whether to limit the staffing restructure to nonmanagement positions or set an upper limit on the base salary in order to effectively decrease the number of less-skilled employees. Last but not least, organizations should consider their own pension plans in setting the eligibility criteria of early retirement. As suggested by Feldman (2003), the rates of acceptance of early retirement incentives in defined contribution plans might be lower than those in defined benefit plans because of the increased level of risk and uncertainty involved in the defined contribution plans.

In sum, employers need to make sure that the criteria of eligibility will satisfy the target headcount that needs to be reduced. Because of organizations' lack of knowledge regarding the actual accruement in employees' retirement saving accounts, it is usually difficult for organizations to predict or control how many employees will accept the early retirement incentive offer (Feldman, 2003). In this situation, low criteria may result in a large eligibility group, leading more employees to take early exits than expected, while high criteria may select out most employees from participation and may not satisfy the downsizing goal.

What to Offer: The Content of an Early Retirement Incentive Program
ECONOMIC INCENTIVES

Extensive economic literatures have examined the impacts of economic policies on early retirement (e.g., Blundell, Meghir, & Smith, 2002). In designing an early retirement incentive package, economic incentives are constantly considered as the most important component that impacts the attractiveness of such package to eligible workers. The three most common forms of economic incentives include pension enhancement, termination incentive bonus, and health insurance coverage.

Pension enhancement. An early retirement pension can be used as a tool for employers to persuade employees to leave their employment before normal retirement age. This usually means that employers need to give employees stronger pension incentives to retire. Many employers in the private and public sectors have offered selected groups of employees bonuses for early retirement in the form of adding years to an individual's age or service. This has been shown consistently to be an effective economic incentive in facilitating early retirement. For example, Hogarth (1988) modeled early retirement decisions and demonstrated that an early retirement bonus affected the average probability of acceptance by 10% (i.e., from 0.30 to 0.33). Recently, Hallberg and Eklof (2010) conducted a study to examine the effect of "buyouts" by modeling the influence of offering a generous pension program by employers on the early retirement behavior of individuals between 60 and 64 years old. Their results indicated a substantially important role of early retirement pensions, such that early retirement hazards would be reduced by 14%–28% for males and 7%–18% for females if no early retirement pensions were issued.

Termination incentive bonus. Employers may provide a termination incentive bonus in the form of a lump-sum payment in order to attract older workers to accept early retirement packages. The lump-sum payment is usually based on some percentage of salary or on the number of years of service with the organization (Feldman, 2003). While the amount may vary, the early retirement incentive bonus has been shown to be effective in impacting employees' retirement decisions. For example,

Bidewell, Griffin, and Hesketh (2006) examined the effect of an early retirement incentive in influencing people's early-exit decision. Supporting the delay discounting perspective, which suggests that a subjective devaluation of a later reward encourages people to prefer a small but immediate reward to avoid potential loss while waiting, their findings showed that early retirement incentives could be viewed as an immediate reward that was preferred by individuals approaching but not yet at the retirement age at which they are eligible for maximized Social Security and pension benefit.

Health insurance coverage. One of the major factors that prohibit individuals from retiring prior to age 65 in the United States is health insurance, as state Medicare plans are not available until an individual reaches 65 years old (Hayden & Pfadenhauer, 2005). The increases in the cost of health care, prescription drugs, and health insurance premiums may lead to high levels of uncertainty and anxiety. Therefore, providing extended health insurance coverage is an attractive factor to encourage early retirement (Feldman, 2003). To contrast, in countries where citizens are covered by publicly funded health systems (e.g., Canada), this component may not be present in the ERIP.

FURTHER EMPLOYMENT OPPORTUNITIES

Employment opportunities after retirement have been shown to be an important component in early retirement incentive programs. Organizations may offer outplacement services and further employment opportunities as a part of their early retirement incentives. For example, they may introduce phased retirement, which allows fewer work hours and has limited job demands (Greller & Stroh, 2003), or bridge employment, which involves the rehiring of retired employees on full-time or part-time contracts or for a guaranteed number of substitute days (Shultz, 2003).

Further employment or bridge employment opportunities have been consistently shown to be positively related to acceptance of early retirement incentive offers (Kim & Feldman, 1998). This might be due to both financial and sociopsychological reasons. Bringing in additional financial income, bridge employment allows older workers to make up some of the difference between their monthly pension benefits and their monthly salary in full-time jobs (Doeringer, 1990). In other words, individuals who claim benefits before their normal retirement age but continue to work or return to the labor force can reduce the early retirement penalty and

improve the valence of early retirement by suspending the collection of monthly benefits (Benítez-Silva & Heiland, 2007).

Further employment opportunities do not serve only as financial incentives. In terms of the sociopsychological benefit of bridge employment, opportunities for bridge employment could lead to better reception of early retirement incentive programs. Given the risk involved in early retirement decision making, knowing that one will have the opportunity to be re-employed temporarily after retirement may help to reduce perceived risk and uncertainty. In addition, bridge employment helps individuals adjust to retirement by allowing employees to maintain their work role identity, social connection, and life routine (Atchley, 1989; Feldman, 1994; Wang, Adams, Beehr, & Shultz, 2009). Thus, the transition from full-time employment to full retirement is less stressful and will result in better retirement satisfaction (Wang, 2007; Zhan, Wang, Liu, & Shultz, 2009).

In addition to rehiring retired employees, organizations may want to provide outplacement services for employees who are eligible for early retirement incentives. For example, they may organize information exchange sessions that offer bridge employment information external to the organization. Also, an outplacement counseling program could be offered to eligible employees to help them better understand their career path and career mobility (Feldman, 2007) or future employment possibilities in their preferred industries.

SOCIOPSYCHOLOGICAL CONSIDERATIONS

As described earlier in the chapter, employees' acceptance of early retirement incentive offers is influenced by a variety of factors, many of which involve their expectation of sociopsychological well-being after retirement. According to the Socioemotional Selectivity Theory (SST), individuals are motivated to achieve different goals across different life stages (Carstensen, 1991). Specifically, different from younger people who are future-oriented and aim toward knowledge acquisition, career planning, and the development of new social relationships, older ones have more present-oriented goals and focus more on socio-emotional outcomes such as regulating their emotions to be positive, pursuing emotionally gratifying relationships with others, and engaging in activities that will benefit them relatively immediately (Carstensen, 1991). Therefore, when designing early retirement incentive programs, organizations should always pay attention to factors that may facilitate employees' well-being. First, retirement counseling or planning programs (e.g., Shuey, 2004) could be offered to employees. Such programs not only help to clarify the criteria and content of early retirement incentive programs but also help employees to better evaluate their status and plan for retirement. Psychologically, retirement counseling programs may help to remove some uncertainty involved in retirement decision and minimize the feeling of anxiety toward retirement. Second, when crafting the eligibility and designing the content of early retirement incentive programs, organizations should be aware of the impacts of family status of employees on their early retirement intentions. Research has shown that individuals with retired spouses are more likely to retire early, and dual-career couples prefer to retire around the same time. Although organizations have little control over employees' marital status or the employment status of employees' spouses, they should be aware of these tendencies in estimating the number of employees who may accept early retirement incentives. Third, organizations' support for retirement may also be enhanced by their participation in community services. In order to increase the acceptance rate of early retirement incentive programs, organizations may be able to enhance the pull factors outside organizations. For example, organizations may show high social responsibility by supporting a local retirement house or retiree activities. By doing so, employees may see a stronger link between their organizations and the community and perceive less risk and more certainty involved in their early retirement decision. This may also lead to a more satisfying retirement transition.

How to Implement: The Process of an Early Retirement Incentive Program

In designing an early retirement incentive program, attention should be paid not only to the content of the incentives but also to the process of how such a program is designed and delivered to employees (Feldman, 2003). According to organizational justice literatures (e.g., Cropanzano & Greenberg, 1997; Colquitt, Conlon, Wesson, Porter, & Ng, 2001), procedural justice concerns fairness in the way or process in which organizational decisions are made (Thibaut & Walker, 1975). To be specific, fair process should follow consistent procedures across people, use and provide accurate information and appear unbiased, provide opportunity to participate and voice, and welcome appeals of the procedure (Leventhal, 1980). Consistent with the concept of

procedural justice, Bowen and Ostroff (2004) have also emphasized the importance of process in human resource practices. It has been proposed that strong and effective human resource practices should be visible and relevant (i.e., distinctiveness), convey unambiguous and consistent messages (i.e., consistency), and treat everyone in an unbiased manner (i.e., consensus). Literatures have shown that a fair process may lead to better reception of an organization's decisions and human resource practices.

Applying Bowen and Ostroff's (2004) suggestions to the implementation of an early retirement incentive program, organizations are recommended to elaborately consider several issues in order to reach the expected goal of the program. First of all, a need analysis should be conducted, and employees should be consulted before the program is finalized to ensure the program's relevance. It may help decision makers to design the incentives more effectively by knowing the diverse needs and preferences of employees. In some situations, outplacement services and phased retirement opportunities might be more important and attractive than a sizable one-time termination bonus, and vice versa in other situations. Better understanding of employees' needs helps organizations to better incorporate them in the early retirement incentive programs.

Second, it is necessary to make sure everyone is aware of the opportunity of the early retirement incentive program and understands the eligibility criteria and benefits. Organizations should make sure that all employees are able to access the resources offered to them. To improve the visibility and the degree of clarity of the early retirement incentive program, top management should show a certain level of commitment to support the implementation of the program. Also, organization may facilitate relevant communication by having workshops and retirement counseling hours. These practices ensure that the accurate and specific information about financial benefits and other incentives is being conveyed to employees and help to reduce employees' anxiety about their future.

Third, given the risk involved in the decision making regarding whether to accept an early retirement incentive package, organizations should provide information as accurate as possible regarding the incentive window (i.e., the period of time that employees are given to consider participating in the program) as well as future plans of offering an early retirement incentive program. Employees' expectation of future early retirement incentive programs may influence their decision of whether to accept a present early retirement incentive offer. For example, Kim and Feldman (1998) found that employees who were ambivalent about early retirement tended to put off the difficult decision to a later date if they expected future implementation of similar programs, while a low expectation led to high probability of accepting the present early retirement incentive offer.

In addition to the influence on employees who are eligible to participate in early retirement programs, having an appropriate process for implementing an early retirement incentive program may also improve the remaining employees' attitude toward their organizations. During the implementation process, organizations may deliver a message of consideration of older employees' well-being and enhance employees' sense of belongingness. This message is likely to be supported by crafting a process that is fair, transparent, and consistent. So far, little research attention has been paid to the impacts of the process of early retirement incentive programs.

Future Research Directions

Research on early retirement incentive programs has been largely focused on the factors that may influence employees' acceptance of the offers. In the following section, several future research directions are recommended. First of all, most existing studies have focused on the one-time decision made by employees regarding whether or not to accept an early retirement incentive package or the acceptance rate of early retirement incentive programs. However, because of the difficulty in predicting and controlling the number of employees participating in the program, organizations always need to make multiple offers in order to reach their strategic goal. Therefore, a longitudinal and dynamic perspective should be taken in future research in order to understand the effectiveness of the whole early retirement incentive program. From a practical perspective, a relevant question for the decision makers is to decide how much to adjust the eligibility criteria in designing a new round of the early retirement program. This question is important because it determines whether the organization may reach its staffing goal, and it may result in perception of injustice if successive programs are not designed in a fair manner.

Another relevant question is how one's early retirement incentive acceptance decisions at different time points influence each other. To be specific, how do employees' prior early retirement decisions influence their present acceptance? How do employees' expectations of future incentives influence their present acceptance? The only empirical work addressing these questions was conducted by Kim and Feldman (1998). Their study examined the participants' actual acceptance of three successive early retirement incentive offers and found that individuals who had previously declined an early retirement incentive offer were more likely to decline early retirement incentives in the future, and individuals with greater expectations of future early retirement incentives were more likely to decline the present early retirement incentive offer. Specifically, one's decisions regarding whether to accept an early retirement incentive offer may not be independent of each other among successive multiple opportunities. In other words, the attractiveness of an early retirement incentive offer might be shaped by one's prior decisions. One is likely to confirm an earlier decision without rational considerations even if the specific contextual factors (e.g., age, retirement saving, workplace age composition, etc.) have changed since the last decision.

Second, few studies so far have been conducted to explore the influences of the implementation process of early retirement incentive programs. As discussed earlier in this chapter, like other human resource practices, the process should be fair and consistent in order to make sure that the incentive program is highly visible and accessible to every employee. For employees, a well-designed implementation process helps them better understand the eligibility criteria and benefits involved in early retirement incentive programs and reduces their anxiety about facing the uncertainty, and thus they may make more rational decisions. For organizations, a justified process may enhance the sense of control in predicting the reactions of employees and in predicting the acceptance rate of early retirement incentive offers. Furthermore, the process of how such a program is implemented may also influence the perception of employees who are not currently eligible for early retirement. Their perceived exchange relationship with their organizations may be enhanced or harmed based on the organizations' treatment toward older employees during the implementation process.

Third, in studying the determinants of acceptance of early retirement incentive programs, little attention has been paid to personality or individual traits of employees. Given the uncertainty involved in early retirement, accepting early retirement incentive programs is likely to be viewed as a risk-taking behavior that leads to the discontinuity of one's role identity and lifestyle, as well as the possibility of being ineligible for Social Security benefits. In this situation, the financial incentives offered in an organization's early retirement incentive package may to some extent alleviate the expected risk. Taking another perspective, for employees who expect an involuntary layoff in the near future, accepting an early retirement incentive program may also be viewed as one way to avoid the risk of being laid off without any financial compensation. Therefore, relevant personality or individual traits, such as risk-taking and risk-aversive characteristics and tolerance of uncertainty, are expected to influence the perceived weights of the prospective value of accepting versus declining an early retirement incentive offer, which may in turn impact employees' acceptance of early retirement incentives.

Fourth, while many studies have been conducted to seek determinants of early retirement incentive acceptance, few studies have explored the individual outcomes of accepting early retirement incentive offers. Although early retirement incentive programs give employees a feeling of control over their future decisions, many employees still view early retirement as involuntary because the only potential alternative to early retirement is being laid off in the near future. It is important to study the different adjustment processes of employees with different levels of voluntariness perception in accepting early retirement incentive offers. In addition, employees who choose to accept the offers and employees who choose to decline the offers may experience different levels of satisfaction and well-being when they compare themselves with their counterparts. Different emotional reactions (e.g., regret, hindsight) may mediate the association between such comparison and long-term psychological outcomes. For example, it is possible that individuals who have accepted early retirement incentive offers may experience negative emotions when an expected layoff does not occur. The emotional mechanism of individual outcomes of early retirement incentive acceptance is speculation, but certainly could be tested empirically.

Conclusion

As a result of the aging population and disproportionate age composition at the workplace, early retirement incentive programs are introduced as financial inducements that organizations offer older workers to retire before their desired retirement age (Feldman, 2003). As was reviewed in this chapter,

from an organizational perspective, early retirement incentive programs function as a part of human resource management that helps organizations to reach their strategic goals, such as downsizing and labor composition restructure. From an employee perspective, these programs provide flexibility regarding the timing of retirement and introduce a decision-making process for eligible employees. For some employees, such programs offer good opportunities to leave the workplace and start a new stage of life earlier without losing all financial benefits of a full-time job. However, the flexibility or voluntariness is risk involved and may not be desirable for all employees. On the one hand, early retired employees may face an off-time transition when they have not planned much for retirement either financially or psychologically. In addition, in spite of the flexibility, employees may feel that they have no other choice but to take an early exit because the only alternative might be being laid off before they reach their normal retirement age.

In general, early retirement incentive programs have been shown to be effective in helping organizations to reach their staffing goals. Three key elements should be considered in designing an effective early retirement incentive program: the eligibility criteria, the content of incentives, and the process of implementation. Prior literatures have been largely focused on the eligibility and content of the programs. This chapter tends to draw more attention to the implementation process, which should deliver clear, accurate, and consistent information in a justified manner. It is influential to the acceptance decisions of eligible employees and the organization-related perception of the rest of the employees.

References

Alley, D., & Crimmins, E. (2007). The demography of aging and work. In K. S. Shultz & G. A. Adams (Eds.), *Aging and work in the 21st century* (pp. 7–23). Mahwah, NJ: Lawrence Erlbaum.

Atchley, R. C. (1989). A continuity theory of normal aging. *The Gerontologist, 29,* 183–190.

Avery, D. R., McKay, P. F., & Wilson, D. C. (2007). Engaging the aging workforce: The relationship between perceived age similarity, satisfaction with coworkers, and employee engagement. *Journal of Applied Psychology, 92,* 1542–1556.

Baillargeon, R. (1982). Determinants of early retirement. *Canada's Mental Health, 30,* 20–22.

Benítez-Silva, H., & Heiland, F. (2007).The Social Security Earnings Test and work incentives. *Journal of Policy Analysis and Management, 26,* 527–555.

Benítez-Silva, H., & Heiland, F. (2008). Early claiming of social security benefits and labour supply behaviour of older Americans. *Applied Economics, 40,* 2969–2985.

Bidewell, J., Griffin, B., & Hesketh, B. (2006). Timing of retirement: Including delay discounting perspective in retirement model. *Journal of Vocational Behavior, 68,* 368–387.

Blakeley, J. A., & Ribeiro, V. E. S. (2008). Early retirement among registered nurses: Contributing factors. *Journal of Nursing Management, 16,* 29–37.

Blekesaune, M., & Solem, P. E. (2005). Working conditions and early retirement: A prospective study of retirement behavior. *Research on Aging, 27,* 3–30.

Blundell, R., Meghir, C., & Smith, S. (2002). Pension incentives and the pattern of early retirement. *The Economic Journal, 112,* 153–170.

Bowen, D. E., & Ostroff, C. (2004). The "strength" of the HRM system, organizational climate formation, and firm performance. *Academy of Management Review, 29,* 203–221.

Carstensen, L. L. (1991). Selectivity theory: Social activity in life-span context. In K. W. Schaie (Ed.), *Annual review of gerontology and geriatrics* (Vol. 11, pp. 195–217). New York, NY: Springer.

Clark, R. L., & Hammond, P. B. (2001). Introduction: Changing retirement policies and patterns in higher education. In R. L. Clark & P. B. Hammond (Eds.), *To retire or not? Retirement policy and practice in higher education* (pp. 1–20). Philadelphia, PA: University of Pennsylvania Press.

Cleveland, J. N., & Lim, A. S. (2007). Employee age and performance in organizations. In K. S. Shultz & G. A. Adams (Eds.), *Aging and work in the 21st century* (pp. 109–137). Mahwah, NJ: Lawrence Erlbaum.

Colquitt, J. A., Conlon, D. E., Wesson, M. J., Porter, C. O. L. H., & Ng, K. Y. (2001). Justice at the millennium: A meta-analytic review of 25 years of organizational justice research. *Journal of Applied Psychology, 86,* 425–445.

Cropanzano, R., & Greenberg, J. (1997). Progress in organizational justice: Tunneling through the maze. In C. Cooper & I. Robertson (Eds.), *International review of industrial and organizational psychology* (pp. 317–372). New York, NY: Wiley.

Doeringer, P. B. (1990). *Bridges to retirement.* Ithaca, NY: Cornell University ILR Press.

Ebbinghaus, B. (2006). *Reforming early retirement in Europe, Japan and the USA.* Oxford: Oxford University Press.

Elovainio, M., Forma, P., Kivimaki, M., Sinervo, T., Sutinen, R., & Laine, M. (2005). Job demands and job control as correlates of early retirement thoughts in Finnish social and health care employees. *Work and Stress, 19,* 84–92.

Feldman, D. C. (1994). The decision to retire early: A review and conceptualization. *Academy of Management Review, 19,* 285–311.

Feldman, D. C. (2003). Endgame: The design and implementation of early retirement incentive programs. In G. A. Adams & T. A. Beehr (Eds.), *Retirement: Reasons, processes, and results* (pp. 83–114). New York, NY: Springer.

Feldman, D. C. (2007). Career mobility and career stability among older workers. In K. S. Shultz & G. A. Adams (Eds.), *Aging and work in the 21st century* (pp. 179–197). Mahwah, NJ: Lawrence Erlbaum.

Greller, M. M., & Stroh, L. K. (2003). Extending work lives: Are current approaches tools or talismans? In G. A. Adams & T. A. Beehr (Eds.), *Retirement: Reasons, processes, and results* (pp. 115–135). New York, NY: Springer.

Hagan, R., Jones, A. M., & Rice, N. (2009). Health and retirement in Europe. *International Journal of Environmental Research and Public Health, 6,* 2676–2695.

Hallberg, D., & Eklof, M. (2010). Do buy-outs of older workers matter? Estimating retirement behavior with special early retirement offers. *International Journal of Manpower, 31,* 337–359.

Hanks, R. S. (1990). The impact of early retirement incentives on retirees and their families. *Journal of Family Issues, 11,* 424–437.

Hardy, M. A., & Quadagno, J. (1995). Satisfaction with early retirement: Making choices in the auto industry. *Journal of Gerontology: Social Science, 50B,* S217–S228.

Hayden, H. S., & Pfadenhauer, D. M. (2005). Implementing early retirement incentive programs: A step-by-step guide. *HR Advisor,* September/October, 12–20.

Higgs, P., Mein, G., Ferrie, J., Hyde, M., & Nazroo, J. (2003). Pathways to early retirement: Structure and agency in decision-making among civil servants. *Aging and Society, 23,* 761–778.

Hogarth, J. M. (1988). Accepting an early retirement bonus: An empirical study. *Journal of Human Resource, 23,* 21–33.

Keefe, J. (2001). Intangible and tangible retirement incentives. In R. L. Clark & P. B. Hammond (Eds.), *To retire or not? Retirement policy and practice in higher education* (pp. 128–137). Philadelphia, PA: University of Pennsylvania Press.

Kim, S., & Feldman, D. C. (1998). Healthy, wealthy, or wise: Predicting actual acceptances of early retirement incentives at three points in time. *Personnel Psychology, 51,* 623–642.

Leventhal, G. S. (1980). What should be done with equity theory? New approaches to the study of fairness in social relationships. In K. Gergen, M. Greenberg, & R. Willis (Eds.), *Social exchange: Advances in theory and research* (pp. 27–55). New York, NY: Plenum.

Mein, G., Martikainen, P., Stansfeld, S., Brunner, E., Fuhrer, R., & Marmot, M. (2000). Predictors of early retirement in British civil servants. *Age and Ageing, 29,* 529–536.

Ng, T. W. H., & Feldman, D. C. (2008). The relationship of age to ten dimensions of job performance. *Journal of Applied Psychology, 93,* 392–423.

Posthuma, R. A., & Campion, M. A. (2009). Age stereotypes in the workplace: Common stereotypes, moderators, and future research directions. *Journal of Management, 35,* 158–188.

Quinn, J. F. (2010). Work, retirement, and the encore career: Elders and the future of the American workforce. *Generations, 34,* 45–55.

Robertson, A. (2000). "I saw the handwriting on the wall": Shades of meaning in reasons for early retirement. *Journal of Aging Studies, 14,* 63–79.

Shuey, K. M. (2004). Worker preferences, spousal coordination, and participation in an employer-sponsored pension plan. *Research on Aging, 26,* 287–316.

Shultz, K. S. (2003). Bridge employment: Work after retirement. In G. A. Adams & T. A. Beehr (Eds.), *Retirement: Reasons, processes, and results* (pp. 214–241). New York: Springer.

Shultz, K. S., Morton, K. R., & Weckerle, J. R. (1998). The influence of push and pull factors on voluntary and involuntary early retirees' retirement decision and adjustment. *Journal of Vocational Behavior, 53,* 145–157.

Thibaut, J., & Walker, L. (1975). *Procedural justice: A psychological analysis.* Hillsdale, NJ: Lawrence Erlbaum.

Tyers, R., & Shi, Q. (2007). Demographic change and policy responses: Implications for the global economy. *World Economy, 1,* 537–566.

Wang, M. (2007). Profiling retirees in the retirement transition and adjustment process: Examining the longitudinal change

patterns of retirees' psychological well-being. *Journal of Applied Psychology, 92,* 455–474.

Wang, M., Adams, G. A., Beehr, T. A., & Shultz, K. S. (2009). Bridge employment and retirement: Issues and opportunities during the latter part of one's career. In S. G. Baugh & S. E. Sullivan (Eds.), *Maintaining focus, energy, and options over the career* (pp. 135–162), Charlotte, NC: IAP.

Wang, M., & Shultz, K. (2010). Employee retirement: A review and recommendations for future investigation. *Journal of Management, 36,* 172–206.

Wang, M., & Zhan, Y. (2012). Employee-organization relationship in older workers. In L. M. Shore, J. A.-M. Coyle-Shapiro, & L. Tetrick (Eds.), *The employee-organization relationship: Applications for the 21st century* (pp. 427–454). New York, NY: Psychology Press.

Zhan, Y., Wang, M., Liu, S., & Shultz, K. S. (2009). Bridge employment and retirees' health: A longitudinal investigation. *Journal of Occupational Health Psychology, 14,* 374–389.

Health Care and Health Insurance in Retirement

Karoline Mortensen *and* Jennifer Villani

Abstract

This chapter discusses the current states of health care and health insurance practice for retirees. The retired population has important public policy significance for the health care sector. Retirees over age 65 are less healthy than the younger population, use more health care services, have higher health expenditures, and are a powerful voting and lobbying force in politics. This chapter details the health insurance options available to retirees and use of health care services in retirement, and offers future directions for research. Medicare is the primary insurer for virtually all retirees over age 65, so the benefits, financing, eligibility, enrollment, quality, access, and utilization of health care services covered by Medicare are described in detail. Retirees will be affected in many ways by the Patient Protection and Affordable Care Act (PPACA) of 2010. The changes will be highlighted throughout the chapter and discussed in depth in the Future Directions section.

Key Words: medicare, health, insurance, health care utilization, PPACA, chronic conditions

The retired population has important public policy significance for the health care sector. Retirees over age 65 are less healthy than the younger population (Case & Deaton, 2005), have more chronic conditions (Thorpe & Howard, 2006), use more health care services and have higher health expenditures (Stanton, 2006), tend to have fixed incomes, and are a powerful voting and lobbying force in politics. This chapter details the health insurance options available to retirees and use of health care services in retirement, and offers future directions for research. Retirees will be affected in many ways by the Patient Protection and Affordable Care Act (PPACA) of 2010. The changes will be highlighted throughout the chapter and discussed in depth in the Future Directions section. Health insurance during retirement has important implications for retirees' financial and physical well-being. If retirees do not plan carefully, they may encounter financial difficulties as a result of both acute and chronic health conditions.

Medicare

Unlike their younger counterparts in the United States, virtually every individual over retirement age is enrolled in a health insurance program. Medicare is the social public insurance program for individuals over age 65 and some younger people with permanent disabilities. Medicare was established in 1965 under Title XVIII of the Social Security Act (Iglehart, 1999), after many failed attempts for national health insurance (Blumenthal, 2006). It is administered by the Centers for Medicare & Medicaid Services (CMS), an agency under the U.S. Department of Health and Human Services. It is not a means-tested or welfare program; Medicare is available to, and covers almost all, U.S. citizens and legal permanent residents (who have been in the country for five continuous years) over age 65 regardless of income or pre-existing conditions. It is a federal program with uniform standards.

In 2010, Medicare provided coverage to 47 million people: 39 million individuals over age 65 and 8 million people with permanent disabilities (Kaiser Family Foundation, 2010a). Only about 1.5% of Americans over age 65 lack Medicare coverage (Schiff, 2002). Medicare benefit payments were estimated to be $504 billion in 2010, which comprised 12% of the federal budget and more than 20% of total national health expenditures (Kaiser Family Foundation, 2010a). Prior to Medicare's passage in 1965, 50% of the group age 65 and older, most of whom were no longer actively employed, had hospital insurance (Gornick, Greenberg, Eggers, & Dobson, 1985).

Eligibility, Benefits, and Financing

Medicare comprises four parts, identified as Parts A through D. Part A is the Hospital Insurance (HI) program, Part B is the Supplementary Medical Insurance (SMI) program, Part C is the Medicare Advantage program that allows beneficiaries to enroll in a private plan, and Part D is the outpatient prescription drug benefit administered by private insurance plans. Eligibility, covered benefits, cost sharing, and financing of each part are discussed in this section.

Part A. Part A covers inpatient hospital care, skilled nursing facilities, home health, and hospice care. Enrollment is automatic if the individual is already receiving benefits from Social Security or the Railroad Retirement Board. Part A and Part B start on the first day of the month the enrollee turns 65. The red, white, and blue Medicare card arrives in the mail three months before the individual's 65th birthday. Those not receiving Social Security or Railroad Retirement Board benefits must sign themselves up for Medicare.

Entitlement is automatic if individuals or their spouses have made payroll contributions for 40 quarters (10 years). There is no premium for Part A for those who paid payroll taxes; those who did not can pay a monthly premium for Part A benefits. In 2011, the monthly premium for those who worked between 30 and 39 quarters was $248, and for those working fewer than 30 quarters the premium was $450 (http://www.medicare.gov). Individuals who are not automatically entitled to Part A face up to a 10% penalty if they do not sign up when they are first eligible. An increased premium will be charged to the beneficiary for two times the number of years they delayed enrollment.

The benefit structure under Part A is complex. Hospital and nursing home stays are classified by benefit periods, which begin on the day the beneficiary is hospitalized and end when he or she has not been in a hospital or skilled nursing facility for 60 days. The number of benefit periods is unlimited in Medicare, but a benefit period has 90 days of maximum coverage. Beneficiaries are provided with a lifetime reserve of 60 additional hospital days that they can use once they have reached the 90-day maximum in the benefit period. These additional 60 days can be used for multiple benefit periods that have reached the 90-day maximum. Once this reserve is used, the beneficiary's days in the hospital after 90 days are not covered by Medicare.

Medicare entails substantial deductibles, coinsurance, and copayments for Part A covered benefits. A deductible is the amount the insured must first pay before any benefits of the plan are payable (Shi & Singh, 2009). Deductibles in 2011 were $1,132 for a hospital stay of 1–60 days, $283 per day for days 61–90, $566 per day for days 91–150, and the enrollee pays all costs for each day beyond 150 days (http://www.medicare.gov).

The financing of each part of Medicare varies. Part A is a "pay-as-you-go" program, meaning taxes collected from current workers are used to finance Part A obligations of current retirees. Part A is a compulsory program in that employees and employers must each contribute a special Social Security payroll tax on earnings of 1.45% each (2.9% total). The self-employed bear the entire 2.9% tax. Since 1994, there is no cap on wages subject to the tax. In 2010, this tax financed 85% of Part A revenue (Kaiser Family Foundation, 2010c). The Affordable Care Act increases the payroll tax by 0.9 percentage points for higher-income taxpayers to 2.35% beginning in 2013 (Cubanski, Huang, Damico, Jacobson, & Neuman, 2010). The remainder is financed by small payments from states, interest, and other smaller contributions. Part A accounted for about 36% of total Medicare benefit spending in 2009 (Kaiser Family Foundation, 2010a).

Part B. Part B covers physician visits, hospital outpatient care, and other services including preventive screenings such as colorectal screening and mammography. Part B also covers clinical laboratory services, ambulance services, outpatient mental health care, durable medical equipment, and diagnostic tests. Enrollment in Part B uses an opt-out method rather than an opt-in method; if the individual is automatically enrolled because he or she receives Social Security or Railroad Retirement Board benefits but chooses to opt out of Part B coverage, he or she returns the Part B card to Medicare.

Under the Medicare law, the standard premium is set to cover one-fourth of the average cost of Part B services incurred by beneficiaries aged 65 and over. The remaining 75% of Part B costs are financed by federal general revenues (htt://www.cms.gov). Since the premium is calculated to increase as Medicare costs increase, and the remainder is financed by general revenues, Part B of Medicare is not in jeopardy of insolvency, although the substantial price tag does have opportunity costs of alternate uses of those tax dollars.

The actual Part B premium paid varies for beneficiaries. The Medicare Prescription Drug, Improvement, and Modernization Act of 2003 (MMA) allowed higher premiums to be charged to higher-income Medicare beneficiaries. Individuals making over $85,000 and couples making over $170,000 face higher premiums (these income thresholds are frozen between 2011 and 2019 by the Affordable Care Act, causing more beneficiaries to be charged higher premiums over time) (Kaiser Family Foundation, 2010b). The Part B premium in 2011, for those who had the premium deducted from their Social Security check, or about 75% of beneficiaries, was $96.40 per month for most beneficiaries (same as the 2009 and 2010 premiums) (http://www.medicare.gov). The premium was $110.50 for new beneficiaries that enrolled in 2010. Premiums increased by income level, up to $369.10 per month if individual income was above $214,000 or if joint income was above $428,000.

Medicare historically did not cover routine annual exams in a physician's office. In 2005, Part B began covering a one-time "welcome to Medicare" physical exam within the first 12 months of enrolling. During the exam, the physician records the patient's medical history; checks blood pressure, vision, height, and weight; and checks to be sure the patient is up-to-date with preventive screenings and services. An annual wellness exam was added to Medicare on January 1, 2011, as a result of the Affordable Care Act. Beneficiaries are now entitled to a wellness visit once every 12 months (http://www.medicare.gov).

Part A and Part B of Medicare were structured off of Blue Cross (hospital insurance) and Blue Shield (physician insurance) policies as they existed in the 1960s. Developing an insurance program for the elderly based on insurance policies designed for healthy working adults readily results in gaps in benefits. Medicare does not cover many services and items that are necessities for many older adults, including long-term care, routine dental care,

dentures, acupuncture, hearing aids, and exams for hearing aids (Centers for Medicare & Medicaid Services, 2010a). Medicare did not cover outpatient prescription drugs until 2006.

Part C. The Medicare Advantage (MA) program (formerly known as Medicare + Choice) comprises Part C of Medicare. Part C replaces the benefits from "original" Medicare Parts A, B, and D with enrollment in an MA private insurance plan. These private plans include at a minimum the benefits associated with original Medicare. Private plans offered include plans such as a health maintenance organization (HMO), preferred provider organization (PPO), or even a fee-for-service plan (original Medicare is a fee-for-service plan).

Medicare beneficiaries have the option of enrolling in a Medicare Advantage program or remaining in original Medicare. In 2010, 24% of beneficiaries (11.4 million) were enrolled in a Medicare Advantage Plan; enrollment more than doubled between 2005 and 2010 (Cubanski et al., 2010). HMOs were by far the most popular plans, with 65% of total Medicare Advantage enrollment in 2010 (Kaiser Family Foundation, 2010d). Many Medicare Advantage Plans provide supplemental benefits in addition to Medicare-covered benefits. Benefits include lower cost sharing, and added benefits such as vision exams, hearing tests, or preventive dental exams (Cubanski et al., 2010).

There is substantial variation across Medicare Advantage Plans, and thus variation in premiums for these plans. Some plans assist beneficiaries with their Part B premiums. The average enrollment-weighted premium for plans covering Part D benefits in addition to Part A and B benefits was $48 per month in 2010 (Cubanski et al., 2010). Almost half of Medicare Advantage drug plan beneficiaries were in plans that did not charge an additional premium for coverage (Cubanski et al., 2010). Medicare payments to Medicare Advantage Plans were estimated to total $116 billion in 2010 (Kaiser Family Foundation, 2010d).

Medicare Advantage and its predecessor, Medicare + Choice, are strategies to infuse market forces and competition into Medicare. Medicare + Choice was created in 1996 when both houses of Congress came under Republican control (Brown & Sparer, 2003). Private plans were paid a fixed monthly amount of 95% of average Medicare fee-for-service costs in each county for each beneficiary (since beneficiaries enrolling in these plans were typically healthier than average) (Kaiser Family Foundation, 2010d). Managed care plans entered the market to build market share. However, when payments were not satisfactory and the costs of covering beneficiaries were unexpectedly higher than insurers had anticipated, plans abandoned the market and left many beneficiaries without managed care coverage (Brown & Sparer, 2003). The MMA renamed Medicare + Choice to Medicare Advantage and structured it carefully to avoid the previous mistakes.

In an effort to avoid the earlier payment issues, payments to MA plans per beneficiary average 109% of original Medicare fee-for-service-costs in 2010 (Kaiser Family Foundation, 2010d). These federal payments to private plans were frozen in 2011 and reduced in 2012 under the Affordable Care Act, bringing them more in line with the average costs of care under original Medicare. The majority of beneficiaries, enrolled in original Medicare, will not be affected, but those in MA plans may find plans cutting ancillary benefits such as vision and dental. However, bonuses to top-performing MA plans are implemented in 2012 under the Affordable Care Act. U.S. Department of Health and Human Services actuaries predict a decline in enrollment between 2011 and 2019 and an erosion of extra benefits, but long-run implications for the viability of MA plans remain to be seen (Gold et al., 2010).

Part D. Part D is a voluntary program for enrollees of Part A and/or Part B that provides insurance coverage for prescription drugs for a separate, additional premium. Part D of Medicare was created under the MMA. Beneficiaries can elect to receive drug benefits through their Medicare Advantage Plans, if they offer coverage at least comparable to Part D coverage ("creditable coverage"), or through stand-alone Part D prescription drug plans (PDPs). Before Part D was established, more than 30% of beneficiaries lacked insurance coverage for prescribed medications (Duggan, Healy, & Morton, 2008), and 3.3% of beneficiaries reported failing to fill or refill one or more prescriptions (Kennedy, Tuleu, & MacKay, 2008).

In 2010, 90% of Medicare beneficiaries had prescription drug coverage. Almost 40% had coverage via a PDP; 21% had coverage through a Medicare Advantage drug plan; 18% had retiree drug coverage; 13% had coverage from state assistance programs, Medigap, and other sources; and 10% had no drug coverage (Kaiser Family Foundation, 2010e). The number without coverage has been steady since 2006 (Neuman & Cubanski, 2009), and those beneficiaries report being in good health and having little need for medications (Neuman

et al., 2007; Regan & Petroski, 2007). Part D enrollment is concentrated; according to the Kaiser Family Foundation, five firms accounted for 54% of enrollees in 2010.

Part D spending was estimated to total $55 billion in 2010 (Kaiser Family Foundation, 2010e). Part D is predominantly financed by general revenues. General revenues accounted for 82% of Part D revenues in 2010, beneficiary premiums accounted for 10% of revenue, and payments from states accounted for 7% (Kaiser Family Foundation, 2010c). Similar to Part B, the financing mechanism ensures that the program does not face insolvency issues.

Beneficiaries who choose to enroll in Part D must do so within the six-month period surrounding their date of eligibility (i.e., three months before and three months after). Failure to enroll in that time frame may result in a late enrollment penalty. The penalty is calculated as 1% of the national Part D base premium times the number of months without coverage, and the resulting amount is added to the beneficiary's monthly premium. Congress felt the premium penalty was necessary to avoid adverse selection, since politics necessitated the Part D program be voluntary rather than mandatory.

The MMA specifies a minimum standard benefit structure for drug plans. For 2011, the standard benefit included an annual deductible of $310, followed by 25% coinsurance until drug costs reach the initial coverage limit of $2,840. Then enrollees enter the coverage gap (also known as the "donut hole"). In previous years, enrollees incurred 100% of their prescription drug costs while in the coverage gap. The coverage gap began to close with the passage of the Affordable Care Act. As of 2011, beneficiaries who enter the coverage gap will receive discounts from pharmaceutical manufacturers of 50% off brand-name drugs and 7% off generic drugs to be paid by their plans. Effectively, this left beneficiaries with 50% coinsurance for brand-name drugs and 93% coinsurance for generics. Additional discounts will be phased in each year until 2020, when coinsurance will remain at 25% in the coverage gap for both brand-name and generic drugs. When a beneficiary's total drug costs exceeded $6,447.50 in 2011, they received catastrophic coverage.

In 2009, the majority of Medicare drug plans, 75% of stand-alone plans, and 49% of Medicare Advantage Plans did not offer coverage of the "donut hole" gap (Neuman & Cubanski, 2009). Gap coverage is primarily limited to generic drugs; only two insurers offered coverage for brand-name drugs in the gap in 2006, and they withdrew those plans after the first year because of adverse selection (Neuman & Cubanski, 2009).

Not all PDPs offer the standard benefit as defined above. In 2011, 40% of PDPs charged the standard $310 deductible, 18% charged a smaller deductible, and 42% had no deductible at all (Hoadley, Cubanski, Hargrave, Summer, & Neuman, 2010). All PDPs charge monthly premiums. Hoadley et al. (2010) estimated that beneficiaries would experience a 10% increase in monthly premiums from 2010 to 2011. The projected weighted-average premium for PDPs was $40.72 per month. However, premiums vary based on region. The range for 2011 was from $14.80 (in all states) to $133.40 (in Delaware, Maryland, and the District of Columbia) (Hoadley et al., 2010).

For newly eligible Medicare beneficiaries, choosing whether to enroll in Part D can be difficult if there is not a current or anticipated need for prescription drugs. However, the late enrollment penalty must be factored into their decision. An analysis by Federowicz (2008) concluded that it is best for newly eligible beneficiaries to avoid the penalty and enroll in Part D. In doing so, beneficiaries will reduce lifetime out-of-pocket spending for prescription drugs, even if they do not require prescription medications in the short term.

Choosing a drug plan has remained challenging for beneficiaries. Many beneficiaries have argued that the benefit is too complex (Avorn, 2006; Polinski, Bhandari, Saya, Schneeweiss, & Shrank, 2010). Not only must they comprehend Part D's complex benefit structure, but they also need to anticipate future drug expenses in order to select the most optimal drug plan. Beneficiaries are focusing too much on monthly premiums when choosing plans, often disregarding other out-of-pocket spending (Abaluck & Gruber, 2009). Ultimately, choosing a suboptimal plan may lead to poorer coverage and higher total out-of-pocket spending. It is anticipated that eventually CMS will standardize these options to assist beneficiaries with the complex array of choices.

The number of plans to choose from has declined each year since 2007. On average, beneficiaries have 33 PDPs to choose from for 2011 (Hoadley et al., 2010). Limiting the number of plans offered will actually make it easier for enrollees (Hanoch, Miron-Shatz, Cole, Himmelstein, & Federman, 2010). Hanoch et al. (2010) found a positive correlation between number of plans offered and difficulty in selecting the plan with the best coverage at the lowest cost.

Selecting the most optimal plan one year does not necessarily mean that same plan will be the best fit the following year. In addition to annual fluctuations in deductibles and monthly premiums, PDPs often change their drug formularies each year. Beneficiaries should reassess their plan choices each year; however, most are reluctant to make changes (Jackson & Axelsen, 2008; Polinski et al., 2010; Walberg & Patel, 2009). Changes can be made during the enrollment period each year, either online via the Medicare Drug Plan Finder, or via telephone. Beneficiaries are automatically disenrolled from their old plan once the new plan's coverage begins. However, if a beneficiary is enrolled in a Medicare Advantage Plan and then enrolls in a PDP, they will be disenrolled from their Medicare Advantage Plan and returned to original Medicare (Centers for Medicare & Medicaid Services, 2010a).

Although the coverage gap is slowly being phased out, it has historically been more burdensome for certain groups. About one out of every six enrollees entered the coverage gap in 2006 (Ettner et al., 2010). Enrollees with chronic pulmonary disease, dementia, depression, incontinence, and/or Parkinson's disease were more likely to reach the coverage gap since they are more likely to rely on brand-name drugs for treatment (Ettner et al., 2010). Reaching the coverage gap often results in cost-related medication non-adherence for the sickest enrollees (Madden et al., 2008; Zivin, Madden, Graves, Zhang, & Soumerai, 2009).

Other Sources of Insurance Coverage

Although Medicare covers virtually all individuals age 65 and over, there are several other sources of health insurance coverage in retirement as well as early retirement (Figure 29.1). Some of these options are supplemental to the coverage that Medicare provides, such as Medicare-Medicaid dual eligible coverage, Medigap policies, and employer-sponsored retiree health insurance, whereas others fill in the gaps for retirees not eligible for Medicare, such as employer-sponsored early retiree coverage. This section describes each of these supplemental options in turn. Beneficiaries may also receive supplemental assistance through the military (TRICARE), the Veterans Administration (CHAMPVA), and other local, state, and federal government programs. TRICARE and CHAMPVA are always the secondary payers for Medicare beneficiaries, meaning these programs pay most of the cost sharing and deductibles not covered by Medicare.

EARLY RETIREMENT (before age 65)
- Employer-sponsored retiree health benifits (own or spouse's)
- Early Retiree Reinsurance Program (ERRP) (until program ends on Janaury 1, 2014)
- COBRA (for up to 18 months after retirement)
- Union or membership organization
- TRICARE for retired military and their dependents
- CHAMPVA for disabled veterans and their dependents
- Individual market

EARLY RETIREMENT (age 65 and over)
- Medicare (basic coverage under Parts A and B)
- Part C/Medicare Advantage
- Part D prescription drug coverage
- Medigap supplemental coverage
- Dual eligibilty with Medicaid (if low income)
- Employer-sponsored retiree health benifits

Figure 29.1 Health Insurance Options in Retirement

Dual Eligibles

Medicare beneficiaries who meet the income and asset requirements for receiving Supplemental Security Income (SSI) and are aged, blind, or disabled are also eligible for Medicaid coverage. Unlike federally standardized Medicare, Medicaid benefits vary by state. Depending on their income, dual eligibles receive either full or partial assistance via Medicaid. Full dual eligibles have Medicare and are entitled to full state Medicaid benefits if they meet the income threshold in their state. They receive assistance from Medicaid for their Medicare Part A and Part B premiums, other cost-sharing expenses, and subsidies for their Part D premiums. They are also eligible for additional services not covered by Medicare such as long-term care, vision, dental, and hearing benefits (Cubanski et al., 2010).

Dual eligibles with partial benefits do not get full Medicaid benefits. They are enrolled in one of several Medicare Savings Programs administered by Medicaid ("Seniors & Medicare and Medicaid Enrollees," n.d.). Qualified Medicare Beneficiaries (QMBs) have an income of no more than 100% of the federal poverty level and resources less than twice the SSI limit. Medicaid pays for their Medicare premiums, deductibles, coinsurance, and copayments for Parts A and B. The Specified Low-Income Medicare Beneficiary (SLMB) program is for beneficiaries with an income between 100% and 120% of the federal poverty level and resources not exceeding twice the SSI limit. Medicaid pays only for Medicare Part B premiums in most cases. Qualifying Individuals (QIs) have slightly higher incomes, between 120% and 135% of the federal poverty level, and resources less than twice the SSI limit. QIs are eligible for Medicaid assistance

for their Medicare Part B premium ("Seniors & Medicare and Medicaid Enrollees," 2012).

There were 5.6 million dual eligibles over age 65 in 2005 (Kaiser Family Foundation, 2009). Although there have been numerous studies on chronic disease, comorbidity, and utilization of services among dual eligibles (Coughlin, Waidmann, & Watts, 2009; Kasper, Watts, & Lyons, 2010; Moon & Shin, 2006), this group also includes disabled individuals under age 65, so the characterizations are not generalizable to the low-income retired population.

Medigap Policies

Beneficiaries who are enrolled in original Part A and Part B may opt to purchase Medicare supplemental insurance to cover, to varying degrees, out-of-pocket costs associated with using services, including deductibles, coinsurance, and copayments. All of the plans offer additional benefits that are not paid by Medicare, such as preventive care and blood for transfusions. Some plans also cover emergency care while traveling abroad. The coverage offered via these policies is still not comprehensive, as Medigap policies do not cover long-term care, vision, or dental services. Supplemental coverage plays a significant role in protecting Medicare beneficiaries from financial risk (Atherly, 2001).

These Medigap policies are sold by private insurance companies but are standardized by CMS. Every insurer must follow federal and state laws, and the benefits in any Medigap supplement plan must be the same for any insurance company. When the plans were originally conceived, they were not uniform and beneficiaries were faced with an array of options (Rice & Thomas, 1992). The plans are now standardized alphabetically to simplify choices; as you move through the alphabet, the plans become more comprehensive in the benefits they provide. Before the Affordable Care Act, there were twelve policies that were available for purchase, identified by letters A through L. As of 2010, there are ten policy options labeled A through N. Two new policy options were added, M and N, and several (E, H, I, and J) could no longer be sold, although beneficiaries with those plans could opt to remain in them (Centers for Medicare & Medicaid Services, 2010b). Benefits and coinsurance in some of these plans has changed, adding a layer of complexity for beneficiaries' decision making.

Individuals who purchase Medigap coverage must pay their Part B premium in addition to the Medigap policy premium. Policies cover individuals only; spouses must purchase their own plan. The cost of Medigap coverage varies widely. It largely depends on the level of coverage provided but also may be influenced by one's age, health status, location, and insurer preferences. If a Medicare beneficiary applies for Medigap coverage during the open enrollment period when he or she first becomes eligible for Medicare Part B, then medical underwriting cannot be used to set his or her Medigap premium.

Medigap plans share the costs of Part A and Part B services via original Medicare fee-for-service only. They are completely separate from Medicare Advantage Plans. Beneficiaries enrolled in a Medicare Advantage Plan do not need and in general cannot be sold a Medigap policy. New Medigap plans do not cover pharmaceuticals, as drugs have been covered by Part D since 2006. Although its effects on utilization of health care services are not entirely clear, Medigap insurance provides important financial protections for many low- and moderate-income beneficiaries (Lemieux, Chovan, & Heath, 2008).

Employer-Based Retiree Health Insurance

Employers are not required by law to provide health insurance coverage for their employees or their retirees. The proportion of large employers offering retiree health insurance in the United States has declined by half over the last twenty years (Strumpf, 2009). The declines are in large part due to changes approved by the Financial Accounting Standards Board in December of 1990. The board issued a financial accounting statement that required companies to record unfunded retiree health benefit liabilities on their financial statements beginning in December of 1992. The share of employers with at least 200 employees offering any type of retiree health benefits dropped from 66% in 1988 to 35% in 2006 (*The Retiree Health Care Challenge*, 2006).

Large employers are more likely to offer retiree health benefits than small employers; 34.2% of employers with over 1,000 workers offer them, compared to less than 1% of employers with fewer than ten workers (Employee Benefit Research Institute, 2010). About 35% of workers age 45 to 64 expect to receive retiree health benefits, despite only 21.5% of Medicare-eligible retirees actually having them in 2005 (Fronstin, Salisbury, & VanDerhei, 2008). Retiree health benefits supplement the coverage provided by Medicare.

Early Retiree Insurance

Unlike Social Security, early retirees under age 65 are not eligible for Medicare coverage. Retirees under age 65 who are not offered employer-sponsored retiree coverage have limited and potentially prohibitively expensive options. Coverage options include Consolidated Omnibus Budget Reconciliation Act (COBRA) health benefits from their pre-retirement employer; group-based coverage via a union, spouse's employer, or membership organization; purchasing individual private coverage; or enrolling in public coverage such as military coverage or Medicaid if they are eligible. Early retirees are eligible for COBRA for only eighteen months, and for many, bearing the employers' full cost of the premium plus administration fees is prohibitively expensive. Coverage on the individual market can also be expensive, and few retirees under age 65 are eligible for Medicaid, so for many early retirees these choices are not an option.

In fact, a retiree health insurance offer may increase the probability of early retirement by over one-third for both men and women (Strumpf, 2009). About one-quarter of early retirees have employer-sponsored retiree health benefits (Fronstin et al., 2008). In 2009, 6.2% of private-sector establishments offered health benefits to early retirees, a drop from 11.3% in 1997 (Employee Benefit Research Institute, 2010).

The Affordable Care Act authorized a new program called the Early Retiree Reinsurance Program (ERRP). ERRP provides reimbursement to participating employer-based plans for a portion of the costs of health benefits for early retirees and their spouses, surviving spouses, and dependents (www.errp.gov). As of October 2010, nearly 3,600 employers and unions were approved by

HHS to participate in the program ("Early Retiree Reinsurance Program," 2010). ERRP serves as a temporary bridge for employers and unions offering early retiree insurance. The program ends January 1, 2014, when the competitive private health insurance exchanges begin operation. The state-level health insurance exchanges will allow early retirees to purchase insurance coverage on the individual market at competitive prices.

Access, Utilization, and Chronic Conditions

Characteristics of Medicare Beneficiaries

Medicare beneficiaries are predominantly non-Hispanic whites (78%); almost 10% are black, 8% are Hispanic, 2% are Asian, and 3% are some other race (Cubanski et al., 2010). Cubanski et al. (2010) project that by 2050, this population will be more racially and ethnically diverse, and Hispanics will account for 42% of the over-age-65 population. Females (56%) outnumber males (44%). In 2006, the average annual median income among beneficiaries was $22,800, and nearly half of all beneficiaries had family incomes of $20,000 or less (Cubanski et al., 2010). Few beneficiaries had incomes exceeding $80,000. About 25% of beneficiaries have less than a high school education (Cubanski et al., 2010).

Health status varies significantly in the Medicare population. Approximately 28% of beneficiaries report being in fair or poor health. Racial and ethnic minorities are more likely to report worse health than whites (Cubanski et al., 2010). Those with lower incomes are generally in poorer health than beneficiaries with higher incomes. While 42% of beneficiaries with incomes below the federal poverty level report their health as fair or poor, only 18% of those three times above the federal poverty level do so (Cubanski et al., 2010).

Health Care Access

Despite fears that physicians may begin to stop accepting Medicare patients, currently Medicare beneficiaries generally do not experience significant difficulties in getting access to care. In 2008, only 4% of Medicare beneficiaries reported having difficulty finding a doctor who accepts Medicare (Cubanski & Neuman, 2010), which is similar to the privately insured population (Hackbarth, 2009). Medicare Payment Advisory Commission (MedPAC) data from 2007 show that 92% of office-based physicians who receive more than 10% of their practice revenue from Medicare were accepting new Medicare patients, and the share of physicians engaged in

participation agreements with Medicare was 95% (Hackbarth, 2009).

However, findings from surveys of physician offices suggest that beneficiaries' access to primary care is limited and varies significantly by region, population size, and provider type, and that primary care physicians are more likely than specialists to restrict Medicare patients (Chou, Cooney, Van Ness, Allore, & Gill, 2007). Availability of primary care has been associated with greater quality medical care for Medicare beneficiaries (Weiss & Blustein, 1996), but access and use of primary care alone do not guarantee better health outcomes (Goodman, Brownlee, Chang, & Fisher, 2010). There is valid concern that access issues may worsen in the future, with potentially negative effects on quality of care (this issue will be discussed in depth in the Future Directions section).

Access to hospital services continues to be good for beneficiaries. The volume of hospital outpatient services provided to beneficiaries has grown, indicating that access is strong, and quality of care measures are generally improving (Hackbarth, 2009). However, subgroups of the Medicare population, including black and Hispanic beneficiaries, those with low incomes, and those living in rural areas, have higher rates of access problems (Hackbarth, 2009). Beneficiaries without supplemental insurance coverage are more likely than those with supplemental coverage to report access problems (Cubanski et al., 2010).

Although over 90% of beneficiaries have Part D prescription drug coverage, they report some issues with access to medications. In 2008, 18% of Part D enrollees reported that they had to switch to a different medicine because a drug was not covered by their plan. Some enrollees (13%) were unable to get a prescription medicine because it was not covered by their plan, and 15% had to get prior authorization or special permission from the plan to continue using a medication (Cubanski & Neuman, 2010).

Health Care Utilization

Since the health care needs of Medicare beneficiaries vary significantly, there are variations in health care utilization. The majority of beneficiaries access preventive services. In 2008, 57% reported a complete physical exam in the previous twelve months, 68% reported a flu vaccination, 61% had a vision exam, and 47% had a dental exam (Cubanski & Neuman, 2010). Among women, 56% had a mammogram in the previous year, and 26% had a pap smear. Among men, 54% had a prostate exam (Cubanski & Neuman, 2010).

In 2006, 82% of all beneficiaries had one or more physician visits, 21% were hospitalized, 30% had one or more emergency room visits, and 8% had home health visits with a median number of seventeen visits (Cubanski et al., 2010). Some beneficiaries use services intensively; in 2008, 15% had six or more physician visits in the previous six months (Cubanski & Neuman, 2010).

Studies have consistently found that the creation of Part D has led to both an increase in drug utilization for the elderly and a reduction in their out-of-pocket drug expenses (Ketcham & Simon, 2008; Yin et al., 2008; Zhang, Lave, Newhouse, & Donohue, 2009; Duggan & Morton, 2010). Medicare Part D was found to reduce user cost among the elderly by 18.4%, to increase their use of prescription drugs by about 12.8%, and increase total usage in the United States by 4.5% in 2006 (Lichtenberg and Sun, 2007). Only 7% of Part D enrollees reported not taking any medications in 2008. Almost 20% reported taking one or two prescription drugs, 35% reported taking three to five prescription drugs, and fully one-third reported taking six or more medications (Cubanski & Neuman, 2010).

Chronic Conditions

Between 80% and 90% of Medicare beneficiaries have at least one chronic condition (Anderson, 2005; Cubanski et al., 2010). Nearly half (46%) have three or more chronic conditions, and roughly one-third (31%) have a cognitive or mental impairment (Cubanski et al., 2010). There has been a pronounced increase in the prevalence of chronic conditions in this population over the last few decades (Thorpe, Ogden, & Galactionova, 2010). The treated prevalence of hypertension rose from 35.2% in 1987 to 51.3% in 2006. In the same time period, the occurrence of mental disorders tripled from 7.2% to 22.6%, and diabetes nearly doubled from 11.3% to 20.5%. Hyperlipidemia, high lipid (fat) levels in the blood, climbed from 2.7% to 34.1% (Thorpe et al., 2010).

As the number of comorbidities increases, the complexity of care also increases. Patients with multiple chronic illnesses are more likely to see more physicians in a year. Medicare beneficiaries with 0–2 chronic conditions have a median of 3 providers, those with 3 to 4 conditions have a median of 5 providers, those with 5 to 6 conditions have a median of 7 providers, and those with 7 or more conditions have a median of 11 providers (Pham, Schrag, O'Malley, Wu, & Bach, 2007). Moreover, patients with more chronic conditions are more likely to require longer stays in inpatient and skilled nursing facilities, as well as more home health visits (Schneider, O'Donnell, & Dean, 2009).

Effects on Spending

Much of the recent growth in Medicare spending is attributable to rising spending on chronic conditions (Thorpe et al., 2010). The growth in Medicare spending stems largely from the increased spending for physician office visits and prescription drugs (Thorpe et al., 2010). Schneider et al. (2009) explored the cost of six chronic conditions that are prevalent among the Medicare fee-for-service population. They studied cancer, chronic obstructive pulmonary disease, depression, diabetes, heart failure, and kidney disease. The estimated average annual cost of a Medicare beneficiary without any of these conditions was $2,820, compared to $26,671 for a beneficiary with kidney disease. Furthermore, average yearly Medicare payments per capita rise as the number of comorbidities increases from one chronic condition ($7,172), to two chronic conditions ($14,931), to three or more chronic conditions ($32,498) (Schneider et al., 2009).

In 1987, 31% of Medicare beneficiaries had five or more chronic conditions that accounted for 52% of total health care spending. Ten years later, almost 40% of Medicare enrollees had five or more chronic conditions and were responsible for 65% of total spending. By 2002, the proportion of Medicare beneficiaries with five or more chronic conditions grew to 50%. Medical care for these patients comprised 75% of total health care spending (Thorpe & Howard, 2006). The treatment of these beneficiaries is likely to be a high-cost item until they die (Anderson, 2005). Spending on end-of-life care during the last year of life comprised 25% of Medicare spending in 2006, and this share has held relatively constant since Medicare was enacted (Riley & Lubitz, 2010).

Gaps in Coverage

There are individuals over age 65 living in the United States who fall through the gap and do not have Medicare coverage. The Social Security Act that created Medicare originally excluded state and local government employees from coverage because of uncertainty concerning whether the federal government could legally tax state employers (Schiff, 2002). Congress removed this exclusion in 1986, but only for public employees hired after 1986. It is illegal for public employees who began work before 1986 to contribute and participate in the regular Medicare payroll deduction program, so those public employees would have to individually purchase Medicare out of pocket (Schiff, 2002). In addition, individuals who are not in the United States legally are not eligible for Medicare coverage. Legal permanent residents must have resided in the United States for five consecutive years before they are eligible for Medicare.

Even those on Medicare may struggle with affordability. Health care costs have risen faster than beneficiaries' income; median out-of-pocket health spending has increased from 11.9% of income in 1997 to 16.2% in 2006 (Kaiser Family Foundation, 2010c). Cost-related major or minor problems accessing care in the previous twelve months affected 13% of the elderly in 2008, with 18% of beneficiaries over age 65 reporting problems paying for health care services (Cubanski & Neuman, 2010).

Medicare does not pay for many routine services or some expensive services such as long-term care. Many seniors are concerned about their ability to pay for long-term care and are disappointed that it is not a covered benefit under Medicare. Long-term care encompasses a broad range of services from home health care to assisted living facilities and skilled nursing facilities. Under certain circumstances, Medicare will pay for temporary nursing home and home health care. However, most beneficiaries must pay for long-term care using their own resources. If they have exhausted their resources and meet the eligibility criteria, then Medicaid may pay for their long-term care.

Long-term services and supports can be very expensive. National spending on long-term care in 2005 was $206.6 billion, which does not include informal care provided by family and friends (U.S. Department of Health and Human Services, 2010). Medicare pays for about 20% of national spending on long-term care, Medicaid pays for 49%, private insurance covers 7%, and out-of-pocket expenditures account for 18% of spending. The average cost of a private room in a nursing home in 2009 was $219 per day, or almost $80,000 per year (U.S. Department of Health and Human Services, 2010).

Demand for long-term care is strong and rising. An estimated 70% of individuals over age 65 will require at least some type of long-term services over their lifetime (U.S. Department of Health and Human Services, 2008). Approximately 9 million seniors needed some type of long-term care services in 2008. It is anticipated that that number will increase to 12 million by 2020 (U.S. Department of Health and Human Services, 2008). About 5% of beneficiaries (2.2 million) live in a nursing home or assisted living facility (Cubanski et al., 2010).

The Affordable Care Act created the Community Living Assistance Services and Supports (CLASS) Act. This act establishes a national, voluntary insurance program for purchasing community living assistance services and supports. Once vested for five years, the program will provide individuals with functional limitations an average of $50 per day to purchase supports necessary to maintain community residence. All working adults will be automatically enrolled in the program; however, they may choose to opt out. The program is financed via voluntary payroll deductions (Kaiser Family Foundation, 2010b). This program will likely assist future retirees in their long-term care expenses and may prevent many of them from relying on Medicaid for assistance. (In October of 2011, the Obama administration announced that the administration would not proceed with the CLASS Act because it was not financially solvent. However, the administration stopped short of repealing the act, so its future is uncertain.)

Conclusions

Medicare is a critical source of health and financial security for Americans age 65 and older. Compared to individuals under age 65 with private employer coverage, Medicare beneficiaries report fewer problems obtaining medical care, less financial hardship due to medical bills, and higher overall satisfaction with their coverage (Davis, Guterman, Doty, & Stremikis, 2009). Medicare is so popular among the elderly that politicians who are seen as threatening it put themselves in political jeopardy (Iglehart, 1999). Despite this security and popularity, there are significant issues with Medicare that must be faced. The benefits that are covered require significant cost sharing via deductibles, coinsurance, and copayments. The complexity of the program can make it difficult for beneficiaries to enroll in the most efficient plan arrangement. There are also major gaps in coverage, and not all beneficiaries have supplemental insurance to fill those gaps. Finally, seniors are living longer, have more comorbidities, and have greater utilization of costly health care services, which jeopardize the financial security of the program.

There are many health insurance options for retired Americans. If an individual retires prior to age 65, then they may be able to obtain coverage through an employer-sponsored plan (their own or their spouse's). Through 2013, ERRP incentivizes qualified employers to offer coverage for retirees. Alternatively, COBRA provides temporary insurance coverage through one's employer if the individual can afford to pay the full, unsubsidized cost of the premium. Retirees can also obtain health insurance through unions or membership organizations. In addition, if the individual served in the military, then he or she can get coverage through TRICARE or CHAMPVA. Lastly, a retiree can acquire health insurance on the individual market.

After age 65, Medicare becomes the primary source of health insurance for most Americans. For those that continue to work past age 65, Medicare works with other payers to coordinate benefits and may serve as either primary or secondary payer, depending on firm size (Centers for Medicare & Medicaid Services, 2010c). Controversially, beneficiaries can't opt out of Part A unless they also opt to forfeit their Social Security benefits ("Forced into Medicare," 2011). Part A provides hospital insurance at no cost for most beneficiaries. Part B is for medical insurance, and Part D is for prescription drug coverage; individuals must pay monthly premiums and other cost-sharing expenses for coverage. Many seniors purchase Medicare Advantage Plans, under Part C, which bundle coverage for Part A, Part B, and sometimes Part D. Others may opt for Medigap supplemental coverage to help pay out-of-pocket costs associated with using health care services, including deductibles, coinsurance, and copayments for Parts A and B. Individuals with low incomes may qualify for dual eligibility, with Medicaid covering some or all of the out-of-pocket expenses of Medicare-covered services. Also, eligible individuals may continue to receive benefits under TRICARE, CHAMPVA, and employer-sponsored retiree health plans in addition to the coverage provided by Medicare.

Future Directions

The first of the baby-boomer generation reached age 65 in 2011. When the last baby boomer turns 65 in 2030, 78 million beneficiaries are projected to be on Medicare (Kaiser Family Foundation, 2008). It has been argued that Medicare poses the single greatest future challenge to taxpayers of all government programs (Shi & Singh, 2009). Future directions of research should explore solutions to some of the major issues Medicare faces, including the financing of the program, the physician

reimbursement strategy, racial and ethnic disparities in access to care, as well as analyze the sweeping reforms implemented by the Affordable Care Act.

Financing of Medicare

Medicare revenues came mainly from general revenue (43%), payroll taxes (37%), and beneficiary premiums (13%), with the remaining 7% of revenues from taxation of Social Security benefits, payments from states, and interest in fiscal year 2010 (Cubanski et al., 2010). In 1970, total spending on Medicare was $6.8 billion, about 3.5% of the total federal budget, and in 1990, Medicare outlays were $107 billion, representing 10.5% of the U.S. budget (Moon, 1996). Expenditures on Medicare in 2010 were over $500 billion (Kaiser Family Foundation, 2010c). The Congressional Budget Office (CBO) estimates that Medicare spending will grow at an average of 7% each year from 2010 to 2018, rising to $879 billion annually (Thorpe et al., 2010).

Medicare is a pay-as-you go system, so taxes on current workers are financing the Part A benefits for current retirees. Just as the demands on the worker base are increasing, the tax base of current employees is shrinking. The ratio of workers per beneficiary is expected to decline from 3.5 in 2010 to 2.3 in 2030 (Kaiser Family Foundation, 2010c). The Social Security taxes that fund Part A are credited to the Part A trust fund, or the Hospital Insurance Trust Fund (Office of the Chief Actuary, 2010; Part B also has a trust fund, but it is financed by premiums and general revenues, so it is not reliant on the tax base.)

Part A spending has exceeded income since 2008, so the program expenditures are greater than its revenues. The trust fund reserves provide the additional revenues. However, the Part A trust fund fails both short-range and long-range financial adequacy tests. The projected date of the trust fund exhaustion is 2029, largely due to a boost in solvency from the Affordable Care Act (Office of the Chief Actuary, 2010). The predicted exhaustion date in 2009 was 2017 (Office of the Chief Actuary, 2010). Part B and Part D of Medicare are both projected to remain adequately financed into the indefinite future because current law automatically adjusts the next year's premiums based on costs.

With Medicare expenditures showing no signs of slowing and a doubling of the number of beneficiaries over 65 in the next twenty years, there is significant concern about the financial sustainability of Medicare. The Affordable Care Act creates an Independent Payment Advisory Board comprising fifteen members to generate recommendations to reduce the per-capita rate of growth in Medicare spending if spending exceeds a specific target rate. Future research should examine the demonstration pilot projects in the Affordable Care Act to determine which strategies are effective in stemming the growth of costs in Medicare. Demonstration projects include an Independence at Home program to provide high-need beneficiaries with primary care services in their home, and a Bundled Episode Payment Pilot program to develop and evaluate making bundled payments for acute, inpatient services, outpatient hospital services, and post-acute care services for an episode of care (Kaiser Family Foundation, 2010b).

Physician Reimbursement

Arguably, one of the biggest issues Medicare grapples with is how to reimburse physicians. The current method, using a formula known as the Sustainable Growth Rate (SGR), is wrought with controversy. The SGR, implemented in 1998, created a physician fee schedule designed to ensure adequate access to physicians' services and control spending for physician services provided under Part B (Congressional Budget Office, 2006). The SGR sets an overall target amount of spending for Part B services, and payments are adjusted annually to reflect differences between actual spending and the spending target. The number of services delivered to beneficiaries (volume) and the average complexity and costliness of services (intensity) determine spending (U.S. Government Accountability Office, 2006). Between 2000 and 2005, Medicare physician fees rose by only 4.5%, while spending on physician services per beneficiary grew by 45%. During this time period, there were significant increases in both volume and intensity of physician services, with the volume and intensity of imaging and diagnostic tests driving the bulk of the increases (U.S. Government Accountability Office, 2006). Medicare payment rates are about 80% of the amount of private insurance payment rates (Hackbarth, 2009).

If actual spending exceeds target spending, fee updates in future years must be lowered sufficiently to offset both the accumulated excess spending as well as to slow expected spending for the coming year (U.S. Government Accountability Office, 2006). Payments for physician services were reduced by 5.4% for 2002 as a result of the SGR formula. Since 2002, the SGR mechanism has called for reductions in payment rates. However, Congress and the President enacted various legislative actions that prevented the fee decreases, and in some years actually increased fees, leaving substantial accumulated spending (U.S. Government Accountability Office, 2006). In 2010, a 21.2% payment reduction was pushed back until December 1, and then again until January 2011. President Obama's 2012 budget proposal called for a two-year delay of a 25% cut, postponing the delay until January 1, 2014.

As the relative payment declines, Medicare beneficiaries' access to care becomes jeopardized. Primary care physicians are more likely than specialists to restrict Medicare patients (Chou et al., 2007). The opportunity cost of a physician's time, or the cost to the physician of not spending his or her time doing something else of value, influence a physician's decision to accept a new Medicare patient (Chou et al., 2007). The main determinants of opportunity cost are reimbursement rates and the amount of time required to see a patient. Chou et al. (2007) found that only 68% of primary care physicians surveyed unconditionally accepted all new Medicare patients, and 20% accepted new patients but restricted new Medicare patients using policies of non-acceptance or conditional acceptance. Thus, there is concern that inadequate reimbursements cause physicians to drop out of the Medicare program, thereby hurting seniors' access to care (Congressional Budget Office, 2006).

The inherent limitation in the SGR is that it does not affect the incentives of individual physicians regarding the rate of use of services (Ginsburg, 2008). No individual physician has an incentive to control growth in the volume of the services he or she provides. The formula is inequitable for physicians who do not unnecessarily increase the volume of their services (U.S. Government Accountability Office, 2006). The substantial reductions in payment dictated by the SGR could have severe effects on physician participation in Medicare. The Medicare Payment Advisory Commission (MedPAC) has recommended replacing the SGR with a system that separates efforts to control aggregate spending from the mechanism used to update fees (U.S. Government Accountability Office, 2006).

Despite being unpopular with policymakers and physicians alike, the SGR has been relatively successful at stemming costs in Medicare, although not as much as the formula calls for. The by-product of the compromises required to keep the cuts from taking effect is that the reimbursement rate for physicians in 2010 was about 17% below the rate paid in 2001 after adjusting for inflation (Horney & Van de Water, 2009).

Considering the SGR has proven to be an ineffective tool for reimbursing physicians (Ginsburg 2008), and there are legitimate fears that physicians may stop accepting Medicare patients, future research should examine better alternatives to the SGR and the effects of substantial reductions in Medicare physician fees on beneficiary access to care.

Medicare's Potential to Reduce Racial/Ethnic Barriers

Before Medicare was enacted, elderly blacks and those with the lowest incomes made fewer office visits and were admitted for inpatient care less frequently than whites and individuals who were more economically advantaged (Gornick, 2008; Starr, 1982). Despite near-universal access to health insurance coverage, low-income elderly, minorities, and those living in rural areas use fewer health care services relative to other groups (Davis & Rowland, 1986). The origins of Medicare are deeply rooted in a federal effort to improve health care in the African American community. The Social Security Act that established Medicare mandated that hospitals comply with the Civil Rights Act of 1964 in order to receive federal payments for Medicare patients, which spurred desegregation of hospitals (Eichner & Vladeck, 2005).

Minority beneficiaries are at a disadvantage relative to white beneficiaries because of lower income and socioeconomic status as well as institutional and individual racism (Zhou, Dominici, & Louis, 2010). More than two-thirds of black and Hispanic beneficiaries live on an income below twice the poverty level (Cubanski et al., 2010). An 80-year-old African American beneficiary from the southern United States is likely to have spent half of his or her life in a segregated health care system, so it is not surprising that minority beneficiaries might be in worse health than whites of the same age (Jost, 2005). There are wide disparities between whites and blacks in the use of many Medicare services (Gornick et al., 1996). Sizable racial and ethnic disparities exist even after adjusting for socioeconomic differences and other factors related to access (Smedley, Stith, & Nelson, 2003).

After implementation of Medicare, the rate of physician visits and inpatient utilization for blacks and the poor approached the rates for whites and higher-income individuals (Ruther & Dobson, 1981). As more detailed Medicare data became available, researchers found substantial disparities by race and socioeconomic status in the use of many services provided in the hospital and in ambulatory care settings (McBean & Gornick, 1994). Specifically, blacks are found to use fewer preventive and health promotion services (such as influenza immunizations and physician office visits), receive fewer tests to diagnose illness (such as colonoscopy and cardiac catheterization), and undergo fewer procedures (such as hip replacement and coronary artery bypass surgery) to treat disease than whites (Gornick, Eggers, & Riley, 2001).

Although racial and ethnic minorities generally receive fewer medical interventions than whites, their end-of-life costs are substantially higher. In the final six months of life, costs for black Medicare beneficiaries averaged 32% higher than those of whites, and costs for Hispanic beneficiaries were 57% more than those of whites (Hanchate, Kronman, Young-Xu, Ash, & Emanuel, 2009). Hanchate et al. (2009) found that more than half of these differences are related to geographic, sociodemographic, and morbidity differences.

These disparities in access and utilization of care are persistent and troubling in a program expected to equalize access to care; the challenge is to determine what society can do to lessen disparities in health care (Gornick et al., 2001). Medicare's leverage as the largest U.S. purchaser and regulator provides a unique opportunity to reduce racial and ethnic disparities, yet Medicare has not realized its potential as a catalyst in reducing health disparities (Eichner & Vladeck, 2005). Quality initiatives aimed at identifying factors contributing to racial and ethnic disparities, coupled with a plan to reduce them, and altering benefit and cost-sharing structures in Medicare are among several suggested solutions to reduce disparities in Medicare (Eichner & Vladeck, 2005).

The Affordable Care Act

The Patient Protection and Affordable Care Act of 2010 (as amended by the Health Care and Education Affordability Reconciliation Act of 2010) has numerous sections that directly affect Medicare. It expands prescription drug and prevention benefits, removes cost sharing for preventive services, introduces new programs designed to improve quality and delivery of care, reduces growth of Medicare Advantage programs, phases out the donut hole in Part D, and creates an independent payment advisory board, among many other things. The Congressional Budget Office estimates that the legislation will result in net reductions in Medicare direct spending of approximately $390 billion between fiscal years 2010 and 2019 (Davis, Hahn, Morgan, Stone, & Tilson, 2010).

Prevention. There is an emphasis on wellness and improving access to preventive services for beneficiaries in the Affordable Care Act. Beginning in 2011, beneficiaries were given access to a comprehensive risk assessment and personalized prevention plan, and encouraged to participate in a behavior modification program if applicable. All cost sharing was eliminated in 2011 for Medicare-covered preventive services that receive a United States Preventive Services Task Force (USPSTF) rating of A or B. Primary care physicians treating Medicare patients receive a bonus payment of 10% between 2011 and 2015. Primary care physicians and general surgeons practicing in health professional shortage areas will also receive a 10% bonus payment (*PPACA P.L. 111–148*, 2010).

Quality. Key provisions to improve the quality care are included as well. Medicare payments to hospitals will be reduced to account for preventable readmissions and hospital-acquired conditions. Physicians submitting data on quality measures to the Physician Quality Reporting System and those who maintain board certification will receive incentive payments through 2014. Those physicians who do not satisfactorily report may be penalized or subject to a payment adjustment beginning in 2015.

Delivery reform. The Affordable Care Act includes numerous demonstration grants and pilot projects. A Medicare pilot program will be set up to test "bundled payments" to encourage integrated care during a hospitalization episode to improve the coordination, quality, and efficiency of health care services (*PPACA P.L. 111–148*, 2010). This approach would align physicians' incentives to work together, unlike the current fee-for-service model, which creates financial incentives to provide more service since each service receives an additional payment. If this pilot project proves effective, the bundled payment system could be adopted more generally through the U.S. health services system and has the potential to slow cost growth and improve quality through coordinated care.

Accountable Care Organizations (ACOs) will be created to promote team-based health care under a "shared savings" program. ACOs create delivery systems that encourage and support teams of physicians, hospitals, and other health care providers to work together to manage and coordinate care for beneficiaries (Centers for Medicare & Medicaid Services, 2010d). If quality and efficiency benchmarks are met, these providers may receive a share

of any savings generated from productivity improvements and cost efficiency.

Medicare Advantage Plans. One of the controversies surrounding Medicare has been the inefficiency of overpayments to the private Medicare Advantage Plans. In 2009, it was estimated that these overpayments totaled $11.4 billion, or $1,138 per beneficiary (Families USA, 2010), with no measurable difference in health outcomes (Centers for Medicare & Medicaid Services, 2010d). The Affordable Care Act restructures payments to Medicare Advantage Plans by first freezing 2011 payments at the 2010 benchmarks. Phased changes in the benchmarks will then reduce payments over subsequent years. Benchmarks will vary from 95% of Medicare spending in areas with high fee-for-service rates to 115% of Medicare spending in low-cost areas, and bonuses for high-quality plans beginning in 2012 (Democratic Policy Committee, 2010). There are some concerns that reducing the overpayments will lead some plans to leave the market, similar to the experiences of Medicare + Choice. This may lead to some beneficiaries returning to original Medicare and losing the additional benefits of Medicare Advantage.

There are many changes that have been implemented or will be implemented through the Affordable Care Act that affect Medicare beneficiaries; not all have been discussed in this chapter. The effects of the legislation offer fertile ground for future research for many years to come.

References

Abaluck, J., & Gruber, J. (2009). Choice inconsistencies among the elderly: Evidence from plan choice in the Medicare Part D program. *SSRN eLibrary*. Retrieved from http://papers.ssrn.com/sol3/papers.cfm?abstract_id=1349592.

Anderson, G. F. (2005). Medicare and chronic conditions. *New England Journal of Medicine, 353*, 305–309.

Atherly, A. (2001). Supplemental insurance: Medicare's accidental stepchild. *Medical Care Research and Review, 58*, 131–161. doi:10.1177/107755870105800201.

Avorn, J. (2006). Part "D" for "defective"—the Medicare drug-benefit chaos. *New England Journal of Medicine, 354*, 1339–1341.

Blumenthal, D. (2006). Employer-sponsored health insurance in the United States—origins and implications. *New England Journal of Medicine, 355*, 82–88.

Brown, L. D., & Sparer, M. S. (2003). Poor program's progress: The unanticipated politics of Medicaid policy. *Health Affairs, 22*, 31–44. doi:10.1377/hlthaff.22.1.31.

Case, A., & Deaton, A. (2005). Broken down by work and sex: How our health declines. In D. Wise (Ed.), *Analyses in economics of aging* (pp. 185–212). Chicago, IL: University of Chicago Press.

Centers for Medicare & Medicaid Services. (2010a). *Medicare & you handbook—a guide to Medicare*. Retrieved from http://www.q1medicare.com/PartD-MedicareAndYouCMS GuideToMedicare.php.

Centers for Medicare & Medicaid Services. (2010b). *Choosing a Medigap policy.* Retrieved from http://www.medicare.gov/ Publications/Pubs/pdf/02110.pdf.

Centers for Medicare & Medicaid Services. (2010c). *Medicare and other health benefits: Your guide to who pays first.* Retrieved from http://www.medicare.gov/publications/pubs/ pdf/02179.pdf.

Centers for Medicare & Medicaid Services. (2010d). *Affordable Care Act update: Implementing Medicare cost savings.* Retrieved from http://www.cms.gov/apps/docs/ACA-Update-Impleme nting-Medicare-Costs-Savings.pdf.

Chou, W. C., Cooney, L. M., Van Ness, P. H., Allore, H. G., & Gill, T. M. (2007). Access to primary care for Medicare beneficiaries. *Journal of the American Geriatrics Society, 55,* 763–768. doi:10.1111/j.1532–5415.2007.01154.x.

Congressional Budget Office. (2006). *The sustainable growth rate formula for setting Medicare's physician payment rates* (Economic and Budget Issue Brief). Retrieved from http:// www.cbo.gov/ftpdocs/75xx/doc7542/09–07-SGR-brief.pdf.

Coughlin, T., Waidmann, T., & Watts, M. O. (2009). *Where does the burden lie? Medicaid and Medicare spending for dual eligible beneficiaries* (No. 7895–02). Kaiser Family Foundation. Retrieved from http://www.kff.org/medicaid/ upload/7895–2.pdf.

Cubanski, J., Huang, J., Damico, A., Jacobson, G., & Neuman, T. (2010). *Medicare chartbook.* Kaiser Family Foundation. Retrieved from http://www.kff.org/medicare/upload/8103. pdf.

Cubanski, J., & Neuman, P. (2010). Medicare doesn't work as well for younger, disabled beneficiaries as it does for older enrollees. *Health Affairs, 29,* 1725–1733. doi:10.1377/ hlthaff.2009.0962.

Davis, K., Guterman, S., Doty, M. M., & Stremikis, K. M. (2009). Meeting enrollees' needs: How do Medicare and employer coverage stack up? *Health Affairs, 28,* w521–w532. doi:10.1377/hlthaff.28.4.w521.

Davis, K., & Rowland, D. (1986). *Medicare policy.* Baltimore, MD, and London, England: Johns Hopkins University Press.

Davis, P., Hahn, J., Morgan, P., Stone, J., & Tilson, S. (2010). *Medicare provisions in the Patient Protection and Affordable Care Act: Summary and timeline.* Congressional Research Service. Retrieved from http://aghealthreform.com/ wp-content/uploads/2010/11/CRSmedppaca.pdf.

Democratic Policy Committee. (2010). *Affordable Care Act implementation timeline.* Retrieved from http://dpc.senate. gov/healthreformbill/healthbill65.pdf.

Duggan, M., Healy, P., & Morton, F. S. (2008). Providing prescription drug coverage to the elderly: America's experiment with Medicare Part D. *The Journal of Economic Perspectives, 22,* 69–92.

Duggan, M., & Morton, F. S. (2010). The effect of Medicare Part D on pharmaceutical prices and utilization. *The American Economic Review, 100,* 590–607.

Early Retiree Reinsurance Program. (2010, October). Retrieved from http://www.healthcare.gov/news/factsheets/early_retiree_ reinsurance_program.html.

Eichner, J., & Vladeck, B. C. (2005). Medicare as a catalyst for reducing health disparities. *Health Affairs, 24,* 365–375. doi:10.1377/hlthaff.24.2.365.

Employee Benefit Research Institute. (2010). *Employers offering retiree health benefits to early retirees: How has it changed?* (Fast

Facts No. 182). Retrieved from http://www.ebri.org/pdf/ FFE182.26Oct10.EarlyRets.Final.pdf.

Ettner, S. L., Steers, N., Duru, O. K., Turk, N., Quiter, E., Schmittdiel, J., & Mangione, C. M. (2010). Entering and exiting the Medicare Part D coverage gap: Role of comorbidities and demographics. *Journal of General Internal Medicine, 25,* 568–574. doi:10.1007/s11606–010–1300–6.

Families USA. (2010). *Lower costs, better care: Medicare cost savings in the Affordable Care Act.* Retrieved from http://familie-susa2.org/assets/pdfs/health-reform/in-perspective/In-Perspe ctive-Medicare-Cost-Savings.pdf.

Federowicz, M. (2008). Should healthy Medicare beneficiaries postpone enrollment in Part D? *Findings Brief: Health Care Financing & Organization, 11,* 1–4.

Forced into Medicare [Editorial]. (2011, March 24). *The Wall Street Journal.* Retrieved from http://online.wsj.com/article/S B10001424052748704461304576216872954763388.html.

Fronstin, P., Salisbury, D., & VanDerhei, J. (2008). *Savings needed to fund health insurance and health care expenses in retirement: Findings from a simulation model* (Issue Brief No. 317). Washington, DC: Employee Benefit Research Institute.

Ginsburg, P. (2008, February 12). Bitter medicine: Prescription to fix SGR requires a commitment to major Medicare reform. *Health Affairs Blog.* Retrieved from http://healthaf-fairs.org/blog/2008/02/12/bitter-medicine-prescription-to-fix-sgr-requires-a-commitment-to-major-medicare-reform/.

Gold, M., Jacobson, G., Damico, A., & Neuman, T. (2010). *Medicare Advantage 2011 Data Spotlight* (No. 8117). Retrieved from http://www.kff.org/medicare/upload/8117.pdf.

Goodman, D., Brownlee, S., Chang, C., & Fisher, E. (2010). *Regional and racial variation in primary care and the quality of care among Medicare beneficiaries.* The Dartmouth Institute for Health Policy and Clinical Practice. Retrieved from http://www.rwjf.org/files/research/68508.pdf.

Gornick, M. E. (2008). A decade of research on disparities in Medicare utilization: Lessons for the health and health care of vulnerable men. *American Journal of Public Health, 98*(Suppl.1), S162–S168.

Gornick, M. E., Eggers, P. W., & Riley, G. F. (2001). Understanding disparities in the use of Medicare services. *Yale Journal of Health Policy, Law, and Ethics, 1,* 133–158.

Gornick, M. E., Eggers, P. W., Reilly, T. W., Mentnech, R. M., Fitterman, L. K., Kucken, L. E., & Vladeck, B. C. (1996). Effects of race and income on mortality and use of services among Medicare beneficiaries. *New England Journal of Medicine, 335,* 791–799.

Gornick, M. E., Greenberg, J. N., Eggers, P. W., & Dobson, A. (1985). Twenty years of Medicare and Medicaid: Covered populations, use of benefits, and program expenditures. *Health Care Financing Review, Suppl.,* 13–59.

Hackbarth, G. M. (2009). *Report to Congress: Medicare payment policy.* Medicare Payment Advisory Committee. Retrieved from http://www.medpac.gov/documents/Mar09_ March%20report%20testimony_WM%20FINAL.pdf.

Hanchate, A., Kronman, A. C., Young-Xu, Y., Ash, A. S., & Emanuel, E. (2009). Racial and ethnic differences in end-of-life costs: Why do minorities cost more than whites? *Archives of Internal Medicine, 169,* 493–501. doi:10.1001/ archinternmed.2008.616.

Hanoch, Y., Miron-Shatz, T., Cole, H., Himmelstein, M., & Federman, A. D. (2010). Choice, numeracy, and physicians-in-training performance: The case of Medicare

Part D. *Health Psychology, 29*, 454–459. doi:10.1037/a0019881.

Hoadley, J., Cubanski, J., Hargrave, E., Summer, L., & Neuman, T. (2010). *Part D plan availability in 2011 and key changes since 2006*. Kaiser Family Foundation. Retrieved from http://www.kff.org/medicare/upload/8107.pdf.

Horney, J. R., & Van de Water, P. N. (2009). *House-passed and Senate bills reduce deficit, slow health care costs, and include realistic Medicare savings*. Center for Budget and Policy Priorities. Retrieved from http://www.cbpp.org/files/12–4-09health.pdf.

Iglehart, J. K. (1999). Medicare. *New England Journal of Medicine, 340*, 327–332.

Jackson, E. A., & Axelsen, K. J. (2008). Medicare Part D formulary coverage since program inception: Are beneficiaries choosing wisely? *The American Journal of Managed Care, 14*(Suppl. 11), SP29–SP35.

Jost, T. (2005, March). *Racial and ethnic disparities in Medicare: What the department of Health and Human Services and the Centers for Medicare and Medicaid Services can, and should, do*. Retrieved from http://www.nasi.org/sites/default/files/research/Jost.pdf.

Kaiser Family Foundation. (2008). *Medicare spending and financing* (No. 7305–03). Retrieved from http://www.kff.org/medicare/upload/7305_03.pdf.

Kaiser Family Foundation. (2009). *Dual eligibles: Medicaid's role for low-income Medicare beneficiaries* (No. 4091–06). Retrieved from http://www.kff.org/medicaid/upload/4091_06.pdf.

Kaiser Family Foundation. (2010a). *Medicare: A primer* (No. 7615–03). Retrieved from http://www.kff.org/medicare/upload/7615–03.pdf.

Kaiser Family Foundation. (2010b). *Summary of the new health reform law* (8061). Retrieved from http://www.kff.org/healthreform/upload/8061.pdf.

Kaiser Family Foundation. (2010c). *Medicare spending and financing* (No. 7305–05). Retrieved from http://www.kff.org/medicare/upload/7305–05.pdf.

Kaiser Family Foundation. (2010d). *Medicare Advantage* (No. 2052–14). Retrieved from http://www.kff.org/medicare/upload/2052–14.pdf.

Kaiser Family Foundation. (2010e). *The Medicare prescription drug benefit* (Fact Sheet No. 7044–11). Retrieved from http://www.kff.org/medicare/upload/7044–11.pdf.

Kasper, J., Watts, M. O., & Lyons, B. (2010). *Chronic disease and co-morbidity among dual eligibles: Implications for patterns of Medicaid and Medicare service use and spending* (No. 8081). Kaiser Family Foundation. Retrieved from http://www.kff.org/medicaid/upload/8081.pdf.

Kennedy, J., Tuleu, I., & MacKay, K. (2008). Unfilled prescriptions of Medicare beneficiaries: Prevalence, reasons, and types of medicine prescribed. *Journal of Managed Care Pharmacy, 14*, 553–560.

Ketcham, J. D., & Simon, K. I. (2008). Medicare Part D's effects on elderly patients' drug costs and utilization. *The American Journal of Managed Care, 14*(Suppl. 11), SP14–SP22.

Lemieux, J., Chovan, T., & Heath, K. (2008). Medigap coverage and Medicare spending: A second look. *Health Affairs, 27*, 469–477. doi:10.1377/hlthaff.27.2.469.

Lichtenberg, F. R., & Sun, S. X. (2007). The impact of Medicare Part D on prescription drug use by the elderly. *Health Affairs, 26*, 1735–1744. doi: 10.1377/hlthaff.26.6.1735.

Madden, J. M., Graves, A. J., Zhang, F., Adams, A. S., Briesacher, B. A., Ross-Degnan, D.,…Soumerai, S. B (2008). Cost-related medication nonadherence and spending on

basic needs following implementation of Medicare Part D. *JAMA, 299*, 1922–1928. doi:10.1001/jama.299.16.1922.

McBean, A. M., & Gornick, M. (1994). Differences by race in the rates of procedures performed in hospitals for Medicare beneficiaries. *Health Care Financing Review, 15*, 77–90.

Moon, M. (1996). *Medicare now and in the future*. Washington, DC: The Urban Institute.

Moon, S., & Shin, J. (2006). Health care utilization among Medicare-Medicaid dual eligibles: A count data analysis. *BMC Public Health, 6*, 88. doi:10.1186/1471–2458-6-88.

Neuman, P., & Cubanski, J. (2009). Medicare Part D update—lessons learned and unfinished business. *New England Journal of Medicine, 361*, 406–414.

Neuman, P., Strollo, M. K., Guterman, S., Rogers, W. H., Li, A., Rodday, A. M. C., & Safran, D. G. (2007). Medicare prescription drug benefit progress report: Findings from a 2006 national survey of seniors. *Health Affairs, 26*, w630–w643. doi:10.1377/hlthaff.26.5.w630.

Office of the Chief Actuary. (2010). *Summary: Reports from the Board of Trustees*. Retrieved from http://www.ssa.gov/oact/trsum/index.html.

Pham, H. H., Schrag, D., O'Malley, A. S., Wu, B., & Bach, P. B. (2007). Care patterns in Medicare and their implications for pay for performance. *New England Journal of Medicine, 356*, 1130–1139.

Polinski, J. M., Bhandari, A., Saya, U. Y., Schneeweiss, S., & Shrank, W. H. (2010). Medicare beneficiaries' knowledge of and choices regarding Part D, 2005 to the present. *Journal of the American Geriatrics Society, 58*, 950–966. doi:10.1111/j.1532–5415.2010.02812.x.

PPACA P.L. 111–148. (2010). Retrieved from http://frwebgate.access.gpo.gov/cgi-bin/getdoc.cgi?dbname=111_cong_bills&docid=f:h3590enr.txt.pdf#page=281

Regan, J. F., & Petroski, C. A. (2007). Prescription drug coverage among Medicare beneficiaries. *Health Care Financing Review, 29*, 119–125.

The retiree health care challenge. (2006). TIAA-CREF Institute. Retrieved from http://www.tiaa-crefinstitute.org/ucm/groups/content/@ap_ucm_p_tcp_docs/documents/document/tiaa02029356.pdf.

Rice, T., & Thomas, K. (1992). Evaluating the new Medigap standardization regulations. *Health Affairs, 11*, 194–207.

Riley, G. F., & Lubitz, J. D. (2010). Long-term trends in Medicare payments in the last year of life. *Health Services Research, 45*, 565–576.

Ruther, M., & Dobson, A. (1981). Equal treatment and unequal benefits: a re-examination of the use of Medicare services by race, 1967–1976. *Health Care Financing Review, 2*, 55–83.

Schiff, G. (2002). An unsuspecting American with no Medicare coverage—me! *Health Affairs, 21*, 202–206. doi:10.1377/hlthaff.21.6.202.

Schneider, K. M., O'Donnell, B. E., & Dean, D. (2009). Prevalence of multiple chronic conditions in the United States' Medicare population. *Health and Quality of Life Outcomes, 7*, 82–82. doi:10.1186/1477–7525-7-82.

Seniors & Medicare and Medicaid enrollees.(N.D.) Retrieved from: http://www.medicaid.gov/Medicaid-CHIP-Program-Information/By-Population/Medicare-Medicaid-Enrollees-Dual-Eligibles/Seniors-and-Medicare-and-Medicaid-Enrollees.html.

Shi, L., & Singh, D. A. (2009). *Essentials of the U.S. health care system*. Burlington, MA: Jones & Bartlett Learning.

Smedley, B. D., Stith, A. Y., & Nelson, A. R. (2003). *Unequal treatment: Confronting racial and ethnic disparities in health care*. Washington, DC: National Academies Press.

Stanton, M. W. (2006). *The high concentration of U.S. health care expenditures*. Research in Action, Issue 19. (AHRQ Publication No. 06–0060). Agency for Healthcare Research and Quality, Rockville, MD. http://www.ahrq.gov/research/ria19/expendria.htm.

Starr, P. (1982). *The social transformation of American medicine*. New York, NY: Basic Books.

Strumpf, E. (2009). Employer-sponsored health insurance for early retirees: Impacts on retirement, health, and health care. *International Journal of Health Care Finance and Economics, 10*, 105–147. doi:10.1007/s10754–009–9072–4.

Thorpe, K. E., & Howard, D. H. (2006). The rise in spending among Medicare beneficiaries: The role of chronic disease prevalence and changes in treatment intensity. *Health Affairs, 25*, w378–w388. doi:10.1377/hlthaff.25.w378.

Thorpe, K. E., Ogden, L. L., & Galactionova, K. (2010). Chronic conditions account for rise in Medicare spending from 1987 to 2006. *Health Affairs, 29*, 718–724. doi:10.1377/hlthaff.2009.0474.

U.S. Department of Health and Human Services. (2008). *Understanding long term care*. Retrieved from http://www.longtermcare.gov/LTC/Main_Site/Understanding/Index.aspx.

U.S. Department of Health and Human Services. (2010). *Paying for long term care*. Retrieved from http://www.longtermcare.gov/LTC/Main_Site/Understanding/Cost/Index.aspx.

U.S. Government Accountability Office. (2006). *Medicare physician payments: Trends in service utilization, spending, and fees prompt consideration of alternative payment approaches* (No. GAO-06–1008T). Retrieved from http://www.gao.gov/new.items/d061008t.pdf.

Walberg, M. P., & Patel, R. A. (2009). Potential opportunity cost of neglecting to annually reassess Medicare Part D standalone prescription drug plan offerings: The price of contentment? *Journal of the American Pharmacists Association: JAPhA, 49*, 777–782. doi:10.1331/JAPhA.2009.09017.

Weiss, L. J., & Blustein, J. (1996). Faithful patients: The effect of long-term physician-patient relationships on the costs and use of health care by older Americans. *American Journal of Public Health, 86*, 1742–1747. doi:10.2105/AJPH.86.12.1742.

Welcome to Medicare Preventive Visit. (2010). Retrieved from http://www.medicare.gov/navigation/manage-your-health/preventive-services/medicare-physical-exam.aspx.

Yin, W., Basu, A., Zhang, J. X., Rabbani, A., Meltzer, D. O., & Alexander, G. C. (2008). The effect of the Medicare Part D prescription benefit on drug utilization and expenditures. *Annals of Internal Medicine, 148*, 169–177.

Zhang, Y., Lave, J. R., Newhouse, J. P., & Donohue, J. M. (2009). How the Medicare Part D drug benefit changed the distribution of out-of-pocket pharmacy spending among older beneficiaries. *The Journals of Gerontology, Series B: Psychological Sciences and Social Sciences, 65B*, 502–507. doi:10.1093/geronb/gbp111.

Zhou, Y., Dominici, F., & Louis, T. A. (2010). Racial disparities in risks of mortality in a sample of the US Medicare population. *Journal of the Royal Statistical Society: Series C (Applied Statistics), 59*, 319–339.

Zivin, K., Madden, J. M., Graves, A. J., Zhang, F., & Soumerai, S. B. (2009). Cost-related medication nonadherence among beneficiaries with depression following Medicare Part D. *The American Journal of Geriatric Psychiatry, 17*, 1068–1076. doi:10.1097/JGP.0b013e3181b972d1.

Learning and Training in Retirement

Jerry W. Hedge *and* Victoria A. Albright

Abstract

Retirement in the twenty-first century can take multiple forms. The current chapter adopts this broader perspective and examines what is known about learning and training for those who remain in a career job after reaching retirement eligibility, pursue some re-careering direction, opt for bridge employment or other work-related endeavors, engage in volunteer activities, or follow some personal educational/intellectual pursuits. Our findings suggest that this is an area of research and application that is broad, scattered, under-researched, and relatively unexplored. The adult education literature is vast but fragmented. The older adult work-related training literature is nearly invisible, and little is known about the extent or effectiveness of training programs that target older workers. The volunteer domain may provide the best example of organized approaches to training and learning opportunities for retirees. As the population of late career and retirement-eligible persons increases, learning and training programs—formal and informal—will become increasingly critical for supporting advancement along these varied retirement pathways. Learning and training in retirement is a fertile but relatively untapped area for research and development.

Key Words: training in retirement, learning, re-careering, volunteerism

Since the introduction of Social Security in 1935, the age of 65 has been considered the benchmark for retiring from paid employment. When Social Security was introduced, though, the average life expectancy was not much above 65. When the first Social Security check was written in 1940 for $22.54, there were fewer than a million persons who turned 65 that year. Moving forward to the present time, it is projected that between 3 and 4.5 million persons will turn 65 *each year* between 2010 and 2025, each with an average life expectancy of almost twenty more years. This demographic shift in the population will also impact the age composition of the labor force. By 2018, 39.8 million workers will be aged 55 or older and represent almost 24% of the workforce (Toossi, 2009).

Over much of the past fifty years, retirement was viewed as a discrete and abrupt discontinuation of paid employment, but as Shultz and Henkens (2010) have noted, today's "retirement" is a process that can take multiple forms. There are increasing signs that a significant proportion of retirement-eligible people will delay retirement or work in some capacity during their retirement years. Between 2007 and 2018, labor economists predict that the labor force participation rate of the 55+ age group will rise from 38% to 43.5% (Toossi, 2009). Some of these workers will remain in their pre-retirement careers, perhaps on a scaled-down basis. Others will leave their old jobs for new ones, possibly part-time. Some of those new jobs will be long term and others will be stepping stones ("bridge employment") to other work or full retirement. Some will stop working for pay but begin working in other capacities, such as volunteering. Some volunteer activities will be part-time and others will be as demanding as career jobs. Some retirees may undertake additional training to prepare for new jobs, be they paid or voluntary; others will enjoy learning for learning's sake alone.

While retirement planning may seem to be a matter of personal choice, as noted by Ekerdt (2010), the literature identifies a number of exogenous factors that influence individuals' decisions about what to do with their retirement years. These include the end of mandatory retirement, changes to public and private retirement benefits, organizational restructuring and job displacement, increased economic/financial uncertainty, a healthier and more educated workforce, fewer jobs with physical demands, coordination of retirement plans in dual-earner households, expanded options for part-time and more flexible forms of work, and new attitudes for work in later life. In a recent survey of those "working in retirement," Brown, Aumann, Pitt-Catsouphes, Galinsky, and Bond (2010) identified factors that pushed people out of the workforce and factors that pulled or attracted them to a new life in retirement. Pushes out of the workforce included poor health; being fired, laid off, or offered a buyout; and job/workplace constraints (e.g., could not reduce job demands, could not arrange for flexible hours). Pulls into a new life included the personal desire to pursue other interests, the opportunity to claim benefits not offered until after retirement, and the desire to be available to care for older family members or grandchildren.

For some people the decision not to retire is easy—they simply cannot afford to retire. The most recent Retirement Confidence Survey (RCS; administered annually by the Employee Benefit Research Institute) found that Americans' confidence in their ability to afford a comfortable retirement has dropped to a new low, and workers continue to change their expectations about how they will transition from work to retirement. More than one-quarter of workers (27%) in the 2011 RCS say they are not at all confident that they will have enough money to live comfortably throughout their retirement years. In addition, the percentage of workers who expect to retire after age 65 has increased, from 11% in 1991 and 1996 to 20% in 2001, 26% in 2006, and 36% in 2011 (Helman, Greenwald, Copeland, & VanDerhei, 2011).

For some people the decision to retire, at least from their old career, is made for them. As noted by Sweet (2007), older workers are particularly susceptible to personnel cuts because they are often among the more highly paid employees in an organization.

Also, while older employees may have developed a set of unique skills because of their tenure in an organization, they also are among the most likely to lack the technological skills to match the needs of rising industries. Then, once jobs are lost, older workers often face greater challenges in finding new jobs than do their younger workers. Recent Bureau of Labor Statistics (BLS) data (i.e., April 2011) indicate that in the U.S. the average period of unemployment for job seekers aged 55+ was 53.6 weeks, or more than one year. This is compared to 39.4 weeks for the younger unemployed (Rix, 2011).

Retirement Pathways

Szinovacz (2003) discussed the concept of pathways into retirement as a way to convey the notion that retirement decisions reflect long-term and sequential processes over the life course. Shultz and Wang (2011) recently suggested that retirement is not a single event but rather a process that older individuals go through over time. This dynamic view of retirement suggests that transitions are embedded in societal and organizational structures and tied to experiences in individuals' lives. Thus, retirement decisions evolve not only from occupational and employment experiences but also from a variety of contextual influences and lifelong experiences in work and non-work realms (Hedge, Borman, & Lammlein, 2006).

Wang (2012) described retirement as an adjustment process, viewing retirement as incorporating both the retirement transition (i.e., from employment to retirement) and post-retirement trajectory (i.e., individual development during retirement). Thus, it is not the decision to retire but the characteristics of the retirement transition process that are of most importance in influencing the retirement outcome. In addition, this conceptualization recognizes retirement as a longitudinal developmental process characterized by adjustment, which provides a more realistic depiction of retirement and guides the selection and investigation of retirement outcomes.

This frame of reference is important to a discussion of the education and training activities of individuals in retirement, as an increasing number of retirement pathways and trajectories can be supported by retirement training applications. For many, being retired offers the opportunity to pursue new directions but does not necessarily mean extensive leisure. For example, using the first five waves of the HRS data, Maestas (2007) showed that nearly half of retirees followed a retirement path that involved only partial retirement or unretirement.

In the pages that follow, work and non-work activities after retirement are explored in terms of educational and training opportunities and demands. Because retirement is so much more amorphous than it once was, we take a broader perspective here, to gain insight into multiple options, whether that be remaining in a career job after reaching retirement eligibility, following some re-careering direction, pursuing some bridge employment or other work-related behaviors, engaging in volunteer activities, or opting for personal educational/intellectual pursuits.

Working in Retirement

For many years the general notion of retirement was as a phase of life that combined, to varying degrees, enjoyment of leisure time, caring for family members, possibly volunteering to help with local community services, and a variety of other unpaid activities. New attitudes and expectations about work and aging have been emerging, however. For many older workers, delaying retirement does not necessarily mean continuing in the same occupations in which they have spent much of their adult lives. Rather, many leave their old jobs for new careers. This change has been referred to by Johnson et al. (2009) and others, as "re-careering." These shifts may involve seeking employment opportunities that may be more personally fulfilling but often less financially rewarding than previous jobs. In addition, many older workers may change occupations after losing their jobs—whether fired, laid off, downsized, or bought out with early retirement packages. They may also involve moves from wage-and-salary jobs to self-employment. Or they may represent a gradual shift into retirement, with workers moving from demanding, full-time work into less stressful part-time work.

The probability that older workers will change jobs and careers is influenced by a number of factors, including education, gender, and pension coverage. When other factors are controlled for, high school graduates are more likely to change jobs late in their work lives than are older workers who have completed college or those who did not complete high school. Among job changers, women and men do so at comparable rates. However, late-life *occupational* change is more common among men because women are less likely than men to continue working if they leave an employer in their 50s (Johnson et al., 2009).

These re-careering patterns may also be a result of the industry within which the career job has been located. For example, according to data reported by Johnson et al. (2009), older job changers tend to move out of manufacturing and into services industries. Only 36% of older men and 39.2% of older women remain in the manufacturing industry after they change jobs. These exits from manufacturing may reflect older job changers' preferences for jobs with a) more flexible employment arrangements than available with manufacturing jobs, or b) less physically demanding work options. The industry's decline over the past several decades may also push many older workers out of manufacturing (Johnson et al., 2009).

Training and Older Workers

Many older adults in the labor force, with or without a current job, could benefit from participation in some form of refresher training or re-skilling. The training of older workers remains a concern from a work-life continuity perspective because older workers have traditionally been viewed as not participating adequately (or not being allowed to participate) in training. This reduces their value in the marketplace and potentially reduces their re-employment opportunities. As Greller and Stroh (2003) noted, some of this may relate to stereotypic views about the learning capabilities and reluctance of older workers to seek out training opportunities, and some may relate to economic thinking about return-on-investment tied to years remaining in the workforce. Still, as the 55+ portion of the workforce continues to grow, it appears that some of these views are gradually subsiding.

Unfortunately, research on training in later life is limited. The literature on older people and training tends to assume that training will increase the employability of older people, but few empirical studies can be cited as examples. The literature on the older labor market, and especially on labor market exit, rarely comments on training as an issue. The larger body of literature on the role of training in returning unemployed older people to the labor market suggests that training may be helpful if linked to other strategies, such as recruitment or job placement.

Similarly, Beier, Teachout, and Cox (2012), in discussing the training and development of an aging workforce, noted that although practical implications of designing training for older learners have been derived from basic research on age, abilities, and motivation throughout the life span, there is little applied research that specifically addresses how to best design training interventions for older learners. Rather, most current research on training and the effectiveness of different training interventions is done with college student samples, which brings into question its generalizability to working-age adults, especially those in late career or who have already retired. They also pointed out that much training research, and most basic research on learning, uses laboratory-based experimental designs, which is useful for understanding the individual differences in ability that lead to learning but may not generalize well to work contexts.

Preparing for Tomorrow's Jobs

Recent economic, demographic, and policy developments have created new training challenges and opportunities for workers and employers. According to Mikelson and Nightingale (2004), older workers may be more likely to be laid off from industries suffering permanent structural declines. The structure of the economy has changed, with less demand than in previous decades for workers in manufacturing and greater demand for highly skilled, technologically savvy workers. Jobs stemming from growth of the health care industry are also expected to require special training. Thus, as noted by Charness and Czaja (2006), when preparing for an aging workforce and understanding the type of training programs to develop and deliver, it is important to consider the types of jobs that are likely to be available in the future and the types of skills that are needed.

FASTEST GROWING OCCUPATIONS

According to BLS projections, the thirty occupations with the fastest rates of growth will likely each increase by almost 30% from 2008 to 2018 (Lacey & Wright, 2009). Professional and related occupations account for seventeen of these (seven of which are in the health care practitioners and technical occupations occupational group). Ten of the thirty fastest growing occupations are service occupations (including seven occupations from the health care support occupations occupational group). Finally, three are management occupations or business and financial operations occupations. As such, a substantial portion of the thirty fastest growing occupations are directly related to *health care*. As elderly individuals account for an increasing proportion of the U.S. population, and as new developments allow for the treatment of a broader range of medical conditions, demand for health care services is expected to grow quickly. For fourteen of the thirty fastest growing occupations, a bachelor's or higher degree is the most significant source of education or training. Seven are in the postsecondary vocational award or associate degree category, one is categorized under work experience in a related occupation, and the remaining eight are in an on-the-job training category.

OCCUPATIONS IN DECLINE

Decreases in employment occur for a variety of reasons, including reduced demand for some goods or services on the one hand, or productivity gains on the other. The thirty occupations with the largest projected numerical declines each will likely lose at least 12,500 jobs between 2008 and 2018. These occupations are clustered in two occupational groups: production occupations (12) and office and administrative support occupations (11). As for the rest, three are transportation and material moving occupations, two are sales and related occupations, and one each is a management and agricultural occupation. None of these thirty occupations is classified in an education or training category that involves postsecondary education. For twenty-nine of them, the most significant form of education or training involves some on-the-job training. For the other occupation, the most significant form of education or training is work experience in a related occupation (Lacey & Wright, 2009).

Many 55+ individuals have either retired from or still work in many of these industries that are likely to experience growth, and so there are opportunities for continued employment. However, this does not necessarily mean that employment opportunities will expand for older workers, as a variety of factors (e.g., job and skill requirements; receptivity to older workers by employers and organizations) influence the eventual outcome. It is expected that almost two-thirds of the projected job openings in the next ten years will require specialized education and on-the-job training.

Work-oriented Training

For retirees interested in pursuing work opportunities, what training options might be available? Prior to the economic downturn that started around 2007, Mikelson and Nightingale (2004) worked with the Department of Labor (DOL)/ Employment and Training Administration (ETA) to estimate expenditures on occupational training in the U.S. While these estimates are not limited to programs that exclusively target older workers, they do provide a good perspective on training expenditures and who provides the training. In summary, they characterized the occupational training landscape this way:

- Federal expenditures on training in 2002 at between $3.2 and $5.3 billion, split about equally between DOL programs, Pell Grants (at two-year and proprietary postsecondary schools), and dozens of other programs in six other federal departments.
- Within the federal government, DOL programs represented about one-third of all training expenditures. These include the Workforce Investment Act (WIA) Adult Programs and Dislocated Worker Programs (representing 50% to 56% of all job training spending in the DOL), followed by Job Corps (which represents about 12% to 18% of the DOL's training expenditures). Aside from DOL and Pell Grants, the next highest spending on training was through Vocational Rehabilitation and the Perkins Act Vocational and Technical Programs and Tech Prep Program.
- States were estimated to have spent $500 to $700 million a year on training, less than 15% as much as what the federal government spent.
- The private sector spent between $46 and $54 billion a year on training for employees—perhaps more than ten times as much as the federal and state governments combined.

Mikelson and Nightingale (2004) estimated that roughly $50 to $60 billion is spent on job training in the United States annually (excluding DoD training and training paid for by individual workers themselves). The majority of that—perhaps over 90%—is spent by private companies and employers to train their employees. The federal government represents about 6% to 8% of the total training expenditures, and states contribute about 1%.

While the private sector is the primary source of funds for training, it is important to remember that higher-level and higher-income workers are considerably more likely to receive employer-funded training than other workers. There is also some evidence that private spending on training has declined in the past few years, perhaps due to the slowing economy after 2001. The federal government and, to a much lesser extent, state governments are the primary sources of training funds for retraining dislocated workers and training lower-level workers and, especially, new labor force entrants. Again, the states have been hit hard by the economic downturn, and

there are reasons to believe that fewer training dollars will be available.

Federal Government Training Programs

Because the DOL is the primary distributor of federal training dollars, we look more closely at their training programs and targeted groups. The DOL's training programs serve many different target groups, including dislocated and incumbent workers, adults, youth, older workers, migrant and seasonal workers, unemployed/underemployed/hard-to-employ workers, native Americans/Hawaiians/Alaskans, veterans, persons with physical and mental disabilities, and other miscellaneous groups. Dislocated and incumbent workers receive more of the DOL's federal funding for occupational training than any other group.

In 1998, Congress established a framework for the nation's workforce development system under the Workforce Investment Act (WIA). The law replaced multiple existing training programs with state formula grants and created a nationwide network of locally administered "one-stop centers" where both workers and employers could access training, employment, and support programs administered through the DOL and other agencies, such as the U.S. Departments of Education and Health and Human Services.

According to Mikelson and Nightingale (2004), approximately 4% to 5% ($42 to $83 million) of the DOL's funds for job training in 2002 were through the program specifically for older workers (55+), that is, the *Senior Community Service Employment Program (SCSEP)*. The SCSEP is the only federal program specifically targeting older adults. This 4% to 5% is in addition to older workers served through WIA adult and dislocated worker programs.

SENIOR COMMUNITY SERVICE EMPLOYMENT PROGRAM (SCSEP)

The SCSEP is a community service and work-based training program for older workers. Authorized by the Older Americans Act, the program provides subsidized, service-based training for low-income persons 55 or older who are unemployed and have poor employment prospects. Participants have access to both SCSEP services and other employment assistance through One-Stop Career Centers. Participants work an average of twenty hours a week. They are placed in a wide variety of community service activities at nonprofit and public facilities. The goal is for community service training to serve as a bridge to unsubsidized employment opportunities, placing 30% of its authorized positions into unsubsidized employment annually.

- *Available Services:* Services available through the SCSEP include (a) *Community Services*—the program provides over 40 million community service hours to public and nonprofit agencies, allowing them to enhance and provide needed services; and (b) *Participant Services*—Individual Employment Plan (IEP) development, orientation, community service placement, training specific to community service assignment, other training as identified in the IEP, supportive services, wages, fringe benefits, annual physicals, assistance in securing unsubsidized employment, and access to local One-Stop Career Centers.
- *Eligible Participants:* Program participants must be at least 55, unemployed, and have a family income of no more than 125% of the federal poverty level.
- *Program Funding:* The SCSEP is currently funded at approximately $571.9 million. All funds are allocated by a formula; 22% of funds are allocated among states and territories, and 78% to national organizations that compete to provide services.
- *Number of Participants:* 77,758 authorized positions are funded for the program year of 2009, with an additional 12,321 authorized positions funded by the American Reinvestment and Recovery Act of 2009.

THE WORKFORCE INVESTMENT ACT

Administered at the federal level by the Employment and Training Administration (ETA) in the DOL, the WIA is the largest single source of federal funding for workforce development activities. WIA Title I addresses the needs of job seekers who are adults, dislocated workers, and youth; other sections of the law cover adult basic education and literacy programs (Title II), state employment services under the Wagner-Peyser Act (Title III), and vocational rehabilitation programs (Title IV). Each is described briefly below.

Title I

Title I of the WIA provides access to employment and training programs through a nationwide network of one-stop centers administered through state and local Workforce Investment Boards (WIBs).

- *Federal Funding:* About $2.97 billion in fiscal year 2010 for adult, dislocated worker, and youth formula grants.

- *Participants Served:* More than 8 million individuals received WIA-funded services in the twelve-month period ending June 30, 2010.
- *Funded Activities:* (a) *Core services* for all job seekers (e.g., skills assessments, job listings, careers, and local labor market conditions); (b) *intensive services* for individuals who have not obtained employment through core services or who are employed but require intensive services (e.g., skills assessments, career counseling, development of IEPs, and short-term prevocational services) to retain or obtain employment allowing for self-sufficiency; and (c) *training services* for individuals who have been unable to obtain or retain employment through core and intensive services (e.g., occupational skills training, on-the-job training, job readiness training).

Title II

Administered by the Office of Vocational and Adult Education (OVAE) in the U.S. Department of Education (DOEd), the Adult Education and Family Literacy Act's (AEFLA) state-administered grant program is the primary source of federal support for adult basic skills programs. AEFLA funding supports instruction in reading, numeracy, general educational development (GED) preparation, and English literacy.

- *Federal Funding:* $628.2 million in fiscal year 2010 for state formula grants.
- *Participants Served:* More than 2.4 million individuals were served in AEFLA state grant-funded programs in program year 2008–2009.
- *Funded Activities:* (a) *Adult education and literacy services*, including workplace literacy services; (b) *family literacy services*, including interactive literacy activities between parents and their children, training for parents so they can help teach their children, parent literacy training that leads to economic self-sufficiency, and age-appropriate education to prepare children for success in school and in life experiences; and (c) *English literacy programs* for individuals with limited English proficiency.

Title IIIa, The Wagner-Peyser Act

Administered by the U.S. Department of Labor's (DOL) Employment and Training Administration (ETA), the Wagner-Peyser Act funds Employment Service (ES) offices to provide employment-related labor exchange services. These services include job search assistance, job referral, and placement assistance for job seekers; re-employment services for unemployment insurance (UI) claimants; and recruitment services for employers with job openings. The WIA of 1988 required Wagner-Peyser funded services to become part of the one-stop system. The Wagner-Peyser statute also authorizes the development and operation of a nationwide employment statistics system. In addition, as part of its role under the law, the ETA has developed and disseminated electronic job search tools, such as America's Job Bank and the CareerOneStop portal.

- *Federal Funding*: $715.9 million in formula grants to states, plus $33.4 million in national activities funding in FY06.
- *Institutions Funded*: More than 1,800 local offices of state employment security agencies.
- *Population Served:* About 13.3 million job seekers in FY05.

Beyond these standard training programs that have been operating for a number of years, the U.S. Labor Department also recently awarded $10 million to organizations that connect older workers to jobs. The money was designated to retrain workers age 55 and older for jobs in high-growth industries such as health care and green jobs. The ten grants with approximately $1 million each were given to organizations in Indiana, Louisiana, Maine, Maryland, Michigan, Pennsylvania, Texas, Vermont, Washington, and Wisconsin. The Atlantic Philanthropies also invested $3.6 million in this effort (Brandon, 2009). The grants targeted older workers who have been laid off and are seeking re-employment who need to stay in the workforce beyond the traditional retirement age, or workers who face barriers to finding a new job such as a disability or a low level of English proficiency. This three-year initiative has recently been completed, and reports of its success should be forthcoming.

An Uncertain Future for Federal Funding to Support Older Worker Training

With the U.S. federal deficit getting increased attention from Congress and the public, some training-oriented spending may begin to wane. According to Whoriskey (2011), details of the budget compromise in the spring of 2011 show that federal funding for job training programs will be significantly affected, with reductions of more than $870 million in total. Included are cuts to occupational training grants at community colleges, green jobs classes, and a program to help low-income older people acquire work skills, the latter program

receiving the single largest cut (reduced by 45%, or $376 million).

In addition, government spending on training has come under renewed criticism of late because of the general lack of program evaluation data that exists (or is reported). According to Corte (2010), the federal government spends $18 billion a year on forty-seven separate job training programs run by nine different agencies, and the GAO found that little was known about the effectiveness of the programs because half have not had a performance review since 2004, and only five have ever had a study to determine whether job seekers in the program do better than those who do not participate.

Still, according to Davidson (2010), enrollment in job training initiatives across the United States has significantly increased since the recession began, as dislocated workers in shrunken industries such as manufacturing, construction, and real estate look to gain the necessary re-training to move into growing fields such as health care, renewable energy, and computers. Also, participation in worker retraining funded by the federal WIA jumped 70% to 672,000 in June 2009, according to the DOL. But the portion of those in jobs related to their training one year after graduating fell to 67.6% from 83.2% in 2006.

Academic Training/Re-training (Higher Education)

As has been mentioned elsewhere, academic training is becoming more of an option these days for retirees, whether it be in pursuit of another career or for the sake of learning, or something in between. Welte (2010) reported that a large number of students 55 and older are enrolling and majoring in education and training, business, health science, and information technology—all sectors that have been hiring. Workers with just a high school degree that have been laid off are pursuing some sort of postsecondary education that will make them suitable for jobs in growth sectors.

The American Association of Community Colleges (AACC), with funding from the Atlantic Philanthropies developed a nationwide program to retrain the expanding group of older adults who want and need to find new work after traditional retirement age. While many older students already attend community college to prepare for new careers, the association saw a need for a more formal program to help them retrain en masse, especially as the oldest baby boomers begin turning 65 in 2011. The organization, which represents 1,200 community colleges across the United States, received a $3.2 million grant from the Atlantic Philanthropies to develop programs to retrain adults 50 and over so they can re-enter the workforce or find volunteer opportunities doing something new (Kornblum, 2007). Called "The Plus 50 Initiative," funding was supplied to a pilot group of 13 community colleges to develop or expand campus programs in one or more of the following tracks: learning and enrichment, workforce training/career development, and volunteering. A recent review of the program for AACC suggests numerous successes in all three of the learning tracks (LFA Group, 2012).

Older Adult Learning

As notions of retirement change along with other conceptions of the social patterns of life for older adults, lifelong education after retirement is beginning to become a serious social, political, and economic enterprise. In addition to those adults engaged in work-related learning, many older adults want to learn simply for the sake of learning, and others because of the social contacts they can achieve by joining a community of learners (Hebestreit, 2006).

What Do We Know About Older Adults and Learning?

Schaie and others (e.g., Schaie, 1983, 1993, 1994) demonstrated that, on average, most cognitive abilities have begun to decline as people reach their late 50s. This is especially true for perceptual speed and numerical ability. The emphasis here, however, should be *on average*; there are large individual differences in when and how much these mental abilities decline among older persons. In addition, in summarizing the learning literature, Charness and Czaja (2006) noted that for activities that require new learning and problem solving (i.e., "fluid" intelligence), performance peaks when individuals are in their 20s or 30s, followed by a gradual decline. For activities that rely on stored knowledge (i.e., "crystallized" intelligence), performance peaks as individuals reach their 40s and 50s and then shows modest decline, with increases in the rate of decline in the 80s. They also suggested that older individuals are typically slower to acquire those skills than younger adults. Some of this may be attributable to older adults' preference for accuracy over speed, with the reverse being true for younger adults.

The evidence that older people learn differently or require teaching differently from younger ones, however, is sparse (McNair, 2010; Withnall,

McGivney, & Soulsby, 2004). There have been numerous attempts over the past several decades to identify techniques that are best suited to older learners, but few instances of interaction between training technique and age have been uncovered. While many techniques for training may be effective for older adults, there is not yet an adequate research base to determine whether some training techniques are differentially beneficial for older workers on a consistent basis. In part, this may be a result of the fact that, as people age, individual difference in learning styles, preferences, and attitudes is likely to outweigh any purely age-related factors.

When looking at performance variability by age group, Charness and Czaja (2006) distinguished two major types: interindividual variability and intraindividual variability. In terms of interindividual differences, younger persons tend to vary less from each other than do older persons. This is due, at least in part, to the fact that older individuals have had more of an opportunity to develop and thus differentiate from one another than have young adults. For intraindividual differences, older adults tend to be more variable in performance, thus prediction of performance becomes less certain as people age.

Barriers that Prevent Older Adults from Continuing with Lifelong Learning

Historically, research suggests that, on average, older adults participate less in learning than other groups, and Findsen (2002) suggested that participation rates could be explained by particular barriers that older adults frequently encounter. These include (a) *situational barriers* (these relate to an individual's life context at a particular time, that is, the realities of one's social and physical environment; e.g., older adults tend to be less physically mobile); (b) *institutional barriers* (barriers tied to learning institutions or agencies that exclude or discourage certain groups of learners; e.g., non-user-friendly enrollment procedures, high fees, inappropriate venues or unexciting methods of teaching); (c) *informational barriers* (students' lack of awareness regarding the availability of learning opportunities; e.g., lack of adequate information about the educational opportunities available for older learners may contribute to their poor participation); and (d) *psychosocial barriers* (individually held beliefs, values, attitudes, or perceptions that inhibit participation in organized learning activities; e.g., a negative view of oneself or low self-esteem due to a poor or negative educational background or previous experience at school).

Who Is More Likely to Pursue Learning Opportunities?

In a series of studies, Gorard and colleagues (e.g., Gorard, Rees, & Fevre, 1999; Gorard, Rees, Fevre, & Welland, 2001) examined patterns or trajectories of participation in education and training across the life span using age cohorts. They hypothesized that educational trajectories would be determined by individuals' early experiences in school and by certain socioeconomic factors. They assumed that the relatively stable *learner identities* formed early in life would be shown to carry through into later life. They found that early experiences in school tended to predict participation in education in later life.

Hebestreit (2006) suggested that this is a persistent theme in the adult education literature, and she pointed to a National Institute of Adult Continuing Education (NIACE) survey (1999) where it was found that social class continues to be the key discriminator in understanding participation in learning, and the length of initial education continues to be the best single predictor of participation in adult learning. The researchers concluded that the vast majority of adults attracted to continued learning are already well educated, middle class, and white. In sum, the higher the level of formal education, the higher the likelihood of participation.

In a review of how older adults are portrayed in the "adult education journals," Chen, Kim, Moon, and Merriam (2008) noted that, with few exceptions, the literature has portrayed older adults as a homogeneous group free from age-related physical and cognitive decline, thus allowing them unlimited access to learning opportunities. Hebestreit (2006) emphasized that this description of older adults in adult education is not surprising, as it reflects the *typical profile* of participants in formal adult education activities—that is, middle class, white, male or female, with higher levels of previous education. Low-income older adults and those living on reduced income in retirement are less likely to be participants and accordingly have tended to be somewhat invisible in this literature.

McNair suggested that a large proportion of work-related learning is informal and embedded in the structure and processes of the workplace, including learning from and with colleagues, from manuals, and simply by trial and error. Consequently, the accessibility and quality of the learning, and its impact on productivity, will depend on the workplace context, on the attitudes about learning and behaviors of managers and coworkers, and on broader cultural expectations. For example, Fuller and Unwin (2005) identified five key dimensions of workplace context related to employee learning: (a) organizational culture and history, (b) job design, (c) how work is organized, (d) the way people are managed, and (e) how their performance is judged.

Further, Fuller and Unwin characterized two types of learning environments—"expansive" and "restrictive" working environments. These are based on two distinct models of learning—"learning as participation" and "learning as acquisition" (Felstead, 2005). The notion is that an expansive environment offers a sense of community that is critical to effective learning in the workplace; that is, for all forms of learning and development, the social bonds between employees are crucial determinants of individual and group performance. Conversely, a high proportion of what is described as "training" focuses narrowly on compliance and conformity in a "restrictive" working environment, including basic socialization into the organization and procedures, health and safety training, and compliance with specific regulatory requirements.

Serious Leisure

Interest from the academic community in education for older adults is a relatively recent phenomenon, but one that has been gaining momentum over the last several decades (Hebestreit, 2006). Jones (2000) observed that some of the appeal of formal education to the retiree may be related to what many miss about working: structure, achievement, creative challenge, and social interaction. For some older learners, participation in education resembles the kind of commitments they make to various organizations. Jones and Symon (2001) agreed that lifelong learning as serious leisure is a bridge for older adults between work and leisure. Serious leisure may provide retired adults with many of the noneconomic benefits of work that are missed in retirement, such as purpose, personal identity, and a social milieu of like-minded peers. Those who pursue active leisure in retirement often participate in educational programs, primarily for their social aspects.

Interest in "serious leisure" extends beyond mere classroom education, having grown in the last few decades into big business. There are now a number of these "educational models" in many countries, developed specifically to meet the needs of older adults—for example, Elderhostel (now known as Road Scholar), Institutes for Learning in Retirement (ILR), and Universities of the Third Age (U3A).

One of the best-known models, Elderhostel, was founded in 1975, as a campus-based program, and within the first twenty-five years evolved into an organization teaching courses at universities, colleges, and organizations worldwide—including numerous educational travel opportunities that include in-depth learning and cultural tours (Kressley & Huebschmann, 2002). In 2010 the organization changed its name to Road Scholar, and continues to expand it programs to meet the growing market, with programs supported by a wide variety of host institutions, including universities, museums, research centers, and national parks.

A campus-based program, generically known as Institutes for Learning in Retirement (ILR), or more recently as Lifelong Learning Institutes (LLI) operates as an independent organization affiliated with a college or university and offers college-level courses to older adults on an audit or tuition-waiver basis. The members of LLI organizations are groups of people who have retired and who are seeking learning opportunities. They meet to plan, participate in, or conduct educational courses for their community. The program's focus is on pursuit of collegial learning for pleasure and stimulation (see for example, Kidahashi & Manheimer, 2009).

Universities of the Third Age (U3A) are self-help, self-managed lifelong learning cooperatives for older people no longer in full-time work. They are designed to provide opportunities for their members to share learning experiences in a wide range of interest groups and to pursue learning not for qualifications, but for fun (Formosa, 2010).

Volunteering

While a significant number of the baby-boom cohort expect to continue working in retirement, many will look to volunteerism to meet their desire to stay active and engaged. Volunteering is the practice of people working on behalf of others or a particular cause without payment for their time and services. Volunteering is both an altruistic activity intended to promote good or improve human quality of life and an individualist activity undertaken to advance learning and insight, develop skills, enjoy social interactions, and for a variety of other reasons.

Volunteering is expected to be an important component of retirees' activities as they enter retirement age for both individuals who continue working at paid employment and those who do not. According to the Bureau of Labor Statistics (U.S. Department of Labor, 2011), older adult (65+) volunteering has been on an upward trajectory through the last three decades, going from 14.3% in 1974 to 23.5% in 2005, and older adults are the most likely to serve 100 or more hours a year (Grimm, Dietz, Foster-Bey, Reingold, & Nesbit, 2006).

The increase in volunteering is driven in part by an increased demand for volunteers from nonprofit organizations. Between 1989 and 2004, the number of operating public charities and other nonprofit organizations more than doubled (Hager, 2004). While most have some professional staff, over 81% of nonprofit organizations utilize volunteers to provide services as well as to help them administer and manage their operations. Based on the approximately 215,000 charities that filed Form 990 or 990EZ with the IRS in 2000 (required of those charities with over $25,000 in annual gross receipts), an estimated 174,000 nonprofit organizations use volunteers.

Formal volunteerism has been an essential component of the American social, political, spiritual, and economic life as far back as the late nineteenth century and early twentieth century. Many well-known volunteer organizations trace their founding back many years (e.g., YMCA—1851; the Salvation Army—1880; the American Red Cross—1881; Volunteers of America—1896; the Junior League—1901; Goodwill Industries—1915; and Boys Town—1917, to name a few). The Great Depression broadly affected the entire nation and, accordingly, the period saw one of the first large-scale, nationwide efforts to coordinate volunteerism for a specific need. By 1940, twenty-eight cities had volunteer bureaus. During World War II, thousands of volunteer offices supervised the volunteers who helped with the many needs of the military and the nation, including collecting supplies, entertaining soldiers on leave, and caring for the injured.

After World War II, the passion of volunteers to help others shifted focus to other areas (e.g., the Nature Conservancy, 1951) and volunteering overseas (e.g., Peace Corps, 1961). President Lyndon B. Johnson's "War on Poverty" in 1964 spawned a new set of volunteer organizations focused on helping the poor (e.g., Volunteers in Service to the Poor or VISTA, 1964). Over the next few decades, volunteer opportunities continued to expand, e.g., Habitat for Humanity (1976), Feed the Children (1979), and AmeriCorps (1990).

The process for finding volunteer work became more institutionalized with the passing of the National Service Act (1990) and the National and

Community Service Trust Act (1993), the latter creating the Corporation for National & Community Service (CNCS), an independent agency of the U.S. government. The mission of the CNCS is to "support the American culture of citizenship, service, and responsibility." While a government agency, the corporation acts much like a foundation, and it is the nation's largest grant-maker supporting service and volunteering. Programs include AmeriCorps, Learn and Serve America, Senior Corps, USA Freedom Corps, the President's Volunteer Service Award program, and the Presidential Freedom Scholarship Program.

Specifically targeted at involving older persons, *Senior Corps* serves to link volunteers over 55 with individuals, nonprofits, and faith-based and other community organizations. Typical roles include mentoring, coaching, and contributing existing skills and expertise to community projects and organizations. Senior Corps currently links more than 500,000 Americans to service opportunities. Senior Corps ensures that volunteers receive pre-service orientation, project-specific training from the organization, and supplemental insurance while on duty.

The three primary subprograms of Senior Corps include (a) the *Foster Grandparent Program,* which provides mentoring to children and young people with special needs (Foster Grandparents serve up to forty hours per week and may qualify to earn a tax-free, hourly stipend); (b) the *Senior Companion Program,* which provides companions to help out on a personal level by assisting with shopping and light chores, interacting with doctors, and providing socialization; and (c) *RSVP,* the nations' largest volunteer network for people age 55 and over. With thousands of local and national organizations, RSVP volunteers tutor children, renovate homes, teach English, assist victims of natural disasters, provide independent living services, and recruit and manage other volunteers. RSVP capitalizes on the volunteering features known to be important to older persons. Volunteers may choose how and where they will serve as well as the amount of time they will offer. Volunteers are also offered the option of drawing on their existing skills or developing new ones. Volunteers do not receive monetary incentives, but sponsoring organizations may reimburse them for some costs incurred during service, including meals and transportation.

Capturing Available Volunteer Talent

All types of organizations that utilize volunteers, even small ones, are becoming more sophisticated in terms of locating, managing, and retaining volunteers. Training—for the paid staff as well as volunteers—is recognized as a critical "best practice." Training for paid staff of the organization as well as volunteers serves to both prepare the organization to locate, select, and utilize volunteers and make volunteers better able to serve in significant and productive roles. One way that training is brought to the multitude of small, local organizations is through programs offered by umbrella organizations. The central office for Senior Corp, for example, working in concert with Temple University, prepared in 2009 a series of training exercises titled "The Boomers Are Here! A Station Training Toolkit." The training is targeted at the managers of volunteer activities in member organizations (Corporation for National & Community Service, 2009).

A number of nonprofit organizations have made it their organizational objective to develop community capabilities for creative and productive volunteering. This type of organization is typified well by the national nonprofit Civic Ventures. One of their principal undertakings is called the *Next Chapter Initiative*, which is described as both a philosophy and a training "blueprint" to guide local communities in the development of approaches and programs to help older adults make choices for their next stage of life and make substantive contributions to their communities (Adler, Goggin, & Peterson, 2005). The four-pronged approach recommended in the *Blueprint* includes the development of life planning programs to help older adults assess their current status and strengths, networking programs to help them locate and assume public service roles, resource programs to provide learning options to enrich their lives and help them prepare for significant undertakings in either the business or nonprofit sectors, and programs to foster interactions with peers and other community members.

A signature program of Civic Ventures is Experience Corps, a program to link those 55+ with children in urban public schools and after-school programs, where they help teach children to read and develop the confidence and skills to succeed in school and in life. The umbrella organization for this multi-city program has invested in researching and compiling advice on best practices for recruiting, training, and retaining older volunteers (Experience Corps, 2005).

Another way that nonprofits are preparing to attract volunteers is by advertising their opportunities online. Operating like a traditional online job search service, websites are available where volunteer opportunities are posted and can be searched. Prospective volunteers click on a posting to be connected with the organization. One prominent website, VolunteerMatch.org, was originated in partnership with Senior Corp. Another site, Serve. gov, is managed by the Corporation for National and Community Service. The website boardnetusa.org advertises "job openings" for people that are interested in serving on a board of a nonprofit. Many standard online job posting sites have a feature to search for only volunteer positions.

Types of Volunteering Opportunities Available

The choice of volunteering formats available today is extensive. Among traditional venues are church-based groups where volunteers provide services to the church itself or lend support to the church's outreach services. School-based volunteering is also popular, and there are many opportunities available in the school system for volunteers to take advantage of that require no specialized skills. Many nonchurch-based opportunities exist in most communities that facilitate contributing one's time to provide hands-on services to needy persons in the local community. Training offered through such organizations is typically project-specific and involves becoming familiar with the specific services or activities performed. In some instances, organizations will enlist professional service organizations to provide management training to paid staff and volunteers. These training activities might involve, for example, weekend retreats focused on team building.

A majority of the *Fortune* 500 companies allow their employees to volunteer during work hours. These formalized Employee Volunteering Programs (EVPs) are regarded as a part of the companies' sustainability efforts and their social responsibility activities (Boccalandro, 2009). These activities typically involve direct service provision and do not require specialized skills related to the volunteers' employment.

Skills-based volunteering refers to a situation in which the volunteer has expertise in the area in which he or she volunteers. For individuals with more general academic backgrounds, numerous opportunities exist for volunteers to capitalize on their existing skill base. Born with the advent of the internet, a newer format for volunteering is *micro-volunteering*, which refers to performing work via the internet. Micro-volunteering websites give individuals an opportunity to match skills, such as

writing and editing, instructional design, or budgeting and finance, with volunteer challenges posted by nonprofits around the world. These micro-tasks take a small amount of time and can be performed long distance. Micro-volunteering also offers volunteers an introduction to an organization, role, or issue in which they might be interested for their own career transition purposes and to practice skills that may be valuable in other volunteer contexts.

Some opportunities rely on a combination of the volunteer's general background and varying amounts of project-specific training. For example, RSVP and Foster Grandparents, two programs targeted at volunteers 55 and older, seek out volunteers with appropriate literacy and social skills and provide training in mentoring and relationship building. Disaster relief workers must have completed training programs before being dispatched to sites.

Some types of volunteering require professional backgrounds. For example, lawyers have a long tradition of providing pro bono services either through corporately subsidized programs or personal involvement. Opportunities for doctors and other health professionals are available through broad-based groups such as Doctors Without Borders and Mercy Ships. In the business sector, programs like SCORE and the International Executive Service Corps enlist volunteers with business expertise to provide consulting services to small businesses. The private nonprofit sector has parallel opportunities offered by organizations whose objective is to facilitate ways to bring business expertise into the nonprofit world. An excellent example is Taproot, itself a nonprofit whose goal is to strengthen nonprofits by connecting them with business professionals. Currently operating in five metropolitan areas, Taproot recruits individuals with appropriate backgrounds, provides additional assignment-specific training as needed, matches these individuals with nonprofits, and helps manage the relationship between the volunteer consultant and the client.

Training and Learning Available through Volunteering

VOLUNTEERING THAT BUILDS SKILLS AND KNOWLEDGE

Training volunteers is considered a "best practice" in nonprofit management. Training serves to increase the value of volunteers' inputs, while highlighting the significance of the work being done. Training through nonprofits is immensely diverse, ranging from building skills that enhance the organization itself (e.g., fundraising, group facilitation) to highly specialized services such as providing paralegal advice or basic medical services. Combining training with hands-on work, The Red Cross, for example, advertises opportunities leading to skill development in fundraising, administrative duties, graphic design, photography, community and media relations, volunteer management, presentation and speaking skills, and partnering with other organizations. Once considered just for young volunteers, older persons are taking advantage of internship programs offered by organizations such as the American Folklife Center, the Congressional Research Service, and the Library of Congress. Most private and public museums have programs whereby volunteers become docents (guides). Many national forests and parks have programs for volunteers to guide tours and provide in-depth historical information. Fisheries enlist volunteers to serve as cruise guides. With the expected boom in health care employment opportunities, many health facilities now offer volunteer opportunities that provide training and hands-on experience in specific clinical areas such as behavioral care, cancer, diabetes, emergency, occupational/physical therapy, and rehabilitations as well as administrative areas such as admitting and patient representation.

VOLUNTEERING TO GAIN CERTIFICATIONS

On a more formal basis, many volunteer organizations offer training leading to certification that can subsequently be used to qualify for employment or more sophisticated volunteering. Certification for training is particularly important to older persons who are moving out of the area where they can point to years of experience and do not otherwise have credentials to evidence their capability. In locations across the country, the Red Cross and other disaster relief agencies offer Lay Responder Instructor courses, which can result in certification as CPR, first aid, and AED instructor. The Internal Revenue Service (IRS) sponsors locally based programs to provide free assistance doing tax returns for people with low incomes, disabilities, and seniors. Volunteers are offered online, self-paced training in the IRS TaxWise software. At the conclusion of training, volunteers may qualify to become IRS-certified tax preparers. The training itself is provided by previous volunteers.

FORMAL TRAINING TO PREPARE
FOR VOLUNTEERING

Requiring a significantly higher time investment, a number of universities across the nation have developed programs targeted at providing the mentoring, knowledge, hands-on experience, and networking resources that are needed to prepare volunteers for significant roles in government, civic organizations, and educational organizations. For example, the North Carolina Center for Creative Retirement (NCCCR), a department of the University of North Carolina at Asheville, offers programs in the arts and humanities, the natural world, civic engagement, wellness, life transition and retirement relocation planning, intergenerational co-learning, and research on trends in the reinvention of retirement. Several years ago NCCCR developed a "Certificate of Merit" for those who successfully completed its Blue Ridge Naturalist program. The rigorous program requires at least 240 hours of classroom study, monthly evening seminars, various six- and eight-week-long mini-courses in basic sciences related to the natural environment, and monthly day-long field studies. Enrollees work with a mentor and must complete a community service project. Certificate holders are expected to continue giving back to the community through education and service opportunities that enhance the environment of Western North Carolina (e.g., develop and teach education courses, host environmental education programs for children, train volunteers to work with visitors at local environmental sites, develop new habitats).

Another excellent example is the Legacy Leadership Institute at the University of Maryland that offers programs leading to certification in the areas of the environment, fundraising for nonprofit organizations, humor practices (e.g., teaching older persons to use humor to present public health messages to school-age children), public policy, and municipal government. Specifically targeted at preparing students to transition from paid employment into new careers as volunteer service leaders, these programs require significant classroom instruction, mentoring, and a practicum. The Legacy Leadership Institute on Fundraising, for example, requires five weeks of classroom instruction and 250 hours service in a local Community Mediation Center under the mentorship of experienced fundraisers, mediation center staff, and University of Maryland faculty.

Conclusions

Persons aged 55 and older are becoming a significant proportion of the population—and a growing part of the labor pool. Retirement patterns are also changing, offering an increasingly wider array of options for these individuals. The current chapter examines what is known about learning and training for those who remain in a career job after reaching retirement-eligible age, follow some re-careering direction, pursue bridge employment or other work-related endeavors, engage in volunteer activities, or opt for personal educational/intellectual pursuits.

What our review of retiree training research and application found was an area that is broad, scattered, under-researched, and relatively unexplored. The adult education literature is vast but fragmented. The older adult work-related training literature is nearly invisible. Little is known about the extent or effectiveness of training programs that target older workers. What we do know is that in many respects older learners are no different from other types of learners. While some older learners may be less able to learn, many experience negligible declines in their capacity. What distinguishes older learners, though, is that after spending most of their adult lives in paid employment, as they become retirement eligible, they are confronted with a variety of decisions about how to spend their remaining years. And, for supporting advancement along many of these available pathways, training can play an important role, but historically and currently this has not been the case.

What little we do know about training for retirement-eligible individuals suggests that most of the training dollars are spent by the private sector and for current employees (many of whom are likely to be white, educated, and financially secure). Interestingly, this relatively narrow segment of the population tends to be reflected in the research cited in the adult education literature. Conversely, those most in need—the displaced, unemployed, people with language problems, those with a high school education or less—have become the primary target of the federal government's training budget.

Compared to the training programs in public and private sectors, the volunteering community appears to be much further along in identifying training needs and developing training programs, and much better prepared to offer training and learning opportunities. Granted, their target population has always been a bit older than that of the workforce in general, but it appears that they are better equipped to attract and identify requisite individual competencies, as well as place and provide the necessary training support for retirees. As the population of late-career and retirement-eligible persons increases, learning and training programs—formal and informal—will become an increasingly

critical support mechanism for this growing segment of the world's population. It is a fertile but relatively untapped area for research and development.

Future Directions

Nininger and Scourtoudis (2003) observed that organizations have constructed extensive "scaffolding" for new employees designed to orient, integrate, and develop them, but suggested that almost no attention is given to the need to create similar scaffolding to support older employees entering the final phase of their careers. Certainly, there is a growing realization of the integral role that late-career workers and retirees can play in the labor force of the future. However, while there are a variety of programs, educational institutions, internships, and training activities available for young people pursuing career development options, career services for people beyond middle age are hard to find (Bass, 2005). Career planning, career counseling, career placement, and career training are extensive in American institutions for this younger age group. Unfortunately, for an older worker or an older person wanting to return to work, these pathways are remarkably inaccessible, even though the decisions that older people have to make are no less complex or impactful—involving financial, health, education, and lifestyle decisions.

While we have noted that several federal/state programs exist that offer training, they tend to target those displaced, or those in low-skill, low-pay jobs. And even these programs tend to miss some intended targets. For example, as suggested by Johnson et al. (2009) and McNair (2010), re-careering rates are significantly lower for certain ethnic minorities, women, and those who did not complete high school than for other workers. Expanding public workforce development initiatives for older adults with limited skills or little work experience could improve their employment options. More training for older adults with limited education could give them the skills and confidence they need to move into new careers, enabling them to extend their working years, increase their retirement income security, and improve the quality of their lives. Training programs for the large majority of older individuals in search of new skills or updating are scarce, and the human resource enterprise to support this group is nonexistent. As a result, a large number of older Americans—those who are quite able and have some financial security—are unlikely to be supported in their training endeavors.

A concerted effort will be required—by government (at all levels) and by the private sector—to develop the type of "scaffolding" needed to capitalize on this growing pool of expertise represented by the aging workforce. The development and availability of training programs designed to offer appropriate re-skilling or refresher training to large numbers of retirement eligibles are crucial.

Bass (2005) suggested that there are essentially three key players for the creation of new programs designed to engage or re-engage the able older workers: (a) the government, (b) the philanthropic community, and (c) the private sector—or some combination of these three. One public organization that should be well-positioned to increase the critical (re)training of older workers is the higher education community. Community colleges and continuing education programs should be interested in offering market-responsive programs designed for mature workers or new retirees. Many of these institutions also receive government subsidies and could provide career enrichment to this special segment of the workforce.

Established foundations (e.g., Sloan, Carnegie, Ford, or Kellogg) could create programs to support learning and training in retirement. Such support might include partnering with the government to offer education grants to expand work opportunities, serious leisure learning, or volunteer activities. This would also appear to be a fertile area for new nonprofits to enter.

If for no other reason than the size of their training budgets, the private sector may hold the most promise for developing new training models for older workers. Companies established by older entrepreneurs designed to assist with job re-training or placement may find willing clients—individuals seeking placement and companies needing skilled labor (Bass, 2005). In addition, as companies seek to recruit older workers to join their firms, it would make sense to have training programs in place to provide the necessary re-skilling or refresher training to quickly bring these experienced workers "up to speed." In sum, training can play an important role in preparing people for changing roles and expanding skills and knowledge to pursue new opportunities.

References

Adler, R., Goggin, J., & Peterson, N. (2005). *Blueprint for the next chapter*. San Francisco, CA: Civic Ventures. Retrieved from www.civicventures.org

Bass, S. A. (2005). New models for post-retirement employment. In P. T. Beatty & R. M. S. Visser (Eds.), *Thriving on an aging workforce: Strategies for organizational and systematic change* (pp. 161–169). Malabar, FL: Krieger.

Beier, M. E., Teachout, M. S., & Cox, C. B. (2012). The training and development of an aging workforce. In J. W. Hedge & W. C. Borman (Eds.), *The Oxford handbook of work and aging* (pp. 436–453). New York, NY: Oxford University Press.

Boccalandro, B. (2009). *Mapping success in employee volunteering: The drivers of effectiveness for employee volunteering and giving programs and Fortune 500 performance*. Boston, MA: Center for Corporate Citizenship, Boston College.

Brandon, E. (2009, August 3). Planning to retire: Labor department awards $10 million to retrain older workers. *Money*. http://money.usnews.com/money/blogs/planning-to-retire/2009/08/03/labor-department-awards-10-million-to-retrain-older-workers.

Brown, M., Aumann, K., Pitt-Catsouphes, M., Galinsky, E., & Bond, J. T. (2010, July). *Working in retirement: A 21st century phenomenon*. Boston, MA: Families and Work Institute.

Charness, N., & Czaja, S. J. (2006, October). *Older worker training: What we know and don't know* (Report No. 2006-22). Washington, DC: AARP Public Policy Institute.

Chen, L., Kim, Y. S., Moon, P., & Merriam, S. B. (2008). A review and critique of the portrayal of older adult learners in adult education journals, 1980–2006. *Adult Education Quarterly, 59,* 3–21.

Corporation for National and Community Service. (2009). *The boomers are here! A station training toolkit*. Washington, DC: Center for Intergenerational Learning Training Division and Corporation for National & Community Service. Retrieved from www.nationalserviceresources.org/news/boomers-are-here

Davidson, P. (2010, June 4). Laid-off workers retrain but end up in same spot: Jobless. *USA Today*. http://www.usatoday.com/money/economy/2010-06-04-retrain04_CV_N.htm.

Ekerdt, D. J. (2010). Frontiers of research on work and retirement. *Journal of Gerontology: Social Sciences, 65B,* 69–80.

Experience Corps. (2005). *Appealing to experience: Zeroing in on the right message*. Washington, DC: Civic Venture. Retrieved from www.experiencecorps.org/

Felstead, A. (2005). Surveying the scene: Learning metaphors, survey design, and the workplace context. *Journal of Education and Work, 18,* 359–383.

Findsen, B. (2002, June). Older adults and learning: A critique of participation and provision. *Proceedings of a Lifelong Learning Conference, 2,* 172–180.

Formosa, M. (2010). Lifelong learning in later life: The universities of the Third Age. *The LLI Review, 5,* 1–12.

Fuller, A., & Unwin, L. (2004). Expansive learning environments: Integrating personal and organizational development. In H. Rainbird, A. Fuller, & A. Munro. (Eds.), *Workplace learning in context* (pp. 126–144). London, England: Routledge.

Gorard, S., Rees, G., & Fevre, R. (1999). Patterns of participation in lifelong learning: Do families make a difference? *British Educational Research Journal, 25,* 517–532.

Gorard, S., Rees, G., Fevre, R., & Welland, T. (2001). Lifelong learning trajectories: Some voices of those in transit. *International Journal of Lifelong Education, 20,* 169–187.

Greller, M. M., & Stroh, L. K. (2003). Extending working lives: Are current approaches tools or talismans? In. G. A. Adams & T. A. Beehr (Eds.), *Retirement: Reasons, processes, and results* (pp. 115–135). New York, NY: Springer.

Grimm, R., Dietz, N., Foster-Bey, J., Reingold, D., and Nesbit, R. (2006, December). *Volunteer growth in America: A review* of trends since 1974. Washington, DC: Corporation for National & Community Service. Retrieved from www.nationalservice.gov/

Hager, M. A. (2004). *Volunteer management capacity in America's charities and congregations: A briefing report*. Washington, DC: The Urban Institute. Retrieved from http://www.urban.org/UploadedPDF/410963_VolunteerManagment.pdf.

Hebestreit, L. K. (2006, November). *An evaluation of the role of the University of the Third Age in the provision of lifelong learning* (Doctoral thesis). University of South Africa, Pretoria, South Africa.

Hedge, J. W., Borman, W. C., & Lammlein, S. L. (2006). *The aging workforce: Realities, myths, and implications for organizations*. Washington, DC: APA Books.

Helman, R., Greenwald, W., Copeland, C., & VanDerhei, J. (2011, March). *The 2011 Retirement Confidence Survey: Confidence drops to record lows, reflecting "the new normal"* (EBRI Issue Brief No. 355). Washington, DC: Employee Benefit Research Institute.

Johnson, R. W., Kawachi, J., & Lewis, E. K. (2009, August). *Older workers on the move: Recareering in later life* (AARP Report No. 2009-08). Washington, DC: AARP Public Policy Institute.

Jones, L., & Symon, G. (2001). Lifelong learning as serious leisure: Policy, practice, and potential. *Leisure Studies, 20*, 415–427.

Jones, S. (2000). Older people in higher education: A personal perspective. *Education and Ageing, 15*, 339–351.

Kidahashi, M., & Manheimer, R. J. (2009). Getting ready for the working-in-retirement generation: How should LLIs respond? *The LLI Review, 4*, 1–8.

Kornblum, J. (2007). Community colleges take lead in retraining retirees. *USA Today*. http://www.usatoday.com/news/education/2007-10-02-retrain-retirees_N.htm.

Kressley, K. M., & Huebschmann, M. (2002). The 21st century campus: Gerontological perspectives. *Educational Gerontology, 28*, 835–851.

Lacey, T. A., & Wright, B. (2009). Occupational employment projections to 2018. *Monthly Labor Review, 132*, 82–123.

Maestas, N. (2007, April). *Back to work: Expectations and realizations of work after retirement* (WR-196–2). Rand Labor and Population Working Paper. Santa Monica, CA: Rand.

McNair, S. (2010, August). *A sense of a future: A study of training and work in later life: A report for the Nuffield Foundation*. Leicester, England: National Institute of Adult Continuing Education.

Mikelson, K. S., & Nightingale, D. S. (2004, December). *Estimating public and private expenditures on occupational training in the United States* (UI Project No. 07389-005-00). Washington, DC: U.S. Department of Labor, Employment and Training Administration.

NIACE. (1999). What motivates people to learn? (Briefing Sheet, No. 2). Leicester, United Kingdom: National Institute of Adult Continuing Education.

Nininger, J. R., and Scourtoudis, L. (2003, April). *Moving beyond the workplace: Exploring life's journey*. Ottawa, Canada: Canadian Centre for Management Development.

Rix, S. (2011, May). *The employment situation, April 2011: Average duration of unemployment for older jobseekers exceeds one year* (AARP Fact Sheet 225). Washington, DC: AARP Public Policy Institute.

Schaie, K. W. (1983). The Seattle longitudinal study: A 21-year exploration of psychometric intelligence in adulthood. In K. W. Schaie (Ed.), *Longitudinal studies of adult psychological development* (pp. 31–44). New York, NY: Springer.

Schaie, K. W. (1993). The Seattle longitudinal studies of adult intelligence. *Current Directions in Psychological Science, 2*, 171–175.

Schaie, K. W. (1994). The course of adult intellectual development. *American Psychologist, 49*, 304–313.

Shultz, K. S., & Henkens, K. (2010). Introduction to the changing nature of retirement: An international perspective. *International Journal of Manpower, 31*, 265–270.

Shultz, K. S., & Wang, M. (2011). Psychological perspectives on the changing nature of retirement. *American Psychologist, 66*, 170–179.

Sweet, S. (2007). The older worker, job insecurity, and the new economy. *Generations, 31*, 45–49.

Szinovacz, M. E. (2003). Contexts and pathways: Retirement as institution, process, and experience. In G. A. Adams & T. A. Beehr (Eds.), *Retirement: Reasons, processes, and results* (pp. 6–52). New York, NY: Springer.

Toossi, M. (2009). Labor force projections to 2018: Older workers staying more active. *Monthly Labor Review, 132*, 30–51.

U.S. Department of Labor. (2011). *Volunteering in the United States—2010 economic news release*. Washington, DC: Bureau of Labor Statistics, Retrieved from www.bls.gov/news.release/volun.toc.htm

Wang, M. (2012). The health, fiscal, and psychological well-being in retirement. In J. W. Hedge & W. C. Borman (Eds.), *The Oxford handbook of work and aging* (pp. 570–584). New York, NY: Oxford University Press.

Welte, M. S. (2010, December 29). Retirement out of reach, seniors seek new job skills. *Community College Week*. http://www.ccweek.com/news/templates/template.aspx?articleid=2266&zoneid=3.

Whoriskey, P. (2011, April 15). Job training programs cut in budget deal. *The Washington Post*. http://www.washingtonpost.com/business/economy/job-training-programs-cut-in-budget-deal/2011/04/15/AFclE3kD_story.html.

Withnall, A., McGivney, V., & Soulsby, J. (2004). *Older people learning: Myths and realities*. Leicester, England: NIACE.

Technology and Retirement Life: A Systematic Review of the Literature on Older Adults and Social Media

Bo Xie, Man Huang, *and* Ivan Watkins

Abstract

The increasingly ubiquitous adoption of technology in contemporary society brings both opportunities and challenges for older adults in retirement. This chapter examines how one specific type of technology, social media, can assist older adults in living a happy and productive life, helping them to cope with retirement transition and the challenges that older adults face in a technology-oriented world. A systematic review of the literature of twenty-nine databases in eight fields was conducted in September–November 2010 to identify existing research on older adults and social media. After four rounds of careful screening, ten articles were selected from these databases. Combined with two additional articles obtained through professional contacts, a total of twelve articles reporting fifteen independent studies was included in the final sample for qualitative analysis. While these existing studies are small in sample size and exploratory in nature, they shed light on the intersection of older adults and social media. Key themes identified in these articles are discussed and future research directions are proposed.

Key Words: social media, Web 2.0, social networking, information and communication technology, aging

Technology is increasingly ubiquitous in contemporary society. This ubiquity brings both opportunities and challenges for older adults in retirement. For instance, with the development of information and communication technologies (ICTs), it is now possible to access vast amounts of high-quality, up-to-date information about health, social security, taxes, and local communities via computers, and communicate and interact with family and friends far away or make new friends around the world with relatively low cost (Xie, 2003). However, to take full advantage of new ICTs, one needs to have sufficient knowledge and skill about these technologies. Older adults' adoption of new technology traditionally lags behind that of younger people. For instance, while the older population's adoption of e-mail is catching up with the adoption rate of other age groups (Jones

& Fox, 2009), older adults' adoption of newer web applications such as social media still lags behind (Lenhart, 2009).

What are older adults' perceptions and uses of newer internet applications like social media? Answers to this question can help develop a better understanding of the impact of social media on older adults, providing a lens to recognize the opportunities and challenges in retirement associated with new technology. Toward this end, we conducted a systematic review of the literature to identify the themes in peer-reviewed articles that address older adults' use of social media. We focus on social media instead of technology in general for two main reasons: first, the impact of technology in general on older adults has previously been examined (e.g., Charness & Schaie, 2003), and second, social media is a new domain that has just begun to emerge during the past few years. This new domain has great potential and requires more systematic examination.

Below, we will first review the brief history of social media to establish an understanding of what social media are and what opportunities—and challenges—they might bring to individuals and society. We then report the procedure and results of our systematic literature review on older adults and social media, followed by the discussion and future research directions.

Literature Review

Social media support user participation, peer-to-peer interaction, information sharing and collaboration, community building, and development (Meraz, 2009; O'Reilly, 2004). While traditional forms of mass media like radio, newspaper, and television feature asymmetric information dissemination and control between the broadcaster and the public, social media are "many-to-many media" that "now make it possible for every person connected to the network to broadcast as well as receive text, images, audio, video, software, data, discussions, transactions, computations, tags, or links to and from every other person" (Rheingold, 2008, p. 100).

The emergence of social media is an inherently dynamic phenomenon, characterized by rapid development and frequent technological and behavioral changes (Hogan & Quan-Haase, 2010). Social media websites typically evolve over time in response to their users' needs and preferences (Hogan & Quan-Haase, 2010). Describing the history of social media is no easy task: The scope of social media can hardly be specified, and no commonly accepted definition of social media precisely describes the types of communication, interaction, and services that social media comprise. Kaplan and Haenlein (2010) define social media as "a group of Internet-based applications that build on the ideological and technological foundations of Web 2.0, and that allow the creation and exchange of User Generated Content" (p. 61). However, the fuzzy boundary between social media and related concepts (e.g., Web 2.0, user-generated content) makes it challenging to define exactly what social media are or when they began to be distinguishable from precedent technologies (Hogan & Quan-Haase, 2010).

Despite the definitional difficulties, different forms of social media do share certain characteristics. In particular, all social media rely on computer-mediated communication (CMC) as a platform, and the history of social media is closely in line with that of CMC. Until the late 1990s, CMC was primarily text-based (Herring, 2004); web pages displayed few of the dynamic characteristics associated with contemporary social media websites (Ha & James, 1998). Users needed a mailer system to access e-mail; similarly, a newsreader was necessary to access Usenet newsgroups (Herring, 2004). Despite the "crude and fragmented" nature of CMC at that time (Herring, 2004, p. 27), these services, along with listservs, became especially popular on college campuses (e.g., in 1979, students from Duke University created Usenet as the first online discussion platform; Kaplan & Haenlein, 2010). Between 2000 and 2005, CMC migrated to web browsers, corresponding with the increasing availability in broadband/high-speed internet. Synchronous chat (instant messaging) and web-accessible e-mail gained popularity during this period. With the wide adoption of ICTs among the general public, CMC is no longer a privilege among the technologically more experienced professionals (Herring, 2004).

In 2004, the concept of "Web 2.0" emerged from the industry (O'Reilly, 2004). Web 2.0 is frequently associated with social media, and oftentimes the phrases are used interchangeably (O'Reilly, 2004). Similar to social media, no commonly accepted definition for the Web 2.0 concept exists. Rather, Web 2.0 is best understood in contrast with Web 1.0. Compared with Web 1.0, Web 2.0 "offers more interactivity, faster feedback, pageless designs, in-context controls, personalization, and access to social networks" (Chadwick-Dias, Bergel, & Tullis, 2007, p. 868). Core Web 2.0 components include the following: First, Web 2.0 serves as a "platform" for broad user participation, in contrast to Web 1.0 as a passive information source (O'Reilly, 2004). Second, user initiative and participation on Web 2.0 sites involve content generation (i.e., user-generated content such as profile pages, user review, status updates) and social networking (e.g., searching for "friends" on the web, recommending "friends"), made possible through numerous technological applications (Cormode & Krishnamurthy, 2008). Third, the versatility of the technologies and subsequent social practices is another key component of Web 2.0. Diverse and fast-changing Web 2.0 techniques provide users with "new ways of using the Internet that are quickly developing into new social practices and new forms of knowledge exchange" (Song, 2010, p. 250).

Since 2005, there has been an enormous rise in the popularity of social networking sites (SNSs). By

September 2009, nearly half of U.S. adult internet users used SNSs (Lenhart, 2009). This number is even higher with younger people: While 55% of teenagers used SNSs in 2006, this number reached 65% in 2008 and 73% in 2009; 75% of internet users age 18–24 maintain a profile on an SNS (Lenhart, Purcell, Smith, & Zickuhr, 2010). Nearly one-third of adult internet users in the United States contributed self-generated content online in 2009, up from 21% in 2007 (Lenhart, 2009). Video sharing sites (e.g., YouTube) are becoming almost ubiquitous with younger people, with 89% of internet users between the ages of 18 and 29 using such sites (Madden, 2009). Facebook stands out as one of the most popular SNSs among high school and college students (Ellison, Steinfield, & Lampe, 2007).

Although new technologies typically offer significant benefits for improving the independence and quality of life for older adults, educational, cognitive, physiological, and experiential factors present challenges to older adults' use of technology (Charness & Schaie, 2003). Age-related differences to information-processing capabilities may impair older adults' relationship with the complicated contemporary technological environment (Schieber, 2003). Previous life experiences may have left older adults unprepared for contemporary technology (Charness & Schaie, 2003). Despite these challenges, advancements in communication technology and technology integrated into the living environment offer numerous benefits to older adults by easing transportation demands and physical limitations, and creating an online network of social contacts (Charness & Schaie, 2003).

Table 31.1 below illustrates key features of three prominent social media applications: (1) Facebook,

Table 31.1 Exemplar Social Media Sites: Facebook, YouTube, and Twitter

Site	Social Networking Feature	Multimedia Functionality	Personalization Feature
Facebook	• Users can establish a network of connections with other users—all called "friends." • Users indicate their interests on their profile. If "friends" share an interest, Facebook will highlight the shared interest. • Users can form groups based on shared interests. • Via interactive calendar (called "events"), "friends" can respond to these "events." • Users can interact privately via instant messaging (chat), e-mail, or "poking." Users can also leave public messages on another user's profile that will be publicly displayed (i.e., posting on another user's "wall")	• Facebook allows users to upload digital photographs & share media from other internet platforms (e.g., video). • Facebook serves as a platform for interactive games (e.g. Farmville).	• Facebook allows users to choose a picture that is prominently displayed when someone visits their profile. • Facebook users can indicate their interest in different things ("likes").
YouTube	• User profiles are called "channels." Users can "subscribe" to channels. Subscribers are notified when a channel uploads new video content. • Users can establish a social network of "friends" through Google friends. • Users can post text comments for each video.	• Users can upload video onto the site. • Users can create "tags" (descriptive keywords) for the video they upload.	• Users can customize their "channel." • Users can create a list of their favorite videos, along with creating playlists of videos. • Users can rate videos that they have viewed.
Twitter	• Users establish connections by "following" other users, which means that users will receive the messages ("tweets") posted by the users they follow. • Users can post messages or "tweets" of up to 140 characters. When a user posts a "tweet," the message appears on that user's profile.	• Twitter itself does not support multimedia; however, users can post links in their messages to other forms of media available on the web (e.g., YouTube videos).	• Users can choose an icon that displays on other users' profiles to represent themselves. Users can customize their profiles by changing the background or theme of their Twitter page.

an SNS; (2) YouTube, a video sharing site; and (3) Twitter, a micro-blogging site.

Social Media Use: Opportunities and Challenges

As a reflection of the dramatic development and wide adoption of social media applications in contemporary society, during the past few years there have been a large—and rapidly growing—number of studies on the impact of social media on individuals and society. There is evidence that online social networks are significantly larger than offline social networks (Acar, 2008). It is suggested that social media can create a wide range of opportunities for individual users, communities, and society at large, including:

• providing emotional support and developing and maintaining social relationships (Baym & Ledbetter, 2009; Greenhow & Robelia, 2009)
• facilitating integration and socialization into a community (Halavais, 2009)
• promoting information sharing and learning (de Almeida Soares, 2008; Greenhow & Robelia, 2009; Paus-Hasebrink, et al., 2010; Luckin et al., 2009; Selwyn, 2009) and knowledge creation (Jones, 2008) among individuals
• facilitating self-expression, self-presentation, and identity construction (Livingstone, 2008; Rettberg, 2009)
• developing social capital (Sargent, 2009), including generating social capital for people with low self-esteem (Steinfield, Ellison & Lampe, 2008)
• promoting civic and political participation (Langlois, 2009; Smith, Schlozman, Verba, & Brady, 2009)
• improving the ability of government to provide efficient information services to citizens (Chun & Warner, 2010); e.g., facilitating the communication and dissemination of health information to the public (Chou, Hunt, Beckjord, Moser, & Hesse, 2009)
• affecting business models, marketing strategies and public relations, by, for instance, facilitating organizations of varying sizes to provide more efficient, timely, inexpensive, and direct customer services (Kaplan & Haenlein, 2010; Ong & Day, 2010; Foster, Francescucci, & West, 2010; Isakson, 2010)

Social media also create challenges, particularly for privacy-related concerns. Research suggests that younger people disclose personal information in SNSs without sufficient awareness of the potential dangers associated with disclosure (Taraszow, 2010). Concern exists among educational professionals and parents that personal disclosures in SNSs facilitate sexual solicitation and cyberbullying (Brandtzæg, 2009), though this danger might be exaggerated (Holmes, 2009). Further, doubt exists about whether social media actually empower users if site developers still maintain significant control over users (Pauwels & Hellriegel, 2009). Zajicek (2007) questions whether Web 2.0 can truly facilitate participation and interaction across all social groups, arguing that the increasingly ubiquitous use of multimedia in Web 2.0/social media applications may exclude, for instance, visually impaired individuals.

Few studies have examined older adults' interaction with social media. The majority of existing studies on older adults and internet applications focus on earlier forms of ICTs such as online forums or discussion groups (e.g., McCormack, 2010; Thomas, 2007; McMellon & Schiffman, 2002; Nahm et al., 2009; Xie, 2006, 2008a, 2008b). A notable trend, though, is that older adults, while still largely lagging behind their younger counterparts, have begun to adopt newer applications such as blogs, Facebook, and Wikis. By September 2009, 7% of internet users in the United States age 65 or older had maintained a profile on an SNS (Lenhart, 2009). While this percentage is small compared with the 73% of the younger population, it nonetheless gives some ground for some to argue that SNSs have "matured" to the "age-neutral" stage where internet users regardless of age can all use these sites to meet daily needs (Stroud, 2008). It has been argued in the gerontology literature that SNSs are "not just for kids anymore" (Creamer, Stripling, & Heesacker, 2009, p. 280). Yet to date little is known about older adults' perceptions of and experience with social media. The study described below aims to address this gap.

Method

Multiple rounds of procedures were performed during September–November 2010 to select relevant research articles for the sample.

Round 1: Database Selection

Databases available through the library of the University of Maryland, College Park were used to perform the search queries. Given the focus of this literature review, databases listed under eight fields most relevant to the topic under investigation—*Anthropology, Communication, Computer Science, Education, Health and Medicine, Library Science,*

Psychology, and *Sociology*—were selected to be the starting point for investigation. The following inclusion/exclusion criteria were used to select the 148 databases listed under these eight fields:

1. A database must contain journals that publish peer-reviewed research articles to be included; databases that contain only encyclopedia, doctoral dissertations or master theses, magazines, book reviews, news articles, or videos were excluded.

2. A database must allow searches within keywords, abstract, or full text to be included.

3. A database must provide English language coverage to be included.

4. A database must appear to be relevant to the subject under investigation to be included (e.g., the Geology database in the Anthropology category or

databases in the Health and Medicine category that deal with basic and clinical medical research were deemed irrelevant and thus excluded).

This round of the selection resulted in a total of twenty-nine databases being selected (Table 31.2) from the databases listed under the eight fields; these twenty-nine databases were used for further examination.

Round 2: Keyword Search

During September to November, 2010, the following combination of keywords was used to search in the twenty-nine selected databases:

("social media" OR "social networking" OR "social computing" OR "Web 2.0" OR Facebook OR blog OR

Table 31.2 Databases Selected from the 148 Databases Listed in the Eight Selected Fields

Field	Database
Anthropology	1. Academic Search Premier 2. Anthropology Literature 3. AuthroSource 4. Article First 5. JSTOR
Communication	6. Communication & Mass Media Complete 7. PsycINFO
Computer Science	8. Computer and Information Systems Abstracts 9. Computer and Applied Science Complete (EBSCO) 10. Computer Reviews 11. IEEE Xplore 12. Lecture Notes in Computer Science 13. ScienceDirect 14. Springer Online Journal Archive
Education	15. Education Research Complete
Health and Medicine	16. PubMed
Library Science	17. ACM Digital Library 18. ERIC 19. Library Literature and Information Science Full Text 20. LISTA 21. Social Sciences Citation Index—Web of Science
Psychology	22. PsycARTICLES 23. Psychology & Behavioral Science 24. Abstracts in Social Gerontology
Sociology	25. Contemporary Women's Issues 26. Family Studies Abstracts 27. GenderWatch 28. Ingenta ConnectComplete 29. JSTOR Sociology

wiki) AND (aging OR "older adult*" OR elder* OR retire* OR "baby boomer*" OR senior*)

To obtain search results as inclusive as possible, no other search limit was used during this round of the selection. Due to differences in the twenty-nine selected databases, keywords contained in the above search query may appear in any field of an article, including the article title, abstract, or full text. This round of the selection resulted in a total of 3,025 articles from the twenty-nine selected databases.

Round 3: Screening the Titles and Abstracts

The title and abstract of each of the 3,025 articles were examined to determine whether both *older adults* and *social media* were within the scope of the article. Three inclusion/exclusion criteria were used in this round of the selection:

1. The concept of *social networking* must incorporate technological aspects on how social networking via computers and the internet may affect older adults' social life. Articles that focus on social networking solely in an offline environment were excluded (e.g., Boneham & Sixsmith, 2006; Kondo et al., 2007; Russell, 2004).

2. The technological aspect studied in an article must be relevant to the core components of social media or Web 2.0 as discussed in the Literature Review section above (e.g., Cormode & Krishnamurthy, 2008; O'Reilly, 2004). If an article does not address the core components of social media or Web 2.0, it would be excluded. For example, an article that investigated game experience of older adults (Nacke, Nacke, & Lindley, 2009) was excluded because the gaming technology mentioned in the article did not embrace any component of social media or Web 2.0. Articles examining forum-based online communities that feature little social networking or user profiling were also excluded (e.g., Nimrod, 2010, 2011; Zaphiris & Sarwar, 2006).

3. While the focus of this literature review was on older adults' use of social media, the authors had anticipated that the number of research articles on this topic would be small. To broaden the scope of the search, the authors decided that older adults need *not* be the only age group examined in a study. Articles that compare the usage of social media or Web 2.0 applications among younger and older users were thus included. One exception

was the West, Lewis, and Currie (2009) article, which involved only younger adults as research participants. However, the explicit focus of the study was on "the extent to which older adults, especially parents, are accepted as Facebook friends, and the attitudes towards such friendships and potential friendships and what these reveal about notions of privacy" (p. 615). This article was included.

This round of the selection resulted in a total of eighty-eight articles that meet these criteria.

Round 4: Screening the Full Text

The full text of each of these eighty-eight articles was further examined to verify if each article indeed met the above three criteria used in Round 3 and to determine if each met the final criterion of reporting original, empirical research data. Articles examining the relationships between family or social relationships and basic internet use (e.g., e-mail), instead of social media or Web 2.0, were excluded (e.g., Hogeboom, McDermott, Perrin, & Osman, 2010; Sum, Mathews, Hughes, & Campbell, 2008; Sum, Mathews, Pourghasem, & Hughes, 2009). Articles that did not report original, empirical research data (e.g., meeting abstract, news report, book chapter, book review, magazine review article, or magazine cover story) were also excluded. One short conference proceedings paper reported the results of the same study as reported in a journal article. The conference proceedings paper, which provided less empirical data than the journal article, was excluded from further analysis (Khoo et al., 2006). A total of ten articles remained in the final sample. Table 31.3 below illustrates the selection procedures, criteria, and search results.

Results

All ten of the articles selected from the four rounds of screening were published between 2007 and 2010; together they reported a total of thirteen independent studies (the Cornejo et al. [2010] article reported two studies, and the Karahasanovic et al. [2009] article reported three studies). These are summarized in Table 31.4 below. Note that Table 31.4 also includes two additional articles: one recently accepted publication that reports our own recent study (Xie, Watkins, Golbeck, & Huang, 2012) and the other brought to our attention via professional contacts (Gibson et al., 2010). These two articles did not appear in the systematic searches due to their

Table 31.3 Selection Procedures and Criteria

Round	Criterion	Result
1: Database selection: 148 databases in eight fields	• Contains journals that publish research articles • Allows searches within keywords, abstract, or full text • Provides English language coverage • Relevant to the subject under investigation	29 databases were selected
2: Searching with keywords	• Search keywords: *("social media" OR "social networking" OR "social computing" OR "Web 2.0" OR Facebook OR blog OR wiki) AND (aging OR "older adult*" OR elder* OR retire* OR "baby boomer*" OR senior)*	3,025 articles were selected
3: Screening the titles and abstracts	• Technology-mediated social networking (research covering only conventional, offline social networking was excluded) • Covers core components of the social media concept • Research topic covers issues related to older adults, including intergenerational interaction and relationships	88 articles were selected
4: Screening the full text	• The same three criteria used in Round 3 • Reports original, empirical research data	10 articles selected

newness. They were nonetheless included in the final analysis due to their direct relevance to the scope of this literature review and the scarcity of relevant work. Together, this final sample consists of a total of twelve articles reporting fifteen independent studies. This final sample was used in the remaining analyses of this study.

In general, the sample sizes of these existing studies were small: the majority of these studies had 5–57 participants (the only exception was Study 1 reported in the Karahasanovic et al. [2009] article, which had 500 survey participants). Consistent with the qualitative, exploratory nature of these studies, the primary research methods used in these studies were interviewing (either individual interviewing or focus group interviewing) and observation. Two studies were quantitatively driven, consistent with their use of large volumes of online content generated by users (user profiles or blog posts). The majority of these published studies (9 out of 15) were based on European populations in Norway, Belgium, Finland, and the United Kingdom. Four were based on North America populations, including three in the United States and one in Mexico; one Asian (Singapore); and one Australian population. The smaller number of U.S. studies compared with the number of European studies is especially striking given that the databases used in this literature review were largely U.S.-based, and one would have expected to find more relevant studies conducted in the United States than other places in the world. More attention is necessary to understand how older adults in the United States interact with social media.

Four studies examined knowledge about perceptions and use of social networking sites in general. Over two-thirds of these studies (11 out of 15) focused on a specific SNS: either a freely available commercial site (Facebook; MySpace; Netlog; My Age Site; MyFriendsOnline; Blogger—Facebook was the only site being studied in multiple studies) or a proprietary site available only to certain users (Age Invader and ePortrait/eBowl, which are under development; and TouchTown, which is already in use). Regardless of the scope of these existing studies, several common themes can be identified, including:

1. Older adults generally have insufficient experience with and knowledge about social media applications and have difficulties using the technologies.

2. Older adults' initial perceptions of social media are typically negative and appear to be in large part influenced by mass media reports of negative incidents associated with social media use (e.g., cyberbullying among teenagers).

3. Despite these experiential and perceptual barriers, older adults can still be highly motivated to learn to use social media applications—if the circumstances are right.

4. An important type of the "right circumstances" that can motivate older adults' learning and use of social media is when it becomes

Table 31.4 Existing Studies on Older Adults and Social Media—in Alphabetical Order by First Author's Last Name

Author, Year	Publication venue	Technology application	Research topic	Participant age	Participant location	Sample size	Research method	Key finding
Ballantyne et al., 2010	Quality in Ageing and Older Adults	An Internet-based SNS: the About My Age site	Effects of an SNS on older adults' experience of loneliness	69–85	South Australia	6 (two dropped out; four completed the program)	Interview	Use of an SNS helped reduce loneliness, opened a door to new experience, and increased connectivity to others and the world. The one-on-one learning approach was key to the success and long-term sustainability of the outcomes.
Brandtzaeg et al., 2010	International Journal of Human-Computer Interaction	Facebook	Content sharing, sociability, and privacy	Younger age group: 16–33 (mean = 22); Older age group: 40–64 (mean = 48)	Norway	Younger people: 8; older adults: 8; Total: 16	Interview; usability testing	Older and younger users differed in motivations and use patterns; older users had more difficulties in understanding and using the site.
Chadwick-Dias et al., 2007	Universal Access in HCI	Web 2.0 applications in general	The changing nature of the web and older users; design considerations	65+	U.S.	5	Interview	Older users have insufficient knowledge and skills to use Web 2.0 applications.
Cornejo et al., 2010	Collaboration Researchers International Working Group (CRIWG) 2010	A prototype SNS consisting of two ambient displays: ePortrait and eBowl	The role of communication and interaction in maintaining emotional ties with family members (Study 1), and how social networking technology can be designed to help (Study 2)	Study 1: older adults: 65–97; caregivers or family members: age not reported; Study 2: age of all participants not reported	Mexico	Study 1: 10 older adults, 7 caregivers or family members; Study 2: 4 older adults, 4 younger adults	Study 1: interviews; Study 2: field trial followed by interviews	Ambient displays can monitor older adults' living environment, provide continuous information about their social ties in nonintrusive ways, which may help older adults feel more integrated with their families.

Study	Source	SNS	Focus	Age	Country	Sample	Method	Findings
Gibson et al., 2010	BCS Conference on Human Computer Interaction—HCI2010	MyFriendsOnline and Facebook (used in demonstrations)	Factors affect older adults' use of SNSs, including offline social networks and understanding of and knowledge about SNSs.	63–86	U.K. (Scotland)	Focus group interviews: 17; individual interviews: 4	Focus group and individual interviews	Offline social networks are in transition in old age; older individuals have negative perceptions of SNSs due to mass media reports, lack experience with and knowledge about SNSs, and have concerns about privacy.
Karahasanovic et al., 2009	Computers in Human Behavior	SNSs in general	Study 1: Participation in online communities & the consumption, sharing, and co-creation of user-generated content (UGC)	15–74	Norway	500	Survey (using a national representative sample)—macro-level	Older adults rarely participate in online communities or share audiovisual UGC.
			Study 2: Social factors in the offline community that affect use of SNSs to consume, share, and co-create UGC	Not reported	Belgium	87 houses in a neighborhood community with a total of 233 residents (unclear how many of these residents were studied)	Ethnographic: Interviews, participant observation, diary, online monitoring—group level	Older adults can be highly motivated to contribute UGC, under the right circumstances: e.g., for digitizing/sharing collective memory, to be in control of the technology, and to monitor online/offline activities.
			Study 3: Individual factors that affect use of SNSs	50+	Belgium	34	Interviews (via telephone, e-mail, or blog), diary, survey—individual level	Being able to use SNSs is important to older adults; usability is important; anxiety impedes use.

(Continued)

Table 31.4 (Continued)

Author, Year	Publication venue	Technology application	Research topic	Participant age	Participant location	Sample size	Research method	Key finding
Khoo et al., 2007	International Federation for Information Processing (IFIP) ICEC 2007	Age Invader—a virtual/physical reality interactive game platform for intergenerational entertainment	User testing of the Age Invader system	Group 1: mean = 19; Group 2: mean = 11.7; Group 3: mean = 68.7 (range: 58–80)	Singapore	Group 1: 37; Group 2: 10; Group 3: 10; Total: 57	Observation; pre-/post-intervention survey; focus group and individual interviews	Supporting evidence for intergenerational interaction using the Age Invader system
Lehtinen et al., 2009	HCI 2009—People and Computers XXIII	A commercial SNS: Netlog (www.netlog.com)	Older adults' understanding of SNSs, use of Netlog, and design implications	58–66	Finland	8	Interviews	The Internet is understood as "a dangerous place," and SNSs are "places of socially unacceptable behavior"; these understandings hinder use of the technology. Design implications: introduce the technology through social events and provide good privacy management on the sites.
Pfeil et al., 2009	Computers in Human Behavior	MySpace	Age differences and similarities in the use of MySpace and social capital	Teenagers: 13–19; Older adults: >60	Not reported	Around 6,000 MySpace user profiles	Content analysis of data collected from MySpace user profile pages	Compared with teens, older adults have smaller networks of friends, are friend with a more diverse age range of people, and use less multimedia and self-references on MySpace.
West et al., 2009	Journal of Youth Studies	Facebook	Friendship; Privacy; Attitudes toward older adults as Facebook friends	21–26 (mean = 22)	U.K. (London)	16	Interviews (via computer)	Mixed attitudes; blurring boundary between the public/private spheres

Wilson & Nicholas, 2008	Proceedings of the 2008 ACM Workshop on Search in Social Media (ACM SSM)	TouchTown—a web portal providing e-mail and blog services to retirement community residents	The topologies (structural properties of the network) of online social networks	65+	U.S.	1,260 blog posts from the TouchTown blog during Jan.–Dec. 2007	Topological analysis (using 3 statistical measures: degree distribution, clustering coefficient, and average path length)	The most common topological shapes were chains instead of stars, indicating blog use more for the purpose of seeking and disseminating information and less for interaction among blog users.
Xie, Watkins, Golbeck, & Huang, in press	Educational Gerontology	Facebook; blogs (blogger.com)	Older adults' perceptions and learning of social media	61–83 ($M =$ 71.4, $SD =$ 8.3)	U.S.	10	Focus group interviews	During the 7-week period of the study, older adults' perceptions of SNSs changed from the initial unanimous, strong negative to the more positive but cautious and to the eventual willingness to actually contribute their own content to a blog site created for them. Privacy was the primary concern and key barrier to participants' adoption of SNSs. Several educational strategies developed during the process appeared to be effective in overcoming their privacy concerns, including: (1) introducing the concepts (what are social media) before introducing the functions (what can social media do); (2) adjust the curriculum to accommodate privacy concerns; and (3) make explicit how social media tools can be relevant to participants' personal lives.

clear to them how the technology is relevant to and useful in their personal lives, which could include, for instance, digitizing and sharing individual and collective memory and staying in touch with family and friends.

5. Another important type of the "right circumstances" is when older adults develop a sense of being in control of the technology, instead of the other way around, which can help ease their anxiety about the technology and concerns about, in particular, privacy.

6. Design and educational interventions, which focus on establishing the "right circumstances" for older adults, are essential in promoting older adults' learning and use of social media applications.[1]

Discussion

The small number of existing studies on the topic of older adults and social media and the newness of these publications (all within the past three years) reflect not only the brief history of social media in contemporary society but also the slow adoption of new technology by older adults compared with younger people: younger people have rapidly adopted social media during the past few years (Lenhart, Purcell, Smith, & Zickuhr, 2010), and their use of social media has been studied quite extensively (while not reported in this paper, in our searches of the literature we found a greater number of studies on younger people's use of social media). In comparison, while older adults are catching up with younger people on use of earlier internet applications such as e-mail (Jones & Fox, 2009), their use of newer applications such as social media still lags (Lenhart, 2009). While the digital generation gaps related to older technology are closing, new gaps have emerged as technology evolves.

Resolving these gaps is important because social media may help to address unique social networking issues facing older adults. Ballantyne et al. (2010) found that social media helped older adults meet new people online, in addition to strengthening offline ties between older adults interested in using social media. As a result, social media may be effective in ameliorating the sense of loneliness experienced by older adults with decreased social contact (Ballantyne et al., 2010), similar to how the internet can help facilitate the formation of offline relationships (Xie, 2007b). Recognizing the unique social challenges facing older adults is essential to understanding how social media can benefit older adults. As older adults transition to retirement, changes

typically occur in how they view their social contacts (Gibson et al., 2010; Wang & Shultz, 2010; Shultz & Wang, 2011). This perceptual change may result from losing social contacts established through employment, geographic disbursement of contacts, death or illness, or other transformative life events like divorce (Gibson et al., 2010). Social media provides a new platform for peer-to-peer interaction and community building for geographically disbursed individuals (Meraz, 2009; O'Reilly, 2004). Therefore, social media could potentially transform how older adults view their social life as they transition into retirement (Wang, Henkens, & van Solinge, 2011).

In addition to addressing older adults' social needs, social media provide a new platform for older adults to share knowledge and information. Wilson and Nicholas (2008) found that older adults using blogs tended to use them to search for and disseminate information rather than for socializing. This finding may be in part a result of the specific social media tool used, as each type of social media tool may be more supportive of certain features than others (e.g., Facebook may be better than blogs in promoting socialization, while blogs may be better than Facebook in facilitating explicit knowledge and information transfer). Education about the different functions of different social media tools is essential for older adults to fully realize the affordances of social media (Xie, 2007a; Xie, et al., 2012). Specifically, older adults may need explicit instruction on using social media to communicate information, especially for social media they already use for socialization. For example, a group of older adults may be enthusiastic users of Facebook to convey affective messages, not realizing that Facebook can also be a powerful tool for sharing information and knowledge. As with socialization, a prerequisite for use of social media for information sharing is an understanding of how a particular social medium can be relevant to older adults' life (Xie, et al., 2012).

In designing technologies for older adults, one common pitfall is to not include older adults in the design process, making older adults a "relevant but absent" social group in the technological development process and, subsequently, making the technology incompatible with older adults' needs and preferences (Paquette & Xie, 2010). To ensure older adults' adoption and use of a new technology, it is essential to gain a good understanding of their needs and preferences early on in the process and to use this understanding to guide the design and development. Cornejo et al. (2010) provided a good example: In that study, researchers first identified via in-depth interviews the main factors (e.g., geographic distances, cognitive declines, being unable to use SNSs) that weaken older adults' emotional ties with their younger family members who communicate frequently through SNSs. Based on this understanding, the researchers designed two ambient displays—ePortrait and eBowl—as physical objects to connect older adults with the virtual world in social media. The ePortrait device retrieves photos from younger family members' Facebook profiles and then displays the photos in a digital frame; the eBowl device enables older adults to share jokes with family members and give feedback on their photos. Meanwhile, older adults' presence is monitored by placing a digital ball into a bowl connected to a computer system. By integrating these everyday physical objects with social media applications, the ePortrait/eBowl system creates easy, nonintrusive ways for older adults to stay connected to and involved in family lives. Such new interaction patterns provide an innovative way to incorporate social networking technology into older adults' lives without imposing excessive cognitive load.

Effective technological design for older adults should always consider the unique safety issues facing this population. In the context of online communication, safety concerns include privacy, security, and fraud (Ji et al., 2010). Older adults traditionally experienced the highest levels of fraud for any age group when using more traditional telecommunications technology like the telephone (Princeton Research Survey Associates, 1996). Responsible technological design requires careful consideration of this population's vulnerability to fraud. Designers, educators, and older adult users should work together to strike a balance between the freedom and opportunities made possible by social media and the accompanying potential dangers.

Additionally, privacy, safety, and fraud concerns can make using social media an anxious experience for older adults. Improving older adults' social media literacy could improve their understanding of the privacy, safety, and fraud issues involved in social media use, reducing anxiety in the process. Older adults' perception of social media is typically based on traditional media reports that emphasize the danger of using social media (Xie, et al., 2012). For example, Gibson et al. (2010) described how a group of older adults formed a negative perception of social media based on a news story reporting

that social media use led to unwanted party guests destroying a house. Unfortunately, safety and fraud concerns do exist (Ji et al., 2010; Princeton Research Survey Associates, 1996), though educating older adults to identify legitimate concerns could help prevent fraud and reduce anxiety. Reducing anxiety is essential because anxiety can impede social media use (Karahasanovic et al., 2009; Lehtinen, Näsänen, & Sarvas, 2009), preventing older adults from enjoying the potential benefits of SNSs (Chen, Wen, & Xie, 2012).

Interventions designed to educate older adults about social media should account for the inherently dynamic nature of the technology. Although certain concepts between different social media applications are consistent (e.g., the ability to establish connections with other users), the technology is constantly changing and adapting to users' needs (Hogan & Quan-Haase, 2010). Simply teaching older adults to use a specific application, such as Twitter, may offer only limited utility. A better approach would be to educate older adults about the fundamental concepts behind social media, along with developing skills that can be transferred across applications as they evolve. Privacy provides an instructive example. Older adults educated about the fundamentals of privacy protection using social media could transfer this ability to the new applications they encounter.

It is important to recognize that despite the safety and literacy challenges facing older adults' use of social media, motivation to use these applications is strong. Karahasanovic et al. (2009) found that older adults were highly motivated to contribute user-generated content (UGC) under the right circumstances (e.g., digitizing collective memory). Similarly, Xie et al. (2012) found that older adults were eager to contribute content to a blog once it became clear how contributing content could be relevant to their lives. Therefore, as application design increasingly accounts for older adults' unique needs and abilities, and pedagogical strategies improve, the motivation to use social media will likely be realized through the broader adoption of social media by older adults.

On a final note, although certain characteristics may adhere to older adults as a group, it is important to note that the older population is diverse (Xie, 2003); individual differences in, for instance, education, socioeconomic background, or culture may also influence online behavior (Ji et al., 2010). Future research of older adults and social media should investigate how the use (or non-use) patterns of older adults with varying characteristics may differ (or be similar).

Conclusion

A systematic review of twenty-nine databases in eight fields found only a total of ten articles reporting thirteen independent studies of older adults' interaction with social media. Adding our own recently accepted article and one additional article found through professional contacts, we included in the final sample a total of twelve relevant articles reporting fifteen independent studies on the topic of older adults and social media. These studies were small in sample size and exploratory in nature. Nonetheless, they provide valuable insights about the intersection between the older population and social media applications. Several key themes were identified in these studies and shed light on issues related to older adults' current state of knowledge about and perceptions of social media and their potential in learning to make use of the technology in the future. Key to older adults' learning and use of social media is creating the "right circumstances" in which older adults can associate the technology with their personal lives and feel in control of the technology instead of the other way around. Design and educational interventions are important in creating these right circumstances.

Taken together, these existing studies suggest that major barriers to older adults' adoption of social media are both technological and social/cultural. Pedagogical interventions focusing on training older adults in the basic, technical aspects of computer operation can help reduce perceived technological barriers (e.g., Xie, 2011; Xie, et al., 2012). Similarly, innovative design techniques can help make social media more closely aligned with how older adults experience the world (e.g., Cornejo et al., 2010). Social and cultural barriers (e.g., negative perceptions of social media), by coloring older adults' understanding of social media, have negative effects on adoption and use. Current studies suggest conflicting perceptions of social media by older adults, as evidenced in studies reporting that older adults are highly motivated to learn about social media applications, even though they associate such applications with unethical behavior like bullying. These conflicts may result from the reported lack of knowledge among older adults about social media, or they may simply reflect a broader cultural confusion experienced across all age groups as a result of the rapidly evolving nature of the technology.

Social and cultural barriers should be understood as interdependent, rather than exclusive, of technological barriers. As pedagogical and design techniques improve, older adults' perceptions of social media will develop and evolve in response to their new experiences.

Future Directions

With the very limited number of existing studies on older adults and social media, much more remains unexplored. Even the common themes identified from these few existing studies, due to the small sample size and exploratory nature of the studies, will need to be examined more systematically before more firm conclusions emerge. Some specific future directions are listed below:

1. What are the general older population's experience with, perceptions of, and knowledge about social media applications, and how might demographic, socioeconomic, cultural, and other factors predict their experience, perceptions, and knowledge about the technology?

2. How might mass media affect older adults' use of social media? If the one-sided, negative reports in mass media have negative effects on older adults' use of social media, how might mass media reports provide a more balanced view of the technology?

3. What other factors may facilitate or impede older adults' use of social media applications?

4. What are the benefits—and risks—associated with older adults' use of social media?

5. What design considerations should be taken into account when designing social media applications for older adults?

6. What learning strategies can be effective in promoting older adults' learning of the technology?

Additionally, future research should examine these issues in the context of intergenerational socialization and information sharing through social media. As researchers learn more about effective social media design and pedagogical strategies for older adults using social media, it will be important to ensure that older adults can fully communicate with younger generations through social media. Intergenerational communication may be especially important for older adults, who typically enjoy socialization with younger relatives and friends. Older adults' integration with the broader social media community will likely influence a variety of subjects requiring investigation. For example, how will the adoption of social media by older adults influence how they perceive social media? What design issues will need to be addressed to facilitate intergenerational communication over social media? These important questions will need to be addressed in the future once a better understanding of older adults' relationship with social media is developed.

Acknowledgements

We thank the Institute of Museum and Library Services for awarding a Faculty Early Career Development grant to Bo Xie. Man Huang and Ivan Watkins were funded as Graduate Research Assistants on this grant during the development of this chapter.

Notes

1. While not included in the final sample of articles (due to, for instance, lack of empirical research data), some researchers have begun to address design-related issues and advocate for a "senior-friendly" Web 2.0 environment (Chadwick-Dias et al., 2007; Jaeger & Xie, 2009). Additional educational strategies for older adults' learning of technology can be found in, e.g., Xie, et al., (2012), Xie and Bugg (2009), Xie and Jaeger (2008), and Xie (2007a).

References

Acar, A. (2008). Antecedents and consequences of online social networking behavior: The case of Facebook. *Journal of Website Promotion, 3*(1), 62–83.

Ballantyne, A., Trenwith, L., Zubrinich, S., & Corlis, M. (2010). "I feel less lonely": What older people say about participating in a social networking website. *Quality in Ageing and Older Adults, 11*(3), 25–35.

Baym, N. K., & Ledbetter, A. (2009). Tunes that bind? *Information, Communication & Society, 12*(3), 408–427.

Boneham, M. A., & Sixsmith, J. A. (2006). The voices of older women in a disadvantaged community: Issues of health and social capital. *Social Science & Medicine, 62*(2), 269–279.

Brandtzæg, P. B., Lüders, M., & Skjetne, J. H. (2010). Too many Facebook "friends"? Content sharing and sociability versus the need for privacy in social network sites. *International Journal of Human-Computer Interaction, 26*(11), 1006–1030.

Brandtzæg, P. B., Staksrud, E., Hagen, I., & Wold, T. (2009). Norwegian children's experiences of cyberbullying when using different technological platforms. *Journal of Children and Media, 3*(4), 349–365.

Chadwick-Dias, A., Bergel, M., & Tullis, T. (2007). Senior surfers 2.0: A re-examination of the older web user and the dynamic web. *Universal Access in Human Computer Interaction, 4554*, 868–876.

Charness, N., & Schaie, K. W. (Eds.) (2003). *Impact of technology on successful aging*. New York, NY: Springer.

Chen, Y., Wen, J., & Xie, B. 2012). "I communicate with my children in the game": Mediated intergenerational family relationships through a social networking game. *Journal of Community Informatics, 8*(1). Retrieved from http://ci-journal.net/index.php/ciej/article/view/802.

Chou, W. S., Hunt, Y. M., Beckjord, E. B., Moser, R. P., & Hesse, B. W. (2009) Social media use in the United States: Implications for health communication. *Journal of Medical Internet Research, 11*(4). Retrieved from http://www.jmir.org/2009/4/e48/.

Chun, S., & Warner, J. (2010). Finding information in an era of abundance: Towards a collaborative tagging environment in government. *Information Polity, 15*(1–2), 83–103.

Cormode, G., & Krishnamurthy, B. (2008).Key differences between Web 1.0 and Web 2.0. *First Monday, 13*(6). Retrieved from http://www.uic.edu/htbin/cgiwrap/bin/ojs/index.php/ fm/article/view/2125/1972.

Cornejo, R., Favela, J., & Tentori, M. (2010). Ambient displays for integrating older adults into social networking sites. *Collaboration and Technology, 6257*, 321–336.

Creamer, A., Stripling, A. M., & Heesacker, M. (2009). Social networking sites, not just for kids anymore: How to recruit older adults online. *Gerontologist, 49*, 280.

de Almeida Soares, D. (2008). Understanding class blogs as a tool for language development. *Language Teaching Research, 12*(4), 517.

Ellison, N. B., Steinfield, C., & Lampe, C. (2007). The benefits of Facebook "friends:" Social capital and college students' use of online social network sites. *Journal of Computer Mediated Communication, 12*(4), 1143–1168.

Foster, M. K., Francescucci, A., & West, B. C. (2010). Why users participate in online social networks. *International Journal of e-Business Management, 4*(1), 19.

Gibson, L., Moncur, W., Forbes, P., Arnott, J., Martin, C., & Bhachu, A. S. (2010, September). Designing social networking sites for older adults. In *Proceedings of the 24th BCS Conference on Human-Computer Interaction* (pp. 186–194), Dundee, Scotland.

Greenhow, C., & Robelia, B. (2009). Old communications, new literacies: Social networking sites as social learning resources. *Journal of Computer Mediated Communication, 14*(4), 1130–1161.

Ha, L., & James, E. L. (1998). Interactivity re-examined: A baseline analysis of early business websites. *Journal of Broadcasting & Electronic Media, 42*, 457–474.

Halavais, A. (2009). Do dug diggers dig diligently? *Information, Communication & Society, 12*(3), 444–459.

Herring, S. C. (2004). Slouching toward the ordinary: Current trends in computer-mediated communication. *New Media & Society, 6*(1), 26–36.

Hogan, B., & Quan-Haase, A. (2010). Persistence and change in social media. *Bulletin of Science, Technology & Society, 30*(5), 309–315.

Holmes, J. (2009). Myths and missed oppurtunities: young people's not so risky use of online communication. *Information, Communications & Society, 12*(8), 1174–1196.

Hogeboom, D. L., McDermott, R. J., Perrin, K. M., Osman, H., & Bell-Ellison, B. A. (2010). Internet use and social networking among middle aged and older adults. *Educational Gerontology, 36*(2), 93–111.

Isakson, C. (2010). Australian book publishing and the internet: How two Australian book publishing companies are using the internet to engage with customers. *Asia Pacific Public Relations, 11*, 65–74.

Jaeger, P. T., & Xie, B. (2009). Developing online community accessibility guidelines for persons with disabilities and older adults. *Journal of Disability Policy Studies, 20*, 55–63.

Ji, Y. G., Choi, J., Lee, J. Y., Han, K. H., Kim, J., & Lee, I.-K. (2010). Older adults in an aging society and social computing: A research agenda. *International Journal of Human-Computer Interaction, 26*(11), 1122–1146.

Jones, J. (2008). Patterns of revision in online writing. *Written Communication, 25*(2), 262.

Jones, S., & Fox, S. (2009). *Generations online in 2009.* Washington, DC: Pew Internet & American Life Project. Retrieved from http://www.pewinternet.org/Reports/2009/Generations-Online-in-2009.aspx.

Kaplan, A., & Haenlein, M. (2010). Users of the world, unite! The challenges and opportunities of social media. *Business Horizons, 53*, 59–68.

Karahasanovic, A., Brandtzæg, P. B., Heim, J., Lüders, M., Vermeir, L., Pierson, J.,... Jans, G. (2009). Co-creation and user-generated content-elderly people's user requirements. *Computers in Human Behavior, 25*(3), 655–678.

Khoo, E., Merritt, T., Cheok, A., Lian, M., & Yeo, K. (2007). Age Invaders: User studies of intergenerational computer entertainment. *Entertainment Computing–ICEC 2007, 4740*, 231–242.

Khoo, E. T., Lee, S. P., Cheok, A. D., Kodagoda, S., Zhou, Y., & Toh, G. S. (2006). Age invaders: Social and physical inter-generational family entertainment. In *Proceedings of the CHI'06* (pp. 243–246). Quebec, Canada.

Kondo, N., Minai, J., Imai, H., & Yamagata, Z. (2007). Engagement in a cohesive group and higher-level functional capacity in older adults in Japan: A case of the mujin. *Social Science & Medicine, 64*(11), 2311–2323.

Langlois, G., Elmer, G., McKelvey, F., & Devereaux, Z. (2009). Networked publics: The double articulation of code and politics on Facebook. *Canadian Journal of Communication, 34*(3), 415–434.

Lehtinen, V., Näsänen, J., & Sarvas, R. (2009). A little silly and empty-headed: Older adults' understandings of social networking sites. In *Proceedings of the 2009 British Computer Society Conference on Human-Computer Interaction* (pp. 45–54). Cambridge, United Kingdom.

Lenhart, A., & Fox, S. (2009). *Twitter and status updating.* Washington, DC: PEW Internet & American Life Project. Retrieved from http://www.pewinternet.org/Reports/ 2009/Twitter-and-status-updating.aspx.

Lenhart, A., Purcell, K., Smith, A., & Zickuhr, K. (2010). *Social media and young adults.* Washington, DC: Pew Internet & American Life Project. Retrieved from http://pewinternet.org/Reports/2010/Social-Media-and-Young-Adults/Part-3/1-Teens-and-online-social-networks.aspx?r=1.

Livingstone, S. (2008). Taking risky opportunities in youthful content creation: Teenagers' use of social networking sites for intimacy, privacy and self-expression. *New Media & Society, 10*(3), 393.

Luckin, R., Clark, W., Graber, R., Logan, K., Mee, A., & Oliver, M. (2009). Do Web 2.0 tools really open the door to learning? Practices, perceptions and profiles of 11–16-year-old students. *Learning, Media and Technology, 34*(2), 87–104.

Madden, M. (2009). *The audience for online video-sharing sites shoots up.* Washington DC: Pew Internet and American Life Project. Retrieved from http://pewinternet.org/Reports/2009/13-The-Audience-for-Online-VideoSharing-Sites-Shoots-Up.aspx.

McCormack, A. (2010). Individuals with eating disorders and the use of online support groups as a form of social support. *Cin-Computers Informatics Nursing, 28*(1), 12–19.

McMellon, C. A., & Schiffman, L. G. (2002). Cybersenior empowerment: How some older individuals are taking control of their lives. *Journal of Applied Gerontology, 21*(2), 157–175.

Meraz, S. (2009). Is there an elite hold? Traditional media to social media agenda setting influence in blog networks. *Journal of Computer-Mediated Communication, 14*(3), 682–707.

Nacke, L. E., Nacke, A., & Lindley, C. A. (2009). Brain training for silver gamers: Effects of age and game form on effectiveness, efficiency, self-assessment, and gameplay experience. *CyberPsychology & Behavior, 12*(5), 493–499.

Nahm, E. S., Resnick, B., DeGrezia, M., & Brotemarkle, R. (2009). Use of discussion boards in a theory-based health web site for older adults. *Nursing Research, 58*(6), 419–426.

Nimrod, G. (2010). Seniors' online communities: A quantitative content analysis. *The Gerontologist, 50*(3), 382–392.

Nimrod, G. (2011). The fun culture in seniors' online communities. *The Gerontologist, 51*(2), 226–237.

Ong, C.-S., & Day, M.-Y. (2010). An integrated evaluation model of user satisfaction with social media services. *Information Reuse and Integration (IRI)* (pp. 195–200). Las Vegas, NV: 2010 IEEE International Conference.

O'Reilly, T. (2004). *The architecture of participation.* Retrieved from http://www.oreillynet.com/pub/a/oreilly/tim/articles/architecture_of_participation.html.

Paus-Hasebrink, I., Wijnen, C. W., & Jadin, T. (2010). Opportunities of Web 2.0: Potentials of learning. *International Journal of Media and Cultural Politics, 6*(1), 45–62.

Pauwels, L., & Hellriegel, P. (2009). Strategic and tactical uses of internet design and infrastructure: The case of YouTube. *Journal of Visual Literacy, 28*(1), 51–69.

Pfeil, U., Arjan, R., & Zaphiris, P. (2009). Age differences in online social networking—A study of user profiles and the social capital divide among teenagers and older users in MySpace. *Computers in Human Behavior, 25*(3), 643–654.

Princeton Research Survey Associates. (1996). *Telemarketing fraud victimization of older Americans: An AARP survey.* Stanford, CA: Stanford Center on Longevity.

Rettberg, J. W. (2009). "Freshly generated for you, and Barack Obama": How social media represent your life. *European Journal of Communication, 24*(4), 451–466.

Rheingold, H. (2008). Using participatory media and public voice to encourage civic engagement. In W. L. Bennett (Ed.), *Civic life online: Learning how digital media can engage youth* (pp. 97–118). Cambridge, MA: MIT Press.

Russell, R. (2004). Social networks among elderly men caregivers. *Journal of Men's Studies, 13*(1), 121–142.

Sargent, C. (2009). Local musicians building global audiences. *Information, Communication & Society, 12*(4), 469–487.

Schieber, F. (2003). Human factors and aging: Indentifying and compensating for age-related deficits in sensory and cognitive function. In N. Charness & K. W. Schaie (Eds.), *Impact of technology on successful aging* (pp. 42–84). New York, NY: Springer.

Selwyn, N. (2009). Faceworking: Exploring students' education-related use of Facebook. *Learning, Media and Technology, 34*(2), 157–174.

Shultz, K. S., & Wang, M. (2011). Psychological perspectives on the changing nature of retirement. *American Psychologist, 66*, 170–179.

Smith, A., Schlozman, K., Verba, S., Brady, H. (2009). *The internet and civic engagement.* Washington, DC: Pew Internet &

American Life Project. Retrieved from http://pewinternet.org/Reports/2009/15—The-Internet-and-Civic-Engagement.aspx.

Song, F. W. (2010). Theorizing Web 2.0. *Information, Communication & Society*, *13*(2), 249–275.

Steinfield, C., Ellison, N., & Lampe, C. (2008). The benefits of Facebook "friends": Social capital and college students' use of online social network sites. *Journal of Applied Developmental Psychology*, *29*(6), 434–445.

Stroud, D. (2008). Social networking: An age-neutral commodity—social networking becomes a mature web application. *Journal of Direct, Data and Digital Marketing Practice*, *9*(3), 278–292.

Sum, S., Mathews, R. M., Hughes, I., & Campbell, A. (2008). Internet use and loneliness in older adults. *CyberPsychology & Behavior*, *11*(2), 208–211.

Sum, S., Mathews, R. M., Pourghasem, M., & Hughes, I. (2009). Internet use as a predictor of sense of community in older people. *CyberPsychology & Behavior*, *12*(2), 235–239.

Taraszow, T., Aristodemou, E., Shitta, G., Laouris, Y., & Arsoy, A. (2010). Disclosure of personal and contact information by young people in social networking sites: An analysis using Facebook profiles as an example. *International Journal of Media and Cultural Politics*, *6*(1), 81–101.

Thomas, C. M. (2007). Bulletin boards—A teaching strategy for older audiences. *Journal of Gerontological Nursing*, *33*(3), 45–52.

Wang, M., Henkens, K., & van Solinge, H. (2011). Retirement adjustment: A review of theoretical and empirical advancements. *American Psychologist*, *66*, 204–213.

Wang, M., & Shultz, K. (2010). Employee retirement: A review and recommendations for future investigation. *Journal of Management*, *36*, 172–206.

West, A., Lewis, J., & Currie, P. (2009). Students' Facebook "friends": Public and private spheres. *Journal of Youth Studies*, *12*(6), 615–627.

Wilson, M., & Nicholas, C. (2008). Topological analysis of an online social network for older adults. In *Proceedings of the 2008 ACM Workshop on Search in Social Media* (pp. 51–58). Napa Valley, CA.

Xie, B. (2003). Older adults, computers, and the internet: Future directions. *Gerontechnology*, *2*(4), 289–305.

Xie, B. (2006). Perceptions of computer learning among older Americans and older Chinese. *First Monday*, *11*(10). Retrieved from http://firstmonday.org/htbin/cgiwrap/bin/ojs/index.php/fm/article/view/1408/1326.

Xie, B. (2007a). Information technology education for older adults as a continuing peer-learning process: A Chinese case study. *Educational Gerontology*, *33*(5), 429–450.

Xie, B. (2007b). Using the internet for offline relationship formation. *Social Science Computer Review*, *25*(3), 396–404.

Xie, B. (2008a). Multimodal computer-mediated communication and social support among older Chinese. *Journal of Computer-Mediated Communication*, *13*(3), 728–750. Retrieved from http://onlinelibrary.wiley.com/doi/10.1111/j.1083-6101.2008.00417.x/pdf.

Xie, B. (2008b). The mutual shaping of online and offline social relationships. *Information Research*, *13*(3), paper 350. Retrieved from http://informationr.net/ir/13-3/paper350.html.

Xie, B. (2011). Older adults, e-health literacy, and collaborative learning: An experimental study. *Journal of the American Society for Information Science and Technology (JASIST)*, *62*(5), 933–946.

Xie, B., & Bugg, J. M. (2009). Public library computer training for older adults to access high-quality internet health information. *Library & Information Science Research*, *31*, 155–162. [PMCID: PMC2818317; NIHMSID: NIHMS136066]

Xie, B., & Jaeger, P. T. (2008). Computer training programs for older adults at the public library. *Public Libraries*, *47*(5), 42–49.

Xie, B., Watkins, I., Golbeck, J., & Huang, M. (2012). Understanding and changing older adults' perceptions and learning of social media. *Educational Gerontology*, *38*, 282–296.

Zajicek, M. (2007, May). Web 2.0: hype or happiness? Web accessibility (W4A). In *Proceedings of the 2007 International Cross-disciplinary Workshop on Web Accessibility*, Banff, Canada (pp. 35–39).

Zaphiris, P., & Sarwar, R. (2006). Trends, similarities, and differences in the usage of teen and senior public online newsgroups. *ACM Transactions on Computer-Human Interaction (Tochi)*, *13*(3), 403–422.

Retirement Practices in Different Countries

José María Peiró, Núria Tordera, *and* Kristina Potočnik

Abstract

The present chapter aims to explore and present different retirement practices around the world. Retirement patterns, and especially early retirement, have gained considerable attention in many societies because of the aging of the population. In response to this, many countries are redesigning their pension laws and changing their policies toward retirement. In spite of the development of those national policies, organizations still have a considerable amount of discretion regarding retiring and/ or retaining their older workforce. This chapter focuses on a cross-national review of retirement practices. After highlighting different trends in retirement between countries, we discuss how organizational management influences individual transition to retirement in different societies by implementing human resource practices. The issues of retirement timing, flexibility in the retirement process, and human resource practices directed toward older workers are discussed. The chapter concludes with implications and future directions in this field.

Key Words: retirement practices, retirement timing, flexibility in the retirement process, early retirement, phased retirement, human resource practices, cross-national comparison

The aging of the population is affecting many geographical areas. Indeed, according to the four major findings highlighted by the World Population Aging report of the United Nations, population aging in the world is unprecedented, pervasive (affecting nearly all the countries in the world), profound (having major consequences), and enduring (United Nations, 2009). In spite of this situation, there is a common trend of early retirement in industrialized countries, resulting in a decrease in the participation of older men and women in the labor market. This trend is also present in some transitional economies (United Nations, 2009). The combination of both trends (the aging process on one hand and low participation of older workers in the labor market on the other) has challenged countries in many aspects, such as in the viability of their pension systems and potential shortages in their workforces.

Several factors may impact how this process of workforce reduction takes place or will take place in different countries. The role of international migration and migratory policies, for instance, could be moderating the process of aging in the workforces of different geographical areas. People in the least developed countries are expected to migrate more, and usually the younger workers are the most ready to do so. On one side, some countries such as Canada or Australia have been adjusting their immigration policies to attract highly skilled workers, while others, such as United States, are receiving immigration mainly from less qualified or trained workers (Burke & Ng, 2006). On the other side, the countries exporting human capital could be suffering an important brain drain. In its World Migration Report, the International Organization of Migration (OIM) prospected that by the year

2050, migrations will double their current level due to overpopulation in some territories or to the consequences of climate change. Moreover, some developing economies are expected to increase their level of reception of those migrations.

Changes in technology could also be affecting countries differently. Those countries with a high development of new technology could have more opportunities in terms of competitiveness and growth, but at the same time high-tech countries will probably need a smaller and more skilled workforce (Burke & Ng, 2006). Together with the changes in technology, the globalization of the economy and more concretely the processes of outsourcing and offshoring in many companies are also challenging the ways in which countries respond to new workforce distribution across the world.

Several voices in different countries have acknowledged the need to respond to this situation, suggesting the need to reform pensions systems or sources of retirement income and change the actual patterns in early retirement. In this sense, there have been different political responses from the Organisation for Economic Co-operation and Development (OECD), the European Union, the United Nations, and several entities at the national levels that advocate for reversal in early retirement (Organisation for Economic Co-operation and Development, 2000; Ebbinghaus, 2006). As a result, there are several ongoing reform processes oriented to reform the pension systems and reverse the early retirement trends in the entire industrialized world and most parts of the developing countries. Research has suggested that each country should find its own way and develop its own policies to help older workers. To begin with, some communalities and differences can be identified in this process between and within countries. The identification of such differences and how they affect and/or are being affected by each country's characteristics could be a key aspect in the understanding of the process of retirement (National Research Council, 2001).

There are many ways in which nations can be differentiated. For instance, the United Nations distinguishes between developed, developing, and least developed countries to classify the global process of aging. Extant cross-national research about retirement and pension systems in the world has mainly followed the well-known Esping-Andersen (1990, 1999) differentiation between welfare regimes. In order to be consistent and offer the reader a coherence with the rest of the literature, in the present chapter we follow this classification and distinguish

between Liberal countries (e.g. the United States, the United Kingdom, Ireland, Australia, Japan, Singapore, Hong Kong), Social-Democratic countries (Norway, Sweden, Denmark, and Finland), Central European countries (Germany, France, the Netherlands, Belgium), and South European countries (Italy, Portugal, Spain, and Greece). We also include some developing countries that are experiencing similar changes with regard to aging and participation of older workers in the workforce under the label of Transitional economies. In spite of the great variability inside each group of countries, the communalities between them in terms of their welfare regime and their cultural or historical proximity prompted us to present them together. We also include specific references to countries when we consider it to be more explicative. This review does not aim to be exhaustive of retirement in the entire world, since such an overview surpasses the scope of this work, but rather our aim is to offer some insight into differences and similarities between some of the countries that are facing challenges with regard to aging and retirement in their societies. There are many ways in which different characteristics of each country could be influencing the retirement process at different levels: at the individual level, individuals in different countries might differ in their beliefs, values, preferences, and behaviors about work and working in old age; at the institutional level, countries vary in policies and laws (for instance, mandatory age for retirement, social security systems, private pension plans, health insurance, as per Hedge, Borman, & Lammlein, 2006); at the societal level, we find different cultures and stereotypes about age and working; and finally, at the organizational level, we find different organizational policies and practices, downsizing through layoffs and early retirement programs, and the existence of cultures oriented toward older workers.

Surprisingly little research has assessed how organizations influence this critical life transition. More importantly, the research that has addressed this issue has primarily been carried out in Western societies, whereas comparatively less research has been carried out in countries of emerging economies. It is important to understand how organizations manage older workers and their transition from work to retirement in different countries to get a clear picture of the dynamics of retirement in this context. Previous chapters in this handbook, especially Yao and Peng, have already addressed the current states of different countries' practices in social security, pension systems, and retirement savings and how these influence retirement-related behavior. In contrast, this chapter explores retirement practices related to human resource management in different parts of the world.

We begin with a description of the differences in participation rates of older workers and basic retirement legislation in different countries to provide some insight into how retirement takes place globally. Next, we analyze retirement practices that organizations implement in different parts of the world with regard to three parameters: retirement timing, flexibility in the retirement process, and human resource practices oriented toward older workers. Then, we provide a review of practices that organizations use to retain or motivate older workers to continue working and delay retirement. We sum up the chapter with conclusions, challenges, and directions for future research and practice.

Social, Legal, and Economic Contexts of the Retirement Transition
Population Aging and Workforce Participation of Older Workers in Different Regions and Countries

Adele Hayutin, director of the Global Aging Program at the Stanford Center on Longevity, states that there are four trends in the aging population: (1) population aging is a universal problem; (2) it is a major force with influences on different aspects of life; (3) it is a quickly growing and accelerating process; and (4) it is taking place at different rates in various areas of the world (AARP, 2009). This process of aging is mainly seen as a result of a decrease in fertility and mortality rates. There has been considerable variation in the timing, levels, and patterns of population aging. The United Nations (2009) distinguishes between three main world areas where this process is taking place: developed countries, developing countries, and least developed countries. Although the proportion of older persons is much higher in developed countries (a fifth of the population) than in developing countries (nearly 8% of their population), the growth rate of the increase of older persons is much faster in the latter. Currently, the average annual growth rate of the population aged 60 years or over is 3% in the less developed regions and 1.9% in the more developed regions (United Nations, 2009); by 2045–2050, the growth rate of the older population in the less developed regions is projected to be over five times as high as that in the more developed regions. It could be argued that the aging process is not currently occurring in South Asia, the Middle East, or Sub-Saharan

Africa (Heller, 2006), but, following the UN prospects for these least developed countries (United Nations, 2009), the proportion of the population aged 60 years or over is projected to increase to 11% by 2050 (surpassing the 5% that has remained stable for years).

At the same time, in most developed and developing countries, there is a common trend of decreased participation of older workers in the workforce. Taking the world all together, Africa shows clearly the highest proportion of older individuals who continue to be economically active after age 65, while Europe shows the lowest. In other geographical areas, such as Oceania and North America, the participation rates of older workers are relatively low. Conversely, in Asia, Latin America, and the Caribbean, this participation rate is considered by the United Nations to be relatively high (United Nations, 2009). Ebbinghaus (2006), comparing tendencies in ten different OECD countries, found that the Central and South European countries (France, Germany, and Italy) showed the highest level of workforce inactivity among women and men between 54 and 65 years old. In a similar vein, Gruber and Wise (1999) identified the lowest rates of workforce participation among older men in Belgium (here, only about a quarter of men are working at the age of 60). On the other side, in some Liberal countries such as Japan, almost half of the population is still working at the age of 69, and in other Liberal (the United States) and Social-Democratic countries (Denmark and Sweden), participation rates in the ages between 50 and 59 are about 80% (Gruber & Wise, 1999).

Although industrialized countries showed a clear decreasing trend in their retirement age during the 1980s and 1990s, national policies have proved to be effective in changing this trend so that the pace of early retirement has slowed down. The latest report of the OECD (2010) suggests a continued growth of the employment of older workers during the recession (2008–2009). While this trend is at least partially due to the recession, it is likely not just a response to a circumstantial situation (Daly, Hobijn, & Kwok, 2009). Indeed, this situation contrasts with previous economic recessions in which older workers were the first to lose their jobs and the first to have difficulties finding employment (OECD, 2011).

There are also important cross-national differences in the level reached and the growth of this trend. Central and South Europe have the lowest rates of older worker workforce participation;

meanwhile, Social-Democratic and Liberal countries have comparably relatively high participation rates (Hofäcker, Buchholz, & Pollnerová, 2010). More concretely, the trends show that Liberal and Social-Democratic countries show slow (the United States, Norway, and Sweden) and medium (the United Kingdom and Denmark) decreases in the rates of older worker workforce participation, while Central European countries (Germany and France) show fast decreases, and South Europe shows medium decreases.

Thus, contrary to the general tendency, some industrialized countries show a slowing of the decrease in older workers' participation rates and even a reversal of this trend, as older worker workforce participation rates begin to increase. According to the U.S. Department of Labor, one out of six Americans aged 65 and older is working today, up from one in eight a decade ago. In Norway in 2000, 73% of older men (ages 55–64) and 61% of older women were employed. Although they had a decrease in the employment of older workers during the 1980s and 1990s, between 1993 and 1998 they experienced some increases in the workforce participation of older adults. Nowadays the average exit age is 64 for both Norwegian men and women.

Some transitional economies are facing problems related to a rapidly growing aging population and a relatively low retirement age as well (Ling & Chi, 2008). For instance, the group of developing countries collectively known as BRIC (Brazil, Russia, India, and China) is facing both an aging population and a decrease in the workforce participation of older workers (Burke & Ng, 2006). Moreover, this population aging is progressing much more quickly than in more industrialized nations. Aging is also expected to have a stronger impact in these economies, since they will reach a similar level of aging in their societies as in industrialized countries without having reached the same level of wealth (United Nations, 2009). Moreover, their old age support systems are close to collapse. For instance, in China, the current retirement policy age is 60 years of age for men and 55 for women working in State Owned Enterprises (SOEs) or for a formal sector employer in the urban areas. However, the average age of retirement in China is only 51.2 years. There are also important differences between urban and rural areas. Most people in rural areas continue working after 60 mostly because there is no formal pension scheme available (Pang, DeBrawl, & Rozelle, 2004). Moreover, aging in rural areas of China is particularly accelerated due to high levels

of migration of younger people from rural to urban areas (Adamchak, 2001).

In Brazil, approximately 90% of the population between ages 60 and 64 was working in the 1950s. In the year 2000, only 65% of people in this age group were still in the workforce (Queiroz, 2007). This situation is even worse for public employees, who reportedly had a mean retirement age of 54 in 2002 (Queiroz, 2007). In general, there are differences between women and men in each geographical area. There is more clear information for patterns in men than women since the employment patterns of women are more difficult to follow (Ebbinghaus, 2006). The general trend indicates that in the industrialized world there has been a decrease in the participation of male older workers and an increase of participation in female older workers (United Nations, 2009). However, when we consider separately different cohorts of women, trends look different. Younger cohorts of women have higher levels of participation in the labor market at all ages. However, when taking into account the cohort-by-cohort patterns of retirement, these match up more closely to those of their male counterparts (Ebbinghaus, 2006; National Research Council, 2001). More concretely, in the statistics offered by the National Research Council (2001), if we observe the evolution in employment rates of the group of women that were aged 55–59 in the year 1976 (about 58% employed), they decrease at a similar pace as men of the same age group in the year 1981 (only 42% employed). These patterns can also be differentiated by countries. Whereas there is a strong decrease of workforce participation rates among female workers in Central European countries (Belgium and France), such rates have been increasing in some Social-Democratic countries (Sweden) and some Liberal countries (the United States). Indeed, in Social-Democratic countries women's workforce participation has been reported to be equal to that of men (OECD, 2006). In urban China, the decrease in the workforce participation begins five years earlier for women than for men (Giles, 2009). As has been the case in other post-communist countries, China has one of the highest female labor force participation rates in the world. The decrease in female worker participation rates seems to be showing some gender bias during state sector restructuring and could suggest some gender bias in employment (Giles, 2009). For instance, while during the pre-reform period the state was protecting women from discrimination in remuneration schemes, the advent of economic reform seems to have opened the gap between genders. In this sense, Maurer-Fazio and Hughes (2002) found gaps in the wages of men and women less favorable for women following economic reform.

National and gender differences in patterns of retirement show that although workforce participation rates appear to be an individual decision phenomenon, there are other factors to be considered, such as socioeconomic contingencies, national policies, and legislation.

Legal and Socioeconomic Contingencies of Cross-national Differences in Retirement Patterns

Some authors have stressed that although the ongoing globalization process in the world could be the main cause for the general trend of older worker withdrawal from the workforce, different characteristics at the national level—such as welfare state policies, education and training, and models of labor regulation—have changed the intensity of this process (Hofäcker et al., 2010). In this sense, Ebbinghaus (2006) points out three institutional characteristics that could explain different retirement patterns in each country: welfare regimes, production systems, and labor relations. Indeed, some studies have found that countries that are rather similar economically and demographically can display considerable variation in retirement patterns (National Research Council, 2001).

It is widely accepted that governmental policies and early access to retirement income contribute to the decrease in the retirement age (Gruber & Wise, 1999; Ebbinghaus, 2006). In contrast, the OECD (2010) suggests that labor supply responses to large losses in retirement savings and the lesser availability of early retirement options are reasons for the employment growth of older workers during the recession. In a recent UN report (2009), it was argued that because of limited access to pension programs and reduced incomes in developing countries, people tend to retire later than in developed countries. Only 14% of men aged 65 years or over are economically active in the more developed regions, whereas 35% are in the labor force of the less developed regions. For women, the difference is 8% for older women in the more developed regions and 19% in the less developed regions. However, the fact that a decline in older worker labor force participation also occurs in developing countries points to other factors such as shortage of employment opportunities, skill obsolescence, and deficient knowledge and training to keep abreast of new

developments (United Nations, 2009). Moreover, some reports also suggest that in some of the states with more generous welfare regimes, workers prefer to retire later (Esser, 2005; OECD, 2003).

In the Yao and Peng chapter of this book, the pension systems and their influences on retirement patterns are analyzed. However, in the present section we aim to summarize the main legal and socioeconomic features that could be affecting retirement decisions in different countries.

As can be seen in Table 32.1, Central European countries all have mandatory retirement ages set at 65 years, though in the case of France and Germany this will increase to 67 within the next decade. However, in these two cases older workers can actually draw a state pension at an earlier age, whereas in the Netherlands they cannot. In all countries, older workers can delay retirement past 65 years of age. Finally, whereas France and the Netherlands have implemented the mandatory redistributive part within their pension system coupled with mandatory savings, in Germany only the latter is implemented (the second-tier points system[1]).

Regarding South European countries, the retirement age is also set to 65 in Greece and Spain, whereas in Italy women can retire earlier. Apart from Greece, older workers can start receiving pension benefits before the normal retirement age, and in all cases they can postpone their retirement. As for the pension system, we observe the same two-part structure in Greece and Spain, whereas in Italy only the mandatory savings part is implemented (through public national accounts).

Considerable variation can be observed within the group of Liberal countries. Whereas Australia, Canada, and the United States abolished mandatory retirement age for most occupations, European Liberal countries as well as Japan still have mandatory retirement ages. In addition, we can observe that whereas in Japan the official retirement age for men is 62 years of age, older workers in the United States start drawing their pension at the age of 66. However, there is also empirical evidence showing that in the United States there are two spikes in retirement, one at the age of 62 (early retirement age) and another at the age of 65 (normal retirement age; Dong, 2008). Only Canada and the United States show no difference in the official retirement age in terms of gender. Finally, in all the Liberal countries, early and late retirement is possible. As for the pension systems, we can see that only the United States does not have any first-tier system implemented, whereas the rest of the countries do.

Table 32.1 Retirement Systems in Different Countries

Group	Country	Official retirement age	Planned changes in official retirement ages	Pension system	Earliest age retirement income available	Changes in age retirement income available	Possibility to defer pension claim (late retirement)	Age discrimination actsa
Central Europe								
	France	65	67	1st Tier (minimum) 2nd Tier (public DB + points)	60	62	Yes	Age discrimination laws (criminal law and labor law)
	Germany	65	67 by 2029	2nd Tier (points)	63 (men) 60 (women)	A gradual rise for women, reaching the age of 65 and afterward 67 for both gender groups	Yes	General equal treatment act
	The Netherlands	65	/	1st Tier (basic) 2nd Tier (private DB)	65	/	Yes	Equal Treatment in Employment age discrimination act
South Europe								
	Greece	65	/	1st Tier (minimum) 2nd Tier (public DB)	65	/	Yes	Law 3304/2005
	Italy	65 (men) 60 (women)	/	2nd Tier (public NA)	57	/	Yes	Constitution and the Statute
	Spain	65	67 in the future	1st Tier (minimum) 2nd Tier (Public DB)	61	/	Yes	Workers' Statute (article 17)

(Continued)

Table 32.1 (Continued)

Group	Country	Official retirement age	Planned changes in official retirement ages	Pension system	Earliest age retirement income available	Changes in age retirement income available	Possibility to defer pension claim (late retirement)	Age discrimination acts[a]
Liberal countries								
	Australia*	65 (men) 63 (women)	65.5 (as of July 1, 2017) 67.0 (as of July 1, 2023) for both gender groups	1st Tier (resource-tested) 2nd Tier (private DB)	55	Gradual increase to 60 by 2025	Yes	Age Discrimination Act
	Canada*	65	/	1st Tier (resource-tested, basic) 2nd Tier (public DB)	60	/	Yes	/
	Japan	62 (men) 60 (women)	65 by 2025 for men and by 2030 for women	1st Tier (basic) 2nd Tier (public DB)	60	/	Yes	Anti-age discrimination law
	United Kingdom	65 (men) 60 (women)	A gradual rise for women, reaching 65 by 2020	1st Tier (resource-tested, basic, minimum) 2nd Tier (public DB)	60	/	Yes	Employment Equality (Age) Regulations
	USA*	66	Gradually increased to 67 in the future	2nd Tier (public DB)	62	/	Yes	Age Discrimination in Employment Act (ADEA)

Social-Democratic countries							
	Denmark	65	67 (by 2027)	1st Tier (resource-tested, basic) 2nd Tier (private DC)	65	/	Yes	Anti-discrimination act
	Finland	65	/	1st Tier (minimum) 2nd Tier (public DB)	62	/	Yes	Non-discrimination in employment directive
	Norway	67	/	1st Tier (basic, minimum) 2nd Tier (public points, private DC)	62	/	Yes	Employment act
	Sweden	65	/	1st Tier (minimum) 2nd Tier (public NA + private DC)	61	/	Yes	Discrimination act
Transitional economies							
	Brazil	65 (men) or 35 years MC 60 (women) or 30 years MC	/	1st Tier (resource-tested, basic, minimum)	60 (men) 55 (women)	/	No information	Anti-discrimination included in the labor law
	Chile	65 (men) 60 (women)	/	2nd Tier (private DC)	65 (men) 60 (women)	/	No information	Anti-discrimination law

(Continued)

Table 32.1 (Continued)

Group / Country	Official retirement age	Planned changes in official retirement ages	Pension system	Earliest age retirement income available	Changes in age retirement income available	Possibility to defer pension claim (late retirement)	Age discrimination acts[a]
China	60 (men) 55 (women)[c]	/	1st Tier (basic) + voluntary personal retirement accounts	60 (men) 55 (women)	60 (men) 55 (women) if working continuously for 10 years	No information	/
Mexico	65	/	1st Tier (basic and minimum) 2nd Tier (private DC)	60	/	Yes	Law for the Rights of Older Adults
Russia	60 (men) 55 (women)	65 (men) 60 (women)	Mandatory retirement age abolished for almost all occupations *				

Notes: DC—defined contribution; DB—defined benefit; NA—national accounts; MC—minimum contribution

[a] the information provided here is basic, in some cases, such as the United States, retirement at the earlier age implies reductions in pension. It is above the scope of this chapter to deal with such specific issues.

[b] in countries with mandatory retirement age, these acts state that retiring an individual reaching the mandatory age is not discriminatory.

[c] In China there are many contingencies that have to be taken into account; for instance, the differentiation between urban and rural workers and also the differentiation between different provinces (e.g., in Shanghai, the retirement age is lower than 60 years for men). Moreover, women in lower hierarchical positions can retire at the age of 50. In cases of those occupations that can be characterized by hard physical demands; e.g., miners), the retirement age is set to 55 for men and 45 for women. Finally, it is important to distinguish between stated-owned enterprises (SCEs) and privatized companies.

* Mandatory retirement age abolished for almost all occupations

Sources: Pensions at a glance 2009: Retirement income systems in OECD countries (at http://www.oecd.org/document/13/0,3746,en_2649_34757_473056:3_1_1_1,00.html): Aging and employment policies: Live longer, work longer (http://www.oecd.org/document/42/0,3343,en_2649_34747_36104426_1_1_1,00.html); Pensions panorama (http://www.oecdbookshop.org/oecd/display. asp?K=5L4W2SVLJ18T&LANG=EN); Latin America's aging challenge (http://csis.org/publication/latin-americas-aging-challenge); Shi (2007); Queiroz (2007) http://www.agediscrimination.info/Pages/Home.aspx

Moreover, we can see that all Liberal countries have implemented either public or private defined benefit schemes in their mandatory savings tier.

With regard to Social-Democratic countries, we observe the highest official retirement age in Norway at 67; however, in Denmark the official retirement age will also increase to 67 by 2027. Apart from Denmark, older workers can start drawing their pension earlier, and they can also postpone receiving a pension. As for the pension system, all Social-Democratic countries have some type of first-tier component implemented, and all but Finland (with public defined benefits) have private defined contributions in the second tier.

Finally, considerable variation is observed within emerging countries, with the lowest official retirement age present in China. Apart from Mexico, retirement ages in this group of countries differ in terms of gender. Pensionable ages tend to be higher in developed than in developing countries (United Nations, 2009). Indeed, in most developing countries, no more than 20% of older individuals receive a pension or adequate health care (United Nations, 2002). Thus, most developing countries, such as China, do not have a comprehensive social security system (Adamchack, 2001). The majority of Chinese rely on savings after retirement (Dong, 2008). Moreover, two pillars of old-age support can be identified: pension systems and family support. However, Adamchack (2001) calculated that in 2005 in China only 20% of the elderly were receiving a pension. For some years, pensions were available for people working in the state and urban collective systems in a pay-as-you-go system (70.9% of those who had pensions were employees of SOEs, 16.1% were from urban collectives, and 13% were from other private and self-employed persons; Ling & Chi, 2008). In urban areas the situation is changing due to the economic and social reforms that are being undertaken related to the privatization of the urban welfare system. Recently, the government launched a rural pension plan to which individuals, the state, and the government all contribute. Instrumental and social support from family has also been decreasing because of the one-child policy and migration from rural to urban areas. In Brazil and Mexico, older workers can draw their pension at an earlier age, and in Mexico they can also postpone their retirement. With the exception of Chile (with private defined contributions), they all have the first tier implemented in their systems. Mexico also tops its system with private defined contributions.

Retirement Patterns in Different Countries

In this section we describe retirement patterns in different countries, taking into consideration retirement timing and flexibility in the retirement process. As a follow-up of the participation rates of older workers in different countries discussed previously, a literature review reveals that indeed, in some countries, a predominant pattern is early retirement (e.g., South European countries), whereas in others the mean retirement age is relatively high (e.g., Social-Democratic countries). Similarly, a flexible retirement pattern is more common in Liberal countries compared to South European or Central European countries. Next, we present more detailed data regarding these trends for each group of countries separately.

Retirement Timing

Retirement timing has received a great deal of attention in the retirement literature, most likely because of its widespread societal implications. We can distinguish between early, on-time, and late retirement, taking into account the moment when the retirement occurred compared to the expected or standard age.

Early retirement. Early retirement occurs when an older worker retires before the legally established retirement age or before the standard retirement age of the employing organization (Vickerstaff, 2006). Such early exits are sometimes triggered by the older employees themselves, or they can be stimulated by the employers. Moreover, as Armstrong-Stassen and Schlosser (2008) have recently pointed out, early retirement incentives have even been supported by labor unions, who promote the early retirement of older employees to preserve the jobs of their younger counterparts. Early retirement has been very frequently used across European countries (Siegrist, Wahrendorf, Von dem Knesebeck, Jürges, & Börsch-Supan, 2006), since pension laws (see Table 32.1) across European countries allow early retirement arrangements.

According to Ebbinghaus (2006), different pathways toward early retirement can be identified: the early pension pathway (providing benefits before the age of 65), such as the provision of special pre-retirement schemes and long-term unemployment benefits for older workers; the organization-sponsored pathway, including severance pay and occupational pensions; and the disability pathway. There are cross-country differences in these pathways. Whereas the first pathway can be considered as an individual right, it requires some minimum contribution and is financed by the state, special pre-retirement programs, and age-related unemployment pensions that have been implemented as part of labor market policies and often go hand in hand with job replacement conditions. Hence, this first pathway also implicates in some cases the role of employers (dismissal of older workers so that a younger workforce can be hired). Similarly, organization-sponsored early-exit policies, such as occupational policies and severance pay, are dependent on the specific HR strategies of each organization. Finally, the disability pathway toward early exit is granted on the basis of individual health status and is granted in all ten countries analyzed by Ebbinghaus (Germany, Sweden, Denmark, the United Kingdom, Ireland, France, Italy, the Netherlands, the United States, and Japan). Because disability benefits used to be more generous than unemployment benefits, in the past the disability route has been frequently used by employers to lay off elderly employees in countries such as the Netherlands (De Vos & Kapteyn, 2004). Due to high costs, however, nowadays the disability pathway to retirement is subjected to more rigorous screening of loss of working capacity.

With regard to Central European countries, Ebbinghaus (2006) reports that in France and the Netherlands, high early exit rates of older workers can be explained by the early pension pathway. At the same time, unemployment benefits for older adults could be the cause for early retirement in France. Regarding the organization-sponsored pathway, this author reports that in the Netherlands there are state regulations that protect older workers who cannot be easily dismissed. Nevertheless, a recent study shows that almost 28% of the managers in the Netherlands and 22% in Germany report that they stimulate early retirement (Leber & Wagner, 2007). In South European countries such as Italy, high early exit rates also seem to be attributed to the early pension pathway (Ebbinghaus, 2006). Also, unemployment benefits to early exit seem to explain why a high percentage of Italian older workers prematurely leave the labor market.

As for Liberal countries, Ebbinghaus (2006) found that in Ireland, the United Kingdom, and the United States, a relatively low percentage of older workers leave the workforce earlier than expected through the early pension pathway. Moreover, in these countries, the state provides only low, short-term unemployment benefits, which could also explain low early retirement prevalence. As for the organization-sponsored pathway, Ebbinghaus (2006) states that employers in the United States have discretion to hire and fire at will, as there are no age- or service-related rules at the federal level. Indeed, early retirement incentive programs have been widely used in North America as a human resource tool to manage organizational size, composition, and labor costs; that is, to carry out downsizing (Appelbaum, Patton, & Shapiro, 2003; Clark & D'Ambrosio, 2005; Farr & Ringseis, 2002). Moreover, Luchak (1997) found that generous early retirement incentives might stimulate older Canadian workers to retire earlier.

In Social-Democratic countries such as Sweden and Denmark, a relatively low percentage of older workers leave the workforce earlier through the early pension pathway (Ebbinghaus, 2006). In Finland, early retirement is frequently granted to older employees on the basis of ill health, providing new retirees with early retirement disability pensions. Surprisingly, however, these two countries are at the same time characterized by a high prevalence of unemployment benefits to early exit. As for the organization-sponsored pathway, Ebbinghaus (2006) highlights Sweden, where older workers are protected by the state regulations and cannot be easily dismissed.

As for developing countries, we found studies showing that a trend of early retirement seems to be present in urban China. Whereas the normal retirement age in urban Chinese sectors is 60 for men and 55 for women, the effective retirement age is much lower. The acceleration of the process of restructuring for SOEs promotes the use of early retirement for older workers and retrenchment with generous benefits (*xiagang*) to reduce the workforce in this sector (Giles, 2009). Moreover, Price and Fang (2002) examined a group of older discouraged workers in a large sample of unemployed Chinese and found that they exhibited significantly higher motivation to retire compared to the rest of the groups observed. The authors conclude that "Older discouraged workers may see retirement as a refuge from the financial strain and lack of career mobility they are experiencing in their lay-off status" (Price & Fang, 2002, p. 424). Within the context of economic reform in China and the downsizing of SOEs, this study suggests that older workers are a particularly vulnerable group experiencing high emotional and financial strains. This evidence suggests that older Chinese workers with little human capital might react to the emerging market economy with resignation, eagerly anticipating retirement. Giles (2009) asserts that substantial shares of retirees do return to the labor force.

On-time retirement. On-time retirement takes place when an older employee retires as it is expected from him or her to retire, that is, when he or she reaches the established, standard, normal, or default retirement age (Flynn, 2010). Whereas in European countries there is a legally established or mandatory retirement age, in other countries, such as in the United States or Canada, there is no such retirement age. However, in these latter cases, there is an expected retirement age established in the occupational pension schemes that can be considered a reference of retirement timing (see Table 32.1). In other words, if an older worker retires at the age established in the pension scheme, he or she retires on time. Quite frequently, older employees are denied continuation in the workforce once they reach the official or normal retirement age, even if they prefer to continue working. Thus, on-time retirement can also be viewed as compulsory or obligatory, since older workers do not have control over the possibility to continue working (Manfredi & Vickers, 2009). This observation is supported by the evidence from different countries.

Regarding Liberal countries, Flynn (2010) reports that in the United Kingdom employers are the ones who decide whether to accept or deny an older worker's request to continue working after having reached the age of 65 years, as long as the correct procedures are followed (as specified in the age regulations).

It is also important to note that in Central European as well as in South European, Liberal, and Social-Democratic countries, the mandatory age is progressively being raised. For instance, in Germany, Spain, the United Kingdom, Japan, and Denmark, the mandatory retirement age for women is being equalized with their male peers, whereas they could have retired earlier before (Ebbinghaus, 2006). In the same vein, Germany and Spain have proposals to raise the mandatory retirement age from 65 to 67. Thus, these regulations will probably delay retirement, coupled with other measures described next.

Late retirement. Late retirement occurs when exit from the workforce occurs after the established or standard retirement age. With the exception of Liberal countries with no mandatory retirement age

(such as the United States, Canada, and Australia), the mandatory retirement age of 65 is a main cause for the rapid decline in workforce participation rates of people over 65. Nevertheless, we must highlight that although mandatory retirement age legislation determines the retirement practices of organizations to a large extent, recently more restricted laws such as those in European countries have been modified to allow older employees to continue in the labor force if desired. That is, many countries have started to implement legislation offering incentives to older workers to continue in the workforce once they have reached the retirement age (apart from delaying the official retirement age as noted in Table 32.1).

In Central European countries, the recent analysis of the older working population by Ebbinghaus (2006) reveals that only 3.1% of older men between 65 and 69 are actively employed in France, whereas this figure is higher in Germany (7.1%) and the Netherlands (8.4%). Also, in the case of women from 65 to 69 years of age, the lowest participation rate is observed in France at 1.3%, whereas 2.4% of women from this age group are actively employed in the Netherlands and 3.3% in Germany.

As for the South European region, the participation rates of men in the 65–69 age group are slightly higher compared to Central European countries. Concretely, the evidence shows that 10.4% of workers between 65 and 69 years of age in Italy are still actively employed. As for women, the data shows that only 2.8% of Italian women in this age group are taking part in the labor market.

Liberal countries, in contrast, show much higher participation rates. Whereas 50.7% of Japanese men between 65 and 69 years of age are actively employed, this figure drops to 30.1% in the United States, and down to 24.2% in Ireland and 15.6% in the United Kingdom. In the case of older women, we can observe a similar trend: 25.4% of older Japanese women are still actively employed, followed by 18.8% in the United States, 6.1% in Ireland, and 8.9% in the United Kingdom. As previously mentioned, recent research shows that employees from the United Kingdom aged 65 or older continue working more on the basis of individual arrangements with their immediate managers, as opposed to changes in an organization's policies and practices (Flynn, 2010). Finally, a recent study by Merline, Cull, Mulvey, and Katcher (2010) on a sample of U.S. pediatricians aged 50 and older shows that almost half of the surveyed respondents reported that they would provide or were planning to provide patient care past age 65.

Relatively high older workforce participation rates are also observed in Social-Democratic countries. In Sweden, for instance, 17.6% of men in the 65–69 age group are actively employed, whereas in Denmark this figure drops to 8.3%. In the case of women between 65 and 69 years of age, we can observe a similar declining trend as in other groups of countries: only 4.5% in Denmark and 4.8% in Sweden.

As for developing countries, Giles (2009) has recently noted that more than 10% of Chinese men and women continue in the labor force after reaching the mandatory retirement ages of 60 and 55, respectively. Also, a recent study reports that peasants in rural China continue working into late old age due to economic difficulties (Shi, 2007). Although the level of pension income varies significantly between different areas of the country (for instance, rural residents in Shanghai enjoy higher pensions than those from Qingdao area or even Beijing), the rural population receives much lower pension income compared to their urban counterparts. Thus, rural peasants have a necessity to retire later than expected.

The current analysis suggests that in some countries, older employees would like to continue working, but their organizations prefer them to fully retire when it is expected of them. In other countries, older employees feel obliged to continue working longer due to financial reasons. As highlighted previously, the issue of delaying retirement is very important in all countries with increasing proportions of the older population on one hand and decreasing proportions of the younger workforce on the other, to sustain the viability of social welfare systems. However, it should also be noted that perhaps delaying retirement can best be achieved with implementing practices that allow older workers more flexible transition to retirement, such as part-time work or phased retirement. In the context of Liberal countries, Nusbaum (2009) recently argued that part-time work arrangements could be effective for delaying the retirement of U.S. physicians. Moreover, Kelly, Dahlin, Spencer, and Moen (2008) have argued that many older workers would like to continue working, thus delaying their retirement, but under different working arrangements (e.g., part-time work). Next, we review retirement flexibility in the process of exiting the workforce.

Flexibility in the Transition to Retirement

Literature regarding flexibility in retirement transition types highlights the different human resource practices that organizations implement, within the limits established by the country laws and regulations, to gradually retire their personnel. Given the changing nature of employment relationships, nowadays retirement should not be considered necessarily as an all-at-once transition from full employment to no employment (Calo, 2005; Hedge, 2008). In this line of thought, many countries have started to implement different types of retirement practices, such as flexible retirement, phased or gradual retirement, or part-time retirement in addition to the traditional full-time retirement practice. The latter represents the least flexible way of retirement, in which human resource strategy focuses on completely retiring all the personnel when they reach a certain age. As noted previously in the section on retirement timing, such practices are quite common across Central European, South European, Social-Democratic (with Sweden as the exception), and European Liberal countries where there is a legally established retirement age. In contrast, in some cases, organizations opt for more flexible practices, allowing retirees a more gradual exit from the workforce. Leber and Wagner (2007) report that across twenty-one EU countries, phased retirement is offered more frequently in larger organizations than in smaller or medium-sized ones. Moreover, they found that phased retirement is more frequent in periods of financial difficulty. Finally, they showed that organizations offering part-time working arrangements and having flexible working hours offer the option of phased retirement more frequently compared with organizations without part-time or more flexible working arrangements. According to Ebbinghaus (2006), flexible pensions that allow part-time work are a common pathway toward retirement in OECD countries, although there are substantial differences between and within each group of countries under consideration. For instance, within Social-Democratic countries, flexible pathways seem to have been widely employed, especially in Sweden, whereas in Denmark such methods did not receive much success (probably because of more attractive full-time exit options). In Central European states, flexible retirement options have received mixed support. In the Netherlands, part-time working arrangements have been widely accepted, whereas in Germany flexible retirement pathways have not triumphed to date. Flexible retirement practices, such as flexible working hours, have not been accepted in the South European area. For instance, Greek trade unions view them with suspicion (Taylor et al., 2000). Moreover, within Liberal countries, Ebbinghaus (2006) noted that flexible retirement can be granted in the United States starting at the age of 62, with pension benefits drawn from private occupational pensions. However, as we will discuss below, many U.S. organizations implement different types of flexible retirement options on a more informal basis. Finally, regarding developing countries, the transition of most of the older peasants in China could be considered flexible on the basis of recent analysis by Shi (2007). As noted previously, although older Chinese workers can start receiving pension benefits at the age of 55, most of them prefer to continue working to complement these benefits with additional income. Heller (2006) has recently suggested that in order to avoid a collapse of the urban pension system in China, the phased retirement system should be seriously considered. In the next paragraphs we will analyze in more detail the various transition types and their use in different countries as well as their implications for organizations and individuals.

Immediate full-time (permanent) retirement. Immediate full-time retirement occurs when an individual permanently leaves the workforce (either earlier than expected, on time, or after having reached the official retirement age). These types of practices are present mainly in nations in which flexible retirement arrangements are not yet implemented in legislation. Research in different geographical areas has focused on analyzing the role of timing in workers' adjustment to retirement. In examining the South European context, Potočnik, Tordera and Peiró (2010) collected data from a sample of Spanish retirees who permanently retired and found that retirement timing did not play any role in retirees' satisfaction or psychological well-being. However, voluntariness of retirement transition did have a strong influence on their subsequent adjustment to retirement (Potočnik et al., 2010; Potočnik, Tordera, & Peiro, in press).

Similar findings can be observed in a group of Liberal countries. For instance, a recent Australian study (De Vaus, Wells, Kendig, & Quine, 2007) found control over retirement transition to be a more important factor in retirees' well-being than whether the transition was gradual or immediate. In the same line of thought, Calvo, Haverstick, and Sass (2009) suggested that although older workers frequently prefer gradual retirement to immediate, abrupt retirement from the workforce, what is most important for retirees' well-being is not the way they left the labor market (either through immediate full-time retirement or gradual retirement), but rather their perception of the workforce exit as

voluntary or obligatory. That is, while retiring gradually allows time for people to make changes to their lifestyle, having control over the timing and manner of exiting the work role has a greater positive impact on psychological and social well-being. Thus, although "conventional wisdom promotes gradual retirement rather than an abrupt end to the working life" (De Vaus et al., 2007, p. 667), empirical findings suggest that having control over one's transition to retirement is more important than the factual flexibility in this transition. Finally, we should highlight that in the United States, where gradual forms of retirement are very popular, Kantarci and Van Soest (2008) reported evidence from the Health and Retirement Study (HRS) showing that in reality almost 38% of surveyed participants in all waves of the survey made a transition from full-time work to full retirement in the next wave (waves 1992–1994; 1994–1996; 1996–1998; 1998–2000).

Phased retirement. In comparison with full-time retirement, phased retirement allows employees to gradually "phase" into retirement by reducing their work hours (through shorter workdays or fewer days per week) until retirement (Hedge, 2008; Kelly et al., 2008; Sheaks, 2007). In Liberal countries, phased retirement is a human resource management strategy frequently used by many U.S. organizations (Clark & D'Ambrosio, 2005; Hedge, 2008). Hutchens (2003) found that while only a few U.S. organizations have formal phased retirement policies, many are willing to permit phased retirement on an informal basis. In either case, we can conclude that phased retirement is indeed a very popular retirement strategy for many North American organizations as well as individuals. As for the former, it is less costly, and as for the latter, it provides new employment options, such as part-time work or callback arrangements for the previous employer (Armstrong-Stassen, 2005; Armstrong-Stassen & Lee, 2009). Research indicates that employees and organizations view these phased plans as being beneficial. For instance, Armstrong-Stassen (2005) found that Canadian nurses prefer partial or phased retirement. Moreover, Clark and D'Ambrosio (2005) reported results from the Survey of Changes in Faculty Retirement Policies suggesting that more than one-third of the surveyed U.S. institutions used phased retirement plans. They examined plans that provided prorated compensation for faculty who gave up tenure and accepted a fixed-term contract for part-time employment, arguing that the value of phased retirement plans to institutions is that they provide certainty of information regarding when senior faculty will finally leave the university. The value to the faculty members is that they have a new retirement option (Clark & D'Ambrosio, 2005). Moreover, Merline et al. (2010) showed that engaging in part-time work is increasingly common with age and may represent a step toward retirement for many older U.S. pediatricians. The authors concluded that gradually reducing the work hours or introducing other types of phased retirement could benefit the practice of U.S. pediatrics by extending the career length of the most experienced pediatricians. Other evidence from the United States shows that phased retirement is more likely to be seen as a possibility in workplaces having more experience with flexible schedules, job sharing, and extended family leaves and is more common in higher education and in the public sector, largely because these sectors are regulated by different, and more flexible, pension laws (Hutchens & Grace-Martin, 2004; Kelly et al., 2008; Perun, 2002; Willett, 2005). Finally, most U.S. organizations prefer that phased retirees work part-week compared to part-day or part-year (Hutchens, 2003).

In European countries, especially those with Social-Democratic economies, the idea of gradually exiting the workforce is gaining more and more popularity (Kantarci & Van Soest, 2008). In Sweden, the current system permits workers older than 61 to reduce working hours up to 50%, and to get 100%, 75%, 50%, or 25% of the full pension (Belloni, Monticone, & Trucchi, 2006). As noted previously, flexible retirement arrangements have been very common in Sweden, particularly due to the high proportion of older workers taking on part-time work (Ebbinghaus, 2006). In Denmark, workers between 60 and 65 years of age who satisfy some conditions regarding their past participation in the labor market can apply for gradual retirement. They can reduce their working hours and receive a partial pension proportional to the reduction in working time. The Finnish system entitles workers between the ages of 58 and 67 to reduce their working hours to 16–28 hours per week and replace 50% of forgone earnings with a partial pension.

Gradual retirement is also available in Central European countries (Belloni et al., 2006). Their systems all allow workers aged 60 or 61 and older to reduce working hours and receive a corresponding partial pension that depends on having contributed enough time to the social security system (Kantarci & Van Soest, 2008). Naegele and Krämer (2001) found that gradual retirement schemes or different part-time work arrangements have started to be implemented in German companies with support at the state level. Moreover, in the Netherlands, human resource management strategies are shifting from standardized collective trajectories for older workers toward more flexible, individualized transitions to retirement (de Vroom, 2004, as cited in Gardiner et al., 2007). For instance, in 2004, about one-third of former and current Dutch employees reported that their (last) employer offered them the option of phased retirement (Van Soest, Kapteyn, & Zissimopoulos ., 2006).

Bridge employment. Bridge employment is defined as a pattern of labor force participation of older employees as they exit their career job and undertake another job (either part-time, self-employment, or temporary employment) before fully retiring (Wang, Zhan, Liu, & Shultz, 2008). Thus, whereas phased retirement refers to the reduction of working hours for the same employer (Kelly et al., 2008), bridge employment implies taking on a different job in another organization. Another term for this type of gradual retirement is partial retirement (Kantarci & Van Soest, 2008).

Regarding Liberal countries, evidence from the United States suggests that a substantial proportion of older workers take on bridge jobs (e.g., shifting to part-time work, or shifting to a job in a different field) after leaving their career employment before they fully retire from the workforce (Cahill, Giandrea, & Quinn, 2006; Nusbaum, 2009). Kantarci and Van Soest (2008) found that 14.5% of employees in the Health and Retirement Study (HRS) who had at least ten years of tenure held a bridge job in 1992. This proportion increased to 29.3% in 1998 and then decreased to 25.3% in 2002. Moreover, this tendency of bridge employment seems to have a U-shaped pattern, with the most common bridge employment seen in low-wage employees (likely due to economic necessity) and in high-wage employees (likely due to desired quality of life related to workforce participation).

As for the South European nations, a recent study indicates that 13.5% of Greek workers between 50 and 60 years of age take on bridge employment (Topa, Depolo, Moriano, & Morales, 2009). In other areas, such as Central European countries and particularly in France, this percentage drops to only 0.8% (Topa et al., 2009). Overall, Topa et al. (2009) showed that on average, the population in this age range from twelve European countries worked 18.6 hours a month in their bridge employment positions.

The Role of Employers in Retirement Patterns: Human Resource Management Practices

In order to accurately describe the process of retirement in different geographical areas, it is important to understand the role of employers in the process of the early exit of older workers, or its reversal, the process of their retention and maintenance. Most research examining this has focused either on the macro-level (such as differences in the welfare state systems) coming mostly from economics, or on the micro-level (such as individual decision making) coming mostly from psychology. Explanations of early exit from work as a result of the incentive of public social policies are clearly insufficient (Costa, 1998; Ebbinghaus, 2006). Other aspects such as the conditions of the production systems or the role of unions have important roles as push or pull factors to retire or maintain older workers in their work roles (Ebbinghaus, 2006). Moreover, changes in governmental policies should also be followed by changes at the organizational and individual level that would increase the willingness of employers and employees to delay retirement. Situations in which individuals who do not wish to keep working are forced to work, or in which organizations who do not want older workers are forced to maintain them, could be very detrimental, not only for the general adjustment and health of those individuals but also for the productivity and efficiency of those organizations and countries (Gaillard & Desmette, 2010). On the other side, the evaluation of retirement as an individual decision-making process ignores that these decisions occur in a social context. A critical part of this social context is the type of policies and practices employers implement for older workers. Indeed, some authors have pointed out that the trend in the decrease of older workers' participation in the workforce is much related to company policies (for instance, policies of not hiring older workers, or layoffs; Guillemard, 2001). It is true that many of those variables are narrowly interwoven. However, it should be noted that it is difficult to understand the policies and practices of employers with regard to recruiting and hiring older employees without taking into account public policies affecting different aspects, such as the flexibility and adaptation of the labor market, discrimination practices, or the level of skills and competencies of older workers.

Little has been reported about how organizations push their workers toward retirement and early retirement (intentionally or unintentionally). Further, considerably little research has focused on how organizations retain and recruit older workers, and even less on how those practices might differ from one country to another. Some studies have shown that organizational context has an important impact on workers' decisions to retire. For instance, Hardy and Hazelrigg (1999) examined a sample of workers in General Motors employees in the United States and found that workers employed in plants that were scheduled to close were more likely to retire early than workers working in plants not expected to close. Some characteristics related to organizational culture have also shown to influence early exit from the work role: human resources practices oriented toward early exit, organizational pressures, or the maintenance of age-based negative stereotypes being among these (Crego & Alcover, 2008; Potočnik et al., 2009, 2010; Gaillard & Desmette, 2010). For instance, Potočnik and colleagues (2009, 2010) found that early retirement enhancement practices (such as retirement plans, actions toward the preparation for retirement, and economic incentives for taking retirement) increased early retirement intentions, whereas organizational pressures toward early retirement decreased the retirement age. So there is some evidence that, together with legal and socioeconomic conditions, the way that organizations manage their human resources may influence worker behavior to remain in or exit the workforce. However, different voices are also acknowledging that few employers are finding and/or implementing long-term solutions to prevent the consequences in terms of labor shortages and brain drain that may be emerging from widespread early retirement (e.g., Manpower, 2007).

Yeatts, Folts, and Knapp (2000) distinguished between two different models of human resource practices related to workers and their aging process: the maintenance model and the depreciation model. On one hand, the maintenance model considers workers at any age as valued *assets* for the organization if they are well trained, educated, and managed. In the context of this model, organizations develop human resource practices oriented toward the retention of older workers. These practices are directed toward four aspects: recruitment and selection of older workers, the enhancement of workers' performance (training, development, and promotion), the improvement and personalization of working conditions through the redesign of jobs, and the flexibilization of the retirement process (phased retirement, bridge employment, part-time retirement) that we have previously reviewed.

In contrast, the depreciation model is based on the idea that the highest value that an individual may have for an organization is at the beginning of his or her career, and this value begins to decline and finally end at the time of his or her retirement. From this perspective, any investment in older workers is seen as a *cost*, and the organization's policy toward them is focused on promoting their exit through early retirement plans (Henkens, 2000; Lin & Hsieh, 2001; Remery, Henkens, Schippers, & Ekamper, 2003). Furthermore, as older workers start to be considered as less valuable, organizations stop integrating them within the common practices of human resource management, such as selection, training, or career development (Hedge et al., 2006). Moreover, sometimes those practices are manifested in the form of pressures or difficulties that obstruct the development of the work role, and there is a lack of actions oriented to adjust the job to the special needs or conditions of the older workers.

To our knowledge there has been no previous systematic attempt to identify cross-country differences in the models of human resource practices with regard to age. Nonetheless, Hofhäcker et al. (2010) have distinguished between governmental policies approaching age management from a depreciation model (employment exit-dominated strategy) and from a maintenance model (maintenance-dominated pathway). They consider Central and South European countries to adhere to the depreciation model, while Liberal and Social-Democratic countries tend to approach age management from a maintenance model perspective. Our review seeks to examine whether differences in public policy parallel the methods employers use to implement different human resource practices regarding older workers.

Evidence from the Perspective of the Depreciation Model in Different Countries

A number of studies suggest that the depreciation model has been prominent in industrialized nations during the past decades. Indeed, there is a large amount of evidence showing the lack of practices designed to promote or maintain older workers in organizations (OECD, 2006). The prevalence of early retirement, together with the existence of discriminatory practices and organizational pressures, characterizes most of the patterns of behavior in human resource practices during the last forty years. These practices may be artifacts of widespread stereotypical thoughts regarding older workers in these countries, although these stereotypes have not received empirical support (Harper, Khan, Saxena, & Leeson, 2006). In Central and South European countries, workers over 50 simultaneously experience economic difficulties in leaving employment and a widespread early workforce exit form. For instance, in France, which has one of the lowest mean retirement ages in the world, survey data collected in 1992 found that managers supporting early exit policies were more likely to do so as a means of dealing with the aging workforce than as a method of attracting and integrating older workers (Guillemard, 2001). More concretely, enforced retirement was preferred by 47.4% of the managers, followed by the incentives for early exit (37.8%) and dismissal (12.7%). Only 22.5% considered internal reorganization of working practices as preferable. There is a rapidly increasing unemployment rate of workers over 50 in these regions, and this type of unemployment tends to last over time. In 1992, one out of three dismissals in France involved wage earners over 50. Guillemard (2001) also noted that in this region, later career stages are becoming progressively more discriminatory and precarious. The majority of early retirees go through a trajectory of unemployment (20%) or pre-retirement (23%) before accessing actual retirement. So, compared to previous generations, where 54% of older workers went directly from job to retirement, nowadays only 34% follow that trajectory. With regard to performance-enhancement practices, Aventur (1994) has shown that only a very small number of employees aged 45 and over received any form of on-the-job training. Moreover, training opportunities diminish significantly after 40.

In the Netherlands in 1996, the National Bureau of Age Discrimination organized a national claim reporting day for experienced age discrimination. Discrimination was experienced by the majority (62.8%) of the 2,538 respondents in one survey study (de Vroom, 2004). In a study examining managers' attitudes toward retirement in public and private sectors in the same region, Henkens (2000) found that managers were influenced by negative age stereotypes of older workers' productivity, reliability, and adaptability.

In South European countries, the existence of age discrimination in the workplace has also been an issue. For instance, Potočnik et al. (2009) found that retirees in Spain perceived that performance-enhancement practices (such as training, selection, promotion, etc.) were almost nonexistent for older workers in the companies from which they retired. Moreover, organizational pressures for retirement and coworkers' norms toward retirement were the main causes of retirement. Also in Spain, Suso (2004) found that older workers had a greater probability of leaving the workforce, being unemployed for a longer time, not receiving training, and experiencing more obstacles and prejudices when applying for a job.

We also found reports of discriminatory practices in the Liberal countries. In the United States, the Equal Employment Opportunity Commission (Taylor et al., 2000) saw an increase in age discrimination charges between 1990 and 1993 (from 14,700 to almost 20,000). However, this number had declined by 1997 (around 15,800). Shore et al. (2009) reviewed research addressing the existence of discriminatory human resource practices against older workers and found that, in general, older workers are disadvantaged with regard to different human resource practices (selection, performance appraisal, training and development opportunities, promotion opportunities, consequences of poor performance), especially when they are in the minority compared to younger workers. The existence of age norms with regard to different aspects of the working life (e.g., age of retirement, age for promotion) has been suggested as an influence of the existence of discriminatory practices. For instance, age norms in the electric sector have been found to influence employee attitudes and performance appraisal (Lawrence, 1984, 1988). Further, in her review about the evolution of retirement in the United States, Costa (1998) points out that although the probability of entering unemployment did not increase with age, the probability of leaving unemployment has declined with age.

In the United Kingdom, Taylor and Walker (1994) found that relatively few managers had policies benefitting older workers (1995, 1998). Harper (2006) found that in 90% of the downsizing processes ongoing in the United Kingdom, older workers have been targeted for early retirement or redundancy. With regard to training, Dibbden and Hibbett (1993) showed that those aged 16 to 24 and those aged 25 to 49 were respectively three times more likely and twice more likely to receive training than those aged over 50. Later on, Metcalf and Meadows (2006) conducted a survey of employers' policies, practices, and preferences relating to age and found that although three-quarters of employers recognized the desirability and potential benefits of training older workers, they did not exhibit preferences or promote older worker-targeted policies because of stereotypes regarding those workers. In

Australia, employers' perceptions of older workers also continue to be stereotypically negative (Shacklock & Shacklock, 2005; Taylor et al., 2000). For example, respondents in a survey study regarding employers' perceptions of older workers found that employers expressed poor interest in recruiting workers over 56. In spite of anti-discrimination laws, the majority of age discrimination complaints received by the Australian Human Rights Commission in 2008–2009 were made by people over 45 and were related to employment (Southam, 2010).

Finally, discrimination against older workers is also reported in Social-Democratic countries. Even in those countries with higher participation rates of older workers in the workforce, such as Norway, age discrimination remains an issue. For instance, Mykletun et al. (2000) found that 61% of local government employees reported age discrimination in their workplaces (cf. Solem & Overbye, 2004). Older workers are generally given less challenging jobs and are kept away from daily hassles and new demands (Solem & Overbye, 2004). In general, they are seen as less attractive in terms of recruitment and selection than younger workers. Moreover, although early retirement has been framed as a method of combating the unemployment of younger workers, Solem & Overbye (2004) reported that in a study from 1971–73, even when unemployment rates were about 1% in Norway, older workers felt pressure from managers and fellow workers to retire early because of youth unemployment.

Age discrimination has also been reported in the Finnish workforce. The Working Life Barometer survey indicated in 1997 that 8% of the surveyed older workers (55–64 years old) had noticed some form of age discrimination in their workplaces (Tillsley, 2000). More concretely, they reported reduced promotion and training opportunities and negative attitudes among coworkers. Other studies have also reported discrimination in access to jobs, reporting age limits for jobs, and negative comments from employers in the selection process (Taylor et al., 2000). With regard to retirement patterns, when retirees in Finland stated that their access to some practices such as early retirement or part-time retirement was voluntary, further inquiry showed that these decisions were typically based on more complex factors than simple individual choice. Although Takala (1999) found that a majority of respondents had retired voluntarily, a deeper analysis revealed that at the time of the survey there was a strong recession in Finland, which could have reduced retiring employees' alternatives and options. Indeed, some of the respondents said that the alternative to part-time retirement was redundancy.

In transitional economies, especially in those countries facing a transition from a post-communist economy to a market economy, conditions such as the lack of anti-discrimination laws are resulting in discrimination practices (Samodorov, 1999). In a recent report by HelpAge International (2010)[2] in which conditions and challenges faced by older workers in developing countries were documented, the conclusion reached was that predominant modes of age discrimination in developing and least developed countries included denying older workers access to employment and training opportunities. In spite of the higher rates of participation in the workforce of older workers in these nations, age discrimination seems to be an even bigger issue than in developed countries. As workers get older they have a greater probability of experiencing unfair pay, poorer working conditions, and job insecurity. Indeed, the majority of older workers in these less developed regions are employed in informal jobs that are less secure and lower paid (for instance, in India in 2004–2005, 80% of older workers were self-employed and 16% were casual workers; HelpAge, 2010).

Evidence from the Perspective of the Maintenance Model in Different Countries

A shared claim in most industrialized countries is the need to develop policies and practices addressed toward the maintenance and attraction of older workers together with a change in pervasive attitudes toward older workers and their participation in the workforce (Patrickson, 2003). Although there are some indicators that organizational managers are beginning to focus on retention of older workers, there is not much evidence that organizations are proactively addressing these issues (Armstrong-Stassen, 2008). For instance, in a survey developed by Manpower (2007) with a sample of 28,000 employers in 25 countries, only 21 of the employers reported that they were implementing some kind of strategy directed toward the maintenance of older employees in their organizations.

Most of the literature adhering to the maintenance model is prescriptive in nature and is directed to the determination of best practices, identifying and reducing barriers and formulating recommendations for enhancing the engagement and contributions of older adults. Thus, the first question that various institutions have tried to answer

is what the best practices for age management are. In the European context this has been defined as those measures that combat age barriers and/or promote age diversity (Walker & Taylor, 1999). In the United States, AARP has tried to determine which characteristics should compose an ideal job for older workers (AARP, 2008). It has also been pointed out that the key to engagement of the older adult in the workforce is to focus on the same issues that are important to other age groups (Manpower, 2007). For instance, people who feel valued and respected are more likely to remain in an organization, are more productive, and are more likely to show citizenship behaviors, regardless of age (Peterson & Spiker, 2005, as cited in Armstrong-Stassen & Lee, 2009). It could also be argued that in less developed countries, a good practice could be considered as being something more basic. For instance, in China, researchers have suggested a need to reduce the obsolescence of older workers. HelpAge International (2010) suggests that in developing countries the priority is to assure the right of older workers to decent work: regular pay, acceptable working conditions, and access to social security.

Armstrong-Stassen (2008) has suggested three major reasons that employers are not being proactive in the retention of older workers in Western countries. First of all, she noted the continued existence of negative stereotypical views of older workers and their discrimination due to those views. Second, workforce aging research has been centered more on reasons to retire early than on discovering which employment practices will encourage workers to remain in the labor market. Third, there is a lack of knowledge about how to effectively develop and implement HR practices relevant to older workers. In their survey about the future of retirement, Harper et al. (2006) identified several reasons that managers reported for not implementing practices directed to retain and recruit older workers, including no need, no urgency, too expensive, and the fact that work is physically demanding. Globally (except in Saudi Arabia), older employees are perceived as more expensive than their younger counterparts, although this was not mentioned as a main reason that employers do not do more to attract or retain older workers. It is especially noteworthy that in most of the regions considered (all the industrialized countries such as North America, Europe, Japan, Hong Kong, and Singapore, and some transitional economies such as China), employers do not perceive older worker retention to be an urgent issue. Moreover, in populations with higher proportions of young workers, employers tend to think of older workers leaving as a method of making room for younger workers to enter (Harper et al., 2006). On the contrary, in Liberal, Social-Democratic, and Central and South European countries, the loss of older workers is associated with the perception of a loss of knowledge and skills.

Focusing on a more positive side of worker retention, Walker and Taylor (1999) proposed three causes that lead organizations to develop policies and practices oriented toward the retention and maintenance of older workers. The first is the labor shortage in some economic areas (such as qualified nursing staff). The second is changes in public policies, such as reduction of early exit subsides or the support of training grants and support for job creation. The third driver is organizational culture. The first and the third are highly related to the awareness of availability of skills and demographic changes in the workforce, as well as to the attitudes of employers toward older workers. Labor and skill shortages have been suggested as being the main drivers of employer attempts to retain older workers. In this sense, Flynn and McNair (2008) stated that in some regions, such as London and southeast Britain, employers have been particularly eager to delay retirement for their older workers because of labor shortages. However, employers of other countries, such as China, that are experiencing increasing levels of labor shortages do not seem to be much aware of the problem (BSR, 2010).

Several factors could be influencing the development of an organizational culture directed toward older workers. One factor could be the proportion of workers of different ages. For instance, in their examination of a Canadian sample of older employees, Armstrong-Stassen and Lee (2009) found that the age distribution within an organization could be a main predictor of the organization developing policies and practices oriented toward age management. Shore et al. (2009) identified that the existence of discriminative practices toward older workers was predominant in those organizations with higher proportions of young employees. In a similar vein, but at the national level, Harper et al. (2006) found that in countries with higher proportions of older workers, employers are more aware and have more favorable attitudes toward older workers and are more likely to implement human resource practices oriented toward older workers.

Several research projects in Western countries have addressed the identification of good practices toward older workers. In the United Kingdom, some researchers have attempted to identify what older workers expect from their jobs and organizations. For instance, the CROW survey (Centre for Research into the Older Workforce) was conducted in order to examine the experience of people aged 20–69 in terms of their job transitions (McNair et al., 2004). In this survey, older workers were asked about job characteristics that could persuade them to defer retirement. The majority of older workers pointed out more flexible ways of working (87%) and opportunities to work closer to home (57%) as the main job characteristics that would cause them to consider deferring retirement. Other human resource management practices, such as providing training and information about job opportunities (66%) and career and life planning (38%), were also identified as attractive job characteristics for older workers. In addition, this survey identified factors related to a later planned retirement age. Job content, work-life balance, financial considerations such as pensions and benefits, and an expectation that work would be missed in retirement were related to later retirement planning.

The examination of organizational and individual factors that lead older workers to continue working has been undertaken by other researchers as well. More concretely, Flynn and McNair (2008) distinguished three types of older workers following a cluster analysis of their job characteristics and preferences: enthusiasts, detachers, and stressed. The enthusiasts are defined by higher degrees of satisfaction with work and are the ones most likely to continue working longer. The detachers find their work less challenging and are more likely to feel undervalued. The stressed have enjoyable jobs with the greatest autonomy and tend to have good social positions, but they tend to experience difficulty balancing home and work commitments, and many find downshifting or reducing hours either unattractive or unfeasible. Flynn and McNair (2008) found that while enthusiastic older adults consider training and career advice to be the most useful job characteristics in their decision to extend their working lives, detachers were more motivated by flexible and home-working options. The stressed group is divided between those who would clearly want, and definitely do not want, to work after retirement. One of the biggest barriers for this group may be job design.

The European Union has developed a European Code of Good Practice regarding aging and employment. This code intends to serve as a guide for employers in order to help them manage the aging of the workforce productively. The code was prepared following a research initiative developed by the European Commission on age barriers in employment. Different countries participated in the elaboration of the draft (Germany, Spain, France, Italy, the Netherlands, the United Kingdom, Sweden, and Finland), which was later discussed with employers, employers' organizations, trade unions, and government officials in each of the participating countries. Good practice is defined as a combination of two elements: the consideration of different measures that could limit age barriers for employment and general management, and HR policies that contribute to the development of a work environment in which every worker can achieve his or her potential regardless of age.

Two European research projects have been developed with the aim of identifying good practices in age management: the Combating Age Barriers Project and Eurowork Age (Walker & Taylor, 1999). The Combating Age Barriers Project has been the first European research project directed to identify examples of good practices in the employment of aging workers (Walker & Taylor, 1999). This project was launched in 1994 and considers the following dimensions in age management in organizations: job recruitment and exit, training, development and promotion, flexible working practices, ergonomics, design, and changing attitudes toward older workers. The initiatives with regard to good practices in age management range from some specific measures to the most comprehensive ones that comprise an integrated age management strategy. Most of the initiatives reported in this European project refer to flexible working practices and job training. Fewer examples can be found with regard to selection and recruitment, and this project prescribes almost nothing regarding changing organizational attitudes toward older workers (Walker & Taylor, 1999).

In the United States, AARP (formerly the American Association of Retired Persons) has also contributed to research attempting to define what a good practice with regard to older employees in organizations is. Different surveys have been conducted in order to ascertain older workers' experiences, opinions, and expectations regarding their work and careers (AARP, 2003, 2008). The aim of AARP is to serve as a guide for employers responding to the challenges of an aging workforce in the coming years. Moreover, AARP yearly awards the label of "Best Employers for Workers Over 50" to those organizations that show best practices for workers aged 50 and above. In the 2002 and 2007 surveys,

they asked older worker what the main features of the ideal job would be. Adequate paid time off and having a flexible work schedule were indicated by the highest percentage of respondents (86% and 76%, respectively). A restructured job or environment was another of the main elements. Many of the respondents considered working part-time and working from home (53% and 41%, respectively) as essential elements as well (Manpower, 2007).

Other projects have focused on specific economic sectors or industries. This is the case for the Workforce Aging in the New Economy (WANE) project. This is a cross-national project that aims to study information technology employment of older workers in small and medium-sized firms. This project is being developed in Australia, Canada, the United States, and three European countries (the Netherlands, the United Kingdom, and Germany) and aims to provide guidance for public institutions, firms, and employees.

Taken together, these projects and studies convey the essential need of a combination of human resource policies and practices that combat age barriers in work and that specifically target older workers for recruitment and selection, training and lifelong learning, personal development, and flexible job arrangements.

There is a scarcity of research addressing cross-national research with regard to employers' actual human resource practices toward older workers, some exceptions being OECD reports (OECD, 2006, 2009), the Future of Retirement Survey (Harper et al., 2006), and the Manpower Survey (Manpower, 2007). The Future of Retirement Survey is a global, cross-sectional, and longitudinal survey conducted in twenty-one countries (developed and developing) in 2004 and 2005. This survey was designed to investigate the attitudes and behaviors of employers with regard to older employees. The Manpower Survey (2007) asked 28,000 employers in twenty-five countries about specific strategies designed to recruit and retain older workers. In addition, other surveys have addressed older workers' perceptions of human resource practices and/or preferences that could help to review these issues (e.g., AARP 2003, 2008; Eurofound, 2008, 2010).

In general, those countries that are showing an increase in older adult workforce participation are the ones implementing more HR practices oriented toward the retention and recruitment of older workers. However, the situation is becoming progressively more disadvantageous for developing economies that are experiencing an aging of their population at faster paces than developed countries and where only a small proportion of employers are implementing HRM practices toward older workers.

Overall, organizational research and practice adhering to the maintenance model has been focused on the retention of older workers rather than on their recruitment. However, in the Manpower Survey (2007), most of the employers sampled did not report having any strategy to either retain (72%) or recruit older workers (80%).

Trends of Specific HRM Practices for Older Workers in Different Countries

Human resource management policies and practices are the predominant tools and mechanisms that companies use to manage older workers. Research conducted in different countries (mostly in those included in the Liberal group) has linked specific organizational human resource practices and the retention or early leave of older workers.

With regard to the Liberal countries, Gough (2003) conducted a study on British workers between 55 and 67 years old and concluded that organizations seeking to retain older workers should implement career-planning programs targeted toward building career opportunities as well as establishing new occupational opportunities. Moreover, in a study on Australian older IT employees, Brooke (2009) found that promoting continuity in work and postponing retirement could be achieved by wider use of flexible hours, contracting back to firms, and teleworking (the author termed this practice home-based "E-work"). She also argued that obsolete age stereotypes should be abandoned and new proactive human resource policies and practices introduced to prolong the working lives of older IT employees. Another study suggested that promoting late careers of older workers in the United States (particularly in the state of Massachusetts) could be achieved through training (Doeringer, Sum, & Terkla, 2002). In the same direction, McNamara and Williamson (2004) pointed toward training programs and employer flexibility as crucial practices to enhance later retirement of the U.S. population between 60 and 80 years of age. Recently, Armstrong-Stassen (2005) carried out a study on Canadian nurses aged 50 and over to examine human resource management strategies that are most important in retaining older nurses in the workforce. Practices such as flexible work schedules, compensation (improving benefits,

offering incentives for continued employment), and recognition and respect (showing appreciation for a job well done; recognizing the experience, knowledge, skills, and expertise of older nurses; ensuring that older nurses are treated with respect by others in the organization) were the practices that were most effective in preventing older nurses from leaving the workforce. In a similar line of thought, it has been argued that employers' policies and practices toward older workers influence earlier exit in the United Kingdom (Taylor et al., 2000).

Taken together, these studies show that human resource practices have a clear influence on retirement behaviors and intentions of older workers. However, more systematic analysis is needed of specific practices and how they tend to be used and how they operate in different types of countries. In addition, more studies are needed in other regions to see if the results from Liberal countries can be generalized to other regions.

In the next section we will focus on reviewing the evidence available on how the most relevant human resource management practices—such as selection, retention, training and personal development, and flexible work arrangements and new kinds of work—tend to be implemented in different countries. Further, we will explore their implications for older workers' continuation in or early retirement from the workforce.

Recruitment and selection. Manpower (2007) reports that some liberal countries, such as Singapore, show a relatively high proportion of employers having a strategy to recruit older workers. Harper et al. (2006) showed that in the Liberal countries, and more concretely in the United Kingdom, efforts have been made in order to recruit older workers; 44% of employers in the United Kingdom recognize a need to develop those practices. A third of the employers surveyed in Canada, the United States, Japan, Hong Kong, and Brazil indicated that they seek to recruit older workers. In some developing countries such as Russia, Indonesia, and China, less than 10% of employers actively attempt to recruit older workers. Although Chinese organizations are experiencing problems due to a lack of younger workers to hire (Meng & Bai, 2007) and a lack of awareness of serious labor shortages (Harper et al., 2006), a relatively low proportion of them actively try to recruit older workers.

Harpers' data are coherent with an OECD (2006) report that shows that hiring rates of older workers are highest in Liberal countries (Australia, Canada, the United Kingdom, and the United States) as well as one post–communist economy, the Slovak Republic. On the contrary, the lowest rates (only about 4%) were found in Central and South Europe (the Netherlands, Belgium, Italy, and Portugal). Moreover, those unemployed for a year or more had a higher chance of finding a new job in the United Kingdom (40%) than in Social-Democratic, Central, South, and East European countries (Belgium, Finland, France, Germany, Greece, Poland, and Sweden). In the United States, the AARP found an increase in the time period between 2002 and 2007 in older workers' expectations of finding a job after unemployment (AARP, 2008).

It has been argued that these cross-national differences could be related to the cost of wages related to age, as those countries with low costs associated with age are the countries in which older workers have a greater probability of being recruited and hired. However, the low proportions of recruitment and hiring of older workers in some developing countries with low wages associated with age seem to challenge this assertion. It is also noteworthy that in the United Kingdom, recruitment procedures are more regulated than in other countries, such as the United States or Australia (McNair & Flynn, 2005). In Singapore, the government has taken an active role in enhancing the employability of the mature workforce, which may help to explain relatively high levels of older worker recruitment (AARP, 2009; Manpower, 2007). Thus, nations with higher rates of older worker recruitment and selection are also those that have developed governmental policies and practices aimed at increasing the recruitment and selection of older workers. For instance, Canada has increased job-assistance programs targeted specifically to older workers. At the same time, Canada is also providing additional training funding for older unemployed persons in order to increase their employability (OECD, 2009).

Retention. In their cross-national research, Harper et al. (2006) found that in developed countries, employers are more aware of the importance of retaining older workers than in developing countries. This is most probably due to the fact that in the latter, there are higher proportions of young employees. However, it is also true that in some of these developing countries, the pace of aging seems to be much faster than in developed countries. This poses a potential problem because the aging of the population will reach higher proportions under a lower level of development compared to industrialized countries.

More favorable levels of practices and attitudes directed toward the retention of older workers have been reported by employers in Liberal countries (the United States, Canada, Hong Kong, and Singapore), with employers showing the highest levels of encouragement of older workers to continue working (almost 80% of the employers) and the most attempts to retain older workers with hard-to-replace skills (Harper et al., 2006; Manpower, 2007). In China, Egypt, India, Indonesia, Japan, Malaysia, Poland, and Russia, less than half of employers reported that they encourage older workers to continue working (Harper et al., 2006). Conversely, in the Manpower Report (Manpower, 2007), Japan showed the highest rates of older worker retention strategies (80%). Again, the authors of the report referred to a governmental initiative in Japan to explain the high rates in those retention practices, pointing out the close relationship between macro-level initiatives (governmental and employer policies and practices) and policies promoting the retention of older workers.

As previously noted, although the proportion of employers encouraging full early retirement is relatively low in all nations, Europe in general shows the highest percentage of employers encouraging this practice (19% of employers), while managers from Denmark report the least encouragement of early retirement in this geographical area (Leber & Wagner, 2007). Latin America closely follows Europe in the proportion of managers encouraging early retirement (17.7%), and the next highest rate comes from Asia (15.2%), followed by some Liberal countries (the United States and Canada, at 14.5%). Employers in Africa and in the Liberal countries of Asia have the lowest levels of such encouragement (8.8%).

In some transitional economies in Asia, results of these surveys show a critical situation. Although the encouragement of full early retirement is not very common, they show one of the lowest levels of recruitment of older workers (19.5%) together with the lowest levels of actions addressed to retain older workers with hard-to-replace skills (52.7%) and encouragement of older workers to continue working (49.5%). In those areas, employers do not seem to encourage older workers to leave the work role but also fail to employ specific actions addressed to retain them, which could be interpreted by older workers as a lack of interest in and need for their work roles.

Training and personal development. The OECD (2006) report showed that the incidence of training decreased with employee age in all of the industrialized countries surveyed. However, some industrialized countries seem to be achieving some advances in this area. For instance, findings from the fifth European Working Conditions Survey (Eurofound, 2010) show that, although there is still a decrease in the opportunities of training with age, opportunities for older workers have increased more sharply for older workers than for younger workers, alleviating some of the discrepancy between them.

In both the Harper et al. (2006) and OECD (2006) surveys, important discrepancies between countries have been found. In the OECD report, training for workers between 50 and 64 years of age (specifically, the percentage of employees who participated in education or training during the previous twelve months) was higher in some of the Liberal and Social-Democratic countries (specifically Sweden, Denmark, Norway, Australia, Switzerland, and the United Kingdom). The lowest percentages were reported for some East (Hungary) and South European countries (Italy, Portugal, and Spain). Cross-national differences in training opportunities for older workers paralleled those of younger workers. In the Eurostat Labour Force Survey (1997), it was reported that European countries that clearly show higher rates of training opportunities within the work environment are the ones showing higher participation rates of older workers in the workforce in recent years (Sweden, Denmark, the United Kingdom, and Austria) and are also the ones that have begun to notice a reversal in the trend toward early exit from the workforce (e.g., Finland and the Netherlands).

The OECD (2006) report also suggests that even in those countries with higher levels of training for older workers, there are some groups of workers that are disfavored in this regard. For instance, although in the United States the training opportunities for older workers are quite good compared to other countries, for low-skilled workers levels of training are low regardless of employee age. The same trend appears in other countries such as Australia.

The Globalife project,[3] which analyzed late-stage careers in eleven OECD countries, also showed the highest rates of participation in training of older workers in Social-Democratic countries (Hofäcker et al., 2010) while showing that Central and South European countries had the lowest levels of participation in training for older workers. Less than 5% of older employees in Germany, Spain, and Italy reported that they had received job- or career-related training in the previous four weeks (Hofäcker et al., 2010). This situation seems to be changing, since the latest findings in the Eurofound Survey on working conditions (Eurofound, 2010) indicate an improvement in educational opportunities for older workers in some of the South European and Central European countries (Spain, Italy, Germany, the Netherlands), while there is a decrease in some others (Belgium, Luxemburg, France). It could be expected that in the near future practices are going to change with regard to older worker training opportunities because governments are introducing different measures to increase them. For instance, in France, since 2009, firms are required to provide career plans, including training for older workers.

In their employee survey, Harper et al. (2006) found higher percentages of employers offering older workers the opportunity to learn new skills in Liberal countries (more than 80% of employers in the United States, Canada, and the United Kingdom), while in some Transitional economies, such as China and Russia, the proportions decreased to 15%. In this sense, Messinis and Cheng (2007) found in a sample of migrant workers in Hangzhou of the Zhejiang province that those with high education, high income, and high work effort tended to get more training opportunities, while older workers tended to get less. This situation is clearly linked to the worsening rates of workforce participation among older workers in those countries, since obsolescence of skills has been argued as one of the main causes for their low participation rate (United Nations, 2009).

Personal growth and development is identified by workers in the United States (AARP, 2003, 2008) and in the EU (Eurofound, 2008) as one of the main features of an ideal job. In a similar vein, in a recent study in Belgium, older workers from various organizations reported that in order for them to desire staying in the workforce longer, organizations would have to implement practices that would enhance older workers' job involvement and career aspirations (Buyens, Van Dijk, Dewilde, & De Vos, 2009). In the survey conducted by Harper et al. (2006), in those countries that had already been showing a trend toward an increase in the participation of older adults in the workforce (the United States, the United Kingdom, Canada, and Sweden), a majority of employers (80%) said that they were offering older workers the possibility to guide and teach younger workers. Moreover, in those countries, almost no employer reported offering no possibilities with regard to this issue. Conversely, in some Transitional economies such as Russia, only

26% of employers reported offering these mentoring opportunities. About one-third of employers in China and a quarter in Russia reported offering no training opportunities for older workers at all.

Flexible work arrangements and new kinds of work. Research developed in European countries and in the United States has shown longer working hours to be a push factor into retirement for older workers (Eurofound, 2008; Gustman & Steinmeir, 2004; Penner, Perun, & Steuerle, 2002). This is a particularly strong predictor of retirement in Liberal countries such as Australia, the United States, Canada, Switzerland, and the United Kingdom, where the proportion of male employees that work fifty hours or more per week is higher than in other countries (Manpower, 2007; OECD, 2006). Further development of this idea can be found in the previously mentioned cluster analysis developed by Flynn and McNair (2008). The workers included in the "stressed" cluster were identified as those who simultaneously presented more favorable and unfavorable attitudes toward retirement. The researchers concluded that unfavorable attitudes could be caused by the very demanding characteristics that those workers face in their work (e.g., difficulty balancing home and work commitments due to difficulties downshifting or reducing hours). European Union reports have shown that longer working hours affect mainly southern countries in Europe, while central and northern countries show the shortest number of hours worked in general (Eurofound, 2008).

The results of Harper et al.'s survey (2006) revealed that globally only 28% of employers offer the possibility for older workers to work fewer hours. The researchers also identified several differences by country, ranging from a very high percentage of organizations offering this accommodation (the United Kingdom, 71%), to a medium percentage (the United States 49%, Sweden 50%, Germany 58%, and Canada 53%), to a very low percentage in Transitional economies (such as China, with a percentage of 7% of its urban employers). A similar situation was found with regard to opportunities offered to pursue new kinds of work. The highest proportion of employers offering this opportunity were found in Liberal countries (70% in the United Kingdom and the United States), followed by the industrialized economies of Europe, Canada, Hong Kong, Japan, and Singapore (50%). In China and Russia, only 10% of employers offered this possibility. Another characteristic of work identified by the Eurofound (2008) as highly related to personal growth was the access to a "high-performance work organization" (HPWO) (Eurofound, 2008). Involvement in HPWOs has shown a high impact on the development of professional and relational skills, mental functioning capacity, and workers' satisfaction. Conversely, workers aged 55 and over usually show low involvement in HPWOs, which also might hinder their development possibilities.

In a recent cross-country comparison, DiPierro and Villosio (2009) found that ideal organization forms for older workers were found mostly in the most Liberal countries of the EU (Ireland and the United Kingdom), in the Social-Democratic countries, and in the Netherlands. Work organization forms in those countries are characterized by low work intensity conditions, high autonomy levels, and a widespread incidence of HPWOs. On the contrary, in South Europe they found low intensity conditions and almost no possibility of HPWOs.

Summary. The differences found between employers' practices in different countries seem to show that in some developed countries there is a slow but growing awareness that older workers are important assets for organizations, and thus employers are increasing their efforts to maintain and retain older workers through different human resource policies and practices. Supporting this idea, the survey conducted by Harper et al. (2006) shows that 49% of managers in most developed countries consider the early retirement of older workers to be related to the loss of valuable knowledge and skills for their organizations. Nonetheless, there are still important differences between countries that reflect to a great extent the differences in the trends of their retirement patterns. Indeed, developing countries showing low levels of implementation of human resource practices addressed to retain and recruit older workers also show a lack of awareness of the implications of an aging workforce.

Main Conclusions: Trends and Challenges for Research and Practice

The aim of this chapter was to identify patterns of aging workers' retention and/or retirement practices in companies and to show how these practices are aligned with more macro-socioeconomic, political, demographic, and labor market trends in different groups of countries. To achieve this aim, we have first differentiated five groups of countries: Liberal, Social-Democratic, Central European, South European, and Transitional economies, taking into account socioeconomic, legal, labor market, and demographic trends. Then, we have presented relevant features of retirement analyzing differences between the groups of countries. Differences have been identified in aging rates of the population in different regions and also in the participation of older workers in the workforce. Moreover, we pointed out legal and socioeconomic contingencies of cross-national differences in retirement patterns.

A general trend has been established during the last decades in most developed and developing countries toward an aging of the workforce together with a decrease in the retirement age. Under conditions of labor shortage and economic welfare, early retirement of aged employees was promoted through the development of pension schemes, and a compulsory retirement age was established in a large number of countries. In other countries with low or no retirement support policies, older employees still have fewer opportunities to work or access to decent work because of discrimination. However, recently this trend appears to be evolving with a number of demographic changes (decreased birth rate, longer life expectancy, etc.), and the costs of pensions are rapidly increasing in developed and developing countries. Hence, the decrease in retirement age is slowing down and a reversed trend is occurring in some countries where continuity of older workers in the workforce is becoming an important strategic aim.

Taking into account these different realities, we have analyzed retirement patterns in different countries with attention to retirement timing (early, on time, and late) in the groups of countries considered. Consistencies between socioeconomic, legal, and labor markets and the prevalence of these patterns have been noted. However, the central aim of this chapter is to identify, from a multilevel perspective, some of the policies and practices of companies (meso-level) regarding aging workers' retirement, and to what extent human resource practices are consistent with national characteristics and policies (macro-level). In doing so, we have first analyzed the implementation of different types of transition-to-retirement patterns in terms of their flexibility (immediate full-time permanent retirement, phased retirement, and bridge employment). Although important differences across countries within the same group exist, trends are clear and consistent between groups of countries considered, and those trends are coherent with the political and economic situations and policies used to manage national labor market and production demands.

Moreover, we examined two potential frameworks underlying human resource management practices toward older workers (the depreciation and the maintenance model) and analyzed existing evidence for the different groups of countries. Interestingly, based on this analysis, we can conclude that while depreciation practices are well implemented in general, maintenance practices are not so prevalent. In this way, the evidence available regarding the maintenance model is mainly on practices and characteristics of older workers who prefer to continue working instead of going into early retirement. Although the prevalence of these practices is generally low, we identified differences across groups of countries indicating that the Liberal and Social-Democratic countries are the most advanced in implementing these practices. Finally, we analyzed more specifically how the use of different human resource practices—such as recruitment and selection, retention, training and personnel development, and flexible work arrangements and new forms of work—are implemented in organizations across different countries. We found differences on how these practices are being used in different countries for "pushing" aged workers from work or for "pulling" and retaining them in the workforce.

In general, we observed that in the socioeconomic and labor contexts where there is a shortage of workers and the cost of pensions is high, governments are promoting policies to retain older workers at work and to delay retirement. However, appropriate practices in companies aiming to retain older workers are not clearly established. Several national governments in Europe are trying to reverse the policies supporting early retirement, but few employers are changing their attitudes and practices in a similar direction. In Liberal countries, retaining policies are also promoted, but in developing countries this trend is not yet occurring although often older workers continue working under poorer conditions because of financial reasons.

Changing the trends from early retirement toward retention of aged workers at work requires the involvement of all social agents: governments, employers, trade unions, and employees. Such a shift requires not only changing national policies and laws but also implementing new human resource policies and practices at the organizational level. Moreover, it implies changing societal and organizational culture in a way that reduces stereotypes and discriminatory practices. In addition, an effort must be made to reorganize and redesign work systems in their content and context in a way that makes them more suitable for older workers to contribute with the best of their resources in a culture in which they perceive value, appreciation, and recognition for their contributions. There is a large repository of knowledge about preferences of older workers, and some good practices have been put in place. However, generalized implementation of these practices in different companies has still to be developed and evaluated. Researchers should continue the identification of more suitable human resource policies and practices for older workers and their effective participation and performance at work. Design, implementation, monitoring, and evaluation of these practices in different contexts are strongly needed. Moreover, as the proportion of older workers increases in organizations all over the world, it will become increasingly important to manage intergenerational cooperation and appropriate fairness and justice in these relations within the organizations.

More research is also needed on the complex relationships between national and supranational policies. Specifically, researchers should examine the way organizations implement and moderate these policies in their own human resource policies and practices concerning retirement age and the improvement of older workers' work content, context, performance, and well-being. Given shifts in workforce gender composition as well as age, gender differences should also be considered in research on these issues.

In sum, profound changes in work context, work activities, and workers themselves call for strong, cutting-edge research to help researchers and practitioners better understand how to manage these shifts, as well as how to guide the design implementation and evaluation of strategies and practices that will allow older workers to remain productive and integral pieces of the global workforce.

Author Note

The authors are grateful for the financial support of the Spanish Agency of Science and Technology (BSO2002-04483-C03-01) and the Spanish Agency of Education and Science (SEJ2005-05375, within the CONSOLIDER project SEJ2006-14086).

Notes

1. Retirement income systems are diverse and difficult to classify. The most common classification to understand this variability divides pension systems into two mandatory tiers (OECD, 2011). The *first-tier* pension is intended primarily to provide a minimum standard of living to all pensioners in a country. Its form can vary widely from one country to another but usually is publicly organized and based in a pay-as-you-go system. Three main types can be differentiated: resource tested or targeted plans, basic schemes, and minimum pensions. The *second tier* is designed to achieve a similar standard of living to the one before retirement. It can be publicly or privately managed and funded in advance or pay-as-you-go. Four types can be identified: defined benefit plans, points schemes, defined contribution plans, and notional account schemes. Private pensions, savings, and other investments shape a non-mandatory *third tier* of the system.

2 HelpAge is a network of organizations that aims to help older people claim their rights, challenge discrimination, and overcome poverty. http://www.helpage.org.

3 The basic idea of the Globalife project is to study the influence of global processes on life courses in OECD-type societies.

References

AARP. (2003). *Staying ahead of the curve 2003: The AARP Work and Career Study.* Washington, DC: AARP Knowledge Management. Retrieved from http://www.nasra.org/resources/aarpexecsumm.pdf.

AARP. (2008). *Staying ahead of the curve 2007: The AARP Work and Career Study.* Washington, DC: AARP Knowledge Management. Retrieved from http://assets.aarp.org/rgcenter/econ/work_career_08.pdf.

AARP. (2009). *Reinventing retirement in Asia. Employment and active engagement beyond 50.* (No. 8-9). Retrieved from http://www.aarpinternational.org/usr_doc/1.pdf.

Adamchak, D. J. (2001) The effects of age structure on the labor force and retirement in China. *The Social Science Journal 38,* 1–11.

Appelbaum, S. H., Patton, E., & Shapiro, B. (2003). The early retirement incentive program: A downsizing strategy. *Journal of European Industrial Training, 27,* 22–35.

Armstrong-Stassen, M. (2005). Human resource management strategies and the retention of older RNs. *Canadian Journal of Nursing Leadership, 18,* 50–66.

Armstrong-Stassen, M. (2008). Human resource practices for mature workers—And why aren't employers using them? *Asia Pacific Journal of Human Resources, 46,* 334–352.

Armstrong-Stassen, M., & Lee, S. H. (2009). The effect of relational age on older Canadian employees' perceptions of human resource practices and sense of worth to their organization. *The International Journal of Human Resource Management, 20,* 1753–1769.

Armstrong-Stassen, M., & Schlosser, F. K. (2008). Taking a positive approach to organizational downsizing. *Canadian Journal of Administrative Sciences, 25,* 93–106.

Aventur, F. (1994). La formation continue des salariés à partir de 45 ans [Life-long learning of employees over 45 years of age]. In L. Salzberg & A. M. Guillemard (Eds.), *Emploi et Vieillissement* (pp. 89–95). Paris, France: LA Documentation Française.

Belloni, M., Monticone, C., & Trucchi, S. (2006). *Flexibility in retirement: A framework for the analysis and a survey of European countries.* Turin, Italy: European Commission, CeRP.

Brooke, L. (2009). Prolonging the careers of older information technology workers: Continuity, exit or retirement transitions? *Ageing and Society, 29,* 237–256.

BSR. (2010). *A study on the labor shortage and employment guidelines for manufacturers in China* (BSR Report). Retrieved from http://www.bsr.org/research/reports-by-category.cfm?DocumentID=6.

Burke, J. B., & Ng, E. (2006). The changing nature of work and organizations: Implications for human resource management. *Human Resource Management Review, 16*, 86–94.

Buyens, D., Van Dijk, H., Dewilde, T., & De Vos, A. (2009). The aging workforce: Perceptions of career ending. *Journal of Managerial Psychology, 24*, 102–117.

Cahill, K. E., Giandrea, M. D., & Quinn, J. F. (2006). Retirement patterns from career employment. *The Gerontologist, 46*, 514–523.

Calo, T. J. (2005). The generativity track: A transitional approach to retirement. *Public Personnel Management, 34*, 301–312.

Calvo, E., Haverstick, K., & Sass, S. A. (2009). Gradual retirement, sense of control, and retirees' happiness. *Research on Aging, 31,* 112–135.

Clark, R. L., & D'Ambrosio, M. B. (2005). Recruitment, retention, and retirement: Compensation and employment policies for higher education. *Educational Gerontology, 31*, 385–403.

Costa, D. L. (1998). *Evolution of retirement: An American economic history, 1880–1990*. Chicago, IL: University of Chicago Press.

Crego, A. & Alcover, C. M. (2008). *Vidas reinterpretadas. Una aproximación psicosocial a las experiencias de prejubilación. [Reinterpreted lives: A psychosocial approach to the early retirement's experiences]* Madrid: Dykinson.

Daly, M., Hobijn, M., & Kwok, J. (2009). Labor *supply responses to changes in wealth and credit* (FRBSF Economic Letter No. 2009–05). Retrieved from http://www.frbsf.org/publications/economics/letter/2009/el2009-05.pdf.

De Vaus, D., Wells, Y., Kendig, H., & Quine, S. (2007). Does gradual retirement have better outcomes than abrupt retirement? Results from an Australian panel study. *Ageing and Society, 27*, 667–682.

De Vos, K., & Kapteyn, A. (2004). Incentives and exit routes to retirement in the Netherlands. In J. Gruber & D. A. Wise (Eds.), *Social security programs and retirement around the world: Micro-estimation* (pp. 461–498). Chicago, IL: University of Chicago Press.

De Vroom, B. (2004). The shift from early to late exit: Changing institutional conditions and individual preferences: The case of the Netherlands. In T. Maltby, M. L. Mirabile, E. Overbye, & B. De Vroom (Eds.), *Ageing and the transition to retirement: A comparative analysis of European welfare states* (pp 120–153.). New Perspectives on Ageing & Later Life. Hants, England: Ashgate.

Di Pierro D., & Villosio, C. (2009, May). *State and evolution of the organisation of work with an age perspective.* Paper presented at the 4th European Workshop on "Labour Markets and Demographic Change" Vienna, Austria. Retrieved from http://www.oeaw.ac.at/vid/lmdc/download/sess4_4_dipierro_villosio_paper_4lmdc.pdf.

Dibbden, J., & Hibbett, A. (1993, June). Older Workers: An overview of recent research. *Employment Gazette, 101*, 237–250.

Doeringer, P., Sum, A., & Terkla, D. (2002). Devolution of employment and training policy: The case of older workers. *Journal of Aging and Social Policy, 14*(3–4), 37–60.

Dong, Y. (2008). *The early retirement decision and its impact on health: What the Chinese mandatory retirement reveals* [Ongoing research at California State University, Fullerton].

Retrieved from http://business.fullerton.edu/Economics/ydong/Research/RetirementHealth_YDong.pdf.

Ebbinghaus, B. (2006). *Reforming early retirement in Europe, Japan and the USA*. Oxford, United Kingdom: Oxford University Press.

Esping-Andersen, G. (1990). *The three worlds of welfare capitalism*. Princeton, NJ: Princeton University Press.

Esping-Andersen, G. (1999). *Social foundations of postindustrial economies*. New York, NY: Oxford University Press.

Esser, I. (2005). *Continued work or retirement. Preferred exit age in Western European countries*. Stockholm, Sweden: Arbetsrapport/Institutet för Framtidsstudier.

Eurofound. (2008). *Working conditions of an ageing workforce*. Dublin, Ireland: European Foundation for the Improvement of Living and Working Conditions. Retrieved from http://www.eurofound.europa.eu/pubdocs/2008/17/en/2/EF0817EN.pdf.

Eurofound. (2010). *Changes over time—First findings from the fifth European Working Conditions Survey*. Dublin, Ireland: European Foundation for the Improvement of Living and Working Conditions. Retrieved from http://www.eurofound.europa.eu/pubdocs/2010/74/en/2/EF1074EN.pdf.

Farr, J. L., & Ringseis, E. L. (2002). The older worker in organizational context: Beyond the individual. In C. L. Cooper & I. Robertson (Eds.), *International review of industrial and organizational psychology* (pp. 31–75). Chichester, England: John Wiley.

Flynn, M. (2010). The United Kingdom government's "business case" approach to the regulation of retirement. *Ageing and Society,30*, 421–443.

Flynn, M., & McNair, S. (2008). What would persuade older people to stay longer in work? In A. Chiva & J. Manthorpe (Eds.), *Older workers in Europe* (pp. 24–37). Berkshire, England: Open University Press.

Gaillard, M., & Desmette, D. (2010). (In)validating stereotypes about older workers influences their intentions to retire early and to learn and develop. *Basic and Applied Social Psychology, 32,* 86–98.

Gardiner, J., Stuart, M., Forde, C., Greenwood, I., MacKenzie, R., & Perrett, R. (2007). Work-life balance and older workers: Employees' perspectives on retirement transitions following redundancy. *International Journal of Human Resource Management, 18,* 476–489.

Giles, J. (2009). *Economic restructuring and retirement in urban China* [Working Paper]. Boston, MA: Center for Retirement Research at Boston College. Retrieved from : http://crr.bc.edu/wp-content/uploads/2009/01/wp_2008–24.pdf.

Gough, O. (2003). Factors that influence voluntary and involuntary retirement. *Pensions: An International Journal, 8,* 252–264.

Gruber, J. & Wise, D. (1997) *Social security programs and retirement around the world*. NBER working paper series. Retrieved from http://www.nber.org/papers/w6134.

Guillemard, A. M. (2001, November). *Reforming employment and retirement in an ageing society: Difficulties in finding a way out of the end of career inactivity trap in France*. Paper presented at the Millennium Project toward Active Ageing in the 21st Century Conference, Japan Institute of Labor, Tokyo, Japan. Retrieved from http://www.jil.go.jp/jil/seika/fr.pdf.

Gustman, A. L., & Steinmeier, T. L. (2004). *Minimum hours constraints, job requirements and retirement* (NBER Working Paper No. 10876). Cambridge, MA: National Bureau of Economic Research.

Hardy, M. A., & Hazelrigg, L. (1999). A multilevel model of early retirement decisions among autoworkers in plants with different futures. *Research on Aging, 21,* 275–303.

Harper, S. (2006). *Ageing societies: Myths, challenges and opportunities.* London, England: Hodder Arnold.

Harper, S., Khan, H. T. A., Saxena, A., & Leeson, G. (2006). Attitudes and practices of employers towards ageing workers: Evidence from a global survey on the future of retirement. *Ageing Horizons, 5,* 31–41.

Hedge, J. W. (2008). Strategic human resource management and the older worker. *Journal of Workplace Behavioral Health, 23,* 109–123.

Hedge, J. W., Borman, W. C., & Lammlein, S. E. (2006). *The aging workforce. Realities, myths, and implications for organizations.* Washington, DC: American Psychological Association.

Heller, P. S. (2006). *Is Asia prepared for an aging population?* (Working Paper No. 06/272). International Monetary Fund. Retrieved from www.imf.org/external/pubs/ft/wp/2006/wp06272.pdf

HelpAge. (2010). *Forgotten workforce: Older workers work longer, for less.* London: HelpAge International. Retrieved from http://www.cardi.ie/publications/forgottenworkforceolderworkersworklongerforless.

Henkens, K. (2000). Supervisors' attitudes about early retirement of subordinates. *Journal of Applied Social Psychology, 30,* 833–852.

Hofäcker,D., Buchholz, S., & Pollnerová, S. (2010, July) .*Employment and retirement in a globalizing Europe – reconstructing trends and causes from a life course perspective.* Paper for the 2010 Social Policy Association Conference, University of Lincoln, UK, July 5–7, 2010. Retrieved from http://www.social-policy.org.uk/lincoln/Hofaecker.pdf.

Hutchens, R. (2003). *The Cornell study of employer phased retirement policies: A report on key findings.* Ithaca, NY: School of Industrial and Labor Relations, Cornell University.

Hutchens, R., & Grace-Martin, K. (2004). *Who among white collar workers has an opportunity for phased retirement? Establishment characteristics* (IZA Discussion Papers No. 1155). Bonn, Germany: Institute for the Study of Labor.

Kantarci, T., & Van Soest, A. (2008). Gradual retirement: Preferences and limitations. *De Economist, 156,* 113–144.

Kelly, E. L., Dahlin, E. C., Spencer, D., & Moen, P. (2008). Making sense of a mess: Phased retirement policies and practices in the United States. *Journal of Workplace Behavioral Health, 23,* 147–164.

Lawrence, B. S. (1984). Age grading: The implicit organizational timetable. *Journal of Occupational Behavior, 13,* 181–191.

Lawrence, B. S. (1988). New wrinkles in the theory of age: Demography, norms, and performance ratings. *Academy of Management Journal, 31,* 309–337.

Leber, U., & Wagner, A. (2007). *Early and phased retirement in European companies: Establishment survey on working time 2004–2005.* European Foundation for the Improvement of Living and Working Conditions. Luxembourg: Office for Official Publications of the European Communities.

Lin, T. C., & Hsieh, A. T. (2001). Impact of job stress on early retirement intention. *International Journal of Stress Management, 8,* 243–247.

Ling, D.C. & Chi, I. (2008) Determinants of work among older adults in urban China. *Australasian Journal on Ageing, 27,* 126–133.

Luchak, A. L. (1997). Retirement plans and pensions: An empirical study. *Relations Industrielles, 52,* 865–886.

Manfredi, S., & Vickers, L. (2009). Retirement and age discrimination: Managing retirement in higher education. *Industrial Law Journal, 38,* 343–364.

Manpower. (2007). The New Agenda for an Older Workforce (Manpower White Paper). Retrieved from http://www.manpower.com.tw/pdf/older_worker_2007_en.pdf.

Maurer-Fazio, M., & Hughes, J. (2002). *The effects of market liberalization on the relative earnings of Chinese women* (William Davidson Working Paper No. 460). Retrieved from http://ideas.repec.org/p/wdi/papers/2002-460.html.

McNair, S., & Flynn, M. (2005). *The age dimension of employment practice: Employer case studies.* London, England: Department of Trade and Industry. Retrieved from http://www.bis.gov.uk/files/file11436.pdf.

McNair, S., Flynn, M., Owen, L., Humphreys, C., & Woodfield, S. (2004). *Changing work in later life: A study of job transitions.* Guildford, England: University of Surrey, Centre for Research into the Older Workforce (CROW). Retrieved from http://www.swslim.org.uk//downloads/sl2088.pdf.

McNamara, T. K., & Williamson, J. B. (2004). Race, gender, and the retirement decisions of people ages 60 to 80: Prospects for age integration in employment. *International Journal of Aging and Human Development, 59,* 255–286.

Meng, X., & Bai, N. (2007). *How much have the wages of unskilled workers in China increased? Data from seven factories in Guangdong, 2000–2004* (Mimeo). Department of Economics, RSPAS, Australian National University.

Merline, A. C., Cull, W. L., Mulvey, H. J., & Katcher, A. L. (2010). Patterns of work and retirement among pediatricians aged ≥50 years. *Pediatrics, 125,* 158–164.

Messinis, G., & Cheng, E. (2007). *The value of education and job training in the developing world: New evidence from migrant workers in China* (Working Paper No. 36).Center for Strategic Economic Studies. Retrieved from http://www.cfses.com/documents/wp36.pdf.

Metcalf, H., & Meadows, P. (2006). *Survey of employers' policies, practices and preferences relating to age.* Department of Work and Pension (Research Report No. 325, DTI Employment Relations Research Series No. 49). London, England: The Stationary Office. Retrieved from http://campaigns.dwp.gov.uk/asd/asd5/rports2005-2006/rrep325.pdf.

Mykletun, A., Mykletun, R. J. & Solem, P. E. (2000). *Holdninger til alder og arbeid i kommunesektoren. Muligheter for å motvirke tidlig yrkesavgang* [Attitudes towards age and work in the municipality sector. Possibilities of counteracting early exit]. Oslo: KLP forsikring. KLP rapport 2000.

Naegele, G., & Krämer, K. (2001). Recent developments in the employment and retirement of older workers in Germany. *Journal of Aging and Social Policy, 13,* 69–92.

National Research Council Panel on a Research Agenda and New Data for an Aging World Staff. (2001). *Preparing for an aging world: The case for cross-national research.* Washington, DC: National Academies Press.

Nusbaum, N. J. (2009). Commentary: Physician retirement and physician shortages. *Journal of Community Health, 34,* 353–356.

Organisation for Economic Co-operation and Development. (2000). *Reforms for an ageing society A Progress Report to G8 Employment Ministers.* Paris, France: Author.

Organisation for Economic Co-operation and Development. (2003). *Retirement behaviour in OECD countries: Impact of old-age pension schemes and other social transfer programmes* (OECD Economic Studies no. 37). Paris, France: Author. Retrieved from http://www.oecd.org/dataoecd/12/23/34561950.pdf.

Organisation for Economic Co-operation and Development. (2006). *Live longer, work longer*. Paris, France: Author.

Organisation for Economic Co-operation and Development. (2010). *Employment outlook. Moving beyond the job crisis*. Paris, France: Author.

Organisation for Economic Co-operation and Development. (2011). *Pensions at a glance. Retirement-income systems in OECD and G20 countries*. Paris, France: Author.

Pang, L., de Brauw, A., & Rozelle, S. D. (2004). Working until you drop: The elderly of rural China. *The China Journal*, 52, 73–94.

Patrickson, M. (2003). Human resource management and the ageing workforce. In R. Weisner & B. Millett (Eds.), *Human resource management: Challenges and future directions* (pp. 33–43). Brisbane, Australia: Wiley.

Penner, R. G., Perun, P., & Steuerle, C. E. (2002). *Legal and institutional impediments to partial retirement and part-time work by older workers* (Urban Institute Research Report). Washington, DC: Urban Institute.

Perun, P. (2002). Phased retirement programs for the twenty-first century workplace. *John Marshall Law Review, 35*, 633–672.

Potočnik, K., Tordera, N., & Peiró, J. M. (2009). The role of human resource practices and group norms in the retirement process. *European Psychologist, 14*, 193–206.

Potočnik, K., Tordera, N., & Peiro, J. M. (2010). The influence of the early retirement process on satisfaction with early retirement and psychological well-being. *International Journal of Aging and Human Development, 70*, 251–273.

Price, R. H., & Fang, L. (2002). Unemployed Chinese workers: The survivors, the worried young and the discouraged old. *The International Journal of Human Resource Management, 13*, 416–430.

Potočnik, K., Tordera, N., & Peiro, J. M. (in press). Truly satisfied or just resigned? A study of pathways towards different patterns of retirement satisfaction. *Journal of Applied Gerontology*. doi:10.1177/0733464811405988.

Queiroz, B. (2007). The determinants of male retirement in urban Brazil. *Nova Economia, Belo Horizonte, 17*, 11–36.

Remery, C., Henkens, K., Schippers, J., & Ekamper, P. (2003). Managing an aging workforce and a tight labor market: Views held by Dutch employers. *Population Research and Policy Review, 22*, 21–40.

Samodorov, A. (1999). *Ageing and labor markets for older workers* (Employment and Training Papers No. 33). Geneva, Switzerland: Employment and Training Department. International Labour Office Geneva. Retrieved from http://www.ilo.org/wcmsp5/groups/public/@ed_emp/documents/publication/wcms_120333.pdf.

Shacklock, K., & Shacklock, A. (2005, December). *The ageing workforce: Ethical implications for HRM practitioners*. ANZAM Conference Proceedings, Canberra, Australia. Retrieved from http://www98.griffith.edu.au/dspace/bitstream/10072/2881/1/29406_1.pdf.

Sheaks, C. (2007). The state of phased retirement: Facts, figures, and policies. *Generations, 31*, 57–62.

Shi, S. J. (2007). *Old-Age pensions and life course in rural China: The emergence of modern retirement?* (Unpublished doctoral dissertation). Faculty of Sociology, University of Bielefeld, Germany. Retrieved from http://bieson.ub.uni-bielefeld.de/volltexte/2007/1076/pdf/Dissertation.pdf.

Shore, L. M., Chung-Herrera, B. G., Dean, M. A., Ehrhart, K. H., Jung, D. I., Randel, A. E., & Singh, G. (2009). Diversity in organizations: Where are we now, and where are we going? *Human Resource Management Review, 19*, 117–133.

Siegrist, J., Wahrendorf, M., Von dem Knesebeck, O., Jürges, H., & Börsch-Supan, A. (2006). Quality of work, well-being, and intended early retirement of older employees—baseline results from the SHARE study. *European Journal of Public Health, 17*, 62–68.

Solem, E., & Overbye, E. (2004). Norway: Still high employment among older workers. In T. Maltby, M. L. Mirabile, E. Overbye, & B. De Vroom (Eds.), *Ageing and the transition to retirement: A comparative analysis of European welfare states* (pp. 18–40). New Perspectives on Ageing & Later Life. Hants, England: Ashgate.

Southam, K. (2010). *Australia "ageist against mature age workers."* Retrieved from http://advertisers.careerone.com.au/hr/hr-best-practices/recruiting-hiring-advice/screening-job-candidates/report-labels-Australia-ageist-against-mature-age-workers.aspx.

Suso, A. (2004). Ageing and work in Spain. The end of working life? In T. Maltby, M. L. Mirabile, E. Overbye, & B. De Vroom (Eds.), *Ageing and the transition to retirement: A comparative analysis of European welfare states* (pp. 260–281). New Perspectives on Ageing & Later Life. Hants, England: Ashgate.

Takala, M. (1999). *The part-time pension programme in Finland*. Paper presented at the Active Strategies for an Ageing Workforce Conference, Turku, Finland.

Taylor, P., Tillsley, C., Beausoleil, J., Wilson, R., & Walker, A. (2000). *Factors affecting retirement* (Age and Employment Reports 2000–2004). UK Department for Work and Pensions. Retrieved from http://campaigns.dwp.gov.uk/asd/asd5/agepositive2001-2004.asp#far.

Taylor, P. E., & Walker, A. (1994). The aging workforce—Employers' attitudes towards older people. *Work, Employment and Society, 8*, 569–591.

Tillsley, C. (2000). *Factors affecting retirement: Executive summary*. Research report (Great Britain. Department for Education and Employment); no. 236.

Topa, G., Depolo, M., Moriano, J. A., & Morales, J. F. (2009). Empleo puente y bienestar personal de los jubilados. Un modelo de ecuaciones estructurales con una muestra Europea probabilística [Bridge employment and retirees' personal well-being. A structural equation model on European probabilistic sample]. *Psicothema, 21*, 280–287.

United Nations. (2002, March). *Decent jobs: Social inclusion and social protection*. United Nations Department of Public Information DPI/2264. Retrieved from http://www.globalaging.org/waa2/articles/decentjobs.htm.

United Nations. (2009). *World population ageing 2009*. New York, NY: Author. Retrieved from http://www.un.org/esa/population/publications/WPA2009/WPA2009_WorkingPaper.pdf

Van Soest, A., Kapteyn A., & Zissimopoulos J. (2006). Using stated preferences data to analyze preferences for full and partial retirement, *DNB working paper* 081, Netherlands Central Bank, Research Department. Retrieved from http://arno.uvt.nl/show.cgi?fid=57901.

Vickerstaff, S. (2006). I'd rather keep running to the end and then jump off the cliff. Retirement decisions: Who decides? *Journal of Social Policy, 35,* 455–472.

Walker, A., & Taylor, P. (1999, Winter). Good practices in the employment of older workers in Europe. *Ageing International, 25*(3), 62–79.

Wang, M., Zhan, Y., Liu, S., & Shultz, K. S. (2008). Antecedents of bridge employment: A longitudinal investigation. *Journal of Applied Psychology, 93,* 818–830.

Willett, M. (2005). Early retirement and phased retirement programs for the public sector. *Benefits and Compensation Digest, 42*(4), 31–35.

Yeatts, D. E., Folts, W. E., & Knapp, J. (2000) Older workers' adaptation to a changing workplace: Employment issues for the 21st century. *Educational Gerontology, 26,* 565–582.

PART 5

Future Trends and Conclusions

The Changing Nature of Work and Retirement

Kenneth S. Shultz *and* Deborah A. Olson

Abstract

We begin this chapter with a discussion of the macro-level changes, such as globalization, diversity, and technological advancements, that are changing work in the twenty-first century. Then, we discuss the more prominent micro-level changes influencing the nature of work, such as opportunities for lifelong learning and rewards; changes with regard to employee expectations, particularly with regard to work-life balance and personal flexibility; and an increased focus on the use of talents. Next, we shift to discussing the changing nature of retirement, examining how individual attributes, job and organizational factors, family factors, and socioeconomic factors are all changing the way we think about retirement. We next focus on two emerging concepts, work ability and bridge employment, and examine how they are shaping how we think about retirement in the twenty-first century. The need to look at both the antecedents and outcomes of retirement from a multilevel perspective is discussed next, before we conclude with several recommendations for future research.

Key Words: retirement, bridge employment, work ability, use of talents, older workers, mid- and late career

Cascio (1995) discussed the "changing world of work," outlining factors such as increased global competition, the information technology explosion, re-engineering of business processes, the shift in mature economies from manufacturing products to providing services, and how the concept of a "job" (as a distinct bundle of tasks) may quickly become a thing of the past. While most of the issues that Cascio discussed still ring true more than a decade and a half later, new and emerging trends in the changing world of work are also surfacing. For example, work itself is generally becoming less physical but more psychologically demanding (Johnson, Mermin, & Resseger, 2007). The pace of technological advancement is accelerating even faster than was imagined in the 1990s. In addition, the nature of careers and the expectations of individuals (e.g., for work-life balance and flexibility regarding when/how work is completed) are rapidly changing. However, while Cascio focused on how the changing world of work was impacting the field of industrial and organizational psychology, we will focus on how the changing nature of work is redefining how the process and expectations of retirement are being reshaped in the twenty-first century.

We begin this chapter by discussing both the broad macro-level changes that impact how work is completed (e.g., increased globalization and the impact of diversity in working relationships) as well as more micro-level factors (e.g., the need for lifelong learning, use of talents, and finding meaning in work and retirement) that are impacting the nature of work in the twenty-first century. We focus predominantly on how these changes are impacting individuals in their mid- and late careers and, thereby, their subsequent transition to retirement.

In particular, we note how these various factors are changing the meaning of working for individuals, especially at older ages. We then explore how retirement itself is changing. Specifically, we delineate how the way individuals prepare for, make decisions about, and adjust to retirement is being impacted by the rapid pace of change. We will also discuss several pioneering topics that should be particularly relevant to the changing nature of retirement in the twenty-first century, including the concepts of bridge employment and workability. We begin, however, with a discussion of the changing nature of work more generally.

The Changing Nature of Work

Significant changes have occurred not only in how organizations have evolved and how work is completed but also in what people expect from work and retirement. In light of these changing expectations, organizational leaders have had to identify ways to adapt the organizational culture and human resource practices to accommodate and support these new expectations to attract and retain employees (Noe, Hollenbeck, Gerhart, & Wright, 2009). For example, creating and nurturing an organizational culture that supports work-life balance, lifelong learning, and flexible scheduling to accommodate workers' personal needs and preferences are more important than ever to attract and retain top performers, particularly those in their mid- and late careers (Wang, Olson, & Shultz, 2013). While there are many factors that could be discussed when we reflect on the changing nature of work, we will focus especially on those factors that directly impact workers in their mid- and late careers, and thus the expectations that individuals have for their retirement.

Macro-level Changes in Work and the Work Context

GLOBALIZATION

Globalization is a given in the world in which we live (Guillen, 2001). Even if an organization does not have facilities, offices, or employees in other countries, it probably has suppliers who are producing goods and providing services that originate in countries outside its own. Globalization specifically refers to the economic, cultural, and social interfaces among people who occupy geographically separate locations (Ohmae, 2005; Wolf, 2004). To operate successfully in a global environment, leaders and employees in those organizations need to be able to develop meaningful relationships with people in other countries who may have different

cultures and expectations. Technology and transportation advances have also accelerated the global interdependence and connectivity among organizations. With a broader reach, organizations have been able to access new markets to sell their goods and services, but they also have access now to a wider pool of people from which to recruit new talent, who are able to perform tasks and create new products, services, and processes (Van der Heijden, 2002). The trend toward outsourcing and offshoring has increased the competitive nature of finding and keeping jobs for individuals in all sectors. This trend can put even greater pressure on those who are seeking work in their mid- and late careers to continue to develop and keep their skills up to date and regularly use technology and other tools that will make them attractive candidates for employers, wherever they are located (House, Javidan, & Dorfman, 2001).

THE IMPACT OF DIVERSITY AND TECHNOLOGY

Along with globalization, the focus on diversity and how to integrate individuals who have divergent values, beliefs, traditions, and experiences has been paramount (House et al., 2001). To address these challenges, organizational leaders need to continue to develop and refine selection and training strategies to facilitate workplace diversity and build relationships among people so that they can work together to achieve organizational goals (Molleman, 2005). When organizational leaders focus on diversity, they often are referring to surface-level factors that are typically clearly observable, for example, race, age, gender, ethnicity, and physical abilities (Richards, 2000). The evolution in the workplace, however, has taken this to a deeper level to include diversity in terms of geographic location, behavioral style, parental status, educational level, religion, first language, and life experiences (van Knippenberg, De Dreu, & Homan, 2004). All of these factors impact how individuals perceive problems, make decisions, and communicate with others, as well as their beliefs and attitudes about what is "right" and "wrong." Of course, as individuals age and progress through mid- and late careers, their individual diversity will continue to grow as their life experiences continue to accumulate and expand.

In an attempt to streamline costs, more organizations are using virtual teams, having individuals in a variety of jobs and in different locations, all of whom need to be able to seamlessly share information and integrate their work. This change indicates the need to have strong technology skills (Charness

& Boot, 2009; Noe et al., 2009). Again, individuals in their mid- and late careers who have developed their technology skills and maintained their "knowledge expertise" will have the greatest number of available options to choose from and will have the most flexibility in terms of when and how they do their work. The internal motivation to learn and continue to develop and refine their skills would directly contribute to individuals' success in their mid- and late careers (Shultz & Wang, 2008).

For individuals in their mid- and late careers, a unique form of diversity that needs to be addressed is when a younger supervisor has an individual in his or her mid- or late career as a direct report. As individuals continue to work longer, the likelihood of older workers having younger supervisors is going to become more prominent. To understand the dynamics of this relationship, Van der Heijden (2010) examined the impact of age differences between supervisors and employees on performance ratings. The results indicated that having a high-quality working relationship between the supervisor and the employee had a positive impact on perceptions of performance when there was a significant age difference between the supervisor and the employee. The practical implications of these results underscore the importance of developing and maintaining positive working relationships with others. Individuals who have positive working relationships with their supervisors can also have greater access to training and development opportunities. Developing new skills and/or refining existing skills can be highly motivating for those individuals who seek out lifelong learning opportunities (Van der Heijden & Van der Heijden, 2006). As the workforce is becoming older on average, age diversity will invariably increase, as older workers will bring a wider variety of experiences, personal characteristics, and talents to organizations. Working in an organizational culture in which individuals are valued even as they reach their retirement years will contribute to feelings of career success. The evaluation of having completed a successful career will in turn make a positive contribution to feelings of a successful retirement (Wang & Shultz, 2010).

Micro-level Changes in Work
OPPORTUNITIES FOR LIFELONG LEARNING AND REWARDS

Individuals at all stages of their careers and work life engage in work activities to receive specific rewards and outcomes. Financial rewards are highly valued outcomes for individuals in their early and mid-careers since they often are paying mortgages, raising children, managing debt, and saving for retirement. However, for individuals in their late career, the financial rewards may become less important, and the ability to work in organizations and in jobs that provide continued opportunities for growth and development may become more important (Loi & Shultz, 2007). Thus, creating a culture within organizations that values diversity and continued personal growth, and working with leaders who support and encourage individuals in their late career to stay engaged, are more important than financial rewards (Deal, 2007).

Many trends have impacted the type of skills and abilities that are needed to be effective in today's organizations. The emphasis today in most organizations is on knowledge workers and the unique skills that they possess. This shift to the value of knowledge requires that individuals stay current in their areas of expertise and identify trends and changes that can impact the work they are doing and the product or service their organization provides (Calo, 2008; Drucker, 2001). The shift from physical skills required in a manufacturing-based economy to cognitive and interpersonal skills required in a knowledge-based economy has direct implications for knowledge workers in their mid- and late careers (Wang, Olson, & Shultz, 2013), as well as for the training and development systems in all organizations (Shultz & Wang, 2008). For example, the decrease in the physical demands of work makes it easier for older workers to continue work, and thus delay retirement. However, increased cognitive and social demands may be particularly stressful for older workers (Shultz, Wang, Crimmins, & Fisher, 2010).

This shift to the importance of knowledge workers also has a direct impact on recruiting and hiring practices in organizations as well, including older workers who may be engaging in bridge employment during retirement (Taylor, Shultz, & Doverspike, 2005). The emphasis has now shifted to identifying cognitive skills (complex problem solving and decision making) and the importance of interpersonal skills (to work effectively with a wide range of other knowledge workers) and also selecting for specific skills (e.g., operating equipment or programming skills), many of which require the use of technology (Charness & Boot, 2009). Greller (2006) found that for individuals in their late career who were motivated and satisfied in their work roles, they were more likely to continue to engage in training and development activities to build new skills. This result emphasizes the importance of having meaningful work and the ability of older workers to use their talents at work in order to remain engaged and committed.

Today, individuals place greater emphasis on the ability to use their talents in meaningful ways on a daily basis as they complete their work and achieve significant goals for the organization (Buckingham & Clifton, 2001; Peterson & Seligman, 2003). Individuals expect that their managers will be facilitators, mentors, and supporters, rather than planners, organizers, and controllers of the work process and outcomes (Drucker, 2001; Wellins, Byham, & Wilson, 1991). As a result, the organizational context can directly impact the opportunities given to individuals in their mid- and late careers and the quality of the work that they are assigned. For example, role autonomy and freedom to make decisions have a direct impact on workers' perceptions of their work. The research of Kohn and Schooler (1983) demonstrated that the ability to have occupational self-control (defined as autonomy, decision-making latitude, task variety, and developmental opportunities) was directly related to the level of work identification, job commitment, and centrality of work in employees' lives.

Without a supportive organizational culture and management practices, individuals often make the decision to leave their position and seek new opportunities. In relationship to individuals in their mid- and late careers, Johnson, Kawachi, and Lewis (2009) found that for workers over 50 who decided to change jobs, they were willing to accept positions in which they made less money and were offered fewer pension and health benefits. In their new positions, these workers who were over 50 reported higher levels of satisfaction because their new positions offered more flexible work hours and were less stressful than their previous positions. Further, older workers who make the decision to change careers are most likely to move out of managerial jobs and move into sales and operations positions. The majority of individuals who downshifted reported that even though their new jobs were less prestigious and had a lower social standing, they enjoyed their new jobs more than the previous jobs they held (Johnson et al., 2009).

Research on the transition between full-time work and retirement has shown that individuals who evaluated their pre-retirement work to be satisfying tended to seek out activities that satisfied them in similar ways in retirement and were more likely to work in roles that were in their profession, rather than starting over in roles that required different skills and talents (Gobeski & Beehr, 2009; Wang, Zhan, Liu, & Shultz, 2008). Thus, it is reasonable to propose that the ability to continue to learn and develop the skills and talents that had been honed and nurtured during one's career, and to continue to experience self-efficacy by achieving outcomes that one finds personally rewarding, would positively impact the transition to retirement (Wang, Adams, Beehr, & Shultz, 2009). Accordingly, one factor in how work has changed over the past several decades is that individuals expect to learn and continue to develop new skills throughout their careers.

EMPLOYEE EXPECTATIONS: WORK-LIFE BALANCE AND FLEXIBILITY

Work-life balance has become one of the most important factors in attracting and retaining high-performing people. No matter what the individual worker's age, ethnicity, parental status, or educational level, one of the most important employee benefits is the ability to have flexible schedules and policies/practices that will allow the worker to work and meet his or her overall needs in life (Bennis & Thomas, 2002; Fugate, Kinicki, & Ashforth, 2004). With the expansion of technology and the range of tools that employees can use, they have the ability to be in touch with their work 24/7. This has caused a reaction on the part of employees who want to have flexibility to complete their work in a way that allows them to meet their personal needs as well. For example, it may well be easier for someone to leave work early to take care of personal business and then at 8:00 p.m. turn on his or her computer and finish the work that he or she started earlier that day. Flexible work schedules not only facilitate the ability of employees to meet their work-life needs but are also essential to address the challenges posed by globalization, where coworkers in Europe may be just ending their workday as workers in the United States are beginning theirs. For workers of all ages, the ability to respond flexibly and identify new options and alternatives that contribute to organizational performance is essential. The stereotype of older workers is that they can be resistant to change (Shultz & Wang, 2008).

NOT JUST WORK: MEANINGFUL WORK AND USE OF TALENTS

Work satisfies a range of needs: economic stability, financial security, skill development, social status, a sense of belonging to a group, recognition for superior work, and the ability to develop one's talents. While all of these elements are important, there is a growing expectation that work will provide value beyond financial and social, by giving workers meaning and a sense of purpose that permeates their lives. Research conducted on the meaning of work over the past fifty years has shown that the vast majority of people (up to 95%) report that they would continue to engage in work activities even if they did not need to do so for economic reasons (Harpaz & Fu, 2002). These results are consistent regardless of culture, age group, occupation, or gender of the participants. The meaning that individuals experience through their work could emanate from the importance of the work being completed, or the engagement of individuals' talents through their work, or the feeling that their work contributes to the greater good. Pratt and Ashforth (2003) state that one of the most consistent findings is that those who find meaning in their work are more satisfied with their jobs.

As individuals move through their career, their definition of what is meaningful can change and evolve (Baltes, Rudolph, & Bal, 2012). Meaning does not come from the *kind* of work one is doing, but from the *relationship* one has with the work being completed. Wrzesniewski (2003) argues that meaningful work can be created and enhanced through the process she defines as job recrafting. The actual process of recrafting one's work could take several forms: individuals can (1) change the way they approach the tasks that need to be completed in their work, (2) decrease the type and/or number of tasks that they need to complete, or (3) change the number of interactions they have with others in the process of completing their work. Creating a culture in which individuals have freedom to decide which tasks to emphasize and how to complete those tasks allows individuals to make choices about how to use their talents to complete their work in the best way for them. Also, for individuals who are performing the same tasks, they can collectively determine the optimal way to complete those tasks, thereby creating meaning for each individual and optimizing performance for the organization (Gaillard & Desmette, 2010; Wrzesniewski, 2003).

Meaningful work, by definition, would engage the energy and focus of the individuals performing the work tasks and activities. Buckingham and Clifton (2001) have discussed in detail the importance of engaging one's talents at work and the experience that creates for individuals. Individuals who are using their talents at work are naturally energized and engaged when learning information that draws on their talents and facilitates their ability to achieve higher levels of performance. Creating and changing the accountabilities in specific jobs in a way that allows individuals to use their talents, and giving them the freedom to make their own decisions about what steps need to be taken to achieve those results, will optimize the results accomplished. For example, formal job descriptions can undermine the ability of individual workers to use their talents and find meaning in the work for which they are responsible. Instead, organization leaders can determine what *must be* done in a specific way for safety or other legal reasons, and then define what approaches are "recommended" to achieve results. This approach will encourage people to find meaning in their work and optimize their creativity and engagement in the process (Buckingham & Clifton, 2001; Peterson & Seligman, 2003).

Understanding how individuals perceive meaning in their work is very different than understanding how individuals respond to specific jobs (Baltes et al., in press). Research conducted across cultures shows that older workers who report higher levels of identification with work describe work as a positive experience and value the outcomes they achieve through work (Meaning of Work International Research Team, 1987). When individuals find meaning in their work, it has a positive impact on the achievement and maintenance of their self-esteem and sense of accomplishment over their life course (Harpaz & Fu, 2002). Individuals who choose to work at older ages do so because work provides them with positive social interactions and a sense of meaning that satisfies their needs (Baltes et al., 2012). The willingness and interest in working longer and remaining engaged in meaningful tasks has dramatically impacted the traditional definition of retirement. For example, there is no longer a defined period of time in which individuals completely stop working and engage in purely leisure pursuits. This has led to the need to explore the changing nature of retirement (Shultz & Wang, 2011).

The Changing Nature of Retirement

While retirement has traditionally been thought of as a noun (e.g., Are you enjoying your retirement?) or a verb (e.g., Did you hear she is retiring next week?), it has evolved over time into much more. Retirement has clearly progressed in the last several decades from being more than a single event of working one day and not the next. In addition, the process of retirement has become more blurred over time (Mutchler, Burr, Pienta, & Massagli,

1997), to the point of researchers being unable to agree on a single definition of what constitutes retirement. As Ekerdt (2010) recently noted, "The designation of retirement status is famously ambiguous because there are multiple overlapping criteria by which someone might be called retired, including career cessation, reduced work effort, pension receipt, or self-report" (p. 70). In fact, Denton and Spencer (2009) recently identified eight different common ways that researchers from across the globe have identified individuals as retired: (1) nonparticipation in the labor force, (2) reduction in hours worked and/or earnings, (3) hours worked or earnings below some minimum cutoff, (4) receipt of retirement/pension income, (5) exit from one's main employer, (6) change of career or employment later in life, (7) self-assessed retirement, and (8) some combination of the previous seven. How retirement was defined in the various studies reviewed by Denton and Spencer depended in large part on the research question being addressed and the researcher's discipline.

Adding confusion to the complexity of defining retirement is the fact that individuals can "un-retire" or "re-retire" by rejoining the workforce and starting a new career after they retire, which has become a relatively common phenomenon in the last few decades (Alley & Crimmins, 2007; Wang et al., 2009). Thus, there are individuals now who retire multiple times throughout their working life. While starting a second career at midlife has always been common in some professional fields (e.g., professional sports, the military), it is now becoming the norm for many older workers, both professionals and nonprofessionals. Employment after retirement is typically referred to as bridge employment. We will discuss bridge employment more extensively later in this chapter. As was discussed in the chapter by Cahill, Giandrea, and Quinn, bridge employment is a positive phenomenon that allows older workers to continue to engage in meaningful, productive activities and provides them with financial stability. Cahill et al. note that retirement is no longer the one-time event it has been traditionally; it is now a process that ebbs and flows based on individual choices, needs, and preferences.

Retirement as a Process

Wang and Shultz (2010) recently presented an extensive review of the retirement literature. In their review, they offered a temporal model of retirement, which is presented in Figure 33.1, that begins with retirement planning, then progresses through retirement decision making (including early retirement incentive offers and considerations of bridge employment), and ends with the retirement transition and adjustment processes. In addition, the model depicted in Figure 33.1 of the retirement process examines how individual attributes, job and organizational factors, family factors, and broader socioeconomic factors all influence the process of retirement.

What is clear from examining Figure 33.1 is that retirement is not a single event. Instead, retirement represents a longitudinal, sequential process that occurs over the course of many years. As depicted in the right side of Figure 33.1, retirement begins with informal thoughts and ideas of retirement in one's early and mid-career, and progresses to more deliberate and overt formal retirement planning as one approaches the retirement decision phase. The retirement decision phase can last for several years or, if one is presented with an early retirement incentive package from their employer, may happen within weeks. In addition, as noted previously, the retirement decision process may occur several times as individuals move in and out of the paid workforce toward the end of their work life. Once the decision to retire is made and enacted, then the retirement transition and adjustment process begins. This third and final phase of the longitudinal retirement process can last for many years or even decades, as retirees adjust to their evolving family and personal situation (e.g., loss of a spouse, onset of a chronic and possibly debilitating medical condition).

In another recent conceptual paper, Shultz and Wang (2011) discuss the changing nature of retirement and how retirement is not a uniform and lockstep process for all older workers. That is, while the vast majority of older workers will go through the temporal progression of retirement planning, retirement decision making, and retirement adjustment depicted in the right side of Figure 33.1, disadvantaged groups (e.g., women, minorities, the disabled, low-income workers, the chronically unemployed) are likely to have very different retirement experiences than individuals with stable, uninterrupted, professional careers. The factors that drive this differential process are depicted in the left side of Wang and Shultz's (2010) temporal model of retirement shown in Figure 33.1. Below we discuss each of these four sets of factors in detail, with particular attention to how they are changing the way retirement has traditionally been prepared for, experienced, and adjusted to.

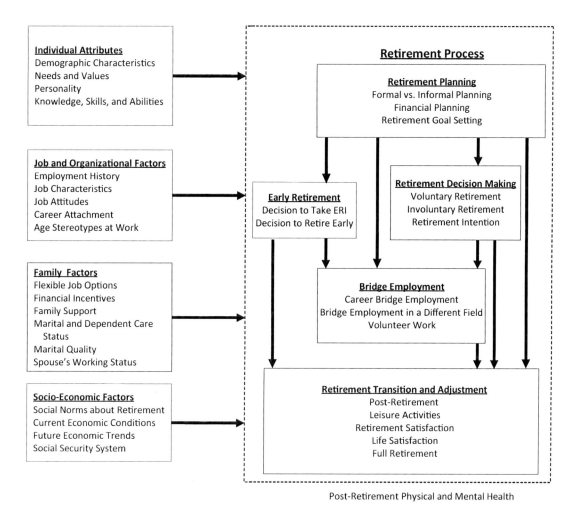

Figure 33.1 The Process of Retirement and Potential Impact Factors (Reprinted with permission from M. Wang and K. S. Shultz [2010]. Employee retirement: A review and recommendation for future investigation. *Journal of Management, 36,* 172–206).

INDIVIDUAL-LEVEL FACTORS

Various demographic factors, such as age, gender, social class, and race, will all impact the nature of the retirement experience for individuals. For example, women are more likely to have interrupted careers (for childbearing and meeting family demands) and are also more likely to work part-time (thus being less likely to be covered by pension plans) compared to men, and as a result are likely to have fewer retirement savings and assets than men as they approach traditional retirement age (Goldberg, 2007). Consequently, women are likely to have fewer options as they approach both retirement planning and retirement decision making when compared to men. These fewer options are also likely to affect women's retirement adjustment and satisfaction relative to men. Specifically,

women would be more likely to experience retirement adjustment difficulties due to the less voluntary nature of their retirement (Shultz, Morton, & Weckerle, 1998).

Taylor and Geldhauser (2007) discussed the plight of low-income older workers in general. They also noted that women and minorities are overrepresented in the low-income group of older workers, and thus the issues of race, gender, and income all become intertwined with one another. In particular, they focus on two paths for enhancing the status of low-income older workers. These include financial planning and increasing mobility into better jobs. Both of these issues, of course, have strong implications for how older workers will experience retirement. For example, strong financial planning and better jobs (which not only pay better but also have better working conditions and benefits) will lead to more options for those older workers who were in low-income jobs for much of their work lives. As a result, these low-income older workers who are able to plan financially for retirement and also transition into better jobs before they retire will be less likely to experience the difficulties when compared to their counterparts who were not able to plan and/or transition into better jobs before they retired.

In addition, individuals' attitudes toward work and retirement can have a strong impact on their likelihood of engaging in retirement planning and decision-making behaviors (Adams & Beehr, 1998). Such attitudes can also influence their likelihood of accepting early retirement incentive offers. Additionally, older workers' knowledge, skills, and abilities (also referred to as their competencies) will impact retirement-related behaviors. For example, older workers with more up-to-date competencies are more likely to want to remain in the workforce compared to older workers who do not have up-to-date competencies. This relates strongly to the concept of workability, which we will discuss in more detail later in this chapter.

Much has been written on the influence of health and wealth factors in retirement (Barnes-Farrell, 2003; Shultz & Wang, 2007). These are two clearly important proximal factors that influence retirement preparation and decision making. Specifically, if individuals experience poor health during their late career, they are much more likely to be "forced" to retire. In addition, as individuals accumulate more wealth, they have less need to work as retirement approaches. However, assuming that one is in adequate health to continue to work and that he or she has enough money to be comfortable, then other factors such as attitudes toward work and retirement will become increasingly influential in the retirement planning and decision-making process (Barnes-Farrell, 2003).

Taken together, these various individual attributes are changing the way retirement is planned for, enacted, and adjusted to in the twenty-first century. With the removal of forced retirement for almost all jobs in the late twentieth century (at least in the United States), workers will have more say regarding when and how they retire. As a result, retirement research in the twenty-first century will need to examine a wide variety of individual-level factors that impact the retirement process in order to capture the dynamic nature of retirement today. In addition, researchers will also have to incorporate factors at various levels of analysis, including job and organizational-level factors, which we discuss next.

JOB AND ORGANIZATIONAL FACTORS

At the job and organizational level, individuals' current job characteristics (e.g., physically demanding work, high travel requirements) will impact their attitudes toward retirement, as will the organizational climate toward older workers (e.g., age stereotypes and biases). For example, as noted earlier, Johnson et al. (2009) recently found that older workers are willing to step down from more prestigious and well-paying positions if the tradeoff is less travel and less physically demanding work. In fact, these workers often report enjoying the lower level of work more due to reduced stress and pressure. In addition, organizational climates that promote and foster ageism and age bias in the workplace are likely to lead workers to want to retire in order to escape these toxic work environments. As Finkelstein and Ferrell (2007) pointed out, however, there does not need to be blatant age bias to have an impact on older workers. Expressions of negative age stereotypes (cognitions), disliking of older workers (affect), and/or negative behaviors (discriminatory decisions) can all lead older workers to accelerate their pursuit of retirement versus continued employment. Thus, the organizational climate with regard to older workers may have just as important an impact on retirement planning, decision making, and adjustment as the individual-level factors discussed earlier.

In addition, the organizational and career attachment levels of the older workers themselves will impact their attitudes toward retirement, retirement planning, and retirement decision making (Adams, 1999). That is, older workers who are more attached to their current organization and their career are going to be less likely to engage in retirement planning and decision-making activities. Conversely, those older workers who may be disenchanted with their current employer and/or career will be much more likely to engage in active retirement planning and decision making in order to find other activities (maybe including bridge employment in a different field) that better match their desires.

Feldman (2007) recently discussed how older workers become embedded in their careers. Building on the concept of job embeddedness (Mitchell, Holtom, Lee, Sablynski, & Erez, 2001), Feldman discussed how individuals in their late career become entrenched in a particular career or occupational path due to *fit* (i.e., the match between personal and occupational characteristics), *links* (i.e., the extent of social and personal ties individuals have within their occupation), and *sacrifices* (i.e., the totality of losses individuals would incur if they left their occupation or career). In addition, individuals' mobility is dependent on both their *motivation* to change careers, as well as their *ability* to change careers. Thus, career change in late career, which may include retirement, is a function of internal forces as well as external forces related to fit, links, and sacrifices. As a result, the concept and enactment of retirement will be impacted by the level of organizational and career attachment older workers experience.

The financial and work options that older workers' organizations provide will also impact retirement-related behaviors. For example, if an organization provides opportunities for phased or partial retirement, older individuals may be more likely to continue with their organization, as opposed to retiring completely or securing other employment (Wang et al., 2009). Of course, phased and partial retirements are precursors to full retirement; some would even say they are instigators of full retirement. However, to the extent that organizations are able to retain critical talent, even for a few more years, they are likely to remain more competitive and also provide older workers with desired work options. Thus, organizations need to consider options for recruiting and retaining valuable older workers (Taylor et al., 2005).

Similarly, flexible work options such as reduced hours, job sharing, and part-year employment are also likely to help retain older workers, albeit for potentially longer and in a larger capacity than might be experienced with phased or partial retirement schemes. Older workers consistently report the desire for more flexible work options (Johnson et al., 2009) in order to provide more balance in their life and to pursue other opportunities outside of work, be it leisure travel, spending more time with family and friends, or caring for elderly parents or a disabled spouse. Thus, to the extent that organizations provide these desirable characteristics, they will be better positioned to attract and retain older workers who might otherwise retire (Loi & Shultz, 2007; Rau & Adams, 2005; Taylor et al., 2005).

In a recent meta-analysis examining the antecedents and outcomes of retirement planning and decision making, Topa, Moriano, Depolo, Alcover, and Morales (2009) examined more than 341 independent samples from 99 primary studies with 188,222 participants. They found that the work

and organizational-level factors of work involvement and job satisfaction were two of the strongest predictors of retirement planning activities, while negative working conditions and positive attitudes toward retirement had smaller, but still meaningful, effects on retirement planning. In addition, the predictive efficiency of these variables in predicting actual retirement decisions was much smaller. Thus, it is clear based on meta-analytic findings that a variety of work- and organizational-related factors can have an impact on retirement planning and, to a lesser extent, retirement decision making.

All told, the various job- and organizational-level factors discussed above appear to have a consistent relationship with both retirement planning and decision-making outcomes. In addition, as these factors continue to evolve in the twenty-first century, their impact on the dynamic and changing nature of retirement will also continue to transform how researchers investigate their impact on the retirement process. Thus, those interested in examining retirement from a dynamic and multilevel perspective will need to be sure to include job- and organizational-level factors in their investigations for retirement planning, retirement decision making, and retirement adjustment.

FAMILY FACTORS

Family support networks, as well as marital quality and satisfaction, also have an impact on individuals' attitudes toward work and retirement. For example, older workers who have spouses or significant others who are not supportive of their continued employment will be less likely to continue to work or seek out bridge employment jobs after retiring from a career job. These individuals are also likely to have a more difficult time adjusting to retirement once they do retire (Wang, 2012). On the other hand, older workers who have supportive family members may or may not continue to work, but will be much more likely to be satisfied with their decision and adjust better to retirement when they do decide to retire, given the more perceived voluntariness of their retirement decision (Shultz et al., 2008).

Similarly, individuals who have a poorer perceived martial relationship may continue to work in order to distract themselves from their adverse marital relationship. Conversely, individuals who express having a strong and vibrant relationship with their spouse would be more likely to try to time their retirement to coincide with that of their spouse so that they could continue to foster their relationship.

Thus, spouses' working status will have an impact on how individuals prepare for and execute their desired retirement plan, as well as how they may adjust once they themselves retire.

Additional family factors such as the number of dependents one has will also impact retirement planning and decision making. For example, many couples are waiting longer to have children, thus, while traditionally most individuals of retirement age are empty nesters, today individuals approaching retirement may still have children in high school or college because of starting a second family later in life, whether through remarriage or making the choice to defer having children until they are in their 30s or 40s. In addition, workers approaching retirement may also be responsible for young grandchildren or aging parents, which can dramatically impact plans for retirement, as well as retirement decision making. For instance, having young grandchildren in the home may require postponing a planned retirement, while suddenly having to care for an infirm parent may require taking an unplanned early retirement. As a result, individuals' retirement planning and decision-making activities will be influenced by factors at the family level.

Taken together, the changing nature of workers' family dynamics in the twenty-first century is going to impact how they prepare for and carry out their retirement. In addition, these factors are likely to have an even bigger impact on the retirement adjustment process, compared to factors at the other levels discussed so far, due to the fact that the family situation will remain a strong proximal factor, while job and organizational factors, for example, will fade to having a more distal impact on retirement adjustment (Shultz, Taylor, & Morrison, 2003).

SOCIOECONOMIC FACTORS

Broad macro-level factors such as the current unemployment rate (particularly among older workers), future economic trends, and changing government policies and programs are all likely to have a significant impact on older workers' attitudes and decisions with regard to retirement. For example, when current unemployment rates increase dramatically (as they did between 2007 and 2010), older individuals may perceive that they have no option but to retire if they lose their job. In addition, perceptions of future economic growth or decline are also going to impact older workers' perceptions of the relative attractiveness of continued employment versus opting for retirement. Economic data has consistently shown that while older workers are less

likely to lose their job compared to younger workers, when they do they are typically out of work more than twice as long. As a result, these discouraged older workers will be more likely to begin tapping into retirement savings and filing for Social Security benefits if they are eligible (AARP, 2005).

In addition, Shultz and Wang (2011) recently noted that government policies regarding retirement have shifted from a "pro-retirement" to a "pro-work" perspective. That is, in the early and mid–twentieth century, governments provided strong incentives to encourage older individuals to retire at relatively young ages. However, starting in the late twentieth century and continuing in to the twenty-first century, government policies (including those in Europe; van Dalen, Henkens, Henderikse, & Schippers, 2010) have encouraged older workers to stay in the workforce. For example, in the United States, the age to receive full retirement benefits from Social Security is slowly raising from 65 to 67 years old. In addition, financial penalties in Social Security for continuing to work past age 65 no longer exist. Thus, the U.S. government has removed the traditional disincentives to work at older ages and instead now provides strong incentives to remain active and employed (McNamara, Sano, & Williamson, 2012).

While explicit government policies have some effect on retirement timing and experiences, more implicit societal-level norms about retirement also impact retirement timing. For example, in the early twentieth century, the expectation was that individuals would work until they were simply no longer physically able to do so. Thus retirement was viewed in a negative light, reserved only for the infirm elderly. However, by the mid–twentieth century, the increased availability of company pensions and full implementation of Social Security retirement benefits led to a cultural shift in attitudes toward retirement, where retirement had become an earned rite of passage and something that individuals should look forward to after a long career toiling at paid labor. However, in the twenty-first century, the cultural expectations with regard to retirement are again shifting. Expectations for continued part-time work, or at least some form of productive involvement, whether paid or unpaid, are increasing (Ekerdt, 2010; Shultz & Wang, 2011).

Taken together, the various implicit and explicit societal-level impacts on retirement planning and decision making are likely to be substantial. As societal attitudes toward retirement change, so do the government policies that impact retirement (e.g., raising the age to obtain full Social Security benefits). In addition, as macroeconomic conditions ebb and flow, societal attitudes toward older workers and retirement are also likely to change. Thus, as retirement becomes a more dynamic and volitional process on the part of older workers and their family, explicit societal-level policies, as well as implicit societal-level norms, are going to continue to shape how individuals prepare for, make decisions about, and ultimately adjust to retirement.

Retirement in the Twenty-first Century

The four sets of multilevel factors noted above, and depicted in the left side of Figure 33.1, are helping to reshape how individuals think about retirement, plan for retirement, implement their retirement decision, and adjust to the changes retirement brings to their lives. In addition, two relatively new concepts, workability and bridge employment, are helping to redefine what it means to be retired and how retirement is enacted in the twenty-first century. As the nature of retirement continues to become more dynamic and in the control of the older workers themselves, the concepts of workability and bridge employment will become even more important. Thus, we discuss each of these concepts in more detail below.

Workability

In Europe, Finland in particular, the concept of *workability* has been studied for the last several decades (cf. Ilmarinen, 2006; Kumashiro, 2009). Workability addresses the ability of older workers to maintain their employability as they age, thus allowing them more say in both the timing and form that their retirement will take. Simply put, workability is "a balance between a person's resources and work demands" (Ilmarinen, 2009, p. 61). Ilmarinen (2009) recently summarized the research on workability by using the analogy of a house, where the ground floor is one's functional capacity (e.g., physical and mental health). Without basic functional capacity, older workers will have little say in how their retirement will play out. Next, competence (e.g., up-to-date knowledge, skills, and abilities) is needed. That is, older workers need contemporary competencies to remain employable in today's capricious workplace. Continuing the house analogy and moving upward, the third level represents values (e.g., attitudes and motivations). Thus, positive attitudes toward work and sufficient motivation to continue working are needed to remain employable. The final element is the work itself, including the

environment, demands, and management and leadership attitudes and behaviors (i.e., this would be analogous to the weather surrounding the house). Finally, the roof of the house represents the workability of the older workers themselves based on the combination of characteristics represented by the floors below, which also allows individuals to withstand the outside "weather." This of course all takes place within the context of a given society and, for a given individual, with regard to the personal resources he or she possesses (e.g., wealth, social support from family and friends). Thus, the concept of workability has implications for both continued work at older ages and the transition to retirement.

As noted throughout this chapter, retirement in the twenty-first century is much more dynamic than in the past. As a result, workers have the potential to have much more say and impact on their retirement experience than they did previously. However, to the extent that workers lack workability factors, the influence they have on their retirement experience will be rather limited. Conversely, to the extent that older workers are able to maintain strong physical and mental health, up-to-date competencies, and positive attitudes and motivations toward work and retirement, they are much more likely to be able to guide their own retirement, rather than have it dictated to them by others or their less-than-optimal circumstances. To the extent that that is true, options for various forms of bridge employment will be more realistic.

Bridge Employment

Bridge employment represents a transition phase when older workers begin to disengage psychologically from working life but are not quite ready to begin a life as a retiree with no work responsibilities at all (Shultz, 2003; Wang et al., 2009). Thus, bridge employment is an opportunity for organizations to retain important talent and achieve successful knowledge transition, while also leading to positive adjustment outcomes for retirees during their post-retirement transition. The empirical research on bridge employment has demonstrated that beyond demographic, health, and financial variables, job-related psychological variables (e.g., job attitudes and work-role stressors) are important predictors of bridge employment decisions (e.g., Davis, 2003; Pengcharoen & Shultz, 2010; von Bonsdorff, Shultz, Leskinen, & Tansky, 2009; Wang et al., 2008), whereas various forms of bridge employment may be beneficial for retirees' physical and mental health (e.g., Zhan, Wang, Liu, &

Shultz, 2009). Thus, retirement is no longer analogous to the cessation of paid employment. Instead, we see many older workers continuing to work after retiring from career jobs, and on the whole, these bridge employment experiences appear to have positive benefits.

Bridge employment has also been described as another career stage by some researchers (Wang et al., 2009). That is, bridge employment can take many forms, from continued employment in a very similar job to that held just prior to retirement, to a totally different line of work completely unrelated to one's previous career field. Thus, bridge employment serves as an important transition strategy for a growing number of older workers, helping them to maneuver through the increasingly dynamic retirement process in the twenty-first century.

Retirement Outcomes from a Multilevel Perspective

Beehr and Bennett (2007) discuss the need to examine how retirement impacts a wide variety of outcomes from a multilevel perspective. Up to this point we have focused on the factors that influence the process of retirement. However, we also need to look at how the retirement process impacts a wide variety of outcomes as well. That is, we need to not only look at how retirement affects individuals but also examine how retirement affects the retirees' families, organizations, and society at large. As the process of retirement continues to change and evolve, the need to look at the changing nature of both the antecedents and outcomes associated with retirement from a multilevel perspective becomes even more important. At the individual level, much research has focused on why people retire, different types of retirement (e.g., partial, phased, full), and the factors that impact retirement adjustment. However, a good deal of this research was completed when retirement was much more homogeneous and predictable. The rapidly changing nature of work and retirement necessitates that we look at additional factors at the individual level that impact why individuals retire and their impact on retirement adjustment and satisfaction.

Recent research has also demonstrated that retirement is influenced by and influences factors at the family level as well (Wang & Shultz, 2010). For example, given the increasing number of dual-career couples, older couples must now consider both their and their spouse's retirement timing and form (e.g., will work be in the retirement equation?). In addition, with human longevity increasing and

modern-day couples delaying childbearing, many individuals of retirement age may well be sandwiched between both child-care demands and elder-care demands (Neal & Hammer, 2007). Such family-related considerations are likely to make the retirement decision-making and adjustment process that much more complicated, as the retirement decision is no longer (assuming it ever truly was) an individual-level decision, but rather a decision that impacts entire families and social networks.

At the organizational level, retirement of older workers can have an immediate impact on the workers who remain, as well as on the company's pension system. That is, those who remain may well have to absorb the work that was formerly carried out by those workers who retire. In addition, with the mass retirements of the large baby-boomer cohort in the next several decades, company pension and health plans will also see this immediate burden. Employee retirements are also likely to have longer-term impacts in terms of the loss of organizational-specific knowledge and history, as well as in terms of succession planning. Again, these issues will become increasingly prominent as the large cohort of baby boomers begin to retire en masse over the next several decades.

At the broader societal level, the mass exit of the baby-boom generation from the workforce will have a dramatic impact on social insurance plans such as Social Security and Medicare. In addition, individuals often migrate when they retire, so the large exodus of the baby-boomer cohort from paid employment may result in accelerated migration patterns to warmer climates. Thus, while we discussed earlier the impact of societal-level factors on individuals' retirement planning and decision making, there is clearly a recursive process at work as well, where older workers' retirement planning and decision making have a cumulative effect, thus impacting society as well.

Conclusion

The nature of both work and retirement has changed dramatically in the last few decades. There are a myriad of factors at both the micro- and macro-level that are impacting how individuals carry out their work and progress toward retirement. In addition, the concept and process of retirement have changed dramatically over the course of the last century. What was once a process primarily dictated by organizations is now for the most part a function of the older workers themselves. In particular, the concepts of workability and bridge employment are becoming more prominent in discussions of retirement in the twenty-first century. Below, we outline several directions for future research in order to more fully capture and understand the dynamic nature of retirement (cf. Shultz & Henkens, 2010).

Future Directions

1. **How can older workers best use their talents in retirement?** As in building cardio health by using interval training, in retirement individuals have many options they can seek out or create that will allow them to expand the use of their preferred talents. This can occur through volunteer activities in the community that use specific talents, bridge employment, continued engagement in personal interests and hobbies, or providing care to loved ones and friends, all of which will allow individuals to continue to hone and expand their talents. In retirement, the key is to understand one's talents and that there are many venues in which they can be demonstrated. Future research will need to explore the issues of maximizing talents in both late career and during retirement.

2. **How can we best study the dynamic nature of retirement?** As noted throughout this chapter, retirement in the twenty-first century is more dynamic than ever. Therefore, many of the procedures used in the past to study retirement (e.g., cross-sectional research designs) may no longer be viable today. Thus, contemporary researchers will need to examine a wider variety of issues and use a larger set of procedures in order to fully capture the dynamic nature of retirement today (e.g., Wang, 2007). We discuss several of these issues below.

3. **What is the best way to maintain workability as retirement approaches?** As the nature of retirement has become more volitional on the part of older workers, the concept of workability has become increasingly salient. That is, in order for older workers to seize the opportunity to control the ever more dynamic nature of retirement in the twenty-first century, they need to continue to maintain their workability. Maintaining workability includes making sure one has the basic physical and mental capacity to work, as well as up-to-date competencies and the right attitudes and motivations with regard to continued work at older ages. However, while Ilmarinen and his colleagues have mapped out the key concepts of workability, there is much less definitive research on how

best to maintain workability in the increasingly dynamic workplace of the twenty-first century.

4. **How can we study the dynamic nature of bridge employment?** The psychosocial predictors and outcomes associated with bridge employment have been studied only for the last decade or so. However, much of this research has looked at bridge employment as a relatively static event, where older workers either do or do not engage in bridge employment in one form or another. However, it is clear that bridge employment in the twenty-first century will be much more dynamic in nature. That is, individuals may engage in multiple forms of bridge employment during the retirement years. Thus, what might have predicted the first occurrence of bridge employment may be very different from what predicts later occurrences of bridge employment. As a result, researchers in the twenty-first century will need to examine the bridge employment process over an extended period of time in order to fully understand the various antecedents and outcomes associated with multiple occurrences of bridge employment.

5. **How best to study retirement from an interdisciplinary perspective?** There are multiple disciplines that study retirement. These disciplines include various subfields of psychology (e.g., life span developmental, industrial and organizational, clinical and counseling), as well as sociology, social work, economics, and other social, behavioral, and organizational sciences. Thus, retirement has always been a multidisciplinary topic, much as gerontology has been. However, in order to better understand the dynamic nature of retirement in the twenty-first century, researchers from the multiple disciplines that study retirement will need to work together in a truly interdisciplinary fashion in order to fully delineate and understand the dynamic retirement process. Unfortunately, it is still unclear on how best to accomplish this goal.

6. **How best to study retirement from an international and cross-cultural perspective?** Not only do researchers from multiple disciplines study retirement, but researchers from numerous countries and cultures also study retirement. Most of these researchers, however, are studying data from only their particular country or cultural perspective. However, more large-scale, longitudinal databases are becoming publicly available that allow researchers to make comparisons across countries and examine the differing influence of various contexts and processes with regard to retirement in different

cultures. For example, researchers can now compare data from the Health and Retirement Study (HRS) in the United States to the Study of Health, Ageing and Retirement in Europe (SHARE) data in Europe to the English Longitudinal Study of Ageing (ELSA) in Britain. In fact, we have seen several recent examples of this in other areas of gerontology (e.g., gender differences in health at older ages; Crimmins, Kim, & Solé-Auró, 2010). Hopefully, we will soon see examples of this in the area of retirement as well.

7. **How to take a broad methodological perspective when studying retirement?** Much of the study of retirement relies on large-scale, longitudinal databases such as the ones noted above. However, we cannot forget about the importance of qualitative studies that allow us to dig deeper into emerging and dynamic concepts with regard to the changing nature of retirement in the twenty-first century. Thus, combining quantitative and qualitative analyses in the study of retirement can provide richer and deeper understanding with regard to the underlying mechanisms that influence retirement planning, decision making, and adjustment, particularly given the increasingly individualistic nature of the retirement transition and adjustment process.

8. **How to examine retirement from multiple levels and perspectives?** Most of the research on retirement in the social and behavioral sciences has focused on the perspective of the individual. The same is mostly true of the organizational sciences; however, some researchers in the organizational sciences, and to some extent sociology and economics, have also occasionally looked at retirement from the organizations' perspective (e.g., Taylor, Brooke, McLoughlin, & Di Biase, 2010; van Dalen et al., 2010). Given the increasingly dynamic nature of retirement in the twenty-first century, it will be increasingly important for researchers to examine retirement from a multilevel perspective in terms of the antecedents leading up to retirement and the consequences of retirement.

References

AARP (2005). *The business case of workers age 50+: Planning for tomorrow's talent needs for today's competitive environment.* Washington D C: Author.

Adams, G. A. (1999). Career-related variables and planned retirement age: An extension of Beehr's model. *Journal of Vocational Behavior, 55,* 221–235.

Adams, G. A., & Beehr, T. A. (1998). Turnover and retirement: A comparison of their similarities and differences. *Personnel Psychology, 51,* 643–665.

Alley, D., & Crimmins, E. M. (2007). The demography of aging and work. In K. S. Shultz & G. A. Adams (Eds.), *Aging and work in the 21st century* (pp. 7–23). Mahwah, NJ: Lawrence Erlbaum.

Baltes, B. B., Rudolph, C. W., & Bal, A. C. (2012). A review of aging theories and modern work perspectives. In J. W. Hedge & W. C. Borman (Eds.), *The Oxford handbook of work and aging* (pp. 117–136). New York, NY: Oxford University Press.

Barnes-Farrell, J. L. (2003). Beyond health and wealth: Attitudinal and other influences on retirement decision-making. In G. A. Adams & T. A. Beehr (Eds.), *Retirement: Reasons, processes, and results* (pp. 159–187). New York, NY: Springer.

Beehr, T. A., & Bennett, M. M. (2007). Examining retirement from a multi-level perspective. In K. S. Shultz & G. A. Adams (Eds.), *Aging and work in the 21st century* (pp. 277–302). Mahwah, NJ: Lawrence Erlbaum.

Bennis, W. G., & Thomas, R. J. (2002). *Geeks and geezers.* Boston, MA: Harvard Business School Press.

Buckingham, M., & Clifton, D. O. (2001). *Now, discover your strengths.* New York, NY: Simon & Schuster.

Calo, T. J. (2008). Talent management in the era of the aging workforce: The critical role of knowledge transfer. *Public Personnel Management, 37,* 403–416.

Cascio, W. F. (1995). Whither industrial and organizational psychology in a changing world of work? *American Psychologist, 50,* 928–999.

Charness, N., & Boot, W. R. (2009). Aging and information technology use. *Current Direction in Psychology Science, 18,* 253–258.

Crimmins, E. M., Kim, J. K., & Solé-Auró, A. (2010). Gender differences in health: Results from SHARE, ELSA, and HRS. *European Journal of Public Health.* Early Access—March 17, 2010. doi:10.1093/eurpub/ckq022.

Davis, M. A. (2003). Factors related to bridge employment participation among private sector early retirees. *Journal of Vocational Behavior, 63,* 55–71.

Deal, J. J. (2007) *Retiring the generation gap: How employees young and old can find common ground.* San Francisco, CA: Jossey-Bass.

Denton, F., & Spencer, B. (2009). What is retirement? A review and assessment of alternative concepts and measures. *Canadian Journal on Aging, 28,* 63–76.

Drucker, P. F. (2001, Nov. 1). The next society. *The Economist.* Retrieved from http://www.economist.com/node/770819.

Ekerdt, D. J. (2010). Frontiers of research on work and retirement. *Journal of Gerontology: Social Sciences, 65B,* 69–80.

Feldman, D. C. (2007). Career mobility and career stability among older workers. In K. S. Shultz & G. A. Adams (Eds.), *Aging and work in the 21st century* (pp. 179–197). New York, NY: Psychology Press.

Finkelstein, L. M., & Farrell, S. K. (2007). An expanded view of age bias in the workplace. In K. S. Shultz & G. A. Adams (Eds.), *Aging and work in the 21st century* (pp. 73–108). Mahwah, NJ: Lawrence Erlbaum.

Fugate, M., Kinicki, A. J., & Ashforth, B. E. (2004). Employability: A psycho-social construct, its dimensions, and applications. *Journal of Vocational Behavior, 65,* 14–38.

Gaillard, M., & Desmett, D. (2010). (In)validating stereotypes about older workers influences their intentions to retire early and to learn and develop. *Basic and Applied Social Psychology, 32,* 86–98.

Gobeski, K. T., & Beehr, T. A. (2009). How retirees work: Predictors of different types of bridge employment. *Journal of Organizational Behavior, 30,* 401–425.

Goldberg, C. (2007). Diversity issues for an aging workforce. In K. S. Shultz & G. A. Adams (Eds.), *Aging and work in the 21st century* (pp. 51–72). New York, NY: Psychology Press.

Greller, M. M. (2006). Hours invested in professional development during late career as a function of career motivation and satisfaction. *Career Development International, 11,* 544–559.

Guillen, M. F. (2001). Is globalization civilizing, destructive or feeble? A critique of five key debates in the social science literature. *Annual Review of Sociology, 27,* 235–260.

Harpaz, I., & Fu, X. (2002). The structure of meaning of work: A relative stability amidst change. *Human Relations, 55,* 639–667.

House, R., Javidan, M., & Dorfman, P. (2001). Project globe: An introduction. *Applied Psychology: An International Journal, 50,* 489–505.

Ilmarinen, J. (2006). *Towards a longer worklife! Ageing and the quality of worklife in the European Union.* Helsinki, Finland: Finnish Institute of Occupational Health.

Ilmarinen, J. (2009). Aging and work: An international perspective. In S. J. Czaja & J. Sharit (Eds.), *Aging and work: Issues and implications in a changing landscape* (pp. 51–73). Baltimore, MD: The Johns Hopkins University Press.

Johnson, R. W., Kawachi, J., & Lewis, E. K. (2009). *Older workers on the move: Recareering in later life.* Washington, DC: AARP Public Policy Institute.

Johnson, R. W., Mermin, G. B. T., & Resseger, M. (2007). *Employment at older ages and the changing nature of work* (Public Policy Institute Report No. 2007–02).Washington, DC: AARP. Retrieved from http://www.urban.org/Uploaded PDF/1001154_older_ages.pdf.

Kohn, M. L., & Schooler, C. (1983). *Work and personality: An inquiry into the impact of social stratification.* Norwood, NJ: Ablex.

Kumashiro, M. (Ed.). (2009). *Promotion of workability toward productive aging.* The Hague, The Netherlands: CRC Press/ Taylor and Francis Group.

Loi, J. L. P., & Shultz, K. S. (2007). Why older adults seek employment: Differing motivations among subgroups. *Journal of Applied Gerontology, 26,* 274–289.

McNamara, T., Sano, J. B., & Williamson, J. B. (2012). The pros and cons of pro-work policies and programs for older workers. In J. W. Hedge & W. C. Borman (Eds.), *The work and aging handbook* (pp. 663–683). New York, NY: Oxford University Press.

Meaning of Work International Research Team (MOWIRT). (1987). *The meaning of working.* London, England: Academic Press.

Mitchell, T. R., Holtom, B. C., Lee, T. W., Sablynski, C. J., & Erez, M. (2001). Why people stay: Using job embeddedness to predict voluntary turnover. *Academy of Management Journal, 44,* 1102–1121.

Molleman, E. (2005). Diversity in demographic characteristics, abilities, and personality traits: Do faultlines affect team functioning? *Group Decision and Negotiation, 14,* 173–193.

Mutchler, J. E., Burr, J. A., Pienta, A., & Massagli, M. P. (1997). Pathways to labor force exit: Work transitions and work instability. *Journals of Gerontology, Series B: Psychological Sciences and Social Sciences, 52B,* S4–S12.

Neal, M. B., & Hammer, L. B. (2007). *Working couples caring for children and aging parents: Effects on work and well-being.* Mahwah, NJ: Lawrence Erlbaum.

Noe, R. A., Hollenbeck, J. R., Gerhart, B., & Wright, P. M. (2009). *Fundamentals of human resource management* (3rd ed.). New York, NY: McGraw-Hill Irwin.

Ohmae, K. (2005). *The next global stage.* Philadelphia, PA: Wharton School Publishing.

Pengcharoen, C., & Shultz, K. S. (2010). The influences on bridge employment decision. *International Journal of Manpower, 31,* 322–336.

Peterson, C. M., & Seligman, M. E. P. (2003). Positive organizational studies: Lessons from positive psychology. In K. S. Cameron, J. E. Dutton, & R. E. Quinn (Eds.), *Positive organizational scholarship* (pp. 14–28). San Francisco, CA: Berrett Koehler.

Pratt, M. G., & Ashforth, B. E. (2003). Fostering meaningfulness in working and at work. In K. S. Cameron, J. E. Dutton, & R. E. Quinn (Eds.), *Positive organizational scholarship* (pp. 309–327). San Francisco, CA: Berrett Koehler.

Rau, B. L., & Adams, G. A. (2005). Attracting retirees to apply: Desired organizational characteristics of bridge employment. *Journal of Organizational Behavior, 26,* 649–660.

Richards, O. C. (2000). Racial diversity, business strategy, and firm performance: A resource-based view. *Academy of Management Journal, 43,* 164–177.

Shultz, K. S. (2003). Bridge employment: Work after retirement. In G. A. Adams and T. A. Beehr (Eds.), *Retirement: Reasons, processes, and results* (pp. 214–241). New York, NY: Springer.

Shultz, K. S., & Henkens, K. (2010). Introduction to the changing nature of retirement: An international perspective. *International Journal of Manpower, 31,* 265–270.

Shultz, K. S., Morton, K. R., & Weckerle, J. R. (1998). The influence of push and pull factors on voluntary and involuntary early retirees' retirement decision and adjustment. *Journal of Vocational Behavior, 53,* 45–57.

Shultz, K. S., Taylor, M. A., & Morrison, R. F. (2003). Work related attitudes of naval officers before and after retirement. *International Journal of Aging and Human Development, 57,* 261–276.

Shultz, K. S., & Wang, M. (2007). The influence of specific physical health conditions on retirement decisions. *International Journal of Aging & Human Development, 65,* 749–161.

Shultz, K. S., & Wang, M. (2008). The changing nature of mid- and late careers. In C. Wankel (Ed.), *21st century management: A reference handbook* (Vol. 2, pp. 130–138). Thousand Oaks, CA: Sage.

Shultz, K. S., & Wang, M. (2011). Psychological perspectives on the changing nature of retirement. *American Psychologist, 66,* 170–179.

Shultz, K. S., Wang, M., Crimmins, E. M., & Fisher, G. G. (2010). Age differences in the demand-control model of work stress: An examination of data from 15 European countries. *Journal of Applied Gerontology, 29,* 21–47.

Taylor, M. A., & Geldhauser, H. A. (2007). Low-income older workers. In K. S. Shultz & G. A. Adams (Eds.), *Aging and work in the 21st century* (pp. 25–50). New York, NY: Psychology Press.

Taylor, M. A., Shultz, K. S., & Doverspike, D. (2005). Academic perspectives on recruiting and retaining older workers. In P. T. Beatty and R. M. S. Visser (Eds.), *Thriving on an aging workforce: Strategies for organizational and systemic change* (pp. 43–50). Malabar, FL: Krieger.

Taylor, P., Brooke, L., McLoughlin, C., & Di Biase, T. (2010). Older workers and organizational change: Corporate memory versus potentiality. *International Journal of Manpower, 31,* 374–386.

Topa, G., Mariano, J. A., Depolo, M., Alcover, C. M., & Morales, J. F. (2009). Antecedents and consequences of retirement planning and decision making: A meta-analysis and model. *Journal of Vocational Behavior, 75,* 38–55.

van Dalen, H. P., Henkens, K., Henderikse, W., & Schippers, J. (2010). Do European employers support later retirement? *International Journal of Manpower, 31,* 360–373.

Van der Heijden, B. I. J. M. (2002). Age and assessments of professional expertise in small and medium-sized enterprises: Differences between self-ratings and supervisor ratings. *International Journal of Human Resource Development and Management, 2,* 329–343.

Van der Heijden, B. I. J. M. (2010). Supervisor-subordinate age dissimilarity and performance ratings: The buffering effects of supervisory relationship and practice. *International Journal of Aging and Human Development, 71,* 231–258.

Van der Heijden, C. M., & Van der Heijden, B. I. J. M. (2006). A competence-based and multidimensional operationalization and measurement of employability. *Human Resource Management, 45,* 449–476.

Van Knippenberg, D., De Dreu, C. K. W., & Homan, A. C. (2004). Work group diversity and group performance: An integrative model and research agenda. *Journal of Applied Psychology, 89,* 1008–1022.

von Bonsdorff, M. E., Shultz, K. S., Leskinen, E., & Tansky, J. (2009). The choice between retirement and bridge employment: A continuity and life course perspective. *International Journal of Aging and Human Development, 69,* 79–100.

Wang, M. (2007). Profiling retirees in the retirement transition and adjustment process: Examining the longitudinal change patters of retirees' psychological well-being. *Journal of Applied Psychology, 92,* 455–474.

Wang, M. (2012). Health, fiscal, and psychological well-being in retirement. In J. Hedge and W. Borman (Eds.), *The Oxford handbook of work and aging* (pp. 570–584). New York, NY: Oxford University Press.

Wang, M., Adams, G. A., Beehr, T. A., & Shultz, K. S. (2009). Career issues at the end of one's career: Bridge employment and retirement. In S. G. Baugh & S. E. Sullivan (Eds.), *Maintaining focus, energy, and options over the life span* (pp. 135–162). Charlotte, NC: Information Age.

Wang, M., Olson, D. A., & Shultz, K. S. (2013). *Mid and late career issues: An integrative perspective.* New York, NY: Routledge Academic Press.

Wang, M., & Shultz, K. S. (2010). Employee retirement: A review and recommendations for future investigation. *Journal of Management, 36,* 172–206.

Wang, M., Zhan, Y., Liu, S., & Shultz, K. (2008). Antecedents and health outcomes of bridge employment: A longitudinal investigation. *Journal of Applied Psychology, 93,* 818–830.

Wellins, R. S., Byham, W. C., & Wilson, J. M. (1991). *Empowered teams: Creating self-directed work groups that improve quality, productivity, and participation.* San Francisco, CA: Jossey-Bass.

Wolf, M. (2004). *Why globalization works.* New Haven, CT: Yale University Press.

Wrzesniewski, A. (2003). Finding positive meaning in work. In K. S. Cameron, J. E. Dutton, & R. E. Quinn (Eds.), *Positive organizational scholarship* (pp. 296–308). San Francisco, CA: Berrett Koehler.

Zhan, Y., Wang, M., Liu, S., & Shultz, K. (2009). Bridge employment and retirees' health: A longitudinal investigation. *Journal of Occupational Health Psychology, 14,* 374–389.

Collision Course: The Impending Impact of Current Immigration and Retirement Trends

Derek R. Avery, Sabrina D. Volpone, *and* Aleksandra Luksyte

Abstract

Three concurrent societal trends are collectively placing immigration and retirement on a collision course of sorts: (a) the largest age segment in many societies (i.e., the baby-boomer generation) is approaching or reaching conventional retirement age, (b) many employers are experiencing significant difficulties attracting and retaining qualified personnel, and (c) immigration rates in many industrialized nations are increasing. In this chapter, we consider how growing immigration and retirement can coexist either in collaboration or competition with one another. In doing so, we consider this impending collision from the perspectives of both natives and immigrants. We conclude the chapter by identifying several avenues for future research to determine ways through which the two might coincide more fruitfully.

Key Words: Immigrants, retirement, conflict, repatriation, diversity management

The purpose of most book chapters is to review empirically established links among clearly related trends. Though we certainly see the point in such an undertaking, we embody a somewhat different approach, as the connections we draw between immigration and retirement (a) extend beyond the existing evidence and (b) are often far from intuitive. On the one hand, immigration involves the transition of an individual or individuals from one national context to another. On the other hand, retirement is the semipermanent physical departure of employees from the workplace. Despite the seeming independence of these constructs, however, we believe that three societal trends help to illustrate the association between immigration and retiring employees, placing the two on a collision course of sorts. We briefly review these three trends prior to introducing our central premise.

First, members of the largest generational cohort in many industrial societies (i.e., baby boomers) are reaching conventional retirement ages in large numbers. The baby-boomer generation includes individuals born between 1943 and 1960 (Beinhocker, Farrell, & Greenberg, 2009; McNeese-Smith & Crook, 2003; Stuenkel, Cohen, & de la Cuesta, 2005; Zemke, 1999). This age cohort includes nearly 80 million people in the United States (U.S.), which represents roughly a quarter of the population and current workforce (Beinhocker et al., 2009; Grossman, 2008). Moreover, populations in Canada and around Europe are aging similarly (Dychtwald, Erickson, & Morison, 2006). Given their age, baby boomers are retiring in large numbers, and the oldest among them are now eligible to begin collecting from 401(k) retirement savings plans without any tax penalties. In addition, the youngest of the baby-boomer generation will have reached 66 years of age by the year 2030, and the number of retirees is expected to double between 1995 and 2025 (Doverspike, Taylor, Shultz, & McKay, 2000). As Cappelli (2005) states, "the baby boomers are expected to live longer and be more active than any previous cohort, which creates concerns for society, such as how we will pay for their retirements" (p. 144). Given the impending retirement of such a large number of baby boomers, it is not surprising that a number of experts anticipate a significant labor shortage to occur as they exit the workforce (Cappelli, 2005; Dohm, 2000; McNabb, Gibson, & Finnie, 2006; Phillips, 2004; Toossi, 2005). For instance, baby-boomer representation in the U.S. labor force is expected to decline from a recent high of nearly half to 28% by 2020 (Myers, 2008; Toossi, 2002).

Second, many organizations are experiencing challenging labor shortages, resulting in considerable difficulties locating necessary human resources. Despite the growing unemployment resulting from the global recession that took hold in 2008, many employers continue to find a shortage of the skilled labor they require (Simpson, 2009). This results in a mismatch between the skills of the ever-growing available labor market and those employers desperately need to succeed. Much of this labor shortfall is a direct result of the number of retiring baby boomers. To elaborate, when the boomers began entering the U.S. workforce in 1965, their workforce participation rate was 59%. By 1995, this rate had risen to 67% (Beinhocker, Farrell, & Greenberg, 2009). Presently, their workforce participation rate has dropped 28 points from the year 2000 (Myers, 2008). These declining workforce participation rates will continue to impact businesses, as baby boomers will compose only 6% of the workforce by 2030. In short, this represents the withdrawal of more than 30 million baby boomers from 2000 to 2030 (Callanan & Greenhaus, 2008).

Third, immigrant populations in many industrial nations continue to grow. For example, the flow of immigrants to industrial nations increased 3% during the 1990s, as compared to a 0% increase of immigrants to the nonindustrial, or developing world (United Nations, 2004). Further, of the approximately 200 million immigrants (i.e., the people that live outside of their country of birth), 60% immigrated to industrial nations (Global Commission on International Migration [GCIM], 2005). As such, approximately 1 out of every 10 people that live in an industrial nation is an immigrant (United Nations, 2006). Evidence of increasing immigrant populations is apparent in the statistical reports published by the governments of various developed countries. For instance, 12% of the U.S. population, or roughly 38 million people, are immigrants, a proportion that has doubled since 1980 (Camarota. 2011). Australia has admitted over 6.8 million immigrants from well over 200 countries since 1945 (Department of Immigration and Citizenship, 2007; Murphy, 1993), resulting in 30% of Australia's population being immigrants (Australian Bureau of Statistics [ABS], 2008). Likewise, Germany has seen a rise in immigrant populations, such that they document 100,000 to 200,000 immigrants a year (e.g., 99,003 in 2007; Segal, Elliott, & Mayadas, 2009).

The collective impact of these occurrences is that many employers are turning to immigrants to fill their current and future vacancies. Though this might seem like a perfect partnership between employers in need of personnel and laborers in need of work, the reality is a complex set of pros and cons for both sides. To explore both of these perspectives, we split this chapter into two halves, with the first section focusing on the vantage point of natives and the second centering on the immigrant outlook. Subsequently, we outline several ideas for future research in order to facilitate a more productive union between immigration, employment, and retirement.

The Native's Perspective on Immigration and Retirement

We begin by examining the native's perspective. That is, we explore potential viewpoints that retiring employees may develop in response to the three current societal trends discussed in the previous section (i.e., baby-boomer retirement, labor shortages, and increased immigrant populations). Specifically, we explore organizational responses to these trends and retiring employees' reactions to these responses. Subsequently, we move on to examine possible factors that could exacerbate tensions between immigrants and retirees.

Organizational Responses

Finding a cheaper alternative. In response to labor shortages caused by mass levels of baby-boomer retirement, organizations are further relying on the burgeoning immigrant population to fill their human resource needs. Labor shortages create human resource dependencies that increase the likelihood of organizations turning to nontraditional sources of labor such as women, minorities, or immigrants (Fields, Goodman, & Blum, 2005; Rynes & Barber, 1990). Additionally, turning to immigrants to fill labor shortages is often an economically sound choice for organizations. Specifically, immigrant employees often cost less than the more senior retiring employees they are most likely to replace. This is because many of the retiring baby boomers are experienced, highly educated, and have been with companies for a long time, whereas immigrants have not established the pay grade that typically accompanies seniority status.

Research supports the notion that relying on immigrants during labor shortages is often an economically savvy decision. In fact, studies demonstrate that a negative relationship exists between immigrant status and pay (Longman, 2005). There is a gap, often referred to as "wage-gap decomposition," between pay levels of similar native-born and immigrant employees. For example, Asians in the United States are paid less on average than their white counterparts, despite having more education than native-born white employees (Hurh & Kim, 1989; Tang, 1993, 2000). Therefore, in response to the current societal pressures found in the United States today, organizations are turning to a comparatively cheaper labor source (i.e., immigrants) for their human resource needs.

Forced retirement. However, not all organizations stop at relying on immigrants to fill their labor shortages. Some companies, having identified a cheaper source of labor (i.e., immigrants), opt to replace their incumbent, costlier employees with immigrants before these individuals reach the decision to retire on their own. In fact, research documents a trend of forced retirement, as many older employees report that they feel that their companies prematurely forced them into retirement (Shultz, Morton, & Weckerle, 1998; Szinovacz & Davey, 2005). Specifically, these employees express sentiments that their retirement decision was made for them instead of by them (Heckhausen & Schulz, 1995).

Forced retirement is not only a result of the fact that immigrants are cheaper for organizations in regards to paying salaries; immigrants do not cost the company as much in health insurance costs. As employees age, their health care needs also may increase. Because Medicare does not cover health care needs until persons 65 years of age and older retire, employers are still responsible for covering these older workers' increasing health care costs (Beinhocker et al., 2009). Consequently, employing older workers costs organizations more than it would cost to employ immigrants due to older employees' typically higher salaries and health insurance costs. Thus, organizations tend to benefit financially when they are able to (a) rely on immigrants to fill their labor shortages, and (b) replace

older employees with immigrants through forced retirement initiatives.

Additional factors to consider. In addition to cost considerations, other factors may prompt organizations to prefer immigrant employees to older employees. For example, social expectations surrounding retirement and age discrimination could prevent older workers from continuing employment beyond retirement age (Beinhocker et al., 2009). First, because it is a socially constructed institution, retirement as a social expectation could influence organizations' desires to employ immigrants over employing older workers past typical retirement age. The social expectation for workers to retire around 65 years of age is common, despite the fact that there is no longer a mandatory retirement age for most occupations in the United States. Research supports this notion, as studies show that older employees receive more pressure to retire and more social support for retirement than their younger counterparts (Greller, 2006). As such, social expectations regarding retirement are stronger for older workers, typically those past 65 years of age.

Second, stereotypes about older employees also could influence organizations' desires to employ younger immigrants over older workers. The term "ageist" describes those who have a negative bias toward the aged (Keene, 2006). Examples of negative age-related stereotypes often embraced by ageists include views of older workers as resistant to change, unable to learn new skills, less productive, less innovative, overly expensive to employ, and more prone to accidents than are younger workers (Swift, 2004; Wrenn & Maurer, 2004). These stereotypes can fuel age-related discrimination (Keene, 2006), which often results in denied opportunities and resources for older workers (Glover & Branine, 2001; Levy & Banaji, 2002). For example, research demonstrates that older workers are rated lower on performance evaluations as compared with younger workers (Finkelstein, Burke, & Raju, 1995). Unfortunately, age discrimination is prevalent, even though studies have demonstrated that performance is not affected substantially by age (Hansson, DeKoekkoek, & Neece, 1997; Ng & Feldman, 2008).

Retirees' Responses

Wanting to work. Next, we turn our attention to how retirees (or those nearing typical retirement age, hereafter referred to as retirees) are responding to societal trends such as a bad economy and increasing immigration and retirement. Many baby-boomer employees say they are willing to continue working.

Specifically, surveys have found that as many as 50% to 85% of baby boomers suggested that they would continue to work beyond the traditional retirement age (MetLife Foundation, 2008). As compared to even ten years ago, when a majority of employees planned to retire by age 62, today this number has risen to 65 years of age. Further, almost a quarter of baby boomers (i.e., 24%) plan to retire at 66 years of age (or later). An even greater number of older workers would like to continue working past the traditional retirement age if they can partake in flexible working arrangements (e.g., part-time work, work from home, decreased hours; Beinhocker et al., 2009). Because organizational responses to current societal trends favor immigrant employees instead of older employees, many older workers may not be given the chance to keep their jobs, irrespective of their desires to do so. Consequently, immigrants could be seen as posing a threat to the jobs older workers of retirement age both want and need.

Retirees' desire to continue working can be explained by continuity theory (CT; Atchley, 1989), which suggests that older employees seek to maintain structure in their lives by participating in activities they value (e.g., working at their jobs). Specifically, working maintains structure in retirees' lives by providing daily routines, normal activities, and social contact to which they have grown accustomed (Atchley, 1989; Kim & Feldman, 2000). Not surprisingly, continuing to work past typical retirement age has shown positive effects for older employees (e.g., increased psychological well-being; Atchley, 1998; Zhan, Wang, Liu, & Shultz, 2009).

Needing to work. Older workers who are near retirement age may not merely want to keep working; they might need to continue to work. In particular, it may be a financial imperative. People are living longer than they have in previous generations (Montalto, Yuh, & Hanna, 2000), which means retirees will need more money for longer periods of time during retirement (Beinhocker et al., 2009). However, due to the recent bad economic conditions (and some say a lack of financial planning and savings), only one-third of baby boomers are left prepared for retirement (Beinhocker et al., 2009), which is a marked decline from the 42% estimate only twelve years ago (Yuh et al., 1998). As such, many employees want to delay retirement to add to their retirement savings (Beinhocker et al., 2009). However, organizations may favor immigrants as lower-cost employees for the jobs that retirees want to keep. These dynamics can fuel intergroup conflict (Dixon, 2006) between immigrants and retirees as

the latter see the former as stealing their jobs and livelihoods.

At least three theoretical perspectives help explain why this conflict may arise. First, group threat theories suggest that as an area becomes more diverse (e.g., an increased immigrant presence), native inhabitants (e.g., retirees) feel threatened (e.g., Blumer, 1958; Blalock, 1967; Coser, 1956; Quillian, 1995). Specifically, natives feel that their social, economic, and political power is threatened. In the case of natives and immigrants, many natives see immigrants as a threat to their valued resources (e.g., jobs; Espenshade & Hempstead, 1996). As such, native persons may engage in a variety of responses to this threat. For example, retirees may actively exclude immigrants and express prejudiced attitudes toward them (Fetzer, 2000; Jackson et al., 2001; Scheepers, Gijsberts, & Coenders, 2002; Stephan, Ybarra, & Bachman, 1999). Moreover, the reactive defensive attitudes and behaviors such bias often provokes typically fuel the situations until intergroup conflict emerges (Valentova & Alieva, 2010). In fact, group threat can lead to intergroup conflict with immigrant populations. For example, white Americans favor immigration restrictions when they believe that the groups that will be immigrating are likely to infiltrate their neighborhoods (Alba, Rumbaut, & Marotz, 2005). Further, studies in European countries show that native persons who live in areas that contain large immigrant populations commonly hold more negative attitudes toward immigrants than native persons who do not live in areas with large immigrant populations (McLaren, 2003; Quillian, 1995). Therefore, research supports the effects of group threat processes for immigrant populations.

Second, social identity theory (SIT; Tajfel, 1982; Tajfel & Turner, 1986) further reinforces the tenets of group threat theory. Specifically, SIT states that individuals tend to have a positive bias favoring the groups to which they belong and identify. As such, when individuals identify with a group (e.g., retirees), they tend to hold negative biases about "others" that do not belong to their group (e.g., non-retirees, immigrants; Mummendey et al., 2001). This negative bias toward others leads to discriminatory attitudes and behaviors against those who are not in the group. Therefore, retirees may have a tendency to dislike immigrants because they are not viewed as part of the retiree in-group.

Third, perceived group deprivation (PGD) is consistent with the positions of group threat theory and SIT. PGD describes native groups' desire to distance immigrant groups to preserve the material and nonmaterial aspects of their group, which are a part of their identity. Triggers, such as bad economic situations or scarce resources, can instigate intergroup conflicts between the group that perceives deprivation and the group they hold responsible for the deprivation. Thus, when older workers perceive that their group is being deprived of resources (e.g., jobs) due to the actions of another group (e.g., immigrants), retirees are prone to move to preserve their group's interests.

In sum, these theories suggest that when native persons feel threatened, they may respond in ways that include negative attitudes and behaviors toward the threatening group. As a result of these negative attitudes and behaviors, intergroup conflict emerges. There are, however, factors that may attenuate or exacerbate this conflict. Consequently, we now build on these aforementioned theories and examine how high immigrant group visibility and a poor economy can aggravate this intergroup conflict.

Factors Exacerbating Existing Tension between Immigrants and Retirees

Visibility. When immigrants are highly visible (due to their size or power), retirees are more likely to have negative attitudes toward them than when immigrants are not as visible. This is because as the threatening group increases (in size or power), competition for resources also increases (e.g., Kunovich, 2002; Scheepers et al., 2002; Semyonov, Raijman, & Gorodzeisky, 2006, 2008; Schneider, 2008; Quillian, 1995). This implies that as the immigrant population in the United States grows, retirees are more likely to perceive them as a threat. Consequently, their attitudes toward immigrants are apt to become increasingly negative.

Research bears out this relationship between the increased size of an immigrant population (or out-group members) and natives' (or in-group members) increasingly negative attitudes toward the foreign group. For example, multiple studies show that when blacks are considered an out-group in a city, the natives' anti-black attitudes increase with the population of blacks in that city (Fossett & Kiecolt, 1989; Giles, 1977). Therefore, as supported by this research, when an immigrant group is highly visible, it is more likely that natives' attitudes and behaviors toward them will be negative.

Economy. The economic climate also may be a factor. When the economy is bad, retirees are more likely to have negative attitudes toward immigrants than when the economy is good. In challenging economic times, retirees perceive threats more easily, especially if those perceived threats are from groups that seek to take their resources (e.g., jobs; Coenders, Lubbers, & Scheepers, 2008; Lahav, 2004; Semyonov et al., 2008). Further, research finds that discrimination and prejudice are closely related to economic conditions (e.g., King, Knight, & Hebl, 2010). Therefore, as economic conditions worsen, retirees are more likely to perceive immigrants as a threat. Consequently, their attitudes and behaviors toward immigrants become increasingly negative.

Individual differences. It is equally important to consider that immigrants pose more of a threat to some retirees than to others. Specifically, retirees falling into the following groups are more likely to see immigrants as threats: those with unspecialized skills, those planning to unretire, and/or those who want to engage in bridge employment. As such, in this section, we describe these three groups of retirees and examine why immigrants are more or less threatening for these individuals.

Competition for jobs is a main contributor to immigrants' threat to retirees. As such, employees with unspecialized jobs and skills are more likely to be threatened by immigrants because a majority of immigrants possess unspecialized skills (Dustmann & Preston, 2000). In fact, research shows that most immigrants in economically advanced societies such as the United States are nonspecialists (Scheve & Slaughter, 2001). This creates a situation wherein retirees with nonspecialist skills, or those in nonspecialist jobs, are facing greater competition from immigrants who have unspecialized skills and want those unspecialized jobs (Esses, Dovidio, & Jackson, 2001; Semyonov et al., 2006, 2008; Quillian, 1995). Therefore, retirees with unspecialized skills are more likely to feel threatened by immigrants than retirees with highly specialized skills.

Unretirement, where employees who previously retired want to re-enter the workforce, is common, especially for those who retired earlier rather than later (Han & Moen, 2001). In fact, Maestas (2007) found that of those who retired at the age of 54 years or younger, 35% returned to work within two years of their initial retirement. Nevertheless, retirees who plan to unretire are more likely to be threatened by immigrants than their counterparts who do not plan to unretire. Older workers are more likely to unretire by accepting jobs that offer flexibility and reduced responsibility. These jobs often make use of unspecialized skills. As discussed previously, retirees looking to work in nonspecialist jobs face more competition from immigrants with unspecialized skills seeking work (Esses et al., 2001; Semyonov et al., 2006, 2008; Quillian, 1995). Therefore, retirees looking to unretire are more likely to feel threatened by immigrants than retirees planning to remain retired.

Another increasingly popular option for retired employees who still desire to participate in the workforce is to find bridge employment opportunities after retiring. In fact, a study found that more than half of all persons that retired by age 60 did not retire fully (Ulrich, 2006). Instead, they continued employment through options like bridge employment. Bridge employment is a transitional work position wherein employees work as they did before they retired. The difference is that retired employees tend to have more flexibility in bridge jobs than in their pre-retirement positions (e.g., fewer hours, less responsibility; Ulrich, 2006). Therefore, bridge employment offers a way for retirees to transition from career jobs to retirement without completely withdrawing from the workforce at a single point in time. Retirees planning to find bridge employment are more likely to be threatened by immigrants than their counterparts who do not plan to engage in bridge employment after retiring. The reasoning is parallel to that of those planning to unretire. Specifically, older workers are more likely to unretire by accepting jobs that offer flexibility and reduced responsibility, and that make use of nonspecialist skills. Thus, retirees looking to maintain bridge employment often face competition from immigrants who also want nonspecialist jobs (Esses et al., 2001; Semyonov et al., 2006, 2008; Quillian, 1995). Therefore, retirees who are looking for bridge employment are more likely to feel threatened by immigrants than retirees who are not looking for bridge employment.

Immigrant Perspectives on Retirement

We now turn our attention to the immigrant perspective on these issues. Immigrant workers close to typical retirement age face unique retirement dilemmas and challenges with which their native counterparts are largely unfamiliar. Specifically, immigrant careers and incomes are usually disrupted (especially for those who immigrated as adults), which reduces their capacity to save sufficient retirement funds (Hu, 2000; Hum & Simpson, 2010; Stanford & Usita, 2002). We integrate several immigration- (e.g., assimilation) and expatriation-related (e.g., push and pull factors) theories to explain various dilemmas (i.e., financial and ethical) facing immigrant workers when pondering retirement choices.

Immigrant employees near retirement age (non-retired people aged 45 to 59; Schellenberg & Ostrovsky, 2008) can be categorized into three groups: (a) those having host country citizenship, (b) noncitizens (e.g., expatriates and self-initiated expatriates), and (c) illegal immigrants (Nguyen, 2008). Although all older immigrant workers experience similar challenges and concerns regarding their retirement (e.g., when to leave the workforce, adequacy of the retirement income to maintain one's standard of living, possibility of working post-retirement; Schellenberg & Ostrovsky, 2008), those without host country citizenship face unique retirement dilemmas (e.g., "have to leave after building a life here"). We will begin by discussing various retirement dilemmas that are commonplace for all immigrant workers, followed by an overview of unique challenges for immigrants without host country citizenship and illegal immigrants.

Retirement Location

One of the central dilemmas of immigrant retirees refers to the location of their retirement. Specifically, freshly minted immigrant retirees or near-retirees ponder whether they should come back to their country of origin, stay in the host country, or choose going back and forth between the two countries. From a theoretical perspective, three theories have been utilized to explain the decision making of immigrant retirees: assimilation (Waters & Jiménez, 2005), transnational behavior (Aguilera, 2004), and the pull/push factors perspective (Tharenou & Caulfield, 2010).

Assimilation theory. The assimilation framework has been the predominant theory to explain how immigrants adjust to social, economic, and cultural aspects of the host country (Waters & Jiménez, 2005). The theory posits that immigrants gradually take on values, customs, and the language of the host country; the longer the immigrants stay in the country, the more integrated they are in the host society (Waters & Jiménez, 2005). In the retirement context, the theory posits that the more ties and the better assimilated a person is into the economic, social, and cultural context of the host country, the greater the likelihood of opting to retire there. Consistent with this theory, highly acculturated immigrants likely seek out retirement plans that are most prevalent in the host country. Despite the informative nature of the assimilation theory, it falls short explaining why even those immigrants who are fully integrated in the host society (e.g., they self-identify as Americans) might decide to retire in their home country.

Transnational behavior theory. Transnational behavior (i.e., transmission of people, goods, information, and money across nations; Aguilera, 2004) theory may provide an answer to this potentially paradoxical situation. The theory suggests that immigrants who have been maintaining multiple connections with their home countries (e.g., frequent visits, owing property, having family, and maintaining business networks there) while assimilating into the host country will either choose to retire in their home country or prefer going back and forth between the two locations. Notably, these two theories are not necessarily mutually exclusive, but "assimilation does occur within a transnational social field" (Aguilera, 2004, p. 356). Alternatively stated, depending on the strength of the host and home countries' bonds, immigrants may debate whether they should retire in their home country or travel between the two nations. For example, immobile aging parents that require day-to-day care likely encourage immigrants to retire in their home country. Yet, the decision to retire in the home country is complicated by other considerations such as children who perceive the host country as their motherland (Bonebright, 2010), deeply rooted social connections (e.g., friends, hobbies), and overall superior quality of life and health care of the host society (Ley & Kobayashi, 2005). Based on transnational theory, many immigrants resolve this dilemma by splitting their retirement between the host and home countries. Although transnational theory addresses weaknesses of the assimilation framework in explaining immigrants' choice of the retirement locale, it does not specify factors that influence these decision-making processes. The pull/push framework may help to fill this gap.

Pull/push factors perspective. The multiple factors that influence immigrants' decision to retire in a particular geographic location can be categorized as either pulling people to stay in the host country or pushing them away from the host society. For example, self-initiated expatriates are more likely to repatriate if they are weakly embedded into their host country (e.g., career and community links do not pull them to remain abroad or low income; Kangasniemi, Winters, & Commander, 2007) and if they have a strong push to go back to their home country (e.g., easiness of re-adaptation, family, friends; Tharenou & Caulfield, 2010). In addition to this deliberate decision-making process, immigrant workers may decide to retire in their home country if they experience shocks—particular, jarring events that facilitate quitting a job (Holtom, Mitchell, Lee, & Inderrieden, 2005) or leaving a host country, such as deteriorating health of aging parents or more attractive career prospects (Tharenou & Caulfield, 2010). Further, cost-benefit considerations include social welfare benefits, the quality of health care, the cost of living, familial considerations such as the location of children's or elderly living, and property ownership (Aguilera, 2004; de Coulon & Wolff, 2010).

Challenges for immigrants without citizenship. The decision about where to retire may pose additional challenges for immigrants without host country citizenship or illegal immigrants. On the one hand, concerns over the retirement location may be an easy decision for them. Due to the absence of prerequisite documents or status for receiving retirement benefits in the host country, these people will be forced to retire in their home country. On the other hand, this decision likely imposes additional financial and psychological challenges for the immigrants. Being forced to depart from the host country after building a life there likely entails leaving behind the social and business networks, which may be difficult if not impossible to replicate in the home country. For example, research on repatriation suggests that upon returning to their home countries, many expatriates feel heightened misfit because their old friends and coworkers lack interest in learning about their experience and are reluctant to accept their multicultural identity (Sanchez, Spector, & Cooper, 2000).

Cultural Considerations and Retirement Living Conditions

Not only do immigrant retirees face various dilemmas (e.g., retirement location), but their children also have similar concerns. Often, the children of the immigrant retirees (e.g., South Koreans, Taiwanese) assume the responsibility of providing financial and emotional support as well as housing assistance for their aging parents (Chiang-Hanisko, 2010; Yoo & Kim, 2010). For many immigrant retirees (especially for those from collectivist societies; Hofstede, 1999), a retirement plan is closely related to their children's financial stability. This strategy is based on cultural expectations of filial piety (sense of responsibility for one's aging parents) and a desire to repay their parents for all the hardships they had to endure to provide a better life for their progeny. Because of these deeply ingrained cultural values, many Asian immigrants relocate their aging parents from home countries to a host society (e.g., the United States, Chiang-Hanisko, 2010). Lack of English language proficiency, absence of social life, high cost of medical services, and unfamiliarity with American lifestyle, however, make such a reunion a stressful experience for immigrant parents. Consequently, some choose to return to their home country, and others move to senior apartments where they stay affiliated with the local community and have easier access to transportation and health care as well as wider social networks (Chiang-Hanisko, 2010).

Challenges for immigrants without citizenship. For immigrants who do not have host country citizenship, the decision to relocate their aging parents to the host country may be particularly stressful. Specifically, in addition to difficulties associated with the cultural adjustment of their parents, the immigrant children likely experience heightened uncertainties and worries regarding the status of their parents. Not surprisingly then, research suggests that a need to take care of aging parents serves as a powerful shock for self-initiated expatriates to leave the host country (Tharenou & Caulfield, 2010). The cross-cultural challenges may not exist for illegal immigrants, who, because of their status, are unable to move their parents to the host country. Instead, they help them by remitting their income.

Financial Dilemmas

Financial dilemmas (e.g., paying into a social security system in which immigrants cannot participate) may pose additional concerns for immigrant retirees. From a societal perspective, immigration boosts social security finances (Gustman & Steinmeier, 1998) because the majority of immigrants tend to be of the working age and buy houses, cars, and open saving accounts for their retirement upon arrival to the host country (Danies, 2010; Nguyen, 2008). For immigrants (especially those without host country citizenship), this situation may be associated with possible losses. Specifically, the retirement plan is considered to be a three-legged stool (i.e., social security, employee pensions, and personal savings; Stanford & Usita, 2002). Often, immigrants without host country citizenship decide to retire in their home country, which likely inflicts financial challenges. For immigrants forced to retire in their home country, this stool has one firmly planted leg—personal savings—and two unsteady legs because the remaining two retirement sources are likely to be either nonexistent or are associated with additional difficulties of claiming the host country's social security and employee pension's funds.

Illegal immigrants represent a particularly unique challenge from both societal and individual standpoints. The former perspective views illegal immigration positively, wherein illegal immigrants help to boost social security finances because they are unlikely to collect the pension and other social benefits (Porter, 2005). Yet for illegal immigrants this situation poses more long-term losses than gains because their retirement plan has only one leg (i.e., personal savings), whereas the other two legs are absent.

Bridge Employment as a Possible Solution for Immigrant Retirees

Retirement for immigrants is a particularly stressful experience due to the frequent absence of professional activities that would have compensated for deficiencies in other life domains (e.g., language, sense of history; Akhtar & Choi, 2004; Stanford & Usita, 2002). This raises the question of what immigrant near-retirees can do to alleviate the potentially worsened psychological well-being, financial burden, and overall quality of life they stand to encounter during their retirement. Further, if immigrants will have to leave post-employment, can bridge employment as an expatriate help to phase transition back? Drawing on assimilation and transnational behavior theories, we believe the answer to this question is yes.

Although there are many reasons why people pursue bridge employment (e.g., individual differences, job factors, familial status; Kim & Feldman, 2000), its existence and prevalence among immigrant retirees has gone largely ignored. Drawing on the combination of the assimilation and transnational behavior theories, we argue that immigrant retirees may be best positioned to obtain bridge employment in their local host communities (e.g., working as a family child care provider; Schnur, Koffler, Wimpenny, Giller, & Rafield, 1995). Specifically, immigrant retirees have an in-depth knowledge of the host country's economic, social, and cultural systems; they also understand challenges that their fellow immigrants face. Hence, immigrant retirees' cultural background and experience with the host society's values and systems may be helpful in facilitating adjustment of newly arrived immigrant families to the style of living in a new country. Bridge employment will benefit not only the society but the immigrant retirees as well, by increasing their retirement and life satisfaction (Kim & Feldman,

2000) and by giving them additional time to decide on the location and financial conditions of their retirement.

The decision to pursue bridge employment may be motivated further by economic considerations. Specifically, the Personal Responsibility and Work Opportunity Reconciliation Act (PRWORA) of 1996 toughened the eligibility criteria of Supplemental Security Income (SSI)—a policy that was used by many elderly immigrants (especially those who arrived in the United States as adults) as an additional retirement income (Kaushal, 2010). These policy changes resulted in a decline (23% in 1995 to 7% by 2006) of SSI receipt among noncitizens aged 65 to 74 and encouraged them to seek bridge employment (Kaushal, 2010). Financial challenges also encourage many immigrants to delay their retirement (Schellenberg & Ostrovsky, 2008). Financially, bridge employment (even when forced) likely boosts the economic prosperity of immigrant retirees. Yet it may have deleterious consequences for their mental and physical well-being. In particular, immigrant retirees' health may constrain their ability to further participate in the workforce, or it may interfere with their plans to pursue other valued activities (e.g., volunteering, travel, hobbies).

Ethical Dilemmas

In addition to the retirement location and financial challenges, immigrants may be plagued by an ethical dilemma: Should they go back to their home country and apply skills they obtained abroad to fostering their motherland's economic development, or should they retire in the host country? The former decision is based on the idea of paying back one's country for educational and social benefits, and the latter is rationalized based on people's intrinsic motivation to maximize their benefits. This ethical dilemma not only concerns individual choices but also has societal implications. In particular, should host countries take other nations' "best and brightest" at a time when those countries might need them? Does brain drain (i.e., talent transfer from mainly developing to developed countries; Beine, Docquier, & Rapoport, 2008; Danso, 2009) have only negative consequences for the sending country, or are there any prospective benefits? Is it always beneficial for a receiving country?

Although it is widely accepted that the country of origin suffers from the brain drain in terms of losing outstanding human capital (Beine et al., 2008; Danso, 2009), negative consequences also can exist for the receiving countries. Specifically, the country

of destination may experience significant opportunity costs because many immigrants are underemployed or they do not fully utilize all their human capital (e.g., skills, education, work experience, and other credentials; Lianos, 2007). For example, Lianos (2007) reported that in Greece 40% of natives are overeducated, which is a relatively low figure in comparison with immigrants (66%). The prevalence of underemployment among immigrants may be explained by several factors, such as a lack of proficiency in the official language, ignorance of the local labor market and its laws, and difficulty verifying the home country's diplomas in a host educational system (e.g., Lianos, 2007). Because of these barriers, underemployment among immigrants may be a long-term phenomenon. Consequently, underemployed immigrants accumulate fewer retirement savings and pay less money into social security than their native counterparts employed in comparable positions. Additionally, these savings and payments are lower than they could have been if immigrants had been employed in positions for which they are adequately qualified. Yet some research suggests that brain drain can be beneficial for a sending country because of the money that immigrants remit to their home countries, return migration with additional skills and qualifications obtained abroad, and extended scientific and business networks (Guth & Gill, 2008; Kangasniemi et al., 2007). Further, brain drain is beneficial for human capital formation in the sending country because people are encouraged to invest more in their education in order to compensate for the loss of the migrated human capital (Beine et al., 2008).

From an organizational perspective, the host country also may experience brain drain when their elderly immigrant workers decide to retire in their home countries. In particular, by retiring in their home countries, immigrant employees are unable to transfer job-related knowledge and professional skills to their younger coworkers. Alternatively, a sending country may benefit by brain drain if retired immigrants decide to retire and pursue bridge employment in the home country. In doing so, they can share accumulated valuable knowledge, skills, and work experience with both younger and similarly aged coworkers.

Future Research Directions

Having covered both the native and immigrant perspectives of this potential collision, we now turn our attention to delineating a few goals for future consideration. First, given the potential tension between immigrants and retiring employees, it is logical that future research investigates ways to ameliorate tension when members of these groups work together in a singular location. Research has established that increased interaction between groups in conflict relates to increased intergroup harmony. Specifically, contact theory (Allport, 1954, 1979; Dixon, 2006; Pettigrew & Tropp, 2008) describes that the increased contact allows the conflicting groups to gain a deeper understanding of the other group. As such, intergroup conflict is decreased. However, we could locate no studies examining how these two groups (i.e., immigrants and retirees) can overcome the barriers that might serve to hinder initial intergroup contact. We encourage future inquiry to consider means through which intergroup cooperation might be enhanced while conflict is minimized (e.g., diversity training, cross-cutting role assignments for immigrants and prospective retirees).

Second, future research could also examine the effect of demographic similarity between immigrants and retirees on the tension experienced between members of these groups during intergroup contact. Previous research and theory demonstrate that demographic similarity commonly fosters interpersonal liking (Byrne, 1971; McPherson, Smith-Lovin, & Cook, 2001). The similarity-attraction paradigm (Byrne, 1971) argues that greater similarity of values, beliefs, and experiences results in the reinforcing outcome of mutual validation (Byrne, 1961, 1971), and relational demography (Tsui & O'Reilly, 1989) stipulates that individuals' level of demographic similarity to other organizational members positively influences outcomes. Each of these theories suggests that if the retiree and immigrant share a demographic characteristic (or multiple demographic characteristics), then less negative reactions to the other party will result. For instance, when an immigrant is of the same sex as the retiree, there is apt to be a greater sense of perceived solidarity between the two. This feeling of solidarity could lead the retiree to be more personally connected to the immigrant, viewing him or her personally as opposed to as an abstract threat. This proposition, however, has not been tested empirically and would benefit greatly from subsequent investigation.

Third, the role of an organization's diversity climate should be investigated in future research concerning immigrants and retirees. Diversity climate, the degree to which an organization maintains a fair and inclusive workplace (McKay et al., 2007), can affect the relationship between immigrants and retirees. For example, an organization with a strong diversity climate often has considerable demographic diversity and strives to promote diversity efforts (Avery & McKay, 2010). Theoretically, if organizations are able to maintain a supportive climate for diversity, they demonstrate to their employees that diverse employees (e.g., immigrants) are valued, despite their demographic differences (Kossek & Zonia, 1993). As such, retiring employees are less likely to demonstrate hostile behaviors toward immigrants in organizations with supportive diversity climates because they know that the company supports these employees and will not tolerate discrimination toward these groups. Likewise, prospective retirees will see that their relative uniqueness is also valued by the company, which should reduce the likelihood of them perceiving immigrants as a threat to their jobs. Practically, no research that we are aware of has examined empirically the role of diversity climate as a way to decrease tension in the workplace between immigrants and retirees.

Fourth, most of the research that examines the tension existing between immigrants and retirees has been investigated in Western settings (e.g., the United States). This is unfortunate, as cultural values and standards likely moderate the relationship between retirees and immigrants. For example, cultures with strong collectivist values tend to value and respect older individuals in society. Due to these values, retirees in collectivist societies may not feel as threatened by immigrants because they have an established, respected position within the society in which they live. Thus, cultural differences may moderate the tension between immigrants and retirees. This proposition has yet to be tested in the literature.

Fifth, the double jeopardy hypothesis examines the notion that those who belong to two demographic minority groups experience discrimination based on each of their minority statuses (Berdahl & Moore, 2006). Research on the double jeopardy hypothesis has not examined the intersection of immigrant and retirement statuses, despite reason to anticipate such a phenomenon. Future studies could examine both versions of the double jeopardy hypothesis found frequently in the literature (i.e., additive and multiplicative). The first version, which describes additive effects, proposes that immigrant and age discrimination occur independently. For example, immigrants perceive more discrimination than non-immigrants perceive. Likewise, minority older individuals perceive more discrimination than younger individuals. Hence, the added effects of immigrant and age discrimination result in older immigrants facing more discrimination than other groups. Furthermore, future research could examine the effects of the multiplicative version of the double jeopardy hypothesis, which proposes that immigrant and age discrimination interact to generate a cumulative effect (Vernon, 1999). This effect is larger than the simple combination discussed in the additive model (Greene, 1994; Reid & Comas-Diaz, 1990). Therefore, the discrimination immigrants perceive based on their immigrant status could interact with the discrimination perceived for belonging to an older age group.

Finally, future research might examine perceptions of immigrants who return to their host country after an extended stay in another country. Specifically, whether immigrant employees returning to their host country are returning to work or to retire, they could experience discrimination as a result of having been abroad. For example, coworkers in the host country could view returning immigrant as "different," or traitors, or be threatened by their new knowledge and experience. Research supports the notion that discrimination may play a role in immigrants returning. For example, Sanchez, Spector, and Cooper (2000) discussed how returning to the host country is often the most stressful part of having an international or expatriate assignment. Part of this stress could be a result of discrimination.

Conclusion

As this chapter illustrates, the concurrent trends of increasing immigration and retirement provide both opportunities and threats for organizations, individuals, and society at large. As retirees attempt to balance the transition out of the workplace along with their financial needs in a precarious economy, immigrant workers experience a complex set of unique challenges throughout their immigration. To the extent that immigrants are able to replace the human resources of departed employees without employing organizations placing undue pressure on their aging employees to retire, the trends may prove complementary. Such a synergistic coexistence, however, will not occur serendipitously. Organizations need subsequent scholarship to continue examining the intersection of immigration and retirement. Hopefully, this chapter will help to stimulate such research.

References

Aguilera, M. (2004). Deciding where to retire: Intended retirement location choices of formerly undocumented Mexican migrants. *Social Science Quarterly*, 85, 340–360. doi:10.1111/j.0038-4941.2004.08502008.x.

Akhtar, S., & Choi, L. (2004). When evening falls: The immigrant's encounter with middle and old age. *The American Journal of Psychoanalysis*, 64, 183–191. doi:10.1023/B:TAJP.0000027272.64645.f2.

Alba, R., Rumbaut, R., & Marotz, K. (2005). A distorted nation: Perceptions of racial/ethnic group sizes and attitudes toward immigrants and other minorities. *Social Forces*, 84, 901–919.

Allport, G. W. (1954). *The nature of prejudice*. Reading, MA: Addison-Wesley.

Allport, G. W. (1979). *The nature of prejudice: 25th anniversary edition*. Reading, MA: Addison-Wesley.

Atchley, R. C. (1989). A continuity theory of normal aging. *The Gerontologist*, 29, 183–190.

Atchley, R. C. (1998). Activity adaptations to the development of functional limitations and results for subjective well-being in later adulthood. *Journal of Aging Studies*, 12, 19–38. doi:10.1016/S0890-4065(98)90018-4.

Australian Bureau of Statistics. (2008). *2006 Census quickstats: Australia*. Canberra, Australia: Author. Retrieved from http://www.abs.gov.au/websitedbs/censushome.nsf/home/Data.

Avery, D. R., & McKay, P. F. (2010). Doing diversity right: An empirically based approach to effective diversity management. In G. Hodgkinson and J. K. Ford (Eds.), *International review of industrial and organizational psychology* (Vol. 25, pp. 227–252). West Sussex, England: Wiley.

Beine, M., Docquier, F., & Rapoport, H. (2008). Brain drain and human capital formation in developing countries: Winners and losers. *Economic Journal*, 118, 631–652. doi:10.1111/j.1468-0297.2008.02135.x.

Beinhocker, E., Farrell, D., & Greenberg, E. (2009). Why baby boomers will need to work longer. *McKinsey Quarterly*, 1, 118–127.

Berdahl, J., & Moore, C. (2006). Workplace harassment: Double jeopardy for minority women. *Journal of Applied Psychology*, 91, 426–436.

Blalock, H. M. (1967). *Toward a theory of minority-group relations*. New York, NY: John Wiley & Sons.

Blumer, H. (1958). Race prejudice as a sense of group position. *Pacific Sociological Review*, 1, 3–7.

Bonebright, D. A. (2010). Adult third culture kids: HRD challenges and opportunities. *Human Resource Development International*, 13, 351–359. doi: 10.1080/13678861003746822.

Byrne, D. (1961). Interpersonal attraction and attitude similarity. *The Journal of Abnormal and Social Psychology*, 62, 713–715. doi:10.1037/h0044721.

Byrne, D. (1971). The ubiquitous relationship: Attitude similarity and attraction: A cross-cultural study. *Human Relations*, 24, 201–207.

Callanan, G., & Greenhaus, J. (2008). The baby boom generation and career management: A call to action. *Advances in Developing Human Resources*, 10(1), 70–85. doi: 10.1177/1523422307310113.

Camarota, S. A. (2011). A record-setting decade of immigration: 2000–2010. Retrieved May 12, 2012, from http://cis.org/2000–2010-record-setting-decade-of-immigration.

Cappelli, P. (2005). Will there really be a labor shortage? *Human Resource Management*, 44, 143–149. doi:10.1002/hrm.20056.

Chiang-Hanisko, L. (2010). Paradise lost: How older adult Taiwanese immigrants make decisions about their living arrangements. *Journal of Cultural Diversity, 17,* 99–104.

Coenders, M., Lubbers, M., & Scheepers, P. (2008). Support for repatriation policies of migrants: Comparisons across and explanations for European countries. *International Journal of Comparative Sociology, 49,* 175–194.

Coser, L. (1956). *The functions of social conflict.* Glencoe, IL: Free Press.

Danies, C. (2010). Banking on newcomers. *Marketing Magazine, 115,* 42–43.

Danso, R. (2009). Emancipating and empowering de-valued skilled immigrants: What hope does anti-oppressive social work practice offer? *British Journal of Social Work, 39,* 539–555.

de Coulon, A., & Wolff, F. (2010). Location intentions of immigrants at retirement: Stay/return or go "back and forth?" *Applied Economics, 42,* 3319–3333. doi:10.1080/00036846.2010.482518.

Department of Immigration and Citizenship. (2007). *Key facts in immigration.* Canberra, Australia: Author. Retrieved from http://www.immi.gov.au/media/fact-sheets/02key.htm.

Dixon, J. C. (2006). The ties that bind and those that don't: Toward reconciling group threat and contact theories of prejudice. *Social Forces, 84,* 2179–2204.

Dohm, A. (2000). Gauging the labor force effects of retiring baby boomers. *Monthly Labor Report, 123*(7), 17–25.

Doverspike, D., Taylor, M. A., Shultz, K. S., & McKay, P. F. (2000). Responding to the challenge of a changing workforce: Recruiting nontraditional demographic groups. *Public Personnel Management, 29,* 445–457.

Dustmann, C., & Preston, I. (2000). Racial and economic factors in attitudes to immigration. *Bonn Institute for the Study of Labor, IZA Discussion Paper,* 190–202.

Dychtwald, K., Erickson, T., & Morrison, R. (2006). *Workforce crisis: How to beat the coming shortage of skills and talent.* Cambridge, MA: Harvard Business School Press.

Espenshade, T. J., & Hempstead, K. (1996). Contemporary American attitudes toward U.S. immigration. *International Migration Review, 30,* 535–570.

Esses, V., Dovidio, J., Jackson, L., & Armstron, T. (2001). The immigration dilemma: The role of perceived group competition, ethnic prejudice, and national identity. *Journal of Social Issues, 57,* 389–403.

Fetzer, J. (2000). *Public attitudes toward immigration in the United States, France and Germany.* New York, NY/Cambridge, United Kingdom: Cambridge University Press.

Fields, D. L., Goodman, J. S., & Blum, T. C. (2005). Human resource dependence and organizational demography: A study of minority employment in private sector companies. *Journal of Management, 31,* 167–185. doi:10.1177/0149206304271601.

Finkelstein, A. M., Burke, M. J., & Raju, N. S. (1995). Age discrimination in simulated employment contexts: An integrative analysis. *Journal of Applied Psychology, 80,* 652–663.

Fossett, M. A., & Kiecolt, K. J. (1989). The relative size of minority populations and white racial attitudes. *Social Science Quarterly, 70,* 820–835.

GCIM. (2005). *Migration in an interconnected world: New directions for action.* Report of the Global Commission on International Migration, Switzerland. Retrieved from www.gcim.org

Giles, M. W. (1977). Percent black and racial hostility: An old assumption re-examined. *Social Science Quarterly, 58,* 412–417.

Glover, I., & Branine, M. (2001). Introduction: The challenge of longer and healthy lives. In L Glover & M. Branine (Eds.), *Ageism in work and employment* (pp. 3–21). Burlington, VT: Astute.

Greene, B. (1994). Lesbian women of color: Triple jeopardy. In L. Comas-Diaz & B. Greene (Eds.), *Women of color: Integrating ethnic and gender identities* (pp. 389–427). New York, NY: Guilford Press.

Greller, M., & Richtermeyer, S. (2006). Changes in social support for professional development and retirement preparation as a function of age. *Human Relations, 59,* 1213–1234.

Grossman, R. (2008). Older workers: Running to the courthouse? *HR Magazine, 53,* 62–70.

Gustman, A., & Steinmeier, T, (1998). *Social security benefits of immigrants and U.S. born.* Retrieved from http://www.nber.org/papers/w6478.

Guth, J., & Gill, B. (2008). Motivations in East-West doctoral mobility: Revisiting the question of brain drain. *Journal of Ethnic & Migration Studies, 34,* 825–841. doi:10.1080/13691830802106119.

Han, S.-K., & Moen, P. (2001). Coupled careers: Pathways throughwork andmarriage in the United States. In H.-P. Blossfield & S. Drobnic (Eds.), *Careers of couples in contemporary societies: A cross-national comparison of the transition from male breadwinner to dual-earner families* (pp. 201–231). Oxford, UK: Oxford University Press.

Hansson, R. O., DeKoekkoek, P. D., Neece, W. M., & Patterson, D. W. (1997). Successful aging at work: Annual review 1992–1996: The older worker and transitions to retirement. *Journal of Vocational Behavior, 51,* 202–233. doi:10.1006/jvbe.1997.1605.

Heckhausen, J., & Schulz, R. (1995). A life-span theory of control. *Psychological Review, 102,* 284–304.

Hofstede, G. (1999). Problems remain, but theories will change: The universal and the specific in 21st-century global management. *Organizational Dynamics, 28,* 34–44.

Holtom, B., Mitchell, T., Lee, T., & Inderrieden, E. (2005). Shocks as causes of turnover: What they are and how organizations can manage them. *Human Resource Management, 44,* 337–352. doi:10.1002/hrm.20074.

Hu, W. Y. (2000). Immigrant earnings assimilation: Estimates from longitudinal data. *American Economic Review, 90,* 368–372.

Hum, D., & Simpson, W. (2010). The declining retirement prospects of immigrant men. *Canadian Public Policy, 36,* 287–305.

Hurh, W. M., & Kim, K. C. (1989). The success image of Asian Americans: Its validity and its practical implications. *Ethnic and Racial Studies, 12,* 512–538.

Jackson, J. S., Brown, K. T., Brown. T. N., & Marks, B. (2001). Contemporary immigration policy orientations among dominant-group members in Western Europe. *Journal of Social Issues, 57,* 431–568.

Kangasniemi, M., Winters, L., & Commander, S. (2007). Is the medical brain drain beneficial? Evidence from overseas doctors in the UK. *Social Science & Medicine, 65,* 915–923. doi:10.1016/j.socscimed.2007.04.021.

Kaushal, N. (2010). Elderly immigrants' labor supply response to supplemental security income. *Journal of Policy Analysis & Management, 29,* 137–162. doi:10.1002/pam.20482.

Keene, J. (2006). Age discrimination. In J. H. Greenhaus & G. A. Callanan (Eds.), *Encyclopedia of career development* (Vol. 1, pp. 10–14). Thousand Oaks, CA: Sage.

Kim, S., & Feldman, D. C. (2000). Working in retirement: The antecedents of bridge employment and its consequences for quality of life in retirement. *Academy of Management Journal, 43*, 1195–1210.

King, E. B., Knight, J. L., & Hebl, M. R. (2010). The influence of economic conditions on aspects of stigmatization. *Journal of Social Issues, 66*, 446–460. doi:10.1111/j.1540-4560.2010.01655.x.

Kossek, E. E., & Zonia, S. C. (1993). Assessing diversity climate: A field study of reactions to employer efforts to promote diversity. *Journal of Organizational Behavior, 14*, 61–81.

Kunovich, R. M. (2002). Social structural sources of anti-immigrant prejudice in Europe. *International Journal of Sociology, 32*, 39–57.

Lahav, G. (2004). *Immigration and politics in the new Europe: Reinventing borders.* Cambridge, United Kingdom: Cambridge University Press.

Levy, B. R., & Banaji, M. R. (2002). Implicit ageism. In T. Nelson (Ed.), *Ageism: Stereotypes and prejudice against older persons* (pp. 49–75). Cambridge: MIT Press.

Ley, D., & Kobayashi, A. (2005). Back to Hong Kong: Return migration or transnational sojourn? *Global Networks, 5*, 111–127. doi:10.1111/j.1471-0374.2005.00110.x.

Lianos, T. (2007). Brain drain and brain loss: Immigrants to Greece. *Journal of Ethnic & Migration Studies, 33*, 129–140. doi:10.1080/13691830601043562.

Longman, P. (2005). Vanishing jobs? Blame the boomers. *Harvard Business Review, 83*, 21–22.

Maestas, N. (2007). *Back to work: Expectations and realizations of work after retirement* (RAND Labor and Population Working Paper No. WR-196-2). Santa Monica, CA.

McKay, P., Avery, D., Tonidandel, S., Morris, M., Hernandez, M., & Hebl, M. (2007). Racial differences in employee retention: Are diversity climate perceptions the key? *Personnel Psychology, 60*, 35–62. doi:10.1111/j.1744-6570.2007.00064.x.

McLaren, L. M. (2003). Anti-immigrant prejudice in Europe: Contact, threat perception, and preferences for the exclusion of migrants. *Social Forces, 81*, 909–936.

McNabb, D., Gibson, L., & Finnie, B. (2006). The case of the vanishing workplace. *Public Performance & Management Review, 29*, 358–368.

McNeese-Smith, D., & Crook, M. (2003). Nursing values and a changing nurse workforce: Values, age, and job stages. *Journal of Nursing Administration, 33*, 260–270.

McPherson, M., Smith-Lovin, L., & Cook, J. (2001). Birds of a feather: Homophily in social networks. *Annual Review of Sociology, 27*, 415–444. doi:10.1146/annurev.soc.27.1.415.

MetLife Foundation (2008). *Americans seek meaningful work in the second half of life.* Retrieved May 12, 2012, from: http://www.encore.org/files/Encore_Survey.pdf.

Montalto, C. P., Yuh, Y., & Hanna, S. (2000). Determinants of planned retirement age. *Financial Services Review, 9*, 1–17.

Mummendey, A., Klink, A., & Brown, R. (2001). Nationalism and patriotism: National identification and out-group rejection. *British Journal of Social Psychology, 40*, 159–172.

Murphy, B. (1993). *The other Australia: Experiences of migration.* Cambridge: Cambridge University Press.

Myers, D. (2008). Aging baby boomers and the effects of immigration and rediscovering the intergenerational social contract. *Generations, 32*, 18–23.

Ng, T. W. H., & Feldman, D. C. (2008). The relationship of age to ten dimensions of job performance. *Journal of Applied Psychology, 93*, 393–423.

Nguyen, B. (2008). Tomorrow's workforce: The needs for immigrant workers and strategies to retain them. *Public Personnel Management, 37*, 175–184.

Pettigrew, T., & Tropp, L. (2008). How does intergroup contact reduce prejudice? Meta-analytic tests of three mediators. *European Journal of Social Psychology, 38*, 922–934. doi:10.1002/ejsp.504.

Phillips, K. W., Mannix, E. A., Neale, M. A., & Gruenfeld, D. H. (2004). Diverse groups and information sharing: The effects of congruent ties. *Journal of Experimental Social Psychology, 40*, 497–510. doi:10.1016/j.jesp.2003.10.003.

Porter, E. (2005). Not on the radar: Illegal immigrants are bolstering social security. *Generations, 29*, 100–102.

Quillian, L. (1995). Prejudice as a response to perceived group threat: Population composition and anti-immigrant and racial prejudice in Europe. *American Sociological Review, 60*, 586–611.

Reid, P., & Comas-Díaz, L. (1990). Gender and ethnicity: Perspectives on dual status. *Sex Roles, 22*, 397–408. doi:10.1007/BF00288160.

Rynes, S. L., & Barber, A. E. (1990). Applicant attraction strategies: An organizational perspective. *Academy of Management Review, 15,* 286–310.

Sanchez, J., Spector, P., & Cooper, C. (2000). Adapting to a boundaryless world: A developmental expatriate model. *Academy of Management Executive, 14*, 96–106.

Scheepers, P., Gijsberts, M., & Coenders, M. (2002). Ethnic exclusionism in European countries: Public opposition to civil rights for legal migrants as a response to perceived group threat. *European Sociology Review, 18*, 17–34.

Schellenberg, G., & Ostrovsky, Y. (2008). The retirement plans and expectations of older workers. *Canadian Social Trends, 86,* 11–34.

Scheve, K. F., & Slaughter, M. J. (2001). Labor market competition and individual preferences over immigration policy. *Review of Economic Statistics, 83*, 133–145. doi:10.1162/003465301750160108.

Schneider, S. L. (2008). Anti-immigrant attitudes in Europe: Out-group size and perceived ethnic threat. *European Sociological Review, 24*, 53–67.

Schnur, E., Koffler, R., Wimpenny, N., Giller, H., & Rafield, E. (1995). Family child care and new immigrants: Cultural bridge and support. *Child Welfare, 74*, 1237–1248.

Segal, U. A., Elliott, D., & Mayadas, N. S. (2009). *Immigration worldwide.* Oxford, UK: Oxford University Press.

Semyonov, M., Raijman, R., & Gorodzeisky, A. (2006). The rise of antiforeigner sentiment in European societies, 1988–2000. *American Sociological Review, 71*, 426–449.

Semyonov, M., Raijman, R., & Gorodzeisky, A. (2008). Foreigners' impact on European societies. *International Journal of Comparative Sociology, 49*, 5–29.

Shultz, K. S., Morton, K. R., & Weckerle, J. R. (1998). The influence of push and pull factors on voluntary and involuntary early retirees' retirement decision and adjustment. *Journal of Vocational Behavior, 53*, 45–57. doi:10.1006/jvbe.1997.1610.

Simpson, B. (2009). Labor shortage! Help wanted. *Manufacturing Engineering, 142*, 176–176.

Stanford, E., & Usita, P. (2002). Retirement: Who is at risk? *Generations, 26*, 45–48.

Stephan, W., Ybarra, O., & Bachman, G. (1999). Prejudice toward immigrants. *Journal of Applied Social Psychology, 29,* 2221–2237.

Stuenkel, D. L., Cohen, J. & de la Cuesta, K. (2005). The multi-generational nursing work force. *Journal of Nursing Administration, 35,* 283–285.

Swift, J. (2004). Justifying age discrimination. *The Industrial Law Journal, 35,* 228–244.

Szinovacz, M. E., & Davey, A. (2005). Predictors of perceptions of involuntary retirement. *The Gerontologist, 45,* 36–47.

Tajfel, H. (1982). Instrumentality, identity, and social comparison. In H. Tajfel (Ed.), *Social identity and intergroup relations* (pp. 483–507). Cambridge, England: Cambridge University Press.

Tajfel, H., & Turner, J. C. (1986). The social identity theory of intergroup behavior. In S. Worchel and W. G. Austin (Eds.), *Psychology of Intergroup Relations* (pp. 7–24). Chicago, IL: Nelson-Hall.

Tang, J. (1993). The career attainment of Caucasian and Asian engineers. *Sociological Quarterly, 34,* 467–496.

Tang, J. (2000). *Doing engineering: The career attainment and mobility of Caucasian, black, and Asian American engineers.* Lanham, MD: Rowman & Littlefield.

Tharenou, P., & Caulfield, N. (2010). Will I stay or will I go? Explaining repatriation by self-initiated expatriates. *Academy of Management Journal, 53,* 1009–1028.

Toossi, M. (2002). A century of change: The U.S. labor force, 1950–2050. *Monthly Labor Review, 125,* 15–29.

Toossi, M. (2005). Labor force projections to 2014: Retiring boomers. *Monthly Labor Review, 128,* 25–44.

Tsui, A. S., & O'Reilly, C. A., III. (1989). Beyond simple demographic effects: The importance of relational demography in superior-subordinate dyads. *Academy of Management Journal, 32,* 402–423.

Ulrich, L. B. (2006). Bridge employment. In J. H. Greenhaus & G. A. Callanan (Eds.), *Encyclopedia of career development* (Vol. 1, pp. 49–51). Thousand Oaks, CA: Sage.

United Nations. (2004). *World economic and social survey 2004: International migration.* Department of Economic and Social Affairs of the United Nations Secretariat, New York, United Nations Publication Sales No. E.04.II.C.3. Retrieved from http://www.un.org/esa/policy/wess/wess2004files/part2web/preface.pdf.

United Nations. (2006). *International migration 2006.* Department of Economic and Social Affairs, Population Division. Retrieved from http://www.un.org/esa/population/publications/2006Migration_Chart/Migration2006.pdf.

Valentova, M., & Alieva, A. (2010). *Immigration as a threat: The effect of gender differences among Luxembourg residents with and without a migration history.* Unpublished manuscript.

Vernon, A. (1999). The dialectics of multiple identities and the disabled people's movement. *Disability and Society, 14,* 385–398.

Waters, M., & Jiménez, T. (2005). Assessing immigrant assimilation: New empirical and theoretical challenges. *Annual Review of Sociology, 31,* 105–125. doi:10.1146/annurev.soc.29.010202.100026.

Wrenn, K., & Maurer, T. (2004). Beliefs about older workers' learning and development behavior in relation to beliefs about malleability of skills, age-related decline, and control. *Journal of Applied Social Psychology, 34,* 223–242.

Yoo, G., & Kim, B. (2010). Remembering sacrifices: Attitude and beliefs among second generation Korean Americans regarding family support. *Journal of Cross-Cultural Gerontology, 25,* 165–181. doi:10.1007/s10823–010–9116–8.

Yuh. Y., Hanna, S., & Montalto, C. (1998). Mean and pessimistic projections of retirement adequacy. *Financial Sciences Review, 7,* 175–193.

Zemke, R. (1999). Service recovery: Turning oops into opportunity. In R. Zemke & J. Woods (Eds.), *Best practices in customer service* (pp. 279–288). New York, NY: AMACOM, AMA Publications.

Zhan, Y., Wang, M., Liu, S., & Shultz, K. (2009). Bridge employment and retirees' health: A longitudinal investigation. *Journal of Occupational Health Psychology, 14,* 374–389.

Generational Differences in Older Workers and Retirement

Jesse Erdheim *and* Michael A. Lodato

Abstract

This chapter discusses generational differences in individual attributes between baby boomers and Gen Xers and provides proposed linkages between those differences and specific retirement processes. Time-lagged multigenerational research suggests that differences exist, on average, in personality characteristics, work values, and mental health variables between baby boomers and Gen Xers. We postulate that these differences in individual attributes will lead to generational differences in the accepting of early retirement incentives, deciding whether to retire early, and taking a bridge position. Implications for the study of generational differences are discussed, along with practical strategies for human resource managers to retain retirement-eligible and near-retirement-eligible employees.

Key Words: retirement, retirement processes, generational differences, baby boomers, Generation X

Retirement has traditionally been defined as a permanent exit from the workforce during which time leisure is financed by personal savings, defined contribution plans, and/or pensions (Wang, Adams, Beehr, & Schultz, 2009). However, the concept of retirement has been rapidly evolving in recent years (Beehr & Bowling, 2002), as those approaching it are now faced with a variety of choices, ranging from a complete withdrawal from work to the pursuit of another full-time career, with countless options in between (Wang et al., 2009). Indeed, within the next decade, the workforce over age 50 (those closest to full retirement) is predicted to grow at a rate of almost four times that of the workforce as a whole (Shultz & Wang, 2008). It is important to note that this trend is occurring alongside an ever-changing workplace that includes a predominant shift toward knowledge-based jobs, which, despite diminishing the physical burden of work, brings with it heavy cognitive and psychosocial demands. In addition,

the modern workforce is more geographically dispersed as well as more ethnically, culturally, and gender diverse than ever before. Moreover, global competition, outsourcing and offshoring of jobs, and an ongoing technological boom will continue to affect the makeup of the twenty-first century workforce in the years to come (Wang et al., 2009). All of these changes are occurring as the baby boomers (those currently age 46–65) approach retirement, and it is likely that they will continue into the future as Gen Xers (those currently 29–45) move toward retirement.

The organizational sciences literature has responded to the emergence of these issues by producing an abundance of research on retirement planning, retirement decision making, early retirement, retirement transition and adjustment, and bridge employment, which considers how individual, job and organizational, familial, and socioeconomic factors affect these retirement processes (Wang & Shultz,

2010). In Wang and Shultz's (2010) comprehensive review of the literature, the authors describe a multitude of individual attributes that affect retirement processes, which include demographic characteristics, needs and values, personality, knowledge, skills and abilities, attitudes toward retirement, and health and financial circumstances. However, despite the wealth of variables studied, to the authors' current knowledge, no research has looked at the relation between individual attributes in the context of generational differences and retirement. This is a significant omission because generational differences have been found in a variety of psychological variables, including personality characteristics (for a review, see Twenge & Campbell, 2008, 2010), work values (for a review, see Twenge, 2010), job attitudes (Kowske, Rasch, & Wiley, 2010), and mental health disorders (for a review, see Twenge & Campbell, 2008, 2010), and these variables are a sizeable part of the list of individual attributes that have been linked to retirement processes. Therefore, studying individual attributes in the context of generational differences may provide a more comprehensive picture of certain retirement processes.

Accordingly, the primary goal of this chapter is to consider how differences in individual attributes between baby boomers and Gen Xers affect retirement processes that fall predominantly under an organization's control (e.g., offering early retirement incentives [ERIs]), thereby viewing retirement from a human resource management lens. We focus on this perspective because our major practical application goal is to offer organizations retention strategies that may delay the impending retirement of valued employees. The two generations mentioned above were selected as the focus of this chapter because baby boomers are the generation closest to full retirement, and Gen Xers will begin entering the aging workforce (55 years or older) over the next decade, thereby becoming retirement eligible. Indeed, Bureau of Labor Statistics' (BLS) projections have shown that by 2012, nearly 20% of the total U.S. workforce will be 55 years old or older (Toossi, 2004), which will lead to a sizable increase in the number of people who may transition into retirement in the next decade. As such, one of the biggest challenges for organizations to manage in the coming years will be the potential wave of retirement of more than 75 million older workers (Twenge, Campbell, Hoffman, & Lance, 2010a), and therefore it will be important for them to develop retention strategies around how this new set of retirement-eligible personnel (Gen Xers) differs

from those who entered retirement in the previous generation (baby boomers). Such retention strategies will be particularly important given the grave state of retirement planning among pre-retirees today. For example, according to a Harris Interactive Survey, on average, respondents indicated that they will need to postpone their retirement by 4.2 years due to inadequate financial planning, and just 18% believe that they have actively planned enough for their retirement (Age Wave, 2009).

This chapter can be considered a first step in addressing the generational differences gap in the retirement decision-making literature and offering organizations practical strategies for retaining retirement-eligible (baby boomers) and near-retirement-eligible (Gen Xers) employees. Our chapter is structured in the following format: first, we define the theoretical basis for studying generational differences (referred to as generational cohort theory); second, we describe the four predominant generations working today (veterans, baby boomers, Gen Xers, and millennials); third, we describe time-lagged design, which is the preferred methodology for studying generational differences; fourth, we review the literature on generational differences in individual attributes; fifth, we link generational differences in individual attributes to retirement processes; sixth, we discuss the theoretical and practical implications of our review and proposed linkages; and last, we discuss future directions for research in this area.

Generational Cohort Theory

As a construct, the term "generational cohort" refers to a group of people of similar age living in a similar location who experience significant life events (e.g., sociocultural, socioeconomic, political) at similar critical stages in their development (Kupperschmidt, 2000), which are often adolescence and/or early adulthood (Arsenault, 2004; Schuman & Scott, 1989). Belonging to the same age group places individuals in a common historical location, limiting them to a specific range of potential experiences and predisposing them to a characteristic mode of thinking and experiencing the world (Sessa, Kabacoff, Deal, & Brown, 2007). According to Wyatt (1993), a generational cohort is formed and bounded when the following causes or determinations are present:

1. a traumatic or formative event, such as an assassination of a political leader (e.g., John F. Kennedy) or a war (e.g., Vietnam)

2. a dramatic shift in demography that influences the distribution of resources in a society (e.g., the size of the baby-boomer generation)

3. an interval connecting a generation to success or failure (e.g., the Great Depression)

4. the creation of a sacred space that enables the sustainment of a collective memory (e.g., Woodstock)

5. mentors or heroes who give impetus and voice by their work (e.g., Martin Luther King)

6. innovators who know and support each other (e.g., Steven Jobs and Bill Gates)

As a result of these factors, generational cohorts form personas that include attitudes, values, and beliefs about family life, religions, gender roles, and lifestyles that are relatively stable over time and distinguish one cohort from another (Strauss & Howe, 1991). For example, baby boomers grew up embracing the psychology of entitlement, expecting the best from life, whereas Gen Xers grew up witnessing high divorce rates among their parents and, consequently, tend to value a stable family unit (Kupperschmidt, 2000) and crave mentorship (Jurkiewicz & Brown, 1998). Although identifying the exact boundary years that define a generation is imprecise (Strauss & Howe, 1991), most researchers generally agree that there are four broad generations of employees currently working in the workplace: veterans (1925–1944), baby boomers (1945–1964), Gen Xers (1965–1981), and Gen Yers, referred to as millennials (1982–2000) (Wong, Gardiner, Lang, & Coulon, 2008). Despite the focus of our chapter being baby boomers and Gen Xers, to be comprehensive we describe each generation below.

Four Generations at Work
Veterans
According to the BLS, in 2011, veterans make up 5% of the workforce. Events that define this generation include the Great Depression, the New Deal, World War II, and the Korean War. In addition, public figures that profoundly impacted veterans include Franklin D. Roosevelt and Charles Lindbergh (Sessa, Kabacoff, Deal, & Brown, 2007).

Baby Boomers
The BLS estimates that baby boomers account for 38% of the workforce in 2011. Their attitudes and values were affected by the Vietnam War, the civil rights and women's movements, the Kennedy family, the Kennedy and King assassinations, Watergate, the first walk on the moon, the sexual revolution, and Woodstock (Arsenault, 2004; Sessa et al., 2007).

Gen Xers
According to the BLS, in 2011, Gen Xers are estimated to account for 32% of the workforce. Gen Xers came of age during the social and economic turmoil that followed the baby-boomer generation and were profoundly influenced by MTV, AIDS, the global economy, the widespread use of computers and video games, the *Challenger* incident, Rodney King, and the fall of communism (Arsenault, 2004).

Gen Yers
Millennials make up about 25% of the workforce in 2011. They are the first generation to be born into a "wired" world in which technology, such as cell phones, automatic teller machines (ATMs), and laser surgery, is a part of everyday life. Millennials are very familiar with scandals, both political (e.g., Clinton/Lewinsky) and economic (e.g., bankruptcy of Enron and Lehman Brothers), natural and environmental disasters (e.g., Hurricane Katrina; Gulf oil spill); and terrorism on American soil (e.g., Oklahoma City bombing; 9/11) (Sessa et al., 2007).

As previously mentioned, the focus of our chapter will be to consider generational differences in individual attributes between baby boomers and Gen Xers. However, before reviewing this literature, it is first necessary to discuss the preferred methodology for multigenerational studies, a time-lagged design that addresses the criticisms of cross-sectional research and therefore is used in all the studies included in our review.

Preferred Generational Research Method: Time-Lagged Design
Generational research continues to receive criticism in the organizational sciences literature (see Macky, Gardner, & Forsyth, 2008) because it often employs a cross-sectional methodology, such as an organizational survey, which cannot distinguish whether differences are due to age or generation (Schaie, 1965). In order to draw generation-based conclusions from research, studies must separate effects due to generation from effects due to age. The best research design to isolate generation effects is a time-lagged design, which compares samples of the same age at different points in time. For example, if comparing baby boomers to Gen Xers using

a college sample, one may compare data on a scale completed by a sample of college freshman in 1968 (baby boomers) to a sample of college freshman who completed the same scale in 1988 (Gen Xers). With age controlled, differences can be attributed to either generation or the specific time period (change over time that affects all generations). Time period effects are often weaker than age or generation effects because attitudes tend to be formed early and retained through life (Low, Yoon, Roberts, & Rounds, 2005). Therefore, a time-lagged design has significant advantages over a cross-sectional design in isolating generational differences.

One specific example of a time-lagged design is cross-temporal meta-analysis, where journal articles and dissertations that administer a psychological scale (e.g., the Internal-External Locus of Control Scale, the State-Trait Anxiety Inventory, etc.) are gathered and analyzed, and the average scores of different samples at different points in time are compared. With age held constant, differences can more confidently be attributed to generation (Twenge & Campbell, 2008). Results describe changes in how the average member of one generation compares to the average member of another generation. On average, the effects of generational changes in personality characteristics are about 0.20 standard deviations for each 10-year difference in birth year. Thus, employees 25 years apart in birth years will, on average, differ on many personality characteristics by 0.50 standard deviations, a moderate effect size. Employees 50 years apart in birth years will, on average, differ by a full standard deviation, a large effect size (Twenge & Campbell, 2010).

Studies have also used time-lagged designs other than cross-temporal meta-analysis to investigate generational differences. For example, Smola and Sutton (2002) replicated a study conducted in 1974 and then compared means on items assessing desirability of work outcomes, pride in craftsmanship, and moral importance of work for 27- to 40-year-olds and 41- to 65-year-olds across the two time periods. In a study examining generational effects in work attitudes, Kowske et al. (2010) used a hierarchical age-period-cohort model using repeated cross-sectional individual data to examine generational differences. This method controlled not only for age effects but also for time period as well. It is important to implement such rigorous time-lagged designs because it is otherwise difficult to attribute significant effects to generational differences. In most time-lagged studies, results have shown that generational changes are linear (Twenge

& Campbell, 2008, 2010); however, some studies have found evidence for curvilinear change (e.g., Twenge & Im, 2007).

Now that we have reviewed the preferred research design for studying generational differences, we will review the literature on generational differences in individual attributes found to be antecedents of retirement processes. We focus on studies that used time-lagged designs so that the results we discuss cannot be attributed to age.

Generational Differences in Individual Attributes

In general, research has looked at generational differences in the following individual attributes: personality characteristics, work values, job attitudes, and mental health variables. We begin our review below with personality characteristics.

Personality Characteristics

Personality is typically defined as a person's characteristic pattern of thinking, feeling, and acting (Myers, 1992). Many theories of personality have been developed over the years, but two that are most relevant to studying behavior in a workplace setting are trait theory and cognitive social learning theory. Trait theorists attempt to label patterns in people's thinking, feeling, and acting with adjectives, or factors that are typically identified through factor analysis. One of the most popular representations of trait theory is the Five-Factor Model of personality (Costa & McCrae, 1992), which consists of Extroversion, Agreeableness, Conscientiousness, Neuroticism, and Openness to Experience. Proponents of this model have argued that personality is stable from about the age of 30 through the rest of adulthood (Costa & McCrae, 1997).

Another common theory of personality applied to research in the workplace is cognitive social learning theory. According to this theory, personality is defined by the cognitive strategies people use to make sense out of the world and interact with others (Kelly, 1955). Examples of such strategies are self-efficacy, which is the competence a person feels he or she has to complete a task (Bandura, 1977), and locus of control, which is the degree to which a person feels he or she has control over his or her destiny (Rotter, 1966). These strategies are said to be learned and more subject to change than traits; however, Twenge (2000) suggests that the social environment of different time periods may produce differences that can be associated with generational membership.

A number of cross-temporal meta-analyses identifying generational differences in personality characteristics have been conducted over the last ten years. First, we discuss studies that look at individualistic traits, such as extroversion, assertiveness, agency, self-esteem, and narcissism, before turning our attention to other important personality characteristics, such as locus of control and need for social approval.

Positive individualistic traits, as a whole, appear to have risen between the baby-boomer generation and Gen X. Regarding extroversion, Twenge (2001a) studied college student scores on the extroversion scales of the Eysenck Personality Inventory and Eysenck Personality Questionnaire between 1966 and 1993. Correlations between the scores and year of data collection were positive and strong (≥ 0.65), which suggests that extroversion increased from the baby-boomer generation to Gen X. The increase is large, near one standard deviation, explaining 14% to 19% of the variance in personality over this time period. This increase in extroversion has occurred alongside a rise in self-esteem. For example, Twenge and Campbell (2001) examined changes in baby-boomer and Gen X college students' scores on the Rosenberg Self-Esteem Scale, with results indicating that self-esteem increased from a mean of 29.82 in 1968 to a mean of 32.86 in 1994, representing a change of $d = 0.62$.

Assertiveness and agentic traits in women have also increased between the two generations. Regarding assertiveness, Twenge (2001b) found that college women's self-reports of assertiveness fell 0.39 standard deviations in the baby-boomer generation from where they had been in the veteran generation. Alternatively, college women's self-reports of assertiveness rose 0.46 standard deviations among those in Gen X. In terms of agency, Twenge (1997) studied data on the Bem Sex-Role Inventory and Personal Attributes Questionnaire and found that women's scores on the masculine scales, which include traits such as assertiveness, independence, leadership, and self-reliance, have increased steadily over the generations.

In addition to positive individualistic traits, narcissism also rose between the baby-boomer generation and Gen X. For example, Twenge, Konrath, Foster, Campbell, and Bushman (2008) studied college students who completed the Narcissistic Personality Inventory (NPI) between 1979 and 2006. The authors found that between the early 1980s and 2006, NPI scores rose 0.33 standard deviations, such that an average student in the early 1980s scored in the 50th percentile and an average student in 2006 scored in the 65th percentile. In other words, two-thirds of recent college students have narcissism scores that fall above the mean 1979–1985 score, representing a 30% increase in narcissism over this time period.

Beyond a rise in individualistic traits, studies suggest that there are differences in locus of control and need for social approval between baby boomers and Gen Xers. In terms of locus of control, Twenge, Zhang, and Im (2004) found that Gen Xers have a stronger external locus of control than baby boomers, such that they have less expectancy in their ability to control events and outcomes associated with their lives. Specifically, between 1960 and 2002, external locus of control scores rose about 0.80 standard deviations in college students, with the average college student in 2002 having a greater external locus of control than 80% of college students in the early 1960s. Although Gen Xers, on average, may feel less able to control the events of their lives than baby boomers, results of another study indicate that they also score lower than baby boomers on need for social approval (i.e., concern with others' viewpoints and impressions), and therefore are more likely to question authority and challenge the status quo (Twenge & Im, 2007). Findings from this study are particularly interesting because need for social approval actually decreased sharply across the baby-boomer generation up to Generation X, and has since leveled off. A decline in the need for social approval also fits with the rise in individualistic traits demonstrated by Gen Xers. Overall, the average member of Gen X seems much more inclined to act in his or her best interests, without regard for social approval, than the average baby boomer.

Personality characteristics summary. Taken altogether, this research shows that between the baby-boomer generation and Gen X, there has been an increase in self-esteem, narcissism, extroversion, external locus of control, and assertiveness and agency in women, and a decrease in the need for social approval.

Work Values

Work values refer to the outcomes and activities people seek to attain through their professional work (Brief, 1998). Work values help to determine how people perceive their role in the workplace, and they influence a number of different outcomes, such as employee attitudes and behaviors, job decisions, and problem solving (Twenge et al., 2010a).

Research on work values acknowledges the distinction between the following values: those that are extrinsic, such as income, status, and opportunity for promotion; those that are intrinsic, such as valuing work because it is inherently interesting or provides an opportunity to grow and develop (Ryan & Deci, 2000); those based around autonomy in decision making, job stability, or security; those related to altruism or helping behaviors; those providing social benefits, such as improved interpersonal relationships at work; and those that are related to leisure, such as the opportunity for free time and vacation (Johnson, 2002; Miller, Woehr, & Hudspeth, 2002).

To our knowledge, there have been three time-lagged studies that have examined work values and how they may differ across generations. In Smola and Sutton's (2002) study that compared data collected in 1974 to data collected in 1999, results indicated that work ethic and work centrality decreased from the baby-boomer generation to Gen X, as evidenced by decreases in mean ratings for items such as "a worker should do a decent job whether or not his supervisor is around," "a good indication of a man's worth is how well he does his job," and "work should be one of the most important parts of a person's life." Alongside this decline in work being the central focus of life, the authors found that Gen Xers were more "me" oriented and less loyal to the their organization than baby boomers, which supports the rise in narcissism across the generations that Twenge's research (e.g., Twenge et al., 2008; Twenge & Foster, 2010) has found.

A study conducted by the Families and Work Institute (2006) provides further evidence for the decline in work centrality between baby boomers and Gen Xers. This study included data from surveys of several thousand U.S. workers in 1977, 1992, and 2002, drawn from the National Study of the Changing Workforce and the Quality of Employment Survey. Results suggest that baby boomers are more likely than Gen Xers to be work-centric (i.e., place a higher value on work than family), whereas Gen Xers are more likely than baby boomers to be family-centric (i.e., place a higher value on family than work). Specifically, 22% of baby boomers reported that they were work-centric compared to 13% of Gen Xers, and 52% of Gen Xers indicated that they were family-centric compared to 41% of baby boomers.

The Families and Work Institute (2006) study also showed a decline in work ethic across the generations, with results suggesting that the desire to move into a job with more responsibility has declined over time because people are deciding that they do not want to work longer hours. For example, in 1992, 80% of workers under 23 eventually wanted to assume a job with more responsibility, but that number dropped to 60% in 2002. In addition, those 23–27 years old and 38–57 years old also showed declines. For this 23–27 years old, this decline fell from 69% (1992) to 54% (2002), and for those 38–57 years old, it slid from 41% (1992) to 31% (2002).

Twenge et al. (2010a) also conducted a time-lagged study examining work values, which was based on a sample of graduating high school seniors in the United States between 1976 and 2006 ($N = 16,507$) who were part of the "Monitoring the Future" data collection (Johnson, Bachman, & O'Malley, 2006). This was the first study to use this database to study generational differences, and it focused on work centrality, job stability, and other job characteristics, such as leisure values (e.g., working in a job that allows more vacation or leaves time for leisure) and extrinsic rewards (e.g., working in a job that has high status or that pays well). In order to compare data across generations, Twenge and her colleagues focused on data from 1976 (baby boomers), 1991 (Gen Xers), and 2006 (millennials). Overall, this study found further support for many of Smola and Sutton's (2002) findings. For example, Twenge et al. (2010a) found evidence for a decrease in work centrality as well as a steady increase in leisure values over time. Interestingly, results of this study also indicated that the value placed on extrinsic rewards increased from the baby-boomer generation to Gen X, but then reached its peak and decreased for Gen Y (although it is still higher for millennials than baby boomers).

Work values summary. Overall, these studies suggest that baby boomers place greater value on work ethic and work centrality than Gen Xers, and Gen Xers place greater value on leisure and extrinsic rewards than baby boomers.

Job Attitudes

Kowske et al. (2010) examined generational differences in job attitudes using data collected from a diverse sample of U.S. employees ($N = 115,044$) obtained from eighteen years of repeated administrations of the Kenexa Work Trends™ employee opinion survey. The authors studied several job attitudes, including overall company and job satisfaction, satisfaction with pay and benefits, recognition, career development and advancement, and job security. When controlling for age and time period, the authors (2010) found that millennials reported higher job satisfaction, more satisfaction with career development, and more confidence in job security than Gen Xers (these effects vary between $d = 0.24$ and $d = 0.28$). Although millennials reported higher levels of job satisfaction than Gen Xers, no significant differences between Gen Xers and baby boomers were reported. Currently, this is the only time-lagged study that has been conducted on generational differences in job attitudes.

Mental Health

The available evidence suggests that two of the most common mental health disorders, anxiety and depression, are on the rise in America (Twenge & Campbell, 2008). Specifically, a cross-temporal meta-analysis conducted by Twenge (2000) found that anxiety in college student samples from 1952 to 1993 increased almost a full standard deviation, explaining about 20% of the variance. As for depression, Twenge, Gentile, et al. (2010) conducted a cross-temporal meta-analysis looking at college students between 1938 and 2007 and found increases in their psychopathology on every clinical subscale of the Minnesota Multiphasic Personality Inventory, including depression.

Conclusion. Time-lagged studies have revealed a variety of differences between baby boomers and Gen Xers in a number of individual attributes. These attributes can be organized by personality characteristics, work values, and mental health disorders (differences in job attitudes have yet to be found between baby boomers and Gen Xers using a time-lagged design). In Table 35.1, we summarize the findings across these three types of individual attributes based on the research studies described above.

Now that we have reviewed the literature on generational differences in personality traits, work values, job attitudes, and mental health, we turn our attention to discussing retirement, viewing it through a human resource management perspective.

Retirement as a Human Resource Management Approach

Although there are numerous theoretical conceptualizations of retirement, such as retirement as decision making, retirement as an adjustment process, and retirement as a career development stage (see Wang & Shultz, 2010), we focus our efforts by conceptualizing retirement as a part of human resource management because one of the primary

Table 35.1 Comparison of Baby-Boomer Generation and Generation X on Personality Characteristics, Work Values, and Mental Health Variables

Personality Characteristics	
Extroversion	Gen X > Baby Boomers
Self-Esteem	Gen X > Baby Boomers
Assertiveness in Women	Gen X > Baby Boomers
Agentic Traits in Women	Gen X > Baby Boomers
Narcissism	Gen X > Baby Boomers
External Locus of Control	Gen X > Baby Boomers
Need for Social Approval	Baby Boomers > Gen X
Work Values	
Work Ethic	Baby Boomers > Gen X
Work Centrality	Baby Boomers > Gen X
Leisure Values	Gen X > Baby Boomers
Extrinsic Rewards	Gen X > Baby Boomers
Mental Health	
Anxiety	Gen X > Baby Boomers
Depression	Gen X > Baby Boomers

aims of this chapter is to provide practitioners with practical strategies for retaining employees approaching retirement. Conceptualizing retirement from this perspective suggests that organizations play a key role in influencing employees' decisions whether to retire or continue working. Much of this research has focused on who will accept ERIs, why people make the decision to retire early, and who will accept bridge employment. As we discuss this research, we intermix propositions linking generational differences in individual attributes to these retirement processes.

ERIs

ERIs are typically offered by organizations to encourage employees at or near retirement age to retire earlier than planned. Typical ERIs include severance packages, continuance of health insurance coverage, and increases in the value of a pension plan (Hayden & Pfadenhauer, 2005). Although organizations have control over what financial incentives they offer, the decision to accept ERIs can be quite complex (Wang & Shultz, 2010). For example, a variety of factors such as self-esteem (Gowan, 1998), personal health, current salary, or a spouse still in the workforce can influence the decision to take or delay accepting ERIs (Kim & Feldman, 1998).

Considering time-lagged research indicates that, on average, baby boomers are more work-centric (Families and Work Institute, 2006) and loyal to their organization (Smola & Sutton, 2002) than Gen Xers, baby boomers may feel more negativity toward accepting ERIs. This reaction may grow out of a sense of abandoning their organization when they still feel like they can contribute to its effectiveness, as well as not wanting to give up their primary focus in life earlier than necessary. In addition, on average, Gen Xers have a stronger external locus of control than baby boomers (Twenge et al., 2004), which suggests that when they are offered ERIs, they may tend to believe that they have little control over their future in the organization, and therefore may be more likely to accept the incentives.

Proposition 1: On average, Gen Xers will be more likely to accept ERIs than baby boomers.

Decision to Retire Early

Although the majority of research on early retirement has looked retrospectively at who accepts ERIs and for what reasons, research has also investigated the intention to retire early, which is an important antecedent to the act of actually retiring. For example, several studies report that those who perceive their jobs as being stressful and having higher workloads intend to retire early (Lin & Hsieh, 2001; Elovainio et al., 2005). Just because a person intends to retire early, though, does not mean that he or she actually does, but research suggests that intentions are one of the strongest predictors of actual behavior (Prothero & Beach, 1984).

Time-lagged studies indicate that, on average, Gen Xers are more likely to suffer from higher rates of anxiety (Twenge, 2000) and depression (Twenge, Gentile, et al., 2010) than baby boomers. This suggests that work may serve as a greater stressor for Gen Xers, and therefore they may be more likely to intend to retire at a younger age. Time-lagged studies also suggest that Gen Xers, on average, are more "me" oriented (Smola & Sutton, 2002) and place greater value on leisure (Twenge et al., 2010a) than baby boomers. This suggests that Gen Xers, on average, may be more likely to value taking care of their individualistic needs and enjoying life outside of work than baby boomers, and therefore may have a greater intention to retire.

Proposition 2: On average, Gen Xers will be more likely to decide to retire early than baby boomers.

Bridge Employment

Bridge employment refers to the employment tendencies of older workers as they transition from the jobs they have held for much of their careers to their complete withdrawal from the workforce (Shultz, 2003). Wang, Zhan, Liu, and Shultz (2008) categorized bridge employment decisions into three types: career bridge employment (i.e., individuals who accept bridge employment in the same industry/field as their career jobs), bridge employment in a different field, and full retirement. Empirical studies on bridge employment focus on addressing what the desirable jobs or organizational characteristics are of bridge employment that attract retirees (Wang & Shultz, 2010). For example, Rau and Adams (2005) found that scheduling flexibility and a targeted equal employment opportunity statement positively influenced older workers' attraction to the organization. Older workers may also favor bridge employment because they perceive premature retirement negatively and as involuntary (Shultz, Morton, & Weckerle, 1998).

Time-lagged studies have found that baby boomers, on average, are higher in work ethic and work centrality (Smola & Sutton, 2002; Families & Work Institute, 2006; Twenge et al., 2010a). This suggests that they may feel a stronger need for a gradual withdrawal from the workplace than Gen Xers. In addition, baby boomers, on average, have a higher need for social approval than Gen Xers (Twenge & Im, 2007). Perhaps a social pressure to be active and productive is more likely to keep them in the workplace after they retire from their main career.

Proposition 3: On average, baby boomers will be more likely to pursue bridge employment than Gen Xers.

Discussion

In this chapter, our main focus has been on generational differences in individual attributes between baby boomers and Gen Xers, and their potential relation to retirement processes, such as the acceptance of ERIs, the decision to retire early, and the likelihood of accepting bridge employment. In summarizing the literature on generational differences in individual attributes, we focused primarily on baby boomers and Gen Xers for the following reasons: (1) they are the generations currently retiring (baby boomers) and next to retire (Gen X), and (2) more research and archival data exists on baby boomers and Gen Xers in comparison to millennials, who are still relatively new to the workforce and in many cases have yet to even enter the workforce. As for retirement outcomes, we chose to focus on ERIs, decisions to retire early, and bridge employment because of their implications for human resource management as well as a belief that findings from existing time-lagged research on generational differences suggested that this was a good place to start. We feel that by presenting the existing research in both areas and making a linkage between the two, we have laid the groundwork for research that can strengthen our theoretical conceptualizations of both the generational construct and important retirement processes.

As a start in broadening our theoretical understanding of multigenerational research and retirement, we developed three propositions. These propositions are based on recent findings from time-lagged studies that looked at generational differences as well as current research on retirement processes. Our first proposition states that Gen Xers will be more likely to accept ERIs than baby boomers. The study of ERIs is important because of its impact on both employees and the organization. When offered ERIs, employees may be facing a difficult decision to retire earlier than they intended. Organizations, on the other hand, may be able to target ERIs at the needs of particular generations. This could help to increase the likelihood that they are accepted, thereby helping the organization to function more effectively and efficiently. For example, if an organization wishes to reduce overhead and/or increase job flexibility by becoming more virtual, it may be in their best interest to offer ERIs to veterans and baby boomers.

However, organizations should not develop an ERI package for veterans or baby boomers and assume it will be effective for Gen Xers as well. As stated earlier, Gen Xers differ on work values (i.e., they tend to value more extrinsic rewards as well as leisure) and other individual attributes (such as greater narcissism and self-esteem) from baby boomers, which could impact their likelihood of accepting ERIs. Therefore, Gen Xers may place the highest value on increases in financial incentives, such as pension plans, severance packages, and separation bonuses, whereas baby boomers may place the highest value on transitional professional development practices, such as career coaching, that will help them to stay active in their careers after they retire from their current organization, Overall, by learning how the average members of different generations differ and how this relates to the likelihood of accepting ERIs, this understanding can provide valuable information to organizations, which can greatly assist with workforce planning efforts.

Our second proposition states that Gen Xers will be more likely to retire early than baby boomers. Again, this is an important question for workforce planning purposes. This proposition is heavily based on generational research focusing on mental health and leisure, which suggests that, on average, Gen Xers are more likely to feel work-related stress and value the opportunity to have more leisure time than baby boomers, and therefore they may have stronger intentions to retire at a younger age. A well-publicized concern in today's workforce is the potential loss of knowledge and skill due to baby-boomer retirement (Kiyonaga, 2004). If Gen Xers and perhaps even millennials intend to retire younger than baby boomers, future losses of institutional knowledge may be even greater. Therefore, it is important that research be conducted that focuses on how future generations think about retirement, and that the results be used to help organizations with workforce planning and the development of retirement policies and plans.

The third proposition we developed states that, on average, baby boomers will be more likely to pursue bridge employment than Gen Xers. Like ERIs, bridge employment is an important area of study from both the perspective of the organization and the individual. Not only does bridge employment provide workers with an opportunity to gradually withdraw from the workplace, but it can also provide older workers with an opportunity for career growth or the chance to regain enthusiasm for work simply by trying something new (Wang et al., 2009). From the organization's perspective, bridge employment provides employers with an avenue for retaining older workers with experience, technical skills, and institutional knowledge that would otherwise be lost if full retirement was the only option. For this reason, it is important that organizational decision makers understand why people choose to accept bridge employment, and what types of programs older workers find most attractive. Also, it is important to understand how taking a bridge position can differ by generation. Due to their differences in personality and work values, baby boomers and Gen Xers may differ in not only their overall likelihood to accept bridge employment but also the types of bridge employment they perceive to be most attractive.

In sum, there are a variety of research questions that may be explored that link generational differences in individual attributes to retirement processes. In this chapter, we have developed three propositions that can help to strengthen our understanding of the generational construct and different retirement processes, and at the same time provide insight into expected differences in retirement choices by members of retirement-eligible (baby boomer) and near-retirement (Gen X) generations. This information will be very useful to human resource managers who are responsible for workforce planning because it will aid their forecasting of who will be likely to retire and who will be likely to remain working. Future research examining these propositions, as well as other potential relations between the generational construct and retirement, will provide greater support for the importance of studying generational differences in individual attributes as well as the value of studying retirement processes.

Challenges in Conducting Generational Research

Generational research has been a controversial topic for many years. Authors have challenged whether generational differences are more of a popular culture topic than actual science, questioned which birth years to use to delineate generations, and debated whether all people born within a certain time frame actually experience the same events (Giancola, 2006; Macky et al., 2008). As discussed earlier, a common criticism of generational research is that the differences found are truly due to age rather than generation. This argument has stood for some time, given the prevalence of generational research conducted with cross-sectional designs (e.g., Wong et al., 2008; D'Amato & Herzfeldt, 2008; Jurkiewicz, 2000; Cennamo & Gardner, 2008) that do not rule out effects due to age instead of generation. In order to control for the age-generation confound, there has been a movement in recent generational research led by Jean Twenge and colleagues that uses time-lagged designs (e.g., Twenge, 2000; Twenge & Campbell, 2001; Twenge & Im, 2007; Twenge & Foster, 2010). The difference between a time-lagged design, like cross-temporal meta-analysis, and a traditional cross-sectional design is that samples are surveyed at the same age at different points in time, thereby eliminating age effects. For example, a cross-temporal meta-analysis is based on data from studies of the same scale or measure at different years, so an effect size may be calculated based on the comparison of the mean of a measure administered to 20-year-olds in 1970 (baby boomers) and 20-year-olds in 1990 (Gen Xers). The additional methodological rigor provided in this research provides great promise for the future scientific validity and acceptance of generational research.

In this chapter, we have focused almost exclusively on generational research that has used time-lagged rather than cross-sectional designs. In cross-sectional designs, surveys are administered at one point in time to people of all ages, and then the means from the different age groups on that measure are compared. For example, in a cross-sectional study conducted by Cennamo and Gardner (2008), it was found that millennials were more likely to report that they had thoughts about leaving their company than baby boomers. It is difficult to draw definitive conclusions from this finding because it may be that younger workers have yet to settle into the workplace and are perhaps still "shopping around" for the right career. At the same time, older workers may be more engrained in the company, have longer tenure, and have less interest in starting over at a new organization. In other words, it is impossible to know whether this finding is due to the age of the participants or their generation.

Age effects are not the only potential confound to beware of when conducting generational research. Previous multigenerational studies, for example, have examined generational differences in different countries (e.g., D'Amato & Herzfeldt, 2008; Yu & Miller, 2005). Conducting generational research across countries introduces the question of whether generations are actually the same across cultures. It may be that people from different cultures have experienced different sociocultural events that define their generation, and therefore have different shared attitudes, values, and beliefs. More research is needed in these areas to determine if the same generational differences are found across cultures.

Lastly, any findings regarding generational differences should be taken with caution, as they are based on averages. All people are different, and just because Gen Xers, on average, may value leisure more than baby boomers, it does not mean every individual baby boomer will be less likely to desire more vacation time than every individual Gen Xer. In general, effect sizes comparing generations in cross-temporal meta-analyses are small as well (Twenge et al, 2010a), so more research in this area is needed to further support the findings discussed in this chapter. In sum, it is important for generational research to be conducted with a high degree of methodological rigor, with a time-lagged or longitudinal design, so that there are fewer questions about its validity and/or ability to accurately characterize the generations.

Implications for Human Resource Management

Much has been made in recent years of the impending retirement of baby boomers and the resulting loss of institutional knowledge and technical skill (Rothwell & Poduch, 2004; Crumpacker & Crumpacker, 2007). In fact, studies have estimated that about 50% of the federal government workforce will be eligible for retirement in the next several years (Liebowitz, 2004). On the face of it, this issue presents a great challenge for human resource managers who must identify ways to maintain a fully staffed and skilled workforce while also retaining the valuable institutional knowledge held by retirees. However, developing programs to keep retirement-eligible workers in the workplace longer or allow them to pass on valuable knowledge and skills to younger workers will create new opportunities for interaction and collaboration across generations. With these opportunities may come new workforce challenges. Research focusing on older workers and retirement should therefore (1) focus on how organizations can benefit from programs designed to retain or involve older workers in the workplace, and (2) investigate the implications of these programs on the workforce. Below, we discuss these two areas in more detail.

One way that organizations are looking to retain skilled workers and lessen the impact of baby-boomer retirements is through programs that keep retirees in the workplace. Liebowitz (2004) surveyed members of the NASA Goddard Retirees and Alumni Association as well as members of the National Institute of Standards and Technology (NIST) Retirees and Alumni Association to learn more about the types of programs federal retirees are most interested in that are designed to keep them involved in the workplace. Table 35.2 presents a list of these programs along with brief definitions.

Phased retirement was the most highly favored of the programs, which supports the notion that today's retirees (baby boomers) are attracted to bridge employment. The retirees in Liebowitz's survey also rated "facilitator of an online community of practice" and "knowledge capture/retention programs" lowest, which suggests that the baby boomers currently retiring are still not quite comfortable

Table 35.2 Examples of Different Programs for Including Retirees in the Workforce

Phased Retirement	Retirement-age employees continue in their old jobs but with scaled down hours, typically 20–29 hours per week.
Retiree Job Bank	Allows retired employees to work up to a certain number of hours each year without adversely affecting their pensions.
Emeritus Program	As a federal retiree, you still keep an office and e-mail address at your organization so you can come in periodically.
Part-Time Retired Annuitant/ Project Team Consultant	Be part of a project team on a limited basis to share your expertise with the team in solving a specific problem.
Mentoring Program	Serve as a mentor in a formal mentoring program in your organization.
Knowledge Sharing Forums	As an experienced individual, you would meet once a month in a small group of up-and-coming individuals to share stories, lessons learned, and insights.
Rehearsal Retirement/Boomerang Job	An employee retires for a few months or a year, and then bounces back to the organization with limited hours.
Job Sharing	More than one person shares a job.
Facilitator of an Online Community of Practice	You would act as a moderator of an online community in your area of expertise.
Knowledge Capture/Retention Program	You would be interviewed via video, and your video nuggets would be accessible over the web in your organization.

Adapted from Liebowitz (2004)

with the latest forms of technology. Given this trend, offering reverse mentoring to retirement-eligible baby boomers, in which a younger employee (often a millennial) shares knowledge and prowess of technology with an older employee, may help persuade baby boomers to remain working into retirement.

Because millennials were born into the information age and have had the opportunity to grow accustomed to advanced communication technology (e.g., social networking) at a young age, the work programs preferred by eligible retirees are likely to change over time. Studying differences by generation in how to engage retirement-eligible workers and keep them in the workplace will be important for planning for future labor shortages or surpluses. Perhaps even more importantly, human resource managers need to begin planning for the issues that Gen Xers, and even millennials, will be facing when they are eligible to retire.

Although the programs to keep retirees in the workplace listed in Table 35.2 are geared toward federal employees, many can be applied to a variety of work settings. It is important for future research to further investigate each of these types of programs, specifically focusing on which are most successful and why, how these programs should be marketed to baby boomers, how this approach should differ when Gen Xers are eligible for retirement, and how the extended involvement of baby boomers in the workforce will impact the dynamics of the workplace.

In addition to programs that have been developed to address potential skill shortages, organizations are also implementing succession planning initiatives to prepare, train, and mentor younger generations of workers. These programs are also developed so that members of the workforce with many years of institutional knowledge, technical skill, and management experience have an opportunity to pass that knowledge on to younger workers, and human resource managers are not left scrambling to fill positions that are absolutely essential to the success of the organization. Succession planning creates a dynamic where interaction between generations is integral to success. Older generations must put their biases aside and seek to identify what makes a Gen Xer stand out from other Gen Xers, or what makes a millennial stand out from other millennials. Older generations must also mentor and support the younger generations and pass on critical institutional knowledge, and they must train younger generations in the skills necessary to lead an organization.

The result of programs designed to keep eligible retirees in the workforce longer and succession planning programs is that there will be more interaction and collaboration across generations in the workplace. Differences in individual attributes such as personality and work values may result in conflicts that could impact job satisfaction and job performance. In a multigenerational workplace, you may have baby boomers perceiving Gen Xers as too impatient, Gen Xers perceiving baby boomers as too traditional and inflexible, and both Gen Xers and baby boomers perceiving millennials as self-absorbed (Dittmann, 2005). Studies should consider what types of conflicts may occur and how to avoid or address them. Human resource managers may consider developing training on topics such as awareness of generational differences, active listening, communication, and conflict resolution (Dittmann, 2005; Notter, 2002).

Lastly, social security reform, companies moving from defined benefit pension plans to defined contribution 401(k) plans, and the recent economic downturn and prolonged recession have impacted baby boomers' ability to retire. Not only does this have an impact on how human resource managers structure retirement plans and assist baby boomers with retirement issues, but it could impact retirement planning for younger generations as well. For example, Dickinson and Emler (1992) found that the perceptions that younger workers have of work is heavily influenced by their parents' employment and economic circumstances. It will be interesting to see how the retirement challenges facing baby boomers impact how younger generations perceive and plan for retirement. It is also important that human resource managers understand how younger generations perceive retirement and what their retirement intentions are, so that retirement plans may be developed accordingly. Perceptions of retirement plans may not only have ramifications for workforce planning, but they can also impact a potential job candidate's likelihood to apply or accept a job offer from an organization as well.

Areas for Future Research

Future research should begin by studying the propositions developed for this study. This will help to expand the literature and our theoretical conceptualizations of both multigenerational research and retirement processes. In addition to the individual attributes studied across generations that are summarized in this chapter, future research should investigate how other personality characteristics, work values, and job attitudes differ across generations using time-lagged designs. To an extent, cross-temporal meta-analyses are limited by the archival data that we have available on measures that are still administered today. However, researchers should identify new individual attributes and begin collecting data from baby boomers, Gen Xers, and millennials now so that human resource managers can be prepared for the workforce challenges of tomorrow.

Although studying how generational differences in individual attributes relate to accepting ERIs, the decision to retire early, and taking a bridge position serves as a fruitful place to begin this area of research, there are a multitude of other retirement processes that are also important to study. Wang et al. (2009) discuss a number of different retirement processes, including retirement planning, which includes formal versus informal planning, financial planning, and retirement goal setting; retirement decision making, which includes voluntary and involuntary retirement; and retirement transition and adjustment, which includes post-retirement leisure activities, retirement satisfaction, and post-retirement physical and mental health. In short, it is important that future research address how generations differ in how they perceive and approach the retirement process at all stages, not just the outcomes specified in our propositions.

Future research on retirement should also begin to study millennials in more detail. Although this may seem counterintuitive, considering that many millennials are just entering the workforce and far from retirement age, if we have learned anything from the workforce challenges associated with baby-boomer retirement, it is that planning for the future is of the utmost importance. Millennials may even consider the retirement package offered by an organization to be an important factor when choosing a place to work, as a result of the widespread emphasis placed on retirement planning in the popular media. As such, future research should further investigate how the retirement packages that organizations offer impact the decisions of millennials to accept job offers.

It is also common to hear how millennials are different from baby boomers and Gen Xers in a negative way, such that they have a sense of entitlement, are less loyal, and are me-oriented (Twenge et al., 2010a). However, studies have also found that millennials exhibit some positive attributes in greater amounts than older generations, such as working well in teams, being motivated to make an impact on their organizations, favoring open and frequent communication with their supervisors, and being at ease with communication technologies (Myers & Sadaghiani, 2010). Future research should focus more on the positive attributes that millennials bring to the workplace, and how millennials, along with other generations, are making the workplace more productive. In fact, it may be that differences in personality characteristics and work values, and the various sociocultural experiences that help to create generations, can actually make generationally diverse teams and organizations more productive. Thus, we also suggest that future research examine the impact of generational diversity on performance.

Conclusion

Empirical studies across generations are still a relatively new undertaking. Studying how differences between generations relate to retirement outcomes will not only help broaden our theoretical understanding of the generational construct but can also inform retirement research and have strong implications for human resource management. Also, applying a high degree of methodological rigor when conducting multigenerational research will increase scientific validity and help the field become more accepted as a legitimate and important area for research. To truly reap the benefits of multigenerational research, studies should be less concerned with whether generations exist at all, and more concerned with how the study of generations can help us to understand retirement processes, solve existing workforce challenges, and plan for the workforce of the future. In conclusion, we offer the following questions for researchers in the fields of generational research and retirement research to consider:

• Is generational membership associated with retirement processes, such as the likelihood to accept early retirement incentives, the decision to retire early, or the likelihood to pursue bridge employment?

• What other individual attributes differ by generation and may be related to retirement outcomes?

• How do human resource initiatives, such as programs to keep retirees in the workforce and succession planning, impact baby boomers, Gen Xers, and millennials in the workplace?

• How can the study of generational differences prepare human resource managers for future workplace challenges?

- How can studying the retirement challenges facing baby boomers prepare younger generations for future challenges, and how will it impact how Gen Xers and millennials plan for retirement?
- How do current retirement issues, tendencies, and challenges impact generational diversity in the workplace, and what is the impact of generational diversity on performance?

References

Age Wave. (2009). *Retirement at the tipping point: The year that changed everything.* New York, NY: Harris Interactive.

Arsenault, P. M. (2004). Validating generational differences: A legitimate diversity and leadership issue. *The Leadership & Organization Development Journal, 25,* 124–141.

Bandura, A. (1977). *Social learning theory.* Englewood Cliffs, NJ: Prentice Hall.

Beehr, T. A., & Bowling, N. A. (2002). Career issues facing older workers. In D. C. Feldman (Ed.), *Work careers: A developmental perspective* (pp. 214–244). San Francisco, CA: Jossey-Bass/John Wiley & Sons.

Brief, A. (1998). *Attitudes in and around organizations.* Thousand Oaks, CA: Sage.

Cennamo, L., & Gardner, D. (2008). Generational differences in work values, outcomes and person-organization values fit. *Journal of Managerial Psychology, 23,* 891–906.

Costa, P.T., & McCrae, R. R. (1992). *Revised NEO Personality Inventory (NEO-PI-R) and NEO Five-Factor Inventory (NEO-FFI) Professional Manual.* Odessa, FL: Psychological Assessment Resources.

Costa, P. T., & McCrae, R. R. (1997). Longitudinal stability of adult personality. In R. Hogan, J. A. Johnson, & S. Briggs (Eds.), *Handbook of personality psychology* (pp. 269–290). San Diego, CA: Academic Press.

Crumpacker, M., & Crumpacker, J. M. (2007). Succession planning and generational stereotypes: Should HR consider age-based values and attitudes a relevant factor or a passing fad? *Public Personnel Management, 36,* 349–369.

D'Amato, A., & Herzfeldt, R. (2008). Learning orientation, organizational commitment and talent retention across generations: A study of European managers. *Journal of Managerial Psychology, 23,* 929–953.

Dickinson, J., & Emler, N. (1992). Developing conceptions of work. In J. Harley & G. Stephenson (Eds.) *The psychology of employment relations* (pp. 19–43). Oxford, England: Blackwell.

Dittmann, M. (2005). Generational differences at work. *Monitor on Psychology, 36,* 54–69.

Elovainio, M., Forma, P., Kivimaki, M., Sinervo, T., Sutinen, R., & Laine, M. (2005). Job demands and job control as correlates of early retirement thoughts in Finnish social and health care employees. *Work & Stress, 19,* 84–92.

Families and Work Institute. (2006). *Generation and gender in the workplace.* American Business Collaboration. Retrieved from http://familiesandwork.org/site/research/reports/main.html.

Giancola, F. (2006). The generation gap: More myth than reality. *Human Resource Planning, 29,* 32–37.

Gowan, M. A. (1998). A preliminary investigation of the factors affecting appraisal of the decision to take early retirement. *Journal of Employment Counseling, 35,* 124–140.

Hayden, H. S., & Pfadenhauser, D. M. (2005). Implementing early retirement incentive programs: A step-by-step guide. *HR Advisor Journal, September/October,* 12–20.

Johnson, L. D., Bachman, J. G., & O'Malley, P. M. (2006). *Monitoring the future: A continuing study of the lifestyles and values of youth* [Computer file]. Conducted by the University of Michigan, Survey Research Center. 2nd ICPSR ed. Ann Arbor, MI: Inter-university Consortium for Political and Social Research.

Johnson, M. K. (2002). Social origins, adolescent experiences, and work value trajectories during the transition to adulthood. *Social Forces, 80,* 1307–1341.

Jurkiewicz, C. L. (2000). Generation X and the public employee. *Public Personnel Management, 29,* 55–74.

Jurkiewicz, C. L., & Brown, R. G. (1998). GenXers vs. boomers vs. matures: Generational comparisons of public employee motivation. *Review of Public Personnel Administration, 18,* 18–37.

Kelly, G. A. (1955). *The psychology of personal constructs.* New York, NY: Norton.

Kim, S., & Feldman, D. C. (1998). Healthy, wealthy, or wise: Predicting actual acceptances of early retirement incentives at three points in time. *Personnel Psychology, 51,* 106–125.

Kiyonaga, N. B. (2004). Today is the tomorrow you were worried about yesterday: Meeting the challenges of a changing workforce. *Public Personnel Management, 33,* 357–361.

Kowske, B. J., Rasch, R., & Wiley, J. (2010). Millennials' (lack of) attitude problem: An empirical examination of generation effects on work attitudes. *Journal of Business and Psychology, 25,* 265–279.

Kupperschmidt, B. R. (2000). Multigeneration employees: Strategies for effective management. *The Health Care Manager, 19,* 65–76.

Liebowitz, J. (2004). Bridging the knowledge and skills gap: Tapping federal retirees. *Public Personnel Management, 33,* 421–448.

Lin, T., & Hsieh, A. (2001). Impact of job stress on early retirement intention. *International Journal of Stress Management, 8,* 243–247.

Low, K. S. D., Yoon, M., Roberts, B. W., & Rounds, J. (2005). The stability of vocational interests from early adolescence to middle adulthood: A quantitative review of longitudinal studies. *Psychological Bulletin, 131,* 713–737.

Macky, K., Gardner, D., & Forsyth, S. (2008). Generational differences at work: Introduction and overview [Guest editorial]. *Journal of Managerial Psychology, 23,* 857–861.

Miller, M. J., Woehr, D. J., & Hudspeth, N. (2002). The meaning and measurement of work ethic: Construction and initial validation of a multidimensional inventory. *Journal of Vocational Behavior, 60,* 451–489.

Myers, D. G. (1992). *Psychology* (3rd ed.). New York, NY: Worth.

Myers, K., & Sadaghiani, K. (2010). Millennials in the workplace: A communication perspective on millennials' organizational relationships and performance. *Journal of Business Psychology, 25,* 225–238.

Notter, J. (2002). *Mixing and managing four generations of employees.* Retrieved from www.fdu.edu/newspubs/magazine/05ws/generations.htm

Prothero, J., & Beach, L. R. (1984). Retirement decisions: Expectations, intentions, and action. *Journal of Applied Social Psychology, 14,* 162–174.

Rau, B. L., & Adams, G. A. (2005). Attracting retirees to apply: Desired organizational characteristics of bridge employment. *Journal of Organizational Behavior, 26,* 649–660.

Rothwell, W. J., & Poduch, S. (2004). Introducing technical (not managerial) succession planning. *Public Personnel Management, 33,* 405–419.

Rotter, J. B. (1966). Generalized expectancies for internal versus external control of reinforcement. *Psychological Monographs, 80,* 1–28.

Ryan, R. M., & Deci, E. J. (2000). Self-determination theory and the facilitation of intrinsic motivation, social development, and well-being. *American Psychologist, 55,* 68–78.

Schaie, K. W. (1965). A general model for the study of developmental problems. *Psychological Bulletin, 64,* 92–107.

Schuman, H., & Scott, J. (1989). Generations and collective memories. *American Sociological Review, 54,* 359–381.

Sessa, V. I., Kabacoff, R. I., Deal, J., & Brown, H. (2007). Generational differences in leader values and leadership behaviors. *The Psychologist-Manager Journal, 10,* 47–74.

Shultz, K. S. (2003). Bridge employment: Work after retirement. In G. A. Adams & T. A. Beehr (Eds.), *Retirement: Reasons, processes, and results* (pp. 214–241). New York, NY: Springer.

Shultz, K. S., Morton, K. R., & Weckerle, J. R. (1998). The influence of push and pull factors on voluntary and involuntary early retirees' retirement decision and adjustment. *Journal of Vocational Behavior, 53,* 45–57.

Shultz, K. S., & Wang, M. (2008). The changing nature of mid and late careers. In C. Wankel (Ed.), *21st century management: A reference handbook* (Vol. 2, pp. 130–138). Thousand Oaks, CA: Sage.

Smola, K. W., & Sutton, C. D. (2002). Generational differences: Revisiting generational work values for the new millennium. *Journal of Organizational Behavior, 23,* 363–382.

Strauss, W., & Howe, N. (1991). *Generations: The history of America's future, 1584 to 2069.* New York, NY: William Morrow.

Toossi. M. (2004). Labor force projections to 2012: The graying of the U.S. workforce. *Monthly Labor Review, 127,* 3–22.

Twenge, J. M. (1997). Changes in masculine and feminine traits over time: A meta-analysis. *Sex Roles, 36,* 305–325.

Twenge, J. M. (2000). The age of anxiety? Birth cohort change in anxiety and neuroticism, 1952–1993. *Journal of Personality and Social Psychology, 79,* 1007–1021.

Twenge, J. M. (2001a). Birth cohort changes in extraversion: A cross-temporal meta-analysis, 1966–1993. *Personality and Individual Differences, 30,* 735–748.

Twenge, J. M. (2001b). Changes in women's assertiveness in response to status and roles: A cross-temporal meta-analysis, 1931–1993. *Journal of Personality and Social Psychology, 81,* 133–145.

Twenge, J. M. (2010). A review of the empirical evidence on generational differences in work attitudes. *Journal of Business Psychology, 25,* 201–210.

Twenge, J. M., & Campbell, S. M. (2008). Generational differences in psychological traits and their impact on the workplace. *Journal of Managerial Psychology, 23,* 862–877.

Twenge, J. M., & Campbell, S. M. (2010). Generation me and the changing world of work. In A. P. Linley, S. Harrington, & N. Garcea (Eds.), *Oxford handbook of positive psychology and work* (pp. 25–35). New York, NY: Oxford University Press.

Twenge, J. M., Campbell, S. M., Hoffman, B. J., & Lance, C. E. (2010a). Generational differences in work values: Leisure and extrinsic values increasing, social and intrinsic values decreasing. *Journal of Management, 36,* 1117–1142.

Twenge, J. M., & Campbell, W. K. (2001). Age and birth cohort differences in self-esteem: A cross-temporal meta-analysis. *Personality and Social Psychology Review, 5,* 321–344.

Twenge, J. M., & Foster, J. D. (2010). Birth cohort increases in narcissistic personality traits among American college students, 1982–2009. *Social Psychological and Personality Science, 1,* 99–106.

Twenge, J. M., Gentile, B., DeWall, N. C., Ma, D., Lacefield, K., & Schurtz, D. R. (2010). Birth cohort increases in psychopathology among young Americans, 1938–2007. A cross-temporal meta-analysis of the MMPI. *Clinical Psychology Review, 30,* 145–154.

Twenge, J. M., & Im, C. (2007). Changes in the need for social approval, 1958–2001. *Journal of Research in Personality, 41,* 171–189.

Twenge, J. M., Konrath, S., Foster, J. D., Campbell, W. K., & Bushman, B. J. (2008). Egos inflating over time: A cross-temporal meta-analysis of the Narcissistic Personality Inventory. *Journal of Personality, 76,* 875–901.

Twenge, J. M., Zhang, L., & Im, C. (2004). It's beyond my control: A cross-temporal meta-analysis of increasing externality in locus of control, 1960–2002. *Personality and Social Psychology Review, 8,* 308–319.

Wang, M., Adams, G. A., Beehr, T. A., & Shultz, K. S. (2009). Career issues at the end of one's career: Bridge employment and retirement. In S. G. Baugh and S. E. Sullivan (Eds.), *Maintaining focus, energy, and options through the life span* (pp. 135–162). Charlotte, NC: Information Age.

Wang, M., & Shultz, K. (2010). Employee retirement: A review and recommendations for future investigation. *Journal of Management, 36,* 172–206.

Wang, M., Zhan, Y., Lin, S., & Schultz, K. (2008). Antecedents of bridge employment: A longitudinal investigation. *Journal of Applied Psychology, 93,* 818–830.

Wong, M., Gardiner, E., Lang, W., & Coulon. L. (2008). Generational differences in personality and motivation: Do they exist and what are the implications for the workplace? *Journal of Managerial Psychology, 23,* 878–890.

Wyatt, D. (1993). *Out of the sixties: Storytelling and the Vietnam generation.* Cambridge, MA: University Press.

Yu, H., & Miller, P. (2005). Leadership style: The X Generation and baby boomers compared in different cultural contexts. *Leadership & Organization Development Journal, 26,* 35–50.

Retirement and Creativity

Ryan Fehr

Abstract

In this chapter I examine retirement through the lens of creativity and explore how retirement can exert a positive impact on retirees through the provision of novelty. With a focus on retirement planning, decision making, and adjustment, I propose that creativity influences retirement through three interrelated perceptions and actions: (a) openness to role transitions, (b) divergent thinking, and (c) goal persistence. Through an interactionist approach, I then examine personality variables and social contexts likely to lead retirees to approach retirement creatively. In the discussion I offer key questions to guide future theoretical and empirical research.

Key Words: retirement, creativity, openness, divergent thinking, role transitions

Across the life span, few experiences are as ubiquitous, dramatic, and life-altering as the transition into retirement. Whether an individual retires at age 40, 60, or 80, he or she will inevitably confront a host of new challenges, from financial insecurity and social isolation to feelings of lost identity (Davidson, 2011; Schlossberg, 2009; Wang & Shultz, 2010). Demographic trends in the United States and across the globe suggest that the number of individuals approaching retirement worldwide is rising dramatically. According to a recent study by the Pew Research Center, over 10,000 Americans are currently turning 65 every day. By 2030, 18% of the population in the United States is expected to be 65 or over. Even higher percentages are projected in many European and Asian countries (Tugend, 2011). Thus, there is a growing need for scholars and practitioners to deepen their knowledge of the retirement process and the predictors of smooth retirement transitions.

As the chapters in this handbook attest, organizational scholars have offered multiple theoretical perspectives to enhance our understanding of how retirement influences individual well-being. Among these perspectives, resource-based models have received particularly consistent attention in recent years (Wang & Shultz, 2010). According to the resource-based approach, retirement often produces dramatic deficits in personal resources. To overcome these deficits, retirees' resource pools become increasingly important. Thus, financial deficits are best addressed through financial resources (e.g., retirement savings; family financial support), social network deficits are best addressed through social resources (e.g., stronger community and family ties), and identity deficits are best addressed through identity-building resources (e.g., bridge employment; post-retirement leisure activities). To quote Wang and Shultz (2010), "when people have more resources to fulfill the needs they value in retirement, they will experience less difficulty in adjusting" (p. 3). Research to date has generally supported the validity of the resource-based approach. All else held constant, resources—financial, social, or otherwise—enhance retirees' well-being during and after the transition into retirement, leading to

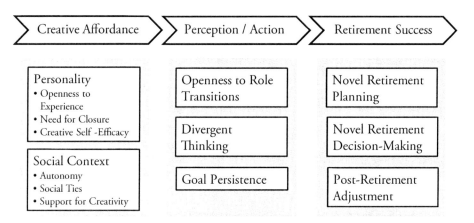

Figure 36.1 Antecedents, Content, and Consequences of a Creative Approach to Retirement

greater post-retirement adjustment and increased life satisfaction (Kim & Feldman, 2000; Kubicek, Korunka, Raymo, & Hoonakker, 2011; Wang & Shultz, 2010).

Although the resource-based perspective broadly allows for the examination of how retirement both enhances and compromises retiree well-being, research to date has overwhelmingly focused on the needs produced by retirement-related stressors, with shifts in well-being attributed to the comparative presence or relief of pre- and post-retirement stress (Wang & Shultz, 2010). Reduced well-being after retirement is therefore attributed to retirees' lack of sufficient resources to overcome financial, social, and other deficits. Conversely, enhanced well-being after retirement is attributed to the presence of sufficient post-retirement resources. In this chapter I propose a complementary, alternative view—that enhanced well-being after retirement can also emerge through the creation of new challenges and novel roles that energize and excite retirees. In this way I draw from current themes in positive organizational scholarship, emphasizing the potential for retirement to become a path to positive identity construction (Dutton, Roberts, & Bednar, 2010) and imbue retirees' lives with enhanced meaning. To build a foundation for this new perspective, I examine retirement through the lens of creativity (Fehr, 2012). I begin with a review of what it means to "retire creatively" and follow with an analysis of three phenomena that represent the core of a creative approach to retirement: (1) openness to role transitions, (2) divergent thinking, and (3) goal persistence. Building upon this framework, I then argue for an interactionist perspective on the predictors of creative approaches to retirement, incorporating both individual differences (e.g., openness

to experience; need for closure) and social contexts (e.g., weak social ties; organizational climate; see Figure 36.1). In the discussion, I present several hereto unexamined questions at the intersection of research on retirement and creativity to stimulate further theoretical and empirical analysis.

What It Means to "Retire Creatively"

In a global marketplace characterized by ever-growing competition, creativity represents a key competitive advantage for organizations that is difficult for rivals to imitate. To quote George (2007), "Creativity is being increasingly recognized as a critical means by which organizations and their members can create meaningful, lasting value for their multiple stakeholders in today's dynamically changing environment" (p. 439). Nations, industries, and organizations alike are increasing the resources they devote to fostering creativity, hoping to find new solutions to a myriad of problems (Hennessey & Amabile, 2010). Thus, it is not surprising to find a concomitant interest among scholars in the antecedents and consequences of creativity in the organizational sciences. Empirical research supports the claim that employees' creative actions "can substantially contribute to organizational innovation, effectiveness, and survival" (Shalley, Zhou, & Oldham, 2004, p. 933). A wide range of dispositional and situational factors have in turn been shown to facilitate organizations' creative efforts, from personality (Feist, 1999, 2010) to organizational climate (Amabile, Conti, Coon, Lazenby, & Herron, 1996).

Over the past several decades, scholars have converged upon a definition of creativity as the production of ideas that are both novel and useful in a given context or setting (George, 2007; Hennessey

& Amabile, 2010). Within organizations, an idea is therefore considered creative to the degree that it is original and holds the potential to facilitate a desirable individual or organizational outcome (e.g., employee satisfaction; organizational performance). At one end of the spectrum are radical ideas that dramatically shift the trajectory of an organization or industry. At the other end of the spectrum are more incremental ideas that, while novel, can be expected to exert less dramatic effects on the organization (Madjar, Greenberg, & Chen, 2011). In contrast to creativity is habitual action, which is typically associated with established routines that produce a relatively invariant set of outcomes (Ford, 1996). Researchers in turn measure creativity through managers' ratings of employee creative performance (e.g., George & Zhou, 2001) or behavioral outcomes such as patent applications (Sørensen & Stuart, 2000), submissions to employee suggestion systems (Verworn, 2009), and ideas generated during brainstorming sessions (De Dreu, Baas, & Nijstad, 2008).

But what does it mean to *retire* creatively? Put differently, what does it mean to take a novel yet useful approach to retirement? Following from the existing retirement literature, I examine the concept of creative retirement through the lens of three well-established constructs at different phases of the retirement transition: retirement planning, retirement decision making, and post-retirement adjustment (Wang & Shultz, 2010). First, I link planning and decision making to the novelty component of creativity by emphasizing the potential for retirees to construct approaches to the retirement transition that are unique in their industry, job, or organization (Csikszentmihalyi, 1999). Then, I link retirement adjustment to the "usefulness" component of creativity. Through this model I argue that creativity emerges during the retirement process when retirees adopt unique, original planning and decision-making processes that facilitate their post-retirement adjustment.

Retirement Planning and Decision Making

Retirement planning and decision making transcend a retiree's tenure at an organization, from the first day of employment to the last. To retire creatively, an individual must develop and enact an approach to retirement that is novel—i.e., fundamentally distinct from the norms of a given culture, industry, or organization (Csikszentmihalyi, 1999). To understand how such novelty might emerge, I draw from Feldman and Beehr's (2011) retirement

decision-making framework and examine how retirees both construct a vision of their post-retirement future and decide when to let go of their workplace identities.

In the early phases of one's employment, retirement planning and decision making are primarily future-oriented. Individuals develop abstract conceptualizations of their future selves and base their initial planning processes on the attainment of long-term goals associated with these abstract future selves. At this phase, opportunity for creativity first comes in the initiation of an imagined future self. Previous research suggests that people typically fail to consider retirement early in their careers, absent external factors (e.g., poor health) that might enhance the salience of retirement (Feldman & Beehr, 2011). Thus, the mere dedication of effort to retirement early in one's career could be conceptualized as inherently novel. By considering retirement early on in their careers, individuals build and recognize the potential for multiple positive identities across the life span (Roberts & Dutton, 2009). Of particular importance is the content of retirees' imagined future selves. Continuity theory suggests that retirees are typically motivated to maintain a consistent self-image both before and after retirement (Atchley, 1999). Thus, if an individual is social before retirement, he or she will seek to remain social after retirement. A creative approach to retirement emphasizes the potential value of drafting new, discontinuous future selves. Given a myriad of environmental opportunities and constraints (e.g., shifts in technology), it may prove difficult to maintain a consistent image over several decades. Retirees who imbue their self-concepts with creativity can conversely embrace the frequently shifting landscape and adapt accordingly. This might entail shifting not only one's personal identity but also one's social identity, as in the case of a British retiree who moves to China and seeks to assimilate into an entirely novel cultural context.

As an individual nears retirement, retirement planning and decision making become increasingly relevant to daily life (Feldman & Beehr, 2011). To be creative at this phase, retirees must counteract inclinations that bias their decisions toward prevailing norms. Consider the question of when an individual chooses to retire. In the United States, workers can apply for Social Security benefits at 62 years of age (Social Security Administration, 2011). However, 62 is unlikely to be the most appropriate retirement age for the entire employed population. Many workers would likely benefit from a retirement age that is substantially lower or higher. A successful investment banker might choose to retire at age 38 and focus entirely on other pastimes such as raising a family or donating time and money to charitable causes. An engaged schoolteacher might conversely choose to remain employed until age 80 to enjoy the job's associated benefits, including financial stability and frequent social interaction. In each of these cases the retiree is adopting a novel approach to the retirement decision by diverting from prevailing norms. Another example can be found with respect to *how* people retire. Just as it is normative to retire within a certain age range, it is also normative to retire abruptly. Yet recent studies suggest that bridge employment, whereby individuals retire gradually through part-time work, often provides retirees with a smoother transition out of the workforce (Zhan, Wang, Liu, & Shultz, 2009). Thus, retirees can benefit from adopting comparatively novel approaches to both the timing and form of their retirement transitions.

Post-retirement Adjustment

Retirees who approach retirement planning and decision making in uncommon ways meet one requirement for creativity by imbuing their actions with novelty. However, to be considered creative, their planning and decision making must also be useful (Hennessey & Amabile, 2010). Within the context of retirement, novel retirement planning and decision making must more specifically contribute to the retiree's post-retirement well-being. Scholars generally acknowledge that increased well-being is the primary goal of retirees' actions, organizations' retirement-focused services, and retirement research in academia (Wang & Shultz, 2010). Thus, constructs such as financial planning and social ties are of interest to the extent that they facilitate a smooth retirement transition. Similarly, organizations develop retirement planning seminars and 401(k) programs to alleviate potential stressors during the retirement transition (Davidson, 2011).

Drawing from past research, I adopt a broad operationalization of post-retirement adjustment with a focus on both physiological and psychological outcomes. Thus, specific intentions and behaviors (e.g., early retirement) can be considered creative only if they diverge from normative retirement behaviors and exert a positive impact on key outcomes such as the retiree's overall health or life satisfaction. In the next section I present a tripartite model of how creativity shapes retirement. As shown in Figure 36.1, I presume that each of these factors is desirable to

the extent that it facilitates novel ideas during the planning and decision-making phases of retirement transitions and ultimately exerts a positive impact on retirees' well-being. These factors include openness to role transitions, divergent thinking, and goal persistence.

How Creativity Shapes Retirement: A Tripartite Model

As previously reviewed, the quality of retirees' retirement-related behaviors holds lasting implications for their financial, psychological, and even physiological well-being (Wang & Shultz, 2010). Although creativity has been linked to a wide range of desirable outcomes for employees and their organizations (Shalley et al., 2004), there is little substantive research on the link between creativity and retirement planning, decision making, and adjustment. To the extent that creativity scholarship can illuminate paths to novel retirement planning and decision-making processes, it can likewise illuminate previously unexamined paths to retiree adjustment. Thus, the central question is: what perceptions and behaviors are most likely to facilitate novel, useful approaches to retirement? As I elaborate below, a creative approach to retirement is theorized to begin with an open approach to role transitions. Following this attitudinal shift, divergent thinking and goal persistence serve as proximate predictors of novel retirement planning and decision making.

Openness to Role Transitions

"The first sense of emotion is loss, [particularly a] loss of identity. The second is a sense of fear of 'how am I going to replace the kind of affirmation that I got.' You lose who you are. You lose the work identity and the work context."
—Dr. *Dwight Moore*, Moore & Associates (Keck, 2007)

In practical writings on the retirement transition, the challenge of identity is a prevailing theme (e.g., Schlossberg, 2009). As in the quote above, retirees frequently express discomfort in the loss of careers that served—at least in part—as a way for them to define themselves and their place in the world. Within the academic literature, role theory speaks most directly to this issue (Wang & Shultz, 2010). Briefly summarized, role theory posits that feelings of self-worth and self-esteem are strongly tied to individuals' ability to fulfill roles that they view as important and central to the self. Well-being is therefore determined at the intersection of individuals' role-based self-concepts and their competence within those roles. For instance, people are most likely to derive well-being from their job roles when they define themselves through their jobs and perform them well (Ashforth, 2001). Role theory is relevant throughout workers' careers. However, it is a particularly salient issue among employees in transition—employees who switch jobs within one organization, join a new organization, switch career paths, or become unemployed or underemployed.

As a theoretical framework that examines employees in transition, role theory is as relevant for retirement as it is for other types of career changes. Just as employees must build new role identities when they switch firms or careers, so too must retirees build new role identities when they transition into retirement. Consistent with the role theory perspective, previous research indicates that post-retirement well-being is directly related to the quality of retirees' work and non-work role identities. Wang (2007) found that retirees who experience a drop in well-being upon retirement display low levels of marital satisfaction and tend to retire earlier than planned when compared against their more well-adjusted peers. In other words, retirees' well-being suffered when they were lacking high-quality non-work role identities (e.g., family roles) and were psychologically unprepared to give up their work role identities (e.g., did not intend or wish to retire). Taylor, Shultz, Spiegel, Morrison, and Greene (2007) similarly found that post-retirement adjustment among naval officers was significantly predicted by the officers' perceptions that their post-retirement work roles would meet their expectations. When retirement did not produce meaningful new role identities, their well-being again suffered.

To date, retirement scholars have generally focused on whether or not certain role identities exist among retirees—for instance, whether or not they have strong family ties, strong community ties, or fulfilling post-retirement work opportunities—rather than on how and why role identities emerge over time. Yet role identities are fluid phenomena that are actively built and deconstructed throughout the course of one's life. In other words, individuals can and do play an active role in identity construction (Roberts & Dutton, 2009). They can *choose* to take on new identities and let go of old identities as a product of individual dispositions and the context in which the individual is situated. Every day, people construct new identities and deconstruct old identities by switching careers, building families, volunteering, and engaging in the local community.

Drawing from research on role transitions broadly construed, the extant literature implicates openness to role transitions as a latent predictor of the tendency to be open to new identities throughout the life course and build them accordingly. More than their peers, people who are open to new possibilities and experiences switch careers, perspectives, and identities throughout their lives. They are willing to challenge their own assumptions and identities to forge new realities about the self. In a fifteen-year cross-lagged study of college graduates, Wille, De Fruyt, and Feys (2010) examined vocational interests and the Big Five personality variables as predictors of work-based role transitions, defined as the frequency with which participants changed jobs within the same company (internal mobility) or into a different company (external mobility). The authors first found that role transitions were positively associated with being investigative and artistic—vocational interest constructs associated with wide interests, creative tendencies, and preference for new experiences. Conversely, they found that role transitions were negatively associated with conventionality—a preference for familiarity and routine. Each of these constructs is consistent with the creative personality. According to Feist (1999, 2010), the creative personality entails a preference for novelty, new experiences, and wide interests.

Within the Big Five personality domain, multiple studies have linked role transition tendencies with openness to experience—a willingness to adjust one's attitudes and behaviors when exposed to new information or situations (Digman, 1990). Wille et al. (2010) found that openness to experience—and openness to ideas and actions at the facet level—predicted role transitions across a fifteen-year career span. Vinson, Connelly, and Ones (2007) found a similar relationship among employees across eleven organizations. Earlier studies demonstrated parallel effects across samples and cultures (e.g., Barton & Cattell, 1972; Creed, 1999). Insomuch as openness to experience is consistently linked with creative tendencies (McCrae, 1987; Runco, 2004), the link between openness and role transitions strongly supports the idea that creativity facilitates a willingness to take on new work roles across the life span. Further theoretical evidence for the creativity-role transition relationship is provided by Ng, Sorensen, Eby, and Feldman (2007), who examined role transitions through a cultural values lens (Schwartz, 1994). Building upon previous research on values and workplace behavior, the authors hypothesized that role transitions are negatively associated with conformity and tradition (values that emphasize consistency and familiarity) and positively associated with stimulation and universalism (values that emphasize novelty and creativity; Schwartz & Bardi, 2001). When employees' identities are threatened, open and creative employees react more positively and are better adjusted after the change occurs. Likewise, Wanberg and Banas (2000) found that employees who were open to the reorganization of a work environment were more satisfied with the workplace and less likely to quit. Mignonac (2008) found that openness to experience was a significant predictor of willingness to change job roles among older workers as well.

Taken together, the evidence implicates openness to role transitions as a criticalpredictor of actual transitions across the life course. When employees are open to the idea of adopting new work roles, they are more likely to switch roles and, after a role switch, are better able to adjust to their new identity. Conversely, when employees possess a negative attitude toward role transitions, they are less likely to switch roles across the life course and less well-adjusted when role transitions do occur. Given the inevitability of retirement for the vast majority of the labor force, these data implicate openness to role transitions as a critical force in ensuring that retirees are not resistant to the idea of retirement. Thus, openness to role transitions can be seen as a critical prerequisite toward identifying the most opportune moment to retire and the most fruitful path to post-retirement adjustment. Yet even the most open retiree will fail to adjust without a plan for approaching the retirement transition. To draft and enact a plan for retirement that is both novel and useful (i.e., creative), retirees must also possess the cognitive capacity for divergent thinking and persist in achieving their creative goals.

Divergent Thinking

"If you retire from a job that has been your entire identity and you don't have some kind of plan or goal, something you want to do, it is dangerous … I've seen people who have sunk into depression because they didn't have anything to do in retirement and their sense of self-worth was pulled out from under them."

—*Terryl Paiste*, retiree (Hinden, 2000, p. H1)

Since the early work of Torrance (1962) and Guilford (1967), scholars have exhibited a lasting interest in divergent thinking as a central marker of creativity (Runco, 2010). Briefly defined, divergent thinking refers to the process whereby an individual generates a wide variety of loosely connected ideas and concepts in an effort to produce creative outcomes (Torrance, 1962). Although divergent thinking is not synonymous with creativity per se, it is central to both creative thinking and the production of creative outcomes (Guilford & Hoepfner, 1971). To quote Woodman, Sawyer, and Griffin (1993), divergent thinking has "long been considered the cognitive key to creativity and has continued to be a major consideration in creativity research" (p. 298). In contrast to convergent thinking, divergent thinking mirrors the context of real-world retirement planning and decision making, wherein there is no single right answer to the task at hand. Divergent thinking is characterized by three primary qualities: fluency, originality, and flexibility. Fluency refers to the total number of ideas an individual develops. Originality in turn refers to the uniqueness of one's ideas, while flexibility refers to the total number of themes or categories that emerge from the idea generation process. Measures of divergent thinking assess these categories in various ways. For example, Torrance's (1962) alternative uses task asks participants to come up with new and unusual uses for an everyday object, such as a tin can. Fluency is assessed by the total number of ideas created, novelty by their uniqueness (e.g., a novel solution is to make a toy robot), and flexibility by the number of categories (e.g., toys vs. containers vs. clothing accessories).

Empirical research indicates that individuals who exhibit positive attitudes toward divergent thinking and perform better on divergent thinking tasks tend to ultimately produce highly creative outcomes. In contrast, individuals who exhibit poor attitudes toward divergent thinking or fall short in their performance on divergent thinking tasks tend to produce routine, commonplace outcomes (Basadur, Graen, & Green, 1982; Williams, 2004). Furthermore, there is evidence to suggest that divergent thinking exerts a direct impact on performance in organizational contexts where creativity is needed. For example, high performance on divergent thinking tasks is positively correlated with entrepreneurial success (Ames & Runco, 2005) and predicts active Army officers' ability to solve complex military leadership problems (Mumford, Marks, Connelly, Zaccaro, & Johnson, 1998; Vincent, Decker, & Mumford, 2002). Research furthermore suggests that divergent thinking enables individuals to identify interesting problems and enact creative solutions (Basadur, 1994).

When applied to the context of retirement, divergent thinking can be expected to enhance the breadth and novelty of retirees' retirement planning and decision-making processes, allowing them to develop and enact behaviors most likely to facilitate their post-retirement adjustment. In this way, divergent thinking is more proximal to retirement than openness to role transitions, and represents a series of cognitive actions that follow from positive attitudes toward divergent possibilities in general. Two examples of approaches to retirement that are more likely to be adopted following divergent thinking and can likewise enhance adjustment during the retirement transition are bridge employment and early retirement. It is important to note, however, that these examples are only illustrative. Given that creativity is fundamentally tied to the context in which the individual exists (Csikszentmihalyi, 1999), divergence itself will depend upon the prevailing norms in a given organization, industry, or culture. For instance, early retirement may be novel in industries where longer tenures are more commonplace, as in academia. Conversely, early retirement may be normative in industries with shorter tenures are more commonplace, as in jobs that present significant physical demands (van den Berg, Elders, & Burdorf, 2010).

Bridge employment. Although retirees often transition into retirement by fully withdrawing from employment overnight, it is becoming increasingly common for them to engage in bridge employment—to work fewer hours and/or switch industries as they transition into retirement (Shultz, 2003). Broadly speaking, research suggests that bridge employment is beneficial to individuals' well-being. Zhan et al. (2009) demonstrated that bridge employment is associated with greater physical and mental health; Kim and Feldman (2000) similarly found that bridge employment is associated with greater life satisfaction and satisfaction with the retirement process. Previous research has demonstrated that one of the strongest predictors of bridge employment is the perceived availability of relevant opportunities (Gobeski & Beehr, 2009). In other words, people will seek bridge employment only when they believe that it is a viable option. An important question, then, is when these types of opportunities are perceived. Davis (2003) demonstrated that individuals with entrepreneurial orientations were more likely than their peers to engage in bridge employment. This link implies a direct role of divergent thinking in the recognition of bridge employment opportunities.

As Davis (2003) and others have noted, entrepreneurial orientation is associated with a tendency to develop and enact new ideas. With respect to divergent thinking, it is particularly likely that creativity will enable individuals to bridge into new career paths, further freeing them from the constraints of the labor market in their previous career.

Early retirement. Although it is growing in popularity, early retirement remains a less traveled path to retirement. Oftentimes, the decision to retire early is driven by early retirement incentives (i.e., ERIs; Wang & Shultz, 2010). As with other retirement constructs, research on the antecedents of early retirement has to date focused on financial and demographic constructs, demonstrating that individuals who are in poor health, earn lower salaries, and have higher pensions tend to accept ERI packages (Kim & Feldman, 1998). Although research on the antecedents of early retirement decisions is limited, research suggests that attitudes toward early retirement are central predictors of its downstream consequences (Shultz, Morton, & Weckerle, 1998). Furthermore, negative perceptions of early retirement are extremely common (Gowan, 1998), especially when they are perceived as part of an organization's efforts to downsize or cut costs (Mein & Ellison, 2006). Certainly, it is inevitable for retirees to resent early retirement and ERIs when they are perceived as driven by a desire to force an individual out of the organization. However, creative retirees may be less likely to perceive early retirement negatively. Retirees who think divergently about retirement should be readily able to develop new goals and new roles to compensate for the financial and psychological repercussions of early retirement. In addition, they should be less concerned with the counter-normative aspects of early retirement than their peers. In other words, divergent thinking facilitates a willingness to retire early by enhancing both the perceived possibilities of post-retirement life and the acceptability of an early retirement age, even if it is counter-normative in a given organization or industry.

Goal Persistence

"We went from a very structured world—a world really that had been structured since we were in kindergarten—to one in which the structure almost totally disappeared. You have to have a lot of discipline to manage the time and space without just idling away the days."

—*Mark Skeie*, retiree (Schoolmeester, 2004, p. A1)

Existing research on creativity suggests that retirees can reap benefits from openness to role transitions and divergent thinking when planning for retirement and engaging in retirement decision making. However, the existing creativity literature likewise suggests that openness and divergent thinking are not sufficient to ensure a truly creative approach to retirement. Rather, it is also important for retirees to exert effort toward their retirement goals—in other words, retirees must exhibit persistence (De Dreu et al., 2008). Multiple streams of research support the importance of persistence in creative achievement. When individuals invest cognitive resources and focus their attention on a creative task, they tend to produce outcomes that are both more original and more useful (De Dreu et al., 2008; Shalley, 1991). Put differently, hard work and motivated effort play a significant role in both the quality and quantity of individuals' creative outputs (Eisenberger & Rhoades, 2001; Hirt, Levine, McDonald, Melton, & Martin, 1997). Historiometric data suggest that the chance of an individual producing a truly creative outcome (e.g., a new scientific theory) is strongly associated with the number of attempts that individual makes (Simonton, 2003).

One organizational example of the role of persistence in creativity is George and Zhou's (2002) application of mood-as-input theory to creativity. In a cross-sectional study, the authors demonstrated that when clarity of thought and perceived rewards for creativity are high, employees use negative moods as a signal that something is wrong in the organization and persist in their efforts to be creative. Similarly, scholars have theorized that conscientiousness can facilitate persistence toward creative goals (Fehr, 2009). Self-determination theory furthermore suggests that extrinsic rewards for creativity might encourage persistence and thus enhance creative performance (Eisenberger & Rhoades, 2001). Indeed, a lack of persistence has been used to explain the minimal empirical relationship between psychosis and creativity despite the former's effect on indicators of novel thought, such as latent inhibition (Carson, Peterson, & Higgins, 2003). Broad constructs such as activation—the sustained engagement of motivational systems toward goal-related activities—have been shown to facilitate creative performance regardless of the form of the motivational system itself (e.g., whether an individual adopts a promotion or prevention orientation; Baas, De Dreu, & Nijstad, 2011).

Retirees can benefit from goal persistence throughout the processes of retirement planning and decision making. When developing their long-term retirement goals, persistence—in tandem with openness to role transitions and divergent thinking—can enable retirees to consider the widest possible array of post-retirement paths, from part-time work to complete role changes that shift focus to family, community, or an entirely new career. Likewise, persistence can ensure that retirees don't simply set creative goals but also achieve them. When faced with difficult financial or social challenges, persistence can help retirees meet their goals and overcome obstacles. For example, persistence can help retirees develop expertise in new career domains during bridge employment, forge new community relationships after retirement, and work within a budget to maintain financial stability. Several retirement studies hint at the role of persistence in achieving retirement-relevant goals. The planning literature in particular demonstrates that when retirees plan more for their retirement, they report greater adjustment across diverse settings (e.g., Taylor & Doverspike, 2003; Mutran, Reitzes, & Fernandez, 1996). Furthermore, they are more likely to exit the workforce early (Taylor & Shore, 1995), suggesting that persistence enables the attainment of new resources and identities. It is important to note, however, that persistence is not a sufficient source of creativity. An uncreative retiree could exhibit admirable persistence toward a traditional retirement savings plan yet exhibit poor adjustment due to a failure to consider novel options such as bridge employment. Rather, persistence must exist in tandem with an openness to new identities and divergent goal setting (De Dreu et al., 2008).

Lessons from the Creativity Literature: Predictors of Post-Retirement Well-Being

Thus far, I have spoken only in general terms about the dispositional and situational indicators of creativity. Numerous well-written reviews have covered these topics in depth (e.g., Feist, 1999; Hennessey & Amabile, 2010; Shalley et al., 2004) and I do not attempt such broad scope here. Rather, my intention is to propose several illustrative constructs that might be utilized in future empirical research to explore the effects of creativity on post-retirement adjustment. In doing so I adopt an interactionist perspective on creativity, emphasizing the importance of both the individual retiree and the context in which the retiree is embedded (Shalley et al., 2004; Woodman et al., 1993). I begin with a discussion of the creative person, reviewing openness to experience, need for closure, and creative self-efficacy as three dispositional indicators of creative ability. Then I present autonomy, social ties, and support for creativity as three situational constructs that are likely to predict of a creative approach to retirement.

The Creative Retiree

Individuals possess varying capacities for creativity (Feist, 2010). Taken together, the confluence of traits and abilities that determine an individual's capacity for creativity is referred to here as *creative ability*. Research focused on the precise demographics, personality traits, and skills associated with creative ability can be conceptualized as the person approach and has received widespread attention among creativity scholars (Rhodes, 1961/1987; Runco, 2004).

Barron and Harrington (1981) succinctly summarized the creative individual as one who has "high valuation of aesthetic qualities in experience, broad interests, attraction to complexity, high energy, independence of judgment, autonomy, intuition, self-confidence, ability to resolve antinomies or to accommodate apparently opposite or conflicting traits in one's self concept, and finally, a firm sense of self as 'creative'" (p. 453). Compared to their peers, creative individuals exhibit a number of adaptive tendencies. They tend to be particularly good leaders (Sternberg, 2003) and as employees are rated as high overall performers by their supervisors (e.g., Zhang & Bartol, 2010). Across the life span, creative individuals furthermore tend to achieve high levels of eminence in the sciences and arts (Simonton, 2003).

Openness to experience. Within the Big Five taxonomy of personality, openness to experience stands to yield important relationships with retirement, especially to the extent that it extends to an openness to role transitions. As previously reviewed, openness to experience is associated with the tendency to switch between career roles throughout the life span (e.g., Wille et al., 2010). It is defined as the willingness to adjust one's attitudes and behaviors when exposed to new information or situations, and is more closely associated with creativity than the other dimensions of the Big Five (Digman, 1990; McCrae, 1987). Whereas open people prefer variety and novelty in their lives, people lower on openness to experience prefer familiarity and routine. People high on openness to experience tend to be curious, broad-minded, intelligent, and artistic (Barrick & Mount, 1991). Furthermore, they are less risk

averse than their peers and more apt to change their opinions over time (George & Zhou, 2001). Across many years of research, openness to experience has been shown to predict interracial attitudes (Flynn, 2005), adaptation to change (LePine, 2003), entrepreneurialism (Zhao & Seibert, 2006), leadership (Judge, Bono, Ilies, & Gerhardt, 2002), and performance during transitional job stages (Thoresen, Bradley, Bliese, & Thoresen, 2004). With respect to creativity, openness to experience has been linked to a wide range of laboratory and field creativity metrics (George & Zhou, 2001; McCrae, 1987). Given these findings, an examination of openness to experience represents a clear first step in the analysis of creativity and retirement success.

Need for closure. Beyond openness to experience, another construct that can be theorized to produce creative retirement planning and decision making is need for closure, otherwise referred to as epistemic motivation. Kruglanski (1990) defines need for closure as a desire for "an answer on a given topic, any answer, ... compared to confusion and ambiguity" (p. 337). Research supports the notion of stable individual differences in need for closure (Webster & Kruglanski, 1994). Compared to their peers, individuals high on need for closure make up their minds quickly when performing tasks, are confident in these decisions, and avoid disconfirming information (Kruglanski & Webster, 1996). High need for closure contexts in turn lead to a wide array of outcomes that imply the suppression of divergent thinking, including cultural conformity (Fu et al., 2007), a preference to interact with similar others (Kruglanski, Shah, Pierro, & Mannetti, 2002), and an overweighting of early information (i.e., a primacy effect) in impression formation (Webster & Kruglanski, 1994). Research furthermore confirms a negative relationship between need for closure and creativity. When need for closure is high, individuals demonstrate less creative idea production in group discussions and brainstorming sessions (Chirumbolo, Mannetti, Pierro, Areni, & Kruglanski, 2005; Chirumbolo, Livi, Mannetti, Pierro, & Kruglanski, 2004). Taken together, these findings suggest that need for closure should exhibit a negative impact on divergent thinking during retirement planning and decision making by predisposing retirees to seize upon only the most salient retirement strategies.

Creative self-efficacy. The final dispositional construct I consider here is creative self-efficacy, which can be theorized to directly relate to goal persistence. Broadly defined, self-efficacy refers to one's level of confidence with respect to goal attainment and task performance (Bandura, 1986). Although generalized self-efficacy exists as an independent construct, scholars have also noted the importance of efficacy constructs tailored to specific content domains (Gist, 1987). Creative self-efficacy—confidence in one's ability to perform well on creative tasks—is an example of one such construct (Tierney & Farmer, 2002). To quote Tierney and Farmer (2002): "creative self-efficacy appears to provide … momentum in that strong efficacy beliefs enhance the persistence level and the coping efforts individuals will demonstrate when encountering challenging situations" (p. 1140). Thus, whereas openness to experience and need for closure should influence retirement planning and decision making through openness to role transitions and divergent goal setting, creative self-efficacy can be theorized to primarily influence creative goal persistence. A growing compendium of scholarship supports the predictive validity of creative self-efficacy with respect to individuals' creative behaviors and manager-rated creative performance (Gong, Huang, & Farh, 2009; Li & Wu, 2011; Tierney & Farmer, 2002, 2010).

The Creative Context

In recent years, scholars have begun to emphasize the importance of an interactionist approach to organizational creativity (Shalley et al., 2004). According to this perspective, creative achievement is best predicted at the intersection of creative individuals and environments that enable and encourage creative behavior to be expressed. For example, George and Zhou (2001) demonstrated that openness to experience best predicts creativity in organizational contexts characterized by autonomy and support. Along similar lines, creativity in retirement should be best predicted when situations afford creative approaches to the retirement process and individuals possess the requisite knowledge, skills, abilities, and personalities to take advantage of these situational affordances. Three situational contexts that can be theorized to consequently enable creative approaches to retirement are autonomy, social tie availability, and support for creativity.

Autonomy. Organizations vary in the degree to which they provide employees with the freedom to conduct their day-to-day work activities as they see fit. Whereas high-autonomy organizations allow individuals to control their daily activities, lower-autonomy organizations provide employees with significantly less freedom. Autonomy is central to Amabile et al.'s (1996) measure of climate for creativity. Additional studies have demonstrated that autonomy enables employees to take advantage of their situations and dispositional inclinations to be more creative (Amabile & Gitomer, 1984; Liu, Chen, & Yao, 2010; Wang & Cheng, 2010). For example, Wang and Chen (2010) found that job autonomy moderates the impact of benevolent leadership on employee creativity, such that the benefits of benevolent leadership are realized only when job autonomy is high. Within the context of retirement, autonomy can be theorized to exert a parallel impact on retirees' ability to approach retirement planning and decision making creatively. For instance, retirees are unlikely to delay their retirement if their organizations limit their freedom to retire when and how they wish.

Social tie availability. Previous research supports the notion that creativity is facilitated by individuals' social ties. In particular, employees appear to reap creative benefits from ties with individuals that possess unique social connections or knowledge. Thus, creativity is best facilitated by weak ties (Perry-Smith, 2006; Perry-Smith & Shalley, 2003) that provide access to diverse information and new social circles (Baer, 2010). Interestingly, Baer (2010) found that employees who are open to experience reaped the greatest benefits from access to diverse social ties, supporting the interactionist perspective. With respect to the retirement domain, social ties can likewise be expected to provide access to different modes of retirement (e.g., bridge employment; early retirement) and novel post-retirement roles (e.g., career changes; family roles; community roles). Therefore, organizations that allow retirees to build and maintain a variety of social ties are more likely to facilitate creative approaches to retirement than organizations that inhibit the breadth and diversity of social tie development.

Support for creativity. Support and encouragement of creativity has been described as "by far, the broadest and most frequently mentioned [contextual predictor of creativity] in the literature" (Amabile et al., 1996, p. 1158). As an aspect of the organizational context, it can emanate from organizational practices, supervisors, and coworkers. At the organizational level, support for creativity has been assessed with respect to multiple practices including explicit reward programs for creativity and supportive evaluation of new ideas. At the core of these practices is an organizational climate that encourages risk taking and idea generation. Through rewards, encouragement, and other signs of approval, organizations encourage creativity by making their expectations for creativity clear and, through positive feedback, enhancing employees' feelings of competence and worth. Similar processes occur at the supervisory level. By making expectations for creativity clear, supervisors can enhance employees' goal clarity. Likewise, by demonstrating support for employees' creative efforts, they can reduce employees' fear of reprisal and enhance their feelings of competence and worth. Most proximally, support for creativity can occur among coworkers. By developing norms for a mutual openness to new ideas and commitment to organizational goals, coworkers in teams and other units can reduce evaluation apprehension and build employees' intrinsic motivation.

Discussion

In an era in which the number of retirees continues to grow, it is increasingly important for scholars to understand the precise dispositional and situational factors that facilitate smooth transitions into retirement and post-retirement adjustment. The purpose of this chapter has been to provide a new direction in this domain by examining the link between retirement and creativity. What does it mean to retire creatively? Retirement is not creative in and of itself—the vast majority of people ultimately retire from their careers. Rather, it is the *approach* to retirement that holds the potential for creativity. Retirees must engage in planning and decision-making processes that are novel when compared to prevailing norms in their organizations and industries (Csikszentmihalyi, 1999). Furthermore, retirees must engage in planning and decision-making processes that facilitate their post-retirement adjustment. To explore the perceptions and actions associated with a creative approach to retirement, three factors were considered: openness to role transitions, divergent thinking, and goal persistence. Through openness to role transitions, retirees can consider the possibility of new post-retirement roles that enable them to fulfill such fundamental needs as the need to belong (Baumeister & Leary, 1995) and the need for significance. Through divergent thinking, retirees can develop broad, varied goals and consider novel possibilities as they plan out their retirement transitions. Two examples of goals that diverge from dominant retirement norms yet have positive effects on post-retirement adjustment are bridge employment and early retirement. However, there are certainly many more divergent goals, and these are only illustrations. Retirees could also develop unique financial planning programs or build new businesses and transition into entrepreneurial roles. In tandem with openness and divergent goal setting, retirees must lastly be persistent. Through goal persistence, retirees can work toward their retirement-related goals and direct their efforts to ensure that their goals are attained. Together, these three factors stand to make a lasting impact on the quality of individuals' lives during and after the transition into retirement.

Future Directions

As noted in the introduction, research explicitly linking creativity and retirement is essentially nonexistent (Fehr, in press). To move forward, scholars must begin to empirically test the ideas put forth in this chapter. In the third section of this chapter, I presented several dispositional and situational constructs that can be theorized to facilitate retirement transitions. Drawing from an interactionist perspective, these transitions should be most effective when dispositionally creative people are embedded in organizations that likewise encourage and support creative behavior. Clearly, an examination of these constructs and their impact on the retirement transition represents a key first step in scholars' empirical understanding of the retirement-creativity link. To further illuminate potential directions for future research, several key questions should be considered:

1. *What does it mean to be novel and useful?* Creativity scholars have long noted that novelty and utility—the hallmarks of creative production—are highly context-dependent. What is novel and useful in one realm might easily be mundane or useless in another. For example, as bridge employment becomes increasingly common, it might no longer qualify as novel. On the other hand, bridge employment might be extremely novel in specific industries and cultural contexts. Building on the systems perspective on creativity (Csikszentmihalyi, 1999), future research must be explicit in modeling the novelty of specific planning and decision-making processes. Existing research on creativity measurement hints at some possibilities. As in research on divergent thinking during brainstorming exercises, scholars can utilize consensual assessment techniques to rate the novelty of retirees' planning and decision making. More objectively, they could examine the relative frequency of each approach within a given organization or industry.

2. *What is the dark side of approaching retirement creatively?* Scholars tend to assume that creativity

is a wholly desirable phenomenon, yet there is research to suggest that it does have a "dark side" with negative consequences for individuals and their organizations (Cropley, Cropley, Kaufman, & Runco, 2010). For example, recent research has pitched creativity as a form of moral deviance, suggesting that it might entail ethical violations (Mainemelis, 2010). In the context of retirement, creativity might backfire in the presence of organizational resistance. Employers might balk at retirees' attempts to retire early, fostering resentment and withdrawal. It is also true that creative approaches to retirement bear risks. Retirees might fail in entrepreneurial ventures or find their new non-work social ties unsatisfying. Future research must consider these and related possibilities to draw meaningful, practical recommendations for organizations seeking to craft organizational practices that maximize retiree well-being and adjustment.

3. *At what level of analysis do creative retirement practices emerge?* Throughout this chapter, I have presented individuals' reactions to and approaches toward retirement as wholly individual-level, with organizations exerting top-down pressures that interact with retirees' creative abilities. Yet retirement perceptions could also be theorized to emerge at higher levels of analysis. For instance, work groups or hospital units might develop their own retirement norms and plans. Thus, entire units or organizations could be characterized as creative, with cross-level analyses examining the implications of inter-organizational differences on retiree behavior. Future research must be careful to consider these issues and the levels at which retirement norms and behaviors emerge.

Conclusion

Retirement is a varied and complex process, fraught with a broad array of challenges and choices. Creativity is one means through which these challenges can be met. By empowering retirees to "think outside the box," an emphasis on creativity can help even the most reluctant retiree find continuity and meaning in new roles and novel transitional pathways. For organizations, this means building a creative environment—supporting creative pursuits, providing employees with autonomy, and enabling employees to construct diverse social ties. For retirees, this means actively seeking to be creative—approaching the retirement process openly, setting novel goals, and persisting in their attainment.

References

Amabile, T. M., Conti, R., Coon, H., Lazenby, J., & Herron, M. (1996). Assessing the work environment for creativity. *Academy of Management Journal, 39*, 1154–1184.

Amabile, T. M., & Gitomer, J. (1984). Children's artistic creativity: Effects of choice in task materials. *Personality and Social Psychology Bulletin, 10*, 209–215.

Ames, M., & Runco, M. A. (2005). Predicting entrepreneurship from ideation and divergent thinking. *Creativity and Innovation Management, 14*, 311–315.

Ashforth, B. (2001). *Role transitions in organizational life: An identity-based perspective.* Mahwah, NJ: Erlbaum.

Atchley, R. C. (1999). Continuity theory, self, and social structure. In C. D. Ryff & V. W. Marshall (Eds.), *Families and retirement* (pp. 145–158). Newbury Park, CA: Sage.

Baas, M., De Dreu, C. W., & Nijstad, B. A. (2011). When prevention promotes creativity: The role of mood, regulatory focus, and regulatory closure. *Journal of Personality and Social Psychology, 100*, 794–809.

Baer, M. (2010). The strength-of-weak-ties perspective on creativity: A comprehensive examination and extension. *Journal of Applied Psychology, 95(3)*, 592–601.

Bandura, A. (1986). *Social foundation of thought and action: A social cognitive theory.* Englewood Cliffs, NJ: Prentice-Hall.

Barrick, M., & Mount, M. K. (1991). The Big Five personality dimensions and job performance: A meta-analysis. *Personnel Psychology, 44*, 1–26.

Barron, F., & Harrington, D. (1981). Creativity, intelligence, and personality. *Annual Review of Psychology, 32*, 439–476.

Barton, K. and Cattell, R. B. (1972). Personality factors related to job promotion and turnover. *Journal of Counseling Psychology, 19*, 430–435.

Basadur, M. S. (1994). Managing the creative process in organizations. In M. A. Runco (Ed.), *Problem finding, problem solving, and creativity* (pp. 237–268). Norwood, NJ: Ablex.

Basadur, M. S., Graen, G. B., & Green, S. G. (1982). Training in creative problem solving: Effects of ideation and problem finding in an applied research organization. *Organizational Behavior and Human Performance, 30*, 41–70.

Baumeister, R. F., & Leary, M. R. (1995). The need to belong: Desire for interpersonal attachments as a fundamental human motivation. *Psychological Bulletin, 117*, 497–529.

Carson, S. H., Peterson, J. B., & Higgins, D. M. (2003). Decreased latent inhibition is associated with increased creative achievement in high-functioning individuals. *Journal of Personality and Social Psychology, 85*, 499–506.

Chirumbolo, A., Livi, S., Mannetti, L., Pierro, A., & Kruglanski, A. (2004). Effects of need for closure on creativity in small group interactions. *European Journal of Personality, 18*, 265–278.

Chirumbolo, A., Mannetti, L., Pierro, A., Areni, A., & Kruglanski, A. W. (2005). Motivated closed-mindedness and creativity in small groups. *Small Group Research, 36*, 59–82.

Creed, P. A. (1999). Personality characteristics in unemployed Australian males—implications for "drift" hypothesis in unemployment. *Psychological Reports, 84*, 477–480.

Cropley, D. H., Cropley, A. J., Kaufman, J. C., & Runco, M. A. (2010). *The dark side of creativity.* London, England: Cambridge Press.

Csikszentmihalyi, M. (1999). Implications of a systems perspective for the study of creativity. In R. J. Sternberg (Ed.), *Handbook of creativity* (pp. 313–335). New York, NY: Cambridge University Press.

Davidson, L. (2011). Triple threats to retirement. *Forbes.* Retrieved from http://www.forbes.com/sites/financialfinesse/2011/09/29/triple-threats-to-retirement/

Davis, M. A. (2003). Factors related to bridge employment participation among private sector early retirees. *Journal of Vocational Behavior, 63,* 55–71.

De Dreu, C. K. W., Baas, M., & Nijstad, B. A. (2008). Hedonic tone and activation level in the mood-creativity link: Toward a dual pathway to creativity model. *Journal of Personality and Social Psychology, 94,* 739–756.

Digman, J. M. (1990). Personality structure: Emergence of the Five-Factor Model. *Annual Review of Psychology, 41,* 417–440.

Dutton, J. E., Roberts, L. M., & Bednar, J. (2010). Pathways for positive identity construction at work: Four types of positive identity and the building of social resources. *Academy of Management Review, 35,* 265–293.

Eisenberger, R., & Rhoades, L. (2001). Incremental effects of reward on creativity. *Journal of Personality and Social Psychology, 81,* 728–741.

Fehr, R. (2009). Why innovation demands aren't as conflicted as they seem: Stochasticism and the creative process. *Industrial and Organizational Psychology: Perspectives on Science and Practice, 2,* 344–348.

Fehr, R. (2012). Is retirement always stressful? The potential impact of creativity. *American Psychologist, 67,* 76–77.

Feist, G. J. (1999). Personality in scientific and artistic creativity. In R. J. Sternberg (Ed.), *Handbook of creativity* (pp. 273–296). New York, NY: Cambridge University Press.

Feist, G. J. (2010). The function of personality in creativity: The nature and nurture of the creative personality. In J. C. Kaufman & R. J. Sternberg (Eds.), *The Cambridge handbook of creativity* (pp. 113–130). New York: Cambridge University Press.

Feldman, D. C., & Beehr, T. A. (2011). A three-phase model of retirement decision making. *American Psychologist, 66,* 193–203.

Flynn, F. J. (2005). Having an open mind: The impact of openness to experience on interracial attitudes and impression formation. *Journal of Personality and Social Psychology, 88,* 816–826.

Ford, C. M. (1996). A theory of individual creative action in multiple social domains. *Academy of Management Review, 21,* 1112–1142.

Fu, J., Morris, M. W., Lee, S., Chao, M., Chiu, C., & Hong, Y. (2007). Epistemic motives and cultural conformity: Need for closure, culture, and context as determinants of conflict judgments. *Journal of Personality and Social Psychology, 92,* 191–207.

George, J. M. (2007). Creativity in organizations. *Academy of Management Annals, 1,* 439–477.

George, J. M., & Zhou, J. (2001). When openness to experience and conscientiousness are related to creative behavior: An interactional approach. *Journal of Applied Psychology, 86,* 513–524.

George, J. M., & Zhou, J. (2002). Understanding when bad moods foster creativity and good ones don't: The role of context and clarity of feelings. *Journal of Applied Psychology, 87,* 687–697.

Gist, M. E. (1987). Self-efficacy: Implications for organizational behavior and human resource management. *Academy of Management Review, 12,* 472–485.

Gobeski, K. T., & Beehr, T. A. (2009). How retirees work: Predictors of different types of bridge employment. *Journal of Organizational Behavior, 30,* 401–425.

Gong, Y., Huang, J., & Farh, J. (2009). Employee learning orientation, transformational leadership, and employee creativity: The mediating role of employee creative self-efficacy. *Academy of Management Journal, 52(4),* 765–778.

Gowan, M. A. (1998). A preliminary investigation of the factors affecting appraisal of the decision to take early retirement. *Journal of Employment Counseling, 35,* 124–140.

Guilford, J. P. (1967). *The nature of human intelligence.* New York, NY: McGraw-Hill.

Guilford, J. P., & Hoepfner, R. (1971). *The analysis of intelligence.* New York, NY: McGraw-Hill.

Hennessey, B. A., & Amabile, T. M. (2010). Creativity. *Annual Review of Psychology, 61,* 569–598.

Hinden, S. (2000). Another choice for the "leisure" years: A second career. *Washington Post,* p. H1.

Hirt, E. R., Levine, G. M., McDonald, H. E., Melton, R., & Martin, L. L. (1997). The role of mood in quantitative and qualitative aspects of performance: Single or multiple mechanisms? *Journal of Experimental Social Psychology, 33,* 602–629.

Judge, T. A., Bono, J. E., Ilies, R., & Gerhardt, M. W. (2002). Personality and leadership: A qualitative and quantitative review. *Journal of Applied Psychology, 87,* 765–780.

Keck, K. (2007). Emotional changes of retirement can tarnish golden years. *CNN.* Retrieved from http://articles.cnn.com/2007-01-09/us/law.emotional_1_retirement-golden-years-identity?_s=PM:US

Kim, S., & Feldman, D. C. (1998). Healthy, wealthy, or wise: Predicting actual acceptances of early retirement incentives at three points in time. *Personnel Psychology, 51,* 623–642.

Kim, S., & Feldman, D. C. (2000). Working in retirement: The antecedents of bridge employment and its consequences for quality of life in retirement. *Academy of Management Journal, 43,* 1195–1210.

Kruglanski, A. W. (1990). Motivations for judging and knowing: Implications for causal attribution. In E. X Higgins & R. M. Sorrentino (Eds.), *Handbook of motivation and cognition: Foundations of social behavior* (pp. 333–368). New York, NY: Guilford Press.

Kruglanski, A. W., Shah, J. Y., Pierro, A., & Mannetti, L. (2002). When similarity breeds content: Need for closure and the allure of homogeneous and self-resembling groups. *Journal of Personality and Social Psychology, 83,* 648–662.

Kruglanski, A. W., & Webster, D. M. (1996). Motivated closing of the mind: "Seizing" and "freezing." *Psychological Review, 103,* 263–283.

Kubicek, B., Korunka, C., Raymo, J. M., & Hoonakker, P. (2011). Psychological well-being in retirement: The effects of personal and gendered contextual resources. *Journal of Occupational Health Psychology, 16,* 230–246.

LePine, J. A. (2003). Team adaptation and postchange performance: Effects of team composition in terms of members' cognitive ability and personality. *Journal of Applied Psychology, 88,* 27–39.

Li, C., & Wu, J. (2011). The structural relationships between optimism and innovative behavior: Understanding potential antecedents and mediating effects. *Creativity Research Journal, 23,* 119–128.

Liu, D., Chen, X., & Yao, X. (2010). From autonomy to creativity: A multilevel investigation of the mediating role of harmonious passion. *Journal of Applied Psychology, 96,* 294–309.

Madjar, N., Greenberg, E., & Chen, Z. (2011). Factors for radical creativity, incremental creativity, and routine, noncreative performance. *Journal of Applied Psychology, 96,* 730–743.

Mainemelis, C. (2010). Stealing fire: Creative deviance in the evolution of new ideas. *Academy of Management Review, 35(4)*, 558–578.

McCrae, R. R. (1987). Creativity, divergent thinking, and openness to experience. *Journal of Personality and Social Psychology, 52*, 1258–1265.

Mein, G., & Ellison, G. T. H. (2006). The impact of early retirement on perceptions of life at work and at home: Qualitative analyses of British civil servants participating in the Whitehall II Retirement Study. *International Journal of Aging and Human Development, 63*, 187–216.

Mignonac, K. (2008). Individual and contextual antecedents of older managerial employees' willingness to accept intra-organizational job changes. *International Journal of Human Resource Management, 19*, 582–599.

Mumford, M. D., Marks, M. A., Connelly, M., Zaccaro, S. J., & Johnson, J. F. (1998). Domain-based scoring of divergent-thinking tests: Validation evidence in an occupational sample. *Creativity Research Journal, 11*, 151–163.

Mutran, E. J., Reitzes, D. C., & Fernandez, M. E. (1996). Factors that influence attitudes toward retirement. *Research on Aging, 19*, 251–273.

Ng, T. W. H., Sorensen, K. L., Eby, L. T., & Feldman, D. C. (2007). Determinants of job mobility: A theoretical integration and extension. *Journal of Occupational and Organizational Psychology, 80*, 363–386.

Perry-Smith, J. E. (2006). Social yet creative: The role of social relationships in facilitating individual creativity. *Academy of Management Journal, 49*, 85–101.

Perry-Smith, J. E., & Shalley, C. E. (2003). The social side of creativity: A static and dynamic social network perspective. *Academy of Management Review, 28*, 89–106.

Rhodes M. (1961/1987). An analysis of creativity. In S. G. Isaksen (Ed.), *Frontiers of creativity research: Beyond the basics* (pp. 216–22). Buffalo, NY: Bearly.

Roberts, L. M., & Dutton, J. E. (2009). *Exploring positive identities and organizations: Building a theoretical research foundation.* New York, NY: Routledge.

Runco, M. (2004). Creativity. *Annual Review of Psychology, 55*, 657–687.

Runco, M. A. (2010). Divergent thinking, creativity, and ideation. In J. C. Kaufman & R. J. Sternberg (Eds.), *The Cambridge handbook of creativity* (pp. 413–446). New York, NY: Cambridge University Press.

Schlossberg, N. K. (2009). *Revitalizing retirement: Reshaping your identity, relationships, and purpose.* New York, NY: American Psychological Association.

Schoolmeester, R. (2004). Retirement isn't just a date—it's a new life. *USA Today*, p. A1.

Schwartz, S. H. (1994). Beyond individualism/collectivism: New cultural dimensions of values. In U. Kim, H. C. Triandis, C. Kagitcibasi, S. Choi, & G. Yoon (Eds.), *Individualism and collectivism: Theory, method, and applications* (pp. 85–119). Thousand Oaks, CA: Sage.

Schwartz, S. H., & Bardi, A. (2001). Value hierarchies across cultures: Taking a similarities perspective. *Journal of Cross Cultural Psychology, 32*, 268–290.

Shalley, C. E. (1991). Effects of productivity goals, creativity goals, and personal discretion on individual creativity. *Journal of Applied Psychology, 76*, 179–185.

Shalley, C. E., Zhou, J., & Oldham, G. R. (2004). The effects of contextual and personal characteristics on creativity: Where should we go from here? *Journal of Management, 30*, 933–958.

Shultz, K. S. (2003). Bridge employment: Work after retirement. In G. A. Adams & T. A. Beehr (Eds.), *Retirement: Reasons, processes, and results* (pp. 214–241). New York, NY: Springer.

Shultz, K. S., Morton, K. R., & Weckerle, J. R. (1998). The influence of push and pull factors on voluntary and involuntary early retirees' retirement decision and adjustment. *Journal of Vocational Behavior, 53*, 45–57.

Simonton, D. K. (2003). Scientific creativity as constrained stochastic behavior: The integration of product, person, and process perspectives. *Psychological Bulletin, 129(4)*, 475–494.

Social Security Administration. (2011). *Retirement benefits.* Retrieved from http://www.ssa.gov/pubs/10035.html

Sørensen, J. B., & Stuart, T. E. (2000). Aging, obsolescence, and organizational innovation. *Administrative Science Quarterly, 45(1)*, 81–112.

Sternberg, R. J. (2003). WICS: A model of leadership in organizations. *Academy of Management Learning and Education, 2*, 386–401.

Taylor, M. A., & Doverspike, D. (2003). Retirement planning and preparation. In G. A. Adams & T. A. Beehr (Eds.), *Retirement: Reasons, processes, and results* (pp. 53–82). New York, NY: Springer.

Taylor, M. A., & Shore, L. F. (1995). Predictors of planned retirement age: An application of Beehr's model. *Psychology and Aging, 10*, 76–83.

Taylor, M. A., Shultz, K. S., Spiegel, P. E., Morrison, R. F., & Greene, J. (2007). Occupational attachment and met expectations as predictors of retirement adjustment of naval officers. *Journal of Applied Social Psychology, 37*, 1697–1725.

Thoresen, C. J., Bradley, J. C., Bliese, P. D., & Thoresen, J. D. (2004). The Big Five personality traits and individual job performance growth trajectories in maintenance and transitional job stages. *Journal of Applied Psychology, 89*, 835–853.

Tierney, P., & Farmer, S. M. (2002). Creative self-efficacy: Its potential antecedents and relationship to creative performance. *Academy of Management Journal, 45*, 1137–1148.

Tierney, P., & Farmer, S. M. (2010). Creative self-efficacy development and creative performance over time. *Journal of Applied Psychology, 96*, 277–293.

Torrance, E. P. (1962). *Guiding creative talent.* Englewood Cliffs, NJ: Prentice Hall.

Tugend, A. (2011). Final fears, and opportunities, on the road to retirement. *New York Times*, B5.

van den Berg, T. J., Elders, L. M., & Burdorf, A. (2010). Influence of health and work on early retirement. *Journal of Occupational and Environmental Medicine, 52*, 576–583.

Verworn, B. (2009). Does age have an impact on having ideas? An analysis of the quantity and quality of ideas submitted to a suggestion system. *Creativity and Innovation Management, 18*, 326–334.

Vincent, A. S., Decker, B. P., & Mumford, M. D. (2002). Divergent thinking, intelligence, and expertise: A test of alternative models. *Creativity Research Journal, 14*, 163–178.

Vinson, G. A., Connelly, B. S., & Ones, D. S. (2007). Relationships between personality and organization switching: Implications for utility estimates. *International Journal of Selection and Assessment, 15*, 118–133.

Wanberg, C. R., & Banas, J. T. (2000). Predictors and outcomes of openness to changes in a reorganizing workplace. *Journal of Applied Psychology, 85*, 132–142.

Wang, A., & Cheng, B. (2010). When does benevolent leadership lead to creativity? The moderating role of creative role identity and job autonomy. *Journal of Organizational Behavior, 31*, 106–121.

Wang, M. (2007). Profiling retirees in the retirement transition and adjustment process: Examining the longitudinal change patterns of retirees' psychological well-being. *Journal of Applied Psychology, 92*, 455–474.

Wang, M., & Shultz, K. S. (2010). Employee retirement: A review and recommendations for future investigation. *Journal of Management, 36*, 176–206.

Webster, D. M., & Kruglanski, A. W. (1994). Individual differences in need for cognitive closure. *Journal of Personality and Social Psychology, 67*(6), 1049–1062.

Wille, B., De Fruyt, F., & Feys, M. (2010). Vocational interests and Big Five traits as predictors of job instability. *Journal of Organizational Behavior, 76*, 547–558.

Williams, S. D. (2004). Personality, attitude, and leader influences on divergent thinking and creativity in organizations *European Journal of Innovation Management, 7*, 187–204.

Woodman, R. W., Sawyer, J. E., & Griffin, R. W. (1993). Toward a theory of organizational creativity. *Academy of Management Review, 18*, 293–321.

Zhan, Y., Wang, M., Liu, S., & Shultz, K. S. (2009). Bridge employment and retirees' health: A longitudinal investigation. *Journal of Occupational Health Psychology, 14*, 374–389.

Zhang, X., & Bartol, K. M. (2010). The influence of creative process engagement on employee creative performance and overall job performance: A curvilinear assessment. *Journal of Applied Psychology, 95*, 862–873.

Zhao, H., & Seibert, S. E. (2006). The Big Five personality dimensions and entrepreneurial status: A meta-analytic review. *Journal of Applied Psychology, 91*, 259–271.

Retirement Research: Concluding Observations and Strategies to Move Forward

Mo Wang

Abstract

This last chapter of the handbook attempts to discuss the potential challenges faced by the field of retirement research. These challenges include: (1) lack of communication among multiple disciplines' research on retirement, (2) great complexity in conceptualizing retirement and retirement processes, (3) great need to accumulate knowledge of causality, and (4) lack of consideration for the research context. The chapter then offers a five-step systematic research paradigm to overcome these challenges and move the retirement research forward.

Key Words: challenges, strategies, systematic research paradigm

As I noted at the outset of this volume, retirement research has arrived as an established interdisciplinary research area with a thriving scientific community. With the aging of America and many other countries, we soon will have perhaps the largest proportion of our society classified as retired than we have ever had. This is one of the fundamental driving forces for studying retirement as an institutional and society-wide phenomenon. Indeed, in the past two decades, retirement has attracted much attention from policymakers, employers, popular media, and academic researchers. So far, retirement researchers have made tremendous progress in understanding the nature of retirement and issues related to retirement. In addition, great advances have been made in terms of identifying the kinds of interventions that are effective and necessary to address those issues. Much of this body of knowledge is summarized in various chapters of this volume.

With this great progress in mind, what are the important next steps in the scientific research of retirement? In this last chapter of the handbook, I attempt to discuss my observations regarding the challenges faced by this field and offer some suggestions to overcome these challenges and move the retirement research forward. It should be noted that my observations and suggested strategies are largely bounded by my own experience of conducting retirement research, serving as a reviewer and action editor for related academic journal submissions, and reading of the existing literature. Therefore, by all means, these do not represent the only ways to move the field forward or the best answers to questions we may encounter in retirement research or practice. My main intention here is to simply inspire more strategic thinking about retirement research as a field and to suggest approaches to further improve the scientific quality and merit of our research product.

The Challenges Faced by the Field

In this section, I aim to discuss four challenges that the field of retirement research faces. They are (1) lack of communication among multiple disciplines' research on retirement, (2) great complexity in conceptualizing retirement and retirement processes, (3) great need to accumulate knowledge of causality, and (4) lack of consideration for the research context. Having a comprehensive understanding and appreciation of these challenges could help us to improve the quality of retirement research and better translate the knowledge to practices.

Lack of Communication among Multiple Disciplines

Retirement as a multidisciplinary research topic attracts scholars from a wide variety of research fields. These research fields may include economics, policy studies, gerontology, sociology, psychology, public health, and management (Wang & Shultz, 2010). Each of these fields also has multiple different subfields or branches that may generate research on retirement. For example, within the field of management, scholars from human resource management, organizational behavior, organizational theory, and strategic management may all view retirement as a relevant research topic and generate research about retirement rooting from their unique perspectives and paradigms.

This multidisciplinary nature of retirement research certainly has its benefits for knowledge generation. For example, it inspires diverse ideas and approaches for studying retirement and its related phenomena. Indeed, encouraging the diversity in research perspectives, questions, and methods is a critical and effective way to match and tackle the complexity of retirement phenomena. Further, the multidisciplinary nature of retirement research ensures good coverage on issues that are of practical importance, helping to maintain an informative transformational and translational relationship between science and practice. However, these advantages of multidisciplinary research cannot really be fully realized if the multiple disciplines involved are not communicating with each other. Although more and more multidisciplinary research teams have been formed to study retirement-related issues (e.g., as evident in the calls for grant proposals on retirement research issued by the National Institute on Aging in the United States), I suspect that there is still much need for such effort.

The lack of communication among multiple disciplines creates several important issues for retirement research. First of all, different disciplines may use different terminologies for describing the same essential constructs. For example, what economists often refer to as happiness is typically termed as satisfaction or subjective well-being by psychologists. Consequently, when economists develop measures of collective happiness at the country level for policy purposes, they run into the same problems that psychologists had encountered many years ago and had accumulated much knowledge about, such as issues in calibration of magnitude, cultural bias, and attribution errors (Judge & Kammeyer-Muller, 2011). However, due to the difference in terminology, most economists are not aware of the existence of this vast literature in psychology, and the process of "reinventing the wheel" becomes inevitable. In the field of retirement research, an example of similar issues exists in the study of employment after retirement. Researchers have used terms like "bridge employment," "encore career," and "retirement jobs" to describe employment status after retirement (e.g., Brown, Aumann, Pitt-Catsouphes, Galinsky, & Bond, 2010; Quinn, 2010; Wang, Zhan, Liu, & Shultz, 2008). Although these terms largely refer to the same phenomenon (i.e., working after retirement) and represent constructs that are operationalized in similar ways, it is not clear whether researchers and practitioners who use these terms are connecting the literature behind them and are fully utilizing the bodies of knowledge generated under these terms.

Block (1995) has reviewed the issue of terminological diversity in personality research and pointed out that such diversity reflects a commendable desire to bring fresh perspectives to the literature, and innovating thinking certainly may generate new antecedents, outcomes, interventions, processes, etc. However, terminological diversity comes with costs; as Block bluntly states, useless concept redundancy is a waste of time; scholars often wind up rediscovering the same basic phenomena over and over. Block characterized the issue in part as a lack of historical knowledge. However, in the age of electronic literature searches, terminology arguably become even more important—as choosing the wrong search term (or the wrong search database) can lead a scholar to draw incorrect conclusions about a topic even before reading any of the relevant literature. These problems present significant challenges to most scientific disciplines, but are particularly problematic in fields involving scholars from multiple disciplines (retirement research being a prototypical example). The result is that scientific advancement occurs at a much slower pace than what might otherwise be possible, and a lot of scrutiny is needed before scientific knowledge can be translated to improve practice. Moreover, the inability of a field to settle on clear labels for constructs could further escalate the communication challenges both among researchers in different disciplines and between researchers and practitioners.

Second, the lack of communication among multiple disciplines may also lead to barriers in connecting different research perspectives and developing comprehensive understanding of the phenomenon of interest. For example, when studying retirement adjustment, researchers from the field of psychology often take a stress perspective, emphasizing retirement as a critical life transition event and thus focusing on understanding how successful people may be in dealing with the stress during the retirement adjustment process (Wang, Henkens, & van Solinge, 2011). Economists, on the other hand, often take a resource-consumption perspective (Gourinchas & Parker, 2002) to study retirement adjustment, thus focusing on how successful people may be in maintaining the balance between the resources they have and their consumption needs. Although it is not difficult to see that the resource-consumption imbalance could be an important source of stress for retirees, previous research has only limited the connection between the two perspectives by studying how changes in financial states during retirement adjustment could influence changes in retirees' psychological well-being (e.g., Wang, 2007). It could be more fruitful if researchers can further connect the two perspectives by applying the resource-consumption perspective to a more extended scope to study the resource-consumption imbalance in the socioemotional aspects of life, as well as its impact on the stress experienced during the retirement adjustment process. This way, the resource-consumption perspective does not have to be limited only to the understanding of financial adjustment to retirement, and the stress perspective can also be enriched by incorporating a new angle for searching for and understanding stress-inducing factors. Obviously, such mutual inspiration and extension of research perspectives between two disciplines cannot happen if there is a lack of communication between researchers from these disciplines.

Third, the lack of communication among multiple disciplines may also lead to inconsistencies in methodological practices in retirement research. It is well known that different disciplines have different acceptable practices in terms of research methods. For example, in conducting survey research, economists and public health researchers often put more emphasis on sampling methods such that they can effectively manage sampling error in their findings. However, they often pay less attention to measurement error, assuming that the survey instruments they use could reliably and accurately capture the theoretical constructs they wish to measure. On the other hand, psychologists often put more emphasis on measurement error, paying a lot of attention to the reliability and validity of the instruments they use to measure theoretical constructs (Schmidt, 2011). However, psychologists often rely on small samples and convenience samples in empirical studies, which leads to concerns regarding the generalizability of their findings (Hanges & Wang, in press). Ideally, we should of course strive to simultaneously control for sampling error and measurement error in conducting retirement research. Thus, improving the communication among multiple disciplines could help us realize each discipline's strength and weakness in research methods and inspire the development of complementary approaches to maximize the benefit from interdisciplinary research.

The lack of communication regarding different practices in research methods across disciplines may also create unwarranted bias toward the findings generated by a certain research methodology. For example, qualitative research methods have often been viewed as too subjective and less scientific in terms of informing cause-effect conclusions (Schonfeld & Mazzola, in press). However, if used rigorously and correctly, qualitative research methods can complement quantitative research methods and offer numerous strengths in (a) instrument development for quantitative studies, (b) theoretical development and hypothesis generation, (c) the discovery of new phenomena, (d) the development of explanations of difficult-to-interpret quantitative findings, (e) insight into why interventions succeed or fail, and (f) the accumulation of rich descriptions of the complex dynamic process behind observed phenomena (Schonfeld & Mazzola, in press). As such, it is important for researchers from different disciplines to clearly communicate with each other on the reasons and philosophy behind their methodological choices in studying retirement. This way, knowledge generated from certain methodological traditions will not go overlooked by the field. It will also be easier to facilitate overall knowledge accumulation in the field.

Great Complexity in Conceptualizing Retirement and Retirement Processes

The second challenge I aim to discuss here regards the great complexity in conceptualizing retirement and retirement processes. For any research field, it is important to provide conceptual taxonomy to decide how researchers describe the concept in question and in turn ground the study in relevant knowledge bases that lay the foundation for tackling specific research questions (Shultz & Wang, 2011). However, in the field of retirement research, there have been many different ways to analyze and understand retirement, thus making the theoretical conceptualization much more complicated (see Beehr and Bowling's chapter and Shultz and Olson's chapter in this handbook). In fact, Denton and Spencer (2009) identified eight different common ways that researchers from across the globe measured retirement: (a) nonparticipation in the labor force, (b) reduction in hours worked and/or earnings, (c) hours worked or earnings below some minimum cutoff, (d) receipt of retirement/pension income, (e) exit from one's main employer, (f) change of career or employment later in life, (g) self-assessed retirement, and (h) some combination of the previous seven. These different ways to measure retirement reflect the different approaches through which researchers conceptualize retirement and form their research questions. As Wang and Shultz (2010) summarized, across different disciplines that study retirement, there generally are four types of theoretical conceptualizations of retirement: retirement as decision making, retirement as an adjustment process, retirement as a career development stage, and retirement as a part of human resource management practice. Therefore, researchers may conceptualize or operationalize retirement in different ways, which may yield dramatically different findings.

For example, if a researcher wishes to study retirement as a decision made with the intention to withdraw from the workforce, it may be best to measure retirement via self-assessment, but not receipt of retirement/pension income. This is because a person may be eligible to receive retirement/pension income but still be engaged in some form of employment and have no intention to exit the workforce. In addition, in this situation, it may not even be ideal to use nonparticipation in the labor face or hours worked as indicators of retirement status, because people may cease their participation in the workforce or cut down their work hours involuntarily. As such, these indices may not sufficiently capture the active withdrawal intention from the workforce that the researcher aims to operationalize. However, if a researcher wishes to study changes in retirees' financial statuses and how these changes may be associated with changes in their health statuses, then using receipt of retirement/pension income as a measure of retirement status may provide a more accurate investigation of the financial status that could generate policy implications. Finally, if a researcher wishes to study how retirement-related HR practices help to streamline organizations' strategic workforce planning process, then exit from one's organization may be used as the more relevant operationalization of retirement.

Similar complexity also exists in conceptualizing retirement processes. As Shultz and Wang (2011) recently pointed out, researchers typically view retirement as a temporal progression process (including retirement planning, early retirement and retirement decision making, bridge employment, and retirement transition and adjustment). Within these broad phases, of course, are smaller and shorter segments through which individuals go as they approach retirement, transition through the retirement decision-making process, and begin life as a self-designated retiree. Thus, researchers will often focus on a specific phase of the retirement process in a given study, all the while realizing that they are studying just one piece of the larger retirement puzzle. As such, this temporal progression process implies that retirement is not a single event. Instead, it is a sequential process that occurs over the course of many years, which makes it difficult to grasp how the whole process of retirement is intertwined with one's later life development and experience.

Adding complication to conceptualizing and understanding the retirement process, recent conceptual development (Shultz & Wang, 2008, 2011) has discussed the changing nature of retirement and how retirement is becoming less a uniform and lockstep process for all older workers. That is, while the vast majority of older workers will go through the temporal progression of retirement planning, retirement decision making, and retirement adjustment, disadvantaged groups (e.g., women, minorities, the disabled, low-income workers, the chronically unemployed) are likely to have very different retirement experiences than individuals with stable, uninterrupted, professional careers. In addition, the changing natures of work, careers, family structures, the organization of work, and government policies all have important impact on how the retirement process is enacted as well (Shultz & Wang, 2011). For example, as Shultz and Olson discussed in their chapter in this volume, both the macro-level changes in work and work context (e.g., globalization, increased diversity, and technology development) and micro-level changes in work (e.g., improved opportunities for lifelong learning and rewards, growing demands for work-life balance and flexibility, and desire to engage in meaningful work) have led to fundamental changes in the process of retirement. In fact, individuals can "un-retire" or "re-retire" by rejoining the workforce and starting a new career of their desire after they retire, which has become a relatively common phenomenon in the last few decades (Alley & Crimmins, 2007; Wang, Adams, Beehr, & Shultz, 2009). As such, retirement researchers have to pay great attention to selecting their research timing and samples so that they can capture the specific phase of the retirement process in which they are interested. Further, retirement researchers cannot just limit their research scope to the retirement process alone, but have to consider the broad context of retirement (e.g., work, life history, family, organization, etc.) to better understand the embedded complexity.

Great Need to Accumulate Knowledge of Causality

The third challenge I aim to discuss here regards the great need we face to accumulate causal knowledge in the field of retirement research. On the one hand, to solve real-world problems, retirement-related interventions, practices, and policy decisions at individual, organizational, and societal levels all have to rely on causal knowledge. On the other hand, given that retirement is largely an enactment of the government policy and social institution, it is extremely difficult for us to isolate it from its context and study it with experimental design. Indeed, it is quite impossible for us to manipulate people's retirement status and rely on random assignment to remove alternative explanations for interpreting research findings. Thus, we need to invest much more effort when it comes to designing retirement studies and conducting data analysis.

In terms of research designs, the vast majority of previous studies in the field of employee retirement research have relied on cross-sectional designs (Wang et al., 2008; Wang et al., 2011). Although cross-sectional designs may be useful in establishing correlations between variables, it is difficult to make sound causal inferences based on such findings. To understand the causal processes, we will also need to understand the time sequence of the changes in variables as well as rule out alternatives. Accordingly, retirement research should use more longitudinal designs to provide more information for understanding the causal processes. Specifically, improving the internal validity of the research, we can assess the time-lagged effect between predictors and outcomes while controlling for the baseline of the outcome variables (Hanges & Wang, in press). We can also rule out the possibility of reversed causality by directly test it. Another advantage for using longitudinal designs is that it provides an examination of within-individual change trends in variables, which reveals how time influences variables of interest (Wang, 2007).

In addition to applying a longitudinal design, researchers should also pay attention to whether their studies omit theoretically relevant variables (Antonakis, Bendahan, Jacquart, & Lalive, 2010). Typically, when using a correlational research design (i.e., using one variable to predict another variable), there are three types of omitted variables that could jeopardize the development of causal knowledge. They are (1) the common causes shared by the predictor and the outcome, (2) the variables that directly capture the underlying mechanisms between the predictor and the outcome (i.e., mediators), and (3) the important boundary conditions for the association between the predictor and the outcome (i.e., moderators).

Regarding the first type of omitted variable, when it is reasonable to believe that the predictor and the outcome variables may share some common causes that are not directly captured by the research design, the problem of endogeneity may be present. In other words, the estimated relationship between the predictor and the outcome will be biased by not partitioning out the effects of unmeasured causes. Therefore, researchers should pay attention to including all known theoretical controls on the outcome variable. However, in reality, controlling for all sources of variance in the context of social science is probably not feasible because the researchers have to identify everything that may cause variations in the outcome variable, and sometimes these causes are unknown. As such, the instrumental-variable approach with simultaneous estimation equations (e.g., two-stage least squares [2SLS] regression) may be more preferable for researchers to consider. Interested readers can refer to Antonakis et al. (2010) and Foster and McLanahan (1996) for details about how to use the instrumental-variable approach to address the endogeneity problem, which is standard practice in economics but is often not familiar to other social science disciplines such as psychology and management.

Regarding the omission of mediators, this often creates a discrepancy between the argued theoretical mechanisms and the actual operationalization of these mechanisms in a study. For example, a researcher may argue that older workers are more likely to take incentives to retire early because they are more frequently subjected to age discrimination in the workplace. As such, when testing the association between workers' age and their decision to take early retirement incentives, it is important to directly measure their perceived age discrimination in the workplace to test whether this theoretical explanation is supported. Without directly testing age discrimination in the workplace as the mediator, even when there is reliable association between the workers' age and their decision to take early retirement incentives, the causal mechanism will still remain unclear. In addition, omitting mediators often reduces the possibility of recognizing important intervention opportunities. Oftentimes, the distal causes (e.g., age, gender, personality, level of education) of retirement-related phenomena (e.g., retirement planning, retirement decision making, and retirement adjustment) are less changeable or trainable than more proximal causes (e.g., motivation and perception). Therefore, directly testing mediators could provide useful causal knowledge to inform intervention effort.

In establishing a causal relationship, boundary conditions often address issues of "for whom," "when," and "where" the relationship is amplified or attenuated (Whetten, 1989). As such, moderators often serve to provide a comprehensive understanding regarding the necessary conditions that dictate a certain causal effect. Consequently, omitting moderators from studies may yield mis-specified statistical models (Antonakis et al., 2010) and ignore the theoretical nuance in observed causal relationships (Wang & Hanges, 2011). For example, until recently, most studies in the field of retirement have ignored the possibility that great heterogeneity may exist in the retiree population. In other words, the retiree population may consist of multiple subpopulations that are closely associated with the multiple pathways underlying the retirement processes (Wang, 2007). As both Pinquart and Schindler (2007) and Wang (2007) have shown, this heterogeneity cannot be fully accounted for by simply examining demographic differences among retirees. Therefore, traditional analyses based on separating and comparing data from multiple observed groups

may not be able to sufficiently examine this heterogeneity in the retiree population. As such, retirement researchers may want to take advantage of recent methodological advancements in latent class procedures (e.g., Wang & Bodner, 2007; Wang & Chan, 2011; Wang & Hanges, 2011) to identify unobserved moderators associated with heterogeneity in statistical estimates of causal relationships.

Finally, although a large number of empirical studies have been conducted in the field of retirement, few studies have used a meta-analytic approach to quantitatively summarize and review previous findings. This may be due to the multidisciplinary nature of retirement research. Not every discipline related to retirement research requires researchers to provide basic statistics (e.g., means, standard deviations, and correlations) in their articles that would be useful for conducting meta-analysis. Therefore, compared to other research fields, it is probably more difficult for retirement researchers to recover enough statistical information from published studies to conduct a meta-analysis. However, meta-analysis is extremely useful for summarizing and scrutinizing the cumulative knowledge about interested causal effects. Specifically, meta-analysis can help us understand the distribution of the sizes of these causal effects, remove sampling and measurement errors in recovering the true estimates of the causal effects, and identify potential moderators that shape the causal effects. As such, we recommend that retirement researchers from all disciplines be diligent in providing basic statistical information in their manuscripts to facilitate further synthesis and comparison of causal knowledge.

Lack of Consideration for the Research Context

The fourth challenge I would like to discuss here regards the lack of consideration for the context in conducting retirement research. As Szinovacz pointed out in her chapter (in this volume; also see Szinovacz, 2003), retirement processes cannot be well understood without consideration of the contexts in which they occur. Specifically, she identified three levels of structures that form the contexts for retirement-related policies, practices, and behaviors. At the macro-level, these contexts include culture, population structures such as the age composition of the population, fertility and marriage or divorce rates, as well as the economy in general and labor markets in particular. Meso-level structures refer to the local and regional environment, including infrastructure as well as economy and labor markets.

Micro-level structures consist foremost of organizations, families, and social networks.

Despite this recognition of the important contexts, retirement research has not really put an emphasis on studying the complex contexts that shape retirement-related phenomena. For example, when researchers study a retirement-related phenomenon or effect in a specific social institution of retirement (e.g., the retirement structures in the United States), rarely are the findings interpreted with the specific context of the social institution in mind. In fact, researchers rarely tie their findings back to the specific social institution to generate context-based insights. However, it is very reasonable to expect that similar findings may not replicate in another country where the social institution of retirement is very different from the United States. Yao and Peng's chapter in this volume reviewed different systems of social security, pension, and retirement saving across four countries (i.e., the United States, Germany, China, and India). Their review provides a good foundation for us to be cautious in overgeneralizing what we know from research conducted in one particular country to other countries. For instance, retirement may mean very different things between older workers who live in a country that implements mandatory retirement age (e.g., Germany) and those who live in a country where mandatory retirement is not a part of the retirement institution (e.g., the United States). With the implementation of mandatory retirement age, it is quite possible that older workers will engage in their retirement planning in a more organized way, as there is little ambiguity in the timing of retirement. Further, for people who are not covered by social security systems (e.g., farmers in China and India), retirement may literally mean losing their major income source. As such, they should be more likely to engage in post-retirement employment than their counterparts who are covered by social security systems.

Important contextual effects can also be expected from employer practices. Peiró, Tordera, and Potočnik's chapter (in this volume) reviewed various human resource management practices as contexts for retirement based on the distinction between a depreciation model and a maintenance model. I do not intend to replicate their review, but one thing that is clear from their review is that these employer practices are intertwined with the social institution of retirement in influencing older workers' retirement patterns. As such, the macro-, meso-, and micro-level contexts do not work in isolation, but indeed jointly shape retirement-related phenomena. Therefore, researchers need to consider carefully the contexts of their research. Oftentimes, although researchers may not be able to fully empirically investigate those contextual effects due to the specific samples they have, it would not hurt to at least discuss the potential implications of those contextual factors in leading to the particular findings. This is certainly beneficial in terms of establishing the theoretical generalizability of the findings and offering more information regarding the boundary conditions of the findings. In turn, such discussion will also be beneficial for practitioners who wish to apply the research findings to better match their issues and contexts at hand to the appropriate collection of knowledge. To achieve this goal, qualitative research methods such as interviewing the research participants regarding the impact of contextual factors may be a particularly efficient way to help understand and speculate on the potential contextual influences. The key is to investigate whether some contextual factors may be interacting with the theoretical model of interest and whether the findings are driven by taking a snapshot of such interaction.

Finally, it should be noted that when researchers have the luxury to directly examine the contextual effects (e.g., when data from multiple countries or organizations are available), they need to pay special attention to both the theoretical development and statistical procedures. Theoretically, choosing a theoretical perspective that could logically accommodate multiple layers of contexts is particularly important (e.g., the life course perspective; see Wink and James's chapter and Szinovacz's chapter in this volume), as it allows for the flexibility to investigate the interactions between factors at different contextual levels. Statistically, specific statistical procedures, such as multilevel modeling, are often needed to analyze data that contains clustering of observations that correspond to multiple layers of contexts.

Strategies to Move Forward

Now that I have discussed my observations regarding the challenges faced by this field, I attempt to offer some suggestions to overcome these challenges and move the retirement research forward. As I mentioned earlier, retirement is a multidisciplinary research topic. Thus, it is important to keep in mind that any strategies that we use to move the field forward must recognize and appreciate the weak paradigm nature of the retirement research.

That is, retirement as a multidisciplinary research field is unlikely to converge to a unified paradigm that would yield consensus on key research questions and research methodologies. Although having a unified paradigm may lead to greater ability to have a cumulative science and the likelihood of greater respect outside the field itself (Pfeffer, 1993), the field of retirement research probably functions best as a garden with many flowers, keeping a spirit of openness to various views and positions. Indeed, the diversity in research perspectives, questions, and methods provides a good match to the structural and dynamic complexity of retirement phenomena.

Thus, with this weak paradigm nature in mind, the strategies I suggest below aim to champion a more systematic paradigm to conduct retirement research. In particular, I am arguing that even without unifying the key research questions and research methodologies, retirement researchers can still improve the ability to have a cumulative science of retirement by implementing systematic steps in conducting their research. The purpose of this systematic paradigm is not to eliminate diverse ideas or approaches but rather to systemize how diverse ideas should be implemented and diverse approaches should be applied to make contributions to retirement research. As such, following this systematic research paradigm may help researchers to effectively manage uncertainty and randomness in the connection between research decisions and actions and their consequences (i.e., contribution and utility of the research product to the field). Below, I detail the five sequential steps for implementing this systematic paradigm.

Step 1: Determining Research Questions

When determining research questions for a study, retirement researchers should consider not only whether there is sufficient public and academic interest but also the true novelty of the research question. Here, a broad literature search across multiple disciplines is recommended to both gauge the prevalence of interest and see how researchers in other disciplines approached similar research questions. In this way, the issues due to lack of communication among multiple disciplines can be effectively dealt with. In addition, researchers can better understand the depth of the research question by considering literature from different countries and occupations, such that the context of the interested phenomena could enter the formation of research questions at the beginning of a study. The ideal end product of this step would be

to construct a relatively comprehensive knowledge base about what is already known regarding the interested retirement-related phenomena, which naturally leads to surfacing of the unsolved research questions.

Step 2: Clarifying Research Contributions

After the potential research questions are determined, retirement researchers need to take time to decide in which ways they intend to make a contribution to the literature by answering these research questions. In other words, although answering the research questions generates previously unknown knowledge and insights, researchers still need to make sure that filling the specific knowledge gap makes a meaningful contribution to the literature, such as offering broader theoretical and empirical implications that go beyond the specific findings themselves. As such, the knowledge generated will not be isolated from the larger literature but can meaningfully inform future development of the scientific research of retirement.

In the literature, there are typically four ways for a study to make such contributions. The first way is to test and extend existing theories/findings, which probably characterizes most studies in scientific research (Whetten, 1989). This is typically done via two research approaches, separately or combined. First, if a theory is already well established, then applying it to understand unknown phenomena may confirm its generalizability or yield inconsistent findings that inspire refinement and revision to the theory. Second, if a theory lacks certain details, such as clear specification of underlying mechanisms or boundary conditions, then testing potential underlying mechanisms or boundary conditions could help to confirm or refute them as important parts of the theory. As consequences of both approaches, novel empirical findings will result either as a product of studying less known phenomena or as a product of studying newly developed parts of theoretical components, or both. It should be noted that when taking these approaches for conducting research, the associated contributions are often viewed as incremental in nature (Hollenbeck, 2008).

A second way to make meaningful contributions to the literature is through studying new constructs or phenomena and developing new theories about them. According to Locke (2007), this type of research often combines the following components: (1) developing a substantial body of observations or data about novel phenomena; (2) on the basis of observations and data, formulating valid concepts that capture the phenomena; and (3) indentifying causal mechanisms relevant to the concepts and integrating them into a noncontradictory whole (i.e., theory building). One example of this type of research in the field of retirement is Feldman's (1994) seminal paper in establishing a decision-making model for understanding early retirement. In that paper, he first reviewed evidences that documented early retirement as a stable and meaningful trend among older workers. He then conceptualized the concept of retirement, distinguishing it from early-career-stage job change and ordinary job turnover, as well as emphasizing its underlying withdrawal intention from the workforce. Based on this conceptualization, he further developed a decision-tree framework that specified a set of factors that may influence older workers' early retirement decisions and a set of theoretical assumptions that underlies and informs the structure of the decision tree. Because this type of research typically tackles issues that have not been systematically conceptualized and examined, when done successfully, its contribution to the literature is substantial and often opens doors for future streams of research on the novel phenomena.

A third way to make meaningful contributions to the literature is through summarizing empirical findings and informing theory building on a particular research question. This type of research can be done with a qualitative review or a quantitative review (e.g., meta-analysis). The key is to summarize the commonalities and contradictions among previous findings regarding a particular research question. The commonalities are typically retained to form the basic premises of the theory about the research question. The contradictory findings, on the other hand, are often used to inform future research regarding theory refinement and identifying boundary conditions of the theory. This type of research is often facilitated by taxonomy generation, which involves categorizing previous research in terms of the aspects addressed regarding the particular research question. For example, when reviewing theories used in studying retirement, Wang and Shultz (2010) first provided taxonomy of retirement conceptualizations (i.e., retirement as decision making, retirement as an adjustment process, retirement as a career development stage, and retirement as a part of human resource management practice) and then summarized the commonalities in theoretical mechanisms used for studying each category of retirement conceptualization. Given that this type of research often provides a useful and organized summary about what we know and what needs to be done in the future, it typically has significant impact to the field.

Finally, a fourth way to make meaningful contributions to the literature is through integrating existing theories and reconciling inconsistent findings. This is often referred to as a "consensus creation" way of making a contribution (Hollenbeck, 2008). Specifically, consensus creation occurs when authors show a lack of consensus in the literature (e.g., in the forms of previous contradictory findings) and either clarify the lines of debate or resolve the conflict by offering new empirical insights. Research that makes this type of contribution typically provides a stand-alone "mini-summary" of the particular research question at the beginning of the paper by clearly positioning the research question in the relevant literature and identifying the importance of the phenomena being examined. Then, the previous inconsistent findings regarding the research question are highlighted and theoretical/empirical insights are introduced to establish the approach for reconciling these inconsistent findings. Given the "consensus creation" nature of this type of research, it often settles debates on important research phenomena, thus moving the field forward. For an example of this type of research, interested readers can refer to Wang (2007).

In summary, the goal of this second step of the systematic research paradigm is to clearly explain why answering the chosen research questions is important in terms of moving the field forward. Researchers should clarify what types of contributions they intend to make with the study, which helps to better position the study and connect it to the existing literature, thus adding to the cumulative science of retirement.

Step 3: Conceptualizing Key Constructs

After researchers clarify the intended contributions of their studies, they need to provide clear conceptualizations of the key constructs that they wish to study. There are several advantages to doing so in terms of addressing the research challenges I discussed earlier. First, given the complexity in conceptualizing retirement and retirement processes, it is extremely important to consider perspectives from different research disciplines and scrutinize the meanings of the constructs within the particular research scope. Second, providing clear and appropriate conceptualizations of the key constructs can help researchers to communicate their interpretation of the phenomena and select corresponding theories for generating hypotheses. Thus, it can decrease the potential disassociation between the theoretical framework and the operationalizations of the key constructs. Third, when conceptualizing the key constructs, researchers are also offered the opportunity to define the key constructs in the specific research context, such as specific sample characteristics (e.g., demographics and occupations) and social institutions of retirement. As such, the research context can be integrated into the theoretical development stage of the study, thus avoiding having to enter the consideration in a post hoc way.

In essence, the goal of this research step is to ensure that the key constructs are defined in a way that logically matches the theoretical framework and the research context of the study. Consequently, it can facilitate later interpretation of the findings and translation of the findings to inform real-world practice. For interested readers, van Solinge and Henkens's conceptualizations of involuntary retirement (2007) and retirement adjustment vs. retirement satisfaction (2008) are good examples of defining key constructs in retirement research.

Step 4: Establishing Theoretical Framework

In this step, researchers should select theories that best inform the investigation regarding the research question. Sometimes, one theory may be sufficient to supply the causal mechanisms needed to establish hypotheses regarding the research question. Other times, multiple theories are needed to jointly provide causal mechanisms if there is an extended research scope and the studied constructs are linked in complex ways. This is particularly necessary when researchers aim to establish a new theoretical perspective on a research question that has been investigated before. In this case, it is important to show that the causal mechanisms deduced from the new theoretical perspective can work above and beyond the causal mechanisms that have been previously established on the same research question. For some retirement research examples, interested readers can refer to Adams, Prescher, Beehr, and Lepisto (2002), Adams and Rau (2004), Gobeski and Beehr (2008), and Wang (2007).

Selecting the most appropriate theories to form the theoretical framework is also important in terms of avoiding the omitting variable problems discussed earlier. This is because each theory's unique causal mechanisms are manifested with a specific scope of variables. Therefore, the most appropriate theories would be those that offer not only clear process variables that pinpoint underlying mechanisms but

also good guidance for identifying boundary conditions. By using theories with these qualities, detailed causal knowledge can be generated with regard to the research question.

After selecting the theories to construct the theoretical framework, researchers need to gather both theoretical logics and empirical evidences that inform the relationships among the studied constructs to form specific hypotheses. The qualities of the evidences can be evaluated in terms of how much they can contribute to establishing causal relationships among the studied constructs. For example, empirical evidence from experimental design should probably be preferred over correlational evidence based on cross-sectional design. Similarly, theoretical logics that have accumulated consistent empirical support should probably be preferred over those that have not been extensively tested. It is also important to pay attention to alternative explanations for the expected relationships at this stage and generate testable hypotheses that could rule out those alternative interpretations.

Step 5: Research Design and Data Analysis

In this step, researchers should strive to employ a research design that can help establish causal inferences. Typically, longitudinal design and quasi-experimental design in naturalistic settings are great options for studying retirement-related phenomena, as I mentioned earlier that these phenomena are not easily manipulated in lab settings. In addition, researchers need to take cautious procedures to prevent and address potential issues that may threaten the ability of the study to make causal inferences, such as omitted selection, measurement error, and common method bias. Omitted selection typically manifests in a situation that involves comparing entities that are grouped nominally where selection to the group is not random (e.g., comparing older workers and retirees on physical conditions where the processes leading to their different employment statuses are not equivalent). One way around this problem is to estimate a Heckman-type two-step selection model (Heckman, 1979) to include instrumental variables in the research design to predict participation in the group membership. Then, the unobserved heterogeneity in the group selection can be controlled for by removing the variance from the error term due to selection in the substantive predictive equation. Measurement errors are typically caused by including imperfectly measured variables in the research design and not by modeling error variance of the measures in the analyses. This problem can be addressed by using statistical modeling methods that take measurement errors into account when analyzing the data (e.g., structural equation modeling; Bollen, 1989) or by using the 2SLS regression I mentioned earlier. Common method bias usually refers to the method variance overlap between independent and dependent variables that are gathered from the same rating source with the same data collection method (e.g., self-report). It is well-known that common method bias distorts the relationship estimates between variables. Podsakoff, MacKenzie, Lee, and Podsakoff (2003) offered several design and analytical suggestions for minimizing such bias in research. Interested readers may refer to that paper for a comprehensive review.

Considering the specific research context, researchers should also articulate the target population to which they would like to generalize their findings, because the sample characteristics and the social institution of retirement may interact with the theoretical mechanisms that are examined. To address this issue, the constructive replication approach would always be beneficial for researchers to use to cross-validate their findings in different samples. Further, in data analysis, as I mentioned earlier, there are a number of statistical procedures that researchers can use to ensure that good measures are used (e.g., reliability analysis, exploratory and confirmatory factor analysis) and that there is no endogeneity problem that jeopardizes causal inferences (e.g., simultaneous equation models; regression discontinuity models, dynamic modeling and nested data modeling; Antonakis et al., 2010; Hanges & Wang, in press). The goal, again, is to best use the available statistical procedures to remove the threat for generating causal knowledge.

Final Thoughts: What Do We Gain as Retirement Researchers?

Given that each chapter included in the current volume has pointed readers to future directions related to specific topics in retirement research, it would be redundant for me to reiterate their points. However, I will use this final space of the book to share some of my personal thoughts about the benefits and rewards we receive as researchers who conduct retirement research. I do hope that these points are intrinsically motivating for attracting the next generations of retirement researchers.

First of all, I need to emphasize that this is a field in which a scientist-practitioner model is likely to thrive. In other words, most of the time our research questions map directly to issues emerged in the real world, whether at the socioeconomic level, organizational level, family level, or individual level; and our research findings have a good opportunity to inform these issues and eventually impact our day-to-day life. This direct match between science and practice results in great meaningfulness and constant feedback to us as researchers. Given that these factors have long been recognized as critical job features that lead to job satisfaction (Hackman & Oldham, 1976, 1980), it is reasonable to expect that retirement research itself is intrinsically motivating.

Further, as discussed throughout this chapter, a lot of retirement-related phenomena are fundamentally intertwined with their specific socioeconomic and policy contexts. Changes have often occurred in these contexts over time (e.g., economic boom due to technology innovation, Social Security reform, health care reform, and early retirement incentive practices), which can alter the research questions investigators ask (Wang & Shultz, 2010). For example, at the end of the 1990s and in early 2000, a lot of effort had been invested in studying early retirement because there was a clear trend that workers were retiring earlier and earlier. However, largely due to the recent economic depression, this trend has somehow reversed, and more and more older workers choose to postpone their retirement and stay in the workforce. As such, bridge employment becomes a focal research topic for investigation. This type of shift in research phenomena makes it never boring to study retirement, as new issues surface constantly. In addition, given the context changes, the same phenomena are likely to be influenced by different factors at different points in time, which often facilitates theoretical and methodological innovations in tackling those issues and creates the innate forces to move the field forward.

Finally, given the weak paradigm nature of retirement research, multiple values and views are appreciated and encouraged in this field. This gives retirement researchers more autonomy to nurture a research profession that combines one's passion, interest, and curiosity. Corresponding to the multiple values and views, there are also a lot of publication outlets that suit the different types of retirement research. As such, it is relatively more efficient for researchers to disseminate the knowledge and experience fewer hurdles for establishing a research career in the field of retirement. Quoting Beehr and Adams (2003, p. 298), "Retirement has proven to be an interesting and yet vexing research topic that should attract the curious, the adventurous, and the concerned."

Author Note

Correspondence regarding this article should be addressed to Mo Wang, Department of Management, University of Florida, Gainesville, FL 32611. Emails should be sent to mo.wang@warrington.ufl.edu.

References

Adams, G., & Rau, B. (2004). Job seeking among retirees seeking bridge employment. *Personnel Psychology, 57,* 719–744.

Adams, G. A., Prescher, J., Beehr, T. A., & Lepisto, L. (2002). Applying work-role attachment theory to retirement decision-making. *International Journal of Aging & Human Development, 54,* 125–137.

Alley, D., & Crimmins, E. M. (2007). The demography of aging and work. In K. S. Shultz & G. A. Adams (Eds.), *Aging and work in the 21st century* (pp. 7–23). Mahwah, NJ: Lawrence Erlbaum.

Antonakis, J., Bendahan, S., Jacquart, P., & Lalive, R. (2010). On making causal claims: A review and recommendations. *Leadership Quarterly, 21,* 1086–1120.

Beehr, T. A., & Adams, G. A. (2003). Concluding observations and future endeavors. In G. A. Adams & T. A. Beehr (Eds.), *Retirement: Reasons, processes, and results* (pp. 293–298). New York, NY: Springer.

Block, J. (1995). A contrarian view of the five-factor approach to personality description. *Psychological Bulletin, 117,* 187–215.

Bollen, K. A. (1989). *Structural equations with latent variables.* New York, NY: Wiley.

Brown, M., Aumann, K., Pitt-Catsouphes, M., Galinsky, E., & Bond, J. T. (2010). *Working in retirement: A 21st century phenomenon.* New York, NY: Families and Work Institute.

Denton, F., & Spencer, B. (2009). What is retirement? A review and assessment of alternative concepts and measures. *Canadian Journal on Aging, 28,* 63–76.

Feldman, D. C. (1994). The decision to retire early: A review and conceptualization. *Academy of Management Review, 19,* 285–311.

Foster, E. M., & McLanahan, S. (1996). An illustration of the use of instrumental variables: Do neighborhood conditions affect a young person's chance of finishing high school? *Psychological Methods, 1,* 249–260.

Gobeski, K. T., & Beehr, T. A. (2008). How retirees work: Predictors of different types of bridge employment. *Journal of Organizational Behavior, 37,* 401–425.

Gourinchas, P., & Parker, J. (2002). Consumption over the life cycle. *Econometrica, 70,* 47–89.

Hackman, J. R., & Oldham, G. R. (1976). Motivation through the design of work: Test of a theory. *Organizational Behavior and Human Performance, 16,* 250–279.

Hackman, J. R., & Oldham, G. R. (1980). *Work redesign.* Reading, MA: Addison-Wesley.

Hanges, P., & Wang, M. (in press). Seeking the Holy Grail in organizational science: Uncovering causality through research design. In S. W. J. Kozlowski (Ed.), *The Oxford handbook of industrial and organizational psychology.* New York, NY: Oxford University Press.

Heckman, J. J. (1979). Sample selection bias as a specification error. *Econometrica, 47,* 153–161.

Hollenbeck, J. R. (2008). The role of editing in knowledge development: Consensus shifting and consensus creation. In Y. Baruch, A. M. Konrad, H. Aguinus, & W. H. Starbuck (Eds.), *Journal editing: Opening the black box* (pp. 16–26). San Francisco, CA: Jossey-Bass.

Judge, T. A., & Kammeyer-Mueller, J. D. (2011). Happiness as a societal value. *Academy of Management Perspectives, 25,* 30–41.

Locke, E. A. (2007). The case for inductive theory building. *Journal of Management, 33,* 867–890.

Pfeffer, J. (1993). Barriers to the advance of organizational science: Paradigm development as a dependent variable. *Academy of Management Review, 18,* 599–620.

Pinquart, M., & Schindler, I. (2007). Changes of life satisfaction in the transition to retirement: A latent-class approach. *Psychology and Aging, 22,* 442–455.

Podsakoff, P. M., MacKenzie, S. B., Lee, J.-Y., & Podsakoff, N. P. (2003). Common method biases in behavioral research: A critical review of the literature and recommended remedies. *Journal of Applied Psychology, 88,* 879–903.

Quinn, J. F. (2010). Work, retirement, and the encore career: Elders and the future of the American workforce. *Generations, 34,* 45–55.

Schmidt, F. L. (2011). An interview with Frank L. Schmidt. *The Industrial-Organizational Psychologist, 48,* 21–29.

Schonfeld, I. S., & Mazzola, J. J. (in press). Strengths and limitations of qualitative approaches to research in occupational health psychology. In R. Sinclair, M. Wang, & L. Tetrick (Eds.), *Research methods in occupational health psychology.* New York, NY: Psychology Press.

Shultz, K. S., & Wang, M. (2008). The changing nature of mid and late careers. In C. Wankel (Ed.), *21st century management: A reference handbook* (Vol. 2, pp. 130–138). Thousand Oaks, CA: Sage.

Shultz, K. S., & Wang, M. (2011). Psychological perspectives on the changing nature of retirement. *American Psychologist, 66,* 170–179.

Szinovacz, M. E. (2003). Contexts and pathways: Retirement as institution, process, and experience. In G. E. Adams & T. A. Beehr (Eds.), *Retirement: Reasons, processes, and results* (pp. 6–52). New York, NY: Springer.

van Solinge, H., & Henkens, K. (2007). Involuntary retirement: The role of restrictive circumstances, timing, and social embeddedness. *Journal of Gerontology: Social Sciences, 62B,* S295–S303.

van Solinge, H., & Henkens, K. (2008). Adjustment to and satisfaction with retirement: Two of a kind? *Psychology and Aging, 23,* 422–434.

Wang, M. (2007). Profiling retirees in the retirement transition and adjustment process: Examining the longitudinal change patterns of retirees' psychological well-being. *Journal of Applied Psychology, 92,* 455–474.

Wang, M., Adams, G. A., Beehr, T. A., & Shultz, K. S. (2009). Career issues at the end of one's career: Bridge employment and retirement. In S. G. Baugh and S. E. Sullivan (Eds.), *Maintaining focus, energy, and options through the life span* (pp. 135–162). Charlotte, NC: Information Age.

Wang, M., & Bodner, T. E. (2007). Growth mixture modeling: Identifying and predicting unobserved subpopulations with longitudinal data. *Organizational Research Methods, 10,* 635–656.

Wang, M., & Chan, D. (2011). Mixture latent Markov modeling: Identifying and predicting unobserved heterogeneity in longitudinal qualitative status change. *Organizational Research Methods, 14,* 411–431.

Wang, M., & Hanges, P. (2011). Latent class procedures: Applications to organizational research. *Organizational Research Methods, 14,* 24–31.

Wang, M., Henkens, K., & van Solinge, H. (2011). Retirement adjustment: A review of theoretical and empirical advancements. *American Psychologist, 66,* 204–213.

Wang, M., & Shultz, K. S. (2010). Employee retirement: A review and recommendations for future investigations. *Journal of Management, 36,* 172–206.

Wang, M., Zhan, Y., Liu, S., & Shultz, K. (2008). Antecedents of bridge employment: A longitudinal investigation. *Journal of Applied Psychology, 93,* 818–830.

Whetten, D. A. (1989). What constitutes a theoretical contribution? *Academy of Management Review, 14,* 490–495.